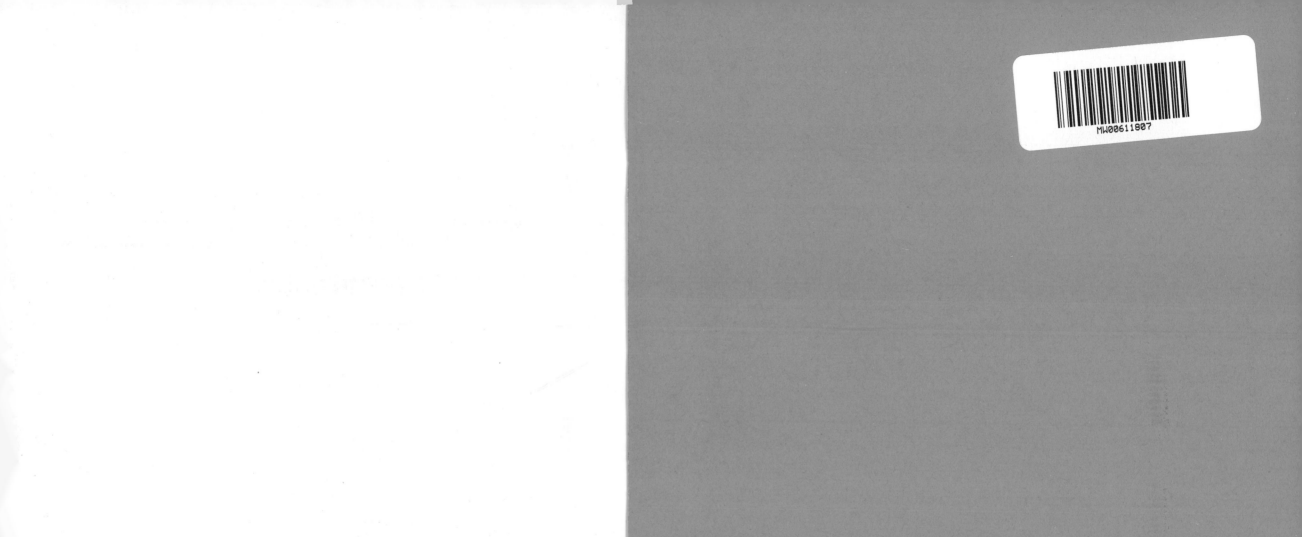

Fortress Commentary on the Bible

THE
NEW TESTAMENT

Fortress Commentary on the Bible

THE
NEW TESTAMENT

Margaret Aymer

Cynthia Briggs Kittredge

David A. Sánchez

Editors

Fortress Press

Minneapolis

Advisory Board: Walter Brueggemann, William R. Herzog II, Richard A. Horsley, Elisabeth Schüssler Fiorenza, Gale A. Yee

Fortress Press Publication Staff: Neil Elliott and Scott Tunseth, Project Editors; Marissa Wold, Production Manager; Laurie Ingram, Cover Design.

Copyeditor: Jeffrey A. Reimer

Typesetter: PerfecType, Nashville, TN

Proofreader: David Cottingham and Linda Maloney

Library of Congress Cataloging-in-Publication is available

ISBN: 978-0-8006-9917-8

eISBN: 978-1-4514-8955-2

The paper used in this publication meets the minimum requirements of American National Standard for Information Sciences— Permanence of Paper for Printed Library Materials, ANSI Z329, 48-1984. Manufactured in the U.S.A.

CONTENTS

CONTRIBUTORS

Volume Editors

Margaret Aymer
Associate Professor of New Testament and Chair of Biblical Studies
    Interdenominational Theological Center
Rootlessness and Community in Contexts of Diaspora

Cynthia Briggs Kittredge
Dean and President and Professor of New Testament
Seminary of the Southwest
Romans

David A. Sánchez
Associate Professor of Theological Studies
Loyola Marymount University
The Apocalyptic Legacy of Early Christianity

Eric D. Barreto
Associate Professor of New Testament
Luther Seminary
Philemon

David L. Bartlett
Professor of New Testament Emeritus
Columbia Theological Seminary
1 Peter

Jennifer G. Bird
Independent Scholar
Portland, Oregon
Ephesians

Robert L. Brawley
Professor of New Testament Emeritus
McCormick Theological Seminary
Luke

Timothy B. Cargal
Coordinator for Preparation for Ministry and
    Assistant Stated Clerk
Office of the General Assembly, Presbyterian
    Church (U.S.A.)
James

Warren Carter
Professor of New Testament
Brite Divinity School
Matthew

Jaime Clark-Soles
Associate Professor of New Testament
SMU Perkins School of Theology
1, 2, 3 John

David A. deSilva
Trustees' Distinguished Professor of New Testament and Greek
Ashland Theological Seminary
Hebrews

Michal Beth Dinkler
Assistant Professor of New Testament
Yale Divinity School
The Acts of the Apostles

Neil Elliott
Acquiring Editor, Biblical Studies
Fortress Press
Situating the Apostle Paul in His Day and Engaging His Legacy in Our Own
Introduction to Hebrews, the General Epistles, and Revelation

Julia Lambert Fogg
Associate Professor of New Testament and Early Christianity, Chair of Religion
California Lutheran University
Philippians

David E. Fredrickson
Professor of New Testament
Luther Seminary
2 Corinthians

Brigitte Kahl
Professor of New Testament
Union Theological Seminary in the City of New York
Galatians

Sylvia C. Keesmaat
Adjunct Professor of Biblical Studies
Trinity College in the University of Toronto
Colossians

Deborah Krause
Academic Dean and Professor of New Testament
Eden Theological Seminary
1, 2 Timothy
Titus

Kwok Pui-lan
William F. Cole Professor of Christian Theology and Spirituality
Episcopal Divinity School
Reading the Christian New Testament in the Contemporary World

Raquel S. Lettsome
Itinerant Elder
African Methodist Episcopal Church
Mark

Laura S. Nasrallah
Professor of New Testament and Early Christianity
Harvard Divinity School
1 Corinthians

Pheme Perkins
Professor of Theology (New Testament)
Boston College
2 Peter
Jude

Raymond Pickett
Professor of New Testament
Lutheran School of Theology at Chicago
Jesus and the Christian Gospels

Edward Pillar
Minister of Evesham Baptist Church
Evesham, UK
1, 2 Thessalonians

Adele Reinhartz
Professor of Classics and Religious Studies
University of Ottawa
John

Barbara R. Rossing
Professor of New Testament
Lutheran School of Theology at Chicago
Revelation

Demetrius K. Williams
Associate Professor of Comparative Litera-
    ture and Associate Professor of Religious
    Studies
University of Wisconsin Milwaukee
Acts as a History of the Early Church

Lawrence M. Wills
Ethelbert Talbot Professor of Biblical Studies
Episcopal Divinity School
*Negotiating the Jewish Heritage of Early
    Christianity*

ABBREVIATIONS

General

AT	Alpha Text (of the Greek text of Esther)
BOI	Book of Isaiah
Chr	Chronicler
DH	Deuteronomistic History
DI	Deutero-Isaiah
Dtr	Deuteronomist
Gk.	Greek
H	Holiness Code
Heb.	Hebrew
JPS	Jewish Publication Society
LXX	The Septuagint
LXX B	Vaticanus Text of the Septuagint
MP	Mode of production
MT	Masoretic Text
NIV	New International Version
NRSV	New Revised Standard Version
OAN	Oracles against Nations (in Jeremiah)
P.	papyrus/papyri
P	Priestly source
PE	Pastoral Epistles
RSV	Revised Standard Version
TI	Trito-Isaiah

Books of the Bible (NT, OT, Apocrypha)

Old Testament/Hebrew Bible

Gen.	Genesis
Exod.	Exodus
Lev.	Leviticus
Num.	Numbers
Deut.	Deuteronomy

Josh.	Joshua
Judg.	Judges
Ruth	Ruth
1 Sam.	1 Samuel
2 Sam.	2 Samuel
1 Kgs.	1 Kings
2 Kgs.	2 Kings
1 Chron.	1 Chronicles
2 Chron.	2 Chronicles
Ezra	Ezra
Neh.	Nehemiah
Esther	Esther
Job	Job
Ps. (Pss.)	Psalms
Prov.	Proverbs
Eccles.	Ecclesiastes
Song.	Song of Songs
Isa.	Isaiah
Jer.	Jeremiah
Lam.	Lamentations
Ezek.	Ezekiel
Dan.	Daniel
Hosea	Hosea
Joel	Joel
Amos	Amos
Obad.	Obadiah
Jon.	Jonah
Mic.	Micah
Nah.	Nahum
Hab.	Habakkuk
Zeph.	Zephaniah
Hag.	Haggai
Zech.	Zechariah
Mal.	Malachi

Apocrypha

Tob.	Tobit
Jth.	Judith
Gk. Esther	Greek Additions to Esther
Sir.	Sirach (Ecclesiasticus)

Bar.	Baruch
Let. Jer.	Letter of Jeremiah
Add Dan.	Additions to Daniel
Pr. Azar.	Prayer of Azariah
Sg. Three.	Song of the Three Young Men (or Three Jews)
Sus.	Susanna
Bel	Bel and the Dragon
1 Macc.	1 Maccabees
2 Macc.	2 Maccabees
1 Esd.	1 Esdras
Pr. of Man.	Prayer of Manasseh
2 Esd.	2 Esdras
Wis.	Wisdom of Solomon
3 Macc.	3 Maccabees
4 Macc.	4 Maccabees

New Testament

Matt.	Matthew
Mark	Mark
Luke	Luke
John	John
Acts	Acts of the Apostles
Rom.	Romans
1 Cor.	1 Corinthians
2 Cor.	2 Corinthians
Gal.	Galatians
Eph.	Ephesians
Phil.	Philippians
Col.	Colossians
1 Thess.	1 Thessalonians
2 Thess.	2 Thessalonians
1 Tim.	1 Timothy
2 Tim.	2 Timothy
Titus	Titus
Philem.	Philemon
Heb.	Hebrews
James	James
1 Pet.	1 Peter
2 Pet.	2 Peter
1 John	1 John

2 John	2 John
3 John	3 John
Jude	Jude
Rev.	Revelation (Apocalypse)

Journals, Series, Reference Works

ABD	*Anchor Bible Dictionary.* Edited by David Noel Freedman. 6 vols. New York: Doubleday, 1992.
ACNT	Augsburg Commentaries on the New Testament
AJA	*American Journal of Archaeology*
AJT	*Asia Journal of Theology*
ANET	*Ancient Near Eastern Texts Relating to the Old Testament.* Edited by J. B. Pritchard. 3rd ed. Princeton: Princeton University Press, 1969.
ANF	*The Ante-Nicene Fathers.* Edited by Alexander Roberts and James Donaldson. 1885–1887. 10 vols. Repr., Peabody, MA: Hendrickson, 1994.
ANRW	*Aufstieg und Niedergang der römischen Welt: Geschichte und Kultur Roms im Spiegel der neueren Forschung.* Edited by Hildegard Temporini and Wolfgang Haase. Berlin: de Gruyter, 1972–.
ANTC	Abingdon New Testament Commentaries
AOAT	Alter Orient und Altes Testament
AbOTC	Abingdon Old Testament Commentary
AOTC	Apollos Old Testament Commentary
A(Y)B	Anchor (Yale) Bible
BA	*Biblical Archaeologist*
BAR	*Biblical Archaeology Review*
BDAG	Bauer, W., F. W. Danker, W. F. Arndt, and F. W. Gingrich. *Greek-English Lexicon of the New Testament and Other Early Christian Literature.* 3rd ed. Chicago: University of Chicago Press, 1999.
BEATAJ	Beiträge zur Erforschung des Alten Testaments und des Antiken Judentum
Bib	*Biblica*
BibInt	*Biblical Interpretation*
BJRL	*Bulletin of the John Rylands University Library of Manchester*
BJS	Brown Judaic Studies
BNTC	Black's New Testament Commentaries
BR	*Biblical Research*
BRev	*Bible Review*
BSac	*Bibliotheca sacra*
BTB	*Biblical Theology Bulletin*
BZAW	Beihefte zur Zeitschrift für die alttestamentliche Wissenschaft
CAT	Commentaire de l'Ancien Testament

CBC	Cambridge Bible Commentary
CBQMS	Catholic Biblical Quarterly Monograph Series
CC	Continental Commentaries
CH	*Church History*
CHJ	*Cambridge History of Judaism.* Edited by W. D. Davies and Louis Finkelstein. Cambridge: Cambridge University Press, 1984–.
ConBNT	Coniectanea biblica: New Testament Series
ConBOT	Coniectanea biblica: Old Testament Series
CS	Cistercian Studies
CTAED	*Canaanite Toponyms in Ancient Egyptian Documents.* S. Ahituv. Jerusalem: Magnes, 1984.
CTQ	*Concordia Theological Quarterly*
CurTM	*Currents in Theology and Mission*
ExpTim	*Expository Times*
ETL	*Ephemerides Theologicae Lovanienses*
ExAud	*Ex auditu*
FAT	Forschungen zum Alten Testament
FC	Fathers of the Church
FRLANT	Forschungen zur Religion und Literatur des Alten und Neuen Testaments
HAT	Handbuch zum Alten Testament
HBT	*Horizons in Biblical Theology*
HNTC	Harper's New Testament Commentaries
HR	*History of Religions*
HSM	Harvard Semitic Monographs
HTKAT	Herders Theologischer Kommentar zum Alten Testament
HTR	*Harvard Theological Review*
HTS	Harvard Theological Studies
HUCA	*Hebrew Union College Annual*
HUCM	Monographs of the Hebrew Union College
HUT	Hermeneutische Untersuchungen zur Theologie
IBC	Interpretation: A Bible Commentary for Teaching and Preaching
ICC	International Critical Commentary
Int	*Interpretation*
JAAR	*Journal of the American Academy of Religion*
JAOS	*Journal of the American Oriental Society*
JBL	*Journal of Biblical Literature*
JBQ	*Jewish Bible Quarterly*
JECS	*Journal of Early Christian Studies*
JJS	*Journal of Jewish Studies*
JNES	*Journal of Near Eastern Studies*

JNSL	*Journal of Northwest Semitic Languages*
JQR	*Jewish Quarterly Review*
JRS	*Journal of Roman Studies*
JSem	*Journal of Semitics*
JSJ	*Journal for the Study of Judaism in the Persian, Hellenistic, and Roman Periods*
JSNT	*Journal for the Study of the New Testament*
JSOT	*Journal for the Study of the Old Testament*
JSOTSup	Journal for the Study of the Old Testament Supplement Series
JSQ	*Jewish Studies Quarterly*
JSS	*Journal of Semitic Studies*
JTI	*Journal of Theological Interpretation*
JTS	*Journal of Theological Studies*
JTSA	*Journal of Theology for Southern Africa*
KTU	*Die keilalphabetischen Texte aus Ugarit.* Edited by M. Dietrich, O. Loretz, and J. Sanmartín. AOAT 24/1. Neukirchen-Vluyn: Neukirchener, 1976.
LCC	Loeb Classical Library
LEC	Library of Early Christianity
LHB/OTS	Library of the Hebrew Bible/Old Testament Studies
LW	*Luther's Works.* Edited by Jaroslav Pelikan and Helmut T. Lehmann. 55 vols. St. Louis: Concordia; Philadelphia: Fortress Press, 1958–1986.
NAC	New American Commentary
NCB	New Century Bible
NCBC	New Cambridge Bible Commentary
NedTT	*Nederlands theologisch tijdschrift*
Neot	*Neotestamentica*
NICNT	New International Commentary on the New Testament
NICOT	New International Commentary on the Old Testament
NIGTC	New International Greek Testament Commentary
NovT	*Novum Testamentum*
NPNF[1]	*The Nicene and Post-Nicene Fathers*, Series 1. Edited by Philip Schaff. 14 vols. 1886–1889. Repr., Grand Rapids: Eerdmans, 1956.
NTL	New Testament Library
NTS	*New Testament Studies*
OBT	Overtures to Biblical Theology
OTE	*Old Testament Essays*
OTG	Old Testament Guides
OTL	Old Testament Library
OTM	Old Testament Message
PEQ	*Palestine Exploration Quarterly*
PG	Patrologia graeca [= Patrologiae cursus completus: Series graeca]. Edited by J.-P. Migne. 162 vols. Paris, 1857–1886.

PL	John Milton, *Paradise Lost*
PL	Patrologia latina [= Patrologiae cursus completus: Series latina]. Edited by J.-P. Migne. 217 vols. Paris, 1844–1864.
PRSt	*Perspectives in Religious Studies*
QR	*Quarterly Review*
RevExp	*Review and Expositor*
RevQ	*Revue de Qumran*
SBLABS	Society of Biblical Literature Archaeology and Biblical Studies
SBLAIL	Society of Biblical Literature Ancient Israel and Its Literature
SBLDS	Society of Biblical Literature Dissertation Series
SBLEJL	Society of Biblical Literature Early Judaism and Its Literature
SBLMS	Society of Biblical Literature Monograph Series
SBLRBS	Society of Biblical Literature Resources for Biblical Study
SBLSCS	Society of Biblical Literature Septuagint and Cognate Studies
SBLSP	*Society of Biblical Literature Seminar Papers*
SBLSymS	Society of Biblical Literature Symposium Series
SBLWAW	SBL Writings from the Ancient World
SemeiaSt	Semeia Studies
SJT	*Scottish Journal of Theology*
SNTSMS	Society for New Testament Studies Monograph Series
SO	Symbolae osloenses
SR	*Studies in Religion*
ST	*Studia Theologica*
StABH	Studies in American Biblical Hermeneutics
TD	*Theology Digest*
TAD	*Textbook of Aramaic Documents from Ancient Egypt.* Vol. 1: *Letters.* Bezalel Porten and Ada Yardeni. Winona Lake, IN: Eisenbrauns, 1986.
TDOT	*Theological Dictionary of the Old Testament.* 15 vols. Edited by G. Johannes Botterweck, Helmer Ringgren, and Heinz-Josef Fabry. Translated by David E. Green and Douglas W. Stott. Grand Rapids: Eerdmans, 1974–1995.
TJT	*Toronto Journal of Theology*
TNTC	Tyndale New Testament Commentaries
TOTC	Tyndale Old Testament Commentaries
TS	*Theological Studies*
TZ	*Theologische Zeitschrift*
VE	*Vox evangelica*
VT	*Vetus Testamentum*
VTSup	Supplements to Vetus Testamentum
WBC	Word Biblical Commentary
WSA	Works of St. Augustine: A Translation for the Twenty-First Century
WUANT	Wissenschaftliche Untersuchungen zum Alten und Neuen Testament

WUNT	Wissenschaftliche Untersuchungen zum Neuen Testament
WW	*Word and World*
ZAW	*Zeitschrift für die alttestamentliche Wissenschaft*
ZBK	Zürcher Bibelkommentare
ZNW	*Zeitschrift für die neutestamentliche Wissenschaft und die Kunde der älteren Kirche*

Ancient Authors and Texts

1 Clem.	*1 Clement*
2 Clem.	*2 Clement*
1 En.	*1 Enoch*
2 Bar.	*2 Baruch*
Abot R. Nat.	*Abot de Rabbi Nathan*
Ambrose	
Paen.	*De paenitentia*
Aristotle	
Ath. Pol.	*Athēnaīn politeia*
Nic. Eth.	*Nicomachean Ethics*
Pol.	*Politics*
Rhet.	*Rhetoric*
Augustine	
FC 79	*Tractates on the Gospel of John, 11–27.* Translated by John W. Rettig. Fathers of the Church 79. Washington, DC: Catholic University of America Press, 1988.
Tract. Ev. Jo.	*In Evangelium Johannis tractatus*
Bede, Venerable	
CS 117	*Commentary on the Acts of the Apostles.* Translated by Lawrence T. Martin. Cistercian Studies 117. Kalamazoo, MI: Cistercian Publications, 1989.
Barn.	*Barnabas*
CD	Cairo Genizah copy of the Damascus Document
Cicero	
De or.	*De oratore*
Tusc.	*Tusculanae disputationes*
Clement of Alexandria	
Paed.	*Paedogogus*
Strom.	*Stromata*
Cyril of Jerusalem	
Cat. Lect.	*Catechetical Lectures*
Dio Cassius	
Hist.	*Roman History*

Dio Chrysostom
    Or.   *Orations*
Diog. *Diognetus*
Dionysius of Halicarnassus
    Thuc.   *De Thucydide*
Epictetus
    Diatr.   *Diatribai (Dissertationes)*
    Ench.   *Enchiridion*
Epiphanius
    Pan.   *Panarion (Adversus Haereses)*
Eusebius of Caesarea
    Hist. eccl.   *Historia ecclesiastica*
Gos. Thom.   *Gospel of Thomas*
Herodotus
    Hist.   *Historiae*
Hermas, *Shepherd*
    Mand.   *Mandates*
    Sim.   *Similitudes*
Homer
    Il.   *Iliad*
    Od.   *Odyssey*
Ignatius of Antioch
    Eph.   *To the Ephesians*
    Smyr.   *To the Smyrnaeans*
Irenaeus
    Adv. haer.   *Adversus haereses*
Jerome
    Vir. ill.   *De viris illustribus*
John Chrysostom
    Hom. 1 Cor.   *Homiliae in epistulam i ad Corinthios*
    Hom. Act.   *Homiliae in Acta apostolorum*
    Hom. Heb.   *Homiliae in epistulam ad Hebraeos*
Josephus
    Ant.   *Jewish Antiquities*
    Ag. Ap.   *Against Apion*
    J.W.   *Jewish War*
Jub.   *Jubilees*
Justin Martyr
    Dial.   *Dialogue with Trypho*
    1 Apol.   *First Apology*

L.A.E.	*Life of Adam and Eve*	
Liv. Pro.	*Lives of the Prophets*	
Lucian		
Alex.	*Alexander (Pseudomantis)*	
Phal.	*Phalaris*	
Mart. Pol.	*Martyrdom of Polycarp*	
Novatian		
Trin.	*De trinitate*	
Origen		
C. Cels.	*Contra Celsum*	
Comm. Jo.	*Commentarii in evangelium Joannis*	
De princ.	*De principiis*	
Hom. Exod.	*Homiliae in Exodum*	
Hom. Jer.	*Homiliae in Jeremiam*	
Hom. Josh.	*Homilies on Joshua*	
Pausanias		
Descr.	*Description of Greece*	
Philo		
Cher.	*De cherubim*	
Decal.	*De decalogo*	
Dreams	*On Dreams*	
Embassy	*On the Embassy to Gaius (= Legat.)*	
Fug.	*De fuga et inventione*	
Leg.	*Legum allegoriae*	
Legat.	*Legatio ad Gaium*	
Migr.	*De migratione Abrahami*	
Mos.	*De vita Mosis*	
Opif.	*De opificio mundi*	
Post.	*De posteritate Caini*	
Prob.	*Quod omnis probus liber sit*	
QE	*Quaestiones et solutiones in Exodum*	
QG	*Quaestiones et solutiones in Genesin*	
Spec. Laws	*On the Special Laws*	
Plato		
Gorg.	*Gorgias*	
Plutarch		
Mor.	*Moralia*	
Mulier. virt.	*Mulierum virtutes*	
Polycarp		
Phil.	*To the Philippians*	

Ps.-Clem. Rec.	*Pseudo-Clementine Recognitions*
Pss. Sol.	*Psalms of Solomon*
Pseudo-Philo	
L.A.B.	*Liber antiquitatum biblicarum*
Seneca	
Ben.	*De beneficiis*
Strabo	
Geog.	*Geographica*
Tatian	
Ad gr.	*Oratio ad Graecos*
Tertullian	
Praescr.	*De praescriptione haereticorum*
Prax.	*Adversus Praxean*
Bapt.	*De baptismo*
De an.	*De anima*
Pud.	*De pudicitia*
Virg.	*De virginibus velandis*
Virgil	
Aen.	*Aeneid*
Xenophon	
Oec.	*Oeconomicus*

Mishnah, Talmud, Targum

b. B. Bat.	*Babylonian Talmudic tractate Baba Batra*
b. Ber.	*Babylonian Talmudic tractate Berakhot*
b Erub.	*Babylonian Talmudic tractate Erubim*
b. Ketub.	*Babylonian Talmudic tractate Ketubbot*
b. Mak.	*Babylonian Talmudic tractate Makkot*
b. Meg.	*Babylonian Talmudic tractate Megillah*
b. Ned.	*Babylonian Talmudic tractate Nedarim*
b. Naz.	*Babylonian Talmudic tractate Nazir*
b. Sanh.	*Babylonian Talmudic tractate Sanhedrin*
b. Shab.	*Babylonian Talmudic tractate Shabbat*
b. Sotah	*Babylonian Talmudic tractate Sotah*
b. Taʿan.	*Babylonian Talmudic tractate Taʿanit*
b. Yev.	*Babylonian Talmudic tractate Yevamot*
b. Yoma	*Babylonian Talmudic tractate Yoma*
Eccl. Rab.	*Ecclesiastes Rabbah*
Exod. Rab.	*Exodus Rabbah*
Gen. Rab.	*Genesis Rabbah*

Lam. Rab.	*Lamentations Rabbah*
Lev. R(ab).	*Leviticus Rabbah*
m. Abot	*Mishnah tractate Abot*
m. Bik.	*Mishnah tractate Bikkurim*
m. Demai	*Mishnah tractate Demai*
m. 'Ed.	*Mishnah tractate 'Eduyyot*
m. Git.	*Mishnah tractate Gittin*
m. Pesaḥ	*Mishnah tractate Pesaḥim*
m. Šeqal.	*Mishnah tractate Šeqalim (Shekalim)*
m. Shab.	*Mishnah tractate Shabbat*
m. Sotah	*Mishnah tractate Sotah*
m. Ta'an.	*Mishnah tractate Ta'anit*
m. Tamid	*Mishnah tractate Tamid*
m. Yad.	*Mishnah tractate Yadayim*
m. Yebam.	*Mishnah tractate Yebamot*
m. Yoma	*Mishnah tractate Yoma*
Num. Rab.	*Numbers Rabbah*
Pesiq. Rab.	*Pesiqta Rabbati*
Pesiq. Rab Kah.	*Pesiqta Rab Kahana*
S. 'Olam Rab.	*Seder 'Olam Rabbah*
Song Rab.	*Song of Songs Rabbah*
t. Hul.	*Tosefta tractate Hullin*
Tg. Onq.	*Targum Onqelos*
Tg. Jer.	*Targum Jeremiah*
y. Hag.	*Jerusalem Talmudic tractate Hagiga*
y. Pesaḥ	*Jerusalem Talmudic tractate Pesaḥim*
y. Sanh.	*Jerusalem Talmudic tractate Sanhedrin*

Dead Sea Scrolls

1QapGen	*Genesis apocryphon* (Excavated frags. from cave)
1QM	*War Scroll*
1QpHab	*Pesher Habakkuk*
1QS	*Rule of the Community*
1QSb	*Rule of the Blessings* (Appendix b to 1QS)
1Q21	*T. Levi*, aramaic
4Q184	Wiles of the Wicked Woman
4Q214	Levi[d] ar (*olim* part of Levi[b])
4Q214b	Levi[f] ar (*olim* part of Levi[b])
4Q226	psJub[b] (4Q *pseudo-Jubilees*)
4Q274	Tohorot A

4Q277	Tohorot B^b (*olim* B^c)
4Q525	*Beatitudes*
4QMMT	*Miqsat Maʿaśê ha-Torah*
4QpNah/4Q169	4Q Pesher Nahum
4Q82	*The Greek Minor Prophets Scroll*

Old Testament Pseudepigrapha

1 En.	*1 Enoch*
2 En.	*2 Enoch*
Odes Sol.	*Odes of Solomon*
Syr. Men.	*Sentences of the Syriac Menander*
T. Levi	*Testament of Levi*
T. Mos.	*Testament of Moses*
T. Sim.	*Testament of Simeon*

INTRODUCTION

The *Fortress Commentary on the Bible*, presented in two volumes, seeks to invite study and conversation about an ancient text that is both complex and compelling. As biblical scholars, we wish students of the Bible to gain a respect for the antiquity and cultural remoteness of the biblical texts and to grapple for themselves with the variety of their possible meanings; to fathom a long history of interpretation in which the Bible has been wielded for causes both beneficial and harmful; and to develop their own skills and voices as responsible interpreters, aware of their own social locations in relationships of privilege and power. With this in mind, the *Fortress Commentary on the Bible* offers general readers an informed and accessible resource for understanding the biblical writings in their ancient contexts; for recognizing how the texts have come down to us through the mediation of different interpretive traditions; and for engaging current discussion of the Bible's sometimes perplexing, sometimes ambivalent, but always influential legacy in the contemporary world. The commentary is designed not only to inform but also to invite and empower readers as active interpreters of the Bible in their own right.

The editors and contributors to these volumes are scholars and teachers who are committed to helping students engage the Bible in the classroom. Many also work as leaders, both lay and ordained, in religious communities, and wish this commentary to prove useful for informing congregational life in clear, meaningful, and respectful ways. We also understand the work of biblical interpretation as a responsibility far wider than the bounds of any religious community. In this regard, we participate in many and diverse identities and social locations, yet we all are conscious of reading, studying, and hearing the Bible today as citizens of a complex and interconnected world. We recognize in the Bible one of the most important legacies of human culture; its historical and literary interpretation is of profound interest to religious and nonreligious people alike.

Often, the academic interpretation of the Bible has moved from close study of the remote ancient world to the rarefied controversy of scholarly debate, with only occasional attention to the ways biblical texts are actually heard and lived out in the world around us. The commentary seeks to provide students with diverse materials on the ways in which these texts have been interpreted through the course of history, as well as helping students understand the texts' relevance for today's globalized world. It recognizes the complexities that are involved with being an engaged reader of the Bible, providing a powerful tool for exploring the Bible's multilayered meanings in both their ancient and modern contexts. The commentary seeks to address contemporary issues that are raised by biblical passages. It aspires to be keenly aware of how the contemporary world and its issues and perspectives influence the interpretation of the Bible. Many of the most important insights of contemporary biblical scholarship not only have come from expertise in the world of antiquity but have also been forged in modern struggles for dignity, for equality, for sheer survival, and out of respect for those who have died without seeing justice done. Gaining familiarity with the original contexts in which the biblical writings were produced is essential, but not sufficient, for encouraging competent and discerning interpretation of the Bible's themes today.

Inside the Commentary

Both volumes of *The Fortress Commentary on the Bible* are organized in a similar way. In the beginning of each volume, **Topical Articles** set the stage on which interpretation takes place, naming the issues and concerns that have shaped historical and theological scholarship down to the present. Articles in the *Fortress Commentary on the Old Testament* attend, for example, to the issues that arise when two different religious communities claim the same body of writings as their Scripture, though interpreting those writings quite differently. Articles in the *Fortress Commentary on the New Testament* address the consequences of Christianity's historic claim to appropriate Jewish Scripture and to supplement it with a second collection of writings, the experience of rootlessness and diaspora, and the legacy of apocalypticism. Articles in both volumes reflect on the historical intertwining of Christianity with imperial and colonial power and with indexes of racial and socioeconomic privilege.

Section Introductions in the Old Testament volume provide background to the writings included in the Torah, Historical Writings, Wisdom, Prophetic Writings, and a general introduction to the Apocrypha. The New Testament volume includes articles introducing the Gospels, Acts, the letters associated with Paul, Hebrews, the General Epistles, and Revelation. These articles will address the literary and historical matters, as well as theological themes, that the books in these collections hold in common.

Commentary Entries present accessible and judicious discussion of each biblical book, beginning with an introduction to current thinking regarding the writing's original context and its significance in different reading communities down to the present day. A three-level commentary then follows for each sense division of the book. In some cases these follow the chapter divisions of a biblical book, but more often contributors have discerned other outlines, depending on matters of genre, movement, or argument.

The three levels of commentary are the most distinctive organizational feature of these volumes. The first level, "The Text in Its Ancient Context," addresses relevant lexical, exegetical, and literary aspects of the text, along with cultural and archaeological information that may provide additional insight into the historical context. This level of the commentary describes consensus views where these exist in current scholarship and introduces issues of debate clearly and fairly. Our intent here is to convey some sense of the historical and cultural distance between the text's original context and the contemporary reader.

The second level, "The Text in the Interpretive Tradition," discusses themes including Jewish and Christian tradition as well as other religious, literary, and artistic traditions where the biblical texts have attracted interest. This level is shaped by our conviction that we do not apprehend these texts immediately or innocently; rather, even the plain meaning we may regard as self-evident may have been shaped by centuries of appropriation and argument to which we are heirs.

The third level, "The Text in Contemporary Discussion," follows the history of interpretation into the present, drawing brief attention to a range of issues. Our aim here is not to deliver a single answer—"what the text means"—to the contemporary reader, but to highlight unique challenges and interpretive questions. We pay special attention to occasions of dissonance: aspects of the text or of its interpretation that have become questionable, injurious, or even intolerable to some readers today. Our goal is not to provoke a referendum on the value of the text but to stimulate reflection and discussion and, in this way, to empower the reader to reach his or her own judgments about the text.

The approach of this commentary articulates a particular understanding of the work of responsible biblical interpretation. We seek through this commentary to promote intelligent and mature engagement with the Bible, in religious communities and in academic classrooms alike, among pastors, theologians, and ethicists, but also and especially among nonspecialists. Our work together has given us a new appreciation for the vocation of the biblical scholar, as custodians of a treasure of accumulated wisdom from our predecessors; as stewards at a table to which an ever-expanding circle is invited; as neighbors and fellow citizens called to common cause, regardless of our different professions of faith. If the result of our work here is increased curiosity about the Bible, new questions about its import, and new occasions for mutual understanding among its readers, our work will be a success.

Fortress Commentary on the Old Testament

Gale A. Yee
Episcopal Divinity School

Hugh R. Page Jr.
University of Notre Dame

Matthew J. M. Coomber
St. Ambrose University

Fortress Commentary on the New Testament

Margaret Aymer
Interdenominational Theological Center

Cynthia Briggs Kittredge
Seminary of the Southwest

David A. Sánchez
Loyola Marymount University

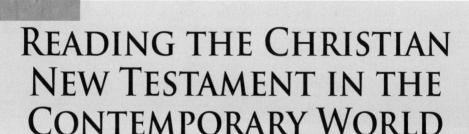

READING THE CHRISTIAN NEW TESTAMENT IN THE CONTEMPORARY WORLD

Kwok Pui-lan

On Ascension Sunday in May 2012, the faculty and students of my school who were taking part in a travel seminar to China attended the worship service at the Shanghai Community Church. We arrived half an hour before the service began, and the church, which can accommodate about two thousand people, was already filled to capacity. Another two thousand people who could not get into the sanctuary watched the worship service on closed-circuit TV in other rooms in the church building. Through this experience and while visiting churches in other cities, we learned about and encountered the phenomenal growth of the Chinese churches in the past twenty-five years. The official statistics put the number of Chinese Christians at around 30 million, but unofficial figures range from 50 to 100 million, if those who belong to the unregistered house churches are counted. China is poised to become the country with the highest number of Christians, and China has already become the largest printer and user of the Bible in the world. In 2012, the Amity Printing Company in Nanjing celebrated the publishing of 100 million Bibles since its inception in 1987 (United Bible Societies 2012).

Besides China, sub-Saharan Africa has also experienced rapid church growth, especially among the African Independent Churches, Pentecostal churches, and Roman Catholic churches. By 2025, Africa will be the continent with the greatest number of Christians, at more than 670 million. At the turn of the twentieth century, 70 percent of the world's Christians were European. By 2000, that number had dropped to 28 percent (Flatow). The shift of Christian demographics to the South and the prospect of Christianity becoming a non-Western religion have attracted the attention of scholars and popular media (Sanneh 2003; Jenkins; Johnson and Ross). According to the *World Christian Encyclopedia*, almost two-thirds of the readers of the Bible are Christians from Africa, Asia, Latin America, and Oceania (around 1.178 billion) as compared to Europe and America (around 661 million) and Orthodox Eastern Europe (around 158 million) (Patte, xxi).

These changing Christian demographics have significant implications for reading the Bible as global citizens in the contemporary world. To promote global and intercultural understanding, we can no longer read the Bible in a narrow and parochial way, without being aware of how Christians in other parts of the world are reading it in diverse linguistic, cultural, and social contexts. In the past decade, biblical scholars have increasingly paid attention to global perspectives on the Bible to prepare Christians to live in our complex, pluralistic, and transnational world (Patte; Wicker, Miller, and Dube; Roncace and Weaver). For those of us living in the Global North, it is important to pay attention to liberative readings from the Global South and to the voices from the majority world. Today, the field of biblical studies has been enlivened and broadened by scholars from many social locations and culturally and religiously diverse contexts.

The New Testament in Global Perspectives

The New Testament touches on many themes highly relevant for our times, such as racial and ethnic relations, religious pluralism, social and political domination, gender oppression, and religious movements for resistance. The early followers of Jesus were Jews and gentiles living in the Hellenistic world under the rule of the Roman Empire. Christianity developed largely in urban cities in which men and women from different linguistic, cultural, and religious backgrounds interacted and commingled with one another (Theissen; Meeks). Christians in the early centuries lived among Jews and people devoted to emperor cults, Greek religion, and other indigenous traditions in the ancient Near East. Jesus and his disciples spoke Aramaic, the common language of Palestine. The New Testament was written in Koine Greek, the lingua franca of much of the Mediterranean region and the Middle East since the conquest of Alexander the Great. Living under the shadow of the Roman Empire, early Christians had to adapt to the cultures and social structures of empire, as well as resist the domination of imperial rule.

From its beginning in Palestine and the Mediterranean, Christianity spread to other parts of the Roman Empire and became the dominant religion during Constantine's time. Some of the notable early theologians hailed from northern Africa: Origen (c. 185–254) and Athanasius (c. 300–373) from Alexandria, Tertullian (160–225) from Carthage, and Augustine (354–431) of Hippo. While Christianity was persecuted in the Roman Empire prior to 313, it found its way to the regions east of the Tigris River possibly as early as the beginning of the second century. Following ancient trade routes, merchants and missionaries brought Christianity from the Mediterranean to the Persian Gulf and across central Asia all the way to China (Baum and Winkler, 8). In the early modern period, Christianity was brought to the Americas and other parts of the world, with the help of the political and military power of colonizing empires. Even though Christianity was a world religion, the study of church history in the past tended to focus on Europe and North America and to marginalize the histories in other parts of the world. Today, scholars of world Christianity have contested such Eurocentric biases. They have produced comprehensive accounts that restore the peoples of Africa, the Near East, and Asia to their rightful place in the rich and multilayered Christian tradition (Hastings; Irvin and Sunquist 2001; 2012; Sanneh 2007).

The translation of the Bible, especially the New Testament, into the native and vernacular languages of different peoples was and remains an important strategy of Christian missions. The United Bible Societies (2013) report that the complete Bible has been translated into at least 451 languages and the New Testament into some 1,185. The Bible is the most translated collection of texts in the world. There are now 2,370 languages in which at least one book of the Bible has been produced. Although this figure represents less than half of some 6,000 languages and dialects presently in use in the world, it includes the primary means of communication of well over 90 percent of the world's population.

Most Christians are more familiar with the New Testament than the Hebrew Bible. The New Testament is read and preached throughout the world in liturgical settings and worship services, taught in seminaries and church Sunday schools, studied in private devotions, and discussed in Bible study groups, women's fellowships, college campuses, and grassroots religious organizations and movements. Christians, Jews, Muslims, and atheists debate the meaning of Jesus and the gospel in books, mass media, and on the Internet. The life and the story of Jesus Christ have been depicted and interpreted in popular culture, such as films, songs, music videos, fiction, blogs, websites, photographs, paintings, sculpture, and other forms of art. The study of the New Testament is not limited to the study of the biblical text, but includes how the text is used in concrete contexts in Christian communities, popular media, and public spheres.

The Bible is taken to mean many things in our contemporary world. Christian communities regard the Bible as *Scripture*, and many Christians think that it has authority over their beliefs and moral behavior. In the academy, the Bible is treated more as a *historical document*, to be studied by rigorous historical criticism. Increasingly, the Bible is also seen as a *cultural product*, embedded in the sociocultural and ideological assumptions of its time. The meaning of the Bible is not fixed but is continually produced as readers interact with it in different contexts. The diverse understanding of what the Bible is often creates a clash of opinions. For example, Christians may think Lady Gaga's "Judas" video (2011) has gone too far in deviating from orthodox teaching. There is also a wide gap in the ways the Bible is read in the church and academy. The experts' reading may challenge the beliefs of those sitting in the pews.

In the field of biblical studies, Fernando F. Segovia (34–52) delineates three stages in the development of academic biblical criticism in the twentieth century. The historical-critical method has been the dominant mode of interpretation in academia since the middle of the nineteenth century. The meaning of the text is seen as residing *behind* the text—in the world that shaped the text, in the author's intention, or both. The second stage is literary criticism, which emerged in the middle of 1970s in dialogue with literary and psychoanalytic theory. The literary critics emphasize the meaning *in* the text and focus on genre, plot, structure, rhetoric, levels of narration, and characterization as depicted in the world of the text. The third stage is cultural studies or ideological criticism of the Bible, which developed also in the 1970s, when critics from the two-thirds world, feminist theologians, and racial and ethnic minority scholars in North America began to increase their numbers in the guild. They have increasingly paid attention to the flesh-and-blood readers *in front of* the text, who employ different methods, such as storytelling and reader-response criticism, in their interaction with the text to construct meaning in response to concerns arising from their communities.

The shift to the flesh-and-blood reader contests the assumption that there is a "universal" reader and an "objective" interpretation applicable to all times and places. The claim of an "objective" and "scientific" reading is based on a positivistic understanding of historiography, which presumes that historical facts can be objectively reconstructed, following established criteria in Western academia. But the historical-critical method is only one of the many methods and should not be taken as the "universal" norm for judging other methodologies. Its dominance is the result of the colonial legacy as well as the continued hegemony of Eurocentric knowledge and cultural production of our time. Nowadays, many methods are available, and biblical critics have increasingly used interdisciplinary approaches and a combination of theories and methods, such as postmodern theory, postcolonial theory, and queer studies, for interpretation (Crossley; Moore 2010).

What this means is the democratization of the study of the Bible, because no one group of people has a monopoly over the meaning of the Bible and no single method can exhaust its "truths." To understand the richness of the biblical tradition, we have to learn to listen to the voices of people from multiple locations and senses of belonging. Eleazar S. Fernandez (140) points out, "real flesh-and-blood readers assume a variety of positions—in relation to time, geography, geopolitics, diaspora location, social location, religion, ethnicity, gender, sexuality, and so on—in the power-knowledge nexus that inform their readings and cultural or religious discursive productions in the global market." Interpreting the Bible in global perspectives requires us to pay attention to the contextual character of reading and the relationships and tensions between the global and the local.

Reading the New Testament in Diverse Contexts

The shift from the author and the text to the reader means that we need to understand the ways the Bible functions in diverse sociolingusitic contexts (Blount 1995). Our critical task must go further than analyzing the text and the processes for production and interpretation, to include the cultural and social conditions that influence the history of reception. Let us go back to the examples of reading the Bible in the Chinese and African contexts. When Christianity arrived in China, the Chinese had a long hermeneutical tradition of interpreting Confucian, Buddhist, and Daoist texts. The missionaries and biblical translators had to borrow from indigenous religious ideas to translate biblical terminologies, such as God, heaven, and hell. The rapid social and political changes in modern China affected how the Bible is read by Christians living in a Communist society (Eber, Wan, and Walf). When the Bible was introduced to the African continent, it encountered a rich and complex language world of oral narratives, legends, proverbs, and folktales. The interpretation of oral texts is different from that of written ones. In some instances, the translation of the Bible into the vernacular languages has changed the oral cultures into written cultures, with both positive and negative effects on social development (Sanneh 1989). And if we examine the history of translation and reception of the English Bible, we will see how the processes have been affected by the rise of nationalism, colonial expansion, and the diverse forms of English used in the English-speaking world (Sugirtharajah 2002, 127–54).

Some Christians may feel uneasy about the fact that the Bible is read in so many different ways. For the fundamentalists who believe in biblical inerrancy and literal interpretation, multiple ways of reading undermine biblical authority. Even liberals might wonder if the diversity of readings will open the doors to relativism. But as James Barr has pointed out, the appeal to the Bible as authority for all doctrinal matters and the assumption that its meaning is fixed cannot be verified by the Bible itself. Both Jesus and Paul took the liberty to repudiate, criticize, and reinterpret parts of the Hebrew Bible (Barr, 12–19). Moreover, as Mary Ann Tolbert has noted, since the Reformation, when the doctrine of *sola scriptura* was brought to the forefront, the invocation of biblical authority by various ecclesiastical bodies has generally been negative and exclusive. "It has been used most often to *exclude* certain groups or people, to *pass judgment* on various disapproved activities, and to *justify* morally or historically debatable positions [such as slavery]" (1998, 142). The doctrinal appeal to biblical authority and the insistence on monocultural reading often mask power dynamics, which allow some groups of people to exercise control over others who have less power, including women, poor people, racial and ethnic minorities, and gay people and lesbians.

Multiple readings and plurality of meaning do not necessarily lead to relativism, but can foster deeper awareness of our own interpretive assumptions and broaden our horizons. In his introduction to the *Global Bible Commentary*, Daniel Patte (xxi–xxxii) offers some helpful suggestions. (1) We have to acknowledge the contextual character of our interpretation. There is no context-free reading, whether in the past or in the present. (2) We have to stop and listen to the voices of biblical readers who have long been silenced in each context. (3) We have to learn the reading strategies and critical tradition developed in other parts of the world, such as enculturation, liberation, and inter(con)textuality. Contextual readings do not mean anything goes or that interpreters may proceed without self-critique. (4) We have to respect other people's readings and assume responsibility for our own interpretation. (5) Other people's readings often lead us to see our blind spots, and invite us to notice aspects of the Bible we have overlooked. (6) We have to learn to read *with* others in community, rather than reading *for* or *to* them, assuming our reading is superior to others.

We can use the different readings of the story of the Syrophoenician woman (Matt. 15:21-28; Mark 7:24-30) to illustrate this point. Many Christians have been taught that the story is about Jesus' mission to the gentiles, because Jesus went to the border place of Tyre and Sidon and healed the gentile woman's daughter and praised her faith. Japanese biblical scholar Hisako Kinukawa (51–65), however, does not emphasize gentile mission but Jesus' crossing ethnic boundaries to accept others. She places the story in the cultic purity and ethnic exclusion of first-century Palestine and draws parallels to the discrimination of Koreans as minorities living in Japan. We shall see that the generalization of first-century culture may be problematic. Nevertheless, Kinukawa argues that the gentile woman changed Jesus' attitude from rejection to affirmation and created an opportunity for Jesus to cross the boundary. Jesus has set an example, she says, for Japanese people to challenge their assumptions of a homogeneous race, to overcome their prejudice toward ethnic minorities, and to respect other peoples' dignity and human rights.

On the African continent, Musa W. Dube, from Botswana, emphasizes the importance of *reading with* ordinary readers. She set out to find out how women in the African Independent Churches in Botswana read the Matthean version of the story (2000, 187–90). She found that some of the women emphasized that Jesus was testing the woman's faith. They said the meaning of the word "dog" should not be taken literally, as Jesus often spoke in parables. Several women did not read the story as if Jesus had insulted the woman by comparing the Canaanites as "dogs" to the Israelites as children. Instead, they saw the Canaanite woman as one of the children because of her faith, and the "dogs" referred to the demonic spirits. This must be understood in the context of the belief in spirits in the African religious worldview. The women interpreted the woman's answer to Jesus, that even the dogs eat the crumbs from the master's table (Matt. 15:27), to mean that no one is permanently and totally undeserving. The women believed that Jesus had come for all people, without regard for race and ethnicities.

These two examples show how social and cultural backgrounds affect the interpretation of the story and the lessons drawn for today. The majority of interpreters, whether scholars or ordinary readers, have focused on the interaction between Jesus and the woman. I would like to cite two other readings that bring to the forefront other details of the text that have been overlooked. Laura E. Donaldson reads the story from a postcolonial Native American perspective and places the "demon-possessed" daughter at the center of her critical analysis. In the text, the daughter does not speak, and her illness is considered taboo and stigmatizing. Donaldson challenges our complicity in such a reading and employs the insights of disabilities studies to demystify the construction of "able" and "disabled" persons. She then points out that the Canaanites were the indigenous people of the land, and the daughter might not be suffering from an illness pejoratively identified as "demon possession" by the Christian text. Instead, the daughter may be in an altered state of consciousness, which is a powerful form of knowing in many indigenous spiritual traditions. For Donaldson, the daughter may "signify a trace of the indigenous," who has the power to access other sites of knowledge (104–5).

While many commentators have noted the lowly position of dogs in ancient Mediterranean and Near East culture, Stephen D. Moore, who grew up in Ireland and teaches in the United States, looks at the Matthean story through the prism of human-animal relations. He contrasts the construction of the son of man with the dog-woman in Matthew. While the son of man is not an animal and asserts power, sovereignty, and self-control, following the elite Greco-Roman concept of masculinity, the dog-woman of Canaan embodies the categories of savages, women, and beasts. Jesus said that he was sent to the lost sheep of the house of Israel and it was not fair to take the children's food and throw it to the dogs. The problem of the dog-woman is that she is not a sheep woman. The image of Canaan as heathen, savage, and less than human justified the colonization of non-Christian people in Africa, the Americas, and other regions. Moore notes that the image of "heathens" in nineteenth- and twentieth-century biblical commentary conjured up the reality of "unsaved" dark-skinned people in need of Christ and in need of civilizing, and hence in need of colonizing (Moore 2013, 63). Moore's reading points out that mission to the gentiles may not be benign, and might mask colonial impulses.

These diverse interpretations of the Syrophoenician woman's story illustrate how reading with other people can radically expand our imagination. We can see how a certain part of the story is emphasized or reinterpreted by different readers to address particular concerns. Sensitivity to contextual and cross-cultural interpretation helps us to live in a pluralistic world in which people have different worldviews and assumptions. Through genuine dialogue and listening to others, we can enrich ourselves and work with others to create a better world.

Interpretation for Liberation

In the second half of the twentieth century, people's popular movements and protests led to the development of liberation theologies in various parts of the world. In Africa and Asia, anticolonial struggles resulted in political independence and people's demand for cultural autonomy. In Latin America, theologians and activists criticized the dependence theory of development, which continues to keep poor countries dependent on rich countries because of unequal global economic structures. Women from all over the globe, racial and ethnic minorities, and lesbian, gay, bisexual, and transgender people have also begun to articulate their theologies. People who are multiply oppressed began to read the Bible through the intersection of gender, race, class, sexuality, religion, and colonialism. I focus on liberative readings from the Global South here.

Following Vatican II (1962–1965), Latin American liberation theology began to develop in the 1960s and focused on social and economic oppression and the disparity between the rich and the poor. Using Marxist analysis as a critical tool, liberation theologians in Latin America argued that the poor are the subjects of history and that God has a preferential option for the poor. They insisted that theology is a reflection of social praxis, which seeks to change the oppressive situation that the majority of the people find themselves in. Juan Luis Segundo (9) developed a hermeneutical circle that consists of four steps: (1) our way of experiencing reality leads to ideological suspicion, (2) which we apply to the whole ideological superstructure, and especially theology, (3) being aware of how prevailing interpretation of the Bible does not take important data into account, resulting in (4) the development of a new hermeneutic.

Latin American theologians contested the formulation of traditional Christology and presented Christ as the liberator. The gospel of Jesus Christ is not about saving individual souls, without import for our concrete lives. In *A Theology of Liberation*, Gustavo Gutiérrez (102–5) argues that Christ is the liberator who opts for the poor. Jesus' death and resurrection liberates us from sin. Sin, however, is not private, but a social, historical fact. It is the absence of fellowship of love in relationship among persons and the breach of relationship with God. Christ offers us the gift of radical liberation and enables us to enter into communion with God and with others. Liberation, for Gutiérrez, has three levels: political liberation, liberation in the course of history, and liberation from sin and into communion with God.

Latin American women theologians have criticized their male colleagues' lack of attention to women's issues and *machismo* in Latin American culture. Elsa Tamez, from Mexico, is a leading scholar who has published extensively on reading the New Testament from a Latin American feminist perspective (2001; 2007). She has raised questions about Jesus' relation with women in the Gospels and the class difference between rich and poor women in the early Christian movement. The discussion of the Bible in the base Christian communities and women's groups helped spread the ideas of liberation theology among the populace. A collection of discussions of the gospel by Nicaraguan peasants who belonged to the Christian community of Solentiname was published as *The Gospel in Solentiname* (Cardenal). The peasants approached the Bible from their life situation of extreme poverty, and they connected with Jesus' revolutionary work in solidarity with the poor of his time. Some of the peasants also painted the scenes from the Gospels and identified biblical events with events leading to the 1979 Sandinista revolution (Scharper and Scharper). In response to the liberation movement, which had spread to the whole continent, the Vatican criticized liberation theology and replaced progressive bishops with conservative ones. But second-generation liberation theologians continue the work of their pioneers and expand the liberation theological project to include race, gender, sexuality, migration, and popular religions (Petrella).

Unlike in Latin America, where Christians are the majority of the population, Christians in many parts of Africa and Asia live among people of other faith traditions. Here, interpretation of the Bible follows two broad approaches. The liberation approach focuses on sociopolitical dimensions, such as the fight over poverty, dictatorship, apartheid, and other social injustice. The enculturation or the indigenization approach brings the Bible into dialogue with the African or Asian worldviews, popular religion, and cultural idiom. The two approaches are not mutually exclusive, and a holistic transformation of society must deal with changing the sociopolitical structures as well as the culture and mind-sets of people.

One of the key questions for those who read the Bible in religiously pluralistic contexts is how to honor others who have different religious identities and cultures. Some of the passages in the New Testament have been used to support an exclusive attitude toward other religions. For example, Jesus said that he is the way and no one comes to the Father except through him (John 14:6) and charged his followers with the Great Commission, to "make disciples of all nations" (Matt. 28:19). But as Wesley Ariarajah (1989) has said, the universality of Christ supports the spirit of openness, mutual understanding, and interfaith dialogue with others. In Acts 10:9-16, Peter is challenged in a vision to consider nothing unclean that God has made clean. He crosses the boundary that separates Jews and gentiles and meets with Cornelius, the Roman centurion, which leads to his conversion. When Paul speaks to the Athenians, he says that they are extremely religious, and he employs a religious language different from that when he speaks to the Jews (Acts 17:22-31). Ariarajah argues that openness to others and dialogue does not contradict Christian witness.

In their protests against political oppression and dictatorship, Asian Christians have reread the Bible to empower them to fight for human rights and dignity. *Minjung* theology arose in South Korea during the 1970s against the dictatorship of the Park Chung Hee government. The word *minjung* comes from two Chinese characters meaning the masses of people. New Testament scholar Ahn Byung Mu points out that in the Gospel of Mark, the *ochlos* ("crowd or multitude") follows Jesus from place to place, listens to his teachings, and witnesses his miracles. They form the background of Jesus' activities. They stand on Jesus' side, against the rulers of Jerusalem, who criticize and challenge Jesus (Mark 2:4-7; 3:2-22; 11:8; 11:27; 11:32). Jesus has "compassion for them, because they were like sheep without a shepherd" (6:34). Jesus proclaims to them "the kingdom of God has come near" (1:15). He identifies with the suffering *minjung* and offers them a new hope and new life. *Minjung* theology developed a political hermeneutics not for the elite but for the people, and spoke to the Korean reality at the time.

In India, the caste system has subjected the Dalits—the "untouchables"—to the lowest rank of society. Dalits are the oppressed and the broken. They are discriminated against in terms of education, occupation, social interaction, and social mobility. The prejudice against the Dalits is so deep-seated that they face a great deal of discrimination even in Indian churches. Dalit theology emerged because of the insensitivity of the Indian churches to the plight of the Dalits and to give voice to Dalits' struggle for justice. In constructing a Dalit Christology, Peniel Rajkumar (115–26) finds Jesus' healing stories particularly relevant to the Dalit situation. Jesus touches and heals the leper (Mark 1:40-45), and transcends the social norms regarding purity and pollution. Afterward, Jesus asks the man to show his body to the priest (Mark 1:44) to bear witness that he has been healed and to confront the ideological purity system that alienates him. Jesus is angry at the system that maintains ritual purity to alienate and classify people. In coming to ask for healing, the leper also shows his faith through his willingness to break the cultural norm of purity. Again, we will find that the generalization of Jewish culture and purity taboo may be open to criticism. Jesus' anger toward injustice and his partnership with the leper to create a new social reality would help Dalits in their present struggles. The emphasis of Jesus' crossing boundaries is a recurrent theme in other Dalit readings (Nelavala). Many of the Dalit women from poor rural and urban areas are illiterate and do not have access to the written text of the Bible. The use of methods such as storytelling and role-play has helped them gain insights into biblical stories (Melanchthon).

In Africa, biblical scholars have addressed poverty, apartheid, religious and ethnic strife, HIV and AIDS, and political oppression, all of which have wreaked havoc in the continent. During apartheid in South Africa, a black theology of liberation was developed to challenge the Western and white outlook of the Christian church and to galvanize people to fight against apartheid. Itumeleng J. Mosala developed a historical-materialist reading of the Bible based on black history and culture. Mosala and his colleagues from Africa have asserted that Latin American liberation hermeneutics has not taken seriously the history of the blacks and Indians. His reading of Luke 1 and 2 brings out the material condition of the text, focusing on the colonial occupation of Palestine by Rome and the imperial extraction from peasants and the poor. He then uses the history, culture, and struggle of black people as a hermeneutical tool to lay bare the ideological assumptions in Luke's Gospel, showing it to be speaking for the class interest of the rich and eclipsing the experiences of the poor. He charges that some of the black theologians have continued to use Western and white hermeneutics even as they oppose the white, dominant groups. What is necessary is a new hermeneutics based on a black working-class perspective, which raises new questions in the interpretative process and enables a mutual interrogation between the text and situation.

In order to develop this kind of hermeneutics, biblical scholars must be socially engaged and read the Bible from the underside. With whom one is reading the Bible becomes both an epistemological and an ethical question. Several African biblical scholars emphasize the need for socially engaged scholars to read the Bible with ordinary poor and marginalized "readers." Gerald O. West maintains that if liberation theology begins with the experience of the poor and the oppressed, then these persons must be invited and included in the dialogical process of doing theology and reading the Bible. He describes the process of contextual Bible study among the poor, the roles of engaged biblical scholars, and lessons gleaned from the process. In the contextual reading of Luke 4:16-22, for instance, the women living around Pietermaritzburg and Durban related the meaning of setting the prisoners free, healing of the blind, and the relief of debts to their society. They discussed what they could do following the insights from the story to organize their community and create social change.

The Circle of Concerned African Women Theologians, formed in 1989, has encouraged Christian women from the African continent to produce and publish biblical and contextual hermeneutics. Some of the contributions have been published in *Other Ways of Reading: African Women and the Bible* (Dube 2001). The authors discuss storytelling methods, reading with and from nonacademic readers, toward a postapartheid black feminist reading, and the divination method of interpretation. The volume demystifies the notion of biblical canon, showing how women of the African continent have read the Bible with the canon of various African oral cultures. Aspects of African cultures serve as theories for analyzing the Bible. The volume is also conversant with feminist readings from other parts of the world, and in particular with African American women's hermeneutical approaches.

The HIV and AIDS epidemic brings enormous loss of life and suffering in the African continent, and the virus has spread mostly among heterosexual people. There is an increasing concern that in the sub-Saharan region, HIV infects more women than men. Musa Dube has played a key role in helping the African churches and theological institutions in addressing HIV and AIDS issues. In *The HIV and AIDS Bible* (Dube 2008), she implores scholars to develop biblical scholarship that is prophetic and healing. She challenges patriarchy and gender justice, and urges the churches to move beyond their comfort zone to respond to people affected by the virus. The church is HIV positive, she claims. Reading with people living with AIDS allows her to see the potential of the Bible to liberate and heal. She brings new insights to reading the miracles and healing stories of Jesus, such as the healing of Jairus's daughter (Mark 5:21-45). Her reading breaks the stigma and silence around HIV and AIDS while calling for adequate and compassionate care, and placing the HIV and AIDS epidemic within the larger context of other social discrimination.

The biblical readings from the Global South contribute to a global scholarship that takes into account other religious texts and classics in what is called intercultural and cross-textual reading (Lee). It is also interpreted through the lens of oral texts and retold and performed through storytelling, role-play, and skits. The exploration of these methods decentralizes Eurocentric modes of thinking that have gripped biblical studies for so long. It allows us to see the Bible and the world with fresh perspectives and new insights.

Contemporary Approaches to the New Testament

Books that introduce the wide array of contemporary methods used to interpret the New Testament are readily available (Anderson and Moore; Crossley). I have selected a few approaches that have global significance, as scholars from both the Global North and the Global South have used them and commented on them to illustrate current discussions shaping biblical scholarship. We will look at feminist approaches, social scientific approaches, racial and ethnic minority approaches, and postcolonial approaches.

Feminist Approaches

The New Testament was written by authors who lived in a patriarchal world with androcentric values and mind-sets. For a long time, churches have used parts of the Bible to deny women's full participation and treat them as second-class citizens in church and society. For example, churches have denied women's ordination based on the argument that all of Jesus' disciples were male. People have also cited the household codes (Col. 3:18—4:1; Eph. 5:21—6:9; 1 Peter 2:18—3:7) to support wives' submission to their husbands. Paul's teaching that women should be silent in the church (1 Cor. 14:34-35) has often been used to deny women's religious leadership. It is little wonder that some Western feminists have concluded that the Bible is irredeemably sexist and have become post-Christian. But feminist interpreters around the globe have developed ingenious ways to read against the grain and to find the Bible's liberating potential.

Christian feminists in many parts of the world have focused on stories about women in the Gospels. They have shown that women followed Jesus, listened to his preaching, and were healed because of their faith. Even when the disciples deserted Jesus at the cross, women steadfastly showed their faith. Scholars have drawn from some of these Gospel stories of women to illuminate how the gospel may speak to women's liberation of our time (Kinukawa; Tamez 2001). Christian women have also reclaimed and retold these stories, imagining dialogues, and supplying different endings. For example, I have heard from Christian women that the ending of Mary and Martha's story (Luke 10:38-42) should not end in Jesus' praising Mary over Martha, but the sisters' inviting Jesus to help in the kitchen so that all could continue the dialogue.

Other scholars find that the focus on biblical women is rather limited, for it does not provide a comprehensive framework to interpret the whole New Testament and still gives primacy and authority to the biblical text. Elisabeth Schüssler Fiorenza's influential book *In Memory of Her* (1983) presents a feminist historical-reconstructionist model, which places women at the center of the reconstruction of the Jesus movement and early Christianity. She shows that women were apostles, prophets, missionaries, as well as founders of household churches. She suggests that the radical vision of Jesus' movement was the praxis of inclusive wholeness and "discipleship of equals" (105–59). But women's leadership was increasingly marginalized in the second century, as patriarchalization set in when the church became more institutionalized. Schüssler Fiorenza's feminist model of critical interpretation insists that women should have the authority to judge whether a particular text is liberating or oppressive in the context of its reception.

Another approach is to use historical data and social theories to investigate the social world of early Christianity and to present a feminist social history. These studies look at women's marriage, status in the family, work and occupation, slave women and widows, and women's resistance in the Roman Empire (Schottroff; Yamaguchi). The parable of the leaven, for instance, makes visible women's work and uses a woman baking bread to describe the kingdom of God (Matt. 13:33; Luke 13:20-21). These works examine the impact of Roman persecution on women, the exploitative economic system, and Jewish resistance movements to provide a wider context to read the New Testament. Influenced by liberation theology, Elsa Tamez (2007) employs class analysis to study the Pastoral Letters. She describes how the rich people had challenged the leadership of the elders and presbyters in the church to which 1 Timothy was addressed. The injunction that women should be silent and submissive (1 Tim. 2:11-12) targeted the rich women, who used their power and status to cause troubles in the church.

Feminist scholars have also used literary and rhetorical approaches. For example, Ingrid Rosa Kitzberger uses a literary approach to examine the women in the Gospel of John, paying attention to the characterization of the Samaritan woman, Mary Magdalene, Mary and Martha, and the mother of Jesus, the intention of the narrator, narrative devices and rhetorical strategies, and the sequential perception of the reader in the reading process. Her goal is to present a reading against the grain—a feminist hermeneutics that empowers women. Antoinette Clark Wire reconstructs a picture of the women prophets in the church of first-century Corinth by analyzing Paul's rhetoric in 1 Corinthians. She suggests that the Corinthian women prophets claim direct access to resurrected life in Christ through the Spirit. These women sometimes conflicted with Paul, but they were known for proclaiming God's thought in prophecy and responding for the people to God (11:5; 14:1-38). Others use rhetorical criticism not to reconstruct historical reality but to focus on the persuasive power of the text to motivate action and shape the values and ethos of the community. Schüssler Fiorenza (1992, 40–50) has suggested a rhetorical approach that unmasks the interlocking system of oppression because of racism, classism, sexism, and colonialism. She coins the term *kyriarchy* (from *kyrios*, the Greek word for "lord" or "master") to describe these multiple systems of domination and subordination, involving more than gender oppression. Her goal is to create an alternative rhetorical space that respects the equality and dignity of women and is defined by the logic of radical democracy. She uses the term *ekklēsia gynaikōn* or "wo/men church" to denote this political hermeneutical space. The Greek term *ekklēsia* means the democratic assembly, and "wo/men" signifies not the feminine gender (as ladies, wives, mothers, etc.) but full decision-making political subjects. She argues that "one can theorize *ekklēsia* of wo/men not only as a virtual utopian space but also as an already partially realized space of radical equality, as a site of feminist struggles to transform social and religious institutions and discourses" (2007, 73). Feminist biblical scholars have also begun to unpack the structures of masculinity in the ancient world and how they were embedded in the biblical text (Moore and Anderson).

Social-Scientific Approaches

As mentioned above, biblical interpreters have used social sciences to learn about the social and cultural world of New Testament texts. One of the early important figures is Gerd Theissen, who studied the sociology of early Palestinian Christianity by focusing on the three roles of the Jesus movement: the wandering charismatics, their supporters in local communities, and the bearers of revelation. The use of social scientific methods has broadened the scope and sources of the third quest or newest quest of the historical Jesus since the 1980s. Billed as interdisciplinary research, scholars claim to possess at their disposal the latest archaeological knowledge, sociological analysis, cultural anthropology, and other newest social-scientific tools. Scholars have employed theories from the study of millennial movements, Mary Douglas's theory of purity and pollution, and non-Western medicine, magic, and charismatic religion to scrutinize the Jesus movement (e.g., Gager; Crossan 1991; Borg).

Schüssler Fiorenza has criticized the social-scientific quest of Jesus. She notes that the emergence of this third quest coincided with conservative politics of the Reagan and Thatcher era and with growing right-wing fundamentalist movements. She chastises the restoration of historical positivism as corresponding to political conservatism and the proliferation of the historical Jesus books as feeding "into literalist fundamentalism by reasserting disinterested scientific positivism in order to shore up the scholarly authority and universal truth of their research portrayal of Jesus" (2000, 46). While these Jesus books are written for popular consumption with their authors featured in mass media, the works of feminist scholars are sidelined and dismissed as being too "political" and not "objective" enough.

From a South African perspective, Mosala asks whether the social-scientific approaches to the Bible are "one step forward, two steps back" (43). On the one hand, the social-scientific approaches are useful, he says, because they help us to see biblical texts as ideological products of social systems and power relations. Far too often, middle-class Christians have the tendency to psychologize or use an individualist lens while reading the Bible. On the other hand, the social-scientific approaches as practiced in the white, liberal, North American and European academy often reflect bourgeois interests. Many scholars, for example, have adapted interpretive sociology and structural-functionalist analysis to study the social world of the New Testament. The structural-functionalist approach looks at how social systems are related to one another so that society can function as a whole. Focusing more on integration, stability, and unity, it is less prone to analyze social confrontation and conflict. Using Theissen's study of Palestinian Christianity as an example, Mosala points out that Theissen fails to provide an adequate structural location of the Jesus movement in the political economy of the Roman Empire and does not deal with the real economic and political contradictions of the time (64–65). As such, Theissen's study will be of limited use for the black South Africans struggling against apartheid and other social oppression. Mosala challenges biblical scholars to be open about their own class interest and the limitations of their methods.

One of the important dimensions of social-scientific criticism is the introduction of models from social and cultural anthropology. In addition to the ancient Jewish, Hellenistic, and Roman cultures that biblical scholars have been studying, Bruce J. Malina, Jerome H. Neyrey, and others suggest a pan-Mediterranean culture, with values and ethos markedly different from those in North American culture. The pivotal characteristics of Mediterranean culture in the first century included honor and shame, patronage and clientele, dyadic personality, and rules of purity. They apply the study of Mediterranean culture to interpret the group development of the Jesus movement and Paul's Letters. Scholars have questioned whether it is appropriate to impose models of contemporary societies onto the ancient Mediterranean. They remain doubtful whether the pivotal values of honor and shame are so different from the values in North American and northern European cultures. James G. Crossley also notes that "the Mediterranean frequently blurs into the contemporary Arab world, an area of renewed interest in American and European politics and media in the past forty years" (27).

As a discipline, anthropology emerged during the colonial time and often served the interests of empire. The hypothesis of a distinct Mediterranean culture and personality as contrasted with those in Western society reinforces a binary construction of the colonizers and the colonized. Malina and others have imported twentieth-century anthropological studies to the study of first-century Galilean and Judean society, assuming that Mediterranean cultures had remained unchanged over the years. Furthermore, the honor and shame code is attributed to a strong division of sexual and gender roles in the region and to the anxiety of Mediterranean men over their manhood. Female scholars such as Marianne Sawicki have voiced concerns that the study of honor and shame has largely followed a masculinist script and that women's experiences are overlooked and different. She suggests that the honor-shame sensibility might simply be an ethnocentric projection of the Euro-American male researchers onto the people they are studying (77).

R. S. Sugirtharajah, from Sri Lanka, has criticized Orientalism in the work of biblical scholars who use social-scientific methods. In *Orientalism*, Edward W. Said questions the representation of the Middle East as inferior, exotic, and stagnant in Western scholarship. Sugirtharajah notes prevalent Orientalist tendencies and the recycling of Orientalist practices in biblical scholarship, especially in the study of the social and cultural world of Jesus. He surmises that designations such as "Israel," "Judah," "the Holy Land," "Mediterranean," "world of Jesus," and "cultural world of Jesus" are "ideologically charged rhetoric and markers of Eurocentric and Christian-centric conceptualizations of that part of the world" (2012, 103). New Testament scholars have reinscribed Orientalist messages by suggesting the idea of a static Orient, by generalizing and reducing complex Mediterranean cultures to a few essentials, by gender stereotyping, and by highlighting the contrast between the East and the West. Jesus is depicted as one who is secure in his culture and yet critical of it through redefining honor culture and rearranging Mediterranean values. Since the publication of Said's work, many disciplines have become cautious about Orientalist methods and tendencies. But such methods have resurfaced in biblical studies and books that display Orientalist biases. Sugirtharajah points out that some of them have even become best sellers in mainstream culture (102–18).

Racial and Ethnic Minority Approaches

Racial and ethnic minorities in the United States began to develop their hermeneutical approaches to the Bible during the struggles of the civil rights movement in the 1960s. The development of black theology, Hispanic/Latino theology, and Asian American theology in the United States could not be separated from the ferment and protest against imperialism and apartheid in the Global South. Tat-siong Benny Liew (2013) characterizes racial and ethnic minority readings of the New Testament as "border crossing"—transcending the border of theology and biblical studies and the border between biblical studies and other disciplines. He also succinctly delineates the different stages of the development of such readings. In the first stage, racial and ethnic minority theologians and biblical scholars interpreted the biblical message through their social realities and experiences. For example, James Cone's black theology (1969; 1973) relates the gospel of Jesus to black power and freedom and argues that Christ is black, because Christ identifies with the powerless in society. Mexican American theologian Virgilio Elizondo relates the story of the marginalized Galilean

Jesus who came from the borderland area of Galilee to the story of Hispanic/Latino people as a new *mestizo* people. Asian American Chan-Hie Kim sees parallels between the Cornelius story in Acts 10–11 and Asian immigrant experience because both Cornelius and Kim are outsiders. Other scholars began to find minority subjects in the Bible and presented positive images of them or more complex pictures, such as the Ethiopian eunuch in Acts 8:26-40 (C. J. Martin 1989), and discussed slavery in early Christianity and modern interpretations (Lewis; Martin 1991).

In the current, second stage, racial and ethnic minority scholars do not simply employ different methods of biblical criticism with a racial inflection; they are more thoroughly informed by scholarship in ethnic studies and cultural studies. Their interpretation of the New Testament no longer begins with the biblical texts but with their experience as racial and ethnic minorities living in the United States. Liew characterizes this shift of emphasis as the move from "reading Scripture reading race" to "reading race reading Scripture" (2013, 183). Instead of finding "race" in the biblical text, new frameworks and paradigms of engaging with the Bible are sought. This shift can clearly be seen in *African Americans and the Bible* (Wimbush), which considers the Bible in contemporary African American culture, including poetry, aesthetics of sacred space, gospel music and spirituals, rap music, folk oratory, and many other contexts. Liew's own volume *What Is Asian American Biblical Hermeneutics?* (2008) reads all the major genres of the New Testament with Asian American literature, ethnic studies, and current events. David A. Sánchez's study of Revelation includes significant resources from Latino/a studies and Chicana/o studies.

Another significant development in the second stage is the move beyond a unified and essentialized notion of race to an acknowledgment of internal diversity within each racial and ethnic minority group. African American women articulate the issues of womanist interpretation of the Bible, placing gender at the intersection of race, class, and other anthropological referents. Demetrius K. Williams examines the biblical foundation of understanding of gender in black churches, while Rachel Annette Saint Clair presents a womanist reading of Mark's Gospel. Within the Asian American community, heterogeneity can be seen not only in the addition of women's voices but also in readings by diverse ethnic groups, intergenerational interpretations, and readings by Asian American adoptees and queer people (Foskett and Kuan; Cheng). Likewise, the diversity of the Hispanic/Latino people has been highlighted, and notions of borderland and *mestizaje* differ among different ethnic groups. Manuel Villalobos has combined the insights from feminist and queer theories to read the Ethiopian eunuch in Acts to bring hope and affirmation to Latino queer bodies.

Moving into the third stage, racial and ethnic minority theologians and biblical scholars have begun collaboration across minority groups. The move from articulating minority experience vis-à-vis the white dominant culture to conversing with other racial and ethnic minorities signals a new awareness, which is much needed to prepare for 2040, when, if current trends continue, there will be no racial and ethnic majority in the United States. An important example of such endeavor is the volume *They Were All Together in One Place? Toward Minority Criticism*, coedited by African, Asian, and Hispanic Americans (Bailey, Liew, and Segovia). This collaboration shows a desire for mutual learning and communication across color lines. In the future, more attention needs to be paid both to engaging Native American readings and, given our transnational world, to linking minority criticism with readings in the Global South.

Postcolonial Approaches

Emerging in the late 1970s, postcolonial studies has had significant influence in the fields of the humanities and social sciences. The prefix *post-* does not simply signify the period after colonialism in a chronological sense, but also refers to reading and social practices that aim at contesting colonialism and lifting up the voices of the suppressed and formerly colonized. Postcolonial criticism has drawn from many disciplines and was introduced to biblical studies in the 1990s, particularly through the works and encouragement of R. S. Sugirtharajah (1998; 2002). Other scholars have included a postcolonial optic in the study of the New Testament; for example, Tat-siong Benny Liew (1999), Fernando F. Segovia, Musa W. Dube (2000), Laura D. Donaldson, Stephen D. Moore (2006), and me (2005).

During Jesus' time, Galilee was under Roman imperial occupation and ruled by Herod Antipas (4 BCE–39 CE), and the early Christian communities lived under the whims of empire. Postcolonial critics of the New Testament share common interests with those contributing to the emerging subfield of "empire studies," promoted enthusiastically by Richard A. Horsley (1997; 2002) and other scholars (e.g., Carter; Crossan 2007). This subfield consists of books and articles with the recurrent words *empire* or *imperial* in their titles and with the intention of using the theme of empire to reframe New Testament interpretation. While the authors of works in empire studies are interested in the ancient imperial contexts, and some have related their work to contemporary contexts, they may or may not use postcolonial studies to aid their research and few have shown particular interest in affixing the label "postcolonial" to their works (Moore 2006, 14–19).

Postcolonial critics emphasize that biblical texts are not innocent. Sugirtharajah, for instance, understands postcolonial criticism as "scrutinizing and exposing colonial domination and power as these are embodied in biblical texts and in interpretations, and as searching for alternative hermeneutics while thus overturning and dismantling colonial perspectives" (1998, 16). Postcolonial criticism shares similarities with liberation hermeneutics, but also diverges from it because postcolonial critics are more suspicious of the historical-critical method that many liberation critics use. Postcolonial critics see biblical texts as more complex and multilayered and do not construct rich/poor, colonizer/colonized, and oppressor/oppressed in binary and dichotomous ways, as some liberation theologians do. Liberation theologians from Latin America tend to be Christocentric, while postcolonial critics engage more fully with religious pluralism and popular religions (Sugirtharajah 2002, 103–23).

Applying postcolonial criticism to the Gospels, Sugirtharajah (2002, 86–91) finds that there is no mention of Jesus' explicit resistance against the colonial occupiers. Yet Jesus' critique of local profiteers who colluded with the Romans and some of his sayings about earthly rulers (Matt. 11:8; Luke 7:25; 13:32) suggest that his alternative vision was against those in power. Horsley (2002) takes a stronger stance that Jesus was against empire. He places the Jesus movement within the context of popular resistance movements in Judea and Galilee, and says that the anti-imperial nature of Jesus' movement can provide a basis for theological critique of the Roman Empire in the past and the American empire in the present. Postcolonial studies of Paul's letters have also appeared; for example, Joseph A. Marchal applies feminist and postcolonial theories to the study of Philippians. The 2011 volume *The Colonized Apostle: Paul through Postcolonial Eyes* (Stanley) is the most comprehensive study to date, discussing Pauline agency, Paul's supposed social conservatism, hybrid identity and ethnicity, gender and colonialism, and Paul's relation to struggles in South Korea and the Philippines, among other topics. Moore (2006) uses postcolonial theorist Homi Bhabha to read apocalypse in Mark and John and the book of Revelation and argues that these texts mimic to a certain extent Roman imperial ideology, even when resisting and eroding it. *A Postcolonial Commentary on the New Testament Writings* (Segovia and Sugirtharajah), published in 2007, showcases the diversity of approaches and is an invaluable resource for further studies.

Postcolonial feminist interpretation challenges white male and female metropolitan readings for ignoring the issues of colonialism and imperialism and shows how their readings might collude with empire (Dube 2000). As we have discussed, Dube has lifted up the readings of ordinary female readers in African Independent Churches. Other critical concerns of postcolonial feminist criticism include the investigation of how the deployment of gender and symbolization of women relate to class interests and colonial domination in the Bible and studying women in the contact zones and the borderlands, such as Rahab, Ruth, and the Syrophoenician woman (Kwok, 81–85).

The publication of *Postcolonial Perspectives in African Biblical Interpretations* (Dube, Mbuvi, and Mbuwayesango) in 2012 pushes the envelope of postcolonial criticism even further. It raises the possibilities of "unthinking Eurocentrism" in biblical studies and developing Afrocentric criticism. The volume discusses the politics of translation of the Bible, the Bible as read in and through African creative writings, the relation of the Bible and "the scramble of Africa," HIV and AIDS, and the roles of socially engaged biblical scholars. The volume offers much insight and food for thought for interpreters in other parts of the Global South as well as in metropolitan areas who want to decolonize their minds and their methods when approaching the Bible.

Contemporary Issues

In this final section, I would like to take up some contemporary issues to see how they have led to new readings of the New Testament from fresh angles. First, the Holocaust has prompted many scholars to be conscious of the long history of anti-Jewish and antisemitic biases in the history of biblical interpretation. Scholars have proposed new ways to interpret New Testament texts so that they will not be construed as anti-Jewish. Second, the vigorous debates on same-sex marriage in the United States and elsewhere require us to reexamine the teachings on marriage, family, and same-gender relationships in the New Testament. Third, the study of "Gnosticism" and other writings in early Christianity has made us keenly aware of the politics of inclusion and exclusion surrounding the New Testament canon. A group of scholars has produced a new version of the New Testament combining both traditional and newly discovered texts.

Anti-Judaism and Antisemitism

Anti-Jewish attitudes and prejudices have contributed to antisemitism and the tragic genocide in modern times of Jewish people in Europe. Jews have been blamed for killing Jesus. Jesus' accusations against the scribes and Pharisees as hypocrites and his polemical sayings about the Jews in

John's Gospel have been used to cast Jewish people as the other, who did not accept the good news of Jesus Christ. Jesus has been seen as the founder of a new religion, separate from his Jewish background. Paul's contrast of law and gospel has been taken as the foundational difference between the covenant of the old and the new. Christianity has often been hailed as a universal religion, accepting gentiles into its mix, while Judaism has been cast in a negative light as a religion belonging to a particular group. Many Christians continue to harbor a supersessionist viewpoint, believing that Christianity ultimately triumphs over Judaism.

Interpreters sensitive to the charges of anti-Judaism and antisemitism have presented alternative views and interpretations different from those often taught in Christian churches. New Testament scholars have emphasized Jesus' Jewishness and interpreted Jesus' movement as a movement *within* Judaism. For example, Géza Vermes regards Jesus as a Jewish Galilean charismatic, while E. P. Sanders sees Jesus as an eschatological prophet who believed that the promises to Israel would soon be fulfilled and restoration would be at hand. Jewish New Testament scholar Amy-Jill Levine (2011) calls Jesus "the misunderstood Jew," and her work helps Jews and Christians understand the Jewish context of the first century. In *The Jewish Gospels*, Daniel Boyarin, a professor of talmudic culture, argues that Jesus' teachings can be found in the long-standing Jewish tradition and the coming of the Messiah was imagined in many Jewish texts. Many also point out that Jesus' arguments with the Pharisees and Jewish leaders were not conflicts between Christian and Jews, but intra-Jewish arguments (Wills, 101–32).

Jewish scholars such as Judith Plaskow and Levine (2000) have cautioned against the blanket generalizations of Jewish culture as misogynist in order to construct Jesus as a feminist over against his cultural background. Sometimes, Christian feminists have used Jesus' critique of his culture to support their challenge of patriarchy in their own cultures. To heed these scholars' call, we must avoid generalization and not imagine "the Jews" as the same transhistorically and transculturally. Some of the characterizations of "purity" discussed earlier would seem to fall under this criticism. More attention must be paid to local practices, regional history, and religious views and political ideologies of different groups and factions in first-century Judaism. Levine also suggests reading in community so that we can be exposed to our biases and blind spots in our reading.

An exciting development is the publication of the volume *The Jewish Annotated New Testament* (Levine and Brettler) in 2011, a collaborative effort of an international team of fifty Jewish scholars, which presents Jewish history, beliefs, and practices for understanding the New Testament. The New Testament is interpreted within the context of the Hebrew Bible and rabbinic literature. Each book of the New Testament is annotated with references, and the volume includes thirty essays covering a wide range of topics, including the synagogue, the law, food and table fellowship, messianic movements, Jewish miracle workers, Jewish family life, divine beings, and afterlife and resurrection. It also addresses Jewish responses to the New Testament and contemporary Jewish-Christian relations. The book will facilitate Jewish-Christian dialogue because it helps Christians better understand the Jewish roots of the New Testament and offers Jews a way to understand the New Testament that does not proselytize Christianity or cast Judaism in a negative light.

It should be pointed out that there is a difference between antisemitism and the critique of the policies of the state of Israel and its unequal treatment of Palestinians. Some Jewish thinkers and leaders, such as Judith Butler and Rabbi Michael Lerner, have criticized political Zionism, the dispossession of land, and hard-line policies of the Israeli state. Palestinian liberation theologian Naim Stifan Ateek has challenged Christian Zionism, adherents of which believe that the Jews must return to the Holy Land as a prerequisite for the second coming of Christ. Ateek draws from the example of Jesus to discuss the relation between justice and peace, nonviolent resistance, and the peacekeeping imperatives of the church.

Same-Sex Marriage

Debates on same-sex marriage in United States, Europe, Latin America, and Asia saw both supporters and opponents citing the Bible to support their positions. In the United States, the influential conservative Christian leader James Dobson defends what he calls the biblical definition of marriage, and blames homosexuality and gay marriage for all kinds of social decline. A cursory search on the Internet can find numerous posts citing biblical passages to defend heterosexual marriage and label homosexual passions and acts as unnatural, shameful, and contrary to God's will. These posts usually cite the creation of Adam and Eve in Genesis and the views of Jesus and Paul on marriage and sexuality as support.

Many Christians believe that the modern nuclear family represents the Christian ideal, but the current focus on heterosexual nuclear family dates back only to the 1950s. Dale B. Martin argues that there are more sources in the New Testament to criticize the modern family than to support it. Jesus was not a family man, and the Gospels present Jesus as living in alternative communities that shared his vision of divinely constituted family. He refused to identify with his natural family, saying, "Whoever does the will of God is my brother and sister and mother" (Mark 3:35; cf. Matt. 12:50; Luke 8:21). Jesus forbade divorce, even though Mosaic law allowed it (Matt. 19:4-9; Mark 10:6-12). But Matthew follows this with the saying about those who have "made themselves eunuchs for the sake of the kingdom of heaven" (Matt. 19:12), which might imply that the avoidance of marriage and of procreation is preferable. Jesus also says in the Gospels that in the resurrection, marriage will be obsolete (Matt. 22:30; Mark 12:26).

Paul in 1 Corinthians 7 did not promote marriage or traditional family and preferred Christians to follow his example and remain single and celibate. He thought that marriage would become a distraction from the life of faith "in Christ." But he allowed marriage for those who were weak and could not control their passions, saying "it is better to marry than to be aflame with passion" (1 Cor. 7:9). In Paul's time, passion and sexual desires were associated with the body and had to be put under severe control. The letters to the Colossians and Ephesians contain the household codes, which propose the hierarchy and order of a patriarchal family. But these letters are generally considered deuteropauline and were written during the increasing patriarchal institutionalization of the church.

Opponents to same-sex marriage often cite Rom. 1:23-27 to support their claims that homosexual acts are unnatural. Scholars have offered different explanations of the context of this text to argue that it is not against homosexual relations as we have come to know them in the present day (Goss, 198–202). Some suggest that homosexual acts were considered part of unclean gentile culture and were condemned by Paul for that reason. Others claim that Paul was not speaking about adult homosexual relations but pederasty in the Greco-Roman world. Some even proffer that Paul might have in mind oral or anal sex as unnatural sexual intercourse, among opposite-sex partners as well. Bernadette J. Brooten comments that Paul's injunction against female homosexual relations was due to his understanding of gender roles. Paul did not want women to exchange their supposedly passive and subordinate desire for an active role (216). Feminist scholars have challenged the androcentric mind-set and patriarchal ideologies of Pauline and other New Testament writings.

The New Testament thus cannot be easily enlisted to support a reductionistic understanding of "Christian marriage" or "family values," as if these have not changed over time. While same-sex marriage has become a rallying cry for marriage equality and recognition of human rights, some lesbians and gay men have also expressed concerns that the legislation of marriage would give too much power to the state, which can legitimize one form of sexual relationship while excluding others. Dale B. Martin belongs to this latter group and encourages queer Christians to expand their imaginations to "allow scripture and tradition to inspire new visions of Christian community free from the constraints of the modern, heterosexual, nuclear family" (39). Tolbert (2006) adds that same-sex couples can find the ideals of friendship in the New Testament supportive of their relationship. In John, Jesus told the disciples that they were his friends and shared with them his deepest knowledge of God. The New Testament, Tolbert says, does not promote marriage, heterosexual or not, as the bedrock of Christian community, but rather values friendship; as Jesus says, "No one has greater love than this, to lay down one's life for one's friends" (John 15:13). Even though the notion of friendship in the ancient world might be quite different from ours, the shift from promoting marriage to friendship opens new horizons.

A "New" New Testament

In 1945, local peasants in Nag Hammadi in Egypt discovered papyrus codices in a clay sealed jar consisting of fifty-two gnostic writings that were previously unknown. Though the papyrus dated back to the fourth century, some of the texts in the manuscripts can be traced back to as early as the first or second century. The Nag Hammadi library contains texts such as the *Gospel of Thomas*, the *Gospel of Philip*, the *Gospel of Truth*, and writings attributed to Jesus' followers, such as the *Secret Book of James*, the *Apocalypse of Paul*, and the *Apocalypse of Peter* (Pagels). The discovery of these texts greatly expanded our knowledge of religious writings in the early centuries.

Just as Jewish scholars have challenged us to reexamine our assumptions about Christian origins and the Jewish roots of Christianity, the discovery and study of the Nag Hammadi library raised new issues about the conceptualization of the history of the early church. Before the discovery, all we knew about "Gnosticism" was that the orthodox heresiologists, especially Irenaeus and Tertullian, vilified it. Karen L. King (2003) argues that these polemicists had constructed the category "heresy" as part of their project of identity formation and to exclude Jews and pagans as outsiders. The Nag Hammadi writings show what scholars have called "Gnosticism" as highly pluralistic and the boundary between Christianity and "Gnosticism" as more permeable than previously assumed. Both the so-called orthodox and the heretical writings belonged to a common body of tradition and represented "distinct varieties of Christianity developed in different geographical areas, at a time when the boundaries of orthodox and heresy were not at all fixed" (152). Moreover, certain texts were excluded from the

New Testament canon because of ideological reasons, such as to marginalize women's authority and leadership. For example, the *Gospel of Mary*, which was excluded, depicts Mary Magdalene as having received special knowledge from Jesus and serving as a leader among the disciples after Jesus' resurrection. This portrait of Mary should be considered together with the depiction of her as one of Jesus' followers and a key witness to his resurrection in the New Testament (King 1998).

In addition to the Nag Hammadi library, other texts have been discovered in the nineteenth and twentieth centuries and scientifically verified to be almost as old as the manuscripts of the traditional New Testament. A group of scholars, pastors, and church leaders under the leadership of Hal Taussig have produced a New Testament for the twenty-first century that includes with the established canon a selection of some of the texts outside the canon and called it "a new New Testament." The newly added documents include ten books, two prayers, and the *Odes of Solomon*, which consists mostly of prayers. Now, within the same volume, we can read about Mary Magdalene in the traditional Gospels as well as in the *Gospel of Mary*. In contrast to the traditional book of Revelation, the *Secret Revelation of John* offers a different picture of how Christ rescues the world, not through apocalyptic battles, but by teaching about God's light and compassion. Taussig hopes that this new New Testament can offer readers a chance to form new opinions about the earliest traditions of Christianity and be inspired by the teachings, songs, prayers, letters, and meditations of Jesus' early followers (xviii–xix).

Conclusion

The New Testament has shaped human cultures for millennia and is read by Christians, people of other religious traditions, and secular people in different tongues, cultural backgrounds, social contexts, and life circumstances. As global citizens living in the twenty-first century, we have to remember how the gospel of Jesus Christ has been misused to oppress and construct the other, whether the other is Jewish people, women, racial and ethnic minorities, colonized people, or queer people, so that history will not be repeated. The availability of so many new resources and methods in New Testament studies and the addition of underrepresented voices from all over the world are cause for celebration. New Testament reading in the contemporary world has become more global, multicentered, and plurivocal, and contributes to interreligious understanding. The interpretation of the New Testament has also been brought to the public square, as people look for insights from the Bible to address problems of our day. I hope that those among the younger generation who profess that they are "spiritual but not religious" will also appreciate the wisdom in the New Testament, as one of the most fascinating and influential religious and spiritual literatures of humankind.

Works Cited

Ahn, Byung Mu. 1981. "Jesus and the Minjung in the Gospel of Mark." In *Minjung Theology: People as the Subjects of History*, edited by Kim Yong Bock, 136–52. Singapore: Commission of Theological Concerns, Christian Conference of Asia.

Anderson, Janice Capel, and Stephen D. Moore, eds. 2008. *Mark and Method: New Approaches in Biblical Studies*. 2nd ed. Minneapolis: Fortress Press.

Ariarajah, Wesley. 1989. *The Bible and People of Other Faiths*. Maryknoll, NY: Orbis.

Ateek, Naim Stefan. 1989. *Justice, and Only Justice: A Palestinian Theology of Liberation*. Maryknoll, NY: Orbis.

Bailey, Randall C., Tat-siong Benny Liew, and Fernando F. Segovia, eds. 2009. *They Were All Together in One Place? Toward Minority Biblical Criticism*. Atlanta: Society of Biblical Literature.

Barr, James. 1983. *Holy Scripture: Canon, Authority, Criticism*. Oxford: Clarendon.

Baum, Wilhelm, and Dietmar W. Winkler. 2003. *The Church of the East: A Concise History*. London: RoutledgeCurzon.

Blount, Brian K. 1995. *Cultural Interpretation: Reorienting New Testament Criticism*. Minneapolis: Fortress Press.

Borg, Marcus J. 1994. *Jesus in Contemporary Scholarship*. Valley Forge, PA: Trinity Press International.

Boyarin, Daniel. 2012. *The Jewish Gospels: The Story of the Jewish Christ*. New York: New Press.

Brooten, Bernadette J. 1996. *Love between Women: Early Christian Responses to Female Homoeroticism*. Chicago: University of Chicago Press.

Butler, Judith. 2012. *Parting Ways: Jewishness and the Critique of Zionism*. New York: Columbia University Press.

Cardenal, Ernesto. 1976–1982. *The Gospel in Solentiname*. Translated by Donald D. Walsh. 4 vols. Maryknoll, NY: Orbis.

Carter, Warren. 2001. *Matthew and Empire: Initial Explorations*. Harrisburg, PA: Trinity Press International.

Cheng, Patrick S. 2002. "Multiplicity and Judges 19: Constructing a Queer Asian Pacific American Biblical Hermeneutic." *Semeia* 90–91:119–33.

Cone, James H. 1969. *Black Theology and Black Power*. New York: Seabury.

———. 1975. *God of the Oppressed*. New York: Seabury.

Crossan, John Dominic. 1991. *The Historical Jesus: The Life of a Mediterranean Jewish Peasant*. San Francisco: HarperSanFrancisco.

———. 2007. *God and Empire: Jesus against Rome, Then and Now*. New York: HarperCollins.

Crossley, James G. 2010. *Reading the New Testament: Contemporary Approaches*. London: Routledge.

Dobson, James C. 2004. *Marriage under Fire: Why We Must Win This War*. Sisters, OR: Multnomah.

Donaldson, Laura E. 2006. "Gospel Hauntings: The Postcolonial Demons of New Testament Criticism." In *Postcolonial Biblical Criticism: Interdisciplinary Intersections*, edited by Fernando F. Segovia and Stephen D. Moore, 97–113. London: Continuum.

Dube, Musa W. 2000. *Postcolonial Feminist Interpretation of the Bible*. St. Louis: Chalice.

———, ed. 2001. *Other Ways of Reading: African Women and the Bible*. Atlanta: Society of Biblical Literature.

———. 2008. *The HIV and AIDS Bible: Selected Essays*. Scranton, PA: University of Scranton Press.

Dube, Musa, Andrew M. Mbuvi, and Dora R. Mbuwayesango, eds. 2012. *Postcolonial Perspectives in African Biblical Interpretations*. Atlanta: Society of Biblical Literature.

Eber, Irene, Sze-kar Wan, and Knut Walf, eds. 1999. *The Bible in Modern China*. Nettetal, Germany: Steyler.

Elizondo, Virgilio. 1983. *Galilean Journey: The Mexican-American Promise*. Maryknoll, NY: Orbis.

Fernandez, Eleazar S. 2013. "Multiple Locations-Belongings and Power Differentials: Lenses for Liberating Biblical Hermeneutic." In *Soundings in Cultural Criticism: Perspectives and Methods in Culture, Power, and Identity in the New Testament*, edited by Francisco Lozada Jr. and Greg Carey, 139–49. Minneapolis: Fortress Press.

Flatow, Sheryl. 2009. "Christianity on the Move." *Bostonia*. http://www.bu.edu/bostonia/fall09/christianity.

Foskett, Mary F., and Jeffrey Kah-Jin Kuan, eds. 2006. *Ways of Being, Ways of Reading: Asian American Biblical Interpretation*. St. Louis: Chalice.

Gager, John G. 1975. *Kingdom and Community: The Social World of Early Community*. Englewood Cliffs, NJ: Prentice-Hall.

Goss, Robert E. 2002. *Queering Christ: Beyond Jesus Acted Up*. Cleveland: Pilgrim.

Gutiérrez, Gustavo. 1988. *A Theology of Liberation: History, Politics, and Salvation*. Translated by Caridad Inda and John Eagleson. Rev. ed. Maryknoll, NY: Orbis.

Hastings, Adrian, ed. 1999. *A World History of Christianity*. Grand Rapids: Eerdmans.

Horsley, Richard A., ed. 1997. *Paul and Empire: Religion and Power in Roman Imperial Society*. Harrisburg, PA: Trinity Press International.

———. 2002. *Jesus and Empire: The Kingdom of God and the New World Disorder*. Minneapolis: Fortress Press.

Irvin, Dale T., and Scott W. Sunquist. 2001. *History of the World Christian Movement*. Vol. 1, *Earliest Christianity to 1453*. Maryknoll, NY: Orbis.

———. 2012. *History of the World Christian Movement*. Vol. 2, *Modern Christianity from 1454 to 1800*. Maryknoll, NY: Orbis.

Jenkins, Philip. 2007. *The Next Christendom: The Coming of Global Christianity*. Rev. ed. New York: Oxford University Press.

Johnson, Todd M., and Kenneth R. Ross. 2009. *Atlas of Global Christianity, 1910–2010*. Edinburgh: Edinburgh University Press.

Kim, Chan-Hie. 1995. "Reading the Cornelius Story from an Asian Immigrant Perspective." In *Reading from This Place*. Vol. 1, *Social Location and Biblical Interpretation in the United States*, edited by Fernando F. Segovia and Mary Ann Tolbert, 165–74. Minneapolis: Fortress Press.

Kinukawa, Hisako. 1994. *Women and Jesus in Mark: A Japanese Feminist Perspective*. Maryknoll, NY: Orbis.

King, Karen L. 1998. "Canonization and Marginalization: Mary of Magdala." In *Women's Sacred Scriptures*, edited by Kwok Pui-lan and Elisabeth Schüssler Fiorenza, 29–36. London: SCM.

———. 2003. *What Is Gnosticism?* Cambridge, MA: Harvard University Press.

Kitzberger, Ingrid Rosa. 1998. "How Can This Be? (John 3:9): A Feminist Theological Re-Reading of the Gospel of John." In *What Is John?* Vol. 2, *Literary and Social Readings of the Fourth Gospel*, edited by Fernando F. Segovia, 19–41. Atlanta: Society of Biblical Literature.

Kwok Pui-lan. 2005. *Postcolonial Imagination and Feminist Theology*. Louisville: Westminster John Knox.

Lady Gaga. 2011. "Judas." Posted on May 3. http://www.ladygaga.com/media/?meid=6765.

Lee, Archie C. C. 1998. "Cross-Textual Interpretation and Its Implications for Biblical Studies." In *Teaching the Bible: The Discourses and Politics of Biblical Pedagogy*, edited by Fernando F. Segovia and Mary Ann Tolbert, 247–54. Maryknoll, NY: Orbis.

Levine, Amy-Jill. 2000. "Lilies of the Field and Wandering Jews: Biblical Scholarship, Women's Roles, and Social Location." In *Transforming Encounters: Jesus and Women Re-viewed*, edited by Ingrid Rosa Kitzberger, 329–52. Leiden: Brill.

———. 2006. *The Misunderstood Jew: The Church and the Scandal of the Jewish Jesus*. San Francisco: HarperSanFrancisco.

Levine, Amy-Jill, and Marc Z. Brettler, eds. 2011. *The Jewish Annotated New Testament*. New York: Oxford University Press.

Lewis, Lloyd A. 1991. "An African American Appraisal of the Philemon-Paul-Onesimus Triangle." In *Stony the Road We Trod: African American Biblical Interpretation*, edited by Cain Hope Felder, 232–46. Minneapolis: Fortress Press.

Liew, Tat-siong Benny. 1999. *The Politics of Parousia: Reading Mark Inter(con)textually.* Leiden: Brill.

———. 2008. *What Is Asian American Biblical Hermeneutics?* Honolulu: University of Hawai'i Press.

———. 2013. "Colorful Readings: Racial/Ethnic Minority Readings of the New Testament in the United States." In *Soundings in Cultural Criticism: Perspectives and Methods in Culture, Power, and Identity in the New Testament,* edited by Francisco Lozado Jr. and Greg Carey, 177–89, Minneapolis: Fortress Press.

Malina, Bruce J. 1981. *The New Testament World: Insights from Cultural Anthropology.* Atlanta: John Knox Press.

Marchal, Joseph A. 2008. *The Politics of Heaven: Women, Gender, and Empire in the Study of Paul.* Minneapolis: Fortress Press.

Martin, Clarice J. 1989. "A Chamberlain's Journey and the Challenge of Interpretation for Liberation." *Semeia* 47:105–35.

———. 1991. "The *Haustafeln* (Household Codes) in African American Interpretation: 'Free Slaves' and 'Subordinate Women.'" In *Stony the Road We Trod: African American Biblical Interpretation,* edited by Cain Hope Felder, 206–31. Minneapolis: Fortress Press.

Martin, Dale B. 2006. "Familiar Idolatry and the Christian Case against Marriage." In *Authorizing Marriage? Canon, Tradition, and Critique in the Blessing of Same-sex Unions,* edited by Mark D. Jordan, 17–40. Princeton: Princeton University Press.

Meeks, Wayne A. 1983. *The First Urban Christians: The Social World of the Apostle Paul.* New Haven: Yale University Press.

Melanchthon, Monica Jyotsna. 2010. "Dalit Women and the Bible: Hermeneutical and Methodological Reflections." In *Hope Abundant: Third World and Indigenous Women's Theology,* edited by Kwok Pui-lan, 103–22, Maryknoll, NY: Orbis.

Moore, Stephen D. 2006. *Empire and Apocalypse: Postcolonialism and the New Testament.* Sheffield: Sheffield Phoenix Press.

———. 2010. *The Bible in Theory: Critical and Postcritical Essays.* Atlanta: Society of Biblical Literature.

———. 2013. "The Dog-Woman of Canaan and Other Animal Tales from the Gospel of Matthew." In *Soundings in Cultural Criticism: Perspectives and Methods in Culture, Power, and Identity in the New Testament,* edited by Francisco Lozada Jr. and Greg Carey, 57–71. Minneapolis: Fortress Press.

Moore, Stephen D., and Janice Capel Anderson, eds. 2003. *New Testament Masculinities.* Atlanta: Society of Biblical Literature.

Mosala, Itumeleng J. 1989. *Biblical Hermeneutics and Black Theology in South Africa.* Grand Rapids: Eerdmans.

Nelavala, Surekha. 2006. "Smart Syrophoenician Woman: A Dalit Feminist Reading of Mark 7:24-31." *ExpTim* 118, no. 2: 64–69.

Neyrey, Jerome H. 1990. *Paul, in Other Words: A Cultural Reading of His Letters.* Louisville: Westminster John Knox.

Pagels, Elaine. 1979. *The Gnostic Gospels.* New York: Random House.

Patte, Daniel. 2004. Introduction to *Global Bible Commentary,* edited by Daniel Patte, xxi–xxxii. Nashville: Abingdon.

Petrella, Ivan. 2005. *Latin American Liberation Theology: The Next Generation.* Maryknoll, NY: Orbis.

Plaskow, Judith. 1980. "Blaming the Jews for the Birth of Patriarchy." *Lilith* 7:11–12, 14–17.

Rajkumar, Peniel. 2010. *Dalit Theology and Dalit Liberation: Problems, Paradigms, and Possibilities.* Burlington, VT: Ashgate.

Roncace, Mark, and Joseph Weaver, eds. 2013. *Global Perspectives on the Bible.* Upper Saddle River, NJ: Pearson.

Said, Edward W. 1978. *Orientalism.* New York: Pantheon.

Saint Clair, Rachel Annette. 2008. *Call and Consequences: A Womanist Reading of Mark*. Minneapolis: Fortress Press.

Sánchez, David A. 2008. *From Patmos to the Barrio: Subverting Imperial Myths*. Minneapolis: Fortress Press.

Sanders, E. P. 1985. *Jesus and Judaism*. Philadelphia: Fortress Press.

Sanneh, Lamin O. 1989. *Translating the Message: The Missionary Impact on Culture*. Maryknoll, NY: Orbis.

———. 2003. *Whose Religion Is Christianity? The Gospel beyond the West*. Grand Rapids: Eerdmans.

———. 2007. *Disciples of All Nations: Pillars of World Christianity*. New York: Oxford University Press.

Sawicki, Marianne. 2000. *Crossing Galilee: Architectures of Contact in the Occupied Land of Jesus*. Harrisburg, PA: Trinity Press International.

Scharper, Philip, and Sally Scharper, eds. 1984. *Gospel in Art by the Peasants of Solentiname*. Maryknoll, NY: Orbis.

Schottroff, Luise. 1995. *Lydia's Impatient Sisters: A Feminist Social History of Early Christianity*. Translated by Barbara Rumscheidt and Martin Rumscheidt. Louisville: Westminster John Knox.

Schüssler Fiorenza, Elisabeth. 1983. *In Memory of Her: A Feminist Theological Reconstruction of Christian Origins*. New York: Crossroad.

———. 1992. *But She Said: Feminist Practices of Biblical Interpretation*. Boston: Beacon.

———. 2000. *Jesus and the Politics of Interpretation*. New York: Continuum.

———. 2002. "The Ethos of Biblical Interpretation: Biblical Studies in a Postmodern and Postcolonial Context." In *Theological Literacy for the Twenty-First Century*, edited by Rodney L. Petersen, 211–28. Grand Rapids: Eerdmans.

———. 2007. *The Power of the Word: Scripture and the Rhetoric of Empire*. Minneapolis: Fortress Press.

Segovia, Fernando F. 2000. *Decolonizing Biblical Studies: A View from the Margins*. Maryknoll, NY: Orbis.

Segovia, Fernando F., and R. S. Sugirtharajah, eds. 2007. *A Postcolonial Commentary on the New Testament Writings*, New York: T&T Clark.

Segundo, Juan Luis. 1976. *Liberation of Theology*. Translated by John Drury. Maryknoll, NY: Orbis.

Stanley, Christopher D., ed. 2011. *The Colonized Apostle: Paul through Postcolonial Eyes*. Minneapolis: Fortress Press.

Sugirtharajah, R. S. 1999. *Asian Biblical Hermeneutics and Postcolonial Criticism: Contesting the Interpretations*. Maryknoll, NY: Orbis.

———. 2002. *Postcolonial Criticism and Biblical Interpretation*. Oxford: Oxford University Press.

———. 2012. *Exploring Postcolonial Biblical Criticism: History, Method, Practice*. Malden, MA: Wiley-Blackwell.

———, ed. 1998. "Biblical Studies after the Empire: From a Colonial to a Postcolonial Mode of Interpretation." In *The Postcolonial Bible*, edited by R. S. Sugirtharajah. Sheffield: Sheffield Academic Press.

Tamez, Elsa. 2001. *Jesus and Courageous Women*. New York: Women's Division, General Board of Global Ministries, United Methodist Church.

———. 2007. *Struggles for Power in Early Christianity: A Study of the First Letter to Timothy*. Translated by Gloria Kinsler. Maryknoll, NY: Orbis.

Taussig, Hal, ed. 2013. *A New New Testament: A Bible for the Twenty-First Century Combining Traditional and Newly Discovered Texts*. Boston: Houghton Mifflin Harcourt.

Theissen, Gerd. 1978. *Sociology of Early Palestinian Christianity*. Translated by John Bowden. Philadelphia: Fortress Press.

Tolbert, Mary Ann. 1998. "Reading the Bible with Authority: Feminist Interrogation of the Canon." In *Escaping Eden: New Feminist Perspectives on the Bible*, edited by Harold C. Washington, Susan Lochrie Graham, and Pamela Thimmes, 141–62. Sheffield: Sheffield Academic Press.

———. 2006. "Marriage and Friendship in the Christian New Testament: Ancient Resources for Contemporary Same-Sex Unions." In *Authorizing Marriage? Canon, Tradition, and Critique in the Blessing of Same-Sex Unions*, edited by Mark D. Jordan, 41–51. Princeton: Princeton University Press.

United Bible Societies. 2012. "Celebrating 100 Millions Bibles printed in China!" November 12. http://www.unitedBiblesocieties.org/news/2902-celebrating-100-million-Bibles-printed-in-china.

———. 2013 "About UBS Translation Work." http://www.ubs-translations.org/about_us.

Vermes, Géza. 1973. *Jesus the Jew: A Historian's Reading of the Gospels*. London: Collins.

Villalobos, Manuel. 2011. "Bodies *Del Otro Lado* Finding Hope in the Borderland: Gloria Anzaldúa, the Ethiopian Eunuch of Acts 8:26–40, *y Yo*." In *Bible Trouble: Queer Reading at the Boundaries of Biblical Scholarship*, edited by Teresa Hornby and Ken Stone, 191–221. Atlanta: Society of Biblical Literature.

West, Gerald O. 1999. *The Academy of the Poor: Towards a Dialogical Reading of the Bible*. Sheffield: Sheffield Academic Press.

Wicker, Kathleen O'Brien, Althea Spencer Miller, and Musa W. Dube, eds. 2005. *Feminist New Testament Studies: Global and Future Perspectives*. New York: Palgrave Macmillan.

Williams, Demetrius K. 2004. *An End to This Strife: The Politics of Gender in the African American Churches*. Minneapolis: Fortress Press.

Wills, Lawrence M. 2008. *Not God's People: Insiders and Outsiders in the Biblical World*. Lanham, MD: Rowman & Littlefield.

Wimbush, Vincent L., ed. 2000. *African Americans and the Bible: Sacred Texts and Social Textures*. New York: Continuum.

Wire, Antoinette Clark. 1990. *The Corinthian Women Prophets: A Reconstruction through Paul's Rhetoric*. Minneapolis: Fortress Press.

Yamaguchi, Satoko. 2002. *Mary and Martha: Women in the World of Jesus*. Maryknoll, NY: Orbis.

NEGOTIATING THE JEWISH HERITAGE OF EARLY CHRISTIANITY

Lawrence M. Wills

Any discussion of the dialogue between Jews and Christians in the twenty-first century must begin with some historical perspective as to what the traditional Christian view has been concerning the relations of Jews and followers of Jesus in the first century. In the first half of the twentieth century, for instance, the dominant Christian view was the following: on the one hand, there was one clear Judaism—viewed through the lens of Paul's critique of the law and represented by the Pharisees as depicted in Matthew—and on the other hand, one clear Christianity as a new entity that had separated from Judaism. If there was any disagreement among the first Christians, it was only that between the "correct" party—those who followed Paul—and the "incorrect" party—those who followed James in retaining Jewish law. How the divorce between Judaism and Christianity took place is treated in the book of Acts, which was taken as a historically accurate record of the intransigence of Jews in the face of Paul's preaching of the message of Christ. True, there were ambiguous passages throughout the Gospels, such as:

> When Jesus saw that he [the scribe] answered wisely, he said to him, "You are not far from the kingdom of God." (Mark 12:34)
>
> Jesus said to them, "The scribes and the Pharisees sit on Moses' seat; therefore, do whatever they teach you and follow it." (Matt. 23:2-3)

But these could be explained away by interpreting them in light of Paul's letters and Acts.

Over the last century, scholars have moved away from this simple view of the relation of ancient Judaism and early Christianity to a much more complex view, questioning almost every part of the description above. In the first half of the twentieth century, some Christian scholars argued that the variety of early Christian groups did not evolve out of one unified body of followers of Jesus, or even from the two divergent paths of "Paul Christians" and "James Christians." Rather, from the earliest period, there were already widely divergent practices and beliefs, without any clear sense of an agreed-on center. This challenge to a trunk-with-branches view of early Christian groups gave more weight to the "branches," groups formerly regarded as smaller, marginal, too Eastern, or heretical. Walter Bauer was a leading figure in this development; more recent scholars who exemplify this approach include James Robinson and Helmut Koester; Jack Sanders; and Stephen Wilson.

For instance, whereas it was traditionally assumed that the four Gospels were narrative depictions of a Jesus who taught essentially what Paul said in his letters using different language, now one had to take seriously the differences among the authors and audiences of these texts. The varied emphases that were found among the four Gospels, or between Paul's letters and Revelation, or between Acts and Jude, or between canonical texts and early Christian texts from outside the canon, came to be seen as reflective of widely divergent movements and eddies in this new religious movement. Scholars might retain the theological preferences of their own traditions, but in colleges and universities, and even in seminaries, the historical narrative no longer seemed like a tree with a clear trunk and branches, but followed the pattern of tubers and vines—widely propagating members with little clear order or lines of development.

In this process, Christian texts from outside the New Testament canon, even those that had been considered "heretical," came to be viewed as having an equal claim in the *historical* reconstruction of early Christianity, regardless of their theology. There was a larger and larger patchwork of groups, and a clear history of origins and development became ever more difficult to reconstruct. Very basic questions about the history of Judaism and Christianity were also introduced: Has the early Eastern history of Judaism and Christianity, all the way from Syria to India and later to China, been ignored as a result of the Western focus of much of the Christian church and of Judaism? To be sure, the Eastern church also included Paul in its canon, but was the relation between eastern Christians and Jews vastly different from that of their Western counterparts (Foltz)?

But another, parallel shift was also underway. In the last half of the twentieth century, scholars proposed a similar proliferation in the number of Jewish groups as well. Before about 1960, many scholars would have described Judaism in the first century as divided into three parties—Sadducees, Pharisees, and Essenes—based on a description of Judaism by the first-century Jewish historian Josephus (*J. W.* 2.117–66). But the discovery of the Dead Sea Scrolls, a new appreciation for the differences among the many Jewish texts of the period, and a growing realization that early rabbinic views were not authoritative for all Jews compelled scholars to recognize the wide variety of Jewish groups, beliefs, and practices (see Cohen 2006; J. J. Collins; Nickelsburg). The classic nineteenth-century history of the Judaism of this period by Emil Schürer (1886–1890) was enlarged in each of the many subsequent editions by the inclusion of more variety in terms of texts, theology, and practices.

Jewish scholars were also motivated by a desire to participate fully in the public discourse on the nature of religions. Judaism, they argued, should be studied in our colleges and universities as an important religious tradition alongside Christianity and other world religions. After World War II and the Shoah, or Holocaust—the genocide of six million Jews—there was an added motivation for both Jews and Christians: a more searching engagement about the origins of Jewish-Christian relations in the ancient world. If the historical assumptions behind a presumed Christian superiority could be challenged, then Christians, Jews, and others would have a chance of living in peace in the twentieth century and afterward without the corrosive effects of stereotypes derived from a misreading of ancient evidence.

Corresponding to the recognition of ancient variety was a new variety among the modern scholars who were studying it as well. During the twentieth century, there arose a full participation of Christian scholars in the study of Judaism and Jewish scholars in the study of Christianity—along with scholars from other religious backgrounds or with no religious affiliation at all. By the second half of the twentieth century, it came to be quite expected that New Testament scholars would know something about rabbinic literature and that Jewish historians of the Roman period would know something about the New Testament and early church. By the end of the twentieth century, there was not just one or two but a number of important studies on the New Testament by Jewish scholars and a number of important studies on rabbinic Judaism by Christians.

The situation at the end of the twentieth century, then, was drastically different from that at the beginning. Influenced by challenges in the social sciences, philosophy, and literary criticism, new issues came to be raised that only made the comparison more complicated, but in many cases, more interesting to modern audiences. Formerly, scholars compared Judaism and Christianity as two clearly defined bodies of people with separate identities, but increasingly many scholars realized that more elite voices within Judaism—for instance, the chief priests, Josephus, or Philo—were being unfairly compared to the less elite forms of Christianity—Mark or the sayings source of Matthew and Luke. The nonelite layers of the Christian movement seemed more revolutionary when compared with the aristocratic voices within Judaism, yet a comparison of Jewish prophetic movements (such as those reported in Josephus) to more elite Christian texts like Hebrews would look very different. Which is the "proper" comparison? Should popular movements among Christians be compared with popular movements among Jews, and more elite texts among Christians with elite Jewish authors, say, Hebrews with Philo? And further, would a female Christian who was the slave of a Christian master have had more in common with her master, or with a Jewish woman who was the slave of a Jewish master, or a female worshiper of Isis who was the slave of a master who worshiped Isis? The effects of geographical distance were also relevant, as both Jews and followers of Jesus were found in communities stretching well over a thousand miles, from Spain to the East, assimilating in each case to vastly different local customs. It was becoming increasingly difficult to define clearly separate bodies of "Jews" and "Christians."

The earlier consensus, then, might have compared the "three parties" of Judaism—Sadducees, Pharisees, and Essenes—and the "two parties" within Christianity—Pauline Christians and "Jewish Christians"—a comparison that could be depicted in this way:

| Jewish groups: | 1 1 1 |
| Followers of Jesus: | 1 1 |

But by the end of the twentieth century, in recognition of the great variety of subgroups, the comparison would appear more like this:

| Jewish groups: | 1 1 1 1 1 1 1 1 1 1 1 1 1 |
| Followers of Jesus: | 1 1 1 1 1 1 1 1 1 1 1 |

If many Jewish groups maintained strict observance of Torah, so did many followers of Jesus. If many followers of Jesus believed that the end of time was near, so did many Jewish groups. If many followers of Jesus believed that the community of believers was bathed in the holiness of God in a way that made the Jewish temple superfluous, so did some Jews. And finally: If the death of Jesus was the theological affirmation that supposedly separated Christians from Jews, what do we make of the fact that some followers of Jesus did not emphasize his death and some Jewish texts (for example, 4 Maccabees) did emphasize the death of Jewish heroes? Similarities and differences among the groups in *both* rows above introduced new challenges for comparing "Judaism" and "Christianity." The Gospel of Matthew, for instance, was clearly critical of Pharisees—*one* of the Jewish groups in the row above—but was it possible that Matthew was actually more similar to Pharisees than he was to Paul? The simple question of the relation of "Jews" and "Christians" could no longer be answered without pressing a more specific question: *Which* Jews? *Which* Christians?

Incorporating this new consensus concerning a variety of groups among Christians and among Jews, some scholars toward the end of the twentieth century began charting the history of the "partings of the ways" or the "divorce" between Judaism and Christianity (e.g., Dunn 1991; Townsend). A title that exemplified the new consensus of variety was James D. G. Dunn's *The Partings of the Ways* (1991), but challenges to the "new consensus" were, of course, inevitable. Dunn's title was countered by a collection of conference papers called *The Ways That Never Parted* (Becker and Reed; see also Boyarin). This volume asked: At what point were the followers of Jesus thoroughly parted from "Judaism" or "Israel"? True, differences among Jewish or Christian subgroups could be discerned, but could the line above of Christian subgroups really be clearly distinguished from the Jewish line? Thus it is somewhat ironic that, after a century of new studies emphasizing the distinctions among different Jewish groups and different Christian groups, some of the heirs of that consensus would amend it by deemphasizing the boundary line *between* Judaism and Christianity. As more and more subgroups were divided off, they began to fill out the *overall* circle of "Judaism and Christianity" approximately equally. It is even suggested that texts that seem at first to affirm a clear, separate identity are in some cases overstating the distinction, or even creating the illusion of separation, imposing distinctions that may barely exist, in order to instill a clearer sense of identity. (This may be true, for example, of Matthew.) As we learn from modern identity studies, the strongest assertions of difference, or the strongest assertions of a good "We" and an evil "Other," often appear between groups that are similar to each other, and almost indistinguishable by outsiders (Wills). Although this newest development appears at first to undo the previous consensus about variety and difference, it actually carries it forward by demonstrating that there is a wide, overlapping spectrum of beliefs and practices among Jews *and* followers of Jesus, and yet the differences that we perceive among groups and subgroups does not result in one clear line *between* Jews and followers of Jesus. Some Christian groups would admittedly be more clearly separated from Judaism—for example, the implied audience of the Letter to the Hebrews—but others would be more ambiguous in their separation than once thought. Again, it is as if the two lines of groups above should be merged into one indistinct set.

The Continuing Demand for Comparison, Despite the Complexity of the Data

While recognizing all of these challenging new questions, the effort to draw general conclusions about the relations of Jews and Christians continues, and is indeed necessary for a dialogue between Jews and Christians in the twenty-first century. The demands of modern Jews and Christians for dialogue have required some general observations about the first century in order to proceed. Some of the older conclusions still inform the present, more complex discussions among Jews, Christians, and others, and can be used as starting points.

Douglas R. A. Hare, for instance, divided the different assessments of Judaism found in the New Testament into three types. Some polemic in the Gospels is simply a critique of Jewish institutions by people who were, after all, also Jews. This he termed "prophetic anti-Judaism," the critique by a prophetic figure of his or her own institutions. (Even this use of the term *anti-Judaism* seems to separate the prophet from the people and imply that the prophet is *not* Jewish; it is tantamount to referring to Martin Luther King's "anti-Americanism." George Michael Smiga [12–13] tried to address this terminological problem.) According to Hare, Jesus himself would have fit in this category, and might be compared to figures such as Socrates, who, although he criticized his fellow Athenians, was not "un-Greek" or "anti-Greek." Nor did his students suggest that they must create a new entity in which to explore his philosophy (though Plato did eventually leave Athens to advise the king of Syracuse in a failed experiment to establish a "philosopher's state"). Other polemic in the New Testament, however, became progressively harsher, and pronounced a final condemnation on those Jews who did not accept Jesus as the Messiah. Hare termed this "Jewish-Christian anti-Judaism." Unlike the previous category, this type represents a division of groups within Judaism that is at the point of divorce, and the polemical language reflects the tension of being "mid-divorce" (Townsend). A third type is "gentilizing anti-Judaism," and is truly postdivorce: the critique of Judaism as a whole by gentile Christians (Wilson, 110–42, 258–84). Authors in this category are no longer realistically concerned with the conversion of Israel. It can be debated which texts of the New Testament or the early church would fall into these categories, but many scholars would consider the Gospel of Matthew as the first type, a prophetic critique of some (or even most) Jews from within Judaism; the Acts of the Apostles as a text of the second type, which condemns Jews for not accepting the message of Jesus as Messiah; and the Epistle to the Hebrews as an example of gentilizing anti-Judaism. But any of these might be and have been debated. Only if we could interrogate the authors could we be sure where they stood on key questions of the relations of the subgroups in a constantly differentiated Judaism.

In addition to historians and biblical scholars, theologians also entered into the dialogue and introduced terminology to define the various positions that Christians have taken in regard to their relation to Judaism. "Supersessionism" describes the traditional Christian view that in Jesus and Paul we find the belief that Judaism was superseded by God's new dispensation in Christ and the church. (Some New Testament scholars use the compound term rejection-replacement.) But even a doctrine of supersessionism can be more or less negative about the validity of the Jewish covenant. Does the old covenant have any continuing role in God's dispensation, or is it simply the precursor to Christianity (Novak; see also Soulen)? A so-called dual-covenant theology has arisen among liberal Christians, which is the notion that God's new dispensation in Christ did not cancel out the existing covenant with Jews. In this view, there are still two covenants operative, and thus there is no supersessionism, but rather a continuing coexistence of parallel covenants. Some passages from early Christian authors might be adduced in support of this position (see below concerning Paul).

Yet this overture only calls forth new questions. Even if Christians developed a benign view of the continuing validity of God's covenant with Jews, that does not begin to address the relations of Christians with religions other than Judaism. Jewish-Christian dialogue is an important beginning, but only a beginning, to dialogues with other faiths, and this should not be forgotten in discussions of the history of Jewish-Christian relations. Although it is understandable that Jewish leaders have often engaged in dialogue with Christian leaders in order to ameliorate the effects of antisemitism, for many Jews it would be unacceptable to achieve a recognition of God's continuing covenant with Jews if other religions still remained in a less favored status. In the twenty-first century, a broader notion of religious acceptance, beyond a "dual-covenant theology," has often arisen.

With these and similar analyses in mind, in the late twentieth century, scholars of the New Testament, including many Jewish scholars, proposed sweeping changes in regard to how the New Testament texts themselves evaluated Judaism. Vermes, Fredriksen, and Levine (17–52) returned to the Gospel accounts and Acts and argued that recoverable evidence about the historical Jesus depicts a teacher who may have *argued* about Jewish law—not surprising for a Jewish teacher—but who probably remained fairly observant to the end. A great deal of consensus has gathered around this view. If Jesus did reject certain aspects of Jewish law that were advocated by others, such as the Pharisees—again, not surprising for any non-Pharisaic Jew—he never made a blanket rejection of the markers of Judaism. Otherwise, why would Paul have been forced to argue so strongly with the disciples who actually knew Jesus (Galatians 1–2)? Some of Jesus' claims in the Gospels might actually constitute a *stricter* than usual observance of Jewish law, an "ultraorthodox" position! (These cases are sometimes ambiguous, and identifying something or someone as more or less orthodox is always a relative question—who defined the norm? Yet Jesus' rejection of divorce in Mark 10:2-12, or his constraints on accepted Jewish law in Matt. 5:17-48, could be considered a stricter "fence around the Torah" than that which became the norm in rabbinic literature. See also Vermes [80–81], and on the apparent exception in Mark 7:19, see below.)

It is likely that any observer in the year 30 CE would not have considered Jesus a "Reform" Jew (admittedly an anachronistic term), but more probably, a "strict" or "pious" Jew. As noted above, a compelling argument was also made that the Gospel of Matthew, although formerly viewed as "anti-Jewish" ("Scribes and Pharisees, hypocrites!" Matt. 23:13), was actually more anti-*Pharisaic* (Harrington, 1–3; Wills, 101–32). That is, Matthew does not perceive the movement of the followers of Jesus as opposing Judaism, but as opposing some within Judaism, especially Pharisees. To be sure, it is stated in Matthew that at the end, the gentiles will come in (28:19), but that is true of many Jewish texts as well. Matthew does not betray a "Pauline" critique of Jewish law and remains observant to the end.

Even if Jesus and the Gospel of Matthew assumed a continuing adherence to Jewish law, it has been assumed that Paul had irrevocably altered this situation by instituting a mission to gentiles without the law. But now this assumption as well has come in for a major reevaluation. The so-called new perspective on Paul has questioned the chasm that Christians have traditionally perceived between this apostle and the Judaism of his day (Dunn 1983). For the new-perspective scholars, Paul was more a missionary theologian than an abstract theologian or a psychologist of the human condition, and was rarely setting up an opposition between "Jews" and those in Christ. Rather than critiquing and rejecting Judaism as a form of legalism and "works righteousness" at odds with God's plan, almost all of Paul's apparent references to "Jews" are more likely referring to those *in the Jesus movement*, whether originally Jewish or gentile, who oppose his mission to gentiles without the law. This raises a challenging question: If gentiles had been allowed to enter freely into his churches without adhering to Jewish law, would Paul have voiced any reservations about the law for Jews at all?

The debate over the new perspective has been significant. The new perspective represents a direct challenge to strongly held tradition, and yet has achieved a large following. Still, conservative Protestant theologians have opposed it, and even those scholars who have self-identified as part of the new perspective can be divided into two groups, a moderate new perspective and a radical new perspective (Wills, 179–82). The distinction is based on how far they would push the questioning of the older consensus. The moderate new-perspective scholars hold that Paul was much less critical of Judaism than once thought. Says E. P. Sanders (552), whom we might consider a moderate new-perspective scholar: "In short, this is what Paul finds wrong in Judaism: it is not Christianity." That is, God (in Paul's view) is not "displeased" with Jews, Judaism, or Jewish law, but has simply, by the death of Christ, created a new door for all, both Jews and gentiles, to enter into the graces of God. The *discontinuity* between Judaism and Christianity is thus drastically reduced. This shift alone unsettled much Protestant tradition.

But the radical new-perspective scholars go further and argue a version of the dual-covenant theology mentioned above. For Paul, the death of Christ did indeed open a new door of access for gentiles that did not require Jewish law, but the old door for Jews remained open as well—without Christ and with the law still in effect! God was not closing one door to open a new one, but was opening an option for gentiles parallel to the one for Jews (Eisenbaum). Paul's letters are ultimately unclear on this question, but Eisenbaum's conclusions may be correct. However, as above with dual-covenant theology, the same demurral still applies: even if Paul envisioned a two-door access, for gentiles in Christ without the law and for Jews with the law only, he is quite explicit that gentile religion (apart from belief in Christ) is degraded and alienated from God (Rom. 1:2; Gal. 4:8; see

Wills, 179–82). There is no "newer perspective" on Paul that could soften his condemnation of the gentile religions, and in the twenty-first century this becomes a fundamental challenge for interfaith dialogue. (It would be speculative to try to imagine what Paul's views of Islam might have been, although the parallels to Paul's theology are significant. In Islam, Jesus is the Messiah of God, born of a virgin, who performed miracles, and the revelation in Islam came to a prophet who was also "last of all, as to one untimely born" [cf. 1 Cor. 15:8]. But even if, continuing this imaginative exercise on the analogy of the "two-covenant" understanding described above, we were to imagine Paul countenancing a third covenant, with Islam, what would we say of the status of other religions?)

Now, many passages in Paul, especially in Romans, would appear to fly in the face of the radical new-perspective scholars, but in each case an alternative interpretation is possible that would at least make this dual-covenant reading a plausible option. Consider the much-discussed case of Rom. 10:4: "For Christ is the end [*telos*] of the law so that there may be righteousness for everyone who believes." Like the English "end," *telos* can be translated as either "point of cessation" or "goal"; does Paul mean that Christ will bring the covenant of law to an end, or that Christ will constitute the goal of that law *for gentiles*? The interpretation of individual passages sometimes also comes down to whether Paul is speaking principally about Christ or God. For example, in Rom. 9:33, Paul quotes Isa. 8:14-15; 28:16.

> See, I am laying in Zion a stone that will make people stumble, a rock that will make them fall,
> and whoever believes in him will not be put to shame.

Is Paul referring here to Christ, as Christian tradition has generally held, or, like the Isaiah passages he quotes, to *God's* role in establishing Jerusalem? Note here that the Greek pronoun for "him" could equally be "*it*," that is, the stone (a masculine noun in Greek). Which is the center of Paul's vision, Christ or God? Is it necessary for Jews to have faith *in Christ*, or faith *in the promises of God for gentiles*? The radical new-perspective scholars point out that in Romans, Paul speaks of both.

Quite often, we see that the debate narrows to a microanalysis of individual verses. Indeed, interpretation can only proceed one passage at a time, and yet, if at each stop alternative understandings are possible, then the decision about the whole becomes more difficult to adjudicate. But for this, as for any important and difficult issue, the positions of scholars and of laypeople will likely not be based on "decoding" one or two passages, but rather on general dispositions to the texts. However, it is possible that the undisputed letters of Paul, really only about seventy-five pages in the English translations, simply do not unambiguously reveal Paul's view on this question. That in itself would still be news. If the supersessionist position were really so central to Paul's theology, should it not be easy to establish it in the letters without question? If the overall impression of ambiguity is sustained, does that not at least suggest that the assurance with which earlier interpreters spoke of Paul in supersessionist ways was unwarranted? If one sets aside the *later* Christian tradition on supersessionism, does the same view disappear in Paul's letters?

The issues found in the Gospel of John have also come under scrutiny. Unlike Matthew, which focuses its polemic stridently on the Pharisees, John equally insistently refers to opponents as "Jews"—*Ioudaioi* in Greek—which can also be translated "Judeans" (that is, those from Judea, where

Jerusalem was located). How does one explain the intense anti-Judaism of John, where it is stated that *Ioudaioi* are the "children of the devil" (8:44)? Was the audience of John an "introversionist sect," which turned the promise of salvation inward to a small group of followers who no longer identified with the *Ioudaioi*, meaning Jews who revered the temple authorities in Judea (Wills, 133–66; Reinhartz, 25; Kittredge, 49–63)? Or is the Galilean origin of the Gospel of John at play here, and should *Ioudaioi* be translated not as "Jews" but as "Judeans," those members of Israel who lived in Judea and exercised some control over the members of Israel (which may include Samaritans) who lived in Galilee and Samaria? Whatever sociological theory is asserted to explain the *Ioudaioi* in the Gospel of John, the text seems to express a polemical separation that is different from Matthew on one hand or Paul on the other. The distinction between good and bad people, or even good and evil people, is even stronger in John than in Paul or Matthew.

For twenty-first-century audiences, it is difficult to come to terms with the strong polemics voiced in our sacred texts. Should modern readers, both Christian and Jewish, simply conclude that the ancient writers of the now-sacred texts took group identity too far? Consider a passage from the Hebrew Bible and a passage from the New Testament.

> When the LORD your God brings you into the land that you are about to enter . . . and he clears away . . . the Hittites, the Girgashites, the Amorites, the Canaanites, the Perizzites, the Hivites, and the Jebusites, . . . then you must utterly destroy them. (Deut. 7:1-2)

> You [Jews] are from your father the devil, and you choose to do your father's desires. He was a murderer from the beginning and does not stand in the truth. . . . He is a liar and the father of lies. (John 8:44, referred to above)

One can imagine asking, "If you knew a Hittite well (or a Jew well), would you say that?" (On the ambiguity of these designations, see Wills, 21–51, 133–66.) But the many varieties of early followers of Jesus means that *different* lines were being drawn in the sand to differentiate groups, and while they defined the fissures between most Jews and followers of Jesus, they also defined serious breaches among different followers of Jesus. Would Paul, Matthew, or John have placed *each other* among the saved, or among the damned?

The Gospel of Mark as a Test Case

At the same time that bold new assessments were being raised in regard to the relations of Jews and followers of Jesus in Matthew, Paul, and John, there was relatively little rethinking of the situation in the Gospel of Mark, and this Gospel could become a test case for the *old* view. It has long been assumed that, *regardless of the original meaning of Paul's letters*, Mark understood Paul as Paul's followers did. The following assumptions seemed secure:

1. Mark was influenced by Paul and inherited a Pauline doctrine of faith.
2. Mark reflected a mission that was like Paul's; in Mark, Jesus moved into gentile territory to demonstrate an openness to gentile converts (Mark 7–9).

3. Mark must have been a gentile, because there are inaccuracies in regard to Jewish practice in the passion narratives and elsewhere, and Mark explains basic Jewish practices, often inaccurately (7:3-4).

4. Jesus is depicted as rejecting kosher laws across the board (7:19).

Now, however, these conclusions have also been challenged. First, it is not at all clear that Mark knew Paul's theology of faith *in contrast to law*. Faith was a constant element in the Hebrew Bible and also in the Jewish discourse of the period. The Hebrew word *'aman* ("to believe, have faith") and its related forms (in Aramaic as well) can be found behind the use of "amen" in liturgy and are related to the word truth (*'emet*, derived from *'aman*), and to the "faithful ones" (*ne'emanim*) among the Pharisees (*m. Demai* 4:6). In Neh. 9:38, the restored community in Jerusalem joins in a "faith covenant" (*'amanah*). The use of this root by Jews speaking Hebrew or Aramaic, and of the *pist-* root by those speaking Greek, only increases in the Hellenistic period. Thus, although the use of the language of "faith" and "believing" in Mark is pronounced, *it was also common in Judaism*, a fact that is almost totally ignored in assessments of Jewish-Christian relations in the first century. Further, the language of "faith" and "believing" in Mark is not explicitly contrasted with law as Paul would have it; it is used in the same way as other Jews were using it. (Parallels between Mark and Paul are often listed, but the Pauline passages are almost all found in Romans. Were Paul's words in this letter carefully chosen to respond to the *Jewish* discourse on faith in which that community would have been schooled?)

Second, although in Mark, Jesus does move into territories occupied by gentiles, these were also (with one exception, 7:1) part of the ancient borders of Israel. The Maccabees and their descendants had already conquered these lands in order to reestablish the boundaries of ancient Israel; so might we regard Jesus' itinerary in Mark as also reconstituting "Israel"? Jesus also heals gentiles, but so had the prophet Elisha (2 Kings 5); was the latter also "gentilizing" Israel? Third, Mark's Gospel does seem to include many *apparent* inaccuracies concerning Jewish practices, but these, too numerous to mention, are in some cases found in other Jewish texts or taken over in the "Jewish" Gospel Matthew, and other cases are much less clear than once thought (A. Y. Collins).

Last, we come to the argument that has often seemed conclusive: Mark's apparent cancellation of all kosher laws in Jesus' debate with the Pharisees and scribes at 7:1-23. The relevant verses are displayed here side by side with the equivalent section of Matthew. The parallel columns allow one to read Mark's words closely while at the same time noting the differences found in Matthew's treatment of this important issue. (Luke and John do not include this passage.)

Mark 7:1-23 (in part)	**Matthew 15:1-20** (in part)
[1] When the Pharisees and some of the scribes who had come from Jerusalem gathered around him, [2] they noticed that some of his disciples were eating with defiled hands, that is, without washing them.	[1] Then Pharisees and scribes came to Jesus from Jerusalem,
[3] For the Pharisees, and all the Jews, do not eat unless they thoroughly wash their hands, thus observing the tradition of the elders;	
[4] and they do not eat anything from the market unless they wash it; and there are also many other traditions that they observe, the washing of cups, pots, and bronze kettles.	
[5] So the Pharisees and the scribes asked him, "Why do your disciples not live according to the tradition of the elders, but eat with defiled hands?"	and said, [2] "Why do your disciples break the tradition of the elders? For they do not wash their hands before they eat?"
[Several scriptural and legal arguments follow here.]	[Several scriptural and legal arguments follow here.]
[14] He called the people to him again and said, [15] "There is nothing outside a person which by going in can defile, but the things which come out are what defile.	[10] He called the people to him and said, [11] "It is not what goes into the mouth that defiles a person, but what comes out of the mouth, this defiles.
[18] Do you not see that whatever goes into a person from outside cannot defile, [19] since it enters not the heart, but the stomach, and goes out into the sewer?" Thus he declared all foods clean [literally, "Thus he cleansed all foods"].	[17] Do you not see that whatever goes into the mouth enters the stomach, and goes out into the sewer?
[20] And he said, "It is what comes out of a person that defiles. [21] For it is from within, from the human heart, that evil intentions come: fornication, theft, murder, [22] adultery, avarice, wickedness, deceit, licentiousness, envy, slander, pride, folly.	[18] But what comes out of the mouth proceeds from the heart, and this is what defiles. [19] For out of the heart come evil intentions, murder, adultery, fornication, theft, false witness, slander.
[23] All these evil things come from within, and they defile a person."	[20] These are what defile a person, but to eat with unwashed hands does not defile."

Mark's words here are traditionally interpreted in a "Pauline" way, that is, that Jewish law now no longer applies among the followers of Jesus. However, challenges to that interpretation of this passage have also arisen. Jesus' debate with Pharisees about eating food with unwashed hands may not be a rejection of Jewish law but a debate *within* Judaism. Mark here may actually have Jesus endorse the majority Jewish position against the stricter Pharisees. Was the view Mark attributes to Jesus actually more typical of Jewish practice in the first century than the Pharisees'? One also notices that the run-on sentence in 7:3-4 may have resulted from the combination of a simple, and accurate, statement about Pharisees and additional comments about practices of "all the Jews" that were added later. (Note that these verses are not present in Matthew.) But Mark's explanation of Jewish customs may also not be as out of place in Jewish discourse as once thought (A. Y. Collins, 345; Regev 2000, 180–81, 188–89). To be sure, the passage indicates (if it was not inserted later in its entirety) that Mark is including gentiles in the audience of the Gospel, but it does not necessarily reveal a gentile *author*. Mark's reference to the practices of "all the Jews" certainly seems to distance himself from them, but we encounter here a hidden problem with English that affects interpretation. An English-speaking Jew might say, "All Jews do such-and-such," but not "All *the* Jews do such-and-such." The English definite article has the power in this construction to separate off the group in question and to distance the speaker from the group. In Greek, however, usage of the definite article is often quite different from English, and it is not clear that it would distance the speaker in this way. Did Mark mean, "All Jews wash their hands"—which could include Mark—or "All *the* Jews wash their hands"—which seems to distance the Markan Jesus from the Jews?

The last half of this passage has also been reassessed. The central statement—"There is nothing outside a person which by going in can defile, but the things which come out are what defile"—may not be a rejection of purity concerns, as long supposed, but simply an insistence that *moral* purity is as important, or even more important, than *ritual* purity. The prioritizing of moral motives over observance was well known in the Jewish background (Mic. 6:6-8, Hosea 6:6), but the insistence that Jewish observance remains in effect as well is also found in New Testament texts: "You Pharisees tithe mint and rue and herbs of all kinds, and neglect justice and the love of God. It is these you ought to have practiced, *without neglecting the others*" (Luke 11:42; Klawans, 147–48).

But Mark also broadens the discussion by the insertion of 7:19c, "thus he declared all foods clean" (*katharizōn panta ta brōmata*). This awkward and intrusive phrase, which does not appear in Matthew (the section as a whole, as noted, is lacking in Luke and John), may have been inserted later in the textual history of Mark (Booth, 49–50, 62–65), but even if these were Mark's own words, it is also possible that this clause has an entirely different meaning. The Greek literally says, "Jesus *cleansed* all foods," but translators, stumped by what that would mean, have chosen a paraphrasing translation that made perfect sense in the twentieth-century consensus: "Jesus declared all foods clean." This translation means that the "Pauline" Jesus was instituting a new policy canceling all kosher laws. However, in the ancient period, it was sometimes stated, in both Jewish and Christian texts, that at the end of time, for the special, saved community, there would be a *cleansing* of foods, vessels, or people. From Ezekiel (36:22-31) to Zechariah (14:16, 20-21) to *1 Enoch* (10:17—11:2) to Qumran (1QS 4:20-21), there are discussions of a shower of purity on the saved community, however that community is described (see also *Jub.* 1:17, 23; 4:26; 50:5; *Abot R. Nat. B* 42; *b. Erub.*

100b; Regev 2000; 2004). Indeed, with this notion in mind, one may look at other passages in Mark as well. Consider Jesus' healing of a leper, phrased in terms of "cleansing" (the *kathar* root in Greek).

> A leper came to him begging him, and kneeling he said to him, "If you choose, you can cleanse me [*katharisai*, cf. 7:19, discussed above]." Moved with pity, Jesus stretched out his hand and touched him, and said to him, "I do choose. Be cleansed [*katharistheti*]!" Immediately the leprosy left him, and he was cleansed [*ekatharisthe*]. After sternly warning him he sent him away at once, saying to him, "See that you say nothing to anyone; but go, show yourself to the priest, and offer for your cleansing [*katharismos*] what Moses commanded, as a testimony to them." (Mark 1:40-44)

Although this passage is often understood, from the perspective of *later* Christianity, as the rejection of purity laws about leprosy, a close reading reveals that Jesus miraculously returns the leper to a state of being clean, but does nothing to alter the Jewish laws concerning purity. In fact, the man is instructed to go to the temple to make the offering that Moses commanded (Leviticus 14). The point is important. Technically, in Jewish law, a leper is not pure until after the temple offering is made, but the point of Mark's story is that purity is now made miraculously available as an eschatological event (see Regev 2000; 2004). In the similar but not identical case in the Hebrew Bible mentioned above (2 Kings 5), the prophet heals Naaman the Syrian from his leprosy. But just as it is not generally suggested in Jewish or Christian tradition that Elisha is opening Israel to gentiles, it is also not suggested that he is canceling Jewish purity laws concerning leprosy. And Mark is not the only Christian text to describe an end-time cleansing of the saints; in an otherwise puzzling passage, Paul finds a new cleansing in the community members themselves; note the juxtaposition of "cleansing" with holiness language (the *hag-* root in Greek):

> The unbelieving husband is made holy [*hegiastai*] through his wife, and the unbelieving wife is made holy through her husband. Otherwise, your children would be unclean [*akatharta*], but as it is, they are holy [*hagia*]. (1 Cor. 7:14; see Johnson Hodge)

So just as the leper in Mark 1:40-45 is *cleansed*—purity rules are *not* abrogated—and in 1 Corinthians 7 an unbelieving spouse is made holy and the children cleansed, so in Mark 7 it is likely that in anticipation of an eschatological change, Jesus *cleanses* foods, as the Greek actually states. Thus, even if this verse was in Mark's original text, it may not have meant that Jewish kosher laws were being rejected, but that for this community, there is at the end of time a dispensation of purity that overwhelms impurity, and also defeats "impure spirits," Mark's more Jewish term for "demons." If, as Zech. 14:20 says, all vessels can be rendered pure at the end of time, and if, as 1 Corinthians 7 says, spouses can be rendered holy, why not lepers in the community, and foods? At the end of time, all heaven breaks loose, but only on the holy community, the *hagioi* ("saints"). There is a division of humanity for a simultaneous cleansing and judgment. The canceling of Jewish food laws, which is how Acts 10, for instance, has been traditionally interpreted, has been too hastily read back into Mark (see also Rom. 14:20).

This passage, then, which had been treated by scholars as a clear confirmation of the Pauline theology at the center of Mark, is much more ambiguous than was once supposed. Paul's letters were often used to justify a gentile mission and identity, but was Mark part of that development (as were Luke and Acts), or was it, like Matthew, part of that segment of the movement, perhaps the larger part, that had not abrogated Jewish law? What was once considered unlikely in regard to Mark now seems quite possible.

Conclusion

A common theme here is that Matthew, Paul, John, and Mark were likely much more rooted in Jewish tradition than Christians have generally assumed. The net effect of these newer investigations is to make discussions among Jews, Christians, and others much more unsettled, but also much richer. Much uncertainty has arisen about each old consensus, and this may seem daunting to contemporary audiences. But there is now a possibility of a wholly *new* dialogue, one that goes back to both the Jewish and Christian sources and asks again what the texts might have meant and what the relations were—both within each body and between the two bodies. The seeds of modern anti-Judaism and the Holocaust can still be seen in some of the ancient texts, but the varied relations also reveal the truth that the story is complex, and it includes many alternative visions of how religious subgroups could respond to each other. There is not just one blueprint for "the relations of Judaism and Christianity" in the first century.

Works Cited

Bauer, Walter. 1934. *Rechtgläubigkeit und Ketzerei im ältesten Christentum.* Tübingen: Mohr. Translated as *Orthodoxy and Heresy in Earliest Christianity.* Philadelphia: Fortress Press, 1979.

Becker, Adam H., and Annette Yoshiko Reed, eds. 2007. *The Ways That Never Parted: Jews and Christians in Late Antiquity and the Early Middle Ages.* Minneapolis: Fortress Press.

Booth, Roger P. 1986. *Jesus and the Laws of Purity: Tradition History and Legal History in Mark 7.* Sheffield: JSOT Press.

Boyarin, Daniel. 2004. *Border Lines: The Partition of Judaeo-Christianity.* Philadelphia: University of Pennsylvania Press.

Cohen, Shaye J. D. 2006. *From the Maccabees to the Mishnah.* 2nd ed. Louisville: Westminster John Knox.

Collins, Adela Yarbro. 2007. *Mark: A Commentary.* Hermeneia. Minneapolis: Fortress Press.

Collins, John J. 2000. *Between Athens and Jerusalem: Jewish Identity in the Hellenistic Diaspora.* 2nd ed. Grand Rapids: Eerdmans.

Dunn, James D. G. 1983. "The New Perspective on Paul." *BJRL* 65:95–122.

———. 1991. *The Partings of the Ways: Between Christianity and Judaism and Their Significance for the Character of Christianity.* London: SCM.

Eisenbaum, Pamela. 2009. *Paul Was Not a Christian: The Real Message of a Misunderstood Apostle.* New York: HarperOne.

Foltz, Richard. 2010. *Religions of the Silk Road: Premodern Patterns of Globalization.* 2nd ed. New York: Palgrave Macmillan.

Fredriksen, Paula. 1995. "Did Jesus Oppose Purity Laws?" *BR* 11:18–25, 42–48.

Hare, Douglas R. A. 1967. *The Theme of Jewish Persecution of Christians in the Gospel according to St. Matthew.* Cambridge: Cambridge University Press.

Harrington, Daniel J. 1991. *The Gospel of Matthew*. Sacra pagina. Collegeville, MN: Liturgical Press.

Johnson Hodge, Caroline. 2007. *If Sons, then Heirs: A Study of Kinship and Ethnicity in the Letters of Paul*. Oxford: Oxford University Press.

———. 2010. "Married to an Unbeliever: Households, Hierarchies, and Holiness in 1 Corinthians 7:12-16." *HTR* 103:1–25.

Kittredge, Cynthia Briggs. 2007. *Conversations with Scripture: The Gospel of John*. Harrisburg, PA: Morehouse.

Klawans, Jonathan. 2000. *Impurity and Sin in Ancient Judaism*. Oxford: Oxford University Press.

Levine, Amy-Jill. 2006. *The Misunderstood Jew: The Church and the Scandal of the Jewish Jesus*. San Francisco: HarperSanFrancisco.

Nickelsburg, George W. E. 2005. *Jewish Literature between the Bible and the Mishnah: A Historical and Literary Introduction*. 2nd ed. Minneapolis: Fortress Press.

Novak, David. 2004. "The Covenant in Rabbinic Thought." In *Two Faiths, One Covenant? Jewish and Christian Identity in the Presence of the Other*, edited by Eugene B. Korn, 65–80. Lanham, MD: Rowman & Littlefield.

Regev, Eyal. 2000. "Pure Individualism: The Idea of Non-Priestly Purity in Ancient Judaism." *JSJ* 31:176–202.

———. 2004. "Moral Impurity and the Temple in Early Christianity in Light of Ancient Greek Practice and Qumranic Ideology." *HTR* 97:377–402.

Reinhartz, Adele. 2001. *Befriending the Beloved Disciple: A Jewish Reading of the Gospel of John*. New York: Continuum.

Robinson, James M., and Helmut Koester. 1971. *Trajectories through Early Christianity*. Philadelphia: Fortress Press.

Sanders, E. P. 1977. *Paul and Palestinian Judaism: A Comparison of Patterns of Religion*. Philadelphia: Fortress Press.

Sanders, Jack T. 1993. *Schismatics, Sectarians, Dissidents, Deviants: The First One Hundred Years of Jewish-Christian Relations*. London: SCM.

Schürer, Emil. 1886–1890. *Geschichte des jüdischen Volkes im Zeitalter Jesu Christi*. 2 vols. Leipzig: Hinrichs.

Smiga, George Michael. 1992. *Pain and Polemic: Anti-Judaism in the Gospels*. Mahwah, NJ: Paulist.

Soulen, R. Kendall. 1996. *The God of Israel and Christian Theology*. Minneapolis: Fortress Press.

Townsend, John. 1979. "The Gospel of John and the Jews: The Story of a Religious Divorce." In *Antisemitism and the Foundations of Christianity*, edited by Alan T. Davies, 72–97. New York: Paulist.

Vermes, Géza. 1991. *Jesus the Jew: A Historian's Reading of the Gospels*. Philadelphia: Fortress Press.

Wills, Lawrence M. 2008. *Not God's People: Insiders and Outsiders in the Biblical World*. Lanham, MD: Rowman & Littlefield.

Wilson, Stephen G. 1995. *Related Strangers: Jews and Christians, 70–170 C.E.* Minneapolis: Fortress Press.

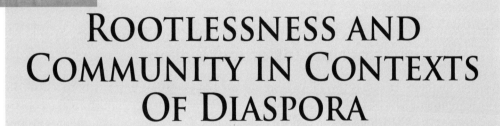

ROOTLESSNESS AND COMMUNITY IN CONTEXTS OF DIASPORA

Margaret Aymer

Rootlessness wanders through Christian imagination today as it has for thousands of years. Even today, hymns proclaiming "this world is not my home," and "I am a poor pilgrim of sorrow, I'm lost in this wide world alone," are sung by women and men whose families can trace their ancestry on any given land mass back multiple generations. Often, the Hebrew Scriptures are credited as the origin of themes of rootlessness, wandering, pilgrimage, and dispersion. However, the New Testament also contains themes of rootlessness and of the creation of community in times of diaspora.

Perhaps it takes an uprooted soul to notice these themes, this ongoing trope in the New Testament. Perhaps it takes the eyes of a woman between cultures, not fully American, and unquestionably not Caribbean—except when I unquestionably am—who emigrated as a child and has functioned as an interpreter of cultures for both my home and host cultures. Some Asian Americans call this the phenomenon of being "the 1.5 generation," the generation that stands between the deep memory of the first-generation immigrant who grew to adulthood in the country of origin and the deep acculturation of the second generation, born in the country of migration. As 1.5-generation people, we stand between homelands, always on a journey, negotiating when possible, turning away when endangered, forging a third way when necessary, and always being in the midst of creating and re-creating culture in ways that are at once rooted in the old, transplanted into a strange land, and bearing hybrid, sometimes nourishing fruit that may at times be unrecognizable as the result of transplantation.

I often read the New Testament with 1.5-generation eyes, eyes not only of an immigrant but also of an immigrant of color. And when I do, I notice that many of these New Testament texts bear marks of migration: evidence of negotiating one's way between home and host cultures, and of the work of forging culture and making meaning in the midst of displacement.

(Re)Considering the History and Rhetoric of New Testament Writings

To argue that the New Testament writings bear marks of migration is to make both a historical and a rhetorical argument. The historical argument is grounded in the accepted historical reconstruction of the creation of these writings by the majority of scholars. The rhetorical argument is grounded in the way in which the authors describe their displacement, their own rootlessness, and that of their community; and how they use that rhetoric to construct strategies of interaction with the wider world. Take, for example, the general consensus that Mark is the oldest canonical Gospel, written after the siege of Jerusalem (of which Mark 13 is understood as description after the fact rather than foretelling), and that it was not written in Judea or Galilee. Already that history suggests displacement, the Gospel narrative written in migration. This would not be the case if the story were an invention out of the imagination of "Mark" the Gospel writer. But if, as biblical scholars have claimed, "Mark" uses oral sources as well as written ones to construct a narrative that he believes to be factually true at least in part, then the ultimate origin of those oral sources would have had to be persons from Judea or Galilee whose bodies, or stories, had migrated to Mark's location. Thus we know with some certainty that at the very least, the stories are migratory.

Mark gives us more clues to suggest that the cultural home of his narrative is not his current audience. He includes and, of even more importance, he *translates* a number of Aramaic sayings of Jesus, among them *Talitha kum* (5:41), *Ephphatha* (7:34), and the cry from the cross, *Eloi, Eloi, lama sabachthani* (15:34). That there is Aramaic in Mark should come as no surprise. After all, Aramaic was one of the languages of Judea and the Galilee. The surprise is Mark's need to translate the Aramaic. This suggests, first, that either Mark or his oral source knows Aramaic, for the short passages are translated correctly. This makes Mark at least bilingual; the Gospel of Mark was composed in Greek. Second, it suggests that Mark is writing to an audience that is, at most, only partially literate in Aramaic.

All of these are traces, hints of the possible origins of the Gospel of Mark, which are, in reality, largely lost. However, these traces suggest a Gospel written in displacement and a writer bridging the distance between a story perhaps told in Aramaic and one written in Greek with Aramaic traces, translating the first generation to the second generation. If this is the case, Mark's Gospel not only tells the good news of Jesus Christ but also, like the older exilic writings of the Hebrew Scriptures, tells a story about a homeland and a home culture no longer accessible to a generation that may be in danger of forgetting. It is an immigrant's tale, a tale of which, if Mark 16:8 can be believed, Mark alone is the only faithful teller.

The other Gospels and the Acts of the Apostles might take issue with Mark's monopoly on faithful discipleship. As second- and third-generation readers (see Luke 1:1-2), they take the traditions of the migrants and rework them for their contemporaries, not unlike the transformation of English plum pudding into Caribbean Christmas cake or the twenty-first-century hip-hop recensions of Bob Marley's twentieth-century reggae hits. Some translation still needs to take place. Some original language still remains in place. And depending on the nature of the community, more of the home culture (Matthew) or more of the host culture (Luke) is emphasized. But the history remains the same: communities of persons outside of Judea and Galilee, and distant from the events of Jesus' life, inheriting a story told and retold in migration, a story possibly even recounted and written by migrants.

With the writings of Paul, one can demonstrate a case for their historical marks of migration much more simply. Paul is, after all, a wandering preacher writing to assemblies in cities and villages outside of his natal Tarsus. This alone is enough to make these writings migrant writings. But Paul, too, is engaging in translation: in this case, not translation from Aramaic to Greek, but the cultural work of translating a primarily Jerusalem-based, Jewish sect into an assembly that denies the distinctiveness between Jew and Greek, slave and free, perhaps even man and woman (Galatians 3). This is an assembly not just for gentiles, but even more powerfully for Diaspora Jews, those who for generations have lived away from but never completely separated from Jerusalem and Galilee. This group would have maintained some traditions and let others go, particularly others that would have made them peculiar or abhorrent to their majority-gentile neighbors. Indeed, by the time he writes to Philippi, Paul radically begins to imagine these assemblies not merely as bodies of believers gathered to pray but also as political entities in which those assembled had status, citizenship, and inheritance (Phil. 3:20). Paul's writing bears marks not only of his own migrant life but also of the diasporic migrant lives of his communities, and of a migrant imagination that forms new communities of migrants—persons living in one place with their citizenship in another.

Paul's interpreters, those who wrote the deuteropauline and Pastoral Epistles, are similarly involved in a work of translation: translation as cultural accommodation of the majority culture. Once Paul's apocalyptic insistence on the imminent return of Christ proves to be premature, these interpreters, perhaps a generation removed from Paul's migrant fervor, use their second-generation status to re-create a Christianity less dangerous to the empire in which it must survive.

Like Paul, John of Patmos seems to be a migrant, perhaps an involuntary migrant, if we take his self-description in Revelation 1:9 as evidence that he is in exile. His epistolary apocalypse then takes on the work of migrant writing, a writing both in migration (he is on Patmos) and to migrant communities. The letter does what John can no longer do, moving from place to place encouraging communities to hold fast and to remember that their final dwelling place is not the place where they currently abide and that their allegiances are not to the beasts of land and sea or to the dragon who gives them power. Rather, their allegiances are to the lion/slaughtered lamb on the throne and their true home is the new Jerusalem, which will come down from the new heaven on the new earth. They are thus to live as citizens of "an-other" place, as migrants in an evil world, waiting, like the souls under the altar, until all is accomplished and their nomadic God migrates to the new Jerusalem and pitches the divine tent among them (Rev. 21:3).

The writings attributed to John the Gospel writer and his community (the Gospel and the three pseudonymous epistles) betray a similar orientation to the world in which the community lives.

John 9, famously, has been held up by Raymond Brown and others as a narrative of the community's forced exile, its forced (e)migration from its community of origin (the synagogue/formative Judaisms) to an-other place, a location somehow outside of both "world" and "home" (John 1). Those who leave this other place are castigated in the first of the Johannine Epistles as antichrists. Within the Johannine community, forced migration on the basis of belief is virtuous; voluntary migration out of the community is satanic.

Migration as an underlying physical and/or rhetorical concern is thus evident in many of the New Testament writings. However, only two make it explicit: James and 1 Peter. James may well be a letter to, rather than by, migrant communities. Indeed, James's letter, addressed "to the twelve tribes in the Diaspora," strongly resembles other such Jerusalem-to-Diaspora missives sent by the Sanhedrin contemporary with this writing (Bauckham, 19–20). James's sermon-in-a-letter, or homiletic epistle, reminds those outside of the immediate influence of Jerusalem of the particular ethics expected of those who gather in synagogues (James 2), claim to follow the "royal law" (2:8), and consider themselves to be followers of the Lord Jesus Christ (2:1). Primarily, these communities should not resemble the stain of the world, but should be separate entities marked by an ethical concern for the workers, the widows and orphans, and the poor (1:27). However, they are not to consider their status permanent. They will continue in their involuntary migration only until the Parousia of the Lord (5:7). At that time, the injustices experienced in their exile will be adjudicated by the Lord of Sabaoth (5:4).

First Peter takes a similar tack. Writing specifically to those Diasporan exiles in Asia Minor, the advice of 1 Peter to these migrant communities is twofold. First, the author insists on the identity of these migrants as displaced royalty, exiled priests, and a people belonging to God (1 Peter 2). Their dispersal does not change their identity. Rather, it requires prudent interaction with the dominating culture of their exile until they can regain their inheritance as heirs to the kingdom of God. Second, the author requires that the migrant congregation act in ways that would be considered blameless during the time of their exile. For this author, this means that the community of faith must adopt even the norms of the kyriarchy of their community of exile. "Kyriarchy," a neologism coined by Elisabeth Schüssler Fiorenza, describes "the rule of the emperor, lord, slave master, husband, or the elite freeborn, propertied, educated gentleman to whom disenfranchised men and all wo/men were subordinated" (Schüssler Fiorenza, 9). Acceptance of such norms moved 1 Peter's Christian community away from less hierarchical structures such as those intimated by Galatians 3 and toward the more accommodationist stance of the second generation of the Pauline school. It was, among other things, a way for these migrants to "fit in." This kyriarchy-as-camouflage was, of course, counseled uncritically by a member of the literate class (or at least one who could pay for an amanuensis). Those who bore its burden most profoundly were the migrant community's least powerful members: women, children, and slaves.

Other New Testament writings give us far fewer clues about their migrant status. Yet even these reference comings, goings, and their impact on community identity. The pseudonymous letters of 2 Peter and Jude, for example, are unlikely to be of Galilean or Judean origin, although this is impossible to know. As such, they would also be migrant writings, strictly speaking. However, their discourse focuses less on the community's migrant nature and more on the danger of the immigration of other people—with other ideas about Christian identity—into their communities (2 Pet. 2:3; Jude 4). Even without a specific focus on the community's movement or clear evidence of displacement, these writings seek to create and strengthen communities that are outside the general population (e.g., not pagan, not Jewish, not licit), and there is still a sense of migration about them.

Hebrews, of course, stands as the New Testament enigma, giving its readers very few clues about authorship, dating, placement, or any other historical data. Yet even if one argues for Hebrews as an early Judean or Galilean document (as does DeSilva in this volume), there is still an overlay of migration in its rhetoric. For even if one depicts Hebrews as a letter/sermon written to, by, and in Judea or the Galilee, one cannot escape the trope of community-as-migrants and the rhetorical journey toward rest that wends its way through the homiletics of the unknown preacher. Hebrews too, although less explicit, bears the marks of migration.

Thus a phenomenon often overlooked marks at least a significant plurality of New Testament literature. The bulk of it, and perhaps all of it, could be categorized as migrant writing. As a result, although rootlessness is most frequently considered a concern of James and 1 Peter, and perhaps to a lesser extent of the rhetorics of Hebrews and Philippians, in truth, underlying all of the New Testament canon is a sense of rootlessness, of dispersion, and of the need to survive in a place that is not home, whether physically or culturally. The rest of this essay seeks to explore the implications of this underlying rootlessness, both in the New Testament writings and for those who appropriate these writings as Scriptures.

New Testament Writings as Diaspora Spaces

What difference might it make if the New Testament writings were considered to be migrant writings? Here, a brief consideration of theory about "diaspora spaces" might be helpful. Sociologist Avtar Brah proposes that diaspora space is that place

> where multiple subject positions are juxtaposed, contested, proclaimed or disavowed; where the permitted and the prohibited perpetually interrogate; and where the accepted and the transgressive imperceptibly mingle even while these syncretic forms may be disclaimed in the name of purity and tradition. [It is a space where] *tradition is itself continually invented even as it may be hailed as originating from the mists of time.* (Brah, 208, emphasis added)

This thick description reflects the struggle and promise of diaspora spaces, those spaces where migrants and host communities enter into the never-ending dance of self-definition. But what does it have to do with the New Testament? Simply this: If the New Testament writings are, indeed, migrant writings, these migrant rhetorics might be expected to create texts that are diaspora spaces, texts/spaces in which migrant writers and migrant communities struggle with the nature of faithfulness to their understanding of the new Christian movements while living in a majority-pagan world.

So, if the New Testament writings are migrant writings, one might expect to note the juxtaposition, contestation, proclamation, and/or disavowal of multiple subject positions (Brah, 208). Perhaps the quintessential example of such struggle is bound up in the person and history of Saul/Paul of Tarsus. He names himself a Jew, born of the tribe of Benjamin, circumcised and a Pharisee (Phil. 3:5). However, he is also named a citizen of the pagan, primarily Greek-speaking Roman Empire, and claims that status by birth rather than through financial or military transaction (Acts 22:25-28). He is Saul, named after the first king of Judea, but without fanfare becomes Paul as he begins his gentile evangelism, no doubt because his Hebrew name is transliterated *saulos* in Greek (Acts 13:9), and *saulos* is an adjective that describes "the *loose, wanton* gait of courtesans or Bacchantes" (Liddell and Scott, s.v. "*saulos*"). This is a person who claims to himself and to his entire community, Jew and Greek, the promises of the particularly Jewish Abrahamic covenant (Gal. 3:1-9). This same person claims to become "all things to all people" for the sake of his Christian evangelism (1 Cor. 9:22).

Of course, Paul is not alone in this place of juxtaposition, of negotiation between cultures. Other characters carry two names, two identities: consider Tabitha/Dorcas and John/Mark (Acts 9; 12). Neither is Paul alone is standing between cultures and negotiating different subject positions: consider Joanna, the wife of Chuza, Herod's steward, who stands between Roman client privilege in Herod's household and her support of Jesus—who would, no doubt, have been understood as a wandering Jewish prophet and social critic, and who was killed for sedition against the Roman Empire (Luke 8). However, not every New Testament figure makes the same choices that Paul makes when faced with this negotiation between cultures. The author of the Epistle of James, for instance, in his counsel to the "twelve tribes of the diaspora" (James 1:1), calls for withdrawal and self-preservation (1:27). Similarly, the seer on Patmos island, echoing the prophet's jeremiad, calls his people to "come out" of Babylon (Rev. 18:4, cf. Jer. 51:45). In a different response to the same question of positionality with respect to one's own culture and to "the world," John's Gospel suggests a third way, a way that is neither of the world nor of the home culture of the migrant outsiders. This way is signified by the Johannine phrase, "sons of God," and represents the formation of an-other position in society (John 1).

In addition to matters of the subject's positionality, New Testament writings also reveal the ongoing interrogation of permitted and prohibited, the mingling of accepted and transgressive, and ultimately the creation of syncretic forms that Brah describes as characteristics of diaspora space. Perhaps the most obvious New Testament example of the interrogation of the permitted and prohibited is the conflict regarding the inclusion of gentiles into the early churches without requiring of them the rite of circumcision. This early church-dividing conflict emerges in many of the undisputed Pauline writings, and differently in the Acts of the Apostles. Paul is usually the anticircumcision champion in his own writings; but the author of Luke-Acts makes Peter the standard-bearer after a theophany and an encounter with a gentile named Cornelius (Acts 10; 15). However, circumcision is not the only New Testament example of the interrogation and re-creation of traditions and forms. The "healing on the Sabbath" crisis seen in many of the Gospels is also part of this ongoing interrogation of what is and is not permitted to be done by faithful people during the Sabbath rest. Table fellowship is yet another example of the New Testament interrogation of permitted and prohibited: not merely who was admitted to the table (thus the Syrophoenician woman's protest in Mark 7) but even more the question of whether meat was to be served (1 Corinthians 8; Revelation 2). After all, meat was almost always sacrificed to the gods, whom Christians and Jews saw as idols. Should, then, Christians eat meat at their symposia, or was this a tacit acceptance of idolatry

(Taussig)? These discussions and debates about the interaction between the permitted and transgressive likely preceded the advent of Christianity among the Jewish migrants in Diaspora around the greater Mediterranean world. However, a new urgency in response to these questions would have been felt after the Roman destruction of the Jerusalem temple in 70 CE. After this destruction of the ritual and political center of Judaism, all claimants to the traditions of Abraham and Moses were in ongoing debates regarding what it might mean to be Jewish in a post-temple diasporic reality. This was not specific to the Gospel writers—or even to Christian writers. The rabbis, too, were beginning to argue about the nature of faithfulness after the fall of the temple.

Circumcision, Sabbath observance, and table fellowship were some of the more blatant ways in which this kind of cultural interrogation between permitted and transgressive took place. Other questions also arose, even if they were more subtly addressed. Should slavery persist in the Christian community, and how could one argue for slavery and yet argue that all have one master (see Col. 3:22-23)? What is the appropriate role of women, particularly of wives, in the early church and how might that intersect with the wider society's understanding of Christians (1 Cor. 7:12-13)? The answers are not straightforward. There are clear moves, particularly among the later Christian writings, to preserve kyriarchy, but the rationale for it is often a subtle rebuke of the dominating structures of the society, even if that rebuke does nothing to alleviate the distress of women, children, or slaves. In Colossians, for example, the command that slaves should obey their masters is followed by counsel to these slaves to perform their tasks "as for the Lord and not for your masters" and a promise that "the wrongdoer will be paid back for whatever wrong has been done" (3:23-25). When there is no rebuke, often there is a call for kyriarchal structuring of society as a mark of purity of the church, purity that makes the otherwise illicit church gathering unassailable by the pagan majority. Thus in 1 Timothy, slaves are told to obey their masters "so that the name of God and the teaching may not be blasphemed" (6:1).

Ultimately, as Brah posits, these ancient migrant writings represent the invention of a new tradition, a tradition we have come to call Christianity. For an example of this, one need look no further than to the name given to this ancient collection of writings: "New Testament." New Testament is an appropriation of the language of the Christian meal found in 1 Cor. 11:25 and Matt. 26:28. While most contemporary translations present this as a "new covenant," the Greek word *diathēkē* can be used either for "covenant" or "testament" (as in "last will and testament," see Galatians 3). So, "New Testament" also means "new covenant," and this in turn cannot be understood without reference to the "old covenant," as the early Christians would have understood it.

For many of these migrant groups, the "old" or Abrahamic covenant between God and God's people functioned not only as tradition but also as a fundamental identifier of the people (*ethnos*—the basis for the concept "ethnic group"). This identifier was traced primarily through the Abrahamic bloodline but could be extended to those who adhered to the identity markers of the covenant, among which were circumcision and the keeping of *kashrut*. So, when Paul and the Gospel writers, quoting the oral tradition that both trace to Jesus, speak of the table meal of the early church as a "new covenant" or "new testament," they are not only relating an important story in the birth of the church but also reinventing tradition, reinventing, not exorcising it. To speak of these stories and letters as a "new *diathēkē*" is both to invent a new way of being a covenant people in the world and to appropriate to the church—made increasingly of people from outside of the Abrahamic bloodline and covenant practices—the ancient *diathēkē* of the Abrahamic era.

Paul and the author of Luke-Acts do not explicitly value the new covenant as superior to the old covenant. However, for the writer to the Hebrews, the "new covenant" or "new testament" clearly supersedes the older. As the author of Hebrews argues, "if that first covenant had been faultless, there would have been no need to look for a second one" (Heb. 8:7). Yet even this assertion is premised on a reinterpretation of the received Scriptures of the people, the "Old Testament." The author to the Hebrews would probably not be claiming to invent tradition any more than would Paul or the author of Luke-Acts. Instead, he would assert that this new covenant is the real, heavenly variety—and thus ultimately more ancient than the human copy. And yet he, like Paul and Luke-Acts, is engaging in that diaspora-space activity of inventing, and claiming ancient provenance for, traditions (Brah).

All of this briefly suggests that, as a collection of primarily migrant writings, the writings of the New Testament can be shown to be diaspora space. The examples above are intended to be representative rather than exhaustive, and self-evident rather than nuanced. The struggle with subject positionality, juxtaposition of the permitted and transgressive, and (re)invention of tradition all appear in some of the most important theological discussions in the collection: discussions around identity, around who and what these Christians will be. However, to say that the New Testament writings constitute a kind of literary diaspora space is not to claim some uniformity of migrant reaction to their host cultures or their home culture. Rather, in the next section, four such possible migrant reactions will be explored, both for their presence or absence within the New Testament canon of writings and for their implications for the migrants who hold them.

New Testament Migrant Strategies

Just because one can argue that the New Testament writings constitute a kind of literary diaspora space, this does not mean that their migrant strategies for life as Christians in migration were identical. Psychologist John Berry's work proves helpful for unpacking these strategies. Berry outlines four migrants' strategies for interacting in their places of migration. He calls these four categories marginalization, separation, assimilation, and integration (Berry, 619).

Three of these strategies are readily observable in the New Testament writings. However, the strategy of assimilation is absent. Assimilation requires that migrants reject their home culture in favor of the host culture in which they find themselves. In twenty-first-century terms, this is the immigrant who intentionally loses her accent, forgets her native language, and claims only the nationality and culture of the nation in which she finds herself. Such assimilation does not exist in the New Testament canon; for, if it did, the writings would be pagan, extolling the virtues of the goddess Roma or the God Zeus/Jupiter. Indeed, an assimilationist of this time would have been found marching with the silversmiths of Ephesus crying out, "Great is Artemis of the Ephesians" (Acts 19:28).

In retaining their monotheistic theologies, both Jews and Christians set themselves apart from the majority-pagan polytheism of the ancient world in ways that were seen as misanthropic by their neighbors, regardless of how much else they mimicked the cultural norms of their host country. There seem to have been some Christians who did aspire to assimilate. To do so, they claimed a higher knowledge that allowed them to participate in pagan religiosity in all of its forms (including eating meat sacrificed to pagan gods) while at the same time claiming the faith of the early Christian church (see 1 Corinthians 7; Revelation 2). Such practices were condemned by those whose writings are preserved in the New Testament as misguided at best and satanic at worst. In fact, no New Testament writing counsels migrant assimilation; none offers a theology of assimilation. In the face of migration, each of the New Testament writings, regardless of how much they appear to mimic the greater society, preserves some separation from that society.

Liminal, or as Berry calls them, "marginalized" migrants take as their response to migration the rejection of both their home culture and their host culture. To determine that a migrant writing counsels such a stance for its audience, one must show *both* its rejection of the home culture, which in the case of early Christianity is Judaism and/or temple culture, *and* its rejection of the host culture in which it finds itself, which in many New Testament writings is simply called "the world." The Gospel according to John contains both of these kinds of counsel for its audience. Consider first this quotation:

> Then Jesus said to the Jews/Judeans who had believed in him, "If you continue in my word, you are truly my disciples; and you will know the truth, and the truth will make you free." They answered him, "We are descendants of Abraham and have never been slaves to anyone. . . .
>
> . . . Jesus said to them, "If you were Abraham's children, you would be doing what Abraham did, but now you are trying to kill me, a man who has told you the truth that I heard from God. This is not what Abraham did. You are indeed doing what your father does." They said to him, "We are not illegitimate children; we have one father, God himself." Jesus said to them, "If God were your Father, you would love me, for I came from God and now I am here. . . . You are from your father the devil, and you choose to do your father's desires." (John 8:31-33a, 39b-42b, 44a)

In this quotation, part of Jesus' longer diatribe against the "Jews" or the "Judeans," the author of John's Gospel, through Jesus, is disavowing any cultural consonance with those who would seem to be his own people, his home culture. There is no plea, here, that those who self-identify as Jews/Judeans are of the same family tree as the community to which John is writing. Raymond Brown posits that John's community has been forcibly removed from the synagogue worship out of which it sprang because of its assertion of the messianic nature of Jesus. This seems to suggest that the audience of John's Gospel has separated itself from its home culture.

However, in turning from its home culture, John's audience has not uncritically embraced its host culture. To the contrary. As part of the symposium dialogue in the fifteenth chapter, the Gospel of John records the following teaching of Jesus:

> If the world hates you, be aware that it hated me before it hated you. If you belonged to the world, the world would love you as its own. Because you do not belong to the world, but I have chosen you out of the world—therefore the world hates you. (John 15:18-19)

Here, John's Gospel is depicting Jesus, and through Jesus, his community, as rejected by its host culture, "the world."

In all fairness, a careful reader of John realizes this at the very outset of the Gospel. In the first chapter, John describes the incarnate Word (*logos*) and the community of those who accepted him this way:

> He [the Word/*logos*] was in the world, and the world came into being through him; yet the world did not know him. He came to what was his own, and his own people did not accept him. But to all who received him, who believed in his name, he gave power to become children of God, who were born, not of blood or of the will of the flesh or of the will of man, but of God. (John 1:10-13)

Perhaps no verse better illustrates John's liminality, the stance of a community leader—and thus of a community—rejected both by the world (host culture) and by his own people (home culture). The audience shaped by John's Gospel reflects such a liminality, neither being part of the world nor part of the home culture, a stance that requires the community of faith to strike out into unknown territory, creating an ostensibly brand-new culture apart from either of these cultural anchors.

The Gospel according to John is joined by the Johannine Epistles (1, 2, and 3 John) and possibly the Gospel according to Mark in this liminal stance. However, most New Testament writings do not use this migrant strategy to interact with their home and host cultures. The Epistle of James is illustrative of a more popular strategy: separation. Consider the following:

> Religion that is pure and undefiled before God, the Father, is this: to care for orphans and widows in their distress, and *to keep oneself unstained by the world*. (James 1:27, emphasis added)

and

> Those conflicts and disputes among you, where do they come from? Do they not come from your cravings that are at war within you? You want something and do not have it; so you commit murder. And you covet something and cannot obtain it; so you engage in disputes and conflicts. You do not have, because you do not ask. You ask and do not receive, because you ask wrongly, in order to spend what you get on your pleasures. [Adulterous women]! Do you not know that *friendship with the world is enmity with God*? Therefore whoever wishes to be a friend of the world becomes an enemy of God. (James 4:1-4, emphasis added)

Like the Gospel of John, the Epistle of James stands firm in its dismissal of the world. As in the Gospel of John, so here also the host culture is rejected. However, unlike John, James also says this:

> Do not speak evil against one another, brothers and sisters. Whoever speaks evil against another or judges another, speaks evil against the law and judges the law; but if you judge the law, you are not a doer of the law but a judge. (James 4:11)

Law, in this case, must be understood as Torah, the law of James's own people and community. James thus is not advocating a liminal migrant strategy. Instead, James is advocating a strategy of separation.

Luke Timothy Johnson has demonstrated that James is very possibly a letter written from the earliest Christians in Jerusalem, through the brother of Jesus, to the earliest diasporic communities of Jews/Judeans who have accepted Jesus as the Christ and son of God. From Jerusalem, James writes to migrant Christ-communities still worshiping in synagogues (James 2). He counsels the earliest believers to adopt a migrant strategy of separation: not to adopt gentile ways in their time of migration. Rather, they are to continue their adherence to the law, to be wary of accepting worldly ways, and to keep themselves unstained from the world.

The Epistle of James is not alone in this counsel. The Gospel of Matthew provides a similar strategy to its readers, almost until the Great Commission at the end; and even that commission is less about befriending the world and more about recruiting it to the "home culture" (Matthew 28). Likewise, the enigmatic book Hebrews, with its focus on Christian endurance, seems to counsel separation from the things of the world in favor of the "race that is set before us" (Hebrews 12). Jude, the often overlooked polemic toward the end of the canon, embraces this sort of strategy; and it is central to the theology of the Revelation to John with its admonition to "come out of" Babylon (Revelation 18). In each of these cases, the migrant strategy of separation calls the community of faith back to its roots and away from the world.

Liminality and separation define strategies in some of the more pivotal New Testament writings. However, the predominant migrant strategy within the literary diaspora space called the New Testament is accommodation. Consider, for example, these quotations from the writings of Paul of Tarsus:

> As many of you as were baptized into Christ have clothed yourselves with Christ. There is no longer Jew or Greek, there is no longer slave or free, there is no longer male and female; for all of you are one in Christ Jesus. And if you belong to Christ, then you are Abraham's offspring, heirs according to the promise. (Gal. 3:27-29)

and

> To the Jews I became as a Jew, in order to win Jews. To those under the law I became as one under the law (though I myself am not under the law) so that I might win those under the law. To those outside the law I became as one outside the law (though I am not free from God's law but am under Christ's law) so that I might win those outside the law. To the weak I became weak, so that I might win the weak. I have become all things to all people, that I might by all means save some. (1 Cor. 9:20-22)

These writings indicate a shift in strategy. Paul's overt inclusion of persons both from within and outside his own migrant culture, and his willingness to accommodate gentile inclusion in his ministry, suggests that he does not advocate a total avoidance of the gentile world. However, Paul simultaneously claims that his mixed community of Jews/Judeans and gentiles, a community comprising migrant Jesus-believers, somehow inherits the benefits reserved specifically for the Jews/Judeans: the covenant blessings of Abraham (Galatians 3). Paul thus not only invites "the world" in but also continues to embrace some of his home culture, a culture steeped in the Abrahamic covenant and the Mosaic law.

This Pauline migrant strategy I have termed accommodation, following sociologist Margaret Gibson, rather than using Berry's term *integration* (Berry, 618; Gibson, 20). According to Gibson, accommodation is marked by "the deliberate preservation of the homeland culture, albeit in an adapted form more suitable to life in the host country" (Gibson, 20–21). To argue that Paul is engaged in accommodation and not integration is to argue that he has deliberately preserved the Jewish narrative while adapting it so that faith communities may include gentiles. The result is an uneasy tension of a migrant strategy that both accepts and critiques home and host cultures. This uneasy tension is most clearly evident in Romans 12 and 13. In chapter 12, Paul famously counsels, "Do not be conformed to this world, but be transformed by the renewing of your minds, so that you may discern what is the will of God—what is good and acceptable and perfect" (Rom. 12:2). However, in Romans 13, this same Paul calls for a certain amount of conformity to the world *as a way to fully comply with the requirements of the Mosaic law.* Here, I quote Paul at length:

> Let every person be subject to the governing authorities; for there is no authority except from God, and those authorities that exist have been instituted by God. Therefore whoever resists authority resists what God has appointed, and those who resist will incur judgment. For rulers are not a terror to good conduct, but to bad. Do you wish to have no fear of the authority? Then do what is good, and you will receive its approval; for it is God's servant for your good. But if you do what is wrong, you should be afraid, for the authority does not bear the sword in vain! It is the servant of God to execute wrath on the wrongdoer. Therefore one must be subject, not only because of wrath but also because of conscience. For the same reason you also pay taxes, for the authorities are God's servants, busy with this very thing. Pay to all what is due them—taxes to whom taxes are due, revenue to whom revenue is due, respect to whom respect is due, honor to whom honor is due. Owe no one anything, except to love one another; for the one who loves another has fulfilled the law. The commandments, "You shall not commit adultery; You shall not murder; You shall not steal; You shall not covet"; and any other commandment, are summed up in this word, "Love your neighbor as yourself." Love does no wrong to a neighbor; therefore, love is the fulfilling of the law. (Rom. 13:1-10)

Despite the counsel in Rom. 12:1-2, one must read Romans 13 as advice to conform to the world—at least in part—even as you also attempt to conform to the law. Here Paul, deliberately holding to the law, counsels the Romans to adapt a form of his adherence better suited to accommodate the host culture in which they find themselves and the home culture to which they must cling.

Paul is not alone in his use of the migrant strategy of accommodation. Along with the thirteen writings written either by him or by imitators of him, this strategy is adopted by the writer of the Gospel of Luke and the Acts of the Apostles, and by the authors of the Petrine letters. This constitutes the majority of the New Testament writings, both by number of writings and by size of corpus.

These three migrant strategies—liminality, separation, and accommodation—reflect three competing New Testament canonical responses to the historical reality of migration and the literary trope of displacement encoded in this canon. It would be a mistake to read this description as though it were intended to denote some kind of progression from "unrealistic" to "realistic"; nor a decline from "purity" to "admixture." Liminality, separation, and accommodation are survival strategies in the face of displacement and dispersion adopted by these different migrant writings. Each adds to the Pentecost-like cacophony (Acts 2) of the diaspora space called the New Testament.

Migrant Writings as Twenty-First-Century Scriptures

Considering the extent to which New Testament writings may also be migrant writings is certainly of interest for the historical study of these texts, as well as for their academic and, perhaps, theological interpretation. But how might this information allow us better to understand the role of these writings in the twenty-first century? To respond, one must first consider the nature of Scriptures themselves: specifically, one must consider what makes certain cultural productions (writings, recitations, songs, etc.) into Scriptures.

Here, the work of Wilfred Cantwell Smith will be a helpful conversation partner. Smith's seminal work *What Is Scripture? A Comparative Analysis* traces the human activity of Scripture-making and Scripture-using across a variety of religious communities and traditions. He finds that

> scripture is a human activity. . . . The quality of being scripture is not an attribute of texts. It is a characteristic of the attitude of persons—groups of persons—to what outsiders perceive as texts. *It denotes a relation between a people and a text.* Yet that too is finally inadequate. . . . at issue is the relation between a people and the universe, in the light of their perception of a given text. (Smith, 18, emphasis added)

Smith's definition makes explicit that those who consider New Testament writings to be Holy Scripture are living in a particular relationship with these ancient texts. This relationship involves more than just a people and their Scripture. The relationship stretches "between a people and the universe, in light of their perception of a given text" (Smith, 18). To use another metaphor, for people of faith, their Scriptures function as a lens through which all things are considered. Scripture helps people of faith to clarify their proper relationships with one another, with the God of their understanding, and with the world.

For the New Testament, an added complication is that not every person of faith has considered every text as equally scriptural, or as scriptural at all. This conflict between what is and is not truly "Scripture" dates as far back as the early second century CE, when Marcion of Sinope rejected those Scriptures he considered "Jewish." Later Christians have had similar reactions to particular books. Reformers like John Calvin and Martin Luther had no love for the Revelation to John and the Epistle of James, respectively. As twentieth-century theologian Howard Thurman revealed, among African Americans descended from US chattel slavery, New Testament writings in favor of slavery were held in low esteem, and even "read out" of the Bible (Thurman, 30–31). In *Jesus and the Disinherited*, Thurman tells a story of his grandmother who would not let him read from the Pauline Epistles, with the exception, on occasion, of 1 Corinthians 13. Thurman recounts:

> What she told me I shall never forget. "During the days of slavery," she said, "the master's minister would occasionally hold services for the slaves. . . . Always the white minister used as his text something from Paul. At least three or four times a year, he used as a text: 'Slaves be obedient to them that are your masters as unto Christ.' Then he would go on to show how it was God's will that we were slaves, and how, if we were good and happy slaves, God would bless us. I promised my Maker that if I ever learned to read and if freedom came, I would not read that part of the Bible." (Thurman, 30–31)

Thurman's grandmother's quite candid assessment of the New Testament caused her to determine not to treat the proslavery writings of the New Testament as Scripture, even if she had to omit almost every word attributed to the apostle Paul. She refused, in so doing, to use the proslavery New Testament writings as Scripture—as lenses to help her negotiate her relationship to the universe.

Like Marcion, Luther, Calvin, and even Thurman's grandmother, Christian practitioners still very often select which among the New Testament writings they will treat as Scripture, although they may not do so consciously. More commonly, even among those who claim inerrant divine inspiration for all of the biblical writings, certain texts are seen as "favorites," or as "the heart of the gospel." As noted above, each of these writings is also a migrant writing. As a result, unsurprisingly, people of faith very often also end up incorporating into their scriptural lenses not only the theological concepts that the texts propose but also the migrant strategies toward home and host cultures embedded in them. Those for whom John's Gospel is paramount might find themselves valuing liminality as the ideal interaction with their world. Those who privilege the Revelation to John might find themselves valuing separation. Those who hold to Paul's letters might find themselves valuing accommodation. These migrant strategies become inseparable from scriptural lenses. As a result, Christians of the dominant culture of a particular country, whose families may not have experienced migration for many generations, may still interact with that culture as though they were migrants in a host culture because of their scriptural lenses.

Within twenty-first-century civic life, this adaptation of migrant strategies may take the form of groups that stay to themselves and are viewed with suspicion because they privilege a separate migrant strategy. In a society in which every detail of human life is readily accessibly through the Internet, the choice of such groups to distance themselves from society at large may be seen as inviting or, by contrast, quite suspicious. Alternatively, it may take the form of groups that vilify both Christian religion as it is typically practiced and the society at large, turning instead to an alternative way of being entirely. Certainly such practices might go unnoticed. On the other hand, when in positions of power, Christians adopting liminal migrant strategies might have profound impact on schools, political parties, and social policy—whether they are found on the left or right wing of the political spectrum. This may seem oxymoronic. However, the liminality in this case is not actual societal power. Rather, these persons adopt a liminal stance toward society because of the Scriptures through which they refract their world, and which counsel them regarding their appropriate interaction with the world.

However, perhaps the migrant strategy that has had the strongest historical stance and still continues to be heard from among Christian practitioners is that of accommodation. In the United States and the Western north, this is in part due to the outsize influence of the writings of Paul in the Protestant churches. It is this strategy that brings us the abolitionist and civil rights movements among African Americans and many other movements for social justice. It is also this strategy that brings us the proslavery movement within the church and the twenty-first-century church's willingness to accommodate unjust policies regarding poverty and human rights. In each of these opposing cases, Christian interaction with the world is governed not only by what the Scriptures say but also by the scriptural stance of holding on to tradition while finding a way to engage the "world," which may appear to be hostile. Thus an abolitionist holds on to one set of scriptural sayings and a slaveholder to another set; however, both take the Pauline tack that both holds to the tradition and engages the society. At stake is the argument over what aspects of the dominant culture shall be accommodated and what resisted. Faithful Christians have, over time, responded very differently to these questions.

Each of these strategies persists today, strengthened by the migrant strategies in these ancient writings that continue to be Scripture for twenty-first-century Christians. As students of these texts, paying attention to these strategies may help us to unpack some of the Christianity-related arguments in our civic commons. Pay attention, also, to the sense of rootlessness that undergirds some of the music and culture, particularly of the United States: the sense that "there's no place like home," but also that "we're not in Kansas anymore" that can emerge in the rhetoric even of people whose families have been resident since the days of European colonialism. For this is not simply a product of changing times; times have always changed. In a culture so steeped in these migrant writings, this literary diaspora space called the New Testament, surely some of that rootlessness, some of those uncritically employed migrant strategies can be traced back to these ancient writings, these migrant Scriptures of the Christian church.

Works Cited

Bauckham, Richard. 1999. *James.* New Testament Readings. New York: Routledge.

Berry, John W. 2001. "A Psychology of Immigration." *Journal of Social Issues* 57, no. 3:615–31.

Brah, Avtar. 1996. *Cartographies of Diaspora: Contesting Identities.* New York: Routledge.

Brown, Raymond. 1979. *The Community of the Beloved Disciple: The Lives, Loves, and Hates of an Individual Church in New Testament Times.* Mahwah, NJ: Paulist.

Gibson, Margaret A. 2001. "Immigrant Adaption and Patterns of Acculturation." *Human Development* 44:19–23.

Johnson, Luke Timothy. 2004. *Brother of Jesus, Friend of God: Studies in the Letter of James.* Grand Rapids: Eerdmans.

Schüssler Fiorenza, Elisabeth. 2009. "Introduction: Exploring the Intersection of Race, Gender, Status, and Ethnicity in Early Christian Studies." In *Prejudice and Christian Beginnings*, edited by Laura Nasrallah and Elisabeth Schüssler Fiorenza. Minneapolis: Fortress Press.

Smith, Wilfred Cantwell. 1993. *What Is Scripture? A Comparative Approach.* Minneapolis: Fortress Press.

Taussig, Hal. 2009. *In the Beginning Was the Meal: Social Experimentation and Early Christianity.* Minneapolis: Fortress Press.

Thurman, Howard. 1976. *Jesus and the Disinherited.* Boston: Beacon.

THE APOCALYPTIC LEGACY OF EARLY CHRISTIANITY

a•poc•a•lyp•tic (adj): of, relating to, or involving terrible violence and destruction: of or relating to the end of the world

leg•a•cy (noun): something transmitted by or received from an ancestor or predecessor or from the past

(Merriam-Webster Dictionary, 2003)

Introduction: The Problem of a Suppressed Legacy

We twenty-first-century Christians find ourselves in a strange place in relationship to our apocalyptic biblical inheritance. In many of our churches, apocalyptic literature, especially the Revelation to John, is treated with benign neglect, yet its images continue to fascinate us, as witness the tremendous success of novels like the *Left Behind* series. This is especially true from my perspective as a Roman Catholic: the book of Revelation remains liturgically peripheral in my tradition (with the exception of December 12—the Feast of the Virgin of Guadalupe, when Revelation 12 is a focal reading—and, on occasion, during the Lenten season). Yet Roman Catholics, like most twenty-first-century Christians, remain remarkably vulnerable to conjuring apocalyptic scenarios, under the right circumstances.

Meanwhile, over the last several decades, a great deal of ink has been spilled by scholars attempting to specify matters like the genre, form, and content of those ancient texts that qualify as "apocalyptic" and thus have contributed to this legacy. As one might expect, the book of Revelation has been the most obvious focal point in those conversations. Indeed, according to the most learned biblical specialists, this is the *only* writing in the New Testament that meets the scholarly criteria regarding the form of the genre apocalypse. I, for one, am in total agreement with this assessment, but I remain unsatisfied with the emphases of the scholarly conversation because something tells me, deep in my soul, that there is more to our Christian apocalyptic legacy than is addressed by such formal considerations.

In this essay, I would like to suggest an alternative point of entry, other than the Revelation to John, for discussing our apocalyptic inheritance. I would like initially to consider the Synoptic Gospels, not, however, as we usually read them, conflated together, as if they are telling roughly the same story; that keeps us from seeing something important—that from the very beginning, Christians have struggled with the troubling legacy of a genuinely apocalyptic vision. The Gospel tradition has embedded within it, specifically within the Gospel of Mark, what functions as a genuinely apocalyptic text. By examining how Matthew and Luke altered that text, we see how early Christians negotiated the first apocalyptic legacy in their tradition by altering its eschatological moorings. More precisely, Matthew and Luke demonstrate how a Christian *apocalyptic* moment was turned into an ecclesiastical movement with the alteration to a less imminent expectation of the Parousia of Jesus Christ.

To start with, this less obvious biblical apocalyptic moment serves several purposes. (1) It prevents us from isolating the book of Revelation as if it were the only example of an apocalyptic worldview in the Christian canon, and from sequestering it in the category of prophetically anomalous literature, rendering it so much easier to ignore. (2) It demonstrates that Matthew and Luke believed they needed to domesticate the apocalyptic agenda of the Gospel of Mark in the wake of the delayed return of Jesus Christ. And (3) it challenges us to bring to consciousness, in a cultural-psychoanalytic sense, the way other scriptural sources, in addition to Revelation, are embedded in our psyches and contribute to our perduring fascination with apocalyptic solutions, prompting us to "act out" apocalyptically under the right circumstances.

Apocalypticism

At this point it is critical to be clear how I am employing the term *apocalyptic*, especially because much scholarly ink has been spilled on the contentious question of categorization. I rely on David Aune's summary in an illuminating 2005 article.

> "Apocalyptic eschatology" is the narrative theology, characteristic of apocalypses, centering in the belief that (1) the present world order, regarded as both evil and oppressive, is under temporary control of Satan and his human accomplices, and (2) that the present evil world order will shortly be destroyed by God and replaced by a new and perfect order corresponding to Eden before the fall. During the present evil age, the people of God are an oppressed minority who fervently expect God, or his specially chosen agent the Messiah, to rescue them. The transition between the old and the new ages will be introduced with a final series of battles fought by the people of God

against the human allies of Satan. The outcome is never in question, however, for the enemies of God are predestined for defeat and destruction. (Aune, 236)

What I find most compelling in this definition—for the purposes of this essay and for my own personal relationship to apocalypticism—are the notions of cosmological dualism (with a war of heavenly proportions affecting, and afflicting, human actors), the introduction of the messianic agent (i.e., Jesus Christ), and the sense of temporal urgency. The present world order will be destroyed *soon*. It is this temporal consideration that I find most compelling when looking at an apocalyptic text like the Gospel of Mark—and at the Matthean and Lukan responses to Mark's acute temporality.

Excavating Mark as Another Example of Christian Apocalyptic

With this working definition of apocalypticism in mind, how does the Gospel of Mark function apocalyptically? Our first consideration is the moment in history when the Gospel of Mark was written. The majority of New Testament scholars date the Gospel between 66 and 70 CE, that is, squarely during the Jewish War with Rome, or shortly after the destruction of the Jerusalem temple. Thus Mark was written during a time of *real* political and cultural crisis (cf. Adela Yarbro Collins's language of *perceived* crisis; A. Y. Collins, 84–110) that may have indeed been an impetus for an apocalyptic response. Second, the Christology of the Gospel of Mark foregrounds the messiahship of Jesus. This is made explicit in the very first verse of the Gospel: "The beginning of the gospel of Jesus Christ" (i.e., Messiah). This christological emphasis is maintained throughout the Gospel (e.g., in the messianic secret motif: see the commentary on Mark). The relationship of a messianic figure to different apocalyptic scenarios is still under scholarly debate. I defer to Aune's assessment, noted above, which highlighted the expectation of God's oppressed people that an agent of God would act on their behalf at the critical and ultimate moment.

Other features of the Gospel of Mark that add to its apocalyptic tenor include its explicit cosmological dualism, as represented in the temptation of Jesus, after his baptism, by Satan (1:12-13) and the multiple exorcisms in the Gospel (e.g., 1:21-28; 5:1-20; 9:14-29). In comparison, the Gospel of John, arguably the least apocalyptic of the four canonical Gospels—has not one exorcism.

The Gospel of Mark also maintains a unique relationship to time. It is by far the most compressed of the four Gospels, narrating the ministry of Jesus from baptism to empty tomb. The Gospels of Matthew and Luke each begin with narratives of Jesus' birth, and end with accounts of his ascension into heaven. The Gospel of John goes even further, beginning "in the beginning" and ending with an ascension account. The Gospel of Mark employs the phrase "and immediately" some forty-one times in its narrative, twelve times in the first chapter alone. (The Greek phrase *kai euthys* occurs only nineteen times in the rest of the New Testament.) The phrase gives the reader/hearer the impression of a story moving very rapidly, and may remind the reader, ancient and modern alike, of the initial words uttered by Jesus in the Gospel: "The time is fulfilled, and the kingdom of God has come near" (1:15). Further, aspects of Mark's story reveal aspects of sectarian groups, as identified by modern theory: the requirement of severance of ties with one's biological family (e.g.,

1:16-20; 2:13-14; 10:28), the creation of a new eschatological family (3:31-35), and the mandatory renunciation of personal wealth for the benefit of the group (6:7-13; 10:17-27).

These observations crystallize the argument that Mark has apocalyptic features. This "excavation" goes beyond the usual characterization of Mark 13 as the "Little Apocalypse" to reveal that an apocalyptic character pervades the Gospel, and thus to foreground another apocalyptic moment in early Christian history; the Revelation to John does not stand in isolation. But consider next how both Matthew and Luke, unsatisfied with Mark's apocalyptic moorings some ten to fifteen years after the fact, chose to domesticate Mark when they incorporated his Gospel into their own. By means of this domestication, the legacy of Christian apocalypticism has been canonically offset, if not altogether suppressed, by the consequent conflated readings of the Gospel narratives.

Domesticating Mark: Matthew and Luke-Acts

I often imagine Matthew and Luke separately clinging to their manuscripts of Mark's Gospel and wondering just what on earth they were going to do with such an apocalyptically urgent Gospel. It is a humorous scene in my mind's eye, considering that apocalyptic movements have a short shelf life. How long can a preacher and/or teacher keep saying that deliverance is just around the corner? Thus I imagine Matthew and Luke questioning the validity of Mark's Gospel and how their Christian movements should proceed. In the wake of the delayed Parousia, with its delayed fulfillment of prophecy, do they quit the movement? Weren't the words of imminence placed on the very lips of Jesus himself (see esp. Mark 9:1; 13:30)? Perhaps they should bring about their own apocalypse, as subsequent Christian groups have done throughout the Christian era? Surely even slight provocation of Roman might accomplish that end. Or what if they took Mark's expected imminent Parousia and moved it into the distant future (by what scholars call "reserved eschatology")? If, as I contend here, this last was the option they chose, what were they to do with the rest of Mark, and even more acutely, what were they to do in the interim before the deferred Parousia?

These are fascinating questions that require some parsing. Note, first, that almost 90 percent of the Gospel of Mark is absorbed into Matthew's account. But how could one domesticate so apocalyptic a Gospel while absorbing so much of the original? Perhaps the best approach to this question is to assess how Matthew employed his sources. Arguably, the Gospel of Matthew can be reduced to three source-rich divisions. Chapters 1–2 are composed of material known as special M, biblical material unique to Matthew. This special source includes the (Matthean) birth narrative, the visitation of the magi, and the holy family's escape to Egypt in the wake of Herod's execution of Jewish male infants. This material accomplishes various purposes for Matthew, but most importantly for my point here, it expands the story of Jesus' life by almost three decades. Recall that the Gospel of Mark begins at Jesus' baptism, approximately one year before his death in his early thirties. Thus Matthew expands narrative time.

Matthew also proceeds in a much less rushed manner. The next section of the Gospel is made up primarily of materials gleaned from the sayings source Q. (See the essay on Jesus and the Gospels.) Embedded in this layer is a collection of words and teachings of Jesus apart from his deeds. In this material, we find the Sermon on the Mount, which takes up three chapters of Matthew's Gospel (chapters 5–7), and includes the Beatitudes and the Lord's Prayer. This saturation of Jesus' teachings in the middle of Matthew shifts the focus from Mark's apocalyptic Jesus to a more refined, rabbinic Jesus, one who certainly has much more time to teach and instruct his disciples on how to interact with the world in the interim before the Parousia.

We are finally introduced to the bulk of the Markan material as it is embedded in Matthew 12–28 (esp. after ch. 16). However, we have already been lulled into a more tranquil state of consciousness by the birth narrative and teaching discourse, so already the apocalyptic materials appear much more distant and future. The apocalyptic predictions imported from chapter 13 of the "Markan apocalypse" (Matthew 24) will come to pass (i.e., the destruction of the Jerusalem temple, wars and rumors of wars, persecution of the faithful, the desolating sacrilege, the appearance of false prophets, astronomical chaos, and the return of the son of man), but without the imminent tones of Mark's composition. This is also the case in the Lukan parallel to Mark 13 (Luke 21).

Even more brilliantly, Matthew incorporates ascension materials (28:16-20) to place Jesus back in heaven in the interim, thus overcoming what is, to Matthew, the more than slightly problematic lack of any indication where Jesus is during the interim according to the original ending of Mark (Mark 16:8, which, in my estimation, is a perfect ending for an *apocalyptic* Gospel). By conjoining it to the "Great Commission" in 28:18-20, Matthew has reframed Mark's apocalypticism into a template for a fledgling church movement that has much to accomplish before Christ's return. It is a brilliant piece of editorial work that simultaneously honors the primacy of Mark, by using so much of it as a source, *and* shifts Mark's emphasis from crisis and end-time speculation to an expanded story of the life of Jesus, with an emphasis on Jesus as aphoristic teacher and founder of a church. However, the point must not be overlooked that Matthew also felt the need for a complete eschatological overhaul of the Gospel of Mark, one that would privilege an emerging church. In my view, this was perhaps the most compelling reason for Matthew's privileged position in the New Testament canon. To place Mark at the beginning of the canon—noting its primacy among the Gospels—would have created an apocalyptic inclusio for the New Testament that would begin with Mark and end with the book of Revelation! The rhetorical brilliance of the canon as it now stands, however, is that the apocalypticism of the book of Revelation is now viewed as a futuristic culmination of the age of Matthew's developing and spreading church.

Luke, like his Synoptic cousin Matthew, had to make a tough decision regarding what to do with Mark's Gospel. I have always found it fascinating that both Luke and Matthew chose to retain and employ material from the Gospel of Mark. Surely, one avenue each author could have taken was to ignore the Gospel of Mark altogether and start from scratch. But neither did. Luke, as did Matthew, also employed special materials unique to his own Gospel, identified today as special L, and employed the 235 sayings of Jesus from Q. Unlike Matthew, however, the author of the Gospel of Luke used approximately one-half of the Gospel of Mark in the composition of his own Gospel (a large percentage even in relation to Matthew). Like Matthew, Luke also expanded the narrative time frame by introducing narratives of Jesus' birth and ascension. However, unlike any of his Gospel counterparts, Luke wrote a second contribution that would find its way into the New Testament canon, the Acts of the Apostles, which maps out the earliest years of the post-Easter church and the spread of the gospel from the Jewish world (foregrounding the apostleship of Peter) to the worldwide spread of the gospel to the gentiles (foregrounding the apostleship of Paul). In Lukan terms, this was the interim age of the Holy Spirit. The Parousia was delayed and Luke was prepared to encounter the delay, not as an unfulfilled prophecy, but as an opportunity to spread the gospel to the world. As in Matthew, the Gospel of Mark is relegated to the apocalyptic drama that would occur in the eschaton in the indeterminate future (again, reserved eschatology). Luke even hinted at an eschatology that we find most pronounced in the Gospel of John (that is, realized eschatology) when he hints at the benefits of the Parousia being accessible already, in the present, in Luke 17:20-21.

> Once Jesus was asked by the Pharisees when the kingdom of God was coming, and he answered, "The kingdom of God is not coming with things that can be observed; nor will they say, 'Look here it is!' or 'There it is!' For, in fact, the kingdom of God is among you."

It is evident from this brief analysis of both Matthew and Luke that both Gospel writers thought enough of the tradition of Mark to incorporate it into their literary productions while simultaneously toning down Mark's apocalyptic sensibilities to make it more palatable for Christians living in the 80s or later. Both spent much intellectual energy doing so. Matthew and Luke found themselves at least a decade removed from Mark's imminent apocalyptic prediction. The apocalyptic rhetoric had to shift because you cannot be an imminent apocalyptic preacher or sustain an apocalyptic community year after year after year.

Thus the Gospels present us with this curious combination of competing eschatologies. Because it has been a Christian interpretive practice to conflate our readings of the Gospels, emphasizing their presumed unity, the apocalypticism of Mark has been absorbed into the grander "gospel story." It is lost, or ignored, or projected into the undetermined future. The Markan legacy is a painful one, to be sure, because embedded within it is an unfulfilled prophecy of the imminent second coming of Christ, and so we can understand the energy that wants to avoid or defer it. But the presence of Mark among the Gospels means that even if we sequester the book of Revelation as some sort of apocalyptic anomaly, the intellectual fodder for subsequent apocalyptic movements and imaginings remains. Apocalypticism is embedded in our Gospel tradition itself, right in front of us, even if we choose not to acknowledge it. We may suppress it—and then act entirely surprised when apocalyptic inklings manifest themselves in us, like any other neurosis or psychosis would, given the right circumstances.

Expanding the Apocalyptic Landscape: The Pauline Tradition

Even the Pauline tradition—where scholars have long recognized the strength of apocalyptic influence on the apostle's thought—is not immune from a similar apocalyptic suppression. Paul's response to the church in Thessalonica regarding the fate of deceased Christians is illuminating:

> But we do not want you to be uninformed, brothers and sisters, about those who have died, so that you may not grieve as others do who have no hope. For since we believe that Jesus died and rose again, even so, through Jesus, God will bring with him those who have died. For this we declare to you by the word of the Lord, that we who are alive, who are left until the coming of the Lord, will

by no means precede those who have died. For the Lord himself, with a cry of command, with the archangel's call and with the sound of God's trumpet, will descend from heaven, and the dead in Christ will rise first. Then we who are alive, who are left, will be caught up in the clouds together with them to meet the Lord in the air; and so we will be with the Lord forever. (1 Thess. 4:13-17)

Here, Paul speaks to the faithful in Thessalonica in no uncertain terms—imminent apocalyptic terms. Paul expects to be at the Parousia of Jesus Christ. And just as we saw in the Synoptic tradition, Paul faced a period of time (approximately five or six years, if we accept the dating of 1 Thessalonians c. 49 CE and Romans c. 55 CE) in which he personally was confronted with the delayed Parousia. Although Romans was written to a different congregation on a completely different set of issues, it is nevertheless surprising how completely lacking are apocalyptic tones in the letter. If we regard Pauline Christianity as an apocalyptic movement like other apocalyptic groups throughout history, we should expect apocalypticism to be the theological lens through which all things are assessed. How could it be otherwise? But then the absence of apocalyptic elements in Romans is altogether curious.

It appears, then, that any assessment of the apocalyptic legacy of early Christianity must begin with an expansion of the scriptural materials we delegate as apocalyptic. To continue to focus our consideration of apocalyptic material solely on the book of Revelation allows us to compartmentalize our assessment of early Christian apocalyptic wholly on the last book of the Christian canon. Thus any subsequent appropriation of apocalyptic worldviews by Christian groups is easily marginalized by placing the hermeneutic blame on simplistic and/or overly literal readings of the book of Revelation. The first step in recovery is acknowledgment: in this case, acknowledgment that our apocalyptic roots run much deeper than the book of Revelation. Therefore, the work of intellectually excavating texts such as the Gospel of Mark and Paul's First Letter to the Thessalonians is a positive first step in parsing how and why Christian apocalypticism has endured over two millennia. It is in our biblical DNA, present in the earliest letter from the apostle Paul and in the first Gospel ever written. And indeed, it is there, in all of its pure genre form, in the book of Revelation. It is more pervasive than we choose to admit, and scholarly discussions on matters of proper form have only distracted us from that fact. But Matthew, Luke, and Paul have left evidence not only of the prevalence of apocalyptic expectation but also of some measure of its unsustainability: that is, evidence that they tried to distance themselves from a perspective that had such a short shelf life. It appears that individuals and communities simply can't be perpetually apocalyptic. Nevertheless, our apocalyptic memories are short, and we Christians find ourselves bouncing to and fro, from postures of apocalyptic fervor to more tranquil, reserved eschatological expectation. It is a rhythmic dance that has played out over two Christian millennia.

The Book of Revelation and the Explicit Legacy of Christian Apocalypticism

Acknowledgment of the comprehensive influence of the book of Revelation on the Western Christian imagination goes unchallenged even with attempts by some denominations to altogether suppress it. It is, according to both form and content, the only true apocalypse in the New Testament (Collins 1979, 9; see the commentary on Revelation). Its rich imagery, full of beasts, martyrs, heavenly interlocutors, plagues, mysterious gematria, natural disasters, whores, and a great descending city is almost too much for the senses to comprehend, yet simultaneously hypersensual enough to draw even the casual reader into a hypnotic state of attention. It is like the car wreck on the highway that simultaneously repels and irresistibly attracts at least a momentary gaze as we cautiously pass by. It has been the source of Christian apocalyptic ambivalence and anxiety for the last two millennia. A summary of that interpretive history will bear out the alternating rhythm described above, in which our collective traditions have tried to come to terms with the last entry in the New Testament.

The apocalyptic legacy of the book of Revelation began early in the second century of the Common Era. According to Robert M. Royalty Jr. and Arthur W. Wainwright, proto-orthodox Christians like Justin Martyr (c. 100–165) and Irenaeus (c. 130–200) represented an interpretive position known as chiliasm (i.e., millenarian, from the Greek *chilia*, "thousand"). Chiliasm, which represented a literal interpretation of the book of Revelation, was theologically "mainstream" in the early second century. This position is best defined as the theological system that "believed literally in the thousand-year reign of the saints in Rev. 20:4 and the actual, physical new Jerusalem in Rev. 21–22" (Royalty, 285). Wainwright argues that "the chiliasts lived in an age of persecution. It was for such an age that they believed the Apocalypse was written. . . . During this period Chiliasm provided an antidote to the fear of persecution. When people are oppressed, they find consolation in dreams of a better life and focus their anger on the institutions and leaders that threaten them" (Wainwright, 22). Thus Wainwright makes the interpretive assumption that the Apocalypse functioned as a rhetorical call for endurance during times of persecution.

One of the first challenges to literal chiliastic readings of the book of Revelation came from Phrygia in Asia Minor. The "New Prophecy" (c. 150–175), or Montanism (as it was called by its opponents), was founded by Montanus, Prisca, and Maximilla. According to the New Prophecy, the new kingdom would be inaugurated by Christ—but in Pepuza, the geographical epicenter of the New Prophecy movement, and not Jerusalem. The New Prophecy thus challenged "normative" chiliastic expectations through a very selective literal approach to the text by its protagonists (including Tertullian, c. 160–220).

The chiliastic certainty of the of the mid-second century was also countered by emerging late second-century and early third-century allegorical interpretations of the book of Revelation forwarded by the likes of Dionysius, bishop of Alexandria (third century), Clement of Alexandria (c. 150–215), and Origen (c. 185–254). These allegorical readings came to full fruition under Augustine of Hippo (ca. 354–430), who himself was first a proponent of chiliasm until his "eschatological conversion" later in his career. Dionysius, Clement, and Origen began to challenge aspects of chiliasm, especially the literal interpretation of the new Jerusalem as a *physical* and earthly place where "the redeemed would eat, drink, marry, have children, and exercise dominion over other people" (Origen, *De princ.* 2.11.2–3). Thus the early challenges to the literal interpretations focused primarily on the location of the new Jerusalem (New Prophecy) and its physical nature, as depicted in Revelation 21–22. These challenges were just enough to begin to dislodge the mainstream chiliastic interpretations that nevertheless prevailed until the reign of Constantine, in the fourth century of the Common Era. That is a fascinatingly long tenure for literal apocalyptic musings. In some ways, the first three centuries of the Christian era mirror the apocalyptic tension that existed in the now emerging canon, representing both movements with apocalyptic sensibilities and those that countered them. Our ambivalence regarding apocalypticism and the variety of divergent interpretive possibilities were beginning to take shape in these earliest Christian centuries.

It could be argued, if one follows the logic of Wainwright, that the fourth century, with the shift in Rome's relationship to Christianity from one of indifference to persecution, then to tolerance and ultimately acceptance, also marked a shift in the Christian rhetorical posture toward apocalyptic literature in general, and the book of Revelation in particular. Violently imaginative and passive-aggressive fantasies of revenge of the Apocalypse were no longer necessary with Christianity's new and prominent relationship to the empire. This was especially the case after 381, when Emperor Theodosius endorsed orthodox Nicene Christianity over Christian Arianism and banned all pagan religious ritual. What was once peripheral was now central, and the Christian relationship to its apocalyptic legacy needed to be reevaluated. On this matter, Royalty notes, "after the Roman emperors moved from tolerance to acceptance and promotion of orthodox Christianity, millenarian views were even more strongly challenged. No imperial ruler, political or ecclesiastical, eagerly anticipated the destruction of the empire they now controlled" (Royalty, 286).

The influence of Augustine's allegorical reading of the Apocalypse was comprehensive and dominated orthodox circles from the fifth through thirteenth centuries of the Common Era. Perhaps the greatest challenge to traditional readings of the Apocalypse was Augustine's hesitance in speculating about the date of the end. Recall that Aune's working definition of apocalypse (see above) identified one of the key elements of literal apocalyptic readings as the expectation of the imminent end. This was not the case for Augustine, however, and in essence, by his very hesitation, he lowered the expectation of what is probably the most important aspect of apocalyptic eschatology: imminence. To challenge literal chiliastic views on the imminent apocalypse, derived from Revelation 20,

> Augustine offered two key interpretive points in the *City of God*, Book 20. First, the thousand year period is symbolic of "the whole duration of the world," the earthly fullness of time. Thus Augustine tried to put an end to speculations about dates and times for this millennium to start and end, a point for which he had plenty of biblical proof texts. Second, this symbolic millennium has already begun in the time of the church for that is what binds Satan until the final end. . . . And as for the final, *final* end, do not count the days, for the thousand year period is symbolic. (Royalty, 286–87)

Thus, with one powerful, stunning theological gesture, Augustine succeeded in shifting the emphasis from literal readings of the apocalypse to spiritual and nonmillennial readings that would last through the thirteenth century—until a Calabrian abbot named Joachim of Fiore (c. 1135–1202) would once again shift our relationship and understanding of the Apocalypse.

In contrast to Augustine's symbolic reading of the Apocalypse, Joachim of Fiore insisted on what he believed was a historical reading of the text. Joachim alleged that the persecution of Christians in his lifetime was evidence that the signs predicted in the book of Revelation were being realized.

Thus Joachim countered the allegorized reading promoted by Augustine by renewing a historicized reading of the Apocalypse similar to those first endorsed by Justin and Irenaeus. After his spiritual conversion and time spent in the Holy Land on pilgrimage, Joachim returned to Calabria and became a recluse, devoting his study and prayer time to deciphering the book of Revelation. Completely frustrated with his attempt to come to terms with the text, he reported that upon awakening one Easter morning, the meaning of the Apocalypse was revealed to him. Thus, unlike Augustine, Joachim is best understood—like John of Patmos—as an apocalyptic seer.

Joachim's primary contribution as a mystical seer was formulating a system (*concordia*) that divided human history into three historical epochs or states (*status* in Latin). The first *status* was the period from Adam to Jesus Christ, which Joachim called the period of God the Father, corresponding to the Hebrew Scriptures (and to the layperson's church). The *status* from Jesus Christ to 1260 was the period of God the Son and of the Christian Testament (corresponding to the papal church). This was the period in which Joachim himself lived. The third and final *status* began in 1260 and was the period of the Holy Spirit. This third epoch corresponded to the Friars' church. This age, according to Joachim, was the age of the new millennial kingdom:

> [The third epoch] was to be inaugurated by a new Adam or a new Christ who would be the founder of a new monastic order. The transition between the Papal Church of the second age and the Spiritual Church of the third age would be a time of great troubles during which the period of the Papal Church was to endure all the sufferings that corresponded to Christ's passion. The Papal Church would be resurrected as the Spiritual Church in which all men would live the contemplative life, practice apostolic poverty, and enjoy angelic natures. To this level Joachim's ideas were debased and popularized during the thirteenth century by a series of pseudo-Joachimite writings, which probably originated amongst the spiritual Franciscans themselves. St. Francis was identified with the messiah that Joachim prophesied. During the later Middle Ages Joachimism and the Apocalypse preserved their ideological union. (Phelan, 14)

Again, in contrast to Augustine's more domesticating and spiritual reading of the Apocalypse, Joachim revisited subversive interpretations of the text that were more at home in a historical interpretive framework. On this matter, Royalty notes, "Joachim reenergized historicized and potentially politically subversive readings of the Apocalypse, with one result being ideological challenges to ecclesiological and civil authorities in Europe within some monastic and mendicant religious communities" (Royalty, 289). And like the historicized readings of the first century, Joachim employed the powerful rhetoric of persecution. The echoes of his historicized reading reverberated most prominently from the thirteenth through the sixteenth centuries in Western Christendom and, in a few select traditions, are palpable even today (Sánchez).

The Protestant Reformation was also not immune from the perduring legacy of the Apocalypse to John. The onetime Roman Catholic German monk Martin Luther (1483–1546) also had an ambivalent relationship with the book of Revelation. In his early career, Luther remarked,

> I miss more than one thing in this book, and this makes me hold it to be neither apostolic nor prophetic . . . there is one sufficient reason for me not to think highly of it—Christ is neither taught nor known in it. (Luther 1960a, 399)

On a disenchanting trip to Rome, Luther felt betrayed by the "corruption" of the Catholic Church. This initiated an intense search of the Scriptures, which led him to conclude that salvation was a function of his own personal faith rather than derived from any corporate church entity—especially a church that he now found so dismaying. Luther set his own course with the posting of his Ninety-Five Theses in Wittenberg, Saxony, which ultimately led to his excommunication from the Roman Catholic Church.

One of the most significant appropriations of the book of Revelation among Protestant Reformers, including Luther, was the equating of the papacy with the beast(s) of the Apocalypse. Wainwright notes that Luther himself promoted "that . . . the papacy was the beast of the land [Rev. 13:11-18], [and] the empire was the beast of the sea [Rev. 13:1-10]. But the pope, he [i.e., Luther] argued, had control over the empire" (Wainwright, 61). Luther was not the first or the only critic of the papacy who employed negative apocalyptic accusations at Rome: "Some of the sharpest criticism came from Bohemia and England. In Bohemia John Milicz (d. 1374), Mathias of Janow (d. 1394), and John Hus (1369–1415) implied the pope was Antichrist" (Wainwright, 59).

Roman Catholicism in general and the papacy in particular came under a severe Protestant challenge. The need for a swift Catholic response was clear. In some circles, the Catholic response was simply to employ the same apocalyptic polemic against the Protestants. Catholic bishops like Bertold Pürstinger (1463–1543), bishop of Chiemsee (Germany), "explained that the locusts of the sixth trumpet vision [Rev. 9:13-19] were Lutherans. Serafino da Fermo described Luther as the star falling from heaven [Rev. 9:1] and the beast from the land [Rev. 13:11-18]" (Wainwright, 61).

Two other lines of interpretation employed by Catholics against Protestant antipapal interpretations were futurism, championed by the Spanish Jesuit Francisco Ribera (1537–1591), and preterism, developed most fully by the Portuguese Jesuit Luis de Alcazar (1554–1613). "Futurists contended that most of the prophecies in the Apocalypse were still unfulfilled, Preterists argued that most of them had been fulfilled already" (Wainwright, 63). Both methods of interpretation were effective. Futurism was attractive to Catholics, "because it dissociated the pope from Antichrist. It was cogent because it recognized the connection of the beast and the harlot of Rome, although it was a Rome of the future. Futurism challenged both the antipapal interpretation and the assumption that the Apocalypse provided a survey of church history" (Wainwright, 63). Preterism, by arguing that most of the prophecies of the Apocalypse had already been fulfilled, "was congenial to Catholics because it rejected the suggestion that the pope was Antichrist and it gave honor to the Roman Catholic Church" (Wainwright, 63).

One interesting offshoot of the Reformation era was the contemporary emergence of a group known as the Anabaptists. The name Anabaptist was not claimed by the group itself but rather came from other Christian groups opposed to their rejection of infant baptism (a common practice in Roman Catholic circles). The name is derived from the Greek *anabaptismos*, which is loosely translated as "being baptized (over) again." The Anabaptists were part of a movement classified today as the Radical Reformation, and it should be noted that both Protestant and Catholics persecuted Anabaptists. Beyond their baptismal practices, Anabaptists rejected organized religious hierarchies in favor of an idealized theocratic state. This ideology led to a faction of their membership occupying the German city of Münster, which they likened to the new Jerusalem (Revelation 21), to await the return of the heavenly Christ. Within the Anabaptist ranks, a Dutch national named Jan Bockelson declared himself the Messiah of the end times, and coins were minted that referenced the imminent apocalypse. The siege of Münster ended violently in 1535.

In the nineteenth century, three religious movements emerged that also took a historical interpretive approach to the Apocalypse. Those groups are the Church of Jesus Christ of Latter-Day Saints (Mormons) founded by Joseph Smith (c. 1830) shortly after the publication of the Book of Mormon; the Seventh-Day Adventists (Millerites), founded by William Miller (c. 1833); and the Jehovah's Witnesses, founded by Charles Russell (c. 1872). These three US-born movements are relevant for the current discussion because all three movements predicted an imminent apocalypse in their initial years, survived those unrealized predictions, and continue to remain with us today. Therefore, all three movements are interesting examples of how to negotiate an evolving apocalyptic expectation.

Latter-Day Saints (LDS) are an interesting example of a religious group that expanded on the Christian canon by including the Book of Mormon, *The Pearl of Great Price*, and the *Doctrine and Covenants* as church Scripture. LDS members also accept the prophecies of their church leadership as authoritative. (The head of the LDS Church at any given time in its history is recognized as prophet.) This combination of Scriptures and "[prophetic] pronouncement of their leaders has led them to expect both the rebuilding of Jerusalem in the old world and the erection of the New Jerusalem [Revelation 21] in North America. They look forward to the return of Christ to inaugurate his millennial reign over the earth" (Wainwright, 99). This bifurcated manner of dividing the old and new worlds is consistent with the LDS belief that Jesus Christ also visited the Americas shortly after his resurrection, in the first century CE.

Seventh-Day Adventists, like the earliest apocalyptic Christians, also had to deal with their own version of the delay of the Parousia. Their founder, William Miller, predicted that Christ would return in 1843. When his prophecy was not fulfilled, he changed the date to 1844, but that too was not realized. This unrealized prophecy was cause for the earliest Adventists to reconsider and reconfigure their intense apocalyptic hopes. What does an apocalyptic group do when their dated expectation is not realized? As noted above, these groups can abandon their expectations, they can initiate their own (violent) apocalypse (see below for modern examples of this option), or they can adjust the anticipated date—thereby adjusting their imminent expectation much as Matthew and Luke adjusted the Markan apocalyptic time frame. Such was the case with the Adventists; and the denomination still thrives today, some 170 years after the original apocalyptic prophecy. The rhetorical shift they made was to the notion that "another divine event, invisible to human eyes, had occurred in 1844. Christ, they said, had entered the heavenly sanctuary (Heb. 9:24-28)" (Wainwright, 99; cf. Froom, 889–99).

Note that the domesticating of apocalyptic imminence among Adventists did not sway the denomination away from their allegiance to the Apocalypse itself. Wainwright notes, "In arguing for the observance of Saturday as the holy day, they quoted the statement that those who did not keep God's commandments have the mark of the beast (Rev. 14:9-12). The Adventist John Nevis Andrews (1829–83) identified the beast from the land with the United States, whose two horns were civil and religious liberty. The beast from the sea and the whore of Babylon represented the papacy" (Wainwright, 99–100). Thus the continued Adventist appropriation of the Apocalypse shifted away from imminent temporal concerns toward an applied cosmological dualism, a trait common in most apocalyptic literature (as expressed, e.g., in the explicit distinction of insiders from outsiders, saved from unsaved, sinners from righteous).

At the forefront of Jehovah's Witness appropriations of the Apocalypse is their privileging of the 144,000 elect referenced in Revelation 7 and 14. Revelation 7:4-8 reads:

> Then I heard the number of those who were sealed: 144,000 from all the tribes of Israel.
>
> > From the tribe of Judah, 12,000 were sealed,
> > from the tribe of Reuben 12,000,
> > from the tribe of Gad 12,000,
> > from the tribe of Asher 12,000,
> > from the tribe of Naphtali 12,000,
> > from the tribe of Manasseh 12,000,
> > from the tribe of Simeon 12,000,
> > from the tribe of Levi, 12,000,
> > from the tribe of Issachar 12,000,
> > from the tribe of Zebulun 12,000,
> > from the tribe of Joseph 12,000,
> > from the tribe of Benjamin 12,000.

And Rev. 14:1 again refers to the 144,000: "Then I looked, and there before me was the Lamb, standing on Mount Zion, and with him 144,000 who had his name and his Father's name written on their foreheads." According to Jehovah's Witnesses, "the United Nations and the world's religious leaders will be on Satan's side in the Battle of Armageddon. Against them will be ranged the 144,000 and the other sheep, but Christ's heavenly army will actually win the victory, and the only survivors of the battle will be the Jehovah's Witnesses" (Wainwright, 100). This position is consistent with founder Charles Russell's original teaching that the 144,000 will constitute the foundation of God's people during the Christian millennium and will do battle with people marked with the mark of the beast (Wainwright, 100). Again, the acute dualism of this apocalyptic appropriation is evident in this end-time narrative. And like the Adventist Church, Jehovah's Witnesses have survived the crisis of unrealized apocalyptic prophecy.

> Mistaken prophecies have not daunted the Jehovah's Witnesses. Joseph Franklin Rutherford, who succeeded Russell as their leader, predicted that Abraham, Isaac, Jacob and other faithful Israelites would return to earth in 1925. More recent Witnesses have entertained the hope that the millennium might begin about 1975. In spite of the failure of these expectations, the organization continues to thrive. (Wainwright, 101)

The Apocalyptic Legacy Today

Looking back on this succinct review of how the apocalyptic legacy has endured over the Christian centuries, I, for one, am perplexed—yet not surprised—by the apocalyptically saturated culture in which we continue to live today. Over the last several decades, myriad films on the imminent end have been produced. Examples include *The Seventh Seal* (1958), *Fail Safe* (1964), *Planet of the Apes* (1968), *The Omega Man* (1971), *The Omen* (1976), *Apocalypse Now* (1979), *Pale Rider* (1985), *The Seventh Sign* (1988), the *Terminator* series (1984, 1991, 2003, 2009, and possibly a fifth episode in the series in 2015), *Independence Day* (1996), *The Matrix* series (1999, 2003, 2003), *Apocalypto* (2006), *Knowing* (2009), *The Road* (2009), *The Book of Eli* (2010), and *The Colony* (2013). At best, this is just a small representation of the hundreds of films produced in the recent past on an apocalyptic and catastrophic "end."

A great deal of apocalyptic music has also emerged over the same period: *The End*, by the Doors, 1967; *Burn,* by Deep Purple, 1974; *It's the End of the World as We Know It (And I Feel Fine)*, by R.E.M., 1987; *Idioteque*, by Radiohead, 2000; *When the Man Comes Around*, by Johnny Cash, 2002; and *Radioactive*, by Imagine Dragons, 2013.

From the literary world, one need look no further than Hal Lindsey and Carla C. Carlson's best-selling *The Late Great Planet Earth* (1970) and Tim LaHaye and Jerry B. Jenkins's sixteen books in the *Left Behind* series (1995–2007). Both pairs of authors were greatly influenced by another form of futurism known as dispensationalism, a term coined by British author John Nelson Darby (1800–1882) that "refers to the idea that all time can be divided into [seven] separate periods known as dispensations. The present dispensation spans the time between the first and second comings of Christ, and the next great dispensation will be the millennium" (Koester, 275). The reading and composition strategy of Lindsey and Carlson was to cut and paste a series of biblical passages to give the reader a comprehensive view of the end-time scenario. According to Craig Koester, "Hal Lindsey's *Late, Great Planet Earth* . . . linked the biblical text used in Darby's system [esp. Genesis 15; Daniel 9; 1 Thessalonians 4; 2 Thessalonians 2; 1 John 2; and the entirety of Revelation] to current newspaper headlines, giving readers the impression that scripture had predicted the dominant political trends of the Cold War. The *Left Behind* novels . . . present Darby's system through the medium of fiction" (Koester, 275).

Examples of Lindsey and Carlson's interpretation of current events as correlative of apocalyptic biblical scenarios include, but surely are not limited to examples like these:

> The seal visions . . . predict the outbreak of war in the Middle East. . . . They tell of economic distress, shortage of food, and the death of a quarter of the human race as a result of these disasters. . . . The sixth seal vision may describe the beginning of nuclear war, and the trumpet visions may foretell the disasters of that war. . . . The bowl visions describe the fearful punishment that will be inflicted on those who reject the Christian Gospel. (Wainwright, 84)

Unrealized scenarios, in Lindsey and Carlson's schema, are considered "still yet to come" rather than failed. Jack Van Impe, a popular apocalyptic and "historical" dispensationalist preacher on the Trinity Broadcasting Network, is another outstanding example of the ongoing hermeneutic tradition initiated by Darby and executed by Lindsey and Carlson. He too postpones unfulfilled prophetic expectations and continues to look to contemporary events as potential signs of imminent fulfillment.

The *Left Behind* series, as noted above, correlates apocalyptic biblical themes with fictional events (although the narrative can include real-world entities). For example, the first novel

> opens against a context of international food shortages, inflation (Rev. 6.5-6) and conflict (Rev. 6.4) in the Middle East. Amidst the upheaval, the rapture occurs. Children and Christian adults are taken up, but a few of those left behind appreciate what has occurred; most prefer the explanations offered by United Nations Secretary General Nicolae Carpathia, who promises a solution to the world's problems, heads a new ten-member (evoking the "ten crowns" of Rev. 13.2) Security Council, and brokers a peace deal for Israel. Carpathia is hailed as a great leader and replaces the United Nations with a totalitarian Global Community, as nations seeking peace and security willingly surrender their sovereignty. (Rev. 13; Wright, 2009, 81)

The popularity of the *Late Great Planet Earth* and the *Left Behind* series cannot be overstated. Combined sales of the books are well into the tens of millions. These books are, for many Christians, the primary source for their understanding of Christian apocalyptic. As Koester has noted, "The view of the future presented in [*Left Behind*] affirms that God is sovereign despite ominous world conditions. . . . The novels show that simple believers, who know the biblical script, are far better informed about global developments than the commentators on television" (Koester, 278). An appealing script for the apocalyptically inclined, indeed.

No survey of the apocalyptic legacy of Christian Scripture is complete without an acknowledgment of three of the most sensational and horrific demonstrations of that legacy in recent memory: Jonestown (1978), the Branch Davidians (1993), and Heaven's Gate (1997). As noted in the beginning of this essay, one generalized way to categorize the trajectories of apocalyptic groups is according to their responses when initial prophecies of an imminent event have been delayed. The group in question can disband; they can move the date of the end into the undefined future; or they can initiate a violent end within the parameters of their apocalyptic rhetoric. The three groups just named all chose the last option, under different circumstances. These three groups (and several others like them) pique our imaginations when we discuss modern apocalyptic groups. They represent the most extreme cases.

It may very well be that my own interest in apocalyptic groups began with the images I witnessed, as an eighteen-year-old, of the Jonestown debacle. The photos and film sent over the newswire were shocking: piles of bodies (many of whom were children) stacked up and grouped together in a jungle in Guyana, a dead US Congressman and reporters executed point blank lying on an airstrip, and syringes and vats of cyanide-laced, purple Kool Aid. Over 900 people died on a single day, March 18, 1978.

What we learned about the group and its leaders after the mass suicide was equally sensational. Pastor Jim Jones (1931–1978) had led his flock from its roots in Indianapolis, Indiana, to Redwood Valley, California, then to San Francisco, and ultimately to their final "utopian" location in Jonestown, Guyana. The group's migration to Jonestown began in 1977 and was executed in several stages: survey, development, occupation. Dominant in the group's rhetoric were themes of persecution, suffering, and potential martyrdom for the cause. The echoes of Christian apocalyptic are not difficult to discern in this rhetoric. Jones and his flock were committed to fighting what they perceived as "the injustices of a racist, classist, and capitalistic society" (Moore, 95). Jones believed that the group's new location in the jungles of Guyana would allow for the free exercise of their religion and the development of a socialist utopia.

The utopian beginnings of the relocated group were hounded by reports as early as 1972—the San Francisco years—"when a religion reporter for the *San Francisco Chronicle* wrote that a member wanting to leave the group had died under suspicious circumstances" (Moore, 97). Moore also reports that "the apostate group called the Concerned Relatives publicized an 'accusation of Human Rights Violations,' which detailed abuses that they believed were occurring in Jonestown" (Moore, 97). These accusations were the impetus for the visit of US Congressman Leo Ryan's visit to Jonestown in 1978. These accusations, combined with some current members desiring to leave Jonestown in conjunction with Jones's elevated paranoia (which may have included an increasing dependence on narcotics), fueled the volatile mix of the rhetoric of persecution and suffering and perceived external pressures. The pressure and paranoia became so acute that the infamous "white nights" (actual rehearsals of mass suicide) became more common in the latter stages of the group's existence. The actual performance was executed on the evening of March 18, 1978. In the words of the self-proclaimed messiah Jones, it was an act of "revolutionary suicide," an act no doubt influenced by apocalyptic ideation.

Fifteen years after the events of Jonestown, another apocalyptic group, the Branch Davidians, appeared on our apocalyptic landscape. The forensic analysis of the global press and the emerging World Wide Web allowed us our closest and most detailed look at an apocalyptic group and its violent end. Led by David Koresh (Vernon Howell, born 1959), another self-proclaimed messiah (Koresh is the Hebrew transliteration of Cyrus, a reference to the Persian king proclaimed messiah by the prophet Isaiah in Isa. 45:1), the Branch Davidians—an offshoot of the Seventh-Day Adventists Church—engaged in a lethal gun battle with US federal agents on April 19, 1993, in which their compound was destroyed by fire and seventy-six Davidians lost their lives. The source of the fire is still under debate: the two competing theories are that federal tear-gas canisters started the fire in the compound, or that members of the Davidians started the fire from within.

What is especially fascinating about this group was their explicit employment of the book of Revelation to map out their perceived apocalyptic destiny. Kenneth Newport argues, "The text [i.e., the book of Revelation] was at the very least an important factor . . . in the decision of the Branch Davidians to self-destruct (or 'act out their biblical destiny' as they would more probably have seen it)" (Newport, 213). He continues, "The community read the Book of Revelation (together with numerous other parts of the Bible, especially the Psalms) and what they read there, I suggest, together with the context in which they read it, led to the group's planned for and well executed apocalyptic self-destruction" (Newport, 213). Certainly texts like Rev. 10:7 were used by Koresh to depict himself as the seventh angel of the Apocalypse. The description of a lamblike beast in Rev. 13:11-18 was used to demonize the US government. Such passages were vital to group awareness. Thus, for the Branch Davidians, "the arrival of the ATF and then the FBI on the morning of 28 February, 1993, was highly significant and prophetically charged" (Newport, 219). For the Davidians (especially Koresh), as for Jonestown, all pressures from outside the group were biblically prophesied signs of the apocalyptic times. So when the *Waco Tribune-Herald* began publishing a critical exposé on Koresh, called "The Sinful Messiah," the day before the first day of the siege on the Davidian compound, all signs pointed to their impending end.

An interesting variation on the modern apocalyptic group coming to an abrupt end is Heaven's Gate. Founded in 1972 by Marshall Applewhite (1932–1997) and Bonnie Lu Nettles (1928–1985), the group chose to end their lives via ritualistic suicide by consuming a lethal combination of Phenobarbital (an anticonvulsant barbiturate) mixed with applesauce and chased with vodka. After law-enforcement authorities received an anonymous tip, thirty-nine bodies were discovered in a mansion in Rancho Santa Fe (an affluent suburb of San Diego), twenty-one women and eighteen men of various ages from twenty-six to seventy-two. The ritualistic suicides were performed over several days in 1997: fifteen on March 22, fifteen on March 23, seven on March 24, and the final two somewhere between March 24 and their eventual discovery on March 26.

The bodies (known as "vessels" by Heaven's Gate members) were all dressed in black shirts and trousers, black Nike sneakers, and a purple cloth covered their upper torsos. Each had an armband with the words "Heaven's Gate Away Team" embroidered on the band. The majority of the deceased had in their possession a five-dollar bill and three quarters.

The impetus for this ritualistic suicide is uniquely different from the rhetoric of persecution, suffering, and martyrdom commonplace in Jonestown and in Waco, Texas, among the Branch Davidians. Benjamin Zeller concludes that "while the movement surely experienced a sense of persecution and failure . . . these conditions are not in themselves sufficient to cause self-violence" (Zeller, 175). What motivated this group ritualistically to end their lives was their belief (according to their still-active website: heavensgate.com) that humanity needed to move beyond human existence to their rightful place at the "next level above human," the realm of God. For the members, the imminent timing of this transition was critical because it was their belief that the earth was soon to be "recycled."

It should be noted, however, that ritualistic suicide was not always a part of the group's theology. Rather, "for the first decade of the group's history it flatly rejected the very notion of suicide, arguing instead for the need to transition into the heavens while still embodied" (Zeller, 175). So what mechanism triggered the shift from embodied to disembodied transformation? The matter is still up for debate, but it should be noted that the death of cofounder Bonnie Lu Nettles of liver cancer in 1985 caused some cognitive dissonance among the membership. This period also marked the beginning of the group's devaluation of the body (from this point on, referred to as "vessels") that may have been a first step in their formulation of ritual suicide as spiritual release to the next level above human. This new understanding of the body, in combination with the belief that the earth was soon to be "recycled," played out when the comet Hale-Bopp manifested itself in the late-March skies of 1997. For Applewhite and the members of the Heaven's Gate group, this was *the sign*. A hypothesis was promoted by the group that located behind this comet was a spaceship that would gather the "elect" for the trip to the level above human. Although Zeller argued (as mentioned above) that the experienced sense of persecution and failure was not sufficient to explain the ritualistic violence that the group enacted, members were convinced in the days leading up to their end of "a massive government conspiracy to hide an extraterrestrial flying saucer trailing the comet" (Zeller, 177).

Epilogue

This essay began by questioning whether the book of Revelation was the sole source for the rich apocalyptic legacy in Western Christendom. It is, according to this essay, no doubt a tour de force in that history. Yet the history also reveals that Western Christians have had an ambivalent relationship with Revelation. The post-Augustinian shift from historical to spiritual readings is demonstrative of that point. That shift was, like Matthew and Luke's appropriation of Mark, a domestication of the apocalyptic tradition. And from roughly that point in history, Christians have both foregrounded and retreated from that position based on our interpretive agendas. The biblical tradition and the interpretive legacy have embedded within them *both* potentialities, for historicizing or for spiritualizing readings, and we are their inheritors.

With this inheritance comes great responsibility. History shows how easy it is for those enthusiastic for a final, definitive ending to risk actions that bring about lesser, still devastating ends. Today, however, more is at stake than the welfare of the members of an apocalyptic group. Apocalyptic scripts and a highly weaponized world make for a volatile mixture. As Catherine Wessinger observes, for example,

> In the 1980s Americans learned that President Reagan (Republican, served 1981–1989) had been influenced by [Hal] Lindsey's predictions about the roles of Israel and nuclear war in the final events. Throughout the Reagan administration Americans who did not believe in these apocalyptic prophecies contemplated the danger of having a Dispensationalist President as commander of the American nuclear arsenal. (Wessinger, 428; cf. Boyer, 140–43)

Apocalyptic scripts also make it much too easy to separate the world into sheep and goats, "axes of evil" and "elect nations"—perpetually seeking to identify antichrists for destruction. For example, George W. Bush's war on terror was often framed in the totalizing language of good versus evil. Again, Wessinger notes that the Bush administration's response to the attacks of 9/11 by Islamic jihadists was an act of "apocalyptic mirroring" (see Rosenfeld) in which "the radical dualism of the Bush administration matched that of jihadists, and Bush's apocalyptic war rhetoric mirrored that of bin Laden and colleagues" (Wessinger, 436). In a speech delivered on September 14, 2011, Bush declared that it was America's responsibility "to answer these attacks *and rid the world of evil*" (italics added; see Räisänen, 155). It should also be noted that the lyrics of hymns such as "Onward Christian Soldiers" and "The Battle Hymn of the Republic"—the musical selections for the Day of Prayer and Remembrance for the victims of 9/11 on September 14, 2001—reflect the anticipation of some fully to participate in the apocalypse on their time rather than God's. But all such appropriations are irrational and zealous impositions on the biblical texts—*all* of the texts we have identified as apocalyptic within the Christian canon (Jewett).

Perhaps it is our role as scholars, theologians, ministers, priests, and simply as rational human beings to remind those in our midst of the consequences of such human impositions on our sacred texts. The models of Jonestown, the Branch Davidians, and Heaven's Gate are just a few examples of the potential for disaster when we set the apocalyptic clock on our time. One could readily add other events and groups to an ever-expanding list (e.g., the Manson Family, Aum Shinrikyo, and the Solar Temple). Against the reflex to expedite the apocalyptic clock, we would do well to heed what the biblical texts actually have to say about the time frame of the end; for example, Jesus' words in Mark 13:32: "But about that day or hour no one knows, not even the angels in heaven, nor the Son, but only the Father." What is most tragic, however, is that our self-imposed acceleration of the apocalyptic clock has also accelerated the dangers of which the seer John issues an awesome warning against anyone who adds to his prophecy.

> I warn everyone who hears the words of the prophecy of this scroll: If anyone adds anything to them, God will add to that person the plagues described in this scroll. And if anyone takes words away from this scroll of prophecy, God will take away from that person any share in the tree of life and in the Holy City, which are described in this scroll. (Rev. 22:18-19)

The reflex to accelerate an apocalyptic schedule has actualized the calamities of which John warns. With or without explicit appeal to apocalyptic texts, the effort to determine the course of history through force has already begun to inflict plagues of biblical proportions on our world: the plague of war, the plague of famine, the plague of disease, the plague of a deteriorating ecosystem, and the plague of abject poverty are just a few prime examples. The time has come to stop and recognize the gravity, both explicit and implicit, of the scriptural inheritances that inform our apocalyptic legacy. Only then will we be able to begin to neutralize it.

Works Cited

Aune, David E. 2005. "Understanding Jewish and Christian Apocalyptic." *WW* 25, no. 3:233–45.

Boyer, Paul. 1992. *When Time Shall Be No More: Prophecy Belief in Modern American Culture.* Cambridge, MA: Harvard University Press.

Cameron, Averil, ed. 1989. *History as Text: The Writing of Ancient History.* Chapel Hill: University of North Carolina Press.

Chilton, Bruce. 2013. *Visions of the Apocalypse: Receptions of John's Revelation in Western Imagination.* Waco, TX: Baylor University Press.

Collins, Adela Yarbro. 1984. *Crisis and Catharsis: The Power of the Apocalypse.* Philadelphia: Westminster.

Collins, John J. 1979. "Introduction: Towards the Morphology of a Genre." *Semeia* 14:1–20.

———. 1984. *The Apocalyptic Imagination: An Introduction to Jewish Apocalyptic Literature.* New York: Crossroad.

Froom, LeRoy E. 2009. *The Prophetic Faith of Our Fathers.* Vol. 4. Hagerstown, MD: Review and Herald Publishing Association.

Hanson, Paul. 1979. *The Dawn of Apocalyptic: The Historical and Sociological Roots of Jewish Apocalyptic Eschatology.* Philadelphia: Fortress Press.

Jones, Ken Sundet. 2005. "The Apocalyptic Luther." *WW* 25, no. 3:233–45.

Koester, Craig R. 2005. "Revelation and the *Left Behind* Novels." *WW* 25, no. 3:274–82.

Kovacs, Judith L. 2005. "The Revelation to John: Lessons from the History of the Book's Reception." *WW* 25, no. 3:255–63.

Moore, Rebecca. 2011. "Narratives of Persecution, Suffering, and Martyrdom: Violence in Peoples Temple and Jonestown." In *Violence and New Religious Movements*, edited by J. R. Lewis, 95–111. Oxford: Oxford University Press.

Jewett, Robert. 1973. *The Captain America Complex: The Dilemma of Zealous Nationalism*. Philadelphia: Westminster.

Luther, Martin. 1960a. "Preface to the Revelation of John [I]." In *LW* 35.

———. 1960b. "Preface to the Revelation of John [II]." In *LW* 35.

Newport, Kenneth. 2009. "Be Thou Faithful Unto Death (cf. Rev. 2.10): The Book of Revelation, The Branch Davidians and Apocalyptic (Self-)Destruction." In *The Way the World Ends? The Apocalypse of John in Culture and Ideology*, edited by W. J. Lyons and Jorunn Økland, 211–26. Sheffield: Sheffield Phoenix.

Perkins, Judith. 1995. *The Suffering Self: Pain and Narrative Representation in the Early Christian Era*. London: Routledge.

Phelan, John Leddy. 1970. *The Millennial Kingdom of the Franciscans in the New World*. Berkeley: University of California Press.

Räisänen, Heikki. 2009. "Revelation, Violence, and War: Glimpses of a Dark Side." In *The Way the World Ends? The Apocalypse of John in Culture and Ideology*, edited by W. J. Lyons and Jorunn Økland, 211–26. Sheffield: Sheffield Phoenix.

Rosenfeld, Jean E. 2011. "Nativists Millennialism." In *The Oxford Handbook of Millennialism*, edited by Catherine Wessinger, 89–109. New York: Oxford University Press.

Royalty, Robert M., Jr. 2005. "The Dangers of the Apocalypse." *WW* 25, no. 3:283–93.

Sánchez, David A. 2008. *From Patmos to the Barrio: Subverting Imperial Myths*. Minneapolis: Fortress Press.

Wainwright, Arthur W. 1993. *Mysterious Apocalypse: Interpreting the Book of Revelation*. Nashville: Abingdon.

Wessinger, Catherine. 2014. "Apocalypse and Violence." In *The Oxford Handbook of Apocalyptic Literature*, edited by John J. Collins, 422–40. New York: Oxford University Press.

Wright, Melanie J. 2009. "Every Eye Shall See Him": Revelation and Film. In *The Way the World Ends? The Apocalypse of John in Culture and Ideology*, edited by W. J. Lyons and Jorunn Økland, 76–94. Sheffield: Sheffield Phoenix.

Wright, Stuart A. 2011. "Revisiting the Branch Davidian Mass Suicide Debate." In *Violence and New Religious Movements*, edited by J. R. Lewis, 113–31. Oxford: Oxford University Press.

Zeller, Benjamin E. 2011. "The Euphemization of Violence: The Case of Heaven's Gate." In *Violence and New Religious Movements*, edited by J. R. Lewis, 173–89. Oxford: Oxford University Press.

JESUS AND THE CHRISTIAN GOSPELS

Raymond Pickett

Jesus in History and Interpretation

This is an essay about Jesus, about the significance of who he was and what he said and did. Any interpretation of Jesus' significance is based primarily on the narrative interpretations of his ministry, death, and resurrection in the four canonical Gospels in the New Testament. The operative word here is *interpretation*. The Gospels interpret the significance of Jesus' words and actions for his followers in order to shape the practices and beliefs of communities of faith, and hence they presume a faith commitment from the intended audiences. Although the Gospels recount select events in Jesus' life, they do not purport to be objective accounts of what happened. Therefore, reading them as straightforward historical reports of what Jesus did and said not only misconstrues the nature and purpose of the Gospels but also obscures the fact that history is itself always a matter of interpretation.

That there are four canonical Gospels and several Gospels that are not in the canon indicates that the memory and early traditions about Jesus were interpreted in various ways. A close comparison of the birth narratives in Matthew and Luke, the chronology of Jesus' ministry in the Gospels of Mark and John, or the resurrection narratives in all four canonical Gospels demonstrate how key events were interpreted differently. Not everything the Gospels depict Jesus saying and doing happened exactly as reported. Later in this essay, we will explore the character and purpose of the Gospels and various approaches to interpreting them in ancient and contemporary contexts. First, however, we investigate how these narrative interpretations of Jesus' significance have been used by modern scholars for historical reconstructions of the figure of Jesus based on critical analysis of the Gospels.

In 1906, Albert Schweitzer wrote a book that evaluated the works about the historical figure of Jesus that had been written in the previous two centuries. The English translation of the title of Schweitzer's book was *The Quest of the Historical Jesus*. The first quest began in the late eighteenth century, when a German scholar by the name of H. S. Reimarus, a philosopher who maintained that reason could arrive at knowledge of God and ethics from the study of nature, questioned the historicity of the Gospel accounts of Jesus' miracles. He was followed by David F. Strauss and others who sought to distinguish what they regarded as purely historical accounts of the life of Jesus from the faith perspective that originally shaped the Gospels. This first quest for the historical Jesus was influenced by Enlightenment-era rationality, which rejected certain aspects of the Gospel accounts of Jesus as problematic because they contradicted the laws of nature.

Schweitzer's review of this historical scholarship of Jesus demonstrated that the lives of Jesus produced during this era using historical-critical methods were themselves not objective, factual accounts. Rather, they reflected the interests and ideals of those who wrote them. In other words, the portraits of Jesus that emerged during the first quest betrayed the worldview and outlook of their authors. Just as the depictions of Jesus in the Gospels were conditioned by the cultural milieu in which they were written and by the faith convictions of their authors, so were the eighteenth- and nineteenth-century accounts of Jesus invariably shaped by the Zeitgeist of that historical period. Schweitzer's critique of historical Jesus research marks the close of what is often referred to as the first quest. However, Schweitzer's own contribution to the endeavor would have an enduring effect on historical Jesus studies. His interpretation of the Gospels in the context of early Judaism led him to conclude that Jesus was an apocalyptic figure who, along with his followers, expected the imminent arrival of God's kingdom. Unlike the liberal portraits of Jesus of the previous two centuries, which preserved his ethical message even as they stripped away the elements that were not consistent with a worldview that discarded the supernatural, Schweitzer's Jesus belonged more to the first-century world of apocalyptic Judaism and was therefore less familiar to Christians at the turn of the twentieth century. Schweitzer concluded that Jesus expected the imminent arrival of the kingdom of God. He wrote that Jesus "in the knowledge that he is the coming Son of Man lays hold of the wheel of the world to set it moving on that last revolution which is to bring all ordinary history to a close. It refuses to turn, and he throws himself upon it. Then it does turn; and crushes him" (Schweitzer, 369).

The first quest for the historical Jesus resulted in a number of important developments that significantly shaped subsequent study of Jesus and the Gospels. First, Mark came to be regarded as the earliest Gospel by scholars and hence was used as a primary historical source in historical Jesus scholarship. However, in 1901, Wilhelm Wrede's book *The Messianic Secret* contended that the secrecy motif was a literary device created by the author of Mark's Gospel to project the apostolic post-Easter faith in Jesus as Messiah back onto the Jesus of history. Although, according to Wrede, Jesus himself had actually made no claim to be messiah, Mark had incorporated this postresurrection belief into his narrative. Wrede's work highlighted the fact that the early Jesus traditions were creatively adapted to convey particular theological convictions. It also called attention to the literary quality of the Gospel, that is, the artistry of constructing such a narrative. These insights resulted in the development of new approaches to studying the Gospels. Redaction criticism, on the one hand, concentrated on how the Gospel writers used and edited source materials, and what this disclosed about the theological perspectives of the respective Gospels. The aim of form criticism, on the other hand, was to ascertain the earlier forms of the oral traditions used to craft the Gospel narratives. It asked questions about the function of the oral traditions in their original contexts and was interested in tracing the development of the Gospel tradition.

Another important consequence of the first quest for the historical Jesus was the distinction made between the "Jesus of history" and the "Christ of faith." One reaction to Schweitzer's historical reconstruction, which made Jesus as apocalyptic prophet less theologically relevant, was for others increasingly to emphasize the Christ of faith. Martin Kähler's book *The So-Called Historical Jesus and the Historical Biblical Christ*, published in German in 1892, claimed that the true Christ is a Christ of faith detached from the Jesus of history. However, the most important champion of this perspective, and one of the most famous New Testament scholars of the twentieth century, was Rudolf Bultmann. For Bultmann, Christianity begins with Easter, and so he downplayed the importance of the Jesus of history for theology. From Bultmann's perspective, it was God's action in the death and resurrection of Jesus that was decisive rather than what Jesus had said and done (Theissen and Merz, 6–7).

The "new quest for the historical Jesus," initiated by Bultmann's students, was interested in establishing a continuity between the Christ of faith and the historical Jesus that Kähler and Bultmann had so persuasively distinguished. In contrast to the first quest, which sought to strip away the theological elements of the traditions about Jesus used by the Gospels, the new quest was interested in supporting the connection between the Christ of faith and the historical Jesus (Theissen and Merz, 7). It was guided by the conviction that the Gospels presuppose the identity of the earthly Jesus and exalted Christ. Bultmann had made the case that presuppositions always influenced the interpretation of New Testament texts. This new quest was intentional in being guided by what they regarded as a foundational presupposition of the tradition, namely, the continuity between the earthly Jesus and the risen Christ. This more explicitly christological approach put history in the service of theology and resulted in representations of Jesus that were more Christian and therefore less Jewish.

In the early 1980s, a third quest for the historical Jesus, catalyzed by new approaches to the study of Judaism, used a variety of ancient Jewish sources. This produced a revitalized picture of early Judaism as much more diverse and nuanced than the caricature of the Pharisees in the Gospels that had been operative in much previous scholarship. Scholars such as E. P. Sanders, John Dominic Crossan, Géza Vermes, Marcus Borg, and many others in the last three decades have written books about the historical Jesus that depict him as thoroughly embedded and engaged in the Judaism of his day. One of the main insights that has emerged from this third quest is that Jesus was the leader of a renewal movement within Judaism (Sanders 1985). The debate has focused on the question of what kind of Jew Jesus was, and the relationship between his particular interpretation and embodiment of Jewish tradition to other forms and expressions of Judaism. This quest has been characterized by greater methodological variety and sophistication, including the use of social-science and anthropological models and, in many instances, greater awareness of the Roman Empire as an important part of the context to which Jesus was responding.

Inasmuch as there continues to be a proliferation of scholarly books on Jesus, we are still in the midst of this third quest. Although no consensus about the historical Jesus is forthcoming, a much more richly textured understanding of the Jewish and Greco-Roman contexts of Jesus and the Gospels has advanced the conversation. Nonetheless, what Schweitzer observed about earlier lives of Jesus reflecting the interests and biases of their authors is also true of more recent scholarship. Historical investigation is always guided to some extent by the presuppositions of those interpreting these texts and traditions. The Gospels are not objective historical accounts of what Jesus said and did. Jesus probably spoke Aramaic, lived in an oral culture, and never wrote anything himself. Remembrances of his teaching and activity were profoundly influenced by the belief that God had raised from the dead this Galilean Jew who had been crucified, and had made him both Lord and Christ. The task of reconstructing from the Gospels a purely historical account of Jesus, unencumbered by the perspectives and presuppositions of those who composed and preserved the traditions about him, seems unattainable. Nonetheless, there are important reasons not only for historians but also for those interested in the importance of Jesus for contemporary life to preserve the connection between the Christ of faith and what can be known about the significance of what Jesus said and did in his own historical context.

The Hermeneutical Circle

There are four canonical Gospels. Matthew, Mark, and Luke are referred to as the Synoptic Gospels because there is a literary relationship between them. The Gospel of John is different in many respects, and is typically not used in historical Jesus research. All four Gospels are a blend of faith and history. That is to say, followers of Jesus recounted the story of his ministry, death, and resurrection for the express purpose of fostering faithful disciples. In this essay, we want to use the methods of historical criticism to investigate how Jesus engaged his own cultural and religious context in a way that makes it possible to explore his significance for our world today. Although it is possible to take a strictly historical approach to an investigation of Jesus and the Gospels, our task calls for a strategy of interpretation that employs historical-critical methods but recognizes that any interpretation is shaped by the social location and cultural context of the interpreter. The hermeneutical circle provides a model, illustrated in figure 1, of what happens in the interpretive process.

To interpret the Gospels is to be drawn into the narrative *world of the text*. The world of the Gospels is a narrative world that has been constructed by the author using existing oral and written traditions to tell the story of Jesus. The *world behind the text* is the historical and cultural context in which the Gospels were originally written and heard as well as the cultural world of the historical Jesus. Although the cultural and religious norms of the world behind the text are reflected in the narrative world of the Gospels, the world of the text takes on a life of its own apart from its original historical context once it is disseminated to be read in other times and places.

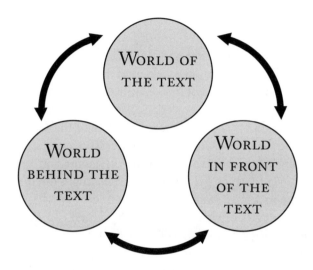

FIGURE 1. *The worlds behind, in front of, and in the text.*

The *world in front of the text* refers to subsequent interpretations of the text, which are always shaped by the social world of the interpreter. This includes the Gospels of Matthew and Luke, which reinterpret the Gospel of Mark in the light of their particular social situations, as well as contemporary interpretations of the Gospels that invariably construe the text through different cultural lenses. Every interpretation of the Gospel narratives about Jesus is influenced by a cultural context that is different from the ancient world in which it was produced and read. This is the reason that all reconstructions of the historical Jesus bear some resemblance to those who write them.

The arrows in the diagram illustrate the dynamic character of the interpretive process. The interpreter enters into the narrative world of the Gospels, but to some extent construes the story of Jesus in terms of the norms and conventions of his or her own social world. For example, modern American society values individual rights and tends to be guided by the ideal of the self-made person, who creates his or her own identity and determines his or her own fate. In the ancient world, however, a person's identity was defined by the group(s) to which he or she belonged and was thought to be vulnerable to numerous external forces, both terrestrial and celestial. So the predominant perception of Jesus as an itinerant charismatic leader held in scholarship on the historical Jesus today seems to reflect more modern ideas about the individual than the more communitarian ethos that was commonplace in antiquity.

The value of the hermeneutical circle is that keeping the worlds *of, in front of,* and *behind* the Gospels ever before the interpreter serves to promote awareness of the distinctive cultural values, conventions, and perspectives involved, and hence to magnify the difference between the world from which they come and the contemporary cultural contexts in which they are being interpreted.

Interpretations of Jesus and the Gospels that are interested primarily in their significance for life in today's world unwittingly collapse the distance of time and space between the worlds *in front of* and *behind* the text to make Jesus more relevant. But this is precisely how Jesus gets made over in our own image. The tools of historical criticism are used to travel the long, winding road from our world to the strange and wonderful world of first-century Judea, to better understand Jesus and the Gospels in their context.

It is, of course, impossible that we could somehow transcend the social milieu that formed us to fully fathom what it was like to live as a Galilean Jew under Roman rule in the decades leading up to the Jewish revolt. However, due diligence in attempting to understand Jesus in his context can also yield new insights into his significance for today. Just as visiting a foreign country casts one's own country in different light upon return, so efforts to better understand Jesus within the world that he inhabited can facilitate new angles of vision on our own cultural contexts and allow Jesus to speak to them in fresh and creative ways. The three worlds of the hermeneutical circle represent the three interacting contextual realities that are always in play in interpretation. In our attempts to grasp the significance of Jesus, we must navigate and negotiate the narrative or literary world of the text to ascertain the substance and force of what Jesus said and did in the world behind the text, and we are circumspect in this endeavor because we are mindful that our own social location colors what we see. Reflection on the significance of Jesus' words and actions for contemporary contexts should be predicated on our attempts to understand their force in their original historical and cultural context.

The Historical Figure of Jesus

The hermeneutical circle emphasizes the importance of context in interpreting the Gospel narratives about Jesus, and the primary task in this first portion of the essay is to place Jesus in his historical context. Any explanation of the significance of Jesus' teachings and actions should be based on an account of the circumstances and issues to which he was responding. However, before outlining the particulars of the historical and cultural framework for our sketch of Jesus, the content of and criteria for what should be regarded as historical need to be considered. This is a more challenging task than one might imagine because of the paucity of sources about Jesus outside the Gospels that can be used to verify the historicity of the tradition. The two basic aspects that need to be assessed historically are the sayings of Jesus and the actions of Jesus. Establishing the historical probability of what Jesus did is the less disputed of the two tasks, though it is complicated by how to interpret the healings, exorcisms, and other deeds of power attested by the Gospels.

In *The Historical Figure of Jesus*, E. P. Sanders offers a list of statements about Jesus that are almost beyond dispute and belong to the framework of Jesus' public career (Sanders 1993, 10–11).

- Jesus was born *c.* 4 BCE, near the time of the death of Herod the Great;
- he spent his childhood and early adult years in Nazareth, a Galilean village;
- he was baptized by John the Baptist;
- he called disciples;
- he taught in the towns, villages and countryside of Galilee (apparently not in the cities);

- he preached "the kingdom of God";
- about the year 30 he went to Jerusalem for Passover;
- he created a disturbance in the Temple area;
- he had a final meal with the disciples;
- he was arrested and interrogated by Jewish authorities, specifically the high priest;
- he was executed on the orders of the Roman prefect, Pontius Pilate.

Sanders adds another short list of what he regards as equally secure facts about the aftermath of Jesus' life:

- his disciples at first fled;
- they saw him (in what sense is not certain) after his death;
- as a consequence, they believed that he would return to found the kingdom;
- they formed a community to await his return and sought to win others to faith in him as God's Messiah.

With some qualifications, these lists serve as a foundation of most of the recent accounts of the historical Jesus. Jesus' birth is usually dated somewhere around 4 BCE. The birth narratives in the Gospels of Matthew and Luke are very different and are best seen as theological interpretations rather than historical accounts. The historical starting point for a reconstruction of Jesus' life and ministry is his baptism by John. The other historical bracket is his death by crucifixion. However, the Gospel traditions of both his baptism and death provide examples of historical traditions that have been expanded on. The Gospel accounts of the baptism highlight the superiority of Jesus to John and the voice from heaven, which announces that he is "Son of God." These, again, are theological appraisals that cannot be validated historically. The crucifixion, which is also on solid historical ground, is intertwined with chronicles of his trial which indicate that the Jewish authorities are ultimately responsible for his death. As Sanders suggests, it is likely that members of the priestly aristocracy were complicit in the trial and execution of Jesus, but from a historical perspective, Jesus was executed for sedition as an enemy of the Roman order. Historical information from other sources shows that Pilate summarily executed thousands of Jews and therefore was probably not as tentative in sending Jesus to his death as he is portrayed in the Gospels.

What the above comments demonstrate is that even the most basic historical information is interpreted in the Gospels in ways that reflect the circumstances and perspectives of faithful followers of Jesus. The four different accounts of the resurrection in the Gospels are further evidence of the interpretive process from the vantage point of such followers. All four Gospels narrate in different ways the common conviction that God raised Jesus from the dead, but that claim cannot be validated by historical investigation as such. What is clearly historical is the disciples' belief that they saw him after his death. So the resurrection faith of the first followers of Jesus is itself historical in some sense, but it is impossible to get behind the tradition to ascertain exactly what happened. What is historical is their conviction that the risen Jesus was alive and present to them and through them, and this conviction had an impact on the continued expansion and growth of the Jesus movement.

Probably the most challenging aspect of efforts to reconstruct the historical Jesus is deciding which words and deeds are authentic to Jesus. It is generally acknowledged among scholars that the Gospel of Mark was the first Gospel, and was written around 70 CE, shortly after the destruction of the Jerusalem temple. So there is approximately a forty-year period between the historical Jesus and the earliest narrative of his ministry, death, and resurrection. During that forty-year period, the memory of Jesus was first preserved and passed on in oral tradition and then written down in collections of Jesus' sayings, deeds of power, suffering and death, and resurrection before being crafted into a narrative of his ministry, death, and announcement of his resurrection by whomever wrote the Gospel of Mark. As the memory of what Jesus said and did passed through these various stages, it was transformed. The question is, How can what the historical Jesus said and did be ascertained from the narrative accounts in the Gospels, where the memory of him has been shaped by forty years and more of adapting the tradition to new contexts, and by the perspectives of the Gospel writers themselves?

Significant advances in the study of memory and orality in recent years have contributed to an understanding of the development of the tradition behind the Gospels. On the one hand, oral cultures tend to preserve traditions with more accuracy than literary cultures such as ours. On the other hand, memory is always selective and involves imagination. Since the Gospels and the traditions they used cannot be read uncritically as unvarnished historical records, scholars have developed criteria to determine what in the Gospels should be regarded as historical and what should be regarded as a creative reworking of the tradition. A brief consideration of a couple of these criteria illustrates the difficulty of getting behind the Gospels to establish a historical substratum of the Jesus tradition.

The *criterion of dissimilarity* was at first applied to posit that if a saying of Jesus could not be attributed to Judaism or to the early church's theological reflection on Jesus, then it was deemed to be something Jesus probably said. The problem with this approach is that it breaks off the lines of continuity with both Judaism and the earliest communities of his followers to put forward a minimal collection of genuine sayings of Jesus that depict him as unique. This approach reinforced a portrait of Jesus that is at the very least non-Jewish, and in some instances anti-Jewish. The *criterion of multiple attestation* maintains that if a saying of or tradition about Jesus is attested in multiple independent sources, it is likely authentic. Although this is a historically sound approach, there is still much debate about the relationship of the Gospels and their underlying sources. One of the main debates concerns the hypothetical document Q. Q is from the German word *Quelle*, for "source," and refers to the sayings of Jesus common to the Gospel of Matthew and the Gospel of Luke. Although Q is not an extant document, many scholars regard this hypothetical source as the earliest collection of Jesus' sayings from Galilee. Given the ongoing debate about the status of Q in scholarship, the material common to Matthew and Luke will be referred to as the *double tradition* in this essay.

Evaluation of what in the Gospel traditions goes back to the historical Jesus is a complex enterprise that requires a repertoire of tools and approaches. Although there have been gains from the application and refinement of these historical-critical methods to the study of the historical Jesus over time, they are typically focused on a particular aspect of the tradition. One of the most difficult challenges in these historical reconstructions of Jesus is that no single one of them can account for all the data in the tradition. Every interpreter of the Gospels, expert and nonexpert alike, brings to their reading of the text a working portrait of Jesus that privileges certain sayings or deeds and then interprets everything else in the Gospel tradition through that lens. In some instances, what one privileges in the tradition is the basis for bracketing something in the Gospel tradition as being less important or even inauthentic. Historical investigation is by its very nature circular inasmuch as it begins with a minimal amount of historical data and then builds a case informed by underlying assumptions that will inevitably have blind spots. The use of the various historical methods can contribute to this phenomenon because they tend to be used in ways that confirm one's preconceptions about Jesus. In other words, interpreters tend to find the Jesus they are looking for.

In view of this methodological impasse, I would propose that more emphasis should be placed on a holistic reading of the Gospel narratives of Jesus applying the *criterion of historical plausibility*. Theissen and Merz succinctly define the criterion of historical plausibility in this way: "Whatever helps to explain the influence of Jesus and at the same time can only have come into being in a Jewish context is historical in the sources" (116). The Gospels are realistic narratives that depict Jesus as a Judean, conversing and interacting mostly with other Judeans. Given the thicker and more richly textured view of first-century Judaism that has emerged in recent years, the primary task is to make sense of what the Gospels depict Jesus doing and saying *within his Jewish context*. This also pertains to the depiction of his contemporaries. For example, the portrait of the Pharisees in the Gospels is something of a caricature. It more likely betrays a conflict between them and the followers of Jesus after the destruction of the temple in 70 CE, which was then projected back onto the ministry of Jesus.

It is unlikely that there will ever be a definitive reconstruction of the historical Jesus that everyone will agree on. However, a critical reading of the Gospels, paired with a good working understanding of Judaism in its imperial context, provides the most promising path to a historically plausible interpretation of Jesus. Such an interpretation must account for the particularities of the Gospel tradition in relationship to a broader comprehension of what Jesus was trying to accomplish in Galilee and then Jerusalem. The attempt to construct a contextually credible account of Jesus' words and deeds will also benefit from the use of social-science models to examine the socioeconomic dynamics of Jesus' Galilean context. An important premise of this discussion of Jesus' significance is that he was addressing concrete circumstances in his own local context, and hence his message had practical significance for those who heard and followed him. The force of Jesus' teaching and ministry are more discernible when viewed against the backdrop of the local situation in Galilee, and so are those elements of the tradition that have been shaped by later theological reflection. From the standpoint of the hermeneutical circle, this requires greater awareness of and appreciation for the historical distance and cultural difference between Jesus' world behind the text and the interpreter's world in front of the text. Interpretations of Jesus' significance for contemporary contexts will be more socially relevant and less abstract when he is viewed as a Galilean Jew engaging local religious and social issues in Galilee.

The Jesus Movement in Galilee

This concise consideration of the historical Jesus will use the Gospel of Mark and the early-sayings source Q to present a historically plausible explanation of the significance of Jesus' words and actions in Galilee in the early 30s of the first century CE. The task of differentiating what the historical Jesus said and did from secondary interpretations of the tradition after the resurrection is complex. As has been noted, every reconstruction of the historical Jesus privileges certain aspects of the tradition that tend to reinforce one's preconceptions of Jesus. There are tensions in the Gospel tradition that cannot be resolved without positing that certain parts of it are the result of later theological reflection. Instead of beginning by outlining a method to distinguish what is authentic to Jesus from what is the product of later christological reflection, the priority here is to succinctly reconstruct the Galilean context as a framework for interpreting the earliest layer of the Jesus tradition. Context is the key to interpretation, and even a compact description of Jesus' Galilean environment elucidates the force of his words and deeds.

Jesus was born in the early years of the Roman Empire, which began when Augustus was declared emperor in 27 BCE. Herod the Great was the client king of the Roman Empire. Herod's allegiance to Rome was evident in his grand building projects, which included the rebuilding of the Jerusalem temple in Hellenistic-Roman style as well as temples dedicated to the divine Augustus. He also appointed high priests to replace the Hasmoneans, and together with other Herodians they formed a powerful aristocracy that collaborated with Rome. Herod's massive building program may have brought honor to him and his Roman patrons, but it was the cause of considerable economic distress for those living in Roman Palestine. It is not surprising that when Herod died in 4 BCE, there were rebellions in Galilee, Judea, and Perea that had to be suppressed. The Jewish historian Josephus relates the views of a delegation that went to Rome to complain about the repercussions of Herod's rule.

> He had indeed reduced the entire nation to helpless poverty after taking it over in as flourishing condition as few ever know. . . . In addition to the collecting of the tribute that was imposed on everyone each year, lavish contributions had to be made to him and his household and friends and those of his slaves who were sent out to collect the tribute because there was no immunity at all from outrage unless bribes were paid. (Josephus, *Ant.* 17.307–8)

The Roman Empire was an aristocratic empire. The example of Herod illustrates the dynamics in which the majority of resources are controlled by elite families who live off the labor of peasants. Roman Palestine was divided after Herod's death, and his son Antipas was given control of Galilee by Augustus. Herod Antipas was client king during Jesus' ministry, and the economic hardship that characterized his rule is reflected in the Gospels. The Jesus movement was a Galilean movement, and Galilee was an agrarian peasant society. Galileans were subjected to a triple tax system that consisted of a temple tax, a Roman tax, and a tax from the Herodian aristocratic administration that placed almost unbearable economic pressure on them. The political facet of this predicament was that this agrarian society was controlled by a ruling aristocracy, mostly from the neighboring cities of Sepphoris and Tiberias, who exploited local peasants through debt slavery. John's baptism of repentance and Jesus' message and enactment of the kingdom of God should be seen as responding to this social crisis in Galilee. Figure 2 is a graphic representation of an agrarian tributary society (from Lenski, 284; see Crossan 1991, 45–46).

The first task is to situate Jesus in his Galilean context in the 30s. All the Gospels agree that Jesus' ministry begins with his baptism by John in the Jordan River. John was an apocalyptic prophet announcing God's imminent judgment unless Israel repented. In the Gospel tradition, John's role is described as forerunner to Jesus. However, the Israelites who submitted to his baptism probably understood it as a reenactment of the exodus, as Crossan and Reed suggest, "taking penitents from the desert, through the Jordan, into the Promised Land, to possess it in holiness once again" (117–18). John's baptism, then, ritualized a hope for liberation from the political and economic oppression that characterized life in Galilee at this time. Jesus began his ministry under the auspices of John the Baptist, and whatever message and ministry he had was, initially at least, aligned with John's.

One of the main challenges in appreciating the significance of John and Jesus in their Galilean setting is the tendency to regard them simply as religious figures. However, in the ancient world,

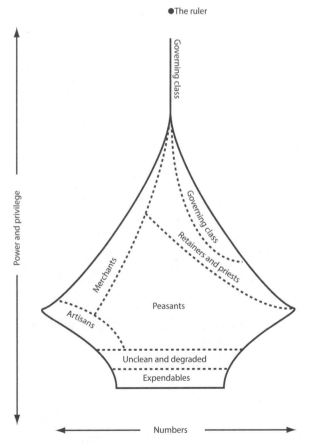

FIGURE 2. *Agrarian tributary society (after Lenski, 284).*

religion, politics, and economics were inextricably bound together. For Israelites, fidelity to God's covenant encompassed every dimension of life. The fact that Herod Antipas killed John indicates that he viewed John as a political threat. A passage from the Jewish historian Josephus elucidates both what John was doing and why Herod was concerned.

> For Herod had put him to death, though he was a good man and had exhorted the Jews to lead righteous lives, to practice justice towards their fellows and piety towards God, and so doing to join in baptism. When others too joined the crowds about him, because they were aroused to the highest degree by his sermons, Herod became alarmed. Eloquence that had so great an effect on mankind might lead to some form of sedition. (*Ant.* 18.117–18)

The Gospels report that Herod expressed the same concern about Jesus when he heard that Jesus had cast out demons and healed the sick.

> King Herod heard of it, for Jesus' name had become known. Some were saying, "John the baptizer has been raised from the dead; and for this reason these powers are at work in him." But others said, "It is Elijah." And others said, "It is a prophet, like one of the prophets of old." But when Herod heard of it, he said, "John, whom I beheaded, has been raised." (Mark 6:14-16)

Later when Jesus is in Jerusalem, Luke says that some Pharisees warned Jesus,

> "Get away from here, for Herod wants to kill you." He said to them, "Go and tell that fox for me, 'Listen, I am casting out demons and performing cures today and tomorrow, and on the third day I finish my work.'" (Luke 13:31-32)

The activity of John the Baptist and Jesus occurred in Galilee and surrounding villages, where taxation and subsistence agriculture served Herod Antipas's project of urbanization (Oakman). Richard Horsley has made the connection between the exploitation of the populace in these agrarian villages and the numerous incidents of resistance and rebellion that occurred around the time of Jesus. A related observation is that during Second Temple times most inhabitants of Galilee were descendants of the northern Israelite peasantry, and stood in the northern prophetic tradition calling for the revitalization of Israelite village communities and a return to covenantal principles as a means of redressing social, political, and economic injustices (Horsley 2003). Both John the Baptist and Jesus were shaped by this prophetic tradition and were committed to the renewal of village life in the face of these harsh circumstances. However, while Jesus was initially identified through baptism with John's more apocalyptic hope of God's coming in judgment to rectify matters, he is depicted throughout the Gospel tradition as having a different strategy of grappling with the distress and discontent that Galileans experienced.

Jesus and John the Baptist

In a passage common to Luke and Matthew, Jesus compares his reputation to that of John: "For John the Baptist has come eating no bread and drinking no wine, and you say, 'He has a demon'; the Son of Man has come eating and drinking, and you say, 'Look, a glutton and a drunkard, a friend of tax collectors and sinners!'" (Luke 7:33-34 // Matt. 11:18-19). Moreover, in this same passage, Jesus draws another sharp distinction between himself and John: "I tell you, among those born of women no one is greater than John; yet the least in the kingdom of God is greater than he" (Luke 7:28 // Matt. 11:11). Even as he affirms John's prophetic ministry, he signals that God is now present and active anew through him. The contrast between Jesus and John in this passage provides an important clue to understanding the distinctive character of Jesus' ministry, the focus of which was the kingdom of God. How do we account for Jesus' transition from participant in John the Baptist's ascetic movement, with its standard covenantal emphasis on repentance and cleansing from sins, to being stigmatized for keeping company with those in need of reform?

John's imprisonment and execution had a traumatic effect on Jesus, but another passage common to Luke and Matthew suggests that Jesus' views were developing in a different direction even before that. When John sends his disciples to ask Jesus, "Are you the one who is to come, or are we to wait for another?" Jesus replies:

> Go and tell John what you have seen and heard: the blind receive their sight, the lame walk, the lepers are cleansed, the deaf hear, the dead are raised, the poor have good news brought to them. And blessed is anyone who takes no offense at me. (Luke 7:22-23 // Matt. 11:4-6)

Paul Hollenbach proposes that this shift was caused by Jesus' experience of God's power being mediated through him to exorcise and heal, which he interpreted as the kingdom of God being present in some sense. The Gospels do consistently portray Jesus as having a distinct authority to enact the kingdom in word and deed that is markedly different from John's apocalyptic vision of awaiting God's approaching judgment.

As we attempt to situate Jesus in the Galilean context of his ministry, one question we must ask is: How did Jesus' message and embodiment of the kingdom of God deal with the hardship of that village populace? This is a difficult question for at least two reasons. First, as Bultmann famously said, already in the earliest strata of the tradition the proclaimer has become the proclaimed. That is to say, the kingdom of God is the primary focus of Jesus' activity, but in the Gospels, Jesus himself, his identity and significance, is the center of attention. The second complication follows from the first. Once Jesus' teaching about the kingdom of God became a set of beliefs about him, the metaphor of the kingdom of God became more abstract and spiritualized. A Galilean or Judean audience in the first century would have heard the phrase "kingdom of God" as a political metaphor and would have grasped the implicit contrast with the client kingdoms that were an extension of imperial rule, such as that of Herod Antipas. To examine Jesus' message and enactment of the kingdom of God in relation to the sociopolitical landscape of Galilee is to explore the politics of the kingdom, that is, how Jesus was organizing and mobilizing his followers to embody divine power in their local context.

Jesus and the Renewal of Local Community

In an article titled "Jesus and the Renewal of Local Community in Galilee," Jonathan Draper challenges the dominant scholarly perspective that Jesus was an itinerant charismatic leader and argues that more attention should be given to group formation in the Jesus movement as a response to the economic and social disintegration and threatened landlessness in Galilee. He contends that Jesus was attempting to "renew local community in villages and towns, to strengthen and renew family and community relations and reverse the downward spiral of violence" (40). Except for a few passages that describe specific instances in which disciples are sent out, the Jesus tradition presupposes the existence and support of settled local communities. Geographically, Jesus moves within a limited radius of a few villages until he goes to Jerusalem. Hence the emphasis on Jesus' itinerancy may be more a consequence of superimposing post-Enlightenment individualism on the Gospel tradition so that a focus on Jesus as a unique religious figure eclipses his "concrete program of action for social transformation" (Draper, 38).

A brief consideration of meals and some of Jesus' teachings as practical expressions of the kingdom of God will illustrate Jesus' strategy for the renewal of community life in Galilee. A place to start is the passage mentioned above that describes Jesus as "a friend of tax collectors and sinners." This phrase occurs with reference to Jesus in all three of the Synoptic Gospels, where it is leveled by scribes and Pharisees as a criticism of Jesus (Matt. 9:10; Mark 2:15; Luke 5:30; 7:34). This complaint about Jesus reflects his opponents' perception of him, and may come from an early stratum of the tradition rather than from Jesus himself. Nonetheless, the criticism preserves a reminiscence of Jesus as a social deviant that probably has some basis in history. In the world in front of the text, "sinner" has a moral connotation, but in the context of Judaism, a sinner is one who is not compliant with Torah. What sinners and tax collectors have in common is that while they represent opposite ends of the socioeconomic spectrum, both were dishonored and therefore socially marginalized. Douglas Oakman has made the interesting suggestion that the word for "sin" in Aramaic, which was the language Jesus spoke, was *hōvayin*, the word for "debtors." He points out that these debtors could have been farmers or fishers in heavy debt, women enslaved in prostitution, or members of trades endangered by taxes. According to Oakman, "In this understanding, Jesus dines with just these people in order to broker relief" (98).

Meals were an integral part of Jesus' enactment of the kingdom of God, and they play a prominent role in the Gospel tradition. In addition to their obvious material significance in satisfying the hunger of a preponderance of people who worked to eke out a subsistence living, they also had symbolic import on a number of levels. Crossan has interpreted the significance of Jesus' meals as a central aspect of what he calls a "brokerless kingdom" marked by "the just sharing of food as the material basis of life, of life that belongs to God" (Crossan, 1991, 341–44; 1994, 66–70). He sees this sharing of meals (commensality) as part of Jesus' program to restore, from the bottom up, a society fractured by urbanization and commercialization and, on a symbolic level, as a confrontation between the divine realm of God's kingdom and the temporal realm of Herod Antipas within the wider realm of the Roman Empire. The feeding stories in the so-called miracle tradition also operate at both material and symbolic levels. On the one hand, the appetites of five thousand and four thousand people respectively are satisfied by the multiplication of the loaves and fishes (Mark 6:30-44; 8:1-10). On the other hand, they also serve to declare God's abundant provision in the midst of ostensible scarcity.

Another important aspect of the kingdom of God signified by Jesus' meals is the manner in which social norms, boundaries, and social relations are reconfigured. According to Dennis Smith, there are four categories of meals in the Gospels: (1) meals with Pharisees, (2) miraculous feedings, (3) meals with "tax collectors and sinners," and (4) meals with disciples (D. E. Smith, 223). Smith maintains that only meals with "tax collectors and sinners" and with disciples offer a high degree of historical probability. "Sinner" and "tax collector" are both terms of slander that refer to two groups on the fringes of Jewish society, albeit at opposite ends economically. The scandal in Jesus' eating with them was his inclusion of two groups who were normally excluded by their social location. In eating with sinners and tax collectors, Jesus exemplified the kingdom of God as encompassing those on the margins of society.

Meals are a prominent theme in the Gospel of Luke, but what is striking about many of Luke's meal scenes is that they are depicted in the style of a Greco-Roman symposium, which provides the occasion for Jesus to teach (see Luke 7:36-50; 11:37-44; 14:1-24; 22:7-30). Formal meals in Greek or Roman settings were a microcosm of society, and meal etiquette served to reinforce the rigidly stratified Greco-Roman social order. In Luke's meal scenes, Jesus often challenges this hierarchical social ranking and teaches the "biblical" virtue of humility. For example, Jesus tells a parable that is only in Luke in which he gives this advice about the seating arrangement at a marriage feast.

> But when you are invited, go and sit down at the lowest place, so that when your host comes, he may say to you, "Friend, move up higher"; then you will be honored in the presence of all who sit at the table with you. For all who exalt themselves will be humbled, and those who humble themselves will be exalted. (Luke 14:10-11)

While the disregard for social honor and stratification evident in this passage is consistent with what is known about the historical Jesus, the challenge to social convention has been recontextualized for Luke's Greco-Roman audience. The historical Jesus' meals with "sinners and tax collectors" and Luke's meal scenes both subvert social convention and act out an inclusive vision of the kingdom of God. However, the original cultural context of Jesus' meals is Jewish, while Luke has set them in a Greco-Roman context, where they challenge conventions of status and honor.

The meal scenes in the Gospels illustrate just how difficult it is to separate history from tradition, to differentiate what Jesus said and did from their symbolic interpretations by his first followers. The prominence of meals in the Gospel tradition indicates that table fellowship was an important aspect of Jesus' ministry and that it had symbolic significance. However, what table fellowship with Jesus meant in the Jewish context of rural Galilee is somewhat different from the symbolic function of the meal tradition in the Gospels, which reflect a more Greco-Roman setting. In the agrarian context of Galilee under Antipas's rule, eating with sinners and tax collectors, and even the feeding stories, can be seen as dealing with the crisis of poverty and dispossession materially and socially through both a concrete and symbolic representation of the kingdom of God. Whatever meaning was originally ascribed to the meals Jesus had with Galileans, once they became a part of memory and tradition about him, their significance was largely symbolic. Jesus was eating with Galilean peasants who may not have kept all of Torah, or at least the traditions of the elders (Oral Torah), as the debate about his disciples' eating with defiled hands indicates (Mark 7:1-23). In the Gospel tradition, "sinners" and "tax collectors" become terms of slander used by Jesus' opponents, who accuse him of transgressing social and religious boundaries. The audiences of the Gospels were communities that included gentiles, who were de facto "sinners," and others who would not have been considered part of the covenant community. These communities were on the margins of Judaism and Greco-Roman society, so a key role of the meal tradition was to legitimate the inclusion of those on the fringe and to depict Jesus' inclusive vision of the kingdom of God as a reordering of social relationships.

Many if not most of the references to meals in the Gospels indicate a symbolic interpretation that connects them with communal meals shared by communities of Jesus' followers. The Lord's Supper tradition is the most obvious example (Mark 14:22-25 // Matt. 26:26-29 // Luke 22:15-20), but the feeding stories and other meal scenes also have eucharistic overtones. The "breaking of the bread" signifies the presence of the Lord at community meals, and this is also tied to an eschatological interpretation. Jesus expresses the eschatological significance of the last meal he eats with his disciples when he says: "Truly I tell you, I will never again drink of the fruit of the vine until that day when I drink it new in the kingdom of God" (Mark 14:25 // Matt. 26:29 // Luke 22:18). The meal anticipates a banquet at the end of time, which is described by Isaiah.

> On this mountain the LORD of hosts will make for all peoples
>> a feast of rich food, a feast of well-aged wines,
>> of rich food filled with marrow, of well-aged wines strained clear.
> And he will destroy on this mountain
>> the shroud that is cast over all peoples,
>> the sheet that is spread over all nations;
>> he will swallow up death forever.
> Then the LORD GOD will wipe away the tears from all faces,
>> and the disgrace of his people he will take away from all the earth,
>> for the LORD has spoken. (25:6-8)

These images were associated with a future messianic banquet: victory over primordial enemies (e.g., death), eternal joyous celebration, abundance of food, the presence of the Messiah, and the pilgrimage of the nations (D. E. Smith, 169). All of these are important themes in the Gospels, but because the meal tradition is so entangled with communal meal practices that celebrate the presence of the risen Jesus and look forward to his return as Messiah, it is difficult to ascertain what exactly in these meal stories goes back to Jesus himself.

Jesus as Prophet

Jesus is depicted in the Gospel tradition as announcing the approach of God's future kingdom, which in some sense is experienced in the present through deeds of power such as exorcisms and healings, as well as gathering followers around particular covenantal practices. Although he is referred to as Son of God and Messiah in the Gospel narratives, these are honorific titles attributed to him by others that he does not explicitly use of himself. The designation that may best represent what Jesus was doing and saying in Galilee, and then in Jerusalem, is that of prophet. The Gospel of Mark indicates that Jesus regarded himself as a prophet. He tells those who took offense at him in his hometown synagogue at Nazareth, "Prophets are not without honor, except in their hometown, and among their own kin, and in their own house" (Mark 6:4). It is unlikely that the epithet "prophet" would have originated with the early church. A passage common to Luke and Matthew says that Jesus regarded John as a prophet, and so he was also linked to this role by virtue of his identification with him.

> When John's messengers had gone, Jesus began to speak to the crowds about John: "What did you go out into the wilderness to look at? A reed shaken by the wind? What then did you go out to see? Someone dressed in soft robes? Look, those who put on fine clothing and live in luxury are in royal palaces. What then did you go out to see? A prophet? Yes, I tell you, and more than a prophet." (Luke 7:24-26)

Jesus here associates John's prophetic activity with "wilderness," and contrasts it with powerful elites such as Antipas. A number of passages in the Gospels suggest that people surmise Jesus is a prophet: "But others said, 'It is Elijah.' And others said, 'It is a prophet, like one of the prophets of old'" (Mark 6:15).

There were different kinds of prophets in early Judaism, but Jesus and John the Baptist fit the profile of popular prophets who led movements of resistance and renewal, which were not uncommon in the first century (Horsley and Hanson). As William Herzog observes, this type of prophetic leader emerges because he or she embodies the values of the group they represent. As a peasant artisan in the village of Galilee, Jesus would have been steeped in the prophetic traditions of Israel (Herzog, 23). In contrast to the scribal subculture within Judaism, characterized by texts and interpretations, Jesus inhabited an oral cultural that related the foundational biblical stories and figures to their own local context. These popular messianic movements, as Horsley calls them, often began in the wilderness as reenactments of the foundational acts of God's deliverance in the exodus and the formation of the covenant community (Horsley 2012, 93). Moses was regarded as the prototypical prophetic leader (Deut. 18:15), and Elijah and Elisha were especially revered figures in the Galilean milieu of Jesus. They were prophets who responded to a crisis in the northern kingdom by challenging political authority. The prophetic renewal movement led by Elijah and "the children of the prophets" has left an indelible mark on the Gospel tradition and may even have provided inspiration for Jesus himself (Brodie).

It would be difficult to overstate the significance of the exodus as the defining event in Israel's history, especially in the popular imagination of Judeans who had lived under imperial rule since the Babylonian exile. John the Baptist's call to prepare the "way of the Lord" evokes Isaiah's theme of a new exodus signaling that God was acting anew through Jesus to effect the liberation of God's people (Mark 1:2-6 // Matt. 3:1-6 // Luke 3:1-7). While the new exodus is a scriptural motif used by the Gospel writers to characterize the movements initiated by John and Jesus respectively, it also symbolizes the phenomenon of power associated with the focus of Jesus' message and activity, namely the kingdom of God. The phrase "kingdom of God" is a political metaphor that has its roots in the biblical notion of God as king. However, it is also a spatial metaphor that highlights a tension between the principal conviction of Judaism, that God is the sovereign creator who rules the universe, and the reality of the Roman control of Palestine. Since Jesus was proclaiming God's reign in a Galilee that was under Roman rule, he was, in some sense, exemplifying an order or an experience of power different from and incompatible with the machinations of imperial power.

Given the anachronistic connotations of kingdom language in contemporary contexts, a constructive alternative translation that conveys the phenomenon expressed is "power." Oakman maintains that "when Jesus spoke of 'Kingdom of God,' his reference was to the presence and reality of the Power, the Power's ultimacy" (76). So, for example, when Jesus says to a group of Pharisees, "The kingdom of God is not coming with things that can be observed; nor will they say, 'Look, here it is!' or 'There it is!' For, in fact, the kingdom of God is among you" (Luke 17:20-21), he was speaking of the power "among you" or "in your midst." The language of power pervades the Jesus tradition and is used in a variety of ways. Jesus' healings are referred to as "deeds of power," and he is described as teaching with "authority." The Greek word translated "deeds of power," and erroneously in some translations as "miracle," is *dynamis* (e.g., Mark 5:20; 6:2, 5, 14; 9:1, 39; 12:24; 13:25-26; 14:62). The Greek term translated "authority" is *exousia* (e.g., Mark 1:22, 27; 2:10; 3:15). This is the same power that the Israelites identified with the one who delivered them from bondage in Egypt in the exodus (Horsley 2011, 45). It is also the power that formed the Israelites into a people, and the template for how that power was to operate among the people was set out in the Mosaic covenant. Principles of political-economic cooperation and justice distinguish it as a power shared in community (Horsley 2011, 43). Jesus uses the metaphor of "father" to speak of this power in personal terms as beneficent and merciful, as well as caring and providing for all creatures (see Luke 6:35-36; 11:2-4; 12:22-34).

The Gospel of Mark introduces the ministry of Jesus by announcing, "Now after John was arrested, Jesus came to Galilee, proclaiming the good news of God, and saying, 'The time is fulfilled, and the kingdom of God has come near; repent, and believe in the good news'" (Mark 1:14-15). Matthew and Luke follow Mark in making Jesus' assertion of the imminence of this "power" the central focus of the narrative by describing its effects. Although the plot of these narratives is a construction of the authors using a variety of traditions about Jesus, the major facets of what the Gospels describe Jesus doing and saying are historically consistent with the portrait of him as a popular prophet leading a local renewal movement that dealt with the severe social and economic conditions of Galilean life. "Kingdom of God" is a biblical catchphrase encompassing the various representations of power featured in the narratives.

If these portrayals of kingdom power in the Gospels are set within the exigent circumstances of Jesus' Galilean context, the shape of Jesus' prophetic program of renewal and the various responses to it become more intelligible as a historical phenomenon. Of primary importance are Jesus' efforts to gather the people of God. The gathering of the scattered people of God is a major theme in Israel's Scriptures, especially among the prophets (see Deut. 30:1-5; Isa. 11:12-13; 58:6). As Gerhard Lohfink observes, "gathering" Israel is often parallel to "liberating," "saving," "healing," and "redeeming" Israel (Lohfink, 60). The twelve disciples Jesus chooses represent the twelve tribes of Israel that were scattered; more importantly, it underscores the point that a primary purpose of the power is the formation of a community. In other words, "the reign of God must have a people" (Lohfink, 48). At the conclusion of an episode common to Luke and Matthew in which Jesus is accused of casting out a demon by Beelzebul, the prince of demons, he asserts: "Whoever is not with me is against me, and whoever does not gather with me scatters" (Luke 11:23). In a character-istically prophetic mode, he holds people accountable to the power operative through him to gather, restore, and heal.

The scene in which we find this saying, about participation in God's power at work in and among the people Jesus was gathering, is one of many exorcisms in the Gospel. Exorcisms can themselves be understood as episodes in a struggle for power. In commenting on the accusation in Luke 11:15 that Jesus "casts out demons by Beelzebul the prince of demons," Halvor Moxnes emphasizes that his response reveals assumptions about space and boundaries underlying the chal-lenge: "Every kingdom divided against itself becomes a desert, and house falls on house. If Satan also is divided against himself, how will his kingdom stand?" (Luke 11:17-18). Moxnes sees the challenge that identified Jesus with Beelzebul as an attempt by opponents to put him outside the boundaries of "civilized" society, outside Israel. The household was the center of social and economic life, and it was at the intersections of household and kingdom that the people around Jesus lived their lives and experienced the power that "the strong man" (Luke 11:21-22) could use to exercise control (Moxnes, 338). Anthropological studies of exorcism in other societies suggest that there is a connection between spirit possession and forms of imperial domination, but such experiences of being occupied by an alien power were interpreted cosmologically rather than politically (Hors-ley 2011, 113–17). These exorcism stories allude to experiences of release from the effects of the oppressive and hegemonic powers that controlled people's lives as a consequence of Jesus imparting a restorative divine power.

Interpreting the exorcism and healing stories in the Gospels as a demonstration and experience of power that challenges existing structures of power not only demystifies the confrontation with cosmic forces but also sheds light on the conflict with the religious authorities. From a literary perspective, conflict drives the plot of the Gospel narratives just as it does any good story. Dif-ferentiating between conflict on the literary level of the narrative and in Jesus' Galilean context is complicated by the fact that the Gospels are written after the destruction of the Jerusalem temple. So the depiction of the conflict between scribes and Pharisees in the Gospels reflects post-70-CE disputes between Jesus' followers and Jewish leaders because the portrait of scribes and Pharisees is something of a caricature that does not completely fit with Jesus' Galilean context. However, if Jesus was mediating a power from outside the socioreligious system, then it follows that as its brokers, scribes and Pharisees would likely have regarded him as a disturbance and a threat.

In Mark's narrative, the conflict between Jesus' authority and scribal authority is introduced at the outset of his ministry where, in the context of teaching in a synagogue, he delivers a man with an unclean spirit (Mark 1:21-28). While it is the narrator who contrasts Jesus' authority to teach with that of the scribes, this passage points to the crux of the conflict between Jesus and the religious authorities both in Jesus' Galilean ministry and in the Gospels, namely the interpretation of Torah. First, it is important to note the setting of many of these conflicts is the local synagogue, which was a center for community life organized around the Torah. In a village context such as Galilee, scribes acted as administrators who related Torah to legal matters and the affairs of people's everyday lives. As prophetic leader of a renewal movement in Galilee, Jesus embodied the values of the people who followed him, and those values were rooted and grounded in Torah. Despite a long-standing view that Jesus transgressed or abrogated Torah, he is depicted in the earliest layers of the tradition as upholding the Decalogue in its entirety (Mark 12:28-31), espousing many of its individual demands (Mark 7:9-13, 21-23; 10:17-19), observing Levitical rule (Mark 1:44), confirming that the whole of Torah is binding (Luke 16:17), and refuting criticism that his behavior is lawless (Mark 2:23-28; 3:1-6; see Allison 2010, 165). What distinguished his interpretation of Torah from the more traditional interpretations of scribes and Pharisees was the conviction that God was speaking and acting through him. This prompted a prophetic approach to Torah that drew on its traditions of justice and judgment and was responsive to the socioeconomic stresses in Galilee.

The two nodal issues at the center of the dispute between Jesus and the scribes about how to interpret Torah were Sabbath observance and purity regulations. In Mark 2:23—3:6, there are two consecutive Sabbath controversy accounts. In the first, Pharisees complain that Jesus' disciples are violating Sabbath by plucking grain, and in the second, Jesus responds to those who are watching to see if he will heal on the Sabbath. Anticipating their criticism, he asks, "Is it lawful to do good or to do harm on the Sabbath, to save life or to kill?" (Mark 3:4). Both episodes have likely been embellished in the context of Mark's narrative, but even so they disclose the underlying issues in Jesus' historical context and a key interpretative principle for him. The matter in question in both incidents is the priority he gives to human distress—hunger and physical affliction, respectively. The purpose of Torah for Jesus was to support the health and well-being of human beings, and this is consistent with how Torah has been interpreted within historic Judaism. Similarly, in the conflict focused on Jewish purity regulations, he does not disregard purity so much as reinterpret it as a matter of interpersonal ethics rather than ritual practice (Mark 7:1-23).

Jesus' habit of fraternizing with "sinners and tax collectors" was also a matter of concern for those scribes and Pharisees who saw themselves as guarding the boundaries of the Mosaic covenant (Mark 2:15-17; Luke 5:30-32; 7:34, 39; 15:1, 7, 10; 18:13; 19:7). "Sinners" were by definition people who behaved contrary to the covenant, or, as Crossley remarks, to someone's definition of law and covenant (87). The most historically accurate aspect of the portrait of the Pharisees in the Gospels is their emphasis on purity or holiness. Some of the people who come to Jesus are depicted as being impure. While it is plausible that Jesus and his followers may have been somewhat lax in their observance of purity regulations, impurity was not regarded as a "sin" per se in early Judaism. Nonetheless, people who were ritually impure could be marginalized socially. The Gospel tradition does not elaborate on the specific reasons some around Jesus were deemed "sinners." Given that a majority of the people in Galilee would have lived around subsistence level, lack of time and resources may have impeded many from observing Torah according to the standards of local religious authorities. Those who were designated "sinners" give the impression of being on the margins of society for economic or social reasons, and Jesus was reintegrating them into the covenant community.

In contrast to the Pharisees, who stressed purity and boundaries, Jesus' teaching was more oriented to economic and social relations, and focused specifically on issues of poverty and debt. Followers were exhorted to give without expectation of return to everyone who begs (Luke 6:30-35). Several passages, including the prayer Jesus teaches his disciples, feature the problem of debt and emphasize the importance of release from indebtedness (Matt. 6:12 // Luke 11:4; Luke 7:41; 16:5, 7; Matt. 18:28, 30, 34). Jesus also instructs his followers regarding their relationship to possessions.

He urged them not to be anxious about material needs and to trust God's care for them. He enjoined them, "Sell your possessions, and give alms. Make purses for yourselves that do not wear out, an unfailing treasure in heaven, where no thief comes near and no moth destroys" (Luke 12:33; 14:33). Jesus also had a lot to say about the deleterious effects of wealth, and in several passages challenges the rich. In addition to aphoristic sayings such as "woe to you who are rich" (Luke 6:24) and "you cannot serve God and wealth" (Luke 16:13), the parables of the rich fool (Luke 12:13-21), the story of the rich man (Mark 10:17-22 // Matt. 19:16-22 // Luke 18:18-23), the parable of the great banquet (Luke 14:15-24), the parable of the dishonest steward (Luke 16:1-8), the parable of the rich man and Lazarus (Luke 16:19-31), the story of Zacchaeus (Luke 19:1-9), and the parable of the pounds (Luke 19:11-27) all challenge the prosperous in a manner that implies their fiscal habits were a cause of economic distress and oppression for others, and so he required them to repent and amend their ways.

Since Jesus lived in an oral culture, he did not regularly cite or refer to biblical texts, but his teaching is grounded in Israel's Scriptures. In the parable of the rich man and Lazarus, the rich man implores Abraham to warn his family so they can repent, but Abraham replies, "If they do not listen to Moses and the prophets, neither will they be convinced even if someone rises from the dead" (Luke 16:31). In a passage common to all three Synoptic Gospels, a scribe asks Jesus, "which commandment is the first of all?" Jesus answers by quoting Deut. 6:4-5 and Lev. 19:18.

> The first is, "Hear, O Israel: the Lord our God, the Lord is one; you shall love the Lord your God with all your heart, and with all your soul, and with all your mind, and with all your strength." The second is this, "You shall love your neighbor as yourself." There is no other commandment greater than these. (Mark 12:29-31)

This double command, as it is sometimes called, is the central precept in Jesus' interpretation and appropriation of Torah in the economically distressed milieu of Galilee. The parable of the good Samaritan in Luke 10:25-37 is an example of how Jesus illustrates the practical implications of these commandments in ways that promote inclusivity, beneficence, and accountability to others, especially those in need.

Jesus refers to the Torah and the prophets mostly in the context of debating with scribes and Pharisees. His disputes with them were predicated on some shared convictions, such as the authority of Torah and the importance of the Mosaic covenant. What differentiated Jesus from these other teachers and precipitated most of their disagreements, however, was his concern to connect the power of God's kingdom to the struggles of a peasant underclass who, for various reasons, found themselves on the periphery. Parables were his preferred medium for imparting the message of the kingdom. A parable is a short, narrative fiction that draws on the concrete particulars of nature and everyday life to subvert the status quo and reimagine the world (Scott 2001, 13–15). Jesus' parables employed poetic metaphors to engage hearers' imagination by painting a vivid a picture of kingdom power that was often set in contrast to grandiose images of power. A good example is the parable of the mustard seed.

> He [Jesus] also said, "With what can we compare the kingdom of God, or what parable will we use for it? It is like a mustard seed, which, when sown upon the ground, is the smallest of all the

seeds on earth; yet when it is sown it grows up and becomes the greatest of all shrubs, and puts forth large branches, so that the birds of the air can make nests in its shade." (Mark 4:30-32 // Matt. 13:31-32 // Luke 13:18-19)

As the parable indicates, the mustard plant is more like a "shrub," which the ancient writer Pliny says, "grows entirely wild" and, once it has been sown, it "is scarcely possible to get the place free of it" (*Natural History* 29.54.170). This is a strange and provocative image for the kingdom of God, but Jesus was likely invoking a comparison with the mighty cedar of Lebanon, which was a common image for empire in Israel's Scriptures (see Ezek. 17:22-23; Dan. 4:10-12). The mustard shrub is a metaphor for an emergent phenomenon that was organic, recalcitrant, and disruptive. Moreover, it was the very antithesis of imperial power as control and order.

While it is not possible to comment on or categorize all of Jesus' parables, they are all part of a strategy to evoke the possibility of another reality, the world as it should be over against the world as it was. Some critique greed, patronage, preoccupation with status, and other Greco-Roman values (e.g., Luke 7:41-43; 12:16-20; 14:15-24; 16:19-31; 19:12-27), and others suggest counter-cultural dispositions and practices such as hospitality, generosity, mercy, forgiveness, vigilance, and so on (Matt. 18:10-14, 21-35; Mark 13:34-36; Luke 10:30-35; 15:11-32). All the parables, along with Jesus' other teachings, were inextricably tied to his effort to gather people into a cooperative form of life that would enable them to stand firm in the face of severe political and economic stress. The immanent power he mediated was the basis for a popular sovereignty, and as the movement organized around it galvanized and gained momentum, tensions with established authorities also intensified.

Journey to Jerusalem

The turning point in the Synoptic Gospel narratives and in the prophetic ministry of the historical Jesus was his journey to Jerusalem, where he caused a disturbance in the temple that eventually led to his trial and execution. Most scholars acknowledge the historicity of the temple incident and the subsequent trial and execution, but the interpretation of these incidents has been heavily shaped by later reflection on them from the perspective of Jesus' postresurrection appearances and in the light of the destruction of the Jerusalem temple in 70 CE. Therefore, the task is to distinguish a historically plausible account of what happened when Jesus went to Jerusalem from later interpretations of these events. This is a challenge because event and interpretation are inextricably woven together from very early in the history of the tradition. They key, however, is establishing the continuity of Jesus' prophetic ministry in Galilee with what he said and did in Jerusalem, and explaining the reaction of the authorities that resulted in his crucifixion. Then it will be possible to elucidate the development of the Gospel traditions about Jesus' passion and resurrection into their current canonical form.

From a historical point of view, Jesus went to Jerusalem as a prophet leading a renewal movement. In a passage from the tradition common to Luke and Matthew, Jesus laments over Jerusalem. The narrative context in which the saying occurs is different in the two Gospels. In Luke's version, some Pharisees warn Jesus that Herod wants to kill him.

He said to them, "Go and tell that fox for me, 'Listen, I am casting out demons and performing cures today and tomorrow, and on the third day I finish my work. Yet today, tomorrow, and the next day I must be on my way, because it is impossible for a prophet to be killed outside of Jerusalem.' Jerusalem, Jerusalem, the city that kills the prophets and stones those who are sent to it! How often have I desired to gather your children together as a hen gathers her brood under her wings, and you were not willing!" (Luke 13:32-34)

This passage is significant both because it contains a saying of Jesus that links the portrayal of his prophetic ministry in Galilee with his presence in Jerusalem, and because it shows how the tradition has been appropriated in the narrative strategies of the Gospel writers. For the purpose of our historical reconstruction, it is noteworthy that Jesus depicts himself as a prophet who is attempting to gather the covenant community. In Luke's account, Jesus is still en route to Jerusalem, so this is not the proper setting for his lament. It is also questionable that Herod is seeking to kill Jesus before he even arrives. The point where history and interpretation converge in this passage is Jesus' reference to himself as a prophet, belonging to a long-standing tradition of Israelite prophets who confronted the authorities and suffered a similar fate in Jerusalem as well as outside Jerusalem. Joseph Fitzmyer observes that behind this statement lies a traditional belief about the fate of various prophetic figures in the city of Jerusalem. He suggests that the killing of the prophet Uriah in Jerusalem by King Jehoiakim might be envisaged (Jer. 26:20-23), or the attempt on Jeremiah's life in Jerusalem (Jer. 38:4-6). However, there are many other examples of prophets who meet a similar fate (Fitzmyer, 1032).

In Mark's Gospel, Jesus enters Jerusalem as he approaches the city from the Mount of Olives. Although this event, like many of the incidents in the passion narratives, is recollected as a performance of Israel's Scriptures, especially the prophets and psalms, Mark's account preserves the historical kernel of a symbolic action typical of prophets. The crowd construes his arrival as the coming kingdom of David and shouts,

> Hosanna!
>   Blessed is the one who comes in the name of the Lord!
>   Blessed is the coming kingdom of our ancestor David!
> Hosanna in the highest heaven! (Mark 11:9-10)

However, in this passage as well as the story of blind Bartimaeus (Mark 10:46-52), the view of Jesus as Davidic Messiah is rejected. Rather, Jesus' action in Mark and in its original historical context is best understood as a parody of royal processions common in antiquity. In contrast to political or military rulers who entered a conquered city in a war chariot or on a ceremonial steed, the symbols of violent power, Jesus entered on a donkey (Crossan and Reed, 220). The fact that this satirical public action was performed during Passover, when Israel celebrated liberation from its oppressors, made it even more provocative, and in itself could have been enough to result in crucifixion (Crossan and Reed, 220).

Upon his arrival in Jerusalem, this symbolic act was followed by another disruptive action in the temple itself. According to Mark, Jesus "entered the temple and began to drive out those who were selling and those who were buying in the temple" (Mark 11:15). In the Synoptic Gospels, this is the incident that leads to Jesus' arrest, trial, and execution. Although Jesus' action in the temple is recognized by most scholars as having some basis in history, the significance of this event is a matter of some debate. The episode is often referred to as the "cleansing of the temple," but that is a misnomer because it does not accurately indicate the focus of Jesus' critique. Jesus is portrayed here as teaching, and the words he uses to convey the reason for his indignation are from Isa. 56:7 and Jer. 7:11: "Is it not written, 'My house shall be called a house of prayer for all the nations'? But you have made it a den of robbers" (Mark 11:17). Although it is improbable that Jesus quoted Scripture verbatim on this occasion, the Jeremiah text in particular associates Jesus' outburst with Jeremiah's temple sermon and is used to interpret the underlying issue in a manner consistent with the focal point of his prophetic praxis in Galilee, namely economic hardship.

The verse from Jeremiah is taken from the prophet's oracle against the temple and its priests. Jeremiah indicts them for presuming that sacrificial worship in the temple could be the basis of the covenantal relationship with God without upholding its standards of justice and moral obligations to the most vulnerable.

> For in the day that I brought your ancestors out of the land of Egypt, I did not speak to them or command them concerning burnt offerings and sacrifices. But this command I gave them, "Obey my voice, and I will be your God, and you shall be my people; and walk only in the way that I command you, so that it may be well with you." (Jer. 7:22-23)

As in Jeremiah, in condemning the temple Jesus was denouncing a priestly aristocracy who presided over it by accusing them of acting like "thieves" who have turned the temple into a "den" where they hide out. Their administration of the temple system disclosed their own elite interests at the expense of the people. As Herzog puts it, the wealth of the temple, which was also a treasury, was an inevitable corollary of the poverty of the peasantry (167). The temple extracted tribute from people through the temple tax, tithes, and sacrifices. It was an economic institution with the priestly aristocracy bearing responsibility for collecting tribute to Rome, so in opposing the ruling class of Jerusalem Jesus was by implication opposing Roman rule (Horsley 2012, 144).

The Gospel of Mark, followed by Luke, suggests that Jesus' prophetic action in the temple was the cause of his subsequent arrest and execution. Within the narrative, after Jesus expresses his dissatisfaction with the temple using the words of Isa. 56:7 and Jer. 7:11, the narrator observes: "And when the chief priests and the scribes heard it, they kept looking for a way to kill him; for they were afraid of him, because the whole crowd was spellbound by his teaching" (Mark 11:18; Luke 19:47). While this is the narrator's interpretive perspective, it is also the most plausible historical explanation. Not only did Jesus' pronouncement against the temple challenge the authority of the priestly aristocracy, but it also roused the multitude of pilgrims in Jerusalem for Passover. In Luke, the narrator's report of the chief priests' and the crowd's response to Pilate's acclamation of Jesus' innocence echoes a similar sentiment: "He stirs up the people by teaching throughout all Judea, from Galilee where he began even to this place" (Luke 23:5). Therefore, even though passages are constructions of the Gospel writers, they underline the fact that Jesus was leading a movement that may have gained momentum in Jerusalem as the Jewish people were celebrating liberation from slavery in Egypt. If so, then Roman authorities would likely have regarded his behavior as seditious and therefore as deserving of execution.

The Gospel accounts of the arrest and trial of Jesus, and of the role of the different Jewish groups in these events, are at variance with one another. This indicates that details of what happened to Jesus in Jerusalem are highly interpreted and cannot be taken at face value historically. The traditions about Jesus' trial and crucifixion have been comprehended through the lens of Israel's Scriptures and shaped both by the experiences of his followers and the destruction of the temple in 70 CE. The development of the passion narratives in the Gospels will be discussed in the next section. What can be established beyond reasonable doubt is that Jesus was arrested and taken before Pilate, the Roman prefect of Judea, who authorized his crucifixion. Temple authorities may have played a role in handing him over, but the trial before the Sanhedrin is historically questionable. There is no historical precedent for such a trial, and the high priest's question, "Are you the Messiah, the Son of the Blessed One?" (Mark 14:61), reflects later christological reflection and debate. Moreover, the charge of blasphemy brought against Jesus by the high priest was not an offense punishable by death (Mark 14:64).

One aspect of the trial before the Jerusalem council that may be historically accurate is the false accusation that Jesus said he would destroy the temple (Mark 14:58). Jesus is also reported to have spoken against the temple earlier in the long discourse set on the Mount of Olives, in Mark 13. He tells his disciples who marvel at the grandeur of the temple, "Do you see these great buildings? Not one stone will be left here upon another; all will be thrown down" (Mark 13:2). Jesus then goes on to predict the tribulation that will occur before the son of man returns. Mark 13 is a dense and complicated passage that has been heavily redacted by Matthew and Luke (Matt. 24:1-44; Luke 21:5-38), and it is difficult to disentangle what might be authentic in these sayings of Jesus from material that was retrojected into the story after the destruction of the temple and in anticipation of Jesus' return. There are, however, two elements in the passage that are important to our historical reconstruction and can serve as points of transition to a discussion of the development of the Gospel tradition. On the Temple Mount, Jesus tells his disciples that "not one stone will be left here upon another; all will be thrown down" (Mark 13:1). Although Jesus does not say that he would destroy it, when he is taken before the chief priests and the council some falsely testify that they heard him say, "I will destroy this temple that is made with hands, and in three days I will build another, not made with hands" (Mark 14:57-58). Jesus' prediction that the temple would be destroyed may have been ascribed to him after the fact. However, given that the ruling class of Judea presided over a long-standing situation of economic distress that eventually resulted in the Jewish wars and the destruction of Jerusalem, it is conceivable that a prophet like Jesus could have foreseen the eventual downfall of the city (Goodman).

Jesus' prophetic warning about the impending destruction of the temple in Mark 13 is associated in this section with his sayings about the return of the son of man. This raises what is probably the most disputed aspect of historical Jesus studies, the eschatological or apocalyptic dimension of Jesus' proclamation and enactment of the kingdom of God. There are essentially two basic views. One view regards Jesus as more of a sage or teacher who propounded a subversive practical wisdom, and attributes the eschatological material to a later layer of the tradition that has its origins in the early church. On this view, what Jesus says about judgment, tribulation, and the imminence of God's kingdom is best explained as the result of Jesus' earliest followers interpreting his memory and tradition in the light of the resurrection, which was itself viewed as an apocalyptic event. This perspective is shaped more by social analysis of the Gospel tradition, which understands Jesus' sayings to be responding to the concrete realities of the local Galilean milieu, and therefore regards sayings more oriented to the future as inauthentic.

Concentrating on the Galilean context tends to highlight the social and pragmatic force of Jesus' words and deeds, but this perspective also tends to downplay Judaism as the framework of his teaching and activity. On the other hand, those who emphasize the apocalyptic or eschatological aspects of the Jesus tradition tend to regard Jesus primarily as a religious figure and make sense of his sayings and activity in relation to other voices and groups in Judaism. Both perspectives have merit and use different approaches to call attention to important but divergent facets of the Jesus tradition that should be held together, even if there is an ostensible tension. As noted in the outset of this essay, the distinction between social, religious, political, and economic dimensions of life is anachronistic and artificial when projected onto the Jesus tradition, because they were correlative facets of Jewish life. The portrait of Jesus as leading a renewal movement in Galilee needs to be combined with the view that regards him as an eschatological prophet within Judaism. As Dale Allison (1998, 100) points out, if Jesus did prophesy the temple's demise and replacement, then he was operating within the framework of restoration eschatology.

The role of prophet in Judaism encompasses the message and praxis of Jesus' Galilean ministry as well as his prophetic pronouncements and actions in Jerusalem. It is impossible to do justice to the complexity of the issues surrounding the debate about whether Jesus had an apocalyptic outlook, but much of what has been construed as apocalyptic in the tradition can also be explained as part of Israel's prophetic tradition. The term "apocalyptic" comes from the Greek word *apokalypsis*, which means "revelation"; and "eschatology" comes from the Greek word *eschatos*, which means "last" or "coming at the end or after all others." Both words denote an orientation to the future. Crossan represents the common understanding of "apocalyptic eschatology" when he says that it refers to "the darkening scenario of the end of the world" with an expectation of divine intervention (1991, 238). Along with a majority of scholars, he sees John the Baptist as a harbinger of an imminent apocalyptic intervention by God, who will enact eschatological judgment on those who don't repent. Those who downplay the eschatological aspects of Jesus' message want to dissociate Jesus from John's apocalypticism. But as Horsley contends (2012, 18), the message that on "the day of the Lord" God would come in judgment to either deliver or punish was typical of the prophets.

Both John and Jesus were prophets who called people to repent as part of a summons to covenant renewal, and this involved holding people accountable, especially those in power, through pronouncements of judgment. Themes of reversal, final judgment, resurrection of the dead, restoration of Israel, and the great tribulation are stock prophetic themes that run throughout the sayings of Jesus (e.g., Mark 10:31; Luke 14:11; 17:33). A good example of a saying that includes themes of tribulation, covenant, eschatological banquet, judgment, and the restoration of Israel is a passage in Luke.

> You are those who have stood by me in my trials; and I confer on you, just as my Father has conferred on me, a kingdom, so that you may eat and drink at my table in my kingdom, and you will sit on thrones judging the twelve tribes of Israel. (Luke 22:28-30; see Matt. 19:28)

The Greek verb translated as "conferred" means "to make a covenant with." Jesus speaks as an eschatological prophet mostly in the context of Jerusalem, where he must face his own imminent end, but this was consonant with his prophetic activity in Galilee. As Allison suggests (1998, 110), eschatology is, among other things, an expression of dissatisfaction with the present. Jesus went to Jerusalem as prophet, addressing issues of poverty and exploitation in Galilee, and there his focus shifted from a strategy of renewal in the present to future judgment. What is not a part of his prophetic warnings, however, was an emphasis on the end of the world. This is a misunderstanding of the message of Jesus and of Jewish apocalyptic.

Mark 13 is sometimes referred to as the "little apocalypse" because it is regarded as the most explicitly apocalyptic passage in the Gospels, with parallels in Matthew and Luke. Jesus speaks to his disciples about tribulations that include wars, earthquakes, famines, trials, betrayal, and false prophets and messiahs, and then exhorts them to stay vigilant. Since many of the particulars in this passage could allude to the Jewish wars that began in 66 CE, ascertaining which parts of the discourse can be traced back to Jesus is difficult. Although many interpreters read the passage with an accent on the end-time scenario, Jesus emphasizes that "the end is not yet. . . . This is but the beginning of the birth pangs" (Mark 13:7-8). After he warns his disciples of these impending disasters, he then assures them that after the ordeal "they will see 'the Son of Man coming in clouds' with great power and glory. Then he will send out the angels, and gather his elect from the four winds, from the ends of the earth to the ends of heaven" (Mark 13:26-27). These words in quotation marks are from Dan. 7:13. Daniel is an apocalyptic book in the sense that it contains "revelation." That revelation assured Jewish people during the reign of Antiochus Epiphanes that "one like a son of man" would mediate divine sovereignty by judging the empires of the world and gathering the elect. However, Daniel 7 is not about a judgment that signals the end of the world, but rather, as Horsley puts it, a judgment that "leads to the renewal of the world as the place where the restored people can finally live in justice" (2012, 49).

The Synoptic Gospels tell the story of Jesus in two parts. In the first part, Jesus is a popular prophet leading a renewal movement in the exploited environs of Galilee, and in the second part, he goes as a prophet to the capital city of Jerusalem to confront those in charge of the temple. Jesus' engagement with the authorities in Jerusalem continued to be on behalf of the Jewish populace. By invoking the apocalyptic vision of Daniel 7, he reiterated and reinforced the connection between the reign of God and the people of God that characterized his Galilean ministry. In that vision, a heavenly court is assembled to judge all the world empires, especially the beasts. The symbols of lion, bear, leopard, beast, and finally "son of man" represent successive societies. Lohfink's comments about the political force of this vision are worth quoting at length.

> The fifth society is, of course, very carefully dissociated from those that precede it. It is no longer brutal, no longer bestial but finally a human society. Therefore it is symbolized not by beasts but by a human being. . . . The fifth society does not arise out of the sea of chaos but comes from

heaven. It comes "with the clouds of heaven" (Dan 7:13). Thus the new, eschatological society comes from above. It cannot be made by human beings. It is God's gift to the world. It is the end of violent rule. (43)

Along with a number of scholars, Lohfink understands "son of man" as a symbol for the ultimate and final royal rule of God, but at the same time a figure for the true Israel or eschatological Israel that serves God alone. Jewish and Roman authorities recognized that Jesus' pronouncements against and demonstration in the temple were, like his proclamation of God's kingdom, patently political. The Gospel accounts of the trial(s) that led to his execution may vary, but what is beyond dispute is that the historical reason for the Roman prefect Pilate sentencing him to death by crucifixion was the charge of sedition.

Crucifixion was a form of execution reserved primarily for slaves and criminals; it was meant to make an example of those who would dare to subvert the imperial order, the *Pax Romana*. This is precisely what was indicated by the inscription on the cross, "The King of the Jews" (Mark 15:26). Although obviously intended to mock Jesus as falsely claiming to be ruler of the Jewish people even while they lived under Roman rule, it nonetheless betrayed Pilate's grasp of the seditious potential of Jesus and the community forming around him. The portrayal of Pilate as a principled official, reluctant to allow the crucifixion but ultimately succumbing to the pressure of the crowd, is in tension with what is known about him from other sources. Philo and Josephus, ancient Jewish writers from the first century, describe incidents that took place during Pilate's tenure that caused near insurrections among the Jews because of his insensitivity to Jewish customs. Philo describes him as "a man of a very inflexible disposition, and very merciless as well as very obstinate" (Philo, *Embassy* 38.299–305). He was removed from office two to three years after the death of Jesus, accused of murdering innocent Samaritans (Josephus, *Ant.* 18.4.1–2). Despite the fact that Pilate authorized Jesus' execution, all of the Gospels shift responsibility for the death of Jesus to the Jewish authorities and, to some extent, the Jewish crowd assembled at his trial. Therefore, it is with the stark and bleak reality of the crucifixion ordered by Pilate that this historical account of Jesus comes to a close and we begin to focus on the interpretive process.

Throughout this account of Jesus in his historical context, it has been evident that the details of events are so tightly interwoven with their interpretation that it is difficult to disentangle them. The most effective approach to ascertaining the historical contours of Jesus' public ministry is setting out a plausible account of the Synoptic Gospels' narrative of Jesus in the cultural-historical milieu of Galilee and Jerusalem. The next step is to show how the memory of what Jesus said and did was preserved and shaped by the first followers of Jesus. After the death of Jesus, his followers continued the movement he initiated and developed the tradition into what became the four literary productions known as the Gospels.

Followers of Jesus and the Development of the Gospel Tradition

The memory of what Jesus said and did, of his trial, and of his crucifixion was preserved by his followers. Also inscribed into each of the four canonical Gospels is the conviction that God raised him from the dead. The Gospel accounts of Jesus' postmortem appearances to his disciples were not included in the discussion of the historical Jesus because resurrection intimates an experience of transcendence that cannot be verified by historical method. What can be explored historically are the effects that belief had on his followers, and on the formation of the Gospels. In the Gospel of Mark, the risen Jesus does not appear to his disciples. Rather, a young man tells the women who go to the tomb, "He has been raised; he is not here. Look, there is the place they laid him. But go, tell his disciples and Peter that he is going ahead of you to Galilee; there you will see him, just as he told you" (Mark 16:6-7). The Gospels of Matthew, Luke, and John all have different appearance stories, which betokens not only multiple encounters with the risen Jesus but also that the narration of the event is itself an interpretation of its significance (see Matt. 28:1-20; Luke 24:1-53; John 20:1-29; 21:1-23). The earliest reference to the resurrection of Jesus is the tradition Paul cites in 1 Corinthians, which says that the risen Jesus "appeared to Cephas, then to the twelve. Then he appeared to more than five hundred brothers and sisters at one time, most of whom are still alive, though some have died" (1 Cor. 15:5-6). Paul goes on to mention Jesus' appearance to James and to himself, and then asserts that in raising him from the dead God had inaugurated the general resurrection of the dead (1 Cor. 15:12-13).

An important element of the resurrection accounts in all four Gospels that is absent from Paul's discussion is the empty tomb tradition. The empty tomb tradition belongs to the earliest conceptualization of Jesus' resurrection. In all four Gospels, it features women who go to the tomb where Jesus was buried to anoint his body, only to discover that it is not there. The initial message from the young man in the tomb in Mark's account, who become angels in Matthew and Luke, is that Jesus is not here because he has been raised. The interpretation of the empty tomb is not self-evident, and indeed raises the question of how an ancient audience would have understood this tradition. Daniel Smith contends that a first-century person (Jewish or Greek) would have interpreted an inexplicably disappearing body or an unaccountably empty tomb as evidence, not of "resurrection," but of "assumption" (D. A. Smith, 4). He notes this is an idea found in almost every ancient culture that, in certain special cases, God or some divine being or beings could take a person immediately and bodily into the divine realm. The significance ancient audiences would have inferred from the empty tomb tradition in the Gospels is that God had vindicated Jesus. In other words, since Jesus was executed as an enemy of the Roman order for sedition, the view that he had been raised from the dead was regarded as a divine response that validated his prophetic message and activity.

The various accounts of Jesus' postmortem appearances have a different function from the empty tomb tradition in the Gospel narratives. The phrase "he appeared" in 1 Corinthians 15 likely denotes a visionary experience of the risen Jesus, but in the Gospels, Jesus' appearances to his disciples are depicted as more than an apparition or a resuscitation. In Matthew, Luke, and John, the risen Jesus walks and talks, and in Luke and John, he even eats with his disciples, thus providing narrative accounts of what in Paul's discussion of resurrection he describes as a "spiritual body": "It is sown a physical body, it is raised a spiritual body. If there is a physical body, there is also a spiritual body" (1 Cor. 15:44). One concern addressed by the appearance stories, especially in Luke and John, may have been the belief, which came to be known as docetism, that Jesus only seemed to be human, and that his physical body was a phantasm. The primary purpose of the appearance stories in all the

Gospels, however, was to show Jesus commissioning his disciples to carry on with his mission. Those who had seen the risen Jesus could claim distinctive authority for leadership in the movement. In the shorter ending of Mark's Gospel, which does not include an appearance account, the young man instructs the women to "go, tell his disciples and Peter that he is going ahead of you to Galilee; there you will see him, just as he told you" (Mark 16:7). Galilee here is not just a geographical location but also symbolic of any place where the ministry of Jesus was continued by his followers. There-fore, within the narrative strategy of the Gospels, appearances of the risen Jesus serve to validate his message and mission vis-à-vis the imperial system that executed him and to inspire his followers to continue the movement he initiated in Galilee.

The empty tomb and the appearance traditions first circulated orally among Jesus' followers. They were related and handed down in the context of instruction or proclamation. These traditions were shaped by the conviction that Jesus was risen from the dead, and then woven together with other traditions about Jesus to form the narrative accounts that are the canonical Gospels. The memory of Jesus was, from the very beginning, shaped by followers who reflected on the signifi-cance of his message and actions for their own lives in diverse contexts. The earliest traditions about him were transformed as they were appropriated by communities of his followers throughout the Roman Empire. Form usually follows function, and this is no less true of the Jesus tradition, as fol-lowers made use of them to define their identity and develop practices of communal patterns of life.

Jesus was crucified sometime around 30 CE, and there is general agreement that Mark was written shortly after the destruction of the temple in Jerusalem in 70 CE. In this forty-year period between the time of Jesus and the time of the Gospels, stories and sayings circulated as oral tradi-tion in what was an oral culture. In contrast to Western societies predominated by written media, the fundamental dynamic of communication in the ancient world was between speaker and hearer. The literacy rate was low, somewhere between 5 percent and 10 percent, and most written texts were scripts to be performed in public. Performative storytelling was the ordinary medium of literary production in the Greco-Roman world. As Michael White puts it, written texts served as scripts *of* and *for* oral presentations (White, 92). Stories about and sayings of Jesus that were disseminated in an oral culture were not static or fixed in the same way written texts are. Oral tradition is conserva-tive in seeking to preserve authentic memories, but it is also malleable in that it changes with each new performance. As the Jesus tradition was transmitted in new contexts, it reflected the interests, values, and ideals of the community in which it was performed (White, 101–3). In this respect, the constructed memories of oral tradition do not simply relate the facts of what happened. They are also scripts for communal practice and belief.

During the forty or so years between Jesus and the Gospel of Mark, the memory of Jesus circu-lated orally. However, Mark and the other Gospels used sources, some of which were written down. There were likely collections of stories about Jesus' deeds of power, aphoristic sayings and parables, accounts of his suffering, death, and resurrection, and eventually nativity stories. As noted earlier in this essay, the sayings of Jesus common to Matthew and Luke are regarded by many scholars as an example of such a sayings collection, and are together referred to as Q. The sayings are not identical in the two Gospels because they were edited by the Gospel writers, but the sayings in Luke are gen-erally regarded as closer to the original than Matthew (Robinson, Kloppenborg, and Hoffmann).

Q contains some of the most memorable sayings of Jesus and is important because it is purported to be an example of an early source for the Gospels; the best guess for its date would be somewhere between 50 and 70 CE. But because there is no manuscript evidence for Q or any references to it in any ancient Christian texts, this dating is at best a working theory that has been questioned by a growing number of scholars (e.g., Goodacre).

What is interesting about scholarship on the Q sayings source is that it provides a window, albeit one based on conjecture, onto the period of oral tradition between Jesus and the Gospels. While there are no extant copies of Q, the *Gospel of Thomas* is an analogous example of a collection of Jesus' sayings that has no narrative structure. The *Gospel of Thomas* is one of the most famous of the cache of texts found in 1945 in the Egyptian town of Nag Hammadi. It is an extant sayings collection that contains 114 logia, or sayings, of Jesus. Half of the sayings have parallels in the Gospels, and half were formerly unknown. So whether there was an actual Q document or not, the *Gospel of Thomas* is an example of a collection of Jesus sayings that makes no allusion to the passion or resurrection. This would suggest that the individuals and communities for whom this document was of value probably tried to live in accordance with these particular sayings of Jesus. Similarly, scholars who work on Q maintain that it describes a particular way of life of Jewish disciples of Jesus, who regarded themselves as itinerant prophets, moving from town to town and announcing, "The kingdom of God has come close to you." Many of the sayings in Q also imply that these followers of Jesus called for repentance and experienced persecution.

There are a number of observations to be made from this brief treatment of collections of sayings during the period between Jesus and the Gospels before we turn to discuss the canonical Gospels. Although there is no evidence for the existence of the Q sayings source as a document, it is probable that this collection, or ones like it, existed as oral tradition. In other words, whether there is a Q source or not, the *Gospel of Thomas* confirms that collections of Jesus' sayings did circulate and were a source for the narratives of Jesus constructed by the Gospel writers. Perhaps even more significant for understanding the development of these Jesus traditions into the Gospels is how the tradition was simultaneously preserved and modified as Jesus' followers sought to embody his teachings. For some communities in the Jesus movement, the sayings functioned as practical wisdom to live by. Not only was the Jesus tradition being performed for followers, followers were themselves performing the tradition with their lives. The Jesus movement was, in its first decades, a messianic movement within Judaism that, if Paul's letters are any indication, included an increasing number of gentiles so that by the end of the first century they were a majority. Jews and gentiles alike were drawn into the movement by the communal pattern of life, predicated on Jesus' teaching and prophetic praxis and on the conviction that, though he had been executed for sedition, God had raised him from the dead and hence had inaugurated the new age.

The Genre and Relationships of the Gospels

As works of ancient literature, the canonical Gospels do not fit neatly into any particular genre. Some have stressed their Jewish character, especially their continuity with the narrative traditions and themes of Israel's Scriptures, while others look for analogies in Greco-Roman literature.

Although the oral qualities of the Gospels have been underlined so far, when the story of Jesus was committed to writing in the second half of the first century CE, the authors made use of literary forms available in the culture. Before the Gospel of Mark, the memory of Jesus was preserved and recounted orally in story and ritual. The Gospel of Mark is the first known attempt to render into a cohesive narrative the oral legacy of Jesus. In this respect, the Gospel of Mark signals an important transition in which a more fluid oral tradition was transformed into a more fixed literary tradition that became the standard and primary source for subsequent narrative interpretations of Jesus. Since the Gospels emerged from a Jewish messianic movement, Israel's Scriptures provided a lens for interpreting the Jesus tradition, and also served as a literary template. At the same time, to communicate the message of and about Jesus to a growing number of followers and would-be followers, it was essential to find some common cultural ground. So there are points of connection with both Jewish and Greco-Roman literary forms.

As Richard Burridge has argued, there are similarities between the Gospels and Greco-Roman biographies (Burridge, 185–211). The structure of the Gospels is broadly biographical, tracing Jesus' public ministry in chronological sequence. However, the disproportionate amount of narrative space devoted to the last week of Jesus' life distinguishes it from the typical Greco-Roman biography. Some elements from the ancient biography genre, such as anecdotes and sayings of particular teachers, known as *chreiai*, bear some resemblance to Justin Martyr's description of the Gospels as "the memoirs of the apostles," but, as Loveday Alexander points out, "the precise literary form adopted by Mark's performance of the Jesus story is hard to match in the Greek biographical tradition" (Alexander, 27). She suggests that the Gospel narratives have more in common with the folktale, which blends some characteristics from biographical tradition with oral traditional literature. The folktale is more a mode of composition and performance than a genre. Like folktales, the Gospels are focused to a remarkable degree on the action of the hero (Alexander, 18). This is especially true of the Gospel of Mark. Alexander cautions against drawing too firm a distinction between action and teaching in the Gospels because many of the action episodes are didactic. Nonetheless, the narratives as a whole give prominence to Jesus' public activity, and this is different from Hellenistic biographies of the philosopher or poet whose life exemplified virtues to be emulated. The Gospels provide virtually no information about Jesus' private existence nor insight into his interior life. A counterpart to the Greco-Roman biography in Jewish literature is the "biography of the prophets," which was concerned with office and function. Helmut Koester has suggested that the Gospel of Mark in particular follows the framework of the "biography of the prophets" because the primary concern in the story of Jesus' suffering and death is the legitimation of his office (Koester, 27–28).

A strong case can be made for the literature of the Hebrew Bible having the greatest influence on the literary form of the Gospels. Much of the narrative of the Hebrew Bible is composed of biographical "story cycles" that feature the exploits and achievements of key protagonists such as Abraham, Moses, or Elijah (Alexander, 27). The paradigmatic significance of the Moses and Elijah traditions in the depiction of Jesus as a prophet has already been discussed, but another critical aspect of the Hebrew Bible narratives is that the tales of these heroic figures were, in Alexander's words, "subordinated to the overall narrative style and goals of a purposeful religious, ethical, and national work" (Alexander, 27). Like the biblical narratives on which they are patterned, the Gospels tell the story of Jesus as a continuation of the story of Israel after the destruction of the Jerusalem temple. They are organized around key themes from the Hebrew Bible such as covenant, kingdom, exodus, prophecy, Suffering Servant, Messiah, Son of God, son of man, and so on, which were pressed into service to cast Jesus as the divinely appointed leader of the covenant community

Among the various reasons the Gospels were written, the destruction of the temple in 70 CE was a watershed event that profoundly influenced the composition of all four canonical Gospels. There is general agreement that the Gospel of Mark was written shortly after Jerusalem was conquered. The rebellion against Rome that began with the wars that broke out in 66 CE culminated with the burning of the temple in Jerusalem. There is general agreement that the Gospel of Mark was written around this time, either just before or after 70 CE, the date that marks the end of Second Temple Judaism. For more than five hundred years, the temple stood not only as the main religious institution of Judaism but also the axis around which its view of reality revolved. Jews regarded it as the *axis mundi*, the center of the cosmos, and believed that when the temple liturgy was performed properly it perpetuated a symmetry between heaven and earth. So the end of the temple not only raised theological questions about faithfulness, both God's and the covenant people's, but also ignited a debate about the future of Israel.

Mark's story of Jesus engaged this debate by presenting Jesus as the leader of the covenant people and therefore as the key to Israel's future after the destruction of the temple. At the beginning of the narrative, at his baptism by John in the Jordan, Jesus is described as being anointed by the Spirit and hearing a divine voice from heaven that declared, "You are my Son, the Beloved; with you I am well pleased" (Mark 1:11). These words are a conflation of Ps. 2:7 and Isa. 42:1. Psalm 2 is an enthronement psalm acclaiming the newly anointed king as God's son. So before Jesus even began his renewal movement in Galilee and the surrounding villages, hearers are informed that he has already been designated as the one through whom God will lead the people. (The "son of God" title ascribed to Jesus defines his role as God's representative who mediates divine power and sovereignty; it should not be confused with later creedal formulations in which language of Jesus as "Son" is interpreted to mean that he has a divine nature.) Mark's story operates on two levels. On one hand, historical sources are used to recount Jesus' activity in Galilee and Jerusalem. But the story is told from a post-70-CE perspective, after Jesus, having been executed by that same imperial power that destroyed the temple, is believed to have been vindicated and appointed by God to lead Israel and the nations in the "way of the Lord" (Mark 1:3). The phrase "way of the Lord" comes from Isaiah and is an allusion to the hope and promise of a new exodus. But in Mark, the "way," as in, Jesus and the disciples were "on the way," is also a metaphor for the pattern of life taught and modeled by Jesus (e.g., Mark 4:4, 15; 8:27; 9:33; 10:32).

The word that is translated "Christ" (*christos*) simply means "anointed one." It has the connotation of "messiah," and occurs in the opening line of Mark with the other term for political leader of Israel, "The beginning of the good news of Jesus *Christ*, the *Son of God*" (Mark 1:1). The use of the designation "Christ" or "messiah" is contested in Mark because it was typically associated with a national model of leadership. The turning point in Mark's narrative is when Jesus begins his journey to the capital city of Jerusalem. At Caesarea Philippi, he redefines the role of messiah for his followers by associating it with his impending suffering and death. Three times in Mark 8–10, Jesus explains that it is necessary for the "son of humanity," his preferred self-designation, to be delivered to the authorities and condemned, only to rise after three days (Mark 8:31-33; 9:30-32; 10:32-34). However, the main thrust of these predictions of his passion and resurrection is to teach his disciples that his path of rejection, suffering, death, and resurrection is the new paradigm of faithfulness for the covenant community in a post-70 imperial world.

Jerusalem is the setting for Mark 11–16, and the predominance of the temple theme in this section takes on new significance in light of the audience's knowledge that the temple has recently been destroyed. Jesus criticizes the temple establishment and forecasts the ruin of a temple that for the audience no longer exists. After Jesus is arrested, he is taken before the chief priests and the council who, according to the narrator, bear false witness against him, saying, "We heard him say, 'I will destroy this temple that is made with hands, and in three days I will build another, not made with hands'" (Mark 14:58). Although the testimony is false in the sense that within the narrative Jesus never said that he would destroy the Jerusalem temple and replace it with a temple "not made with hands," the audience understands that this new temple that will replace the one that has been destroyed is the covenant community. It seems likely that the word "temple" here echoes Paul's metaphor of the "body of Christ," which could also be translated "body of the Messiah." The inscription on the cross that sarcastically acclaims Jesus as "the king of the Jews" also has ironic force because, for the audience, Jesus has been divinely appointed to lead the lead the people of God into a new future and way of life at variance with the imperial power and social order. Finally, as Jesus breathes his last, "the curtain of the temple was torn in two, from top to bottom," and a centurion exclaims, "Truly this man was God's Son!" (Mark 15:38-39). Having a Roman centurion, someone implicated in Jesus' execution, acknowledge that Jesus is God's anointed leader portends that gentiles will also be included in the movement as it spreads throughout the empire.

Matthew and Luke as Interpreters of Mark

In the transition from oral tradition to written narratives about Jesus, the Gospel of Mark established the basic plot of the story followed by Mathew and Luke. Together, these three Gospels are referred to as the Synoptic Gospels. The term *synoptic* comes from two Greek words, *syn* ("with") and *optikos* ("seeing"), and denotes the literary relationship between them. There is an ongoing debate about whether the Gospel of John also used Mark as a source or is an independent Gospel tradition. All four Gospels were likely written in last third of the first century, though some scholars would date Luke and John early in the second century. The earliest traditions about the four canonical Gospels stem from the second century and are reflected in the titles prefaced to the Gospels. Matthew and John were attributed to apostles, and Mark and Luke were attributed to companions of the apostles. However, the names of the apostles were attached to the Gospel manuscripts much later. The oldest witness is Bishop Papias of Hierapolis, who is quoted by Eusebius (*Hist. eccl.* 3.39.3–4). Papias's writings are dated between 100 and 150 CE. Helmut Koester makes three important observations about the Papias tradition. First, Papias does not use the term "Gospel," but says that Matthew composed "the sayings." Second, in their written form, these traditions about Jesus do not carry any greater authority for Papias than what was transmitted orally: in other words, these texts are not regarded as Scripture. Third, Papias shows that these written documents came with the names of apostolic authors, or of men who had followed the apostles, which guaranteed the trustworthiness first of the oral tradition and then of the written documents (Koester, 33).

A close reading of the Synoptic Gospels side by side in a Gospel parallel shows that while they have a great deal in common, there are also a number of inconsistencies and contradictions in details. The birth narratives of Matthew and Luke, for example, are completely different, as are the resurrection narratives. The tendency throughout church history was to harmonize the differences, which had the consequence of minimizing the distinctiveness of each Gospel. In the second century, an early Christian apologist by the name of Tatian combined the four Gospels into a single narrative called the *Diatesseron*. But as scholars began to compare the four Gospels and study them critically, it became evident that the authors were not eyewitnesses. New theories about the interrelationship of the Gospels emerged.

In the eighteenth century, scholars realized that the parallels in the Gospels are so similar in wording that one of the three Synoptic Gospels must have been the basis for the others. Since Luke states in the preface to his Gospel that he made use of other narrative accounts (Luke 1:1-4), this Gospel must have been dependent on either Matthew or Mark. From the time of Augustine in the fourth century, the canonical order of the Gospels was regarded as the order of dependence, so Matthew was thought to have been written first. According to Papias, the Greek version of Matthew was a translation of an earlier Hebrew edition. So, for centuries, the common view was that Mark abbreviated Matthew. Toward the end of the eighteenth century, however, J. J. Griesbach proposed a theory, based on the early view that Matthew was the first Gospel, which claimed that Mark used both Matthew and Luke for his abbreviated version. The main problem with the Griesbach hypothesis is that it is difficult to account for why Mark would omit material in the double tradition common to Matthew and Luke. Therefore, the theory that is most widely accepted by scholars is the two-source theory, which posits that Matthew and Luke depended on Mark and wrote independently of each other. The other main source used by both Matthew and Luke was Q. The distinctive material in Matthew and Luke is designated "M" and "L" respectively. Although the theory posits four sources, it is called the two-source theory because Matthew and Luke both use Mark and Q as primary sources. The two-source theory is illustrated in figure 3.

There is no one solution that solves all the difficulties, but since 80 percent of Mark is reproduced in Matthew and 65 percent in Luke, Markan priority is seldom questioned. The existence of Q, however, continues to be debated, with the majority of scholars who question the existence of Q maintaining that Luke used both Mark and Matthew.

One of the main benefits of the study of the relationships among the Gospels is that it led to a deeper appreciation for the distinctive narrative vision of each Gospel. Although the study of the use of sources in the Gospels involves a certain amount of conjecture, it has also put more emphasis on how the evangelists redacted and shaped the Jesus tradition to address particular contextual and theological issues. In using Mark as a source, Matthew and Luke can be read as the first interpreters of Mark, or better, as performances of Mark. A close analysis of how Matthew and Luke modify Mark's narrative provides some insight into their respective narrative strategies. This, along with an examination of the material unique to Matthew and Luke and the distinct themes and uses of

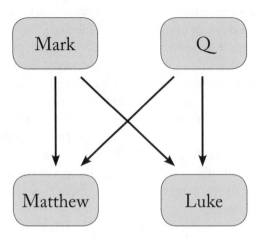

FIGURE 3. *The Two-Source Hypothesis*

Israel's Scriptures, suggests how Matthew and Luke adapted Mark's story of Jesus to shape the convictions and practices of audiences negotiating particular concerns and circumstances. While there is no external information outside the Gospels themselves that would make it possible to situate them geographically, the overarching perspective and key emphases of each Gospel can be inferred from the narrative itself.

Matthew and Luke both follow the basic framework of Mark's Gospel, and both also add infancy narratives to set the stage and introduce the story. Since it is only possible to touch on the broad contours of their narratives in this essay, the main point to be inferred from the divergent accounts of Jesus' birth, including irreconcilable genealogies, is that in different ways they are at the outset connecting their respective stories of Jesus to the history of Israel. Matthew establishes that Joseph belongs to the house of David so as to depict Jesus as the Davidic Messiah. Throughout the Gospel, Matthew makes a point to show that Jesus' ministry, death, and resurrection were a fulfillment of Israel's Scriptures. Luke's genealogy goes back to Adam to underline the universal scope of Jesus' mission. The main themes of Luke's Gospel are set out in the canticles of Mary (Luke 1:46-56) and Simeon (Luke 2:25-35), and the prophecy of Zechariah (Luke 1:67-80). The focus in all three passages is on the redemption of Israel, in particular the restoration of Israel that includes the nations. This central theme of the restoration of Israel is woven throughout the narrative and expressly highlighted in the final scene as two disciples, walking on the road to Emmaus with the risen Jesus whom they do not yet recognize, say, "we had hoped he was the one to redeem Israel" (Luke 24:21). This theme is then carried over into Acts, the only sequel to a Gospel in which the mission of Jesus is continued by his followers.

In each Gospel, there are key passages vital for understanding the narrative as a whole, and that also provide a window on the communal context of the Gospel. Matthew's Gospel is organized around five major discourses that include the Sermon on the Mount (Matthew 5–7), the discourse on mission (Matthew 10), parables of the kingdom (Matthew 13), discourse on community life (Matthew 18), and an eschatological discourse (Matthew 24–25). The Sermon on the Mount contains material that is also in Luke, but Matthew's Jesus is portrayed as the authoritative interpreter of Torah who teaches and models a righteousness characterized by "meekness" (Matt. 5:5; 11:29; 21:5) and "mercy" (Matt. 5:7; 9:13; 12:7; 23:23). Since Jesus tells his followers, "Do not think that I have come to abolish the law or the prophets; I have come not to abolish but to fulfill. . . . For I tell you, unless your righteousness exceeds that of the scribes and Pharisees, you will never enter the kingdom of heaven" (Matt. 5:17, 20), a number of scholars have inferred that the setting for this Gospel was a Torah-observant community of Jesus' followers that was involved in a dispute with scribes and Pharisees (who are likely represented by the religious authorities in Matthew's context). The vitriolic diatribe against scribes and Pharisees in Matthew 23 acknowledges their authority but criticizes them because they "do not practice what they teach" (Matt. 23:3). Matthew's story of Jesus can be read as a narrative portrayal of a righteousness, a central theme in Torah, that can be practiced by all. Hence the final authoritative command of the risen Jesus to "Go therefore and make disciples of all nations . . . *teaching* them to obey everything that I have commanded you" (see Matt. 28:19-20).

Luke's story of Jesus tells of God fulfilling promises of salvation for Israel and the nations. Only Luke's account of John the Baptist includes the phrase from Isaiah 40, "and all flesh shall see the salvation of God" (Luke 3:6). This vision of salvation is given more specific definition in Jesus' programmatic first speech at his hometown synagogue in Nazareth, where he reads from the Isaiah scroll.

> The Spirit of the Lord is upon me,
>   because he has anointed me
>   to bring good news to the poor [Isa. 61:1].
> He has sent me to proclaim release to the captives
>   and recovery of sight to the blind,
>   to let the oppressed go free [Isa. 58:6],
> to proclaim the year of the Lord's favor. (Luke 4:18-19)

This passage signals to the audience that Jesus' ministry will engage various forms of oppression and injustice. There is more material on economic relations in Luke than any other Gospel, so issues of poverty and marginalization were specific contextual issues facing the author (e.g., Luke 6:20-21, 27-36; 12:13-21, 32-34; 14:15-33; 16:1-13, 19-31). The hope of salvation in Luke is defined as deliverance from social ills, and so Jesus is cast in the role of prophet on the model of Elijah, who was engaged in renewing society. However, the offer of salvation requires a human response of "repentance" that entails participation in Jesus' mission. Luke's story of Jesus offers an alternative vision of life and practice. This vision promises God's deliverance from the dehumanizing effects of imperial society for the covenant community that hears Jesus' words and does them (see Luke 6:46-49).

The Gospel of John

The Gospel of John has not been discussed because its narrative about Jesus is different from and probably independent of the Synoptic tradition. At least we can say it radically departs from it. The literary relationship among Matthew, Mark, and Luke indicates that they share a similar form, structure, and content. All three Synoptic Gospels, on the one hand, use many of the same sources and traditions to tell the story of Jesus. Their authors edited the material in ways that reflected the concerns and interests native to the communities and contexts in which they were writing, but Matthew and Luke are essentially following and adapting Mark's story of Jesus. The Gospel of John, on the other hand, is so different from the Synoptic Gospels that we must begin with what is distinctive so that John's story of Jesus can be interpreted on its own terms.

On a basic level, the chronology and geography of the Gospel of John are at variance with the Synoptic Gospels. In the Synoptic Gospels, the temple incident is the turning point in the plot of the story inasmuch as it leads to his trial before the Sanhedrin and, ultimately, to his death. In the Gospel of John, the incident in the temple occurs at the beginning of the Gospel, in chapter 2. Jesus moves back and forth between Galilee and Jerusalem throughout the Gospel. John and the Synoptic Gospels are obviously referring to the same incident, even though they place it at different points in the chronology. They also interpret its significance in different ways. In the Synoptic Gospels, Jesus' prophetic challenge to the temple administration belongs to a longer section that deals with temple themes and sees his trial and execution as the direct consequence of what he said and did in the temple. In John, the plot to kill Jesus is hatched after Jesus raises Lazarus from the dead (John 11:45-53), something that does not happen in the Synoptics.

Among some of the other important differences between John and the Synoptic Gospels is the fact that in John, Jesus' ministry spans three years, while in the Synoptic chronology it lasts only a year. There are no exorcisms or parables in John. There are fewer healings and other deeds of power in John, and those that are narrated are called "signs." In the Synoptic Gospels, the exorcisms, healings, and other deeds of power are evidence of the presence of the "kingdom of God." But the "kingdom of God" is not the focus of the Gospel of John. Rather, the "signs" serve to reveal the true identity of the one who performs them. Perhaps the most striking difference between John and the Synoptic Gospels is the manner in which Jesus speaks. Instead of short, pithy sayings, or parables, Jesus speaks in long, extended discourses. The metaphors and symbols of John are also different from those in the Synoptic Gospels. Jesus' metaphorical way of speaking is self-referential and does not point to the "kingdom of God," the root symbol of the Synoptic tradition. This is because John depicts Jesus preeminently as the "Revealer." He comes from God and he reveals God. Even the healings are occasions for long monologues in which Jesus "reveals" the deeper significance of his identity and the nature of his work.

The Gospel of John begins with a hymn that succinctly tells the story of Jesus in poetic form. John's prologue sets out many of the main themes and the essential plot of the Gospel. At the outset, the hymn evokes the creation and introduces the "Word" as the central character who "was in the beginning with God. All things came into being through him, and without him not one thing came into being" (John 1:2-3). In Stoic philosophy, *logos*, translated "Word" here, referred to the cosmic reason holding the universe together. The counterpart to this idea in Judaism was the important concept of Wisdom as a preexistent divine being. This personification of Wisdom found in Proverbs 8 and other Jewish literature is probably the frame of reference for this poetic description of the descent of the Word into the world. Wisdom was perceived to be a female figure, present with God at creation, who comes to dwell on earth. In Jewish tradition, she is identified with Torah, but in John, Jesus is the expression of this divine Wisdom.

In the Gospel of John, Jesus is the incarnation of this preexistent divine Wisdom. He came to "take up residence" in the cosmos in order to lead people to life (John 1:14). But as the prologue and the Gospel both attest, this story takes a tragic turn when those who inhabit the cosmos reject this particular embodiment of the divine presence. Another feature that makes this Gospel so different from the Synoptic Gospels is that it is plotted along a vertical axis, whereas the Synoptics are plotted along a more historical, horizontal axis. John's Jesus is the "man from heaven" who "tabernacles" among the people of God, only to return to the Father. Although the Synoptic Gospels affirm the divine presence and power in and through Jesus, they do not go so far as to suggest that he was with God from the beginning. John tells the story of Jesus as a cosmic tale, while in the Synoptic Gospels the story unfolds on the horizontal plane of history (see figure 4).

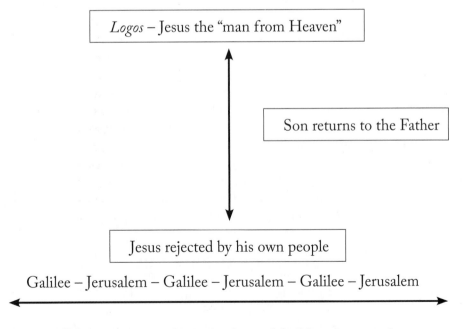

FIGURE 4. *Vertical and horizontal axes of the Johannine narrative.*

So while the Johannine Jesus moves back and forth between Galilee to Jerusalem and interacts with various characters, the main narrative arc is from heaven to earth and then back again. What Jesus says and does, the conflicts he is embroiled in, and even his death and resurrection are presented from the point of view of the cosmological tale set out in the opening hymn. John essentially replaces the Synoptic Gospels' proclamation of the kingdom of God with a present experience of "life" that is "eternal" (see John 3:15-16; 4;14, 36; 5:24, 39; 6:27, 40, 47, 54, 68; 10:28; 12:25, 50; 17:2). The phrase "eternal life" (*zōē aiōnion*) in John virtually replaces the proclamation of the kingdom and denotes a quality of life peculiar to the new age that is experienced in the present.

The clearest window onto the world behind the text of this Gospel is the skillfully narrated healing of the man born blind in John 9. This healing story operates on at least two levels, in the sense that the story of the blind man who receives his sight also discloses something about the story of the Johannine community. After Jesus heals the blind man, he is brought before the Pharisees to be interrogated. Since the Jewish authorities do not believe the man had been blind, they call the man's parents to explain how he now sees. They reply:

> "We know that this is our son, and that he was born blind; but we do not know how it is that now he sees, nor do we know who opened his eyes. Ask him; he is of age. He will speak for himself." His parents said this because they were afraid of the Jews; for the Judeans had already agreed that anyone who confessed Jesus to be the Messiah would be put out of the synagogue. (John 9:20-22)

There are other references in the Gospel to being put out of the synagogue (12:42; 16:2). We should, however, be careful about taking such statements at face value as indicating believers were actually expelled from the synagogue. This Gospel was written fifteen to twenty-five years after the destruction of the Jerusalem temple, during a time when Jewish leaders were shoring up boundaries as they attempted to redefine what it meant to be Jewish in a world without a temple. As a result, there developed some kind of strife between the Johannine community and the local Jewish community. The language of enmity against "the Jews" in this Gospel was born of intense emotional pain and social bereavement due to strained relationships with and perhaps separation from their Jewish compatriots. The Gospel itself suggests that the main issue may have been the community's claims regarding Jesus' unique relationship to God. There was a perception among Jewish rabbis early in the second century that Christians believed that there were "two powers in heaven." This was thought to compromise the foundational monotheistic confession in Judaism that there is one God. There are passages in John that suggest this may have been a point of contention between the Johannine community and the synagogue.

Concluding Summary

This essay about Jesus has shown that, from the beginning of his ministry in first-century Galilee, people have interpreted the significance of what he said and did in various ways. The four canonical Gospels are the primary sources for understanding who Jesus was, but they are not straightforward historical accounts. Rather, they are narrative interpretations that relate Jesus' message and mission to new historical circumstances for followers. The Enlightenment gave rise to historical criticism and attempts to get behind the text of the Gospels to distinguish the Jesus of history from the faith perspectives of his followers. However, as Schweitzer saw at the turn of the twentieth century, interpretations of the Jesus tradition always reflect the social location of the person who is doing the interpreting. History and interpretation are so intertwined in the Gospels that there continues to be a robust conversation and a diversity of views about the historical reliability of the Gospels and how they are used to construct a portrait of the historical Jesus.

This essay has suggested that a thick and nuanced description of the sociohistorical context of Galilee and Jerusalem in the 30s of the Common Era is needed to provide a framework for deciphering the significance of what Jesus said and did in his own context, and for understanding how the Gospel writers adapted the traditions about Jesus to their contexts after the destruction of Jerusalem in 70 CE. The canonical Gospels represent four similar yet different narrative performances of the story of Jesus. Each has its own rhetorical strategy, designed to shape the identity and practices of a particular community, or perhaps multiple communities. In his Galilean context, Jesus was leading a renewal movement that addressed issues of economic and political oppression, and social and religious marginalization. He went to the capital city of Jerusalem as a prophet to challenge the priestly aristocracy that collaborated with Rome, and was executed as an enemy of the imperial order. The four Gospels all attest that his followers experienced him as alive after the crucifixion and commissioned them to continue the movement, which then spread throughout the Roman Empire. The Gospels were all shaped by the conviction that God had raised Jesus from the dead and inaugurated a new messianic age. Each Gospel narrates what Jesus said and did, and the events of his life, as the basis for a distinctive vision of an inclusive and communal pattern of life that was countercultural and had the power to transform the lives of individuals and the world in which they lived.

Works Cited

Alexander, Loveday. 2006. "What Is a Gospel?" In *The Cambridge Companion to the Gospels*, edited by Stephen Barton, 13–33. New York: Cambridge University Press.

Allison, Dale C. 1998. *Jesus of Nazareth: Millenarian Prophet*. Minneapolis: Fortress Press.

———. 2010. *Constructing Jesus: Memory, Imagination, and History*. Grand Rapids: Baker Academic.

Barton, Stephen C., ed. 2006. *The Cambridge Companion to the Gospels*. New York: Cambridge University Press.

Borg, Marcus J. 1994. *Jesus in Contemporary Scholarship*. Valley Forge, PA: Trinity Press International.

———. 1998. *Conflict, Holiness, and Politics in the Teachings of Jesus*. Harrisburg, PA: Trinity Press International.

———. 2008. *Jesus: Uncovering the Life, Teachings, and Relevance of a Religious Revolutionary*. San Francisco: HarperOne.

Brodie, Thomas L. 2000. *The Crucial Bridge: The Elijah-Elisha Narrative as an Interpretive Synthesis of Genesis-Kings and a Literary Model for the Gospels*. Collegeville, MN: Liturgical Press.

Burridge, Richard. 2004. *What Are the Gospels?: A Comparison with Graeco-Roman Biography*. Grand Rapids: Eerdmans.

Crossan, John Dominic. 1991. *The Historical Jesus: The Life of a Mediterranean Jewish Peasant*. San Francisco: Harper.

———. 1994. *Jesus: a Revolutionary Biography*. New York: HarperCollins.

Crossan, John Dominic, and Jonathan L Reed. 2001. *Excavating Jesus: Beneath the Stones, Behind the Texts*. San Francisco: HarperSanFrancisco.

Crossley, James G. 2006. *Why Christianity Happened: A Sociohistorical Account of Christian Origins (26–50 CE)*. Louisville: Westminster John Knox.

Draper, Jonathan. 1994. "Jesus and the Renewal of Local Community in Galilee." *Journal of Theology for Southern Africa* 87:29–42.

Fitzmyer, Joseph A. 1985. *The Gospel According to Luke X–XXIV*. Garden City, NY: Doubleday.

Goodacre, Mark S. 2002. *The Case Against Q: Studies in Markan Priority and the Synoptic Problem*. Harrisburg, PA: Trinity Press International.

Goodman, Martin. 1987. *The Ruling Class of Judaea: The Origins of the Jewish Revolt against Rome, A.D. 66–70*. New York: Cambridge University Press.

Herzog, William R. 2005. *Prophet and Teacher: An Introduction to the Historical Jesus*. Louisville: Westminster John Knox.

Hollenbach, Paul. 1982. "The Conversion of Jesus: From Jesus the Baptizer to Jesus the Healer." In *ANRW* 2.25.1:196–219.

Horsley, Richard A. 2003. *Jesus and Empire: The Kingdom of God and the New World Disorder*. Minneapolis: Fortress Press.

———. 2011. *Jesus and the Powers: Conflict, Covenant, and the Hope of the Poor*. Minneapolis: Fortress Press.

———. 2012. *The Prophet Jesus and the Renewal of Israel: Moving beyond a Diversionary Debate*. Grand Rapids: Eerdmans.

Horsley, Richard A., and John S. Hanson. 1999. *Bandits, Prophets, and Messiahs: Popular Movements in the Time of Jesus*. Harrisburg, PA: Trinity Press International.

Koester, Helmut. 1990. *Ancient Christian Gospels: Their History and Development*. London: SCM; Philadelphia: Trinity Press International.

Lenski, Gerhard. 1966. *Power and Privilege: A Theory of Social Stratification*. Chapel Hill: University of North Carolina Press.

Lohfink, Gerhard. 2012. *Jesus of Nazareth: What He Wanted, Who He Was*. Collegeville, MN: Liturgical Press.

Moxnes, Halvor. 2010. "Ethnography and Historical Imagination in Reading Jesus as an Exorcist." *Neot* 44, no. 2:327–41.

Oakman, Douglas E. 2012. *The Political Aims of Jesus*. Minneapolis: Fortress Press.

Robinson, James McConkey, Paul Hoffmann, and John S. Kloppenborg. 2009. *The Sayings Gospel Q in Greek and English*. Minneapolis: Fortress Press.

Sanders, E. P. 1985. *Jesus and Judaism*. Philadelphia: Fortress Press.

———. 1996. *The Historical Figure of Jesus*. New York: Penguin.

Schaberg, Jane. 2002. *The Resurrection of Mary Magdalene: Legends, Apocrypha, and the Christian Testament*. New York: Continuum.

Schweitzer, Albert. 1910. *The Quest of the Historical Jesus*. London: Black.

Scott, Bernard Brandon. 1989. *Hear Then the Parable: A Commentary on the Parables of Jesus*. Minneapolis: Fortress Press.

———. 2001. *Re-imagine the World: An Introduction to the Parables of Jesus*. Santa Rosa, CA: Polebridge.

Smith, Daniel Alan. 2010. *Revisiting the Empty Tomb: The Early History of Easter*. Minneapolis: Fortress Press.

Smith, Dennis Edwin. 2003. *From Symposium to Eucharist: The Banquet in the Early Christian World*. Minneapolis: Fortress Press.

Theissen, Gerd, and Annette Merz. 1998. *The Historical Jesus: A Comprehensive Guide*. Minneapolis: Fortress Press.

Vermes, Géza. 1981. *Jesus the Jew: A Historian's Reading of the Gospels*. Philadelphia: Fortress Press.

———. 1993. *The Religion of Jesus the Jew*. Minneapolis: Fortress Press, 1993.

White, L. Michael. 2010. *Scripting Jesus: The Gospel Authors as Storytellers and Their Images of Jesus*. San Francisco: HarperOne.

Wrede, William. 1971. *The Messianic Secret*. Trans. J. C. G. Greig. London: James Clarke.

MATTHEW

Warren Carter

Introduction

Matthew's story of Jesus unfolds in six sections. The opening section introduces Jesus (1:1—4:16). He is located in the story of Israel (1:1-17); conceived and commissioned by God to manifest God's saving presence (1:18-25); threatened by Herod, recognized by the magi and a star, protected by Joseph (ch. 2); witnessed to by John the Baptist (3:1-12); sanctioned by God in baptism (3:13-17); tested by the devil (4:1-11); and interpreted by the Scriptures (4:12-16). Then in the second section, Jesus carries out his commission to manifest God's saving presence (4:17—11:1) by announcing God's reign or empire (4:17); calling disciples (4:18-22); teaching (chs. 5–7, 10); and performing actions such as healings and exorcisms (chs. 8–9).

The third section highlights diverse responses to Jesus and his activity of recognition and rejection (11:2—16:20). In the fourth section (16:21—20:34), Jesus announces a further dimension to his commission. The ruling alliance of Jerusalem elite and the Roman governor Pilate will crucify him. In his teaching (ch. 18) and while journeying from Galilee (chs. 19–20), he elaborates the implications of his death for his disciples' "way of the cross." The fifth section narrates his increasing conflict with the ruling powers in Jerusalem, his curses and judgment on their imperially allied world, and his crucifixion as rebel king and death (chs. 21–27). The final section reveals that Roman power does not have the last word as God raises Jesus (ch. 28).

This story of Jesus' birth, activity, teaching, death by crucifixion, and resurrection exhibits standard features of the genre of ancient biography. We do not know its author. Though the Gospel twice mentions a disciple named Matthew (9:9; 10:3), he is probably not the author. This disciple plays a minor role in the Gospel. And the name "Matthew" is not linked with the Gospel until late in the second century, some one hundred or so years later.

The Gospel's references to Rome's destruction of Jerusalem in 70 CE (see below) and its apparent citing by writings from Syrian Jesus-followers early in the second century (e.g., *Didache*, letters of Ignatius) establish a window of c. 80–c. 100 CE for its composition. The Gospel, then, is not an eye-witness account or day-by-day record of Jesus' ministry. It shapes its sources—Mark's Gospel and a collection of Jesus' sayings called Q—to address its audience's circumstances in the 80s or 90s CE. It was written perhaps in Galilee or in Syria, notably the city of Antioch. The prominence of Peter, the surprising reference to Syria in 4:24, and its early citing by writings from Syria suggest the latter.

Narrative Pastoral Theology at Work

Why tell this story of Jesus? The devastating assertion of Roman power in destroying Jerusalem and its temple in 70 CE, events that concluded the 66–70 war of revolt, had momentous consequences for emerging Judaisms. The Gospel's telling of the story of Jesus, one crucified by Rome as a rebel king, functions to interpret these events, to secure the distinct and differentiated identity of the community of Jesus-followers, to discredit other groups, and to envision practices and a societal vision that constitute a way ahead. The Gospel is thus a work of narrative pastoral theology, address-ing its audience's particular circumstances.

These circumstances comprised conflict, competition, pressure, and vulnerability. Syria had sig-nificant involvement in the 66–70 war. In 67, the Roman general and later emperor Vespasian mar-shaled there three or four legions of troops (more than 20,000 troops in a city of perhaps 150,000). Syrian grain was levied to support Titus's troops in the subsequent siege of Jerusalem. The practice of *angaria* requisitioned transport, labor, lodging, and supplies from local people (see Matt. 5:41; 27:32). As Roman presence and pressure increased, conflicts among Jews in Antioch erupted. A highly acculturated member of the Jewish elite by the name of Antiochus accused other Jews of plotting to burn Antioch. Antiochus banned identity-defining practices (Sabbath observance) and required sacrifices to city and/or imperial gods. Some complied, some refused, some were martyred, and some gentiles violently attacked Jews (Josephus, *J.W.* 7.47–53).

After the war, the victorious Roman general and future emperor Titus paraded Jewish captives and booty through Antioch. Some Antiochenes urged him, unsuccessfully, to expel Jews from the city. The emperor Vespasian levied a tax on Jews as a subjugated people, diverting the tax formerly paid to the Jerusalem temple to maintain and rebuild the temple of Jupiter Capitolinus in Rome. This move added insult to injury. Jupiter was the sponsoring deity whose blessing had ensured Roman victory over Judea, its God, and temple.

Jerusalem's devastation made an example out of Jewish people. It reminded the rest of the empire that Roman power was not to be challenged. It also raised significant theological issues and questions about the identity, way of life, and future of Jewish communities in the empire. What was God doing? Had God withdrawn God's presence and blessing? Was the event punishment? If so, was there forgiveness? How should they live so as to prevent such a terrible thing happening again?

And this military-political event posed special challenges for Jesus-followers. They followed one who had been executed on a cross. Rome used crucifixion, a cruel form of the death penalty, to punish runaway slaves, bandits who attacked elite personnel and their property, and insurrectionists against Roman rule. Jesus' death by crucifixion placed him in such company. The alliance comprising the Roman governor Pilate, the face of Roman power in Judea, and the Jerusalem leaders with whom Pilate shared power, had viewed Jesus as a threat for attacking the temple that was the basis for their power, for proclaiming an alternative empire, and for being understood as a king not sanctioned by Rome.

In telling the story of Jesus, Matthew's Gospel interprets and addresses this post-70 situation. How did followers of one crucified by Rome negotiate a world defined by a fresh assertion of Roman power?

One consequence of the 70-CE defeat of Jerusalem was added pressure on and suspicion of the significant Jewish population of Antioch. The reality that when a ruling power exerts downward pressure on a subordinated group, horizontal verbal, structural, and physical violence frequently breaks out among group members is well attested. This phenomenon is evident in Antioch, as noted above, and in Matthew's Gospel. The Gospel exhibits considerable verbal hostility toward and conflict with leaders, at least, of the synagogue or synagogues of which these Jesus-followers were members.

The Gospel explains the destruction of Jerusalem and its temple as punishment on the rulers of Galilee and Judea for rejecting Jesus (22:1-10). Jesus declares the temple leadership (allied with Rome) to be "robbers" or "brigands." Their rule attacks and harms the people's well-being (21:12-13; quoting Jer. 7:11). Through several parables (21:33—22:10; esp. 21:41; 22:7), Matthew interprets Jerusalem's fall to the Romans in 70 CE as God's judging the leaders for rejecting Jesus (21:45-46).

This explanation presents Rome as chosen by God to be agents of this punishment. But following a well-established Hebrew Bible pattern, the Gospel also presents Rome as under God's judgment. Chapter 24 offers the fantasy of Jesus' return to establish God's empire or reign in full, destroying Rome's empire (24:27-31). Rome and other nations will be condemned for not caring for the broken and powerless (25:31-46). The sinful structures of power that benefit elites at the expense of the rest created unjust and harmful circumstances.

Worse, the Gospel presents this Roman-ruled, sinful world as being in the devil's hands. In tempting Jesus, the devil asserts control over all the empires of the world, of which Rome is the leading empire. The devil offers Jesus these empires if he will bow down to the devil (4:8-9). Jesus' exorcisms of demons, the devil's agents, show his victory over the devil's control (8:28-34).

Moreover, the Gospel declares that this judgment on the Jerusalem leaders and Rome is not the end. It presents Jesus as God's anointed agent (Christ/Messiah, 1:1; Son, 3:17). He represents and reveals God's saving presence (1:21-23) and will for the way ahead. Jesus challenges the ruling powers with a different societal vision. He announces and enacts God's empire or kingdom (4:17). He calls disciples to form a new community (4:18-22) and teaches them (chs. 5–7). Many sick people occupy the world of the Gospel (4:23; 9:35) because Rome's imperial structures ensure that the ruling elite have plenty to eat while most struggle for daily sustenance. In such a context, diseases of deprivation and contagion are rife. Jesus' healings, exorcisms, and feedings (see 14:13-21; 15:32-39) enact and anticipate the physical wholeness and abundant fertility that the prophets picture when God's reign/empire is established in full (Isa. 26:6-10; 35:1-7).

Jesus forgives sin (9:1-8; 26:26-29). He also declares that he represents God's presence wherever his followers gather (18:20) and engage in mission (28:18-20). In five teaching blocks, Jesus reveals God's will and purposes, shaping the identity and way of life of his followers (chs. 5–7; 10; 13; 18; 24–25). Jesus' teaching announces the surprising situations in which God's blessing is encountered—among the poor (most of the population!) whose poverty corrodes their being or spirit (5:3), and in deeds of mercy (5:7; 9:13; 12:7; 18:21-35). Mercy is demonstrated in actions that relieve harsh socioeconomic conditions (25:31-46). Quoting from Deut. 6:5 and Lev. 19:18, Jesus declares that the double command to love God and neighbor is central to God's will (22:34-40).

Through this presentation of Jesus' actions and teaching, Matthew's Gospel reassures people after Rome's destruction of Jerusalem and the temple in 70 CE that God has not abandoned them or withdrawn God's presence, forgiveness, and blessing. God's agent, Jesus, provides a future. God has commissioned him to reveal God's purposes in his actions and teaching, shaping their identity and way of life.

How, then, are followers of Jesus, crucified by Rome, to live in this imperial world? Despite opposition (5:10-12), they are to understand that the empire's power is not ultimate. It could not keep Jesus dead. God raised him from the dead (ch. 28), and he will return to establish God's reign (chs. 24–25). Disciples are not to "resist violently" but are to negotiate Rome's power in active, nonviolent ways (5:39-42). They pay taxes while recognizing that the earth belongs to God, not to Rome (17:24-27; 22:15-22). They pray for God's will and rule to be established (6:9-13). They reject hierarchical structures of power (20:20-28). They care for and support one another with practical mercy, love, and forgiveness (5:42; 6:9-13; 18:1-35; 22:34-40; 25:34-36). The Gospel thus shapes the identity and way of living of Jesus-followers in a world often not structured according to God's purposes of abundant life for all people.

Enemies and Verbal Violence

The Gospel's presentation indicates, though, that other members of the synagogue do not accept Jesus' credentials, explanations, and teaching. Considerable tension exists between Jesus-followers and the rest of the synagogue communities. Though Jesus is active in synagogues (4:23; 9:35), he often finds opposition. The Gospel's verbally violent rhetoric associates synagogues with conflict and rejection (12:9-14; 13:54-58). Jesus describes them as full of hypocrites (6:2, 5) and violent toward his followers (10:17-18, as are rulers). Throughout, Jesus is in conflict with leaders such as scribes, Pharisees, and chief priests who, along with the Roman governor Pilate, crucify him (9:2-8; 12:1-14; 16:1-12; 26:3-5, 57-68). They clash over how to interpret the Scriptures and practice God's will in Sabbath observance (12:1-14), elder care (15:1-9), divorce (19:3-12), and paying taxes (22:15-22). They think he is a blasphemer (9:3), the devil's agent (9:34; 12:24), lacking authority for his actions and teaching (21:23-27). In turn, he declares them disqualified from God's purposes (15:6-9), warns against their teaching (15:13-14), and in the terrible chapter 23 curses them as hypocrites who neglect justice, mercy, and faithfulness (23:23).

At the heart of this conflict is the issue of Jesus' identity. Those who oppose him in synagogues do not recognize him as God's agent commissioned to manifest God's will, presence, forgiveness, reign/empire, and purposes. In the difficult situation of post-70 Antioch, perhaps various synagogue leaders and members thought that a group committed to one who had been crucified was likely to attract unwelcome hostile attention. Perhaps they considered the Gospel's analysis of Roman power as diabolical and dangerous. Perhaps they found its certainty about Jesus' return to end the Roman world similarly provocative. Perhaps they found it incredible that a crucified one could manifest God's saving presence and reign/empire. Perhaps they found the eschatological declaration that God had raised him untenable, because clearly the world continued unchanged, with, in fact, Roman power strengthened.

The Gospel, then, tells the story of Jesus so as to address the circumstances of its own time. This situation is marked in part by struggles among synagogue members to make sense of the events of 70 CE and to discern a faithful way ahead. The Gospel sees Jesus as the key figure in offering a way ahead; others in the synagogue do not. The Gospel inscribes this bitter conflict in its story of Jesus.

A word of warning, though, is necessary. This Gospel presents this conflict between Jesus, synagogues, and Jewish leaders in harsh terms. Jesus makes nasty statements that are problematic for contemporary readers (e.g., ch. 23). The history of reading this Gospel over the last two millennia shows that its language has readily been a source of hostile anti-Jewish thought, rhetoric, and actions among Christians. The Gospel provides no warrant for such responses by contemporary readers. Its hostile rhetoric emerges from particular circumstances that no longer apply. And the Gospel holds out a different and greater vision of love for neighbors that accompanies love for God (22:37-40).

In the following commentary, I elaborate this reading and engage the Gospel's contemporary address. In the bibliographies, I regularly cite two quite different commentaries from among many fine Matthean commentaries. One is my own, *Matthew and the Margins*, which elaborates this interpretation of Matthew. The other is the magnificent commentary by Ulrich Luz, from which I have drawn much material in the sections on the interpretive tradition. I wish to acknowledge my debt to this fine work.

Part 1: God Commissions Jesus (Matthew 1:1—4:16)

The first chapters of Matthew make clear that Jesus has been commissioned by God. A new section of the narrative is marked by the statement in 4:17 that "from that time Jesus began to preach . . ."

Matthew 1:1-17: A Genealogy

■ THE TEXT IN ITS ANCIENT CONTEXT

While repeating a formula "*a* was the father of *b*" some thirty-nine times may not strike modern sensibilities as a gripping beginning, first-century readers found this opening genealogy to be of great significance. Genealogies linked the present with the past. They named prestigious ancestors, creating identity through an ancestral line to which some belonged and some did not. Jesus and his followers are set in a line that originates with the eminent figures of David and Abraham.

This genealogy, though, is not primarily about biology. The artificial patterning of 3 × 14 generations, the lack of match between the number of generations and the likely time spans, the false link between Salmon and Rahab (1:5), and missing generations (1:8, 11) indicate a different focus.

Matthew narrates a distinctive version of the biblical story in which the purposes of God are worked out through the ages and generations, and especially through Jesus. Jesus' significance is defined by divine purposes and not, for example, by cultural markers such as elevated social status, noble birth, wealth, and power. The selected biblical traditions provide a theological framework for the rest of the Gospel, where everything and everyone are evaluated in relation to God's workings (Carter 2000, 53–66; Waetjen).

This theological focus is polemical in the context of Matthew's audience. Jewish traditions included various tellings of the biblical story. Matthew's account chooses to highlight the key role of Jesus. Further, in the context of the Roman Empire, Rome's self-presentation in coins, public festivals, buildings, and literature written by elite authors emphasized Rome as chosen by the gods. Jupiter had chosen Rome to manifest the gods' will and blessing throughout the earth. The genealogy's concern with God's purposes contests those claims and offers an alternative. God's purposes are displayed through Israel and Jesus, not Rome.

The genealogy establishes that God intends life for all people, not only the empire's privileged elite. The opening verse ("the book of the origin") evokes God's life-giving act of creation (Genesis 1). Abraham recalls God's declaration of blessing through him for all the nations of the earth (Gen. 12:1-3), a promise elaborated in terms of fertility, food, health, and safety in the covenant blessings of Deuteronomy 28–29. Linking Jesus to David recalls the kingly tradition that was to represent God's reign, justice, and protection for the vulnerable (Psalm 72). The genealogy also uses a common technique in the ancient world involving numbers to emphasize David's importance. The number fourteen, which structures the three sets of fourteen generations, underlines David's importance (1:17). The numerical value of the consonants in David's name in Hebrew adds up to fourteen.

The genealogy demonstrates that God's purposes are wide and inclusive, embracing gentiles (Ur, Babylon) and Jews (Israel, Judah), men and women (five in 1:3, 5-6, 16), the celebrated (Abraham, David) and the nobodies that even the tradition has forgotten (1:3b-4, 13-15), the powerful (kings) and those on the cultural margins (the women). Nor is God bound by human structures such as imperial power (Babylon), patriarchy (the women), or primogeniture (Isaac not Ishmael; Jacob not Esau). God is not confined by human boxes.

▌ THE TEXT IN THE INTERPRETIVE TRADITION

At least two issues have dominated interpretive discussions. Interpreters have long noticed that Matthew's genealogy differs significantly from that of Luke 3:23-38. Tertullian explained the difference by claiming that Matthew offers Mary's genealogy while Luke provides Joseph's. Others have tried to distinguish between a "natural" genealogy and a "legal" genealogy, though which Gospel offers which continued to be debated. Both approaches are unsatisfactory because they do not recognize the theological and narrative functions of the genealogy.

As christological debates and formulations unfolded through the second to fifth centuries, interpreters read the genealogy as underscoring the humanity of Jesus. It showed the birth of the human Jesus. John Chrysostom saw the marvel of the incarnation in observing the skeletons that rattled in

Jesus' closet. These rattling ancestors included sinful characters such as the women, Judah who had sex with an apparent prostitute (his daughter-in-law Tamar), and the adulterer David.

▋The Text in Contemporary Discussion

The genealogy is often regarded as irrelevant for contemporary congregations and is not often utilized in preaching. Yet it contains important perspectives both for the Gospel narrative as a whole and as a subsection of the Gospel.

For example, every name evokes a story of encounter with God and a role in the divine scheme. What emerges from these individual stories is a mosaic attesting that God's work embraces all people through diverse circumstances: faithfulness or sinfulness (many of the kings in 1:6b-11 were unfaithful to the vision of kingship in Psalm 72) or gender (male and female) or ethnicity (Jew and gentile) or imperial power (Babylon cannot thwart God's faithfulness, 1:11-12) or even anonymity when some of the characters, especially in verses 12-15, are unknown. Human sinfulness and assertions of imperial power are caught up in, but cannot derail, God's faithful efforts to be with God's people and enact God's will. Preaching and informed Bible study can explore these numerous stories.

The presence of the women, unusual but not unique in ancient genealogies, provides another point of connection. They also underline God's inclusive and unconventional ways of working. The naming of Tamar (1:3; cf. Genesis 38), Rahab (1:5; cf. Joshua 2), Ruth (1:5; cf. Ruth), the wife of Uriah (Bathsheba, 1:6; 2 Samuel 11–12), and Mary (1:16) disrupt the pervasive and patriarchal "*a was the father of b*" pattern. Why are they included? Numerous suggestions have included their gentile origins or connections, and unconventional sexual roles (Tamar, seducer; also Ruth; Rahab, prostitute; Bathsheba, adulterer; Mary, pregnant virgin) that bypass and even threaten conventional patriarchal structures. They occupy socially marginal and often culturally powerless locations in which they exercise initiative and participate in God's plans. They often exhibit faithfulness lacking from their attendant males (Levine 1998, 340–41).

Matthew 1:18—2:23: Jesus' Conception, Commission, and Vulnerability

▋The Text in Its Ancient Context

Framed by the theological context of the genealogy, the Gospel story commences with the conception, commissioning, and endangerment of Jesus as God's agent (Carter 2000, 66–89).

First, Jesus is conceived at God's initiative. Twice Mary's pregnancy is attributed to the Spirit (1:18, 20), and twice she is said to be pregnant before having sex with Joseph (1:18, 25). Stories of miraculous conceptions involving divine power circulated about great conquering military men and rulers such as Alexander "the Great" and the emperor Augustus. Jesus is placed among heroes, though for very different reasons (Horsley).

Second, God commissions Jesus as the agent of God's purposes. Named "Jesus," he is to save from sin (1:21) and, as Emmanuel, to manifest God's presence (1:23). As God's chosen agent ("son," 2:15), Jesus joins and exceeds other agents such as Moses (5:21-22), David (22:42-43), Solomon

(12:42), as well as chosen places such as the temple (12:6). He also contests Roman claims to be the designated agent of divine purposes, will, and blessings among humans (Carter 2001, 57–107).

Third, the Scriptures interpret Jesus. Five times (1:22-23; 2:5-6, 15, 17-18, 23), the narrator stops the action to underscore God's shaping of events by quoting the Hebrew Bible. Four of these instances involve prophets: Isaiah (1:22-23), Micah (2:5-6), Hosea (2:15), Jeremiah (2:18). The fifth is attributed to the collective entity of "the prophets," with no one particular source able to be identified (2:23). The citations do not mean that prophets predicted events in Jesus' life or his messianic identity centuries ago. None of these texts mentions a messiah. Rather, the prophets addressed a word from the Lord to circumstances in their own time. Matthew, reading with "Jesus-glasses," sees God doing similar things in Jesus' life and uses Hebrew Scriptures to interpret his significance.

Fourth, Jesus is opposed by King Herod. Herod ruled Judea as Rome's client king and agent of Rome's interests. Introducing both Herod (2:1) and Jesus (2:2) as kings sets up the conflict. Herod uses various methods typical of an imperial tyrant to eliminate Jesus as a threat to his and Roman interests. He gains information from his allies, the Jerusalem leaders (the chief priests and scribes; 2:3-6). He tries to turn the magi into spies (2:7-8). He tells lies, claiming that he wants to pay homage to Jesus (2:8). He tries to kill Jesus (2:13), creating misery in killing all the male babies two years and under in the vicinity of Bethlehem (2:16-18). His attempts are thwarted by divine intervention through an angel and dreams (2:13). He dies, an event the narrative attests three times by way of emphasizing God's protection of Jesus and God's purposes being worked out through him (2:15, 19, 20). The threat of imperial power to Jesus continues with Herod's son Archelaus (2:22).

Fifth, the magi and a star witness to Jesus. The gentile magi "from the East" are astrologers, interpreting events in relation to the stars. Stars were commonly associated with important events or the births of important figures such as emperors (Augustus, Nero). Magi often had some marginal and destabilizing role as political advisors. They come to pay homage to Jesus, thereby threatening Herod (2:2-3). They bring gifts for Jesus (2:11), which in Matthew's narrative recalls Hebrew Bible traditions of gentile homage in Jerusalem (Isaiah 60; Ps. 72:10-11). Their witness emphasizes Jesus' significance for gentiles and Jews.

And sixth, Jesus is protected from Herod by the righteous Joseph (1:19). In chapter 2, Joseph's righteousness comprises his receptivity in dreams to the angel's leading and his instant obedience (2:13-15, 19-21, 22). The narrative underscores his obedience by narrating his actions with wording almost identical to the angel's instructions.

▍ THE TEXT IN THE INTERPRETIVE TRADITION

This section has a rich interpretive history (Luz 2007, 89–131). The passage itself engages in reinterpretation of biblical texts, reading them in a new context in relation to Jesus. It also employs numerous echoes of the Moses story—killing male children, conflict with rulers, divine protection, Egypt—thereby linking Moses and Jesus.

In the church's history, Matthew's reading of Hebrew Bible texts in relation to Jesus has often provoked anti-Jewish attitudes in Christian readers. These citations have often been misread in mechanistic, predictive terms with prophets "obviously" referring to Jesus. Accordingly, when Jewish readers of the Hebrew Bible texts did not see references to Jesus, condemnations from Christians have been harsh. Martin Luther, for instance, fumes about "obstinate damned Jews" who did not see Isa. 7:14 (addressing an eighth-century-BCE crisis with Assyria) as a reference to Jesus. As with many readers, Luther fails to see Matt. 1:22 and all Matthew's citations of the Hebrew Bible as distinctively Christian readings.

Mary's conception has been much debated. The Roman Catholic tradition has defended her perpetual virginity, while Protestant interpreters have noted Matt. 13:55's references to Jesus' brothers and sisters. Other interpreters have read this verse in terms of Joseph's children from another marriage (Epiphanius), or cousins (Jerome).

Since the Enlightenment, Mary's virgin birth has been both strongly defended by those who understand God to intervene in human history to accomplish anything and dismissed as improbable by rationalists and those committed to cause-and-effect historical inquiry. The latter can, nevertheless, find meaning in the narrative in terms of God's gracious initiative of the events of Jesus' life.

The magi have spawned extensive traditions (Powell, 131–84). They have been turned into kings, numbered (three? twelve?), named (in the sixth century), celebrated in festivals (thirteen days after Jesus' birth: Augustine), and paid homage in a Middle Ages cult of relics and devotion that was opposed by the Reformers. Their gifts have been interpreted christologically (gold for kingship, frankincense for high priesthood or divinity, myrrh for humanness or death) or as denoting discipleship qualities (variously, prayer, faith, good works, reason, mercy, etc.).

■ THE TEXT IN CONTEMPORARY DISCUSSION

Often read around the Christmas season, this rich text counters popular sentimentality and materialism with a profound theological claim ("God is with us"), a christological revelation of Jesus as agent of God's saving presence, examples of faithful discipleship (Joseph, the magi), and a warning that empires always strike back, resisting to death divine efforts for a transformed world (Herod).

Matthew 3:1—4:16: Witnessed to by John and the Scriptures, Tempted by the Devil

■ THE TEXT IN ITS ANCIENT CONTEXT

Chapters 1–2 have introduced Jesus and his mission as agent of God's saving presence (1:21-23). He is initiated and commissioned by God, interpreted by (as he interprets) the Scriptures, opposed by Herod, ignored by the Jerusalem leaders, attested to by a star and the gentile magi, and protected by Joseph. This section continues to prepare for his public ministry (Carter 2000, 90–116).

In 3:1-12, John the Baptizer appears, a popular prophet, like others in the first-century Judean context (Taylor). His mission is to purify people in preparation for God's coming reign and the agent of that reign. Isaiah 40:3, originally a reference echoing the exodus to describe God's saving the Babylonian exiles, is reinterpreted to sanction John's work. Perceiving life in Rome's empire to be inconsonant with God's empire/kingdom, John demands repentance (3:2), expressed, at least initially, in the cleansing sign-action of baptism (3:6).

His ministry, oriented to God's empire, is opposed by Pharisees and Sadducees. The phrase "coming for baptism" is much more adequately translated "coming against baptism." The exchange is ugly, with John's harsh rebuke and threat of divine judgment (3:7-10). These groups, with the chief priests and scribes (2:4), constitute the religious-societal leaders who, as allies and retainers of Rome, embody a societal vision and practices that Jesus contests throughout. Their presence may reflect post-70-CE debates over societal practices such as observance of the Sabbath, food purity, and interactions with gentiles. The scene ends with John witnessing to Jesus as the dispenser of the Spirit and eschatological judge (Murphy). The Gospel emphasizes the latter role, with Jesus as the agent of God's judgment of a world ruled by Rome, which is allied with the Jerusalem leaders (e.g., 25:31-46).

In 3:13-17, Jesus appears as an adult. His baptism by John is presented as a revelatory occasion with the "heavens opened" (compare Ezek. 1:1-2), the Spirit descending on him, and God speaking (which happens again in 17:5). God endorses Jesus as God's agent or beloved Son, empowered and sanctioned to carry out the mission of manifesting God's saving presence (1:21-23). For first-century readers, the language of "son" employs Hebrew Bible language denoting God's people (Hos. 11:1) and kings (Ps. 2:7) as representatives or agents of God's will. It does not yet bear the high christological meanings that will develop in subsequent centuries.

As God's agent/son, Jesus demonstrates loyalty to God by resisting the devil (4:1-11). Numerous Jewish traditions attest the devil as tempter. The central issue concerns whether Jesus will remain faithful to his identity as God's son/agent (3:17; 4:3, 6), or whether he will be directed by the devil. Even when the temptation has a noble end—turning stones into bread—the issue remains one of authorization. The third temptation positions the devil as the power in control of Rome's empire. Though not the Gospel's only statement about the empire, it is nevertheless an important perspective for Jesus-followers who live in the Roman Empire. While the empire claims to be chosen by the gods (as Jupiter) to manifest their blessings and worldwide rule, this temptation scene "reveals" that the actual power "behind the throne" is the devil. Jesus-followers are cautioned to be careful in ascribing absolute power to the empire.

Witnessed to by John, sanctioned by God, tempted by the devil, Jesus is now interpreted and legitimated by the Scriptures (4:12-16). Prompted by John's arrest (unelaborated until 14:1-12), Jesus withdraws to Galilee and Capernaum in Zebulon and Naphtali. These regions, bearing the names of two Israelite tribes, were land allocations in the promised land (Josh. 19:10-16, 32-39). Jesus thus withdraws to territory that the tradition attests God had given and over which God should have sovereignty. Now Galilee is "of the Gentiles" (4:15). The genitive case indicates possession and suggests translations such as "Galilee under the Gentiles" or "Galilee possessed by the Gentiles." The gentiles are Rome, whose world is described as "darkness" and "death." The citation from Isa. 9:1-2 referred, in the eighth century, to Assyrian domination. Matthew reads it in relation to Roman control and deliverance ("light") in Jesus, the eschatological judge.

▌ THE TEXT IN THE INTERPRETIVE TRADITION

Two of the scenes, Jesus' baptism and his temptation, have presented interpreters with significant challenges (Luz 2007, 133–60). Mark's Gospel narrates Jesus' baptism as a revelatory event without explanation or rationale. Matthew's addition of the dispute between John and Jesus over who should baptize whom (3:14-15) reflects concern or embarrassment among Jesus' followers over Jesus' submission to John, and the implication of Jesus' need for forgiveness. Matthew's solution is to present the event as enacting the divine will and saving action ("fulfill all righteousness"). Subsequent interpreters found the scene difficult for high Christologies, rejecting notions that Jesus the eternal Son was adopted as God's Son at baptism or that the fully incarnated eternal Logos was somehow devoid of the Spirit until baptism. Others, like Calvin, saw the scene witnessing to the triune God with Father, Son, and Spirit acting in concert, with the revelation of Jesus' Sonship not for his benefit but as a public witness. The problem of course is that Matthew presents the revelation of the Spirit's presence as something Jesus alone sees (3:16) even while recasting the heavenly voice. Mark's private word to Jesus ("You are my Son, the Beloved," Mark 1:11) becomes in Matthew a public announcement ("this is my Son, the Beloved").

Interpreters have, predictably, connected the scene with the ecclesial practice of baptism. Ignatius saw Jesus purifying water. Augustine celebrated the connection of water and word. In Eastern traditions, epiphany became the occasion for baptisms. Interestingly, the New Testament writers do not make the argument that believers should imitate Jesus in being baptized. Some have seen this absence as indicating, using the criterion of dissimilarity, the historicity of Jesus' baptism. (The criterion of dissimilarity has been used by scholars questing for the historical Jesus; it states in its classic form that if an action or saying is dissimilar to Jewish culture and to early church practice or teaching, the saying or action probably derives from Jesus.)

■ THE TEXT IN CONTEMPORARY DISCUSSION

The scenes in this section can be difficult for contemporary readers looking for ready guidance for daily living. John the Baptist can seem to us to be something of a caricature: weird and remote, involving anger issues, bad wardrobe, and an obsession with judgment. Clearly Matthew's presentation takes him very seriously. The temptation scene with the devil is also difficult for some readers, many of whom have not found quoting Bible verses to be an effective strategy for countering temptations.

A more useful reading strategy might be found in understanding the scene's roles in the unfolding narrative of the Gospel. Each scene underscores aspects of Jesus' mission and identity in preparation for his public ministry, which begins in 4:17.

Part 2: Jesus' Public Ministry Begins (Matthew 4:17—11:1)

A new section begins with the transitional statement that "from that time, Jesus began to preach . . ." (4:17). In this section Jesus commences his public ministry (Carter 2000, 119-27).

Matthew 4:17—5:48: God's Empire Displayed in Jesus' Actions and Teaching

■ THE TEXT IN ITS ANCIENT CONTEXT

Jesus declares that "the kingdom/empire of the heavens has come near" (4:17, author's translation; cf. 3:2). The term "kingdom/empire" is also used to denote Rome's rule. Jewish traditions used the image of rule to celebrate God delivering God's people (Psalms 47; 72). Here it expresses Jesus' commission to manifest God's saving presence (1:21-23). This reign originates in God's domain, heaven (cf. 6:10); the verb "come near" tensively holds together nearness and arrival.

The following two scenes illustrate the disruptive and restorative impact of God's rule/empire. In 4:18-22, it overturns the lives of four fishermen embedded in the empire's socioeconomic structures of a fishing economy, providing new allegiance, mission, and community (Hanson and Oakman, 106–10). Then Jesus heals numerous sick people (4:23-25). The sick embody the damage of imperial structures, especially elite control on food supply whereby the powerful few ate well while many struggled for regular adequate nutrition, resulting in diseases of deficiency and contagion. God's reign, manifested in Jesus' healings, restores wholeness and anticipates the physical wholeness of the eschaton.

Having enacted God's grace in calling disciples, Jesus instructs them (5:1-2) in the Sermon on the Mount (chs. 5–7; Betz; Patte). The sermon's placement after their call is decisive for its interpretation as an identity-forming, practice-shaping discourse. God's empire (5:3, 10, 19-20; 6:10, 33; 7:21) provides the central image of this first of five major teaching blocks (chs. 5–7; 10; 13; 18; 24–25). Its setting on an unidentified mountain evokes God's giving of the Decalogue to Moses on Mt. Sinai. Other traditions anticipated the establishment of God's reign over all nations at Mt. Zion (Isa. 2:3).

The sermon opens with nine beatitudes or blessings (5:3-12). Beatitudes were common in Greco-Roman writings and in Jewish wisdom and apocalyptic texts. They are not concerned with individual feelings and emotions. The inaccurate translation "Happy are" makes these declarations into the "Be-Happy attitudes." Rather, they announce God's favor on certain situations and actions (see Ps. 1:1-2), both present and future, when God reverses and transforms current injustice (Hanson). They reassure people experiencing distress that God's favor is with them.

They also function to exhort human actions consistent with God's favor. They thereby identify actions characteristic of the community of disciples. These situations (being poor) and practices (being merciful) are commonly not those valued by the Roman elite. Hence a countercultural quality to the community of disciples contests and challenges the status quo.

The first four beatitudes (5:3-6), shaped by Isa. 61:1-3, name situations of oppression and distress in which God's just and transforming favor is already manifested in Jesus' ministry, in anticipation of the future transformation in the eschatological completion of God's purposes. Specifically, these four beatitudes identify God's transformation of the destructive sociopolitical, economic, and religious consequences of Roman rule. The "poor in spirit" are not to be spiritualized. They are the literal poor whose material poverty has crushed their very being (e.g., 4:23-25). They mourn their desperate circumstances. The meek are not what contemporary culture would consider "wimps," but are, in Jesus' citation of Ps. 37:11, 22, 29, the powerless poor who trust God to deliver them from "the wicked" (elite control) by inheriting the basic resource of land. They hunger for justice, transformed societal structures, and access to life-giving resources. They will not be disappointed at the completion of God's purposes.

The second group of five beatitudes (5:7-12) moves from God's reversal of these circumstances to human actions that enact God's purposes. Acts of mercy, integrity of action and worship (evoking

Ps. 24:4), peacemaking and nonviolent dissent from Roman rule, and enduring the backlash result in divine approval and participation in God's good reign (line two of each beatitude).

Two further images of discipleship follow, in 5:13-16. Salt flavors, purifies, transforms. Light, used in 4:15-16 to describe Jesus' manifesting God's saving presence and reign, now describes the continuing lifestyle and mission of the community of disciples.

Six further examples of the actions of "exceeding justice/righteousness" that God's empire shapes follow in 5:17-48. Verses 17-20 indicate that these examples are consistent with and do not abolish "the law and the prophets." Accordingly, the six scenes in 5:21-48 are not antitheses, where Jesus quotes from the biblical tradition and then abolishes it. Rather, he quotes the passage and interprets it. He instructs disciples to be a reconciled community (5:21-26), to curb male lust and power concerning adultery and divorce in a patriarchal society (5:27-32), to speak trustworthy words (5:33-37), to employ active, nonviolent resistance to evil (5:38-42; Wink), and to love neighbors and enemies (5:43-48).

▌The Text in the Interpretive Tradition

Debates about the sermon's meaning have been extensive (Luz 2007, 161–294). Does it offer an impossible ideal, thereby provoking repentance? Is it an interim demand until the kingdom comes in full? Or does it shape discipleship, as Anabaptist traditions, for example, have argued? Particular scenes have caused much controversy especially in relation to other parts of the Gospel. For example, how does the prohibition of divorce cohere with the mercy of new relationships (5:7; 9:13; 12:7)? How does the scathing attack on Jewish leaders in chapter 23 display love for enemies?

▌The Text in Contemporary Discussion

This rich sequence challenges contemporary readers to careful reading, informed reflection, and communal action. If the sermon is practicable, how are contemporary Jesus-followers to live the practices shaped by the identity of being salt and light, of the Beatitudes, or of the examples in 5:21-48? For example, the renouncing of violence in 5:38-42 and urging of love for enemies in 5:43-48 offer the church a practice that is out-of-step with the aggressive assertion of personal will and military power typical of our world. To embody this teaching requires both a firm witness to this alternative, nonviolent practice matched by pragmatic efforts for justice that remove occasions for violence.

Matthew 6:1—7:29: Jesus Continues Teaching on the Mountain

▌The Text in Its Ancient Context

The sermon continues in these two rich chapters (Carter 2000, 158–95; 2007, 8–35). The first section (6:1-18) assumes three conventional Jewish acts of "justice" (misleadingly translated in verse 1 as "piety").

Verse 1 establishes the basic principle. Disciples live for God's approval, not public approval. First-century values of honor and shame required public displays of beneficence by wealthy elite members (funding food distributions, buildings, festivals). These "honorable" actions enhanced power and societal status. Disciples do not imitate this value system.

The first act of justice concerns almsgiving or acts of mercy (the root meaning of the Greek word; 6:2-4; cf. 5:7). Almsgiving was a normal part of Jewish faithfulness (Prov. 25:21-22). The negative example of blowing a trumpet is a caricature (6:2). The polemical tone may suggest strained relationships with synagogues. The "how-to-do-it" of 6:3-4 presents acts of mercy as normative and uncalculated in enacting God's redistributive justice through providing resources for all.

The second act of justice concerns prayer (6:5-15). Matthew 6:5-6 contrasts prayer with the false practice of public performance; 6:7-15 contrasts prayer with a false theology comprising unknowing, uncaring, and vain gods, manipulated by repetition and verbosity. Many gentiles would rightly protest this polemical caricature. Disciples, by contrast, engage God as a knowing and caring Father (6:8; Sheffield) and align themselves with God's purposes for the world.

The Lord's Prayer sets out these purposes (6:9-13). The first petition, hallowing or sanctifying God's name, concerns God's saving will (Lev. 22:31-32; Ezek. 36:22-38). The parallel petition, "Your kingdom/empire come," similarly asks God to accomplish God's life-giving and just reign in Rome's world. Jesus enacts this mission (4:17), as do disciples (10:7-8). This is the doing of God's will, which shapes "earth" in accord with God's domain, heaven (6:10).

The fourth petition requests God's provision of food that is "necessary for existence" (the difficult word translated "daily"). God's forgiveness requires forgiveness of others (6:12, 14-15). The "testing" petition of 6:13 concerns perhaps general temptation, or deliverance from eschatological woes, or God's overcoming of all evil in transforming the world.

The third act of justice concerns fasting (6:16-18). How is divine, not societal, approval gained through fasting? Isaiah 58 emphasizes that fasting participates in the struggle against societal injustice by doing God's will.

The second major section (6:19-34) concerns justice and materialism. Previously, the destructive impact of Rome's empire has been evident on the poor, who are deprived of access to adequate resources (5:3-6). And disciples have been instructed to do economic justice in the three acts of 6:1-18. Now they are warned against pursuit of and distraction by material things (6:19-21), exhorted to focus on God's empire (6:22-23), alerted to the incompatibility of serving God and wealth (6:24), and urged to rely on God's provision of daily necessities (6:25-34).

The third section highlights three characteristics of discipleship. Disciples are to embody compassionate correction, not condemnation (7:1-6), persistent prayer (7:7-11), and indiscriminate love for all as the key interpretation of the biblical tradition (7:12). This "golden rule" exists in both positive and negative forms in various ancient cultures.

The fourth section (7:13-27) contextualizes discipleship in God's future. This eschatological goal provides incentive (reward/inclusion, not punishment/exclusion) and perspective on the present. So 7:13-14 adapts the common "two ways" metaphor (Deut. 30:15-20) to underscore the countercultural way of discipleship. Verses 15-23 warn against false prophets, urge attention to their lifestyle, and provide assurance of their final condemnation. And verses 24-27 contrast two responses to (doing/not doing) and two eschatological consequences (of vindication/condemnation) Jesus' teaching. Verses 28-29 note the crowds' positive responses (cf. 5:1-2) and contrast Jesus' teaching with that of the scribes.

The Text in the Interpretive Tradition

The interpretive traditions concerning this material are extensive (Luz 2007, 295–397). The Lord's Prayer has been used in personal piety (the *Didache* instructs its use three times a day), communal worship, and teaching, both as a summary of doctrine in catechesis and for ethical instruction. Interpretive questions have explored whether the prayer is answered by God's actions alone, or through the actions of disciples, or a partnership of both. Is the prayer answered in the present or in the eschatological future, when God's purposes are finally established?

The passage on trusting God to provide (6:19-34) has posed substantial difficulties. Many in the Matthean world knew degrees of poverty, and hence God's lack of provision, a situation repeated throughout history. The passage has seemed simplistic and naive. Others have found it to exhort laziness, at odds with the apostolic command to work (2 Thess. 3:8-12). Yet others, some hermits, have interpreted it literally—giving away possessions, not working, and not providing for the future. Some have spiritualized it to say that God meets spiritual needs. Others have interpreted it to permit possessions, but focus on their use in almsgiving. Others have read it as forbidding worry about earthly matters but legitimating concern over heavenly matters. Verse 34 has been central for some in pointing to a way of life focused on God's kingdom/empire, a way that is an alternative to seeking security in things, careers, and cultural conformity.

The Text in Contemporary Discussion

Contemporary interpreters interact with this text in a number of productive and often difficult ways. Attention to economic justice, for example, is pressing in a global village where many lack adequate resources. For rich Christians, the petition for daily bread (6:11), for example, recognizes this lack because of human greed, misuse of power, and unjust access to and distribution of resources. The petition, then, counters greed and incessant questing for "more stuff." It requires appropriate actions of redistribution and disinvestment. Along similar lines, we can note the use of debt forgiveness as a strategy of international justice.

Some have experienced "dis-ease" with the eschatological judgment of 7:13-27. Matthew regularly ends teaching blocks with eschatological threats and rewards. For some, this "bullying" tactic imitates the strategy of the empire and stands at odds with the Gospel vision of God's indiscriminate love (5:45).

Matthew 8:1—9:38: God's Empire Displayed in Jesus' Actions

The Text in Its Ancient Context

After three chapters of teaching, chapters 8–9 present Jesus' actions (Carter 2000, 196–231). Miracles dominate with six healings—leprosy (8:1-4), paralysis (2×; 8:5-13; 9:2-8), fever (8:14-15), hemorrhage (9:20-22), blindness (9:27-31)—two exorcisms (8:28-34; 9:32-34), a rescue-epiphany (8:23-27), and a raising from the dead (9:18-26). Two summary passages (8:16; 9:35-36) indicate widespread preaching, healing, and exorcism (Wainwright). There are also dialogue scenes about discipleship—faith (8:9-12), the cost of following (8:18-22), calling (9:9), eating with the marginalized (9:10-13), and not fasting (9:14-17). A well-established tradition of itinerant teachers and miracle workers exists from the ancient world (Meier, 509–1038).

Five perspectives on Jesus' actions emerge.

1. His actions express God's empire (8:11-12; 9:35). They enact his commission to manifest God's saving presence (1:21-23), elaborating the initial presentation of the impact of God's reign in 4:17-25 (proclamation, calling disciples, healing, exorcism). The Scripture citation of 8:17 confirms he does the divine will.

2. Three statements declare Jesus' purposes and motivation. In 9:13, citing Hos. 6:6, his actions perform mercy. In 9:16-17, his actions mean interactions between the old and the new. In 9:36, he enacts compassion for harassed and afflicted people.

3. These displays of the transforming power and wholeness that God's empire effects interfere with and repair Rome's world. A centurion cannot heal his servant (8:5-13). And the demon-possessed empire, depicted by demons named after the central unit of the Roman army, the "Legion," faces inevitable destruction: the boar was the mascot of the tenth Fretensis legion, which played a key role in Jerusalem's defeat in 70 CE (8:28-34). The destruction of the demon-controlled pigs in the sea depicts God's sovereignty and portends Rome's eventual destruction.

4. Elites oppose Jesus. Town leaders ask him to leave (8:34). Scribes (retainers) deny that his ministry enacts God's authority (9:3). Pharisees question his association with "tax collectors and sinners" (9:11) and declare he is the devil's agent, not God's (9:34). Jesus echoes the indictment of Israel's leaders in Ezekiel 34 for failing to provide for the poor and weak. He laments that the Rome-allied Jerusalem leaders oppress, rather than provide for, the people (9:36).

5. By contrast, the marginalized and broken receive Jesus' ministry positively in being healed and exorcized.

Miracle stories dominate the chapter. The prevalence of the sick and demon-possessed is not surprising, given a context of disease-promoting social conditions such as urban and rural squalor, poor water supply, limited medical knowledge, poor nutrition, diseases of deficiency and contagion, overwork, and tough daily living conditions. The miracle scenes often follow a predictable four-fold form. An introduction assembles participants (Jesus, crowd, distressed person) and narrates a respectful request for Jesus' help. Verbal exchanges often elaborate the distress or involve conflict. The miracle takes place, involving touch or word, distance, and a report or demonstration. The scene's conclusion can involve wonder, dismissal, an alternative explanation, secrecy, or spreading the news.

Miracle stories function to demonstrate God's power in a Roman world in which inhabitants experienced the powers of numerous gods and goddesses. They also manifest compassion in a context in which many understood ailments to result from sin, the devil and demons, angry gods, and hostile people. God's empire rules over all forces in compassionate and transformative ways. The emphasis on somatic wholeness anticipates the final transformation effected by God's reign (11:2-6). In the meantime, healings and exorcisms enact the blessing of God's empire on the poor (5:3), transforming destructive economic circumstances (no work, poverty), social isolation, political oppression, and religious marginalization.

▌THE TEXT IN THE INTERPRETIVE TRADITION

Interpretive questions have commonly centered on the nature of miracles (Luz 2001, 1–65). While some readers have readily accepted the stories as accurate accounts of actual events, numerous others have not done so. The latter have adopted various interpretive strategies. Rationalists have looked for natural explanations of events. Others have declared all life to be miraculous, but failed to account for the distinctiveness of miracles. A dominant line has spiritualized the scenes, overlooking the physical or social in favor of spiritual lessons. So Augustine saw in 8:1-5 a man freed from "spiritual leprosy" or the mortal sin of not observing the Sermon on the Mount. The centurion of 8:5-13 exhibits true humility and faith (Chrysostom). For Luther and other Protestant Reformers, the physical healing of the paralyzed man (9:2-8) recedes before the word of forgiving grace understood in antithesis to legalism and works. The raising of the dead daughter (9:18-26) anticipates Jesus' resurrection. On the basis of Romans 11:25-32, she and the hemorrhaging woman have represented the inclusion of both gentiles and Jews in salvation history.

A similar symbolizing strategy has been used for the storm scene in 8:23-27 (Bornkamm). Since Tertullian, this story has been read as depicting the church tossed about by various crises but assured of Jesus' protective presence. Another line of interpretation comprises an individualistic reading with the boat as the human heart that Jesus enters.

▌THE TEXT IN CONTEMPORARY DISCUSSION

Miracle stories remain contentious in contemporary faith communities. Those who read them literally and/or claim contemporary miracles face the challenge of explaining their relative dearth in contemporary society. Hospitals remain full, and most dead people remain so. Those who reject the narrated events and experiences as actual events, but nevertheless find "spiritual" significance in the scenes, face the challenge of explaining why God's healing or liberative action might be experienced spiritually but not materially or somatically. In a faith tradition that affirms the importance of the material and somatic from the perspectives of both creation and incarnation, this ready dismissal of the somatic requires examination.

The emerging discipline of disability studies seeks, among other things, to honor the suffering and physical challenges of people, past and present, whom the Gospel often presents as "photo ops" for the larger christological and theological agenda. This approach, along with imperial-critical studies that locate the Gospel's numerous sick and demon-possessed in a context of imperial power, at least moves attention to responses of compassion and justice (9:13). Jesus' description of his imperial world as "harassed and helpless" by illegitimate leaders and structures (9:36) points similarly toward transformative actions.

Matthew 10:1—11:1: Mission Work for Disciples

▌THE TEXT IN ITS ANCIENT CONTEXT

Jesus has manifested his God-given commission to disclose God's saving presence in calling and teaching disciples (chs. 5–7) and in various, especially miraculous, actions (chs. 8–9). In chapter

10, the mission discourse, Jesus elaborates for disciples their call to mission from 4:19 ("fish for people") and 5:13-16 (salt, light). The ancient world knew numerous individuals and nations who were on missions. Israel was to be God's light to the nations (Isa. 49:6). Zeus sends itinerant Cynic teachers (Epictetus, *Diatr.* 3.22.19–26). The poet Virgil presents Jupiter giving "empire without end" to Rome to be "lords of the world" (*Aen.* 1.254–82) and to "crown peace with justice, to spare the vanquished, and to crush the proud" (*Aen.* 6.851–53).

The disciples' mission continues Jesus' manifestation of God's empire (Carter 2000, 232–46). So in 10:1-4, Jesus calls a community of twelve "apostles" (the only use of "apostle" in Matthew). Peter is named first. Jesus commissions them to continue his mission of repairing imperial damage through proclamation, exorcism, and healing (10:1, 7-8). The community is apostolic in being "sent out" in mission (10:2).

The second section (10:5-15) identifies four aspects of their mission. Its arena is, at this point, Israel (10:5b-6). Its task is to continue Jesus' mission, proclaiming God's life-giving empire, and performing the transformative, miraculous actions Jesus performs in chapters 8–9 (10:7-8a). Their material support is minimal. They give without payment or profit, traveling inconspicuously, being vulnerable and sustained by recipients (10:8b-10). And the impact of the disciples' mission is both positive and negative (10:11-15).

The third section (10:16-23) underscores the challenge of God's empire to the vested interests of the powerful and of households (10:17-22). Suffering and persecution are inevitable consequences. Mission means danger. The image of sheep among wolves (10:16) picks up Jesus' "sheep" description of 9:36, which evoked Ezek. 34:5, 10, where the people are food for "wild beasts," consumed by their rapacious leaders (Matt. 10:17-18). Faithful endurance, sustained by "the Spirit of your Father," is required (10:20-22) until the son of man returns (10:23).

The fourth section identifies the courage, impact, and reward of faithful mission (10:24-42). As Jesus was resisted, so are disciples (10:24-31). But disciples can "fear not" (10:26, 28, 31) because God rules the future (10:28, 32) and the present (10:29-31). The mission's exclusive loyalty to Jesus disrupts households (10:34-39). Yet some will be receptive and vindicated in the judgment (10:40-42).

This mission discourse underscores key features of the community of disciples. As a mission community commanded by Jesus, it imitates and continues his mission. Disciples do so in poverty, single-mindedness, itinerancy, vulnerability, and interdependence. They engage society, neither fleeing from it nor accepting imperial society as normative. Mission comprises transformative practices of proclamation, healing, and exorcisms. It is not a sporadic or optional activity but is central to the community's identity and practice. It requires courage, hope, and conviction about its life-and-death importance in the face of resistance and persecution. The existence of persecution highlights its contestive and conflictual nature.

▌ THE TEXT IN THE INTERPRETIVE TRADITION

This chapter has provoked numerous debates as interpreters have read it in circumstances that differ greatly from its original context concerning itinerant preachers (Luz 2001, 66–128).

In the Reformation and Counter-Reformation, for example, Catholics understood the placement of Peter first in the list of apostles (10:2) as an indication of his superior qualities or merits, and thus found support for the primacy of the papacy. Protestant interpreters have maintained the view (drawing on Chrysostom, from the fourth century) that the placement reflects only Peter's call as the first disciple (4:18-22) and says nothing about his merits or authority.

The restriction of the mission to Israel (10:5-6) stands in contradiction to the Gospel's final command to "Go therefore and make disciples of all nations" (28:19). Some have explained the difference by arguing that 10:5-6 originated from the historical Jesus (pre-Easter) while 28:19 originated from an early believing community some time after Jesus' resurrection (a post-Easter community). Others have seen a reflection of a struggle in the Matthean community between Jewish members favoring mission to Israel, and a growing gentile presence supporting gentile mission. The inclusion of both statements reconciles and endorses both missions. Others have seen the verses reflecting not a community struggle but a succession in the narrative. That is, there is a narrative movement from an initial mission to Israel, in chapter 10, that is subsequently expanded, after the resurrection in chapter 28, into the wider world.

The very difficult instruction in 10:9-10 concerning mission, marked by poverty and defenselessness and unencumbered by money, bag, spare tunic, sandals, or staff has received various interpretations. Some have obeyed it literally. According to one source, St. Francis of Assisi is said to have thrown away his shoes after reading these verses. There is also a long tradition that avoids a literal reading and diminishes the severity of the demands by using the verses in polemic against opponents, especially against their (presumed) pride and greed. The verses also appear in debates over whether clergy should be paid, and if so, how much. Luther supported some modest payment; Calvin disagreed.

The chapter underscores frequent rejection of the mission, hostility to it, and division of households over it. How are disciples to respond? Clearly they are to endure (10:22), even embracing martyrdom (10:28). But how are they to treat hostile and hurtful responders? How are the actions of social (10:14) and eschatological (10:32) reprisals consistent with the demand of love for enemies (5:44)?

■ THE TEXT IN CONTEMPORARY DISCUSSION

The assertion of the church's identity and practice as a mission community challenges all images and practices of contemporary mainline and emerging churches (Luz 1994, 39–55). At least since the Reformation, the marks of the one, holy, apostolic, and catholic church have comprised word (preaching) and sacrament (baptism, Eucharist). But here the marks of the church comprise mission, powerlessness, vulnerability, poverty, suffering. For Matthew, the church is about actions consistent with the mission and qualities of Jesus. The chapter points churches in this direction. In societies where creature comforts, wealth, security, power, and status are so important, this chapter offers the massive challenge for churches to be always moving obediently to embrace active, countercultural mission for others.

Part 3: Responses to Jesus' Ministry (Matthew 11:2—16:20)

Chapter 11 begins the Gospel's third section (11:2—16:20), which narrates a growing division of responses to Jesus' ministry (11:1; Carter 2000, 249–79). The section is bookended with two scenes that pose the question of Jesus' identity (11:3; 16:13). Increasing opposition emerges from scribes and Pharisees (12:2, 14, 24, 38). Along with the issue of Jesus' identity is that of his societal vision and claim to reveal God's will. The section has been understood to reflect a post-70 context of conflict between Jesus-followers and other synagogue members.

Matthew 11:2—12:50: Discerning and Responding to Jesus' Mission and Identity

▌ THE TEXT IN ITS ANCIENT CONTEXT

The opening scene provides both the central question and the means of answering it (11:2-6). Jesus responds to John's disciples by summarizing his activity from chapters 8–9 and evoking visions from Isaiah of a society shaped by God's life-giving reign/empire (Isa. 26:19; 29:18-19; 35:5-6; 42:7; 61:1). Jesus favors the marginalized, repairs elite-inflicted damage, and creates new social participation. Those who perceive his identity and activity as manifesting God's saving presence and empire are blessed (11:6).

In 11:7-15, Jesus asks the crowds six rapid-fire questions about John. The point is that understanding John's mission (3:1-12) prepares one, through repentance and understanding, to receive Jesus. Negative responses, however, dominate, with John misunderstood as demonic (11:18) and Jesus rejected as not God's faithful or wise son (11:19; Deutsch). Jesus curses the unrepentant Galilean towns of Chorazin and Bethsaida, which cannot see the significance of Jesus' actions (11:20-24).

Yet some receive his revelation. Verses 25-27 affirm his identity and role as revealer of God based in intimate relationship of Father and Son. They also affirm, despite 11:20-24, that the "infants" or lowly, the weary and burdened, accept his yoke (God's reign rather than Rome's) and find "rest" (11:28-30; Carter 2001, 108–29). By contrast, the subsequent narrative shows the "wise and intelligent" (powerful leaders and elite) not receiving him.

Chapter 12 opens with rejection. Two scenes concern whether procuring food and healing are acceptable Sabbath practices. Pharisees, retainers in the imperial system with a societal vision extending temple practice to everyday life, protest. The issue is not whether one party observes Sabbath or not, but *how* Sabbath is honored—by mercy (12:7) and doing good (12:12), or by rest, as God did? Anticipating Jesus' passion, they plan to kill him (12:14).

More responses concerning the authority and origin of Jesus' ministry follow. Matthew now applies Isa. 42:1-4, a text originally declaring Israel as God's servant and light to the nations in the midst of the Babylonian Empire, to Jesus' activity in Rome's empire (12:15-21). An exorcism/healing produces three verdicts: from the crowds (Son of David, 12:23), the Pharisees (the devil, 12:24), and Jesus (12:25-37). Scribes and Pharisees demand a sign despite Jesus' previous actions

(12:38-42). Jesus identifies these leaders as an "evil generation." The chapter ends with Jesus identifying true followers, or "family," as those who do God's will, which he reveals.

◼ THE TEXT IN THE INTERPRETIVE TRADITION

Among the interpretive challenges of these chapters (Luz 2001, 129–227), one has concerned the "violence" statement in 11:12. Challenges in translating this verse have produced different meanings. One understanding is that the kingdom is aggressively (violently) breaking in and people readily seize it. Another reading sees violence inflicted on the kingdom as people aggressively embrace its proclamation. A variation of this reading sees gentile believers stealing the kingdom from Israel. Both readings, though, are unsatisfactory, because the verb and noun denoting violence and the violent usually have negative associations.

Another reading sees the kingdom suffering because violent people like Zealots blasphemously co-opt it and force God's hand. This reading, though, ignores the saying's context in chapter 11. A more convincing, fourth reading understands the language and the context to refer to opponents of John, Jesus, and disciples as agents of the kingdom (3:2; 4:17; 10:7-8). Opponents include synagogues, governors, kings (Herod), leaders, and households (10:17-18, 21, 34-36; 12:14).

Matthew 11:27 featured in the fourth-century Arian christological controversy. Arians understood the claim that God had "handed over" all things to the Son to indicate a time when "all things" had not been delivered to him, thereby denying the eternal divinity of the Son. The orthodox either dismissed the reading, thereby preserving a trinitarian understanding, or with Athanasius, saw the handing over as the moment when the eternal Logos became incarnate in the human Christ. Others, notably nineteenth-century Protestant exegetes, abandoned any trinitarian framework to focus on the historical Jesus' special insight into or consciousness of God's plan of salvation.

In 12:32, Jesus declares speaking against the Holy Spirit unforgivable. Interpreters have suggested three explanations for what this speaking consists of. Some see it as denying the divinity of Christ. Others see it as sins committed by Christians despite good knowledge of God's will. And others, such as Augustine, understand it as resisting the unity of church, an especially useful interpretation for denouncing heretics.

◼ THE TEXT IN CONTEMPORARY DISCUSSION

A concern with unforgivable sin remains ongoing among some people. Concern over whether one has committed the unforgivable sin usually indicates one has not. In Matthew's context, its primary sense seems to involve a sustained refusal to see the Spirit at work in Jesus in manifesting God's saving presence and empire (3:16-17).

While conflict between Jesus and the leaders increases in the narrative, Christian readers must be careful not to perpetuate anti-Jewish sentiments and practices in interpretations. Jesus' association of the resisting leaders with demons in 12:43-45 is one such instance. Related to this matter is the understanding that all leaders in the Gospel (Pharisees, priests) are not accurately identified as "religious" leaders akin to contemporary clergy. Rather, they are societal leaders. Their conflicts with Jesus do not involve merely "religious" questions but matters of societal visions and practices.

The Sabbath controversies raise questions about Sunday observance among contemporary believers. In an age of shopping, sports, entertainment, family events, and seven-days-a-week work, in what sense is the day "honored"?

Matthew 13:1-58: Explaining Different Responses to Jesus

■ THE TEXT IN ITS ANCIENT CONTEXT

Chapter 13 comprises seven parables as Jesus addresses alternatively disciples and crowds (Carter 2001, 280–300). Parables were a familiar form in the Hebrew Bible (2 Sam. 12:1-4: the ewe lamb; Ezek. 17:2-21), rabbinic literature, and collections such as Aesop's fables. The word *parable* literally means to "throw something alongside," indicating a comparison in which one thing—God's empire—is compared to the situation of the subsequent, short narrative.

The parables in chapter 13 interpret the division increasingly evident in responses to Jesus in chapters 11–12. While some people discern Jesus' identity as the agent of God's saving presence and empire, others—especially powerful leaders—do not. The parables explain why this division occurs. The lack of receptivity derives not from failure on God's part but from human sinfulness and the devil's activity. The parables also affirm the Gospel audience's welcoming response and further illumine God's empire.

The opening section features the parable of the seed and soils and an allegorical explanation (13:1-23). The sower is compared to Jesus proclaiming God's empire (the seed). Three-quarters of the seed falls on unproductive ground and produces nothing because of the evil one (13:19), opposition (13:21), and the "cares of the world and the lure of wealth" (13:22). These three factors explain in part the dominant negative response to Jesus' ministry. Only a quarter of the seed finds receptive people (13:23).

The second section (13:24-43) comprises three parables. The parable of the weeds and wheat, interpreted allegorically in 13:36-43, depicts God's empire coexisting in Jesus' ministry with evil/the devil (and the devil's agents). Disruptive weeds, sown by the devil, grow together until the final harvest/divine victory.

The parable offers another reason that some/many do not respond positively. They fail to recognize a "now but not yet" dynamic. God's empire is present in part but not yet fully.

The mustard seed (13:31-32) offers a further explanation, namely, the strange and mysterious nature of the reign's present manifestation. The mustard seed denotes invisibility (is anything happening under the ground?), contrast (small seed, big shrub), continuity or inevitability (the seed becomes a shrub), and growth (it takes time). These features describe the present state yet also the future goal of God's work, explaining why some/many fail to see it, but assuring disciples of God's work.

A third parable repeats these factors (13:33). God's reign, like yeast or leaven, works over time, in a hidden manner, yet its transforming work continues inexorably.

A further section (13:44-50) presents three final parables. In the parable of hidden treasure, the focus moves from a contrast of small beginnings and cosmic completion to a person's encounter with the empire. Searching, joy, setting aside all else, commitment, and disruption of priorities mark the encounter, and confirm its great value. The pearl offers a similar experience. The repetition underscores the point (13:45-46). The parable of the fishnet rehearses emphases from the weeds and the wheat. Evil coexists with God's empire, as do negative and positive responses until the final division and God's triumph (13:47-48).

The chapter ends with a rejection scene (13:54-58). People in Jesus' hometown wonder about his teachings, actions, and origin, but cannot recognize God's commission. The scene enacts the rejection that the parables explain.

▌ THE TEXT IN THE INTERPRETIVE TRADITION

One theme that emerges in the diverse and multivalent interpretations of the parables concerns how God works in the church and world (Luz 2001, 228–304). Some interpreters of the sower/seed/soil parable, for example, emphasized the quality of the soil in exhorting lives receptive to the gospel. Others, such as Luther in the Reformation, emphasized the truth of the word sown by preachers even when it does not produce fruit, thereby encouraging disheartened preachers. Some interpretations of the mustard seed equated God's kingdom with the church in its growth to dominance, while others understood the seed as Christ or the preached word at work in an individual.

Interpreters of the wheat and weeds parable have variously understood the field or arena of God's activity to comprise an individual, the church, and the world (cf. 13:38). The weeds have been understood as specific heresy existing alongside the pure doctrine of the church, or the presence of evil coexisting with the gospel, or the presence of sinners within the church. What is to be done about them, and what is the role of church discipline? Chrysostom offers that heretics should be expelled but not killed. Others saw the parable justifying religious wars against enemies (Aquinas). Others saw it justifying patience in recognizing God's role in judgment. Others saw the parable urging a restrained and realistic use of church discipline, and recognizing the futility of expecting a perfect church. People should be wheat and produce good fruit in faithful living.

▌ THE TEXT IN CONTEMPORARY DISCUSSION

Current questions of what, how, and where we understand God to be active in the church and in the world are live ones. Some pieties understand God to be active in arranging all sorts of personal matters and circumstances on a daily basis. When things do not work out well, it is not a matter of divine inactivity but an opportunity to trust and learn whatever God is teaching the individual. The larger world is largely not in view.

Other pieties take a more global perspective and understand themselves to be active partners with God's life-giving and just work in the world. The challenge here often comes with the recognition that, despite much effort, injustice and human needs seem to continue unabated. This situation raises questions about both the power and the will of God. Is God uncaring and/or powerless in the face of vast human need? Why does God's reign not seem more evident? Matthew's chapter offers a range of perspectives on God's current activity, simultaneously recognizing human resistance or indifference, God's persistent and faithful activity in the midst of the world, and the certainty of God's eschatological completion.

Matthew 14:1-36: God's Empire at Work

■ The Text in Its Ancient Context

The emphasis on discerning Jesus' identity and God-given mission to manifest God's saving presence and reign (1:21-23; 4:17) continues in the four scenes of chapter 14 (Carter 2000, 301–13). First, God's empire arouses opposition from Rome's client ruler Herod, who was tetrarch of Galilee until 39 ce (14:1-12). Then Jesus attests the fertility and abundance of God's reign in a feeding (14:13-21). He demonstrates his identity as God's agent in walking on water (14:22-33). He exhibits the healing, restorative work of God's empire in more healings (14:34-36). That is, the divisive effect of his ministry continues. The powerful Herod rejects God's work, the crowds benefit from feeding and healing, and the disciples receive the disclosure of Jesus' identity as God's agent or son (14:33).

The Herod scene elaborates the brief references in 4:12 and 11:2 to John's arrest and imprisonment. John is arrested and executed because of his prophetic criticism of Herod's liaison with Herodias, wife of Herod's brother Philip. Given the close allying of John and Jesus in relation to God's empire (3:2; 4:17), Herod's action against John is consonant with the negative or hostile responses to God's work that are depicted in the divisions in the parables of chapter 13 (between weeds and wheat; different kinds of fish), and in the rejection of Jesus in his home town at the end of chapter 13 (13:54-58).

It is also consonant with the Gospel depiction of kings and rulers as opposing God's work—the disobedient kings of 1:6-11, Herod (ch. 2), Archelaus (2:22), persecuting governors and kings (10:18), the great men of the gentiles (20:25-26), and Pilate and his Jerusalem allies (27:11-26). The powerful elite protect their interests and societal structures against God's empire and its agents. They do so characteristically with violence, as Herod (2:16) and his sons Archelaus (2:22) and Herod Antipas (14:1-12) demonstrate. By contrast, the martyred John remains faithful (10:28).

After the extravagant and violent, elite birthday feast with its grotesque image of John's head on a platter, the next scene presents Jesus compassionately enacting God's will to feed hungry people (Isa. 58:6-7). The act echoes Moses and the exodus wilderness feeding. It also addresses the social reality that a significant proportion of the population struggled for adequate nutrition. And it anticipates the final establishment of God's reign, marked by fertility and abundant food for all (Isa. 25:6-10; Matt. 8:11; 22:1-10).

With the disciples in a boat (14:22), Jesus performs more Godlike actions. He again calms stormy seas (Exod. 14–15; Ps. 69:1-3, 30-36; cf. Matt. 8:23-27) and walks on water (Job 9:8; Ps. 77:16-20). These acts demonstrate God's control over the waters (Gen. 1:6-10) and contest an imperial tradition in which emperors claim sovereignty over land and sea. They also demonstrate God's concern for disciples battered by the storm. Peter imitates Jesus walking on the water, exhibiting both faith and unbelief, and evoking Psalm 69, a psalm of deliverance. The scene ends with the storm calmed and the disciples' confession, for the first time in the Gospel, of Jesus' identity as God's agent (14:33).

The chapter closes with another summary scene of Jesus' healings (14:34-36).

◼ THE TEXT IN THE INTERPRETIVE TRADITION

The scene of Herod's execution of John has drawn attention in various ways (Luz 2001, 305–24). Numerous artists have depicted John's head on the platter. Ironically, it is Herodias's daughter (unnamed in Matthew's version) who has often received attention. Some writers, including Chrysostom and Ambrose, were drawn to yet appalled by her dancing. They dwell on her voluptuous and seductive movement but are equally sure that her dancing is sinful and/or provokes sin. A nineteenth-century tradition gives the daughter a makeover, freeing her from ecclesial condemnation in (re-)presenting her with positive sensuality, in love with John, and appalled at his execution (Oscar Wilde; Richard Strauss). Both images are, of course, fantasies created by men that focus on sexuality, while ignoring other dimensions such as the scene's murderous assertion of imperial power.

Interpretations of the feeding story have often found ways to avoid taking seriously the literal feeding of people. Some interpreters, highlighting echoes of Moses and the wilderness journeys, read it in supersessionist terms of salvation history. The five loaves represent the five books of the Torah, and the twelve baskets represent the apostles. Jesus transforms the tradition into life-giving spiritual food. Another line of interpretation, including a number of current interpreters, reads it as a eucharistic scene, noticing the similarities between the distribution of 14:18-19 and the Last Supper scene of 26:26-27. Yet another approach has extended both lines in an ecclesiological interpretation that sees the disciples as priests or pastors in mediating Christ's benefits and the Eucharist to the laity. Such readings ignore the feeding of people's bodies.

◼ THE TEXT IN CONTEMPORARY DISCUSSION

What does contemporary discipleship look like? This chapter offers various vignettes of discipleship shaped by God's reign. John, for example, loses his head for courageously speaking truth to power. He remains faithful to his word in the face of life-and-death opposition. His speech in the midst of evil embodies dynamics depicted in the parables of chapter 13. And his disciples display their own courage and loyalty, honoring him in burial. Jesus' disciples serve food to the people. Peter emerges from the group of disciples with an initiative that imitates Jesus in walking on the water. In responding to Jesus' command (14:28-29), he courageously and obediently trusts Jesus' word to forsake the safety of the boat and undertake a task that seems impossible. Having started well, however, his faith gives way to fear and doubt, and Peter the rock sinks like a stone. He knows enough, though, to cry out in the words of a psalm of deliverance and experiences rescue through Jesus. In turn, his experience and the calming of the storm provide the occasion for a revelation of Jesus' identity and the disciples' confession. What contemporary situations and experiences do such vignettes address, and how do they shape authentic discipleship?

Matthew 15:1—16:20: Jesus' Authority as God's Agent

◼ THE TEXT IN ITS ANCIENT CONTEXT

Disclosure, conflict, and confession continue (Carter 2000, 314–37). Jesus reveals his authority and identity as God's agent (15:1-20; 16:13-20). He dispenses God's wholeness and abundance to a Canaanite woman's daughter, in healings, and in another feeding (15:21-39). He conflicts with scribes, Pharisees, and Sadducees from Jerusalem (15:1; 16:1-12). Peter confesses Jesus' identity (16:13-20).

Jesus' opponents constitute an alliance of groups with some status, political power, and wealth. Sadducees, absent since 3:7, and scribes, legal agents and interpreters of traditions, have not recognized Jesus' identity (2:4; 12:38). The Pharisees participate in the ruling group centered on the Jerusalem temple and allied with chief priests and Rome's governor (15:1). They have some political power and a religious-societal vision involving table companions (9:11), Sabbath observance (12:1-14), hand-washing (15:2), and support for the temple (15:3-7). They think Jesus is an agent of the devil (9:34; 12:24) and want to kill him (12:14).

Jesus reciprocates the antagonism. He disparages their traditions as "human precepts" contrary to "the commandment" and "word of God" (15:3, 6, 9). He rebukes them for teaching that gifts to God (priests and temple) void parental support (15:5). He declares them to be leaders not sanctioned by God (15:13), blind and unreliable guides (15:14). He accuses them of majoring on minor matters (hand-washing) while ignoring disruptive societal practices (murder, theft, slander; 15:19).

In 16:1-12, things deteriorate when the Pharisees and Sadducees ask Jesus again for a sign (cf. 12:38-42). Their repeated demand shows an unwillingness to listen and learn. Verse 1 presents this request negatively, as a "test." The temptation scene uses the same verb when the devil tempts or tests Jesus (4:1, 3). They thus behave as the devil, tempting Jesus to address their demands rather than maintain his allegiance to God. Jesus rebukes them for failing to discern God's saving presence and empire in his activity. Jesus calls them evil (16:4), the same term he uses for the devil (6:13). They, like Rome (4:8), are agents of the devil.

Jesus follows up this nasty polemic by warning the disciples against the Pharisees' and Sadducees' teaching (16:5-12). Given their position as political-societal leaders, this warning embraces more than limited religious questions. Jesus warns against the societal structures and practices that they uphold.

Between these conflict scenes, Jesus blesses the crowds with further healings (15:29-31) and a feeding (15:32-39). He displays God's care for physical well-being, repairing damage inflicted by imperial structures through inadequate availability of land and food, and diseases of deprivation and contagion. Two confessional scenes—the Canaanite woman who successfully seeks mercy from Jesus for her demon-possessed daughter (15:21-28; Ringe 1985; Levine 2001) and Peter's confession of Jesus as "Messiah, the Son of the Living God" (16:16; cf. 14:33)—counterbalance the conflicts. The section 11:2—16:20 has depicted growing division in response to Jesus' activity.

■ THE TEXT IN THE INTERPRETIVE TRADITION

Perhaps there is no more significant a passage for the disunity of the worldwide church than 16:13-20 (Luz 2001, 325–77). Peter confesses Jesus' messianic identity. Jesus blesses him, announces this answer to be divinely revealed, declares that "on this rock I will build my church," and assigns to him "the keys of the kingdom of heaven" (16:16-19). The interpretive issues, discussion, and tradition are immense; space permits only a brief naming.

One question concerns whether, in confessing Jesus' identity (16:16), Peter functions as a representative or ideal spokesperson for all disciples (appealing to the previous confession of 14:33), or has a unique and preeminent role (appealing to 4:18; 10:2; and 16:18).

Another concerns the meaning of "on this rock" in verse 18. Does it refer to Christ himself or to Peter? Augustine argued for Christ, appealing to 1 Cor. 3:11 and 10:4, among other passages. If it refers to Peter, in what role? One view emphasizes Peter as representative of all believers, particularly in confessing Jesus' identity. This line was favored initially by Origen and Tertullian, and was developed by Reformers like Zwingli and Melanchthon in arguing against the papacy. Another option focused on Peter the model bishop and head of the church succeeded by bishops of Rome. This option had clearly emerged by the mid-third century in relation to the bishop of Rome; in the fifth century, it was developed by Leo the Great in arguing that Peter is present in the bishops of Rome as his successors.

A third issue concerns the identity of the "keys" in verse 19. Does this refer to the authority of the pope and the church (for example, forgiveness from sins and the sacrament of penance) or, as in Protestant interpretation, to preaching and communal confession that reflects Peter's confession?

These centuries-old interpretive debates, of course, continue to influence contemporary ecclesial traditions and practices.

▋THE TEXT IN CONTEMPORARY DISCUSSION

In this rich section is the story of the Canaanite woman who successfully overcomes Jesus' initial indifference and procures healing for her demon-possessed daughter and commendation for her faith. Troubling, though, is both the disciples' (15:23) and Jesus' reluctance to assist a non-Israelite woman (15:24), despite substantial traditions about God's blessing for all people (e.g., Abraham, Gen. 12:1-3). Worse, Jesus dismisses her in a demeaning and sexist fashion by calling her a dog (15:26). As one contemporary commentator has observed, Jesus is caught with his compassion down. Yet despite this treatment, the woman refuses to be humiliated, perseveres, and outwits Jesus in verbal sparring as she turns his metaphor back on him. She affirms Israel's temporal priority in God's purposes along with their universal and inclusive reach (15:27). This "teachable moment" for Jesus results in healing and commendation for this gentile woman's daughter.

The text has proved disturbing for readers who impose on it later christological formulations of Jesus' divinity. Some deny any poor treatment of the woman or that Jesus has anything to learn. Other readers recognize a difficult yet intriguing text, which displays courageous faith and, eventually, inclusive divine mercy.

Part 4: Jesus Will Be Crucified and Raised
(Matthew 16:21—20:34)

The Gospel's fourth major section begins in 16:21 (Carter 2000, 341–60). God has commissioned Jesus to manifest God's saving presence and reign (1:1—4:16). Jesus enacts that commission in his words and actions (4:17—11:1). Responses of division and conflict follow (11:2—16:20). Now, the narrative establishes that Jesus' commission involves his death by Jerusalem's ruling elite and his resurrection by God (16:21—20:34).

Matthew 16:21—17:24: The Way of the Cross for Jesus and Disciples

▌ THE TEXT IN ITS ANCIENT CONTEXT

Jesus' announcement of his imminent suffering in 16:21 provides a plot summary for the rest of the Gospel. His confrontation with the alliance of power in Jerusalem is the inevitable consequence of challenging the status quo with an alternative vision and practices. Yet his opponents do not have the final word or ultimate power. God will raise him from the dead. The understanding of resurrection as God's vindication of those who suffer faithfully, even to death, emerged in the second century BCE under the tyranny of Antiochus Epiphanes (Dan. 12:1-3; 1 Macc. 1–2; 2 Maccabees 7).

Jesus' death has implications for disciples. Peter, the hero of the previous scene, rejects Jesus' teaching; Jesus allies him with the devil against God (16:22-23). Jesus also declares that disciples walk the way of the cross, thereby specifying how he will die (16:24). Crucifixion was a shameful form of execution reserved for those who challenged the imperial status quo. Jesus calls his followers to discipleship of this same style and consequence, continuing his mission until his return (16:27-28).

The transfiguration scene confirms Jesus' instruction in two ways (17:1-8). First, Jesus appears in glory, foreshadowing his resurrection and return (cf. 17:2 and 13:43). Second, God speaks, repeating the intimate blessing from Jesus' baptism (3:17), but adding a key clause, "listen to him" (17:5). With this imperative, God confirms Jesus' disclosure of his forthcoming death, resurrection, and return, and his teaching about discipleship as the way of the cross.

Jesus performs his final exorcism (17:14-20) after the disciples' faith fails in the face of Satan's reign. They are unable to manifest God's liberating and merciful empire, despite Jesus' commission to them (10:8). Jesus again predicts death and resurrection in Jerusalem (17:22-23). The repetition underscores its importance.

The chapter ends with an enigmatic scene about taxes (Carter 2001, 130–44). In the Gospel's post-70-CE context, the scene instructs Matthew's audience to pay an imperial tax (17:24-27). After Rome's destruction of Jerusalem, the emperor Vespasian imposed a humiliating and punitive tax on Jews as a defeated people. Vespasian co-opted the temple tax and used it to rebuild and maintain the temple of Jupiter Capitolinus in Rome, the sponsoring deity of Rome's victory in 70 CE. The scene instructs disciples to pay the tax, though with an understanding that—for disciples in the know—it subverts Roman claims of sovereignty and asserts God's sovereignty. Jesus' instruction in verse 27, about catching the fish and finding in its mouth the tax coin, evokes and counters imperial claims that Rome's sovereignty subdued even wild animals and fish. Jesus' instruction reasserts God's sovereignty over God's creation, represented by the fish (8:23-27; 14:13-21; 15:32-39). God supplies the tax. It is paid to Rome. For disciples in the know, it testifies subversively to God's sovereignty.

▌ THE TEXT IN THE INTERPRETIVE TRADITION

Jesus' statement in 16:28 promises his return before some of his generation die (Luz 2001, 378–420). Various interpretations have arisen to account for its nonfulfillment. The *Gospel of Thomas* (log.

1) individualizes and spiritualizes the saying by claiming that those who understand Jesus' words do not die. An extensive tradition found its fulfillment in the transfiguration scene that immediately follows with the "some" comprising Peter, James, and John. Among the Reformers, it was common to interpret the resurrection as attesting Jesus "coming in his kingdom" (Luther, Calvin, Bucer). For nineteenth-century interpreters, one way of avoiding the problem of Jesus' reliability was to declare that it was not an authentic saying of Jesus.

Not surprisingly, many interpreters understood the transfiguration story as a revelation of, and therefore a confirmation of, the church's subsequent elevated christological teaching regarding Jesus' divine being. Another tradition, though, has seen it as a scene in which believers participate. In believers, too, the glory of God's reign is present, and in Jesus' experience is prefigured the eschatological experience of transformation.

▌The Text in Contemporary Discussion

This passage contains provocative and disparate material about discipleship. The call to self-denial in 16:24 has often been understood to negate the world and personal, somatic existence that God created and declared to be good. As recently as 15:29-39, Jesus has demonstrated in his healings and feeding God's commitment to physical, created, somatic well-being and flourishing. Yet as Bonhoeffer rightly observes, following Jesus requires a way of life out of step with dominant cultural values. To "take up the cross" (16:24) is to commit to a way of life that does not conform to, but challenges, self-serving societal and personal practices and structures. Hence Jesus does not remain transfigured but comes down the mountain (17:9-13) and repeats his declaration about going to Jerusalem to be killed (17:22-23).

Yet such a life is not monolithic in cultural opposition. The chapter recognizes the humanness of disciples (17:19-20). It also includes the scene about paying taxes. Disciples are to pay taxes that signify submission to Roman rule, yet the story reframes them so that payment simultaneously signifies covert dissent. Taxes for contemporary disciples do not necessarily represent submission to ruling power, but they do provide funding for governmental programs that followers of Jesus might decide are contrary to Jesus' teaching. The military provides a center of concern, causing some contemporary followers to withhold or redirect a percentage of taxes as a sign that simultaneously expresses cooperation and dissent.

The juxtaposition of such material indicates the complexities and challenges of discipleship, and the need for communities of discourse to discern together appropriate and intentional practices of faithfulness.

Matthew 18:1-35: A Community of Sustaining Relationships and Practices

▌The Text in Its Ancient Context

Jesus has declared that the way of discipleship is the way of the cross (16:24). The image immediately locates disciples committed to God's empire/reign in the difficult societal place of both being at cross-purposes with Roman power, while also simultaneously accommodating its demands (17:24-27). How, then, to live?

Chapter 18 constitutes the Gospel's fourth block of teaching material (see chs. 5–7, 10, 13; Carter 2000, 361–75). Known as the community discourse, it establishes that the difficult and ambiguous way of the cross is communal. This life is constituted as, and sustained by, a network of practices and interdependent relationships. These practices emerge in Jesus' teaching throughout the chapter.

The first section names humbleness as basic practice among disciples (18:1-5). Empires and "greatness" form a natural pair. Alexander "the Great" and Rome's Pompey "the Great" personified greatness in terms of power (through military subjugation), privileged birth, wealth, office, and status. Jesus rejects such a definition, replacing it with the humbleness of the child (18:4). If we define "child" in terms of our contemporary values—children are pure and innocent—we miss the point. In the ancient world, children were understood to be insignificant nobodies, vulnerable, powerless, and defenseless. By some estimates half died by age ten. They lacked status and resources and were often regarded as unpredictable, even threatening. Matthew 2, particularly verses 13-18, shows children vulnerable in a dangerous political world. They are further depicted as sick (8:6; 9:2), hungry (14:21), demon-possessed (15:22; 17:18), and dead (9:18). The community of disciples knows vulnerability and powerlessness, but also mutual support and protection.

Moreover, disciples do not cause one another to stumble nor despise one another (18:6-9, 10-14; Loader, 20–36). Aware of God's protection through guardian angels, they are vigilant in communal interactions that reflect God's valuing of and vigilance for each one. God, like a shepherd, lovingly searches for any that "go astray" (18:10-14).

Such interactions do not mean, though, that disciples always agree with one another. Verses 15-20 recognize the reality that among human beings, especially among a hard-pressed community, conflict and offense are inevitable (Duling). Typical of numerous groups in the ancient world, the verses set out a general process of communal accountability involving reproof and restoration. The one who is wronged initiates the process with the offender (18:15), perhaps involving witnesses (18:16) and the church (18:17). To be treated as "a Gentile and a tax collector" is not to be shunned but to be the object of restorative efforts that are ratified by God (18:18-20). Verses 21-22 confirm the limitless commitment to reconciliation and forgiveness.

The emphasis on the practice of forgiveness continues with the parable of the unforgiving servant (18:23-35). The point is straightforward in establishing forgiveness as a communal norm— God's forgiveness requires disciples to forgive one another. But the parable sits uneasily here. Verses 21-22 exhort forgiveness, but the parable depicts its opposite with two examples of not forgiving! The king takes back the forgiveness he initially offered (18:27, 32-34), and the forgiven slave refuses to forgive another slave (18:28-30). The parable warns that not forgiving means the loss of God's forgiveness (cf. 6:14-15).

The discourse exhorts a network of community relationships and practices among disciples marked by humble receptivity to the other, mutual support and active respect, accountability, relentless commitment to reconciliation, and repeated forgiveness. Such a communal life sustains and embodies vulnerable discipleship on the way of the cross.

■ THE TEXT IN THE INTERPRETIVE TRADITION

This chapter as a whole has not often played a significant role in discussions about "marks" of the church (Luz 2001, 421–83). The commonly accepted marks of the church—whether "one, holy, catholic, and apostolic," or preaching and sacraments—do not, in and of themselves, highlight the relationships, practices, and structures evident in this chapter.

Yet while the chapter's relative lack of influence as a whole is evident, significant interpretive discussions about many of its subsections exist. Its most striking image concerns the repeated instructions to cut off the hand, foot, or eye if they cause one to stumble (18:8-9). Some have placed the saying in a tradition of ancient medical practice whereby people sacrificed a body part to ensure their own survival. Others note a link to torture and martyrdom traditions (cf. 2 Maccabees 7). Some, reading the passage in relation to Mark 9:43-48 and in the context of Matt. 18:1-5, have seen a warning to protect (literal) children from pederastic activity. Others have seen a more generalized, metaphorical reference that graphically exhorts self-protection against sinful behavior, whether one's own or of others such as evil friends. Another line of interpretation has seen the body imaging, as it commonly did in ancient thinking, an ecclesial or social context (akin to 1 Corinthians 12–14). On this reading, the "cutting off" refers to expelling offending members. There are, though, difficulties with this last reading. Matthew does not use the "body" image for the church, and verses 15-20 and 21-35 exhort reconciliation.

■ THE TEXT IN CONTEMPORARY DISCUSSION

This chapter's insistence on the central place of "church as community" in following Jesus challenges some contemporary understandings of discipleship. Some frame discipleship in terms of individual salvation and emphasize "my personal walk with the Lord" to such an extent that, in actuality, there is no place for or accountability to any community. While such individual understandings protect against manipulative communal practices, they have no room for the sort of humility, accountability, and interdependence envisioned in Matthew 18.

The chapter's vision also challenges ecclesial understandings that see the "true" church constituted by particular rituals, or structures of ministry, order and authority, or doctrinal tests, or positions on social issues. That is not to say these things do not matter; each aspect is important for ecclesial life. But in Matthew's vision, they do not matter as much as relational community that sustains and embodies disciples on the way of the cross. The chapter urges followers to nurture such communities.

Matthew 19–20: Alternative Households Shaped by God's Empire

■ THE TEXT IN ITS ANCIENT CONTEXT

Jesus has declared twice that he must walk the way of the cross (16:21; 17:22-23). In 19:1, he and his disciples leave Galilee for Jerusalem, where the ruling elite will execute him. Chapters 19–20 narrate the journey as he continues to instruct disciples about the way of the cross (Carter 2000, 376–410; Loader , 80–81, 102–20, 127–35).

The content of his instruction concerns household matters: marriage and divorce (19:3-12), children (19:13-15), wealth (19:16-30), a parable about a wealthy householder and day laborers (20:1-16), and being slaves (20:17-28), concluding with a healing story (20:29-34). Why this cluster of material on households?

Various philosophical traditions (Aristotelian, Stoic, neo-Pythagorean) as well as Hellenistic Judaism (first-century writers Philo and Josephus) understood the household as the basic unit of a city or empire. They envisioned ideal households as a microcosm of imperial society. Households were, then, to be patriarchal and androcentric, reflecting and constituting elite imperial society in privileging male "power over." The husband/father/master was to "rule over" wife/children/slaves. He provided the household's economic well-being and represented it in society.

Given this link between households and empires, Jesus' manifestation of "the empire of the heavens" predictably includes instruction on households. The Gospel imitates this cultural pattern, just as it continues to privilege male power in recognizing twelve special male disciples (among other disciple figures, including women). Yet simultaneously, it also contests this dynamic to some extent. The first scene, on divorce and remarriage, while maintaining a male perspective, limits male power in divorce (advocated by Pharisees "for any reason," 19:3) with a vision of "one flesh" reciprocity and mutuality (19:6) and by specifying only one situation of "unchastity" (Allison).

In 19:13-15, instead of maintaining the dismissal and insignificance of "little children" (practiced by disciples, 19:13), Jesus affirms their central place in God's empire (19:15). He identifies all disciples as children ("such as these," 19:14-15). He envisions the community of disciples as comprising only children (brothers and sisters, 12:46-50) and without "power-over" parental figures (18:1-5; 23:9). In 19:16-30, he endorses not the pursuit of wealth but its disinvestment. He instructs the rich man to divest himself of his household wealth and redistribute it to the poor (19:21). The poor, not the elite wealthy, have a special place in God's empire (19:24; cf. 5:3) in anticipation of the abundance of God's new age for all people (19:27-30).

A parable about a wealthy householder and day laborers exemplifies God's empire. It in part treats all people equally (20:12), reversing hierarchy. In 20:17-28, Jesus repeats his explanation about going to Jerusalem and co-opts the exploitative and humiliating image of being a slave to present himself acting for the benefit of others (20:28). His actions contrast those of his disciples and the "great men of the Gentiles" who seek power and "lord it over" others. Disciples are to imitate Jesus and seek each other's good (20:20-27).

The section ends with a display of transforming mercy in response to two determined (faith-full) blind men (20:29-34). The same mercy can empower disciples in unlearning cultural values and structures as they live into societally contestive household structures.

▌THE TEXT IN THE INTERPRETIVE TRADITION

Catholic and Protestant traditions have interpreted the teaching on divorce in 19:9 quite differently (Luz 2001, 484–551). Catholic interpretation has generally read the verse as forbidding divorce and remarriage (complementing 5:32), though recognizing that partners live apart. Protestant interpretation has increasingly come to accept divorce and remarriage without restrictions and increasingly without stigma, although some more conservative expressions are not supportive. The interpretive difficulties multiply. What does "unchastity" mean—adultery, or incestuous marriages as defined by Leviticus 18? Does it modify divorce alone or remarriage also?

The verse assumes a very different world of arranged marriages, younger participants, much shorter life spans, and patriarchal cultural assumptions that only women commit adultery and that men divorce. Contemporary expectations of loving, fulfilling, chosen relationships are not in view. Yet the Gospel values love in urging love for God and neighbor (22:37-39). It also knows the importance of mercy (9:13; 12:7), which surely means, among many things, not only empowering and transforming broken situations (forgiveness), but also the possibility of fresh starts that do not trap people in loveless relationships but sets them free for new life. The verse (19:9) does not seem to be informed by this rich Gospel thread of love and mercy, thereby creating an opportunity for interpreters to put verse and context into conversation.

The saying about eunuchs in 19:10-12 has been read, in the context of 19:3-9, as referring to divorced men who cannot remarry and produce children because of restrictions in verse 9 on remarriage. It has also been read in relation to subsequent ascetic practices of voluntary celibacy, and particularly priestly celibacy as a way of life shaped by God's reign.

▌The Text in Contemporary Discussion

The passage raises numerous issues: male power, gender roles, household and societal structures, and discipleship and cultural practices.

Two further brief comments can be made. The "ransom" saying (20:28) has informed a personal piety concerning Jesus' self-giving death "for me." A reading that points to a much broader societal scope for God's work is possible. The verse's language is plural ("for many"), and "ransom" language often evokes God redeeming or liberating people from imperial powers (Egyptian, Exod. 6:6; Deut. 7:8; Babylonian, Isa. 43:1). Jesus' death and resurrection expose the limits of Roman power and demonstrate God's life-giving work for the world.

Second, the Gospel's concern with wealth and the poor continues in 19:21. This instruction has been read literally, whereby the wealthy should give all their wealth away. The definition of "wealthy" is complex and contested. Interpretation has also moderated the demand to giving, not everything, but something to the poor (almsgiving) and has focused on attitudes to wealth. Clement of Alexandria argued that the threat is not possessions themselves, but emotional attachments to wealth, so the rich who are not attached to wealth can be saved. What do rich, comfortable Christians in a poor global village do with this verse?

Part 5: Jesus in Jerusalem: Conflict and Death (Matthew 21–27)

The Gospel's fifth section (chs. 21–27) centers on Jerusalem and Jesus' fatal conflict with the temple-based rulers allied with the Roman governor Pilate (Carter 2000, 413–31). What Jesus predicted three times now takes place (16:21; 17:22-23; 20:17-19).

Matthew 21: Conflict in Jerusalem

▌ THE TEXT IN ITS ANCIENT CONTEXT

The entry scene is full of irony, imitating celebratory imperial entry processions yet with an "antitriumphal" parody (21:1-11). It borrows features of entry processions that celebrated conquering generals or the arrival of governors and emperors in a city representing imperial grandeur and "power over" subjugated peoples: procession, crowds, hymns, temple worship. Yet it creates street theater to critique imperial practice and mind-set. Entry processions defined greatness in terms of military violence, defeat of enemies, power, plunder, and public gratitude. Jesus, though, rides not a war horse but a donkey, a poor person's working animal, yet also one that evokes the scene in Zech. 9:9 of God's eschatological king, establishing God's reign triumphantly over all enemies in Jerusalem on the Mount of Olives (Zechariah 14; Matt. 21:1, 4-5). Continuing ironically to mimic imperial ways even while reinscribing them, verse 9 reinforces this emphasis by quoting a Passover processional psalm celebrating God's victory over the nations (Ps. 118:10-18).

Jesus does not attack empty temple ritual or the futility of Jewish efforts to encounter God. Rather the scene focuses on the temple's economic practices, which Jesus deems exploitative, turning a place of prayer into a "den for robbers" (21:13; Hanson and Oakman, 99–159). He cites Isa. 56:7 and Jer. 7:11, which condemn injustice and envision just communities. The scribes and priests are angered by his action, healing (21:14), and appreciation from children (21:15-16). A cursed and withered fig tree symbolizes God's judgment on the temple (21:18-20; Jer. 8:12-13), the first of several explanations for Rome's destruction of it in 70 CE. Jesus envisions a different community marked by prayer and faithfulness (21:21-22).

The offended "chief priests and elders" initiate open conflict as they check Jesus' credentials (21:23-27). The conflict is between Jesus and the leaders, not between Jesus and Israel. He prevails in verbal sparring through posing the question of the origin and the legitimacy of John's baptism. To evaluate John is to evaluate Jesus (11:7-19). The chief priests and elders do not recognize either as commissioned by God.

Jesus counterattacks these societal leaders with three parables (the third comprising 22:1-14). Jesus introduces and ends the first parable, concerning two sons, with a question that requires their response (21:28, 31). They correctly identify the one who does his father's will. In so doing, they endorse an important emphasis in Jesus' teaching on obeying God's will (7:24-27; 12:46-50). They condemn themselves, though, as people who do not welcome God's agents—unlike the prostitutes and tax collectors (21:31-32).

The second parable—that of tenants who do not pay rent from a vineyard—interprets Jerusalem's fall to the Romans in 70 CE as punishment on the leaders' violent unfaithfulness in crucifying Jesus (21:33-43). The landowner planting a vineyard evokes the picture of God choosing Israel (Isa. 5:1-7). But the tenants refuse to pay the rent—the good and just works of obedient living—killing slaves (prophets) and the landowner's son (Jesus). The temple leaders correctly identify the tenants' eviction and replacement, thereby announcing their own penalty at the hands of the angry landowner (21:35-41). The vineyard (Israel) is not destroyed, but God replaces the leaders as tenants.

On realizing their condemnation by Jesus, "the chief priests and Pharisees" want to arrest Jesus (21:45-46).

THE TEXT IN THE INTERPRETIVE TRADITION

Across the church's history, interpretation of the chapter has emphasized God's rejection, not of the Jerusalem leaders as in the reading offered above, but the rejection of Israel as a whole from God's story of salvation (Luz 2005, 1–44). Regularly the chapter's scenes have been allegorized to underscore the passing of God's favor from Israel to the church. Even the entry-to-Jerusalem scene was so read. Justin and Origen interpreted the mother donkey as the sin-bound, law-yoked synagogue and the colt as gentiles who leave Jericho (the world) to enter the church (Mount of Olives) and the heavenly Jerusalem. The cloaks on the road are church dogma. In a twist uncommon in the Christian tradition, a few understood the mother donkey (Israel) to follow the colt; she too will enter the heavenly Jerusalem, though after the gentiles. Other interpretations, especially dramatic liturgical reenactments, emphasized Christ as the victorious king, anticipating the Easter victory over sin and death.

The cursed fruitless fig tree was similarly understood, from the second century on, as condemned Israel (not the temple as proposed above). Jesus' hunger depicted his unsatisfied yearning for faith in Israel. Likewise, the parable of the two sons was read, since Origen, as one of salvation history. The second son, who says "yes" but does not go, represents disobedient Jews or Israel (not only leaders), while the son who obeys represents gentiles. The parable of the vineyard was likewise interpreted as a story of Israel's rejection. Some, however, like Calvin, rejected such allegorization and read it as a warning to the church to produce fruit.

THE TEXT IN CONTEMPORARY DISCUSSION

Such interpretations of Christian Scriptures constitute a long, shameful, and tragic tradition of anti-Jewish attitude and practices among Christian groups that should not be forgotten, but should never be replicated. Such readings pose an ongoing challenge to Gospel readers. Has God forever abandoned Israel, revoking covenant with God's people? Has God withdrawn love and grace once and for all? It is both tragic, given the history of interpretation, and hopeful, for a different future, to recognize that these supersessionist or replacement readings are not inevitable or necessary. They can be interrupted. One option is to read against the grain. Another option is to formulate readings such as in the first section above that endorse not a general repudiation of Israel and breaking of covenant but a specific targeting of an institution (temple) and group (leaders).

This solution, though, remains imperfect because of a further issue, namely the notion of judgment that pervades the Gospel (7:24-27; 10:40-42; 13:47-50; 18:21-35; 25:31-46). God the householder acts like an imperial tyrant in destroying the leaders and their temple. The Gospel enacts the imperial practice of requiring acceptance of God's empire or else punishment follows for those who reject and defy. While verses like 5:45 depict God's mercy and goodness extending to all people, the Gospel is not convinced that God's mercy draws everyone into loving relationship with God. Hence judgment plays a significant role. Disturbingly, in this regard, the Gospel constructs God as acting like an emperor.

Matthew 22: Conflict over Jesus' Authority

■ THE TEXT IN ITS ANCIENT CONTEXT

The conflict between Jesus and the Jerusalem-based socioreligious leaders continues from chapter 21 (Carter 2000, 432–48).

The chapter's opening scene comprises the third of three parables Jesus tells against the "chief priests and Pharisees" (not all Israel). After the second parable, they want to arrest him, yet he continues the attack (21:45; 22:1). This parable, concerning rejected invitations to the wedding banquet of the king's son, rehearses the leaders' rejection of Jesus as God's agent and their judgment, enacted in Jerusalem's destruction in 70 CE. Banquets and eating often signal participation in God's purposes, including their full establishment (Prov. 9:1-2; Isa. 25:6-10; Matt. 8:11-12). The reference in verse 7 to the burning city is a particularly Matthean feature, missing from the Q version of Luke 14:21, interrupting the sequence between verses 5 and 8, and creating an improbable scenario of a banquet among the smoldering ashes of the burned city. Josephus records Jerusalem's burning in 70 CE (*J. W.* 6.249–408), and the city's fall was widely interpreted as divine punishment enacted by Rome. The reasons for the punishment differed (*2 Bar.* 1:1-5; *4 Ezra* 3:24-26); Matthew's is explicitly christological: the rejection of the Son. Verses 11-14 extend the reach of the judgment. Guests at the banquet who, once admitted, do not behave in a manner appropriate to that identity (they are not appropriately attired) are also excluded.

Verse 15 narrates the response of Pharisees. They now attempt to trap Jesus. Allied with Herodians, presumably supporters of the Herodian dynasty and Rome, they ask Jesus about tax payment to the emperor. The question is astute. Tax payment expressed submission to Roman rule over God's people and land. Refusal was serious dissent. Coins bore forbidden images of emperors. Most accommodated; a few openly resisted. Jesus dissembles, first not having the tax coin, then with a naive, perhaps mocking question, then with a riddle (21:21). What is the relationship of the two clauses? Does Jesus endorse paying the tax as part of the things of God, or, in privileging the second cause, as a strategy for removing the blasphemous and idolatrous coin from the land, or, reading the "and" in an adversative sense, does he disqualify payment because the land and people belong to God, not to the impostor Rome? It is indeed an amazing answer (22:22).

The conflict scene involves another power group, the Sadducees, and resurrection. Resurrection is not just a religious matter. The notion arose during the second century BCE in the context of the Seleucid tyrant Antiochus Epiphanes' martyrdoms of faithful followers of God's law (1 Maccabees 1-2; 2 Maccabees 7). Resurrection denoted God's faithful justice even through and beyond death. The Sadducees parody resurrection with a ridiculous scenario that utilizes the patriarchal structure of levirate marriage that was concerned to continue a dead man's name (Deut. 25:5-10). Jesus bests them rhetorically, declaring their errors both in their general rejection of resurrection and in their particular construction (22:29-34).

Further conflict follows with the Pharisees (22:34, 41), first in ranking the commandments, then concerning his identity as Messiah. The question about the greatest commandment *could* be a fair one. Various summaries of the tradition prioritize its requirements (Isa. 56:1; Mic. 6:8). But the verb "test" (22:35) recalls previous confrontational scenes (16:1; 19:3) and the devil's testing (4:1, 3).

Jesus' prioritizing of love for God and neighbor draws from the heart of the tradition, envisioning societal interaction at odds with an imperial, hierarchical social structure that favored a few. Unable to answer his question about Ps. 110:1, the Pharisees join the Sadducees in being silenced (22:34). Question time ends (22:46).

▌THE TEXT IN THE INTERPRETIVE TRADITION

The wedding-feast parable has most commonly, and troublingly, been read as another allegory of salvation history (Luz 2005, 45–91). On this reading, Jewish rejection of Jesus (refused invitations) means Israel's rejection by God from the covenant and from their status as God's chosen. Gentiles replace them (22:9-10) in a full wedding hall (22:10b), where there is no room any more for Israel.

While many interpreters have readily found judgment on Israel in 22:1-10, they have been less happy about finding it extended to the wedding guests in the added scene of 22:11-14. The debates are long-standing. Origen engaged the question of this display of God's rejecting anger. Luther called it a "terrible Gospel." The referent for the requisite "wedding robe" has been debated. Initially, the dominant reading identified it with good works, particularly works of love (Augustine). Others, though, saw it as baptism or Christ put on in baptism (Aquinas), or the Holy Spirit. The Reformers (Zwingli, Luther, Calvin) saw it as active faith expressed in works of love. This church-centered reading of 22:11-14 regards Israel's rejection (supposedly presented in 22:1-10) as providing a warning to the church.

▌THE TEXT IN CONTEMPORARY DISCUSSION

The tax-payment scene continues to raise the question of the relation of Jesus-followers to political and civic authority. A long tradition in both Catholic and Protestant traditions reads this scene through a division of responsibilities between the church (spiritual matters, rites and piety, word and Spirit) and civic authorities (civic and political order). However, such a division separates civic and political order from divine accountability as well as from the voices and input of Christian citizens who are rendered quietistic and automatically compliant by such a dualistic schema (contrary to Acts 5:29). For many Jesus-followers, such forced nonparticipation in the processes of government is unacceptable.

The double-love commandment, drawing from Deut. 6:5 and Lev. 19:18, continues to be central for contemporary Christian practice. Always the question of how we love God has to be addressed. This question includes issues of worship, emotion, mind, mystical communion, and obedience. Yet however we answer the question, it cannot be separated from love for neighbor and for oneself.

Matthew 23: Jesus Attacks the Scribes and Pharisees

▌THE TEXT IN ITS ANCIENT CONTEXT

Though none of the Jerusalem leadership "dared to ask him any more questions" (22:46), Jesus is not finished attacking them. In the notorious chapter 23, he curses them with seven woes, while differentiating the practices of the community of disciples (Carter 2000, 449–65).

Three factors indicate that Jesus directs his attack not to all Israel but against its Jerusalem-based, Rome-allied leaders. First, the chapter continues conflict with Israel's leaders evident since

Jesus entered Jerusalem in chapter 21. He has tangled with "chief priests and scribes" (21:15), "chief priests and elders" (21:23), "the chief priests and Pharisees" (21:45), "Pharisees and Herodians" (22:15-16), Pharisees (22:34, 41), and Sadducees (22:23). This sequence parades Israel's leaders in accord with Jesus' passion predictions (16:21; 20:18-19).

Second, this animosity is usually understood to reflect post-70 conflicts with leaders in a synagogue to which Matthew's Jesus-followers belong. Chapter 23 details their unfaithfulness, and distinguishes Matthew's supporters from them. It does not claim God's rejection of all Israel.

Third, the chapter employs common polemical language to identify these leaders as opponents. Just as modern political rhetoric conventionally paints opponents and their policies as too expensive, too late, and too little, ancient polemic had a standard lexicon. It was common to attack enemy groups as snakes, blind persons, hypocrites, sexual and socioeconomic offenders, deceivers, and murderers. We are not reading objective discourse about "all Jews," but polemic against specific enemies.

The opening eight verses present the leaders as hypocrites. The image denotes actors who play a part, who represent someone they are not. Here the leaders lack integrity in the disparity between their living and their teaching. They also love and benefit from their position as retainers in hierarchical, imperial society. Verses 9-12 contrast different social interactions among disciples.

The first two woes against "the scribes and Pharisees" appear in 23:13-15. Woes, especially in prophetic traditions, conventionally announce divine judgment (Isa. 3:9-11). Jesus declares divine judgment on them as hypocrites who hinder access to God's purposes. The third and fourth woes (23:16-24) condemn them as blind for majoring on minor matters and neglecting important societal and covenantal practices, namely the "weightier matters of the law: justice and mercy and faith(fullness)." The fifth and sixth condemn disparities between actions and motivation, especially their greed and self-indulgence, hypocrisy, and lawlessness (23:25-28). The final woe (23:29-36) places them in a long line of leaders who have violently rejected the prophets to preserve the status quo. The woes target their societal leadership concerned with their own position and benefit and not with representing God's justice among the people.

The chapter ends with a lament over Jerusalem, the leaders' city. Again the leaders are in view (not all Israel), with the repeated emphasis on their violent rejection of prophets and of God's agents who manifest God's maternal care and guidance. Verse 38 again interprets the fall of Jerusalem and its temple in 70 CE by Rome as divine punishment. Verse 39, though, offers some relief from the insistent judgment in citing Ps. 118:26 to anticipate Israel's final salvation.

▮ THE TEXT IN THE INTERPRETIVE TRADITION

Early second-century interpretation extended the polemic in chapter 23 against Jewish leaders to target *all* Jews as "hypocrites" in practices of prayer and fasting (Luz 2005, 92–177). This extension enabled Christian interpreters to distinguish Jewish practice from Christian practice (*Didache* 8). But once the separation of gentile Christ-believers and Jews was more widely established, chapter 23 generally (and surprisingly) seems to play little explicit part in expressing hostility toward Jews, though its continued negative influence should not be underestimated. Instead, readings became more ecclesially centered in attacking vices and exhorting virtuous behavior. The chapter is, then, understood textually to rebuke Jews but functionally to teach and warn Christians. Polemical readings continue but are directed against ecclesial opponents or against inappropriate Christian behavior. Scribes and Pharisees, for example, are understood to represent not Judaism but stingy and greedy actions (23:23, 25). Jerome called Christians who seek public applause "scribes and Pharisees" (23:5). In terms of polemic, Dante called Pope Boniface VIII a Pharisee, and Luther labeled Catholic opponents Pharisees. More generally among the Reformers, Pharisees came to represent those who trust in works and are hypocrites. In our time, the *Shorter Oxford English Dictionary* includes "self-righteous" and "hypocritical" in its entry on "Pharisees."

▮ THE TEXT IN CONTEMPORARY DISCUSSION

The presence of the woes of chapter 23 in a canonical Gospel is most troubling (Saldarini). Whatever the interpretive tradition, the chapter has exercised continuing negative influence on Christian anti-Jewish attitudes and practices. Attempts to read the tradition against the grain, in terms of warnings for Christians, have some merit, but they cannot be the only way forward. This dreadful past cannot be glossed over, set aside, and forgotten; repentance is required. Such Christian readings assume in their very language attacks on Jewish practices, and they maintain the hostility by presenting Jews as types of deficient Christian piety.

Moreover, the presence of such language in this Gospel poses the very difficult question of its relationship to the command in 5:44 to love one's enemies. Chapter 23 is as far from 5:44 as the east is from the west. No definition of love stretches to include condemning one's opponents to God's judgment. Yet 23:39 should not be completely forgotten. As much as it offers some hope—the punishment of the leaders' city is not a final dismissal—it compounds the contradictions. What is the relationship between the divine condemnation of the woes and this glimmer of hope?

In a different direction, 23:8-12 continues the vision of the church in chapters 18–20 as an alternative society marked by egalitarian structures (no teacher, no father) and contrary to hierarchical imperial society. In the history of interpretation, its import has been mollified by emphases on humility and against pride in defending ecclesial hierarchy and power. Matthew's vision for different social interactions is more radical, its continued challenge underscored by the theological and christological affirmations of 23:9-10.

Matthew 24–25: Jesus Announces the Final and Full Establishment of God's Empire

▮ THE TEXT IN ITS ANCIENT CONTEXT

Chapters 24–25 continue the conflict and condemnation of Jesus' final days in Jerusalem (Carter 2000, 466–97). The two chapters form the eschatological discourse, the Gospel's fifth major teaching section. Jesus addresses "signs of his coming/return and of the end of the age" (24:3)—his intervention to end Rome's empire and its Jerusalem allies, and fully establish God's reign/empire.

The chapter opens with another reference to the temple's destruction by the Romans in 70 CE. The discourse is located on the Mount of Olives and evokes Zechariah 14, which presents the Mount as the place where God enters the city, overcomes Israel's enemies, and establishes God's reign. The disciples ask about Jesus' "coming" or "arrival" (24:3; Gk. *parousia*), a term that refers to the arrival of generals or emperors parodied in 21:1-11. Now, though, there is no parody as his powerful and triumphant coming outmuscles the empire. The time until his coming, however, is difficult, marked by false agents misrepresenting God (24:4-5), wars (24:6-7a), natural disasters (24:7b-8), persecution, betrayal and faithfulness (24:9-13), mission (24:14), violation of the temple (24:15), flight and false alarms (24:16-26). The son of man's coming, however, will be unmistakable. He overcomes Roman power (represented in 24:28 by eagles, not vultures) and cosmic deities, before gathering God's people (24:27-31; Carter 2003a).

Exhortation takes over, as Jesus underscores the importance of recognizing the signs of his imminent coming with a lesson from the leafy fig tree (24:32-35). Subsequently, several passages warn that while his return is imminent, its timing is unknown and disciples must be ready (24:36-44). Three parables make the same point with slight variations. The first employs the imperial institution of slavery without any questions, and adds a picture of frightful punitive violence (24:45-51). A second parable uses a wedding scenario to show the joy of Jesus' return and the necessity of being ready (25:1-13). The third employs the common imperial scenario of the wealthy absentee landowner who entrusts his estate's management to his slaves (25:14-30). Returning, he holds them accountable for the talents entrusted to them. The faithful slaves are joyfully rewarded (25:21, 23); the unfaithful slave is punished (25:30).

The final scene portrays the judgment of the nations to take place at Jesus' return (25:31-46). Jesus appears as son of man and king in representing God's rule over the nations (25:34). The key interpretive question concerns the criterion for vindication (25:34-40) and condemnation (25:41-46). The participants themselves do not know (25:37-39, 44). One reading sees the nations judged on the basis of how they have treated those in need. Another reading sees the nations judged on the basis of their response to Christian proclamation of the good news. This latter view highlights the mission of 24:14 to all the nations (gathered in 25:31), and understands positive response to "the least of these" (25:40, 45) as referring not to the needy but specifically to receiving disciples and their Gospel message (so 10:40).

▍ The Text in the Interpretive Tradition

Chapter 24 has been read along various, but at times overlapping, lines (Luz 2005, 178–296). One approach, beginning with the *Didache*, and present from Irenaeus through the Reformers, has read it as an eschatological text culminating in Jesus' parousia. Verses 3-26 are understood as depicting the final collapse, with references often focusing on the personification of evil in an antichrist (imported from 1 John 2:18 and not specifically mentioned anywhere in Matthew). The antichrist is identified variously with the "false prophets" (24:11), the "desolating sacrilege" (24:15), and the "false" Messiahs (24:5, 23-24). A second approach, beginning with Chrysostom, has read the chapter historically, not in relation to the end of the age but in relation to the Roman destruction of Jerusalem in 70 CE. This approach understands the "desolating sacrilege" as something done by a Roman to profane the temple, such as introducing an image of the emperor or a legionary standard into the temple. The historical approach handles much of verses 4-31 but struggles with the question of verse 3b and with verses 27-31. To solve these problems, a mixed interpretation emerged with Augustine that notes concerns with both the fall of Jerusalem and the end of the age and tries to read the chapter as moving between these two events. Another line emerging from this approach found connections with contemporary ecclesial and world situations. (Spener, for instance, identified the "desolating sacrifice" with the papacy.) This approach was often combined with a sense that the end was near in the time of the interpreter (true of both Luther and contemporary TV preachers).

■ THE TEXT IN CONTEMPORARY DISCUSSION

These two chapters pose numerous questions for contemporary readers. Perhaps the most basic question concerns how we engage eschatological thinking, both the notion of divine intervention to affect the end of history with the establishment of God's purposes, and its bleak, hopeless perspective on the present. Two thousand years later and counting, the imminent expectation of 24:34 has not materialized. Some parts of the contemporary church live in such thinking; other parts find no resonance with it at all. A related issue is the language in which this divine intervention is described. Throughout, the eschatological discourse borrows imperial language (*parousia*), structures (slavery, absentee landowners), and strategies (punishing violence) to depict divine actions. The ways of Caesar are attributed to God without hesitation. There is no questioning of the violent assertion of cosmic power in 24:27-31 in the defeat of Roman military power (24:28). There is neither critique of slavery in 24:45-51 nor restraint in depicting the horrendous violence of hacking a slave to pieces in 24:51. Violent punishment continues in 25:31-46. How does this strand of violent judgment interact with the depictions of universal divine favor in 5:45 and the elevation of mercy (9:13; 12:7)? And what are we to make of the presentation of judgment by works and the privileging of the poor in the assertion of God's kingly power in 25:31-46?

Matthew 26–27: Jesus Is Crucified

■ THE TEXT IN ITS ANCIENT CONTEXT

After two chapters of eschatological discourse (chs. 24–25), the path to the cross via conflict with the Roman governor and the Jerusalem elite resumes from chapters 21–23. The transition from chapters 25 to 26 is stunning. The king who judges the nations is now judged by their rulers even while he exposes the vicious and self-serving ways of the imperial world.

These two long chapters move quickly with short and interwoven scenes, changing characters, and varied settings (Carter 2000, 498–540). The turning point comes in 26:47-56 as Judas betrays Jesus in Gethsemane, Jesus is arrested, and the disciples flee. From 26:57 to 27:26, Jesus is condemned first by the high priestly leadership and then by governor Pilate (Carter 2003b). Matthew 27:27-66 narrates his crucifixion as "king of Israel" (27:37, 42)—a treasonous claim in Roman rule—death (27:50), and burial in a guarded tomb.

The early Christian movement had to account for Jesus' death by crucifixion and for its own loyalty to one who had been crucified. Doing so clearly posed an enormous challenge. These chapters, as do other New Testament writings, devote considerable effort to offering explanations of that significance both for divine plans and for the life of discipleship. The challenge originates with the act of crucifixion itself.

In the Roman system, the punishment fit the social status of the convicted. Crucifixion, the "most pitiable of deaths" (Josephus, *J.W.* 7.202–3), was reserved for lower-ranked, more marginal, and provincial folks like violent criminals, unruly slaves, and rebellious provincials or foreigners who claimed kingship not sanctioned by Rome and attacked the personnel and property of elites. Crucifixions were carried out publicly along well-traveled roads so as to intimidate as many as possible.

Jesus' death by crucifixion puts him—and his followers—in such company. So, in 27:38-44, two rebels (bandits or brigands) are crucified with Jesus for rebellion against Roman order. Matthew's chapters take up the questions: What was God doing? What is the significance of this event? How does it shape discipleship? The two chapters can be read as a catalog of interpretations of his crucifixion, viewed through the perspective of resurrection. Among Matthew's affirmations are the following:

- Jesus' crucifixion is the inevitable consequence of a prophetic challenge to the imperial powers that be (26:1-5). The empire always strikes back. This is the way of the cross.
- An unnamed woman—a model disciple—recognizes that Jesus dies not in defeat but willingly (26:36-46), in God's service (26:6-13) and will (26:56). This service includes the establishment of a covenant for release from sins in anticipation of the full establishment of God's life-giving will (26:17-30). Jesus' death exposes the sinful nature of the imperial world.
- Jesus' death results from the betrayal by one disciple, Judas (26:14-16, 47-56; 27:3-10), and his abandonment by Peter (26:31-35, 69-75) and all the male disciples (26:56). By contrast, it is witnessed by courageous women followers (27:55-56).
- Jesus' death results from the concerted and effective effort of the alliance of Jerusalem and Roman imperial power to kill a challenger to the imperial status quo. This alliance involves the high priest Caiaphas (26:57-68), the Roman governor Pilate (27:1-2, 11-26), Roman soldiers (27:27-31, 54, 62-66), and the chief priests, scribes, and elders (27:41-43).

▌ THE TEXT IN THE INTERPRETIVE TRADITION

The interpretive tradition concerning Jesus' passion is rich and diverse, expressed through art, drama, music, and theological reflection (Luz 2005, 297–589, with images). One history identifies four broad approaches across the last two millennia. Initial interpretations, viewing crucifixion and resurrection as one connected event, emphasized not its suffering but its triumph (indicated in the eschatological anticipations of resurrection in 27:51-53). A second emphasis emerged in seeing the cross as an act of love (cf. Rom. 5:8). A third emphasis, especially in medieval exegesis, emphasized the suffering of the cross in which believers emotionally share and suffer through various contemplative practices, including self-flagellation, so as to learn love, pity, and thankfulness, and live a world-denying life. Protestant Reformation piety commonly associated with Luther, Calvin, and Melanchthon emphasized the benefits—both judgment and grace—of Jesus' death as *pro me* ("for me") or *pro nobis* ("for us"), encountered through preaching and sacraments, and responded to with faith.

Contemporary strands of interpretation have continued emphases from the past such as ransom theories (Anselm: Jesus' death satisfies God's honor and justice and buys release from sin and the devil), God's wooing love that draws humans into divine relationship (Abelard), *Christus victor* formulations of triumph over sin, and the *pro nobis* benefits of Jesus' sacrificial death. Other contemporary approaches, such as feminist and liberation work, have reacted strongly against sacrificial emphases, regarding "God giving God's son to die" as more akin to child abuse and as encouraging submission to abusive power and suffering. Instead, in focusing on life-giving and liberating dimensions, they have, for example, emphasized Jesus as one who suffers with us and strengthens all who are poor and oppressed. A similar approach has countered spiritualizations of the cross by seeking to restore it to its Roman imperial context. On this approach, the cross exposes human (imperial, systemic) evil, violence, and scapegoating (Girard) in the resistance to Jesus' alternative societal vision and practices.

■ The Text in Contemporary Discussion

Creative reflection on the significance of Jesus' death continues, though often ecclesial communities seem wary of this diversity and favor traditional, especially sacrificial, interpretations without exploring the diversity in the New Testament writings and the tradition across the ages.

These two chapters are full of characters that provide numerous points of entry into discipleship as the way of the cross. These characters include the anointing woman (26:6-13), the betrayer Judas, the overconfident but fragile Peter, the disciples who sleep through the Gethsemane prayer meeting, Caiaphas, who represents Jewish identity and allies with Roman power, Pilate, not spineless but concerned to maintain Roman rule and score a victory over his begging provincial allies (27:22-23), Simon of Cyrene, who is compelled to carry the cross (27:32), and the faithful and brave women at the tomb (27:55-56).

Part 6: God Thwarts Imperial Power and Raises Jesus (Matthew 28)

On normal expectations, the Gospel story should end with Jesus' death and the ruling elites' victory. Chapter 28, though, boldly declares God's miraculous intervention, which creates a different future with the raising of Jesus (Carter 2000, 541–54). The worst that imperial power can do is thwarted and reversed.

Matthew 28: Jesus' Resurrection and the Commissioning of Disciples

■ The Text in Its Ancient Context

Verses 1-10 emphasize this divine intervention. The raising of Jesus is assumed and declared, not described, thereby augmenting its mystery. The narrative focuses on the two women who come to "see" the tomb. Unlike Mark 16, they do not bring spices to anoint a dead body. That omission and the significant verb "see," with which Matthew frequently denotes understanding (Matt. 9:2) and insight into Jesus' mission (13:13-17), suggest they expect resurrection.

The descent from heaven of "an angel of the Lord," the earthquake, and the angel's divine-like appearance and reassuring words "do not be afraid" underscore God's presence and intervention.

God's action renders the empire's military agents powerless, "like dead men," in this place of new life (28:3-5a). The angelic proclamation underscores both divine intervention with its passive, "he has been raised" (28:5-8), and the need to reveal this activity. The notion of resurrection emerged in contexts of imperial tyranny to affirm God's triumph over death caused by imperial tyrants, and to provide assurance of participation in God's eschatological purposes (Dan. 12:1-3; 2 Maccabees 7). With joy and fear, the women obey the instruction to proclaim this message to the disciples in Galilee, an instruction renewed in their worshipful, fearful encounter with the risen Jesus (28:8-11; Cotter).

While the chapter's first section interprets the empty tomb in terms of God's life-giving intervention, its second scene presents the ruling powers' perspective (28:11-15). The now-revived soldiers, representing the power of the alliance of Pilate and the Jerusalem leaders (27:62-66), report "everything that had happened." The chief priests, assuming the governor's support, bribe the soldiers to declare an alternative story: the disciples have stolen the body. Regrettably, the scene presents those who do not believe or accept the angel's story as corrupt, deceiving, greedy—and not very smart.

In this conflictual context, the all-powerful Jesus commissions the disciples (28:16-20). The obedient disciples worship and doubt Jesus on a mountain, echoing Mts. Sinai and Zion. Jesus' massive assertion that God has given him "all authority in heaven and earth" declares a share in God's reign over all creation (contrast 4:8). The assertion both contests yet imitates Roman imperial claims to rule land, sea, and people. Jesus commissions the disciples to worldwide mission, making disciples, baptizing, and teaching Jesus' instruction (evoking the teaching of chs. 5–7, 10, 13, 18, 24–25; Carter 2004). Again the commission contests yet imitates imperial practice. Rome paraded its Jupiter-given mission to be "lords of the world" and to "crown peace with justice, to spare the vanquished, and to crush the proud" (Virgil, *Aen.* 1.254–82; 6.851–53).

The scene closes with Jesus' promise to be present with the small community of disciples as they undertake this mission in the resistant world of 28:11-15 (28:20). The Gospel ends by repeating its opening claim, that Jesus' presence manifests God's saving presence and reign/empire throughout the world (1:21-23; 4:17).

▌ THE TEXT IN THE INTERPRETIVE TRADITION

The four Gospels present significantly different resurrection accounts comprising different characters, events, appearances, and settings (Luz 2005, 590–636). Early interpreters regularly combined these different versions to reconstruct a narrative sequence of "what actually happened." With the Enlightenment emerged new understandings of historical inquiry that dismissed miracles, gave prominence to rationality, and emphasized cause-and-effect explanations and the importance of analogous situations. This approach has meant for much—but not all—contemporary interpretation a shift in focus from the narratives as providing a historical account to their significance or meaning.

Interpreters have found meaning variously in allegorizing the accounts, with a primary focus on hearing the word that the stories narrated. The Reformers urged attention to the "for us" quality of the narratives, particularly focusing attention on the women. Calvin, for example, interprets the women in terms of 1 Cor. 1:27 and God's choice of those who are regarded as weak and foolish. Others have highlighted the emotional, rather than cognitive, components of joy and fear, worship and doubt in Matt. 28:8, 17, as alternative but appropriate, meaning-making responses.

■ THE TEXT IN CONTEMPORARY DISCUSSION

Evangelism is a significant issue for contemporary congregations, both its strong advocates and those troubled by the practice. The history of interpretation shows that 28:19-20, a central text for contemporary debates, gained that central place as recently as the late eighteenth century. Early interpretation and the Reformers interpreted the verses as referring only to the disciples' mission. Catholic practice centered on territorial expansion such as the Spanish and Portuguese missions in the Americas and Asia. It was among Anabaptist and Protestant pietists that a missional interpretation developed. The English Baptist William Carey argued in 1792 for 28:19-20 as a central missional text, commanding worldwide mission to convert non-Christian individuals to Christianity. Such understandings have informed both Protestant and Catholic evangelistic missions.

Others, however, have become increasingly uncomfortable with assertions of ecclesial power and the association of the church with the damage done by colonial powers on local ways of life. Interfaith dialogue has also questioned evangelistic practices as triumphalistic and disrespectful of diverse traditions. Does 28:19-20 authorize such practices, or does its location at the end of the Gospel point to an interpretation in relation to the Gospel's previous teaching, such as Jesus' emphasis on the praxis of love for God and neighbor as demonstrated in "good works" more than words (5:16; 22:37-39)?

The Gospel's final promise raises questions as to how the continuing presence of the risen Jesus is experienced. Interpreters have suggested the Spirit, otherwise not prominent in the Gospel, the Eucharist, and the proclaimed word. Perhaps also this presence is experienced in worship and joy in the midst of fear and doubt.

Works Cited

Allison, Dale. 1993. "Divorce, Celibacy, and Joseph (Matthew 1:18-25 and 19:1-12)." *JSNT* 49:1–10.

Betz, Hans Dieter. 1995. *The Sermon on the Mount*. Minneapolis: Fortress Press.

Bornkamm, Günther. 1963. "The Stilling of the Storm." In *Tradition and Interpretation in Matthew*, by Günther Bornkamm, Gerhard Barth, and Heinz Held, 52–57. London: SCM.

Carter, Warren. 2000. *Matthew and the Margins: A Sociopolitical and Religious Reading*. Maryknoll, NY: Orbis.

———. 2001. *Matthew and Empire: Initial Explorations*. Harrisburg, PA: Trinity Press International.

———. 2003a. "Are There Imperial Texts in the Class? Intertextual Eagles and Matthean Eschatology as 'Lights Out' Time for Imperial Rome (Matt 24:27-31)." *JBL* 122:467–87.

———. 2003b. *Pontius Pilate: Portraits of a Roman Governor*. Collegeville, MN: Liturgical Press.

———. 2004. "Matthew and the Gentiles: Individual Conversion and/or Systemic Transformation?" *JSNT* 26:259–82.

———. 2007. "Power and Identities" and "Embodying God's Empire in Communal Practices." In *Preaching on the Sermon on the Mount: The World That It Imagines*, edited by David Fleer and Dave Bland, 8–21 and 22–35. St. Louis: Chalice.

Cotter, Wendy. 2001. "Greco-Roman Apotheosis Traditions and the Resurrection Appearances in Matthew." In *The Gospel of Matthew in Current Study*, edited by David Aune, 127–53. Grand Rapids: Eerdmans.

Deutsch, Celia. 2001. "Jesus as Wisdom: A Feminist Reading of Matthew's Wisdom Christology." In *A Feminist Companion to Matthew*, edited by Amy-Jill Levine with Marianne Blickenstaff, 88–113. Sheffield: Sheffield Academic Press.

Duling, Dennis. 2012. "'Egalitarian' Ideology, Leadership, and Factional Conflict within the Matthean Group," "The Matthean Brotherhood and Marginal Scribal Leadership," and "Matthew 18:15-17: Conflict, Confrontation and Conflict Resolution in a 'Fictive' Kin Association." In *A Marginal Scribe: Studies in Matthew in a Social-Scientific Perspective*, 145–78, 179–211, and 212–44. Eugene, OR: Cascade.

Hanson, K. C. 1994. "How Honorable! How Shameful! A Cultural Analysis of Matthew's Makarisms and Reproaches." *Semeia* 68:81–111.

Hanson, K. C., and Douglas Oakman. 1998. *Palestine in the Time of Jesus: Social Structures and Social Conflicts*. Minneapolis: Fortress Press.

Horsley, Richard. 1989. *The Liberation of Christmas: The Infancy Narratives in Social Context*. New York: Crossroad.

Levine, Amy-Jill. 1998. "Matthew." In *Women's Bible Commentary: Expanded Edition*, edited by Carol A. Newsom and Sharon H. Ringe, 339–49. Louisville: Westminster John Knox.

———. 2001. "Discharging Responsibility: Matthean Jesus, Biblical Law, and Hemorrhaging Woman." In *A Feminist Companion to Matthew*, edited by Amy-Jill Levine with Marianne Blickenstaff, 70–87. Sheffield: Sheffield Academic Press.

Loader, William. 2005. *Sexuality and the Jesus Tradition*. Grand Rapids: Eerdmans.

Luz, Ulrich. 1994. *Matthew in History: Interpretation, Influence, and Effects*. Minneapolis; Fortress Press.

———. 2001. *Matthew 1–7*. Trans. James E. Crouch. Hermeneia. Minneapolis: Fortress Press.

———. 2005. *Matthew 8–20*. Trans. James E. Crouch. Hermeneia. Minneapolis: Fortress Press.

———. 2007. *Matthew 21–28*. Trans. James E. Crouch. Hermeneia. Minneapolis: Fortress Press.

Meier, John P. 1994. *A Marginal Jew: Rethinking the Historical Jesus*. Vol. 2, *Mentor, Message, and Miracles*. New York: Doubleday.

Moss, Candida R., and Jeremy Schipper, eds. 2011. *Disability Studies and Biblical Literature*. New York: Palgrave Macmillan.

Murphy, Catherine. 2003. *John the Baptist: Prophet of Purity for a New Age*. Collegeville, MN: Liturgical Press.

Patte, Daniel. 1999. *The Challenge of the Sermon on the Mount: A Critical Study of the Sermon on the Mount as Scripture*. Harrisburg, PA: Trinity Press International.

Powell, Mark Allan. 2001. *Chasing the Eastern Star: Adventures in Biblical Reader-Response Criticism*. Louisville: Westminster John Knox.

Ringe, Sharon. 1985. "A Gentile Woman's Story." In *Feminist Interpretation of the Bible*, edited by Letty Russell, 65–72. Philadelphia: Westminster.

Saldarini, Anthony. 2001. "Reading Matthew without Anti-Semitism." In *The Gospel of Matthew in Current Study*, edited by David Aune, 166–84. Grand Rapids: Eerdmans.

Sheffield, Julian. 2001. "The Father in the Gospel of Matthew." In *A Feminist Companion to Matthew*, edited by Amy-Jill Levine with Marianne Blickenstaff, 52–69. Sheffield: Sheffield Academic Press.

Taylor, Joan. 1997. *The Immerser: John the Baptist within Second Temple Judaism*. Grand Rapids: Eerdmans.

Waetjen, H. 1975. "The Genealogy as the Key to the Gospel of Matthew." *JBL* 95:205–30.

Wainwright, Elaine. 2001. "The Matthean Jesus and the Healing of Women." In *The Gospel of Matthew in Current Study*, edited by David Aune, 74–95. Grand Rapids: Eerdmans.

Wink, Walter. 1992. "Beyond Just War and Pacifism: Jesus' Nonviolent Way." *RevExp* 89:171–214.

MARK

Raquel S. Lettsome

Introduction

No one knows exactly who wrote the Gospel of Mark. The ancient church historian Eusebius wrote that Bishop Papias of Asia Minor attributed the Gospel to John Mark (Acts 12:12; Col. 4:10), who was a follower and interpreter of Peter (*Hist. eccl.* 3.39). This would suggest that it was not a first-hand account of Jesus' ministry. The general consensus is that Mark, whoever he may be, wrote the Gospel somewhere in the Roman Empire between 66 and 70 CE. The precise dating of the Gospel hinges on the interpretation of the events prophesied by Jesus in Mark 13. For some scholars, the similarity between Jesus' prediction that there will be left of the temple "no stone upon a stone" and Josephus's narrative of the temple being razed in 70 suggests that Mark should be dated after the fall of the temple (Marcus; Pesch; Theissen). I find this a compelling argument (St. Clair). Therefore, the context of Mark's Gospel is the Jewish War: It is one of several Jewish and Christian responses to the fall of the temple.

The setting first posited for Mark's Gospel was Rome. This is where John Mark was believed to have written it, according to Papias. But the Gospel's use of Latin involves only a few military terms like "legion" (5:9) and "centurion" (15:39); there are no Latin words that reflect the social, domestic, or religious areas of Roman life (Kelber, 129). Based on this evidence, it is more probable that Mark wrote somewhere in the Roman Empire other than in Rome itself. Scholars have since identified Galilee and southern Syria as possible locales, suggestions that would also disqualify John Mark as the author. The viability of each of these locations primarily depends on how well they account for certain characteristics of Mark's Gospel: geographical discrepancies (his knowledge of the Galilean locales is lacking beyond their names, and his topology is often inaccurate: 1977); the use of a number of Hebrew (7:11; 11:9) and Aramaic words in transliteration (5:41; 7:34; 14:36; 15:22, 34), most of them translated into Greek, suggesting that Mark's community included Jews and gentiles in close association (Waetjen, 14); the explanation of Jewish traditions (e.g., 7:3-4) to at least some readers unfamiliar with them; the author's and presumed audience's familiarity with Jewish Scriptures, which are cited on twelve occasions, without further explanation (1:2-3; 4:12; 7:6-7; 10:6-8, 19; 11:17; 12:10-11, 36; 13:24-26; 14:27, 62; 15:34); and the representation of Jesus' ministry to gentiles, suggesting the presence of some gentiles, at least, in the audience. Both Rome and southern Syria had large gentile populations with a significant number of Jewish inhabitants, but given the limited use of Latinisms mentioned above, southern Syria seems more probable. Moreover, the Gospel's setting seems to be more rural than urban. All of Jesus' parables use agrarian imagery, and the majority of Jesus' ministry occurs in the villages, towns, farms, and countryside (1:38; 6:56; 8:27; 11:1, 2, 11, 12; 14:3).

Until the 1800s, Mark's Gospel was neglected, for the most part, by both church tradition and scholarship because it was not a firsthand account and because it was dated after Matthew (Catholic scholars) or after both Matthew and Luke (Protestant scholars). Nevertheless, it boasts some unique literary features. The author highlights key points and narrative themes by "sandwiching" one story in the middle of another, arranging episodes into concentric patterns, using two similar stories to begin and end a large section of the Gospel (Rhoads, Dewey, and Michie 1999). Mark's style is terse and literal. This led Augustine to conclude that Mark was an abbreviated version of Matthew. It was not until 1838 that Mark's priority was established (by C. J. Wilkes and C. H. Weisse). Mark's Gospel then gained popularity because its simplistic style suggested historical accuracy, until form critics argued that the Gospel was not historically accurate but reflected the beliefs of early Christian communities. They examined the literary units to reveal the *Sitz im Leben* of the various forms in the Gospel. Next, the redaction critics focused on the author's arrangement of the tradition, thereby uncovering the author's theological approach to it.

Interest in the Gospel shifted from the historical to the literary. Mark was then primarily viewed as narrative, understood as a "communication event between a writer and an audience" (Juel, 13). The narrative approach to the Gospel drew attention to the contemporary audience or reader and how they engaged the text. This brought to the fore theological concerns that are of importance to people in local churches, rather than only literary and historical issues (Placher, ix–xi). Contemporary Mark scholarship examines the traditional themes of discipleship, Christology, and kingdom of God in the text. However, these are now reexamined through different cultural and theological lenses to expose the liberative strains of Mark's Gospel.

Mark 1:1-13: The Beginning of the Good News

▌THE TEXT IN ITS ANCIENT CONTEXT

According to Mark, his story is "good news" (*euangelion*). Although his tidings of "good news" announce a beginning, they do not stand as an isolated experience. Rather, he connects his story to the story of Israel. Moreover, the content of his story will not focus on a single event but on a singular person: Jesus, whom he labels as both "Christ" and "Son of God." For those in his audience who are familiar with the Hebrew Scriptures, the title Christ brings to fore communal memories of exile and foreign rule under Babylon and subsequent deliverance under Cyrus. According to Isa.

44:28, Cyrus was God's anointed (*christos*), and his release of the captives was seen by Isaiah as a result of God's intervention. By employing the designation "Christ," Mark identifies Jesus as the anointed of God who will be used for a divine purpose. In the context of first-century Palestine languishing under foreign (Roman) rule, it would be hard to walk away from these opening lines without having expectations of deliverance raised. Mark compounds this further by his use of "Son of God." Jesus is more than God's anointed; he is in fact God's Son. Textual experts disagree about whether this title in Mark 1:1 is part of Mark's original text or a later inclusion. The title is missing from a few important manuscripts (e.g., Sinaiticus) and present in others (e.g., Vaticanus). However, the presence of the title in important manuscripts like Vaticanus, along with Mark's penchant for identifying Jesus as God's Son throughout the Gospel (1:11; 3:11; 5:7; 9:7; 12:6; 13:32; 14:61; 15:39), suggests that its inclusion here is the work of an omniscient narrator clearly stating his point of view from the start.

Against the backdrop of Old Testament prophecy, Mark sets the stage for the events that follow. Although he opens with a quote that he ascribes to Isaiah (1:2), the first portion of the quotation ("I am sending a messenger ahead of you") is better attributed to Exod. 23:20 and Mal. 3:1. Exodus 23:20 evokes images of wilderness wanderings in which God sends forth a messenger (*angelos*) to keep watch over the Israelites as they sojourn to the promised land. Malachi 3:1 describes the sending of the messenger prior to the coming of the Day of the Lord. The second portion of the quotation, found in Isa. 40:3 (Mark 1:3), announces the coming of the Lord but without the tones of impending judgment found in Malachi. Instead of condemnation, the prophet heralds the end of the exile and Babylonian captivity.

By detailing both John's proclamation and performance against the landscape of Old Testament prophecy, Mark conveys a sense of hope and expectancy to his original readers. As an introduction to his work, this citation of the prophets implicitly offers the theme of judgment as a means of understanding the destruction of the Jerusalem temple by the Romans and unites it here with a theme of comfort. Just as John preaches and baptizes in preparation of the Lord's arrival (1:3, 7-8), so Mark sets the narrative stage for Jesus' appearance.

The narrative lens then turns to Jesus, who has come to the Jordan to be baptized by John. Mark has already introduced him as "Christ" and, depending on how one interprets the textual evidence for Mark 1:1, also "Son of God," perhaps to counter any negative preconceived notions that his audience may have about the next bit of information that he shares. Jesus is from Nazareth of Galilee, a small village off the main roads that is about seventy miles from Jerusalem. Jesus' hometown has no geographic, religious, or political importance of its own. However, about four miles northwest lies the city of Sepphoris. Not only was Sepphoris highly influenced by Rome, but it also greatly angered the rest of Galilee when it refused to rebel against Rome in 66 CE. Had not Mark given the titles in the first verse, his audience's initial perception of Jesus might be as a "nobody from nowhere," or worse, a Roman sympathizer. The titles "Christ" and "Son of God" help to persuade his readers that it is his personage rather than his address that is significant.

Mark tells us nothing of Jesus prior to this moment. It seems that his baptism is the beginning of his story and nothing before matters. The heavens, the barrier separating the human and divine realms, are torn. The Greek verb, *schizein*, suggests that the tear is irreparable. There will be no mending of this breach: God is now accessible to human beings and human beings are accessible to God (Juel, 34–35). Through this divide comes the Spirit in the form of a dove, perhaps intimating the birth of a new creation (Gen. 1:2; 8:8). Mark notes that the dove descends "into" (*eis*) him—not "upon" (*epi*) him (Matt. 3:16; Luke 3:22). Jesus is indwelled by the Spirit. Finally, a voice speaks from heaven affirming that he is God's Son, who is both "pleasing" and "well loved."

No sooner does the Spirit descend into Jesus than it "drives" him into the wilderness. Jesus is cast out from human company, much like the demons he will cast out in his ministry. Both his location and length of stay are important to note. They allude to the children of Israel's sojourn in the wilderness for forty years. Jesus is also in a place of testing, suggesting that his departure from this place will be the fulfillment of another divine promise. However, it will not be without opposition. Otherworldly lines of demarcation are being drawn: Satan tests him and angels minister to him, leaving his audience to wonder how this will play out in the human realm.

◼ THE TEXT IN THE INTERPRETIVE TRADITION

Questions about Jesus' (divine and/or human) nature have caused Mark's account of Jesus' baptism to be ignored and/or conflated with Matthew's version. Until the late eighteenth century, Matthew was believed to be the first written Gospel. According to Augustine, Mark was Matthew's abbreviator. Therefore, Matthew's Gospel, which included an infancy narrative and an explanation of why Jesus was being baptized (Matt. 3:14), was preferred. Once Markan priority was established, it became clear that the early church had been uncomfortable with Mark's presentation and preferred Matthew, often called the "church's Gospel," because it corrected Mark's lack of episodes such as the infancy narrative, which depicts the miraculous nature of Jesus' birth, and the lack of explanation for Jesus' receiving John's "baptism of repentance," which implicitly called into question early Christian belief in Jesus' sinlessness.

Rather than focus on what this passage says about Jesus' (divine or human) nature, contemporary scholars explore the connection between Jesus' baptism and his ministry. His baptism is understood as Jesus' surrender to God's will, his divine commissioning by God, his rejection of the dominant culture, and/or his identification with sinners. Questions of divine origin hinge more on whether "Son of God" (1:1) was originally included in Mark's manuscript than on an examination of Mark's baptism account alone.

◼ THE TEXT IN CONTEMPORARY DISCUSSION

If we are to follow the trajectory of contemporary scholars and focus on Jesus' ministry, baptism becomes intimately connected to discipleship. We can no longer stop with the question of who Jesus is but must ask, how can others follow him? Matthew, Mark, and Luke record John's proclaiming a "baptism of repentance." It may be helpful for readers of Mark's Gospel to think about repentance as changing one's heart or mind and then read the Gospel with this question in mind: How does Mark's story of Jesus get us to change our minds about the world around us and our participation in it?

Mark 1:14-39: An Invitation to Follow

■ THE TEXT IN ITS ANCIENT CONTEXT

Unlike John, who ministered in the southern region of Judea near the urban center of Jerusalem, Jesus' ministry begins in the northern region of Galilee. Galilee was known for its farming and fishing, both industries sustained through the labor of a predominantly peasant population. It was a largely rural area surrounded by foreign nations whose inhabitants would later be strongly resistant to the Romans during the war (66–70 CE). They reaped none of the benefits Rome bestowed on the Jewish political and religious elites in the south. Instead, their labor fueled an economy that kept them at the lowest economic and social strata of ancient Palestinian society. It is here that Jesus proclaims the impending arrival of God's kingdom.

The first thing Mark shows his community is that the kingdom has both social and economic implications. As Jesus "pass[es] along" the Sea of Galilee, he calls four fishermen to follow him: Simon, Andrew, James, and John (vv. 16-20). Each of them responds without hesitation. They leave behind all ties to their current livelihood, which will affect them economically and affect their relationships with their families. James and John work with their father, Zebedee. We will soon see that Simon is married; he has a mother-in-law (v. 30). If we are to begin to understand the appeal of Jesus' invitation, we must first refrain from equating the modern industry of fishing and our understanding of entrepreneurship with the profession in its ancient Palestinian form. According to K. C. Hanson, the fishing industry was highly regulated and governed by political and kinship ties. The profits routinely made their way to the coffers of the urban elites, leaving many fishermen indebted to brokers for leases and money needed to run their businesses. Fisherman often formed cooperatives to survive. If they did not have enough people in the cooperative, they hired laborers, as Zebedee did (Hanson, 104). In effect, the four men forsake the highly regulated vocation that is controlled by the Jewish elites and accept Jesus' invitation to follow and fish for people.

Next, Mark demonstrates that the kingdom of God is manifest in both Jesus' word and deed (vv. 21-18). When Jesus enters the synagogue and begins to teach, he astonishes the audience with the level of authority he possesses. In the midst of his teaching, a man with an unclean spirit interrupts him and identifies him as the "Holy One of God." The presence of the man is not surprising: the world was believed to be inhabited by spirits, which were mainly malevolent in nature. Both Judaism and the pagan religions of the Greco-Roman world saw the need for people to be freed from the power of unclean spirits/demons. In Judaism, the presence of unclean spirits symbolized the struggle between God and the forces of evil (Mann). Therefore it is ironic that the people who are supposed to be on the side of God, namely, the religious leaders and members of the congregation, are not the first characters in Mark's narrative to recognize who Jesus really is. Instead, it is the unclean spirit who knows what the people of God do not. Jesus responds by silencing and exorcizing the demon with a verbal command, thereby confirming the audience's original assessment of his authoritative teaching. His is a "performative utterance" (Tolbert). Jesus speaks and things happen; demons obey.

Finally, kingdom life involves service. Jesus and his four followers return to Simon's house, where they find Simon's mother-in-law sick with a fever. Jesus takes her by the hand and heals her of the fever. In return, she begins to serve them. She is the second character in Mark's story to serve (*diakonein*) Jesus; the first are the angels in the wilderness (1:13). These acts of service foreshadow Jesus' teaching and example of discipleship as servanthood (10:43, 45).

▌THE TEXT IN THE INTERPRETIVE TRADITION

As early as the Middle Ages, the church interpreted the kingdom (*basileia*) of God as a sphere of influence (reign of God) rather than a spatial reality (physical kingdom). However, they equated God's reign with ecclesial rule (Mann). In the mid-1800s, Albrecht Ritschl awakened scholarly interest in this theological concept. He argued that the kingdom of God was the sociopolitical transformation of this world and that it would result in the overthrow of oppression. His work laid the foundation for the social gospel movement, which peaked in the early 1900s. However, Ritschl's work lacked the apocalyptic edge that other scholars believed was present in the Gospel's articulation of the kingdom of God. Scholars such as Johannes Weiss, Albert Schweitzer, and Rudolf Bultmann maintained the apocalyptic notion of time that is divided into two eras: the now and the not yet. For these scholars, the kingdom is a future reality that is beyond human control. C. H. Dodd rejected this otherworldly, future orientation and advocated a realized eschatology. For him, the kingdom of God was already present whenever and wherever God's rule was established.

In the mid-1900s, the next wave of scholarship sought to mediate between the apocalyptic and realized eschatological thrusts of kingdom language. They attempted to bridge the academic chasm between the now and the not-yet, on the one hand, and the kingdom as beyond human control and the participatory nature of the kingdom, on the other (Blount). In addition, scholars moved away from a "pan-Synoptic" approach to the kingdom, in which they studied the kingdom-of-God concept across the Gospels. Instead, they began to explore how individual Gospels presented the kingdom of God (France). Liberation theologians who have equated the kingdom with sociopolitical acts of liberation have taken the symbol full circle, bringing scholarship back to the groundbreaking work of Ritschl as well as to its critiques (Blount).

▌THE TEXT IN CONTEMPORARY DISCUSSION

During the last few years, the emerging church movement, which has been defined as "a growing, loosely-connected movement of primarily young pastors who are glad to see the end of modernity and are seeking to function as missionaries who bring the gospel of Jesus Christ to emerging and postmodern cultures" (Driscoll 2006, 22), has shown renewed interest in the kingdom of God. They claim that the kingdom of God is, or at least can be, here and now: "Our [principal] desire is to see God's kingdom come on earth as it is in heaven. We believe this happens when God's people are renewed around God's mission of love and justice in the world" (Maddock and Maddock, 80). This mission of love and justice in the world includes addressing ecological, moral, economic, and social ills. The focus is, therefore, communal, as relationships are of primary importance. However, it is not only human relationships that matter but also humanity's relationship with all of creation.

The communal emphasis of the emerging church movement is similar to that of liberation theologians, who see the redistribution of wealth and a sociopolitical reordering of society that brings in those who have been relegated to the margins as part of the kingdom of God agenda. However, liberation theologians believe that the presence of evil is so pervasive that the kingdom agenda as they understand it cannot be brought about completely by human initiative. It will require divine intervention for its fulfillment, including judgment on those people and systems that oppose God's work. For the emerging church movement, the future is bright. Heaven will eventually come to earth as the kingdom of God is manifested through good works.

As we read Mark's presentation of Jesus' proclamation of the kingdom and Jesus' ministry, how are we to articulate its meaning in a postmodern setting? However we define it, we must be mindful that our definitions have implications for both mission and eschatology.

Mark 1:40—3:6: Following beyond the Boundaries

▌THE TEXT IN ITS ANCIENT CONTEXT

Jesus' ministry in Galilee continues to grow. However, it brings to him not only the crowds but also the criticism of the scribes and Pharisees. Mark's presentation of Jesus' ministry and the response of the religious leadership in Galilee show a fundamental difference between the two. By narrating a series of boundary-crossing ministry acts in a concentric pattern, Mark highlights for his audience both the growing tensions between Jesus and the religious leaders in Galilee and the reasons for Jesus' popularity among people in the region.

The first episode in this section (1:40-45) reveals that Jesus' fame has now reached the lowest social strata—the outcasts. A leper approaches Jesus. Despite the hopelessness of his situation, he does not question Jesus' ability to cleanse him. The only barrier the leper perceives to his deliverance is Jesus' willingness to cross the boundaries of ritual purity in order to engage and aid him. Jesus is willing and sends the cleansed man to the priests, commanding that he offer what Moses commanded in the law (Lev. 14:1-7). The leper does not do as Jesus commands, however, but instead tells what Jesus has done for him. Jesus' fame increases to the point that he cannot go into the town but must remain in the country.

As Jesus' popularity grows, so does his conflict with the religious leaders in Galilee. In the remainder of this section of his Gospel (2:1—3:6), Mark shows this by setting up these stories in a series of concentric circles (Rhoads, Dewey, and Michie, 52). He frames this section with two healing stories (2:1-12 and 3:1-6) placed at the beginning and end of this section. The first pericope details the healing of a paralytic. Jesus heals the man so that the scribes who accuse him of blasphemy will know "that the Son of Man has authority on earth to forgive sins" (2:10). In the last, he heals a man with a withered hand. It appears to be a setup since "they watched to see whether he would cure him on the sabbath, so that they might accuse him" (3:2). In both passages, Jesus' power, his "ability to exercise control over the behavior of others" (Pilch, 139), is unquestionable. He has the power to affect the functioning of both men's bodies. The real issue is Jesus' authority, whether he has the "socially recognized and approved ability to control the behavior of others" (Malina, 11). The scribes in 2:1-12 and the Pharisees and Herodians in 3:1-6 do not believe Jesus has the authority to forgive sin or transgress Sabbath law just because he has the power to heal. They do not share the same willingness demonstrated by Jesus when he healed the leper: a willingness to use both power and authority to help those in need. Therefore, Mark shows his audience that if things are left up to the current religious leadership, nothing will change for the vast majority of people.

The second and fourth episodes deal with eating regulations (2:13-17 and 2:23-28). In the second episode, Jesus calls a tax collector by the name of Levi to follow him. Later that evening, he is eating with Levi and many tax collectors and sinners are eating with them. Although the tax collectors represent an economically stable cadre of individuals, they were considered social outcasts and the greatest sinners. They were exploiters of the common people; they raised funds that supported the oppressive regimes of Herod and Rome. Moreover, they increased their salaries by extorting from the people additional money in excess of the tax rate. At first glance, Mark's audience might get the impression that Jesus' table fellowship with tax collectors and sinners implies his approval of them. However, Mark makes it clear to his readers, just as Jesus makes it clear to the scribes that question him, that Jesus is calling sinners because they are the ones in need of assistance. His ministry is directed to those outside the pale of Jewish law, and he goes where they are in order to get them.

The fourth pericope also has to do with eating. In this story, Jesus is criticized for allowing his disciples to eat plucked grain on the Sabbath. Plucking the grain is work and therefore puts them in violation of Sabbath law. Jesus responds to this criticism by reminding his detractors of what David did while fleeing from Saul (1 Sam. 21:1-6). Although there are differences between David's story and the episode at hand (Donahue and Harrington, 111), the reference to David serves to parallel Jesus and David. The implicit argument was a common Jewish technique in which one argues from "light to heavy" (*qal we chomer*). The logic is that if David could claim special authority, then how much more so could Jesus, a point Marks makes explicit in 12:35-37. This special authority extends to his interpretation of what is proper to do on the Sabbath (2:28). He reminds them that the Sabbath was created to serve humans, not the other way around, a notion not foreign to Judaism (Hooker, 104; Juel, 54). This interpretation represents Jesus' basic view of the law—it is to help people, not hurt them.

In the middle of this section is the third episode (2:18-22), which illumines the surrounding stories. In response to questions raised about his disciples' lack of fasting, Jesus compares himself to a bridegroom. A wedding is a time of celebration, not of fasting. In the same manner, his disciples do not fast while he is with them. There will be time to fast when he is no longer there. Right now, a new thing is transpiring. It is symbolized by the images of wine, wineskins, and cloth, highlighting the two very different applications of the faith of Mark's day. The new wine and the new cloth of Jesus cannot fit within the current tradition. If the old does not change, it will cause the two to tear apart. By using the word *schisma* ("tear"), Mark calls his audience's attention back to Jesus' baptism, in which he uses the verbal form of *schisma* to describe the irreparable tearing of the heavens. Mark suggests that just as God ripped through the heavens to destroy the boundary between the Creator and creation, so God will rip through the current religious practices and traditions to destroy the social and economic systems that separate God's people from their God.

This tearing away emphasizes both the severity of the growing conflict between Jesus and the religious leaders and the intensity of the religious leaders' commitment to the prevailing social structure. With each successive story, more people are involved in the conflict. It starts with the scribes, who functioned as low-level officials and religious leaders invested with the authority to interpret Scripture. The Pharisees, who represented perhaps the most influential leadership group among the common people, show up next. It ends with the Pharisees and Herodians, most likely the courtiers of Herod, joining forces to kill Jesus (3:6). Moreover, as Jesus' opponents increase, so has the level of animosity against him. It begins with the scribes questioning in their hearts (2:6) and ends with a conspiracy to assassinate Jesus (3:6). Jesus' response to his challengers also intensifies. He begins by merely responding to their questions and ends with outright anger (5:5), showing that his commitment to change the status quo is just as profound as the religious leaders' opposition.

■ THE TEXT IN THE INTERPRETIVE TRADITION

"Son of man" (*ho huios tou anthrōpou*), first mentioned in Mark 2:10, is the Greek translation of the Aramaic phrase *bar nasha*. The earliest commentators saw the son of man as a reference to the humanity of Jesus as it related to his earthly parentage. In the writings of Tertullian and Ignatius, both qualified "son of man" with the phrase "according to the flesh" to highlight Jesus' humanity and juxtaposed it to "Son of God," which highlighted his divinity. The early church fathers followed the Jewish understanding of the Hebrew form (*ben 'adam*), which refers to humanity in general. Within its Jewish context, "son of man" was believed to highlight the weakness and frailty of humanity. This is where the early church fathers' understanding of son of man differed from the Jewish understanding. For them, Jesus' divinity could in no way be compromised by human weakness.

The understanding of "son of man" as an affirmation of and emphasis on Jesus' humanity continued through the 1600s. However, new theories emerged after the Protestant Reformation. The two most predominant were from scholars who asserted that son of man was a messianic title based on Dan. 7:13 and those that argued that it was simply a self-reference. The understanding of "son of man" as a messianic title gained ground during the 1700s and 1800s. Yet the stress on Jesus' humanity remained. "Son of man" referred to a very human Messiah.

By the mid-1800s, this changed when an Ethiopic manuscript of *1 Enoch* was discovered that mentioned a preexistent heavenly son of man. For nearly a century, scholars asserted that Jesus' use of the phrase was based on this figure (France). During this same time period, scholars posited various theories: namely, that Jesus identified himself with the son of man that he expected to arrive during his lifetime (Joachim Jeremias); that the son of man was an allusion to and Jesus' acceptance of his role as an obedient servant (Morna Hooker); that the phrase was a creation of the early church; and that "son of man" was an idiom meaning "I," and therefore a nontitular self-reference (Géza Vermes). Scholarship remains divided on the theological interpretation of this phrase and whether it should be understood as a title or a simple self-designation. The lack of scholarly consensus has caused son of man studies to be described as "a prime illustration of the limits of New Testament scholarship" (Burkett, 5).

◼ THE TEXT IN CONTEMPORARY DISCUSSION

Scholars identify three types of son of man sayings in the Synoptic Gospels. They refer to (1) Jesus' earthly ministry, (2) his suffering, or (3) his future glory. The initial two son of man sayings in Mark's Gospel (2:10, 28) are located within the controversy cycles and refer to Jesus' earthly ministry. At the heart of the conflict are the boundary-breaking actions of Jesus that upset the social structure of his day. Interestingly enough, twenty-first-century American life reflects this aspect of Mark's world, a world in which 1 to 2 percent of the population controlled the vast majority of resources, leaving the rest barely able to survive (Saldarini, 40–41). We also live in a time and place in which scriptural interpretation and theological perspectives are used to support public policies and practices that deny people equal access under the law and basic forms of societal maintenance. Although we do not use the language of "unclean" to exclude people, we hear the labels "lazy," "deviant," and "dangerous" used to suggest that certain people are undeserving and unworthy of medical care, decent food and housing, equal rights under the law, or quality education because they are morally unfit or unqualified to reap societal benefits. Therefore, the ministry of the son of man in the controversy cycles poses questions to us: Who benefits from our interpretations of Scripture and practices of the faith? Who is excluded?

Mark 3:7-35: Following in Ministry: Expansion and Opposition

◼ THE TEXT IN ITS ANCIENT CONTEXT

Just as Mark recounted the upsurge of Jesus' fame due to the testimony of the leper (1:45), followed by the rise of opposition (2:1—3:6), so the pattern now continues. The crowds from Galilee are joined by those from Judea, Jerusalem, Idumea, beyond the Jordan (Perea), and the area of Tyre and Sidon. Although mentioned cursorily, the expansion of Jesus' following by people in these locales is significant in that it foreshadows the continued antagonism toward Jesus.

Initially of note is the fact that Mark mentions Judea and Jerusalem separately. At this time, the area that had long ago been the kingdoms of Israel and Judah comprised three regions: Judea, Samaria, and Galilee. Jerusalem was located in the region of Judea. However, Mark highlights the fact that people came not only from the smaller Judean towns and villages but also from the urban religious and political center of Jerusalem, the residence and spiritual base of the upper echelon of the Jewish religious leaders. It was also the political domain of the Roman procurator Pontius Pilate and the Roman client king Herod Antipas.

The inclusion of Idumea and Perea ("beyond the Jordan") as key places from which the multitudes have come gives further reason for the Herodians' animosity (3:6). The Herodians were most likely servants, courtiers, and/or officials of Herod. As supporters of Herod's rule, the Herodians would have found Jesus' preaching of a coming kingdom and (if known) his connection to the Davidic royal line to be a threat to their political interests (Meier, 744). At this point in the narrative, Jesus' ministry has been exclusively within the region of Galilee. Both Galilee and Perea were the original provinces given to Herod Antipas by Rome upon the death of his father, Herod the Great. Moreover, Idumea is the ancestral home of the Herodian dynasty.

Joining the people from Galilee, Judea, Jerusalem, Idumea, and Perea are the crowds that come from the area around Tyre and Sidon. Jesus' ministry has now attracted gentiles from two of the leading Phoenician maritime merchant provinces of Rome. Their inclusion suggests that at some point, Jesus will also find himself in conflict with Rome.

The crowd has now swelled to "crushing" proportions. Despite the potentially deadly repercussions, Jesus does not scale back ministry but expands it. He calls twelve people to "be with him" and participate in ministry by preaching his kingdom message and having the authority to exorcize unclean spirits (3:14-15). Again, opposition will follow expansion. One of the twelve whom Jesus has chosen, Judas Iscariot, will betray him (3:19).

The pattern continues into the final portion of this section. Again, Mark notes the size of the crowd (3:20). What follows is a Markan inclusio—one story "sandwiched" between the beginning and end of another story—that highlights the opposition. The first conflict comes from an unexpected place, Jesus' own family. They believe that he is no longer in his right mind and are on their way to get him. Mark then turns the narrative lens to the "scribes from Jerusalem" who accuse Jesus of demon possession. They attribute his power to Beelzebul, the prince of demons. The story shifts back to Jesus' being told that his family is looking for him. Jesus redefines his family as those who "do the will of God" (3:35), which is precisely how Mark has depicted Jesus' ministry. Howard Clark Kee argues that this new eschatological family is a break from the actual family unit that allows followers of Jesus to form a new kinship group. It represents Markan "eschatological existence," which "involves the acceptance of present opportunities and obligations in view of the age to come" (Kee, 109).

The opposition to Jesus has arisen from every possible vantage point. He is confronted by his family and will soon face betrayal from one of his handpicked apostles. The spread of his fame and the increasing number of people drawn to him potentially threaten to exacerbate the tensions between him, the religious leaders in Jerusalem, and the supporters of Herod. Eventually, Jesus' ministry will catch the attention of Rome.

▌ THE TEXT IN THE INTERPRETIVE TRADITION

One of the initial concerns for Roman Catholic interpreters of Mark 3:31-35 was reconciling the presence of Jesus' siblings (also mentioned in 6:3) and the perpetual virginity of Mary. Bede states emphatically, "the brothers of the Lord must not be thought to be the sons of the ever-virgin Mary." Jerome in his treatise *Against Helvidius* argues that Jesus' brothers were actually his cousins. Another argument for the perpetual virginity of Mary asserts that the siblings of Jesus were the children of Joseph from a previous marriage. However, the majority of scholars from the patristic period to the present focus on the formation of Jesus' new family.

John Chrysostom and John Calvin believed Jesus' actions demonstrated the primacy of spiritual relations over fleshly ones. Pseudo-Jerome held that these spiritual relations were not limited by gender. The inclusion of "sisters" in Jesus' new family (Mark 3:35) causes him to conclude: "He [Jesus] discerns us not by sex but by our deeds." Donald Juel avoids spiritualizing Jesus' words. Instead, he points out the controversial nature of denying the most basic social institution of the time, the family, and forging a new one (Juel, 65). Ched Myers articulates the eschatological role of Jesus' new family: it will socialize people into the kingdom just as the natural family socializes individuals into society (Myers, 168).

◼ THE TEXT IN CONTEMPORARY DISCUSSION

The phrase "family values" hit the national political scene in 1976, when the Republican Party decried the "erosion of family structures and family values." At the 1992 Republican National Convention, Pat Robertson and Dan Quayle claimed that "family values" were what the Republican Party stood for. Since then, the GOP has been criticized for its narrow definition of "family," often specified as a mother, a father, and their child/ren, when only 20 percent of US households fit this particular model. The phrase "family values" often works as code to refer to policies opposing reproductive and homosexual rights. But as historian Lawrence Stone observed while delivering the Tanner Lectures on Human Values at Harvard University, family values actually include several wider areas of social life: how children are socialized to fit into definitions of societal and individual roles, and a range of values concerning work, the accumulation of goods, sexual behavior, religion, and race (Stone, 70). In practice, any political party's policies will affect people's lives in all these areas.

In Mark 3:31-35, Jesus redefines his family. How might Mark's story of Jesus shape our behavior and affect our attitudes in terms of "family values," that is, our attitudes toward and behaviors concerning the areas just named?

Mark 4:1-34: Parables of the Kingdom

◼ THE TEXT IN ITS ANCIENT CONTEXT

Chapter 4 opens with the first discourse found in Mark. It contains three parables that use the common images of Galilean agrarian life: seeds and sowers. Jesus uses the parables to explain the kingdom he proclaims. The parables also serve to explain the rejection of Jesus and his kingdom message to Mark's readers.

The first parable describes a sower whose seed falls on four types of soil: a path, thorny ground, rocky ground, and good ground. The sower initially appears to be carelessly scattering seed. He has not identified a particular plot or portion of land to sow; nor is he careful about seed placement. Consequently, the majority of the parable is dedicated to describing the consequences: the seed does not grow from bad soil. However, the good soil produces an unimaginable harvest of thirty, sixty, and a hundredfold. These numbers vastly exceeded the 10 percent increase that a farmer would have considered a "bumper crop." Yet, no explanation is given about why the good soil produces such an unheard-of harvest. The assumption of the parable is that the seed is inherently good and only needs the right or good soil to produce copiously.

Producing a harvest at the level Jesus describes would have been a life-changing event for the masses that listened to him. Those gathered were more than likely dispossessed landowners or day laborers whose lack of employment and/or land enabled them to wander the countryside following Jesus (St. Clair, 105). They were ensnared by debt for their entire lives. The burden of Roman taxes, Jerusalem tithes, and the money required to seed the land and take care of a family left many people living at a subsistence level. The result is that those who had land often lost it because of debt. Those living on the land as tenant farmers could never earn enough to buy the land they worked. However, a harvest of thirty, sixty, or a hundredfold meant not only the difference between life and death but also freedom from a debt system that kept them in financial slavery (Myers, 177).

Although Jesus admonishes the crowd to listen, not everyone understands what he is saying. When the crowds have dispersed, those "around him" ask him to explain the parable. Before giving the explanation, he tells them that what they are in receipt of is the "mystery of the kingdom of God" (v. 11). Something is about to be revealed to them that will remain in parables to those "outside." This mystery is a dividing line that demarcates outsiders and insiders.

Mark's Jesus stresses the insider-outsider distinction by quoting Isa. 6:9-10. Whether the lack of understanding and subsequent repentance is the product of Jesus' intention or the consequence of one's failure to hear and accept Jesus' words depends on one's interpretation of *hina* in the Isa. 6:9-10 quotation as either an expression of purpose ("so that") or of result ("in order that"). Although C. S. Mann argues that determinism is a characteristic of apocalyptic and that an interpretation of purpose would not be surprising to Mark's audience, the subsequent parable in this chapter suggests a reading that implies *consequence*. Mark asserts that the meaning of Jesus' parable is "to be disclosed" and "come to light" (4:22). In addition, Mark will show the repeated misunderstanding of the Twelve, who are recipients of the parable's explanation. Originally cast as insiders, their misunderstanding suggests a refusal on their part to heed what they have been taught. Thus the line Mark draws is traversable. Insiders could be "anyone" who has "ears to hear" and listen (v. 9). These receive the mystery of the kingdom that Jesus is giving to them. However, a refusal to hear and listen can relegate one to the outside.

What follows is an explanation of the parable that is critical for understanding all of the parables in Mark (v. 13). It begins simply: "The sower sows the word" (v. 14). The primary sower in Mark's Gospel is Jesus, whose ministry began with proclaiming the good news of God. His sowing, too, seems wasteful. The vast majority of those who gather around him when he is giving the word are poor, diseased, demon-possessed, or considered sinners. They lack economic means and social acceptance and cannot attain the standards of ritual purity. Although their lack relegates them to the margins of their current society, it will not hinder their participation or production in the kingdom of God. According to the parable, Satan, persecution or trouble, and wealth or worldly desires cause spiritual barrenness. But if people will hear, accept, and act on the word, then they, too, can be fruitful (v. 20).

In short, the kingdom is not what people would expect. It is hidden (vv. 22) like a seed on the earth that is not readily seen but takes time to grow and make its presence known (vv. 26-29). It starts small and looks insignificant but becomes great (vv. 30-32). One could easily dismiss the kingdom and its messenger. For this reason, Jesus admonishes those around him (and Mark, by extension, is telling his readers) to "listen" (v. 22) and "pay attention" (v. 23), lest they too become the bad soil that rejects the seed of this sower.

▉ The Text in the Interpretive Tradition

The earliest interpretations of Jesus' parables were allegorical in nature. The early church read parables as stories that used earthly symbols to communicate heavenly truths. Pseudo-Jerome wrote that Jesus spoke in parables so that "those who could not take in heavenly things, might conceive what they heard by an earthly similitude." The first major departure from an allegoristic approach was by Adolf Jülicher in 1888. He argued that Jesus would not have used coded language; therefore, the allegorical interpretations of the parables were the creation of the Gospel writers. Interestingly enough, the patristic and medieval interpreters had no problem with the coded language of the parables. Although they believed the ability to see or understand was a result of God's grace, the lack of understanding was attributed to human unwillingness (Pseudo-Chrysostom), specifically people "mak[ing] themselves not to see" (Theophylact).

Scholars who followed in the wake of Jülicher, like Joachim Jeremias, believed that by studying the parables one could reconstruct the situation in which they developed and uncover the original sayings of Jesus. The next shift occurred when the focus of study moved from the world behind the text to the narrative world of the text. Contemporary scholars now look at the literary context of the parables to ascertain their meaning and seek to be mindful of the insider-outsider dynamic of the text by acknowledging both the comfort and the discomfort created by the text.

▌The Text in Contemporary Discussion

Parables are tricky. One the one hand, they use familiar imagery to communicate a message. This lends an air of accessibility; it makes one feel like the parables can be easily understood. Yet this is not the case for those around Jesus in Mark's Gospel. He must explain the parables, and then only does so in private, thereby erecting a wall between those on the inside, who understand, and those on the outside, who do not. Coded language separates, and the inevitability of its separating function is often uncomfortable. The first major interpretive shift in the study of parables occurred precisely because of a scholar's discomfort with Jesus' use of coded language. Yet some people are comfortable with coded language. They see the boundaries that the code erects as necessary for survival and communication. The apocalyptic language of Daniel and Revelation and the use of spirituals by African Americans are two examples.

Mark 4:35—6:6: Ministry and Rejection

▌The Text in Its Ancient Context

Writing shortly after the fall of the Jerusalem temple, Mark responds to the religious crisis by encouraging his readers to follow Jesus. In this section, Mark makes it clear to the Jews and gentiles that constitute his audience that following Jesus will require the inclusion of the gentiles as well as Jews like the woman with the hemorrhage, who have found themselves marginalized by Jewish law.

After a day of public and private instruction on the kingdom of God, Jesus decides to take his disciples to the "other side" of the lake (4:35). Before they reach gentile soil, however, a storm arises that threatens to keep them from reaching their destination. It also causes the disciples to fear for their lives (4:38). Within the narrative context, the storm could be symbolic of the Jewish attitudes that oppose the inclusion of the gentiles. Since Jesus is able to subdue nature in the same way he has been able to subdue demons, the disciples do not perish as they follow Jesus' command to cross over. Mark, therefore, shows his readers that this ministerial direction is by divine proclamation and under divine protection.

According to Mark, Jesus and his disciples disembark in the land of the Gerasenes (5:1). Although the name of this region differs from that given in Matthew (Gadarenes, 8:28) and its location is unknown, it is a gentile territory near the Decapolis, a group of ten Greek city-states southeast of the Sea of Galilee. This area represents the height of uncleanness for Jews. The first person Jesus and the disciples encounter is a man possessed by so many demons that they refer to themselves as "Legion" (5:9). He lives among the tombs, a place inhabited by the dead (5:3). There is a "great herd" of pigs nearby (5:11).

It seems that Jesus has entered the "strong man's house" (3:27) by invading enemy territory both spiritually and politically. "Legion" is the name of a Roman military unit composed of about six thousand soldiers. During this time, the soldiers stationed in Palestine displayed a wild boar as their symbol. Although the demons possess the man, their control of him is secondary to their desire to remain within that particular geographical locale. After begging Jesus not to send them out of the region (*chora*, 5:10), they beg him to send them into the swine (5:12). By exorcizing the demons, Jesus has "plundered [the strong man's] property" (3:27). He is strong enough to subdue the demoniac (5:4) because he is the stronger one whom John foretold (1:7). Mark shows his readers that this foray into gentile territory does not result in the demise of Jesus or his disciples. Neither does it contaminate them. On the contrary, it results in the drowning of the demon-possessed pigs in the sea, like Pharaoh's army in Exodus, and produces another disciple who follows Jesus in his preaching ministry (5:20).

Next, Jesus and his disciples return to Jewish soil. Mark now links the stories of Jairus's daughter and the woman with the issue of blood. Both are referred to as "daughter" (5:23, 34), a familial designation that suggests they are part of the Jewish community. Given that the number twelve, the number of Israel's tribes, is used with reference to both women, perhaps Mark intends these two females to symbolize Israel.

This passage begins with Jairus's begging Jesus to heal his daughter. If the two women are meant to represent Judaism in some way, then Jairus's daughter might represent Jews whose lives are properly circumscribed by the law. The little girl is the legitimate offspring of her father (5:23). He speaks on her behalf and solicits the aid she needs. Moreover, he is a leader of a synagogue. He and his family would have been fully included in the community. Furthermore, her age suggests that she is still virginal. Her presence within the home suggests that she is ritually clean. However, none of this prevents her from being sick to the point of death and needing Jesus to heal her.

Before the girl is healed, Jesus is stopped by the touch of a woman who has suffered from hemorrhages for twelve years. She may represent those who have been marginalized by the law. Her condition renders her status as perpetually ritually unclean (Leviticus 15), and she has found no one to help her. Like the little girl, she is sick. She has gone to physicians, but the physicians have not made her better. She too needs Jesus in order to be healed. However, her healing will restore more than her health. It will restore her place within the community. She will no longer be excluded by virtue of her disease.

Critical to each story is Jesus. If these women are meant to represent classes of people, Mark may be showing that Jesus' ministry is needed not only for the gentiles to be delivered (5:1-20) but also for Israel to be healed. By placing the little girl's healing last, perhaps Mark suggests that Israel will not be healed until not only the gentiles but also the Jews who have been marginalized by the law are included. Like the father who was told to "only believe" (5:36) and the woman whose "faith made [her] well" (5:34), Israel must heed Jesus' kingdom message and believe the good news.

Unfortunately, the prospect of this occurring does not look good. Earlier, the gentiles begged Jesus to leave their neighborhood (5:17). Now, although a crowd is pressing in on Jesus, only one person has enough faith to get Jesus' attention (5:30-31). Rather than celebrate the fact that the little girl is not dead, the mourners laugh at Jesus (5:40). Even the people from Jesus' hometown are offended (*skandalizein*) by him (6:3). Their unbelief amazes Jesus (6:6). Yet the only scandalous thing Mark has shown Jesus do is minister to those who have been left out.

■ THE TEXT IN THE INTERPRETIVE TRADITION

This section contains four of the most extraordinary miracles in the Gospel. During the late nineteenth and early twentieth centuries, scholars from the history of religions school began to explore the Hellenistic origins of Christianity. In 1935, Ludwig Bieler published a two-volume work, *Theios Anēr*, which cataloged the characteristics of the Greek "divine man" (*theios anēr*) and listed examples of the divine man in ancient literature including the Bible. One of the characteristics of the divine man was the performance of miracles. Based on the similarities discovered between Hellenistic figures and Jesus, a *theios anēr* or god-man Christology arose. Redaction critics who accepted the existence of a *theios anēr* Christology argued that Mark was written as either a modification of it (Keck) or an outright rejection of it (Weeden). Other scholars, such as Barry Blackburn, deny a *theios anēr* Christology in Mark and argue that the miracle stories are derived from a Jewish rather than a Hellenistic context. Narrative critics, on the other hand, were not concerned about the miracle stories' connection to a cultural milieu. Instead, they looked at how these stories moved Mark's plot forward and attended to the expansion of Jesus' ministry and mission.

■ THE TEXT IN CONTEMPORARY DISCUSSION

On January 20, 2009, Barack Hussein Obama was inaugurated as the forty-fourth president of the United States of America. He was the first African American to hold this nation's highest political office. This led many to conclude that the United States was now a "post-racial" society. Somehow President Obama's election was believed to be the death knell of racism, race-based discrimination, and prejudice. It proved that America was whole, or at the very least no longer divided by race. Yet Sunday mornings remain the most segregated time of the American day, and church pews remain one of the most segregated places.

At the time of President Obama's election, approximately 5 percent of US churches were racially integrated or had 20 percent or more of their members represent a different racial/ethnic background from the majority group. Half of these congregations were trending toward a single ethnic identity, which was a reflection of the basic preference among all racial groups: homogeneity. In order for a congregation to be truly multicultural, no single racial identity can dominate its religious life or practice. This means that more than the face of the congregation must change. The congregation must be prepared for changes in things like leadership, worship practices, mission projects, and financial priorities.

As we reflect on this passage in Mark, it is important for us to consider honestly who the gentiles would be to us—whose racial/ethnic background is not only different from our own but also what separates us from each other. Who would be the outcasts—the people who share a similar racial/ethnic background but whose social, cultural, and/or economic status separates us from them? What storms could potentially arise if we were to "cross over to the other side"? Would our declining and dying congregations be resurrected if we, too, included the modern-day equivalent to Mark's "outsider" (gentile) and "outcast"? What would national policies like immigration, health-care reform, and welfare reform look like?

Mark 6:7-29: Ministry and Murder

▋ THE TEXT IN ITS ANCIENT CONTEXT

Whereas the parable of the sower in chapter 4 focuses on the condition of the soil (4:3-8), this section reveals the possible consequences of sowing the word. The theme began with the sending out of the Twelve whom Jesus called to be with him, proclaim the message, and have authority over unclean spirits (3:14-15). This is the same ministry work that Mark records Jesus doing and that the disciples now perform (6:12-13). Jesus gives them specific instructions on how to govern themselves and what to bring with them. It is clear that Jesus expects the people to welcome the itinerant ministers because he tells them to take nothing with them except a staff (6:8). The *Didache* also shares this expectation of hospitality (*Did.* 11.1–12). However, Jesus is aware that not everyone will receive the Twelve. In this instance, they are to shake the dust from their feet (6:11), thereby disassociating themselves from the bad soil that does not listen and accept the word.

The ministry of the Twelve is apparently successful. People begin to speculate that John the Baptist or Elijah has been raised from the dead (6:14-15). The ministry work of the disciples, work that clearly mirrors the ministry of Jesus, is now connected to John the Baptist. Prior to this point, Mark has told the reader that John was arrested (1:14). Now the reader finds out that John has been beheaded by Herod (6:16) and his death was orchestrated by Herodias (6:19-24). Like Jezebel, who sought to kill Elijah for condemning the worship of her gods and killing her prophets (1 Kings 19:1-2), Herodias wanted John executed for speaking against her marriage to Herod (6:18-19).

At this point in the narrative, one sower is dead, and sowing the word lies at the root of his death. Members of Mark's community, who already know of Jesus' death, would also know that John will not be the only casualty in Mark's story. Jesus will die, and Mark is laying the foundation to connect his death to John's. In Mark's narrative, both men are "handed over" or "betrayed" (*paradothēnai*, 1:14; 3:19; 14:41). The means of death (beheading and crucifixion) are the most shameful ways of executing a person during this time. Mark shows their words to be the precipitating factor in their deaths (6:18; 14:62). The people's assertion that John has been raised from the dead (6:14) prepares Mark's audience for Jesus' prediction of his own resurrection (8:31; 9:31; 10:34).

Upon the disciples' return, Jesus decides that they should get away from the crowds and rest (6:31). However, they cannot escape the multitudes. The people flock to where they are. The scene is reminiscent of Israel in the wilderness, whose hunger is satisfied by manna, bread from heaven. In this instance, Jesus looks up to heaven, blesses and breaks five loaves, divides two fish, and gives them to his disciples to distribute (6:41). At least five thousand people are fed (6:44). Once again, Jesus and his disciples are aligned in ministry. Yet Mark will show that they still do not grasp the significance of who Jesus is, and therefore cannot possibly understand the consequences of following in a ministry like his.

▌ THE TEXT IN THE INTERPRETIVE TRADITION

In 1901, Wilhelm Wrede published his groundbreaking work, *Das Messiasgeheimnis in den Evangelien*. He is credited with being "the first to appreciate the theological nature of the synoptics" (Dunn, 92). His basic thesis was that Jesus' silencing of demons, healed persons, Peter after his confession at Caesarea Philippi, and the disciples after the transfiguration as well as the private instruction, parabolic teachings, and continued misunderstanding of the disciples (like the misunderstanding about the loaves in 6:52 noted above) are all a part of the "messianic secret." The messianic secret was Mark's attempt to resolve the tension between the early church's claim that Jesus is the Messiah and Jesus' not claiming this role for himself in the Gospel. Wrede believed that the messianic secret was not historical in origin, but rather a theological motif created by and imposed on the Gospel by Mark.

James Blevins traces three waves of reactions during the first seventy years after the release of Wrede's monograph. The first decade was characterized by a widespread rejection of his theory. The few who accepted it did so in modified form. For example, Albert Schweitzer accepted Wrede's theory but did not attribute the secrecy theme to Mark. Modifications of the theory continued into the next wave of reactions. During the second and third decades, scholars tried to connect the motif to the historical Jesus. Form critics who accepted Wrede's argument noted that certain elements included in the secrecy motif, like the silencing of demons, was not the work of Mark, but preredaction material. During the years just before and after World War II (fourth and fifth decades), a primary issue was whether the secrecy motif originated with Jesus, and was therefore historical in nature, or with Mark, thereby making the Gospel a wholly theological construction.

This interplay between history and theology also emerges in this section, when Mark lays the death of John the Baptist at the feet of Herodias (Mark 6:19, 24; cf. Matt. 14:8). Mark portrays Herod as easily manipulated and an unwilling partner in Herodias's deadly scheme. However, Josephus attributes John's death to Herod's fear of John's popularity (*Ant.* 18.116–19), not Herodias's "grudge against him" (6:19). According to Bede, it is not Herod's fear but Herodias's fear of Herod repenting of his marriage to her that is the impetus for her murderous designs. Theophylact also implied Herodias's culpability by claiming that lust is what prompted Herod to comply with his wife's wishes. Despite Josephus's assertion and the Herodian rulers' hunger for political power, both biblical scholarship and popular culture have left Herodias's diabolical role in John's death unquestioned.

In medieval Europe, Herodias was said to fly through the night once a year and was purported to be the leader of a cult of witches. During the nineteenth century, Flaubert and Massanet both wrote stories in which Herodias bore all the features of a stereotypical femme fatale. Contemporary Mark scholars pay little attention to the historical Herodias. Their focus tends to be more theological as they note the similarities between John's and Jesus' death, the analogous roles Herod and Pilate played in their respective deaths, and the parallels between John, Herod, and Herodias and Elijah, Ahab, and Jezebel.

▉ THE TEXT IN CONTEMPORARY DISCUSSION

Although much of Wrede's thesis has been dismissed or modified by subsequent scholars, any discussion of Mark's Gospel must take it into consideration. C. S. Mann correctly asserts, "The 'secrecy' motif is too strongly entrenched in the narrative to be dismissed lightly" (Mann, 216). However, it is almost universally agreed that Wrede's "messianic secrecy" is too limiting a category to house such "disparate phenomena" (Donahue and Harrington, 28) that have a "variety of motives" at work (Dunn, 98). Since the World War II years, scholarship remains divided on whether the secrecy motif finds its genesis in Jesus or Mark. On one end of the debate are those who locate the motif's origin with Jesus, who was afraid that revealing himself would incite a military revolt. On the other end are those who say it is a creation of Mark, who seeks thereby to explain why Jesus does not claim to be the Messiah in his Gospel. At the heart of the issue is whether the origin of Mark's Gospel is historical or theological.

Meanwhile, the work of feminists, which has drawn scholarly attention to the negative portrayal of Herodias, struggles with the historical and theological interplay in Scripture. They admonish readers of the biblical text to beware when reading stories about women because historically these have been "stories by men about women" (Schüssler Fiorenza, 50). They reveal the patriarchal language in the text in which Herodias is referred to as a possession belonging to Herod's brother (6:18). They call attention to the contradiction between Herodias's alleged power in having John killed and her absence from Herod's birthday celebration, which suggests she was not important enough to attend. They examine the roles of women within the sociocultural world that shaped the Gospels. This allows them to show how women have been misrepresented, overlooked, or even vilified.

Narrative readings allow scholars to hold the story world of Mark together with its theological import while examining the historical background of the text. Narrative critics see Mark as an author with an important story to tell. In the case of Herodias, narrative critics look at how a woman has been characterized: What does the author show and tell us about her? Does she espouse or reject the evaluative point of view (the belief system or moral disposition) of the narrator? What are her character traits? If the portrayal in Mark's Gospel is negative, it is also important to ask if her role is consistent with Mark's characterization of other women his Gospel, or does he present a variety of female characters? While her story as presented by Mark may not be historically accurate, it can help the reader understand Mark's story better.

Mark 7:1-23: Ministry and Tradition

▌THE TEXT IN ITS ANCIENT CONTEXT

Jesus' popularity among the masses has gotten the attention of the religious leaders in Jerusalem (7:1). Previously, the scribes who had come from Jerusalem accused Jesus of being possessed by Beelzebul (3:22). Now the Pharisees join the scribes. The point of contention is the "tradition of the elders," the oral law that was eventually written in the Mishnah, as it relates to hand washing. The scribes and Pharisees notice that Jesus' disciples do not wash their hands before eating, and question why (7:2, 5). At the root of their concern is more than hand washing; it is the practice of their faith.

Whereas Mark's response to post-temple Judaism is to encourage following Jesus, the Pharisees' response was to bring holiness into everyday life. In their opinion, Jews could uphold God's requirement for holiness (Lev. 11:44, 45; 19:2) by ordering life in such a way that all they did and touched was sanctified. This required avoiding anything that defiled a person. To disregard the practices that helped to cleanse daily life was to dismantle the faith and disregard the oral tradition. This dismantling was, in their eyes, as destructive to Judaism as was the destruction of the temple. For the Pharisee, on the one hand, the Torah as interpreted by the oral tradition mediated the relationship between God and God's people. Mark, on the other hand, sees Jesus fulfilling that role (Juel, 106–7).

According to Mark, Jesus asserts that "human tradition" and the commands of God are at variance with one another (7:8-9). At the heart of Jesus' concern is the inclusion of those heretofore excluded from the practice of the faith. When Mark writes that "all the Jews" do not eat with unwashed hands (7:3), he is using "Jews" to refer to those who adhered to the teachings of Pharisaic Judaism because he has not shown this to be the practice of the Jewish followers of Jesus. It would have been virtually impossible for the five thousand men fed in the wilderness to have washed their hands before eating (6:44). Neither does he record any hand washing before the meal at Levi's house (2:15). Moreover, it is doubtful that many of the people who came to Jesus would have been concerned with, or had the means of maintaining vigilant hand-washing practices, since these persons were predominantly indigent, ill, or demon-possessed. Consequently, Mark's use of "all of the Jews" is inaccurate. However, saying "all the Jews" allows him to separate the practices of his community not only from Pharisaic Judaism but also Judaism in general. Therefore, Jesus' refusal to uphold the tradition of hand washing is no longer a difference of opinion with those from a particular branch of Judaism but represents a rift with Judaism itself. It also allows gentiles and Jews who do not or cannot keep the traditions of the elders to follow Jesus.

Jesus begins his critique of the tradition by quoting Isa. 29:13. He uses the words of the prophet to argue against the practices of the Pharisees. In short, they are hypocritical (7:6). Their tradition actually militates against true worship of God (7:7). Consequently, the Jews in Mark's community need not feel obligated to follow the Pharisees or feel excluded by them. Moreover, the gentiles in Mark's community can reach the same conclusion, as it is clear that Mark is writing to them also. He explains what "defiled hands" mean (7:2), expounds on the "tradition of elders" (7:3-4), and translates the Aramaic word *korban* (7:11).

Jesus pushes his kingdom agenda further by using this opportunity to explain what truly defiles a person. Mark refers to Jesus' teaching here as a "parable" (7:17). As with the telling of the parables in chapter 4, Jesus commands those around him to "listen" (7:14). Moreover, he explains the meaning of the parable to his disciples in private. These similarities intimate that Jesus is telling his listeners something about the kingdom of God.

Specifically, Jesus teaches that an understanding of defilement in terms of the kingdom of God is not about what goes in but what goes out (7:15, 20). There is a difference between the stomach and the heart (7:19). What comes out of the heart corrupts. What goes in the stomach does not have the power to defile, leaving Mark to conclude that Jesus has "declared all foods clean" (7:19). How one eats (whether the hands are washed or unwashed) and what one eats (whether the food is deemed clean or unclean according to dietary laws) no longer has the power to deny persons a relationship with God or prevent participation among the people of God.

■ THE TEXT IN THE INTERPRETIVE TRADITION

Readings of this passage have primarily focused on the dispute between Jesus and the Pharisees over the validity of oral law. Many commentators equated "oral law" with "man-made" law because they were unaware that the Pharisees believed in a dual Torah, written and oral, that was revealed to Moses on Sinai (Donahue and Harrington, 228). However, interpretations became more nuanced as scholars began to examine the Jewish context of Jesus' ministry and no longer to view first-century Judaism in monolithic terms. Instead, scholars began to see the varied strands of Judaism and how they responded to the fall of the Jerusalem temple. Consequently, descriptions of Pharisaic Judaism went beyond labels of "religious legalism." Attention to the sociocultural context of Mark's Gospel filled out the flat characters that Mark presented. It also prompted contemporary scholars to view this passage as breaking the barriers that would have prevented gentile participation in the early church. This passage clarified for Mark's community its stand on issues that would have distinguished it from Pharisaic Judaism.

■ THE TEXT IN CONTEMPORARY DISCUSSION

In almost every religious tradition, there is a belief that certain things or people have the power to defile individuals or the community. There are usually two basic approaches to dealing with the pollutant: washing machine or garbage disposal. At the heart of the washing-machine approach is the conviction that the power to cleanse is greater than the power to contaminate. Therefore, the polluted thing or person can be cleaned up and restored to inclusion. When one opts for the garbage-disposal approach, there is a belief that the power to contaminate is greater than the power to cleanse. Consequently, the pollutant must be removed before it corrupts another individual or community. One's approach depends on the particular contaminant being addressed, and both approaches can be utilized within the same religious tradition. For example, unwashed hands, certain foods, and table fellowship with the wrong people were just a few of the contaminants that first-century Pharisees believed made a person unclean. Hands could be purified by washing (the washing-machine approach) and certain foods and people could be avoided (the garbage-disposal approach).

What are the pollutants that we fear in our contemporary practice of the faith? Which ones do we believe have a power to contaminate that is greater than the power to cleanse (requiring us to use a garbage-disposal approach)? Over what pollutants is the power to cleanse greater than the pollutants' power to defile (so we may use the washing-machine approach)? According to Mark, Jesus redefines what defiles a person and thereby pronounces all food clean (7:19). By so doing, he eradicates the need to employ either the washing-machine or the garbage-disposal models because there no longer exists any need for cleansing. Do we need to amend our understanding of what defiles and therefore our approach to some things and/or some people?

Mark 7:24—8:26: Receptivity and Misunderstanding

▌ The Text in Its Ancient Context

Jesus again journeys into gentile territory. This trip reveals the receptivity of the gentiles to Jesus' ministry and proves that there is room for them to be included. Mark, then, uses the receptivity of the gentiles to highlight the growing lack of perceptivity of the Jews whom Jesus encounters throughout this section.

Jesus' first stop is in the region of Tyre. There, he meets a Syrophoenician woman who begs him to cast a demon out of her daughter (7:26). Initially, Jesus seems disinclined to help her. He dismisses her by insisting that "the children" (Israel) are to be fed (*chortasthēnai*) first (7:27). To do otherwise is tantamount to giving their food to dogs (7:28). Although Jesus calls her a dog (7:27), the woman is not dissuaded. She insists that even the dogs get crumbs (7:28). Jesus validates her statement by casting the demon out of her daughter (7:29-30). However, the veracity of her statement has farther-reaching implications than the fulfillment of an individual request.

By recounting the feeding of the five thousand in a manner that alluded to Israel's experience of manna in the wilderness, Mark had shown that "the children" have already eaten to the point of satisfaction (6:42). There he used the same verb that occurs in 7:27 (*chortasthēnai*) to convey that the desert meal filled them. He also noted that the disciples collected twelve baskets of leftovers, symbolically suggesting a basket from each of the twelve tribes of Israel. Indeed, there are crumbs from the children's table, and now Jesus meets a woman so hungry for his help that she is willing to receive these scraps. Mark further emphasizes the gentile woman's hunger for Jesus' ministry by placing her story immediately after Jesus' confrontation with the scribes and Pharisees. While the Pharisees and scribes were concerned with the purity of one's hands and one's food, the gentile woman is willing to eat off the floor to get what she needs from Jesus. By linking her story to the feeding of the five thousand and positioning it immediately after Jesus' argument with the scribes and Pharisees, Mark argues that the inclusion of gentiles will neither prevent nor lessen what God has for the Jews.

Upon leaving Tyre, Jesus travels to the region of the Decapolis. Mark identifies this place as the locale of the former demoniac's preaching ministry. It is here that he proclaimed what Jesus had done for him (5:20). Earlier, the people of this region begged Jesus to leave (5:17). Now they beg Jesus to heal a deaf and mute man (7:32). Jesus heals the man "in private, away from the crowd"

(7:33) and forbids the people from telling it. Yet they proclaim it "zealously" (7:36), thereby joining the former demoniac in his preaching ministry by again proclaiming what Jesus has done.

The two preceding events occur at the initiative of gentiles. They seek out Jesus and request his aid. The feeding of the four thousand, which is the last act Mark records as occurring on gentile soil, happens at Jesus' initiative. Like the feeding of the five thousand on Jewish soil, the motivation behind this miracle is Jesus' compassion. However, Jesus had compassion for the Israelites because they lacked leaders (6:34). Here, Mark emphasizes the receptivity of the gentiles to Jesus' ministry by noting that the crowd has been with Jesus for three days (8:2). As a result, they are hungry. However, their physical hunger is the direct result of their hunger for Jesus, a hunger that causes them to remain with him for three days without food. Therefore, Jesus responds.

Using seven loaves and a few small fish, he feeds the four thousand gathered around him. Jesus has now used a total of twelve loaves to feed both Jews and gentiles. The number twelve may allude to the twelve tribes of Israel. If this is the case, then Mark is letting his community know that what has been given to Israel is more than enough to satisfy both groups. The supply is so great that neither group can exhaust it. Like the Jews who were fed in the wilderness, the gentiles are filled (*chortasthēnai*) and there are still leftovers (8:8).

After the feeding of the four thousand, Jesus immediately returns to Jewish territory. Here he is met with skepticism and misunderstanding. His first encounter is with Pharisees who demand a "sign from heaven" (8:11). Jesus refuses to oblige them (8:12). However, Mark has answered their question for the reader, with the details he has included in his Gospel. He has recounted the heavens opening (1:10), a voice from heaven at Jesus' baptism (1:11), Jesus looking to heaven as he blessed the five loaves he used to feed five thousand people (6:41), and Jesus looking up to heaven before healing the deaf mute (7:34). Although Mark never mentions the presence of the Pharisees at the aforementioned events, his narrative flow makes the Pharisees appear obtuse to the reader. Because Mark's audience has been given all these "signs from heaven," they are left to assume that the Pharisees should understand rather than argue.

Misunderstanding is not a quality reserved for Jesus' enemies alone. There is much his disciples do not get. Mark shows their lack of understanding in the next episode. Jesus warns them about the "yeast of the Pharisees" and the "yeast of Herod" (8:15). They do not grasp the symbolic use of yeast as a corrupting agent (Donahue and Harrington, 252). Instead, they think Jesus is talking about their lack of physical bread. Even if they could not appreciate the full intent of Jesus' warning, the fact that they think Jesus is troubled by a lack of bread after feeding at least nine thousand people with only twelve loaves shows their imperceptivity.

This section closes with Jesus' healing a blind man. What is unique about this account is that Jesus must lay his hands on the man twice to fully restore his sight (8:23, 25). Given Jesus' command of nature, authority over demons, ability to multiply fish and loaves, and healing virtue that is so strong that touching his garments restores people to full health, the need to touch the blind man twice does not suggest a diminishment of Jesus' power. Instead, it points to the persistent imperceptivity of the disciples. They are blind like this man. They do not get it on the first encounter. They see a little, but they do not yet grasp the whole thing.

▮ THE TEXT IN THE INTERPRETIVE TRADITION

Some of the earliest commentators on the story of the Syrophoenician woman (7:24-30) focus on the woman as model of faithful persistence. Bede describes her reply to Jesus' initial refusal of her request as both "humble and faithful." He asserts that these are the qualities that garnered her request. Calvin observes, "she adhered firmly to . . . [her] sentiment of faith" despite the fact that Jesus "[makes] trial of her faith" (Calvin 1845, 2:266-68). Although he describes her actions as "presumptuous," most early commentators downplay her transgression of social boundaries by finding qualities such as humility and service in her behavior. Pseudo-Chrysostom goes so far as to say her reverence was demonstrated by placing herself at the level of a dog. Feminist and womanist scholars broke from this tradition by highlighting her disregard of social convention and applauding her bold behavior. They point to her "sass" (womanists) and her wit (feminists), rather than traditional female virtues of passivity and submission, as the reason she got what she needed from Jesus.

▮ THE TEXT IN CONTEMPORARY DISCUSSION

Scholars have attempted to soften the impact of Jesus' calling the Syrophoenician woman a "dog," by (1) drawing attention to more positive gentile understandings of "dog" as a house pet (!); (2) pointing out that Jesus actually referred to her and her child as "little dogs" (*kynaria*), which is less offensive than "dog" (*kyōn*); or (3) arguing that Jesus' words represented prevailing Jewish opinion about gentiles, rather than his own perception of the woman, in order to counter opposition to gentile inclusion. The fact remains, however, that this ethnic slur is found on the lips of Jesus.

Now consider how common it has become in some parts of popular culture today to refer to women in general, and African American women in particular, as "bitches" (female dogs). The lyrics of many hip-hop songs equate "bitch" with "woman." Reducing women to the level of animals allows men outright to exploit them or treat them as pets (Collins). Moreover, women are also referred to as "hoes" (whores), thereby relegating them to the status of sex objects, or as "chicken-heads," persons of intellectual inferiority. Social theorists and feminist scholars acknowledge that while it is easy to point out the vulgar references to women in hip-hop and especially its subgenre gangsta rap, these are merely the blatant expression of a wider societal misogyny.

The attempts by Mark scholars to neutralize the "dog" language in the text is akin to the efforts of some women and that of some African Americans to defuse the racist and misogynistic import of the *b* and the *n* word. As people argue both sides of the issue, the question remains: Are there words that are so negative that it is impossible to redeem their meaning or their use? If so, what do we do with a text like Mark 7:24-30?

Mark 8:27—10:52: Following on the Way

▮ THE TEXT IN ITS ANCIENT CONTEXT

Jesus' lessons on discipleship and the misunderstanding of his disciples typify this section. Although Jesus' lessons have the disciples as their narrative audience, Mark shows that anyone can follow Jesus

(Malbon 1986). Like Jesus' original disciples, however, many will misunderstand. Therefore, Mark employs Jesus' passion prediction and lessons to prepare a would-be disciple for both the call and consequences of discipleship (St. Clair 2008).

Discipleship is not for the fainthearted; no one finds it easy (Malbon 1983, 29). Defined primarily in terms of servanthood, discipleship runs counter to a social structure that advances persons with access to wealth, power, authority, and even purity to the highest levels of the social order. Those without access to this social currency remained at the lowest levels. Thus the way of Jesus reverses the honor-shame codes that structure the cultural world in which Mark's audience lives (St. Clair, 109–64).

Mark first attends to Jesus' identity. Peter declares Jesus to be the "Messiah" (*christos*, 8:27), and for the first time within the narrative, someone uses the same title as that found in the opening line of the Gospel (1:1). Jesus' response confirms the veracity of Peter's answer. He orders Peter and the disciples to keep silent for the same reason he forbade the demons to speak: they knew him (1:25, 34; 3:11).

On the heels of Peter's confession, Jesus foretells his suffering, death, and resurrection (8:31). Although Peter has correctly identified Jesus as the Christ, he does not fully grasp the consequences of Jesus' messianic ministry. He therefore attempts to silence Jesus by rebuking (*epitimān*, 8:32) him as Jesus has rebuked the demons. Rather than silencing Jesus, Peter's actions precipitate Jesus' first lesson on discipleship. Jesus teaches that following him will necessitate two things that run counter to the cultural values of ancient Mediterranean society. First, a would-be disciple must deny himself or herself (8:34). For Mark's original audience, self-denial meant leaving behind one's primary group affiliation (usually the family or kinship group) and solely identifying with Jesus and his gospel. The would-be disciple would need to do "the will of God" so that Jesus and his followers become his or her "brother and sister and mother" (3:35). She or he would then seek approval from Jesus rather than their original group or society at large (St. Clair, 135–36). Second, she or he must "take up the cross" (8:34). The cross represented the most painful and humiliating death that Rome could exact on its subjects. Therefore, Jesus' disciples needed to be able to face pain and shame as a result of following Jesus. In short, a follower of Jesus needed to be prepared to die (St. Clair, 138).

Six days later, Jesus takes Peter, James, and John up a high mountain, where he is transfigured in the presence of Moses and Elijah. Their presence with Jesus suggests that the law (Moses) and the prophets (Elijah) reach their fullest expression in Jesus. Their disappearance, leaving Jesus standing alone, suggests that Jesus has the final authoritative word. Once again, Peter misunderstands. Whether he proposes the booths to prolong the mountaintop experience (Donahue and Harrington, 270) or he believes this event signals the time Zechariah foretold (14:12-21) in which the survivors of the war against Jerusalem would celebrate the Feast of Booths (Juel, 128), he knows he stands at a critical moment. However, the correct response is neither speaking nor building: he needs to listen.

Peter, however, is not the only one struggling to follow Jesus. The remaining nine disciples have also been having difficulty. They have been unable to cast a spirit out of a little boy (9:17). Before rebuking the spirit, Jesus criticizes those around him, including his disciples, for their lack of faith. Faithlessness both characterizes their generation (9:19) and reveals the disciples' lack of identification with Jesus and his words. They are more like the people around them than they are like Jesus.

Jesus must start from the beginning. He foretells his suffering and death for the second time (9:31). Rather than ask Jesus for clarification, the disciples argue about who is the greatest (9:34). Jesus' teaching again reverses the honor-shame codes: status comes through service (9:35). The one willing to humble oneself to the level of the least is the greatest. Jesus illustrates this point by taking a child, the person with the least social status, in his arms (9:36). If one can welcome such a person of low estate in Jesus' name, it will be like welcoming Jesus (9:32). Mark then highlights Jesus' lesson by presenting four episodes that deal with the treatment of the least.

The first episode concerns an exorcist who casts out demons using Jesus' name but does not follow Jesus like the disciples (9:38). For this reason, the disciples try to stop him. Jesus forbids them to stop him and warns them about putting a "stumbling block before one of these little ones" (9:42). "Little ones" are the followers of Jesus who are called to be the servant(s) of all (9:35). Though society may view them as small in social stature and having little power, the "little ones" are great in the kingdom. The sin of hindering their discipleship is so egregious that it is better to cut off the offending body parts rather than risk hellfire (9:43-47).

Jesus' description of the "little ones" as those who believe in him suggests that the exorcist is a disciple. The exorcist believes in Jesus enough to use his name successfully. Unlike the disciples, who could not exorcize the demon in the little boy, this exorcist has been able to cast out unclean spirits (9:38). Rather than hinder kingdom work by trying to erect boundaries that exclude, Jesus admonishes his followers to be at peace with one another (9:50).

The next episode addresses another low-status group in Mark's social world: women. When the Pharisees come to test Jesus, their question references the law, which only allows men the right to divorce (10:2-12). This practice leaves women vulnerable because they are financially and socially dependent on their husbands. Jesus declares that Moses allowed divorce because of their hard hearts. Quoting Gen. 1:27 and 2:24, he argues that divorce was not the original plan but a concession made due to their inability to live up to the original intent of Scripture. Jesus' words show that the Pharisees are not in line with teachings of Moses. When Jesus explains divorce to his disciples, he puts men and women on equal footing. His teaching gives both genders the same right to divorce as well as the same culpability should the divorced person remarry (9:10-12). Thus Mark continues to demonstrate the same concern for women he has shown with the positive portrayals of Peter's mother-in-law (1:31), the woman with the hemorrhage (5:25-34), and the Syrophoenician woman (7:26-30), as well as the intentional inclusion of "sister[s]" as part of Jesus' redefined family (3:35).

The narrative moves from the treatment of women to that of children. Jesus reiterates the principle of his last discipleship lesson. Greatness in the kingdom of God will not be the result of wealth, power, or ritual purity. On the contrary, the kingdom belongs to the least (10:14). This is precisely why one must become the least and servant of all to enter it (10:15). Jesus blesses the children (10:16), thereby sealing his reversal of the honor-shame codes. The ones who are blessed are the ones society has relegated to the lowest social level.

The last episode deals with wealth. The underlying issue is the treatment of another group considered least in Mark's social world, the poor. When a rich man approaches Jesus wanting to know how to gain eternal life (10:17), Jesus tells him to sell all he has, give the money to the poor, and then follow him (10:21). His command to give the money from the sold possessions is an attempt to restore to the poor what was unfairly taken from them. These instructions seek to remediate economic practices that consign the majority of the people to poverty. Discipleship that forbids the oppression of the poor protects these who are also among the least. Jesus' teaching about wealth runs counter to the prevailing notions of wealth in Mark's day. Wealth gave people access. Yet Jesus claims it is a hindrance to those who desire to enter the kingdom of God (10:23). Even for those who have little to no wealth, Jesus' declaration is so shocking that the disciples question the possibility of anyone being saved (10:26).

Despite Jesus' teaching on wealth and a third passion prediction, James and John still clamor for status by asking for positions of honor (10:37). Jesus presents his final discipleship lesson and again emphasizes the need to be a servant (10:43). He concludes by pointing out how he has modeled the behavior he is teaching them. He has not come to be served. Instead, he gives his life in service as he ministers to the least. He will give his life in death because the opposition to this ministry will be fatal. However, his service will ransom "many" (10:45), thereby releasing them from the "strong man's" clutches.

Mark finishes this section with the healing of blind Bartimaeus (10:46-52). He is the first person to call Jesus the "Son of David" (10:47-48) and thus to convey the political implications of Jesus' journey to Jerusalem. According to the Hebrew Scriptures, God promised the throne of Israel to David and his descendants forever (2 Sam. 7:16). It was therefore expected that the Messiah would be a descendant (son) of David (Isa. 11:1; Jer. 23:5-6). As son of David, Jesus is a threat to both Roman and Jewish leadership. The blind man sees the very thing that Jesus has foretold in his passion predictions.

▌ THE TEXT IN THE INTERPRETIVE TRADITION

Jesus' passion predictions introduce a new theme into the Gospel: suffering. Since discipleship characterizes this portion of the Gospel, the relationship between suffering and discipleship is worth exploring. Historically, Mark scholars have understood suffering to be a condition or requirement of discipleship. Many interpret *dei* (8:31) as divine necessity. In other words, God sent Jesus to suffer. Others use this section of the Gospel as their interpretive key. They highlight themes of suffering and servanthood, and suffering and death. They claim that the key to understanding Jesus is in relation to his suffering and therefore describe him as a suffering Messiah. Others posit a scriptural necessity for suffering, by interpreting Mark 9:12 and 10:45 as allusions to Psalm 118 and Isaiah 53 respectively. Most recently, Mark scholars have argued for *dei* to be interpreted in terms of inevitability. They cite the opposition to Jesus' ministry in the narrative as the reason for his death. For these scholars, suffering is not a condition but a consequence of discipleship (St. Clair).

▌ THE TEXT IN CONTEMPORARY DISCUSSION

The relationship between suffering and discipleship is especially important for people who have endured personal or communal suffering. Womanist scholars have found it helpful to distinguish between suffering, on one hand, that arises from oppressive systems and circumstances and results in a static condition that will not change until its sources are confronted, and pain, on the other hand, that is a result of challenging the causes of one's oppression and therefore has the possibility of being eliminated. Jesus' passion is then understood in terms of pain. To follow him is not a call to perpetual suffering for the sake of suffering. To follow him is to accept pain as a consequence of discipleship that requires one to participate in boundary-breaking ministry like his (St. Clair, 145).

The work of womanist scholars causes exegetes (1) to be mindful, when interpreting passages about self-denial, of people who have been denied access to basic necessities, and (2) to be aware, when interpreting passages about taking up the cross, of people who have and are functioning as surrogates (persons who take the place of another by performing the roles and responsibilities of said person). How one interprets these passages may justify, prolong, or even sacralize the suffering and oppression that Jesus in Mark's Gospel seeks to eradicate.

Mark 11:1—12:44: Following to Jerusalem

▎THE TEXT IN ITS ANCIENT CONTEXT

Jesus now arrives at Jerusalem, the center of Jewish religious power (11:1). His entry into the city is replete with messianic overtones. Jesus rides into Jerusalem on a colt. The scene depicts the fulfillment of Zech. 9:9. People spread their cloaks for Jesus to tread on like officers did when Jehu was anointed King (2 Kings 9:13). Hosanna, "save, please," conveys the people's desire for deliverance. It is clear from their shouts that they view Jesus' entry into the city as heralding the reinstitution of the Davidic monarchy (10:10). Like Bartimaeus, they recognize Jesus as the promised son of David. They quote Ps. 118:26 as they cry out, "Blessed is the one who comes in the name of Lord!" Yet the second portion of that verse, "we bless you from the house of the LORD," will not be realized. The ministry that has the crowds following him and his entry into the city amid cries of messianic expectation makes Jesus a threat to both Jewish and Roman leaders.

Mark adds new groups to those he has already shown to be arrayed against Jesus. The chief priests and the elders, whose rejection Jesus foretold in 8:31, confront him in the temple (11:27). The Sadducees join the chief priests, elders, scribes, Pharisees, and Herodians as interrogators of Jesus (12:18). The common link among them all is their support of and participation in the temple system, a system Jesus finds corrupt.

The temple is not functioning as intended. Therefore, one of Jesus' first undertakings is symbolically to cleanse the temple. He uses the language of the prophets to describe what has happened to the temple. Instead of being a "house of prayer for all nations" (Isa. 56:7), it has become "a den of robbers" (Jer. 7:11). In Mark, Jesus specifically uses the Greek word for "bandits" (lēstai). He equates temple practices with those of first-century highway robbers who plunder people by force. He also depicts Jesus as the stronger one who enters the strong man's house (3:27). And he uses the language of exorcism (ekballein) to describe the driving out of the buyers and sellers (11:15).

Additionally, Mark shows the temple system to be representative of a tree that does not produce fruit. He does this by "sandwiching" the temple cleansing (11:15-19) between the story of the cursed fig tree (11:12-14, 20-25). The temple is like the fig tree. It was the crowning achievement of Herod's building projects, but it only has the appearance of fruitfulness, like the fig tree in leaf suggests. On closer inspection, however, there is nothing to it. The fig tree imagery alludes to Old Testament Scriptures that compare Israel to barren fig trees (Jer. 13:13; Hosea 9:10; Mic. 7:1). Jesus' cursing of the fig tree, therefore, intimates the destruction of the temple.

The corrupt temple system and its impending demise is the result of corrupt leadership. In the parable of the vineyard (12:1-12), Jesus implicitly compares the scribes, chief priests, and elders to the evil tenants who kill the vineyard owner's beloved son (12:7-8). He warns people about the scribes' pride (12:38-9), unscrupulous financial practices that result in the "devouring" of widow's property (12:40), and hypocrisy (12:40). It is important to note that Mark uses the scribes to connect Jesus' enemies. He lists the scribes with the chief priests and elders (8:31; 11:27; 14:43, 53; 15:1) and with the Pharisees (7:1), whom Mark pairs with the Herodians (3:6; 12:13). Therefore, Jesus' condemnation of the scribes can be applied to all of the Jewish leaders whose opposition has increased in numbers and in intensity as the scribes and chief priests also look for a way to kill Jesus (11:18).

∎ THE TEXT IN THE INTERPRETIVE TRADITION

Couched between Jesus' scathing condemnation of the scribes and his foretelling of the temple's destruction is the story of the widow's offering. Leo the Great, Gregory the Great, and John Chrysostom lifted her as an example of faith and generosity. Based on his interpretation of this story, Calvin concluded that one who "offers to God the little that he has, is more worthy of esteem than that of him who offers a hundred times more out of his abundance" (Calvin, 3:113). From their earliest readings until the present time, scholars have commended the widow whose actions Jesus is believed to have extolled. Most recently, however, scholars have interpreted this story as an indictment of the temple system that victimizes the poor and vulnerable.

∎ THE TEXT IN CONTEMPORARY DISCUSSION

In 2012, the *Chronicle of Philanthropy* reported their findings on giving patterns in the United States by state, city, and zip code. What they found was that people in higher-income brackets gave less to charitable causes than people with less income. Persons earning between $50,000 and 75,000 per year gave 7.6 percent of their income to charity. People earning more than $200,000 per year, and living in areas where at least 40 percent of their neighbors shared their economic status, gave only 2.8 percent to charity. The divide between income and generosity encourages us to take another look at the widow's offering in Mark's Gospel.

Much of contemporary discussion around this text no longer offers a commendation for the widow's gift but rather a condemnation of the systems of oppression, both religious and political, that persuade those with less to give out of their lack and the rich to keep what they have. They note the juxtaposition of Jesus' condemnation of the scribes as those who "devour widows' houses" (12:40) and the story of the widow's offering. The widow is now seen as a victim of predatory practices rather than a woman whose faith in God results in generosity. Her once positive portrayal is threatened as she becomes a passive character who is duped into supporting something that Jesus condemns and predicts will be destroyed.

As we interpret and apply this passage to our current context, it is important to tease out the strands of condemnation and commendation. How we understand the relationship between the woman and the temple influences how we use this passage to either encourage or discourage relationship between giver and the faith community to which they give.

Mark 13:1-37: Following to the End

▌ THE TEXT IN ITS ANCIENT CONTEXT

Chapter 13 contains the largest block of teaching found in Mark's Gospel. Commentators have referred to this chapter as the prophetic discourse, believing it to foretell the future; the eschatological discourse, because it speaks of "the end"; the Olivet Discourse, because Mount Olives is the setting for the passage (Brooks, 204); and the "Little Apocalypse," because it reveals the future and discloses the heavenly realm. The description of this chapter as the Little Apocalypse, however, is often debated because certain apocalyptic features such as visions, resurrection, and final judgment are missing. Neither is there a juxtaposition between heaven and earth, the present age and the age to come, or those inside and outside of the church that characterize Christian apocalyptic writings (Edwards, 384). In addition, there is no heavenly intermediary revealing the future events.

Although Mark 13 is different from most examples of apocalyptic literature, there are enough features to categorize it as such. Since apocalyptic literature is a form of sociopolitical resistance by people who have little chance of achieving the political, economic, or military overthrow of their oppressors, Mark, written in the context of the Jewish War, reflects the exact setting out of which apocalyptic literature develops. Moreover, the description of wars, conflicts among nations and kingdoms, famines, and earthquakes are common Christian and Jewish apocalyptic features. Mark specifies that Jesus teaches from the Mount of Olives, the eschatological location of YHWH's final deliverance of Israel from her enemies (Zech. 14:4). Mark 13:19 parallels Dan. 12:1, which is an undisputed apocalyptic portion of the book. Both Mark and Daniel foretell suffering using the same Greek word, *thlipsis*, and record the magnitude of the suffering in similar fashion. Daniel states that it is "such as never occurred since the nations existed"; Mark says it is "such as has not been from the beginning of the creation."

Because apocalyptic literature arises from situations of oppression and/or persecution, its writers often promote both patient endurance and hope. In a manner of speaking, apocalyptic literature is "good news," not in the sense of a literary genre but in terms of the message it proclaims. There is confidence in the fact that although things look bleak now, God is in control and will be victorious. Therefore, Jesus encourages the disciples to "endure" (13:13) and "keep awake" (13:35, 37). The events Jesus foretells in verses 5-23 are described as "birth pangs" (13:8). Read in this context, Mark communicates to his readers that while their situation will get worse before it gets better, their suffering is connected to a greater purpose (Juel, 176). It is not the end; their salvation is (13:13). Mark thus inspires a present hope in his readers as he communicates Jesus' revelation of future events.

It is important to note that some apocalyptic literature "describes the course of history as well as a climactic cosmic transformation" (Donahue and Harrington, 378). In other words, one of the functions of apocalyptic literature is to explain the current circumstances of its readers in light of God's unfolding plan. As expectations for liberation erupted into social protests such as banditry and messianic movements (Horsley 1984, 482), messianic expectations raised eschatological hope, since the Messiah was expected to arrive before "the end." Therefore, Mark needed to address these first-century Palestinian expectations while protecting his community (13:5-6, 21-22). The warnings against false prophets and messianic pretenders found on Jesus' lips frame the discourse so that Mark's readers will not be led astray (13:6, 22).

According to Mark, Jesus foretells the destruction of the temple (13:2) as well as the persecution of his followers (13:9, 11-12). These prophecies prepare Mark's readers for their current state of affairs. First, they are reassured that the temple was not intended to be the center of the community's faith. Mark presses this point by reminding them (through words he attributes to Jesus) that those in Judea are supposed to flee when the temple's destruction, signaled by the "desolating sacrilege," is about to take place (13:14). In Dan. 9:27, the "desolating sacrilege" referred to the pagan altar set up in the temple by Antiochus Epiphanes. Mark uses the phrase to refer to another desecration of the sacred space. By using the masculine form of the Greek participle for "stand" (*estēkota*) rather than the neuter, Mark informs his readers that the "desolating sacrilege" is not an "it" but a "he." There are three main proposals for identifying this person: (1) Caligula, who ordered the erection of a statue of himself in the temple in 40 CE (Josephus, *Ant.* 18.261), (2) the rebel Eleazar, who used the inner temple as his headquarters from the winter of 67–68 CE until 70 CE, and (3) Titus, who entered the temple in 70 CE as it was being destroyed. Since the "desolating sacrilege" is a sign to flee Judea, Caligula would be too early and Titus would be too late, which leaves Eleazar as the best option (Marcus). The attention Mark pays to the "course of history," namely, the temple's destruction and the desolating sacrilege, provides clues for dating his Gospel as well.

By recounting Jesus' prophecy about the persecution of his followers, Mark parallels his community's suffering with that of Jesus. Like Jesus, they will be "handed over to councils" (15:1), beaten (14:65), brought to trial (14:55-64) and before governors (15:1-15), and betrayed by their own families (14:43-45). Given Jesus' redefinition of family (3:35), the betrayal by family members may not come from one's biological kin but those who are part of the community of disciples.

After twenty-three verses that focus on the "course of history," Jesus' discourse gives way to "cosmic transformation." In the background of Jesus' teaching is the disciples' question of when "these things" will take place (13:4). The contextual referent for "these things" is the destruction of the temple. However, as Jesus answers their question, he speaks of "the end" twice (13:7,13) and concludes with the appearance of the son of man and the gathering of the elect (13:24-27). The son of man's appearance in Mark 13:26 mirrors that of the apocalyptic son of man who also comes in the clouds in Dan. 7:13.

Although his style is not typical of apocalyptic literature, Mark does juxtapose heaven and earth in his own way. The destruction of the temple signals transformation on an earthly scale, but the appearance of the son of man does so on a celestial scale. Famines, earthquakes, and wars are signs on earth that will eventually give way to the heavenly signs of a darkened sun, a lightless moon, falling stars, and shaken heavenly powers. Thus salvation takes on a spiritual, eschatological dimension as those who "endure to the end will be saved" (13:13).

Ultimately, the disciples' question is never answered. Jesus informs them that he does not know when "that day or hour" (13:32) will come. Instead, he tells them how to interpret the events so that they know when he is "near, at the very gate" (13:29). However, Jesus does tell them that it will not happen before the good news is preached to all nations (13:10). This statement extends the timetable of Jesus' return for Mark's readers. It reminds them that the end is imminent but not yet. Therefore, he tells them what to do: "Watch" (13:5, 9, 23, 33, *blepete*).

"Watch" characterizes Mark's ethical stance (Donahue and Harrington, 378). The inclusion of this ethical/exhortation component makes this chapter practical and immediately applicable. It also caused James A. Brooks to conclude that Mark 13 "combines two literary forms, apocalyptic and testamental" (Brooks, 204). This fusion enables Mark to achieve his purpose for this chapter: keep eschatological hope alive while balancing it with vigilance (Donahue and Harrington, 378). His message to his readers is clear: This is not the end. It is only birth pangs, and they are just as unpredictable as labor. So, keep awake!

▌ THE TEXT IN THE INTERPRETIVE TRADITION

In Mark 13:32, Jesus states that he does not know the day or hour of the son of man's return. This statement resulted in three words, "nor the Son," becoming a point of interpretive contention since its earliest readings. For interpreters such as Arius, this verse posed no problems. Instead, they saw it as scriptural affirmation of their theological position that subordinated both the Son and the Holy Spirit to the Father. Using Mark 13:32 (and its parallel Matt. 24:36), they rejected the equal divinity of Jesus with the Father. However, the majority of interpretations of this verse have been fueled by the same discomfort as described by John Calvin: "But since it is manifest that the same kind of ignorance is ascribed to Christ as is ascribed *to the angels*, we must endeavor to find some other meaning which is more suitable" (Calvin, 1845, 3:37).

The quest for a "more suitable" meaning began with Matthew's Gospel. Although the most reliable manuscripts of Matthew's parallel text (Matt. 24:36) include "nor the Son," several omit the phrase due to the doctrinal problems it raised (Harrington, 342). Athanasius, who defended the doctrine of the Trinity against the Arian heresy of subordinationism, affirmed the divinity of Jesus by arguing that Jesus was "speaking according to his humanity" in this verse. Chrysostom, Gregory of Nazianzus, Martin Luther, and John Wesley also espoused this interpretation of Mark 13:32. Ambrose seems to have had the Matthew text with the omission of "nor the Son" since he accused the Arians of inserting the phrase into Mark's text because the other Gospels did not include it.

For Augustine, the issue was not from which nature Jesus' words derived, but an exercise of choice. Jesus chose not to disclose what he knew because "he had not been sent by the Father with this commission, so long as he lived among mortals." Theophylact concurred, reasoning that this concealment was "better for us; for if, now that we know not the end, we are careless, what should we do if we knew it?" Hilary of Poitiers argued that Jesus' apparent lack of knowledge was not a reflection of his ignorance, but that it "must be connected with the hiding of the treasures of wisdom, which are in Him." Contemporary options for those who take Mark literally follow one of the three interpretive trajectories: subordinationism, in which Jesus (and by implication the Holy

Spirit) are ignorant of the Father's timetable; "official ignorance," in which Jesus purposely conceals the day and hour; or what might be called the "nonuse" approach, in which Jesus does not use the omniscience of his divine nature but rather speaks from a human point of view (Carl).

■ THE TEXT IN CONTEMPORARY DISCUSSION

The material in the first twenty-three verses of Mark 13 can be linked easily to events shortly before or after the fall of the Jerusalem temple. However, verses 24-27 foretell the coming of the son of man, an event that has not yet occurred. On one end of a spectrum today are readers who have interpreted Mark 13 in its ancient setting and concluded that Jesus expected the fulfillment of verses 24-27 in his lifetime, but died a failure (Schweitzer). On the other end are premillennialists, who read Rev. 20:1-6 literally and believe that Jesus will physically return to rapture the righteous prior to the tribulation and that he will subsequently inaugurate a thousand-year reign. They see the signs of Jesus' coming in contemporary events.

During the twentieth century, the possibility of nuclear destruction, the reality of ecological collapse, the creation of the state of Israel along with the Six Day and Yom Kippur Wars, and the perceived threats to US exceptionalism fueled premillennial expectations of Jesus' return. Despite the statement in 13:32 that the timing of the son of man's return remains a mystery, some readers still attempt to correlate current events with those listed in Mark 13 so as to describe contemporary timetables that will lead up to Jesus' appearing. Examples in popular culture include *The Late, Great Planet Earth* (Lindsey 1970) and, more recently, the *Left Behind* series (LaHaye and Jenkins 1995–2007).

The underlying premise of such interpretations is the expectation that apocalyptic passages like Mark 13 accurately and precisely predict the future. Should supposedly predicted events not take place as expected, then the passage might become a failed apocalyptic text or proof that Jesus was wrong (Schweitzer). Yet, premillennialists like Tim LaHaye and Hal Lindsey can avoid Schweitzer's conclusion if the events that signal "the end" are seen as still forthcoming. If Jesus does not return as expected, then calendars can be readjusted. This way, the *interpretation of the text*, rather than the text itself, fails. The "prophet," rather than Jesus, is wrong. However, this attempt fails to preserve the integrity of the text. Instead, it risks undermining the text's integrity by using current events to predict the "end," when the historical context of Mark's Gospel points to the events surrounding the Jewish War.

Mark 14:1—15:47: The Cost of Following

■ THE TEXT IN ITS ANCIENT CONTEXT

Mark gives great attention to Jesus' passion. He lays the foundation for his passion narrative with three passion predictions and then devotes one third of his Gospel to detailing Jesus' final days. He takes great pains to highlight what contemporary readers might identify as the sociopolitical reasons behind Jesus' death. Although Jesus is executed by Rome as a criminal, his death does not represent a failure on his part. Rather, Mark shows that there has been a failure of justice, a failure of discipleship, and a failure of sight on the part of Roman and Jewish leadership.

Mark tells the story of Jesus' death against the backdrop of the Passover. The day before the feast, the day of preparation, the chief priests and scribes are preparing to arrest Jesus (14:1). A woman enters the room where Jesus is sharing a meal with Simon the leper and anoints him (14:3). Amid criticisms for wasting the money on the perfume and accusations of neglecting the poor, Jesus defends her actions. Jesus states that the deed was done "for me" (14:6). Just as the disciples' lack of fasting while the "bridegroom" is present (2:18-20) showed an understanding of the significance of Jesus' presence among them, so this woman's kindness highlights the same (Myers, 359). Moreover, acts of kindness can be shown to the poor at any time, but he will not always be with them (14:7). His statement is neither a consignment of people to perpetual poverty nor an encouragement to neglect the poor. Jesus does not set up an "either/or" dynamic. Personal acts of kindness are no substitute for public care of the poor or vice versa, and "one should not be harassed for doing either" (Tolbert, 271). By performing a "good service," this nameless, speechless woman fits the predominant image of women in Mark's Gospel as those who serve and provide for Jesus (1:31; 15:41). Her prophetic act helps to move the reader into Mark's passion narrative. She is not anointing Jesus as king but is preparing his body "beforehand for its burial" (14:8). Jesus will not be given a crown, but a cross.

The Last Supper (14:17-25); Jesus' betrayal (14:41-45), arrest (14:46-49), and trial before the Sanhedrin (14:53-65); his prayer in Gethsemane (14:32-40); the desertion of his disciples (14:50-52); and Peter's denial (14:66-72) all occur on the day of Passover. The Passover is not simply a remembrance of divine intervention, but of divine intervention with sociopolitical implications. It is a Jewish feast that commemorates Israel's liberation from Egyptian slavery or the freeing of God's people from an oppressive government. Just as the Passover celebrates the ransoming of Israel from Egypt (Exod. 6:6, *lytroō*), so Mark presents Jesus' life and death as part of a ransoming work (10:45, *lytron*). This time, the oppressive regime is Rome.

During the Passover meal, Jesus reinterprets the bread and wine in light of his impending death. The bread is his body, which will soon be broken (14:22). The wine is the "blood of the covenant" (14:24). The "blood of the covenant" has two possible references to the exodus story. First, it may refer to the blood that Israelites painted on their doorposts to protect their firstborn from the death angel (Exod. 12:7). According to Exod. 4:22, Israel is God's firstborn. Therefore, Jesus intimates that the deliverance and protection of Israel is tied to his spilled blood. The second reference to the "blood of the covenant" is the blood sprinkled on the Israelites at Sinai to establish their relationship as the people of God and confirm their covenant with God (24:1-8). Jesus' spilled blood verifies that God's commitment to Israel is still in effect. However, Mark shows that what God is doing through the death of Jesus will not be for Israel alone. Instead, he once again pushes for gentile inclusion.

Israel's deliverance from Egyptian slavery was necessary for God to fulfill God's promise of land and progeny to Abraham (Gen. 15:5-7). According to Gen. 17:5, Abraham would not be the ancestor of the Israelites alone, but of "many [*pollōn*] nations" (Gen. 17:5). Mark links the language of the "many" (*polloi*) to Jesus. Jesus will give his life as a ransom for "many" (10:45, *polloi*). His blood is described as being "poured out for many" (14:24, *polloi*).

It is important to note that the Passover language in Mark is not expiatory; it points instead to the sociopolitical dimensions of Jesus' death (Blount). Mark simply states that Jesus' body is broken. Unlike Luke, he does not add "for you" (Luke 22:19). Moreover, the breaking and blessing of the bread alludes to the feeding stories in which Jews (6:33-44) and gentiles (8:1-9) are filled. In addition, the "blood of the covenant" is not specified as being for the "forgiveness of sins" (as in Matt. 26:28). Jesus forgave sin prior to his death (Mark 2:5).

At the heart of the animosity toward Jesus on the part of scribes, Pharisees, and other authorities in Jerusalem are the sociopolitical implications of his ministry. Jesus is a threat to the temple system and their control of the people, both of which ingratiate them to Rome. When Jesus is arrested, the only accusation Mark records is someone claiming that Jesus said, "I will destroy this temple that is made with hands, and in three days I will build another, not made with hands" (14:58). When Jesus drove the animal sellers and money-changers out of the temple, it resulted in the chief priests and scribes looking for a way to kill him (11:18). Jesus has predicted the temple's destruction (13:1-2). Later, when he dies, Mark will report that the temple curtain is torn (*eschisthē*) in two (15:38) like the heavens were ripped asunder (*schizomenous*) during Jesus' baptism (1:10). Because the tearing of the temple curtain occurs during the darkness that covers the land at noonday (15:33), it is probably best read as an omen of God's judgment against the temple. However, Mark's use of *schizein* at both Jesus' baptism and death suggests that the latter event, like the former, grants access to God, rather than the temple system. Moreover, the tearing (*schizein*) of the curtain suggests that the breach between the old way represented by the temple and the new way represented by Jesus is as irreparable as the tear (*schizma*) created from sewing together new and old cloth (2:21).

Such bold political counteractions require authority. At Jesus' trial before the Sanhedrin, the high priest's question is therefore one about identity. He asks if Jesus is "the Messiah [*christos*], the Son of the Blessed One?" (14:61). The high priest's question mimics what Mark has already told his readers is Jesus' true identity. According to Mark, Jesus is the Messiah (*christos*, a political designation), and the Son of God (a theological designation, 1:1). Jesus affirms both by responding with an answer that has political and theological undertones. He begins with "I am" (*egō eimi*), which is a play on the divine name (Exod. 3:14) revealed to Moses during his divine commission to free Israel from Egyptian bondage. Next, Jesus declares that those questioning him will see him "seated at the right hand of the Power" (14:62). For Jesus' interrogators, his position next to God may be seen as a threat to the sovereignty and/or the oneness of God. In either case, they view him as "infringing on God's prerogatives" (Juel, 208–9). Consequently, they charge him with blasphemy, which is punishable by death. Yet they take Jesus to the Roman procurator, Pilate (15:1), where the accusation against Jesus becomes purely political, not theological. In an effort to present Jesus' offense as a crime punishable by Rome, blasphemy disappears from everyone's vocabulary. Instead, the charge is treason: his alleged claim to be a king. Three times Pilate refers to him as "king of the Jews" (15:2, 9, 12). The crowds as well as "the whole cohort" mock him as such (15:16-20). The sign placed over his cross reads the same (15:26). Even the chief priests and scribes refer to him using two political titles: "king of Israel," a variant of "king of the Jews," and "Messiah" (15:32).

Mark further highlights the sociopolitical nature of Jesus' death through his use of bandit (*lēstēs*) language. In first-century Palestine, bandits were typically highway robbers or guerrilla warriors who opposed Rome and Judean collaborators with Rome. They were viewed by Rome and Roman sympathizers as seditious and traitors (Horsley 1985). When taken into custody, Jesus likens his arrest to that of a bandit (14:48). Mark tells us that he was crucified between two bandits (15:27). Moreover, Mark juxtaposes Jesus and Barabbas. Jesus is arrested as if he were the rebel; Barabbas has been arrested for actually participating in an insurrection. There is no historical evidence that attests to the existence of Barabbas or the Passover custom that allows the crowd to choose which man goes free. Jesus and Barabbas may be Mark's way of representing two sociopolitical responses to Roman oppression. Jesus represents those in favor of nonviolent opposition. Barabbas, whom Myers says is described by Mark as a Sicarii operative, is the choice of those who advocate outright rebellion to Rome (Myers, 380). Meanwhile, Jewish leaders who have made the temple a den of bandits (11:17) are behind Jesus' arrest.

In the end, Jesus is crucified. He suffers a horrifically painful and humiliating death reserved for crimes against the state, high treason, and as punishment for slaves, prisoners of war, rebels, robbers, freedmen, and *peregrini*, that is, free persons without Roman citizenship (Hengel). Mark shows Jesus' death to be a failure of justice. The Sanhedrin does not follow jurisprudence found in the Torah (or, later, the Mishnah), nor does Pilate free him when he believes Jesus to be innocent (Juel). Jesus' death highlights the failure of his followers, who cannot stay awake and pray with him in Gethsemane (14:37); who betray him (14:10, 43), desert him (14:50), deny him (14:66-72), turn against him (15:14), and follow only from a great distance (15:40-41). Mark uses verbal irony to reveal the failure of sight on the part of Jewish and Roman leadership. They repeatedly identify him correctly as "King of the Jews," but fail to recognize who he really is.

However, none of these failures come as a surprise to Jesus, nor should they surprise Mark's readers. Jesus has predicted it all, and so it has come to pass. Yet one things remains to be accomplished: a resurrection!

▮ THE TEXT IN THE INTERPRETIVE TRADITION

Readings of Mark's passion narrative have often been influenced by the ransom and the substitutionary/penal-substitutionary theories of atonement. Scholars who argue for a theory of atonement in Mark's Gospel point to 10:45 and 14:24 as justification for their position. In addition, some read Mark's passion narrative against the backdrop of Isaiah 53 and contend that Mark presents Jesus as Isaiah's Suffering Servant. Jesus then becomes one who suffers vicariously for humanity as payment for our sin. Once one assumes an atonement theory is at play, one interprets other portions of the Gospel in light of the theory rather than the narrative context. For example, Morna Hooker interprets Jesus' "cry of dereliction" (15:34) as his experiencing "what Paul elsewhere describes as 'becoming a curse' (Gal. 3:13) or 'being made sin' (2 Cor. 5:21)" (Hooker, 375).

In the last thirty years, however, scholars have argued against the presence of any atonement theories in Mark. Instead, they opt to make meaning of Jesus' death on the basis of evidence within the text rather than by imposing theological constructs formulated outside it (Myers; Tolbert; Blount).

Therefore, Mark 15:34 can be explained within the context of the narrative using the historical reality of the crucifixion as its backdrop. The cry of dereliction becomes "Jesus' final emotional and psychological torment, in addition to his physical suffering" (Powery, 150). By quoting Psalm 22:1 and alluding to Psalm 22 throughout the passion narrative, Mark holds in tension the horrific conditions of Jesus' death and the hope for his vindication as a righteous sufferer.

◼ THE TEXT IN CONTEMPORARY DISCUSSION

The shift to a narrative reading of Mark as described above also enables us to recognize Christian anti-Judaism in Mark's Gospel. Mark portrays the Jewish leadership (3:6; 11:18; 14:1; 15:11) and the crowds (14:43; 15:8-14) as the instigators of Jesus' death, causing some to conclude that Mark's Gospel is inherently antisemitic. William A. Johnson argues that "every kind of Jew" is presented negatively in the Gospel, which he describes as a "carefully devised theological attack on the Jews" (Johnson, 183). He concurs with S. G. F. Brandon that Mark's reader "is led to see Jesus as both rejected by, and in turn rejecting his fellow-Jews" (Brandon, 274). Fortunately, this shift to narrative readings has also sensitized scholars to the potential antisemitic implications of their analyses. Therefore, attention is given to certain aspects of the Gospel in an effort to prevent readers from forming antisemitic attitudes based on Mark's story.

Contemporary scholars note that Mark's Gospel reflects the historical tensions between Jews who followed Jesus and Jews who did not in Mark's day (Hooker, 24). Initially, the dispute between Jews and Jewish Christians was an internal dispute among *Jews* about accepting Jesus as the Messiah. Thus Mark writes about a time when followers of Jesus will be "beaten in synagogues" (13:9).

In addition, scholars highlight Jesus' Jewish background. Indeed, Jesus was a Jew whose ministry was directed to the Jewish people. His use of Scripture and adherence to the law (1:44; 3:4; 10:19; 12:29-31) demonstrate his fidelity to Judaism. The main contention with his opponents over Mosaic tradition was whether he or they were more faithful in interpretation and application (Hooker, 24–25).

Narrative readings of Mark's Gospel are also careful to point out the divergence between historical data and Mark's story. Historically, Jesus' death cannot be attributed to the Jewish leaders as Mark portrays. Scholars appeal to extrabiblical literature to see if the image of the easily manipulated Pilate in Mark's Gospel matches what other writers say about him. It seems highly unlikely that Pilate would have left the decision to execute Jesus to the crowd, especially since there is no extrabiblical evidence of any custom to release a prisoner of the crowd's choosing (15:8). Legally, Pilate would have had to sentence Jesus to death, and the means of Jesus' death—crucifixion—was a Roman practice, not a Jewish one.

Contra Johnson, Mark does not present all of the Jews in a negative light. Mark's Gospel distinguishes itself with a very positive portrayal of women, the majority of which are Jewish, who serve as examples of discipleship (Dewey; Malbon 1983; Miller; Kinukawa; Mitchell). Jairus, a synagogue leader, had enough faith to have his petition granted (5:36) and be allowed to remain in the room after Jesus put everyone out (5:40). Although Jesus' disciples betray, deny, and desert him, he still commands them to meet him in Galilee after the resurrection (16:7).

Mark 16:1-8: Will You Follow?

■ THE TEXT IN ITS ANCIENT CONTEXT

Despite the variety of endings given to Mark, the evidence suggests that the version of Mark's Gospel available to his original readers ended with 16:8 (see below). Chapter 16 begins with three women journeying to Jesus' tomb at first light (16:1-2). Mary Magdalene heads the list of women. Mark tells us that she provided for Jesus' ministry and witnessed his crucifixion (15:40), followed to see where he was buried (15:47), and came to anoint his body (16:1). Absent is any reference to her deliverance from seven demons (Luke 8:2) or any information that would suggest she was the harlot that the later interpretive and especially artistic tradition claimed. There is some inconsistency around the identity of "Mary, the mother of James." It is not certain whether she is also "Mary, mother of James and Joses" (15:40), "Mary, mother of Joses" (15:47), or even Mary, Jesus' mother, who is mentioned with Jesus' brothers, also named James and Joses (6:3). Salome only appears here and in 15:40, among those who provided for Jesus' ministry and were present at the crucifixion. These women anticipate providing for Jesus one last time. They come to anoint his body, apparently oblivious to the fact that he was "anointed beforehand for [his] burial" in Bethany (14:3-9). Yet, even the narration of Jesus' predicting his own death and resurrection three times (8:31; 9:31; 10:33-34), the first being declared "quite openly" (8:32), had not caused them to expect a resurrection, only a dead body.

The timing of the women's visit is also inconsistent. "Early morning" would have been between three and six in the morning. Nevertheless, Mark adds that they came after sunrise, perhaps wishing to assure his readers that the women were able to see clearly what follows. As they journey to the tomb, they worry about the stone at its entrance (16:3). The stone, however, is an afterthought, as they do all the preparations for the anointing and depart for the tomb, thinking about the stone only as they arrive. This afterthought, Hooker asserts, is probably an attempt to emphasize the fact that the tomb was indeed sealed (Hooker, 384) and to confirm that the absence of Jesus' body is due to a resurrection, not a theft.

When the women arrive at the tomb, the stone has already been rolled away (16:4). However, there is no resurrection appearance, only a young man with a message. Mark describes him as a "young man dressed in a white robe" (16:5). Some interpreters identify the young man as an angel, citing his white robe; the similarity between the women's alarm at seeing the young man and the fear that often accompanies angelic appearances (Gen. 21:17; Matt. 28:5; Luke 1:13, 30; 2:10); Luke's (24:4) and Josephus's (*Ant.* 5.277) use of the word "man" (*anēr*) to describe angelic appearances; and the fact that the young man knows about the postresurrection meeting in Galilee (14:28)—information R. T. France argues no human being apart from the disciples would have known (France, 676). Others, however, link the young man in the tomb to the young man in the garden who lost his garment during Jesus' arrest.

The Greek words used for "young man" (*neaniskos*) and "dressed" (*peribeblēmenos*) occur only here (16:5) and in 14:51-52. Mark connected Jesus with the young man in the garden, writing that the latter "followed" (*synēkolouthe*) Jesus. (Throughout the Gospel, Mark uses "follow" [*akolouthein*] to signify discipleship: 1:17, 20; 2:14, 15; 3:7; 5:24, 37; 6:1; 8:34; 10:21, 28, 32, 52; 11:9; 14:54; 15:41. By adding the preposition *syn* to the word, Mark suggests a close relationship between the young man and Jesus.) Both are dressed in linen fabric, the young man wearing a linen cloth (*sindon*) when Jesus is arrested (14:51) and Jesus wrapped in a linen cloth (*sindon)* before Joseph places him in the tomb (15:46). Mark also links Jesus with the young man in the tomb, recording that both appear in white garments: Jesus in "dazzling white" at the transfiguration (9:3) and the young man in the tomb (16:5).

Finally, Mark specifies the location of the young man in the tomb as being "seated on the right" (16:5). Individuals positioned on the right side figure prominently in Mark's Gospel: James and John request to sit at the right and left of Jesus (10:40); the Messiah's place is at the right hand of the Lord according to Ps. 110:1 quoted in Mark 12:36; and Jesus prophesies the coming of the son of man "seated at the right hand of the Power" (14:62). Myers defines the right side as denoting "true power of solidarity" (Myers, 397). Although there is no scholarly consensus on the identity of either young man (in the garden or at the tomb), the connections Mark makes between them and Jesus suggest that the young man was someone close enough to Jesus to have insider information and familiar enough to Mark's community to need no explanation.

The young man tells the women that "Jesus of Nazareth" has been raised (16:5-6). He does not employ a christological title, but rather situates Jesus historically as a real man from a real place. The women are commanded to carry the news to Jesus' disciples "and Peter" (16:7). It is most likely that the young man mentions Peter by name because Peter needs special encouragement (Juel, 232). As one who denied being a disciple by denying Jesus (Hooker, 385), he is specifically welcomed back here into the community of followers.

Unlike the people in the Gospel who are commanded to be quiet but tell what Jesus has done anyway (1:44; 7:36), the women who are commanded to speak here remain quiet. Mark highlights this with a double negative construction in Greek: "they said nothing to no one" (16:8). Instead, the women flee like the disciples (14:50-52). Narratively, there is a failure of discipleship for all who have followed Jesus. Yet the fact that Mark's community has access to his Gospel proves that someone said something. The message was indeed proclaimed.

Neither the absence of a resurrection appearance nor the fear and silence of the women nullifies Mark's description of his work as "good news." Emerson Powery states that for Mark, "hope is not defined by a resurrection or a physical appearance *but* by an empty tomb and a promised re-gathering" (Powery, 152). Herein lies the good news: not only is the tomb empty, but Jesus also has gone ahead of them to Galilee, "just as he said" (14:28; 16:7). There is no need to doubt Jesus' words, as Mark has taken great pains to prove his trustworthiness. His instructions concerning his entry into Jerusalem (11:2-6), the preparation for the Passover meal (14:16), and the events surrounding the passion have all come to pass (Juel, 233). Moreover, Mark has kept his word. He promised to tell "the beginning of the good news of Jesus Christ." Whether by accident or intent, this is exactly what he has done.

▌THE TEXT IN THE INTERPRETIVE TRADITION

Interpretations of Mark's last chapter must contend with a problem unique to his Gospel. The Gospel has four endings: 16:8, the longer ending (vv. 9-20), a shorter ending, and the longer and shorter endings combined. The most reliable codices, Sinaiticus and Vaticanus, end with 16:8. Both Clement of Alexandria and Origen knew only of this ending. However, Eusebius and Jerome report that they are aware of the longer ending, but the longer ending is not found in the majority of Greek manuscripts. Both Irenaeus, who quotes 16:19, and Tatian, who includes the longer ending in his *Diatessaron*, do so without any acknowledgment of its being a later addition. By the second century, either the longer and/or shorter endings were added and were copied onto the majority of manuscripts.

In 1546, the Council of Trent canonized the old Latin Vulgate edition, which included Mark's longer ending. The Protestants also accepted the longer ending by including it in the King James Version. Modern scholarship reverted to the ending at 16:8 after Adolf von Harnack contended, in 1893, that Mark's original ending was lost. The textual evidence above as well as the stylistic, syntactical, vocabulary, and theological differences between the material prior to and after 16:8 have been the basis for contemporary arguments in favor of an ending at 16:8.

Whereas some of the earliest readers of the Gospel felt it necessary to create an ending for Mark's Gospel that is more consistent with the endings of Matthew, Luke, and John, contemporary readers may find the ending at 16:8 to be theologically consistent with the preceding narrative. Unlike von Harnack, they may consider that Mark intentionally ended his Gospel at 16:8. Donald Juel argues that the ending at 16:8 leaves the reader without any reason to trust human response: one "can only trust that God will one day finish the story, as God has promised" (Juel, 235). Others may see the abruptness of 16:8, with its unusual grammatical structure, to be an invitation by the author for readers to finish his story of discipleship for themselves. Early readers did something similar, codifying their supplemental endings by including them in ancient manuscripts. Contemporary readers will have to decide how they will complete "the beginning of the good news of Jesus Christ, the Son of God" (1:1).

■ THE TEXT IN CONTEMPORARY DISCUSSION

Traditional African American preaching lends homiletical support to Mark's Gospel being good news despite the ending at 16:8. In *Celebration and Experience in Preaching*, Henry Mitchell argued that celebration, which has been defined as "the joyful and ecstatic reinforcement of the truth already taught and delivered in the main body of the sermon" (Thomas, 85), is a distinctive of African American preaching (Mitchell 1990). In the overwhelming majority of African American sermons, the moment of celebration centers on the resurrection of Jesus. However, the celebration often begins, like Mark's passion narrative, with a detailed account of the crucifixion. Classic African American preaching often punctuates the story with rhetorical questions like "He died, didn't he die?" and describe how Jesus was "hung high and stretched wide" until "the earth reeled and rocked like a drunken man, and the sun refused to shine." At this point, worshipers are often already standing on their feet, clapping their hands, shouting the preacher on, or engaged in some other form of congregational celebration in response to the Word. This celebration is not a reflection of masochistic or death-glorifying tendencies but a manifestation of the congregant's confidence in the end of the story.

Like Mark's community, the worshipers are not physical witnesses to Jesus' resurrection. However, the proclamation of it is enough to elicit praise because the one who foretold it and the witness of other believers are enough. There is every reason to expect death to give way to life, even in the midst of the darkest circumstances. So, before the preacher can say "early Sunday morning," the celebration has begun. It is not based on what people did but on what God did. They believe God raised Jesus from the dead, even if they have not yet seen the risen Lord. They do not need to end the story. Instead, they can be a part of it, by following the resurrected one.

Works Cited

Blevins, James L. 1974. "Seventy-Two Years of the Messianic Secret: A Review Article." *Perspectives in Religious Studies* 1, no. 2:192–200.

Blount, Brian K. 1998. *Go Preach! Mark's Kingdom Message and the Black Church Today*. Maryknoll, NY: Orbis.

Brandon, S. G. F. 1967. *Jesus and the Zealots*. New York: Oxford University Press.

Brooks, James A. 1991. *Mark*. The New American Commentary 23. Nashville: Broadman & Holman.

Burkett, Delbert. 1999. *The Son of Man Debate: A History and Evaluation*. New York: Cambridge University Press.

Calvin, John. 1845. *Commentary on a Harmony of the Evangelists Matthew, Mark, and Luke* (Vols. 2 and 3). Trans. the Rev. William Pringle. Edinburgh: The Calvin Translation Society.

Carl, Harold F. 2001. "Only the Father Knows: Historical and Evangelical Responses to Jesus' Eschatological Ignorance in Mark 13:32." *Journal of Biblical Studies* 1, no. 3.
http://www.mountainretreatorg.net/articles/only_the_father_knows.shtml.

Collins, Adela Yarbro. 1992. *The Beginning of the Gospel: Probings of Mark in Context*. Minneapolis: Fortress Press.

Dewey, Joanna. 2006. "Women in the Gospel of Mark." *WW* 26, no. 1:22–29.

Donahue, John R., and Daniel J. Harrington. 2002. *The Gospel of Mark*. Sacra Pagina 2. Collegeville, MN: Liturgical Press.

Driscoll, Mark. 2006. *Confessions of a Reformission Rev.: Hard Lessons from an Emerging Missional Church*. Grand Rapids: Zondervan.

Dunn, James D. G. 1970. "The Messianic Secret in Mark." *TynBul* 21:92–117.

Edwards, James R. 2002. *The Gospel according to Mark*. Pillar New Testament Commentary. Grand Rapids: Eerdmans.

France, R. T. 2003. *Divine Government: God's Kingship in the Gospel of Mark*. Vancouver, BC: Regent College Publishing.

Haber, Susan. 2003. "A Woman's Touch: Feminist Encounters with the Hemorrhaging Woman in Mark 5:24-34." *JSNT* 26 no. 2:171–92.

Hanson, K. C. 1997. "The Galilean Fishing Economy and the Jesus Tradition." *BTB* 27:99–111.

Harrington, Daniel J. 1991. *The Gospel of Matthew*. Sacra Pagina. Collegeville, MN: Liturgical Press.

Hengel, Martin. 1977. *Crucifixion*. Minneapolis: Fortress Press.

Hooker, Morna D. 1999. *The Gospel according to St. Mark*. Peabody, MA: Hendrickson.

Horsley, Richard A. 1984. "Popular Messianic Movements around the Time of Jesus." *CBQ* 46:471–95.

———. 1985. *Bandits, Prophets, and Messiahs: Popular Movements at the Time of Jesus*. Harrisburg, PA: Trinity Press International.

Johnson, William A. 1989. "'The Jews' in Saint Mark's Gospel." *Religion and Intellectual Life* 6, nos. 3–4:182–92.

Juel, Donald H. 1990. *Mark*. Augsburg Commentary. Minneapolis: Fortress Press.

Keck, Leander E. 1965. "Mark 3:7-12 and Mark's Christology." *Journal of Biblical Literature* 84, no. 4: 341-48.

Kee, Howard Clark. 1977. *Community of the New Age: Studies in the Gospel of Mark*. Philadelphia: Westminster, 1977.

Kelber, Werner H. 1974. *The Kingdom in Mark: A New Place and Time*. Philadelphia: Fortress Press.

Kinukawa, Hisako. 1994. *Women and Jesus in Mark: A Japanese Feminist Perspective*. Maryknoll, NY: Orbis.

LaHaye, Tim F., and Jerry B. Jenkins. 1995–2003. *Left Behind Series*. Carol Stream, IL: Tyndale House Publishers.

Lindsey, Hal, and Carole C. Carson. 1970. *The Late Great Planet Earth*. Grand Rapids: Zondervan.

Maddock, Sherry, and Geoff Maddock. 2007. "An Ever-Renewed Adventure of Faith." In *An Emergent Manifesto of Hope*, edited by Doug Pagitt and Tony Jones, 79–88. Grand Rapids: Baker Books.

Malbon, Elizabeth Struthers. 1986. "Disciples/Crowd/Whoever." *NovT* 28:104–30.

———. 1983. "Fallible Followers: Women and Men in the Gospel of Mark." *Semeia* 28:29–48.

Malina, Bruce J. 1993. "Authoritarianism." In *Biblical Social Values and Their Meaning: A Handbook*, edited by John J. Pilch and Bruce Malina. 11-17. Peabody, MA: Hendrickson.

Mann, C. S. 1986. *Mark: A New Translation with Introduction and Commentary*. AB 27. New York: Doubleday.

Marcus, Joel. 1992. "The Jewish War and the *Sitz Im Leben* of Mark." *JBL* 111:441–62.

McLaren, Brian. 2004. *A Generous Orthodoxy*. Cajon, CA: Youth Specialties Books.

Meier, John P. 2000. "The Historical Jesus and the Historical Herodians." *JBL* 119:740–46.

Miller, Susan. 2004. *Women in Mark's Gospel*. New York: T&T Clark.

Mitchell, Henry H. 1990. *Celebration and Experience in Preaching*. Nashville: Abingdon.

Mitchell, Joan L. 2001. *Beyond Fear and Silence: A Feminist-Literary Approach to the Gospel of Mark*. New York: Continuum.

Myers, Ched. 1988. *Binding the Strong Man: A Political Reading of Mark's Story of Jesus*. Maryknoll, NY: Orbis.

Pesch, Rudolf. 1976–80. *Das Markusevangelium*, 2 vols. HTKNT. Freiburg: Herder.

Pilch, John J. 1993. "Power." In *Biblical Social Values and Their Meaning: A Handbook*, edited by John J. Pilch and Bruce Malina. 139-42. Peabody: Hendrickson.

Placher, William C. 2010. *Mark*. Belief: A Theological Commentary on the Bible. Louisville: Westminster John Knox.

Powery, Emerson B. 2007. "Mark." In *True to Our Native Land: An African American New Testament Commentary*, edited by Brian K. Blount, 121–57. Minneapolis: Fortress Press.

Rhoads, David, Joanna Dewey, and Donald Michie. 2012. *Mark as Story: An Introduction to the Narrative of a Gospel*. 3rd ed. Minneapolis: Fortress Press.

Saldarini, Anthony J. 1998. *Pharisees, Scribes, and Sadducees in Palestinian Society*. Grand Rapids: Eerdmans.

Schüssler Fiorenza, Elisabeth. 1992. *But She Said: Feminist Practices of Biblical Interpretation*. Boston: Beacon.

Schweitzer, Albert. 2001. *The Quest for the Historical Jesus: The First Complete Edition*. Trans. and ed. John Bowden. Minneapolis: Fortress Press.

Stone, Lawrence. 1994. "Family Values in a Historical Perspective." Tanner Lectures on Human Values, Harvard University, November 16 and 17.

St. Clair, Raquel A. 2008. *Call and Consequences: A Womanist Reading of Mark*. Minneapolis: Fortress Press.

Theissen, Gerd. 1991. *The Gospels in Context: Social and Political History in the Synoptic Tradition*. Translator Linda M. Maloney. Minneapolis: Fortress Press.

Thomas, Frank A. 1997. *They Like to Never Quit Praisin' God: The Role of Celebration in Preaching*. Cleveland: United Church Press.

Tolbert, Mary Ann. 1989. *Sowing the Gospel: Mark's World in Literary Perspective*. Minneapolis: Fortress Press.

Waetjen, Herman C. 1989. *A Reordering of Power: A Socio-Political Reading of Mark's Gospel*. Minneapolis: Fortress Press.

Weisse, Christian Hermann (1838). *Die evangelische Geschichte kritisch und philosophisch bearbeitet*. Leipzig: Breitkopf und Härtel.

Wilke, Christian Gottlob. 1838. *Der Urevangelist oder exegetisch kritische Untersuchung über das Verwandtschaftsverhältniß der drei ersten Evangelien*. Dresden und Leipzig, G. Fleischer.

Weeden, Theodore. 1971. *Traditions in Conflict*. Philadelphia: Fortress Press.

LUKE

Robert L. Brawley

Introduction

Luke's Gospel is embedded in Israel's story of God's relationship with humanity and the world. Though it was canonized sometime after its writing, it extends Israel's scriptural tradition. Special emphasis falls on covenants. Abrahamic promises in particular are synthesized with other covenants in Israel's traditions. Luke is composed from individual episodes that are here arranged in three primary sections: the setting and preparation for Jesus' ministry (1:5—4:13); proclamation and extension of God's commonwealth (4:14—21:28); passion and resurrection (23:1—24:53).

Luke is also embedded in Israel's relationships with surrounding cultures. It participates in Hellenism not only in its language but also in its literary conventions. The Roman Empire especially bleeds through every page (Carter 2006). Luke's audience seldom experienced the empire's upper stratum directly. Rather they confronted systems that flowed down through client kings, governors, and local elite collaborators, including a high-priestly hierarchy, magistrates, and tax collectors. These systems sustained a world divided between unpropertied and propertied populations, those who subsisted from their own labor (90 percent) and those who lived from the labors of others (10 percent) (De Ste. Croix).

Luke's Jesus proclaims God's commonwealth as an alternative to these imperial systems. Anything new in God's commonwealth is also in continuity with Israel's covenant community. Continuity comes with critiques aimed at abuses in imperial systems, but the critiques also aim at renewing Israel's heritage. Luke anticipates extending God's commonwealth to the nations, but this too is grounded in God's promises to bless all the nations of the earth.

An early third-century manuscript, P^{75}, contains most of the Third Gospel, but its first lines, presumably including the title, are missing. Nevertheless, the ending attributes the writing to "Luke." A coworker of Paul bears this name in Philem. 24. But there are two problems with identifying the author. Though early, P[75] already represents development from an original writing, indicated by variants of the title in other manuscripts but also by the standardization of Gospel titles in P[75]. Original writings like the separate Gospels were unlikely to have used the same titular formula. The earliest attribution is at the stage of standardizing the Gospels. Second, the name Luke was common, and it is impossible to determine if the name on the manuscript refers to the same person as Philem. 24. Consequently, we know virtually nothing about the author.

Attempts to locate the place of writing or the destination produce only speculations. Again, we know virtually nothing about the place of writing or destination. When apparent historical allusions and time to allow for the use of sources are considered, a date in the last decades of the first century CE is likely.

A strong consensus takes Acts to be a sequel to Luke. Therefore, at times one volume elucidates the other. Furthermore, just as Luke presumes Israel's prior story, it also presumes a sequel, even beyond Acts.

Luke 1:1-2 acknowledges the use of "many" sources. Close agreement with passages in Mark and Matthew have led to widely accepted hypotheses that Luke used Mark and Q. A minority of scholars rejects the hypothetical source Q without denying the use of sources (e.g., Goulder). This has led to highlighting differences between sources and Luke's use of them in order to discover particular emphases. Here, scholars have encountered difficulties. Literary relationships among the Gospels are too complicated for hypotheses as simple as the use of Mark and Q, indeed too complicated to allow any solution (Sanders and Davies, 97–111). If "many" in 1:1 is literal, other sources may have been oral. Further, when authors use sources, emphases cannot be deduced from differences any more than from duplication. Therefore, reading Luke as a coherent document is a highly valued approach for interpretation today. Interpreters approach reading with constructs of authors and contexts in their minds, but images of authors and contexts ultimately develop from reading.

Note: in the following I translate *Ioudaioi* as "Jewish people." Most of the time in Luke, "Jewish people" are not to be confused either with institutional Judaism or the entire populace. All translations are mine unless otherwise noted.

Luke 1:1-4: Prologue: What and How

▌ THE TEXT IN ITS ANCIENT CONTEXT

Ancient parallels demonstrate that the prologue (1:1-4) follows literary conventions. It orients audiences to the literature they will hear, which the author calls a "narrative." With only hints of the contents as "things that happened," emphasis falls on methods and purposes. The author's involvement is analytical, communal, and dependent on antecedents. The things that happened "among us" (communal), already appeared in "many" other narratives that comprise chains of traditions. If "many" is literal, previous narratives included oral traditions. The purpose, addressed to Theophilus with a noble title, *kratiste,* is to ensure order and increase certainty for people who already have received instruction.

■ THE TEXT IN THE INTERPRETIVE TRADITION

Almost universally, interpreters assume Mark and another written source that Luke shares with Matthew (Q) among antecedent narratives. Whether "the things that have happened" includes events in Acts is debated. If so (this is quite likely), Acts 1:1-2 provides a secondary prologue. Parallels with Josephus and other Hellenistic authors imply that the author is writing history, but only as modified by previous sources and Israel's Scriptures (Alexander).

■ THE TEXT IN CONTEMPORARY DISCUSSION

Traditions that Luke was a physician who accompanied Paul persist. The only reference the author makes to himself is a masculine participle ("having investigated"). Assuming that the author is Paul's companion, therefore, is beyond evidence in the text.

Some interpreters claim that if the genre is history, this enhances Luke's "authority." Readers encounter a narrative, and the prologue notwithstanding, the narrative itself unfolds the kind of literature that audiences perceive. Can authority be determined by the prologue, or does it rest in the power of persuasion in the reading itself?

Luke 1:5—4:13: Setting and Preparation for Jesus' Ministry

Luke 1:5—3:20: Divine Promises, Infancy Narratives, Global and Local Settings

■ THE TEXT IN ITS ANCIENT CONTEXT

Immediately after the prologue, Luke establishes a setting before Herod's death (4 BCE). But more than establish chronology, the narrator starts with a local personal story that is set in global systems of social order, religion, and politics. Zechariah and Elizabeth belong to a priestly order of low status that contrasts with high-priestly elites. Piety makes them exemplary, but in an ethos where children manifest God's blessings, childlessness blemishes them. Sterility *before* menopause and *advanced age* are characteristic of biblical stories of extraordinary births. Their privacy cannot escape the foreground of imperial systems (see also 2:1-2; 3:1-2). Systems involving an imperial client king (1:5) and high-priestly collaborators (implied by Zechariah's status under a priestly hierarchy, 1:5, 8) affect their lives.

The setting jumps inside the Jerusalem sanctuary (1:8). Outside, a multitude prays; inside, incense goes up like prayers. Gabriel has to do with both. Inside, he promises God's remedy for the couple's childlessness. For the outside, his promise is for Israel. Zechariah's question "how will I know" encompasses *both* sides, and his inability to speak until the child's birth is a sign that validates God's promises for Israel as well as for him and Elizabeth.

Dramatically the narrative becomes gendered. It shifts from masculine characters to women. Elizabeth celebrates her pregnancy as God's inversion of disgrace, and the term of her pregnancy links her to Mary in Galilee. Gabriel speaks to Mary, and aside from overarching imperial systems, her impending marriage is the context. Promises to her are also both private and communal—a child for her; restoration of David's commonwealth for Israel. In keeping with 2 Samuel 7, the restoration is everlasting—with a twist. In 2 Samuel, David's "seed" is a collective noun for David's dynasty. Gabriel makes it literally singular. Gabriel promises *Jesus'* everlasting enthronement (1:32-33).

Like Zechariah, Mary asks "how" (1:34). Gabriel's response makes her conception a matter of divine initiative and correlates it with Elizabeth's pregnancy by means of an astounding claim: "Any prediction [thing] will not be impossible with God" (1:37). Mary avows remarkable consonance with Gabriel's announcement: "[I am] the Lord's servant; may it be with me according to your prediction" (1:38).

When Mary journeys to Elizabeth, they join forces. In contrast to mute Zechariah, women deliver the first speeches of consequence. By concealing herself, Elizabeth occupies the social margin but transforms it into creative space by playing a prophet's role. She blesses Mary and Mary's child, and affirms her own place in God's eyes in something greater than themselves.

Mary adds the antiphonal voice of another prophet from the margins. She identifies with the low social class and affirms God's power to bless. This takes the shape of God's "class conversion." Against powerful thrones (implicating imperial systems), God manifests mercy to generations of those who have inadequate access to the earth's resources. Her references to Abrahamic promises also supplement Gabriel's allusions to David's commonwealth (1:46-55).

Then a male prophesies creatively from the margins (the Judean backcountry, 1:68-79). Zechariah reiterates Gabriel's allusions to Davidic promises, synthesizes them with Abrahamic promises, and views God's fidelity to the promises as liberation from oppression. John and Jesus are ways God keeps ancient promises. When Zechariah calls this "forgiveness of sins," he means corporate consequences beyond individual transgressions: in context, complicity in Israel's subjugation. John's role as preparing the way of the Lord, recalling prophecies of Israel's restoration from captivity, likewise embraces liberation from oppression.

Luke 2:1 fills in the foreground of imperial systems. Emperor Augustus and Governor Quirinius in Syria complement the picture of King Herod and an implicit priestly hierarchy in chapter 1. Another imperial agent in Bethlehem, an unmentioned local clerk, awaits Joseph's enrollment. Geographical horizons reflect the interplay between local and global—Herod's Judea (1:5), all the world (2:1) (Wolter, 121). Distinctions in political status between Judea and Galilee also affect the setting, as does the village atmosphere reflected in a manger and shepherds. Augustus's might, contrasted with peasants caught homeless at childbirth, is full of pathos. Irony snags imperial powers, who force a journey that matches divine purposes for Jesus to be born in David's city. Like Mary, shepherds measure low culturally and are unanticipated recipients of the message that a Savior-Messiah is born to *them*. The inauspicious becomes auspicious, and out of character for their marginal status, shepherds become witnesses to others.

Joseph and Mary comply with cultic expectations of circumcision and purification. Offering two turtledoves underlines their peasant status (Lev. 12:8). But the inauspicious is also confirmed in the temple by sagacity, commitment, and hope. This also is gendered. First, venerable Simeon anticipates peace through God's restoration of Israel. He labels Jesus a light of revelation for the nations and for the glory of Israel, but also predicts the falling and rising of many in Israel (Luke 2:34). This reiterates Mary's prophecy about the downfall of the powerful and exaltation of the lowly (1:52) and anticipates conflict between elites and the oppressed. Second, venerable Anna witnesses to God's promises to deliver Jerusalem from oppression.

Most interpreters present 3:1-20 as a new literary unit. A reference to Tiberius's fifteenth year (c. 29 CE) lures many commentators to focus on chronology. But 3:1-2 elaborates and extends the local and global political and economic setting of chapters 1–2 and depicts how Jewish people experienced imperial systems from the emperor to local collaborators. Furthermore, like Elizabeth, Mary, Zechariah, Simeon, and Anna, the Baptizer plays a prophet's role within this imperial setting. His baptism for forgiveness has implications for individuals (3:10-14) but is also tied to Isaiah's message of national restoration (Isa. 40:3; Luke 3:3-6). Individual behavior has communal consequences for Israel in imperial contexts in both Isaiah and Luke. When John deals with instances of behavior in 3:14, they have to do with covenant values of equitable access to resources, economics, and the power of the strong over the weak. By contrast, 3:18-20 portrays another imperial client ruler, Herod Antipas, suppressing covenant values by imprisoning John.

Abraham, who figures in Mary's and Zechariah's prophecies, reappears in John's. First, he challenges Abrahamic descent unless it bears fruit in covenant ethics (3:8). Simultaneously, he espouses God's ability to raise up children of Abraham. Most interpreters take the metaphor of raising up children from stones as devaluing Abrahamic descent. But does it not also, like 1:37, affirm God's power (see 19:40)? In Luke, does God (metaphorically) raise up children of Abraham from stones?

▌The Text in the Interpretive Tradition

Most interpreters underplay the context of imperial systems and social struggles among the elite and the oppressed and focus instead on chronology (1:5; 2:1; 3:1-2). From the beginning of the second Christian millennium, Elizabeth's prophecy concerning Mary and her child became a liturgical prayer, with emphasis on Mary's roles as the mother of the Lord and mediatrix. This reduced the complementarity of the prophecies of Elizabeth, Mary, and Zechariah. The virginal conception also dominated interpretation and eclipsed scriptural traditions of divine initiative in birth wonders; indeed, it overshadowed parallels between Elizabeth's conception and Mary's, and diverted emphasis from God's initiative to Mary's character.

Moreover, emphasis on John as a forerunner and Jesus as Savior tended to write off antecedents in Israel's history and neglected continuity with Israel in portrayals of John and Jesus in the traditions of Elijah, David, and Abraham.

▌The Text in Contemporary Discussion

Debates persist over the virginal conception. The narrative lacks specificity about how conception occurred. When Gabriel predicts that Mary will bear a son, her engagement implies conception in her impending marriage (see Fitzmyer 1973, 566–67). However, Mary presumes not her marriage but her virginal condition (Brown 1979, 298–309). In addition, some deduce that Luke conceals Mary's pregnancy outside marriage. This too can be intensely theological if one assumes pregnancy due to rape or abuse. This intensifies God's inversion of shame among the marginalized (Schaberg). Either option underscores God's initiative in the births of Jesus and John. Such divine initiative, however, remains mysterious. Karl Barth once remarked that the virginal conception is "inconceivable."

Luke's use of sources leads interpreters to emphasize individual episodes, but increasingly, narrative continuity is also accented. Speeches of Gabriel, Elizabeth, Mary, and Zechariah fit together in one story. The context of imperial systems is also overarching.

Mid-twentieth-century interpretations made a sharp break between Jesus' proclamation of God's commonwealth and Israel's heritage (Conzelmann), sharpened even into "anti-Judaism" (J. Sanders). This will come under consideration again, but continuity with God's promises to Israel is undeniable.

Similarly, some interpreters judge Luke deficient in neglecting significant roles for women (Reid). Elizabeth and Mary are prominent exceptions. Interpreters often read the silence imposed on Zechariah as punishment for failing to believe Gabriel and contrast this with Mary's assertion of conformity to divine purposes. Actually, both ask "how?" Further, when it is clear that Gabriel's promises are for Israel as well as for Zechariah and Elizabeth, rather than punishing Zechariah, Gabriel declares that the inability to speak is a sign that confirms predictions both to him *and* to Israel.

How does the serene and contemplative Mary as the servant of the Lord (1:38) in popular piety and art fit her role as a prophet in 1:46-55? As with servants of the Lord in Israel's traditions such as Moses and the prophets, in her role as God's servant she also confronts oppressive powers and correlates God's mercy and promises to the plight of poverty, hunger, and oppressive powers. Today the Virgin of Guadalupe has been used as just such a prophet among the disadvantaged in Mexico, especially among indigenous populations. An image of her accompanied César Chávez and the striking United Farm Workers in the 1960s, and some feminists have adopted her as an advocate of liberation.

Luke 3:21—4:13: Unfolding Jesus' Identity and Endowment with the Spirit

▌ THE TEXT IN ITS ANCIENT CONTEXT

Jesus' baptism unfolds his identity. A heavenly voice declares: "You are my beloved son" (3:22, reiterating 1:32), and he is endowed with the Spirit.

More than monotonous lists, genealogies establish relationships and continuity. Jesus is related to Israelites in whom God was at work: Zerubbabel in Israel's restoration after exile (Ezra 3:2, 8); David in God's promises of rulers on Israel's throne (2 Sam. 7:13; Luke 1:32-33); Abraham, Isaac, Jacob, and Adam—continuity with stories of both Israel and humanity.

The devil (4:1-13) advances Jesus' identity by questioning, "If you are God's son" (4:3, 9). The devil proposes that Jesus dramatize sonship, but Jesus' first words as an adult demonstrate what he is not—he is not what the devil proposes. Forty days in the desert echo Israel's wilderness wandering. Further, allusions to Scripture evoke their larger contexts. Turning stones into bread recalls wilderness feedings of Israel, personified as God's Son. Will God likewise feed Jesus, God's Son? For Jesus, "one does not live by bread alone" (Deut. 8:3) means that Israel's *hunger* rather than the *feeding* taught them to live under God's care. The devil's promise to give Jesus the world's kingdoms for worshiping him (violating monotheism) is a deceitful shortcut to David's throne (Luke 1:32).

Jumping from the temple is a challenge to trust the words of Scripture: "God will keep you" (Ps. 91:11-12). Citing Deut. 6:16, Jesus asserts that testing whether God is "among us or not" is a failure of trust (Brawley 1995, 15–26).

◼ THE TEXT IN THE INTERPRETIVE TRADITION

Some interpreters argue that by reporting Jesus' baptism after John's imprisonment, Luke conceals that Jesus was baptized by John (Conzelmann, 21). This is excessive. In Luke 3, Jesus' baptism stands in continuity with John's baptism of the crowds (3:7). He is baptized along with them (3:21). Many take the devil's claim to exercise power over all kingdoms to mean that Luke thinks all governments are demonic. But the deceptive devil is unreliable! In keeping with Gabriel's interpretation that *Jesus* is David's seed (singular, 1:32-33), the genealogy avoids David's descendants who ruled, and links Jesus more directly to David (2 Sam. 7:8-16) (Wolter, 175).

◼ THE TEXT IN CONTEMPORARY DISCUSSION

Jesus' genealogy is masculine, but the hint about Joseph's paternity ("as was supposed," 3:23) may be the only reference outside the birth narratives to the virginal conception or alternatively, to a problem pregnancy (rape, abuse) (Schaberg). Descent from Adam gives Jesus a role in God's relationship with all humanity. Jesus and the devil challenge each other by interpreting Scripture. When used deceptively, Scripture is false (Brawley 1995, 20–26).

Luke 4:14—21:38: Proclamation and Extension of God's Commonwealth

Luke 4:14-41: Hopes and Manifestations of Jesus' Mission

◼ THE TEXT IN ITS ANCIENT CONTEXT

Interpreters often call Jesus' proclamation in Nazareth his inaugural sermon, but the preceding summary (4:14-15) shows that it is an instance of his ministry already underway. The incident has four foci. Jesus reads Isaiah, announces a word-event that occurs when the congregants hear the reading, implicates himself in this word-event, and provokes a response.

Luke's audience would hardly have understood God's sending Jesus as one anointed with the Spirit in terms of a developed Christology. With thematic emphasis on the Spirit (annunciation, baptism, temptation), they would have heard that where God's Spirit is, God's favor is manifest, like the Jubilee Year (Green 1997, 212–13). The poor who receive good news are the bottom 90 percent, dominated by elites in a two-tiered system. Their social status is that of Rome's vanquished victims. Concretely, debts are annulled, debtors are released from prison, blindness is overcome, brokenness is mended. Jesus assumes the power of God's Spirit in his ministry. This is what God's commonwealth is (4:43).

Blindness plays on Jesus' hearers who fix their *eyes* on him (Green 1997, 211). They see Isaiah's gracious words (originally spoken also in an imperial context), but reject Jesus as sent by God (see "sent" in 4:18, 43). Luke gives no motivation for the people of Nazareth to reject Jesus. However, rejection verifies the proverb demonstrated by Elijah and Elisha: "No prophet is accepted in his own countryside." Their rejection confirms Jesus' prophetic mandate (Brawley 1987, 6–27). Conversely, Jesus' ministry in Capernaum manifests the favor God's Spirit generates (4:31-41).

■ THE TEXT IN THE INTERPRETIVE TRADITION

Since the development of Chalcedonian Christology, Jesus' claim to be anointed has directed attention to his messianic identity, often associated with doctrines of human and divine natures. Emphasis is on his God-sent ministry rather than his ontological essence. Possibly Luke intends only a prophetic anointing (Fitzmyer 1981, 1:529–30). But "anointed" in Acts 4:27 (citing Psalm 2) speaks against restriction to a prophetic anointing.

■ THE TEXT IN CONTEMPORARY DISCUSSION

It is significant that Jesus' ministry has a major focus on release from prison. In Luke's world, prisons were primarily short-term facilities. Debtors, however, were subject to long-term incarceration ("until you have paid the very last penny" [Luke 12:59]). Today "restorative justice" places emphasis on building relationships between victims and offenders and offers the latter opportunities to make restoration—obviously impossible if offenders are incarcerated.

Recent discussion tends toward Jesus' anticipation of his ministry in terms of poverty and exploitation in addition to personal or figurative meanings (Wolter, 192–93). Many interpreters take the Nazarenes' rejection of Jesus as anticipating Jewish rejection of Jesus, even revealing Luke's anti-Judaism in favor of gentiles (J. Sanders). This ignores Jesus' prior successful ministry in Galilean synagogues, his subsequent ministry and acceptance in Capernaum, and his programmatic statement of his *sending* to the *synagogues* of Judea (4:14-15, 31-41, 42-44) (Brawley 1987, 7–11). In Luke, particular Israelites respond positively and negatively to Jesus and his followers. A corporate rejection by Jewish people distorts the data. Given the setting in imperial systems, the citation from Isaiah, and Jesus' claims of fulfillment, the Nazareth incident initiates the realization of the covenant promises claimed by Mary in 1:50-55.

Luke 4:42—5:11: Initial Extensions of Jesus' Mission

■ THE TEXT IN ITS ANCIENT CONTEXT

Luke 4:44 summarizes Jesus' proclamation in synagogues. Then 5:1-11 shifts the setting precipitously to public space, where his auditors are a crowd closely identified with the 90 percent of the subdominant population—earlier called "the poor." Merely the appearance of crowds is a sign of differentiation from reigning imperial systems (Scott, 63). Again, Jesus' proclamation is summarized and gives way to a brief narrative about recruiting coworkers. Following Jesus' suggestion, Simon and his partners net an abundant catch of fish. Sequence alone leads hearers to presume causation by Jesus and to be astonished, like Simon and his companions. Simon then recognizes a manifestation of the numinous that threatens him, a "sinner." Thematically, this has to do with manifesting

God's Spirit in God's commonwealth, a manifestation that dramatizes what God's commonwealth is. Jesus makes it analogous to collaborating in mission—catching people. They leave all and follow.

■ THE TEXT IN THE INTERPRETIVE TRADITION

The catch of fish is often called a nature "miracle." Beyond prescience, little is extraordinary. Abundant catches are remarkable but natural, and Jesus makes this one a parable of mission. Developments of church hierarchy have appealed to Simon's priority and apostolic office. Here, however, there is no "calling" or "sending." The fishermen follow on their own initiative.

■ THE TEXT IN CONTEMPORARY DISCUSSION

This incident culminates in a dramatic change. "Leaving everything" entails striking changes personally (e.g., Peter), economically (the fish are not marketed), socially (relationships are fundamentally altered), and decisively (commitment to mission to the poor/crowds) (4:18; 5:1). These disciples have a special status in Luke and are hardly models for every reader, but the call for change, commitment, and ministry are unavoidable.

Luke 5:12—6:11: Faith and Restorations in Contexts of Oppression

■ THE TEXT IN ITS ANCIENT CONTEXT

Luke 5:12—6:11 presents concrete cases of good news to the poor (4:18) in other Judean cities (4:43). Three incidents focus on Jesus (5:12-14; 5:17-26; 6:6-11), three on his followers (5:29-32; 5:33-39; 6:1-4).

The healing of a leper is a remarkable deed of compassion pared to essentials (5:12-14). Luke's hearers understand the sparse description of leprosy as a skin disorder (not Hansen's disease) that required heartrending exclusion from normal society (Lev. 13:46; Josephus *Ant.* 3.264: "as good as dead" [author's trans.]). Prostration and supplication reflect the gravity of the ailment. Purification is primary; healing, the means to it. The leper links restoration with Jesus' desire: "If you *want to . . .* you can make me clean" (5:12 PHILLIPS). Exceeding mere healing, Jesus proclaims good news: "Certainly I want to." Touching affirms his desire. Thus an instance of God's Spirit that blesses occurs. Luke's hearers cannot understand Jesus' charge not to tell to mean suppressing the deed, since the story itself makes it known. Rather, procedures in the law, rather than rumors, confirm the man's restoration to his community.

The second episode is closely related because it is stimulated by the cleansing of the leper (5:15). The priest's confirmation of the purification should have served as a witness to some Pharisees and teachers of law who show up in 5:17-26. Whereas the leper's purification is a bare-bones account, complex narrative tensions surface in the healing of a paralytic. The paralytic and the men who bring him beat the competition for space by a dramatic act of breaking through barriers to gain access to Jesus. They are virtually pallbearers who let the paralytic down through the roof. When the narrator says that Jesus *saw* their faith(fulness) (5:20), faith(fulness) is not confessed, but dramatized. (Confession does not thereby become irrelevant; see on 12:8-9 below.) Faith(fulness) looks like this. Jesus' reaction to their faith(fulness) is a non sequitur—an assurance of pardon that perhaps reflects beliefs that sin produces maladies. Some scribes and Pharisees create a narrative need by questioning: Who can forgive sins but God alone? Luke's audience understands that Jesus assures *God's* forgiveness (divine passive, 5:20) on the basis of action that overcomes obstacles to life. But Jesus provokes theological considerations by arrogating power (5:24) to grant assurance of pardon on earth (on the basis of the dramatic act) and offers healing as evidence that forgiveness is not in word only but in deed as well. Luke's audience hears Jesus refer to himself as "son of man" for the first time and understands that he claims a special commission from God. When the paralytic arises and carries his bed, he and *everyone*, including scribes and Pharisees, glorify God and acknowledge this as a "sign" with a double meaning—a sign of the power of the Spirit in God's commonwealth, and of Jesus' power to assure God's forgiveness.

Two additional episodes also produce conflict and prepare for what follows—for Jesus' proclamation of God's commonwealth, recruiting followers, and developing themes of mission (5:27-32; 5:33-39). Like the catch of fish (5:4-11), calling Levi is a recruitment story. The first person Jesus "calls" is not Simon, but this tax collector. Like Simon and his partners, he leaves all and *follows*. This does not merely provide a setting for the subsequent conflict over table fellowship. Rather, Levi's banquet is an instance of *following*. For Levi, following Jesus means including in God's commonwealth people who are of questionable repute, like himself, because they participate in systems of economic abuse (see 3:13) and/or transgress social norms. Thus the banquet is an act of following that becomes a conflict story. Pointedly, not the narrator, but critics label the guests "sinners" and question Jesus' inclusive table fellowship. Jesus defends his relationships by a parabolic image associating his "companionship" ("eating bread together") with healing those who are not in good health. Astute hearers of Luke would recognize thematic development on Jesus' mission to proclaim God's commonwealth not only to those who are economically poor but also to people like lepers whose social status is problematic. Jesus then expresses his mission thematically: to call sinners to repentance. This explanation also proclaims God's commonwealth to his critics.

Anonymous interlocutors then question the failure of Jesus' followers to practice special prayer while fasting ("praying and fasting" go together as one act, 5:33-39). The first time Jesus' followers are called "disciples" in Luke is on the lips of interlocutors who compare them with disciples of John and the Pharisees. Thereafter, the name sticks. Jesus responds with two figurations. His answer in the second person plural places his interlocutors at a wedding feast where fasting is absurd; under different conditions, fasting is appropriate (see 22:18). Garments and wineskins old and new depict *preservation* and *innovation* simultaneously.

The fifth incident (6:1-5) is a controversy story. A small amount of harvesting and eating grain on Sabbath raises protests against the behavior of Jesus' disciples. "Some" Pharisees object that harvesting on Sabbath is unlawful. Jesus tacitly affirms their premise, but also makes it contextually dependent by appealing to David's precedent, in which need supersedes regulations. Luke's audience would find Jesus' reference to the "son of man" (6:5) ambiguous. Do needs of *any* human supersede restrictions? Or do Jesus' prerogatives outshine David's?

The sixth episode (6:6-11) is another conflict story that clarifies this question somewhat by refocusing on Jesus. Luke 6:6 makes this incident an instance of Jesus' mission in other synagogues of

Judea (4:44). But his prior activity also invites a test. His examiners are some scribes and Pharisees with ulterior motives to find fault. The only question on the examination is: Will Jesus heal on Sabbath? Jesus' response first restates Sabbath law positively: instead of prohibiting what is unlawful, he proposes that doing good is lawful. *His* only "work" is words: "Stretch out your hand" (6:10). When the man does, Jesus' critics discuss: What are we going to do with Jesus? This question deliberates possibilities, which makes the translation of *anoia* as "fury" (NRSV) unlikely. Rather they lack "understanding" (6:11).

▌ THE TEXT IN THE INTERPRETIVE TRADITION

The cleansing of a leper, the raising of a paralytic, and the restoration of a withered hand are all healing stories, but controversy over forgiveness and Sabbath behavior in the last two also mix with conflict stories about table fellowship and harvesting grain on the Sabbath. Conventionally, the healings are called "miracles." But antiquity does not distinguish between "natural" and "supernatural," as common definitions of miracle imply. The term in 5:26 means "something remarkable." Tradition understands the leper's cleansing as an act of Jesus' authoritative will. But the leper's supplication and Jesus' response are at the level of desire: "If you want to" (5:12-13). When conflict arises with scribes and Pharisees, almost all interpreters presume that Jesus' critics are unyielding. But 5:26 includes them among "all" who glorify God and acknowledge a remarkable deed. The other conflict stories end with Jesus' explanations of his and his followers' behavior. The restoration of a man's hand, however, ends with his critics' reaction: What are we going to do with Jesus? English translations of 6:11 that make his critics "furious" are simply inadequate. Rather, they "misunderstand." This is one among other cases where the interpretive tradition has set Jesus in opposition to his interlocutors in a way that is unjustified.

Interpretations of garments and wineskins have overwhelmingly emphasized innovation to the point of incompatibility between old and new. Both cases depend indispensably on *preservation* of the old. Indeed, the image of the wineskins ends with the value of old wine (5:39) (Green 1997, 250; against Wolter, 232–33).

▌ THE TEXT IN CONTEMPORARY DISCUSSION

Studies of Jesus' remarkable deeds have highlighted features that are prominent in Luke. Virtually all involve descriptions of oppressive restrictions, which either Jesus or persons in need violate in order to produce transformation (Theissen, 134–37; Wire, 109–10). In the healing of the paralytic, sin (not merely personal but also corporate and systemic), the pardon of which Jesus assures, plays a role in oppression. Demonic possession may be psychosocial expressions of domination and protests against social oppression (Theissen, 255–56). Some interpreters portray Jewish society generally as oppressive, against which Jesus produces a new order.

Two features resist such negative portrayals of Israelite communities. One is the larger context of oppressive imperial systems. Although some Jewish people collaborated problematically in these systems, such imperial systems do not represent Israelite covenant communities in general. Second, there is no supplanting of Israelite covenant communities here. Invariably, the transformations reintegrate people into Israelite communities. Violations of barriers are clear in the leper's healing, where

Jesus' touch violates a social quarantine in order to reintegrate the man into his community. Similarly, the healing of the paralytic violates controlled channels of access to divine power. This produces conflict, but the story ends in reintegrating the paralytic and Jesus' critics into common affirmations of God. Controversies over the practices of Jesus' followers highlight behavior appropriate to contexts, and continuity with the old balances innovation. Conflict over Jesus' table fellowship and questions about fasting receive Jesus' explanations of his and his followers' behavior. If Luke finds these responses persuasive for his hearers, should contemporary interpreters not also suppose that some of Jesus' critics were also persuaded? With post-Holocaust sensitivities, it is important to note that only "some" Pharisees scrutinize Jesus and his followers (see 6:2). Interpreters should refrain from taking them as characteristic of all Pharisees. Luke's Gospel is a narrative of persuasion (see 1:4). But unloading on Jesus' interlocutors as irreparable antagonists forestalls possibilities for either the antagonists or readers who are, like them, to be persuaded. Early Jewish tradition, a bit later than Luke, reflects a similar controversy resulting in a ruling that allows crushing small quantities of straw with the hands on Sabbath, without utensils (*b. Shab.* 128a). As Jesus' emphasis on doing good on Sabbath shows, he highlights "doing" over negative restrictions but does not abrogate the Sabbath.

These incidents of healing are also cases of overcoming oppressive conditions related to maladies. Simply identifying maladies today as something "wrong," restricting the sick to confinement or quarantine, or putting people with diseases such as HIV-AIDS under judgment are scarcely any different.

Luke 6:12-49: Life in God's Commonwealth

■ THE TEXT IN ITS ANCIENT CONTEXT

Prayer provides a setting for Jesus' selection of twelve disciples and his subsequent Sermon on the Plain. Praying suggests that Jesus is not independently self-sufficient. Rather, on the basis of his relationship with God, he chooses the Twelve and proclaims God's commonwealth (the program of 4:43). Here the Twelve play no role other than following, but the title "apostles" anticipates that they will be "sent" in the future.

The detail that Jesus looks at his *disciples* is a key to understanding his sermon. He describes their life in God's commonwealth, but the crowds also hear. Jesus highlights the poor from the outset of his speech (6:20), as did Mary (1:46-55), and as he did in his proclamation in Nazareth (4:18-19).

The programmatic 4:43 indicates that the Beatitudes describe life under God's commonwealth. Strikingly, blessings are announced in direct speech to Jesus' hearers ("you"). Luke's audience would likely have heard sympathetically as if Jesus were addressing them. Each blessing is expressed without a verb in the first half (common in Greek), but verb tenses vary in the explanatory half. God's care for the poor is clearly in the present (6:20). Thus it is a performative proclamation of God's blessing for the poor now (reiterating 4:18). Blessings for the hungry and those who weep are future (6:21), but Luke's audience certainly recalls Levi's banquet (5:29) as a present reality and anticipates feasting within Jesus' ministry, not merely beyond. Luke 6:22-23 breaks the terse form of the first three Beatitudes by adding a longer culmination of blessings for disciples as Jesus' marginalized followers when they face opposition, individually and collectively. As in the vindication of Israel's martyrs (6:23 calls to mind Israel's prophets and the Maccabean tradition), blessedness may indeed anticipate a future beyond this life, but the reward in heaven (a metaphor for vindication by God, Wolter, 251) is expressed without a verb and likely includes a relationship of confidence in and succor from God realized in Jesus' proclamation itself. Luke 6:23 also breaks the form by including an imperative: "Rejoice and skip for joy" (6:23, "rejoice and skip" together describe one act).

These blessings are balanced by an antiphony of woes. Again the address is directly to Jesus' hearers ("you"). The explanation of the woe to the rich is accounting language: "You have your receipt for what is due" (6:24). The explanations of the woe to those who eat well and laugh, like the second and third Beatitudes, are future (6:25), presumably near future. The longer, final woe balances the fourth Beatitude. Jesus exposes those who are highly regarded in the present as falsely deceived on the basis of "lessons of history" (6:26).

Jesus then shifts from performative declarations to imperatives. Thus God's commonwealth also includes directives for implementing blessings. Luke 6:27-38 is centered on relationships encapsulated in: "Do to others as you would have them do to you" (6:31). Because this is not "do to others as they do to you," it contravenes even mutuality and inverts retaliation into love, including accommodating to others. Second, it means mercy that surpasses what others deserve. Hearers of both Jesus and Luke would understand this in terms of concrete relationships in village or community life. Enacting this behavior does not depend on individual resolve but is inspired, motivated, and made possible by a relationship with a merciful God, like that between parent and child (6:35-36). Relationships with others involve relationships with God; relationships with God involve relationships with others. To be God's children means that behavior is begotten by God. The "great reward" in 6:35, as in 6:23, is a metaphor for vindication by God.

Luke 6:39-49 deals again with how behavior under God's commonwealth is inspired, motivated, and made possible by a relationship with the teacher (the God of mercy? or Jesus? 6:40), which also "opens one's eyes." The metaphors here turn hindered vision into following a teacher and orient hearers to tend to themselves rather than others. This relationship bears fruit like a tree (6:43-45). Luke's hearers then view Jesus as a mediator of God's commonwealth who proclaims how life is when God rules.

▌ THE TEXT IN THE INTERPRETIVE TRADITION

Studied independently, the Beatitudes are generally understood as exhortations, although Luke's version contains only one imperative ("Rejoice and skip for joy," 6:23). The entire speech has also been interpreted as an "interim ethic" for a period before the imminent parousia (among others, Albert Schweitzer), or as an impossible ethic to demonstrate human inadequacy that evokes dependence upon God's mercy (among others, Luther), or as an intensification of Torah. When the Beatitudes are seen as an integral part of the speech in their Lukan context, they characterize life in God's commonwealth.

▌ THE TEXT IN CONTEMPORARY DISCUSSION

Some interpret the Beatitudes as addressed to the inner group of disciples to whom the blessings of God's commonwealth are proclaimed, whereas the imperatives regarding mutual relationships are spoken to the entire crowd. But the gathering of the crowd with the purpose of hearing Jesus (6:18) and the address of woes directly to the rich speak for an address to the entire group. Cases such as turning the other cheek are "focal instances" (Tannehill 1975) that provoke wide-ranging consideration far beyond one literal incident. They encourage not passive submission but active behaviors for God's children to take initiative from oppressors (Wink, 127).

Jesus' sermon has fueled discussions about the relationship of the indicative (performative declarations of God's blessing) and the imperative (commands). But the proclamation is nothing other than life under God's commonwealth in which relationships with God are integral to relationships with others—two dimensions that are hardly separate. Giving to those who ask (6:30, 34) exceeds mutuality; the initiative and control of goods lies not with the giver but with those in need. The imperative to be merciful in 6:36 is often understood as ethical imitation of God. On the other hand, the context has to do with a parent-child relationship. The relationship is not imitation as such but the behavior that a merciful parent begets in a child, as in the gender-specific proverb "like father, like son."

Inasmuch as peasants at the subsistence level constituted 90 percent of the population in Luke's world, the vast majority of the hearers of both Jesus and Luke were the poor. By contrast, for many of us in the so-called first world today who disproportionately consume the resources of the earth, it is disturbingly difficult to hear the Beatitudes with the ears of the poor (Bovon, 1:223), and we find ourselves bluntly challenged.

Luke 7:1-50: Deeds That Substantiate Jesus' Identity

▮ THE TEXT IN ITS ANCIENT CONTEXT

Luke 7 characterizes Jesus by what he does. Two remarkable deeds precede the Baptizer's question: "Are you the one who is coming or do we expect another?" (7:19-20). Jesus' response is then followed by a short discourse that elaborates his answer, and by the woman in Simon's house. Though the healing of a centurion's slave and the raising of a widow's son appear to drop precipitously into the narrative, they are integral to Jesus' response to the Baptizer. First, Jesus returns to Capernaum, where he previously had a remarkable ministry and achieved prominence (4:31-42). The centurion clearly plays a role in imperial systems—succinctly, he commands subordinates—but here he makes himself subservient to God's commonwealth. His slave exercises no agency but remains hidden behind the centurion and his friends, Jewish elders, and Jesus. The centurion controls everything from offstage, including Jesus' actions. Nevertheless, testimony about Jesus motivates him (7:3). So he sends elders, who present a positive picture of Israelite citizens (Green 1997, 286–87, views their appeal to reciprocity for the centurion's generosity negatively). They also portray the centurion positively. Through other friends, the centurion tells Jesus what to do and says more than Jesus (7:6-8). He acts with "power" in order to access Jesus' power. Jesus names this act "faith(fulness)," exceeding such acts among Israelites. Faith(fulness) is not confessed but dramatized. If hearers recall the men who took a paralytic to Jesus (5:19) and liken the elders to them (7:4-5), the comparison with Israel (7:9) does not indict Israel but produces amazement even for Jesus (there is no "disjunction between this Gentile and Israel" as Green [1997, 288] suggests). Previously, witnesses of Jesus' remarkable deeds were amazed; now Jesus is.

Jesus travels to Nain for another remarkable deed and this time takes the initiative (7:11-17). The incident is a traumatic funeral of a widow's only son. According to customs of patrilineal marriage, the woman's plight eclipses concern for the son. Without a husband or son, she is bereft of subsistence. In keeping with the good news of God's commonwealth, compassion motivates Jesus to touch the coffin. Surprisingly, he speaks to the dead youth with an imperative, commanding him to be raised (7:14-15). A crowd interprets Jesus' command as a prophecy, spoken for God whose favor comes to Israel (7:16), that is, God's commonwealth. This characterizes Jesus as a prophet *before* competing evaluations label him a "drunkard and glutton" (7:34) and Simon's skepticism about his prophetic identity (7:39). God's favor corresponds to Jesus' mission in 4:18, reinforces his prophetic character, and further associates his ministry with Elijah by parallels with 1 Kgs. 17:17-24. God's favor for *Israel* (7:16) speaks against taking the centurion's faith(fulness) in the previous episode as indicting Israel.

These deeds set the stage for the Baptizer's question, conveyed by messengers (*angeloi*, 7:24). The question whether Jesus is "the one who comes" picks up John's announcement in 3:16 of a more powerful one who comes but likely also alludes to general traditions of a figure who comes in God's name (see 19:38; Ps. 117:26 LXX). Jesus' response summarizes his deeds and reiterates his mission from Luke 4:18. Like John, Luke's hearers deduce Jesus' identity, as the one who comes, from what he does. Before Jesus answers, however, the narrator summarizes Jesus' deeds (7:21). In 4:18, Jesus anticipates giving sight to the blind, but the first reference to such an incident occurs in this summary. Thus, when Jesus recaps his deeds in 7:22, he can include restoration of sight as well as the raising of the dead from 7:11-16. The restoration of the centurion's slave, the raising of the dead youth in Nain, and the narrator's summary prepare for Jesus' answer to John.

Jesus' reference to *blessedness* for those who take no offense (7:23) likely picks up Ps. 117:26 LXX again. The negative statement regarding taking no offense expresses its positive counterpart: blessed are those whose actions dramatize their faith(fulness).

Jesus then elaborates his response to John. John's ministry was extraordinary, unlike some trivial reeds blowing in the wind, and was democratic, unlike elite royalty. Conspicuously, John included tax collectors (3:12; 7:29). Jesus reiterates John's task to prepare for one who comes (3:4, 16; 7:27). Demolishing social hierarchies (Wolter, 283), Jesus evaluates John as greater than all others. Second, he makes two comparisons. One is between the least and John in God's commonwealth (7:28). The other is between the way *some* Pharisees and lawyers and *some* tax collectors responded to God. The criterion for the comparison in both cases is God's justice (7:29-30), which John portrayed in socioeconomic terms (3:11-14). These tax collectors celebrated God's justice in forgiving them by accepting John's baptism.

Jesus gives a striking characterization to those who respond negatively to both John and Jesus. When he speaks about "this generation" in 7:31, he does not mean everyone of his epoch. "This generation" is literally "what is born from this." "Rejecting God's purpose" in 7:30 is personified as if it is their "daddy," in contrast to those who are the children of *Sophia*, who also is the personification of "Wisdom" (7:35). Although the reference to Pharisees and lawyers in 7:30 is general, they cannot be identified directly with those in 5:17, because here they are characterized by their response also to *John*. Jesus then consummates his characterization of specific Pharisees and lawyers who are present (addressing them directly in the second person, 7:34) with a proverb: "Sophia/Wisdom is vindicated on the basis of her children" (7:35). Sophia's children respond positively to John and Jesus as the antithesis of rejection by these Pharisees and lawyers. But the use of Sophia leaves room for weighty amplification (see the following section). Sophia's children include tax collectors who celebrated God's justice (7:29), but this also picks up the tradition of Wisdom as an attribute of God (Wis. 9:9-11).

The meal in Simon's house (Luke 7:36-50) also brackets John's question about Jesus' identity. Moreover, it is a case of Jesus' association with tax collectors and sinners. Although Jesus confronts Simon, Luke's audience would not overlook his initial hospitality. Jesus eats not only with tax collectors and sinners but also with Pharisees. But Simon's hospitality is interrupted by a woman with a reputation as a sinner. She performs an acted parable with her hair, tears, and ointment (7:38; e.g., like Jeremiah wearing a yoke [Jeremiah 27–28]). But the acted parable is subject to two interpretations. Simon interprets it as a violation of norms that calls into question Jesus' prophetic identity (Luke 7:39). Jesus interprets it as asserting the woman's restoration.

Simon's interchange with Jesus is marked by civility. He addresses Jesus as "teacher" ("rabbi"). Jesus tells a parable about a debtor who owes ten times as much as another. Proportionally, the greater debtor is more estranged from the creditor than the lesser. Simon participates in agreeing that forgiving both debts transforms the greater estrangement into greater affection. Jesus then contrasts the woman's actions with Simon's. In this comparison, Simon is not rebuked for not bathing Jesus' feet or kissing him or anointing him (7:44-46). Rather, this makes Simon analogous to the small debtor. Then Jesus overwhelmingly emphasizes the woman's forgiveness and indicates that her actions show great love for having been forgiven. In response to Simon's interior monologue (7:39), Jesus does know what kind of woman touched him. As the centurion dramatizes faith(fulness) at the beginning of the chapter, so does the woman at the end. She does not confess faith(fulness) but demonstrates it. The scene ends in restoration and peace for the woman. How does it end for Simon?

▌ THE TEXT IN THE INTERPRETIVE TRADITION

Jesus' comparison of the centurion's faith(fulness) with Israel's is virtually always understood as a judgment on Israel in favor of gentiles. The centurion is a specific character already related to Israel and does not represent gentiles generally.

A strong interpretive tradition takes Jesus' remarkable deeds as manifesting his divinity. In the healing of the centurion's servant and the raising of the widow's son, Jesus does astonishingly little, however. The centurion especially contributes significant action. Both events point especially to Jesus as a prophet (see also 7:39) who speaks and acts for God. Luke's Christology is deduced from Jesus' functions (Cullmann). Similarly, faith(fulness) in this chapter is not confessional. It is deduced from actions.

The NRSV and many commentators take 7:29-30 to be the narrator's voice. It is equally possible that Jesus continues to speak. The word "this" is not in the Greek: Instead of: "All the people who heard *this*," read: "All the people who *heard including* the tax collectors affirmed God's justice . . . but the Pharisees and lawyers who refused John's baptism rejected God's purposes for themselves."

Does Jesus or the narrator affirm John's baptism? Whereas many interpreters take these words as representing Luke's view of Pharisees and lawyers in general, if Jesus is speaking, then it is clear that the Pharisees and lawyers here are individual characters who rejected God's purposes. This resists painting all Pharisees and lawyers in Luke with the same brush.

"This generation" in 7:31 is generally understood as a repetition of "those born of women" in 7:28 (note: the idiom emphasizes "birth"). Such a reading interprets this generation (7:31) apart from the context. Further, the basic meaning of *genea* (7:31) is not a "generation" (time period) but "lineage," "descent." Contextually, "this generation" has a referent—the Pharisees and lawyers who rejected God's purpose (7:30). At the end of the comparison, Jesus speaks of Sophia's children (7:35). The parallel at the beginning of the simile likewise has to do with parent and child: "To what will I compare people whose 'daddy' is 'rejecting God's purpose'?" (John the Baptist similarly characterizes those who reject God's purposes as "children of vipers," 3:7.)

The sudden appearance of Sophia in Jesus' pronouncement in 7:35 draws on a bank of traditions especially from Wisdom literature. In recent decades, the notion of drawing on the background of Wisdom traditions has achieved prominence especially through feminist interpretations. In Wis. 9:9-11 and elsewhere, Sophia has the status of a divine attribute. In Prov. 1:20-33 and 8:1-21, Sophia is a personified voice who calls for followers at the intersection of wisdom and evil.

Prominent interpreters hold that John is outside God's commonwealth (Conzelmann, 18–27; Wolter, 283). Some also consider "blessed is anyone who takes no offense at me" as a rebuke of John. Two matters make both unlikely. John's question and Jesus' response are in interplay with Ps. 117:26 LXX. "The one who comes" in the psalm is in interplay with John's question (Luke 7:19), and "*Blessed* is the one who comes" from the psalm is in interplay with 7:23. Second, the phrase "in God's commonwealth" (7:28) preferably modifies the verb rather than the "least": "In God's commonwealth the least is greater than John." The "least" who is "greater" demolishes hierarchies in God's commonwealth (see 22:26-27).

Simon the Pharisee is generally taken as negatively characterizing all Pharisees and as ironically participating with those who call Jesus a friend of tax collectors and sinners (7:34). Granted, his hospitality pales in comparison with the woman's, but he nevertheless hosts Jesus and Jesus responds actively. Simon's question to himself about Jesus' prophetic identity is answered in the passage. Was Simon convinced that Jesus was a prophet as Luke's hearers would be? Tradition notwithstanding, there is no basis in the text for identifying the woman who anoints Jesus, whom the narrator calls "a sinner," as a prostitute or as Mary Magdalene (see 8:2).

◼ THE TEXT IN CONTEMPORARY DISCUSSION

Many commentators note that the centurion and the widow pair a male and female, characteristic of Luke elsewhere. Nevertheless, the widow's meager characterization pales in comparison with the centurion's extended characterization.

John's question about "the one who comes" has been taken as equivalent to a messianic title (Mowinkel; Hahn, 380). Evidence for a stock title is lacking, but this does not detract from the allusion in 7:19, 23, to Ps. 117:26 LXX (quoted in Luke 19:39).

There is renewed interest today in pre-Lukan traditions. Multiple independent attestation of Jesus' table fellowship with tax collectors and sinners (e.g., Mark and Q) and agreement of friend and foe on such table fellowship (Jesus agrees with opponents, 7:34) make inclusive commensality strongly characteristic of the historical Jesus.

Traditional interpreters have construed Sophia as parallel to Jesus. But Elisabeth Schüssler Fiorenza has interpreted Sophia (Q 7:35) as reflecting an early Christian Wisdom theology in which both John and Jesus are among her children. Jesus in particular is "Divine *Sophia's* eminent prophet"—engendered and derivative from her (Schüssler Fiorenza, 139–44). For her, even Luke equates Jesus' messianic work with divine Sophia's (151). This heightens attention to feminine dimensions of God's character. Such dimensions pour beautifully and profoundly from Bobby McFerrin's "Twenty-Third Psalm" in the feminine. But lack of direct evidence in the text calls for reservation as to what is meant in Luke.

That slaveholders exploited slaves, including sexual exploitation, was a cultural commonplace. If interpreters note the centurion's slave's lack of voice and strain nevertheless to discern it, they might hear overtones of same-sex eroticism (Gowler, 116–18; similarly on Matthew's version; Jennings and Liew). This fits Jesus' inclusive relationships. If, however, such a voice is present, would the Israelite elders, who are positively characterized, also portray the centurion positively (Wolter, 269–70)?

Interpreters often call the woman in 7:37 a prostitute. Feminists and others object that this is gratuitous and prejudicial. Whatever her reputation, Jesus' affirmation of her forgiveness and his blessing of peace mean her restoration to proper communal relationships.

Jesus' interchange with Simon ends without resolution. Two views compete in studies of Pharisees in Luke. One sees them consistently characterized as pejorative even to the extent of reflecting anti-Judaism in Luke and views Simon as completely failing to offer Jesus hospitality—not even comparable to the lesser creditor. Another perspective sees Pharisees as characterized variously (not mere stereotypes), who, like Socrates' sophist interlocutors, are not straw men but competent interlocutors. Given Simon's role as host, the clarification of his doubt about Jesus' prophetic identity, and Jesus' parable, might he (and other guests, 7:49) also be persuaded? Indeed, Robert Tannehill asks, "Should We Love Simon the Pharisee?" (1994). Are interpreters today open to new possibilities for such Pharisees?

Luke 8:1-56: Seed and Soil, Discipleship and Kinship

▎THE TEXT IN ITS ANCIENT CONTEXT

Luke 8:1 recalls 4:43 and makes this section a continuation of proclaiming the good news of God's commonwealth in other towns. New emphases fall on women associates, four of whom are named (see 23:55; 24:10) and who contravene customs by supporting men (8:1-3). Anticipating the parable of the seed and the soil, they correspond to seed growing in good soil.

Unproductive and abundantly productive soils in 8:4-8 echo relationships between plants/fruit and good/evil in 6:43-45. Nevertheless, the disciples request clarification. Jesus responds initially with the riddle of speaking in parables (8:10). God grants (divine passive) insiders knowledge of mysteries of God's commonwealth that are hidden from outsiders. Inconsistently, Jesus shifts from varieties of soil to relationships between seed and soil, corresponding to people shaped by divine or evil powers.

But this allegory is bracketed by metaphors that demand probing reflection. Mysteries of God's commonwealth (8:10) introduce the explanation (8:11-15), and it concludes with a lamp, correlated with hiddenness that will be disclosed and secrets that come to light (8:16-17). The result is a figuration between insider/outsider and mystery/light. Insiders who know mysteries of God's commonwealth are to disclose them to outsiders. Outsiders then become insiders. Insiders who do not disclose the mysteries become outsiders (8:18). Consequently, the mysteries are not esoteric!

Jesus' mother and siblings, who are outside (8:20), provide an instance of what constitutes insiders. Biological kinship warrants no priority over the crowd. Jesus' kinship derives not from human ancestry but from God: whoever derives life from God is God's child and therefore Jesus' kin ("elective kinship," Bovon, 1:315).

Though commonly understood as controlling nature, calming a storm at sea is also related to hearing and doing God's will (8:22-25). The key is two rebukes. Jesus rebukes the storm but also his disciples when he asks, "Where is your faith(fulness)?" The rebuke of the storm produces calm; the rebuke of the disciples produces fear and amazement. Faintness of faith(fulness) positions them perilously close to outsiders. Are they Jesus' kin?

Then a bizarre outsider becomes an insider (8:26-39). For the first and only time, Luke's Jesus leaves Israelite territory. He encounters a demoniac on the eastern side of the Sea of Galilee, likely a gentile, unclean—an extreme outsider who dwells not among the living but in tombs, as good as dead. As in other restorations, violations of norms (this time regarding gentiles and tomb impurity) are formidable. Also the demons name themselves "Legion," which the narrator associates with "many demons." But it is also Latin for many Roman soldiers. Moreover, how this demoniac plays out his insanity involves psychosocial manifestations of oppression (Theissen, 255–56). Indeed, Jewish people named the Romans who subjugated them "swine." They equated Roman legions with herding pigs, and a Qumran text belittles a legion for worshiping the emblem of swine on their standards and weapons (Annen, 184). The demons enter swine that bring about their own demise by jumping in the lake (symbolically?). The man then becomes an insider at Jesus' feet, who makes mysteries of God's commonwealth known to others. He hears God's word, does it, and is Jesus' kin.

Two intercalated healings juxtapose a prominent, named synagogue leader, who comes to Jesus face-to-face, with a nameless woman hidden in a crowd, who approaches from behind (8:41-56). He voices a desperate request for his "only" daughter (reminiscent of the widow's only son, 7:12); she expresses her desperate desire only as an internal monologue to herself. Twelve years of life-draining hemorrhages also juxtapose her to the voiceless twelve-year-old whose life is draining away. Indeed, Jesus calls the woman "daughter." Astonishingly, her healing occurs solely by her action. Jesus, as an enabler, senses it but does nothing. She violates norms about blood taboos and touching. Her internal voice also becomes public, and she tells her story. Jesus calls this "faith(fulness)"—not confessed, but dramatized. The moment her life is restored, the twelve-year-old loses hers. But Jesus implores Jairus not to give in to death. Mourners who do give in to death contrast with Jesus' insistence on life. Again, Jesus does little. Taking the daughter's hand and calling her "child," he entreats her to arise. He is an enabler; she acts and arises.

▌The Text in the Interpretive Tradition

At 8:2-3, social and economic dimensions certainly have to do with women among Jesus' disciples. Responsibility with respect to the "word" is often understood as a verbal message. But 8:15, 21, specifies doing. God's commonwealth is not confined to proclaiming good news. It is realizing good news, as in the Baptizer's call for fruits in socioeconomic terms (3:2-14). God's word for Jesus (5:1) also means restoration of marginalized people to community (4:18; ch. 5). The restoration of the demoniac, understood early and often as an allegory of salvation, includes his proclamation of what God did for him, including his reintegration into family and community.

▌The Text in Contemporary Discussion

Mary Ann Tolbert's interpretation of the parable of the seed and soil in Mark looks for characters in the rest of the Gospel who play out roles described in the parable (1989). The result is a particularly positive characterization of women. This holds also for Luke. The near context in 8:2-3 calls special attention to women disciples who bear fruit. Do their actions correspond to the grateful woman in Simon's house (7:35-50)?

But publicly women also have limited exposure and voice. The voiceless woman with the flow of blood transforms herself and achieves a public voice. When Jesus calls her "daughter," some take it as subordinating her. Alternatively, does this "daughter" anticipate 13:16, where another woman is called Abraham's daughter, which indicates reintegration into Israel's covenant community? Does it fit Jesus' understanding of "elective kinship" in 8:21?

Interpreters debate the relationship of the woman with the flow of blood to purity laws. One outcome is resistance to portraying Israelite culture negatively, so that the woman's healing becomes supersessionism, in which Jesus transcends oppressive Israelite society. But in both Israelite and Hellenistic cultures, a flow of blood was taboo, and as in other restorations in Luke, violation of norms is integral to the healing. But the woman's restoration to her *Israelite* community precludes supersessionism.

Luke 9: Disciples and Mission, Triumphs and Disappointments

▌The Text in Its Ancient Context

In 9:1-6, Jesus enables and sends the twelve to overcome oppressive powers and disease as manifestations of God's commonwealth. The context is clearly communal; they make no provisions for themselves, but live in mutuality with villagers. Jesus also anticipates opposition (recalling 2:34), and endorses a ritual that witnesses against opposition—shaking off the very vestiges of the town, a sign of how serious neglecting God's commonwealth is.

Luke 9:7-9 juxtaposes imperial systems with God's commonwealth by bracketing Herod's perplexity before and after by success in the apostles' mission. Rome's client ruler finds the success sensational enough to take notice (maintaining local order is his charge). Recalling the Baptizer's execution also makes the apostles take Herod seriously. Herod's imperial perspectives evaluate Jesus quite inadequately.

But the twelve are out of step. The feeding of the five thousand (9:12-17) is generally taken as an independent episode, but contextual connections are strong. In 9:3-4, the Twelve live in mutuality with villagers. Luke 9:12 inverts the situation. Villagers need sustenance from the Twelve. Indeed, the incident focuses on Jesus' command to them: "You give them something to eat" (9:13). Jesus enabled the Twelve to liberate and cure (9:1-2); now they claim inability. Jesus' enabling actions are unassuming—blessing and breaking meager provisions, the beginnings of any Israelite meal. This enables the Twelve to complete the task—they give "them" something to eat (9:17).

Characterizations of Jesus and the disciples are interdependent. Rumors provide Jesus a prophetic identity; Peter adds messianic identity (recalling 1:32-33). Jesus, however, immediately associates rejection and suffering with messianism and adds his first passion prediction. Clearly here, as elsewhere in Luke, Israelite leaders, necessarily collaborators with Rome, are involved in his suffering, but not *the people* as such. Identifying Jesus as God's Messiah adds to Peter's prominence, but discipleship is also qualified by following Jesus under the image of a cross. Crucifixion means Roman punishment designed to shame and terrorize resistors of imperial systems severely. Following Jesus does not avoid imperial systems. It means perseverance unto death. In Luke, who meets this qualification?

The transfiguration drives the interdependent characterization of Jesus and the disciples higher (9:28-36). The setting and scene—the mountain, the changed appearance, clothes as bright as "white lightning," Moses and Elijah glorified, Jesus' departure (*exodos*) to be accomplished in Jerusalem, the cloud, and the voice all evoke the numinous, which both reveals and conceals. The voice naming Jesus God's Son and commanding the disciples to heed him advances the identity of both. But the disciples are deficient, in a stupor and terrified. Peter speaks nonsense. At the end, all are dumbfounded.

Meanwhile, disciples at the foot of the mountain fare poorly. Jesus enabled them to cast out demons and cure (9:1-2). Now they are unable to heal another only son. Could Luke's audience discern who is included in Jesus' address to a "faithless and misbelieving generation" (9:41)? The specific charge in the *second person plural* to people who are *present* may include the father, certainly includes the disciples, but not Jesus' contemporaries generally. Again, Jesus is the enabler who heals, and restoration to family and community is explicit (9:42). Luke 9:43 again characterizes Jesus by his functions in relation to God.

Another ominous prediction again characterizes the disciples as fearful and lacking understanding (9:44). The following incident bears this out. They dispute their own prominence (9:46-48). Jesus corrects them by welcoming a child and by encouraging mutuality with people of low status. But then they do not accept another who is enabled in Jesus' *name* but whom John evaluates as an outsider. Again Jesus corrects: "Whoever is not against you is for you" (9:50).

Luke 9:51 shifts to a new period designated as the time for Jesus to be taken up, and Jerusalem emerges as Jesus' destination/destiny. Still, relationships with strangers, qualifications for following Jesus, and enabling disciples for mission follow long-established narrative trajectories (Bendemann 2001). Jerusalem fills in the itinerary that started in 4:43-44. In 9:52-55, James and John express another misunderstanding of relationships with Samaritans. Jesus rebukes them. In 9:57-62, Jesus challenges three potential followers. To the first, he portrays himself as homeless (the unpropertied class). Sharp sayings about the dead burying the dead and someone who looks back while plowing (self-contradictory) anticipate negative responses. Yet Luke leaves room to suppose that they might accept the challenges.

▌The Text in the Interpretive Tradition

The feeding of the five thousand is conventionally understood as a nature wonder. But emphasis falls on enabling the disciples to feed others. The crowd is unaware of and infers nothing about Jesus' power. Many interpreters have taken Peter's naming Jesus Messiah (8:20) as fulfilling Israelite expectations. But Israelite expectations varied greatly, and a suffering Messiah was unexpected. Persistent anti-Jewish interpretations of the transfiguration as showing that Jesus superseded Moses and Elijah are unwarranted. Because Jesus' glory is in the eyes of the beholders (Peter, James, and John), some interpreters shift the transformation to the disciples. But they remain woefully deficient. In spite of views that the transfiguration anticipates later two-nature Christology, it remains awesomely inexplicable.

A strong consensus takes 9:51 as introducing a central section/travel narrative. Alternatively, 9:51 specifies a destiny but continues Jesus' itinerary and mission from 4:43-44 (Bendemann).

▌The Text in Contemporary Discussion

The feeding of the five thousand as the disciples' feeding others shifts the focus from a nature wonder to a gift (Theissen, 45, 251). Luke underplays the multiplication of food, and focuses on mission in God's commonwealth: "You give them something to eat" (9:13). The twelve baskets of remnants signify that Jesus enables the Twelve to fulfill their mission (Fitzmyer 1981, 1:769). This fits thematically with Mary's joy over God's mercy in filling the hungry (1:53), Jesus' mission of good news to the poor (4:18), and blessedness for the poor who are fed (6:21) (see also feasting and eating, e.g., 5:27-39; 6:1-5). The plight of hunger today, exacerbated by using food as a tool for wealth and power over others, certainly indicts those who today claim to be disciples of the Jesus who enables mission: "You give them something to eat."

In Jesus' inversion of a dispute about greatness into welcoming a child with whom Jesus himself identifies, children achieve a paramount place in what it means to follow Jesus.

Jesus makes two separate remarks on discipleship (9:23-27, 57-62) that emphasize God's commonwealth first, last, and always. Between the transfiguration and the second remark, the problem of the need for Jesus to enable the disciples is again at issue in their inability to heal (9:37-43). Nevertheless, at the end of this healing, the greatness of God's commonwealth is apparent.

Luke 10: Manifesting God's Commonwealth in Contexts of Oppression

▌The Text in Its Ancient Context

Luke 10:1-12 extends Jesus' enabling. He commissions seventy-two others (seventy in the NRSV). Like the Twelve, the livelihood of the seventy-two depends on mutuality, and they heal and proclaim God's commonwealth. Three things are new: they go in pairs, they prepare for Jesus' visits, and God's commonwealth is at hand through them. The harvest anticipates success but comes with dangers—they are like lambs among wolves (10:2-3). But rejecting them incurs judgment because it is rejecting God (10:16).

As in the sermon in Luke 6, Jesus addresses woes against the unrepentant directly in the second person, mixing singular and plural (10:13-16). The plural may indicate the cities, and the singular may indict individuals among whom deeds of power are performed. Luke 10:16 legitimates the seventy-two: to listen to those whom Jesus' commissions is to listen to him. In 9:10, the narrator summarizes the apostles' success; in 10:17, they report in direct speech. This evokes Jesus' explanation of their power against hostility. His report of Satan's fall is parallel with the "enemy's" subjugation (10:18-19). Perhaps Luke's hearers construe this as mythological, but it is also contemporaneous with Jesus and the mission of the seventy-two. The enemy's power is tangible. From 1:71, 74, enemies are subjugators and involve imperial systems. In addition, Jesus' assurance that the names of the seventy-two *are written* in heaven (10:20) means that their part in God's commonwealth is not future but a present alternative to imperial systems.

Jesus uses kinship language (parent/child, five times) to confirm the present reality of God's commonwealth. The revelation of Jesus and God is also not future but present. The disciples' blessedness is similarly what they *have seen and heard* (10:21-24).

In contrast, a Torah teacher inquires about his *future*: "What do I do so that I will inherit eternal life?" (10:25). "Inherit" alerts Luke's hearers to God's promises of inheritance to Abraham's descendants (e.g., Gen 12:3; 17:3-8), which Israelite traditions pushed into a future "world to come." "Testing" implies a dialogue to discover answers (Wolter, 392). The lawyer, not Jesus, defines love of God and neighbor as the heart of Torah. In Jesus' response to the lawyer's challenge to delimit "neighbor," Luke's audience presumably hears the parable for the first time. In it, the sequence of a Levite following a priest anticipates a third Israelite who would pass by. But a Samaritan interloper throws open the question about who is neighbor to whom and subverts expectations. If hearers identify with the Samaritan, the parable is an astonishing example of transgressing barriers to help someone. If they identify with the wounded man, as the lawyer likely would, they are the ones needing help from someone deemed deficient. Again, the lawyer gives the answer. Luke's hearers obviously heard the story as persuasive. Did they ponder how the lawyer heard it? Further, this is a concrete story of life in God's commonwealth already.

Sheer sequence invites comparison of Martha and Mary (10:38-42) with the lawyer. Like the women in 8:2-3, Martha offers hospitality as envisioned in 9:4-6; 10:5-9. But she is anxious and troubled. Mary as a female learner is as astonishing as the Samaritan in the previous parable. Jesus affirms Mary's *choice* as "the good part." Linguistically, in comparing two choices, "the good part" may be heard as "the better part" (NRSV). The focus, however, is not on comparing the two women but on the "one thing" that is needful. This is what Mary chose.

■ THE TEXT IN THE INTERPRETIVE TRADITION

The announcement that God's commonwealth is at hand has generated discussions of whether it is already or not yet present. A present qualified by the future takes care of both (Wolter, 380–81).

Satan's fall is often understood as a mythological primordial event. Joel B. Green (1997, 419) pushes it toward the future. But Satan's fall is manifest in the success of the seventy-two, though struggles against evil continue. Interpreters conventionally categorize the parable of the compassionate Samaritan as an example. But if hearers identify with the wounded man, they play the role of needing help rather than providing it. Interpreters have long viewed Martha and Mary in terms of preference for submission to Jesus over hospitality. Emphasis has shifted to a contrast between distraction and listening to Jesus.

■ THE TEXT IN CONTEMPORARY DISCUSSION

Because God's commonwealth is an alternative to Rome's, the dangers for the seventy-two are sociopolitical, like Jesus' crucifixion. Evil, however, exceeds its manifestations in imperialism. The lawyer's test question implies an honor-shame challenge that implies gain for one participant and loss for the other (Malina and Neyrey). But challenges also invite dialogue from which both may gain. The lawyer's attempt to "justify himself" may mean "ensuring what is right" (Robbins, 252). In any case, his interchange with Jesus explodes with astonishing new visions of reality, of inclusion and mutuality beyond ethnic, social, political, and religious differences. Parallels today both local and global are inescapable. Schüssler Fiorenza (62–73) takes Martha's *diakonia* ("serving [tables]" or "ministry") as preserving memories of her office of ministry among the earliest followers of Jesus, which later antifeminism (either Luke's or his precursors') repressed. But the contrast is between listening and distraction, not between listening and *diakonia* (Green 1997, 436).

Luke 11:1—13:9: Praying and Acting, Fairness and Injustice

■ THE TEXT IN ITS ANCIENT CONTEXT

Teaching disciples to pray continues Jesus' enabling and aims at God's commonwealth in fullness—on earth as in heaven. Directly addressing God as "father" as a child to a parent is unusual (but see Sir. 23:1, 4), but fundamental to God's commonwealth. God's commonwealth entails table and community, food (a synecdoche for all of life) and forgiveness (the heart of community). In relation to God, sins are forgiven. In relation to others, debts are released (11:1-4) (Green 1997, 443). Then parables reinforce this parent-child bond—God is contrasted with a friend at midnight who gives, resistance notwithstanding, and with parents with human fallacies who give children good gifts. God's preeminent gift is the Holy Spirit (11:5-13).

Against this parent-child bond, Luke's audience encounters a competing identity for Jesus—an ally of the ruler of demons (11:15). Three arguments counter this: the proverbial civil-war "house divided against itself" (11:18-19), manifestations of God's commonwealth deriving from Jesus' bond with God (11:20), and binding the strong man (11:21-22). Another perspective identifies Jesus by his maternal relationship. Jesus gives preference to kinship with those who obey God (11:27-28; 8:21).

Judgment then invades a short sermon (11:29-36). The "generation" that Jesus characterizes as evil means not just his contemporaries but also their "lineage" from evil as if they are its children. His first point is about signs. As 11:15-16, 20, shows, signs are ambiguous. Interpretations vary. Beyond exorcisms that show his bond with God, Jesus appeals to Jonah and the queen of the South only to claim that God's commonwealth exceeds both. Nineveh's repentance occurred not from Jonah's positive proclamation but his warning of judgment.

Again Jesus eats not only with outcasts but also with Pharisees (11:37). This Pharisee is surprised that Jesus neglects washing, but makes no reprimand. Jesus contrasts body zones—clean outside does not mean clean inside (11:39-41). Suddenly he levels woes at Pharisees. He avoids criticizing their practices but emphasizes matters that they neglect: justice (mercy toward others, 11:41) and love of God (11:42). Assuming status above others incurs another woe (11:43). He characterizes them as covertly unclean, like unmarked graves—metaphorically similar to "clean outside does not mean clean inside" (11:44). He adds three woes against lawyers: loading people with burdens (how is unstipulated, 11:46); participants (vicariously and concretely) in violent treatment of messengers from God's Sophia/Wisdom (11:47-51); obfuscating knowledge in contrast to God's Sophia (11:52). After this, the summary of hostility against Jesus hardly surprises.

Jesus continues preparing disciples in Luke 12, warning them about the Pharisees' "yeast," which Luke glosses as hypocrisy (12:1). Hypocrisy is not merely outward behavior that conflicts with inner realities, but also accepting deceptive views of reality as genuine (see 11:42). Luke 12:2-3 reiterates the saying about hiddenness that will be disclosed from 8:17. There, it refers to positive revelation of mysteries of God's commonwealth; here, it is a negative judgment against hypocrisy. Astoundingly, this judgment is not against Pharisees but against disciples. A double message prepares them for persecution—first, *fearing* death and condemnation, and second, trusting God's care: "Do *not be afraid*; you are of more value than many sparrows" (12:4-7). Confessing Jesus assures his reciprocal affirmation before God; denials beget his denials (12:8-10). The context of interrelated imperial systems is again evident with reference to adjudication before synagogues, rulers, and authorities (12:11-12).

God's care is also the context for orientation toward material goods (12:13-20). First, Jesus refuses to settle a dispute about inheritance. Inheritances from father to son are developments from Abrahamic covenant promises that supposedly resulted in providing equitable access to resources of the land. The dispute means that either the plaintiff wants more or his brother refuses equitable access. Either way, Jesus presumes greed, which he reduces to absurdity with a "you-cannot-take-it-with-you" parable.

Then, analogies from nature illustrate divine provisions for subsistence. Moreover, Jesus distinguishes God's commonwealth from the nations (12:30). Behind this lies Israel's covenant traditions of distribution of land and its resources that are qualitatively distinct from other nations. Here Luke's audience would understand imperial systems that exploited subsistence farmers—90 percent of the population—and funneled resources to the top 10 percent, and especially the top 2 percent (12:22-34). "Alms" as the complement to selling possessions means not mere "donations" but "merciful action" (12:33). This is but half of Jesus' message, which also has exhortations to diligence and warnings of judgment (12:35-59). Even these are punctuated with promises of blessing for fidelity. But figurations shift from nature to master-slave relationships, presuming that masters have prerogatives to bless and punish (12:37-38; 12:42-48). Slavery was a pervasive feature of Roman imperial systems that exploited the have-nots. In contrast to the conventional notion of oppression of slaves by the master, in 12:37 the master serves the slaves. In 12:45, like imperial collaborators, a slave enslaves other slaves. This too is a common feature of imperial oppression in which certain slaves become overseers of others. Both the slave and the master who punishes this slave play roles in oppressive imperial systems (see below on 17:7-10).

Jesus ends by portraying conflicts that God's commonwealth faces (12:49-59). Jesus comes with fire (12:49). The Baptizer associated fire with Jesus' baptism with the Spirit (3:16). But instead of baptizing, Jesus faces baptism (12:50). The range of associations with fire for Luke's audience would stretch from "enthusiasm" to "empowerment" to "purification" to "destruction." Here it is closely associated with division—surprisingly focused on households (12:52-53).

This portrait ends before a magistrate, a local imperial collaborator (12:57-59). Luke's audience would not assume that the accused is in the wrong. Magistrates favored elite Roman citizens over peasants (Garnsey, 128–41; Lintott, 97–123). So Jesus advises prudent accommodation to avoid debtor's prison. Such prudence also transfers to making judgments about God's commonwealth.

Luke 13:1-5 continues themes of judgment and repentance. Jesus' interlocutors report two rumors about unusual suffering and speculate about punishment for guilt. Pilate's massacre of Galileans instantiates imperial violence. The other is an accident at the tower of Siloam. At first glance, Jesus appears to dissociate sin from suffering. Actually, he intensifies it by leveling the playing field to include everyone and warning his hearers of punishment unless they repent.

But the following parable emphasizes "pastoral care" for opportunities to repent (13:6-9). A gardener cultivates and nourishes a tree so that it will bear fruit. The vineyard and fig tree are stock imagery for Israel and shalom. How will listeners transfer the meaning from the planter, the gardener, and the fruit to the situation of Jesus and God's commonwealth?

▌THE TEXT IN THE INTERPRETIVE TRADITION

Jesus claims no additional sign other than Jonah and the queen of the South because manifestations at hand are evident (11:29-32, see 12:54-56). Interpreters vary on whether that which is "here" is Jesus himself or God's commonwealth. Jesus' manifestations of God's commonwealth resolve these alternatives. "Alms" in modern terms inadequately translates *eleēmosynē* (12:33). It means "merciful action" far exceeding "donations." Eschatology is often understood as a map of the future. Eschatology in 12:35-48 functions for living appropriately in the present. The incident of Pilate's slaughtering Galileans at their temple sacrifices is not attested elsewhere, but it fits other acts of his violence that are.

▌THE TEXT IN CONTEMPORARY DISCUSSION

Little in this section is explicit about imperial systems until the end of Luke 12. But responses of subjugated Israelites to Hellenistic and Roman domination heightened certain identity markers (circumcision, Sabbath, purity) above other aspects of Israel's heritage. Social control agents attempted to enforce these (11:46) (Bhabha, 3–5, 37, 41, 58, 162–64; Niebuhr, 21–23). Jesus' woes reflect debates among factions about such identity markers (11:37-54) and lament disregard shown to central aspects of Israel's heritage—justice and the love of God (11:42).

The so-called prosperity gospel takes 12:31 to mean that striving for God's commonwealth engenders wealth. Living in God's commonwealth ("It is your parent's good pleasure to give you the commonwealth," 12:32) in contrast to the world's nations (12:30-31) clearly contradicts this. It is elites in the world's nations that amassed wealth by exploiting the masses. Further, 12:22-31 has to do with subsistence living, not accumulating wealth.

Luke 12:35-59 is predominantly taken as anticipating the parousia. But emphasis still falls on mission in the present. The debtor before the magistrate (12:57-59) is generally understood as a parable of God's judgment. Alternatively, it means prudent accommodation to imperial systems.

Some interpreters view the reference to "one more year" in the parable of the fig tree (13:8) as a *last* opportunity for *Israel's* repentance that, from Luke's retrospective point of view, would no longer be available. This view was strongly supported until the last quarter of the twentieth century, when emphasis on the gardener's care achieved more prominence, but it is still advocated (Egelkraut, 206; Fitzmyer 1985, 2:1005–6).

Luke 13:10-35: Restoration and Inclusion in God's Commonwealth

▌The Text in Its Ancient Context

The context of the *healing* in 13:10-17 is *teaching*. Luke's audience perceives both. As liberation from Satan, the woman's healing manifests God's commonwealth (11:20-22). The synagogue plays a dual role. Under imperial systems, institutions have sociopsychic impact in maladies (Theissen, 255–56). But it also is a place for teaching and healing. The synagogue leader objects not to healing but to violating the Sabbath. Jesus challenges not the synagogue leader but the assembly: "hypocrites" (13:15). Hypocrisy is not playing an artificial role, but the failure to discern *God's work* on Sabbath (Green 1997, 524). Further, the woman emerges from marginality when Jesus names her uniquely "Abraham's daughter"—astonishingly, such a title for a woman is otherwise unknown. Jesus endorses the healing with village analogies about animal husbandry. Reference to Abraham also evokes God's promises to bless (1:54-55) that this healing fulfills. Luke 13:17 implies that Jesus persuades critics to join in rejoicing at *all* his remarkable deeds.

Jesus underscores this woman's liberation as manifesting God's commonwealth with two brief parables (13:18-20). First, a mustard seed produces a nesting place for birds. This may echo Ps. 84:4: "The sparrow finds a home, and the swallow a nest where she may lay her young." Moreover, this recalls God's care that exceeds concern for birds (Luke 12:24). Next, a woman leavens enough flour to feed 150 people (Nolland, 2:730). This also is not mere increase but the woman's accomplishment.

Luke 13:22 reiterates Jesus' programmatic mission to other cities (4:43-44) and his destination/ destiny (9:51). Teaching is emphasized, but it depends on an interlocutor who presumes that Jesus will agree: "Only a few will be saved, won't they?" (13:23). Jesus concurs, but to the interlocutor's peril, Jesus includes him among those left out: "I say to *you* [plural]" (13:24). Then they see ancestors and prophets in God's commonwealth from the outside looking in (13:28). By contrast, numerous people from everywhere are eating inside. Those who imagine that others are excluded in favor of a few are themselves excluded.

Simultaneity links the next incident closely. After the prologue, the first word Luke's audience hears, in 1:5, is "Herod." The same name in 3:1 identifies his son, Antipas, who beheads the Baptizer (3:19-20). Some Pharisees (13:31), who are not antagonistic (Green 1997, 537–38), warn Jesus to avoid him. Herod is not merely curious (9:9) but presumes a ruler's right to dispose of Jesus. Jesus' epithet "fox" is adverse—no concession to shrewdness. His message for Herod (13:32-33) reiterates his itinerant mission and contests Herod's right of disposal over him.

Jesus travels to Jerusalem not to escape Herod's jurisdiction but to contest *Jerusalem's* jurisdiction. Jewish people are heirs of Abrahamic promises whom Jesus longs to *gather* like a hen her chicks. The deeds in 13:32 identify this gathering as God's commonwealth. The "forsaken house" refers to existing systems that are antithetical to God's commonwealth.

■ THE TEXT IN THE INTERPRETIVE TRADITION

The mustard seed and the yeast are often called growth parables, but this highlights only *growth*, whereas the figuration involves the *whole*. The lack of reference to the seed's size or the amount of leaven means that the comparison is not between small and large. Many interpreters take nesting birds in a mustard plant as sheer exaggeration. Still, the plant's specific species is beyond recovery. Some varieties grow as high as ten feet (BDAG). These parables highlight accomplishments of a man and a woman.

■ THE TEXT IN CONTEMPORARY DISCUSSION

A change in setting notwithstanding, the woman's healing stands in continuity with the unfruitful fig tree (13:6-9) as a case of pastoral care for Abraham's descendants (Green 1989, 515). The mother of the seven sons in 4 Macc. 15:28 is identified as "the Abrahamite" (like "Israelite"), but not as Abraham's daughter as in Luke 13:16 (Brawley 1999, 120n36). Schüssler Fiorenza (1992, 209–10) objects that anti-Judaism is inscribed in Jesus' dialogue with the synagogue leader. In the setting, however, everyone is Jewish. Moreover, Jesus' concern is instantiating Israel's covenantal values. The narrow way and the closed door in 13:22-39 are often appealed to as limiting salvation to a devout remnant only. In the text, however, the door is closed for those who limit salvation, whereas the banquet in God's commonwealth is wide open. This raises a question for the popular *Left Behind* series: Who gets left behind?

Luke 14: Changing Social Relationships

■ THE TEXT IN ITS ANCIENT CONTEXT

The primary setting for Luke 14 is a meal. Again a Pharisee hosts Jesus. Close scrutiny at meals regarding social status and ethics was the norm in antiquity. So watching Jesus (14:1) hardly means hostility. Indeed, Jesus likewise scrutinizes his companions (14:7). Meals were also occasions for thought-provoking discussions. It is appropriate, then, that Jesus raises the discussion topic of healing on Sabbath (14:3). He argues by curing a man with dropsy and defends this by giving his interlocutors the perspective of a parent or farmer who would rescue a child or ox from a well on Sabbath (similarly 13:15). The other guests mount no objection.

Luke's "parable" in 14:7 is actually an exhortation against seeking honor over others, based on a proverb that inverts honor and shame (14:11). Further, Jesus challenges his host not to invite elite guests with expectations of reciprocity, but the poor and afflicted, who cannot reciprocate. Astute hearers might note that the host partially complied by inviting Jesus and the man with dropsy, presumably without expecting reciprocity.

As expected, another guest introduces a discussion topic regarding dining in God's common-wealth (14:15). Jesus responds with a parable about someone whose invitation to a banquet is refused by people who are tied to possessions and family (14:18-20). The host replaces them with the poor and afflicted (as Jesus advises, 14:12-14) and demands that his house be filled with street people to the exclusion of the original invitees (14:16-24). Thus this host is "converted." He changes his social relationships by including people of low status (Braun, 98–131). His original invitation built a "fence" that excluded the lowly; now he builds a "bridge" to include them (Braun, 120, 126).

The topic of inclusion/exclusion of disciples then takes an arduous turn (14:25-35). Severe criteria for discipleship exclude virtually everyone. Luke's audience understands the reference to "hate" to mean the necessity to decide between God and family. Still, deciding *against* family members and life itself (14:26) exceeds Jesus' earlier definition of kinship among those who do God's will (8:19-21), but fits his warnings of family divisions (12:51-53). Abandoning all possessions (14:33) appears to con-flict with the support Jesus and his disciples receive from women (8:2-3). Two parables also contradict these severe demands. The first is an analogy of *possessing sufficient economic resources* to complete a tower (14:28-30). The second calls for capitulation to a more numerous army with the supposition that *if resources were sufficient* there would be no capitulation (14:31-33). These analogies demonstrate that actions involve consequences, but poorly serve the specific conclusion of abandoning possessions. Salt that has lost saltiness is absurdly self-contradictory. If relations with family, possessions, and life itself empty salt of its saltiness, and if such salt is not worth a mound of feces, then it would seem that inclusion in discipleship is exceedingly unlikely. There are two hermeneutical clues to the scope of the exhortation: Hating family and life is glossed by reference to crucifixion (14:27), which literally was a consequence for resisting imperial systems. Further, the final comment hints that it is a figuration: "Let anyone with ears to hear listen" (14:35). The juxtaposition of crucifixion with the rejection of family is extreme but still conceivable. Because God's commonwealth requires an unrelenting deci-siveness for Israel's heritage as an alternative to imperial systems, discipleship is arduous.

▌ THE TEXT IN THE INTERPRETIVE TRADITION

Long traditions have supplied allegorical identities to the sequence of those invited to the banquet: for example, (1) Israel's leaders, (2) the Israelite populace, and (3) gentiles. The slaves who bring in the poor and afflicted are commonly understood as allegories of missions, first to Israel and then to gentiles. Alternatively, the parable is not allegorical, but deals with relationships with the poor and afflicted.

Read against a Septuagint background, hating family and life means making a decisive choice between God's commonwealth on one hand and family and life on the other (Wolter, 516–17). Many interpreters struggle in vain to explain how salt loses its saltiness. The saying is simply self-contradictory.

▌ THE TEXT IN CONTEMPORARY DISCUSSION

Dropsy (14:2) causes the body to retain fluid and paradoxically induces thirst. Some interpreters think the reference to dropsy is meant to parody Pharisees, some of whom are "lovers of money"

(16:14) (Braun, 26–42). This is excessive. Dropsy plays no role other than a malady to be cured. Furthermore, in other healings, maladies do not parody characters. Later rabbinic sources allow healing illnesses that are life-threatening on Sabbath (e.g., *m. Yoma* 8.6). Jesus' criterion of doing good on Sabbath is in continuity with such an attitude and extends it.

Willi Braun shows that the host in the parable is converted to change social relationships. "Hating one's life" (14:26) merits consideration that elsewhere in Luke the spirit of life drives *restoration* of health, justice, and peace.

Luke 15: Advocating Inclusion in God's Commonwealth against Resistance

■ The Text in Its Ancient Context

In Luke 15, some Pharisees and scribes murmur against Jesus' association with socially marginalized people. Jesus defends himself with three parables. The first puts his detractors in the shoes of a shepherd who rejoices over finding a lost sheep, makes divine rejoicing over one person who repents analogous, and thereby legitimates Jesus. The second makes a woman's search for a lost coin analogous to Jesus' mission and concludes, again, with divine joy over one person who repents. The first half of the third parable partially corresponds to the first two without an analogy to Jesus' mission. A father rejoices extravagantly over finding his son. All three parables subvert expectations. The shepherd irrationally forsakes ninety-nine sheep in dedication to one. In a patriarchal culture, the second makes female characters analogous to Jesus' mission and God's joy. The third evokes pathos when the desperate son expects to return, but only as his father's laborer. His father's extravagant joy and his restoration to sonship beyond anything he asked or thought are astonishing. This story turns not on the son's return, which fits a son who has learned his lesson, but on the father's welcome. Perhaps this echoes Ps. 103:13: God's love is like a father's.

But the third parable also has a second half. An older brother is contrariwise shocked over the celebration of his brother's return. His refusal to celebrate is reminiscent of those who rejected the banquet invitation (14:18-20; Wolter, 538). The father assures him of his love but gives priority to celebrating the other son's return. Not only has a lost person, like a sheep or coin, been found, but also a family member. This parable ends without closure. Did the older brother enter and celebrate? Can he remain his father's son without welcoming his brother? Were those who murmured in 15:1-2 persuaded?

■ The Text in the Interpretive Tradition

Since Adolf Jülicher (1888), most interpreters have considered the settings for the parables in the Gospels to be secondary. Thus they separate parables from their contexts in order to interpret them from Jesus' perspective. Joachim Jeremias (132) took the setting in 15:1-2 as essentially accurate and argued that these parables were not the gospel, but a defense of it. Other interpreters have reasoned that if these parables did not proclaim the gospel, where else could it be found?

In the third parable, the son's share of the inheritance is his patrimonial heritage, deriving from God's promise of land to Abraham's descendants. Israel distributed land among tribes and families.

Squandering this heritage in a foreign land abandons Israelite identity beyond feeding pigs. The break is not merely with the nuclear family but with the family of Abraham.

■ THE TEXT IN CONTEMPORARY DISCUSSION

Interpreters often note that the older brother characterizes the younger negatively as squandering his possessions with prostitutes and designate his characterization as unreliable (Powell, 274). Typically, this transfers to also regarding as unreliable Luke's portrayal of Pharisees and scribes who unreliably accuse others. But narratives commonly fill in additional information progressively, and this characterization fills in the picture of "reckless living" in 15:13. This "completing analepsis" (later information that fills in an earlier gap) scarcely transfers to Pharisees and scribes.

The ratio of what is lost to the original unity is stepped up with each parable: one sheep of one hundred, one coin of ten, one son of two (Green 1997, 573, 576). Mark Allan Powell (265–87) designates the famine in 15:14 as a crucial detail that is generally disregarded in the prosperous Western world but would have been obvious in Luke's world, where famine was a menacing threat, and often a reality, and the squandering son fails to safeguard against such a world. Nevertheless, in that uncertain world, he is welcomed and safe in his father's house. In the imperial context, Rome's tribute system moved enormous amounts of grain from the East to the capital, often leaving local populations unable to accumulate surpluses against famines, which were thereby exacerbated. Such a world is contrasted with the father's house, a vivid analogy of the contrast between Rome's empire and God's commonwealth.

Luke 16: Children of Mammon and Children of God

■ THE TEXT IN ITS ANCIENT CONTEXT

Luke 16 shifts Jesus' address from critics to disciples. A parable describes an economic delivery system featuring a rich man who acts unlike the father of the prodigal son. His broker squanders his property. So he dismisses him. The broker already manipulated accounts in his own favor and does the same for his patron's creditors so they will favor him. Even the rich patron praises his prudence. Jesus interrupts this story at 16:8 with the comparison typical of Luke's parables: Offspring of "this age"—that is, who derive their behavior from "this age"—are more prudent than offspring of light—who derive their behavior from "light." All the characters in the parable—the rich man, his broker, the debtors—are offspring of this age in contrast to offspring of light. For Luke, mammon in 16:9 is also an "offspring" of this age; that is, mammon is born from injustice. Jesus' exhortation to make friends by means of mammon that is born from injustice hinges on the oxymoron "eternal tents" (16:9). Tents as *temporary* shelters make this scathing irony (Porter; Brawley 1998, 820): Make friends by means of wealth that is born from injustice so that when it fails they will receive you in "eternal temporary shelters" (contra Nolland, 2:806). (Note: the rich man in 16:19-31 winds up *without* supporting friends.)

Jesus continues comparing faithfulness with injustice. In 16:11-12, he explicitly critiques faithlessness with respect to "unjust wealth" belonging to another. This excludes taking the broker's prudence in 16:8 as an example to emulate. Two worlds—mammon and God's commonwealth—are mutually exclusive (16:13).

Some Pharisees overhear and ridicule Jesus. Like the rich man in 16:1-8, their prudence regarding not only wealth but also honor (justifying themselves) makes them offspring of "this age." Jesus' response contrasts self-justification with God's perspective and insists that abominable conventions of honor-shame are incompatible with God's commonwealth (16:14-15).

Although Luke's audience could have taken Jesus' reference to the law and John as being discontinuous with the good news (contrasting "until then" with "now," 16:16), more likely, the law and John are starting points from which good news is now proclaimed. Therefore, Jesus affirms the abiding validity of law (16:17). Indeed, his interpretation of adultery in 16:18 intensifies law. Perhaps Luke's audience puzzled over entering God's commonwealth by force. "Force" could reflect the power of patron-client systems to compel reciprocity, to gain support by favoritism, to gain honor for oneself, and to accommodate to prudent rationales in contrast to the law, the prophets, and God's commonwealth.

This corresponds to the next parable, about a propertied member of the elite who scores splendidly in serving mammon, but poorly in terms of justice according to the law and prophets (16:19-31). He is the foil for a poor man who receives God's promises to Abraham's children. Lazarus is clearly Abraham's descendant; the rich man is not (see 3:8). The rich man pleads for his brothers in vain, because Abraham also affirms the abiding efficacy of the law and the prophets.

▌ The Text in the Interpretive Tradition

Interpreters debate whether the "lord" in 16:8a is the rich man or Jesus. Clearly shifting from third person narration in the parable to first person exhortation, 16:9 begins with the word *kai*, which continues from 16:8b: "Because the children of this age are more shrewd than the children of light, I *also* say to you." Coherence also supports the patron as the lord of 16:8a. There is no verb in 16:16: "The law and the prophets until John" (NRSV supplies "in effect"). Many interpreters have argued that John belongs to a decisively separate time before Jesus. The trend today is toward continuity, supported by the abiding validity of the law (16:17-18). The good news of God's commonwealth is the law and the prophets (Nolland, 2:802).

▌ The Text in Contemporary Discussion

More than dealing with possessions, the parable in 16:1-8 deals with economics in patronage and honor-shame systems. Especially it deals with deriving behavior from injustice. The broker is characterized not by the adjective "unjust" but by the genitive (*tēs adikias*, 16:8), which, as the "offspring of this age" and "offspring of light" (16:8) indicate, is a genitive of origin (Brawley 1998, 819). Another genitive of origin modifies mammon in 16:9. Prudent rationales fit patronage and honor-shame systems but are incompatible with God's commonwealth (similarly Green 1997, 597). Most interpreters value prudence positively here. The parable and Jesus' critique of honor-shame (justifying oneself) among Pharisees devalues prudence as a way of rationalizing injustice (16:15). The rich man and Lazarus is hardly about future judgment. Their deaths are past, and their relationships with Abraham are in the present.

Luke 17:1—18:8: Scandals and Faith(fulness) Less Than a Mustard Seed

▌ THE TEXT IN ITS ANCIENT CONTEXT

Jesus warns his disciples that it is impossible to avoid stumbling (*skandala*). Momentarily, Luke's audience might take this as their own stumbling, but 17:1 quickly shifts to causing another to stumble. A millstone around the neck is a radical punishment metaphor for causing one "little" one to stumble (17:2). This recalls the little children of 10:21, who know their parent and know they are God's children; that is, the "little flock" in 12:32, to whom God gives the commonwealth as fulfillment of promises to Abraham, and Lazarus from the preceding parable. Anyone familiar with Scripture might remember *skandala* that caused Israel to fall away from God. Suddenly Jesus turns to forgiveness. Failing to forgive is an instance of *skandala* (17:3-4).

Does 17:5 skip to another issue, or is faith(fulness) the condition for avoiding *skandala*? Repeatedly, Luke dramatizes faith(fulness) as action. The apostles' request implies a profusion of faith(fulness) beyond what they already have; Jesus reduces what they presume they have to *less than* a mustard seed (17:5-6).

Is the slave who does what is commanded a positive or negative example (17:7-10)? Hearers first occupy the role of a slave owner whose slave comes in from the field. They have a choice: invite the slave to the table or command him to serve the table. If the slave serves, would they, as slave owners, express gratitude? (parallel to 12:37). But precipitously, hearers are made to play roles not of slave owners but of unthanked slaves.

In sorting this out, hearers confront a story about ten lepers who encounter Jesus. Jesus does nothing except to say, "Go and show yourselves to the priests." On the way, they become clean (17:11-14). One returns to give thanks, and the narrator calls him a Samaritan (17:15-19). Jesus calls this faith(fulness); that is, the Samaritan dramatizes faith(fulness). The other nine treat Jesus as an unthanked slave, and now hearers perceive that Jesus' mustard-seed basic minimum is gratitude to God for God's works. Some Pharisees' question of *when* God's commonwealth comes (17:20-21) stands in continuity with this basic minimum. Jesus' answer is *where* as well as *when*. That is, he locates the commonwealth in the cleansed leper's gratitude as manifesting God's commonwealth in their midst.

Jesus then alerts his disciples to adversity in God's commonwealth. One stumbling block (*skandalon*) that leads astray is false messiahs (17:23-24). Jesus predicts a future final manifestation of God's commonwealth in himself, but only after suffering and rejection (17:24-37). This final manifestation is an unforeseen crisis demanding decisions in which some are saved (Noah, Lot) and others destroyed (Sodom, Lot's wife) (17:26-35). This prompts a question from Jesus' disciples: "Where?" Jesus answers in a riddle: where eagles gather around a corpse (17:37). Is it possible to unravel what *eagles* mean? (See below under "The Text in Contemporary Discussion.")

Luke 18:1-8 still addresses Jesus' disciples. Before narrating the parable, Luke interprets it: "It is necessary to pray always and not to despair." Maintaining hope (18:1) responds to the adversity predicted in 17:22-37. The judge, who does not fear God or respect people (18:3) and thus whose behavior is born from "injustice" (genitive of origin, 18:6), refuses to grant justice to a widow. He belongs to imperial systems that contrast with concerns for widows in Israel's Scriptures. Still, the woman's audacity would surprise hearers. The judge finally accedes to the widow's vexing persistence and grants her justice. Luke 18:8 reiterates the theme of faith(fulness) in 17:5-6, 19.

▍THE TEXT IN THE INTERPRETIVE TRADITION

Stumbling in 17:1 initially raises concern for personal failure. Such an element is present in 17:3-4, but in 17:1-2 the issue is causing others to stumble. Stumbling in the Septuagint means falling away from God.

The parable about a slave who does what is commanded, ending with "we are worthless slaves, we have done only what we ought to have done," is widely taken as Jesus' evaluation of his apostles who ask for increased faith, and the slave owner is likened to God, whose gratitude they should not expect. But if the parable is taken with the healing of ten lepers, and with 12:37 in the larger context, the unthanked slave corresponds also to Jesus, who is unthanked by nine out of ten lepers who are healed. Green (1997, 614) asserts that thanking a slave would put a master in debt to the slave. But the Samaritan leper who returns with thanksgiving does not obligate Jesus (17:16).

Interpreters have long debated whether *entos hymōn* in 17:21 means "in one's heart" or "among you." Questioning when God's commonwealth comes diverts some Pharisees from the cleansing of the lepers and searches in the wrong place for the wrong time. The NRSV implies a new setting by beginning 17:20 with "once." An alternate translation, "when he was asked," gives the Pharisees' question continuity with the context. There is no change in setting.

From the early church through the Middle Ages, the eagles in 17:37 were understood to be either angels or believers who are devoted to the body of Christ (O'Day).

Under the notion that parables have *one* central meaning, the parable of the widow and the unjust judge has been taken as *either* valuing the widow's persistence or contrasting God's readiness with the judge's reticence. Neither excludes the other.

▍THE TEXT IN CONTEMPORARY DISCUSSION

Popular eschatology, such as the *Left Behind* series, often takes 17:22-37 to be descriptions of what some call the "rapture." First, the notion of rapture is not taken from any one biblical text but from a selective combination of texts picked here and there and removed from their contexts. Second, the language here is apocalyptic—vivid, imagistic figurations that create a sense of crisis *for the present*. The purpose is not to be a road map of the future (e.g., pilotless airplanes; see 17:34) but to encourage appropriate responsibility now.

Luke 17:37 repeats a Greek proverb (Ehrhardt) but substitutes "eagles" for the proverbial "vultures." Definitively, the text means "eagles" and not "vultures," as in recent English translations. Roman soldiers marched behind standards bearing eagles. Rome, like many nations today, depicted itself as an eagle. Jupiter's mascot was an eagle. Roman emperors likewise associated themselves with eagles, and the Septuagint repeatedly depicts empires that God uses to punish Israel as eagles. But God also brings to naught all such empires to reestablish shalom. Jerusalem's gathering, which Jesus desires in 13:34, is God's commonwealth (see on 13:32-34 above). The gathering of imperial eagles is Rome's kingdom. Christ's final manifestation reestablishes God's commonwealth against imperial systems, which are reduced to feeding on a corpse (Carter 2003).

Feminists and others (e.g., Cotter) champion the widow who asserts her rights against unjust, imperial, patriarchal systems, and they emphasize the way she dramatizes faith(fulness). Imperial studies note the verisimilar depiction of Roman courts, which favored elite Roman citizens over others (Garnsey, 128–41). "The parable is a burlesque of the whole justice system" (Cotter, 342). Praying with confidence that God grants justice is part and parcel of confronting injustice persistently, and vice versa.

Luke 18:9-34: Inclusion in and Exclusion from God's Commonwealth

▌ THE TEXT IN ITS ANCIENT CONTEXT

The parable in 18:9-14 revisits inclusion and exclusion. The addressees (some who trusted that they were right and despised others) are new. A Pharisee and a tax collector pray at the temple. Neither the Pharisee's gratitude for what differentiates him from others nor the tax collector's plea for God's mercy typify prayers of their group (Wolter, 593). Rather, group identity reflects social standing. Reminiscent of 13:23, in which it is presumed few will be saved and many will wind up outside, the first worshiper is not justified, the second is. Jesus, then, inverts honor and shame with a proverb (18:14).

The disciples, dangerously close to having a millstone hung around their necks (17:2), rebuke people who bring infants to Jesus. But following his own remarks in 17:3, Jesus rebukes them and declares that God's commonwealth belongs to little children (18:15-16, similarly 10:21). Three interpretations of receiving God's commonwealth "as a little child" are possible: receiving the commonwealth the way a child would; receiving it the way one accepts a child; receiving it by accepting a child (18:17). Interpreters profit from pondering each possibility without neglecting the others.

A rich ruler, obviously part of imperial systems, then asks the same question as the lawyer in 10:25: "What must I do to inherit eternal life?" (18:18). The question unavoidably interacts with receiving God's commonwealth as a child. Jesus' answer, similar to his response in 10:26, is: "What is written in the law?" (18:20). Jesus tells him to sell "whatever you have" and redistribute it among the poor, recalling 16:13: "You cannot serve God and mammon." The ruler's disillusionment evokes Jesus' parable: It is harder for the rich to enter God's commonwealth than for a camel to go through the eye of a needle (18:24-25). Some listeners deduce that no one can enter. Jesus then reiterates 1:37 with variations: "Human impossibilities are God's mighty deeds" (18:27).

Peter presents Jesus' followers as the rich ruler's counterpart. Jesus promises a double repayment for leaving home and family for God's commonwealth (18:29-30). In the world to come, it is eternal life. Repayment in the present is unspecified but already includes Jesus and present manifestations of God's commonwealth.

At 18:31, Jesus again reveals adversity to the Twelve. He forecasts being handed over to gentiles (Jewish people are not mentioned). A summary of his suffering and death follows. The Twelve do not understand.

▌ THE TEXT IN THE INTERPRETIVE TRADITION

Many interpreters take the parable of two men praying in the temple as addressed to Pharisees. But the Pharisee who prays determines the addressees no more than the tax collector. In Luke 23, Jesus is mocked and Pilate threatens to flog him, echoing terms used in 18:32, though spitting is not mentioned. John Nolland's note (2:895) that handing Jesus over to gentiles breaks Jewish national solidarity fails to consider how indigenous ruling elites collaborate in imperial systems.

■ The Text in Contemporary Discussion

Social identity theory holds that members of groups exaggerate both in-group solidarity and distinctions from out-groups. Further, the social sciences identify honor as the pivotal value in antiquity. In this light, the Pharisee draws honor both from his in-group and by differentiation from tax collectors. The tax collector is inevitably a collaborator in imperial systems, but his prayer disavows norms of his group and implies changing group identity. As one whom God justifies (divine passive), he belongs to God's commonwealth.

Jesus' promise to the ruler of "treasure in heaven" (18:22) is parallel to God's commonwealth (18:24, 29), and it is a figurative circumlocution for God (Wolter, 600). Redistributing wealth as such does not accumulate treasure in heaven (18:22). Rather, the entire statement is a figuration for serving God rather than mammon.

Luke 18:35—19:27: The Commonwealth Jesus Brings and Ruling Systems

■ The Text in Its Ancient Context

Three episodes move toward Jesus' destination/destiny in Jerusalem: he heals a blind man as he approaches Jericho, encounters Zacchaeus in Jericho, and relates a parable as he nears Jerusalem. As Jesus approaches Jericho, a blind man calls him David's son and pleads for mercy, as did the tax collector in 18:13 (18:35-43). He is literally marginalized, off the road, begging. His insistent pleas break through efforts to silence him. Jesus issues only one word commanding him to do something: "See [again]!" The blind man's pleas in spite of protests dramatizes faith(fulness). He does see again and glorifies God, as did the Samaritan in 17:18. Unlike the ruler (18:22-23), he follows Jesus. Perhaps he also "sees" what the Twelve cannot understand (18:34) (Wolter, 607). The crowd, including those who protested the blind man's pleas, also sees anew and praises God (18:48).

In Jericho, Jesus encounters rich Zacchaeus, also marginalized as a chief tax collector/sinner (19:7). His office assures that he is a collaborator in imperial systems. He also wishes to "see" but faces two obstacles: a crowd and his short stature (19:3). He does one thing: he climbs a tree. As Zacchaeus's guest, Jesus enters another relationship with tax collectors/sinners that draws social protests (19:7). Zacchaeus reveals no motivation for changing relationships with mammon by redistributing half of his possessions among the poor and making fourfold reparation for defrauding (19:8-9). Jesus equates this change with salvation and the renewal of Zacchaeus's Abrahamic heritage (19:9-10). Like Abraham's daughter in 13:16, Zacchaeus is Abraham's son.

Jesus relates a story to a crowd traveling to Jerusalem that expects God's commonwealth to appear with Jesus' arrival there (19:11). In the story, a ruler in imperial systems gives ten slaves one mina (traditionally rendered "pound") each, with which they are to do business. Meanwhile, he goes to receive a kingdom (19:12-14), which some compatriots oppose. When he returns, he audits his slaves. Profits garner praise (19:16-23), but he disenfranchises a slave who safeguarded his mina

(19:26). Moreover, he slaughters the delegation that opposed him. The story is hardly about the minas and the slaves. It is a parable of a throne pretender who seeks and tries to maintain power. For Luke's audience, this likely was a gruesome analogy to Rome's empire—exploiting peasants, punishing unproductivity, and slaughtering opponents. Jesus distances himself from such a kingdom.

◼ THE TEXT IN THE INTERPRETIVE TRADITION

From early Christian centuries, the blind man's naming Jesus David's son was understood as a christological confession fulfilling Scripture. It more directly recalls 1:32-33, 54-56, 69-73. Many interpreters emphasize Jesus' healing by the power of his word, but here the word is an imperative for the blind man to act: "look up/again." Some take Zacchaeus's expression of giving in the present tense as informing Jesus of what he already practices customarily (Fitzmyer 1985, 2:1225). But this runs aground on the future fourfold restitution of those he defrauded (19:8; also Wolter, 613–14). Interpreters have long noted parallels to Josephus's account of Herod Archelaus, who promised rewards to those who would support him in his attempts to consolidate power as a king (Josephus, *Ant.* 17.8.4–9.2). But then commentators virtually always take the parable as an allegory in which slaves correspond to people facing Jesus' parousia and judgment, including the eschatological destruction of his opponents, particularly Jerusalem and its rulers.

◼ THE TEXT IN CONTEMPORARY DISCUSSION

Restoring the blind man's sight in 18:35-43 involves defying attempts to keep the marginalized on the margin. Faith(fulness) here is not confessional but consists in persistent violations of impediments. Unlike others for whom Jesus performed remarkable deeds, the blind beggar is not merely reintegrated into community (Theissen, 52–53) but also follows Jesus. Recovery of Israel's covenant traditions is thematic for Luke, and in light of 1:32-33, 54-56, 69-73, "David's son" manifests God's fidelity to Abrahamic promises to bless. In Zacchaeus's case, Jesus overcomes social impediments in order to manifest that even an enlightened tax collector is Abraham's son. In light of how hard it is for a rich man to be saved (18:27), Zacchaeus is an instance of an impossibility in human hands that becomes God's mighty deed (Brawley 1998, 822). Zacchaeus's reversal follows Mary's inversion of rich and poor in 1:52-55, but it directly benefits the poor with something approaching mutuality. Overwhelmingly, interpreters of the parable on the minas and the slaves focus on praise of industrious discipleship. This produces a misfit of a harsh, greedy ruler disciplining unproductive disciples and opponents (cf. Herzog, 162–68). But parallels to Josephus's account of Archelaus make it rather a parable of a throne pretender that is analogous to imperial systems. Jesus presents these systems as the antithesis to God's commonwealth.

Luke 19:28—20:44: Ruling Systems in Jerusalem and the Things That Make for Peace

◼ THE TEXT IN ITS ANCIENT CONTEXT

Riding a donkey over his disciples' clothes, Jesus parodies royal parades and reprises Zech. 9:9 (Luke 19:28-40). In connection with the preceding parable of the throne pretender, this caricatures military acclamations. On the basis of deeds of good news for the poor and oppressed (19:37; cf. 4:18), Jesus' disciples ascribe a benediction to him as the king who comes in God's name (Ps. 117:26 LXX) and chant a doxology of God's peace (20:1). When some Pharisees protest, Jesus persistently follows the example of the blind beggar (18:38-39) and violates their objections (19:39-40).

Jesus is grim. He weeps. Jerusalem has not recognized what makes for peace—but faces disaster under destructive imperial systems (19:41-44).

The so-called cleansing of the temple is nothing of the sort. Rather, Jesus makes a *claim* on it as a house of prayer. The "den of robbers" (Jer. 7:11) insinuates the high-priestly party's place in imperial systems that reward elites and plunder the people (cf. Jer. 7:5-7). Jesus' claim for a place of prayer notwithstanding, he uses the temple for teaching and proclamation such that his teaching remains dramatically public (19:47; 20:1; see also 21:37-38; 22:53), again persistently violating opposition (19:45-48).

Luke 20 primarily reports consequences of Jesus' teaching. In a dispute about Jesus' source of power, Jesus makes his source comparable to John's. Beyond that, he refuses to answer (20:1-8). He narrates a parable, alluding to Isaiah's figuration of Israel as a vine (Isa. 5:1-7), about tenants of a vineyard who produce no fruit for the owner (20:9-19). This targets the high-priestly coterie (20:19). Avoiding a snare about paying tribute to Caesar, Jesus tantalizes hearers to ponder what belongs to God (20:20-25). An interchange with Sadducees on resurrection produces another riposte: "God is not the God of the dead but of the living" (20:27-38). Luke's audience would not consider all Jesus' interlocutors intractable because some agree with him (20:39). The Jesus whom Luke portrays in order to persuade the Gospel's audience also persuades his interlocutors. Jesus then takes his turn at posing a challenge: "How can people say that the Messiah is David's son?" Luke's audience might take this as denying the Messiah's Davidic lineage or as posing a riddle about *how* the Messiah can be both (20:41-44). Since Luke underlines both Jesus' Davidic lineage and his messiahship, a possible answer to how David's son can also be Messiah is by God's power (cf. Patte, 315–16).

■ The Text in the Interpretive Tradition

After 19:39, Pharisees disappear from Luke. Jesus' challengers become the high-priestly coterie. From earliest interpretations, debates have raged about *exousia* ("authority" or "power," 20:2, 8). The high-priestly party actually asks, "By what sort of *power* do you do these things? Who gave you this *power*?" (20:2). The *source of power* is the issue for both John and Jesus. Both lack *authority* (20:2-8).

Many interpreters understand the parable of the wicked tenants as rejecting Israel. But Luke correlates the tenants only with the high-priestly party (20:19), differentiated from the people in 19:48. The introduction for the trick question in 20:20 clearly spells out collaboration with the governor in imperial systems. Jesus' saying about tribute has been taken as indicating what in the United States is now called the separation of church and state. Jesus actually turns the question of tribute back on his interlocutors. The "Tiberius Denarius" of the time bears a "graven image" of the emperor with legends that label him "divine" and "high priest." The coin also belongs to mammon that derives from injustice (16:9, 11), and it recalls: "You cannot serve God and mammon" (16:13; similarly Green 1997, 716). The interlocutors are left to ponder their own question.

▮ THE TEXT IN CONTEMPORARY DISCUSSION

Jesus' disruption in the temple has strong support as a historical factor in his execution (E. P. Sanders, 253–68). The multitude's praise and benediction in 19:37-38 is christological but remains theocentric. That is, Jesus' deeds manifest God's power and produce praise of God. Arguments that the prediction of the siege of Jerusalem is an anachronistic reading of its devastation in 70 CE back into the life of Jesus are dubious. The prediction borrows from scriptural accounts of sieges (19:43-44) and is a logical deduction from imperial domination (Dodd 1947; Wolter, 634–35). Jesus' comparison of himself with John in 20:4 recalls John's economic and political emphases (3:10-14, 19-20). Prominent models for peace today presume that it is dependent on armed strength. In consideration of the larger context of Luke, the things that make for peace in 19:42 are good news for the poor and liberation from oppression.

Luke 20:45—21:38: The Demise of Injustice and God's Commonwealth

▮ THE TEXT IN ITS ANCIENT CONTEXT

Jesus turns to critiques of socioreligious conventions. Luke 20:45-47 does not condemn all scribes, but those who seek honor and abuse widows. The line of thought continues in 21:1-4 with rich people, like the scribes in 20:46, and a poor widow, who is like those abused in 20:47. In destitution, she casts her life (*bios*) into the temple treasury. She outshines the charity of elites but is hardly an example to emulate. Her offering is qualified by scribes who abuse widows and by Jesus' immediate prediction of the temple's destruction (21:4). She casts her *bios* into a collapsing institution.

Jesus' audience is unclear. He addresses disciples in 20:45, but others overhear. In 21:7, "they" ask when the collapse will occur. Nevertheless, the imperatives in 21:8 are directed to his followers. Jesus' response to inquiries about the time of the collapse is indeterminate, but he warns against deception from false claimants (21:8) or portentous events (21:9-11). Jesus warns of persecution in an unspecified period of time from control agents in imperial systems, kings, governors, synagogues, and prisons (21:12). This occasions exhortations for testimony that derives from a continuing relationship with Jesus (21:13-15).

Jesus paints the time of crisis in alarming tones: family and social conflict, military violence, hardships for pregnant women, mothers, and infants (21:20-24)—a time of punishment for, or justice against, evil (*ekdikēsis*). It is likely that Luke's audience had already witnessed some such, but would be puzzled by Jerusalem's rehabilitation after the time of the nations (21:24).

Suspense and uncertainly continue with Jesus' forecast of confusion over cosmic portents, natural disasters, and the shaking of heavenly powers (21:25-26). This becomes the setting for the ultimate manifestation of the son of man (21:27, alluding to Dan. 7:13). Violence and cosmic dissolution then turn into optimism, because as the ultimate manifestation approaches, evil powers fight violently but in vain. Increased violence signals how close they are to defeat (21:28-31). When Jesus says, "This generation will not pass away until all has taken place" (21:32), Luke's audience would have understood "this generation" to mean "the human race." Nolland (3:1009–10) takes "this generation" (21:32) as "Jesus' contemporaries," who obviously would have passed away before

Luke's audience heard these words. But the fundamental meaning of the Greek means "what is born" (= "all who live on earth" in 21:35). Wolter (682) is on track when he takes the Greek to mean the "human race."

▌ THE TEXT IN THE INTERPRETIVE TRADITION

Scribes belong to an established group, but verse 46 is most properly understood as "those scribes who like to walk around in long robes." Rather than characterize all scribes, Jesus specifies those who seek honor but practice abuse (Nolland, 3:975–76; against Green 1997, 725). Abusing widows contravenes Torah stipulations to care for them. What "devouring houses" means is beyond recovery. *Bios* (21:4) means "life" or "sustenance for life." Luke is both looking back on events including the fall of Jerusalem and looking forward beyond his own time (Wolter, 672).

▌ THE TEXT IN CONTEMPORARY DISCUSSION

Although the poor widow's gift shames the rich, feminist and postcolonial interpreters (e.g., Sugirtharajah) correctly resist using her to encourage sacrificial giving. On scribes who abuse widows, Amy-Jill Levine objects appropriately to anti-Jewish attempts to negatively characterize all scribes and temple functionaries (oral presentation at Duke Divinity School, Durham, NC, February 20, 2013). On the other hand, critiques of elite collaborators in favor of preserving Israel's heritage are hardly anti-Jewish.

Luke 22:1—23:56: The Greatest Who Serves and the Power of Violence

▌ THE TEXT IN ITS ANCIENT CONTEXT

Luke's narrative changes abruptly at 22:1. Jesus' didactic encounters with people cease. Execution plots set the tone (22:2). Characters take sides—the high priests, Satan, and Judas over against Jesus, his disciples, and the people (22:2).

Sober realism modifies festivity (Passover recalls liberation *and* oppression). Jesus vows abstinence for the coming of God's commonwealth (22:18), presumably the final manifestation of the son of man from 21:27. Moreover, he interprets his final Passover as the giving of himself and a "new covenant." "New covenant" recollects both the Abrahamic covenant (synthesized with other covenant traditions) and Jer. 31:31, where it means not the replacement of but renewed consecration to Israel's covenant with God. Table solidarity fades, however, when Jesus announces Judas's betrayal (22:22).

Unexpectedly, the apostles reflect not God's commonwealth but imperial rulers—intrigue, betrayal, competition for priority (22:25). Jesus mandates God's commonwealth as a blunt alternative: "Not so for you" (22:26). Second, he inverts hierarchy into mutuality. He himself is "one who serves" (22:27).

Therefore, when Jesus confers his commonwealth on the apostles, Luke's audience understands his redefinition of rulers and thrones as mutuality (22:29-30). But when Jesus forecasts a satanic attack, the apostles' place in God's commonwealth again comes under threat (22:31-34). In 22:35-38, Jesus enigmatically advises his disciples to arm themselves, amending instructions in 9:3; 10:4. Earlier, they lived in mutuality; now they face animosity. Moreover, Jesus connects swords with fulfilling Scripture—they play the role of outlaws (22:37).

In 22:40, 46, Jesus and the apostles retreat to pray that they not enter into temptation, as in 11:4. Jesus himself appeals to God as Father. The cup metaphor for what lies ahead (22:41-42) also looks back to the new covenant (22:20). Both mean consecration to God. Grief already leads the apostles into temptation—instead of praying, they sleep (22:45).

With swords and failure at prayer, things turn topsy-turvy. Judas betrays Jesus with a kiss (22:47-48). All the apostles are willing to engage in swordplay. One actually does. They really do play the role of outlaws and mimic imperial violence. According to 22:37, this fulfills Scripture. By contrast, Jesus manifests God's commonwealth by stopping the swordplay and healing (22:49-51). Jesus' arrest confuses daylight and darkness (22:53).

While Jesus faces the high priest, Peter faces people of insignificant rank, and his promises of fidelity turn into denial (22:33, 54-62). The king who comes in the Lord's name (19:38) is mocked (22:63). The council demands that the one whose deeds manifested God's finger (11:20) confess whether he is the Messiah or not (22:67). When Jesus forecasts the manifestation of the son of man, the council ironically calls him "son of God." The interrogative "Are you the son of God?" can also be declarative: "You are the son of God." Jesus responds: "That [claim] is on your lips" (22:70). The testimony on their lips then becomes evidence against him.

In chapter 23, things remain topsy-turvy. Before Pilate, the high-priestly party accuses Jesus of being an insurgent king (23:2). Recalling the irony of "son of God" on the council's lips, Pilate's question, "Are you king of the Jewish people?" can also be declarative: "You are the king of the Jewish people." Jesus responds as he did to the council: "[That] is on your lips" (23:3). Herod's entrance (23:8) recalls repeated appearances in 3:1, 19-20; 9:7-9; 13:31-32. He and his soldiers mock Jesus as if he were a member of the ruling elite in elegant clothing (23:11).

In 23:22, Pilate declares Jesus innocent for the third time, but then delivers the verdict against him. Luke's audience could hardly have reacted positively to Pilate or Roman justice. Things are still topsy-turvy. Roman (in)justice condemns an innocent man (Lee, 100). Assertions of Jesus' innocence also follow the crucifixion: a victim crucified with him declares that Jesus has done nothing wrong (23:41); a Roman centurion declares him innocent (23:47); observers leave beating their breasts in remorse (23:48). Injustice is what Rome's systems look like. Leaders ridicule Jesus as saving others but unable to save himself, but unwittingly they deny the criterion of life in God's commonwealth: "Those who want to save their life will lose it" (9:24). Soldiers mock him as carnival king (23:36), daylight turns into darkness (23:44), the temple curtain separating sacred from profane is split (23:45). Like other temporary inversions at Jesus' crucifixion, there is no indication in Luke that the temple structure is abrogated. Note the resumption of activity in the temple in 24:53 as well as in Acts.

One thing contests utter absurdity. Quoting Ps. 30:6 LXX, Jesus commits his life to God (Luke 23:46). Luke's audience likely knew the psalm well enough to finish the verse: "Redeem me, Lord

God of truth." A few acquaintances watch, Joseph of Arimathea entombs Jesus' body, and some women prepare to pay last respects (23:49-56).

▌The Text in the Interpretive Tradition

Debates have raged over the meaning of "this is my body" (22:19). Roman Catholicism has held that without changing outward features, sacramental bread is transformed into Christ's body. Lutheranism speaks instead of Christ's presence in, with, and under the bread. Anything similar for the cup is impossible, because in Luke what is poured out is not blood but a new covenant (22:20). Luke attaches "do this in remembrance of me" only to the bread (22:19). Lack of a referent for "this" leaves uncertain what is to be done. Interpreters often take "remembrance" (*anamnēsis*) as making present what is remembered. This interpretation is a post–New Testament development (Brawley 1990a).

Accusations against Jesus before Pilate are political (23:2). Crucifixion was reserved for defiant slaves and unpacified foreigners. The mode of execution means that Jesus and the other two victims were executed as rebels. But Jesus' protest to his arrest as if he were a "brigand" (22:53) means that Jesus was executed "as if" he were a rebel.

▌The Text in Contemporary Discussion

The role of Jerusalem's populace in Jesus' execution is heavily debated. Identifying "the people" as the same group in every instance is problematic. Luke 22:2 separates the people from the high-priestly party. A crowd in 23:4 is the council of 22:66; 23:1. Their concern for "this place" associates them with the temple, and their perspective that Jesus stirs up "the [other] people" subtly differentiates them from "the people" (23:5). In 23:13, the context associates "the people" with the high priests. Pilate also says that he examined Jesus in the presence of this coalition (23:14), and thus they are the crowd of the council associated with the chief priests in 23:4. They are never identified as the Jewish people of Jerusalem (against Green 1997, 791; and Wolter, 745–46; Wolter softens this to "representatives"). The summary of opponents in 24:20 omits the people.

A closely related discussion interprets Luke not only as anti-Jewish but also pro-Roman. Postcolonial perspectives shed new light on this. Rome delegated control of local populations to native elite collaborators, whom Josephus identifies as "the high priests" (*Ant.* 20.251). Native collaborators may resist colonizers out of nationalistic concerns, but also support them in order to maintain privilege in colonial systems. In this light, Jesus' crucifixion is not a matter of theological ideology but of maintaining order (Lee, 95–96). From Mary's song (1:46-55) to Jesus' prescription for disciples in contrast to imperial systems (22:25-26), tensions with imperial systems in Luke is strong (Lee, 97). Although Jesus rejects rebellion, he proclaims God's commonwealth as an alternative to Rome's systems. Rome's systems claimed to bring justice to vanquished nations. By comparison, Pilate's verdict against Jesus in spite of declaring him innocent makes Rome's justice a travesty (Lee). Declarations of innocence also reflect negatively on Jewish people (Wolter, 688), but they are on the lips of Pilate, Herod (as Pilate alleges), a victim on a cross, and a Roman centurion. Pilate attempts to persuade the high priests, but they never treat Jesus as innocent of undermining imperial systems.

In the New Testament, "new covenant" occurs only in 1 Cor. 11:25, its parallel in Luke 22:20; 2 Cor. 3:6 (alluding to Jer. 31:31); and Heb. 8:8, 13, quoting Jer. 31:31-34. In spite of the prominence of "new" in Christian history and the scriptural canon, "covenant" in the New Testament virtually always (if not always) refers to Israel's covenant traditions. Jesus' new covenant as consecration of the heart, as in Jeremiah, is not discontinuous with Israel's heritage (also Green 1997, 763).

Postcolonialists have taken references to ruling (22:30) and swords (22:36, 49-50) as mimicry of Roman domination and violence. But before conferring thrones on the apostles, Jesus subverts imperial hierarchies (22:25-27). This subversion defies mimicry and redefines commonwealth and thrones as mutuality. The apostles' swordplay in 22:49-50 is imperial mimicry, which Jesus stops (22:51).

Luke portrays attempts of Jesus' opponents, from mockery to crucifixion, to reduce him to absurdity. Crucifixion is not only castigation but shaming to the uttermost. The other side of the story resists reduction to absurdity by irony and scriptural figurations (Brawley 1995, 42–60).

The other two victims crucified with Jesus (23:39-43) reflect the division among the people anticipated by Simeon (1:34-35). One mocks Jesus; the other declares him innocent. The second accepts crucifixion as deserved justice (v. 41) and thereby unjustly internalizes the values of the empire. Crucifixion was a vile form of capital punishment designed to terrorize resistors to the empire administered without "equality under the law" (compare executions of "terrorists" today). Traditionally, the second rebel has been called "penitent." But more than confess his deeds (v. 41), he confesses Jesus' commonwealth beyond the crucifixion before anyone else does (Wolter, 760): "Remember me when you come into your commonwealth" (v. 42). Jesus' reference to Paradise (v. 43) is too brief and inexact to build definitive pictures of the afterlife.

Luke 24: Resurrection

■ THE TEXT IN ITS ANCIENT CONTEXT

After Jesus' violent crucifixion, Luke 24 opens with the softness of dawn. Women resume their solemn task, delayed by Sabbath, of anointing Jesus' body (23:56). Quickly, mysteriously, their unenviable but compassionate task is canceled, and incidents pile up for an eventful day. The stone—unmentioned earlier—is rolled away. "The" stone (24:2), with the definite article in its first reference, may presume familiarity with the tomb story or may be a cultural presumption that a stone would close the tomb. Jesus' body is absent. Two men (later called "messengers," *angeloi*, 24:23) in clothes shining like lightning startle them (24:1-4). The men ask a succinct question and jog memories: "Why are you seeking the one who lives among the dead? He is not here but has been raised. Remember what he told you." With the declaration "he is not here," the tomb loses significance (Green 1997, 836). For the women and Luke's audience, an empty tomb does not mean resurrection, and the messengers must interpret it by recalling Jesus' passion predictions (24:5-7). "He is risen" (24:5 NRSV) is a divine passive. "Has been raised" is preferable. Resurrection is God's act. The women's task is redefined. They had sought one who was dead among the dead. Astute listeners might have wondered if Jesus predicted his passion on occasions that are unnarrated because in 9:22; 18:31-34, he informed his disciples, not the women. But when the women remember, the predictions belong to their community just as to Luke's audience.

The women, who are named, report to a small but coherent community. The apostles consider their report nonsense. Because of the reminders of Jesus' passion predictions, made specifically to the apostles, their unbelief cannot be attributed to the low status of women in the culture (Green 1997, 840; against Nolland, 3:1193). Luke's audience knows that they are reliable (Tannehill 1986, 7–8, 21–22, 294). Somehow Peter (and others, 24:24) is a partial exception to the evaluation of the women as unreliable. He visits the tomb, sees some linen cloths, and goes home mystified (24:10-12).

Suddenly the story moves with two "of them" toward Emmaus. Their knowledge of "everything" is irony. They are unaware of Jesus' identity, and this "stranger" knows more than they. Reminiscent of Simeon and Anna (2:25, 38), they recount their hopes for Israel's redemption, now dashed: "We had hoped" (24:21). They reprise the five brothers in 16:31: they are unpersuaded, even though someone has been raised. Still, they ponder the women's report and mention others involved in Peter's experience at the tomb. In spite of the announcement that Jesus had been raised, they do not interpret the empty tomb as resurrection (24:13-24). Jesus, incognito, then provides a key for understanding. He interprets himself from Scripture but also interprets Scripture from himself. The essence of the interpretation is the Messiah's entering into glory after suffering (24:25-27). "Glory" in 24:26 means manifestations of God's power.

The travelers, probably husband and wife, extend the stranger hospitality (see 9:4-5). Reminiscent of Jesus' last supper (22:17-20) and feeding the five thousand (9:12-17), Jesus also plays the role of host in the home where he is the guest, blessing and breaking bread. In this act, they recognize the risen Jesus, but enigmatically, he vanishes (24:28-32). When they immediately return to Jerusalem, they find a coherent group, not scattered, but gathered like a family experiencing death. Luke's audience expects the two from Emmaus to tell their experience. Instead, the two listen as those in the group relate their experiences, including Jesus' appearance to Peter, which otherwise goes unnarrated (24:33-35).

Jesus astonishingly appears among them. He questions doubts, demonstrates his wounds and materiality (nails were unmentioned in Luke's crucifixion narrative), and eats (24:36-43). Then reviewing his ministry, he again interprets Scripture in terms of his suffering and resurrection (24:44-46). He also envisages this group's mission to proclaim repentance and forgiveness, which he universalizes and for which he promises empowerment (24:47-49). Listeners who also hear Acts 1:4-5 might retrospectively pick up allusions to Luke 11:13—God's eagerness to give the Holy Spirit to those who ask (Tannehill 1986, 239).

Luke succinctly recounts Jesus' ascension, accompanied by a benediction (24:50). This becomes the occasion for spontaneous worship reinforced by continual worship of God. Luke begins with Zechariah in the temple and ends with Jesus' followers likewise in the temple. In spite of Luke's quarrels with the high priesthood, his audience could not have taken the Gospel as antitemple.

▌The Text in the Interpretive Tradition

In contrast to the other Gospels, Luke locates all resurrection events in the environs of Jerusalem. Mark has no resurrection appearances, but anticipates them in Galilee. Matthew and John mix the locales. Luke's focus on Jerusalem likely has to do with the biblical perspective on Jerusalem as the center of the world, the point of contact between heaven and earth. When Gabriel appears in the temple, the first locale mentioned in Luke (1:8), he steps down from heaven at the central point of contact between heaven and earth. Although Gabriel also appears to Mary in Nazareth, the appearance in the temple emphasizes the direct contact of heaven and earth. At the end of Luke, Jesus ascends to heaven, also in the environs of Jerusalem. Further, Jesus' followers await the fulfillment of the promise of the Holy Spirit in Jerusalem, which in Acts, indeed, happens in Jerusalem (Brawley 1987, 118–32).

When Acts is taken into consideration, it is popular to argue for a shift of the center from Jerusalem to Rome. True, Paul winds up in Rome, but to make his destiny the destiny of the gospel is simply a category error. Beginning and ending the narrative in the temple, resurrection appearances in and around Jerusalem, and the ascension in the precinct of Jerusalem are part of Luke's emphasis on the validity of the good news as deriving from and centering on God.

◼ THE TEXT IN CONTEMPORARY DISCUSSION

Luke's empty tomb is not the basis for believing Jesus' resurrection. Various explanations for empty tombs are possible, and resurrection is usually not among them. The proclamation of the messengers provides the crucial interpretation. The empty tomb does not explain Jesus' resurrection; Jesus' resurrection explains it (Wolter, 770, 772). Even the proclamation remains incomplete without scriptural interpretations and resurrection appearances.

Schüssler Fiorenza (1992, 213) maintains that even though Luke reports the women at the tomb, he suppresses them by slighting their report (24:11) and ignoring resurrection appearances to them narrated elsewhere. Peter still holds first place in resurrection appearances in 24:34, although no narrative of it exists. The appearance to Peter even takes precedence over the Emmaus couple, likely husband and wife. Those who hear Luke's account of the place of women in Jesus' story should find it hard to understand how proclamation of the resurrection could ever have come about without women.

At the beginning, Luke presupposes and builds on a story of God's deeds that keep divine *promises* alive. The risen Jesus' last words in Luke instruct his followers to wait for what God has *promised* (24:49). Luke's audience waits with Jesus' followers to see how this will come to pass. Even without Acts as a sequel, they would expect the story of God's work to continue.

Works Cited

Alexander, Loveday. 1993. *The Preface to Luke's Gospel*. Cambridge: Cambridge University Press.

Annen, Franz. 1976. *Heil für die Heiden*. Frankfurt: Knecht.

Bendemann, Reinhard von. 2001. *Zwischen ΔΟΣΑ und ΣΤΑΥΡΟΣ*. Berlin: de Gruyter.

Bhabha, Homi. 1994. *The Location of Culture*. London: Routledge.

Bovon, François. 2002. *Luke: A Commentary on the Gospel of Luke*. Vol. 1. Trans. Christine M. Thomas. Minneapolis: Fortress Press.

Braun, Willi. 1995. *Feasting and Social Rhetoric*. Cambridge: Cambridge University Press.

Brawley, Robert. 1987. *Luke-Acts and the Jews*. Atlanta: Scholars Press.

————. 1990a. "*Anamnesis* and Absence in the Lord's Supper." *BTB* 20:139–46.

————. 1990b. *Centering on God*. Louisville: Westminster John Knox.

————. 1995. *Text to Text Pours Forth Speech*. Bloomington: Indiana University Press.

————. 1998. "Offspring and Parent." *SBLSP*, 2:807–30. Atlanta: Scholars Press.

————. 1999. "Abrahamic Covenant Traditions and the Characterization of God in Luke-Acts." In *The Unity of Luke-Acts*, edited by J. Verheyden, 109–32. Leuven: Peeters.

Brown, Raymond. 1979. *The Birth of the Messiah*. Garden City, NY: Doubleday.

Carter, Warren. 2000. *Matthew and the Margins*. Maryknoll, NY: Orbis.

————. 2003. "Are There Imperial Texts in the Class?" *JBL* 122:467–87.

————. 2006. *The Roman Empire in the New Testament*. Nashville: Abingdon.

Conzelmann, Hans. 1960. *The Theology of St. Luke*. New York: Harper & Bros.

Cotter, Wendy. 2005. "The Parable of the Feisty Widow and the Threatened Judge." *NTS* 51:328–43.

Cullmann, Oscar. 1963. *The Christology of the New Testament*. Philadelphia: Westminster.

Dodd, C. H. 1947. "The Fall of Jerusalem and the 'Abomination of Desolation.'" *JRS* 37:47–54.

————. 1961. *Parables of the Kingdom*. New York: Scribner.

Egelkraut, Helmuth. 1976. *Jesus' Mission to Jerusalem*. Frankfurt: Peter Lang.

Ehrhardt, Arnold. 1953. "Greek Proverbs in the Gospel." *HTR* 46:68–72.

Fitzmyer, Joseph. 1973. "The Virginal Conception of Jesus in the New Testament." *TS* 34:541–75.

————. 1981. *The Gospel According to Luke I–IX*. AB 28. Garden City, NY: Doubleday.

————. 1985. *The Gospel According to Luke X–XXIV*. AB 28A. Garden City, NY: Doubleday.

Garnsey, Peter. 1970. *Social Status and Legal Privilege in the Roman Empire*. Oxford: Clarendon.

Goulder, Michael. 1989. *Luke: A New Paradigm*. Sheffield: JSOT Press.

Gowler, David. 2003. "Text, Culture, and Ideology in Luke 17:1-10: A Dialogic Reading." In *Fabrics of Discourse: Essays in Honor of Vernon K. Robbins*, edited by David Gowler, L. Gregory Bloomquist, and Duane F. Watson, 89–125. Harrisburg, PA: Trinity Press International.

Green, Joel B. 1989. "Jesus and a Daughter of Abraham (Luke 13:10-17)." *CBQ* 51: 651–52.

————. 1997. *The Gospel of Luke*. NICNT. Grand Rapids: Eerdmans.

Hahn, Ferdinand. 1969. *The Titles of Jesus in Christology*. New York: World.

Herzog, William. 1994. *Parables of Subversive Speech*. Louisville: Westminster John Knox.

Jennings, Theodore, and Tat-Siong Benny Liew. 2004. "Mistaken Identities but Model Faith: Rereading the Centurion, the Chap, and the Christ in Matthew 8:5-13." *JBL* 123:467–94.

Jeremias, Joachim. 1972. *The Parables of Jesus*. New York: Scribner.

Jülicher, Adolf. 1888. *Die Gleichnisreden Jesu*. Freiburg: J. C. B. Mohr (Paul Siebeck).

Lee, Jae Won. 2011. "Pilate and the Crucifixion of Jesus in Luke-Acts." In *Luke-Acts and Empire*, edited by David Rhoads, David Esterline, and Jae Won Lee, 84–106. Eugene, OR: Pickwick.

Lintott, Andre. 1993. *Imperium Romanum: Politics and Administration*. London: Routledge.

Malina, Bruce, and Jerome Neyrey. 1991. "Honor and Shame in Luke-Acts." In *The Social World of Luke-Acts*, edited by Jerome Neyrey, 25–65. Peabody, MA: Hendrickson.

Mowinkel, Sigmund. 1956. *He That Cometh*. Oxford: Blackwell.

Niebuhr, Karl-Wilhelm. 1992. *Heidenapostel aus Israel*. Tübingen: Mohr Siebeck.

Nolland, John. 1993. *Luke 9:21—18:34* and *Luke 18:35—24:53*. WBC 35b-c; Dallas: Word Books.

O'Day, Gail R. 2004. "'There the ? Will Gather Together' (Luke 17:37)." In *Literary Encounters with the Reign of God*, edited by Sharon H. Ringe and H. C. Paul Kim, 288–303. New York: T&T Clark.

Patte, Daniel. 1987. *The Gospel according to Matthew*. Philadelphia: Fortress Press.

Porter, Stanley E. 1990. "The Parable of the Unjust Steward (Luke 16:1-13)." In *The Bible in Three Dimensions*, edited by David J. A. Clines, Stephen E. Fowl, and Stanley E. Porter, 127–53. Sheffield: Sheffield Academic Press.

Powell, Mark Allan. 2004. "The Forgotten Famine." In *Literary Encounters with the Reign of God*, edited by Sharon H. Ringe and H. C. Paul Kim, 265–87. New York: T&T Clark.

Reid, Barbara. 1996. *Choosing the Better Part*. Collegeville, MN: Liturgical Press.

Robbins, Vernon K. 2004. "The Sensory-Aesthetic Texture of the Compassionate Samaritan Parable." In *Literary Encounters with the Reign of God*, edited by Sharon H. Ringe and H. C. Paul Kim, 247–64. New York: T&T Clark.

Sanders, E. P. 1993. *The Historical Figure of Jesus*. New York: Penguin.

Sanders, E. P., and Margaret Davies. 1989. *Studying the Synoptic Gospels*. Philadelphia: Trinity Press International.

Sanders, Jack. 1987. *The Jews in Luke-Acts*. Philadelphia: Fortress.

Schaberg, Jane. 1987. *The Illegitimacy of Jesus*. San Francisco: Harper & Row.

Schlüssler Fiorenza, Elisabeth. 1992. *But She Said: Feminist Practices of Biblical Interpretation*. Boston: Beacon.

Scott, James. 2004. *Hidden Transcripts and the Art of Resistance*. Atlanta: Society of Biblical Literature.

De Ste. Croix, G. E. M. 1981. *The Class Struggle in the Ancient Greek World*. Ithaca, NY: Cornell University Press

Sugirtharajah, R. S. 1991–1992. "The Widow's Mite Revalued." *ExpTim* 103:42–43.

Tannehill, Robert. 1975. *The Sword of His Mouth*. Missoula, MT: Scholars Press.

———. 1986. *The Narrative Unity of Luke Acts*. Vol. 1. Philadelphia: Fortress Press.

———. 1994. "Should We Love Simon the Pharisee?" *CurTM* 21:424–33.

Theissen, Gerd. 1983. *The Miracle Stories of the Early Christian Tradition*. Philadelphia: Fortress Press.

Tolbert, Mary Ann. 1989. *Sowing the Gospel*. Minneapolis: Fortress Press.

Wink, Walter. 1992. *Engaging the Powers*. Minneapolis: Fortress Press.

Wire, Antoinnette. 1978. "The Structure of the Gospel Miracles Stories and Their Tellers." *Semeia* 11:83–113.

Wolter, Michael. 2008. *Das Lukasevangelium*. Tübingen: Mohr Siebeck.

JOHN

Adele Reinhartz

Introduction

The Fourth Gospel is a study in contradictions: uplifting and infuriating; enigmatic and transparent; artful and inconsistent; profound and superficial; obscure and memorable. Commentators, from the ancient period to the present, often seek to smooth over the Gospel's inconsistencies and difficulties. It is these very contradictions, however, that have permitted readers throughout the centuries to find the Gospel both fascinating and meaningful to their own lives and situations.

The Gospel is most often associated with Ephesus in Asia Minor (today's Selçuk in Izmir province, Turkey), though an early version of the Gospel may have originated in Judea. Until the first publication of the Rylands Library Papyrus 52 in 1935, the Gospel was often dated to the mid-second century CE. P[52] is an Egyptian codex fragment of John 18:31-33, 37-38, which has been reliably dated to 135–160 CE. Allowing for a period of several decades for circulation, a late first-century date for the Gospel's final version is likely.

The Book

The Gospel itself points to the unnamed Beloved Disciple, who makes his first appearance at the Last Supper (John 13), as the author of, or the authority behind, the Gospel (19:26-27, 35; 21:24). Traditionally, this disciple has been identified as John the son of Zebedee. This identification is unlikely, however. The Beloved Disciple is closely associated with Jerusalem and, according to the Gospel, had links to the high priest, an unlikely connection for Galilean fishermen such as the sons of Zebedee. The author of John's Gospel therefore remains unknown.

Another puzzle is John's relationship to the Synoptic Gospels. Clement of Alexandria (c. 150–211/216) asserted that John's Gospel was meant to supplement the Synoptics (Matthew, Mark, Luke; see Eusebius's fourth-century *Hist. eccl.* 6.14.7). Many modern scholars disagree. Although some Johannine stories are paralleled in the Synoptics (e.g., the feeding of the multitudes [6:1-14; cf. Matt. 14:13-21; Mark 16:32-44; Luke 9:10-17], Jesus' stroll on the water [6:16-21; cf. Matt. 14:22; Mark 6:45-51]), most of its episodes (e.g., the wedding at Cana [2:1-13], Jesus' encounter with the Samaritan woman [4:1-42], the raising of Lazarus [11:1-44]) are unique. Also unique is the Gospel's Christology, which emphasizes his existence prior to the world's creation and his identity as God's only-begotten Son. It is therefore unlikely that the Fourth Gospel drew directly on any of the Synoptics (Smith).

Despite the simplicity of its Greek, the Fourth Gospel is a literary masterpiece. It has a clear narrative structure built around Jesus' "signs" (miracle stories) and amplified by thematic discourses. It makes superb use of literary devices such as symbolism, irony, contrast, repetition, and misunderstanding. The book also, however, contains blatant discontinuities. For example, the story of the healing of a lame man, set in Jerusalem (ch. 5), is followed immediately by a note that places Jesus on the "other side of the Sea of Galilee" (6:1) without mentioning how and when he got there. In 14:31, Jesus tells his disciples to "Rise, let us be on our way," and then continues his lengthy discourse for two more chapters.

These awkward transitions suggest that the Gospel was heavily redacted before reaching its present form. The enumeration of two of the signs-stories (the "beginning of the signs," 2:11; "the second sign," 4:54) has been taken as evidence that the Gospel incorporated an earlier source consisting of a series of numbered miracle stories (Fortna; Von Wahlde). Theological inconsistencies may suggest that the Gospel was redacted several times in response to changing circumstances and ideas. There is currently, however, no manuscript evidence of redaction, with one exception: the story of the woman caught in adultery (7:53—8:13), which most scholars consider to be non-Johannine.

In its present form, the book divides easily into two parts: the Book of Signs (1:19—12:50), which is structured around a series of miracles or signs; and the Book of Glory (13:1—20:31), which begins with the Last Supper and ends with the resurrection appearances. The book is introduced by a prologue (1:1-18) and concludes with an epilogue (21:1-25).

The Hero

John's Jesus differs significantly from his Synoptic counterpart. He speaks in long discourses rather than pithy parables. While he heals the sick, feeds the multitudes, and walks on water, as in the Synoptics, he also speaks, only here, with Samaritans (John 4), raises the dead (John 11), and washes his disciples' feet (John 13).

These stark differences, and John's relatively late date, raise the question of this Gospel's value for historical Jesus research. Clement of Alexandria's (150–215 CE) famous description of the Gospel of John as the "spiritual Gospel" may imply that it is valuable for spiritual formation but not for historical understanding (Elowsky 2006, xix). The tendency to discount John as a source for the historical Jesus has been challenged in recent years, however (e.g., Fredriksen; Anderson, Just, and Thatcher).

The Story

The Gospel of John concerns a Galilean who gathers followers, performs miracles, teaches, rouses the ire of the Jewish leadership, and ends up before the Roman governor, who sentences him to death. In literary terms, this story is a tragedy because it ends in the wrongful execution of an innocent man. Because it is set in a specific time—the first third of the first century CE, when Pilate was the Roman governor of Judea and Caiaphas was high priest—and in specific geographical locations—the Galilee, Judea, and Samaria—the story can also be described as a historical tale (which is not to claim that it is historically accurate in its details).

This historical tale, however, is embedded in a larger cosmological story, about God's Son who existed with God before creation, came to dwell among humankind, and returned to God. In contrast to the historical tale, this cosmological tale is not bound in space and time but has the cosmos as its location and eternity as its time frame.

The two tales intersect at the incarnation (1:14) and the passion. The discourses draw the readers into the meanings of Jesus' signs within the cosmological tale. Indeed, the purpose of the Gospel is to help readers discern Jesus' cosmic significance within and through the signs "written in this book" (20:30-31).

The Message

The Gospel's main message is christological. John's Jesus is the preexistent Son of God, whom God sent into the world as God's agent, and the son of man, an apocalyptic figure who exercises judgment on God's behalf. Despite the prevalence of "son" language, the precise relationship between Jesus and God is uncertain. Is Jesus equivalent—in power, in majesty—to God? Does he have authority in himself, or is his authority derived from his relationship to the Father? Christology is closely linked to soteriology (the doctrine of salvation): those who believe in Jesus as the Christ and the Son of God will have "life in his name." John's Jesus insists that believers have eternal life in the present at the same time he promises eternal life in the future.

The most problematic element of John's message concerns the Jews and Judaism. The Gospel refers seventy times to *hoi Ioudaioi* ("the Jews"), far more than any other New Testament book. The Gospel makes ample use of the Hebrew Bible and has parallels to some postbiblical Jewish traditions. Yet its overall depiction of Jews and Judaism is negative. John's Jews are Jesus' archenemies. They interrogate him, challenge him, and pursue him unto death. In 8:44, Jesus tells a group of Jews that they have the devil as their father, an accusation that echoes through antisemitic literature to the present day. These negative statements may reflect a historical tension between the Johannine followers of Christ and the Jews who did not follow Christ, even if the details of their relationship cannot be determined.

The intended meaning and the best English translation of *hoi Ioudaioi* in the Gospel of John remain matters of considerable contention among scholars. Although most English translations use the term "the Jews," some scholars have argued vigorously for other options, such as "the Jewish authorities" (Von Wahlde) or, most prominently, "the Judeans" (Lowe; Mason; cf. Miller). These suggestions are motivated by what is seen as a discontinuity between the ancient *Ioudaioi*, with which the Gospel writer and audiences may have been familiar, and the modern "Jews" as known to contemporary readers and scholars of the Fourth Gospel. Some believe that using the term "Jews" for *hoi Ioudaioi* runs the risk of spreading antisemitism, given that many of the Gospel's references to *hoi Ioudaioi* are negative or even hostile. Translating *hoi Ioudaioi* as "the Jewish authorities," or "the leaders of the people," conveys the clear message that it is not the Jewish people as a whole who opposed Jesus or led to his death. Others argue that the *hoi Ioudaioi* of the first century were an ethnic group rather than a religious group. For that reason, it is preferable to translate the term as "the Judeans," an ethnic and geographic marker, rather than as "the Jews," which, in their view, refers to a group that practices the religion of "Judaism," which, some insist, did not yet exist at the time the Gospel was written (Mason). Both of these proposals are problematic. While in some contexts, such as 19:7, the term appears to refer to the authorities as distinct from the Jewish crowds, there are many passages in which the term clearly refers to the people as a whole (e.g., 2:13; 12:9). And while it may be true that the first-century *Ioudaioi* were distinguished by more than beliefs and practices that might be defined as "religious," the same is true of the modern term "Jew," which identifies not only those who actively engage in Jewish religious practices and customs but also secular Jews who explicitly reject those practices, as well as a broad spectrum of people in between. The best translation, therefore, remains "the Jews" (Reinhartz 2001a; Levine 2006, 162).

The Purpose and Audience

The Gospel's narrative, theology, message, and language suggest that it was written within and for a specifically "Johannine" group, perhaps the same group for which the Johannine epistles were composed (Painter). The community may have included Samaritans and gentiles alongside Jews, given that the Gospel draws on Jewish, Samaritan, and gentile traditions, ideas, and modes of expression.

Attempts at a detailed reconstruction of the community's historical circumstances have been based on the three verses (9:22; 12:42; 16:2) that refer to *aposynagōgoi* (people who are cast out of the synagogue). Some argue that these verses refer to an actual expulsion of Johannine followers from the synagogue on account of their faith in Christ (Martyn; Lincoln, 84). As the present commentary will explain, this hypothesis is problematic on historical and methodological grounds. Yet even if the expulsion theory is tenuous, the Gospel's hostility toward the Jews is real. It likely reflects a process of identity-formation on the part of the community, which also entailed efforts at differentiation from the Jewish community. This perspective does not excuse the Gospel's rhetoric, but it makes it possible to acknowledge the Gospel's place in the process by which Christianity became a separate religion, to appreciate the beauty of its language, and to recognize the spiritual power that it continues to have in the lives of many of its Christian readers.

The Commentary

The Fourth Gospel invites readers to insert ourselves into the text and even to a certain extent encourages us to become particular types of readers: compliant readers who will agree with the worldview it presents, and align themselves unequivocally with the light, life, and Spirit as defined in this Gospel and against the forces of darkness, death, and flesh, again as defined by John. But readers have a choice as to whether and how they insert themselves in this text, and it is often by resisting or challenging a compliant reading that we can truly engage with John's Gospel.

This commentary, like the others in this volume, will have three levels. The first level examines the text in its ancient context. In this level, we will take the position of a late first-century reader, while recognizing that bridging such a profound distance in time, space, culture, and language is ultimately impossible.

The second level, the text in the interpretive tradition, will comment on the text in the interpretive tradition. Because it is not possible in a brief commentary to do an exhaustive survey of the interpretive tradition, the comments here will focus primarily on how patristic readers understood certain key issues. The church fathers were keen and insightful readers of Scriptures. Although they often bent over backward to smooth over the contradictions with the Fourth Gospel and the differences between John and the Synoptics, their approaches to some of the text's difficulties can help illuminate our own understanding.

The third level, the text in contemporary discussion, considers some of the issues and questions raised by this text for our own place and time. The focus here will be on us as real readers. Because every real reader is different, the comments will necessarily reflect my own perspective as a Jewish scholar of the New Testament who is nevertheless respectful of those traditions and communities for which this Gospel is canonical. My starting point is the conviction that while the Gospel attempts to steer us in the direction of compliance, it is by resisting that pull and critical questioning that will lead us to a deeper understanding and engagement with the text, whatever our personal religious beliefs and commitments.

References to "John" are not meant to be taken as statements of authorship but simply as a shorthand for the name of the book. Biblical quotations are from the New Revised Standard Version, unless otherwise stated. References to patristic sources in the second level of commentary are from *The Ancient Commentary to the Scriptures* (Elowsky 2006; 2007), unless otherwise noted.

John 1:1-18: The Prologue

■ THE TEXT IN ITS ANCIENT CONTEXT

The opening of John's Gospel may surprise first-time readers familiar with the opening chapters of Matthew and Luke. Absent are the virgin Mary, the manger, the magi, and all other elements of the "Christmas story." Instead, the prologue situates Jesus within the relationship between God and humankind that begins with Genesis, and proclaims the universal scope and significance of the Gospel's salvation story. The prologue's opening words, "In the beginning," quote the opening of the biblical book of Genesis (Gen. 1:1). The quotation signals that what follows is not just another biography but a story of life-giving significance for all creation.

Poetic Style

The prologue makes use of "staircase parallelism," in which an important word at the end of one line is taken up at the beginning of the next: "In the beginning was the *Word*, and the *Word* was with God" (1:1); "in him was *life*, and the *life* was the *light* of all people. The *light* shines in the darkness" (1:4-5). Some view this poetic style as evidence that the prologue was a pre-Johannine, independent hymn that was incorporated into the Gospel and adapted to serve as its introduction.

Wisdom Imagery

The prologue's "Word," though masculine in both grammatical and human form, is remarkably similar to "Lady Wisdom" of biblical and postbiblical Wisdom literature. In Prov. 8:22-31, Wisdom describes her role in the creation of the world, and the intimate delight of her relationship with God (8:30-31). Wisdom and Logos are closely linked in the writings of the Alexandrian Jewish philosopher Philo (20 BCE–50 CE) and the Aramaic targumim, in which God's assistant is the *memra*, a masculine term meaning "word." This prior linking suggests that the fluidity between feminine Wisdom and masculine Logos is not the Gospel's innovation.

The phrase "lived among us" (NRSV) is more literally, and vividly, translated as "tabernacled among us," thereby preserving the allusion to the Shekinah, the divine presence (cf. *Tg. Onq.* at Deut. 12:5), and the tabernacle that the Israelites constructed in the wilderness (e.g., Exod. 25:9), in which God's presence was uniquely palpable.

The prologue also introduces key metaphors, figures, and themes that will be developed in the Gospel's stories and discourses. The metaphors include "light" and "life" to describe Jesus and the opportunity he will provide to humankind, and "world," a multilayered term—*cosmos*, in Greek— that can refer to the physical world, to humankind, but also more narrowly to those who refuse to believe. John 1:6-8 refers to John the Baptist as the one who testifies to the "light" but is not himself the light. John 1:17 contrasts the law that was given through Moses with the grace and truth now given through Jesus Christ.

Finally, the prologue draws its imagined or ideal audience into the Gospel's narrative and theological world. The first person plural in 1:14—"we have seen his glory, the glory as of a father's only son, full of grace and truth"—situates the reader alongside the narrator as a member of the group that, in contrast to Jesus' own people, "received him, . . . believed in his name," and therefore became "children of God" (1:12-13).

▌ THE TEXT IN THE INTERPRETIVE TRADITION

The church fathers viewed the Johannine account of the Word as complementary to the infancy narratives of Matthew and Luke. Augustine (354–430 CE) commented that Christ's dual nature required two births, one divine—described in John—and one human—described in Matthew and Luke (*Serm.* 196.1; Elowsky 2006, 3). His contemporary Jerome (347–420) stressed his inability to comprehend how the Word was made flesh, admitting, "The doctrine from God, I have; the science of it, I do not have" (*Homily* 87, On John 1:1-14; Elowsky 2006, 41).

The opening lines of the prologue have fired the imagination since ancient times. Their "celestial flights" led to the use of the eagle to represent the Fourth Gospel (R. E. Brown 1966, 18). The words were thought to have healing power, and for that reason were used in long-standing custom of the Western church as a benediction over the sick and over newly baptized children and as amulets to protect against illness (R. E. Brown 1966, 18).

▌ THE TEXT IN CONTEMPORARY DISCUSSION

The poetic beauty of the prologue can make the human spirit soar and provide a glimpse of the cosmic context of our mundane existence. But its binary contrasts—between light and darkness,

Moses and Jesus, law and truth, acceptance and rejection—also construct a polarized worldview that is both supersessionist and hierarchical. The claim that Jesus—the Word—provides the only path to knowledge of God explicitly invalidates any belief system, including Judaism, that does not include faith in Jesus as the Christ and Savior. By occupying the compliant reading position that the prologue, through its use of the first person plural and other techniques, prescribes, we become complicit in this invalidation.

But we are not required to be compliant readers in order to understand the prologue, or the Gospel as a whole, and appreciate its beauty. Although the Gospel narrator steers us relentlessly toward compliance, we as readers are autonomous and therefore free to choose our own subject positions, to resist the prescribed response, accept it, or modify it, to investigate what may lie behind the polarizing rhetoric, and to raise our own questions, at the same time that we appreciate the Gospel's language and ideas.

The Book of Signs (1:19—12:50)

1:19-34: The Testimony of John the Baptist

■ THE TEXT IN ITS ANCIENT CONTEXT

The Book of Signs (1:19—12:50) opens with priests and Levites from Jerusalem interrogating John the Baptist. To their open-ended question, "Who are you?" John responds more specifically that he is neither the Messiah, nor Elijah, nor the prophet. He is merely the forerunner of a far worthier man, "the voice in the wilderness" who cries, "Make straight the way of the Lord." The quotation of Isa. 40:3 is taken from the Greek version (Septuagint) in which *the voice* is "in the wilderness," rather than the Hebrew (Masoretic text) version, in which not the voice but *the way of the Lord* is in the wilderness.

Jesus makes his announced appearance the next day. John continues his testimony by describing a past occurrence: the descent of the Spirit on Jesus, and Jesus' identification as the one who "baptizes with the Holy Spirit" (1:33). The Fourth Gospel does not recount Jesus' own baptism, which in the Synoptics is the occasion on which the dove, or the Holy Spirit, descends on Jesus.

■ THE TEXT IN THE INTERPRETIVE TRADITION

The Gospel's omission of the baptism account may reflect some discomfort with the notion that the one who removes the world's sin (1:29) would have been baptized by John. The church fathers read the baptism back into the Johannine narrative. John Chrysostom (347–407) explained that baptism allowed John to testify publicly, and provided Jesus with his first disciples (*Homilies on the Gospel of John* 17.1–2; Elowsky 2006, 68).

■ THE TEXT IN CONTEMPORARY DISCUSSION

Implicit in John's account is the story of a master—the Baptist—who gradually lost his following to a former disciple. The Baptist is remarkably gracious about Jesus' ascendancy, and anxious that both the authorities and his own followers know the truth. The historicity of this subtext is anyone's guess, but the scenario itself is not uncommon in religious and many other contexts. The passage provides an opening for thinking about how power, authority, and leadership can shift within and between communities, and how such changes are best handled.

1:35-51: Call of the Disciples

▌ THE TEXT IN ITS ANCIENT CONTEXT

John the Baptist testifies to two disciples who then follow Jesus, converse with him, and believe. One of those two disciples, Andrew, testifies to his brother Simon. Simon comes to Jesus, who renames him Cephas (Peter; 1:42). Jesus then travels to the Galilee and finds Philip (1:43), who then testifies to Nathanael. Nathanael is initially skeptical but then comes to Jesus and, astounded by Jesus' prophetic abilities, exclaims: "Rabbi, you are the Son of God! You are the King of Israel!" (1:49). With the exception of Philip, Jesus does not actively recruit the disciples. Rather, one disciple testifies to another, who then comes to Jesus for a personal encounter.

The sequence concludes with a prophecy by Jesus to Nathanael that he "will see heaven opened and the angels of God ascending and descending upon the Son of Man" (1:51), an allusion to Jacob's ladder (Genesis 28). The son of man title is a direct translation from the Aramaic *bar nasha*, which literally means a human being. But in this Gospel, the title refers to Jesus' role in the cosmos and his relationship to God.

▌ THE TEXT IN THE INTERPRETIVE TRADITION

For Chrysostom, Simon's name change (1:42) demonstrates Jesus' divine identity: "He does this to show that it was he who gave the old covenant, that it was he who altered names, who called Abram 'Abraham,' and Sarai 'Sarah' and Jacob 'Israel.'" The difference is that in these cases, each person received a different name, whereas "now we all have one name, that which is greater than any. We are called 'Christians,' and 'sons of God' and 'friends' and [his] 'body'" (*Homilies on the Gospel of John* 19.2–3; Elowsky 2006, 82). Chrysostom's comment alludes to (among other passages) John 5, 10, and 11, in which Jesus calls the dead, his sheep, and Lazarus by name, and in doing so, renews their lives. The same may also be true for Simon, whose life is renewed when he meets Jesus.

▌ THE TEXT IN CONTEMPORARY DISCUSSION

The paradigm of the call, whereby discipleship is initiated through personal testimony, ascribes equal importance to the human witness and to the divine, and it has served as the model for Christian evangelizing activity for almost two millennia. But those on the receiving end today, whether from door-to-door missionaries or from well-meaning acquaintances, can experience evangelizing activities—and the assumption of some that the only route to a good life is faith in Christ—as at best an intrusion and at worst as offensive. Indeed, toward the end of the twentieth century, a number of Christian communions officially renounced the cause of "evangelizing" Jews, thus opening the door to more mutual conversation.

2:1-12: Jesus' First Sign: Wedding at Cana

■ The Text in Its Ancient Context

Jesus' public ministry begins when he turns water into wine at a wedding in the Galilean town of Cana, approximately nine miles (fifteen kilometers) north of Nazareth. In referring to this act as the "first of his signs," the narrator creates an expectation that there will be more signs, perhaps indeed an entire series of them, and also signals that these acts are not mere miracles, designed to demonstrate Jesus' ability to overturn the natural order of things, but signs that point the way to something important: the cosmological tale.

Jesus' mother spurs Jesus into action by mentioning that the wine has run out. She remains unnamed here (as throughout this Gospel), but has confidence in his ability to rectify the problem. Jesus responds: "Woman, what concern is that to you and to me? My hour has not yet come" (2:4). But she is not put off by Jesus' apparent refusal (2:4) and instructs the servants to do whatever Jesus says. Modern readers may bristle at the idea of a young man calling his mother "woman," but as the young man is Jesus, commentators have alternative explanations.

In this case, however, we may safely acquit Jesus of the charge of disrespect. Jesus consistently prefaces his revelations to women—the Samaritan woman (4:21), Jesus' mother again (19:26), and Mary Magdalene (20:13, 15)—in this way. Rather than a marker of social distance, the term "woman" functions like "behold" or "truly, truly I say to you" and parallels the form Jesus uses to address God as Father. Indeed, Jesus makes revelatory statements to individual women perhaps even more frequently, and with less ambivalence, than he does to men. In addition to the three women just mentioned, he reveals his truths to Mary and Martha of Bethany (11:25; 12:7). This motif renders the Gospel of John amenable to feministic historical, literary, and theological interpretation (see the collected essays in Levine 2003).

The passage also introduces the term "hour," which appears in several different formulations throughout the Gospel. The reference is to the time of Jesus' death and glorification. The messianic and salvific echoes in this passage may also be conveyed by the comment that it happened on the third day. While this may simply be a chronological marker indicating that it was the third day after the preceding event—Jesus' comments to Nathanael—it may equally foreshadow the resurrection, just as the wedding may allude to the messianic banquet, the feast that will celebrate the inauguration of God's rule (Kobel, 85–86). The passage shows that first-century Jews practiced ritual hand-washing prior to eating a meal; the practice is otherwise known from later rabbinic sources (*b. Ber.* 53b, *b. Shab.* 62b). The "bridegroom" is a double entendre that refers literally to the Cana bridegroom but, in the cosmological setting of the Gospel, also alludes to Jesus as the eschatological bridegroom (cf. 4:29).

■ The Text in the Interpretive Tradition

Like modern commentators, the church fathers attempted to explain Jesus' apparent rudeness. Bede (672/673–735) stated categorically that "he would not dishonor his mother, since he orders us to honor our father and mother" (*Homilies on the Gospels* 1.14; Elowsky 2006, 95). Chrysostom too insists that Jesus honors his mother, on the basis of Luke 2:51, and provides a helpful general principle governing filial obligation: we must be subject to our parents but only as long as they "throw no obstacle in the way of God's commands." But "when they demand anything at an unseasonable time or cut us off from spiritual things," we are not to comply (*Homilies on the Gospel of John* 21.2; Elowsky 2006, 91).

▌THE TEXT IN CONTEMPORARY DISCUSSION

The fact that this Gospel can proclaim an exalted view of Christ without an annunciation scene raises the question of whether the belief in Mary's virginity is indeed essential to Christian faith.

Also striking in this passage is the notion of abundance. While many are accustomed to bounty in the material aspects of daily life, this passage can serve as a reminder that for some, abundance is an experience as rare as a wedding celebration.

2:13-25: Jesus' Sign of Authority over the Temple

▌THE TEXT IN ITS ANCIENT CONTEXT

In the Synoptics, the cleansing of the temple occurs at the end of Jesus' ministry and spurs the Jewish authorities' decision to press for Jesus' death (Matt. 21:17; Mark 11:15-19; Luke 9:45-48). In John, however, this episode is Jesus' first public appearance. The presence of merchants and money-changers in the temple precinct may seem an affront to the dignity and holy nature of the temple. Prior to the temple's destruction (70 CE), however, Jewish worship was carried out primarily through regular sacrifices. During the three pilgrimage festivals (Tabernacles, Passover, Weeks), pilgrims needed sacrificial animals and birds, and had to change their local currency into the Tyrian half-shekel for the temple tax (Exod. 30:11-16). Merchants and money-changers were needed. Why, then, did Jesus create a scene?

For this Gospel, one answer lies in Ps. 69:9: "Zeal for your house will consume me." The episode asserts Jesus' entitlement to his father's house, by virtue of his role as the Son of God. At the same time, when Jesus challenges the Jews to "destroy this temple, and in three days I will raise it up" (2:19), the narrator explains, he did not intend the physical temple but rather the temple of his body.

▌THE TEXT IN THE INTERPRETIVE TRADITION

To smooth over the contradiction between John and the Synoptics, the church fathers posit two "cleansing" events (Elowsky 2006, 101). Augustine uses the occasion to chastise "those who seek their own interests in the church rather than those of Jesus Christ" and warns: "Let them beware of the scourge of ropes. The dove is not for sale; it is given gratis, for it is called grace" (*Tract. Ev. Jo.* 10.6.1–3; Elowsky 2006, 101).

▌THE TEXT IN CONTEMPORARY DISCUSSION

The temple scene is shocking due to the uncharacteristic violence and hot emotion that it attributes to this otherwise cool, calm, and collected Savior. One cannot but wonder if a less violent act might have served to state Jesus' claim to his Father's house. It may be that the Gospel reflects the post-70 era, when the temple no longer stood, the sacrifices no longer took place, and the evangelist or community had only vague knowledge of the pilgrimage festivals. But the passage raises the more fundamental question of when, if ever, and under what circumstances, if at all, it is appropriate to use a violent act to demonstrate sovereignty, ownership, or entitlement.

3:1-21: Nicodemus

■ THE TEXT IN ITS ANCIENT CONTEXT

Jesus' first extended discourse is a dialogue with a Pharisaic leader named Nicodemus, who comes under the cover of darkness. To him, Jesus utters the now famous words: "No one can see the kingdom of God without being born from above" (3:3), or born again (the source for the term "born-again Christianity"). Interpreting this saying literally, Nicodemus wonders how one can reenter the womb and be reborn. But Jesus was referring to spiritual, not physical, rebirth.

It is difficult to discern where Jesus' discourse ends and the narrator's commentary begins. Greek manuscripts do not include punctuation, but many commentators argue that verses 16-21 belong to the narrator because they refer to "the Son" in the third person. But perhaps this problem does not demand resolution. In this Gospel, Jesus' discourses and the narrator's commentaries are similar in theology and in phraseology, thereby suggesting a complete congruency between Jesus' words and the narrator's comments.

■ THE TEXT IN THE INTERPRETIVE TRADITION

For most church fathers, rebirth was associated with baptism, which, accompanied by repentance, resulted in the remission of former sins (Justin Martyr, *1 Apol.* 61; Gregory of Nazianzus, *On Holy Baptism*, Oration 40.8; Elowsky 2006, 109, 111). Hilary of Poitiers (300–368) attempts to explain how God's sacrifice of his only Son can express divine love for the world: "Gifts of price are the evidence of affection: the greatness of the surrender is evidence of the greatness of the love. God, who loved the world, gave no adopted son but his own, his only begotten [Son]" (*On the Trinity* 6.40; Elowsky 2006, 126).

■ THE TEXT IN CONTEMPORARY DISCUSSION

The idea of human sacrifice—especially of one's own child—as an expression of love seems counterintuitive. Its roots are buried in the sacrificial systems that were the dominant form of worship in many ancient cultures. Yet even in the Hebrew Bible, the idea of sacrificing a beloved child is shocking, as in Judges 11, in which the warrior Jephthah vows to sacrifice the first thing—person— that comes out of his house to greet him if he wins a battle (Judg. 11:31). A closer parallel is the "binding" of Isaac. In Genesis 22, God orders Abraham to sacrifice his only son, the one whom he loves, Isaac, but Abraham receives a last-minute reprieve. By contrast, the Fourth Gospel insists, God went all the way. If Abraham was motivated by love of God to obey such a difficult order, how much more meaningful is God's sacrifice, which was motivated by love of the world? Nevertheless, God's loss is not absolute, because his Son is resurrected, and returns to live with him.

3:22-36: Jesus the Baptizer

▋THE TEXT IN ITS ANCIENT CONTEXT

In John's Gospel, the ministries of Jesus and John the Baptist overlap and, indeed, are competitors. The Fourth Gospel has the Baptist reassure his disciples that it is not only inevitable but actually essential that Jesus' followers outnumber the Baptist's disciples (3:30). From this point onward, the Baptist is absent from the Gospel narrative.

▋THE TEXT IN THE INTERPRETIVE TRADITION

Bede used this text as an opportunity to speak about the church "gathered from among all nations," which he calls "a virgin pure of heart, perfect in love, bound to him in the bond of peace, in chastity of body and soul and in the unity of the Catholic faith. . . . Our Lord therefore committed his bride to his friends who are the preachers of the true gospel" (*Exposition on the Gospel of John* 3; Elowsky 2006, 135).

▋THE TEXT IN CONTEMPORARY DISCUSSION

We may speculate that it may not have been easy to differentiate the followers of Jesus from the followers of other figures such as the Baptist. Non-Christians often have the same difficulty when surveying the Christian landscape today. The Baptist's deferential behavior raises the question of how competing groups are to relate to one another.

4:1-42: The Samaritan Woman

▋THE TEXT IN ITS ANCIENT CONTEXT

Chapter 4 opens on a troubling note: Jesus must leave the vicinity because the Pharisees have heard about his baptizing activity. The narrator clarifies that it was the disciples, and not Jesus himself, who baptized, but the significance of this distinction is unclear given that they were acting on Jesus' behalf. The focus of this chapter, however, is on the rest stop that Jesus takes in the Samaritan town of Sychar en route to the Galilee. Sitting by a well, he asks a Samaritan woman for water, and at the end of their conversation, the woman returns to her city without her water jar, as an apostle of the Messiah (4:29).

Jesus and the woman are alone, as Jesus' disciples had gone into the city to buy food (4:8). The Samaritan woman is surprised by Jesus' request for water, for, as the narrator comments, Jews do not share with Samaritans. Jesus offers her living water—far superior to the well water that she can give him—and then inquires about her husband. He reveals his detailed knowledge of her unusual situation: she has already had five husbands "and the one you have now is not your husband" (4:18). Rather than take offense, the woman proclaims him to be a prophet. She asks about a difference between Jews and Samaritans, concerning the location for worship: Gerizim or Jerusalem? Jesus initially affirms the contrast between Jews and Samaritans: "You worship what you do not know; we worship what we know, for salvation is from the Jews." He then prophesies a time when worship will concentrate in neither location but in Jesus himself. The woman discerns that he may be the Messiah. The disciples return, and, while surprised that he is speaking with a woman, they do not confront him. Their surprise is in itself surprising, for the Gospel gives no indication that Jesus refrained from speaking to women.

The episode is reminiscent of the biblical stories in which boy meets girl at well (4:12; see Gen. 24:15-31; 29:9-13; Exod. 2:16-21). The present encounter does not end in betrothal but in something much greater: the promise, or assurance, of eternal life (Eslinger). In speaking with the Samaritan woman, Jesus transgresses boundaries of both gender and ethnicity. The scene also implies that there may have been Samaritans among the Gospel's intended readership.

The disciples bring food. Just as he redefined water from the mundane to the eternal, so does Jesus elevate the notion of food from physical to spiritual nourishment: doing his Father's will. He continues enigmatically: "Four months more, then comes the harvest," which the disciples will reap though they did not plant the field. The episode draws to a close when the Samaritans to whom the woman has testified invite Jesus to stay with them. Afterward, they declare that their faith is no longer because of her words but because of their encounter. This episode echoes the pattern of the call of the disciples: the Samaritan woman meets Jesus, testifies to others, who encounter Jesus in person and declare their faith. The passage presumes the readers' knowledge that the Samaritans, like the Jews, believed in the eventual coming of a savior figure, whom the Samaritans called *Taheb* (Crown, Pummer, and Tal, 224–26).

▌ THE TEXT IN THE INTERPRETIVE TRADITION

In leaving Judea, Chrysostom explains, Christ aimed "to take away their malice and soften their envy." Although in a confrontation Jesus could have prevented the Jews from hurting him, he preferred to do things "in a human way" so that people would "believe his incarnation" (*Homilies on the Gospel of John* 31.3; Elowsky 2006, 141). Augustine adds that Jesus "wanted to provide himself as an example for believers in time to come, that it was no sin for a servant of God to seek refuge from the fury of persecutors" (*Tract. Ev. Jo.* 15.2; Elowsky 2006, 142).

Scholars who attempt to soften the Gospel's harsh verdict on the Jews point to Jesus' statement in 4:22 that "salvation is from the Jews." The church fathers were not similarly motivated but nevertheless came up with the most logical interpretation of this verse: that it refers to Jesus' own Jewish origins. As Augustine notes, "Of what lineage was Christ born? Of the Jews. . . . He did not say, after all, 'salvation is for the Jews' but 'salvation is from the Jews'" (*Serm.* 375.1; Elowsky 2006, 159).

For Origen, the woman is an apostle and a role model, "for by recording the woman's commendation for those capable of reading with understanding, the Evangelist challenges us to this goal" (*Comm. Jo.* 13.169; Elowsky 2006, 166). Chrysostom admires her for exhibiting "the actions of an apostle, preaching the gospel to everyone she could and calling them to Jesus. She even drew out a whole city to hear him" (*Homilies on the Gospel of John* 32.1; Elowsky 2006, 154).

▌ THE TEXT IN CONTEMPORARY DISCUSSION

The Gospel implies that the message of Jesus as Son of God and Savior is open to all regardless of gender and ethnicity, and overcomes both sets of socially constructed boundaries. Jesus' discourse also decouples true worship from any specific location. In doing so, he establishes a framework for a universal mode of covenantal relationship with God where women and men, Jews, Samaritans and gentiles, can worship where they are, united in a community whose salvific agent came "from the Jews." Christian "universalism" has often been contrasted favorably with Jewish "particularism," suggesting that Christianity is broad and accepting while Judaism is narrow and exclusivistic. Open and welcoming as this message sounds, the insistence on one single path or "way" (cf. 14:6) to covenantal relationship with God in itself is an exclusive message that invalidates other choices.

4:43-54: Second Sign: Healing of the Official's Son

▌THE TEXT IN ITS ANCIENT CONTEXT

After his stay with the Samaritans, Jesus continues his journey to the Galilee, as the narrator maintains a quiet sense of danger with the proverb—"a prophet has no honor in the prophet's own country" (see Matt. 13:53-58; Mark 6:1-6; Luke 4:22-24; *Gos. Thom.* 31).

An official asks Jesus to come down to Capernaum to heal his son. Jesus refuses but assures the man that his son will live. As the man departs, his slaves (or servants) meet him with the good news of his son's recovery, and they all become believers. Jesus has healed the son by words and from a distance. The narrative describes this act as Jesus' second Cana sign—an enumeration important for the hypothesis that the Gospel made use of a preexisting "signs source"—but Jesus criticizes the nobleman for requiring a sign in order to believe: "Unless you see signs and wonders you will not believe" (4:48). Although addressed to an individual, the verb "you see" is not singular but plural. This warning is intended for all readers, not only this distraught father.

▌THE TEXT IN THE INTERPRETIVE TRADITION

Chrysostom comments on the weakness of the official's faith, who needed confirmation before believing fully. Chrysostom dismisses the official's approach to Jesus as "nothing special, for parents often are so carried away by their affection that they consult not only those physicians they depend on, but even people they do not depend on at all." The lesson? Do not wait for miracles or lose faith when prayers are not answered, for those whom God loves he also chastens (*Homilies on the Gospel of John* 35.2–3; Elowsky 2006, 174).

▌THE TEXT IN CONTEMPORARY DISCUSSION

Chrysostom accurately describes the frame of mind of someone whose loved one is ill. But Jesus' rebuke also fits into a major Johannine theme: the tension between hearing and seeing. A second tension, between presence and absence, is also not fully resolved. Despite Jesus' words in 4:48, the Gospel continues to present signs and wonders that, if properly—cosmologically—understood, can be a basis for faith. The tension is by no means limited to this Gospel, or to issues of faith, but permeates our own lives due to the rapid growth of digital communication. Do email and Skype overcome absence or contribute to alienation? Are Facebook friendships real or illusory? Do virtual experiences interfere with or enhance our "real" relationships? Although our digital dilemmas were not even remotely anticipated in the first century, the followers of Jesus who lived after his death had to grapple with presence and absence as well. How is a would-be believer to have a personal encounter with Christ in the years after the crucifixion? And how are leaders such as Paul supposed to interact with the communities they founded throughout the region? For Paul, and many others, it was the written word that would serve as their mode of virtual presence, substituting for the real presence of Jesus, and themselves, in a post-Easter world.

5:1-47: Healing on the Sabbath

▌THE TEXT IN ITS ANCIENT CONTEXT

Although the term *sēmeion* is not used, the healing of the lame man, like the two Cana miracles, is a sign that reveals Jesus' identity and relationship to the Father to those who can understand the cosmological story beneath the narrative's surface. The sign takes place on an unnamed Jewish pilgrimage festival and displays a detailed knowledge of the temple area, corroborated by the modern discovery of a second-century healing sanctuary and pool with five porticoes in this approximate location (Freund, Arav, and Bethsaida Excavations Project). The explanation of how healing took place at the pool—an angel of the Lord used to come down in the pool, the water was stirred up, and the first to enter would be healed (5:3)—was known to Tertullian (160–225) and to Chrysostom, but because it is absent from the earliest manuscripts, it is not considered original to the Gospel.

This sign marks an escalation in the conflict with the Jewish authorities. Jewish law permitted violation of the Sabbath to save a life, but in healing a chronically disabled man, the Johannine Jesus was deliberately provoking the authorities. Indeed, the narrator insists that it was because of such Sabbath activities that the Jews began to persecute Jesus (5:16).

The primary conflict, however, is christological. Jesus' response to the Jews' concerns about Sabbath violation is provocative: "My Father is still working, and I also am working." Because birth, growth, death, and other natural processes did not cease on the Sabbath, Philo of Alexandria commented that though God rested on the seventh day of creation, God works on the weekly Sabbath while Jews do not (Philo, *Cher.* 86–90; *Leg.* 1.5–6). In the context of this ancient debate, Jesus' act of healing shows not that the Sabbath is invalid but that, like his Father, he does not stop his divine work.

For the Jews as presented in John's Gospel, this claim is blasphemy and they sought "all the more to kill him, because he was not only breaking the sabbath, but was also calling God his own Father, thereby making himself equal to God" (5:18). The sign is followed by a discourse devoted to two main topics: the Son's divine work of judgment and raising the dead; and the various witnesses to Jesus' identity as God's Son, such as John the Baptist, God, and the Scriptures. The entire discourse has a forensic, judicial tone to it, and concludes with Jesus' judgment on the Jews who have confronted him: by persecuting Jesus, they show their alienation from God.

▌THE TEXT IN THE INTERPRETIVE TRADITION

Although the Johannine Jesus was not inciting Jews to violate the Sabbath, Cyril of Alexandria (376–444) suggests that with faith and new life in Christ, "it was necessary that the old letter of the law should become of no effect and that the typical worship in shadows and empty Jewish customs should be rejected" (*Commentary on the Gospel of John* 2.5; Elowsky 2006, 183).

As Cyril's comments show, John 5 is often (incorrectly) taken as evidence that Jesus abrogated Sabbath observance. Christians and others often view the Jewish Sabbath regulations as restrictive, overly ritualistic, and outmoded. Far from disrupting modern life, however, the Sabbath provides the rest, respite, and temporary retreat from the noise, rush, and anxiety of daily life. Jews who observe the Sabbath experience it as the sanctification of time, as a foretaste of the world to come, a day of spiritual and physical renewal (Heschel). The restrictions on work, travel, and other activities are what make that experience possible.

6:1-21: A Fifth Sign: Feeding of the Multitudes and Walking on Water

■THE TEXT IN ITS ANCIENT CONTEXT

John 6 begins with a sign (although, again, the term *sēmeion* is not used) familiar from the Synoptic Gospels: the feeding of the multitudes, also known as the feeding of the five thousand (see Matt. 14:13-21; Mark 16.32-44; Luke 9:10-17) or the multiplication of the loaves and fishes. The note that "after this Jesus went to the other side of the Sea of Galilee," also called the "Sea of Tiberias," is puzzling, as in the immediately preceding passage Jesus is in Jerusalem, far from the Galilee. The transition to this passage has often been seen as evidence of a redactional process of composition. By remaining in Galilee for the Passover, Jesus fulfills the prophecy to the Samaritan woman, that soon people would worship God neither on Gerizim nor in Jerusalem, but through Jesus (Reinhartz 1989). As in the Synoptics, the feeding miracle is followed by Jesus' walking on water, suggesting that these two events were linked from a very early point in the tradition.

■THE TEXT IN THE INTERPRETIVE TRADITION

As Chrysostom notes, this sign differs from the others thus far recounted in that Jesus gives thanks before performing the miracle. Chrysostom derives from this the principle that it is proper to give thanks to God before eating, perhaps without realizing that Jesus was following the Jewish practice of blessing the bread before a meal. Chrysostom also criticizes the eagerness of the crowd to eat, when earlier they were ready to kill Jesus for his behavior during the feast (*Homilies on the Gospel of John* 42.3; Elowsky 2006, 214).

■THE TEXT IN CONTEMPORARY DISCUSSION

As at the wedding at Cana, the theme in the feeding story is abundance, stunning in its quality, quantity, and its very existence. Jesus' concern for feeding the crowd comes as a surprise, for there is no sign that they expect him to provide lunch. The story would seem to demonstrate responsibility toward the hungry. The crowd does not ask to be fed; rather, it is Jesus who takes this daunting task upon himself. The story emphasizes the wonder inherent in Jesus' ability to feed such a big crowd with a mere five loaves and two fish, but perhaps the larger miracle is the concern to provide for others in the first place. Many ordinary individuals are capable of doing the same. And yet, the discourse that follows does not address this theme but, on the contrary, directs attention away from human needs and responsibilities and focuses instead on forms of "spiritual nourishment" that many in that same crowd refuse or are unable to digest.

6:22-71: The Bread of Life Discourse

■ THE TEXT IN ITS ANCIENT CONTEXT

Those who had eaten their fill finally catch up with Jesus in Capernaum. Playing on the contrast between material food and spiritual food, Jesus criticizes them for eating their fill without understanding the deeper meaning of the experience. The people cannot accept that the true and divine bread is Jesus himself. Even more shocking, however, is the next revelation: Just as people eat bread to sustain their bodies, so must they eat the bread of life in order to sustain their spirits and gain eternal life. Jesus shocks them by warning: "Unless you eat the flesh of the Son of Man and drink his blood, you have no life in you" (6:51-54).

On the surface, and no doubt also to the incredulous crowds, this assertion sounds uncomfortably cannibalistic. But in Christian theology, the passage has often been interpreted in eucharistic terms. It is difficult, however, to pin this discourse down to a single meaning, for its language is reminiscent also of the Passover as the season of salvation, and of pagan rituals of theophagy—eating of God—associated with the Greco-Roman mystery cults of Demeter and Dionysus (Kobel, 234–36, 247), and because the Eucharist plays no part in the Johannine account of the Last Supper (John 13).

Many followers leave, but the Twelve remain, for they "have come to believe and know that you are the Holy One of God" (6:69). Jesus seems reassured, and in turn reassures them that he has chosen them, but introduces a sinister note: "Yet one of you is a devil" (6:70). The narrator reveals information not yet known to the disciples: the betrayer is one of them, Judas Iscariot (6:71).

■ THE TEXT IN THE INTERPRETIVE TRADITION

The eucharistic interpretation of the discourse was widespread among the church fathers. Cyril of Jerusalem compares the bread of life to the showbread that was part of temple worship. The showbread, however, belonged to the "old covenant" that has now been replaced by the "new covenant" in which "the bread of heaven and the cup of salvation . . . sanctify body and soul" (*Mystagogical Lectures* 4.4–6; Elowsky 2006, 239). He notes that "the person who receives the flesh of our Savior Christ and drinks his precious blood . . . shall be one with him" (*Commentary on the Gospel of John* 4.2; Elowsky 2006, 241).

■ THE TEXT IN CONTEMPORARY DISCUSSION

Eating the body and drinking the blood can also refer to consuming Jesus' words and teachings, which provide the nourishment needed to grow and thrive spiritually (Phillips). Just as the food and drink we ingest have a profound effect on health, state of mind, mood, and ability to function in the world, so can the books we read, the conversations we have, and all our worldly encounters change us, nourish us, and help us make our way in the world. But not all words will be beneficial, or equally beneficial, to all.

7:1-52: Festival of Tabernacles

▌THE TEXT IN ITS ANCIENT CONTEXT

John 7 takes place during yet another pilgrimage festival, Tabernacles. During this harvest festival, families and communities are required to live in booths reminiscent of the temporary dwellings in which the Israelites lived during their forty-year wandering in the desert.

When Jesus' brothers urge him to go, he refuses, "for my time has not yet fully come" (7:8). Yet once his brothers leave, Jesus secretly goes as well. In any other story, this about-face would be seen as deception. Commentators are reluctant, however, to view Jesus in this light, and suggest that his earlier refusal was misunderstood by his brothers: Jesus was not refusing to go to Jerusalem, but asserting that it was not his time to "go up" to his Father (R. E. Brown 1966, 308). This is far from convincing, as it does not account for why he went up to Jerusalem "in secret."

The scene then shifts to Jerusalem, and introduces a refrain that extends throughout this and the following chapters: a division among the Jewish crowds as to Jesus' identity. Some defend him as a good man, others condemn him as a deceiver. When Jesus finally arrives, in the middle of the festival, his teachings astonish the people, but the narrator does not reveal those teachings to the reader. The crowds propose a criterion for discerning whether Jesus is the Messiah: "We know where this man is from; but when the Messiah comes, no one will know where he is from" (7:27). This may be an allusion to the tradition of the "hidden messiah," one of several different strands of messianic expectation in the first century (see *1 Enoch* 46:1-3). Yet, from the point of view of the Gospel and the Johannine Jesus, their knowledge is inadequate and misguided. For Jesus does not fundamentally come from Nazareth but from God. For this reason, he fulfills "hidden messiah" criteria, as the readers, but not the crowds, are aware.

The split in the crowd alarms the Pharisees, and they and the chief priests send the temple police to arrest him (7:32). At the same time, Jesus predicts his imminent departure, and prophesies that "you will search for me, but you will not find me; and where I am, you cannot come" (7:34). In a typically Johannine move, the crowds understand, or rather, misunderstand him to be speaking literally, and wonder whether he intends to "go to the Dispersion among the Greeks and teach the Greeks?" (7:35). The reader knows that Jesus is referring to his return to the Father, but the statement may also be an ironic hint that the Word has spread from Judea and Galilee to the gentile communities of the Diaspora.

Each day of the Tabernacles festival is marked by a procession including prayers for deliverance, called Hosannas. The last day was (and still is) called the "great" Hosanna. On this day, Jesus offers "living water" to all. This may be an allusion to the custom during Tabernacles of carrying a golden pitcher of water from the pool of Siloam to the temple as a reminder of the water drawn from the rock in the desert (Num. 20:2-13) and as a symbol of hope for messianic deliverance (Isa. 12:3).

The temple police, sent by the Jewish authorities to arrest Jesus, return empty-handed but astonished: "Never has anyone spoken like this!" (7:46). Nicodemus urges that Jesus be heard out before judgment is passed. The others mock Nicodemus: "Surely you are not also from Galilee, are you? Search and you will see that no prophet is to arise from Galilee" (7:52). The authorities will not be deterred from seeking his death.

■ THE TEXT IN THE INTERPRETIVE TRADITION

The church fathers were unsure what to make of Nicodemus's behavior. Theodore of Mopsuestia (350–428) believes that Nicodemus did not defend Jesus vociferously enough (*Commentary on John* 3.7.52; Elowsky 2006, 271), but Cyril of Alexandria counts Nicodemus among Jesus' secret believers (*Commentary on the Gospel of John* 5.2; Elowsky 2006, 271).

■ THE TEXT IN CONTEMPORARY DISCUSSION

Jesus' duplicity in relation to his brothers adds unexpected depth to this two-dimensional figure. His duplicity was less of a problem for the Gospel writer than for modern commentators. While the desire for an unsullied Jesus is understandable, it is at odds with a Christology that views him as both human and divine. It is unfortunate that so few commentators allow him any of the foibles that help make human beings interesting, if also at times irritating or exasperating. How refreshing it would be to imagine Jesus deliberately deceiving his brothers because he does not want to go to Jerusalem with them! Would this behavior make Jesus any less Christlike? The point is raised most sharply in comparison with the great figures of the Hebrew Bible—Abraham, Moses, David—all mentioned in the Fourth Gospel, and all of whom are portrayed in the Bible as using guile to achieve their purposes.

7:53—8:11: The Adulterous Woman

■ THE TEXT IN ITS ANCIENT CONTEXT

The story of the adulterous woman is a non-Johannine interpolation, appearing in some ancient manuscripts after Luke 21:38, where it fits the narrative context quite well, and in others at its present spot, where it interrupts the Johannine narrative. In this story, Jesus exposes the hypocrisy of the scribes and Pharisees who intend to stone the woman for adultery yet are themselves sinful. Before confronting the leaders, Jesus bends down and writes something with his finger (8:6). What he actually wrote is unknown, but the mention of writing may allude to Jer. 17:13, which declares that those who depart from God shall be written in the earth. Jesus sends the woman on her way without condemnation but adjures her to refrain from sin.

■ THE TEXT IN THE INTERPRETIVE TRADITION

Augustine, like Jerome, knows that the story is absent from some manuscripts of John but believes that it was excised by weak men who fear that their wives would interpret Jesus' injunction to the woman as "liberty to sin with impunity." He also strongly criticizes men who refuse to accept that the prohibition of adultery extends to them as well (*On Adulterous Marriages* 2.7.6, 2.8.7; Elowsky 2006, 276).

■ THE TEXT IN CONTEMPORARY DISCUSSION

This non-Johannine story provides occasion for further reflection on the imperfections of human nature. There is an irony in the passage that often escapes notice. Jesus challenges the scribes: "Let anyone among you who is without sin be the first to throw a stone at her" (8:7). By challenging anyone "among you," Jesus excludes himself as a potential stone-thrower. Implicit but not stated is that, for the New Testament authors, Jesus himself would have been the only person present who was without sin, and yet he does not lift a finger against her. Rather than judging and sentencing the woman, he judges those who would punish her. Missing from the passage, however, is any attribution of responsibility to the man with whom she committed this transgression. This is striking in light of Deuteronomy's explicit statement that both the man and the woman shall be punished (Deut. 22:22).

8:12-59: Confrontation with the Jews

■ THE TEXT IN ITS ANCIENT CONTEXT

This lengthy polemical discourse revolves around two major issues: Jesus' identity and Jewish identity markers. At stake is the fundamental notion of covenant: on what basis does one enter into and maintain a covenantal relationship with God?

In John, Jesus' Jewish identity is not signaled explicitly—he is called a *Ioudaios* only once (4:9)—but it is implied by his participation in the Jewish festivals, his use of biblical quotations, and the locations of his activity. In 8:17, however, the Johannine Jesus distances himself from Judaism, when he declares to the Pharisees, "In *your* law it is written that the testimony of two witnesses is valid" (emphasis added). Perhaps Jesus is simply declaring that as the preexistent son of God, the Torah does not apply to him.

At the outset, Jesus' interlocutors are described as Pharisees, but soon his partners in dialogue are referred to simply as "the Jews" (8:22). Much of the discourse alludes to the Abraham story and to God's covenantal promises to the patriarch (Genesis 12; 15). In 8:33, the Jews claim that they are children of Abraham (see Gen. 12:2; Deut. 14:1), and that they have never been enslaved. Although commentators contend that the Jews were lying by deliberately ignoring their enslavement in Egypt prior to the exodus, it is likely that their claim refers not to slavery but to idolatry, which involves "serving" gods other than the one God of Israel (see Jer. 2:10-14; Reinhartz 2001b).

The second element concerns Ishmael, the slave Hagar's son, and Isaac, the son who inherits the covenant promises. In Genesis, it is the Israelites who descend from Isaac; postbiblical Jews claimed this lineage as well. Paul, however, argued that it was believers in Christ who descend from Sarah, and nonbelievers who are the slaves (Galatians 4). John does not develop the "allegory," but in 8:35 he describes sonship as a consequence of faith in Christ, not as a birthright. Jesus himself is the true "son" who belongs in the temple, in contrast to the Jews, who serve in the temple but do not inherit it.

Evidence that the Jews have lost their Abrahamic lineage lies in their rejection of Christ, in contrast to Abraham, who welcomed the three divinely sent guests to his tent in Genesis 18. Finally, Jesus claims that because they murder and lie, the Jews are not children of God, but "from your father the devil" (8:44). The argument regarding Abrahamic and divine/demonic sonship rests on the idea that children will behave like their parents, an assumption that is not borne out by experience.

The Jews respond with their own accusations: Jesus is a Samaritan and has a demon (8:48). Jesus does not respond to the Samaritan charge and simply denies that he has a demon. But he makes a shocking statement that persuades them that he is indeed possessed: "whoever keeps my word will never see death" (8:51). This claim turns the conversation back to Abraham, as the Jews ask: "Are you greater than our father Abraham, who died?" (8:52). Jesus declares that Abraham rejoiced at "his day," and that he existed before Abraham. These statements may allude to Jesus' preexistence, as well as to the traditions described in the pseudepigraphical *Testament of Abraham*, in which God gives Abraham a tour of the heavens and provides him with knowledge of the final judgment. Predictably, the chapter ends with the Jews' attempt to stone Jesus.

◼ THE TEXT IN THE INTERPRETIVE TRADITION

The church fathers hope for the conversion of some Jews. Cyril states that "we must not think that all the Jews were utterly immersed in ill-tempered foolishness"; some came to faith while others were dissuaded by the "unholy scribes and Pharisees whose boundless unbelief stirred the others to wrath and intemperately kindled them to bloodthirstiness" (*Commentary on the Gospel of John* 6.1; Elowsky 2006, 309).

In claiming never to have been enslaved, Augustine insists, the Jews were lying ingrates. "Wasn't Joseph sold? Weren't the holy prophets led into captivity? And again, didn't that very nation, when making bricks in Egypt, also serve hard rulers, not only in gold and silver but also in clay? If you were never in bondage to anyone, ungrateful people, why is it that God is continually reminding you that he delivered you from the house of bondage? . . . [and how] were you now paying tribute to the Romans, out of which also you formed a trap for the truth himself, as if to ensnare him?" (*Tract. Ev. Jo.* 41.2; Elowsky 2006, 296).

◼ THE TEXT IN CONTEMPORARY DISCUSSION

The unfortunate link between the Jews and the devil in 8:44 has spawned a potent antisemitic symbol. As a Jew, I would urge Christians to acknowledge and wrestle with this aspect of the text. What does it mean that texts like this are present in canonized literature? Does it make it better to understand these discourses, not as belonging to the historical Jesus, but as reflecting a flawed and ideologically motivated author and community? As some Christian churches have begun to ask, should such texts continue to be read in Christian worship?

9:1-41: A Sixth Sign: Healing of the Blind Man

◼ THE TEXT IN ITS ANCIENT CONTEXT

On seeing a man born blind, the disciples ask Jesus about whose sin caused his blindness: the man or his parents? Neither, says Jesus. The man was born blind so that Jesus might heal him and thereby perform a sign (though, again, the term *sēmeion* is not used) that testifies to the divine glory and his identity as God's Son. The man's journey from blindness to sight symbolizes the journey from unbelief to belief. Like the healing of the lame man, the sign, also done on the Sabbath, causes a division among the people. The formerly blind man is taken to the Pharisees for investigation. As in John 8, the term "Pharisees" for Jesus' interrogators drops out in favor of "the Jews," a change that blurs the distinctions between the general term and the subset of Jewish leaders. The Jews now call the man's parents as witnesses, but they prove reluctant to respond directly to questions, because "they were afraid of the Jews; for the Jews had already agreed that anyone who confessed Jesus to be the Messiah would be put out of the synagogue" (9:22).

Using a two-level reading method, many scholars argue that John 9, and the Gospel as a whole, tell not only a story of Jesus but also the story of the Johannine community, specifically the expulsion of Johannine believers from the synagogue for confessing Jesus to be the Messiah. This expulsion is seen as the rationale for the Gospel's often harsh words about the Jews, as well as an important milestone in the "parting of the ways" between Judaism and Christianity. External corroboration has often been sought in the liturgical "blessing" (curse) on the heretics, *Birkat ha-Minim*, that was added to the daily liturgy. The theory is that in the late first century, Jewish authorities added this curse as a way of flushing undesirables such as Jewish Christ-confessors out of the worship service and thereby from the community as a whole (Martyn).

Recent research, however, has revealed no first-century manuscript evidence for *Birkat ha-Minim*. Nor is there evidence that belief in an individual's messianic identity would have been a basis for exclusion. Indeed, in 132–135 CE, Rabbi Akiva is said to have made similar claims for Simeon Bar Kosiba, yet Akiva's high status did not suffer as a result. Rather than a coded reference to the expulsion of the Johannine community from the synagogue, 9:22 may well be a strategy for forging a community identity outside of and separate from Judaism.

Jesus provides the symbolic, cosmological meaning of this sign: "I came into this world for judgment so that those who do not see may see, and those who do see may become blind" (9:39). The Pharisees—here again, the more specific term is used—object to being called blind, but Jesus insists: "If you were blind, you would not have sin. But now that you say, 'We see,' your sin remains" (9:41).

▌The Text in the Interpretive Tradition

Augustine makes much less of the expulsion in 9:22 than do modern scholars. Reading the complete separation of Judaism and Christianity back into the Gospel, he explains that "it was no disadvantage to be put out of the synagogue since the one they cast out, Christ received" (*Tract. Ev. Jo.* 44.10; Elowsky 2006, 331).

Augustine and Cyril of Alexandria use this Sabbath healing as an opportunity to distinguish between the "carnal" Sabbath observed by Jews and the spiritual Sabbath observed by Christ. Augustine explains that the Pharisees were wrong to accuse Jesus of profaning the Sabbath. "On the contrary, he kept it because he was without sin; to observe the sabbath spiritually is to have no sin . . . But these men, who neither could see nor were anointed, observed the sabbath carnally but profaned it spiritually" (*Tract. Ev. Jo.* 44.9; Elowsky 2006, 330).

▌The Text in Contemporary Discussion

The reference to expulsion, however it is interpreted, provides an opportunity to think about the frequent experience of schism within faith-based or other communities. The separation of a subgroup from the main community may be perceived as a departure by those who remain within and as an expulsion from those who leave. Drawing on our own experiences allows us to consider a range of possibilities that acknowledge the efforts of early groups of Christ-followers to create new communities within which they could give full expression to their convictions.

10:1-42: The Good Shepherd

▮ THE TEXT IN ITS ANCIENT CONTEXT

The Johannine Jesus, unlike his Synoptic counterpart, does not speak in parables. In John 10, however, he employs the "figure" (Gk. *paroimia*) of the shepherd who calls his sheep by name and leads them out of the sheepfold. This is a pastoral, everyday scenario that lends itself readily to a cosmological interpretation.

The shepherd is a well-known biblical metaphor for leaders, divine and human, such as Moses (Exod. 3:1), David (2 Sam. 5:2), and God (Psalm 23). The language (hearing the voice, calling the sheep by name, leading them out) recalls John 5:28, in which Jesus promises that "all who are in their graves will hear his voice and will come out" and anticipates 11:43, in which Jesus calls Lazarus by name out of his grave. These references to death raise the intriguing possibility that the passage alludes to the "harrowing of hell," the belief that Jesus spent the days between his crucifixion and resurrection in Hades bringing the dead to faith (Reinhartz 1992).

Jesus also refers to "other sheep that do not belong to this fold" (10:16), perhaps an allusion to members of the Johannine community—believers—who are not of Jewish origin. This discourse, too, took place during the early winter festival, Hanukkah (Dedication). This festival commemorates the rededication of the temple (164 BCE), after it had been desecrated by the Seleucid king Antiochus IV (1 Macc. 4:52-59). Again the Jews attempt to stone him, this time for blasphemy, "because you, though only a human being, are making yourself God" (10:33). Jesus responds as a true rabbi, with a biblical verse: "Is it not written in your law, 'I said, you are gods'?" (10:35). Here, too, Jesus distances himself from the Torah, even as he brings it as a witness to the truth of his own words and identity.

▮ THE TEXT IN THE INTERPRETIVE TRADITION

The church fathers interpreted the prophecy that in the future "there will be one flock and one shepherd" (10:16) as a reference to gentile Christians. As Theodore of Mopsuestia points out, "many among the Gentiles as well as many among the Jews are destined to gather together into a single church and to acknowledge one shepherd and one lord, who is Christ" (*Commentary on John* 4.10.216; Elowsky 2007, 35).

▮ THE TEXT IN CONTEMPORARY DISCUSSION

The inclusion of other sheep projects the ideal of a single, universal community united by faith in Christ. Yet a similarly universal and totalizing image in the Hebrew Bible, the Tower of Babel, is broken up by God, who is critical of the endeavor. In the twentieth and twenty-first centuries, many Western countries have become ever more diverse, ethnically, religiously, culturally, and linguistically. Some see this development as disturbing. Others, however, view the diversity as enriching and exciting. The principles of acceptance and mutual respect are often lacking in universalizing ideologies or homogeneous communities, but are necessary for living in communities characterized by diversity.

11:1-54: A Seventh Sign: Raising of Lazarus

◼ THE TEXT IN ITS ANCIENT CONTEXT

When Jesus learns of Lazarus's serious illness, he makes the surprising decision to remain where he is instead of rushing to his friend's bedside. As the story proceeds, the reason for the delay becomes clear: Jesus is waiting for Lazarus to die so that he can raise him up and thereby glorify God.

By the time Jesus arrives, Lazarus has been dead and buried for four days. Mary and Martha are mourning in the company of "many of the Jews" (11:19). Each sister reproaches Jesus for not coming sooner. Jesus promises Martha that Lazarus will rise again, and declares famously, "I am the resurrection and the life. Those who believe in me, even though they die, will live, and everyone who lives and believes in me will never die" (11:25-26). Martha responds with a full confession of faith: "Yes, Lord, I believe that you are the Messiah, the Son of God, the one coming into the world" (11:27).

Upon seeing Mary, Jesus "was greatly disturbed in spirit, and deeply moved" (11:33). When he sees the tomb, he weeps (11:35). In the first century, Jews were buried in linen shrouds and their bodies laid in a sealed tomb so that the flesh would decompose. After a period of eleven months, the tomb would be unsealed, and the bones would be placed in an ossuary (bone box) and stored on a shelf in the tomb (Hachlili). In the days after burial, however, removing the stone would release the stench of decomposition. Jesus gives thanks to God and clarifies that his prayer is "for the sake of the crowd standing here, so that they may believe that you sent me" (11:41). In doing so, he attributes the miracle not to his own innate power but to God. He then calls out—like the shepherd would to the sheep in John 10—"Lazarus, come out!" thereby fulfilling the prophecy in 5:28-29, that the dead will hear the voice of the Son of God and come out of their tombs (11:43). Lazarus's revival foreshadows Jesus' own.

Some Jews believe, but others go to the Pharisees, who call a meeting of the council (11:47) out of concern that "Romans will come and destroy both our holy place [the temple] and our nation" (11:48). The Gospel may be suggesting that the Jewish authorities viewed faith in Jesus as a loss of attachment to God, which God would punish by allowing Rome to destroy the temple, just as the Hebrew Bible believed that God had sent the Assyrians and Babylonians to punish the Jews for turning away from the covenant (2 Kgs. 21:14-15). In the Maccabean era, a similar explanation was used to explain how Antiochus IV succeeded in desecrating God's temple (2 Macc. 5:15-20). A second possibility is that widespread belief of Jews in Jesus might make Rome fear rebellion or civil war, and therefore prompt Rome to move quickly by moving against the temple.

In response, Caiaphas (high priest 18–36 CE; Josephus, *Ant.* 18.90–95) reminds the council that "it is better for you to have one man die for the people than to have the whole nation destroyed" (11:50). The narrator interprets this comment as an unwitting prophecy that Jesus would die for the nation (11:51) and "to gather into one the dispersed children of God" (11:52). While Caiaphas is often depicted as the mastermind behind Jesus' death, his comment is a general principle and does not convey animosity toward Jesus. Jesus again withdraws, this time to the town of Ephraim, where he remains with the disciples (11:54).

THE TEXT IN THE INTERPRETIVE TRADITION

Chrysostom saw a contradiction between the expulsion mentioned in 9:22 and the presence of Jews in the home of Mary and Martha. He asks: "How could the Jews console the loved ones of Christ, when they had resolved that whoever confessed Christ should be put out of the synagogue?" He suggests that "perhaps the extreme affliction of the sisters excited their sympathy, or they wished to show respect for their rank. Or perhaps those who came were of the better sort, as we find that many of them believed" (*Hom. Jo.* 62.2; Elowsky 2007, 12).

Origen asks a more theological question: If Caiaphas was wicked, and therefore, by definition, did not possess the Holy Spirit, how could he utter a true prophecy? Perhaps Caiaphas was simply speaking unintentionally, as everyone does at times. In the end, however, he cannot deny that the prophecy was from the Holy Spirit, even as he refuses to commit himself fully to this idea: "I do not in the least maintain that this was the case, but leave it to readers to decide what one must recognize as correct concerning Caiaphas, and the fact that he has been moved by the Spirit" (*Comm. Jo.* 28.191; Origen, 332).

THE TEXT IN CONTEMPORARY DISCUSSION

As with the Gospel as a whole, it is important to remember that the passage is little concerned with accurate reportage but obsessed with Christology. The speech placed in Caiaphas's mouth describes Jesus as the scapegoat. On the annual Day of Atonement, the high priest symbolically cleansed the nation of sin by loading the people's sins onto the goat and sending it into the desert. Caiaphas's words also recall the Christian interpretation of the temple's destruction as a consequence of the Jews' role in the passion and prophesy the messianic ingathering of all peoples joined by faith in Christ.

The congruence of the high priest's words with the Gospel's own theological interests does not of course say anything one way or another about the historicity of the events or words. But they should caution us on the need to read critically, and to remember that even the texts we consider sacred or that mean much to us cannot be disentangled from their historical contexts or the interests of their authors.

11:55—12:11: The Anointing of Jesus at Bethany

THE TEXT IN ITS ANCIENT CONTEXT

Prior to the third and final Passover of Jesus' public ministry, Jesus eats dinner with the Bethany siblings. At this dinner, Mary anoints Jesus' feet with expensive perfume and wipes his feet with her hair. (This story parallels but does not duplicate the Synoptic story of an unnamed woman who anoints Jesus at the home of Simon the Pharisee; see Matt. 26:6; Mark 14:3; Luke 7:36.) Judas protests that it would have been better to sell the perfume and give the proceeds to the poor.

Jesus responds that the anointing foreshadows his impending death; the poor remain, but Jesus will soon depart.

▮ The Text in the Interpretive Tradition

The church fathers struggled with the question of Judas's moral status. If he was always evil, how could he have been chosen as a disciple? If he became evil only at the end, why would not his association with Jesus have saved him from himself? Augustine's view is that "Judas did not become perverted only at the time when he yielded to the bribery of the Jews and betrayed his Lord. . . . But he was already a thief, already lost, and he followed our Lord in body but not with his heart" (*Tract. Ev. Jo.* 50.10-11; Elowsky 2007, 46).

▮ The Text in Contemporary Discussion

Although Jesus rebukes Judas for commenting on the expense of the ointment, the narrator indirectly acknowledges the validity of the concern, but dismisses it due to the source, for Judas "said this not because he cared about the poor but because he was a thief" (12:6). Yet Jesus' rebuke, "you always have the poor with you, but you do not always have me" (12:8), is problematic, as it places a higher priority on the symbolic preparations for his death (12:7) than on the needs of others. In contemporary society, it can also be difficult to balance the desire to honor individuals or occasions with the responsibility to help the less fortunate.

12:12-50: The Triumphal Entry and End of Jesus' Public Ministry

▮ The Text in Its Ancient Context

Jesus' entry (cf. Matt. 21:1; Mark 11:1; Luke 19:28) is the high point of his ministry, as he is greeted by jubilant crowds waving palm branches and proclaiming him the king of Israel (12:13). This demonstration would have given the Romans ample reason to be concerned about the royal claims made for, if not quite by, Jesus, and to justify a verdict of treason punishable by crucifixion. The Gospel puts this act in a cosmological context, which the disciples do not understand until after his death and glorification (12:16), while the alarm of the Pharisees increases (12:19).

Jesus' triumphal entry is witnessed not only by Jewish crowds and authorities but also by "Greeks" who have gone up to Jerusalem to worship at the festival (12:20). Although it is possible that these were Greek-speaking Jews, Jesus' reaction suggests that they were non-Jews. It was not uncommon for gentiles to attend the temple; indeed, Herod's temple included a Court of the Gentiles (Schmidt 2001, 79). These Greeks approach Philip, who in turn tells Andrew, and they both tell Jesus (12:21). In contrast to the call of the disciples and the Samaritan woman, Jesus refuses to encounter them directly but instead announces that "the hour has come for the Son of Man to be glorified" (12:24). The question of whether gentiles can be part of this new movement is therefore postponed until after Jesus' death. In contrast to the Synoptics, in which Jesus prays that the Father remove this cup from him during the dark night at Gethsemane (Matt. 26:39; Mark 14:36; Luke 22:42), John's Jesus braces for his death: "it is for this reason that I have come to this hour" (12:27). He accepts that he must die in order to fulfill his divine mission and return to the Father.

Nevertheless, he does request something from God: "Father, glorify your name" (12:28). God responds immediately: "I have glorified it, and I will glorify it again" (12:28). Jesus gives the people one last chance to understand his cosmological significance (12:32-36), but they refuse. He hides and departs from them. Even so, the narrator states, many authorities did believe in him but were afraid to confess openly for fear of expulsion from the synagogue (12:42).

∎ THE TEXT IN THE INTERPRETIVE TRADITION

Augustine contrasts the Jewish and gentile response to Jesus: "Look how the Jews want to kill him, the Gentiles to see him. But they also were there with the Jews who cried, 'Blessed is he who comes in the name of the Lord, the king of Israel.' Here then are both those of the circumcision and those of the uncircumcision, once so wide apart, coming together like two walls and meeting in the one faith of Christ by the kiss of peace" (*Tract. Ev. Jo.* 51.8; Elowsky 2007, 58). Augustine's interpretation reflects a perspective grounded in the letters of Paul, who provided a theological rationale for the inclusion of the gentiles among God's covenant people (Gal. 4:5; Romans 9–11).

∎ THE TEXT IN CONTEMPORARY DISCUSSION

Some scholars suggest that the gentiles who want to see Jesus represent the gentile members of the Johannine community (R. E. Brown 1979, 55), and can encourage reflection about the challenges involved in heterogeneous communities when it comes to self-definition. The gentiles who became part of the Jesus community encountered a worldview different from their culture of origin, but they also brought new ideas and customs. The challenge is to allow the group identity to expand and change in response. It is likely that the Gospel exposes some of the negotiations that had to take place in order to forge an identity for its ethnically mixed audience, and the same is true of communities today.

The Book of Glory (13:1—20:31)

13:1-38: Final Dinner

∎ THE TEXT IN ITS ANCIENT CONTEXT

Whereas in the Synoptics (Matt. 26:26-29; Mark 14:22-25; Luke 22:13-20) Jesus' final meal with the disciples is a Passover seder—the ritual Passover meal that, in the period when the temple was standing, was convened for the eating of the Passover sacrifice—and is marked by the institution of the Eucharist, the Last Supper in John is not a Passover seder but takes place the day before the Passover begins, and it features not the Eucharist but a ritual foot washing.

The pre-Passover timing of this meal, and of the passion narrative as a whole, transforms Jesus' own death into the Passover sacrifice, as it takes place several hours before the festival begins, at the time when the Passover lamb would be slaughtered (R. E. Brown 1970, 556; *m. Pesach* 5.1). The chronology may therefore be theologically motivated, but at the same time, it is also more plausible historically than the Synoptic timing. The Synoptic narrative indicates that the Jewish council put

Jesus on trial during the night of the Passover festival itself, a highly unlikely circumstance given that this would have constituted a violation of Jewish law (Sanders, 298).

The passage raises the interesting but ultimately unanswerable question of whether there were ancient communities of Christ-confessors who rejected or perhaps were not aware of the eucharistic practices of other churches. The eucharistic allusions in the Bread of Life discourse (John 6) would suggest knowledge of this practice, but its absence from the Last Supper story casts doubt on this group's practices.

The narrator provides three crucial pieces of information in the first two verses: Jesus' hour "to depart from this world and go to the Father" has finally come; Jesus would love "his own" to the end (13:1); and "the devil had already put it into the heart of Judas son of Simon Iscariot to betray him" (13:2).

At the table, Jesus explains that just as he had washed the disciples' feet, so also should they wash each other's feet (13:12-13). This was to be an egalitarian act, for "servants are not greater than their master, nor are messengers greater than the one who sent them" (13:16). Jesus surprises his disciples when he prepares them for the betrayal. Though readers have known the betrayer's identity since John 6 (and, likely, before they read or heard this Gospel at all), not so the disciples.

The narrator now introduces a new character: the disciple whom Jesus loved (13:23). If he is new to the readers, he is not new to Jesus. Indeed, he is an intimate friend, not only because he is loved by Jesus—as all the disciples are—but because he reclines next to Jesus, in his bosom, just as Jesus does with God the Father (1:18). This intimacy is acknowledged by Peter, who asks the disciple to address Jesus on his behalf. Jesus hands bread to Judas, who departs, thereby sealing Jesus' fate.

The Gospel returns to the outline of the story shared by all four Gospels, in which Jesus prophesies that Peter will deny him three times (13:38). Before that point, however, he introduces the commandment to "love one another" (13:34). The love commandment sounds expansive, uplifting, and generous, and in this regard it echoes a saying that the rabbinic tractate *The Sayings of the Fathers* attributes to the Pharisaic teacher Hillel: "Be of the followers of Aaron, loving peace, pursuing peace, loving your fellow human beings and bringing them to Torah" (*Abot* 1.12). Nevertheless, the fact that the commandment is given only to the disciples implies that the love is meant only for those who are within the community (Meier, 559).

▋ The Text in the Interpretive Tradition

The church fathers accepted the identification of the Beloved Disciple as John son of Zebedee and proposed various solutions to the problem of his anonymity in the Gospel. Augustine explains that "it was a custom of the sacred writer, when he came to anything relating to himself, to speak of himself as if he were speaking of another. He would give himself a place in the flow of the narrative so that he became one who was the recorder of public events rather than making himself the subject of his preaching" (*Tract. Ev. Jo.* 61.4; Elowsky 2007, 103).

The more important issue concerns Judas's moral culpability. If the devil had put the idea of betrayal into Judas's heart, to what extent is Judas to blame? Does Jesus bear some responsibility as the one who chose his disciples, including the betrayer? Cyril of Alexandria appeals to the principle of freedom of choice in addressing these questions: "Christ chose Judas and associated him with the holy disciples, since at first he certainly possessed the capacity for discipleship. But when, after the temptations of Satan succeeded in making him captive to base greediness for gain, when he was conquered by passion and had become by this means a traitor, then he was rejected by God. This, therefore, was in no way the fault of him who called this man to be an apostle. For it lay in the power of Judas to have saved himself from falling" (*Commentary on the Gospel of John* 9; Elowsky 2007, 99).

Perhaps the most famous interpretation of John's Last Supper is Leonardo da Vinci's mural painting in the refectory in the convent of Santa Maria Della Grazie, Milan (1495–1498). Leonardo catches the dinner party just at the moment that Jesus declares: "One of you will betray me" (13:21). He captures the astonishment and fear on the disciples' faces and their attempts to excuse themselves. Judas is posed to accept the bread, and the Beloved Disciple, portrayed as a young, beardless man, reclines on Jesus, in a pose that prompted the novelist Dan Brown to speculate that this was really Mary Magdalene (D. Brown; Ehrman).

▌The Text in Contemporary Discussion

Jesus' explanation of the foot washing implies a radical egalitarianism that erases the hierarchies of master-servant and teacher-disciple. This egalitarianism was not incorporated into the institutional structures of the church, but the Johannine passage may open up such possibilities for contemporary communities. Appealing as it might be, however, this model is not without its issues. How does the humility inherent in the act of foot washing mesh with the insistence on Jesus' divine identity? Another issue concerns the question of gender. The text does not specify whether the dinner party also included women, and it therefore lends itself to either interpretation. If the Gospels are to be taken as a source for Christian community—an assumption that is often made but that could be queried nonetheless—John 13 provides some opening for a less hierarchical institution.

14:1—16:33: Farewell Discourses

▌The Text in Its Ancient Context

After dinner, Jesus speaks for three full chapters. These Farewell Discourses prepare his disciples for his death and for moving forward without him.

Images. The discourses contain several images that make his message more vivid. The first describes "his father's house" as a mansion with many rooms. Jesus promises that he will return and take them to this house (14:2). There may be an allusion here to the Jewish *hekhalot* ("palaces") tradition, involving stories in which a seer visits the heavenly realm and explores its different rooms (see the chariot vision in Ezekiel 1 and *1 Enoch* 17–18). More immediately, the verse also alludes to the temple, which Jesus called his Father's house in 2:16, and to the son/slave contrast in 8:35. Jesus insists that this house can be reached in only one way: "I am the way, and the truth, and the life. No one comes to the Father except through me" (14:6).

A second vivid image is found in 15:1-6, in which Jesus declares himself to be the true vine, and God the vine grower. This vividly illustrates the central tenets of Johannine Christology: that God has planted his creation, the vine, in the world and continues to tend it so that it will bear fruit. The branches—the disciples—must not only gather followers but also ensure the quality of the wine, that is, of the faith in Jesus. Those that cannot bear fruit are pruned. This may be a veiled reference to Judas, the disciple who has been removed from the Twelve. Essential to the production is mutual indwelling; the branch cannot bear fruit except as part of the vine. Jesus exhorts: "Abide in me as I abide in you" (15:4).

Finally, Jesus reassures the disciples using a common apocalyptic motif: the woman in labor, e.g., Rev. 12:2; cf. Isa. 13:8). In the short term, they will "weep and mourn" while the hate-filled world rejoices. But in the larger, cosmic context, it is the disciples who will rejoice, like a woman is in pain during labor but rejoices when the child is born (16:21).

The Love commandment. In chapter 13, Jesus adjures the disciples to love one another. This commandment is repeated and amplified in John 15. The greatest love is "to lay down one's life for one's friends" (15:13). Now that he has revealed all to them, his disciples are his friends. Yet he remains their leader, whose commandments—to go and bear fruit that will last (15:15)—must be obeyed. The idea of dying for one's friends is also expressed in Aristotle's extensive comments on friendship in the *Nicomachean Ethics* 9.1169a. The question, however, is, What constitutes love, and who are the friends (cf. Luke 10:29)?

The Paraclete. Those who are addressed by the love commandment, in turn, will receive another "Advocate" (or Paraclete: Gk. *paraklētos*), who will remain with the disciples forever. The Advocate is the Holy Spirit; he will be sent by the Father, and he will teach the disciples, and remind them of what Jesus said to them in his life. He will testify on Jesus' behalf, and prove the world wrong about sin and righteousness and judgment (16:8). For this reason, Jesus' departure is not only necessary but also beneficial; otherwise, the Advocate will not come (16:7). It is unclear whether the Paraclete will work through the community's leadership, through prophecy, or through other "spiritual gifts" as discussed by Paul in 1 Corinthians 12–14. Nevertheless, the promise of the Paraclete implies the existence of a community that already believes it possesses additional knowledge and authority that has come to them through and after Jesus' death and ascension to God.

Persecution. Alongside these benefits, however, the disciples are warned to expect persecution (15:21) and even death (16:2). The context implies Jewish responsibility for this suffering, but this is not supported by the historical record. This section contributes to the arguments some have made that the Gospel is a martyr's text, intended to give comfort and strength to those who face persecution (Moss).

◼ THE TEXT IN THE INTERPRETIVE TRADITION

With regard to 14:2, Augustine suggests that Jesus is "preparing the dwellings by preparing for them the dwellers. As, for instance, when he said, 'In my Father's house are many dwellings.' What else can we suppose the house of God to mean but the temple of God? And what that is, ask the apostle, and he will reply, 'For the temple of God is holy, which temple you are.' This is also the kingdom of God that the Son is yet to deliver up to the Father" (*Tract. Ev. Jo.* 68.2; Elowsky 2007, 121).

◼ THE TEXT IN CONTEMPORARY DISCUSSION

The love commandment is often quoted to assure non-Christians that love is the essence of the Christian message. Yet within its context, in which Jesus, for the first time, is speaking to the disciples alone and not to a crowd, and warning them of persecution, it seems that this love is turning inward, and characterizing friendship within the community rather than humankind more generally.

17:1-26: Jesus' Prayer

▍ THE TEXT IN ITS ANCIENT CONTEXT

After these final words to the disciples, Jesus prays to God, not for his own benefit, or for God's, but for those who are listening in, whether directly, as the disciples, or through the written word, as the book's readers or listeners. In contrast to the Synoptic Savior, the Johannine Jesus anticipates his fate with satisfaction and joy, as it marks his return to the glory that he enjoyed with God before the world existed (17:5). In alluding to the prologue, this prayer provides a brief reprieve from the gritty account of the passion, which they are about to read, and recalls the cosmic significance of the narrative as a whole.

The prayer advocates for the disciples, seeks God's protection for them, and thereby reassures them of the joyous end that will await them after their pain and persecution will end. He gives their credentials—they were given to them by God, they kept God's word (quite literally, perhaps: they have kept Jesus, the Logos, safe, 17:6), and they know that Jesus came from God (17:8). Jesus differentiates sharply between those who are "his own" and those who are not. Though his disciples live in the world, they do not belong to the world.

Jesus concludes with a statement of the unity among Father, Son, and believers, and the prayer that the disciples shall indeed enter into the glory "which you have given me because you loved me before the foundation of the world" (17:24). This concludes the revelatory part of the Gospel, and it ends as it begins, with a statement about Jesus' preexistence and the cosmic context for his earthly mission.

▍ THE TEXT IN THE INTERPRETIVE TRADITION

How does one live in the world but not be of the world? The *Letter to Diognetus* (late second century) explains by analogy: "What the soul is to the body, Christians are to the world. The soul is dispersed through all the members of the body, and Christians throughout the cities of the world. The soul dwells in the body but is not of the body. Likewise, Christians dwell in the world but are not of the world. The soul, which is invisible, is confined in the body, which is visible. In the same way, Christians are recognized as being in the world, and yet their religion remains invisible" (*Letter to Diognetus* 6; Elowsky 2007, 244).

Cyril of Alexandria has a more pragmatic explanation: "Christ does not wish for the apostles to be set free of human affairs or to be rid of life in the body when they have not yet finished the course of their apostleship or distinguished themselves by the virtues of a godly life. Rather, his desire is to see them live their lives in the company of people in the world and guide the footsteps of those who are his to a state of life well pleasing to God. After they have done this, then at last, with the glory they have achieved, they will be carried into the heavenly city and dwell with the company of the holy angels" (*Commentary on the Gospel of John* 11.9; Elowsky 2007, 250).

■ The Text in Contemporary Discussion

Jesus prays that the disciples will transmit Jesus' message to the world after he is gone, perhaps aided by the Paraclete. Yet it is rare, or perhaps impossible, for the message to remain the same over time. The churches that developed after Jesus' death, including the Johannine community itself, may have perceived themselves in continuity with Jesus (even when in conflict with each other), but they departed from his teachings in significant ways, including the egalitarianism implied in chapter 13.

18:1—19:16a: Betrayal, Trials, and Denial

■ The Text in Its Ancient Context

John's account of the events that led directly to Jesus' death are similar in outline, though not always in detail, with the Synoptic versions, suggesting to many scholars that the passion narrative was the first lengthy narrative unit in the Gospel tradition.

Immediately after the prayer, Jesus steps into the garden across the Kidron Valley (18:1), where he is immediately met by Judas, along with a detachment of soldiers and police of the Jewish authorities (18:2-3). There is no "Judas' kiss" (cf. Matt. 26:48; Mark 14:44; Luke 22:47-48). Rather than wait for Judas to identify him, Jesus steps forward and asks, "Whom are you looking for?" (18:4). This echoes the question he first asked of the Baptist's disciples (1:38). Jesus identifies himself simply with "I am he," recalling yet again God's self-identification in Exod. 3:14. Once in custody, he endures an interrogation before a high-priestly authority. In contrast to Mark and Matthew, however, this authority is not the high priest himself—whom Matthew names but Mark leaves anonymous—but Caiaphas's father-in-law, Annas. The episode has led to considerable speculation concerning Annas's ongoing role in and influence over high-priestly matters.

The "high priest" is most interested in Jesus' disciples and teachings. As usual, Jesus responds indirectly: "I have spoken openly to the world; I have always taught in synagogues and in the temple, where all the Jews come together. I have said nothing in secret" (18:20). Jesus' assertion is borne out by his earlier activity. In fact, until the Farewell Discourses, Jesus has taught only crowds, and often in the synagogue or the temple.

Intercut with this interrogation is the story of Peter's denial. By its end, Jesus is presumably in Caiaphas's custody, but what, if anything, occurred between them is not divulged.

The decisive event in the passion sequence, however, is the trial before Pilate. John's Pilate is extremely reluctant to condemn Jesus. He asks Jesus' Jewish captors: "What accusation do you bring against this man?" (18:29). Like Jesus, they do not answer directly, but simply say that had he not been a criminal they would not have handed him over. Pilate suggests that he give Jesus over to them for judgment, but they remind him that it is only Rome that can hand down the death penalty. The narrator points out the necessity of crucifixion to fulfill Jesus' prophecy about his mode of death (18:32).

Because the Jews must remain outside to avoid pre-Passover ritual defilement (18:28), Pilate goes back and forth between them and Jesus. He confronts Jesus with the claim that he is king of the Jews. Jesus poses a question of his own: "Do you ask this on your own, or did others tell you about me?" (18:34). Pilate reminds him that it is his own people who have handed him over, and now asks more generally, "What have you done?" (18:35). Jesus then responds, enigmatically, to the previous question: "My kingdom is not from this world," for his disciples are not fighting on his behalf (18:36). Pilate struggles to comprehend: "So you are a king?" (18:37). But Jesus, as always, avoids a direct answer: "You say that I am a king." As for what he says, "For this I was born, and for this I came into the world, to testify to the truth" (18:37), setting the stage for Pilate's famous but cryptic question: "What is truth?" (18:38). Without awaiting a response, Pilate goes back out to the Jews and declares that he finds no reason to prosecute Jesus.

Instead of releasing Jesus, however, he offers the crowds a choice between Jesus and Barabbas. Although the Gospel describes this as a Passover custom (18:39), there is no evidence for it outside the Gospels' passion accounts (cf. Matt. 27:15; Mark 15.6; Luke 23:17). The Jews insist on Barabbas. Barabbas is described as a *lēstēs* (18:40), which can mean "robber" or "bandit." In the writings of Josephus, the term is used to describe guerrilla fighters who both stole and incited violence against Rome (*War* 2.253–54). The fact that Barabbas was sentenced to crucifixion, a punishment normally reserved for those convicted of treason, may imply that he was such a fighter, rather than a mere thief.

And still the death sentence is not passed. Pilate has Jesus flogged and then finally brings him out to face his accusers: "Behold the man" (19:5 KJV). The chief priests and police cry out for his crucifixion, as Pilate insists a third time: "I find no case against him" (19:6). The Jews again insist that he has broken their law by claiming to be Son of God, a claim that leads Pilate to approach Jesus again: "Where are you from?" (19:9). In this way, the Gospel reminds the reader of the messianic criterion of unknown origins that has been woven through the narrative.

Jesus does not respond until Pilate threatens him: "Do you not know that I have power to release you, and power to crucify you?" (19:10). But Jesus denies that Pilate has any independent power; rather, "the one who handed me over to you is guilty of a greater sin." (19:11). If Jesus' death by crucifixion is essential to the fulfillment of his mission and his return to God, why is Pilate blameless but the Jewish authorities guilty? Finally, Pilate relents and hands Jesus over to be crucified (18:16a).

As in the Synoptics, Pilate is extremely reluctant to condemn Jesus, and uses several tactics—deflection, negation—to extricate himself from the situation. In contrast to the Synoptics, however, John's Gospel suggests that Pilate was more interested in and engaged with Jesus beyond his potential to stir up a crowd. This interest is conveyed, first, by his question: "What is truth?" to which Jesus, continuing his near silence, does not respond (18:38). A second hint is found in the formality with which he presents Jesus, now wearing the crown of thorns and "royal" robe, to the crowd. The King James Version captures the nuance of the Greek, with its translation: "Behold the man" (19:5); even more striking is the famous Latin phrase of the Vulgate: "Ecce homo." The third, occurring in the next section, is the *titulus* that proclaims Jesus the king of the Jews, and his insistence on this wording in the face of the chief priests' protests (19:21-22).

Pilate's interest can be read in two different ways: as a tacit but sincere acknowledgment of Jesus' royal status (with acceptance of Jesus' declaration that he is the head of a kingdom that is not from this world, 18:36), and as irony intended to humiliate Jesus (as the soldiers did when robing and crowning him; 19:2-3) and to mock the royal claims made on his behalf.

■ THE TEXT IN THE INTERPRETIVE TRADITION

Augustine opted for the former view. He not only exonerated the Roman governor but also drew him in as a witness to the "truth," suggesting that the "truth" that Jesus was the king of the Jews was inscribed in Pilate's heart, as it was on the *titulus* (*Tract. Ev. Jo.* 115.5; Elowsky 2007, 294).

Cyril of Alexandria has a less elevated view of the governor: "When he called Jesus king of the Jews, he spoke in jest and tried to abate by ridicule the anger of the furious mob. He also clearly showed that this particular accusation was brought in vain. A Roman officer would never have thought a man condemned of plotting for a kingdom and revolution against Rome worthy to be released. He bore witness, then, to Jesus' utter innocence by the very reasons he gave for Jesus' release" (*Commentary on the Gospel of John* 12; Elowsky 2007, 294).

■ THE TEXT IN CONTEMPORARY DISCUSSION

The trial narrative is a case study on the use of intimidation in legal and political processes. This theme operates not only on the story level—the Jews intimidating Pilate into sentencing Jesus to death—but also in the potential impact of the Gospel on its ideal readers: to leave them with no alternative but to blame the Jews for Jesus' death.

19:16b-42 Crucifixion and Burial

■ THE TEXT IN ITS ANCIENT CONTEXT

The events wind to their inevitable conclusion. The crucifixion field is here called Golgotha, an Aramaic term meaning "The Place of the Skull" (19:17). A trilingual *titulus*—in Hebrew, Latin, and Greek—is placed on the cross, reading "Jesus of Nazareth, the King of the Jews." The chief priests object to the wording, arguing that it should read, "This man said, I am King of the Jews" (19:21), but Pilate refuses to change it, thereby indirectly acknowledging Jesus' sovereignty (19:22). The trilingual nature of the *titulus* testifies to the diversity that the Gospel writer presumed was the case in Jerusalem.

Even on the cross, Jesus maintains his presence of mind. The narrator notes that three women are standing near the cross: his mother, his aunt, and Mary Magdalene (19:25). From the cross, Jesus tells his mother, "Woman, here is your son," and says to the disciple, "Here is your mother" (19:26-27). On the face of it, Jesus is here showing his filial solicitude by ensuring that his mother will be cared for after his death. But interpreters have more often sought symbolic interpretations. It seems clear that the Beloved Disciple represents the ideal believer, but who or what would the mother represent? R. H. Strachan (319) suggests that she symbolizes the Jewish heritage that is now being entrusted to Christians; for Bultmann (673), she represents Jewish Christianity, now entrusted to gentile Christianity. Raymond Brown (1970, 925–26), drawing on the imagery of John 16:21, suggests that she evokes "Lady Zion," who brings forth a new people in the messianic age that Jesus' death ushers in. This interpretation ties in well with the promise that believers will be reborn (3:3) as children of God (1:12-13); nevertheless, the absence of any references to a maternal figure in these other contexts makes it difficult to conclude that this is meaning the evangelist or his first readers would have read into or out of this scene.

At the point of his death, the narrator says, Jesus declares his thirst, to fulfill Scripture (Ps. 69:21). He sips wine from a sponge on a hyssop branch, declares, "It is finished," bows his head, and gives up his spirit (19:30). In this moment, as throughout the Gospel, Jesus fully and calmly accepts the necessity of his death to the fulfillment of God's will and his own return to the Father. Interestingly, despite the numerous scenes involving food and drink, it is only at the moment before his death that Jesus himself explicitly consumes food or drink (Kobel, 301–6). The reference to hyssop recalls the Passover sacrifice, as it was used to mark the doorposts before the exodus (Exod. 12:22). Its mention here recalls the theme, distinct to this Gospel, of Jesus as the Passover sacrifice. This identification of Jesus as the Passover lamb is further strengthened by the fact that, unlike the other men crucified alongside him, Jesus did not have his legs broken (19:31-32). The narrator explains that this was because he was already dead (19:33). But in keeping his legs intact, the Roman soldiers also (inadvertently) ensure his acceptability as a Passover sacrifice, which had to be "without blemish" (Exod. 12:5).

After his death, Jesus' side is pierced, and "at once blood and water came out" (19:34). What this means from a physiological point of view has been much discussed but remains unclear (Wilkinson). Like many other elements of this Gospel, however, the scene has a symbolic meaning, perhaps alluding to the spiritually cleansing role of water in baptism and foot washing. The passage may also link back to 7:38, in which Jesus quotes a Scripture (the source is unclear, but Prov. 18:4; Isa. 58:11; and Sir. 24:30-33 have been suggested)—"Out of the believer's heart shall flow rivers of living water"—that the narrator interprets as a reference to the Spirit. If so, the scene may be christological, proclaiming Jesus as both human (blood) and divine (water). The blood may also suggest a eucharistic interpretation, whereby believers are able to imbibe Christ by virtue of his death on the cross. To emphasize the importance of this event, the narrator stresses the reliability of the witness, referring to the Beloved Disciple (19:35). A secret disciple, Joseph of Arimathea, along with Nicodemus, anoints and wraps Jesus' body and buries it in the garden near Golgotha. This passage lends credence to the view that Nicodemus, too, was a secret disciple. The preparation for Passover, the season of salvation, has been completed; the lamb has been sacrificed, his mission in the world accomplished, and his return to the Father assured.

◼ THE TEXT IN THE INTERPRETIVE TRADITION

Augustine indicates that a trilingual *titulus* was needed: "the Hebrew because of the Jews who gloried in the law of God; the Greek, because of the wise people among the gentiles; and the Latin, because of the Romans who at that very time were exercising sovereign power over many, in fact, over almost all countries" (*Tract. Ev. Jo.* 117.4; Elowsky 2007, 311). He also expands on the motif of Pilate as a convert. The governor was "the wild olive [see Rom. 11:17] to be grafted on, while the leaders of the Jews represented the broken-off branches" (*Serm.* 218.7; Elowsky 2007, 312). In this passage, Augustine is expanding on the Gospel's clues that Pilate was attracted to Jesus' message.

▮The Text in Contemporary Discussion

The crucifixion scene is perhaps the most poignant in the entire Gospel tradition. For John, it is in Jesus' death that he is most completely and profoundly both human and divine. His calm acceptance has served as a model for martyrs—those who must, or choose to die for their beliefs—from the early Christian period to the present day (Chilton), even as the Gospel's eschatology, which assures believers that they will follow Jesus to the rooms he has prepared for them in his Father's house, made it possible for Christians to face death calmly in times of persecution.

20:1-18: Mary Magdalene and the Gardener

▮The Text in Its Ancient Context

The Gospels are silent on the period of time between Jesus' burial and the discovery of the empty tomb, but all depict women as the ones who discover the empty tomb on Sunday morning. In John, Mary Magdalene comes alone, sees that the stone is rolled away, and runs to tell Peter and the "other" disciple that "they" have removed the body (20:2). The two men run to the tomb. The other disciple reaches the tomb first, but it is Peter who enters first. When the other disciple goes in, he believes. *What* he believes, however, is not specified. The narrator does not help clarify matters when he states that "as yet they did not understand the scripture, that he must rise from the dead" (20:9), for there is no specific biblical quotation to this effect. The two men return to their homes, but Mary remains weeping at the tomb. She then looks in and sees two angels (20:11-12), who ask, "Woman, why are you weeping?" She turns and sees Jesus but does not recognize him. He asks, "Whom are you looking for?" the same question he asked the Baptist's followers (1:38) and the forces who had come to arrest him (19:7). Mary mistakes him for the gardener and politely asks him to tell her where he put the body, so that she can take it away. He then calls her by name, as he had called Lazarus, and reveals his identity to her. She responds "Rabbouni!" which the narrator explains as meaning Teacher in Hebrew, though in fact it is Aramaic (20:16). He then tells her not to hold on to him; whether Mary had already touched him, or was merely reaching out to do so, is not stated, but the reason is "because I have not yet ascended to the Father" (20:17). Jesus' reason suggests that he is undergoing a process of change with regard to his corporeality that physical contact might interrupt. At the same time, one cannot ignore the hint of sexual tension in the scene. Mary's search for Jesus' body echoes the language of the Song of Solomon (Song of Songs), in which the female lover searches for her groom (see esp. Song of Sol. 3:1-4). Other parallels include the reference to "peering in" (John 20:5; Song of Sol. 2:9) and the use of spices (John 19:39; Song of Sol. 1:12; 3:6) (Reinhartz 1999). This is not to say that John portrayed Mary and Jesus as physical lovers. Even in the first century, the Song of Songs had acquired a spiritual interpretation as an allegory of the love between God and the covenant people, and it is likely that this allegory lies in the foreground of the Gospel's allusions to the Song of Songs. At the same time, this section has been one source of the speculation found in second-century and later sources of a special relationship between Jesus and Mary Magdalene that is expressed explicitly in the *Gospel of Thomas*, the *Gospel of Philip*, and the *Gospel of Mary* (Schaberg; King).

More important, he gives her a special mission: to go to "my brothers"—the male disciples—and tell them that he is ascending to the Father (20:17). She does so, saying, "I have seen the Lord" (20:18). Their response, if any, is not recorded.

■ THE TEXT IN THE INTERPRETIVE TRADITION

Rufinus of Aquileia (340–410) noted the story's echoes of the Song of Songs, which he interprets, alongside passages from the Psalms, the Prophets, and, indeed, all of Scripture, as a prophecy of the resurrection: "This was foretold in the Song of Songs: 'on my bed I sought the one my soul loves. I sought him in the night and did not find him' [Song of Sol. 3:1]. Of those also who found him and held him by the feet, it is foretold, in the same book, 'I will hold the one my soul loves and will not let him go' [Song of Sol. 3:4]" (*Commentary on the Apostles' Creed* 30; Elowsky 2007, 344).

■ THE TEXT IN CONTEMPORARY DISCUSSION

The Song of Songs allusions subtly place Mary and Jesus in the role of lovers, a hint that is reinforced when he does not permit her to touch him. Whatever their historical relationship was, it has been transformed by his death. More important for contemporary purposes is to note that Mary is an "apostle to the apostles." This description is thought to have originated in the *Commentary on the Song of Songs* 25.6 (Cerrato, 191) written by (or perhaps attributed to) Hippolytus of Rome (170–235) (Haskins, 65; Ernst, 95–117). This point reinforces the theme of egalitarianism found in Jesus' encounter with the Samaritan woman (also an apostle), and in the foot washing at the Last Supper. But in contrast to the Samaritan woman, there is no evidence that Mary's testimony had any effect on the disciples. This silence replicates the difficulty that some women have experienced in being respected and trusted for their knowledge. Even if the (male) disciples' response is not evident, the Gospel itself is a vehicle through which her testimony can be appreciated.

20:19-29: Appearances to the Disciples

■ THE TEXT IN ITS ANCIENT CONTEXT

That evening, Jesus materializes in the room in which the disciples are hiding from the Jews and announces his presence with a traditional greeting: "Peace be with you" (20:19; cf. Tob. 12:47). He identifies himself by showing his hands and side, commissions them to carry on his work (20:21), and, emulating God's act of creating Adam (Gen. 2:7), he breathes the Holy Spirit onto them. One disciple, who has come to be known as "Doubting" Thomas because of this scene, was absent and refuses to believe, "Unless I see the mark of the nails in his hands, and put my finger in the mark of the nails and my hand in his side" (2:25). The following week, Jesus reappears. Whereas Mary was forbidden from touching Jesus, Thomas is now invited to do so, raising the question of Jesus' post-crucifixion corporeality. Throughout the Gospel, Jesus' crucifixion has been described as an exaltation (e.g., 3:14), suggesting that his death is simultaneously his return to the Father. If the ascension is a return to the same preexistent state that the Word had before it (or he) was made flesh (1:14), then it is reasonable to think that it also marks a return to a noncorporeal existence. His ability to enter the room despite the locked doors also implies incorporeality. And yet, he invites Thomas to touch him. The inconsistency with regard to the status of Jesus' body has suggested to some scholars that the Thomas story is a secondary addition (R. E. Brown 1970, 1032). This is certainly plausible, particularly in light of 20:29, which is obviously addressed to the Gospel's audiences. The narrative is silent as to whether Thomas does touch Jesus, but he immediately confesses his faith: "My Lord and my God!" (2:28). Jesus gently chides him: "Have you believed because you have seen me? Blessed are those who have not seen and yet have come to believe" (20:29). This passage brings to fruition the pattern that began with the call of the first disciples: the emphasis on believing through the testimony of others. In chiding Thomas, Jesus is addressing later readers who cannot see Jesus directly but who have access to the reliable testimony of the Gospel (see 19:35) as a basis for faith. The story therefore reinforces the authority of the Gospel as a source for its readers' christological understanding and therefore also their salvation.

▍THE TEXT IN THE INTERPRETIVE TRADITION

Gregory the Great (540–604) suggested that "the unbelief of Thomas is more profitable to our faith than the belief of the other disciples. For the touch by which he is brought to believe confirms our minds in belief, beyond all question" (*Forty Gospel Homilies* 26; Elowsky 2007, 367). Leo the Great (400–461) acknowledges the difficulty of believing without seeing, but argues that "it is the strength of great minds and the light of firmly faithful souls unhesitatingly to believe what is not seen with the bodily sight and to focus your affections where you cannot direct your gaze" (*Sermon* 74.1; Elowsky 2007, 374).

▍THE TEXT IN CONTEMPORARY DISCUSSION

Jesus' remark to Thomas provides space for considering the relationship between the written word and historical, philosophical, and spiritual truths. The norms of historiographical writing have changed since the late first century; we now expect historians and biographers to report the facts and not only their interpretations thereof. Nevertheless, every attempt to convey facts also entails shaping those facts into a story, which in turn complicates its relationship to fact. No wonder that Thomas would not believe something so unusual as resurrection without seeing the evidence for himself. And yet, as the story itself emphasizes, there are many occasions when we must rely on the testimony of others, even in matters of crucial importance to our own well-being.

20:30-31 Conclusion and Statement of Purpose

▍THE TEXT IN ITS ANCIENT CONTEXT

Although it is followed by a final chapter, John 20:30-31 is the conclusion and statement of purpose of the Gospel as a whole. The passage acknowledges that the Gospel presents only a selection of Jesus' many acts and directs our attention to the disciples as the primary witnesses. Like 4:48, the passage is aimed directly at the readers or listeners. What is remarkable about this passage is the important role that it envisages for "this book" in the lives of its audiences.

On the surface, the intent of these verses is clear: to persuade "you" that Jesus is the Messiah, the Son of God, and thereby to lead "you" to eternal life. But the meaning is murkier than one might suppose, due to a textual variant in 20:31: "so that you may [come to] believe" (NRSV). The conjunction "so that" requires a verb in the subjunctive mood (English: "may" or "might"). The oldest manuscripts have the verb "believe" in the present subjunctive form, meaning "that you may continue to believe." This variant implies that the Gospel was written in order to deepen the faith of an audience that already professes belief in Christ. Other manuscripts, however, have the verb in the aorist subjunctive, meaning "that you may come to believe." This variant suggests that the Gospel was written in order to persuade nonbelievers to become believers; in other words, for missionary purposes. Although the New Revised Standard Version has chosen the latter reading in its translation, the scholarly consensus is that the Gospel is not a missionary document, because its language and concepts are better understood as addressing insiders rather than outsiders.

■ THE TEXT IN THE INTERPRETIVE TRADITION

For Origen, reading Jesus' words in the Gospels was tantamount to hearing him directly. He comments that "the Samaritans renounce their faith that was based on the speech of the woman when they discover that hearing the Savior himself is better than that faith . . . Heracleon says, 'People believe in the Savior first by being led by people. But whenever they read his words, they no longer believe because of human testimony alone, but because of the truth itself'" (*Comm. Jo.* 13.353; Elowsky 2006, 170).

■ THE TEXT IN CONTEMPORARY DISCUSSION

The Gospel's statement of purpose, like the prologue, calls on readers to situate themselves within the Gospel, that is, to be the "you" that the Gospel is addressing. This "you" is an idealized, fully compliant reader who will situate him- or herself alongside the narrator, the disciples, the Samaritan woman, and other positive characters. Such a reader will not only accept that Jesus is the Christ and Son of God as described in the Gospel but also take on the negative representation of the unbelieving world—represented by "the Jews"—that runs throughout the narrative. Real readers, however, have a choice as to whether or how much of the Gospel to take on in their own personal faith and spiritual journey. Christian readers may choose to accept some sections and resist others. Non-Christian readers may resist the fundamental message but nevertheless engage with other elements of the Gospel, such as its rich symbolism or its positive representation of women.

21:1-25: Epilogue

■ THE TEXT IN ITS ANCIENT CONTEXT

On the basis of its content and literary style, this chapter has sometimes been viewed as a later, non-Johannine addition. Unlike 7:53—8:11, however, the manuscript evidence does not show that it circulated separately from the rest of the Gospel or that the Gospel originally ended with chapter 20. Nevertheless, it presents a somewhat different image of the disciples than the rest of the Gospel.

The chapter recounts Jesus' third and final postresurrection appearance, during the disciples' fishing expedition by the Sea of Galilee. Until Jesus appears, the fish are not biting, but when he instructs them about where to cast the net, their haul is huge: 153 large fish. They cook and eat some with bread, in a scene that recalls the multiplication of the loaves and fishes (John 6).

After breakfast, Jesus asks Peter three times whether Peter loves him, and instructs him to tend the flock (20:15-17). In doing so, Jesus erases the shame of the threefold denial, and installs Peter as the shepherd who will lead them in Jesus' absence. The reemergence of the shepherd and sheep metaphor clashes with the fishing symbolism, though both sets of images are used in the Gospel to refer to the gathering of believers and followers. Also jarring is the elevation of Peter over the Beloved Disciple, who has been Jesus' closest follower to this point. Jesus concludes his charge to Peter with an enigmatic prophecy: "when you were younger, you used to fasten your own belt and to go wherever you wished. But when you grow old, you will stretch out your hands, and someone else will fasten a belt around you and take you where you do not wish to go" (21:18). The narrator attempts to clarify that Jesus "said this to indicate the kind of death by which he would glorify God" (21:19).

Peter then asks: what about the Beloved Disciple (21:20)? This question elicits an even more opaque response: "If it is my will that he remain until I come, what is that to you? Follow me!" (21:22). The narrator carefully explains that Jesus has used a conditional formulation ("If it is my will . . .") that does not necessarily promise that the disciple will live, but neither does it declare his death. Many have speculated that the Beloved Disciple, while portrayed in an idealized fashion, was the founder and leader of the Johannine community (R. E. Brown 1979). If so, the story suggests that by the time of writing (or perhaps the time of the final redaction), the disciple had already died. Nevertheless, the narrator asserts that "this is the disciple who is testifying to these things and has written them, and we know that his testimony is true" (21:24).

While some have suggested that John 21 was a later addition to the Gospel, the majority opinion views it as original to the final version of the Gospel (for discussion see Köstenberger, 582–86). Even if it was written or redacted by the same person or group that is responsible for the rest of the Gospel, the ending may serve to bring this Gospel closer to the Synoptics, in which Peter is the disciple closest to Jesus.

▌ THE TEXT IN THE INTERPRETIVE TRADITION

The precise number of fish has encouraged considerable speculation. Ammonius (fifth century) suggests that "the hundred can be understood to mean the fullness of the Gentiles. The fifty refers to the elect of Israel who have been saved. And the three set one's mind on the revelation of the holy Trinity, to whose glory the life of the believers who were caught in the dragnet is naturally connected" (*Fragments on John* 637; Elowsky 2007, 381).

Augustine offers a more complex calculation: "When to the number of 10, representing the Law, we add the Holy Spirit as represented by 7, we have 17. And when this number is used for the adding together of every serial number it contains, from 1 up to itself, the sum amounts to 153. . . . All therefore who are sharers in such grace are symbolized by this number. . . . This number has, besides, three times over, the number of 50, and 3 in addition, with reference to the mystery of the Trinity; while, again, the number of 50 is made up by multiplying 7 by 7, with the addition of 1. . . . And we know that it was the fiftieth day after our Lord's ascension that the Holy Spirit was sent, for whom the disciples were commanded to wait according to the promise. It was not, then, without a purpose that these fishes were descried as so many in number and so large in size" (*Tract. Ev. Jo.*122.8–9; Elowsky 2007, 382).

◼ THE TEXT IN CONTEMPORARY DISCUSSION

The epilogue rehabilitates Peter, who had played second fiddle to the Beloved Disciple since chapter 13. This may well be the result of changing circumstances in the Johannine community—the death of its founder—but it also speaks to the ways in which narratives confer authority and how succession is managed.

From beginning to end, this Gospel keeps a steady eye on its readers or hearers. Whether the evangelist envisaged an audience beyond the late first-century community to which it was most immediately addressed is not known. From a vantage point some two millennia later, however, it is clear that the Gospel of John has engaged, inspired, and challenged many readers in many eras, locations, and situations, and continues today to provide ample material for grappling with the fundamental historical, spiritual, and theological questions of human existence.

Works Cited

Anderson, Paul N., Felix Just, and Tom Thatcher. 2007. *John, Jesus, and History*. Atlanta: Society of Biblical Literature.

Brown, Dan. 2003. *The Da Vinci Code: A Novel*. New York: Doubleday.

Brown, Raymond Edward. 1966. *The Gospel according to John I–XII*. AB 29. Garden City, NY: Doubleday.

———. 1970. *The Gospel according to John XIII–XXI*. AB 29a. Garden City, NY: Doubleday.

———. 1979. *The Community of the Beloved Disciple*. New York: Paulist.

Bultmann, Rudolf. 1971. *The Gospel of John: A Commentary*. Philadelphia: Westminster.

Cerrato, J. A. 2002. *Hippolytus between East and West: The Commentaries and the Provenance of the Corpus*. Oxford: Oxford University Press.

Chilton, Bruce. 2008. *Abraham's Curse: The Roots of Violence in Judaism, Christianity, and Islam*. New York: Doubleday.

Crown, Alan David, Reinhard Pummer, and Abraham Tal. 1993. *A Companion to Samaritan Studies*. Tübingen: Mohr Siebeck.

Ehrman, Bart D. 2004. *Truth and Fiction in The Da Vinci Code: A Historian Reveals What We Really Know about Jesus, Mary Magdalene, and Constantine*. Oxford: Oxford University Press.

Elowsky, Joel C. 2006. *John 1–10*. Ancient Christian Commentary on Scripture, New Testament 4a. Downers Grove, IL: InterVarsity Press.

———. 2007. *John 11–21*. Ancient Christian Commentary on Scripture, New Testament 4b. Downers Grove, IL: InterVarsity Press.

Ernst, Allie M. 2009. *Martha from the Margins: The Authority of Martha in Early Christian Tradition*. Leiden: Brill.

Eslinger, Lyle. 1987. "The Wooing of the Woman at the Well: Jesus, the Reader and Reader-Response Criticism." *Literature and Theology* 1, no. 2:167–83.

Fortna, Robert Tomson. 1970. *The Gospel of Signs: A Reconstruction of the Narrative Source Underlying the Fourth Gospel*. London: Cambridge University Press.

Fredriksen, Paula. 1999. *Jesus of Nazareth, King of the Jews: A Jewish Life and the Emergence of Christianity*. New York: Knopf.

Freund, Richard A., Rami Arav, and Bethsaida Excavations Project. 1995. *Bethsaida: A City by the North Shore of the Sea of Galilee*. Kirksville, MO: Truman State University Press.

Hachlili, Rachel. 2005. *Jewish Funerary Customs, Practices and Rites in the Second Temple Period*. Leiden: Brill.

Haskins, Susan. 1994. *Mary Magdalen: Myth and Metaphor*. New York: Harcourt, Brace.

Heschel, Abraham Joshua. 1951. *The Sabbath, Its Meaning for Modern Man*. New York: Farrar, Straus and Young.

King, Karen L. 2003. *The Gospel of Mary of Magdala: Jesus and the First Woman Apostle*. Santa Rosa, CA: Polebridge.

Kobel, Esther. 2011. *Dining with John: Communal Meals and Identity Formation in the Fourth Gospel and Its Historical and Cultural Context*. Leiden: Brill.

Köstenberger, Andreas J. 2004. *John*. Baker Exegetical Commentary on the New Testament. Grand Rapids: Baker Academic.

Levine, Amy-Jill. 2003. *A Feminist Companion to John*. 2 vols. London: Sheffield Academic Press.

———. 2006. *The Misunderstood Jew: The Church and the Scandal of the Jewish Jesus*. San Francisco: HarperSanFrancisco.

Lincoln, Andrew T. 2005. *The Gospel according to Saint John*. Peabody, MA: Hendrickson.

Lowe, Malcolm F. 1976. "Who Were the 'Ioudaioi'?" *NovT* 18, no. 2:101–30.

Martyn, J. Louis. 2003. *History and Theology in the Fourth Gospel*. 3rd ed. NTL. Louisville: Westminster John Knox.

Mason, Steve. 2007. "Jews, Judaeans, Judaizing, Judaism: Problems of Categorization in Ancient History." *JSJ* 38:457–512.

Meier, John P. 2009. *A Marginal Jew: Rethinking the Historical Jesus*. Vol. 4, *Law and Love*. New Haven: Yale University Press.

Miller, David. 2010. "The Meaning of Ioudaios and Its Relationship to Other Group Labels in Ancient 'Judaism.'" *Currents in Biblical Research* 9, no. 1:98–126.

Moss, Candida R. 2010. *The Other Christs: Imitating Jesus in Ancient Christian Ideologies of Martyrdom*. New York: Oxford University Press.

Origen. 1993. *Commentary on the Gospel according to John. Books 13–32*. Translated by Ronald E. Heine. Washington, DC: Catholic University of America Press.

Painter, John. 2010. "Johannine Literature: The Gospel and Letters of John." In *The Blackwell Companion to the New Testament*, edited by David Edward Aune, 344–72. Malden, MA: Wiley-Blackwell.

Phillips, Gary A. 1979. "'This Is a Hard Saying; Who Can Be a Listener to It?' The Creation of the Reader in John 6." In *SBLSP*, edited by Paul Achtemeier, 185–96. Missoula, MT: Scholars Press.

Reinhartz, Adele. 1989. "Great Expectations: A Reader-Oriented Approach to Johannine Christology and Eschatology." *Literature and Theology* 3, no. 1:61–76.

———. 1992. *The Word in the World: The Cosmological Tale in the Fourth Gospel*. Atlanta: Scholars Press.

————. 1999. "To Love the Lord: An Intertextual Reading of John 20." In *The Labour of Reading: Essays in Honour of Robert C. Culley*, edited by Fiona Bladk, Roland Boer, Christian Kelm, and Erin Runions, 56–69. SemeiaSt. Atlanta: Scholars Press.

————. 2001a. "'Jews' and Jews in the Fourth Gospel." In *Anti-Judaism and the Fourth Gospel: Papers of the Leuven Colloquium, 2000*, edited by R. Bieringer, Didier Pollefeyt, and F. Vandecasteele-Vanneuville, 341–56. Assen, the Netherlands: Royal Van Gorcum.

————. 2001b. "John 8:31-59 from a Jewish Perspective." In *Remembering for the Future 2000: The Holocaust in an Age of Genocides*, edited by John K. Roth and Elisabeth Maxwell-Meynard, 2:787–97. London: Palgrave.

Sanders, E. P. 1985. *Jesus and Judaism*. Philadelphia: Fortress Press.

Schaberg, Jane. 2002. *The Resurrection of Mary Magdalene: Legends, Apocrypha, and the Christian Testament*. New York: Continuum.

Schmidt, Francis. 2001. *How the Temple Thinks: Identity and Social Cohesion in Ancient Judaism*. Sheffield: Sheffield Academic Press.

Smith, D. Moody. 2001. *John among the Gospels*. Columbia: University of South Carolina Press.

Strachan, R. H. 1941. *The Fourth Gospel, Its Significance and Environment*. London: Student Christian Movement Press.

Von Wahlde, Urban C. 1989. *The Earliest Version of John's Gospel: Recovering the Gospel of Signs*. Wilmington, DE: Michael Glazier.

————. 2000. "'The Jews' in the Gospel of John: Fifteen Years of Research (1983–1998)." *ETL* 76:30–55.

Wilkinson, John. 1975. "Incident of the Blood and Water in John 19:34." *Scottish Journal of Theology* 28, no. 2:149–72.

ACTS AS A HISTORY OF THE EARLY CHURCH

Demetrius K. Williams

If the Gospel of Luke and the Acts of the Apostles were written by the same person—the view taken here, though it is a controversial matter to which we will return below—the author has the distinction of being the only writer of a Gospel to provide a sequel. Acts offered to the early church an account of Christian origins and an edifying narration of the spread of the gospel, chronicling the notable deeds and challenges of the first generation of Jesus-followers and addressing several issues confronting the early church in its infancy, the most pressing of which were the social and theological challenges resulting from expansion (i.e., the inclusion of gentiles); the early church's relationship with Judaism; and its spread into and navigation of the cultural and political environment of Rome (C. Matthews, 183). The commentary that follows will trace these themes through the work; this essay will discuss Acts as the single historical writing in the New Testament.

The designation "Luke-Acts" considers the Gospel and Acts together as a single two-volume literary project, though these were separated early on in the ecclesial tradition: there are no extant manuscripts or canon lists in which they appear joined together. The patristic writers treated Luke and Acts separately, although they acknowledged their common authorship. Their separation was likely a result of the different literary types and functions of the two documents within the canon (which is organized by genre, Gospels, History, Letters, Apocalypse). The Gospel of Luke is similar to the other Gospels, but Acts more closely resembles other well-known literary genres in the ancient world, historical writings in general, but also the ancient romance genre that included travel, shipwreck, and danger. On the one hand, Luke provides both a kind of ancient "biography" of the founder (Jesus) and as an introduction to the deeds of the first generation of Jesus' followers as depicted in Acts. The latter writing, on the other hand, serves as an introduction to the letters of Paul, even though it was likely written decades later than they. (Note, too, that the letters ordinarily begin with Paul's Letter to the Romans and that Acts ends with Paul in Rome, openly preaching the gospel without hindrance.) Their separation within the canon allows the two writings to perform these different literary and ecclesial functions (Johnson, 187–88).

While Luke-Acts is generally believed to be the work of a single author, the traditional attribution of these writings to Luke—"the beloved physician" and companion of Paul (see Col. 4:14; Philem. 24; 2 Tim. 4:11)—has been challenged. Neither the Gospel nor the Acts includes a name in the superscription of the earliest manuscripts. (Superscriptions were added to the Gospels in the early second century, during heated ecclesial debates concerning to whom "the Scriptures" belonged—the emerging proto-orthodox movement, or the "heretics," or even to Judaism, for that matter, as we see being argued in the *Epistle of Barnabas*.) As in the commentary, I refer here to the author as "Luke" as a matter of convenience (Williams 2007, 213).

Dating the Acts of the Apostles

Different proposed dates for Acts correspond to very different understandings of the character and purpose of the writing. Three distinct periods have emerged as prominent candidates: early (62–70 CE), intermediate (80–90 CE), and late (110–150 CE; Tyson, 1–23; Drane, 245–47).

Those scholars who prefer an early date believe Paul's arrival and sojourn in Rome (Acts 28) most likely occurred between 58 and 60 CE. On this view, the author of Acts, who included ample and detailed descriptions of Paul's earlier trials, did not provide a description of the final trial in Rome or its outcome because Acts was written before that trial took place. This would also explain why Acts does not mention any of Paul's letters, since they had not been collected and circulated at so early a date. Further, the so-called we-sections (Acts 16:10-17; 20:5-15; 21:1-18; 27:1-28), which appear to imply that the narrator was present with Paul as an "eyewitness" on a number of important occasions, are taken as evidence that at least chapters 13–28 depend on a firsthand report, and the character of these chapters is taken to suggest the historical reliability of the book as a whole. The author's intention presumably was to document and describe the spread of the gospel from Jerusalem to Rome, and once Paul arrived at this destination, that task was completed.

Scholars who favor an intermediate date for Acts point out that while the Roman destruction of Jerusalem and its temple in 70 CE is not mentioned in Acts, it is alluded to in the Gospel of Luke (21:20-24). Furthermore, if Luke used the Gospel of Mark, which was arguably written between 66 and 70 CE, Luke-Acts could not have been written before this time. These scholars propose a date before 90 CE, however, because the author does not seem to know of Paul's letters, which were presumably collected and being circulated by that date. This dating, perhaps in the mid-70s to mid-80s, casts doubt on arguments for an "eyewitness" account of the life of Paul. The author is arguably a generation removed from the persons and events about which he writes, and while he devotes considerable attention to Paul, he fails to mention important aspects of the apostle's teaching; for example, his preaching of justification by faith for gentiles (Galatians 3 and Romans 4), or the validity of his identity as an apostle (see 1 Corinthians 9; 2 Corinthians 3; Rom. 1:1). (The criteria for being an apostle in Acts 1:21-22 implicitly exclude Paul, notwithstanding Acts 14:4, 14, where

Paul and Barnabas are called apostles—perhaps reflecting a source used by the author and not his own view.) On this view, it would have been highly unlikely for an author who had been Paul's close associate and companion to have overlooked or excluded these and other essential Pauline concerns. Furthermore, Acts expresses attitudes and beliefs that became common in the postapostolic age and tends to smooth over tensions in the early church, portraying the apostles as unified and in mutual agreement in matters over which Paul's letters indicate tension and debate.

Scholars who prefer a late date for the composition of Acts (110–150 CE) observe that Acts seems to be unknown before the last half of the second century; the first unquestionable witness to Acts is the church leader Irenaeus (fl. c. 180 CE). Further, the author of Acts was apparently acquainted with Josephus's *Antiquities of the Jews* (ca. 93–94 CE): we may compare the mention of Theudas in Acts 5:36-37 and of the Egyptian troublemaker in Acts 21:38 with Josephus's description of related events in *Antiquities* 20.5.1. Positioning Acts between the times of Josephus and Irenaeus yields a period between 110 CE and 150 CE. In contrast to advocates of earlier dating, some recent studies have argued that the author of Acts was quite aware of the Pauline Letters (Pervo 2006), especially Galatians (Leppä). Indeed, it has been argued that Acts was written to subvert at least one possible second-century interpretation of Galatians. Although there are verbal and conceptual similarities between Acts 15 and Galatians 2 (Walker 1985; 1998), there are also marked differences, as Acts conveys more unified and harmonious relationships between Paul and the Jerusalem apostles. One explanation is that the author of Acts sought to counteract the notion of a radical break between law (Torah) and gospel that could be inferred from an "improper" reading of Galatians, as for example by Marcion or his followers. In contrast to Marcion's separation of Jesus from Israel's Scriptures, Acts depicts Peter, Paul, and other believers proclaiming that Jesus as their fulfillment. While Marcion claimed that Paul was the only true apostle, Peter and the others being "false apostles," Acts portrays Paul as in total agreement with the other apostles and even subservient to them; portrays Peter (not Paul) as the first to initiate preaching to the gentiles (Acts 10:1—11:18); and even defines apostleship in a way that excludes Paul (Acts 1:22-24). While Marcion attributed to Paul a radical distinction between law and grace, the dispensation of the law (Torah) having come to an end with the coming of Christ (see Gal. 3:23; Rom. 10:4), Acts characterized Paul as a Torah-observant Jew and a devout Pharisee, even portraying him as circumcising Timothy "because of the Jews" (Acts 16:1-4). Recent studies take these aspects of the narrative as evidence that Acts was written in direct opposition to Marcionite teaching and belongs alongside other anti-Marcionite figures like Justin Martyr (c. 140s CE). Indeed, Acts appears to share aspects of the thought-world of early second-century writings including those of Justin, 4 Maccabees (c. 100 CE), the letters of Ignatius of Antioch (c. 110 CE), and the *Martyrdom of Polycarp* (c. 150 CE), and appears a close relative of the apocryphal *Acts of Paul*, both in terms of genre and dating (S. Matthews, 5–6; see also Gregory; Mount; Tyson; and Skarsaune).

A late date for Acts has obvious implications for its relationship to the Gospel of Luke. The facts (mentioned above) that no extant manuscripts or canon lists ever joined the two writings together and that patristic writers discussed them separately suggest to some scholars that we should exercise caution in claims regarding the assumed unity of authorship (Parsons and Pervo; Walters). Patricia Walters argues that literary seams and redactional summaries in Luke-Acts, which have usually been attributed to a single author's use of different sources, should instead be attributed to the work of different authors. Lexical and theological thematic differences between the writings are too great, she argues, to be accounted for as the result of different genres (gospel, acts) or a shift in narrative style. She proposes dating the Gospel to the first century, but Acts to the second.

The diversity of these arguments means that a precise date for Acts still cannot be determined with certainty. What is certain is that decisions about the date of Acts shape the various ways we read it: as a history of the first Christian generation from the 60s or 70s, incorporating "eyewitness" accounts; as a second-generation (70s–80s) account of Christianity's movement away from its Jewish roots to become a largely gentile movement; or as a second-century (110–150) effort to combat Marcionite teachings.

The Genre of Acts

Traditionally, there was little dispute among New Testament interpreters that the author of Acts was a historian by intention, making Acts the only intentionally historical writing in the New Testament (Conzelmann, xl). As historical-critical perspectives have developed, however, the discussion has become more nuanced. After acknowledging that Luke intended to write a historical narrative, scholars have asked whether he was a good or bad historian (Johnson, 190). Acts has been severely criticized regarding its historical value and accuracy, a dispute that not long ago made it "the storm centre of modern New Testament study" (Marshall, 13, after Unnik). The first criticisms of the historicity of Acts arose from the mid-nineteenth-century Tübingen school, led by Ferdinand Christian Baur, whose stated singular purpose in investigating the New Testament was to "comprehend the historically given in its pure objectivity as far as it is generally possible" (Baur, vi–viii). This new emphasis on "historicity" and historical "objectivity" (though in some tension with Hegel's dialectical philosophy of history) led members of the Tübingen School to assert that Acts was merely a piece of Christian propaganda literature, written in the early second century and entirely unreliable as a historical document (see Munck, lv). This assessment has been reasserted among some contemporary scholars: for example, Gerd Lüdemann wrote that the "straight-line" arrangement of the narrative "clearly oversimplifies the actual order of events," and so "cannot furnish the basis for a valid history of early first-century Christianity" (Lüdemann 2008, 71; 2005). It is perhaps more appropriate, Lüdemann asserts, to view Acts as a combination of both historical fact and historical fiction (Lüdemann 2008, 65). Acts may not be completely unreliable—it appears to have embedded within it traditions that may contain a kernel of historical fact—but each episode must be critically evaluated to ascertain the historical value of the traditions behind it.

Other interpreters have emphasized the entertaining aspect of Acts and classified it among the historical novels of antiquity (Pervo 1987, 11, 137–38); Howard Clark Kee describes it as a "novelistic drama" (Kee, 1). This designation further blurs the characterization of Acts as history because the measure of a genre's entertainment value does not allow us to distinguish works of ancient history from ancient novels. As Emilio Gabba notes in this regard, "in the same climate of paradoxographical literature the 'novel' is born and develops; the novel in antiquity is in fact a form of history"

(Gabba, 15). While accuracy, objectivity, and critical assessment are expected today of the modern historian—"accuracy about the facts together with some accurate, and as far as possible objective, assessment about what the facts signify; in other words, some interpretation of what happened, in the economic and social as well as the political and military spheres" (Grant, 2)—ancient principles of historiography were different. To be sure, in antiquity, the craft of writing history also dealt with events regarded as important and noteworthy. But "ancient history was written according to principles, interests, aims, and tastes of great diversity. Works of history in antiquity were composed according to its intended audience, and different types of history aimed at different readers, had different aims, were composed according to different principles" (Gabba, 3). Ancient historiography, therefore, should not be understood according our contemporary sense of factual reporting, but as "literary artistry," because the first duty of any historian was to be an artist. In Lucian's opinion (120–180 CE), a good historian had to have "powers of expression" (*On Writing History* 34). In short, then, an ancient historian had to weave stories that would, first and foremost, entertain, and for this purpose, historical precision and detailed accuracy were secondary, if not totally disregarded. Even if we measure Acts against the standard of ancient historiography as found, for example, in the works of Thucydides (460–400 BCE)—whose survey of causes and effects, goal of impartiality in securing and evaluating evidence from both sides of an issue, and rigorous accuracy of detail in separating truth from falsehood established ancient scientific standards (though these were not maintained by his successors: "in the end, the demands of artistry gained precedence over those of science" [Grant, 8, 95]) and constitute perhaps the closest approximation to the contemporary ideal of history-writing—Acts suffers in the comparison, for it lacks some of the basic characteristics of a historical work as found in Thucydides. Some scholars have therefore asserted that Acts is not historical, and that its author is not the first Christian historian (Kümmel, 161–62).

Some scholars have asked whether the question of genre would be resolved if the entire literary project of Luke-Acts were considered and assessed together (Rothschild; Ehrman, 155). Attempts to classify the literary genre of Luke-Acts have included "theological history" (Maddox, 16), "apologetic historiography" (Sterling, 374; Doughty), and Greco-Roman biography, composed of an admixture of two subtypes (Talbert, 134). But since the two writings are structured and organized quite differently, as was recognized early on in the ecclesial tradition that treated and placed them separately, efforts to categorize the conjoined work have not proved generally convincing.

It is nevertheless commonly recognized that the book of Acts is concerned, in organization and intention, with a sequential development of the early Christian movement and with recounting the deeds of important figures in that development. The narrative is set within a chronological framework that begins with the origin of the movement, noting its spread and development using "synchronisms" (DeSilva, 349)—that is, attempts to correlate an event with different methods of dating; for example, the reigns of kings, the tenure of governors, or the Jewish high priesthood. In these respects, Acts resembles other kinds of histories produced in antiquity that used similar literary features to recount the lives of key leaders, significant incidents in the life of a particular city or region, or momentous events (major wars, for example) in a nation's history. Such histories could be arranged according to a particular topic, or presented in a chronological sequence (Polybius). This could be restricted to a single, albeit complicated event, such as in Thucydides' account of the

Peloponnesian War, or as a series of interrelated events, as in Polybius's account of Rome's ascendance over the Mediterranean world. Some historical narratives covered the salient events in the memory of a nation, designed particularly to show how the character and identity of a people or nation was established and how they came to be. (For example, Josephus's twenty-volume *Antiquities of the Jews* sketches the significant events, beginning with Adam and Eve and continuing to Josephus's own day, in the history of Judaism.) Contemporary historians sometimes call this genre a "general history" or a "historical monograph." These ancient histories commonly had a number of principal characters and tended to employ a wide range of subgenres, such as travel narratives, anecdotes, private letters, dialogues, and public speeches. For the most part, ancient Greco-Roman histories were creative literary productions and were not concerned necessarily with exacting certitude with regard to dates or facts. Historians exercised creative freedom in how they compiled and communicated their information (Ehrman, 155). Thus the ancient view of history was not unified, and historians in the Greco-Roman world produced a variety of differing literature that was designated as history. Moreover, for many ancient historians, the relevant criteria for historical narratives were similarity, plausibility, and persuasiveness. Acts seems most closely to correspond to these designations in that it provides a single, orderly account that sketches the salient events of the history of the Jesus movement, from its origins to a point in the not-too-distant past, to show how the Christian identity as a new genus or people was established (Palmer).

The act of persuasion requires the use of language intentionally and purposefully crafted to convey meaning and appeal. Contemporary historians increasingly recognize that *language* shapes and creates the past; the basic events of human experience do not in and of themselves possess the qualities of coherence, unity, integrity, connectivity, comprehensiveness, and closure (S. Matthews, 20–24). Human ingenuity and creativity impose these formal narrative qualities on events and experience. Consequently, all written histories, whether ancient or modem, cannot be viewed as objective and unbiased accounts of what "really happened in the past." Ancient and modern historians out of necessity pick and choose what to recount and what to present as significant or noteworthy. In this selection process, it is certain that a historian narrates events, intentionally or not, in such a way that exposes his or her priorities, values, beliefs, and interpretation of those events (Ehrman, 155). In contemporary postmodern thought, it is recognized that *this is the ideological work that ancient (and modern) narratives do* (S. Matthews, 21). This important shift in perspective for understanding ancient historical writings has potential to aid the contemporary reader in reading the Acts of the Apostles.

Contemporary Options for Reading Acts: Ideological, Postcolonial, and Postmodern Perspectives

While standard historical and literary approaches have provided important insights into the text of Acts, the theology of Luke-Acts, and important themes and motifs in the narrative, a number of newer "reading perspectives" and interpretive frameworks offer insights into the ways in which narrators both ancient and modern encode their own (and their group's) priorities, agendas, values, beliefs, and biases into the stories they tell.

Ideological critics help us to understand that the "raw events" of the past are to be distinguished from historical narration about those events, giving them meaning. The writing of history involves perspective, opinion, interpretation, and organization as the historian connects events with a particular purpose in mind. History is not possible without discourse (Dijk, 120–21); "history as a discourse attempts to wrest and provide meaning out of events that inform the development or making of culture, nation building, and processes by which ethnoracial identity is constructed" (S. Matthews, 4). Ancient (and contemporary) historical narratives are perspectival and bound up with views of authority and social order, not always as it is, but as it ought to be. In these ways, historical writings and narratives are ideological—they express vested interests whether consciously or only implicitly. Because "no one can write entirely objective history, we must be ever alert to identify ideology when it plays a recognizable role" in Luke-Acts as well (Lüdemann 2008, 66).

"[As] the basis of a social group's self-image, ideologies organize its identity, actions, and resources as well as its relations to other social groups" (Dijk, 115). So, ideology is not necessarily negative; all human groups are implicated in it. However, the social, political, and religious impact of ideology becomes more acute with regard to empires and imperial or colonial regimes that seek to promote and impose their values on other nations or peoples. Although military power usually was (and is) used to maintain control, the political and social mechanisms of empire are also extended through social, cultural, religious, and political constructs that promote acceptance and a sense that the hegemony is "natural" (Punt, 192). The Roman Empire provides an appropriate example of the material reality through which ideology is imposed, through the use of images (the ancient mass media)—statues, monuments, coins, and temples (Lopez)—and through inscriptions and literature, especially the imperial patronage of historical narratives that promoted and legitimized the empire and imperial prerogatives. Such propagandistic images and historical literature, whether conscious or unconscious or by means subtle or overt, portray the reality, values, and benefits of empire (as natural or divinely instituted), expressed through *a unifying cultural ideal*, or in contemporary postmodern nomenclature, through a "grand-narrative" (Flax). In postmodern thought, a grand-narrative (or meta- or master narrative) is "a global or totalizing cultural narrative schema which orders and explains knowledge and experience" (Stephens and McCallum, 1). All aspects of societies depend on these grand-narratives. Therefore, a grand-narrative is a story that encompasses and explains other "little stories" within totalizing schemes (Lyotard, xxiii–xxiv).

At this point, postmodern thought converges with postcolonial and ideological investigation. Not only social groups but also national and imperial regimes produce grand-narratives that universalize, characterize, and promote their politics, worldviews, identities, and values. These grand-narratives inevitably mask contradictions and inconsistencies inherent in a regime's practice or organization. For example, a grand-narrative is implicit in the statement in the American Declaration of Independence that "We hold these truths to be self-evident, that all men are created equal, that they are endowed by their Creator with certain unalienable Rights, that among these are Life, Liberty and the pursuit of Happiness." The ideal stated here is the foundation of American democratic politics, institutions, and society, but we know that it has also masked inconsistencies of racism, slavery, sexism, and classism (among other things). Postmodern examinations attempt to expose and critique such inconsistencies (Flax, 41). Postcolonial analysis engages in "ideological reflection on the discourse and practice of imperialism and colonialism," recognizing that the shadow of empire stands behind and within the construction of ancient texts (Segovia, 126). An ideological-critical lens is essential to both perspectives because ideological analysis explores the relationship between rhetoric and power (Bible and Culture Collective, 274). Postmodern, postcolonial, and ideological-critical perspectives resonate in biblical studies because the biblical texts were written in the shadow of empire and are at once rhetorical and ideological: that is, they too seek to persuade, they espouse certain values and beliefs, they interpret the meaning of certain events, and they limit and constrain their readers in multiple ways (DeSilva, 678–79). These perspectives allow new angles of vision on Luke-Acts as a historical project.

Luke as a Historian of the Early Church

We may consider Acts a work of ancient ecclesial history. In the prologue to Luke (1:1-4), the author expresses what we may take as his purpose for Acts as well (see Acts 1:1; Stott, 22). He informs his reader that he has examined and explored both written and oral sources (Luke 1:1-3), presumably attempting to use them "critically"; that is, collecting information and relating it to his story (an "orderly account" or "narrative," 1:3). We may also understand Acts as interacting with other grand-narratives. Luke-Acts draws connections among events in the origins of the Christian movement (beginning with characters rooted in Judaism), the teaching and deeds of Jesus, the proclamation and actions of the apostles, and the later experiences of the churches. He relates these, further, to Israel's Scriptures, casting the emergence of Jesus and the early Christian movement as a fulfillment of biblical prophecy and thus continuing the heritage of Israel. He also indicates that his story coincides with the period of the emergent glory of the Roman Empire and its civilizing mission (see Brunt, 25–35), stipulating that Jesus was born under the reign of the first Roman emperor, Caesar Augustus (Luke 2:1); while Quirinius was governor of Syria (2:2) and King Herod the Great ruled Judea (1:5); his ministry began during the reign of Tiberias Caesar (Luke 3:1); and he was crucified under the procurator Pontius Pilate (Luke 23:24-25), while Tiberias was still in power. Acts tells the story of the early church within the framework of the larger Roman context as well, in Judea and Syria (Herod Agrippa, Acts 12:20-22; procurators Antonius Felix, Acts 23:24, and Porcius Festus, Acts 25:1; King Herod Agrippa II, Acts 25:13), Asia Minor (*Asiarchs* or officials in the province of Asia, Acts 19:31), and Europe (the proconsul Gallio, Acts 18:12-17). Luke must have known that Rome, too, had its "gospel" (an inscription from 9 BCE in Priene, Asia Minor references the "good news [*euangelia*] of Augustus"; see Deissmann, 366) that promoted the *Pax Romana* ("peace of Rome"), its "savior" (the reigning Caesar), and a driving mission to dominate and to civilize the world as part of its ideology (as expressed in Virgil's *Aeneid*, 29–19 BCE; Horsley 2003, 12). Indeed, Theophilus, to whom Luke-Acts is dedicated, may have been a Roman patron: the address "most excellent Theophilus" echoes the use "most excellent" used to address a governor of a province (Acts 23:26; 24:3; 26:25). (Theophilus, literally translated "lover of God" or "beloved of God," might also simply be a code name for all Christians: Ehrman, 115–17.) One narrative strategy in the work is to show that, although Judaism (and emerging Christianity) are insignificant in the eyes of Rome, providence is being mediated through the traditions of Israel, *not* those of Rome; it is by means of the gospel of Christ that God is bringing about a new world order, and the apostles are God's agents (Horsley 1997, 206–14, 242–52; 2003, 132–33).

Luke's sources for Acts were limited, so far as contemporary scholars can detect them at all; the whole work is so consistent in style that detecting sources behind the narrative is a matter of deduction (or educated guesswork). Nevertheless, scholars have suspected at least three possible sources: (1) traditions about Peter (and Stephen and Philip) and the Jerusalem church; (2) an "eyewitness" travelogue recounting a portion of Paul's missionary journeys, beginning in chapter 16; and (3) traditions about Paul's conversion and early experiences (Dupont; Hemer, 308–64; Barrett, 1:49–56, 2:xxiv–xxxii). Given the apparent limitations of these sources, Luke can describe some events in detail, but must skip over others, on occasion leaving gaps of several years at a time. This aspect of his narrative resembles the Greek historians Xenophon and Plutarch, who presented a selection of a hero's acts, emphasizing historical vignettes that set forth the hero's character. Most of his narrative is dominated by the towering personalities of Peter and Paul, indicating that Acts is not a simple chronicle, but a portrayal of the character of figures in the early church (Baker, 884).

In piecing together his narrative, Luke exhibits a historian's instinct for chronology and causality: "he makes connections between events, so that a thread of purpose runs through his narrative" (Johnson, 190). That purpose is stated in Acts 1:8, where Jesus tells the disciples, "But you will receive power when the Holy Spirit has come upon you; and you will be my witnesses in Jerusalem, in all Judea and Samaria, and to the ends of the earth." This singular purpose, to explicate the spread of the gospel from Jerusalem to Rome, connects the seemingly disparate pieces into a cohesive whole (Witherington, 1).

Movement from Jerusalem to Rome and the Portrayal of the Apostles

Some scholars have attempted to outline Acts according to the geographical schema in Acts 1:8. But although Luke begins his narrative in Jerusalem, he does not follow the precise sequence in Acts 1:8: Philip's missionary efforts in Samaria (Acts 8:5-25) are narrated before Peter's work in Judea (Acts 9:31—10:48). A little later, the story moves back and forth from Antioch to Jerusalem (11:19-30; 12:1-25). Then, once Paul's missionary work begins, the narrative moves from Europe to Asia, and then back to Jerusalem again. Finally, the book ends with Paul in Rome, which might have been regarded by Luke's readers as the center of the Roman Empire, but certainly not "the ends of the earth." These minor incongruencies are secondary to the overarching theological (or ideological) purpose reflected in the narrative of the gospel's spread from Jerusalem to Rome. This spread represents Luke's conception of salvation history; that is, the sweep of missionary activity throughout the Roman Empire, beginning in Jerusalem and then to the broader Judean regions (chs. 1–8), expands and gains new converts through the Hellenists' mission to the gentiles (which includes Paul and Barnabas, chs. 11–15), and ends with the mission of Paul in Rome (chs. 16–28), thus fulfilling the history of salvation.

This salvation-historical schema has a significant intertextual reference in Isaiah 40–66. Like the postexilic Second Isaiah, Luke is attempting to redefine and rebuild the people of God after the distress and destruction of the first Jewish-Roman War in 66–70 CE (by rewriting the "Isaianic new exodus": Pao). Scholars have noted that Acts often quotes from the Septuagint, and especially Isaiah (Acts 7:49-50; 8:32-33; 13:34, 47; 28:26-27); however, there are other implicit allusions as well. Some of the most important allusions refer to the power of God's word (Isa. 40:6-8; cf. Acts 6:7; 12:24; 19:20), the centrality of Jerusalem (Isa. 40:9-11; cf. Acts 1:4-5), the work and power of the Holy Spirit (Isa. 42:1; 44:1-4; 61:1-2; cf. Acts 2:1-4; 10:38; 13:1-4), and the (re-)creation of God's people that will include both Jews and gentiles (Isa. 43:15-21; 49:6; cf. Acts 10:44-48; 14:1; 15:12-31) and will also include previous outcasts like eunuchs (Isa. 56:4-5, 8; cf. Acts 8:26-40). Interestingly, Acts 1:8 captures a number of the main elements of Isaiah 40–55: "the geographical sequence of the verse signifies the centrality of Jerusalem ('in Jerusalem [first]'), the reunification of Israel ('in all Judea and Samaria'), and the inclusion of Gentiles ('and to the ends of the earth'). This verse is further sandwiched by two references to the focus of the Isaianic new exodus: Israel's restoration or reconstitution" (Liew, 420–21). The disciples' question in Acts 1:6 prompts Jesus' "programmatic promise," and for Luke, the apostles have a signal role in fulfilling that promise.

Given the limited narrative portrayal of all the apostles, the title "Acts of the Apostles" is a bit misleading. The writing could be more accurately titled the "Acts of Peter and Paul" because they play particularly prominent roles, Peter especially in Acts 1–12, 15, and Paul in Acts 9 and 13–28. The apostles James and John play only minor roles, and the other apostles, no significant role at all. If we think of them as implicitly subsumed under Peter, the result is a roughly symmetric presentation in which Peter (and the other apostles) are guarantors of Jesus' ministry and, as authorized witnesses, provide continuity for the church's continuing mission through Paul. Peter is clearly the leader and chief spokesman of the group; his preaching founds the church (Acts 2), authorizes and ordains new leaders (Acts 6), and guards and regulates the transmission of the Holy Spirit (Acts 8). His missionary work, not Paul's, opens the door to gentile integration into the community (Acts 10). The Jerusalem Conference (Acts 15), narrated at the midpoint of the book, represents a pivotal point in the spread of the gospel, separating the Jerusalem period of the church (under the leadership and authority of Peter) from the expanding outreach to the gentiles; it provides the presupposition and legitimacy for Paul's independent mission after his separation from Barnabas (also in Acts 15). Whether or not this narration reflects history "as it actually happened," it gives rhetorical foundation and validation to Paul's mission, showing that it is congruent with and legitimized by the earlier apostles, especially Peter and James (who defend gentile freedom from the law; compare the impression left in Galatians 2). The central place of the Jerusalem Conference has salvation-historical significance (Lüdemann 2003, 68–69).

The Construction of Christian Identity

In Acts, the good news is proclaimed to rich and poor, slave and free, high and low, Greek and Roman, Jew and gentile. Evidently Luke sought to portray the gospel as available to all peoples (cf. Gal. 3:27-28), an agenda expressed most vividly in Acts 2:16-21—a passage that advances the imperative of Acts 1:8. Luke describes the day of Pentecost as the fulfillment of the prophet Joel's prophecy regarding the descent of the Holy Spirit; indeed, that prophecy expresses the "grand narrative" in Luke by promising universal inclusion of all peoples into the covenant people Israel. Through the proclamation and promise of the gospel, the former barriers of age, race and ethnicity, class, status, and gender were eradicated by the coming of the Holy Spirit, thus grounding the new movement's identity and purpose (Williams 2009, 289–93). Although the Pentecost event, like Joel's prophecy, describes the experience of "ethnically diverse" Jews, in Acts the event foreshadows the eventual integration of gentiles in the promise of the Holy Spirit—a theme that receives significant development later in Acts (see 8:26—15:35), perhaps signifying a protracted struggle in the church. The integration of gentiles depends on the giving and receiving of the Holy Spirit (10:34), who also functions as the "eraser" of ethnic difference (15:8-9).

Because Luke also believes that God is faithful to God's promises, however, and that certain patterns in history indicate the regularity of divine providence, the early part of the narrative depicts the work of mission and evangelism as restricted to Palestinian or Hellenistic Jews. Missionary activity is carried out by Jewish figures like Peter, Philip, Barnabas, and Paul (and a few "minor" missionaries like the Hellenist Jews in Acts 11, Priscilla and Aquila, and the Alexandrian Jew Apollos, whom they "instructed more accurately in the faith," 18:1-2, 24-26). Luke never recounts the missionary activity or preaching of any non-Jewish convert. "This ethnic monopoly (a kind of 'glass ceiling' for Gentile followers?) may explain why Paul circumcises Timothy, who has a Greek father and a Jewish mother (16:13). . . . What distinguishes him is that Paul desires to make him a missionary partner (16:3)" (Liew, 422).

In addition, one observes that Luke does not depict the Holy Spirit as bestowed on all converts without distinction. In Acts, faith in Christ without reception of the Holy Spirit represents only incomplete or partial integration into the community (8:14-17; 18:24—19:7). "The presence of the Spirit is seen as the distinguishing mark of Christianity—it is what makes a person a Christian. . . . The Spirit, then, is the *sine qua non* for being a Christian, not merely a means by which one gets a spiritual booster shot subsequent to conversion" (Witherington, 140). The Samaritans experience a delay between their baptism and their receiving of the Holy Spirit (8:16); the Ephesians receive the Holy Spirit closely following their baptism (19:5-6); and the Holy Spirit comes upon the centurion at Caesarea, Cornelius, and his household even before they are baptized (10:44-48; Liew, 420–21), causing some scholars to term this event "the Gentile Pentecost" (Witherington, 134). There is no mention of the Ethiopian convert in chapter 8 receiving the Holy Spirit, however; the Spirit instead moves on Philip as he and the Ethiopian are rising from the baptismal waters, transporting Philip to a new locale (8:38-40). Accordingly, the black Ethiopian's incorporation into Christ appears incomplete, while the nonblack European's incorporation is complete. This may be (as some contemporary scholars have suggested) because Luke seeks to complete the "Acts of Philip" before moving to his next subjects, Paul's "conversion" (ch. 9) and Peter's initiation of the gentile mission (ch. 10; Haenchen, 309–17). Or perhaps Luke used the Ethiopian eunuch positively to express the fulfillment of Isaiah (56:4-5, 8), which promises God's salvation and honor to the eunuch (González, 117–18). Or perhaps we see here an aspect of Luke's ideology regarding authority: although Philip initiated the Samaritan mission, the Holy Spirit was not given until Peter arrived (ch. 8); likewise, although Philip baptized the Ethiopian eunuch, he was not authorized (according to Luke) to transmit or confer the Holy Spirit. These explanations may not mitigate the impression that Luke values the conversion of a European—a Roman centurion—over a black African who presumably "outranks" him—an official of the Candace.

The issue of gender offers another example of Luke's inconsistency. The quotation from Joel names "prophesying daughters," but neither the prophesying of non-Jews nor of women is narrated in Acts; only that of sons of Israel. Luke and Acts are generally held to be the New Testament writings most affirming of women, but as Beverly Roberts Gaventa asks, "What ever happened to the prophesying daughters?" Several women are mentioned by name, like Tabitha, Mary (mother of John Mark), Lydia, and Damaris, among the believers; but they are not given voice. The first woman to speak in the narrative, Sapphira, is also the last (Acts 5:8; Gaventa, 49). When we at last encounter Philip's four unmarried daughters (21:9), we are told that they prophesy, but hear not a word from them; instead, we hear from Agabus, who has come down from Judea, some distance away, to warn Paul of the danger awaiting him in Judea (Acts 21:11). The silence even of prophesying daughters subtly reveals Luke's views of masculinity (Gaventa, 56–58). Women are not independent missionaries and preachers; rather, they support the male apostle's missionary activity as coworkers and patrons (even Prisca/Priscilla must accompany her husband: Schüssler Fiorenza, 161).

Nor does Luke narrate prophesying slaves (the last element in Joel's prophecy). Twice, female slaves are given voice, although briefly. Rhoda, a house slave, encounters Peter, but her testimony about him is initially rejected by those in her owner's household (Acts 12:6-17). Paul exorcizes a spirit of divination from an unnamed slave girl (who stands outside the circle of believers), who declares the truth about his mission and message (though this is not described as prophecy); but she too is silenced and is not offered the message of salvation after the exorcism (Acts 16:16-18). Thus, while Luke includes several accounts of women and of slaves in Acts, his narrative effectively suppresses roles that conflict with his own treatment of the church and his understanding of authority. For him, "male characters circumscribe female identity in the text, developing the 'domestic' characterization of women whereby premium Roman imperial values are demonstrated for leadership" (Penner and Vander Stichele, 198).

A postmodern reading of all these issues recognizes that Luke utilized Joel's prophecy to express his grand-narrative that the bestowal of the Holy Spirit on "all flesh" embraces all racial and ethnic diversity, without regard to geographical location, language, or nationality (Witherington, 71–72). This promise of universal fulfillment nevertheless masked certain inconsistencies: Luke did not understand it to eliminate or radically to realign sex and class barriers, but only to validate the incorporation of gentiles into the covenant promises of the people Israel. In the end, a postmodern reader might critique such inconsistencies by observing that Luke's idea of embracing all ethnic diversity accorded with the values of the Roman Empire: it embraced ethnic diversity without demolishing Roman social convention or the hierarchical ordering of society (Williams 2009).

Luke's project, then, might be described as attempting to redefine and rebuild the people of God after the distress of the first Jewish-Roman War; he attempted to establish the church as the newly constituted Israel, composed of believing Jews and gentiles as the true heirs of Israel (Pao). He pursued this goal by using Joel's prophecy as his grand-narrative. In this endeavor, he also had some other scriptural precedents, for example, Isaiah 40–55. Thus one could also describe Luke's efforts as attempting to present his version of the fulfillment of the promises of Isaiah, which resulted in two distinct social/religious entities called Judaism and Christianity. Although according to Acts 11:26, believers are called "Christian" for the first time in Antioch during the apostolic age, the absence of the term *Christianoi* in any literature, from within or without the Jesus movement, until the early second century leads most scholars to conclude the term was *not* a common name for members of the movement before that point. Luke's effort is an early endeavor to form a distinct identity that will not be firmly established for some centuries (S. Matthews, 7).

Acts and the "Break" with Judaism: "Jews" as Agents of Persecution

Luke's ethnic interests are also exhibited in the way he explains Christianity's move from its Jewish foundations to spread to the gentile world. The process can be described in terms of hierarchical authority: the chain of succession established in Acts moves from God to Jesus, from Jesus to Peter and the other disciples, then from the Jerusalem church to the Hellenistic church, which influences Stephen, and then Paul and Barnabas, who continue the mission to the gentiles. The progression of "the Way" also happens geographically, moving from Jerusalem to Judea and Samaria and unto the ends of the earth. These themes are combined in a narrative in which Christianity emerges and diverges from Judaism quickly and decisively. The Hellenistic wing of the "Way" initiates the development of a new identity for Jewish and gentile followers of Jesus that is different from that of Judaism (Acts 11:26). Paul's final speech to the Jews in Rome represents a decisive break between Jews and gentile followers of the Way, already in the lifetime of Paul himself (28:25-28). Luke marks the beginning of this transition by Stephen's death at the hands of a disorderly and unruly mob of Jews, a device so influential that the fourth-century church leader Eusebius of Caesarea would emulate it, reinscribing the narrative of Acts "by which originary martyrdom is linked to the creation of two distinct social groups," Stephen's death igniting "the 'first and great' persecution of one distinct social group, the Jerusalem *ekklesia* by another, 'the Jews'" (S. Matthews, 9, citing *Hist. eccl.* 2.1.8). Thus Acts constructs the identity of nonbelieving Jews (Acts 14:2) as agents of violence, and Christian identity as those who suffer at the hands of Jews.

Luke's earlier portrayal of his narrative hero, Saul of Tarsus, as a radical defender of (Pharisaic) Judaism and a zealous persecutor of the Christians, places him "present and accounted for" at the murder of Stephen. After his "conversion," in solidarity with his new identity and community with the Hellenists Jews whom he formerly opposed, Paul would suffer at the hands of the (unbelieving) Jews (9:23; 13:50; 14:2, 14, 19; 17:5; 20:3, 19; 21:11, 27; 23:12, 20, 27; 26:21). Luke's construction of two categories, persecutor and persecuted, requires that although Paul is still a Jew (21:39; 22:3), he is a persecuted one (because he believes in Jesus as the Messiah). At the beginning of his missionary travels and preaching, he preached to gentiles only under compulsion, that is, only after the Jews rejected his gospel (13:46-7; 18:5-6). Luke defends Paul against accusations that he preached against Judaism; he did not (Luke insists) teach Jews to abandon their traditions. As a matter of fact, Luke shows that Paul participated in Jewish rituals both in Ephesus and in Jerusalem (Acts 21:17-26; 16:1-3, which may be compared with Gal. 2:1-5, where Paul was *not* inclined to perform such a gesture). Not all Jews are depicted as persecutors of Christians, however; those who at least are willing "to search the scriptures" and withhold judgment are presented as civil and rational (Acts 17:11, 17; 14:4; 19:10). In the end, nonetheless, Luke's portrayal of a break with Judaism, initiated by Stephen's death, is swift and contingent on violence. Luke's distinction between the "persecuting Jew" and the "victimized Christian" has been reinscribed to some degree in modern scholarship, which still buys unsuspectingly into Luke's binary master-narrative of Christian origins (S. Matthews, 8).

Portrayal of Roman Characters

Unlike the depiction in Acts of some Jews as violent persecutors of Christians, some Roman characters are virtually absolved from violence. Roman magistrates and other officials are depicted as reasonable in their comportment and equitable in their judgments (but not all: Gallio does nothing to quell a riot [Acts 18:17]; Felix obstructs justice waiting for a bribe [Acts 24:26]). Even military personnel, for the most part, are depicted quite positively, even when carrying out orders (Acts 22:24-26). This was evident already in Luke, particularly in the trial of Jesus (which prefigures the Roman treatment of Paul in Acts) and his crucifixion. In Luke's account of Jesus' execution (Luke 23), it was "the Jews" who carried out the act—not the Romans. Luke omits the scene in which Jesus was scourged by Romans (cf. Mark 15:14; par. Matt. 27:26); Pilate reluctantly hands Jesus over to the will of the Jews (Luke 23:25), and it is they who lead him away (23:26) and crucify him (23:33). In Luke's narrative, those who call out for Jesus' death also judge and condemn him. As Lüdemann observes, "In literary terms, the way [Luke] uses others to relieve the Roman authorities of responsibility for the condemnation of Jesus and the actual crucifixion is a *tour de force*; in historical and theological terms, it is a *monstrosity*. Indeed, historical truth comes in a distant second to the evangelist's zeal in promoting his ecclesiastical program" (Lüdemann 2008, 71). Note, too, the elimination of the sort of cruelty in the report of Jesus' execution that appears in other reports and descriptions of the Roman practice of crucifixion (Hengel).

While Luke evidently attempted to play down the actual role and brutality of the Romans in such events, he could not simply ignore the death of Jesus. His narrative strategy did allow him to ignore and exclude a portrayal of Paul's death, however, and since Paul suffered like Jesus "at the hand of the Jews," Luke could continue his positive presentation of Roman characters. Having exonerated the Roman participation in the crucifixion of Jesus, Luke depicts the Roman soldiers involved in Paul's arrest in Jerusalem, and the subsequent negotiations, as protective of Paul and reasonable in a threatening situation (except in the two cases noted above). The Jews, on the other hand, are generally portrayed for the most part as hostile and riotous in their behavior, from which the Romans must protect Paul. This idyllic narrative depiction of the Romans masks the actual role and historical realities of Roman imperial power, as well as the violence it unleashed generally against colonized peoples in the Mediterranean world under its dominion (including Jews and "Christians" alike). Although Luke knows that the Roman state eventually executed Paul, he chose not to report the fact, instead closing the narrative of Acts with Paul being privileged by the Romans to preach the gospel without any hindrance. The historical reality was that Paul was never set free but rather was executed under Roman decree. Luke does not recount the story of Paul's violent death, perhaps because he did not consider it edifying, or because ending on the note of Paul's unhindered freedom to preach opened up possibilities for the church even under severe threats to its life. It seems, then, that Luke created a theologically (or ideologically) grounded picture of the Roman state in order to secure present and future privileges of unhindered preaching for the church.

It appears, then, that despite apparent tensions with the Roman imperial grand-narrative, as described above, the author of Luke-Acts also avoids the presentation of episodes that might raise those tensions to the level of an explicit conflict of values. In other ways, the author appears to participate in some of the values of Roman imperial culture. In this regard, Mariann Bonz has observed aspects of a remarkable but seldom-recognized intertextuality with Virgil's *Aeneid*. Virgil presents the legendary Trojan hero Aeneas escaping from the flaming ruins of Troy to bring to Italy the best values of Trojan piety and honor; the explicit consequence is that the Romans of the Augustan age, descendants of Aeneas, are ordained by the gods to act out those values by exercising their divine right to dominate the world. In some ways, Bonz argues, Luke appears to imitate Virgil, presenting the Christians as a new people destined to spread (from east to west, even to Rome) and "conquer" the world. The Christians emerge in Acts as heirs of the very best of the Jewish tradition, who, after the suffering of the first Jewish Revolt and the destruction of Jerusalem, are given the right and privilege to rebuild the nation of Israel (Bonz, 182).

It is in Luke's apparent imitation of Roman values that we gain a picture of his own participation in the Roman construction of masculinity as well. The "imperial atmosphere of masculine comportment and display, quintessential in the formation of [Acts'] narrative flow, also reflects on Luke's own manly performance." Moreover, "the speaking voice in Acts is clearly a powerful male-gendered voice, which finally says something about Luke and the masculine image he projects through inscribing it on the narrative community and especially its leaders, with whom Luke seems to identify the most, given the role they play in proclaiming *his* gospel" (Penner and Vander Stichele, 202 [emphasis original]). On this view, Luke has portrayed the Romans so positively because, although he proposes a narrative in which divine providence is carried forward by another people—the new people created by a restored Israel joined with believing gentiles obedient to Israel's Messiah—he nevertheless ultimately upholds the Roman values of *virtus* and *imperium*, which encompass the virtues of social order and masculinity. Luke depicts acts of speech and behavior that comply with the social values of a (male) Roman elite, which may show us just how closely the author himself comports with those values.

Reading Luke-Acts Today

Luke clearly sought to accomplish several goals in his account of the origins of the early church. The preceding discussion shows that different contemporary interpreters perceive different possible agendas in his writing, both explicit and also the implicit values of conflicting grand-narratives in Luke's environment.

Like the author of Luke-Acts, the modern reader also brings to the reading of this work his or her own view(s) of the world, biases, agendas, and participation in the often implicit grand-narratives of our own time. By attending to these possibilities, we may discover in reading Acts our own values and also our own inconsistencies, for as Louis Althusser has warned: "there is no such thing as an innocent reading, we must say what readings we are guilty of" (Althusser, 14).

Works Cited

Althusser, Louis B. 1975. *Reading Capital.* Translated by Bruce Brewster. London: New Left Books.

Baker, William H. 1989. "Acts." In *Evangelical Commentary on the Bible*, edited by Walter Elwell, 884. Grand Rapids: Baker.

Barrett, C. K. 1994. *Acts of the Apostles.* 2 vols. ICC. Edinburgh: T&T Clark.

Baur, Ferdinand Christian. 1853. *Das Christentum.* Tübingen.

Bible and Culture Collective. 1995. *The Postmodern Bible.* New Haven: Yale University Press.

Bonz, Mariann Palmer. 2000. *The Past as Legacy: Luke-Acts and Ancient Epic.* Minneapolis: Fortress Press.

Brunt, P. A. 1997. "*Laus Imperii.*" In *Paul and Empire: Religion and Power in Roman Imperial Society*, edited by Richard A. Horsley, 433–80. Harrisburg, PA: Trinity Press.

Conzelmann, Hans. 1987. *Acts of the Apostles.* Edited by Eldon Jay Epps and Christopher R. Matthews. Philadelphia: Fortress Press.

Deissmann, Adolf. 1927. *Light from the Ancient East.* New York: Harper & Row.

DeSilva, David A. 2004. *Introduction to the New Testament: Contexts, Methods and Ministry Formation.* Downers Grove, IL: Intervarsity Press.

Dijk, Teun A. van. 2006. "Ideology and Discourse Analysis." *Journal of Political Ideologies* 11, no. 2 (June): 115–40.

Doughty, Darrell J. 1997. "Luke's Story of Paul in Corinth: Fictional History in Acts 18—Historical Criticism or Apologetic Historicizing?" *Journal of Higher Criticism* 4, no. 1 (Spring): 3–54.

Drane, John. 2011. *Introducing the New Testament.* 3rd ed. Minneapolis: Fortress Press.

Dupont, J. 1961. *The Sources of Acts.* Translated by K. Pond. New York: Herder and Herder.

Ehrman, Bart D. 2012. *The New Testament: A Historical Introduction to the Early Christian Writings.* 5th ed. Oxford: Oxford University Press.

Flax, Jane. 1990. "Postmodernism and Gender Relations in Feminist Theory." In *Feminist/Postmodernism*, edited by Linda J. Nicholson, 621–43. London: Routledge.

Gabba, Emilio. 1983. "Literature." In *Sources for Ancient History*, edited by Michael Crawford, 1–79. Cambridge: Cambridge University Press.

Gaventa, Beverly Roberts. 2004. "What Ever Happened to the Prophesying Daughters?" In *A Feminist Companion to the Acts of the Apostles*, edited by Amy-Jill Levine, 49–60. Cleveland: Pilgrim.

Grant, Michael. 1995. *Greek and Roman Historians: Information and Misinformation.* New York: Routledge.

Gregory, Andrew. 2003. *The Reception of Luke and Acts in the Period before Irenaeus: Looking for Luke in the Second Century.* Tübingen: Mohr.

González, Justo L. 2001. *Acts: The Gospel of the Spirit.* Maryknoll, NY: Orbis.

Haenchen, Ernst. 1971. *Acts of the Apostles: A Commentary.* Philadelphia: Westminster.

Hemer, Colin J. 1989. *The Book of Acts in the Setting of Hellenistic History.* Edited by C. Gempf. Tübingen: Mohr Siebeck.

Hengel, Martin. 1977. *Crucifixion in the Ancient World and the Folly of the Cross*. Philadelphia: Fortress Press.

Hodgson, P. C. 1966. *The Formation of Historical Theology: A Study of F. C. Baur*. New York: Harper.

Horsley, Richard A., ed. 1997. *Paul and Empire: Religion and Power in Roman Imperial Society*. Harrisburg, PA: Trinity Press International.

———. 2003. *Jesus and Empire: The Kingdom of God and the New World Disorder*. Harrisburg, PA: Trinity Press International.

Johnson, Luke Timothy. 2010. *The Writings of the New Testament*. 3rd ed. Minneapolis: Fortress Press.

Kee, Howard Clark, 1990. *Good News to the Ends of the Earth: The Theology of Acts*. Philadelphia: Trinity Press International.

Kummel, Werner. G. 1987. *Introduction to the New Testament*. Rev. ed. London: SCM.

Leppä, Heikki. 2002. "Luke's Critical Use of Galatians." PhD diss., University of Helsinki.

Liew, Tat-siong Benny. 2004. "Acts." In *Global Bible Commentary*, edited by Daniel Patte, 419–28. Nashville: Abingdon.

Lopez, Davina C. 2012. "Visual Perspectives: Imag(in)ing the Big Picture." In *Studying Paul's Letters: Contemporary Perspectives and Methods*, edited by Joseph Marchal, 93–116. Minneapolis: Fortress Press.

Lüdemann, Gerd. 1989. *Early Christianity according to the Traditions in Acts*. London: SCM.

———. 2005. *The Acts of the Apostles: What Really Happened in the Earliest Days of the Church*. Amherst, NY: Prometheus.

———. 2008. "Acts of Impropriety: The Imbalance of History and Theology in Luke-Acts." *TJT* 24, no. 1:65–79.

Lyotard, Jean-François. 1979. *The Postmodern Condition: A Report on Knowledge*. Manchester: Manchester University Press.

Maddox, R. 1982. *The Purpose of Luke-Acts*. Edinburgh: T&T Clark.

Marshall, I. Howard. 1984. *Luke—Historian and Theologian*. Exeter: Paternoster.

Matthews, Christopher R. 2001. "Acts of the Apostles." In *The New Oxford Annotated Bible: NRSV with the Apocrypha*, edited by Michael D. Coogan, 1919–71. 3rd ed. Oxford: Oxford University Press.

Matthews, Shelly. 2010. *Perfect Martyr: The Stoning of Stephen and the Construction of Christian Identity*. Oxford: Oxford University Press.

Mount, Christopher. 2002. *Pauline Christianity: Luke-Acts and the Legacy of Paul*. NovTSup 104. Leiden: Brill.

Munck, J. 1986. *The Acts of the Apostles*. AB 31. New York: Doubleday.

Palmer, Darryl W. 1992. "Acts as the Historical Monograph." *TynBul* 43, no. 2:373–88.

Pao, David C. 2002. *Acts and the Isaianic New Exodus*. WUANT 2. Tubingen: Mohr Siebeck.

Parsons, Mikeal C., and Richard I. Pervo. 1993. *Rethinking the Unity of Luke and Acts*. Minneapolis: Fortress.

Penner, Todd, and Caroline Vander Stichele. 2004. "Gendering Violence: Patterns of Power and Constructs of Masculinity in the Acts of the Apostles." In *A Feminist Companion to the Acts of the Apostles*, edited by Amy-Jill Levine, 98–104. Cleveland: Pilgrim.

Pervo, Richard. 1987. *Profit with Delight: The Literary Genre of the Acts of the Apostle*. Philadelphia: Fortress Press.

———. 2006. *Dating Acts: Between the Evangelists and the Apologists*. Santa Rosa, CA: Polebridge.

Punt, Jeremy. 2012. "Postcolonial Approaches: Negotiating Empire Then and Now." In *Studying Paul's Letters: Contemporary Perspectives and Methods*, edited by Joseph Marchal, 191–208. Minneapolis: Fortress Press.

Rothschild, Clare K. 2004. *Luke-Acts and the Rhetoric of History: An Investigation of Early Christian Historiography*. Tübingen: Mohr Siebeck.

Sacks, Kenneth. 1981. *Polybius on the Writing of History*. Berkeley: University of California Press.

Schüssler Fiorenza, Elisabeth. 1989. *In Memory of Her: A Feminist Theological Reconstruction of Christian Origins*. New York: Crossroad.

Segovia, Fernando F. 2000. *Decolonizing Biblical Studies: A View from the Margins*. Maryknoll, NY: Orbis.

Skarsaune, Oskar. 1987. *The Proof from Prophecy: A Study in Justin Martyr's Proof-Text Tradition: Text-Type, Provenance, Theological Profile*. NovTSup 56. Leiden: Brill.

Stephens, John, and Robyn McCallum. 1998. *Retelling Stories, Framing Culture: Traditional Story and Metanarratives in Children's Literature*. New York: Routledge.

Sterling, G. E. 1992. *Historiography and Self-Definition: Josephus, Luke-Acts and Apologetic Historiography*. Leiden: Brill.

Stott, John R. W. 1990. *The Message of Acts*. Leicester: Inter-Varsity Press.

Talbert, C. H. 1977. *What Is a Gospel? The Genre of the Canonical Gospels*. Philadelphia: Fortress Press.

Tyson, Joseph. 2006. *Marcion and Luke-Acts: A Defining Struggle*. Columbia: South Carolina University Press.

Unnik, W. C. van. 1980. "Luke-Acts a Storm Center in Contemporary Scholarship." In *Studies in Luke-Acts*, edited by Leander. E. Keck and J. Louis Martyn, 15–32. Philadelphia: Fortress Press.

Walker, William O., Jr. 1985. "Acts and the Pauline Corpus Reconsidered." *JSNT* 24:3–23.

———. 1998. "Acts and the Pauline Corpus Revisited: Peter's Speech at the Jerusalem Conference." In *Literary Studies in Luke-Acts: Essays in Honor of Joseph B. Tyson*, edited by Richard P. Thompson and Thomas E. Phillips, 77–86. Macon, GA: Mercer University Press.

Walters, Patricia. 2009. *The Assumed Authorial Unity of Luke and Acts: A Reassessment of the Evidence*. Cambridge: Cambridge University Press.

Williams, Demetrius K. 2007. "Acts of the Apostles." In *True to Our Native Land: An African American New Testament Commentary*, edited by Brian Blount, 213–48. Minneapolis: Fortress Press.

———. 2009. "'Upon All Flesh': Acts 2, African Americans and Intersectional Realities." In *They Were All Together in One Place: Toward Minority Biblical Criticism*, edited by Randall C. Bailey, Tat-siong Benny Liew, and Fernando F. Segovia, 289–310. Atlanta: Society of Biblical Literature.

Witherington, Ben, III. 1998. *Acts: A Socio-Historical Commentary*. Grand Rapids: Eerdmans.

THE ACTS OF THE APOSTLES

Michal Beth Dinkler

Introduction

The Acts of the Apostles is unique in the New Testament as the only sequel to a prior narrative (Luke's Gospel). Although the precise relationship between the Gospel and Acts remains under debate, most scholars agree that the same author wrote both volumes. Despite traditional accounts attributing this work to Paul's companion "Luke, the beloved physician" (Col. 4:14), in truth, the historical identity of this anonymous author remains unknown. He will be called "Luke" here simply for convenience.

Though the author was not a historian in any modern sense of the word, he clearly was concerned to give his addressee Theophilus a verifiable, orderly, historiographical account of Jesus' life and the subsequent spread of the early Jesus movement (Luke 1:1-4; Acts 1:1-2; Sterling). He was conversant with Roman administrative practices, and also clearly educated, writing in sophisticated Greek prose and alluding to Greco-Roman literature, as well as Jewish Scripture and traditions.

Recently, scholars have reopened the question of when Acts was written, suggesting that a composition date during the mid-second century CE (c. 110–130) is more likely than the traditional consensus dating Acts between 80–100 CE (Tyson; Pervo). The authorship and date of composition obviously influence our consideration of the historicity of Acts. The traditional view that Luke was Paul's companion lent credence to the sections of Acts that refer to Paul, a view further bolstered by the so-called we-passages, in which the narrator speaks in the first-person plural (16:10-17; 20:5—21:18; 27:1—28:16). In the second century CE, Irenaeus took the we-passages as proof that the author was an eyewitness of the events narrated (*Adv. haer.* 3.1–14). This view reigned until the eighteenth century, when historical-critical scholars (e.g., redaction, source, and form critics) mined the we-passages for evidence of Luke's multiple sources. In the nineteenth century, Bruno Bauer suggested that "we" narration established reliability within a fictional narrative world.

Contemporary scholars tend not to see the we-passages as evidence of historicity, but rather as the conventional ancient style for narrating sea voyages (Robbins), or as a means of legitimating Paul (Campbell). The ambiguities surrounding the historical identity of the author have led most scholars today to reject the previously common practice of using Acts to establish the historicity or chronology of the Pauline Letters.

Like reconstructions of the Lukan author, conjectures about the location of composition and intended audience must be tentative. Commentators have offered intriguing proposals regarding the identity of the "most excellent" Theophilus (Luke 1:3). As Luke uses "most excellent" elsewhere to refer to Roman leaders (Acts 23:26; 24:3; 26:25), perhaps Theophilus is a Roman patron who commissioned these narratives; alternatively, "Theophilus," which literally means "God-lover," could refer symbolically to anyone who loves God. In any case, it seems clear that Luke wrote Acts to be read more broadly than by one person.

Specific scholarly suggestions tend to link Luke's intended audience with a particular rhetorical purpose: Luke wrote to Jewish Christians in order to legitimate Paul, to Christians in Rome to commend the Roman Empire, or to Roman officials to defend Christianity. All we can say with certainty is that Acts can be situated within the first- or second-century-CE Mediterranean world, which means the implied audience would be familiar with basic sociocultural, political, geographical, and religious norms associated with life in the Roman Empire.

Scholars have consistently emphasized one dominant theme in Luke's two-volume work: salvation to the ends of the earth. Typically, Acts 1:8 is viewed as the quintessential Lukan formulation of universal salvation, and as an outline for the book of Acts as a whole. Other themes commonly identified in Luke-Acts include Christians' relationships with marginalized "others" (e.g., the poor, women, and Jews), proper uses of wealth, fulfillment of prophecy, the divine will and human response, the church (its growth, leadership, eschatological role, and ecclesiological practices), and the gift of the Holy Spirit. For more detail on these and other critical debates in Acts scholarship, see the preceding essay in this volume.

Given the extent of the narrative, it is helpful to keep a broad outline of the story in mind:

> Acts 1:1—6:7: The Birth of the Church and Witness to Jerusalem
> Acts 6:8—9:31: Spreading Beyond Jerusalem: Samaria and Judea
> Acts 9:32—12:25: Bridge to the Gentiles: Expansion into Antioch
> Acts 13:1—15:35: Expanding to the "Ends of the Earth": Asia Minor
> Acts 15:36—21:16: Expanding to the "Ends of the Earth": Europe
> Acts 21:17—28:31: At Long Last: The Movement Reaches Rome

1:1-26: Prologue and Introduction

◼ THE TEXT IN ITS ANCIENT CONTEXT

The stereotypically formal Greco-Roman dedication to Theophilus mirrors that of the Gospel (Luke 1:1-4). Thus the foreword (1:1-5) and ascension story (1:6-11; cf. Luke 24:44-53) function as a bridge, establishing continuity with Luke's Gospel and looking ahead to the story's next phase.

Many see Acts 1:8 as programmatic for the entire book: Acts recounts the worldwide spread of the gospel.

Jesus' ascension in Acts (1:6-11) differs slightly from the Gospel account (Luke 24:50-53). This version shifts the focus from Jesus to the apostles and postpones the Parousia (which supports Conzelmann's controversial contention that Luke wrote to explain the Parousia's delay). Acts 1:3 is the only mention in the New Testament of forty days between Jesus' resurrection and ascension (though this may be idiomatic for "a long time").

Continuities exist as well; the account reinforces several key Lukan themes. First, the passive form of the Greek verb *epērthē* ("he was lifted up") establishes that God governs the narrative's events. God's sovereignty is so strong in Luke-Acts that the acts of Luke's characters have been called "the twitching of human puppets" (Haenchen, 361). Second, Jesus promises the Holy Spirit (1:8), whom many consider the main character in Acts. Third, Acts 1:9 recalls Jesus' prediction of the son of man's return (Luke 21:27), and is consistent with other New Testament texts (Matt. 26:64; Mark 14:62; Rev. 1:7; 14:14).

The account resonates with other ancient ascension narratives. For example, Gen. 5:24 implies that Enoch ascends into heaven, and in the Jewish mystical texts *1* and *3 Enoch*, he transforms into an angel. In 2 Kgs. 2:11, the prophet Elijah ascends into heaven on a chariot of fire, and in *Joseph and Aseneth* 17.7–8, an angel rides a chariot to heaven. Acts 1:9-11 especially resembles Josephus's depiction of Moses' ascension in *Antiquities* 4.326.

Following Jesus' ascension, Peter makes the first of twenty-four public speeches in Acts (1:16-22). Speeches in Acts establish Luke's literary artistry, interpret theological themes for readers, and propel the plot. In this, Luke resembles ancient historians, who used speeches to emphasize themes and move the narrative forward.

Peter cites Pss. 69:25 and 109:8, effectively casting Judas as God's enemy and making his replacement a divine necessity. Luke's readers already know that Judas betrayed Jesus (Luke 22:47-53), but here, they learn of Judas's bloody death (cf. Matt. 27:3-10). After praying and casting lots, the disciples choose Matthias (1:21-26), who is otherwise unimportant, as he is unmentioned elsewhere in the New Testament. What matters is the unbroken apostolic witness of Jesus' ministry; the number twelve maintains symbolic continuity with Israel's twelve patriarchs, whom the twelve apostles will eventually judge (Luke 22:30).

▌ THE TEXT IN THE INTERPRETIVE TRADITION

In the second and third centuries, Christian apologists such as Justin Martyr, Tertullian, and Origen further developed the doctrinal and theological importance of Christ's ascension when defending against those who denied that it had happened at all. Athanasius insisted that Jesus' ascent is the natural corollary to the incarnation, as it ends Christ's bodily humiliation and begins his heavenly exaltation. Jesus' ascension also appears repeatedly in early creedal formulas (e.g., the Apostles', Nicene, and Athanasian Creeds). In the Qur'an, Jesus does not die at all; he ascends into heaven alive.

Pictorial renditions through the centuries reflect the inherent difficulties in representing Jesus' ascension. Early Christian artists struggled with how to depict Jesus' earthly absence (which paradoxically points to his heavenly presence), often resorting to static scenes of Jesus on clouds above his disciples. Eventually, a new kind of visual rhetoric arose as artists depicted the scene from below, with only Jesus' feet visible (e.g., Albrecht Dürer's famous sixteenth-century woodcut).

In the thirteenth century, Thomas Aquinas emphasized that Christ's ascension prepares the way for the ascension of all believers. Later, sixteenth-century Reformers picked up on a similar theme; Calvin interpreted Jesus' ascension as evidence that Christians are *already* victorious through Christ (*Institutes* 2.16).

Luther and Zwingli drew different conclusions about the Eucharist based on Jesus' ascension: for Zwingli, Christ's body is located with the Father and therefore cannot literally be present at the Eucharist. For Luther, however, the Father's right hand symbolizes a place of power, not a physical location; thus, Luther argued, Christ is literally present whenever Christians celebrate the Lord's Supper.

▌THE TEXT IN CONTEMPORARY DISCUSSION

The symbolic geographic movement of the Gospel from Jerusalem to Rome presents a hermeneutical challenge for modern interreligious dialogue, since it easily lends itself to a supersessionist theology: Jerusalem (representing Judaism) is superseded by the power of Rome (representing Christianity). Furthermore, twentieth-century evangelist Billy Graham referred to Acts 1:8 when calling Christians to "win the whole world for Christ." Does "winning the whole world for Christ" facilitate Western triumphalism?

Some consider the call to spread the gospel "to the ends of the earth" as an indication that the Christian message is superior to and ought to supplant all other religious traditions. Such religious triumphalism, which was inextricably wedded to Western colonial expansion, often assumes that to do missionary work Christians must be foreigners in a strange land; however, the early Christian movement "begins in Jerusalem," suggesting that empowered by the Spirit, Christians can and should also witness at home (Kanyoro).

Jesus' promise that God's reign transcends expectations can also challenge marginalized people groups today. For example, Justo González warns that if US Hispanics overemphasize God's coming reign, they will neglect their global witness. Does Acts teach that the church should prepare for an imminent Judgment Day, or maintain tradition in the face of an indefinitely delayed eschatology?

Some take Acts 1:12-26 as a fixed prescription for church leadership. According to the Catholic Church, apostolic succession originates here, guaranteeing doctrinal teachings through the bishops' unbroken lineage. In contrast, Ernst Käsemann famously disparaged Acts' "early catholicism" (Frühkatholizismus), by which he meant a departure from the "true" gospel's egalitarianism. Most scholars today emphasize that Acts describes leaders adapting to changing circumstances.

Recently, Luke's contradictory gender constructions have provoked a spate of scholarly studies. On the one hand, Acts 9:36 is the only time a woman is explicitly labeled a "disciple" in the New Testament (Tabitha; cf. Rom. 16:7), and other women play important roles in the Christian community (1:14; 2:17-18; 12:2; 16:13-15; 18:18, 26; see Josephus, *Ant.* 4:219 on rejecting a woman's legal witness). Thus many believe Acts supports women's church leadership (Pierce, Groothuis, and

Fee). However, Acts also silences women: they are rarely quoted, men remain in command, and Peter stipulates that Judas's replacement be male (1:21). Therefore, others find it futile to try and reclaim Acts for feminist causes (Schaberg).

A more basic question underlies these discussions: Should an ancient narrative be a contemporary imperative? If so, how should interpreters discern which narrative elements are relevant and/or normative for their situation(s)?

2:1-47: The Day of Pentecost

◼ THE TEXT IN ITS ANCIENT CONTEXT

The miraculous outpouring of the Holy Spirit on Pentecost (2:1-13) fulfills Jesus' prophecies (Luke 24:49; Acts 1:4-5) and formally inaugurates the messianic community. Luke is beholden to Jewish tradition: Hellenistic Jews gave the name "Pentecost" ("fiftieth") to the Jewish "Festival of Weeks" (Shevuot), which occurred fifty days after Passover. Originally a harvest festival, Pentecost eventually celebrated the giving of the Mosaic law. The onlookers' comprehension of the multiple languages likely echoes the rabbinic legend that God gave the Sinaitic law in seventy languages for the world's seventy nations (compare *glōssolalia*, which requires interpretation; 1 Cor. 14:1-25; see Philo, *De decalogo* 9–11). The sound of rushing wind and the tongues "as of fire" evoke Hebrew Bible theophanies (Gen. 2:7; Exod. 3:2; 13:21; 19:18; Ps. 33:6; cf. Isa. 5:24).

The onlookers are devout Diaspora Jews living in Jerusalem (2:5). This is the first instance in Acts of *Ioudaios*, a difficult word to translate since it has multiple overlapping referents: geographic, religious, and ethnic. The subsequent list of nations (2:9-11) resembles lists found in ancient astrological and historical writings. Scholars have proposed several direct sources (e.g., Genesis 10 and Philo's *Embassy to Gaius* 281–82). Aside from questions of translation and derivation, juxtaposing *Ioudaios* and the list of nations at the start of Acts substantiates the Lukan message that the gospel came first to the Jews, then spread throughout the world.

As is common in Luke-Acts, bystanders misinterpret the events (2:13). In the Gospel, those who misunderstand are typically closest to Jesus (2:43, 50; 9:10-17, 28-36, 37-42, 44-45, 49-50, 54-55, 57-62). In Acts, outsiders misunderstand, often about a character's identity (3:17; 7:25; 8:18-24; 13:27; 14:11-13; 19:14-16; 22:9; cf. 21:17-26). Characters' ignorance frequently introduces dramatic irony (when characters know less than the readers), thus privileging readers and solidifying insider-outsider boundaries. Lukan characters often unwittingly voice the narrator's—and ultimately God's—perspective (cf. 5:39).

Peter instructs the witnesses to "listen carefully" (2:14). Using a complex of seeing- and hearing-related words, Luke consistently commends listening well. Peter interprets Pentecost as a fulfillment of prophecy (2:16; a slightly modified citation from Joel 2:28-32 LXX), thereby connecting the indwelling of the Spirit with the prophetic task established in the Hebrew Bible. As a result of these events, three thousand join the nascent Jesus movement (first labeled "Christian" in Antioch; see 11:26).

◼ The Text in the Interpretive Tradition

Patristic preachers like Cyprian and John Chrysostom used an idealized Acts 2 community to castigate their congregations' divisiveness. Fourth-century monastics like Basil the Great appropriated Acts 2:44-45 for the apostolic life (*vita apostolica*), including a vow of poverty. This passage also inspired Thomas More's *Utopia* (sixteenth century) and Marx and Engels's *Communist Manifesto* (nineteenth century). As a result, it was common in the twentieth-century view to assert that early Christians were "communists." Despite the fact that communist thinkers appealed to early Christian practice to develop and support their ideological system, labeling early Christians "communist" is anachronistic.

By the fifth century CE, the Feast of Pentecost had become a liturgical tradition distinct from Easter; Eastern churches held that the church was born at Jesus' resurrection, while Western churches considered Pentecost the church's birth.

Pentecost has sparked many debates over pneumatology: Post-Reformation theologians (sixteenth century) and Princeton theologians like B. B. Warfield (nineteenth century) advanced a cessationist view (charismata have ceased), whereas others insist that demonic deliverance, divine healing, and ecstatic prophecy continue. According to Charles Parham (1873–1929), missionaries who speak in tongues need not study foreign languages. Pentecostals and members of the Holiness movement (early twentieth century) took glossolalia as evidence of true faith and, often, the dissolution of racial barriers. The Pentecostal movement initially was interracial (e.g., the Azusa Street Revival of 1906–1909).

◼ The Text in Contemporary Discussion

A nostalgic, romanticized image of early Christian unity continues. Commentators often write that Pentecost overturns the Tower of Babel story (Gen. 11:1-9) and that the Holy Spirit brings concord (Acts 2:44-45). Many Christians today assume that while contemporary Christians are divided, the early church enjoyed uncomplicated *koinōnia* ("fellowship": a praised virtue in Hellenistic literature). For instance, the Barna Research Group reports that the "house church movement" is growing worldwide. The movement rejects ecclesiastical structures and ordained clergy in favor of meeting in private homes; this is supposedly modeled on the early Christians (Acts 2:42; 5:42; 12:12; 16:40; 20:20), though advocates of the movement often overlook how Roman households were bustling hubs of activity, with business conducted in the *tablinum* ("office"), and daily offerings left in the *lararium* ("shrine"). The earliest house churches did not meet in solely private spaces. The Holy Spirit's coming also led to believers sharing their resources (Acts 2:44-45); since the 1960s, liberation theologians have referenced Acts 2 to advocate for sharing material wealth with poor people.

For others, Pentecost is not an overturning, but simply a new iteration of Babel, since the disciples speak local dialects (not one common language), and they again scatter throughout the earth. How one interprets Pentecost influences missions and diversity in the church today. For instance, some Christian missionaries seek to assimilate, or "speak the language" of other cultures, while others believe a truly "globalized" Christianity will transcend cultural differences. Does the Holy

Spirit erase ethnic/racial differences and subvert human-made hierarchies? Does Pentecost add a welcoming, multiethnic element to Christianity that churches today should celebrate and emulate?

Relatedly, if Pentecost overcomes humanity's fragmentation, as Rome also purported to do, does this imply that early Christians appropriated Roman imperialistic propaganda (Gilbert)? Does Luke reinscribe hierarchical values? If so, do Christians today perpetuate similarly problematic ideologies?

Luke utilizes the prevailing discourses of his time in his own form of what Denise Buell calls "ethnic reasoning." Recognizing that race and ethnicity are socially shaped, discursive constructions, rather than fixed, stable categories complexifies Luke's universalism. How have Christians used the fluid categories of race/ethnicity apologetically, as evidence of Christianity's multicultural appeal?

In the United States, racial-ethnic minorities are becoming the majority. How does, or should, this influence American churches, which remain predominantly segregated? Are ethnically homogenous congregations blind to their own racialized assumptions and systemic sin, or are they rightly respecting differences between people groups?

3:1—6:7: The Church in Jerusalem

■ THE TEXT IN ITS ANCIENT CONTEXT

Peter's healing of the lame man (3:1-11) provides the first instance of the "wonders and signs" mentioned earlier (2:43). The miracle recalls Jesus' healings (Luke 7:22) and the prophetic tradition that at Israel's redemption the lame will "leap like a deer" (Isa. 35:6). In ancient society, those with disabilities often were ridiculed and associated with sin; Peter communicates that *all* people, regardless of appearance or ability, are welcome in God's kingdom.

Four times, Luke says the witnesses are astonished (3:10-12). This further develops an established Lukan theme: in Luke's Gospel, God amazes people (1:63; 2:18, 33), then Jesus does (4:22, 32, 36; 5:24-26); and now in Acts, the disciples engender amazement, implicitly linking them to God and Jesus, and heightening their authority in the narrative.

Peter's prophetic speech (3:12-26) echoes the one he gave at Pentecost: again, he addresses a misunderstanding, clarifies the miracle's divine origin, and demonstrates that Jesus fulfills messianic prophecies. Contrary to a common Jewish conviction, welcoming gentiles fulfills the Abrahamic covenant (3:25).

While the "people" respond gladly, the Jewish authorities become angry. In Luke's Gospel, the Pharisees *and* Sadducees oppose Jesus, but in Acts, the main opponents are the Sadducees. The descriptions of the Sadducees in Acts (4:1; 5:17; 23:6-8) cohere with Josephus's account that they are the aristocratic temple priesthood, the majority party of the Sanhedrin (*Ant.* 13:297–98). Testifying before the Jerusalem Council (4:1-22), Peter fulfills Jesus' promise (Luke 12:11-12).

Luke then adds to the picture of Christian communal life (cf. 2:43-47). The disciples' prayers are immediately answered (4:23-31), in a clear echo of Pentecost (cf. 2:1-4); unified in "heart and soul" (4:32), they voluntarily share possessions (4:33-37), thereby implementing Jesus' commands (Luke 12:33; 18:22), in contrast to typical Mediterranean patron-client relations (Moxnes). Correct use of possessions is a common Lukan theme (Seccombe). The phrase "heart and soul" may draw on Deuteronomy (4:29; 6:5; 10:12; 11:13; 26:16), and/or echo traditional Greek proverbs (*Nic. Eth.* 9.8.2).

And yet, this idyllic communal portrait does not last. Unlike Barnabas (4:36-37), Ananias and Sapphira refuse to surrender their possessions and lie about their hoarding (5:1-11). Similar to Achan, whose deceit results in his divinely sanctioned death (Josh. 7:16-26), God strikes Ananias and Sapphira dead. Ironically, after refusing to place all their money "at the apostles' feet" (5:2; cf. 4:35-37), this is precisely where Sapphira dies (5:10). The divine retribution legitimates the apostles' authority (5:11).

Acts 5:17-26 is the first of three miraculous prison escapes in Acts (cf. 12:6-11; 16:25-27). Again, the Jerusalem Council attempts to thwart the spread of the gospel. Again, the apostles refuse to be silenced, citing a well-known Greek proverb and common Jewish admonition that they obey God, not humans (5:29; cf. Plato, *Apology* 29D; Deut. 4:30; 8:20; 9:23; 30:2). The Pharisee Gamaliel's intervention pacifies the Jewish authorities (5:39) and immediately proves prophetic, as the apostles continue preaching (5:42).

In line with Jewish practice (Deut. 14:28-29; 24:17-21; 26:12-13; Isa. 1:17-23), the early church cared for widows (6:1-7), who were particularly vulnerable in such a patriarchal culture (Moxnes). Luke's Gospel repeatedly refers to widows (7:11-17; 9:39; 18:1-8; 20:47). Historically, the presence of Greek-speaking Hellenistic Christians and Aramaic-speaking Hebrew Christians is likely, given Jerusalem's diversity and hellenization's long-standing influence throughout the empire (cf. 1 Macc. 1:11-15). When choosing overseers for daily food distribution, the apostles pray (cf. 1:12-26) and lay hands on the seven (6:6), evoking Joshua's commissioning (Num. 27:18-23). They repeat the practice later (8:15-19; 9:12-17; 13:2-3).

Six summary statements like 6:7 punctuate the Acts narrative (cf. 9:31; 12:24; 16:5; 19:20; 28:31), reiterating and deepening the inseparable link between God's unstoppable word and the growth of the church. Each of the six resulting panels shows the movement of the gospel into a different geographical region.

▌The Text in the Interpretive Tradition

Proponents of the traditional view that Luke was a physician long believed Acts 3:1-11 demonstrated unique medical knowledge (e.g., W. K. Hobart [*The Medical Language of St. Luke*, 1882]). However, in 1920, Henry Cadbury convincingly demonstrated that such vocabulary was common in ancient literature.

As with Acts 2:42-47, patristic sermons (e.g., Cyprian, Chrysostom) take the common life described in 4:32-37 as a normative historical reality and a paradigmatic example of Christian generosity and unanimity. In contrast to this ideal, church fathers condemned Ananias and Sapphira as greed personified (e.g., Maximus of Turin).

Patristic interpreters produced panegyrics of Peter based on this section of Acts: Peter is the divinely appointed miracle-worker and defender of the faith nonpareil. Cyprian cites Peter's lack of money (3:6) to denounce greed. The Venerable Bede taught that the church, who "walks upright" (Peter), must raise Israel, who "limps" without the gospel (the lame man). The Catholic Church sees Peter as Rome's first bishop, from whom infallible papal authority descends. Ironically, throughout the sixteenth through the eighteenth centuries, English Dissenters used Acts 4:19 to justify leaving the Church of England (which was originally established to oppose papal authority).

Supporters of the church's rigid hierarchical structure in the Middle Ages used Acts 6:1-7 (and 20:17, 28) to defend formal ecclesiastical offices. For medieval theologians, institutionalization was necessary to stave off false teachings and to manage the church's increasingly differentiated ministries.

■ THE TEXT IN CONTEMPORARY DISCUSSION

Recent advances in disability studies focus on the lame man. Although scholars debate whether first-century-CE laws banned those with disabilities from the temple, in Acts, the man enters the temple only after he is healed. The key question is whether the story demeans or emancipates those with disabilities: Does God overturn human discrimination? Or does Luke reinscribe the polemics of ancient physiognomy (systematically connecting physical features with one's inner disposition) by implying that one must be physically able to be spiritually acceptable?

Although Ananias and Sapphira's deaths offend modern sensibilities, most commentators conclude that they deserved their punishment. Recently, scholars have warned against uncritically accepting the text's ideology that Christian violence is divinely sanctioned "justice," whereas outsider violence against Christians is unjust. The theme of unrighteous outsiders persecuting righteous insiders appears throughout ancient literature, including the Dead Sea Scrolls and the Hebrew Bible. Furthermore, in Acts, violence is gendered: perpetrators (on both sides) are male, but the text effeminizes "outsiders" (e.g., Acts 19:21-41) and glorifies "insider" (i.e., Christian male) violence.

Violence in Acts also raises the complicated question of Jewish-Christian relations. Scholars often single out depiction in Acts of the Pharisees as relatively positive. The *Catechism of the Catholic Church* refers to Acts 6:7 to affirm that Jews are not responsible for Jesus' death. Others challenge what they see as anti-Jewish rhetoric in Acts (e.g., 13:44-52), objecting that those stereotypes are dehumanizing, overly simple, and historically inaccurate.

Acts 6:1-7 both affirms and undermines women: on the one hand, Luke insists that the church must care for socioeconomically disadvantaged women; on the other hand, this perpetuates female dependence on a male-run ecclesiastical institution, perhaps squelching widows' autonomy (Price). Clearly, early Christians were ambivalent over widows' relative power and sexuality (cf. 1 Tim. 5:9-16). Acts 6:1-7 also records divisions of ministerial labors that eventually became gender-based (e.g., ministries of the word are for males, service ministries are for females).

6:8—8:3: The Persecution and Martyrdom of Stephen

■ THE TEXT IN ITS ANCIENT CONTEXT

In the previous section (6:1-7), the disciples in Jerusalem chose seven leaders to resolve an internal conflict. Here, the conflict begins to move outward, as diasporic Jews from Asia Minor (Cilicia and Asia) and Africa (freed slaves from Cyrene and Alexandria) arrest one of the chosen seven (Stephen). The Lukan narrator underscores the injustice of their accusations by emphasizing Stephen's grace and power (6:8), wisdom through the Spirit (6:10), and angelic innocence (6:15)—attributes associated with God's chosen leaders enacting the divine plan (7:22, 25).

Several significant parallels exist between these scenes and Jesus' passion in the Gospel: like Jesus, Stephen is falsely accused of speaking against Moses, opposing Jewish customs, and blaspheming. Both Jesus and Stephen refer to the son of man at God's right hand (7:55; cf. Luke 22:69), both ask God to forgive their tormentors (7:60; cf. Luke 23:34), and Stephen commends his spirit to Jesus (7:59), just as Jesus commended his spirit to God (Luke 23:46). Rhetorically, these recurrences link the sufferings of Christians back to the sufferings of Jesus' passion.

There is a crucial distinction, however. Whereas Jesus himself remains silent before Herod (Luke 23:9), Stephen eloquently refutes the charges against him (Acts 6:9-12); presumably, as Stephen speaks, Jesus is fulfilling his promise to provide the words (Luke 21:14-15). Stephen recounts the establishment of God's covenant, summarizes Israel's history, and draws extensively on the patriarchal stories (with some divergences from Genesis). The attentive reader knows that with Stephen as his mouthpiece, Luke is adding a new layer of meaning to these familiar accounts. For example, Stephen's citation of Deut. 18:15 contains a pun: God fulfilled the promise to "raise up" a prophet like Moses—literally and figuratively—in Jesus (cf. 3:22). Stephen's speech also advances a crucial Lukan theme: the state of one's heart determines whether one will receive the divine word (cf. Luke 8:4-21; 10:24). The Lukan narrator's ideological conviction is placed in Stephen's mouth: the Jews reject Moses, the law, and the prophets due to their "uncircumcised" hearts and ears (7:51). Without Gamaliel to appease the authorities (see 5:34-40), the confrontation escalates and Stephen becomes the first Christian martyr. Ironically, by executing him, the people prove Stephen's point that the Jews reject God's prophets; the narrative rhetoric thereby authorizes Stephen and his message.

Acts 7:58 records the most famous witness of Stephen's killing: Saul of Tarsus in Cilicia, later called Paul (a Roman name). Saul, a member of the Jewish Diaspora and committed Pharisee, most likely was named for Israel's great king. As Acts repeatedly attests, Saul zealously sought to exterminate the early Jesus movement (7:58; 8:1; 9:1-2, 5, 13-14, 21; 22:4-5, 7, 19; 26:9-11, 14). According to the Lukan narrative, Stephen's death inaugurated a "severe persecution," scattering the Jerusalem church throughout Judea and Samaria (8:1).

▮ THE TEXT IN THE INTERPRETIVE TRADITION

Non-Christian martyrdoms symbolically associated crowns with the "victory" of martyrdom and immortality prior to Stephen's execution. Nevertheless, traditional Christian history dubs Stephen (whose name means "crown") the "Protomartyr"—the first in a long line of Christians "crowned" with martyrdom in imitation of Christ. For instance, the early account of the martyrdoms in Lyons and Vienna refers to Stephen (Eusebius, *Hist. eccl.* 5:2:5).

By the fourth and fifth centuries, once Acts was canonized, church fathers like Gregory of Nyssa, Hesychius of Jerusalem, and Augustine of Hippo often referred to Stephen's martyrdom in their homilies, lauding his effective preaching, his service as a deacon, and his patience when persecuted. Though the Catholic Church never officially canonized Stephen, he is recognized as a saint; Christian iconography depicts him with stones and a crown.

The famous *Foxe's Book of Martyrs*, originally published in 1563, chronicles Christian martyrdoms from Jesus through the Inquisitions (twelfth–thirteenth centuries) and the Protestant Reformation (fourteenth–sixteenth centuries); subsequent editions added the Church of England's split from the Catholic Church (1559) and nineteenth-century American missionaries like Adoniram Judson. *Foxe's Book of Martyrs* shaped the West's collective Christian consciousness, including the complex legacy of Christian self-identification as the legitimate heirs and correct interpreters of Jewish traditions and Scriptures. For centuries, claims that the Jews rejected the true Messiah, killing Jesus and then his followers, have fueled antisemitism, including Luther's highly influential *Von den Juden und Ihren Lügen* (*On the Jews and Their Lies*, pub. 1543), and the Nazis' "ethnic cleansings" (1939–1945).

▍The Text in Contemporary Discussion

Acts is particularly virulent in its anti-Jewish polemic. Stephen blames Jesus' crucifixion and early Christian persecution entirely on the Jews (7:51-60). Since passages like this have fueled antisemitic atrocities like the Holocaust, many question whether this is the "word of God," and whether such passages should be read in church. Are the *Lutheran Lectionary for Mass* and *The Revised Common Lectionary* right to include them in the liturgy, or should clergy avoid them?

Recently, scholars have debated the historical origins of the Christian martyrdom tradition. Some, following William Frend, argue that Christian martyrdom accounts have literary precedents in the Jewish Maccabean genre (1965); Glen Bowersock, however, contends that Christian martyrdom was an entirely new phenomenon that arose from early Christian interactions with Romans, who venerated suicide (1995). Still others, such as Daniel Boyarin, argue that the Christian martyrological narratives reveal the contested nature of Jews' and Christians' close interconnectedness at the time, and their efforts to construct separate categories of identity (1999). Relatedly, scholars like Judith Perkins and Candida Moss fundamentally challenge the traditional notion that early Christians faced pervasive, consistent persecution, since most extant accounts come from the church historian Eusebius, who wrote during Constantine's pro-Christian reign and consistently disparaged earlier emperors as anti-Christian (fourth century CE). Other historical records indicate that individual governors held localized freedom regarding Christian persecution, and mass apostasy was far more common than actual martyrdoms. Scholars like Elizabeth Castelli bracket historiographical considerations, focusing on the dynamic role of power negotiations and hagiographical memories in early Christian identity formation (2004).

Nevertheless, the narrative of unjust Christian martyrdom at the hands of outside persecutors remains powerful; Christian self-sacrifice today is often cast in the same mold as the ancient accounts. The Voice of the Martyrs, an American nonprofit organization, seeks to encourage those who are "persecuted for their faith in Christ" and distributes Bibles in "hostile nations"; innocent deaths, as in the Columbine massacre (April 20, 1999) and the World Trade Center attacks (September 11, 2001), are deemed martyrdoms and used as rallying cries against America's "enemies." There is a danger when such views legitimate unethical violence and racial profiling, or perpetuate stereotypes of entire populations as "anti-Christian."

8:4-40: The Ministry of Philip

■ THE TEXT IN ITS ANCIENT CONTEXT

The "severe persecution" begun at Stephen's martyrdom ultimately enables the fulfillment of Jesus' promise in Acts 1:8, since it leads Philip (one of the seven chosen in 6:1-7) to preach in Samaria (8:4). As part of a pervasive motif advocating for the outcasts of society, Luke's Gospel gives special attention to Samaritans, whom Jews despised for insisting that they were the true preservers of the Mosaic law (Luke 10:30-37; 17:11-19). Entrance into Samaria thus establishes connective tissue with the Gospel and represents a significant moment in the expansion of the church.

Simon, Philip's literary foil, has duped the Samaritans with magic, which for Luke represents the cosmic drama between God's forces and the forces of evil (8:4-25). Despite his baptism (8:13), Simon is not transformed; failing to distinguish between miracles and magic, he tries to buy the Spirit's power (8:18-24). The narrative rhetoric here emphasizes two common Lukan themes: the danger of magic and the danger of wealth.

Though the gentile mission does not formally begin until chapter 10, Acts 8:26-40 depicts the first gentile conversion. Philip overhears an Ethiopian eunuch reading aloud (following the ancient custom) from the Isaianic scroll (most likely the Septuagint version). The Ethiopian eunuch is an outsider on multiple counts: In the Greco-Roman geographical imagination, Ethiopia was the end of the world (whereas Rome was its navel, or *omphalos*). The eunuch's conversion fulfills Acts 1:8 and demonstrates that the Spirit reaches all who are "far away" (*makran*, 2:39; in Greek literature, *makran* often refers to Ethiopians). Ancient writers like Herodotus, Strabo, and Homer describe Ethiopians as the original race, handsome and dark. Several ancient physiognomic handbooks, which outline how physical features reflect moral character, depict Ethiopians as cowardly (Parsons, 119).

The term *eunuch* could simply indicate his official title (cf. Gen. 39:1 LXX) as finance minister for the Candace (the title for queens of Ethiopian Meroë). If *eunuch* indicates that he was castrated, then he was "other" physically, as well. First-century society demonized eunuchs, associating honor with masculinity and shame with femininity. Further, if he was castrated, he could not be a Jew, despite his interest in Israel's religion (8:27-28; Lev. 21:20; Deut. 23:1; Josephus, *Ant.* 4.290–91). Overall, the eunuch's conversion epitomizes the Lukan themes of universalism and social justice: the gospel reaches the marginalized.

As elsewhere in Luke-Acts, the Holy Spirit directs events on the Gaza road (8:26, 29, 39). This detail characterizes Philip as a prophet like Elijah, whom the Spirit leads similarly (1 Kgs. 18:46). The passage cited (Isa. 53:7-8) refers to the sacrificial lamb, who (like Jesus before Herod; Luke 23:9) "does not open his mouth" (8:32); in contrast, Philip "opens his mouth" (8:35) and explains the Scriptures, just as the risen Jesus did on the Emmaus road (Luke 24:27). Philip baptizes the eunuch, ritually reversing his debased status. The *katabasis-anabasis* language here (8:38-39) is common in Greco-Roman mythology (e.g., Theseus, Heracles, and Orpheus travel "down" to Hades and "come up" again), and may have contributed to the Christian concept of baptism as a death and rebirth. The eunuch rejoices (8:39), a common response to the gospel in Acts. The Spirit "snatches up" Philip, depositing him in Azotus, a city over twenty miles north (8:38-39). Few instances of miraculous disappearances occur in Luke-Acts (cf. Luke 9:28-36; 24:31; Acts 1:9), though they are common elsewhere in ancient literature (e.g., Mars takes Romulus up into heaven in Dionysius of Halicarnassus, *Ant. Rom.* 2.56.2; Aphrodite "snatches" Paris in Homer, *Il.* 3.380–83). The Hebrew Bible similarly depicts God's Spirit transferring prophets to new locations (1 Kgs. 18:12; 2 Kgs. 2:11-12, 16; Ezek. 3:14; 8:3; 11:1, 24; 43:5). Philip settles in Caesarea, which is where we find him thirteen chapters later (Acts 21:8).

◼ THE TEXT IN THE INTERPRETIVE TRADITION

The church fathers were troubled by Simon's "wickedness" following baptism (8:22). The Venerable Bede posited that Simon feigned receiving the Spirit (CS 117:79), while Augustine concluded that baptizing someone evil results in evil, even if the baptizer is holy (FC 79:19). Simon appears elsewhere in Christian literature as Simon Magus (a Greek title meaning magician), who, traveling with a woman named Helena, was the ultimate heretic (e.g., Irenaeus, *Adv. haer.* 1.23.1-4).

Ferdinand Christian Baur, leader of the so-called Tübingen School of theology (nineteenth century), drew attention to references to Simon Magus in the Clementine literature and Apocryphal Acts, suggesting that Simon Magus was an alternative name for Paul. Building on the Hegelian dialectic, Baur held that the hierarchical "Catholic Christianity" of the second century CE represented the synthesis of Jewish Petrine Christianity (thesis) and gentile Pauline Christianity (antithesis).

Many patristic commentators held that the eunuch exemplifies the ideal response to the Christian message: he studies Scripture and, despite his high political station, humbly asks for help. Later Christian tradition taught that he was the first missionary to Africa. The eunuch's conversion also posed hermeneutical problems, however. Early Christian apologists like Justin recognized that ideal non-Christian readers *should* ask questions like the eunuch's (8:34), but they also believed that only Christian readers *can* ask them.

Acts 8:37 also presents a text-critical issue: though clearly not original, several manuscripts add a liturgical gloss with a baptismal formula: "He said to him, 'If you believe with your whole heart, you may.' He replied, 'I believe that Jesus Christ is the Son of God.'" Modern translations omit the verse number or put it in parentheses.

◼ THE TEXT IN CONTEMPORARY DISCUSSION

Conservative Christians in the West have revived the ancient Christian polemic against magic, believing that popular narratives about magic (e.g., J.K. Rowling's *Harry Potter* series) expose children to evil. African Christians offer a unique perspective on Simon's magical worldview because many Africans generate revenue by practicing magic today; although Simon's attempt to buy the Holy Spirit's power makes good financial sense in such a context, African Christian leaders condemn magic and superstition.

Many African churches uphold the tradition that the Ethiopian eunuch was the first African missionary; we do know the gospel reached the African continent early, and some of the earliest complete Bible translations were produced there.

Often, Christians take the Ethiopian eunuch's conversion as evidence of Christianity's counter-cultural inclusivity. Though the eunuch customarily stands outside acceptable society, the reference to Isa. 53:7-8 (LXX) affirms that foreigners will be restored to the people of God (cf. Isa. 56:3-5). From this perspective, Acts 8:33 commends the pursuit of justice in all contexts of humiliation, including ours today. Some consider this text redemptive for LGBTQ Christians, calling Christian communities to accept those who cannot/do not have children or engage in heterosexual intercourse (Wilson).

Liberation and womanist theologians commend a hermeneutic of suspicion instead. For them, ethnic difference is used as a polemical device marking outsiders, which is especially evident when comparing the Ethiopian eunuch's conversion to that of the Roman Cornelius (Acts 10:1-48). Ethno-political language and heterosexist ideologies suggest that early Christians simply adopted Rome's discursive strategies, marginalizing those outside of Rome.

The same dialectic remains operative today: On the one hand, the eunuch is an example of a marginalized minority who converts to Christianity; the example itself implicitly invites minorities today to imagine themselves as followers of Jesus as well. On the other hand, despite his conversion, the eunuch's marginal status does not change, in the story or in subsequent Christian history.

The overwhelming majority of Christian artwork depicts Jesus and his closest followers as white Europeans, which (despite many beloved iconic images) is historically inaccurate and perpetuates Eurocentric notions of racial superiority. We can see the continued power of this racialized image of Jesus and his followers in the fact that when Barack Obama was elected president of the United States in 2009, Afrocentric depictions of a black Christ that circulated on the Internet provoked the ire of many Americans.

Larger questions thus remain: can Acts 8:26-40 empower contemporary faith communities to challenge all forms of oppression? Or is the text inherently racist and/or sexist? Is Christianity a "white man's religion," as members of the Nation of Islam and others contend? How do biblical tropes that marginalize the "other" function today?

9:1-31: The Call of Saul/Paul

▌ THE TEXT IN ITS ANCIENT CONTEXT

In this highly dramatic episode, Saul, vigorous persecutor of Jesus' disciples, experiences a divine epiphany on the road to Damascus, in Syria. We are not told how the gospel has reached Damascus, only that Saul is on his way there to persecute followers of Jesus, and that his reputation precedes him. Ananias's parallel vision directs him to lay hands on Saul to restore his sight (cf. 4:30; 5:12; 8:17). Ananias's obedience and familial greeting (9:17-19), along with Barnabas's testimony (9:27), corroborate God's acceptance of Saul and validate Saul's claim to apostleship.

Luke's third-person account of Saul's transformation here differs slightly from the first-person versions recounted later in Acts (22:1-16; 26:9-18), and in Paul's letters (1 Cor. 15:3-8; Gal. 1:11-16). The Christophany contains typical features of Jewish theophany-type scenes, including a fall (cf. Ezek. 1:28; Dan. 8:17, 10:9), a bright light (cf. 4 Macc. 4:10, *Joseph and Aseneth* 14.1–2), and a vision only the recipient sees (cf. Dan. 10:7; Ezek. 1:28). There are also verbal echoes of the legend in 2 Maccabees 3, where a persecutor, Heliodorus, falls to the ground in darkness, "converts," and testifies to God's power.

Ironically in light of his previous witness of Stephen's martyrdom (7:58), Saul steps into the gap left by Stephen's death, taking a central leadership role in the Christian community. As such, this represents a major turning point in the narrative. For Luke, Saul's shifting role is inevitable: he is God's "chosen vessel" (9:15), instantiating the Lukan theme of divine necessity (what Cosgrove calls "the divine *dei*").

◼ The Text in the Interpretive Tradition

For some early Christians, Acts 9:1-31 was literally prescriptive: Saul's fast prepared him for baptism, which is necessary for salvation (e.g., Justin, *1 Apol.* 61; Tertullian, *Bapt.* 20). Later commentators often read Saul's conversion story more symbolically. For instance, to the Venerable Bede (seventh century CE), Saul's blindness represents the darkness of sin, which is then overcome by the light of faith. The three days of blindness teach Saul that he was wrong to doubt Jesus' resurrection on the third day.

Many influential Christian theologians have read Saul's Damascus vision as an archetype for Christian conversion. For example, Augustine's own famous garden conversion in 386 CE led him to read Saul's conversion as God's "violent capture of a rebel will." Medieval illustrations portray a wolf changing into a lamb, or a toppled horseman, both of which represent the rebellious human will being forcefully transformed. In the sixteenth century, Luther preached that Saul's conversion is a paradigm of Christian faith: failure to keep God's law leads to deep shame. Conversion, which frees one from the devil's grasp, is the result of God's prevenient grace alone. Luther contrasted Saul's transformation with the so-called papists who, like Saul before his conversion, persecuted the Reformers (the "true" Christians).

◼ The Text in Contemporary Discussion

This passage is at the center of ongoing debates about Saul's identity and how his conversion experience should influence Christianity today (e.g., Longenecker). Luther's depictions of Saul's conflicted conscience contributed directly to current Christian conceptions of sin, grace, and salvation. Still, scholars attuned to anthropological and social-scientific concerns caution Western readers not to overly psychologize Saul's Damascus-road experience; the social implications of Saul's "conversion" were just as important as his interior state. Ananias's astounding willingness to forgive Saul, and Barnabas's commendation, serve as a welcoming entrée into the community of Jesus-followers, some of whom likely suffered at Saul's hands. Accordingly, contemporary readers should be wary of reading an individualized psychological pattern into Saul's transformation as normative, as Luther did.

In colloquial English, we often use the proverbial "Damascus experience" to describe any abrupt change of mind, as when a politician suddenly reverses her position on an issue. Despite idiomatic usage, some scholars object to the word *conversion*, since Saul never denounced his Jewish identity. The new perspective on Paul insists that Saul did not "convert" to a new religion; rather, this prophetic "call" or "commissioning" (akin to Isa. 6:1-13) allowed Saul to maintain his Judaism. By recognizing Jesus as the Jewish Messiah, Saul simply transferred to another Jewish sect (Segal).

For Luke, did Saul's "conversion" liberate his soul from the torturous Mosaic law? Those who interrogate anti-Jewish strains in Christian rhetoric point out that this view easily engenders supersessionism and xenophobia. What is at stake when Christians take Saul's pre-"conversion" violence against Christians as characteristic of all Jews? Relatedly, does Saul's gentile mission *replace* a failed mission to Israel (Sanders)? If so, is Acts inherently antisemitic? Or does the gentile mission *complete* the mission to Israel, as implied in prophetic passages like Isa. 49:6 (Jervell)?

9:32—11:18: The Ministry of Peter

▌ THE TEXT IN ITS ANCIENT CONTEXT

In 9:32, Luke reintroduces Peter, who takes the gospel westward to Lydda (on the Plain of Sharon) and Joppa (9:32, 36). Peter's healing of Tabitha (Dorcas in Greek) fits the form of ancient miracle-type scenes (Bultmann's *Wundergeschichten*): a description of the circumstances (9:37), the miracle (9:40), a corroborating sign (9:40), and/or the witnesses' response (9:42). Raising the dead establishes continuity between prophets in the Hebrew Bible (1 Kgs. 17:17-24; 2 Kgs. 4:32-37), Jesus in the Gospel (Luke 7:11-17; 8:41-42, 49-56), and the apostles in Acts. The story has intertextual resonances with Luke 8:49-56, where Jesus raises Jairus's daughter; Jesus' instruction in the Markan parallel (5:35-43), *Talitha, koum* ("Little girl, I say to you, get up") also sounds similar to Peter's instruction, *Tabitha, anastēthi* ("Tabitha, get up," Acts 9:40).

Acts 9:36 is the only instance of the feminine noun for "disciple" (*mathētria*) in the New Testament (a *hapax legomenon*). Scholars often assume, based on 9:39, 41, that Tabitha was a widow, though the text never explicitly states this. Tabitha cares for the poor (9:36), a description Luke also uses to describe Cornelius in the next section (10:2, 4).

Like Tabitha, Cornelius is a sympathetic character with financial means. As a centurion, he commands one hundred men in the Roman army's Italian cohort (likely an anachronistic reference, since it is not attested elsewhere until 69 CE). Cornelius lives in Caesarea Maritima, the Roman capital of Judea, where Herod the Great had several pet building projects (see Josephus, *Ant.* 15.9.6 [15.331–41]). As an influential paterfamilias, Cornelius commands a large household (10:7).

Described as a devout gentile who "fears God" and prays continuously (10:2), Cornelius may be a "God-fearer," a category of gentiles who worshiped God and followed Jewish customs, without being proselytes. Some question the existence of God-fearers as a distinct historical category, though inscriptional evidence seems to indicate that "God-fearers" were active in synagogues, often as benefactors. In Acts, such gentiles resemble devout Jews (13:16, 26; 16:14; 18:7). Like Mary (Luke 1:26-38) and Ananias (Acts 9:10-17), Cornelius receives an angelic visitation at the ninth hour (three o'clock), the hour of prayer (10:3; cf. 3:1).

When the spotlight shifts to Peter, Luke highlights a main obstacle to gentile inclusion in the messianic assembly: their ritual uncleanness. Although no purity laws forbade Jewish table fellowship with gentiles, social taboos clearly discouraged such associations. Within the narrative, interactions between Jews and gentiles are vigorously contested. Peter's vision leads to the first of four household conversions in Acts (see also 16:11-15, 25-34; 18:1-11), and to Peter's own "conversion" to a new point of view regarding Jew-gentile relations (Parsons, 141); after some reticence, Peter finally grasps God's impartiality (10:34).

The significant amount of repetition throughout chapters 10–11 accentuates the importance of this narrative moment, when gentiles are officially welcomed into the people of God. In a recapitulation of the Pentecost event, the Holy Spirit descends on the gentiles (10:44-48). Upon Peter's return to Jerusalem, he recounts his vision (11:1-18; cf. 10:9-16). Similar to Luke's own storytelling (Luke 1:3), Peter describes events "step by step" (11:4), adding his own interpretive emphasis on God's role in establishing the gentile mission. Just as Jesus' opponents are silenced in Luke's Gospel (Luke 14:1-6), Peter's criticizers are silenced; unlike Jesus' antagonists, however, Peter's interlocutors eventually praise God (11:18).

■ THE TEXT IN THE INTERPRETIVE TRADITION

Chrysostom and Basil the Great enjoined their congregants to emulate Tabitha's virtuous behavior. During the Protestant Reformation, Calvin taught that faith preceded Tabitha's good works.

Cornelius's baptism (10:44-48) appeared in third-century doctrinal debates over the (re)baptism of "heretics," apostates who left the church in the face of Roman persecution. Cyprian ("pope" of Carthage) wrote a letter to Stephen ("pope" of Rome) in which he argued that Cornelius's baptism *after* receiving the Spirit commends (re)baptism (*Epist.* 72). Christian thinkers also referred to the household conversions in Acts to support infant baptism (which was widespread by the third century CE), assuming that children were present whenever entire households are mentioned.

Origen's and Augustine's different readings of Cornelius's angelic visitation were important in theological disputes over free will and divine grace (e.g., the semi-Pelagian controversy). For Origen, Cornelius merits an angelic visitation because he is charitable (10:2), but for Augustine, God's prevenient grace led to Cornelius's good works.

Fierce debates arose in late antiquity between the Antiochene "school" of intellectuals like Chrysostom, Diodore of Tarsus, and Theodore of Mopsuestia, who read Scripture literally, and those of the Alexandrian "school" like Origen and Clement of Alexandria, who read allegorically. Surprisingly, Antiochene interpreters read Peter's vision (10:9-16) allegorically (the animals represent incorporating gentiles into God's people), while Origen took it literally (the animals represent overturned Jewish dietary restrictions).

In the fourth- and fifth-century trinitarian and christological controversies, Western adoptionists took Peter's reference to God's "anointing" Jesus (10:38) as evidence that Jesus is subordinate to the Father; the now-orthodox interpretation is that Jesus' unction concerns only his humanity.

Nineteenth-century African American preachers appropriated Peter's assertions (10:34-36) to denounce prejudice. This text thus undergirded Christian objections to white supremacists, who preferred New Testament texts like Philemon.

▍The Text in Contemporary Discussion

Feminist reception history oscillates between celebrating female difference and insisting females are no different from males. Some feminist scholars celebrate Tabitha's status as a "disciple" (*mathētria*), lamenting "malestream" scholarship's dismissal of this title. Further, Lukan scholars often consider the successive healings of Aeneas and Tabitha (9:32-43) as an instance of the "gender pairs" that are a signature feature of Luke's work (e.g., Luke 1:11-20/26-38, 46-55/67-79; 2:25-35/36-38; 8:40-56; 11:31-32; 13:16/19:9; 13:18-21; 15:3-7/8-10). They reference this so-called dual-witness motif as evidence of Luke's emphasis on gender equality. Acts contains fewer gender pairs, but frequently notes that "both men and women" belong to the Christian community (5:14; 8:3, 12; 9:2, 36; 22:4; cf. 9:2; 17:12). On the other hand, praising Tabitha "has a dark side" when her service-oriented good deeds are contrasted with the depictions in Acts of preaching and teaching as male activities (Anderson, 33).

The baptisms in Cornelius's household continue to factor into disputes over infant baptism versus believers' baptism. Although most churches today (Catholic, Protestant, and Orthodox) baptize infants, certain denominations (e.g., Baptists, Pentecostals) only baptize adults. The Church of Jesus Christ of Latter-day Saints holds that infants are sinless; they do not baptize until the age of eight (*Doctrine and Covenants* 68:27).

House-church advocates consider the conversions of Cornelius's household a missiological model for decentralized, autonomous church planting today. One operative question is whether patriarchy should characterize the church. Some hold that the apostolic home-fellowship model marks the climax of progressive revelation, overturning the patriarchy of the old covenant and erasing all sociocultural and ethnic differences; women lead house churches around the world (e.g., in China, women lead an estimated two-thirds of Christian churches). Others, however, point out that Cornelius remains the paterfamilias, the Roman patriarch in charge of the household; some Christians take this *normal* historical reality as *normative*, believing that Christians ought to embrace God-ordained, male-led hierarchy.

11:19—12:25: God Protects the Jerusalem Church

▍The Text in Its Ancient Context

The summary in 11:19-21 serves several narrative purposes: first, the mention of Stephen's martyrdom subtly reminds readers of Saul (9:1-31). Second, Luke introduces Antioch, Saul's home base during his missionary journeys. As the Roman government's seat in Syria and a cosmopolitan intellectual center, Antioch is an appropriate place for the gospel to reach the "Hellenists"/"Greeks" (manuscripts vary at 11:20). The appellation "Christian" was a label given by outsiders (11:26; cf. 26:28); Luke prefers "the Way" (see 9:2; 19:9, 23; 22:4; 24:14, 22).

Luke seeks to integrate the Christian narrative into Greco-Roman historiographical accounts: in 11:28, he mentions Claudius's reign (41–54 CE) and a famine in Judea (Josephus records one c. 45–48 CE in *Ant.* 20.51–53) that threatens the "whole inhabited world" (11:28); this may be hyperbolic, or it may refer to the Roman Empire, purportedly the "whole world" to its inhabitants (cf. 17:6; 24:5).

The famine-relief mission frames the following unit (11:30—12:25), where God protects Peter from King Herod Agrippa I, son of Herod Antipas and grandson of Herod the Great (both mentioned in the Gospel; Luke 1:5; 3:1, 19-20; 9:7-9; 13:31; 23:8-15). As Rome's vassal king, Agrippa's relationship with the Jews was contentious; he hopes arresting Peter will placate them. The note that this occurred during the Feast of Unleavened Bread alludes to Jesus' arrest (cf. Luke 22:1-7) and explains why Peter's execution is delayed.

The second of three miraculous prison escapes in Acts (12:5-11; cf. 5:17-21; 16:23-40) utilizes exodus language and stock images from prison escapes elsewhere (e.g., chains falling off, angelic intervention, gates opening automatically, walking past sleeping guards). Form critics posit dependence on Euripides' *Bacchae*, Dan. 3:1-30, Artapanus's depiction of Moses, and/or Homer's *Iliad* (MacDonald, 121–45). The scene also recalls Jesus' resurrection (Luke 24). Acts emphasizes God's sovereignty over attempts to arrest (!) the spread of the gospel.

In a uniquely humorous moment, a slave named Rhoda recognizes Peter's voice at Mary's door, but rather than opening the door, she runs to tell the disciples. As happens repeatedly in Luke-Acts, the recipients of good news misconstrue it as nonsense (12:15; cf. Luke 24:11; Acts 2:13-15; 26:24); their response reflects an ancient belief that a guardian angel appears when one dies (12:15). Of course, Peter's miraculous escape story vindicates Rhoda.

The guards' panic at Peter's absence is warranted (12:18; cf. 5:21-24), given Agrippa's tyrannical reaction: he cross-examines and executes them (12:19); following Roman law, guards typically received the punishment intended for escaped prisoners (*Code of Justinian* 9.4.4).

The final scene starring Agrippa (12:20-25) highlights his unexplained anger with the people of Tyre and Sidon on the Phoenician coast, who seek reconciliation (likely bribing the king's assistant) for economic reasons (12:20). In Josephus's account of this event, Agrippa's speech (12:21) occurs at a festival honoring Caesar in Caesarea. As was common in the ruler cult, the crowd declares Agrippa's voice divine (12:22); according to Josephus, they do so because of his silver robes (*Ant.* 19.346). Whereas the apostles redirect praise toward God (see 3:12-13; 10:25-26; 14:13-15), Agrippa accepts the flattery and (ironically, since the crowd considers him immortal) dies by worms (cf. Jth. 16:17; 2 Macc. 9:9). Agrippa's demise reflects the ancient trope of a tyrant's downfall, and fulfills Mary's prophecy (Luke 1:52).

God's word (here, a metonymy for believers) remains unstoppable (12:24). When Barnabas and Saul return (12:25), the episode comes full circle and the main protagonist shifts from Peter (often called "apostle to the Jews") to Saul (usually dubbed "apostle to the Gentiles"). Peter is only mentioned again in 15:7.

■ THE TEXT IN THE INTERPRETIVE TRADITION

Antioch has been called Christianity's birthplace, since believers were first called "Christians" there (11:26) and the Antiochene church sponsored Saul's initial missionary journey (13:1-3). This gave Chrysostom great pride, since Antioch was his hometown. Antiochene Christians also sent many bishops to the Councils of Nicaea and Chalcedon, and generated "canon" lists similar to our contemporary New Testament.

Church fathers emphasized moral formation in this section of Acts. For instance, Chrysostom pointed to the Antiochene church when chastising his congregants for neglecting the poor. This moralizing also led ante-Nicene Christians to wrestle with Agrippa's execution of the innocent prison guards (12:18-19), often concluding that God would overturn such injustices upon Jesus' return. Agrippa's portrayal in Acts contrasts with Jewish tradition, where he is fair and generous (*Ant.* 19.330).

This subunit of Acts gave rise to several important Christian traditions. Postapostolic Christians identified John Mark (12:12) as the author of Mark's Gospel and founder of the Alexandrian church. James (12:17), later called "James the Just," brother of Christ and leader of the Jerusalem church, became legendary for his piety. In the second century, Hegesippus famously reported that James's knees were like a camel's from constant praying. According to Catholic tradition, James is patron saint of Spain, where he was sent to evangelize. Catholics also believe the vague reference to "another place" in Acts 12:17 refers to Rome, where Peter was the first pope. (Later texts explicitly connect Peter with Rome; see 1 Pet. 5:13; *1 Clement* 5.4; *Acts of Peter* 7.)

Despite Baur's distinction between Peter and Paul, Christian tradition venerates them together: iconography depicts them as pillars of the church, often with Jesus giving Peter the keys to the kingdom (the *donatio clavium*) and Paul the law in a scroll (the *traditio legis*).

■ THE TEXT IN CONTEMPORARY DISCUSSION

The summary in 11:19-21 signals a new challenge for the church: community integration. Despite the reference to peaceful growth in 9:31, the bulk of Acts points to barriers to full integration among early Christian converts. Recently, minority biblical criticism has identified similar concerns among minorities today, as their membership in American society hinges on loyalty to ideologies like capitalism or individualism (Liew). What do contemporary Christian groups establish as qualifications for inclusion? How should the Lukan narrative's treatments of cultural integration influence church membership (broadly conceived) today? How can scriptural discourses around insider/outsider boundaries inform ecclesial traditions and practices in today's communities?

An important corollary is whether Luke wrote to bolster insiders' faith, or to defend Christianity's political innocuousness to Roman outsiders (the *apologia pro ecclesia* hypothesis). Here, distinguishing among multiple potential audiences is helpful. Even as stories are embedded within particular communities, they are never fixed in only *one* sociohistorical situation. Readers' presuppositions and experiences predispose them to understand texts in unique ways. While Luke's earliest readers probably all understood Roman imperial practices, "outsiders" likely interpreted the narrative differently from "insiders."

13:1—14:28: Paul's First Missionary Journey

■ THE TEXT IN ITS ANCIENT CONTEXT

Acts 13:1-3 is a pivotal dividing point: chapters 1–12 focus on Peter and Jerusalem, while chapters 13–28 describe Paul's mission to the "ends of the earth," beginning with Asia Minor. Following the biblical topos of name changes consonant with role changes, Saul is called Paul from 13:9; once the

Spirit appoints Paul and Barnabas, they are commissioned in what appears to be a formal ceremony (13:3). Inaugurating the first of three Pauline missionary journeys, Paul and Barnabas travel with John Mark to the island of Cyprus, where they establish a pattern repeated throughout the journeys: they begin in the synagogues, gentiles convert, and Jews drive them out with (threats of) violence.

They arrive in Paphos on the southwestern Cyprian coast—seat of the Roman proconsul Sergius Paulus—indicating they have traversed the entire island. Paul's encounter with the magician Bar-Jesus (whose name, ironically, means "son of Jesus") resembles Stephen's confrontation with Simon (8:4-25). Paul's condemnation echoes the denunciations of magic in the Hebrew Bible. Bar-Jesus' blindness subtly recalls Paul's own temporary blindness (9:1-30) and reinforces the Lukan theme of divine fulfillment. Consider the ironies: Paul, called to open the eyes of the gentiles, casts one into further darkness. Whereas Paul was sent to "Straight Street" (9:6-11), Bar-Jesus makes the Lord's straight paths crooked (13:10). Bar-Jesus' attempts to lead the proconsul astray spiritually result in his own need to be led physically (13:11).

Paul (*sans* John Mark; 13:13) reaches Antioch of Pisidia (distinct from Antioch of Syria), in the Roman province of Galatia. He begins the first of his three major sermons by surveying Israelite history, and ends with the gospel (13:14-52). The parallels between this and other apostles' sermons unify the narrative, establishing and interpreting theological themes for readers (Soards). This episode also recalls Jesus' Nazareth sermon (Luke 4:16-30) in both content and result (13:50-52; cf. Luke 4:28-29). The apostles leave (13:51-52), shaking dust off their feet in protest (cf. Luke 9:5; 12:10-11).

Events in Iconium (14:1-7) repeat what is by now a familiar progression: the "apostles" (the designation extends here beyond the Twelve; 14:4, 14; cf. 1:2; 2:37; 4:33; 5:29; 9:27; 15:2; 16:4) begin in the synagogue, gentiles convert, and some Jews become violent. Paul avoids being stoned in Iconium, but he is not so fortunate in the next vignette, set in the Roman colony of Lystra (14:8-20). Following Jesus' and Peter's examples, Paul heals a lame man (cf. Luke 5:17-26; Acts 3:1-10). These intratextual echoes bolster Paul's legitimacy as God's agent. The witnesses' conclusion that Paul and Barnabas are Hermes and Zeus incarnate (the messenger god and sky god, respectively) is unsurprising in light of the widespread ancient notion—reflected in the Homeric epics and Ovid's *Metamorphosis* 8.611–724—that the gods disguised themselves as strangers.

Paul and Barnabas, rending their clothes in grief, redirect the exaltations to the "living God" (cf. 2 Kgs. 19:4, 16; Dan. 6:20, 26). The Lycaonians and Jews from Antioch and Iconium stone Paul and leave him for dead; ironically, given that Paul rejects attributions of immortality, he inexplicably "gets up" and leaves (14:19-20). This is particularly striking when compared with Agrippa's death (12:20-23).

Paul's first journey ends with many converts and no persecution in Derbe, on the outskirts of imperial territory (14:21-28). Returning to their Antiochene sponsors, Paul and Barnabas bravely revisit Lystra and Iconium, where they had been violently opposed. In a brief (anachronistic?) note, Luke reports that they elect presbyters in every church.

▌ THE TEXT IN THE INTERPRETIVE TRADITION

Paul's evangelistic efforts as a traveling missionary have been reimagined and imitated over time. In the second and third centuries, for example, the apocryphal Acts expanded on the canonical profiles of the apostles. Although the apocryphal Acts tend to reflect the framework of the canonical Gospels rather than the canonical Acts, some were built around a similarly episodic travel-narrative structure, with different itineraries and casts of characters (Bovon). The *Acts of Paul* describes Paul traversing the major Mediterranean cities, where he preaches, performs miracles, and encounters opposition. One excerpt, the *Acts of Paul and Thecla*, contains the earliest extant physical description of Paul (short, bald, with a long nose and large eyes). This description typifies subsequent depictions of Paul in Christian paintings and iconography.

For Chrysostom, Paul epitomized pedagogical prowess, using different rhetorical strategies for different audiences. For instance, Chrysostom explained why Paul blinded Bar-Jesus (13:11) by pointing to the plague of boils in Egypt (Exod. 9:8-12): Paul used blindness just as God used the boils—to teach, not to punish.

Commitment to the Protestant doctrine of *sola scriptura*, along with a desire to model evangelistic efforts on a fixed Pauline paradigm, led nineteenth-century interpreters to divide Paul's travels into three separate "missionary journeys," a threefold division still popular today (but likely foreign to Paul himself).

◼ THE TEXT IN CONTEMPORARY DISCUSSION

Postcolonial scholars recognize that modern missionaries' Eurocentric interpretations of Paul's journeys served their own colonizing interests; they used Acts to construct totalizing binaries—"center versus margins," "civilized versus uncivilized," and "enlightened versus superstitious"—that are too reductionistic to represent the ambivalences inherent in every time and culture. Dehumanizing stereotypes are not limited to earlier generations; some biblical scholars today adopt racialized rhetoric and supersessionist ideologies. For example, stereotypes of the Lycaónians as Mediterranean "hicks" betray scholars' "Orientalizing" tendencies (Wordelman, 205).

Some call Christians to repent and reject racist, anti-Jewish rhetoric in Acts (e.g., 13:44-52), while others point to Paul's blinding of Bar-Jesus (13:11) as another Lukan instance of justified Christian violence against outsiders. These views provoke hermeneutical questions: if we aim to read Acts within its cultural, sociohistorical contexts, but Acts uses fixed categories and essentializing language, should we accept these as evidence of how the implied author or audiences conceptualized their world? Or should we assume that this rhetoric masks Luke's internalization of the imperialist agenda? Should we counter authoritarian claims to hegemony by uncovering the text's unspoken ambiguities? Do these approaches simply represent different readers' goals (i.e., discovering Luke's intentions versus exposing inconsistencies in Acts)? Are these goals at odds with one another, does one presuppose the other, or do or can they complement each other?

15:1-35: The Jerusalem Controversy

◼ THE TEXT IN ITS ANCIENT CONTEXT

The Jerusalem Council (15:1-35) publicly legitimates the gentile mission, which started privately with the Ethiopian eunuch's conversion in Acts 8, and began to spread with Cornelius's conversion and Peter's defense in Acts 10–11. This is the first formal council convened to address the complexities that arose as gentiles increasingly joined the inchoate Christian community; early Christian identity-construction involved significant disputes about covenant-related issues such as food sacrificed to idols, the Mosaic law, and circumcision. The precipitating event is that Pharisaic Judaizers in Antioch want to circumcise gentiles. Paul and Barnabas, unable to resolve this dispute alone, seek the advice of the Jerusalem "apostles and elders" (mentioned five times in the chapter; 15:2, 4, 6, 22, 23).

The account paints a picture of both dissension and decorum. On the one hand, "much debate" occurs (15:7); on the other hand, the apostles listen attentively (15:12), and James waits patiently to speak (15:13). Contrast this insider assembly's dignified tone with outsiders' unruly mayhem and intentional interruptions elsewhere (18:12-17; 19:23-41). Although Luke attests to tensions among early Christians, their mode of resolving disputes adheres to Greco-Roman standards of masculine comportment, including self-restraint and propriety; in this way, Luke's storytelling reflects and reinforces the gendered sociocultural ideologies of the Greco-Roman environment, as he constructs early Christian insider-outsider boundary markers.

Acts 15:6-21 follows a trifold legitimating sequence. First, Peter (absent from the story since Acts 12) reappears with a judicial speech that further develops themes established in Cornelius's conversion story, especially that of divine choice. Salvation comes through grace, as a gift for *both* Jewish and gentile believers, not through the "yoke" of the law (15:11). Peter's speech, recounted in direct discourse for emphasis, appeals to recent events of which the church leaders are well aware. Second, Paul and Barnabas attest to the visible "signs and wonders" (cf. 14:3) that God has performed among the gentiles. In the Gospel and Acts, miraculous "signs" follow and verify God's communication (Luke 2:12, 34; 11:16, 29, 30; 21:7, 11, 25; 23:8; Acts 2:19, 22, 43; 4:30; 5:12; 6:8; 7:36; 8:6, 13; 14:3). Finally, James's speech provides scriptural warrant for the gentile mission, referencing Amos 9:11-12 (LXX), and Lev. 17:8—18:26 concerning "aliens" among the Jews. Rhetorically, each phase in this progression provides a different basis for the gentile mission—experience, miracles, and Scripture. All three point to the gentile mission as God's original plan, and to God's initiative in bringing it about.

The group drafts a letter (15:22-29) stipulating two major decisions: gentile Christians need not be circumcised, but they ought to abstain from fornication, blood, and things strangled or polluted by idols (Exod. 34:15-16; Lev. 3:17; 17:3-14; 18:6-30; Deut. 12:16-27). Though the issue arose in Antioch, the letter is addressed to Antioch, Syria, and Cilicia (15:23), subtly underscoring the Jerusalem church's widespread influence. Paul and Barnabas return to the Antiochene Christians (15:35), who rejoice at the verdict, providing closure for this watershed event in the early church.

∎ THE TEXT IN THE INTERPRETIVE TRADITION

The legacy of James and the Jerusalem Council extended in narrative form into noncanonical accounts like the *Ascents of James* (probably preserved in *Ps.-Clem. Rec.* 1.43–44). The council (15:1-35) also figured prominently in later theological discussions: while some emphasized the council's format as a normative process for handling church conflict, others developed the implications of its resolutions.

Early Christian apologists marshaled Acts 15:1-35 as evidence against so-called heretics. Responding to Celsus's charge that Christianity was disunified, Origen pointed to Acts 15 as proof that the Holy Spirit resolves Christian disputes (*C. Cels.* 3.10–11). Chrysostom considered the account an ecclesiological model for theological decision making: ecumenical councils should be orderly, with all participants submitting to the bishop (*Hom. Act.* 33).

Interpreters' views of the Jews determined their assessment of the Jerusalem Council's decisions. For the Venerable Bede, the council attested to early Christian respect for Judaism. Others took it as a rejection of Judaism. During the Reformation, Luther cited Acts 15 to denounce the Jews' "works-based theology." Relatedly, opponents of infant baptism argued that, since salvation is through grace, unbaptized infants go to heaven (15:11). Catholics point to Acts 15 as evidence of the development of doctrine: contrary to the Protestant principle of *sola scriptura*, in this view, the Holy Spirit reveals truth progressively, which church leaders safeguard through tradition.

During the modern period, the difficulties with reconciling Acts 15 and Gal. 2:1-10 based on modern historiographical standards raised larger issues of the historicity and relationship between Acts and Paul's letters. Some harmonized the two accounts and ignored discrepancies, while others considered them two separate events; still others took the differences as evidence of the story's historical unreliability.

∎ THE TEXT IN CONTEMPORARY DISCUSSION

Missiologists frequently cite Acts 15 when considering how to communicate the gospel across cultural boundaries. Is the Christian message universal, or does every unique culture require its own contextualized form of the gospel message?

Some look to Acts 15 as a hermeneutical model, asking: What is the Holy Spirit's relationship to the Word of God? How do/should Christians appropriate Scripture for new situations like those raised by modern birth control, Internet use, stem cell research, or weapons of mass destruction? Some apply the text directly to contemporary situations, like Jehovah's Witnesses, who refuse blood transfusions based on Acts 15:29: Others believe each new age requires fresh Spirit-led discernment. Interpreters also disagree about whether Acts 15 condones or vilifies interpretive plurality. On the one hand, characters express multiple viewpoints in a respectful dialogue with a peaceful resolution. On the other hand, the leadership's final decision effectively suppresses the other faction's views. Certain scholars believe Acts 15 is a distinctly formative event in the life of the early church, and thus not paradigmatic for today.

Acts 15 has important implications for contemporary Jewish-Christian relations. Many scholars have labeled Acts antisemitic, since repeatedly, Jews oppose the gospel, while gentiles accept it (cf. 13:44-46; 18:6; 28:25-28). The Jerusalem Council also rejects a fundamental distinguishing feature of the nation of Israel (circumcision), and affirms salvation for Jews and gentiles alike (15:11). On the other hand, the council maintains certain purity laws and, although gentiles convert, Luke never shows them as leaders. A few scholars describe Luke as Jewish and pro-Israel.

While twentieth-century scholars found inconsistencies between Acts 15 and Galatians 2 to be problematic, interpreters today recognize that rhetorical exigencies engender different kinds of narratives; thus it can be more productive to ask how each writing functions rhetorically. This, of course, raises larger questions about doing "history" using the New Testament texts. What does it mean to reconstruct historical circumstances with limited sources, especially when ancient concepts of "history" differ from ours?

15:36—18:21: Paul's Second Missionary Journey

▮ THE TEXT IN ITS ANCIENT CONTEXT

Paul's second journey moves through Philippi (16:11-40), Thessalonica and Beroea (17:1-15), Athens (17:16-34), and Corinth (18:1-18). Thus the expansion in the narrative to "the ends of the earth" now extends into Europe. The trip begins inauspiciously: in the so-called Antioch incident, Paul and Barnabas part ways (15:36-40), and Acts does not record them together again. Instead, Paul invites Timothy, who—with a Jewish-Christian mother and a Greek father—embodies Lukan universalism. Paul's unnecessary circumcision of Timothy (16:3; cf. 15:1-35) illustrates how he adapts evangelistic strategies for different audiences (16:1-5). Multiple references to divine guidance (16:6-10) establish that God chooses Paul's destinations.

At 16:10, the narration inexplicably shifts from an anonymous third-person external point of view to a first-person plural internal perspective. Though the Gospel and Acts both begin with first-person direct address (Luke 1:1-4; Acts 1:1), the "we-passages" (see 20:5-21:18; 27:1-28:16) are famously enigmatic. In Acts, they coincide with sea voyages (Robbins).

Luke calls Paul's first destination—Philippi—the "foremost city" of Macedonia (16:11-12), which is odd, since Thessalonica was Macedonia's capital. The Philippian mission is framed by references to Lydia of Thyatira (which had a famous purple dyeing industry; 16:14-15, 40): Lydia deals in purple cloth, a luxury item. She and her household become the first converts in Europe; the reference to her household likely indicates that she is unmarried and wealthy. Her conversion thus illustrates the spread of the gospel to prominent elites. Repeated narrative articulations of the gospel's spread to a variety of people create coherence across Luke's episodic narrative.

Sandwiched between mentions of Lydia is a pericope about someone on the opposite end of the social scale: a slave girl with a "pythonic spirit" whose prophetic abilities generate revenue for her masters (16:16). The pythonic spirit alludes to the oracle of Apollo at Delphi, a staple of popular Roman religion that was inextricably linked to the city's economy. Following Paul and Silas's exorcism of the slave girl against her masters' wishes, the magistrates (the Roman colony's chief officials) imprison the two apostles, who miraculously escape. Unlike the other prison escapes in Acts (see 5:19-21; 12:6-11), this one results in the conversions of the jailor and his household (16:25-34).

In both Thessalonica and Beroea, Christianity draws converts (17:4, 12). However, in Thessalonica, Christians are accused of "turning the world upside down"—an ironic charge, given that *the mob* disturbs the peace (17:5-6). In contrast, Jews in Beroea respond positively, verifying Paul's claims with the Scriptures (17:11).

Athens was a major urban center marked by religious fervor and intellectual curiosity. Luke describes Athens as "full of idols" (17:16) because Athenian public spaces were crowded with statuary, temples, iconography, and altars to the emperor and pagan gods. Unlike other public speeches in

Acts, which are addressed to Jews, Paul addresses the Areopagus, Athens's elite administrative body (17:16-31). Tailoring his apologetic strategies accordingly, Paul speaks in classical Greek oratorical style and addresses Epicurean and Stoic philosophies. His language resembles the Athenians' charge against Socrates in Plato's *Apology* (17:18), and he cites the third-century-BCE Greek poet Aratus (17:24-29). The conversions of members of the Areopagus demonstrate Paul's rhetorical effectiveness (17:34).

Corinth, the Roman capital of Achaia, was a thriving commercial center; strategically located on the Isthmus of Corinth, the city controlled major trade routes between Asia and Rome. Paul's meeting before Gallio (the Roman proconsul governing Achaia c. 51–53 CE) suggests Corinth's administrative importance as well. In a rare temporal marker, Luke reports that Paul stays in Corinth for a year and six months (18:11), where he meets Prisca (Priscilla is the diminutive) and Aquila (18:2-26). Ancient literature rarely lists the woman's name first (18:18, 26); doing so may indicate that Priscilla was of higher social status than Aquila. Paul cuts his hair in Cenchraea (eastern Corinth; 18:18) due to an unknown vow (cf. 21:23-24); it may be the Nazirite vow (Num. 6:1-21).

■ The Text in the Interpretive Tradition

Paul's split with Barnabas (15:39) posed a challenge for those who emphasized early Christian harmony; for Calvin, Paul's refusal to compromise marked his zeal for the gospel.

Proponents of infant baptism supported their case by appealing to the household conversions in 16:11-15 and 16:25-34.

In line with his stereotypically anti-Jewish polemic, Chrysostom insisted that Paul only circumcised Timothy to gain a hearing with the Jews, not because he respected Jewish laws.

Later texts mimicked Paul's Areopagus address, as in the apocryphal *Acts of Philip* 2, where Philip similarly appears before the Athenian philosophers. Others have hailed it as a missiological manifesto, emphasizing that the speech is addressed to non-Jews. Nineteenth-century abolitionists used it (esp. 17:26) as a prophetic call for racial justice. However, early twentieth-century scholars like Martin Dibelius denigrated the Areopagus speech as an un-Pauline capitulation to educated pagan elites.

■ The Text in Contemporary Discussion

Jewish orthodoxy is not the primary issue at stake in Timothy's circumcision (16:1-3; cf. 15:1-35; 16:4-5); texts like Philo's writings and *Joseph and Aseneth* attest that circumcision was already debated in Paul's day. Rather, this passage reminds us that religious identities are always negotiated and configured on the body. How are physical bodies variously employed in Christian discourses today? How do assumptions about the body inform contemporary Christian theology, and how does embodiment influence contemporary Christian practice?

Lydia and the slave girl have been read as "border women" in "land possession type scenes" (a traveling hero and a "native" woman) that simultaneously highlight Paul's foreignness and legitimate his ideological conquest (Staley). Laura Nasrallah suggests another intriguing parallel: Paul's travels create a Christian form of the Panhellenion—a mid-second-century league of Greek cities Hadrian established to promote unity. Expansionist discourses like this helped to shape American concepts like "Manifest Destiny" and divinely mandated territorial expansion, which continue to inform US imperialism and post-9/11 political rhetoric.

For some scholars, Luke subordinates both Lydia (16:13-15) and the slave girl (16:16-18) to Paul, demonstrating that Christian communities do not threaten the patriarchal values of the Roman social order. Merely a pawn in the power contest between her masters and Paul, the slave girl herself is inconsequential. Many African American scholars have pointed out that this reinscribes oppressive slave ideologies.

Some hail Paul's Areopagus speech (17:16-31) as a model for interreligious dialogue. The Native American Lifeway Adult Bible Study argues that unlike early European settlers in America, Paul never forced his beliefs on others; observing them, he developed his approach accordingly (17:22-23). Larger questions arise: How does Paul portray the essence of Christian identity when speaking with the Athenians (17:28-29), and (how) does this differ from the way Christian identity is portrayed elsewhere in Acts? How does/should Christianity influence minority acculturation today? How should Christians from different ethnic and cultural backgrounds relate to one another? Is Christianity a homogenizing force in our world? Should it be?

Paul's upbringing in Tarsus (a university city) and his Roman citizenship presumably increased his stature before the Athenian intellectuals. By adopting their discourse, is Paul practicing effective evangelism, or compromising the gospel? Should Christians regard Paul here as a model to be emulated, or a cause for caution? More broadly, when leaders in education, politics, news and entertainment media, and other forums adapt their message to the medium, are they communicating responsibly, or perpetuating patterns of power and privilege?

18:22—21:16: Paul's Third Missionary Journey

■ THE TEXT IN ITS ANCIENT CONTEXT

Paul's third missionary journey begins in Ephesus, the capital of Asia and probably the third-largest city in the empire behind Rome and Alexandria. Situated on multiple land routes and a major seaport, Ephesus was a center of international trade. Filled with notable buildings and multiple agoras, inscriptions describe Ephesus's great wealth and importance. Paul spends the most time in Ephesus (two years and three months; 19:8, 10), and even if 19:10 is hyperbolic from the perspective of historical reconstruction, the narrative portrays this as the culmination of his evangelistic efforts.

Creating narrative continuity with the foregoing section, where Priscilla and Aquila are mentioned (18:18-21), Luke sets the stage in Ephesus with a story about the couple's ministry to Apollos (18:24-28). Right away, the narrative associates Apollos with the apostles, as he speaks boldly in the synagogue (18:26). Bold speech—*parrēsia*—characterizes true discipleship in Acts (9:27-28; 13:46; 14:3; 19:8; 26:26). Rightly receiving Priscilla and Aquila's instruction, Apollos preaches in Achaia (19:27-28). This progression of the right disposition, correct reception of God's word, and faithful proclamation is a central Lukan paradigm for discipleship.

Acts 19:10-20, framed by references to the "word of the Lord" (19:10, 20), contrasts God's power (e.g., Paul's miracles in 19:11-12) with magic, which was particularly pervasive in Ephesus.

Jewish exorcists, attempting to use Jesus' name as an incantation, are overtaken; the event, like Bar-Jesus' defeat (13:6-11), causes amazement and widespread conversion. Those who practiced magic burn their books (instruction manuals in the art of magic), publicly renouncing that way of life in favor of the Christian Way (19:19-20). As is familiar by this point in Acts, success begets opposition. Employing a common figure of speech called litotes (an understatement using a double negative to make an affirmative statement), Luke describes "no little" public disturbance (19:23; cf. 12:18-19; 15:2; 19:23-24; 20:12; 27:20).

Having established that the Christian God is more powerful than generic magic, Luke turns to the locale-specific goddess Artemis, whose Ephesian cult was well known in antiquity. It would be difficult to overstate the importance of the cult of Artemis to the Ephesian worldview. Numerous inscriptions, coinage, literary artifacts, and the enormous temple of Artemis itself (one of the Seven Wonders of the Ancient World) attest to the Ephesians' conviction that they enjoyed a unique covenant relationship with their patron goddess. Worship of Artemis was considered necessary for the city's economic stability, as she sent the harvest and guarded the city's welfare. The temple was not only a spiritual sanctuary but also a bank, lending money, charging interest, and housing Artemis's own large financial estate (on the temple as a bank, see Strabo, *Geog.* 14.1.21–29).

For economic and spiritual reasons, Demetrius incites a riot (19:24-28). In what becomes a major public spectacle, the believers face a confused (19:29, 32), angry mob in the Ephesian theater (which held nearly twenty-five thousand people and still stands today). The mob exemplifies the opposite of classical Greco-Roman decorum and orderliness (cf. the Christian assembly in 15:1-35). Paul's third great missionary journey ends when the town clerk indirectly vindicates Paul and dispels the crowd.

Paul's journey to Rome parallels the Lukan passion narrative: the reference to the days of unleavened bread (20:6) mirrors references to Passover in Luke 22:1, 7; the mention of breaking bread in an upper room (20:7, 8) recalls Jesus' Last Supper (Luke 22:7-14); Eutychus's sleepiness (20:9) may allude to the disciples' sleeping in Gethsemane (Luke 22:45-46). The believers' failures to dissuade Paul from his inexorable march toward Rome (21:4, 12) parallel Jesus' Spirit-led journey to Jerusalem. Paul is further likened to Jesus (and Peter) when he raises Eutychus from the dead (20:10; cf. Luke 7:15; 8:52-55; Acts 9:36-42).

▌The Text in the Interpretive Tradition

Following the Reformation, early Baptists pointed to John's baptism of repentance (19:3-4) and the baptism of Ephesian believers (19:5) to argue for believers' baptism. They stressed the importance of personal repentance and individual accountability.

Priscilla's apparently prominent role in teaching Apollos (18:24-28) gave rise to several legendary accounts, including the belief that a fourth-century church (Saint Priscae) was built on the site of her house church in Rome (cf. 1 Cor. 16:19). In 1900, Adolf von Harnack even posited that Priscilla wrote the book of Hebrews.

Although Christians officially excluded women from leadership roles for centuries, examples like Lydia and Priscilla demonstrate that there were women leaders even in the early church.

Widespread evidence such as tombstone inscriptions attest to women priests from the third through the ninth centuries, and women prophets were active in early church life. Tertullian (e.g., *De anima* 9.4), Cyprian (e.g., *Epistle* 74.10), and the Nag Hammadi poem *Thunder, Perfect Mind* all mention unnamed women prophets. In the second century, Montanus's female colleagues Prisca and Quintilla influenced the rise of the New Prophecy, or Montanism.

According to the church historian Eusebius in the fourth century (*Hist. eccl.* 3.31.3–4), a tradition dating to the second century held that Philip's daughters of Acts 21:8-9 moved to Hierapolis in Phrygia. Several later traditions claim that the women eventually married.

Twentieth-century advocates of women's ordination proclaimed a theology of liberation based partly on the view that Philip's prophesying daughters fulfilled the prophecy in Joel 2:28 (cf. Acts 2:17) and served as "leaders for the church in Caesarea" (Torjesen, 27–28). Readers in Papua New Guinea were distracted by the description of Philip's daughters as unmarried (21:9), since in that culture, everyone marries (Clark, 208); this illustrates Hans-Georg Gadamer's well-known claim that all interpretations reflect the interpreter's sociocultural situatedness.

◼ THE TEXT IN CONTEMPORARY DISCUSSION

Women's roles in the Christian community continue to garner scholarly and popular attention. Some believe Lydia and Priscilla point to a Lukan emphasis on women's leadership. Others counter that when women are rhetorical tools with which men think, even positive portrayals of women legitimate patriarchal control. Though Luke mentions Philip's prophesying daughters, he quotes only Agabus's prophecy (21:9-11). Note, too, that Philip's daughters remain anonymous, while the male prophet is named (21:10; cf. 11:28). This is unsurprising: although low-status characters played integral roles in society, they generally remain unnamed in ancient literature. The point is to acknowledge that gender-based ideological implications underlie Luke's narrative; Acts both recognizes and represses women's ministries (Seim).

Philip's daughters also raise the issue of virginity, which was much lauded in early Christian contexts (the Greek word *parthenos* can be translated "unmarried" or "virgin," 21:9). Some contemporary scholars argue that praise for female virginity points to negative presuppositions regarding femininity, while affirmations of celibate female leaders in the church subtly reinscribe patriarchal biases.

Many conservatives and liberals accept a unilinear paradigm of "decline," in which early Christians were egalitarians, while later Christians marginalized women as institutionalism increased. Recently, scholars have critiqued three common dichotomies imposed on historical reconstructions of early Christianity: patriarchy versus the discipleship of equals; public versus private; ascetic versus domestic lifestyles. Each category is more complex historically than typically assumed.

These discussions provoke crucial questions: How might understanding early Christian history as ambiguous and polyphonic affect women's roles in churches today? How do biblical translations communicate specific ideologies? For instance, the NRSV, NIV, ESV, NASB, and ASV translate *gynai* (21:5) as "wives" instead of "women." Both are linguistically possible, but "wives" subordinates women to their husbands and limits women's involvement in the early church.

21:17—23:35: Events in Jerusalem

■ THE TEXT IN ITS ANCIENT CONTEXT

Estimates of the number of Jews in Jerusalem at Paul's time range from twenty thousand to fifty thousand. According to Luke, many thousands of these Jews have become believers, but they remain "zealous for the law" (this description recalls the passionate commitment to Yahweh and Israel that typifies many heroic Jewish figures: Num. 25:6-13; Judg. 9:2-4; 1 Kgs. 18:40; 1 Macc. 2:23-27, 49-68; cf. Paul's self-description in 22:3). For them, Paul's teachings threaten Israel's distinctive boundaries, but this does not fit the narrator's characterization of Paul; by Acts 21, he has circumcised Timothy (16:3), shaved his hair (18:18), and observed Jewish holidays (20:16). Still, he agrees to demonstrate his respect for the Mosaic law publicly, so that the Jewish believers might observe him for themselves (21:23-26).

Though Paul appears to appease the Jewish Christians, events repeat themselves when a mob of outsiders (Jews from Asia) challenges him. The description is remarkably similar to the riot in Ephesus: the crowds are in an "uproar," shouting confusedly as they seize Paul and drag him outside the temple (21:30-32; cf. 19:29-32). The two scenes also differ: unlike the proconsul Gallio, who dismissed a similar dispute as an inter-Jewish quarrel and allowed a man to be beaten (18:12:17), officers in Jerusalem control the situation, protect Paul (21:31-35; 23:10), and allow him to defend himself (21:40). Paul chooses his content and his language wisely (first, Greek to the tribune, 21:37, then Aramaic to the crowd, 21:40; 22:2), identifying himself in terms appropriate for each audience. Paul's exchange with the tribune picks up the Lukan motif of misunderstood identity.

Paul's defense in Jerusalem (22:1-21) retrospectively recounts his Damascus experience for the second time (cf. 9:1-31), now from his first-person perspective, and with several changes that appeal to a Jewish audience. Effectively concluding his earlier defense, Paul takes advantage of the well-known dispute between Pharisees and Sadducees over resurrection to provoke violent controversy between them (23:6-10). Even as the Jews accuse Paul of rejecting their teachings (21:28), his intimate knowledge of Jewish teachings protects him. A divine pronouncement that Paul will testify in Rome (23:11) sets the stage for the journey to Rome, which occupies the rest of the narrative.

The Jews then hatch the most elaborate plot yet to kill Paul; whereas Luke briefly describes earlier attempts on Paul's life (9:23-25, 29-30; 14:19; 20:3, 19; 21:31), this premeditated conspiracy—and Paul's escape—are related in much greater detail. The dramatic tension mounts as a large group vows to achieve their goal (23:12-15). Paul's nephew (otherwise unknown in early Christian literature) warns Paul and informs the tribune about the plot (23:16-22). The tribune (whose name, Claudius Lysias, the reader finally learns in 23:26) goes to great lengths to protect Paul: nearly five hundred men—probably Lukan hyperbole to increase suspense—escort Paul through the night to Caesarea, where he appears before Felix (23:23-35).

■ THE TEXT IN THE INTERPRETIVE TRADITION

Second- and third-century martyrdom accounts demonstrate that the right response to suffering was a point of contention for Jesus-followers. Though Christian apologists like Tertullian argued that martyrdom is a Christian duty, Paul's detailed escape plan (23:12-35) supported Christian exhortations *not* to volunteer for martyrdom (e.g., *Mart. Pol.* 4.1).

For Augustine, Paul's claim to Roman citizenship (22:22-29) exemplifies Jesus' injunction to turn the other cheek (Luke 6:29). Augustine viewed the scene as juxtaposing heavenly and worldly values: the tribune disregards the heavenly honor that Paul values most (salvation), but respects the earthly honor that Paul values least (citizenship).

In the nineteenth century, debates raged over whether to translate the Greek word *baptizein* in verses like 22:16 as "wash" or "immerse," with obvious doctrinal implications accompanying each choice. Bible Societies that sought to translate biblical texts "directly" without promoting specific doctrines found this problematic.

▮ THE TEXT IN CONTEMPORARY DISCUSSION

Postcolonial thinkers who interrogate race and ethnicity in biblical texts assert that Acts 21:37—22:29 epitomizes Paul's *hybridity* (the mixtures and interdependences created in liminal spaces of boundary crossings). Paul is a Jew and a Roman citizen, Hebraic and Hellenic—as Daniel Boyarin puts it, he is a "Jewgreek" (1994, 79). Paul speaks Hebrew, claims his education under Gamaliel, and insists on his prior obedience to the Jewish authorities. And yet, he also invokes his Roman citizenship. With great rhetorical skill, Paul strategically highlights certain aspects of his identity based on each discursive situation.

Paul's conversation with the tribune illuminates ancient conceptions of social class. The tribune paid for his citizenship, whereas Paul was born a citizen (22:28). Although we lack statistics on the Roman economy (especially from rural areas, where most poverty exists), historians agree that Roman social status was relatively fluid. Routes for upward mobility such as manumission meant the same person could be assessed using different criteria, such as wealth, juridical status, education, and so on. A slave could be better educated than his master; citizenship did not imply wealth. A more nuanced picture of early Christian socioeconomic realities should inform our readings of Paul's identity claims.

24:1—26:32: Events in Caesarea

▮ THE TEXT IN ITS ANCIENT CONTEXT

Although ancient accounts describe Felix as corrupt, Acts at first characterizes him positively: "well-informed about the Way" (24:22), he gives Paul a fair hearing and liberty while in custody (24:10-24). Still, for two years (24:27), he stalls (24:22), hoping for a bribe (24:26). Luke mentions Felix's wife Drusilla (24:24), whom many readers would have known he pursued while she was married to Azizus of Emesa. And Felix keeps Paul in captivity when Festus succeeds him, hoping to ingratiate himself with the Jews (24:27). Perhaps this explains why Felix becomes "frightened" when Paul describes divine judgment (24:25).

Festus also wants to appease the Jews (25:9), a detail that attests to their power in the region. Nevertheless, in keeping with Luke's positive portrayals of Roman authorities (Luke 23:4, 14, 15,

20, 22, 41, 47; Acts 18:14-16; 19:37-41; 23:29), Festus listens to Paul's defense and agrees to his request to go to Rome (25:8-12). This long-anticipated journey is delayed by the arrival of King Herod Agrippa II (son of Herod Agrippa, cf. 12:1-4) and his sister Bernice (with whom Agrippa reportedly had an incestuous relationship).

Their arrival prompts the fourth cycle of Jewish accusations and Paul's sophisticated rhetorical maneuvering in his own defense (22:1-21; 24:10-21; 25:8-11; 26:2-29). In each case, Paul's forensic rhetoric serves two chief purposes: he depicts Jesus as the Jewish Messiah and legitimates his own apostolic ministry. The accusations levied against Paul instantiate the Lukan theme of Jesus'—and his disciples'—innocence.

Paul's trials before the authorities recall Jesus' trials, albeit with an important distinction: whereas Jesus remains silent before Herod (Luke 23:6-12), Paul, like Stephen in Acts 6:8—8:3, vehemently defends himself; perhaps he receives the words from Jesus himself (Luke 21:12-15).

The recapitulated episodes in Acts 25–26 are not simply the scene repetitions that are common in episodic narratives; rather, a sense of suspense and intrigue accrues as the stature and power of those who hear Paul's defense increases. More is at stake with each successive trial. The elaborate public ceremony (25:23) before King Agrippa and Bernice is the climactic moment on Paul's inexorable journey to Rome, ending with Agrippa's consternation over why Paul appealed to Caesar (26:32).

■ THE TEXT IN THE INTERPRETIVE TRADITION

Early Christian martyrdom accounts conventionally portray the martyr pronouncing judgment on the accusers and/or confessing her or his identity as a Christian. Early Christians did not appear to understand Jesus' silence on trial as a paradigmatic model; they followed Paul's example instead.

Many centuries later, the modern missionary movement drew on Paul's example to legitimize missionary expansion and, concomitantly, European colonization. Parachurch Bible societies, translation efforts, and formal missionary societies were founded and flourished following William Carey's famous sermon in 1793; Carey, along with missionaries like Adoniram Judson, defended the historicity of Acts and appealed to Paul's missionary journeys as an ideal missionizing blueprint: choose destinations strategically, establish churches, train local leaders, and vehemently defend the faith.

■ THE TEXT IN CONTEMPORARY DISCUSSION

Acts 26:12-18 contains the third recounting of Paul's Damascus experience (cf. 9:1-31; 22:1-21). Following Ernst Haenchen, most contemporary scholars abandoned the attempt to identify disparate sources behind the accounts of Paul's Damascus road experience; instead, they consider the differences between the accounts as evidence of the author's specific theological and stylistic emphases at various points in the story. For instance, the third rendition of the story in Acts contains fewer details about the event itself (e.g., Ananias is removed entirely), and a greater emphasis on its symbolic dimensions: Paul draws stark lines between good and evil (and Christian and Jew), extending the description of his prior persecution of Christians (26:9-11), and using the language of light and dark to connect himself with Christ (26:13, 18, 23).

Acts 24:1—26:32 spotlights the Roman governmental authorities (Felix, Festus, Agrippa, and Bernice). Luke-Acts is clearly preoccupied with power; however, whether Luke presents a consistently pro- or anti-imperialist agenda continues to be a site of rigorous scholarly contestation. The crux of the debate is whether Luke is sympathetic toward or fundamentally opposed to Roman rule. Some argue that Acts openly rejects all forms of hegemony; others suggest that like many colonized peoples, Luke internalized and replicated Rome's imperialist ideology, only dissenting via what James Scott famously called "hidden transcripts," or private, everyday speech countering hegemonic discourse.

Postcolonial theorists have challenged the common tendency to portray the Roman Empire and early Christianity as monolithic, reified categories: the antagonistic colonizing Roman authorities as clearly opposed to the (resistant or complicit) colonized Christians. Postcolonial thinkers destabilize the simplistic colonizer/colonized binary by recognizing what Homi Bhabha dubs "colonial ambivalence"—the oscillation between desire and denigration that occurs within colonizer and colonized, invariably implicating both in contested discourses about identity. Colonialism is never unilateral. Like many colonized people today, early Christians lived within multiple contexts; Acts testifies to early Christian attempts to revise inherited stories and negotiate a coherent identity in conversation with other texts and other communities. Furthermore, the relationships between the Roman authorities and "native populations" were inconsistent across the empire. Can we move beyond essentialist caricatures of the oppressive Roman Empire and oppressed Christians? What implications might attention to ambivalence, misrepresentation, and inconsistencies have for marginalized communities across the globe?

27:1—28:31: Paul's Trip to Rome and Conclusion

■ THE TEXT IN ITS ANCIENT CONTEXT

The last two chapters of Acts are recounted almost entirely in the first-person plural (27:1—28:16). Paul's journey to Rome has all the makings of an epic adventure tale—a sea voyage, storms, shipwreck, an exotic location with island "natives," miraculous healings, and heroism in the face of danger. As the voyage begins, the narrator notes that "the Fast" (the Day of Atonement) has passed, indicating the season is autumn. This detail and Paul's prophetic warning (27:10) create a foreboding sense of impending calamity. Indeed, the situation goes from bad to worse when the ship runs aground on Malta, an island south of Sicily (28:1). Luke's harrowing account of the struggle to reach shore is vivid and detailed (27:39-44). The shipwreck and the soldiers' plan to kill all the prisoners (27:42) make it even more astounding that everyone survives (27:44). In the narrative fulfillment of Paul's vision (27:22-26), Luke again demonstrates that God's plan inevitably comes to fruition.

The voyage is rich with intertextual traces of Homeric epic, Greco-Roman literature, the Hebrew Bible (including Isaiah), and Virgil's *Aeneid* (Bonz). In Chariton's ancient Greek novel *Chareas and Callirhoe*, which is roughly contemporaneous to Acts, a travel narrative provides the impetus for plot development. Legal trials fulfill similar functions in the Greek novels and Acts; courtroom scenes are particularly conducive for communicating ideologies because they establish a rhetorical winner and loser. Whereas ancient Greek novels record crimes of passion, Acts records "crimes" against Christianity; Luke uses this juridical trope to emphasize that when the apostles stand trial, the view they espouse is true. Other parallels exist, as well; Petronius's early Latin novel *Satyricon* explicitly references the early Christian rite of the Lord's Supper, while Paul's breaking of bread in Acts 27:35 clearly has eucharistic undertones (cf. Luke 22:19).

On Malta, the "natives" warmly welcome the newcomers (28:2, 7, 10); foreign hospitality extended to shipwrecked protagonists is a trope from the ancient novels that Luke appropriates to illustrate Christian benevolence. Despite the Maltans' misunderstandings (28:4-6), Paul heals their sick (28:8-9). The group departs on an Alexandrian ship probably carrying grain, as Rome imported grain from Egypt (cf. 27:38). Zeus's sons Castor and Pollux ("the Twin Brothers" on the ship's figurehead, 28:11) were thought to provide protection at sea; the irony that an ideal Lukan reader will discern is that only the Christian God provides true protection.

Typical narrative plots follow the climax with a denouement—a falling action that provides closure. Acts ends with Paul under what we today call "house arrest": with only one guard, he enjoys remarkable freedom (28:16). Though tradition tells of Paul's beheading in Rome around 64–65 CE (and Luke alludes to it in 19:21; 20:22-25; 23:11; 26:32; 27:24), this is not how Luke ends his story. Rather, Acts concludes on a triumphant note. The disciples have fulfilled Christ's programmatic commissioning (1:8): the message has finally reached Rome, the capital of the empire and (according to Roman ideology) the center of the *oikoumenē* (the inhabited world).

▌The Text in the Interpretive Tradition

As the first generation of Christians passed away, tradition became the crucial ideological battleground. In response to Marcion and others, proto-orthodox Christians of the second through fourth centuries generated many pseudepigraphical works to build on existing details and fill the lacunae in Acts. For instance, most accounts utilize the depiction in Acts of Paul as a Roman citizen (21:39; 22:25-29; 23:27); however, whereas the canonical Acts implies (but does not state) that Paul is martyred in Rome, in the apocryphal *Acts of Paul*, the beheaded Paul appears to Nero, promising divine vengeance.

Martin Luther's Heidelberg Disputation (1518) coined the terms "theology of glory" and "theology of the cross" to contrast salvation based on human effort (*theologia gloriae*) with salvation based on Christ's sacrifice on the cross (*theologia crucis*). Luke has long been read as a theology of glory, partly because it ends with Paul preaching "without hindrance" in Rome (28:31). Still, persecutions punctuate Paul's journeys; he arrives in Rome because he refuses to avoid suffering, which the Holy Spirit has predicted repeatedly (cf. 20:22-24; 21:11-13).

▌The Text in Contemporary Discussion

Acts 28:27-28 reiterates that God's salvation is for the gentiles. Is the mission to the Jews permanently over, thereby replacing one form of particularism (Jewish salvation) with another (gentile salvation)? Or does this simply reinforce that God has ordained the gentile mission and the gospel must spread to all people?

Our final picture of Paul epitomizes several Lukan motifs—the gentile mission, the unstoppable divine will, rightly receiving God's Word, and boldly proclaiming the gospel as a constitutive component of discipleship. In a sense, then, the final installment provides closure, reinforcing ideological commitments that are discernible throughout the entire narrative.

And yet, Acts also remains famously open-ended. Though ancient historians extolled the virtues of completing one's narrative (e.g., Dionysius, *Thuc.* 16.847), Luke's ending generates openness in several ways. Paul's visitors in Rome have mixed reactions to the gospel (28:24-25), Jesus does not reappear as promised (1:11), and the reader never hears of Paul's fate after his two years in captivity (28:30). Neither does Luke relate the ending of other main characters' stories, like Barnabas or Peter. And although the book begins with a personal address (1:1), there is no concluding second-person farewell, as in the epistles (cf. Rom. 16:21-7; 1 Cor. 16:19-24; Eph. 6:23-24; Phil. 4:20-23; Col. 4:7-18). Does the final word of Acts—a Greek adverb meaning "without hindrance"—hint that the church's work is over, or just beginning?

Discussing this inconclusive ending, some scholars have suggested that Luke intended to write a third volume, that he ran out of space on his scroll, or that he was ignorant of Paul's fate. More generally, if the ending of Acts implies that the gospel will continue to spread, what are the implications for Christian disciples today? What forms of interference limit the spread of the gospel, and how are Christians called to overcome them?

Ancient rhetors like Cicero (*De or.* 2:41:177) and Plutarch (*Mor.* 1.45E) believed open-endedness engaged readers by allowing them to linger longer over the story. In modern psychological terms, this is an instance of the Zeigarnik Effect: what remains unfinished is better remembered. The open-endedness of Acts implicitly situates the reader in Theophilus's position: the reader must decide how to respond to this dynamic, challenging, and beautifully complex early Christian narrative.

Works Cited

Anderson, Janice Capel. 2004. "Reading Tabitha: A Feminist Reception History." In *A Feminist Companion to the Acts of the Apostles*, edited by Amy-Jill Levine, 22–48: New York: T&T Clark.

Bhabha, Homi. 1994. "Of Mimicry and Man: The Ambivalence of Colonial Discourse." In *The Location of Culture*. London: Routledge.

Bonz, Marianne P. 2000. *The Past as Legacy: Luke-Acts and Ancient Epic*. Minneapolis: Fortress Press.

Bovon, François. 2003. "Canonical and Apocryphal Acts of Apostles." *JECS* 11: 165-94.

Bowersock, Glen. 1995. *Martyrdom and Rome*. Cambridge: Cambridge University Press.

Boyarin, Daniel. 1999. *Dying for God: Martyrdom and the Making of Christianity and Judaism*. Stanford: Stanford University Press.

———. 1994. *A Radical Jew: Paul and the Politics of Identity*. Berkeley: University of California Press.

Buell, Denise Kimber. 2005. *Why This New Race? Ethnic Reasoning in Early Christianity*. New York: Columbia University Press.

Campbell, William Sanger. 2007. *The "We" Passages in the Acts of the Apostles: The Narrator as Narrative Character*. Atlanta: Society of Biblical Literature.

Castelli, Elizabeth A. 2004. *Martyrdom and Memory: Early Christian Culture Making*. New York: Columbia University Press, 2004.

Clark, David. 2011. "Linguistic and Cultural Influences on Interpretation in Translations of the Bible." In *The Oxford Handbook of the Reception History of the Bible*, edited by Michael Lieb and Emma Mason, 200–213. Oxford: Oxford University Press.

Cosgrove, Charles. 1984. "The Divine DEI in Luke-Acts." *Novum Testamentum* 26: 168-90.

Frend, W. H. C. 1965. *Martyrdom and Persecution in the Early Church: A Study of a Conflict from the Maccabees to Donatus*. Oxford: Basil Blackwell.

Gadamer, Hans-Georg. 1960. *Wahrheit und Methode*. Tübingen: J. C. B. Mohr.

Gilbert, Gary. 2002. "The List of Nations in Acts 2: Roman Propaganda and the Lukan Response." *JBL* 121:497–529.

González, Justo L. 2001. *Acts: The Gospel of the Spirit*. Maryknoll, NY: Orbis.

Haenchen, Ernst. 1971. *The Acts of the Apostles*. Translated by Bernard Noble et al. Philadelphia: Westminster.

Jervell, Jacob. 1972. *Luke and the People of God*. Minneapolis: Fortress Press.

Kanyoro, Musimbi. 2004: "Thinking Mission in Africa." In *A Feminist Companion to the Acts of the Apostles*, edited by Amy-Jill Levine, 61–70. New York: T&T Clark.

Liew, Tat-siong Benny. 2004. "Acts." In *Global Bible Commentary*, edited by Daniel Patte, 419–28. Nashville: Abingdon.

Longenecker, Bruce, ed. 1997. *The Road from Damascus*. Grand Rapids: Eerdmans.

MacDonald, Dennis. 2003. *Does the New Testament Imitate Homer? Four Cases from the Acts of the Apostles*. New Haven: Yale University Press.

Moxnes, Halvor. 1991. "Patron-Client Relations and the New Community in Luke-Acts." In *The Social World of Luke-Acts: Models for Interpretation*, edited by Jerome H. Neyrey, 241–68. Peabody, MA: Hendrickson.

Nasrallah, Laura S. 2008: "The Acts of the Apostles, Greek Cities, and Hadrian's Panhellenion." *JBL* 127:533–65.

Parsons, Mikael C. 2008. *Acts*. Paideia. Grand Rapids: Baker Academic.

Pierce, Ronald W., Rebecca Merrill Groothuis, and Gordon D. Fee, eds. 2004. *Discovering Biblical Equality: Complementarity without Hierarchy*. Downers Grove, IL: InterVarsity Press.

Pervo, Richard. 2006: *Dating Acts: Between the Evangelists and the Apologists*. Santa Rosa, CA: Polebridge.

Price, Robert. 1997. *The Widow Traditions in Luke-Acts: A Feminist-Critical Scrutiny*. SBLDS 155. Atlanta: Scholars Press.

Robbins, Vernon. 1975. "The We-Passages in Acts and Ancient Sea Voyages." *BR* 20:5–18.

Sanders, Jack T. 1987. *The Jews in Luke-Acts*. London: SCM.

Schaberg, Jane. 1998. "Luke." In *Women's Bible Commentary*, edited by Carol A. Newsom, Sharon H. Ringe, and Jacqueline E. Lapsley, 363–80. Louisville: Westminster John Knox.

Scott, James. 1990. *Domination and the Arts of Resistance: Hidden Transcripts*. New Haven: Yale University Press.

Seccombe, David. 1982. *Possessions and the Poor in Luke-Acts*. Linz: A. Fuchs.

Segal, Alan. 1990. *Paul the Convert: The Apostolate and Apostasy of Saul the Pharisee*. New Haven: Yale University Press.

Seim, Turid Karlsen. 1994. *The Double Message: Patterns of Gender in Luke-Acts*. Edinburgh: T&T Clark.

Soards, Marion L. 1994. *The Speeches in Acts: Their Content, Context, and Concerns*. Louisville: Westminster John Knox.

Staley, Jeffrey L. 1999. "Changing Woman: Postcolonial Reflections on Acts 16:6-40." *JSNT* 73:113–35.

Sterling, Gregory. 1992. *Historiography and Self-Definition: Josephus, Luke-Acts and Apologetic Historiography*. NovTSup 64. Leiden: Brill.

Torjesen, Karen Jo. 1993. *When Women Were Priests: Women's Leadership in the Early Church and the Scandal of Their Subordination in the Rise of Christianity*. San Francisco: HarperSanFrancisco.

Tyson, Joseph. 2006. *Marcion and Luke-Acts: A Defining Struggle*. Columbia: University of South Carolina Press.

Wilson, Nancy. 1995. *Our Tribe: Queer Folks, God, Jesus, and the Bible*. San Francisco: HarperSanFrancisco.

Wordelman, Amy L. 2003. "Cultural Divides and Dual Realities: A Greco-Roman Context for Acts 14." In *Contextualizing Acts: Lukan Narrative and Greco-Roman Discourse*, edited by Todd Penner and Caroline Vander Stichele, 205–32. Atlanta: Scholars Press.

SITUATING THE APOSTLE PAUL IN HIS DAY AND ENGAGING HIS LEGACY IN OUR OWN

Neil Elliott

After Jesus of Nazareth, the apostle Paul is the most significant figure in the New Testament. The letters he wrote, other letters attributed to him, and the portion of the Acts of the Apostles dedicated to him together account for about a third of its pages. In Christian churches that read the Bible according to lectionary cycles, Paul's is the single voice more often heard than any other, as his epistles are read in all three years of a cycle. Throughout Christian history, Paul has been revered as one of the chief witnesses of the risen Christ (1 Cor. 15:3-8) and as his "apostle to the nations" (Rom. 1:1-5, 13; 11:13; 15:16-18; Gal. 2:8). (The Greek word *apostolos* means one "sent," as on a mission; the translation "nations" will be discussed below.)

It is customary in modern scholarship (and in this commentary) to distinguish the letters whose authenticity has only rarely been questioned from other letters that appear under his name but are regarded by many scholars as pseudepigrapha—"falsely attributed" writings by others, after Paul's death, who traded on his name to win acceptance for their ideas. The genuine (or "unquestioned") letters are Romans, 1 and 2 Corinthians, Galatians, Philippians, 1 Thessalonians, and Philemon. (This is their order of appearance in our New Testament, based originally on decreasing length; one reconstruction of their probable chronological order is indicated in the timeline below.) The disputed letters include Colossians, Ephesians, 2 Thessalonians, and the Pastoral Epistles (see the discussions in the introductions to those letters). The genuine letters are premiere sources for understanding the beginnings of Christianity, but they are nonetheless puzzling and paradoxical sources, for reasons to be discussed below. The New Testament collection, however, makes no distinction between "genuine" and pseudepigraphic letters, presenting all alike as "Pauline Epistles" and as Scripture. As a consequence, not only are letters widely regarded as pseudepigrapha routinely read, especially in churches, as if they were from Paul himself, but also ambiguous passages in the unquestioned letters are frequently understood as if Paul "must have" meant the same thing that the disputed letters say.

A Basic Chronology of Paul's Life and Career (after Taylor, 35–40)

33	Crucifixion of Jesus
34	Paul's "conversion" (or better, call)
35–38	Missionary activity in Arabia (including escape from Damascus and from the ethnarch Aretas IV)
38	First visit to Jerusalem
38–48	Missionary activity in Syria and Cilicia
48	Second visit to Jerusalem (the "Apostolic Council")
48–52	Missionary activity in Asia Minor (Galatia), northern Greece (Philippi, Thessalonica, and Beroea), and Achaia (including Corinth)
50–56	Writing of 1 Thessalonians
51–52	Hearing before Gallio
52–55	Missionary activity centered in Ephesus; writing of Galatians, 1 Corinthians, portions of 2 Corinthians, Philemon, perhaps Philippians
55–57	Final missionary activity in Greece (Macedonia and Achaia); writing of other portions of 2 Corinthians and, from Corinth, Romans
57–59	Journey to Jerusalem with offering; arrest and imprisonment
59–60	Journey to Rome as prisoner
60–62	Imprisonment in Rome; perhaps writing of Philippians and Philemon
c. 62	Execution under Nero

Although Paul has been revered down the centuries, he was also opposed from the beginning, and today he is held by many men and women in suspicion, within the churches as much as outside them. Paul has been reviled—and not only in the modern age!—as a religious huckster who betrayed the teaching of Jesus, concocted a mythology of heavenly redemption through his death, and, in his enthusiasm for that religion, imposed on his converts a harsh doctrine of subordination to gender and social hierarchies (famously, Kazantzakis, 473–77). His detractors have regarded him as a spiritual charlatan at worst, a deeply flawed personality at best, and have regarded his letters as a toxic residue still leaching into contemporary culture with harmful consequences. Even in churches where his figure elicits deep devotion, Paul also evokes wariness, even antipathy, among men and women who have suffered real injuries under the invocation of his name.

To the historian of Christian origins, and of the relationship between early Christianity and Judaism in particular, Paul's letters are indispensable. But because the information they provide is partial and far less than the historian would like in producing a convincing picture, we are compelled to fill in the blanks with educated but nonetheless imaginative reconstructions. Not surprisingly, historians draw different conclusions, due to the different weights they give to various aspects of the evidence and to their assumptions about the scope and significance of their subject—assumptions shaped as much by their own social locations as by the scientific aura of historiography.

Paul's letters also present considerable challenges to readers seeking spiritual inspiration or theological clarity. They may be surprised how uninterested Paul actually appears to have been in elaborating metaphors or themes that have subsequently proven important for Christian doctrine. The obvious explanation is that Paul wrote his letters for others, far removed from us in historical circumstance and cultural presuppositions, and simply did not explain what he presumed his readers would understand. But because Paul himself repeatedly declares that Scripture (by which he meant Israel's Scripture) was "written for our sake" and that it provides examples "for us" (1 Cor. 9:8; 10:1-11), and a later Pauline letter declares that "all scripture is inspired by God and is useful for teaching, for reproof, for correction, and for training in righteousness" (2 Tim. 3:16), the rehearsal of such phrases has encouraged many modern readers to expect that his words (which, after all, are "Scripture" for many in our day) should be completely transparent and self-explanatory to the spiritually discerning. These readers will often be disappointed. Christian clergy—who are often familiar with the critical issues involved—would do well not only to mention these issues in their preaching and teaching but also to cultivate an awareness in their communities that reading Paul's letters is a complicated affair.

Beyond the confines of Christian churches as well as within them, statements from Paul's letters have come to be woven into the fabric of social roles and expectations in contemporary life—in the public sphere and domestic spaces alike. Modern readers may well find ourselves chafing against those statements. Much of the contemporary interest in Paul—in scholarly circles as well as beyond them—is driven by concerns to address the sometimes ambivalent, sometimes acutely painful legacy of his remarks, most often by seeking to set them into one or another historical context in Paul's life or the life of one or another assembly. None of these efforts have yet won universal acceptance, however, for reasons that cannot be attributed solely to the agendas—or the obstinacy—of the apostle's various interpreters. Paul's letters themselves present a confounding array of puzzles and problems. Even if a particular reconstruction of the past should prove convincing, its significance for the present would remain a conundrum, for Paul's letters are accorded very different levels of authority in different churches, let alone in a putatively secular society.

This essay will not attempt to resolve these interpretive questions or to set out a definitive portrait of Paul. To the contrary, one of its themes will be the remarkable variety of alternative interpretations on offer today. The task will instead be to identify some of the most important questions raised in the encounter with Paul and to discuss the sorts of decisions readers must make in the attempt to answer them. We will proceed in an order corresponding to the sequence in commentary entries in this volume. First, we will explore aspects of Paul's letters and of his apostolic work in their ancient context. Next, we will consider some of the varied ways Paul has been remembered, and appropriated, through history. And last, we will turn to questions of Paul's legacy and the interpreter's responsibility today.

Historical Puzzles in the Letters

Paul's letters are important to the historian for several reasons. They offer the only direct access to a first-person voice in the New Testament. (Jesus left behind no writings; the Gospel narrators are anonymous; and the epistles that appear under the names of Peter, James, and John are considered by many scholars to be pseudonymous: see the introductions to those writings.) They are also the earliest writings from the nascent movement of believers in Christ (with the possible exception of the hypothetical document Q: see the introduction to the Gospels).

But it is the powerful story that lies implicit behind Paul's letters that attracts and intrigues the historian, no less than the Christian believer. It is the story of a Pharisee, "zealous" for the law and ardent in his opposition to the earliest followers of Jesus, who was caught up short when "God revealed his son" to him and "called" Paul to be Christ's apostle (Gal. 1:13-17). That language evokes Israel's prophets, who were "called" and "sent" to deliver God's word; and if Jeremiah could speak of the word of the Lord like a fire "burning" irrepressibly in his bones (Jer. 20:8-9), Paul could declare that he had been "crucified with Christ; and it is no longer I who live, but it is Christ who lives in me" (Gal. 2:19-20). The intensity of the experience to which Paul repeatedly alludes has long attracted the attention of theorists of religion, whether or not they are sympathetic to Christian belief (Ashton; Meeks and Fitzgerald). Further, Paul's sharp juxtaposition of his "earlier life in Judaism" (Gal. 1:13-14) with his newfound life "in Christ" has long been read as evidence of his "conversion," his abrupt and total reversal from life under Torah to life in a new reality, though that understanding has been challenged and largely undermined, at least in scholarly circles, in the last half of the twentieth century (Stendahl; but see Kim).

Whatever its nature (a question to which we return below), the intensity of Paul's experience is echoed in the intensity of concern he expresses for "all the churches" (2 Cor. 11:28), the assemblies that he founded in various cities in Asia Minor, Macedonia, and Achaia. (The Greek word *ekklēsia* is usually translated "church" in English Bibles, and the Latin loanword *ecclesia* gives us the adjective "ecclesiastical" for all things churchly, but *ekklēsia* was also used in Paul's day for a civic assembly in a Greek city, and so a growing minority of interpreters prefer the translation "assembly.") The letters provide us tantalizing glimpses onto landscapes of community life in very different congregations, landscapes that defy easy description or even harmonization with each other. Because Paul addresses a bewildering assortment of issues in his correspondence with the Corinthian believers, our 1 and 2 Corinthians, which probably represent a compilation of earlier, more fragmentary letters (see the entries for each letter), are irresistible to the historian, and have often been used as the primary evidence for generalizations about "Pauline Christianity" (see Meeks; Theissen). But what situation should we imagine prompted these letters: a rift between Paul and the (more law-observant) Jerusalem apostles and their adherents (Barrett)? The impulses of an incipient Gnosticism among the

Corinthians (Schmithals)? Differences in economic status, reflected in theological conflicts (Theissen)? Tension between Paul's social experience and that of inspired women in the congregations (Wire)? Each of these answers (and there are more!) grasps at real clues in the letters, but none has won universal recognition for its capacity to explain the whole. And the issues Paul encountered in Corinth are quite different from those he addressed in letters to other cities.

And how should we understand Paul himself? To take a single question as an example, Paul tells the Romans that the horizon of his concern for the assemblies is not just the calling to secure "the obedience of faith among all the nations" (Rom. 1:5, my translation): that obligation is based in a deeper anguish for his "own people," that is, "Israelites" (Rom. 9:1-5). It is the clashing juxtaposition of what generations of readers have taken as Paul's "conversion," or from another perspective, his apparent *apostasy* from Judaism, with such expressions of abiding *loyalty* to the people Israel that generates some of the liveliest controversies in biblical scholarship today. Should we understand Paul as having left central aspects of his former life in Judaism behind, or, as a matter of principle, should we interpret his work and thought *within* Judaism? (See Nanos and Zetterholm.)

Stories We Tell about Paul

In the mid-twentieth century, Rudolf Bultmann wrote what stands as a crisp summary of Paul's place in early Christianity:

> Standing within the frame of Hellenistic Christianity, he raised the theological motifs that were at work in the proclamation of the Hellenistic church to the clarity of theological thinking; he called to attention the problems latent in the Hellenistic proclamation and brought them to a decision; and thus—so far as our sources permit an opinion on the matter—became the founder of Christian theology. (Bultmann, 187)

This summary makes clear that Paul did not develop his views from nothing, as some sort of theological genius: he joined a movement already in the lively process of developing beliefs and practices, and he received its most important traditions (see 1 Cor. 11:2, 23-26; 15:3-7). Scholars differ, however, among themselves and with Bultmann, regarding the key phrase in this summary. What *were* "the problems latent in the Hellenistic proclamation"? Bultmann recognized that Paul did not invent a movement that welcomed non-Jews without requiring Torah observance of them; that is, he already stood "within the frame of Hellenistic Christianity." But as Bultmann understood it, that frame appeared more a strategy of opportunity than a theological principle, and talk of freedom from the law could easily be construed by one or another Hellenistic church as mere libertinism. For Bultmann (as for many Protestant interpreters before and after him), Paul's grappling with the Hellenistic church required him to resolve tensions between the characteristically Jewish understanding of the human before God—which *had* been Paul's own understanding—and the understanding to which Paul had been brought "in Christ," especially regarding the role of the law in the human's obedience to God's claim. Even "within the frame of Hellenistic Christianity," then, the apostle was preoccupied in letter after letter by an implicit debate *with Judaism*. The eventual prevalence of a law-free "gentile" church is not a historical accident or an aberration, but the triumph of Paul's own ideas. Thus, although he did not write the Letter to the Ephesians, its calm assurance of the Torah's irrelevance to those who are "in Christ" could be regarded, on this view, as "the quintessence of Paulinism" (Peake).

Here a note on the translation of a Greek term *ethnē* is important. The word, a plural, literally means "peoples" or "nations," and is used throughout Jewish Scripture to mean the nations *other than Israel*. In many English New Testament translations, however, it is rendered "Gentiles." The capitalized form is potentially misleading since it suggests a coherent ethnic identity, like "Scythian" or "Egyptian," though no individuals in the ancient world called themselves "Gentiles." Furthermore, the same word is sometimes translated two different ways in the same Bible. For example, the NRSV uses "nations" in Isaiah, but "Gentiles" in Romans 15:9-12, *even where Paul is quoting the same passages from Isaiah*. The effect is subtle, but meaningful: it suggests that Paul imagines two sorts of people in the world, "Jews" and "everyone else," and is preoccupied with the boundary line that distinguishes them.

Just this understanding of Paul has been hotly contested in the late twentieth and early twenty-first centuries, however. We may broadly distinguish three "stories" that interpreters now tell about the apostle.

Paul as Convert from Judaism

The first story prevailed in Bultmann's day, as it still does today in much of Christianity. Paul received a preeminent education as a Jew. (Acts names him "Saul" in this period and makes him a student of the famed Rabbi Gamaliel II: 5:34; 22:3.) Indeed, his self-professed credentials, "as to the law, a Pharisee; as to zeal, a persecutor of the church; as to righteousness under the law, blameless" (Phil. 3:5-6), "zealous for the traditions of my ancestors" (Gal. 1:14), are an accurate self-appraisal as an exemplary Jew. It is as a representative Jew that he sought "a righteousness of [his] own that comes from the law" (Phil. 3:9), for all Israel characteristically strove for "the righteousness that is based on the law . . . as if it were based on works" (Rom. 9:31-32). On this view, Paul (Saul) the Pharisee persecuted the early believers in Jesus because they had, in some way he found intolerable, flouted or ignored the law. The reversal occasioned by the "revelation" of Christ to him was nothing less than a conversion, a personal about-face from one who now abandoned any effort at achieving his own righteousness through works of law and accepted instead the righteousness "on the basis of faith," meaning trust in Jesus (Rom. 9:32).

From this point on, Paul was opposed by other Jews because he adamantly insisted the law had no positive role in salvation: it provided only the knowledge of sin (Rom. 7:7). His resolve to approach those outside the law "as one outside the law" (1 Cor. 9:19-21) and his judgment that "nothing is unclean in itself" (Rom. 14:14) show his rejection of the Torah's binding authority. Even the Jerusalem apostles (and their delegates) fought Paul on these points, refusing to accept shared meals between Jews and "Gentiles" at Antioch (Gal. 2:11-14; for the view that the law forbade even social "associations" between Jews and gentiles, see Acts 10:28). Paul saw this failure as hypocrisy on the part of the apostles (Gal. 2:14), and could only regard with anguish his fellow Jews' stubborn insistence on that righteousness "as if based on works." Though Paul (in Gal. 2:1-9) and

Acts (15:1-29) agree that the Jerusalem apostles accepted his mission to the "uncircumcision," they apparently acquiesced when Paul was accused by other Jews of flouting the law himself and teaching other Jews to do the same (see Acts 21:17-36). Jewish antagonists further accused Paul (falsely, according to Luke) of bringing gentiles into the temple court, a capital offense—but James and the other apostles play no further role in the narrative. Paul's subsequent pleas before kings and Roman magistrates are eloquent arguments that he represents the true legacy of Israel's Scriptures, but by the end of the story he has convinced only a minority of Jews who hear him. The "parting of the ways" between Judaism and Christianity is already evident in the response to Paul. The anguish he expressed for his "kindred according to the flesh" (Rom. 9:1-4) was his response to their final failure to obey his gospel.

This is the account most familiar to readers today, and it still predominates in Christian preaching. Since the last quarter of the twentieth century it has been challenged, however, because of several landmark developments. One is the discovery in the 1940s and 1950s of the Dead Sea Scrolls, which bore abundant witness to a form of Judaism that could not be identified with the "works-righteousness" Paul presumably opposed, and that often sounded "Pauline," as in its insistence that "by [God's] righteousness alone is a human righteous" (e.g., 1QH 5.18; 8.12). Because the scrolls also included multiple copies of some Jewish texts that had previously been known, but marginalized in biblical interpretation (e.g., *Jubilees*, *1 Enoch*), they sparked renewed interest in such "pseudepigraphic" writings and a growing awareness that Second Temple Judaism was a far richer and more complex array of religious expressions than the traditional account had allowed.

Second, in the wake of the mass murder of European Jews (the Shoah or "Holocaust"), many European and US churches turned to processes of institutional soul-searching, seeking to identify and repudiate aspects of Christian teaching that traded in stereotype and caricature of Jews and Judaism (see, notably, the Roman Catholic document *Nostra Aetate*). In this changed environment, older Jewish objections to Paul's rhetoric suddenly gained new attention from Christian and other interpreters.

Third, these developments provided the space in which new and innovative scholarly monographs appeared that reconfigured the relationship of Paul, Judaism, and the origins of Christianity (Ruether; Stendahl; Sanders). E. P. Sanders's demonstration that the traditional understanding of "works-righteousness" was *not* current in Paul's day issued in a changed climate, sometimes called the "post-Sanders era," in which a "new perspective on Paul" began to take shape (Dunn 1983; 1998).

Paul as the Champion of a Law-Free Church

The "new perspective" (now more than thirty years old) actually includes a variety of different interpretations, united by their acceptance of the agenda posed by Sanders. We may nevertheless sketch the outlines of a coherent second narrative in this array of new-perspective readings. Here, Paul is *not* assumed to have been a representative Jew, but (taking him at his word) is seen to have persecuted the early churches out of an extreme hyperobservance, having been *"far more* zealous for the traditions of my ancestors" than his peers (Gal. 1:13-14, emphasis added). Paul did not suffer the sort of introspective anguish regarding his own salvation that would later preoccupy Martin

Luther and subsequent Western interpreters; rather than being "converted" to a new understanding of redemption, Paul experienced a "call" similar to the call of Israel's prophets (Stendahl). This calling was specifically to bring a *biblical*, that is, *Jewish* message of salvation to the nations (or "gentiles"). The proper focus of interpretation, on this view, is thus not "soteriology" (the salvation of individuals) but the sociological behavior of groups. The "works of law" against which Paul repeatedly inveighed (Gal. 2:16; 3:2, 5, 10; Rom. 3:27-28; 4:2, 4-6; 9:32; 11:6) are now relieved of the burden of summarizing a Jewish theology of redemption; they should instead be identified with specific "boundary-maintaining" practices that distinguished Jews from their non-Jewish neighbors, especially circumcision, kosher diet, and Sabbath observance. Rather than opposing a Jewish understanding of "redemption" or "justification from works," Paul was defending the "gentile church" from Jewish opponents who sought to incorporate Paul's converts into Jewish life according to more traditional channels—the acceptance of circumcision and observance of Torah. The difference between Paul and other Jews, then, involved a question of the scope of salvation, rather than its mechanism. Was the covenant people limited to Israel (and "converts" or proselytes to Judaism), or did it, on Paul's innovation, include non-Jews as full members?

Challenges have been raised to this second narrative as well. Except for a few voices who have concluded that Paul's own thought was "inconsistent" or "incoherent" (Sanders; Räisänen), many new-perspective interpreters still put Paul forward as the pioneer of an intelligible and appropriately inclusive faith—the indispensable ancestor of contemporary Christianity. But this also means that Paul is not infrequently contrasted with negative characterizations of Jewish "ethnocentrism" or exclusivism. His identity as a Jew is affirmed, and his conflicts with other Jews are regarded as "inner-Jewish" controversies, but the often unavoidable implication is that Paul and his associates *alone* represented the open, inclusive, "right" legacy of Judaism, in contrast to the narrow and ill-fated insistence of the rest of his Jewish contemporaries on ethnic boundaries of the covenant people. The "parting of the ways" between Christianity and Judaism still appears here to be foreshadowed in Paul's controversies with other Jews.

Paul as a (Non-Christian) Jew

A third narrative has emerged from a small group of interpreters—many of them Jewish scholars of the New Testament—who seek thoroughly to interpret Paul's work and thought within Judaism, without appeal to a dramatic interruption (Paul's vision of Christ) that somehow set him on a course that necessarily led him away from it. On this account, Paul the Pharisee persecuted the early *ekklēsiai* not because of any deviation on their part from Jewish observance, but because their (thoroughly Jewish) proclamation of a messiah who had been crucified by Rome was potentially threatening to the precarious stability of other Jewish communities under Roman rule (Fredriksen, 133–76). As Alan F. Segal shows, Paul's vision of the crucified Jesus in heaven (as obliquely reported in 2 Corinthians 12) was formally similar to other Jewish visionary experiences. While Segal himself did not pursue the implications, we can extrapolate what such a vision might have meant for Paul, on purely Jewish terms, by examining the consequences for earthly life that other Jewish apocalypses drew from comparable visions of heaven. The confirmation of God's sovereignty in heaven generally informed how the apocalyptists understood the possibilities for living under oppressive Hellenistic or Roman rule (Portier-Young). Similarly, the vision of the crucified Jesus as heavenly Christ likely would have had immediate political implications for Paul (Elliott 1994, 140–80). This vision involved no halakhic "conversion": Paul remained a Jew (and never became a "Christian": Eisenbaum). These interpreters (in his essay in this volume, Lawrence M. Wills calls their view a "radical new perspective") point out that there is no evidence anywhere in his letters that Paul himself relinquished observance of Torah or taught other Jews to do so. (Paul's comment about acting "as one outside the law" in 1 Cor. 9:19-21 does not mean apostasy, on this view, but only a tactical choice to socialize with non-Jews.)

Paul's vision did involve Paul's perception of non-Jewish adherents to the proclamation of Jesus as the fulfillment of biblical prophecy. They were the "nations" who would turn to Israel and Israel's Messiah at the last day. (Note here that the term *ethnē* is given its more natural meaning "nations": Paul's concern is not with the un-Jewish ethnic identity of individuals but with relations between the world's nations and Israel, and with the biblical vision of international harmony to be achieved in the messianic age.) That is, Paul's resistance to the pressure to "normalize" these converts by making them Jews had nothing to do with any perceived insufficiency in Judaism or the law. It had everything to do with his expectation that *morally* converted non-Jews—rare enough, in Diaspora Jewish eyes—*united around obedience to Israel's Messiah, and in solidarity with Israel*—would be as clear a signal to other Jews as they were to him that the messianic age had dawned. His organization of a collection for "the poor among the holy ones" in Jerusalem (Rom. 15:25-28), which he perceived both as a gesture of reciprocity and as a sacred "offering" that he presented as a priestly service (Rom. 15:14-16, 27), was motivated by this expectation.

On this interpretation, already foreshadowed in some ways by Johannes Munck, Paul's disagreements with the Jerusalem apostles (e.g., in Antioch: Galatians 2) are not deep theological fissures but tactical or rhetorical differences (see Nanos 1996; 2002). His differences from Jews outside the assemblies arose, on one side, from his belief that the messianic age has arrived, and on the other, from the concern of Jews who did not share that belief to protect their communities from scrutiny or suspicion—the sort of unwanted attention that messianic agitation on the part of Paul's non-Jewish newcomers might prompt. As to the question of justification from works of law, interpreters in this third perspective hew methodologically to the principle that any of Paul's statements regarding the law *made in letters addressed primarily to non-Jews* should be read narrowly as statements about the significance of the law *for non-Jews*, rather than generalized statements about the Torah's role in salvation. The nature of *Jewish* opposition to Paul is less the focus of attention here than in the preceding two perspectives; on the other hand, the possible motivations of *non-Jews* in Paul's assemblies to adopt *some* Torah observances—but not all (see Gal. 5:2-3)—is a paramount consideration. Here, interpreters explore possible reasons for anxiety on the part of non-Jews who may have seen in the Torah the promise of achieving the goal of "self-mastery" (*enkrateia*) so highly prized in post-Augustan culture (Stowers 1994), or (in Galatia) might have sought to "pass" in Roman society, taking on some of the mystique of the synagogue in order to make their refusal of customary Roman worship ("idolatry") more palatable to their Roman neighbors (Gaston; Nanos

2002, 257–71; Kahl 2010). Paul's resistance to "Judaizing" is seen here as his thoroughly Jewish reaction to aberrant behavior on the part of non-Jews.

Similarly, the Letter to the Romans has been read as an admonitory warning to non-Jews not to show disdain or contempt for Jews. That warning is evident enough in Rom. 11:13-32, but in earlier interpretation, that passage was often seen as an isolated aside. When chapters 9–11 are read as the "climax" of the letter and the whole letter is read as rhetoric directed to a primarily non-Jewish audience, the brief address to a hypothetical Jew in Romans 2–3 is no longer seen as an attempt to "explode Jewish privilege"; rather it supports the overarching purpose of the letter to correct non-Jewish error. Here, too, Paul appears to offer a fundamentally Jewish response to aspects of the emerging Hellenistic church (Elliott 1990; 2008).

Paul against Roman Imperial Ideology

If, in service of the last-named narrative, interpreters have tried in different ways to understand Paul within Judaism, that effort seems also to have involved understanding Judaism not just as a *religion* or an *ethnic identification* (it was, of course, both in Paul's day), but also as participation in an identity construed in different ways by outsiders. The experience of Jews *under Roman rule*—as a minority population seeking civic recognition in different Roman cities and under different imperial regimes—becomes a central concern of such interpretation of Paul (Smallwood). A new field of study has sprung up since the late 1980s around the relationship between "Paul and empire." That scholarship initially sought to challenge the apolitical character of previous "theological" interpretation and to wrest Paul from what had become a fairly tight grip on his legacy on the political right, where Paul was routinely presented as an advocate of political quietism and social conservatism (points to which we return below). "Paul and empire" scholarship and the adjacent field of postcolonial study of Paul have now become themselves the object of scrutiny and debate, which is all to the good (see Horsley 1997; 2000; 2004; Stanley; McKnight and Modica 2013). It bears note, however, that these areas are not only concerned with the ways Paul is interpreted and appropriated for political purposes today. They also inform, and necessarily so, the investigation of Paul as a member of the Jewish Diaspora in the Roman world (Nanos and Zetterholm).

The Paradox of Reading Paul's Letters Today

Many, perhaps most, readers of Paul's letters come to them with religious interest. Paul's letters have long offered Christianity a rich resource for devotion and for theological reflection. As mentioned above, the letters are the most frequently encountered vein of Scripture in many churches. At least some of the more lyrical passages in them, such as Paul's assurance that nothing "will be able to separate us from the love of God in Christ Jesus our Lord" (Rom. 8:28-39) or his praise of love as the "better way" (1 Cor. 12:31—13:13), are among the most cherished passages of Scripture for many people. Metaphors that appear in Paul's arguments have exercised powerful and decisive influence in Christian theology: that of baptism as a "dying with Christ," for example (Rom. 6:3-11), or of the church as the "body" of Christ (Rom. 12:3-7; 1 Cor. 12:4-30), or the Lord's Supper as a proclamation of the death of Jesus (1 Cor. 11:17-34). Paul's use of an apparently preexisting Christian hymn in Philippians has shaped Christian understanding of the divinity of Christ as one who, though "in the form of God," "emptied himself" to accept "the form of a slave" and humbled himself even further, in obedience to God, to the point of "death on a cross" (Phil. 2:6-8).

This familiarity makes for a remarkable paradox: When we read these letters today, we do so with purposes Paul never imagined, and may grant them an importance they never enjoyed in Paul's own day. They are our primary source for understanding Paul; but that was not true for Paul's first readers, for whom he was not a "biblical author" to be "interpreted." The possibility of reading the letters anachronistically inevitably increases when they are incorporated into modern worship as "Scripture."

The Paradox of "Theological" or "Pastoral" Readings

It should strike us as curious that readers today approach even Paul's genuine letters to discover his "theology." After all, we do not have a sample of the message Paul initially proclaimed to gather a community (although many interpreters have tried to read Romans as such). Rather, all of the letters were written to assemblies some time *after* Paul—or, in the case of Romans, others—had founded them. In his letters, Paul sought to strengthen or, occasionally, as he saw it, to correct their adherence to Christ. As a consequence, the letters have a theological character, but they never spell out his convictions in any systematic way. Paul often leaves a key conviction unspoken, since he could presume his audience already had heard, or heard about, his proclamation. The letters are therefore problematic sources, at best, from which the premises and contours of "Paul's theology" might be constructed as an exercise of historical imagination.

The passage from Philippians cited above, for example, shows that Paul's understanding of the death of Jesus already depended on traditions he received from early assemblies that preceded him. He explicitly acknowledged as much when he wrote to the Corinthians, "I handed on to you as of first importance what I in turn had received: that Christ died for our sins in accordance with the scriptures" (1 Cor. 15:3). Note that Paul does not explain here which Scriptures he has in mind, or just what dying "for our sins" meant. In fact, Paul could describe the salvific value of Christ's death in different ways: as a "sacrifice of atonement" (*hilastērion*, Rom. 3:24-25), though Paul never elaborates a comparison with the ritual of the Day of Atonement (as does Hebrews); or as the slaughter (NRSV: "sacrifice") of a Passover lamb (1 Cor. 5:7)—a very different ritual!—or as deliverance from the "curse" of Deut. 21:23, though, again, this reference seems to have played no larger part in his thinking (Gal. 3:13). Surprisingly, amid these diverse and conflicting metaphors, Paul never offers even a rudimentary explanation of just *how* he understands Christ to have "died for our sins." He is more concerned, in Romans, to insist that those who have "died *with* Christ" in baptism (another dramatic metaphor that is simply asserted, not explained) can no longer live in sin, having been joined to Christ's obedience (Romans 5–6).

His purpose in these letters (and in the apostolic work of which they are occasional instruments) has been described as "pastoral." This might also strike us as curious, since Paul was not evidently interested in the sort of long-term spiritual accompaniment of individuals and families in settled congregations that we associate today with pastoral ministry. (Indeed, he seems intentionally to have left such work to others whom he described as his "coworkers," *synergoi*.) The "daily pressure" about which Paul complained to the Corinthians, caused by his "anxiety for all the assemblies" ("churches": 2 Cor. 11:28 NRSV), was less oriented to the self-fulfillment of individuals than to the sanctity in which they were to maintain themselves. ("Saints"—literally, "holy ones" [*hagioi*]—was Paul's preferred designation for members of his assemblies.) Looking at the non-Jewish world through the eyes of a Hellenistic Jew, Paul regarded the hallmarks of such holiness in the avoidance of the vices characteristic of that world—the worship of other gods, using tangible forms ("idolatry"), and a range of sexual transgressions to which he simply referred as "immorality" (*porneia*: see Gaca; Ruden)—and the maintenance of an ethos of affectionate mutual regard characteristic of the idealized Roman household. Paul sought to establish a sort of baseline of such holiness and then, on an ad hoc basis, to perform whatever corrections were needed to maintain it. We might consider Paul "pastoral," then, to the extent that he was an "advisor" who "counseled" his congregations "in order to be able to present them to Christ at his coming, which Paul expected in the near future" (Dahl, 73, citing Rom. 15:16; 1 Cor. 1:8; 2 Cor. 11:2; Phil. 1:10-11; 1 Thess. 3:13; 5:23).

He described his work to the Romans in terms of priestly service (*latreuein*, Rom. 1:9; *diakonos*, *leitourgos*, *hierourgōn*, 15:8, 16, terms associated with public ritual action). He sought to present to God "the obedience of the nations" (Rom. 15:17; see 1:5-6), represented in each city by the holy living of individuals on whom he called to present their bodies as "a living sacrifice, holy and acceptable to God" (Rom. 12:1-2), and on an international scale by the sanctified "offerings [*prosphora*] of the nations" (Rom. 15:16-17). The latter phrase rang with the language of the prophet Isaiah's vision in which the earth's nations streamed to Jerusalem, bearing tribute and joining in the worship of Israel's God (see Isaiah 60, and Paul's quotations in Rom. 15:8-13); but also with echoes of an imperial vision in which conquered peoples offered their gifts to Caesar (e.g., Virgil, *Aeneid* 8.720–23). More prosaically, it referred to the collection of money Paul had gathered from various assemblies in Achaia and Macedonia as "aid for the poor among the saints" in Jerusalem (Rom. 15:25-26). Paul hoped those funds would be received as more than relief, as evidence of a fulfillment of messianic prophecy.

It appears, then, that what might be called the "pastoral" aspect of Paul's work had a much nearer eschatological horizon than many church leaders acknowledge today as they plan decades-long ministerial careers. Even Paul's expression of concern for "all the assemblies" in 2 Corinthians comes at the end of a recital of dangers Paul had faced *in travels abroad* (11:23-27). His letters responded to situations that arose after Paul had *departed* from one city or another, usually after a relatively brief stay—just sufficient to inaugurate an assembly. (Paul's longest stays in a single place, according to the book of Acts, were eighteen months in Corinth and a little more than two years in Ephesus—hardly what many contemporary denominations would consider lengthy "pastorates.") Neither did Paul apply himself to what we might call "church growth." To judge from one admittedly conflictual but nonetheless telling situation, he gave thanks that during his initial stay in Corinth he had baptized only Crispus and Gaius, and the household of Stephanas (1 Cor. 1:14-16); the increase of the Corinthian congregation under the baptismal ministry of Apollos, and the lively competition of perspectives that increase generated, precipitated a crisis for him (1 Cor. 2:1—3:15). Paul seems to have regarded innovation with suspicion: his interventions were intended to preserve the assemblies in an initial, pristine state of "holiness" as they awaited the imminent return of Christ. This aspect of Paul's work shows him ever on the move, eager to establish fledgling congregations and then to move on. He looks back, through his letters or the efforts of his colleagues, to maintain the sanctity of a congregation over what he clearly believes will be the short term.

The culmination of Paul's story, however, was a series of disappointments bordering on the tragic. We cannot say whether his views immediately prevailed in controversies in Corinth or in Rome. We do know, however, that the anxiety he expressed concerning his last journey to Jerusalem, bearing the collection, was more than warranted. The story told in Acts 21 describes controversy in Jerusalem over Paul's allegiance to the Torah and the accusation—which Luke considers false—that Paul had brought some, at least, of his non-Jewish delegates into the precincts of the temple that were reserved for Jews alone (21:28-29). The riot that ensued set Paul on a narrative road that ends in Rome, whither he was sent on charges of civil unrest that he was compelled to appeal before the emperor (Acts 22–28).

The deep symbolic significance Paul attached to the collection, his reason for being in Jerusalem, goes unmentioned in Acts; so also, then, is any hint at the effect of its failure on him. Also missing is any account of Paul's subsequent hearing before Nero, or any reference to Paul's execution, on the emperor's authority, events reported in other sources (*Acts of Paul* 10.6; Eusebius, *Hist. eccl.* 2.25.5). Instead of these catastrophes, Luke offers the reader the triumph of Paul speaking the word of proclamation boldly before assembled philosophers in Athens (17:16-34); before the Roman procurators Felix and Festus and the Judean king Agrippa (chapters 24–26); and—for the first time in the narrative—before an unbiased synagogue audience, in Rome itself (28:17-22). These accomplishments fulfill Jesus' prophecy that his followers would take his word "before kings and governors" (Luke 21:12), and incorporate Paul's last days in Rome within Luke's theme of the inexorable spread of the word "to the ends of the earth" (Acts 1:8). But these triumphant notes come at the cost of what Luke must suppress. The reader will not learn from Acts how much hung, for Paul, on the journey to Jerusalem. Nor does Luke convey the purpose behind Paul's fervent attempts to conform the non-Jews in his assemblies to a life of holiness: namely, in order to impress upon his fellow Jews that they were living in the last days (see Romans 11).

It appears enough for Luke that Paul helped to inaugurate the church of Jews and non-Jews (though he is careful to stipulate that the important first steps were taken by Peter in Joppa, Acts 10). Just so, in the generation after Paul's death, another writer represented the core of Paul's gospel as the "mystery" that God intended Jews and non-Jews to worship together in the name of Christ (Eph. 3:1-6). But while Paul had hoped the "obedience of faith among the nations" would manifest the fulfillment of scriptural promises to Israel, the author of Ephesians understood the Pauline "mystery" to involve the dispensability of Torah itself, its having been "abolished" by Christ (*katargēsas*, Eph. 2:13-16)—an idea that was unthinkable for Paul himself (see Rom. 3:31).

The attention given to reading and interpreting Paul's letters today, especially in churches, may then be described as paradoxical. The paradox lies not just in the fact that these letters were manifestly written to others, centuries ago. It is also a matter of the letters being directed to achieve specific ends that made sense within an eschatological scenario that has not just been "delayed," but has manifestly failed. When Paul is read today simply as the champion of a law-free, "gentile"

Christianity, he is being read through the lens of Ephesians and Acts. But this is to impose onto Paul's letters the "perfect hindsight" that our place "downstream" from him allows us. The temptation for those of us who find our place in the current of gentile Christianity is to imagine that our religion is what Paul sought to found.

The Paradox of Paul's Authority

Some passages in the letters suggest that Paul may have not been the clearest of communicators. In places, Paul seeks to "correct" or manage what he considers his audience's mistaken apprehension of his own earlier teaching (see 1 Cor. 2:1-6; 5:9-13; 1 Thess. 4:13-18), or hints at obligations that were perhaps not explicit earlier (e.g., the master's "duty" in Philem. 8). He admonishes the Corinthians for grievously misunderstanding the nature of the Lord's Supper, though he had passed along to them traditions he obviously considered important (1 Cor. 11:17-34). He is "astonished" at how quickly the Galatians have deserted his teaching (Gal. 1:6-9), though he refers obliquely to having taught something else earlier (did he once "preach circumcision," 5:11? Is he now "building up" what he once "tore down," 2:18?). In none of these passages does Paul admit that he has changed his mind, or that he might not have spoken clearly in the first place—even when his advice appears to remain contradictory (compare his advice on food offered to idols in 1 Corinthians 8 and 10:14-22). Further, his readers may well have been confused when he took a different tack than what they may have heard from the tradition of Jesus' words—regarding questions of marriage and divorce, for example (1 Corinthians 7), or his refusal of the support to which apostles are entitled (1 Corinthians 9). They might have been as vexed by his sometimes cavalier attitude to the authority of other apostles (Gal. 2:11-14; 2 Cor. 11:1-6), or his fierce denunciations of "other" gospels (Gal. 1:6-9; 2 Cor. 11:4). If Paul had such difficulty communicating with his first hearers, perhaps the contemporary reader may be forgiven for not finding the meaning of his letters transparent!

Precisely because Paul's letters have been read, preached, cherished, annotated, and exposited over centuries of Christian practice, they present their contemporary readers with another paradox that we might call a "lexical illusion." Put simply, we *read* Paul, and more, we read Paul as a part of the Bible. We thus may think of him as an influential and articulate *writer*, picking up his pen to express sublime thoughts. This would have surprised many of Paul's contemporaries, however, for whom Paul was not, first of all, a writer. (Some adversaries in Corinth contemptuously declared that his letters were the weightiest aspect of his work, and even these were unimpressive: see 2 Cor. 10:9-10.) Nor would many of those who knew him best have regarded him primarily as a "thinker," and certainly not one whose authority was unquestioned. Indeed, one of the most vivid impressions one gets from these letters is that of an ardent and often scrappy polemicist. Paul appears frequently to argue for a viewpoint or a practice that he expects to be controversial, at least, and likely contested by at least a few of his hearers. The Corinthian correspondence shows that Paul faced considerable opposition from some of the more influential members of that assembly who found his arguments unconvincing. Paul's prominence in our New Testament hardly justifies the assumption that his voice normally prevailed in his own day.

It is a commonplace that as readers of Paul's letters, we are "listening in" on only one half of a conversation, but even this is putting the matter too simply. We are listening to an intensely opinionated correspondent! The reverence Paul is accorded in the Christian tradition for his role as paramount guide into the practices of new life "in Christ" is, in large part, the mirror image of the significance Paul claims for himself as he addresses "his" congregations. They may have many guides in Christ, but "not . . . many fathers," he tells the Corinthians in a characteristic claim (1 Cor. 4:15); he is an example to be imitated (Phil. 3:17). His letters often give a contemporary reader the sense of riding an emotional roller coaster. In the rhetoric of 1 and 2 Corinthians, for example, Paul alternates between assuring a community that the Spirit of Christ dwells among them, guiding them and guaranteeing their holiness, and shaming them for not living up to even the rudimentary standards of the pagan world (1 Cor. 5:1-8). To contemporary readers more accustomed to modern ideals of mutual respect and equality among persons, Paul's rhetoric may come across as authoritarian, perhaps even coercive or abusive.

It is the enduring gift of feminist scholarship to have clarified that in his letters (and, we may presume, in his initial face-to-face efforts as well), Paul might *claim*, but could never *presume*, his authority. Indeed, in correspondences such as the Corinthian letters, he appears to be scrambling to find the rhetorical ground from which to assert a right to a hearing. We must take into account, then, not only the existence of another "half" of a conversation but also the possibility that Paul's construal of one or another situation was a minority opinion and may even, on occasion, have been unintelligible to his readers. The point may seem subtle, but it is an important principle to which feminist interpretation calls much-needed attention. A view of biblical authority that *presumes* Paul's voice would have prevailed, simply because it was his, is anachronistic. It takes Paul's letters "out of the public domain where argument is in order and where Paul's strong arguments could have social impact." Careful attention to the way Paul argued shows that he never presumed his voice was sufficient to settle an issue. Rather, he hoped to gain the assent of his hearers to his arguments "*because they are convincing*" (Wire, 10, emphasis added). Today as well, when various and competing appeals are made to this or that passage in Paul's letters, the same principle suggests that mere resort to biblical authority is insufficient and inappropriate: thoughtful and ethical discernment remains our shared responsibility, within the churches no less than in the public square.

Seeing Paul through a Glass, Darkly

I have been dwelling on the challenges and complications of understanding Paul quite deliberately. Any hope that we will arrive at a single understanding of the apostle that will convince everyone must be tempered by recognizing the divergent responses Paul received in his own day and the significant variety of portrayals of Paul that have been cherished over the centuries—beginning with writings found in our New Testament.

The Pauls in the New Testament

We do not have all of Paul's letters to the assemblies: we do not have what he says he earlier wrote to the Corinthians, for example (1 Cor. 5:9). The reference in Col. 4:16 to a letter to the Laodiceans, not otherwise attested, prompted a Christian in the third or fourth century to produce one by patching together phrases from the available letters of Paul. We have Paul's letters, we may presume, because after they were first given the hearing for which Paul wrote them, some persons in the assemblies thought them worth preserving, exchanging with others (see Col. 4:16 again), and collecting. We should also presume that Paul wrote for the purposes that are evident in the letters themselves; the *subsequent* work of preserving, exchanging, and collecting was done for different purposes. The letter form became a popular device by which others disseminated the apostle's thought, *after* his own letters had won whatever (probably mixed) reception they were given. The *Epistle to the Laodiceans*, a third letter to the Corinthians, and correspondence with the philosopher Seneca are examples of letters written by other Christians, living long after the apostle's death, to achieve results for which Paul should hardly be held responsible (for texts discussed here, see Elliott and Reasoner; for further discussion, Pervo). The technical term for such "falsely signed" writing is *pseudepigraphy*.

Today, many interpreters are convinced that pseudepigrapha appear in our New Testament as well as outside it. The "Pastoral" Epistles (1 and 2 Timothy and Titus) are different enough in vocabulary, writing style, and mood, and seem to address so different a situation from the other letters, that they are the most widely considered to be pseudepigrapha. Ephesians is also widely questioned, and after it, Colossians and 2 Thessalonians (but see the entries on these letters). It is a principle of scholarship that judgments about Paul's own thought should be based first on the genuine (that is, the unquestioned) letters, Romans, 1 and 2 Corinthians, Galatians, Philippians, 1 Thessalonians, and Philemon, and that the other, possibly pseudepigraphic letters should be used only when they corroborate what has been found in the genuine letters. From the scholarly viewpoint, the appearance of some pseudepigrapha in our New Testament should not cloud this principle. After all, various writings that are now universally recognized as pseudepigraphic, like the *Acts of Paul* (in which *Laodiceans* and *3 Corinthians* appear), not only were once popular but also were frequently copied and regarded by some Christians as part of the New Testament. Hebrews was often copied after Romans in collections of Paul's letters, on the assumption (now almost universally rejected) that Paul wrote it; the *Epistle to Barnabas*, a pseudepigraphon bearing the name of Paul's erstwhile companion, was also included in some copies of the New Testament. Furthermore, while the shape of our New Testament gives the impression of continuity, leading some interpreters to describe the "canonical" pseudepigrapha (Colossians, Ephesians, and the Pastorals) as appropriate "adaptations" of Paul's legacy by faithful "Pauline churches" or a "Pauline school," there is no *external* basis for establishing only some pseudepigrapha as the creations of such "faithful" disciples of Paul, and rejecting others as deviations or betrayals (Elliott 1994, 25–54). The scholarly principle holds that each writing should be evaluated in terms of its own similarity to or difference from the genuine letters.

But letters were not the only way Paul's legacy was fashioned and refashioned in early Christianity. At one point in his controversy with some members of the Corinthian assembly, Paul wrote, "I have become all things to all people, that I might by all means save some" (2 Cor. 9:22). His immediate purpose was apparently to defend his refusal of financial patronage from wealthy members of the church; but today his words have floated free of their original context to become something of an emblem for what his sympathizers might consider his strategic skill, and what less charitable interpreters might consider an unscrupulous ambition. Even in the first few centuries of

Christianity, Paul seems, chameleon-like, to have taken on a wide variety of guises, depending on who held him in their gaze.

The Acts of the Apostles was only the first of several narratives that gave Paul, or one version of Paul, pride of place. Written decades after Paul's death, Acts purports to continue the authoritative account begun in the Gospel of Luke of "the things that were fulfilled among us" (Luke 1:1). The narrator is never identified. In some dramatic passages, the narrator suddenly shifts to the first-person plural ("we"), giving rise to the belief that the account is eyewitness testimony of a companion of Paul: traditionally, Luke, the "beloved physician" of Col. 4:14. But the abrupt use of the first-person was a stylistic device in Hellenistic historiography and novels, meant to convey the immediacy of past action. The narrator strikes a number of notes in describing Paul that are not found, or are in some tension, with Paul's own letters. In Acts, Paul is first named "Saul" (many Jews bore both Hebrew and Greek names), and identified as a native of Tarsus (9:11) and a student of Rabbi Gamaliel (22:3), who is revered in the Mishnah as well. Acts reports that Paul's actions as a persecutor of the followers of Jesus were authorized by the high priest (9:1-2). And Acts narrates—three times, twice in recitals by Paul himself!—the dramatic reversal in his course on the road to Damascus, where he is blinded by a bright light and hears the commissioning voice of the risen Jesus (chaps. 9, 22, 26). Here, Paul is also a Roman citizen, a piece of information that arises at a crucial plot point to deliver Paul from an angry mob in the temple and set him on the protracted course that ends in Rome (22:25-29).

All of these pieces of information appear only in Acts, and serve to present Paul dramatically as a faithful and observant Jew. Here he is also an indefatigable missionary, proclaiming Christ in cities in Syria, Cilicia, Galatia, Asia Minor, Achaia, and Macedonia, and at last, in chains, in Rome. In the adventurous style common to Hellenistic novels, his travels are recounted as accompanied by miraculous healings and deliverance from shipwrecks, imprisonments at the hands of corrupt magistrates, and attacks from jealous Jewish rivals, all of which give Paul occasions to make his case in eloquent speeches in synagogues, theaters, and the court of the temple, and before philosophers, governors, and kings (in explicit fulfillment of Jesus' words in Luke 21:12).

What is left unsaid in Acts is just as interesting. As mentioned above, although Acts narrates Paul's final visit to Jerusalem, we learn nothing of his collection or how it was received. Instead, hostile "Jews from Asia" stir up mob action by making a false accusation, that Paul has brought non-Jews into the temple itself (21:27-29). And Acts ends on a triumphant note: Paul has at last reached Rome and has opportunities freely to address the city's Jewish leaders without interference from his antagonists (28:21-22; perhaps mirroring Luke's own narrative purpose). Though living under Roman guard there for two years, he welcomes inquirers and preaches and teaches "without hindrance" (28:30-31). We know from other sources, and Luke's readers must have known, that Paul was martyred under Nero, probably in 64 CE, but that event has no place in the story Luke wants to tell.

Competing Memories

The multiplicity of portraits of Paul—which is to say, the multiplicity of "Pauls" effective in particular historical situations—did not end with the diversity in the New Testament; it was only sparked by that diversity. For example, the author of 1 Timothy assumed Paul's identity (though writing, most scholars agree, decades after his death) to exhort the subordination of women and to extol marriage (2:12-15; 4:1-4)—in some tension with Paul's own commendation of women colleagues (and superiors: Rom. 16:1-7), and his exhortation to the Corinthians that he wished all people could remain unmarried as he was (1 Cor. 7:1-7)! Whether Paul himself encouraged the silencing of women is a matter of still-unresolved controversy around the status of 1 Cor. 14:33-34 (are these lines genuine, or a later interpolation into the text?). Regarding marriage, 1 Timothy and 1 Corinthians seem to offer contradictory advice, but set together in the New Testament as equally letters of Paul, they provide a sort of ranked hierarchy: the ideal is celibacy; second-best, but still good, is a single, monogamous marriage. Other variations—suffering divorce and even remarrying, provided it is within the assembly—are acceptable, but clearly represent failures to achieve the ideal. The "biblical" Paul is effectively conformed to the moral expectations of the Roman household (see the entry on the Pastoral Epistles).

But a different memory of Paul persisted: perhaps a hundred years later, the anonymous author of the *Acts of Paul* described the apostle as teaching a "gospel of virginity" and leading the Iconian noblewoman Thecla, as she then led other women, to break off engagements and even leave husbands. Tertullian repudiated the *Acts of Paul* because it so clearly endorsed the ordained leadership of women, but could not declare the document a forgery (it does not claim to be written by Paul); instead, he attacked the impudence of its author. His attack shows us, however, that in the third century a priest was able to compile such a portrait and do so "out of love for Paul" (*Bapt.* 17). Nor did the *Acts* represent one man's idiosyncratic perspective: it appeared in manuscripts of the New Testament as late as the sixth century and was a widely popular text long afterward, to judge from the proliferation and variety of manuscripts of the writing.

Other such contrasts could easily be multiplied. (1) In the early second century, Marcion championed Paul as "*The* Apostle," who had rightly taught Christians to reject Jewish law and Jewish Scripture. Marcion was condemned as a heretic, but his claim regarding Paul is only a little more extreme than that of Ephesians, where we see formulated another early synthesis of Paul's gospel, now as the unification of Jews and gentiles into one people through the "abolishing" of the law through Christ's death (2:13-16). Decades later, the anonymous author of an early Christian novel apparently shared this basic understanding of Paul as an opponent of the law, but bitterly opposed it, casting a Paul-like figure as the wicked mortal enemy of the properly law-abiding apostles Peter and James in terms that evoke Paul's confrontation with Peter in Galatians 2 (*Ps.-Clem. Rec.* 1.70–71). According to Irenaeus, the Ebionites, too, repudiated the apostle, "maintaining that he was an apostate from the law" (*Adv. haer.* 1.26.2). Another writing, the *Ascents of James*, alleges that Paul was an impostor, a Greek who came to Jerusalem and accepted circumcision only to woo the high priest's daughter; when his prospective father-in-law spurned him, "he became angry and wrote against circumcision and against the Sabbath and the law" (Epiphanius, *Panarion* 16.6–9). Heated arguments about Paul's view of the law are not a recent innovation!

(2) The pseudepigraphic letters between Paul and Seneca depict warm mutual respect between the apostle and the emperor Nero's closest advisor, who even brings Paul's letters to the emperor's attention; they commiserate over the unfairness of Nero's blaming the Christians for the great fire

in 64. Paul counsels a policy of quiet life, rather in keeping with Rom. 13:1-7 and 1 Tim. 2:2. In the *Martyrdom of Paul*, however (which was incorporated in some versions of the *Acts of Paul*, but also traveled separately), the apostle speaks defiantly to the emperor, warning that his lord comes "to wage war upon the world with fire." After being put to death, Paul returns in a resurrected state to warn Nero that he faces eternal judgment; in terror, the emperor releases Paul's companions. The defiant tone stands in contrast to the perception among many contemporary readers of Rom. 13:1-7 as a quietist, even abject endorsement of governing authority as established by God. It is noteworthy, then, that the earliest reports of Christian martyrdoms—apparently composed and circulated to present an "ideal" protocol for extreme circumstances—portray Christians citing or quoting the apostle, indicating that "we have been taught to render honor . . . to princes and authorities appointed by God" (*Martyrdom of Polycarp*); "we give honor to our emperor" (*Acts of the Scillitan Martyrs*), even as they offer resolute defiance. (The site of Paul's own martyrdom and his tomb "outside the walls" were sites of Christian worship from very early on.) Romans 13:1-7 appears to have been read, at least by some Christians, as a script for respectful refusal to obey authority (Schottroff).

(3) Paul's oblique reference to a heavenly vision (2 Corinthians 12), his description of seeing Christ raised in a "spiritual" rather than a "physical" body (1 Cor. 15:50), and his insistence that "flesh and blood cannot inherit the kingdom of God" (1 Cor. 15:50) stand in contrast with the depiction in Acts of Paul's remarkable but clearly terrestrial audition of the heavenly Christ (Acts 9; 22; 26), and in even more pointed contrast with the terrestrial and quite tangible appearances of the risen Jesus to his disciples in Luke 24:36-43 or John 20:26-29 or 21:1-14. We know that some Christians took the language of Paul's own letters further because their opponents appropriated Paul's memory or voice to denounce them. In the *Acts of Paul*, men who declared "that there is no resurrection of the flesh, but that of the spirit only, and the human body is not the creation of God" come to Corinth and trouble Paul's church; the narrator includes a transcript of Paul's response as *3 Corinthians*, universally regarded today as a pseudepigraphon, in which Paul affirms not only the bodily life, death, and resurrection of Jesus but also his miraculous birth from Mary (something Paul never mentions in the unquestioned letters).

(4) As a final example, Paul's own comments on slavery are maddeningly brief and enigmatic. The two-word slogan in 1 Cor. 7:21 is characteristic: "if you can gain your freedom, *mallon chrēsai*"— alternatively translated, "take advantage of the opportunity!" and "make use of your present condition instead!" His letter to the owner of Onesimus is rhetorically powerful but cryptic (see the introduction to Philemon). Later writings sought to clear up the mystery by attributing to Paul a clear endorsement of the master-slave relationship, though tempered with Christian kindness (Eph. 6:5-9; Col. 3:18—4:1), and 1 Timothy went further, insisting that slaves in the churches should not "be disrespectful on the ground that they are members of the church: rather they must serve all the better since those who benefit by their service are believers and beloved" (6:1-2). (The author is also concerned to limit support for widows to only the impeccably worthy: 5:3-16.) The risk that slaves might consider their status changed once they stood alongside their masters in the assembly may have arisen from Paul's own language in Gal. 3:28: "there is no slave nor free . . . in Christ Jesus." Some early Christian communities did in fact practice the manumission of slave members (Hermas, *Mand.* 8.10; *Sim.* 12.8; *1 Clem.* 55.2). But Ignatius, bishop of Smyrna, who presented himself as an

ardent follower of Paul, specifically rejected the practice: "Do not be haughty to slaves, either men or women; yet do not let them be puffed up, but let them rather endure slavery to the glory of God, that they may obtain a better freedom from God. Let them not desire to be set free at the church's expense, that they not be found slaves of desire" (*To Polycarp* 4). Centuries later, John Chrysostom complained from the pulpit that Christian efforts to redeem slaves constituted "violence" against masters, "the subversion of everything." He cited "Paul"—that is, 1 Tim. 6:1—to denounce the practice as inciting "blasphemy" against Christianity (*Homily on Philemon*).

These examples suffice to show that throughout the early centuries of Christianity, Paul was remembered in different ways (Pervo). While a few of these memories have ended up in our New Testaments today, it is just as remarkable that the variety *persisted* so long: there simply was no single, "authoritative" version of Paul from whom all the alternatives could be imagined simply as divergences. Just as remarkable as the fact of diversity is the determination with which Christians have, in so many diverse ways, clung to a perceived continuity with Paul as an important warrant for their own actions. For every bishop like Chrysostom, whose homilies were gathered reverently and published in handsome volumes, we have indirect evidence for other, anonymous Christians (whom we would not know except for Chrysostom's protest!) who practiced the manumission of slaves, quite possibly in Paul's name and quite possibly aware that they were practicing an "alternative" Christianity opposed by their bishop!

Paul the Problem: Apostle of the Status Quo?

Our efforts to understand Paul's thought and work in his historical context and to wrestle with his legacy today are of importance far beyond the bounds of church life. Paul merits thoughtful attention wherever Christianity has played a role in shaping contemporary cultures. My goal here is not to resolve the numerous questions that continue to occupy Paul's interpreters—or even to name them all!—but to describe the most important patterns into which the answers continue to fall.

Many of the apostle's critics—and even a few of his champions, who appear to consider this a virtue—would agree that Paul was largely unconcerned with the social inequities and injustices of his age. To many contemporary ears, the New Testament letters that now appear under his name include some of the most offensively retrograde passages in Scripture. These letters are among the most cited parts of the Bible (and remain influential even when they are not cited!) when a variety of questions regarding civil rights, gender equality, economic justice, and other areas of public life are discussed today.

The Pauline Letters have played a dismal role in many of the most grievous episodes of modern history. For example, the nineteenth-century movement to abolish slavery in the United States faced steep challenges, not least because the Bible nowhere condemns slavery. To the contrary, letters appearing under Paul's name explicitly exhorted slaves to obey their Christian masters (Eph. 6:5-8; Col. 3:22-25; Titus 2:9-10), and not to assume that being members of the church together (literally, "brothers") constituted genuine equality with their masters (1 Tim. 6:1-2). At a time when questions about the authenticity of these letters were rare, the presumption that the apostle Paul condoned slaveholding was inevitably powerful, and for that reason, specific letters proved inestimably useful to slave owners in the US South who recruited preachers to indoctrinate their slaves regarding their spiritual "duties." But this woeful situation cannot be explained simply as resulting from a naive acceptance of letters that many scholars today consider pseudonymous. Even a century after the passage of the Thirteenth Amendment to the US Constitution, the civil rights movement faced fierce opposition among twentieth-century American Christians who read Paul as enjoining quiet submission even to fiercely segregationist government (see Rom. 13:1-7), and exhorting believers to "remain in the state in which [they were] called" (1 Cor. 7: 17-24 RSV). Martin Luther King Jr.'s "Letter from a Birmingham Jail," in which he challenged white clergy not to be "more devoted to 'order' than to justice" and lambasted appeals for Negro "patience," had as one of its targets just this legacy of Paul.

For another example, the women's suffrage movement in the United States faced tremendous obstacles in the clear and ostensibly Pauline admonitions that women should keep silence in the assembly and submit to their husbands (1 Cor. 14:34-35; Eph. 5:22-24; Col. 3:18; 1 Tim. 2:11-15). Almost a century after US women won the right to vote, these passages continue to exercise a baleful influence in the cultural "backlash" against women's ongoing struggle for equality. Advocates for women and their children who suffer violence at the hands of the men in their homes candidly point out that these passages are now woven into a culture of rape, silence, and terror (Faludi), yet Christian clergy are often reluctant to denounce these texts from their pulpits. Like the passages exhorting subordination of slaves, verses encouraging women's subordination continue to hold powerful sway through the presumption, alive and well in some corners of American society, that striving for equality between genders or among races somehow springs from an inordinate self-indulgence. Both these sets of passages are hard to square with Paul's own declaration that in Christ "there is neither slave nor free, neither male nor female" (Gal. 3:28). But this only intensifies the question: *If* Paul wrote all these passages, was he unaware of the tensions between them? Or (as some more conservative Christians today would have it) did Paul wisely see, from the first, that freedom and equality could properly be exercised only within straitened limits?

Paul presents other problems as well, to which I have already pointed. His retrospective comments about his "former life in Judaism" (Phil. 3:4-7; Gal. 1:11—2:10) have often been read as flat dismissals of an obsolete and ineffective religion ("loss," "rubbish"). Alongside Gospel narratives assigning blame for Jesus' death to the "crowds" or "people" of Jerusalem, these passages have provided impetus not just for Christian supersessionism but also for centuries of violence against Jews that came to a terrible climax under Nazism. Yet as the historical record shows, even some Christian pastors in Nazi Germany who recognized that their government was perpetrating grave evils were often reluctant actively to resist it, not only out of fear but also from an exaggerated concern to obey the apostle's admonition to "be subject to the governing authorities" (Rom. 13:1).

Those same words from Romans served to quell Christian resistance to apartheid in South Africa and to the national security regimes of Central America in the 1980s (Brown). They have been cited to deflect pacifism and conscientious objection to combat in every US war to date, and, with Paul's exhortations (as they are usually translated) to "remain in the life the Lord has assigned," the "condition in which you were called" (see 1 Cor. 7:17-24), have proven a powerful inhibition of Christian involvement in every progressive movement down to the present.

But Paul's legacy has not always been read in so monochromatic a way. S. Scott Bartchy has shown that the now-standard reading of those exhortations in 1 Cor. 7:21-24, in which the Christian's "calling" (*klēsis*) is understood as a calling *to a particular social location*, a "state" or "condition," is lexically and exegetically impossible: the Greek simply does not say what the English represents. In subsequent work, he has traced the decisive (mis)translation to the period of the Peasants' Revolt in Germany and Martin Luther's response to it—hardly a situation conducive of objective, dispassionate exegesis! But the translation persists, and exercises decisive control over the assumptions that modern readers bring to Paul. Indeed, we perceive a much narrower range of possible meaning in Paul's letters than our predecessors may have done. For example, some clergy were ranged with the poor in the fourteenth-century Peasants' Rebellion in England, including a bishop who publicly read Paul's declaration that "there are divisions of work, but all of them, in all men, are the work of the one Lord" (1 Cor. 12:6) as showing clearly that God did not intend disparities of wealth in creation (Thomas Brinton, *Sermon* 44). For another example, the words in 2 Thess. 3:10—"if any will not work, neither let them eat!"—have been quoted by right-wing pastors and politicians in order to vilify families seeking state-provided food or medical assistance, with such regularity that the verse has become a banner of what one journalist calls "poverty denialism" in government (Goldberg). But a century ago, Vladimir Lenin quoted the same verse as exemplifying "the prime, basic, and root principle of socialism: 'He who does not work, neither shall he eat.'" It was obvious to Lenin, just as it was to a number of anonymous Russians who made the slogan into banners plastered around Petrograd, that those who "would not work" were the bourgeois profiteers, who exercised monopoly control over grain markets and used their power to suffocate labor. "Every toiler understands that," said Lenin, and "in this simple, elementary and perfectly obvious truth lies the basis of socialism" (Lenin, 391-98).

Particular challenges to a received understanding of Paul's "social conservatism" have been posed especially from Latin American interpreters working in the context of the theology of liberation. One of the earliest in a line of philosophical interpreters of Paul, José Miranda read Romans in terms of the contemporary tension between justice and "law and civilization" (Miranda, 109–200; more recently, Jennings; Frick). Elsa Tamez has argued that "in societies where poverty and marginalization abound," evangelistic misreadings of the Protestant understanding of justification by faith "can be inappropriate and even violent" (Tamez, 23). Paul's thought, she continues, was in fact "markedly utopian: Paul longed for a society of equals where solidarity would reign" (49). Néstor O. Míguez has read 1 Thessalonians in terms of the strategies needed to keep hope vital in a situation of imperial oppression. Indeed, Luise Schottroff argued years ago that the pivotal theme of liberation theology, the preferential option for the poor, was simply an elaboration of Paul's conception of the *ekklēsia* (Schottroff, 249). One of the most important efforts on the part of a North American to synthesize a liberative theology of the New Testament relies on the Pauline language of "powers and principalities" to describe the need to name, engage, and unmask systems of domination in our own day (Wink 1984; 1992; 1993), and others have sought to describe a more emancipatory understanding of Paul's thought (Elliott 1994; Lopez; Zerbe 2012).

The Promise of a Critical Historical Imagination

Such widely divergent interpretations, or appropriations, of a text can leave many a reader perplexed: "but what did Paul really *mean*?" Were the busybodies rebuked in 2 Thessalonians the indolent recipients of some imaginary Roman antecedent of the modern welfare state, or were they people of means who could pursue lives of leisure, presuming that their social inferiors would attend to their needs? (The latter attitude is in fact well documented among the Roman aristocracy.) Was the Letter to Philemon most like the genre of the *amicus* ("friend") letter, which we know from a number of Roman examples, in which a social peer would appeal to an angry slaveholder to extend leniency to a slave who had disobeyed or run away, then had a change of heart? Or was it simply a request to "borrow" a slave's services for a time; or a carefully leveraged appeal to a master to fulfill an otherwise unspecified "duty" by granting a slave his freedom?

On these and many other points of interpretation, the *promise* of historical criticism is to describe a range of possible meanings that may be drawn, through inference, from the available data and, on occasion, to identify some as more or less probable (or even to rule some out as impossible). The *temptation* posed by historical criticism, however, is to exaggerate that promise: to imagine that once the right methods and instruments have been deployed, a single "right" interpretation, *what the text really meant*, can be determined. As the diversity of current interpretations of Paul shows, things rarely work out that way.

One reason is simply the limits of our evidence (and thus of the inferences we can draw from it). Another is that "we" contemporary readers do not agree on what should be done with whatever results might be achieved, because "we" actually encompass a variety of different subjectivities and purposes. Some of us presume the authority of Paul's voice because it is scriptural; we want to use historical-critical method to fix the single, authoritative meaning of his words. Others of us want to qualify or mitigate the consequences of one or another pronouncement in Paul's letters and use historical-critical method to circumscribe Paul as a man of his own age, *rather than* a transcendent voice of revelation, binding on all generations.

And many of us are frankly inconsistent about just when or how historical considerations should matter. For example, Paul is often cited most vociferously today by individuals who insist that *some* of his words, at least, enjoy timeless and universal authority. In the still-roiling debates over equal protection under law and marriage equality for same-sex couples, a few select passages (Rom. 1:24-27; 1 Cor. 6:9-10; 1 Tim. 1:8-11) are regularly invoked by some Christians to argue that God considers homosexuality, and even homosexual persons, an "abomination" (though that specific language is drawn from Leviticus, not Paul). My purpose here is not to adjudicate the issue but to point out that such appeals to Paul are necessarily selective: that is, most of these same Christians would presumably *not* argue analogously that the comments on slavery discussed above had an eternal validity, binding on twenty-first-century American society, any more than the other "abominations" mentioned in Leviticus might. Such appeals also necessarily avoid historical investigation. "Homosexuality" is a modern conception; we know, from abundant and intersecting data, that people in the ancient world did not recognize what we call "sexual orientation," and so Paul simply could not have commented on it (Nissinen). This has not stopped the appearance of some recent Bible translations, however, where Paul's Greek is rendered—quite improbably—with inter-pretive paraphrases like "active and passive partners in homosexual relations." Whatever Paul *did* mean to comment on in these passages (and this remains a matter of debate among scholars: see for example Boswell; Scroggs; Martin, 37–64; Countryman; Ruden) is clearly abusive and outrageous. But this means that equating Paul's target with contemporary same-sex couples who seek a church's recognition of their love seems both exegetically dubious and morally gratuitous. Regrettably, with regard to this unfinished debate, it seems that setting the Pauline Letters in their historical context is the last thing some readers wish to do!

Some of us have used the historical-critical identification of Pauline pseudepigrapha to dis-qualify certain letters, or verses in them, as tendentious adaptations of Paul's own voice, which in contrast is more liberative than has usually been perceived (e.g., Elliott 1994; 2008; Lopez; Zerbe 2011; 2012). Others point out that the attempt to isolate the "genuine" voice of Paul only reinforces the problematic and too-prevalent assumption of "the 'masculine' hegemonic voice inscribed in kyriarchal Pauline or other ancient source-texts" (Schüssler Fiorenza 1999, 187), and the problem-atic aura of Paul himself as a "heroic" figure (Johnson-DeBaufre and Nasrallah). It is worth notice that the plea to "decenter" Paul is based, in part, on a historical-critical argument that contextual-izes Paul precisely as one voice among many on a crowded and complex Roman landscape (Wire). Resistance to "kyriarchal" aspects of Paul's legacy involves recognizing the actual character of Paul's own appeals for obedience, submission, and imitation as rhetoric—patterns that were reinscribed in successive generations (Schüssler Fiorenza 1987; Castelli; Kittredge; Marchal).

Historical criticism, then, is neither a panacea that will reliably deliver us from the tyranny of an oppressive text *or* an obsolete means of holding on nostalgically to the same text—though it can be used for either purpose. The important consideration is what the interpreter's purposes are, for these will determine just how one or another method of biblical study will be used. The twin virtues of responsible interpretation are honesty with regard to the data (or lack of it) on a specific question, and accountability with regard to the purposes toward which we invoke it. In this light, the scientific mystique that the historical criticism of Scripture has long enjoyed has the effect of obscuring, or effacing altogether, the actual role of the interpreter. More recent challenges to classical histori-cal criticism, whether they have gone under the names "postmodern," "postcritical," "contextual," "deconstructive," or "minority" or "minoritized" interpretation, have sought to pull back the curtain to reveal the interpreter's identity, standpoint, and intentions.

Such challenges are still mounted as exceptions to the status quo. Attention to the social loca-tion of the interpreter is most pronounced when members of a marginalized group seek to identify the power relations inscribed in the dominant discourse of biblical scholarship. Greg Carey has observed that in the history of biblical studies in the United States, a "commonsense" interpreta-tion that privileged the biblical text as floating above ambiguity coincided with the culture of white privilege. Thus, he observes, it remains the case today that "'minority' criticism is performed almost exclusively by minorities," while the analysis of white interpreters is also performed, "well, almost exclusively by minorities" (Carey, 7).

Nor is race the only modality in which questions of power relations are usually effaced by the scholarly mainstream. For example, in his slender 2005 book on Paul, N. T. Wright discusses the state of Pauline interpretation by identifying the social location of various alternative viewpoints. Narrative criticism precipitated, as naturally as dew, in "the postliberal and canonical air of New Haven"; secular Copenhagen gave rise, unsurprisingly, to readings of Paul "which owe little to traditional Jewish or Christian ideas and much to first-century pagan philosophy"; and political interpretation distilled, almost inevitably, from the context of "below-the-tracks university" life in Blue-State Massachusetts, where deep suspicion of American empire was presumably at home. Similarly, suspicion of the authenticity of Colossians and Ephesians derived from "a particular kind of German existentialist Lutheranism." But if those specific contexts produced the readings that Wright considers eccentric, social location has nothing to do, so far as he admits, with his own theological approach, except insofar as he speaks from "[his] own acquaintance with Paul." Wright attributes the same innocence to "the vast majority of Christians in the world today" who "read Paul with blissful ignorance" of those other, peripheral, situationally contingent "movements and counter-movements" (16–18).

Such comments would not deserve our attention if they were unusual. The point is that representations of interpretive innocence remain prevalent in biblical scholarship, and not surprisingly. Scholarship on the Bible is often sponsored by churches and church-affiliated educational institutions and continues to be shaped in large part by the interests of Christian ministry. Such sites are likely the context in which many readers will encounter this volume, and are assuredly the context in which many of its contributors work. But just here, many of the critical considerations discussed above run up against the prevalent routines of Christian theology. The habits that may be observed in many a Christian pulpit on a Sunday morning emphasize the unique saturation of the biblical texts with unitary and authoritative sacred meaning. Although some preachers may invite admiration for their virtuosic skill in extracting that meaning homiletically, it is just as important for a preacher to insist that the meaning he or she finds in the text is not their invention. The powerful ethos of "commonsense" interpretation requires that the preacher has only *discovered* the meaning that was somehow, supernaturally packed into the biblical text. Admitting that my own life experience helps to determine what I hear or see in the text suggests more than just that you may hear or see something different. The preceding discussion also shows that, historically, relations of unequal privilege and power have also determined the possibilities for which truths prevail as "common sense" in a particular society, at a particular time.

In contrast, the interpretation to which feminist, postcolonial, African American, and an array of other important voices call all of us will require habits of candid self-awareness. Alongside historical questions about the apostle Paul and lexical, exegetical, and rhetorical-critical questions about the range of possible meanings of his words, we will need to ask what is at stake for our engagement with the apostle and his legacy. In what ways do different parties "use Paul to think with"? What are the consequences of different claims, and why do the people raising those claims seek out the aegis of Paul's authority for them? Are there more direct and honest ways to think through interpreting Paul as a matter of public responsibility?

These questions have their true force only when they are joined with questions about the actual power relationships in our society, the nature of our participation in those relationships, and—to adopt the interpretive principle of the theology of liberation—the effect of those relationships on the poor. This mode of interpretation remains peripheral and contested in scholarship, and is practiced more or less sporadically in different faith communities, but it is avowed in the preparation of this volume and the structure of its various entries, including the entries on Paul's letters that follow. By attending to each letter as a text in an ancient historical context, these entries challenge the "commonsense" assumption that we can read the ancient texts with the directness of their contemporaries. By attending to the various ways one or another text has been heard, or contested, through history, and to the contours of contemporary debate as well, these entries are intended to erode the confidence that any part of the Bible simply "means one thing." But the loss of false confidence can be the occasion for new discovery and, when shared with others, new opportunity for mutual understanding.

Works Cited

Ashton, John. 2000. *The Religion of Paul the Apostle.* New Haven: Yale University Press.

Barrett, C. K. 1963. "Cephas and Corinth." In *Abraham unser Vater: Festschrift für Otto Michel.* Leiden: Brill.

Bartchy, S. Scott. 1971. ΜΑΛΛΟΝ ΧΡΗΣΑΙ: *First-Century Slavery and the Interpretation of 1 Corinthians 7:21.* Chico, CA: Scholars Press.

Boswell, John. 1980. *Christianity, Social Tolerance, and Homosexuality.* Chicago: University of Chicago Press.

Boyarin, Daniel. 1994. *A Radical Jew: Paul and the Politics of Identity.* Berkeley: University of California Press.

Brown, Robert McAfee. 1990. *Kairos: Three Prophetic Challenges to the Church.* Grand Rapids: Eerdmans.

Bultmann, Rudolf. 1953. *Theology of the New Testament.* Vol. 1. Translated by Kendrick Grobel. New York: Charles Scribner's Sons.

Carey, Greg. 2013. "Introduction and a Proposal." In *Soundings in Cultural Criticism*, edited by Greg Carey and Francisco Lozada, 1–15. Minneapolis: Fortress Press.

Castelli, Elisabeth A. 1991. *Imitating Paul: A Discourse of Power.* Louisville: Westminster John Knox.

Countryman, L. William. 2007. *Dirt, Greed, and Sex: Sexual Ethics in the New Testament and Their Implications for Today.* Rev. ed. Minneapolis: Fortress Press.

Dahl, Nils. 1977. *Studies in Paul: Theology for the Early Christian Mission.* Minneapolis: Augsburg.

Dunn, James D. G. 1983. "The New Perspective on Paul." *BJRL* 65:95–122.

———. 1998. *The Theology of Paul the Apostle.* Grand Rapids: Eerdmans.

Eisenbaum, Pamela. 2009. *Paul Was Not a Christian: The Original Message of a Misunderstood Apostle.* San Francisco: HarperOne.

Elliott, Neil. 1990. *The Rhetoric of Romans: Argumentative Constraint and Strategy and Paul's Dialogue with Judaism.* JSNTSup 45. Sheffield : JSOT Press.

———. 1994. *Liberating Paul: The Justice of God and the Politics of the Apostle.* Maryknoll, NY: Orbis.

———. 2008. *The Arrogance of Nations: Reading Romans in the Shadow of Empire.* Paul in Critical Contexts. Minneapolis: Fortress Press.

Elliott, Neil, and Mark Reasoner, eds. 2010. *Documents and Images for the Study of Paul.* Minneapolis: Fortress Press.

Faludi, Susan. 1991. *Backlash: The Undeclared War against American Women.* New York: Crown.

Fredriksen, Paula. 1988. *From Jesus to Christ: The Origins of the New Testament Images of Jesus.* New Haven: Yale University Press.

Frick, Peter, ed. 2013. *Paul among the Philosophers: The Apostle in the Grip of Continental Philosophy*. Paul in Critical Contexts. Minneapolis: Fortress Press.

Gaca, Karen L. 2003. *The Making of Fornication: Eros, Ethics, and Political Reform in Greek Philosophy and Early Christianity*. Berkeley: University of California Press.

Gager, John G. 1985. *The Origins of Christian Anti-Semitism*. New York: Oxford University Press.

Gaston, Lloyd. 1987. *Paul and the Torah*. Vancouver: University of British Columbia Press.

Goldberg, Michelle. 2013. "Poverty Denialism: According to Many in the GOP, the Poor Have It Easy." *The Nation* 297:21 (Nov. 25): 6, 8.

Horsley, Richard A., ed. 1997. *Paul and Empire: Religion and Power in Roman Imperial Society*. Harrisburg, PA: Trinity Press International.

———. 2000. *Paul and Politics: Ekklesia, Israel, Imperium, Interpretation*. Harrisburg, PA: Trinity Press International.

———. 2004. *Paul and the Roman Imperial Order*. Harrisburg, PA: Trinity Press International.

Jennings, Ted. 2009. *Transforming Atonement: A Political Theology of the Cross*. Minneapolis: Fortress Press.

Johnson-DeBaufre, Melanie, and Laura S. Nasrallah. 2011. "Beyond the Heroic Paul: Toward a Feminist and Decolonizing Approach to the Letters of Paul." In *The Colonized Apostle: Paul through Postcolonial Eyes*, edited by Christopher D. Stanley, 161–74. Paul in Critical Contexts. Minneapolis: Fortress Press.

Kahl, Brigitte. 2010. *Galatians Re-Imagined: Reading with the Eyes of the Vanquished*. Paul in Critical Contexts. Minneapolis: Fortress Press.

Kazantzakis, Nikos. 1960. *The Last Temptation of Christ*. New York: Simon & Schuster.

Kim, Seyoon. 2004. *The Origins of Paul's Gospel*. 2nd ed. Eugene, OR: Wipf & Stock.

Kittredge, Cynthia Briggs. 1998. *Community and Authority: The Rhetoric of Obedience in the Pauline Tradition*. HTS 45. Harrisburg, PA: Trinity Press International.

Lenin, Vladimir I. 1918. "On the Famine: A Letter to the Workers of Petrograd." *Pravda* 101 (May 24). ET: *Collected Works*, 391–98. 4th ed. Translated by Clemens Dutt. Edited by Robert Daglish. Moscow: Progress Publishers, 1972.

Lopez, Davina C. 2008. *Apostle to the Conquered: Reimagining Paul's Mission*. Paul in Critical Contexts. Minneapolis: Fortress Press.

Marchal, Joseph A. 2008. *The Politics of Heaven: Women, Gender, and Empire in the Study of Paul*. Minneapolis: Fortress Press.

Martin, Dale B. 2006. *Sex and the Single Savior: Gender and Sexuality in Biblical Interpretation*. Louisville: Westminster John Knox.

McKnight, Scott, and Joseph B. Modica, eds. 2013. *Jesus Is Lord, Caesar Is Not: Evaluating Empire in New Testament Studies*. Downers Grove, IL: InterVarsity Press.

Meeks, Wayne A. 1983. *The First Urban Christians: The Social World of the Apostle Paul*. New Haven: Yale University Press.

Meeks, Wayne A., and John T. Fitzgerald. 2007. *The Writings of Paul: Annotated Texts, Reception, and Criticism*. 2nd ed. New York: W. W. Norton.

Míguez, Néstor O. 2012. *The Practice of Hope: Ideology and Intention in 1 Thessalonians*. Paul in Critical Contexts. Minneapolis: Fortress Press.

Miranda, José. 1974. *Marx and the Bible: A Critique of the Philosophy of Oppression*. Translated by John Eagleson. Maryknoll, NY: Orbis.

Munck, Johannes. 1959. *Paul and the Salvation of Mankind*. Translated by Frank Clark. Richmond: John Knox.

Nanos, Mark D. 1996. *The Mystery of Romans: The Jewish Context of Paul's Letter*. Minneapolis: Fortress Press.

——. 2002. *The Irony of Galatians: Paul's Letter in First-Century Context*. Minneapolis: Fortress Press.

Nanos, Mark D., and Magnus Zetterholm, eds. 2014. *Paul within Judaism*. Minneapolis: Fortress Press.

Nissinen, Martti. 1998. *Homoeroticism in the Biblical World: A Historical Perspective*. Minneapolis: Fortress Press.

Peake, Arthur S. 1918. "The Quintessence of Paulinism." *BJRL* 4:285–311.

Pervo, Richard. 2011. *The Making of Paul: Constructions of the Apostle in Early Christianity*. Minneapolis: Fortress Press.

Portier-Young, Anathea E. 2011. *Apocalypse against Empire: Theologies of Resistance in Early Judaism*. Grand Rapids: Eerdmans.

Räisänen, Heikki. 1983. *Paul and the Law*. Philadelphia: Fortress Press.

Ruden, Sarah. 2011. *Paul among the People: The Apostle Reinterpreted and Reimagined in His Own Time*. New York: Image.

Ruether, Rosemary Radford. 1974. *Faith and Fratricide: The Theological Roots of Anti-Semitism*. New York: Crossroad.

Sanders, E. P. *Paul and Palestinian Judaism: A Comparison of Patterns of Religion*. Philadelphia: Fortress Press.

Schmithals, Walter. 1971. *Gnosticism in Corinth: An Investigation of the Letters to the Corinthians*. Translated by John E. Steely. Nashville: Abingdon.

Schottroff, Luise. 1992. "'Give to Caesar What Belongs to Caesar and to God What Belongs to God': A Theological Response of the Early Christian Church to Its Social and Political Environment." In *The Love of Enemy and Nonretaliation in the New Testament*, edited by Willard Swartley, 223–57. Louisville: Westminster John Knox.

Schüssler Fiorenza, Elisabeth. 1987. "Rhetorical Situation and Historical Reconstruction in 1 Corinthians." *NTS* 33:386–403.

——. 1999. *Rhetoric and Ethic: The Politics of Biblical Studies*. Minneapolis: Fortress Press.

Segal, Alan S. 1990. *Paul the Convert: The Apostolate and Apostasy of Saul the Pharisee* (New Haven: Yale University Press.

Smallwood, E. Mary. 1976. *The Jews under Roman Rule from Pompey to Diocletian*. Leiden: Brill.

Stanley, Christopher D., ed. 2011. *The Colonized Apostle: Paul through Postcolonial Eyes*. Paul in Critical Contexts. Minneapolis: Fortress Press.

Stendahl, Krister. 1976. *Paul among Jews and Gentiles*. Philadelphia: Fortress Press.

Stowers, Stanley K. 1994. *A Rereading of Romans: Justice, Jews, and Gentiles*. New Haven: Yale University Press.

Tamez, Elsa. 1991. *The Amnesty of Grace: Justification by Faith from a Latin American Perspective*. Trans. Sharon Ringe. Nashville: Abingdon.

Taylor, Walter F. 2012. *Paul, Apostle to the Nations: An Introduction*. Minneapolis: Fortress Press.

Theissen, Gerd. 1982. *The Social Setting of Pauline Christianity: Essays on Corinth*. Translated by John Schütz. Philadelphia: Fortress Press.

Wink, Walter. 1984. *Naming the Powers: The Language of Power in the New Testament*. Philadelphia: Fortress Press.

——. 1992. *Engaging the Powers: Discernment and Resistance in a World of Domination*. Minneapolis: Fortress Press.

——. 1993. *Unmasking the Powers: The Invisible Forces That Determine Human Existence*. Minneapolis: Fortress Press.

Wire, Antoinette Clark. 1990. *The Corinthian Women Prophets: A Reconstruction through Paul's Rhetoric.* Minneapolis: Fortress Press.

Wright, N. T. 2005. *Paul in Fresh Perspective.* Minneapolis: Fortress Press.

———. 2013. *Paul and the Faithfulness of God.* Christian Origins and the Question of God 4. Minneapolis: Fortress Press.

Zerbe, Gordon. 2011. "The Politics of Paul: His Supposed Social Conservatism and the Impact of Postcolonial Readings." In *The Colonized Apostle: Paul through Postcolonial Eyes*, edited by Christopher D. Stanley, 62–73. Paul in Critical Contexts. Minneapolis: Fortress Press.

———. 2012. *Citizenship: Paul on Peace and Politics.* Winnipeg, MB: CMU Press.

Zetterholm, Magnus. 2009. *Approaches to Paul: A Student's Guide to Recent Scholarship.* Minneapolis: Fortress Press.

ROMANS

Cynthia Briggs Kittredge

Introduction

The Letter to the Romans, the latest and longest of Paul's undisputed letters, was written from Corinth in about 55 CE to the church in Rome, the capital and center of the Roman Empire. Adapting the conventions of letter writing and employing ancient rhetorical techniques, Paul writes to those who share the faith of Jesus Christ, and throughout the letter he invokes a story of God, the Creator, and the people of Israel that is well known by those to whom he writes. In the argument of Romans, Paul displays dramatically the results and implications of Jesus Christ for the story of God and the people of God. As throughout the New Testament writings, the Scriptures of Israel are the primary fund for Paul's imagination and language in Romans. The first part of Romans (1–8) claims, presents, and elaborates the effects of the death and resurrection of Christ and participation in it through baptism. Romans 9–11 treats the question of the role of Jews and gentiles in the plan of God, and the third part (12–16) exhorts the congregation to a transformed pattern of life.

Another apostle evangelized and established the church in Rome. The first followers of Jesus interpreted his resurrection as God's vindication of a faithful human being and came to understand Jesus as Messiah. Gradually the community around Jesus, which had begun as a popular Jewish movement, spread the "good news" of the crucified Messiah to the cities of the Greco-Roman world, where the message was received by the gentiles. As faith in Jesus as the Messiah, the culmination of Israel's hopes, shifted from a Jewish sectarian context to a majority non-Jewish one, many questions about identity and practice arose. Central was the question of the role of the Torah, or Jewish law, for those in the new movement. The New Testament writings witness in different ways to the disputes and debate about observance of the law, relationships with governments, and organizations of households. Paul, as preacher and writer of letters, came to have a significant role in the ultimate resolution of these issues, both in his own time and in the decades that followed his ministry.

Paul writes the letter to the church at Rome, where he has not preached, to build and strengthen his ties with them as he prepares to deliver the collection of offerings from gentile churches to Jerusalem, the home of the church and the symbolic origin of the gospel. Paul seeks their support as he plans for his mission to Spain. The focus of energy in Romans is the relationship of gentiles and Jews in the plan of God, a subject central to Paul's understanding of his identity and his vocation, essential to the well-being of the community, and of ultimate significance for salvation.

Biblical scholars reconstruct the occasion of the letter and Paul's reasons for writing from clues within the letter itself, especially the information in the opening and closing (Rom. 1:8-15; 15:22-33). One ancient source outside the letter (Suetonius, *Life of Claudius*) appears to refer to the expulsion of the Jews from Rome under the emperor Claudius. On the basis of this passage, it is conjectured that perhaps the return of Jesus-believers of Jewish origin to the community of gentile believers, who now dominated in the Roman house churches, may have caused discord that Paul addressed in the exhortation to forbearance in Romans 14.

Paul, the writer of the letter to Rome, understands himself as an apostle, called to the work of preaching the gospel to the gentiles. (Paul describes his call in Gal. 1:11-12.) The "gospel" or "good news" (*euangelion*) is that Jesus, the Messiah, is the culmination of God's plan to bless all nations through Israel, to rescue the world from sin, and to re-create it to its original glory. The conviction that God, the Creator, was the God of all people originated in the exile and is expressed in the prophetic writings of Second Isaiah (Isaiah 40–54). Paul, a Pharisee who had previously been zealous to oppose those Jews who believed Jesus to be God's anointed one, was called to preach Jesus as Messiah.

At the same time, many others who followed Jesus read the Scriptures together and enacted the story of his death and resurrection in worship. Multiple strands of speculation about divine redeemer figures whom God would send to bring justice or to save the faithful are found in the Hebrew Bible and texts from the Second Temple period (Nickelsburg). However, the execution of the Messiah was not recognized as a conventional part of the script. In the patterns of death and resurrection and exile and restoration within Israel's Scriptures, believers in Jesus found metaphors and images to interpret their own lives and the lives of the nations. Jesus' faithfulness and his death as "sacrifice of atonement" (Rom. 3:25) come to represent the righteousness of God and God's promise of salvation for all. Understanding Romans in its ancient context requires placing it within the shared symbolic universe of the early Christian tradition, furnished with the stories and images from Israel's Scriptures. In order to appreciate the resonance of its language and concepts, it is also necessary to read it in dialogue with the political rhetoric of the Roman Empire, which also declared good news and the coming of rulers who promised peace.

Paul's Letter to the Romans in the Interpretive Tradition

Interpretation of Paul's Letter to the Romans has had enormous impact on Christian theology throughout history. Placed at the head of the canon of Paul's letters, theologians have read Romans as a systematic theology, as the singular apostle's last will and testament. Christian theologians and exegetes have read the dualistic rhetoric concerning Jews and gentiles in the letter as representative of real, historical Jews, as opposed to "Christians," those believers with whom Paul identifies. The antipathy toward "works righteousness," that is, the idea that one can "earn" salvation through effort, good works, or obedience to the law, is prominent in Christian theologies and finds its support in Romans (Rom. 4:1-25; 9:30-33). The polemic of the Reformers that caricatured the Jew, based on the language of Romans, as obsessed with "works righteousness" contributed to the antisemitism in Europe that was complicit in the Holocaust (Ruether; Carroll). Aware of the violent historical effects of the anti-Jewish reading of Romans and informed by more accurate depictions of Second Temple Judaism (Sanders), contemporary interpreters of Romans read the letter within the variegated landscape of Jewish practice and belief of the first century. Biblical scholars seek to interpret Romans with the categories of first-century thought and in terms of the shared cultural language of the time, rather than with anachronistic categories of Judaism and Christianity and concepts of individual salvation (Stowers). In Paul's context, they argue, the question of God's dealings with Jews and gentiles would have been in the foreground. Recent attention to the context of Romans in the Roman Empire has highlighted the ways Paul uses and subverts imperial language and patterns of thought (Wan 2000; Elliott 2008). When Romans is read intertextually with literature of the Roman Empire, new emphases and themes emerge. The rediscovery of the Roman Empire as a context for reading Romans coincides with a self-consciousness about the imperial context of North American biblical interpretation.

Romans in Contemporary Discussion

The transition from reading in the context of the "introspective conscience," that is, in terms of a modern psychological reading, to reading the letter in the historical context of Jewish and Christian self-definition has offered new ways for interpreters to engage with the rhetoric and politics of the letter (Stendahl 1963). Focus on Jews and gentiles, on *peoples* or *communities* with whom God is in relation, suggests analogies with "peoples" in the present with whom God is in relationship. How can Romans 9–11 be put into conversation with the conflicting faith claims in the world? Within Paul's wrestling with the fate of Israel and the nations in the comprehensive plan of God, is there a conviction about God's commitment to all peoples? Within the apocalyptic framework that sees the whole creation groaning as divine purposes work themselves out (Romans 8), there are resources for thinking theologically about ecology and the fate of the earth (McGinn). Paul's language about the power of sin over human beings and within systems is one powerful, first-century diagnosis of those who have been oppressed by sinful systems (Tamez). Paul's counsel to this community to live in a way that does not conform to the world but that requires transformation of values might be read as instruction to Christian people in the present who are negotiating life in a complex and pressured culture. The letter's focus on mission, the trajectory of the gospel to the whole world, and God's ultimate plan to save all people has been read in light of mission in the contemporary world (Jewett).

The attempt to read Romans in its historical context has been fruitful for theological reflection. It has identified the anti-Jewish impact of the previous tradition of interpretation and the limitations of an individualistic focus. At the same time, reading Romans with its own categories and concepts raises difficult questions about how to "translate" the vision of God and humanity from its social and historical context in the first century into a culture with radically different categories of thought and modes of imagination.

Romans 1:1-17: Paul Introduces Himself and the Gospel

▌ THE TEXT IN ITS ANCIENT CONTEXT

In densely packed phrases, Paul conveys how he understands his role. The "gospel of God," for which he is set apart, is continuous with the promises made by the prophets in the Holy Scriptures. Paul's own call is that of a "servant," or literally a "slave," of Jesus Christ. He quotes a traditional confession of faith that may have been valued by the church at Rome (1:3-4) that Jesus was "declared" or installed as Son of God at his resurrection. In tension with other statements in Paul's letters that assert that Jesus was equal to God from the time of creation (Phil. 2:6-11), this formula gives another perspective on Jesus' sonship—that it was revealed in his resurrection. The resonant term, "servant," connotes both humility and honor and evokes the suffering servant figure of Second Isaiah. Paul's purpose, given to him through Jesus Christ, is "to bring about the obedience of faith among all the Gentiles" (1:5). Although in the modern period faith has come to mean assent to a particular truth claim, here *pistis* describes an attitude and way of being that encompasses loyalty and trust. "Faithfulness" is a closer translation. Romans asserts God's faithfulness (3:3), cites the faithfulness of Jesus, and urges faithfulness as the path for gentile followers of Jesus. Those to whom he writes are also "called" to be God's holy people (Rom. 1:6-7).

After the greeting of "grace" and "peace," Paul thanks those in Rome, praises their faith, asserts his unceasing prayers, and expresses his wish to visit them. Just as he has reaped a harvest among the rest of the gentiles, so he wishes to proclaim the gospel to those in Rome. When he states that their faith is known throughout the world, Paul reflects the importance and centrality of Rome in the ancient empire. He explains his unfulfilled desire to visit in order to build a relationship as well as to recognize their independence from him. As he began his self-introduction with a summary of the gospel (Rom. 1:2-4), so he concludes his greeting to the church with another definition of the gospel (Rom. 1:16-17). This summary makes sense within the apocalyptic perspective of the letter: that in Jesus, God's plan for the fulfillment of history is nearing its finale. God's judgment is at hand. "Salvation" denotes the rescue of the world from negative judgment and death. God's rescue will encompass the Jew first and also the Greek.

For Paul and his contemporaries, the categories of Jew and gentile organized the world. Throughout Romans, Paul will argue for both the priority of the Jew and for the inclusion of the gentile. The word "gospel" (*euangelion*) is used in the prophets to speak of the coming of God (Isa. 40:9; 41:27; 52:7; 60:6; 61:1) and in political imperial rhetoric to refer to the victory of a ruler. The gospel reveals the "righteousness" of God, or God's "justice." The root of the Greek word translated "righteousness" is the word meaning "just," or "justice." Through Jesus Christ God is "making right" the relationship between humans and God. Faith, or faithfulness, is the criterion for salvation. Human faith reflects God's faithfulness. Using the conventional formula for citing Scripture, Paul quotes the prophet Habakkuk. In its original context in Hab. 2:4, faith expressed Jewish solidarity in the face of adversity (Nanos 2011). A better translation, noted in the NRSV margin, is "the one who is righteous by faith will live." Righteousness through faith makes life possible. The "righteous one" may also be an allusion to Christ, understood to be the ultimate example of faithfulness to God.

▌The Text in the Interpretive Tradition

Beginning with Augustine and interpreted by Martin Luther, "faith" in 1:16-17 came to be understood as individual "belief." "Faith" was internal assent to a proposition about Jesus as Son of God. As such, faith was what defined a Christian and what was required for the individual to be "saved." This understanding of "faith" continues to dominate in Christian communities who characterize themselves as "evangelical" and who require an experience of "conversion." The sequence of "the Jew first and also the Greek" has been the basis for influential schemes of "salvation history." Dependent on the narrative in Luke-Acts, this construction of the story of the early church imagines that the gospel was offered to Jews first, who rejected it, then given to gentiles instead. The implication of this scenario—that the Jews have surrendered their role as the people of God in favor of the church—does not recognize Judaism as an ongoing religion of faithful people in relationship with God. Recent interpreters of Romans have disputed this conclusion and the exegesis on which it is based. Mark Nanos argues that Paul addressed Romans solely to gentiles and that for Paul, the covenant with God through Torah remained intact for Jews (Nanos 1996).

▌The Text in Contemporary Discussion

Contemporary interpreters of Romans have recontextualized Paul's language in the first-century discussion about Jewish and Christian identity and self-definition, rather than in terms of modern categories of faith and individual salvation. Within this first-century discussion, the obligation of Torah observance was the concrete expression of God's covenant with Israel and the definition of Israel's identity. As a nuanced understanding of the complexity of Judaism in the first century has grown, it has become more and more difficult to make easy analogies between categories in Romans and parties or positions in the time of the contemporary interpreter. Readers of Romans have been confronted with the distance between the ancient and contemporary contexts (Gager), and in some ways, this cultural gap has made interpretation more difficult. However, the recovery of the centrality and priority in the letter of the salvation of peoples, Jews and gentiles, rather than of individuals, has drawn renewed attention to the corporate nature of faith and the impact of the good news on society and nations. Rereading faith as "faithfulness" broadens the practical nature of faith into an orientation of one's whole being rather than a single act of assent. When "justice" is understood as the root of "justification," then the impact of the good news goes beyond the status of individuals and affects the network of relationships in society.

Romans 1:18—3:31: Human Wickedness and God's Justice through Jesus Christ

▮ THE TEXT IN ITS ANCIENT CONTEXT

In a highly structured argument, Paul illustrates how the gospel solves the deadly dilemma of human sin that is shared alike by Jew and gentile. Because sin would prevent any and every person from being declared just at the time of God's judgment, in order to be justified and therefore "saved" or "redeemed," God put forward Jesus Christ as "a place of atonement" (3:25, alternate NRSV reading). The effectiveness of Jesus Christ is compactly summarized in the climax of this section, 3:21-26. Leading up to the dramatic summary of the solution, Paul lays out an extended presentation of the problem: an exposition of the evil of gentiles and then of Jews. Paul and other Jews in the Hellenistic world understood that the law, given to the Jews by God as part of the covenant, was a powerful means of dealing with sin by offering a way to live righteously in accordance with the will of God (Stowers). As he does throughout Romans, Paul argues against the possibility that the law is an adequate solution for sin. He simultaneously wants to maintain the particular and unique relationship of the Jewish people with God and uphold the value of the law, while at the same time arguing that any reliance on the law or on religious identity in an exclusive way will result in failure.

Romans 1:18-32 depicts the evil of those gentiles who do not possess the law, but are able to know God through observation of the creation. Popular philosophers of Paul's time contended that God could be perceived through the natural order. Although they know better, gentiles do not honor God, but worship idols in the form of people and animals. Because of their idolatry, God "hands over" these people (the verb is used three times) to behavior that epitomizes lack of control and chaos, including to "lusts of their hearts" (1:24), "degrading passions" (1:26), and a "debased mind" (1:28). The epitome of disorder is the women's exchange of natural intercourse for unnatural and men's surrender of natural intercourse for passion for one another. In the construction of gender in the ancient world, sexual intercourse reflected the power relationship between male and female. In this arrangement, males were active and females passive (Brooten 1996). The asymmetrical pattern was built into "nature" and into God's creation. When humans fell into idolatry, wrong worship, the result is the violation of these gender patterns. The description of disorder and lack of control is meant to evoke horror.

Paul addresses a question to "you," a person who is judging others (2:1). Asking a rhetorical question to an imaginary opponent is a feature of the diatribe, a form of discourse used by Greek philosopher rhetoricians of Paul's time. Paul asserts that the self-righteous will be judged for their sinful deeds as well. Possession of the law, while a gift, does not prevent sin; it only makes it more visible. Because of sin, God's wrath and fury are the inevitable fate of all. A series of quotations from Scripture is the climax of Paul's portrait of universal sinfulness and its dire consequences (3:9-18). The portrayal of the inescapable plight reaches its turning point in 3:21. Now, without reference to the law, God's righteousness is "through faith in Jesus Christ for all who believe." The Greek genitive phrase translated to mean faith "in Jesus Christ" may also be translated to mean the faithfulness of Jesus, his trust in God exhibited in his life, which discloses God's righteousness. God has created a way for humans to be made right with God, justified, and judged righteous that is available equally to "all."

Images that describe how God's rescue is accomplished come from the worship and language of the early Jesus believers. "Redemption" is a metaphor that comes from the context of slavery and refers to the freeing of a person who is held hostage. God put forward Christ Jesus as a *hilastērion*, a "sacrifice of atonement" or "place of atonement" or "mercy seat." This term refers to an element in the ritual on the Day of Atonement (Lev. 16:3-15). In using this term, Paul alludes to a wider network of meaning that is not explained here but that makes a metaphorical connection between the death of Jesus and the ritual of atonement. While God overlooked sins committed in the past, at this present time, he shows himself to be righteous and makes righteous the one who has faith in Jesus or who has the faith of Jesus (3:26).

◼ THE TEXT IN THE INTERPRETIVE TRADITION

Paul's affirmation that gentiles can know God through the "things he has made" expresses the belief, shared by Stoic popular philosophy, that the order that inheres in all created things reflects a divine order. In the history of interpretation and the development of doctrine these verses have been the locus for development of "natural theology," the idea that nature teaches the order of God. Paul's description of the consequences of idolatry, God's surrendering humans to the chaos of their passions and the exchange of what is natural for what is unnatural, continues to be read as the condemnation in Scripture of homosexuality for women and for men. The horror that the passage is meant to evoke in its ancient context echoes and amplifies the misunderstanding and suspicion of sexual relationships between same-sex couples that has been widespread in culture since that time. This passage gives cultural abhorrence of homosexuality scriptural legitimation. Caricatures of Jewish judgmentalism and hypocrisy as well as gentile debauchery and depravity have remained powerful and harmful throughout history. Paul's statement that "a person is a Jew who is one inwardly, and real circumcision is a matter of the heart—it is spiritual and not literal" (2:29) has led to the spiritualization of the identity of Jew and gentile as symbolic categories, rather than as real historical peoples. Influential theologies of the atonement that explain how Christ's death is a sacrifice for sin have been based in the language of *hilastērion* in this passage.

◼ THE TEXT IN CONTEMPORARY DISCUSSION

Contemporary interpreters have grappled with how to translate the teaching and proclamation of these verses into the worldview and symbolic universe of the present. For example, many question the ancient understanding that the order of active male superiority and passive female subordination is woven into creation. Ideas about gender have changed over time in interaction with culture and religion. In more and more societies, equality of men and women is a fundamental value. Therefore, the logic of the text that understands same-sex intercourse to be a violation of this natural order and therefore an apt example of the consequences of idolatry is no longer accepted. For those who hold more traditional views about the relationship of male and female, its logic remains convincing.

Paul's argument depicts the universal sinfulness of all and the human need for salvation. He condemns self-righteousness and judgment of others on the basis that all sin. Just as sin is not limited to any one group of people, neither is God's salvation. Paul affirms that God's salvation is totally inclusive, of both Jew and gentile. As "justification by faith" came to mean that believing in Jesus was necessary for salvation, "faith" or lack of faith became the new dividing line between people and drew a boundary for God's mercy. However, when faith is reconceived as "faithfulness" and as "trust" modeled on the faithfulness of Jesus, it becomes a holistic orientation that might be mutually understood by Jews and Christians. Faithfulness comprises righteous action and works within the expanse of God's righteous judgment. In Rom. 1:18-32 idolatry is the chief cause of chaos and misery for human beings. While sexual immorality may be more easily recognized, idolatry is ultimately more destructive. Christian readers of this text might ask how to identify idolatrous worship in their own communities and reorient themselves to God.

Romans 4:1-25: Abraham Is Ancestor of Jews and Gentiles

▌ THE TEXT IN ITS ANCIENT CONTEXT

The story of Abraham (Genesis 12–17) provided Second Temple Jews with Scripture from which to draw lessons, preach, and on which to elaborate. In other Jewish writings from this period, Abraham represents a great hero of monotheism, the first Jewish convert from paganism, and the epitome of obedience to Torah. In the New Testament, the author of the Epistle of James extols Abraham as an exemplar of justification by works when he offered his son Isaac (James 2:21).

Paul interprets the Genesis story with his own questions in mind. Developing the question about Jewish identity and circumcision that he raised in 3:1, and offering additional support to his claim in 3:29 that the one God is the God of gentiles as well as Jews, Paul presents Abraham as a model of one who is justified by faith. In this argument, Abraham becomes the spiritual father or ancestor of the gentiles, the people who are symbolically incorporated into his lineage.

Paul employs conventional Jewish techniques of scriptural commentary and argument and builds his commentary around scriptural quotations: Gen. 15:6 (cited in Rom. 4:3, 22); Ps. 32:1-2 (Rom. 4:7-8); Gen. 17:5 (Rom. 4:17); and Gen. 15:5 (Rom. 4:18). He explores the text of Gen. 15:6 from different angles to illustrate the theme, "We know that a person is justified by faith apart from works prescribed by the law" (3:28). Paul plays on the word "reckoned" throughout this part of Romans, first using it in the context of payment to contrast righteousness that comes as wages with that which comes as a gift (3:28; see 3:24). Paul uses the verb "reckon" again in 4:6, citing Ps. 32:1-2 as a second corroborating scriptural support. Paul next argues that Abraham, the patriarch whose covenant with God was represented by the sign of circumcision, actually was "reckoned" righteous before his circumcision (4:9-10). The account of the sign of circumcision in Gen. 17:10-11 occurs after God's "reckoning" of righteousness to Abraham (in Gen. 15:6); therefore, Paul argues, Abraham was to be made the ancestor also of all who are not circumcised, but who follow his example of faith.

God's promise to Abraham that he would be made a great nation (Gen. 12:2) and "the father of many nations" (Gen. 17:5; Sir. 44:19-21) came through faith and rests on grace. The scriptural promise, "I have made you the father of many nations" (Gen. 17:5), is interpreted to mean that Abraham's descendants include all who share his faith. The God in whom Abraham believes, who "gives life to the dead and calls into existence things which do not exist," is the God of resurrection and creation. Abraham's faithful response to God's promise is elaborated in a short vignette portraying his "hoping against hope," his consideration of his own nearly dead body and Sarah's barren womb. He grows strong and gives glory, thus depicting the ideal heroic exemplar of faith. Paul's argument closes with the repetition of the thematic verse and a claim that the words of Scripture "it was reckoned to him" were written not only for his sake but for "ours also," referring to the audience of Romans. The concluding formula is likely an early Christian creedal statement summarizing the belief "in him who raised Jesus our Lord from the dead, who was handed over to death for our trespasses and was raised for our justification" (Rom. 4:24-25).

■ THE TEXT IN THE INTERPRETIVE TRADITION

New Testament evidence shows Abraham to have been a major figure of exegetical and theological speculation for Christian writers (see James 2:21-23; 1 Pet. 3:6; and Hebrews, passim). Abraham's wife Sarah and slave Hagar figure in Paul's Letter to the Galatians as mothers of the slave and the free child, of Mount Sinai and Jerusalem (see Gal. 4:21-31). Later, Protestant theologians understood Abraham to be the representative of justification by faith in opposition to works righteousness, which they regarded as characteristic of the Roman Catholicism they opposed. John Calvin was concerned with questions about Paul's exegesis of the Abraham story that preoccupied his own forebears and contemporaries. These included how to reconcile Paul's portrait of Abraham's faith with his laughter in response to God's promise of a son (Gen. 17:7) and how to resolve the apparent contradiction between Paul's and James's exegesis of the Abraham story. As all exegetes do, the sixteenth-century interpreters looked to the biblical text to address their pressing theological questions (Steinmetz).

■ THE TEXT IN CONTEMPORARY DISCUSSION

Contemporary scholarship sees Paul's argument here within the context of Jewish styles of biblical exegesis in the first century. Extrabiblical and legendary traditions about Abraham's adventures and virtues show the variety and fluidity of scriptural commentary. When Paul constructs the argument that Abraham is the father of both Jews and gentiles, we see theology built up out of story and patterns within God's activity. The presence of other versions and variations within the New Testament in James, Hebrews, and Galatians testifies to the creativity of early Christian theology. The emphasis of scholarly commentators is no longer to harmonize the statements of different New Testament authors or to arrive at one consistent reading of the accounts of Abraham in Genesis.

The negative contrast Paul sets up between being justified by works and justified by faith has been read by Christians to denigrate both ancient and modern Judaism. Recently scholars have corrected that historically inaccurate portrait of Jewish belief and practice. By reading Romans 4 within the context of Second Temple Judaism, contemporary scholarship understands that Paul is not arguing for the replacement of Israel by the church or contrasting grace and faith with the negative foil of the law. Rather, he is finding, within the story of God in Torah, grounds for gentiles being included in God's promises.

Keen awareness of the function of gender in the text and the role of gender in the culture causes some readers to note that Sarah does not play a role as an active agent of faith here in Romans as she does in Hebrews 11 and in Galatians 4 (Trible and Russell). God's sacrifice of his Son Jesus on the cross is able to rearrange genealogical relationships and make gentiles into the patrilineal line of Abraham (Eisenbaum).

Romans 5:1-21: Christ's Gift of Righteousness Brings Life

▮ THE TEXT IN ITS ANCIENT CONTEXT

In Romans 5–8, Paul elaborates the results of justification that were summarized in Rom. 3:21-26. The section begins and ends with an affirmation of the love of God (5:5; 8:39). Paul speaks of justification with the parallel images of "having peace with God" and "being reconciled to God," metaphors that have their meaning in the context of warfare and conflict. The audience of Romans would have recognized the echoes of imperial rhetoric that claimed the peace of the *Pax Romana* as the benefits gained by the emperor (Georgi). Here, however, the peace is gained not through the perpetration of violence. Rather it is Jesus' death ("through his blood"), not on behalf of the righteous, but on behalf of the unrighteous, that is the means of peace and the way to be saved.

In Paul's anthropology, boasting is a characteristic human activity. Boasting and being ashamed are part of the language of honor and shame typical of Greco-Roman culture (Jewett). For a Christian, it is what one boasts about, and on what basis, that matters. While Paul criticizes boasting in 2:17; 3:27; 4:2, here boasting is celebrated as positive and justified. Here the speakers, "we," who are made right with God through faith, as Abraham exemplified in the previous example, may boast in hope and because we are saved from God's wrath (5:3, 11). The phrase "glory of God" alludes to the story of Adam in Genesis (Gen. 1:26-28; Ps 8:5-8), whose transgression caused him to lose the glory of God that he possessed. The sequence of virtues, linked in a chain-like structure, culminates in God's love.

Paul explains how this salvation works through a comparison of Adam and Christ, two corporate figures, men who represent humanity. As a "type" of the one to come, Adam is parallel to Christ, who will rectify the damage caused by Adam's trespass. Paul retells the story of humanity as a sequence of reigns, each dominated by a different ruler. Each ruler personifies the quality of the age and tyrannizes his subjects, here as either death or life. While death, the result of Adam's sin, rules in Adam, through Christ those who have been given the gift of righteousness will rule in life. The verb to exercise dominion (*basileuein*) is translated in the NRSV as both "rule" and "reign." In extrabiblical literature, Adam is held responsible for human death (*4 Ezra* 3:7; Wis. 2:23-24). While Paul's Jewish contemporaries would have understood the giving of the law through Moses to rectify this deadly situation, in the story Paul tells, the law plays a role as a minor character (5:13, 20) that increases the trespass. While the two figures of Adam and Christ are parallel, and one's action cancels the other, Paul stresses how much greater is the gift of Christ. The increasing and abounding of grace leads to eternal life.

▌The Text in the Interpretive Tradition

Augustine found in Rom. 5:12 the locus of the doctrine of original sin that he developed from the phrase *eph' hō*, "in whom." Arguing against his theological adversaries the Pelagians and the Manicheans, Augustine diagnosed the fact of original sin in the human person as a child of Adam. Sin was propagated through Adam to all subsequent descendants, passed down by parents to their children. The baptism of infants, he argued, was necessary to cleanse them from sin. Luther radicalized Augustine's notion of original sin, elaborating that "all humanity sinned with Adam in Adam's sin." Original sin, according to Luther, is "complete lack of righteousness in all the parts of a person, and a predisposition to commit evil, a loathing of what is good, a delight in what is evil" (Reasoner, 49). Augustine and Luther's reading of this part of Romans has profoundly shaped church teaching and Western culture. On the other hand, historical-critical biblical scholars contend that, read in its context, Rom. 5:12 is an incomplete sentence that serves only as the basis for showing the parallel figure of Christ and the positive benefits of Christ's death for human beings to reign in life. As we have seen with other parts of Romans, the history of interpretation emphasizes one part of this passage strongly, while biblical scholars see Paul's emphasis elsewhere.

▌The Text in Contemporary Discussion

Paul uses a variety of terms for salvation that are at home in different semantic settings. Here the metaphors for salvation, synonyms for justification, have their meaning in the setting of warfare and conflict. The rhetoric of this passage can be read as disguised commentary on the language of pacification and imposition of peace of the *Pax Romana* (Elliott 2008; Georgi). In the language of domination and rule, interpreters have seen an apt description of the way in which political and economic systems dominate human life in the present. Focus on imperial language in Romans has alerted interpreters to the contemporary imperial context of interpretation. Paul's mythological scenario might be translated into the present as analogous to global capitalism or globalization (Elliott 2008). The dramatic totalizing language of ruling, "exercising dominion," is apt for the reality of these systems of power. Attending anew to Paul's language of corporate connection and corporate identity can act as an antidote to commonplace assumptions about individualism in contemporary culture. The solidarity of sin in Adam is overcome by a parallel, yet superior "solidarity in grace" through Christ. Jesus "represents the weakness of God and thus the dominion of grace, the sole form of dominion befitting both humanity and God" (Georgi, 100).

Romans 6:1-23: United to Christ in Death and in Resurrection

▌The Text in Its Ancient Context

The argument is advanced with a rhetorical question from an imaginary dialogue partner (6:1). The question appears to draw a conclusion from 5:20: if sin increases and grace abounds all the more, does that mean that one should continue to sin? Paul introduces and expands on narratives of baptism and enslavement to show that the free gift of justification does not give believers license to sin, nor does it cause sin to be impotent. Rather, sin still flourishes as a power with which to contend and not surrender. Paul personifies sin as a ruler, who exercises dominion, rules (*basileuein*), and who demands allegiance. Paul and his audience understand that those who undergo the rite of baptism into Christ are participating in the narrative of Christ's death and resurrection, a two-part movement of dying and rising. Death is in the past and resurrection is still in the future, a hope and expectation. The association of baptism and death is made also in Mark 10:38-40 in Jesus' response to the request of James and John for positions of honor. Jesus' response shows that early believers linked baptism with the death of Jesus. Paul connects the death in baptism to the destruction of the body of sin. He concludes that those he addresses are, just as Jesus, dead to sin and alive to God.

The language of life and death and of freedom and slavery organize this passage, and the categories shift and reverse in the course of Paul's argument. Death and slavery represent negative states that are reversed and overcome in the resurrection and baptism. The exception to this pattern is the conclusion of this passage, where slavery to righteousness is presented as the positive alternative to slavery to sin.

With the military imagery of weapons, Paul exhorts that bodies are to be employed as instruments of righteousness rather than as weapons of wickedness. As in 1:18-32, passions lead to danger and make one out of control. Sharp contrasts structure the argument: dead to sin/alive to God, not present to sin/present to God, not as instruments of wickedness/but instruments of righteousness, not under law/under grace.

In a response to another imaginary question (5:15), Paul uses the analogy of slavery to redescribe the human situation in relationship to Christ. The social world in which Paul lived was a slave society, and Paul used a familiar and extreme image to speak of the alternative between living in the rule of God or the rule of sin. Formerly slaves to sin, now those who are freed from it are slaves to righteousness. While slavery to sin means death (6:21), slavery to God means sanctification and eternal life. Here the alignment of freedom with life shifts to equate slavery to God with life.

▌ THE TEXT IN THE INTERPRETIVE TRADITION

When slavery was a social institution thoroughly embedded in the fabric of society, as it was at the time of the writing of the New Testament, the instructions to slaves to obey their masters were read as Christian teaching about slavery. Because the Bible assumed the existence of slavery, readers who were not slaves concluded that slavery had divine support and approval. The prevalence of slavery in Christian Scripture and the fact that Paul and other authors did not unambiguously speak against it, made it possible to take slavery for granted and to see it as "natural." However, as criticism of the practice of slavery increased within society, readers sought to use the Bible itself to critique the slavery texts within it. When those who were enslaved and their descendants read these scriptural texts, they put their experience of oppression into dialogue with their faith and drew the conclusion that God did not intend for those made in God's image to be enslaved by others. The slave society offered the image of slavery, an apt metaphor for the tyrannical reign of sin (Tamez). On the basis of the conclusion of the passage in which "slaves of righteousness" is the positive alternative to "slaves of sin," some have argued that freedom is not freedom in the modern sense, but enslavement to the proper master. Because there was no alternative to a state of spiritual enslavement, human existence is inevitably some form of obedience (Cranfield, 323; Hays 1996, 38–39, 390).

▌THE TEXT IN CONTEMPORARY DISCUSSION

The Bible's historical role both to support slavery and to abolish it affects the way interpreters read the metaphors of slavery and their meaning in Romans 6. While slavery has been judged immoral by most contemporary societies, the enslavement of people by other human beings continues to be a political reality. "Human trafficking" and "sex trafficking" are the modern synonyms for slavery. Slavery is a state of "natal alienation" (Patterson) and remains the most extreme form of human mistreatment and violence. The spiritualization of slavery, its use as a metaphor, can direct attention away from its physical and bodily effects in real people's lives (Glancy). The reality of physical slavery is masked by the metaphor. On the other hand, to describe sin as an enslaving power highlights sin's total domination and indicates its evil results. The only effective opposition is "slavery" to God. While many interpreters have concluded from this passage that in a Christian perspective there is no state that is not obedience, others point to the images of freedom and equality in other parts of Paul's letters (Schüssler Fiorenza; Kittredge 1998). The concentration of slavery language in Romans 6 raises for readers the ethical question: How is it possible to use the language of "ruling" that so permeates Romans without adopting and reinforcing structures of domination and subordination in the present?

Romans 7:1—8:1: The Role of the Law

▌THE TEXT IN ITS ANCIENT CONTEXT

Paul asserts the holiness and goodness of the law and at the same time insists that it has no positive role in the life of those in Christ. He makes an analogy with marriage. The law of marriage no longer pertains to a woman whose husband has died. Just as Paul's analogies with slavery depend for their meaning on the existence of a slave society, so his use of marriage depends on the assumption of marriage in which the husband owns the wife and rules over her. A person "belongs" to Christ, as a wife "belongs" to her husband.

In denying that the law is sin (7:7), Paul employs the first-person pronoun to explain the relationship between sin and the law. With the "I," Paul is not telling his own story but is using the rhetorical form of a "speech in character" to tell the experience of a typical human being. The story echoes the story of Adam in Genesis 2, who transgressed God's commandment. Sin acts as the serpent (7:11). It alludes also to the story of the people of Israel who rebelled against God when they worshiped the golden calf (Grieb). Philo, a Jewish writer of the Second Temple period, wrote that covetousness or desire is the most basic sin, the source of all others. The dramatic description of the "I" who, because of indwelling sin, is unable to good, but only evil, has a parallel in the Dead Sea Scrolls: 1QS 3–4 identifies an evil impulse dwelling within the flesh that opposes God until God intervenes. Paul sees the person divided between mind and flesh and mind and members, one opposed to the other. In the scope of his argument, his statements about the law are subordinate in importance to the overall story of God's victory in Jesus Christ, and the statements about human slavery are preparatory to the affirmation of freedom and life. The positive turn comes in 8:1, and Paul summarizes the climax of the story in 8:3-4, that God did what the law could not do, by sending his son, to overcome sin.

◼ THE TEXT IN THE INTERPRETIVE TRADITION

The history of interpretation of Rom. 7:7-25 has focused on the identity of the speaker, the "I." Augustine, contesting with Pelagius, in early writings argued that the "I" was the person before he/she was in Christ, later that it was Paul himself, and finally that it was the person after conversion who still struggled with sin. For Augustine, the text denied the perfectibility of the human person. The history of reading Romans 7 as an example of the "introspective conscience of the West" (Stendahl) began with Augustine, who first identified the "I" with his own youthful self who was unable to do good on his own. Martin Luther then identified with Paul, interpreted through Augustine, and saw his own overzealous conscience in Paul's confession of helplessness over sin and the ineffectiveness of the law. The doctrine *simul iustus et peccator* ("at the same time justified and a sinner") summarized his reading of Rom. 7:14-20 as a description of the Christian's ongoing struggle with sin. Paul's description of the bondage of the will and its interpretation in Christian theology has shaped Western views of the human self as incapable of achieving good. Calvin's doctrine of "total depravity" is based on an interpretation of 7:14-21.

Interpreters have also made analogies between the "law" of Romans 7 and other aspects of human life: for Barth, the law was "religion" (Reasoner). When scholars began to read Paul with the cultural and religious milieu of his own time, rather than with the lenses of later Christian systematic theology, Romans 7 was read not as autobiographical but as "rhetorical reinforcement" of the larger argument of God's saving purpose for Jews and gentiles. Here Paul was offering an apology for Torah, a defense of its essential goodness, rather than a condemnation. With this approach, Paul's Letter to the Romans provided a New Testament model for imagining Christianity and Judaism, the descendants of the Torah-abiding Jews and Christ-believers in Romans, as both having a place in the purposes of God. Paul's vision in Romans created the basis for cooperative and appreciative relationships between Christians and Jews in the present.

◼ THE TEXT IN CONTEMPORARY DISCUSSION

Krister Stendahl and his followers succeeded in shifting scholars' interpretations of Romans away from the internal psychological reading to a reading that saw the subject of the letter as the relationship between peoples of the world, Jews and gentiles, in God's saving plan for the whole creation. In a world that had seen the murderous effects of antisemitism and hatred between peoples, the shift to a corporate understanding of Romans spoke eloquently and opened up avenues of dialogue and mutual understanding. However, the individualistic approach to Romans, that it is about the person's helplessness under sin and the need for inner assent and conversion to Christ, remains popular in evangelical Christianity and influential in Christian belief in general. Read as an autobiographical confession, Paul's story of "I do not do the good I want" resonates with contemporary people's own experience. Alcoholics Anonymous, for example, names powerlessness over alcohol as the first step of recovery. The power of sin, personified as a tyrant, describes and diagnoses a reality that many experience. Conversion to Christ within a Christian context or dependence on a "higher power" in Alcoholics Anonymous is effective in opposing and overcoming the force of sin. Others have read Paul's language about sin here to refer to systemic or corporate systems of oppression and enslavement that make "doing good" impossible. The challenge is how to translate the drama of Romans 7 into the contemporary context and find appropriate analogues to "sin," "law," the "good."

Romans 8:1—8:39: Life in the Spirit

■ THE TEXT IN ITS ANCIENT CONTEXT

The argument that began in 5:1 culminates in 8:39, ending as it began on a note of "love." In the scriptural world that supplies the imagery in this passage, God's Spirit is present at creation, linked to the resurrection of Jesus, and given at baptism. History is envisioned as a battle between opposing forces, a struggle at the brink of its conclusion, which is the intervention of God. God's judgment is imminent. Here Paul claims that in the action of Jesus Christ, those who participate in his death and resurrection through baptism will not be condemned, but will become children of God. "Law," *nomos*, has various meanings here that range from the common, "rule," to the specific, "Torah." As in Romans 6–7, the primary opposition is between life and death, and secondarily between freedom and slavery.

In Rom. 8:3-4, Paul expresses how God succeeded in defeating sin, a task that the law failed to do, "by sending his own Son in the likeness of sinful flesh." After God's defeat of sin, the choice is between two ways of living, "according to the flesh" or "according to the Spirit." One is the way of life and the other the way of death. The ethical choice between two ways of behaving is modeled after Moses' challenge in Deut. 11:26-28 to choose between blessing and curse. Here the choices appear as two "spheres of influence," "reigns," "realms," or kingdoms. "Flesh" does not mean physical flesh, but is a term that signifies sin. The one who has faith has already been transferred from the realm of flesh/death to the realm of spirit/life because of the Spirit who dwells within the person. Romans 8:14-17 is a baptismal formula that uses the language of adoption and "sonship" to describe the relationship between God and those baptized/those believers/those in Christ. This relationship is opposed to the spirit of slavery, the antithesis of adoption and sonship. It allows the right of inheritance and the privilege of crying "Abba," the name given by a young child to a father. Traditions about the exodus undergird this passage—the people of Israel are considered children of God whom God creates, elects, and delivers from slavery in Egypt. The redemption in Christ is parallel with the delivery of Israel in the exile. The tradition of Israel's holy war funds these images of conquering and being children of God (Grieb).

Paul understands that the present time of suffering is part of the final struggle between the forces of good and evil that will culminate in victory for God. God's purposes include not only human beings but also the whole creation, described as groaning with labor pains. This culmination is near, but still in the future, a glory for which we "long" and "wait." Just as righteous Israel suffered in preparation for vindication by God, so those who are in Christ suffer as they await the "glory" about to be revealed. Paul's confidence that God will prevail is summarized in the assertion "those he called, he justified." In an allusion to Abraham's near sacrifice of Isaac, "who did not withhold his own Son," Paul connects God's giving up of Jesus with Abraham's giving up of Isaac.

▌ THE TEXT IN THE INTERPRETIVE TRADITION

The overarching oppositions set up in this passage between the realm of the spirit and the realm of the flesh, characteristic of apocalyptic literature and deriving from "the two ways tradition" in the Deuteronomistic history, has been interpreted to denigrate the body and the material world in favor of the nonbodily and "spiritual." Appreciation of the origins of this oppositional language, and a nuanced understanding that what Paul means by "flesh" is not the physical body but is by definition the realm of sin, help readers to contextualize this dualism rather than universalizing or generalizing it. Romans 8:28-30 describes God's relationship with the elect people of God in a stair-step sequence of verbs. In these verses, Paul has transferred the scriptural terminology for Israel, "called," "chosen," "sons," onto those gentiles and Jews who follow Jesus (Reasoner, 86). While these verses originally referred to God's relationship with the people Israel, Luther and Calvin understood them to refer to God's choice of individuals for salvation. In the Protestant Reformation, theologians developed theologies of predestination of individuals from the verbs "predestined," "foreknew," and "called." Liturgically, the acclamation of the inseparability of the faithful from God's love is well known in burial services in both Protestant and Roman Catholic churches. Outside of their context in Paul's Letter to the Romans, these verses—"neither death, nor life, nor angels, nor rulers, nor things present, nor things to come"—have become an expression of faith for those who grieve the death of a loved one. For those who see Romans 1–8 as the theological center of Romans, this exultant affirmation of the love of God is the letter's "climax."

▌ THE TEXT IN CONTEMPORARY DISCUSSION

The proclamation of freedom in Christ in Rom. 8:15-17 functions as a "canon within the canon" for many theologians of liberation. The inclusion of the whole creation in the cooperative struggle toward renewed relationship with God, described in poetic, apocalyptic language, provides a rich resource for readers who seek earth-affirming images in Scripture. The "groaning" of Rom. 8:22-23 evokes the cries of labor and the sounds of speaking in tongues (Stendahl 1976; McGinn). Feminist interpreters resist reading the language of flesh and spirit to create a mind-body or a male-female dualism. The transformation from "slaves" to "sons" and "heirs" describes the move from death to life and from slavery to freedom accomplished in baptism. The NRSV translation of *huioi* as "children" obscures its male referent and masks the patriarchal assumptions of the metaphors of adoption, sons, and heirs. At the same time, society's customs around adoption are not merely reflected by the text, but challenged, as indicated by the use of *teknoi*, "children"—male and female alike (McGinn; Kittredge 2012). Responding to the theological and ethical questions raised by readers after the Holocaust and in the economic and ecological crises at the close of the twentieth century, contemporary readers have turned away from focus on theologies of God's election of individuals and their promised salvation. Rather, interpreters have read Paul's affirmations of God's commitment to rescue the whole creation, and they have attempted to translate that faith into holiness of life in the present.

Romans 9:1-29: God's Promises to Israel Are Sure

■ THE TEXT IN ITS ANCIENT CONTEXT

In Romans 9–11, Paul addresses the success of the gospel among gentiles and its rejection among the majority of Jews. The reversed relationship between Jews and gentiles calls into question the central role of God's elect people and threatens confidence in God's integrity. The stakes are high. In an extended argument that runs through these chapters, Paul draws on Scripture and on analogies from everyday life to speculate about what God is doing. In sending Jesus Christ, God has altered the overall plot of the story, but revised it in a way that makes sense with patterns of divine activity told in Scripture. The phenomenon of gentile acceptance of the gospel and Jewish rejection was an urgent and immediate challenge for Paul because it appeared to undermine the faithfulness of God. Paul's defense of God takes the form of a lament, colored by emotionally charged accusations, questions, challenges, expressions of doubt, and fury, alternating with thanksgiving and praise (Grieb; Hays 1989). Paul uses the "I" pronoun to refer to himself as he identifies with his own people and protests God's decisions. Paul affirms (9:4-5) that Israel possesses all the privileges and gifts of relationship with God and is the source of the Messiah.

In order to defend the word of God from an accusation of failure (9:6), Paul garners a series of arguments that depend on citation and analysis of different verses and images in Scripture. The first is that God specifies that it is through Sarah's child that God names true descendants. The second is that Jacob was chosen over Esau, and the third is that God raises up Pharaoh to show his power and proclaim God's name. The sovereign power of God to choose on whom to have mercy is asserted by this series of scriptural examples. Each one is tinged with irony, surprise, and reversal and emphasizes how God inexorably carries out God's purposes (9:11). Paul upholds God's justice and mercy (9:14) and at the same time asserts God's freedom to act without regard to human expectations. Employing the image of God as the potter (Isa. 29:16; 45:9; Jer. 18:1-11; Wis. 15:7; Sir. 33:13), Paul asks a series of questions (9:19-24) that imply the absurdity of the human creation arguing with the Creator. Citing the words of the prophet Hosea, who speaks of God's choosing Israel and calling her "my people" and "beloved," Paul applies this election to Jews and gentiles. He cites Isaiah's reference to a remnant and to "survivors" or "descendants." Paul's argument in 9:1—11:36 is a series of attempts to address the problem of God's change of plan, and its conclusion is not reached until the end of chapter 11.

■ THE TEXT IN THE INTERPRETIVE TRADITION

When Romans was read as a treatise on Christian doctrine, it was Romans 1–8 that was considered the center of the letter while Romans 9–11 was considered a parenthetical topic of little importance for theologians (Reasoner). With the scholars of the new perspective, Romans 9–11 received renewed attention. While the question of the status of Israel had seemed settled and irrelevant for interpreters during the time when Christianity dominated as a sociopolitical force, it became a critical question in a new way for Christians after the Holocaust. Simultaneously, interest in the letter in its first-century context coincided with application to its contemporary context. Before the modern period, interpreters from Origen through Augustine and the Reformers were chiefly interested in the issue of election, "that God's purpose of election might continue." What is now understood in its historical context to have been an affirmation of God's relationship with a people was then interpreted as applying to individuals who were predestined to salvation or damnation. Interpreters read the "objects of wrath" and the "objects of mercy" as referring to two groups of people, each predestined to salvation or damnation. Augustine in his later work developed a strong predestinarian reading of the text. Karl Barth disputed rigid determinism and talked about God's purposes of election as being more general (Reasoner). Paul's rhetoric about the irony of God's choice and the stress on God's mercy was taken in an absolute and literal sense to speak about the predetermined fate of individuals and their inability to change that status. Commentators who have tried to put this passage into its historical context have read this passage as an argument among Jews about the role of Israel's covenant responsibility in God's overall purpose (Nanos 1996).

▌The Text in Contemporary Discussion

As the question of the ongoing status of the people of Israel was a critical theological issue for Paul, so the relationships between Christians and Jews after the Holocaust were urgent for biblical interpreters. Stendahl and others believed that Paul's argument in Romans 9–11 might give clues to understanding how Jews and Christians can be conceived to coexist within the mystery of God. As theologians grapple with pluralism of faith traditions, the way Paul uses Scripture and analogies with ordinary life may provide a model for how to reflect on what God is doing in the world. The manner in which Paul creatively engages with Scripture in a christological perspective, and in a way that seeks patterns within its narratives, can be used as a model for Christian preachers and theologians who interpret Scripture in the present (Hays 1989).

Although this passage's emphasis on the sovereignty of God appears to limit human choice and decision, the emphasis is not on human helplessness but on the mercy of God. While Paul mocks the idea that the pot would talk back to the potter, he himself is talking back to God out of an experience of anguish and making a bold and creative attempt to ascertain God's purposes.

Romans 9:30—10:21: Trying to Understand Israel and the Gentiles

▌The Text in Its Ancient Context

Opening the next stage of the argument with a rhetorical question, Paul contrasts gentile attainment of righteousness through faith with Israel's lack of success. Paul uses the opposition of faith and works to explain the paradox that gentiles who did not strive succeeded, while those who did strive did not. Behind this explanation lies the metaphor of the footrace in which two runners "chase" (*diōkein*), "strive" or compete. A "stumbling stone" has tripped up one contestant and allowed the other to overtake. A quotation that combines Isa. 28:16 and Isa. 8:14-15 refers to God who lays a stone in Zion. In 1 Cor. 1:23 the word *skandalon*, "stumbling stone," refers to Jesus Christ. Although the identity of the stone is left ambiguous here, Paul implies that Christ is the stone that is laid as an obstacle for Israel. The image of the footrace will be picked up again for further irony in 11:7-8.

In emotional language, appropriate for a lament ("heart's desire"), Paul expresses his wish that Israel be saved. Their "zeal," a quality Paul elsewhere attributes to himself (Phil. 3:6), misunderstands that righteousness through the law is not possible. "God's righteousness" comes through Christ, as the next verse asserts. In the statement "Christ is the end of the law," the word translated "end," *telos*, can mean either "termination" or "goal." "Goal" is the preferred interpretation: Christ is the "point" of the law as expressed in 3:21-26, "apart from the law" (3:21).

Employing a pesher style of scriptural interpretation in 10:5-13, Paul puts into opposition two quotations about the law, one from Lev. 18:5 and the other from Deut. 30:12-14. The text from Deuteronomy is used to interpret Leviticus. While Deuteronomy 30 in its original context asserts the nearness of the word so that the law could be done, here in Romans, by interspersing christological commentary into the quotation, Paul harnesses the original text to support the nearness of "the word of faith that we proclaim." The lips and heart of the quotation now speak of the requirement of assertion of faith with lips and in heart. Paul quotes two more verses from Scripture: Isa. 28:16 and Joel 2:32. Together these texts assert no distinction between Jew and Greek, their sharing of the same Lord, and the availability of salvation to "everyone" who calls on the name of the Lord.

The reference to calling on the name of the Lord leads Paul to address the possible objection that Israel has not been given the opportunity to call on the Lord and to believe. With a sequence of linked phrases in which the second of two becomes the first of a second pair, "believed," "heard," and "proclaimed," Paul presents a series of questions followed by scriptural quotations that demonstrate that God has provided Israel adequate opportunity to hear the good news. Isaiah 50–65 is the source of these quotations, passages where the prophet bewails the stubborn refusal of Israel to repent. Paul applies these prophetic critiques to the present situation of Jewish unbelief in Christ. Divine jealousy explains the current paradox. Deuteronomy 32:21 describes how the people's idolatry causes God to be jealous. In turn, God incites jealousy among his own people by taking on others. Paul attributes this motivation to God to account for Israel's unbelief.

▍ THE TEXT IN THE INTERPRETIVE TRADITION

Paul's reflection on the lack of success of his preaching of Jesus Christ to Israel, his own people, has been read by interpreters in their own historical context. They have understood Paul's words to describe and to diagnose their present. Reading *telos* to mean "end" rather than "goal," Marcion rejected the law as a whole. Others have cited this verse to support antinomianism. The Protestant opposition between faith and works, drawn from Paul and developed by Luther, has shaped Christian perceptions of Jews and Judaism as being motivated by "zeal" and focused on selfishness. Interpreted psychologically, this opposition is understood to be egoism and pathology. When this argument in Romans is read universally or timelessly, "Israel's unbelief" may be equated with ongoing Judaism, so that Judaism represents rejection of Jesus. For centuries, many churches derived from this interpretation of Romans 10 a mandate to convert Jews, but in the wake of the Holocaust many denominations worldwide have explicitly repudiated this view. So pervasive is this mapping of Paul's rhetoric in Romans onto contemporary Judaism that it is invisible and unconscious for many Christians (Levine). For example, Paul's christological interpretation of Deut. 30:12-14 has so defined the passage that Christian readers conclude that, for Jews, God is far away and must be sought across the seas, while for Christians, the word is near. The requirement of verbal confession and belief in the heart has become dominant in evangelical Protestantism as the necessary and critical action for conversion or salvation.

■ THE TEXT IN CONTEMPORARY DISCUSSION

Contemporary interpreters grapple with the legacy of distorted and negative caricatures of Judaism built on Paul's rhetorical arguments about Israel and gentiles. Commentators see a sad irony that the portrait of Israel's unbelief presented by the prophet Third Isaiah to his own people, within their common tradition, to woo them back to faithfulness, has here been taken up by the lips of Paul, enshrined in Christian Scripture, and applied as Christian condemnation of Jews in the present. The agony of Paul's first-century commitment to his own people is lost in translation across history and context. Those who seek to read the letter in a way that honors its first-century context and still finds positive value as Christian Scripture attempt to understand Paul's scriptural interpretation as selective and tendentious; they place it within a wider conversation of interpretation of Scripture in the Second Temple period. At the same time, they try to read it sympathetically and find in it a model for reading Scripture. Richard Hays, for example, suggests that Paul's use of Scripture might provide a model of intertextual theological reflection for Christian readers (Hays 1989). Krister Stendahl developed the motif of "holy envy" to describe the ways that each religion envies the gifts of the other, and that envy is used by God for good (Landau).

Romans 11:1-36: The Restoration of Israel and the Inclusion of the Gentiles

■ THE TEXT IN ITS ANCIENT CONTEXT

In the final stage of the argument of chapters 9–11, Paul refutes the conclusion that might logically be drawn from the portrayal of the people of Israel as "disobedient and contrary" (10:21). He completes his attempt to explain how God is keeping God's promises to Israel while drawing in the gentiles, by looking toward the future and imagining God's future action. He picks up and elaborates in turn on a series of images and metaphors from Scripture: the prophet Elijah's complaint and God's response, the motif of hardening, the dough, the olive tree, and the apocalyptic motif of previously unrevealed mystery.

The aim is to warn against arrogance of gentiles toward Israel, an attitude that ironically may have been provoked by earlier parts of Paul's argument. The lament continues with Paul citing himself and his own story. Implying a parallel between himself and Elijah, Paul recalls that God did not leave Elijah alone, but kept a remnant chosen by grace (1 Kgs. 19:18). This remnant is Paul's community of believers, who will have a role with regard to the salvation/fate of the rest. Citing from Isa. 29:10 and Ps. 69:22-23, Paul claims that God has hardened those who have not accepted the gospel. Returning to the image of stumbling in the footrace, Paul implies that the stumbling is temporary, not permanent, and will make Israel jealous. Here Paul uses again a "how much greater" argument (*pollō mallon*, see Romans 5) to predict the full inclusion of Israel that will be restated at the climax in 11:26. Again using himself as an example and employing the "jealousy" motif, Paul says that his role as apostle to the gentiles will, in a roundabout way, save some of his own. He invokes the images of the dough and roots to speak of the way that holiness "spreads" from the part to the whole. The word for "dough" is the same word as "lump," referring to clay, in 9:21. The image of root and branches leads into an elaborate argument whose central metaphor is the cultivation of an olive tree that is grafted with wild pieces, pruned, and regrafted. "Natural" (*kata physin*) is used to describe the original tree; "unnatural" (*para physin*), the wild branches. With this simile, Paul is able to speak of the relationship between peoples, Jews and gentiles, to speculate on shifting relationships between them, and to urge humility and forbearance toward Jews on the part of gentiles. Wild branches should realize their dependence on the roots. That some branches were broken off should serve as a warning against pride. In the final move, Paul imagines that in time, even the natural branches, formerly separated, will be grafted back in. As in Romans 9, where mercy is the last word, here kindness and mercy have the stress. Paul describes what God is doing using the word for a secret revealed by God: a "mystery." The "hardening" will last until "the full number of the Gentiles has come in. And so all Israel will be saved." The motif, known from the prophets, that the faith of Israel would lead all nations to God takes an unexpected twist: here the disobedience of Israel leads to mercy for one community first, and then for all. The section concludes with a doxology, or hymn of praise to God, that draws on language from Isaiah and from Job. The lament in which Paul complained and wrestled with the attempt to know God's ways and justify them to humans ends with an exclamation of wonder at the impossibility of knowing God or the "mind of the Lord."

▌THE TEXT IN THE INTERPRETIVE TRADITION

What was for Paul an urgent question in the first century, the ultimate fate of Israel in the plan of God, was not an issue for the church fathers and other early interpreters. In their view, the church had replaced Israel as the elect. It was ongoing Jewish practice and belief that posed a threat to them, and with which they disputed. Indeed, in much of its history, Paul's warning against gentile arrogance actually was used to fuel Christian triumphalism! Paul's hopeful conclusion about God's regrafting Israel into the tree did not hold a central place in their reading of Romans. Augustine focused on and developed Paul's negative statements about Israel. Luther understood that his contemporaries, the Jews and the Roman Catholics, exemplified those who lived as God's people by works rather than grace. Forcible conversion of Jews was one response to his reading of Romans 11. Karl Barth interpreted "all Israel will be saved" as speaking of the church. Among contemporary scholars, some interpret "all Israel" to refer to the church and Jesus-believing Jews, while Dunn and others understand it to include Christians and Jews (Reasoner).

▌THE TEXT IN CONTEMPORARY DISCUSSION

It makes sense that in the contemporary reality of religious pluralism, Paul's argument in Romans 9–11, and in Rom. 11:13-36 in particular, is taken up as a model for Christian theological reflection on God's surprising and unpredictable plans for the salvation of the whole world. While Paul claims in 11:34-35 the impossibility of human attempts to know the mind of God, it is exactly this effort that he makes in these verses. He approaches the task by searching for patterns in the Scriptures of Israel, even patterns that undermine traditional patterns of expectation. In addition to drawing on Scripture, Paul calls on images from everyday life—foot-racing, bread making, and horticulture—to attempt to imagine how God can demonstrate both faithfulness to the past and creativity for the future. Paul's surrender to the impossibility of the attempt after his extended effort in the exclamation of praise in the concluding doxology testifies to both human theological creativity and the merciful creativity of God.

Romans 12:1-21: Exhortation to Holy Living

▌ THE TEXT IN ITS ANCIENT CONTEXT

Paul appeals to the audience to practice a particular manner of life based on the argument of Romans 1–11. Several elements tie the content of this exhortation back to the images and stories earlier in the letter. "By the mercies of God" recalls the multiple examples of God's mercy demonstrated in the stories of Pharaoh and others in Romans 9. God's expansive vision of inclusion of the gentiles finds its concrete expression in the life of the community by the exercise of Christian virtues that echo the teaching of Jesus. Out of concern for the whole body, members are to practice forbearance toward the scruples and weaknesses of others (12:14). The language of baptismal renewal from Romans 6–8 recurs in the vocabulary of transformation and renewal (12:2) and of "one body" (12:4-5). Paul weaves together liturgical traditions from the early house churches, the preaching of Jesus, and the ethical teaching of the prophetic and wisdom traditions in Scripture. It is not possible to untangle these strands of teaching. The appeals appear to be general rather than to any specific behavior in the Roman church.

The image of sacrifice underlies the opening appeal "to present your bodies as a living sacrifice" and evokes the complex of meanings surrounding the sacrificial system in ancient Israel. As the drama of Rom. 6:12-19 described the members presented to slavery or to righteousness, here the presentation of the "body," the whole sentient being in community, is made to God. The "spiritual" worship (NRSV) might also be translated "rational" worship (*logikē*) or the worship one owes as a rational being (Byrne). The living sacrifice and the rational worship stand in sharp contrast to the corrupt and perverse worship of the creature rather than the Creator described in Rom. 1:18-32. Paul draws on the prophets who insist on the alignment of ritual and ethics (Isa. 1:10-20; Jer. 6:20; Hosea 8:11-13; Amos 5:21-27).

Believers are not to conform themselves to the current age, but are through baptism (6:4) to be transformed. Renewed minds enable discernment of God's will and, by implication, right decisions about how to live. The ideal of controlled rational discernment here corrects the picture of chaotic depravity in Rom. 1:18-32. Paul warns against arrogance and urges sober assessment of oneself "according to the measure of faith that God has assigned" (12:3). The stress on right proportion and differentiation resembles Stoic teaching about moderation and temperance. The measured tone contrasts with the apocalyptic drama portrayed elsewhere in the letter. The sequence of imperatives to love, zeal, joy, followed by the instruction to "bless," echoes the sayings from Jesus' teaching, particularly those found in the Sermon on the Mount in Matthew 5. The prohibition against taking vengeance cites a text in Deut. 32:35 that restricts the exacting of punishment to God. One feeds one's hungry enemies and gives water to those who are hostile in order to shame them. As in Prov. 25:21-22, "heap burning coals on their heads" (Rom. 12:20) may imply that they will experience remorse in response to one's good deed.

▌The Text in the Interpretive Tradition

Paul's rationale for not taking vengeance—that one's forbearance to enemies would result in heaping "burning coals on their heads"—was interpreted in two directions by patristic commentators. John Chrysostom, on the one hand, understood Paul to mean that nonretaliation by Christians would have the effect of intensifying ultimate punishment by God toward enemies. Origen, Augustine, and Jerome, on the other hand, interpreted the heaping of burning coals to be a provocation to repentance, and hence to divine mercy for the enemies. Modern interpreters take parallel options, some taking the more generous approach: not taking vengeance gives enemies a chance to repent; and others taking the more severe one: that the righteous avoid vengeance so that God's vengeance on the unrighteous can be more severe.

▌The Text in Contemporary Discussion

The potent mixture of Jewish wisdom and prophetic traditions and the inheritance of Jesus' teaching in this rhetorically eloquent exhortation demonstrates the close kinship of what later has been known as "Jewish" and "Christian" teaching. The conviction, held in common by prophets and early Christian writers, that right worship and right action are necessarily aligned, is a basis for ethical and liturgical decision making. Paul's imperative "do not be conformed to this world" (12:2) provides an antidote to the counsel of submission in Rom. 13:1-7 that follows. The apocalyptic sense that this present age is passing away provides leverage for Christians to critique and resist the powers that be in their political context. The exhortation to rational formation and decision making assumes the ability to reason on the part of human beings. Unlike those accounts in Romans that assert human incapacity for doing good (Rom. 7:14-26), here the outlook for human transformation is more hopeful. While a flesh/spirit dualism operates powerfully in other parts of the argument, the presentation of the body here presents a picture of bodily existence as integrated with physical, spiritual, and intellectual dimensions.

Romans 13:1-14: Subjection to Governing Authorities

▌The Text in Its Ancient Context

Paul exhorts, "let every person be subject to the governing authorities." The address appears universal—the word translated "person" is literally "every soul." The tone is absolute as Paul claims that authorities on earth have a divine origin—they are appointed by God and have a purpose from

God. They are to be God's servants, to provoke fear of punishment and to execute God's judgment, symbolized by the sword. The language of the passage is replete with vocabulary of "order"—the roots *tasso-* and *tag-* mean "put," "place," "appoint," and the prefix *hyper* means "over." The symbolic universe assumed by these instructions is a hierarchical one in which human rulers rule with the authority of God, and the role of subordinates or citizens is to be ruled, to be subject, to take one's appointed place. "Fear," *phobos*, is the proper attitude to be shown by a subordinate to a superordinate. Elsewhere in the New Testament Epistles, commands to "be subject" are addressed to women, slaves, and children, who must behave as their appointed station requires (Col. 3:18—4:1; Eph. 5:21—6:9; Titus 2:1-10; 1 Pet. 2:18—3:7). The view of the world presented in Rom. 13:1-7 is closely paralleled in Hellenistic writings such as Wisdom and Josephus. God's judgment and wrath, which have played an important role in the narrative of the letter, are constructed as equivalent to the judgment of the authorities.

Historical-critical scholars have noted the tension, if not contradiction, between the perspective expressed here and Paul's view that the form of the world is passing away (1 Cor. 7:31) and that the rulers of the world are ignorant of the purposes of God (1 Cor. 2:6-8; 15:51-58). The counsel against resistance seems at odds with the exhortation not to conform to the world (Rom. 12:1-2). Some critics have evaluated the counsel to be so out of place that they judge that the passage is not a part of the original letter. Others try to conceive of a historical context in which such a counsel would have made sense. Within the context of imperial propaganda, Paul's instruction to pay taxes may have been made to ensure the safety of Jewish communities in Rome for whom tax revolts caused danger. Arguments about the historical context function to highlight Paul's statement as a historically specific and strategic instruction, rather than a generalizable principle about the relationship of church and state (Elliott 1997).

▌ The Text in the Interpretive Tradition

Discussion of this passage in the history of interpretation has been closely connected with the relationship of the interpreter's community with the political "authorities" of their own historical period. Most readers have had to grapple with the fact that although the text claims that there is an equivalence between the judgment of rulers and of God and that rulers are God's servants, this ideal is contradicted by experience—the experience of Christians under Roman rule in which martyrdom was the fate of many, the experience of blacks under apartheid in South Africa, African Americans under Jim Crow in the United States, and many others. Origen was disturbed by the claim that all governments are from God when some persecute believers (Reasoner, 130). He writes that "authority" can be misused and that God will judge those who violate the laws of God. Martyrdom is a means of overcoming evil governments. Since Luther identified Rom. 13:17 as the ultimate reference point for biblical teaching about the state and developed the doctrine of "two kingdoms," this text has been a center of controversy in theological discussion. For Luther, there were two ways for God's rule to be expressed: in the secular sphere, where the civic authorities ruled, and in the spiritual sphere, where the church ruled. On the basis of this passage, Luther opposed the peasant revolts in Germany. Karl Barth, on the other hand, rejected the equating of any political organization or ideology with the kingdom of God. For Barth, the state was evil, and all governments are under the judgment of God. Barth's insistence on the sovereignty of God above any civic authority appears to undercut the outward implication of the passage that civil authorities derive their legitimacy from God.

▌THE TEXT IN CONTEMPORARY DISCUSSION

The challenges raised by this text for contemporary interpreters come from the history of interpretation, particularly influenced by Luther, in which this text has been used to prohibit resistance or rebellion against state authority. In the "state theology" of South Africa in the time of apartheid, this text was the centerpiece of supporting and legitimizing apartheid and disallowing resistance (West). In order to dispute interpretations that read the text at face value for self-serving ends, engaged biblical scholars have employed different strategies to diffuse the text or to deploy its power in another direction. One strategy is to explain it as a realistic response to a dangerous political environment for Jews—to counsel quiescence for the sake of the safety of others. By contextualizing the text in a particular historical and social place, these readers relativize its absolute and universal-sounding claims. Another strategy is to place this counsel in the larger panorama of Paul's argument about nonretaliation, about overcoming evil with good (12:14-21), and within the wider framework of apocalyptic eschatology. For Christians living in contemporary situations of persecution, rather than being a text that prevents them from possible agency, the plea to be subject and the counsel that follows becomes a source of realism, caution, and hope in God's ultimate judgment against injustice (Tamez; Elliott 2008). Another approach is to recognize that the difficulty comes from the enormous distance between a worldview that sees the hierarchical political realm as a reflection of the hierarchical heavenly realm and a worldview built around democratic debate. Rather than affirming the exhortations to subordinates—citizens, wives, slaves, and children—to submit, readers will critique them on the basis of these democratic values.

Romans 14:1—15:13: Welcome One Another

▌THE TEXT IN ITS ANCIENT CONTEXT

Paul urges tolerance of diverse views and practices within the community by exhorting consideration of those whom he calls the "weak in faith." His rhetoric assumes that he counts himself among the "strong" (15:1), whom he urges not to pass judgment on those who take other positions about eating (15:2) and the observation of "days." It is not possible to identify precisely the early Christian parties or groups behind this dispute, nor is it certain whether Paul knows of specific disagreements about these matters in the church at Rome. One influential theory is that some believers returned to Rome who were more attached to the observance of Torah as part of Christian practice, and they came into conflict with those who did not practice dietary restrictions and other observances. However, vegetarianism, abstention from wine, and consideration of special "days" are not known to be part of Torah regulations. Those who reconstruct the disputes behind Paul's instructions here rely on controversies from other letters—over the eating of idol meat in 1 Corinthians 8–10, circumcision and feasts in Gal. 4:8-11 and Col. 2:20-23—although none of these provides a precise parallel.

Paul argues against judgmentalism on the basis of a series of theological rationales: that they should welcome one another because they have been welcomed by God, that the weak have the same lord/master as the strong (14:3-4), and that both groups do what they do out of full conviction and to honor the Lord (14:5-6).

The passage incorporates traditional elements from liturgical or wisdom settings; for example, 14:7-8 may be a hymn. The blessing/prayer wishes in 15:5-6, 13, 33, may also be traditional. Paul argues that the strong should refrain from eating or drinking in a manner that would injure another and destroy the "work of God," the community. One's own conviction, or one's "faith," makes the difference in discriminating what is sin. Paul cites Christ as a reason for tolerance, arguing that Ps. 69:9 refers to Christ's suffering rather than pleasing himself. Christ is the original source of "welcome" or acceptance. Returning to the theme of the reliability of God's promises and the story of Christ, Paul describes Christ as the servant of the circumcised whose ultimate purpose is the gentiles' glorification of God. A series of four scriptural quotations, from the Law, the Prophets, and the Writings (Ps. 17:50 LXX; Deut. 32:43 LXX; Ps. 117:1 LXX; Isa. 11:10 LXX), affirms Christ's purpose to bring gentiles to God. A prayer wish concludes the exhortation not to pass judgment, but to forbear, to act from faith, and to tolerate a range of diverse beliefs about matters of food and drink and calendar.

■ THE TEXT IN THE INTERPRETIVE TRADITION

Paul's appeal for tolerance, respect for the convictions of others, and inner commitment to one's own faith convictions in 14:1—15:13 has not been given the same attention in the history of interpretation that Romans 1–8 has received. Theologians who have been occupied with questions of predestination and free will have not found this moral exhortation to be of interest. The radical claims about faith in the earlier chapters of Romans appear to be compromised here with the focus on the needs of the "weak in faith." However, this section of the letter has received renewed attention because concern about how those with diverging opinions about Christian practice or belief can best live together is an urgent ethical issue in the current environment of diverse positions within the Christian community and without. In the context of the Roman Empire, this counsel of tolerance would have been an alternative value system (Elliott 2008).

■ THE TEXT IN CONTEMPORARY DISCUSSION

Contemporary interpreters who read Romans as primarily occupied with the relationship between peoples in God's plan for salvation and with holy relationships within the community have developed the principles and theological rationales that are elaborated here. For example, Neil Elliott speaks of this passage as conveying an "ethic of solidarity" in tension with the Roman imperial system of hierarchy and patronage (Elliott 2008). Kathy Ehrensperger shows how a feminist ethic of relationships overlaps with the perspectives of Romans 14. She identifies an ethic of "mutuality and accommodation" rather than hierarchy. As theologians have focused on the relationship between "belief" and "practice," Paul's concrete practical counsel is valued as offering a way of living out the claims of the gospel in a complex and diverse world.

Analysis of the composition of this chapter out of fragments of liturgical and philosophical tradition demonstrates how the commonplace maxim "no one lives unto himself" is incorporated into a letter of Paul and in light of the overarching christological arguments takes on new depth and meaning (O'Neill). The anthropology implied in the exhortation here, with its emphasis on conviction and personal commitment, appears to give human beings more control and intention to their actions than does the anthropology of Rom. 6:12-19, in which every human serves a master. The language of thralldom and slavery seems in contrast to the more rational implications of this quasi-Stoic counsel. In the course of history, interpreters have been drawn to one or the other view more strongly. The choice to interpret one or the other anthropology as primary is a decision that is made on theological, ethical, or political grounds.

Romans 15:14-33: Paul's Reasons for Writing, Plans to Visit Rome, and Delivery of the Collection

▮ THE TEXT IN ITS ANCIENT CONTEXT

These verses give information to reconstruct the "reasons for Romans" or the situation "behind" the letter. While appearing as informative "news" about his plans, the substance of this communication is highly symbolic and theological. Paul's travel and its rationale express his understanding of the relationship between Jews and gentiles and how he understands his identity and his purpose. Paul expresses confidence in the competence of the congregation. This friendship-strengthening rhetoric both reflects and fashions the relationship between the sender and receiver of the letter. At the same time as he underplays the letter as "writing rather boldly," Paul's self-description as a "minister of Christ Jesus to the Gentiles in the priestly service of the gospel of God, so that the offering of the Gentiles may be acceptable, sanctified by the Holy Spirit" (15:16) is a claim of unique status in God's mission. Using cultic language taken from the tradition of Israel's worship, Paul conveys his conviction that by his ministry, he is delivering the gentile believers in Christ as a holy offering to God. While he had begun the letter by saying that he is not ashamed, here Paul admits to having reason to "boast." As in 2 Cor. 2:12 and Gal. 3:5, the action of the Spirit in the community is accompanied by signs and wonders. The map of Paul's preaching extends in a full circle from Jerusalem to Illyricum on the east coast of the Adriatic Sea. The picture of the vast sweep of the gospel is less a reflection of Paul's own individual activity and more a theological portrayal of the inevitable progress of the good news.

Referring to his practice of not preaching where another person has begun the work of evangelism, Paul quotes from Isa. 52:15, words that refer to the work of the suffering servant. By borrowing the prophetic words to describe the recipients of his preaching who have "never been told" and "never heard," he makes an implied parallel between his ministry and that of the Servant of the Lord (Grieb). His missionary travels have occupied him until the present, when he will fulfill his long-held wish to visit them on his way to Spain. In ancient rhetoric, the expression "be sent on by you" may imply financial support. He speaks of his plan to deliver the collection from the churches of Macedonia and Achaia "with the poor among the saints at Jerusalem" (15:26).

The collection from the churches in Greece and its delivery and acceptance by the Jerusalem church represent economically the relationship between Jews and gentiles, the subject of the letter. By contributing to it, gentile churches demonstrate their gratitude to Jerusalem for the spiritual benefits that they have received, and by accepting it, the Jerusalem church acknowledges the rightful role of the gentile churches in God's promises. The successful delivery of the collection equals the confirmation and legitimization of Paul's own mission as apostle to the gentiles. He appeals for their prayers and asks that he be delivered from those unbelievers who would oppose him. Paul's letters refer to the collection for Jerusalem in 1 Cor. 16:1-4; 2 Cor. 8–9; and Gal. 2:10. The survey of Paul's plans concludes with a picture of the anticipated joyful union with the church at Rome.

▌ The Text in the Interpretive Tradition

Before the advent of historical criticism, interpreters took the attribution of the letters to Paul at face value and accepted the presentation of Paul as chief apostle in all the letters and in Acts of the Apostles as factual. Paul's centrality and uniqueness was taken for granted. In the view of modern biblical criticism, the canon of the New Testament gives evidence that the figure of Paul was given increasing authority in the second century. The addition of pseudonymous letters, 1, 2 Timothy and Titus, and the Acts of the Apostles, Luke's theological history of the church, combined to create the persona of Paul. As the rhetorical character of Paul's letters has come to be better appreciated, Paul's own statements about his missionary practice or the views of his opponents or his relationship with the congregation to whom he writes have come to be understood as statements that do not just reflect reality but also contribute to shaping it. Tensions between theological perspectives in the undisputed letters, Ephesians and Colossians, and the Pastoral Epistles were recognized and interpreted as showing the development of the Pauline tradition, the positions that claimed Paul as their authoritative source. Paul's own self-understanding, which he expresses here, while it may have been more complicated or even contested in his own time, came to be accepted by the church. In reconstructing the reasons for Romans, scholarly scenarios develop one or more aspects of what Paul says here: need for support from the church at Rome, fear of the rejection of the collection, or the danger of the mission to Spain.

▌ The Text in Contemporary Discussion

Contemporary interpreters have given attention to the collection for the poor in Jerusalem as a concrete practice that expressed the solidarity (*koinōnia*) of the gentile churches with the mother church in Jerusalem. Within the structure of patronage in the Roman Empire, the collection functioned to communicate an alternative structure of relationship and accountability. Economic exchange and distribution shows the power of economic relations to embody relationships of justice. The collection for Jerusalem provides a model for practices of solidarity that subvert conventional values and create an alternative community. If the collection was a "symbol of resistance and subversion" (Wan, 196) in the context of the Roman Empire, what might be analogous practices of economic solidarity in the current globalized economy?

Romans 16:1-27: Paul Commends Phoebe and Greets His Coworkers

◾ THE TEXT IN ITS ANCIENT CONTEXT

The letter to the Romans concludes with greetings from Paul to members of the church at Rome (16:1-16), a warning against those who cause division (16:17-20), additional greetings, and a doxology (16:25-27). Critics have questioned whether these elements were part of the original Letter to the Romans or were added at later points in its composition. While all editions of Romans contain chapter 16, in some manuscripts the doxology comes after 15:33. In addition to textual evidence, readers have questioned how Paul could have known so many individuals by name in a community that he has not visited. The theory that Romans 16 was not an original part of the letter is no longer widely accepted. Paul's greetings to other leaders and his amplification of their association serve to strengthen the bonds with the community at Rome and to enhance Paul's own reputation and reception. The twenty-six leaders named here give insight into the makeup of the early Christian missionary movement, particularly the activity of other prominent missionaries, and the role of women as leaders. The terms "coworker," "beloved," "relative," and "in the Lord" convey the collaborative role of these individuals in the mission. The women named by Paul are named independently (Mary), paired with a man (Prisca, Junia), paired with another woman (Tryphaena and Tryphosa), or called "mother" (of Rufus) and "sister" (of Nereus). Paul's commendation of Phoebe names her as a deacon, a term that refers to offering service and that later became a formal office. She is a *prostatis*, a benefactor, who has provided Paul and others financial support. Phoebe is the one who delivers the letter to Rome. Prisca and Aquila, a missionary pair who are also mentioned in Acts 18, have demonstrated bravery that has earned the gratitude of all the churches of the gentiles. Andronicus and Junia receive high praise as "prominent among the apostles" and who were "in Christ before I was" (16:7). Paul greets these named coworkers and includes "all the other saints who are with them" (16:15). Paul asks them to greet one another with a holy kiss, a sign of love exchanged in the assembly. Critics disagree about whether the harsh warning that appears to interrupt the series of greetings is original to Romans or was added by a later writer. Its harsh tone appears to be out of place in Romans; however, other letters of Paul include severe warnings in their closing verses: Gal. 6:12-13; Phil. 3:2; and 1 Cor. 16:22.

There is widespread agreement that the doxology which concludes the letter is not original. Textual evidence shows it occurring in different positions (being omitted or included after chap. 14, after chap. 15, or in both positions). Its language concerning "strengthening you" and the disclosing of a "mystery" resembles the language of Ephesians (Eph. 1:9; 3:3-4, 6, 9; 5:32; 6:19). It may have been composed by a later writer who understood Romans itself as part of the "prophetic writings." At the time of the assembling of the canon, the doxology was added as an emphatic response and conclusion to a letter that had attained significance and esteem.

◾ THE TEXT IN THE INTERPRETIVE TRADITION

In the history of interpretation, Paul's centrality was accepted as a given. The presence of other evangelists, missionaries, or apostles, though clearly spelled out here, were not memorialized or celebrated by the ongoing tradition of the church. While Paul habitually greets, thanks, and refers to his coworkers, the singularity of Paul, his independence, and uniqueness are remembered most insistently by the tradition. That among these twenty-six names are recorded the names of nine women, some with titles—"deacon," "benefactor," "apostle,"—and some with epithets—"coworker," "sister"—may account for the fact that this series of coworkers has been overlooked in the history of interpretation and minimized in majority scholarship. Because the exclusion of women from leadership became an element of orthodox teaching, the names of the women here and their participation in the early Christian mission became invisible. The female name *Junia* was amended in the manuscript tradition to the otherwise unattested male name *Junias* to conform to the norm that no women were apostles (Brooten 1977). Phoebe, likely the one who delivered the letter to Rome, becomes a footnote in the story of the Letter to the Romans. In the contest over the authoritative interpretation of Paul in the canon, the position of 1 Timothy, which requires women to learn with all submission (1 Tim. 2:11-13), prevails. The memory of Paul's commendation of Phoebe, deacon of the church at Cenchreae, or Junia, prominent among the apostles and in Christ before Paul himself, fades into obscurity.

▮ THE TEXT IN CONTEMPORARY DISCUSSION

As women have become conscious readers of Scripture and agents aware in the making of history, they have contributed to research into women in the Greco-Roman world and in Jewish and gentile Jesus movements. Readers have questioned the gender asymmetry encoded in Scripture and recognized its complicity in the maintenance of male superiority and female subordination in church and society. Reconstruction of early Christian history to include the presence and leadership of women has made it possible to read restrictive biblical texts differently and has recovered models and exemplars of women's leadership in the early period. Romans 16 gives rich evidence of a missionary movement of women and men in partnership, counters the view of the singular apostle, and nourishes the imagination for reenvisioning the *ecclesia* as a discipleship of equals (Kittredge 2012).

Works Cited

Briggs, Sheila. 1989. "Can an Enslaved God Liberate? Hermeneutical Reflections on Philippians 2:6-11." *Semeia* 47:137–53.

Brooten, Bernadette J. 1977. "Junia—Outstanding among the Apostles (Romans 16:7)." In *Women Priests: A Catholic Commentary on the Vatican Declaration*, edited by J. Leonard and Arlene Swidler. New York: Paulist.

———. 1996. *Love between Women: Early Christian Responses to Female Homo-eroticism*. Chicago: University of Chicago Press.

Byrne, Brendon J., SJ. 1996. *Romans*. Collegeville, MN: Liturgical Press.

Carroll, James. 2001. *Constantine's Sword: The Church and the Jews: A History*. Boston: Houghton Mifflin.

Cranfield, C. E. B. 1975. *The Epistle to the Romans*. Edinburgh: T&T Clark.

Eisenbaum, Pamela. 2004. "A Remedy for Having Been Born of Woman: Jesus, Gentiles, and Genealogy in Romans." *JBL* 123, no. 4:671–702.

Elliott, Neil. 1997. "Romans 13:1-7 in the Context of Roman Imperial Propaganda." In *Paul and Politics: Ekklesia, Israel, Imperium, Interpretation: Essays in Honor of Krister Stendahl*, edited by Richard A. Horsley. Harrisburg, PA: Bloomsbury T&T Clark.

———. 2008. *The Arrogance of Nations: Reading Romans in the Shadow of Empire.* Minneapolis: Fortress Press.

Ehrensperger, Kathy. 2004. *That We May Be Mutually Encouraged: Feminism and the New Perspective in Pauline studies.* New York: T&T Clark.

Gager, John G. 2000. *Reinventing Paul.* New York: Oxford University Press.

Georgi, Dieter. 1991. *Theocracy in Paul's Praxis and Theology.* Minneapolis, Fortress Press.

Glancy, Jennifer A. 2006. *Slavery in Early Christianity.* Minneapolis: Fortress Press.

Grieb, A. Katherine. 2002. *The Story of Romans: A Narrative Defense of God's Righteousness.* Louisville: Westminster John Knox.

Hays, Richard B. 1989. *Echoes of Scripture in the Letters of Paul.* New Haven: Yale University Press.

———. 1996. "The Moral World of the First Christians." *QR* 6, no. 4:13–30.

Jewett, Robert. 2007. *Romans: A Commentary.* Minneapolis: Fortress.

Kittredge, Cynthia Briggs. 1998. *Community and Authority: The Rhetoric of Obedience in the Pauline Tradition.* Harrisburg, PA: Trinity Press International.

———. 2012. "Feminist Approaches: Rethinking History and Resisting Ideologies." In *Studying Paul's Letters: Contemporary Perspectives and Methods*, edited by Joseph A. Marchal, 117–34. Minneapolis: Fortress Press.

Landau, Yehezkel. 2007. "An Interview with Krister Stendahl." *Harvard Divinity Bulletin* 35, no. 1: 29-31.

Levine, Amy-Jill. 2006. *The Misunderstood Jew: The Church and the Scandal of the Jewish Jesus.* San Francisco: HarperSanFrancisco.

McGinn, Sheila E. 2005. "Feminists and Paul in Romans 8:18-23: Toward a Theology of Creation." In *Gender, Tradition and Romans: Shared Ground, Uncertain Borders*, edited by C. Grenholm and D. Patte. New York: T&T Clark.

Nanos, Mark D. 1996. *The Mystery of Romans: The Jewish Context of Paul's Letter.* Minneapolis: Fortress Press.

———. 2011. "The Letter of Paul to the Romans." In *The Jewish Annotated New Testament: New Revised Standard Version Bible Translation*, edited by Amy-Jill Levine and Marc Z. Brettler. New York: Oxford University Press.

Nickelsburg, George W. E. 2003. *Ancient Judaism and Christian Origins: Diversity, Continuity, and Transformation.* Minneapolis: Fortress Press.

O'Neill, John Cochrane. 1975. *Paul's Letter to the Romans.* Baltimore: Penguin.

Patterson, Orlando. 1982. *Slavery and Social Death: A Comparative Study.* Cambridge, MA: Harvard University Press.

Reasoner, Mark. 2005. *Romans in Full Circle: A History of Interpretation.* Louisville: Westminster John Knox.

Ruether, Rosemary Radford. 1974. *Faith and Fratricide: The Theological Roots of Anti-Semitism.* New York: Seabury.

Sanders, E. P. 1977. *Paul and Palestinian Judaism: A Comparison of Patterns of Religion.* Philadelphia: Fortress Press.

Schüssler Fiorenza, Elisabeth. 2007. *The Power of the Word: Scripture and the Rhetoric of Empire.* Minneapolis: Fortress Press.

Steinmetz, David C. 1988. "Calvin and Abraham: The Interpretation of Romans 4 in the Sixteenth Century." *CH* 57, no. 4:443–55.

Stendahl, Krister. 1963. "Paul and the Introspective Conscience of the West." *Harvard Theological Review* 56:3, 199-215.

———. 1976. *Paul among Jews and Gentiles*. Philadelphia: Fortress Press.

Stowers, Stanley K. 1994. *A Rereading of Romans: Justice, Jews and Gentiles*. New Haven: Yale University Press.

Tamez, Elsa. 1993. *The Amnesty of Grace: Justification by Faith from a Latin American Perspective*. Translated by Sharon H. Ringe. Nashville: Abingdon.

Trible, Phyllis, and Letty Mandeville Russell. 2006. "Unto the Thousandth Generation." In *Hagar, Sarah, and Their Children: Jewish, Christian, and Muslim Perspectives*, edited by Phyllis Trible and Letty Mandeville Russell, 1–30. Louisville: Westminster John Knox.

Wan, Sze-Kar. 2000. "Collection for the Saints as Anticolonial Act." In *Paul and Politics: Ekklesia, Israel, Imperium, Interpretation. Essays in Honor of Krister Stendahl*, 191–215. Edited by Richard A. Horsley. Harrisburg, PA: Trinity Press International.

West, Gerald O. 2008. "Contending with the Bible: Biblical Interpretation as a Site of Struggle in South Africa." In *The Bible in the Public Square*, edited by Cynthia Briggs Kittredge, Ellen Bradshaw, and Jonathan Draper, 101–15. Minneapolis: Fortress Press.

1 CORINTHIANS

Laura S. Nasrallah

Introduction

First Corinthians is not the first letter that Paul and his coworkers wrote to those in Christ at Corinth (1 Cor. 5:9), but is part of a pattern of correspondence (7:1; 8:1; 12:1), oral reporting (1:11; 5:1), and visits from travelers (1:11; 4:7). This letter from Paul and Sosthenes to the community was penned from Ephesus (1 Cor. 16:8, 19) and dates to approximately 52 or 54 CE. The gift of the Corinthian correspondence, unique in the New Testament, is that it includes more than one authentic letter, allowing for historical reconstruction of a community's relationship with Paul over time. The letters collected in 2 Corinthians allow us to see that 1 Corinthians did not meet with universal success at Corinth. Second Corinthians 2:4, for example, mentions a letter of tears, and 2 Cor. 10:1—13:20 may be that letter of tears, in which Paul claims he has to act like a fool and boast. The passages 2 Cor. 2:14—6:13 and 7:2-4 together form an *apologia*, or defense, of Paul's apostleship. Because we have multiple letters to Corinth, we can glean more data and form a richer interpretation of productive struggle regarding ideas and practices over time between Paul and the Corinthians, between Paul and other traveling religious teachers, and, likely, among the Corinthians.

After nearly two millennia of study and commentaries on Paul's letters, the task of the commentator is more to curate what she or he thinks are important data and interpretations than to offer something new. But one contribution this commentary makes is that it joins other scholarly work that elucidates not what Paul meant in his communications with the Corinthians but the possible responses of the community in Christ. It considers what the participants in the *ekklēsia* had at hand in Roman Corinth theologically, religiously, politically, and socially. That is, what were the conditions out of which those in Christ developed their rituals and beliefs, made ethical and political choices, and evaluated Paul's critiques and suggestions?

Ekklēsia

If we move the focus away from Paul—ignoring the binary of whether he was a heroic apostle or a traitor to Christ's true message (the latter was Thomas Jefferson's view), and turn instead to the communities to which he wrote (Johnson-DeBaufre and Nasrallah), we must ask what *ekklēsia,* their word for themselves, may have meant. What did it signal about how their community worked or how they ideally envisioned themselves? Some have argued that the term is a translation of the Hebrew *qahal,* a congregation. Certainly, Jewish associations, which used the Greek term *synagōgē,* existed in the Diaspora and attracted gentile converts and allies. Some have argued that *ekklēsia* signals the similarity of these earliest communities in Christ to so-called voluntary associations—guilds of people who gathered based on their employment (a guild of textile workers, for instance)—whose community together included worship of a god, meals, and often financial contributions (Ascough et al.). Some have pointed out similarities to philosophical schools (Stowers 2011b). Recent scholarship has shown that many associations were quite small (Kloppenborg). We should not assume that those to whom Paul wrote understood themselves to be, or to be in the process of becoming, a tight-knit, unified community (Stowers, 2011c). Further, the common translation for *ekklēsia,* "church," risks picturing something anachronistic.

Those who heard the term *ekklēsia* in antiquity may have understood a range of meanings, but certainly a political, civic assembly would have been evoked in an urban context (to which Paul's letters are aimed, after all: Meeks 2003). The term in the classical period had referred to the democratic assembly of the city, usually made up of free adult male citizens. At the time of Paul's writings, political assemblies in Greek cities around the Roman Empire still bore the name *ekklēsiai,* or in the singular, *ekklēsia,* and still met to engage in democratic deliberation about what was best for their cities (Miller). Were the *ekklēsiai* to which Paul wrote places of democratic debate and deliberative discourse, of authoritative speeches and challenges to those speeches, of the busy roil of argument, struggle, and the testing of ideas (Schüssler Fiorenza 1987; 1993)?

In this short commentary, I use the term *ekklēsia* instead of church. I also avoid using the term "Christian," since applying it to Paul's letters would be anachronistic: the term was coined only approximately forty years after the writing of 1 Corinthians (see Pliny, *Ep.* 10.96; the statement in Acts 11:26 represents Luke's significantly later view). Moreover, while Paul had experienced an important change in identity, it was not to a known quantity called Christianity. Paul described himself as a Jew (e.g., Gal. 2:15)—a good Jew (Stendahl; Gager; Eisenbaum)—who had had a revelation of Christ and who was now called to communicate to "the nations" (NRSV: "Gentiles") about the righteousness of God that was available through faith (*pistis*) in this Christ (*christos,* the Greek translation of the Hebrew word that we render "Messiah" in English).

The Sociopolitical Context of Roman Corinth

To better understand the religious, political, and socioeconomic context within which the Corinthian *ekklēsia* developed their new identity in Christ, we must investigate Roman Corinth. In 146 BCE, the forces of the Roman general Mummius destroyed the city. It survived in a diminished form until Julius Caesar reestablished it as a Roman colony in 44 BCE, after which time it again emerged as a leader on the Peloponnesus. Corinth lay on a significant trade route in antiquity, on the isthmus connecting ancient Attica to the Peloponnesus. It nestled inland between its ports of Lechaion to the north and Kenchreai to the south, and near Isthmia, a town renowned for its quadrennial games. To transfer cargo from the Saronic Gulf to the southeast to the Gulf of Corinth to the northwest, ships had to negotiate with Corinth, unless they wanted to circumnavigate the Peloponnesus (Strabo, *Geog.* 8.6.20). Julius Caesar, Nero, and Herodes Atticus all attempted to dig a canal across the isthmus near Corinth, but failed, leaving it to Corinth to control a seven-meter-wide paved roadway (*diolkos*) that allowed oxen to drag ships or cargo across the narrow spit of land. Analysis of ceramic finds indicates Corinth's importance in trade (Slane).

Who made up the new, Roman Corinth? In literature of the first century BCE, the city is characterized by its tragic history and as a site of grief (Cicero, *Tusc.* 3.53; Nasrallah 2012). Some inhabitants remained in the region between 146 BCE and the city's refounding as a Roman colony in 44 BCE, but Corinth was largely resettled at that time. Unlike many Roman colonies, Corinth was repopulated not by military veterans but by ex-slaves. Numismatic evidence indicates that a mix of freedpersons—former slaves—and traders became leaders in Corinth upon the founding of the new colony (Spawforth). Although freedpersons were not usually eligible for magistracies, Caesar made exceptions for colonies he founded (Millis 2010; 2013; Williams). Thus some characterized the city as populated by "a mass of good-for-nothing slaves," in first-century-BCE poet Crinagoras's language (Harrill, 71; Spawforth, 169). Yet the rhetoric about low-status freedpersons may be precisely aimed to discredit the high-status freedpersons who emigrated to Corinth to take advantage of this commercial hub (Millis 2013).

Thus it may not be coincidental that in a letter to Corinth we find the only use in the New Testament of the technical term "freedperson" (*apeleutheros*, 7:22). Some freedmen in Corinth held high civic positions and the Forum was marked by the benefactions of ex-slaves. Paul's words "Let . . . those . . . who buy [be] as though they had no possessions, and those who deal with the world as though they had no dealings with it" (7:29-31) would have been particularly thought-provoking to Corinthians-in-Christ in an urban setting in which buying and dealings with the world were central to civic identity—and in which having been bought and later manumitted were part of the identity of local elites (Nasrallah 2013).

Ethnicity and Identity in Roman Corinth: The City and the *Ekklēsia*

Given this history, what about ethnicity in Roman Corinth? Paul writes as a Jew who both asserts and reframes his ethnicity (9:19-22) to a community that is largely gentile (e.g., 12:2). We should not be surprised that gentiles sometimes wished to affiliate with Jews and even to shift their ethnicity and to become Jewish (Lieu; Cohen). Although archaeological evidence of Jews at Corinth is late and meager (a poorly incised lintel that once read "Synagogue of the Hebrews"; an impost capital with three menorahs), Philo mentions Corinth as having a Jewish population (*Legat.* 281) and Josephus states that Vespasian sent six thousand Jews to Corinth to work as slaves in the canal across the isthmus that Nero was attempting (*J.W.* 3.540; Millis 2010).

Although those to whom Paul wrote at Corinth were mostly gentiles, their choice to affiliate with Jews in Christ meant a shift in their ethnicity. In 1 Cor. 10:1, Paul argues that "our fathers were all under the cloud," referring to the story of Moses leading them through the Red Sea, and thus writing gentiles into the story of Israel. Such shifts in, debates about, and reflections on ethnicity were not rare in Roman Corinth (Concannon); the historical and mythical prestige of the city's Greek past was highlighted, even in the Roman period, through monuments and through the dissemination of iconography associated with the myths of Corinth (Robinson). Yet the city's dominant Romanness is signaled by a vast majority of its public inscriptions that appear in Latin only (Millis 2010).

In 2 Corinthians, Paul fights opponents whom he mockingly calls "super-apostles," but in 1 Corinthians he struggles with the Corinthian community itself, or at least with some members of it. The cause of this struggle has been the subject of debate. A variety of theories have been presented regarding the theological-philosophical inclinations of these Corinthians in Christ and their interest in being "spiritual people." The thesis of F. C. Baur (1831) and others, of Judaizers or other Christian factions as outside opponents, has largely been left behind. In the mid-twentieth century, Walter Schmithals's theory that the Corinthian community tended toward "a pneumatic-libertine Gnosticism," which was at the same time Jewish, was popular. Hans Conzelmann qualified this by calling the Corinthians "proto-Gnostic," employed the label "Corinthian libertinism," and talked about their "enthusiastic individualism." More recent scholarship demonstrates that we cannot discover a pre-Christian "Gnosticism" that may have affected the Corinthians, as Schmithals maintained (Pétrement 1990; K. King).

Scholars have long characterized the Corinthians as gnostics, libertines, Judaizers, and especially individualists, concerned about their private spiritual success rather than that of the community. Such approaches assume that Paul's letter neutrally records events and that his viewpoint is normative (see Wire; Castelli; Schüssler Fiorenza 1999). Instead, 1 Corinthians should be investigated as part of a larger correspondence, some of which is lost to us, that provides data about a community that included men and women, poor persons and those at or above subsistence level, slaves and freedpersons and free, who sometimes accepted and sometimes resisted Paul's characterizations of them. The Corinthian correspondence indicates a context of deliberative debate as happened so often in the civic *ekklēsia*—of back and forth, of struggling together toward a better future. Paul's letters are written to particular communities about particular situations; they are not systematic theology or doctrine in their first instantiation. He uses his rhetorical arts to persuade the Corinthians, and we can use the letter to reconstruct vibrant debates at the very beginnings of what we have come to call Christianity.

Those debates were conducted as the appointed time was "growing short" (7:29-31; 15:51-57). Paul and the communities to which he wrote, like many who framed their lives in terms of Jewish apocalyptic thought, understood themselves to be awaiting the imminent end of the age and the *parousia* ("appearance") of Christ. Nonetheless, their attention is focused in this letter on things great and small: the resurrection of the body, what they should eat, whether they should have sex, to give a few examples.

Paul has been characterized as promoting faith over law and works. Readers often approach 1 Corinthians in light of Paul's emphasis on faith and as a letter enjoining early Christian morality.

Indeed, much of 1 Corinthians *is* about making ethical and practical choices in the world, and faith—faith in Christ, God's faithfulness, a concept that Paul explains in light of God's covenant with Abram (Gen 12:3; see Gal 3:6–18) and in the midst of a Jewish discussion about how God's faithfulness may or may not extend to "the nations," or gentiles—is central to Paul's letters. But when we look more closely, we realize that the binary of faith versus works may need dissolution and that the vague language of morality may not be adequate. Paul's writings about "morality" involve *practices* of communities in Christ, something we could even call "works." Is faith itself a matter of practice, or works? First Corinthians is, after all, very much about sex and eating, and even about whether Paul is owed a wage, as much as it is about things we might label more spiritual or faith-based: wisdom, spiritual gifts, and the resurrection.

The Text

The complex work of reconstructing the Corinthians in Christ is made somewhat easier because, other than some arguments about the place of 1 Corinthians 15 in the letter, most scholars agree that 1 Corinthians is a unified letter. In addition, it has few text-critical issues: its Greek text is remarkably uniform in various manuscripts (Fitzmyer, 63). It employs deliberative rhetoric (Conzelmann; Schüssler Fiorenza 1987; Mitchell 1991), the "political address of recommendation and dissuasion" that focuses on the future time as its subject of deliberation, urging audiences to pursue a course of action for the future, and often employs language of concord or harmony (Mitchell 1991).

Outline of the Letter

Chapters 1–4 of the letter contain the greeting and the *stasis*, or main point of the letter, and are characterized by a discussion of wisdom and an argument regarding how the Corinthians ought to think of themselves: they are not quite as spiritual as they thought themselves to be. In 5:1—11:1, Paul discusses particular case studies in ethical and theological practice, treating especially themes of sex and eating, as well as discussing the marital, ethnic, and social conditions in which persons may have been "called" to be in Christ. In 11:2—14:40, Paul treats further issues of practice in the *ekklēsia*, ranking the spiritual gifts the community experienced and seeking to control their use. Paul grounds these discussions in the political rhetoric of unity and "one body." In chapter 15, Paul turns to the topic of the resurrection of the dead, bringing together the cosmological hints about wisdom and the cosmos in chapters 1–4, together with concerns about the body's purity and practices in 5—11:1 and interest in the spiritual in 11:2—14:40. The epistolary closing comes in chapter 16.

Conclusions

According to the style of this volume, each section of my commentary on 1 Corinthians will be divided into three subsections: "the text in its ancient context," "the text in the interpretive tradition," and "the text in contemporary discussion." These divisions are heuristic. We should not think we have access to an ancient context that is pure data, neither disturbed nor enriched by our contemporary situations and by the long interpretative tradition. There is no true division between what the text meant and what it means today. Rather, we can use our locations of interpretation to open new questions about these ancient texts, and we can turn a critical eye to the limitations of our own locations. That is, we should approach the text with a *disciplined intimacy*, acknowledging the feeling of closeness that we may have with this text, whether as Christians, or because the text communicates important and recognizable ethical or political injunctions, or on account of the sheer pleasure of discovering something about ancient history. But we should also pursue the discipline of distance, acknowledging that the text was written in a time, language, and context not our own and that its values and injunctions, as well as the conditions of the social, political, and economic world in which it was produced, may surprise us.

1:1-17: Letter Writing and Community

◼ The Text in Its Ancient Context

As is typical of ancient letters, 1 Corinthians begins with the *superscriptio*: "Paul, called to be an apostle of Christ Jesus by the will of God" (1:1). In other letters, Paul begins by introducing himself as "Paul, slave [*doulos*, sometimes translated more weakly as "servant"] of Jesus Christ" (Rom. 1:1, a letter in which he likely recommends himself to a community he doesn't know; see also Phil. 1:1) or "Paul, prisoner" (Philem. 1:1). The comparatively forceful *superscriptio* here introduces two key issues that follow in the letter. The first is the term *klētos*, "called" or "chosen." The letter uses this term and its cognates to talk about Paul's and the Corinthians' status. The addressees are described as "*chosen* holy ones" (1:2); "you were *called* into the fellowship of his [God's] son" (1:9). The issue of "calling" arises again in chapter 7. The second is the term *apostolos*, "one who is sent." As the letter ends, in 1 Cor. 15:9, Paul calls himself "least of the apostles," "unfit *to be called* an apostle," yet elsewhere in the letter he asserts his role as laying a foundation (3:10) and as a father (4:14-21), as well as his ability to shape-shift depending on audience (9:19-22).

If we look more closely at the *superscriptio* of this letter and others, we see that the majority are cowritten: Silvanus and Timothy are cowriters of 1 Thessalonians; Timothy again is cowriter of the Letter to the Philippians. Romans 16:22 reveals an amanuensis: "I, Tertius, the writer of this letter, greet you in the Lord." In addition, some delivered letters and traveled on behalf of Paul and various *ekklēsiai*, such as Timothy and Epaphroditus. First Corinthians is cowritten by Sosthenes, "brother." These are not just the letters of Paul; they invoke and evoke an entire network of writers, deliverers, and readers. The writing desk becomes crowded with coworkers and perhaps slaves and freedmen, former slaves, since people of such status were often responsible for penning and delivering letters (Mouritsen).

The extended sentence, which is also a statement of thanksgiving (1:4-8), reveals four key issues of the letter. *Charis* (v. 4), often translated "grace," also means "favor" or "delight." A form of this word appears again at verse 7, *charisma*, often translated "spiritual gift": the idea of gifts of God or God's grace, and the question of how these "gifts" should be used and ranked, become key issues in chapters 11–14. Second, the word *eploutisthēte*, "you were enriched," appears in verse 5; the letter will later challenge the Corinthians precisely on issues of spiritual and material wealth and poverty. Paul will characterize the Corinthians as "what is low and despised in this world" (1:28). Mention of hunger and of some who "have not" indicates that some within the Corinthian community are poor (11:22). Third, the phrase "in speech [*logos*] and knowledge [*gnōsis*] of every kind" (1:5) signals debates about lofty or lowly speech and about what truly constitutes knowledge (1 Corinthians 1–4; 13:2, 9, 12). Fourth, verse 8 signals the letter's concern with the end time (the "day of the Lord"), a theme that arises especially at 1 Cor. 7:29-31 ("time growing short") and in the discussion in 1 Corinthians 15 of material transformation and the last trumpet. Grace and gifts, poverty and wealth literal and metaphorical, word or speech and knowledge, and the coming day of the Lord: these four themes, introduced early in the letter in the traditional epistolary location for a prayer or thanksgiving, will weave their way throughout this letter.

The *stasis*, or main point of the letter, emerges at 1 Cor. 1:10: "Now I appeal to you, brothers and sisters, by the name of our Lord Jesus Christ, that all of you be in agreement and that there be no divisions among you, but that you be united [or "reconciled"] in the same mind and the same purpose." Some take this thesis statement as Paul's description of a historical fact and have attempted to outline various "factions" of the community, following on Paul's characterization of the community as stating "I belong to Apollos" or "I belong to Paul," based on whomever had baptized them. But we do not know if all the Corinthians would have accepted Paul's assessment, and indeed, it seems that Paul has to argue rather hard for his role as the one who "planted" the community (1 Cor. 3:4-23). His arguments may have met with little success, given his admission that others have successfully influenced the community at Corinth (2 Corinthians). Paul turns from this interest in baptism (which will appear elsewhere in the letter) to emphasize "the cross of Christ" and Paul's own preaching, which happens "not in persuasive words of wisdom but in a demonstration of spirit and power" (2:4).

▌ The Text in the Interpretive Tradition

John Chrysostom, a church leader from Antioch, was made archbishop of Constantinople in 397 CE. A well-known champion of Paul (Mitchell 2002), Chrysostom in some ways set forth what would become the mainstream Protestant understanding of a humble, suffering Paul among other apostles. Chrysostom focused on 1 Cor. 1:12 ("I belong to Paul . . .") and emphasized that Paul placed Peter last in this sequence to give Peter greater honor, despising any glory for himself. Chrysostom celebrated Paul's lack of eloquence in good homiletic fashion, with an anecdote: he once heard a "Greek" and a Christian arguing about whether Plato or Paul was superior. The Christian was wrong, Chrysostom argued, in trying "to establish that Paul was more learned than Plato." "For if Paul was uneducated and defeated Plato, the victory (as I have said) was glorious. . . . from this is it clear that his preaching has prevailed not by human wisdom but by the grace of God" (*Hom.* 3; Kovacs, 20–21). Chrysostom emphasizes the uneducated and common nature of early Christians, using Paul as a focal point to develop a well-known Christian trope, geographically widespread, that Christian identity was rooted in humble fishermen yet now elevated even women, fishermen, and the ignorant to a philosophical life (the Syrian Tatian, *Ad gr.* 32.1–3; the Carthaginian Tertullian, *De an.* 3; the Alexandrian Origen, *C. Cels.* 3.44, 50). Paul's rhetoric in 1 Corinthians concerning his own ineloquence and his inversion of wisdom and folly fit well with early Christian self-definition as simple and humble, yet triumphing over the sophistication of the world, even though the early

Christian men who used this trope were themselves quite sophisticated, educated, and powerful. Many Christians today, too, stand in an ambivalent relationship to certain forms of education and knowledge; it may be helpful to recognize that sometimes it is those who are well-educated who use the powerful persuasive trope of Christian simplicity and revelation.

■ The Text in Contemporary Discussion

The Second Vatican Council's "Decree on Ecumenism, *Unitatis redintegratio*" alludes to 1 Cor. 1:13 at its beginning.

> The restoration of unity among all Christians is one of the principal concerns of the Second Vatican Council. Christ the Lord founded one Church and one Church only. However, many Christian communions present themselves to men as the true inheritors of Jesus Christ; all indeed profess to be followers of the Lord but differ in mind and go their different ways, *as if Christ Himself were divided.* ("Decree on Ecumenism, *Unitatis redintegratio* 1)

More recently, the World Council of Churches has declared as the theme for the "Week of Prayer for Christian Unity" the question, "Has Christ been divided?" (1 Cor. 1:1-17).

Paul's evaluation that the Corinthians were divided and his injunction that they must be unified in one body was powerful in the past and is powerful today. This letter's language of unity draws from common political tropes of its time. *Homonoia* in Greek and *concordia* in Latin were terms used by various cities of the Greek East, for example on their coins, to assert a harmony that was the hard-won result of civic power plays. Paul's rhetoric of "one body" takes part in a broader discourse of unity that we know from the political rhetoric of the early Roman Empire (Mitchell 1991). Yet, today, in reading this rhetoric of unity in 1 Corinthians both scholarly and Christian communities often take for granted that Paul's characterization of Corinthian schism was an accurate description of problems at Corinth and do not inquire whether the Corinthians might have disagreed. Rhetoric of schism and unity is powerful whether in antiquity or today; it can be used to affirm community, but it also can be used to exclude or shame those who disagree.

1 Corinthians 1:18—4:21: Spirit and Wisdom

■ The Text in Its Ancient Context

The first four chapters of the letter move contrapuntally among the themes of Paul's role, the Corinthians' identity, spirit, and wisdom. The theme of wisdom was likely part of a long-standing conversation that was ongoing among the Corinthians in Christ; in this letter we find the term "wisdom" (*sophia*) seventeen times in contrast to its scant appearance elsewhere in Paul's genuine epistles (once in Romans and once in 2 Corinthians); so, too, *sophos* ("wise") appears eleven times in 1 Corinthians and four times in Romans, among the Pauline Epistles. Paul's letters reflect and discuss topics important to those to whom he wrote: obviously wisdom was a major theme among those at Corinth (Koester, 55–62). Paul takes an instructive tone in these chapters, one that might lead us to think that the Corinthians did not know much about wisdom or knowledge. Yet chapters 11–14 indicate that the Corinthians engaged in community practices that embodied and demonstrated their links to spirit and wisdom through "spiritual gifts." (I here leave the term "spirit" uncapitalized so that we do not read it through the lens of later Trinitarian ideas.)

Paul uses the rhetorical technique of developing his *ēthos*; that is, as Aristotle discusses it (*Rhet.* 1.2.1356a.4–12), the speaker describes himself in such a way as to make the audience sympathetic to him. Paul says that he did not come offering a testimony with lofty words or wisdom (2:1); he elaborates the common trope in which an orator talks about the simplicity and lack of education of his words over and against others—a simplicity and lack of education that then lends authenticity, truth, and power to his writing or speech. But Paul also may be making lemonade out of a lemon, since his opponents, it seems, characterize his person and speech in person as "weak" and "nothing" (2 Cor. 10:10). Paul places as central "Jesus Christ, and him crucified" (2:2), a "stumbling block" and weakness and scandal; Paul's juxtaposition of his own weakness with Christ's paradoxically elevates Paul: he is like Christ. In addition, with this language he may align himself with some in the community who are being called "weak," who are less educated and have concerns about being invaded by external, polluting forces.

First Corinthians 1:18—4:21 focuses on wisdom, yet questions what it (or she—the word is feminine in Greek: see below) truly is. Paul has just mentioned his role not as baptizer but as someone who preaches the gospel "not with wisdom," "lest the cross of Christ be emptied." Here the historical datum of the cross—a shameful criminal execution that predates the writing of this letter by only twenty years or so—is laid on a cosmological scale. It is understood to represent "the power of God" (1:18). Paul asserts—or perhaps admits—that the "word" (the term *logos* in Greek can mean "word," "speech," or "reason") of the cross is folly. The letter troubles the common sense that wisdom is good while folly is bad. The wisdom and folly of this world or universe (*tou kosmou*, 1:20, 28; also *kata sarka*, "according to flesh," 1:26; and *tou aiōnos toutou*, "of this age," 1:20, referring to the "debater") are contrasted to the wisdom and folly of God. The two are inversely related: God has made foolish the wisdom of this world (1:20); "what we preach" is in fact folly (*mōria*, 1:21).

Because of the emphasis on wisdom and knowledge (*gnōsis*), as well as the labels *sarkikoi or sarkinoi, psychikoi*, and *pneumatikoi*—that is, Paul's labeling certain people according to the terms "flesh," "soul," and "spirit"—in these early chapters of 1 Corinthians, twentieth-century scholars hypothesized either that the Corinthians were "gnostics" or that they were influenced by "gnostic" missionaries (Schmithals). But the language of wisdom and knowledge is not only found in materials we might label "gnostic"—for example, the texts found at Nag Hammadi and the points of view polemically treated by writers like Irenaeus and others—but also in Jewish texts that speculate about the creation of humans (esp. Gen. 2:7), divine inbreathing at creation, and the human potential for knowledge, wisdom, and being like God. Moreover, "Gnosticism" was not an established or unified school in the first century. The term itself is a later invention emerging from early Christian polemics, then reified in modern scholarship (K. King).

The language of wisdom at Corinth emerges in a context of many traditions that honored wisdom and knowledge in the ancient world, whether Jews, members of philosophical schools, or those who honored a goddess like Isis; it emerged in the context of rich philosophical debates and diverse stories about the creation of the world, including much debate over the interpretation of

Plato's *Timaeus*. Paul and the Corinthians perhaps had different understandings of the terminology of wisdom and knowledge, of flesh, soul, and spirit. But in their deployment of such language they stood in a conversation that preceded and would follow them about how creation happened and whether and how humans might know the divine in the present, as Jews and Christians alike debated the meaning and significance of a creation out of the clay or earth in Genesis 2 and reference to creation of the human in God's image in Genesis 1. Such Jewish and Christian debates about wisdom and knowledge, about flesh, soul, and spirit, happened in the context of a culture that produced images of the gods in human form, and happened in conversation with Greek philosophical texts and with the strong traditions of wisdom theology in Judaism, characterized by texts like Ben Sira and the Wisdom of Solomon, among many others.

Scholars have long situated 1 Corinthians within Hellenistic Jewish discourses on wisdom (e.g., Wilckens; Horsley; Sterling). There must have been at Corinth deep and rich debates about the nature of God and creation, about how God works and is manifest in the world, which drew from the wisdom theologies of Judaism. Proverbs 8:22 offers a famously clear statement of Wisdom personified as cocreator of the world with God (the Greek word *sophia* is grammatically feminine; see also Philo, *Cher.* 49 on God as "the husband of Sophia"). Other traditions, exemplified in the early-first-century CE Jewish writer Philo of Alexandria, seem to understand Sophia and Logos as related or interchangeable figures who are divine characters themselves; Philo talks about the Logos of God as the instrument by which God made creation (*Cher.* 127); elsewhere, the Logos is the image of God, in closest proximity to God, and the "charioteer" above all the other divine powers (*Fug.* 100; see also Philo, *Post.* 78; *Fug.* 97; Horsley 1979; Grabbe; Boyarin 2001).

Some (or many) within the Corinthian *ekklēsia* likely considered Sophia—Wisdom personified—to be a power of God that was significant for their theology and for their understanding of themselves. Jesus as Sophia or as a prophet of Sophia is well attested in earliest Gospel traditions (e.g., Luke 7:34-36; Lamp; Schüssler Fiorenza 1994; Johnson-DeBaufre). In 1 Cor. 2:9, we find a quotation that alludes to the Jewish Scriptures and bears a striking resemblance to *Gospel of Thomas* 17 (see also Q/ Lk 10:23-24; Koester, 58–59; Conzelmann, 63–64). Thus the Corinthians and Paul may have shared a source of Jesus sayings that involved wisdom, and perhaps they knew of theological traditions that employed terminology of hiddenness and revelation (see also 1 Cor. 2:7, 10; 3:13; 4:5; Koester, 55–56).

Indeed, the Corinthians may have understood Christ as Wisdom. Paul emphasizes Christ terminology instead and debates the meaning of *sophia*. For Paul, wisdom is not a divine power to be reckoned with, or a power that helps to perfect humans and render them friends of God, as she is depicted in the Wisdom of Solomon (from Alexandria, perhaps first century CE). Wisdom as cocreator of the world leaves only a faint trace in 1 Corinthians.

At Corinth, Wisdom is understood not only in terms of cosmology and theology but also in terms of sociology. The question of who has true wisdom and knowledge percolates throughout the letter. Paul extends a challenge: "Where is the one who is wise?" (1:20). In 1 Cor. 2:6, Paul renders wisdom into something he and others can impart, and only to the "perfect" or "initiates" (*teleioi*).

Paul discusses wisdom in ethnic terms in 1:22: *Ioudaioi* (which we can translate "Jews" or "Judeans"; see Cohen; Hodge) "ask for signs and Greeks seek wisdom." How might Paul's characterization of ethnicity have gone over in Roman Corinth, with its famed Greek heritage, its new Roman status? In this passage, Paul proposes an alternative mixed ethnicity for the *ekklēsia* in Christ at Corinth, aligning them with "those who are the called [*klētoi*], both Jews and Greeks" (1:24). Paul defines the identity of the *ekklēsia* at Corinth as a chosenness that brings Jews and Greeks together.

The community may have understood itself as wise, as "called," and also as *teleioi*, which can be translated "perfect" or "complete" and is also the term for "initiates." "Yet among the *teleioi* we do speak wisdom . . . God's wisdom, secret and hidden, which God decreed before the ages," Paul declares (2:6-7). A Corinthian hearing this might reasonably think that she or he is one of the "perfect" who has received the spirit from God, rather than the "spirit of this cosmos" or world (2:12). Later in the letter it becomes clear that Corinthians engaged in practices of *pneumatika*, spiritual things or spiritual gifts (1 Corinthians 12–14). But Paul introduces another label: the *psychikos*, the "soul" person, who doesn't discern things as the *pneumatikos*, or "spirit person," does (2:14-15). Certainly any reader or hearer of the passage would prefer to fall into the "perfect" and "spiritual" category. The news gets worse: Paul states that he had to address them as *sarkinoi*, "flesh people" (3:1), feeding them only milk. Not only was this true in the past, but also "you are still of the flesh" (3:3) because of "strife" and claims like "I am of Paul, I am of Apollos."

Paul's accusation of dissension because of Corinthian attachment to one apostle or another reprises the thesis of the letter and allows him to segue again to the issue of apostleship and leadership that he had raised earlier (1 Cor. 1:10-16). In 3:5—4:21, he continues to raise questions about the roles he and Apollos played in the community; he depicts himself and Apollos in the language of household managers (3:5: *diakonoi*; 4:1: *hypēretas* and *oikonomous*). These roles are often taken by high-status slaves or freedpersons who have risen in the ranks of a household, promoted by their masters to more authoritative roles (Martin 1990). The Corinthians are depicted as passive, as a field to be planted or as something to be built (Wire).

Paul goes on to depict active, suffering apostles in contradistinction to the Corinthians. The apostles are "as though sentenced to death, because we have become a spectacle to the world, to angels and to mortals" (4:9). The language of death sentence and spectacle reminds us of the very real Roman practice of putting people to death and of spectacle (Frilingos), yet Paul's image does not limit itself to the Roman imperial context; the image he gives is of cosmic battle (so also at 2:8, "rulers of this age"). He contrasts the apostles' role as "refuse of the cosmos" (4:13) to the Corinthians, who are enriched and have come to reign (4:8). The apostles are "fools for the sake of Christ, but you are wise in Christ" (4:10).

Given the language of reversal that has already occurred regarding true wisdom and God's foolishness, the Corinthians would do well to be suspicious of this seeming praise. Indeed, Paul makes it explicit that he speaks to them as "beloved children" in need of admonition and he suggests to them that he is their sole father in the midst of many guides (4:15), a father who might come "with a stick" rather than "with love" (4:21). From chapter 1 to the end of chapter 4, leadership and authority in the Corinthian community has been reduced from four examples of possible mystagogues or leaders ("I am of Cephas," "I am of Apollos," "I am of Paul," "I am of Christ") to two (Paul and Apollos), to one, in his framing of himself as the singular father.

■ The Text in the Interpretive Tradition

Later Christians often used and debated the meaning of the discussion in 1 Corinthians 1–4 of wisdom and knowledge, as well as the question of which humans could be "spiritual," which "psychic" (from the term *psychē*, "soul," not to be confused with our modern meaning of the term!), and which "fleshly" (or, later, "hylic" or "material"). In the decades and centuries after Paul wrote, Christians wished to be *gnostikoi*, which we could woodenly translate "gnostics," but given the historical misuse of that term, perhaps "in the know" is a better translation. They wished to be *pneumatikoi*, spiritual people. These were values common to the ancient world and indeed today.

In the late second century CE, Irenaeus, a Christian writer in Gaul, would accuse some Christians, whom he said were "followers of Valentinus" (a Christian philosopher-theologian who likely lived a few decades prior) of a kind of determinism that assigned people to a certain fixed category, that would gut any motivations for ethical behavior, and that would limit salvation (*Adv. haer.* 1.6.2). In a Christian text such as the *Tripartite Tractate*, found among the so-called gnostic materials at Nag Hammadi, we find the statement:

> Now, humanity came to be according to three essential types—spiritual, physical, and material—reproducing the pattern of the three kinds of dispositions of the Logos, from which sprung material, physical, and spiritual beings. The essences of the three kinds can each be known by its fruit. (*Tripartite Tractate* 118.14–29, in Kocar 2013)

While Irenaeus would accuse such Christians of a determinism that condemned some humans to a permanent state of ignorance of the Father and no possibility of salvation, closer investigation of the *Tripartite Tractate* or indeed Irenaeus himself shows that Paul's writings in 1 Corinthians 1–4 instead inspired a great deal of later theological controversy over what constituted correct Christian practice and thinking, and how one could attain to the status of being spiritual or "in the know," truly *gnostikos*.

We find further evidence of how 1 Corinthians inspired later debates about wisdom in Origen, for example, who in the late second century or early third century explained that what is meant by the "wisdom of the rulers of this world" are the secret and hidden philosophies, astrologies, and magi of various nations, which may lead to demonic invasion. Christians, in contrast, are purified by abstinence and pure practices and receive prophecy and gifts in this way (*De princ.* 3.3). In the early sixth century, someone who took up the name of Dionysius the Areopagite (according to Acts, a convert at Athens after he heard Paul's speech there) and used Paul's language of Greeks seeking wisdom to rehabilitate the truth of Greek philosophy for Christian purposes (Stang, 148–50). A variety of Christians found in 1 Corinthians' language of wisdom and knowledge a foundation from which to debate who could access such wisdom and knowledge and how.

■ The Text in Contemporary Discussion

The November 1993 conference "Re-Imagining: A Global Theological Conference by Women: for Men and Women" was an ecumenical meeting largely organized by U.S. Protestant denominations as part of the World Council of Churches' larger "Ecumenical Decade: Churches in Solidarity with Women," begun in 1988. The repeated chant "Bless Sophia" at this conference, among other things, led to accusations of goddess worship. Organizers are said to have grounded their emphasis on Sophia through recourse to Scriptures in Proverbs, Luke, and 1 Corinthians. Accusations that Sophia rather than Jesus was set forth as a "divine revealer" and concerns that Sophia was elevated to a divine level indicate that some ancient communities in Christ were more flexible and expansive in their Christology and theology than modern communities. We can think, for example, of language of Jesus as "the Sophia of God" in 1 Cor. 1:24 or of the flexibility of ancient Jewish and Christian traditions that describe a Sophia who existed at the beginning of the world with God and created the world with God. An emphasis on Wisdom or Sophia can be controversial in any age, even if canonical texts present Sophia as cocreator with God or as attribute of God, as a figure who sends out prophets like Jesus, and as a divine figure instantiated by Jesus. A theology—thealogy, we could say, emphasizing the possibilities of thinking of a God who transcends gender and/or is sometimes thought of in feminine terms—that takes into account the traditions of Sophia can support two kinds of work. First, it can undergird the work of those theologians, whether ancient or contemporary, who point out that attempts to name God definitively as Father or Mother or to fix our idea of God too firmly are idolatrous. Second, taking into account ancient traditions of Sophia in Judaism and Christianity can aid those who argue for women's leadership in Christian communities.

1 Corinthians 5:1—6:11 Insiders, Outsiders, and Judgment

▌THE TEXT IN ITS ANCIENT CONTEXT

Paul has introduced the idea that the Corinthians are not at the highest state of completion or initiation (*teleioi*) as spiritual people (*pneumatikoi*) and that he as father can correct them with love or with a stick (1 Cor. 4:21). In the pages that follow, Paul expands on the bad news that the Corinthians are not, in his opinion, at the level of spiritual or wise or perfected people. Paul treats particular examples of Corinthian practices that he seeks to correct.

He speaks against *porneia*, a broad term in the ancient world that the NRSV translates "immorality," but that among Jewish and Christian writings has tinges of sexual sin and of idolatry, which is often also sexualized as an improper relationship of a nation with a false god (see, e.g., Hosea 4:11; Revelation 17; Rom. 1:22-32). The theme of *porneia* echoes throughout the passage and reaches its apex in two vice lists at 5:9-11 and 6:9-10, lists that represent cultural understandings of disorder in the world and are typical discourse at the time, whether among those we would label Jews or those we would label Greco-Roman writers. On the one hand, Paul insists that the Corinthians were previously *pornoi* (NRSV: "fornicators") and idolaters (6:9); on the other hand, he describes them as "washed, made holy, made just [or righteous] in the name of the Lord Jesus Christ and in the spirit of our God" (6:11). This new state is called into question by the presence of some who are still *pornoi* among them, and the dangers of idolatry loom large in the following chapters.

Paul's first example is a man who "has" (a sexual euphemism) his father's wife, presumably his stepmother. This discussion of *porneia* reveals something larger about how Paul frames the community's identity. First, he roots the *ekklēsia* at Corinth in a Jewish identity by stating derogatorily that they have *porneia* among them that is not even found among "the nations" (5:1). Framing the man's sin as a contagion that can permeate the community like leaven that "puffs up" a lump of dough, he introduces the idea of Christ as Paschal sacrifice, indicating that he and/or those at Corinth followed early traditions (as in the Gospel of John) of Jesus as having been crucified on Passover. Paul's metaphor also assumes that the community will understand basic Passover practices. Second, Paul introduces explicitly the theme of insiders and outsiders. A quotation from Deut. 17:7, "Drive out the wicked person from among you" (5:13), not only shows that Paul expects the community at Corinth to make sense of references to Scripture, but also makes the point that it's God's business to worry about "those outside" and the Corinthians' business to worry about those "among" or "inside," a theme that will arise again with the question of outsiders' response to speaking in tongues (14:24-25). In 5:3-5, Paul suggests that when those in Christ at Corinth assemble, Paul's spirit is present and the community should deliver the man to Satan so that the man's flesh will be destroyed, but his spirit saved "in the day of our Lord" (5:5). What sort of ritual is imagined is unclear (perhaps even a death penalty? Gaca, 140), but the theme of spirit clearly carries through from the first four chapters into the rest of the letter, in which spiritual gifts are discussed as well as the idea of spiritual bodies.

From the case of the man with his stepmother emerges a larger point about judgment. Paul emphasizes that the Corinthians should be concerned with what is happening inside the community and with adjudicating—"judging"—things there. From the relatively mundane case at hand emerges a larger cosmological vision: the holy ones (*hagioi*, a term Paul and Sosthenes had applied to the Corinthians in 1:2) will judge the cosmos and the angels (6:2-3).

▌ THE TEXT IN THE INTERPRETIVE TRADITION

John Calvin's mid-sixteenth-century commentary on 1 and 2 Corinthians eruditely surveys early church fathers' interpretations of these epistles, as well as offering his opinion, which is marked by the rise of the Protestant Reformation, in which Calvin was a key figure. The insider-outsider language of 1 Corinthians is transferred to his contemporaneous situation of Protestant-Catholic relations and shows the malleability of Paul's text for various situations. Calvin notes that the passage about leaven and the true Passover "will also be of service for setting aside the sacrilege of the Papal mass. For Paul does not teach that Christ is offered daily, but that the sacrifice being offered up once for all, it remains that the spiritual feast be celebrated during our whole life" (Calvin, 189–90). Reference to the exclusion of the one called brother inspired Calvin momentarily to soften his antipapist tone, declaring that "no one may think that we ought to employ equally severe measures against those who, while at this day dispersed under the tyranny of the Pope, pollute themselves with many corrupt rites" (194). Inspired by Paul's line about not taking food with the brother who has offended, Calvin rails against "the Roman antichrist" that prohibits "any one from helping one that has been excommunicated to food, or fuel, or drink or any of the supports of life" (195). The way in which Calvin applies this passage to his own time reminds us of the larger history of interpretation of Paul's letters. Scholars and "lay" alike tend to define early Christianity over and against Jews (who have been characterized as particularistic and law-obsessed) and Catholics (who have been depicted as like "pagans" in their concern with works and ritual), as J. Z. Smith discusses in his *Drudgery Divine*. If we forget that Paul was a Jew and that many of his letters are concerned with very practical things, we may stand in danger of producing interpretations that read as anti-Jewish and anti-Catholic.

▌The Text in Contemporary Discussion

Paul's use of strong language of insiders and outsiders has inspired scholars to discuss 1 Corinthians through the lens of anthropology and sociology, reminding us that contemporary interpreters of Paul's writings include those outside of confessional Christian circles who find the letters useful for comparison with other times and places.

Theissen (1982), for example, explains various theological and ritual stances at Corinth as linked to varieties of socioeconomic status there and suggests that scholars should be in the business of comparing early Christian literatures with other religious phenomena of the world. Taking up such a challenge, Jonathan Z. Smith (2004) and Richard DeMaris (1995) have used anthropological insights to understand 1 Corinthians in a *local* context. The former shows the way in which 1 Corinthians has influenced discussions of "commensalism" (namely, relations with other local religions) and Christian revivalism in the local context of Papua New Guinea. The latter elucidates Corinthian references to spirit in light of ancestor cults and familial practices, evidenced in the archaeological record at Corinth.

Many have found anthropologist Mary Douglas's expounding of how the individual body is controlled and regulated (or not) in relation to the social body (a group) helpful for an analysis of the various viewpoints that might stand behind 1 Corinthians (e.g., Neyrey). Might some members of the *ekklēsia* have perceived the body as dangerously permeable, and sought to control sex, eating, spirit-possession, and relations with outsiders, while some saw the body as less dangerously subject to pollution? Dale Martin (1995) addresses the important question of how these perceptions—theological and medical—of the individual body affected ideas of the communal body.

These comparisons and insights help us to sharpen our understanding that 1 Corinthians deserves close attention and comparison with other phenomena in the history of religions. Paul's letters are not written to "us," whatever our time and place, even if his injunctions about holiness and purity, as well as his exhortations to unity, might be used in church debates today, for example about sexuality or sex acts. There is no "commonsense" reading that respects the complexity of these letters. They require a contextualization in their own time, in light of religious practices and beliefs in the first century, before they can be appropriated today.

1 Corinthians 6:12—7:40: "All Things Are Permitted to Me" and "Stay as You Are"

▌The Text in Its Ancient Context

Having insisted that those in Christ at Corinth were once, and in the present some still are, *pornoi*, Paul continues to treat the theme of immorality by quoting and questioning "slogans" that may be the Corinthians' own or that he assumes they will understand. In 6:12, we find "all things are permitted to me," met by Paul's commentary "but not all things are beneficial"; in 6:13, we find "food is meant for the stomach and the stomach for food," met by Paul's commentary "God will destroy both." With both verses, we find common structure; a rhetorical analysis shows the assertion of an idea, and then its qualification, which leads scholars to think that the assertion is an idea that the Corinthians have set forth, while the qualification is Paul's own response to the idea or slogan (Wire).

Paul takes the theme of his previous chapter and argues that the body (*sōma*) is not meant for *porneia* but for "the Lord" (6:13). *Sōma* in Greek signals the body proper; it signals the body politic (Mitchell 1991); it is also a term sometimes used for "slave." Throughout 1 Corinthians, the political force of the term *sōma* is deployed, as well as the frequent political rhetoric that the body should be unified. In Paul's thought, the Corinthians' bodies become members of, and come to constitute, the body of Christ (6:15), and so should communally maintain the purity of their body. The Corinthian community is also twice asked to think of itself as collectively "on the market," as if a slave body purchased by God. First Corinthians 6:19b-20 reads, "You are not your own; you were bought with a price. So glorify God in your body"; it is echoed by 7:23, "you were bought with a price; do not become slaves of humans." Participants in the *ekklēsia* at Corinth lived in a city steeped in the history of former slavery, refounded as it was by freedpersons; 1 Corinthians 7 makes clear that slaves are part of the community as well. Thus the language of *sōma* resonated at multiple levels, calling to mind the individual body and its morality, the slave body, and the communal body politic.

Paul argues that those to whom he writes should together "shun immorality," including associating with a prostitute. The conversation is framed toward a male audience that might "join" themselves (6:16) to a female. Jennifer Glancy interrogates the passage, wondering whether a slave would necessarily be excluded from the Corinthian body of Christ, since slaves were not able to control their bodies but could be subjected to *porneia* by their masters; ancient texts talk about slaves "used" by their masters as part of the "normal" operations of slavery, or a slave might be forced into prostitution (Marchal).

Paul reinforces his point about not joining one's body with a prostitute by using the metaphor of body as *naos*, or temple to the Lord. What temple is evoked? The Corinthians might be familiar with the kind of thought that Philo, for instance, exhibits when he interprets Genesis 2, describing Adam's body as a "shrine or sacred sanctuary" carrying within it the *agalma*, or "image," of the divine (*Opif.* 137). Given concerns expressed for a collection to be taken to Jerusalem (1 Cor. 16:1-4; 2 Corinthians 8–9), the temple in Jerusalem might be evoked. Given their location, one of the many temples of Corinth might be come to mind (Weissenrieder), each with its own *temenos*, or boundary, within which space is sacralized and only certain activities are allowed.

What are the appropriate practices of the individual body and the "body politic"? First Corinthians 7 extends this question to the circumstances of marriage, enslavement, and circumcision. The main theme of the chapter is to "remain as you are," which is elaborated in 7:17: "Only, let everyone lead the life which the Lord has assigned to him or her, and in which God has called him or her" (see Harrill). Here Paul reprises the significant theme of "call," which resounds throughout the letter and which was part of the unique ethnic and practical identity of the community at Corinth—recall that they are no longer Jews or Greeks, but "the called" (1:24). But this status as "the called" leads to an odd stasis rather than transformation: they may be called, but, depending on their place in society in Roman Corinth, the Corinthians may have been variously surprised, disappointed, or reassured to be told to remain as they are. Scholars still hotly debate the meaning of this passage, however, because of difficulties in understanding the Greek; Scott Bartchy has argued instead, for example, that Paul emphasizes that one's call in Christ is more significant than any social status, but that 1 Corinthians 7 does not encourage members of the community to remain enslaved. If we keep our attention on the question of the interpretation of those who first received the letter, we may reasonably surmise that they too debated the meaning of this section.

Some Corinthians likely understood their identity as "called" by Christ and the transforming ritual of baptism to lead to a present state of resurrection (Wire) and/or to upend the distinctions of a kyriarchal society—a term coined by Elisabeth Schüssler Fiorenza to point to intersecting structural injustices rooted in the rule of masters (*kyrioi*) over slaves, males over females. They might have disagreed with Paul's urgent call to remain in the state in which they had been called.

While marriage is a primary concern in chapter 7, we see all three of the socioeconomic and ethnic binaries of what is likely a pre-Pauline baptismal formula discussed here (marriage [male and female]: 7:1-16, 25-40; ethnicity [Jew nor Greek] in terms of circumcision as its sign: 7:18-20; slavery and manumission [neither slave nor free]: 7:21-24). We know that baptism was important to the community at Corinth (1:13-17) and that they practiced baptism on behalf of the dead (15:29). We can assume that the Corinthians used a standard pre-Pauline baptismal formula, since in 1 Cor. 12:13 Paul partially cites what are likely ritual words that we also know from Gal. 3:27-28: "As many of you as were baptized into Christ have clothed yourselves with Christ. There is no longer Jew or Greek, there is no longer slave or free, there is no longer male and female; for all of you are one in Christ Jesus."

The Corinthians likely had suggested to Paul that "it is good that a man not touch a woman," since he precedes this with "now concerning what you wrote." The Corinthians' practice may be rooted in expectations of an imminent end to time, or to larger cultural and philosophical discussions of desire and its extirpation; the popular philosophical idea of *enkrateia*, or self-control, is evoked in 7:9 with the word "they should control themselves." Philo, a Jew from Alexandria who was a near contemporary of Paul's, interpreted the entire Tenth Commandment as an injunction, "do not desire," and understood the Mosaic dietary laws as ascetic precepts that led to self-control (Svebakken), teaching how to keep the self inured to the buffets of outside attractions, whether of food or sex or prestige. Such philosophical practices as abstaining from sex and marriage might fly in the face of Augustan marriage laws. Later sources characterize the *Lex Julia de maritandis ordinibus* and the *Lex Julia de adulteriis coercendis* of 18–17 BCE as encouraging people to marry, enacting penalties for adultery, imposing financial penalties on unmarried men and women, and seeking to limit marriages so that those of senatorial status would not mix with those of lower status—thus a senator or his children were barred from marrying freedpersons, those involved in certain kinds of theater, and prostitutes (e.g., Dio Cassius, *Hist.* 54.16.1). These harsh reforms, which were presented as part of a family values campaign (Suetonius, *Life of Augustus* 34), were revised in 9 CE in the Lex Papia Poppaea, which used a carrot rather than a stick, preferring political candidates who had more children, allowing freedpersons who had more children substantial freedom from the patron-client relations with their former masters, and relieving from political responsibilities those who had a great number of children.

The discussion of marriage also reminds us that many at Corinth would hear these words in light of their own "mixed marriages" (Hodge), having to negotiate with or to be subject to a spouse who had different ethics and religious practices from their own. Paul's arguments indicate that he and perhaps the Corinthians shared some notion of an extended or communicable health or salvation (Hodge, 16): the one who is made holy can somehow extend that holiness to his or her spouse and render their children "saints" or "holy ones" (Hodge, 14).

Although chapter 7 focuses on marriage, Paul briefly treats circumcision and slavery, the two other categories of the pre-Pauline baptismal formula. He quickly argues that one should seek neither circumcision nor to remove the marks of circumcision. While Jewish men were not the only men to practice circumcision in antiquity, and while Jewish women were not circumcised, circumcision became a kind of metonymy for Jews (Cohen). In Galatians, Paul insists that circumcision is nothing, even though men in antiquity who affiliated with Judaism may have wished to participate fully in the covenants of Judaism, including circumcision: Paul instead offers an extended argument in Galatians that covenantal participation is possible without circumcision, since God brought Abra(ha)m into covenant with him before Abra(ha)m was circumcised.

Paul then proceeds to talk about slaves. Verse 20 asserts the larger theme of the chapter (Harrill), that "everyone should remain in the state in which he [or she] was called." It continues: "Were you a slave when called? Never mind. But if you can gain your freedom, rather use [it] [*mallon chrēsai*]." The last phrase is the subject of much controversy. The object of the Greek verb is unclear. Should they "use" their freedom? Their slavery? If we attend to the immediate grammatical context, we will conclude that they should use their freedom—that is, to seek manumission by some means. If we look at the overall message of chapter 7, with its banging repetition of "remain," we will conclude that we should supply "slavery." The grammatical uncertainty is not due to our weak grasp of first-century Greek: roughly three centuries after the writing of 1 Corinthians, John Chrysostom's community debated whether to supply "freedom" or "slavery" (*Hom. 1 Cor.* 19.5). The Corinthians who received this letter were likely as baffled as we. We may wonder whether they sought clarification from the carrier of Paul and Sosthenes's letter, who was likely a freedperson or slave; such letter carriers were often expected not only to deliver their masters' correspondence but also to voice and to interpret its contents (Mouritsen).

Many attempt to neutralize the passage's revolutionary idea of seeking freedom, on the one hand, or its horrifying quietism of staying enslaved, on the other, by reading the passage as "merely" eschatological or theological (e.g., Conzelmann; Horsley 1998). It is a reasonable choice after Paul's own phrasing in 7:29: "the appointed time has grown short" and the following passage, in which people are encouraged to live "as if not," with the conclusion that "the form of this cosmos [or world] is passing away" (7:31b). Many commentators impute to Paul (and thus to "his" churches) a disinterest in material conditions on account of expectation of an imminent *parousia* or appearance of Christ, but apocalyptic notions could equally lead to concrete political action such as the kind of revolutionary fervor Josephus mentions when he talks about Jewish prophets who led groups that opposed the Romans and were quashed. Others would argue that we should read Paul in light of popular philosophical movements like Stoicism that enjoin that gender and social status and economic opportunity should not matter if one rightly cultivates within oneself a philosophical lack of caring for external events (e.g., Philo, *Every Good Man Is Free*); Epictetus describes the slave who longs to be free, only to be freed and realize that he is enslaved by the need to supply himself with such things as food and clothes (*Diatr.* 4.1.33).

Such an approach misses the opportunity to think about material and social realities of slavery at Corinth (Nasrallah 2013). The Corinthians did not necessarily share Paul's argument to "remain as you are," and they may have debated what he meant by the elusive *mallon chrēsai*, "rather use." Perhaps they wished Paul had offered a clearer statement of social change in the present. Perhaps some of the Corinthians were aware of contemporaneous practices at Delphi and Kalymna, in which a slave was "sold" for freedom to a god and thus manumitted (Deissmann). Perhaps they preferred to think that baptism and their calling "in Christ" transformed ethnicity, gender, and social religions in the present, rather than accepting a present stasis followed by future transformation. Perhaps they found the divine to be inbreaking in the present, as evidenced in spiritual gifts or *pneumatika*, and understood their individual bodies and communal body alike to be based in a new calling rather than an old.

▊ THE TEXT IN THE INTERPRETIVE TRADITION

Over the centuries, Christians have debated the merits of celibacy and marriage in clerical and lay life. While Paul prefers that people not marry, his injunctions in 1 Corinthians 7 allow for marriage, and even suggest that desire be recognized and channeled in marriage—thus that marriage exists not only for procreation but also as a locus of sexual morality. In 1523, Martin Luther wrote a treatise on 1 Corinthians 7, addressing it "to the August and honorable Hans Loser of Pretzsch," as a wedding gift, with the hopes that he will "no longer postpone your marriage" (Luther, 3). A pity for the bride, then, that Luther's treatise proper starts with the words "What a fool is he who takes a wife, says the world, and it is certainly true" (5). Of course, Luther goes on, like Paul, to point out the folly of this worldly wisdom, as well as to use Paul as a tool against the Roman Catholicism of his day. Luther states that he has taken on the task of interpreting 1 Corinthians 7 because "this very chapter, more than all the other writings of the entire Bible, has been twisted back and forth to condemn the married state and at the same time to give a strong appearance of sanctity to the dangers and peculiar state of celibacy" (3).

So too, in the ancient world, Paul's teachings on marriage were used in two opposing directions. Two examples will suffice to show how 1 Corinthians 7 was interpreted in radically different ways soon after it was written. First Timothy, written in Paul's name at the end of the first century or beginning of the second, insists that those who have the task of "bishop" should be married, although only once (3:2), and that "she" (whether Eve or women more generally is unclear) "will be saved through bearing children" (1 Tim. 2:15). The *Acts of Paul and Thecla*, a text embodying traditions circulating in the second century CE, insists that Paul blessed celibacy, and focuses on the story of a young woman, Thecla, who follows Paul and renounces her betrothal for a life of celibacy.

◾ THE TEXT IN CONTEMPORARY DISCUSSION

The phrase "the appointed time has grown short" (7:29) has attracted recent attention by political philosophers and other scholars. Following on Walter Benjamin's *Theses on the Philosophy of History*, they expand on the idea of "messianic time" and find in Paul's writings a sense of crisis that has the potential to inspire new ways of thinking about being in the present. Giorgio Agamben is particularly interested in the use in 1 Cor. 7:29 of the term *synestalmenos* ("drawn together" or "shortened" like a sail) to discuss time (*kairos*) (Agamben, 62). Alain Badiou describes Paul as "poet-thinker of the event" and a "militant figure"; Paul is to Jesus as Lenin was to Marx (as Slavoj Žižek also argues). Even more than Jesus, Badiou argues, Paul marked a break in what he calls "eventual time": that is, for Paul, the resurrection changed everything.

Paul's letters and the sort of apocalyptic thinking we find in 1 Corinthians 7 are worthy resources for political philosophy. But Badiou and others, in part because of their only cursory understanding of Paul's historical context, have misused and mischaracterized Paul as a hero of universalism. For example, while recognizing Paul as a Jew, Badiou has nonetheless supported anti-Jewish interpretation by emphasizing Paul as a universalist thinker above the particulars of Judaism (Badiou, 13, 23); despite his claimed interest in universality, Badiou sweeps Paul's statements about women under the carpet by seeing them as only "cultural" (103–4). Badiou and others have produced a Paul who is an "anti-philosophical theoretician of universality," who is uniquely right over and against the "opinions" of those to whom he writes; they have elaborated a Paul who in relation to messianic or "eventual" time argues for a truth that is produced by the subject, without recognizing that the subject they celebrate looks awfully like a "rational," universal male (Dunning).

The transformative theological and political idea of the *eschaton* and "messianic time," which Agamben, Badiou, and others correctly see in Paul's letters, does not reach full potential in these contemporary philosophical conversations. Contemporary philosophers and cultural critics do not take into account the productive struggle over ideas that occurred between Paul and those to whom he wrote, and they assume that people's experience of an urgent expectation of the Parousia or appearance of Christ allowed for some sort of individualized spiritual transformation that nonetheless had no concrete social or political effects in the world.

1 Corinthians 8–10: Food Offered to Idols, Ethnicity, and Identity

◾ THE TEXT IN ITS ANCIENT CONTEXT

Paul had said that the Corinthians are still "infants" (*nēpioi*) and "people of the flesh" (*sarkikoi* or *sarkinoi*, 3:1). Chapters 5–10 provide examples of the practical ethical outworkings of Paul's chastisement. While chapters 5–7 touched on issues of practices of the *sōma* that had particularly to do with sex and marriage, chapters 8–10 focus on practices regarding food and transformations in ethnic identity that occur for those in Christ.

In 1 Cor. 10:25, Paul uses the word *makellon*, a *hapax legomenon* (a word that appears only once) in New Testament literature (Cadbury): "Eat whatever is sold in the meat market without raising any question on the ground of conscience" (1 Cor. 10:25). The location of the *makellon* (an area primarily for selling meat and fish) in Roman Corinth is unclear, although fragmentary epigraphic evidence confirms that there was a *makellon* at Corinth (Cadbury, 139; Nabers; Kent, n. 321; West, n. 124; Nasrallah forthcoming). Although not all meat in antiquity was sacrificial meat, the markets were locations where trade and religion converged, along with the sale of meat (Ruyt). Divinities were honored there in the Roman imperial period, especially in the central, usually round building (Ruyt; Nabers).

In chapters 8–10, Paul offers somewhat contradictory advice about the eating of meat in sacred precincts or from the market. In chapter 8, on the one hand, he suggests that one shouldn't eat it (in particular not in sacred precincts, *en eidōleiō*), lest one offend the conscience of a "weak" brother or sister. In chapter 10, on the other hand, he indicates that one shouldn't ask about the origins of the sacrificial food (*hierothyton*)—one can go ahead and eat it. Two principles seem to dominate: first, a set of philosophical-theological slogans, likely the Corinthians' own: we know that there is one God, that idols don't really exist, and that the earth is the Lord's and everything in it; in sum: God trumps all, and it doesn't matter what you eat. Second, and in tension with the first, we find a social issue: think about your sibling's conscience, and don't offend your brother or sister by eating sacrificial food. With regard to eating and drinking in Corinth, we can also consider the question of the meals shared by those in Christ; we know that Paul considered these to be handled badly, and his comments indicate that some were likely poor and were certainly hungry (see below on 1 Cor. 11:17-34; e.g., Stowers 2011a). Debates about food in Gal. 2:11-13, in which Paul accuses Cephas of sitting at table with gentiles, then separating from them when some from James (brother of Jesus) came to visit, likely had to do with kashrut or Jewish dietary laws more generally, while the discussion in 1 Corinthians 8–10 seems to have to do more specifically with food associated with sacrifice and sacred precincts.

The Corinthians in Christ were familiar with the intimate connection between food, community, and cult. Meals were eaten in sanctuaries at Corinth. The Asklepieion near the Lerna Fountain at Corinth has some rooms that seem to have functioned for dining. In addition, excavations have revealed fish bones, lentils, and casserole dishes in the sanctuary of Demeter and Kore on the Acrocorinth, which had several structures for dining even in the Roman period (Bookidis and Stroud; Økland). Not only meat but also other sorts of food were sometimes sacrificial, and if not sacrificial, still sacralized by their consumption within sacred precincts (Ekroth), yet not all meat was sacrificial meat (Naiden). Yet Paul tries to convince the Corinthians that the commodity could be drained of its religious force (see discussions in Still; Gooch; Stowers 2011a).

If we ask how various participants in the Corinthian *ekklēsia* would have heard Paul's injunction to "eat whatever is sold in the meat market," we recognize, aided by archaeological materials, that the conditions in antiquity were such that slaves, free, or freedpersons entered into a market that was religiously marked to purchase goods that may or may not have been religiously marked. In addition, literary evidence often depicts slaves sent to the market to purchase food (e.g., *Life of Aesop*). Hearers of 1 Corinthians would have found it difficult to think of *hierothyton* as neutral food, or of their mandated or voluntary entrance into the meat market as religiously neutral. The commodity in question was tagged by religion, whether or not it is called *hierothyton* ("sacred offering") or *eidōlothyton* ("idol" or "image offering"). The food, the eating of it, and the market space are all marked by religious practice and affiliation.

Spliced into the conversations about food and idolatry in chapters 8 and 10 is Paul's own assertion regarding food, one's right (*exousia*), freedom, and his identity in chapter 9. (We also saw how chapters 1–4 contrapuntally treat wisdom and Paul's role within the community.) "Am I not free?!" Paul begins chapter 9. While Paul presents himself at the beginning of 1 Corinthians (and at its end) as an apostle, not slave of Christ (as in Rom. 1:1), Paul here presents himself as analogous to one "employed in the temple" (9:13). Such religious experts were not necessarily (only) high-status priests but also temple slaves and/or public slaves in the employ of the temple (Shaner). Wondering about his own finances, Paul refers to temple religious specialists eating from the altar. This image is easily skimmed over as an odd metaphor, so that we can get to the meat (!) of Paul's self-description in 9:19-23, but it is a crucial tie to the themes of chapters 7–8 and 10–11. In chapters 7–8, real slavery and freedom are at stake, as is the question of eating meat from the temple. In chapters 10–11, eating *hierothyton* is again an issue, and by the end of chapter 11 the *ekklēsia* at Corinth is criticized for how it does its eating and drinking.

What is at stake in these verses is Paul's identity as an apostle, what authority (*exousia*, 9:12b) he has in the community at Corinth, and his wage (*misthos*, 9:18). Paul responds to this by proudly stating that he is a shape-shifter. "For though I am free with respect to all, I have made myself a slave to all, so that I might win more of them. To the Jews I became as a Jew . . . To those outside the law I became as one outside the law . . . To the weak I became weak . . . I have become all things to all people, that I might by all means save some" (9:19-22). The passage is confounding if we look for Paul's biography or an insight into his psychology; we should read it instead as part of Paul's *ēthos*—the rhetorical strategy by which a speaker both defines himself and does so in a way that he hopes will draw the audience's sympathy.

Paul twice pauses in his arguments in chapters 8–9 to refer to Jewish Scripture. In 8:6, he offers a remix of the Shema, the Jewish claim in Scripture and prayer that the Lord is one (Deut. 6:4), expanded by a reference to "one Lord, Jesus Christ," perhaps quoting a common teaching of early Christ-communities and perhaps also sparking, for the Corinthians, the idea of Stoic monotheism (Thiselton, 635–37). That is, Jews were not the only ones in antiquity who argued for one God; some who followed Greek and Roman religions also thought that there was one true God, and various local manifestations or ways of imagining aspects of that God. In chapter 9, speaking of the issue of wage, Paul offers an allegorical interpretation of Deut. 25:4, insisting, in what I think must be a comic tone, that "You shall not muzzle an ox while it is treading out the grain" is a Mosaic statement for "our sake": in the midst of a chapter about Paul's own identity, he briefly takes on the identity of an ox. From these references and from the beginning of chapter 10, we can deduce that the Corinthians understood references to Jewish tradition and that they were a largely gentile community, undergoing an ethnic-religious transformation toward a Jewishness rooted in faith in Christ.

At the beginning of chapter 10, Paul reprises the theme of food and idolatry using the exodus story. "I don't want you to be ignorant, brothers and sisters," he writes—again, a reference to who is in the know—"that our fathers were all under the cloud and all passed through the sea, and all were baptized into Moses in the cloud and in the sea, and all ate the same spiritual food and all drank the same spiritual drink. For they drank from the spiritual rock which followed them, and the rock was Christ" (10:1-4). The passage was perhaps surprising to the Corinthians as they recalled their ethnic change. It asserts that the paternity of those to whom Paul writes is derived from Moses, despite the fact that he later writes "when you were gentiles" (12:2)—that is, from the *ethnē*, or nations, that are precisely not Jews. The story of the exodus through the sea is framed in terms of baptism. This passage reminds us again that the Corinthians considered baptism to be a key ritual, perhaps one that transformed identity, community, and possibilities for present and future. Baptism, as we know from what is likely a pre-Pauline baptismal formula found in Gal. 3:28, included the phrase "neither Jew nor Greek." Here, as in Gal. 3:29, Paul reinforces the idea that baptism does not lead to an ethnically neutral state or to participation in a third or "new race," as some Christians would later assert (*Diogn.* 1.1; Buell), but to being incorporated within the stories, covenants, promises, and responsibilities of God's people, the Jews.

Here Paul offers a midrash on the exodus story that may trade on and shift other interpretations of exodus familiar to those at Corinth. In a roughly contemporaneous text, the Wisdom of Solomon, Wisdom herself leads the people through the sea.

> A holy people and blameless race wisdom delivered from a nation of oppressors. . . . She brought them over the Red Sea, and led them through deep waters; . . . wisdom opened the mouth of the dumb, and made the tongues of babes speak clearly. . . . When they thirsted they called upon thee [Wisdom], and water was given them out of flinty rock, and slaking of thirst from hard stone. (Wis. 10:15, 18, 21; 11:4)

The accounts in 1 Corinthians and the Wisdom of Solomon differ in various ways. The latter is a celebration of Jewish identity over against "the nations" and "the ungodly"; the former brings the nations into a Jewish lineage. The Wisdom of Solomon celebrates Wisdom; Paul may substitute Christ for Wisdom. The triumph of the story of the Wisdom of Solomon becomes a warning in 1 Corinthians: the latter tells the story of the exodus as a warning concerning idolatry, instruction, and trial or temptation, rather than a celebration as we find in the Wisdom of Solomon. Given what we learned in chapters 1–4 of the importance of wisdom/Wisdom to the Corinthian *ekklēsia*, we may reasonably wonder whether Paul is trying to shift the importance of this hypostatized figure in the community at Corinth.

▌ THE TEXT IN THE INTERPRETIVE TRADITION

In 10:26, Paul cites from Ps. 24:1 a kind of cosmological-philosophical slogan: "The earth is the Lord's, and everything in it." Such a way of thinking means that *anything*, even foodstuffs usually considered questionable, taboo, or forbidden due to dietary laws, is reframed as "the Lord's" and is thus acceptable. We find concern about this issue also in Gal. 2:11, framed in terms of Jews eating with gentiles. Written approximately fifty years later, Acts 10 reframes the fundamental insight in terms of dietary law and gives to Peter, not Paul, the vision (literally) that God says he may "kill and eat" all things (10:13). Acts adopts this probably earlier story to provide Peter with the insight that he can travel to the household of Cornelius the gentile, since "God has shown me that I should not call anyone profane or unclean" (10:28). Some recent scholars have argued that the canonical Acts of the Apostles knows Paul's letters and self-presentation, even if Acts presents Paul in quite a different light, as a tremendous speaker rather than one who is weak (Pervo). Acts 10 presents a *different* tradition from Paul's own in 1 Corinthians 8–10 with regard to eating and idolatry and relations with gentiles, so it is an "interpretive context" for Paul's letter in the loosest sense. But it is important to recognize that the community in Christ, whether in the time of Paul or in the century thereafter, picks up Jewish interpretive traditions that declare the Mosaic laws to be allegorizations of *people*, rather than literal injunctions about what to eat. For example, the *Letter of Aristeas* depicts a figure named Eleazar the high priest, who argues that Moses' true aim is *dikaiosynē* ("righteousness" or "justice"), and so Mosaic dietary law is to be interpreted with each animal as a symbol that corresponds to human ethical behavior (see Svebakken, 111–12).

First Corinthians 10:25 is used quite differently by Clement in second-century-CE Alexandria, who employs it in a larger section on eating, both to enjoin people not to "abolish social intercourse" but also to shun "daintiness . . . we are to partake of few and necessary things." A string of citations from 1 Corinthians leads Clement to mark his intended audience as fairly wealthy, since his conclusions have to do both with the host and with moderation at a luxurious table: "We are to partake of what is set before us, as becomes a Christian, out of respect to him who has invited us, by a harmless and moderate participation in the social meeting; regarding the sumptuousness of what is put on the table as a matter of indifference, despising the dainties, as after a little destined to perish" (*Strom.* 4.15). In the community at Corinth and elsewhere, food, status, economic access, and religious practice were intertwined issues. Maybe you aren't what you eat, but you are formed by those with whom you eat.

▋The Text in Contemporary Discussion

Paul presents himself as a shape-shifter in 1 Corinthians 9, as "all things to all people." In other passages in his letters, he presents himself as nurse (1 Thess. 2:7), as father coming with a stick (1 Cor. 4:15-21), as someone having ecstatic experiences (2 Cor. 12:1-11), and as prisoner (Phil. 1:13-14), among many other self-portraits. Paul's presentation in 1 Corinthians, as well as these other self-portraits, has informed two responses. First, Paul offers a self so complex that students of his letters struggle to define his intention: Who *was* Paul? What was his frame of mind? This has led to a scholarly obsession with declaring Paul a hero (often a liberative or postcolonial hero, resisting the Roman Empire and bringing egalitarian community) or a betrayer of Christ's message (from the Pseudo-Clementine literature to Thomas Jefferson and beyond: Johnson-DeBaufre and Nasrallah). A better approach would be (1) to take into account the rhetorical nature of Paul's statements: he is not describing himself, but portraying himself to various communities for various reasons; (2) to consider whether our ideas of authorship and intention might not match those held in antiquity; and (3) to focus not only on Paul as hero but on the broad spectrum of early communities in Christ as well.

Second, some scholars of the past decades have interpreted Paul's shape-shifting in the context of the "new perspective" on Paul, placing Paul as a Jew negotiating his newly Jewish identity *in Christ* in the midst of the diversity within Judaism in the first century CE. They demonstrate that Paul has not invented a new religion, but stands alongside other Jews who try to make a way for gentiles to come into covenant with God.

11:2-34: Veiling and Eating

▌ The Text in Its Ancient Context

In chapter 9, Paul pointed to his own identity as shape-shifter; by the end of chapter 10, he emphasizes that his readers should do all to the glory of God and give no offense to "either Jew or Greeks or the *ekklēsia* of God," even as he himself seeks to please the many. Paul enjoins his audience here to "Be imitators of me, as I am of Christ" (11:1; see also 4:16). The pattern set up in this verse (Christ-Paul-participants in the *ekklēsia*) echoes throughout the following verses, even as the powerful political language of imitation echoes elsewhere in this letter and others (Castelli).

An initial commendation to the community for remembering him and what he has "handed down" quickly shifts to a correction of practices of prayer and prophecy. Paul begins by setting a hierarchy of "headship"—God, Christ, man, wife. This hierarchy undergirds his insistence that a man praying or prophesying should do so with head uncovered, while a woman doing so must cover her head. As Antoinette Clark Wire has shown, Paul then proceeds to offer several disparate logics for his insistence on such a practice. Although scholars have long tried to discover the causes of such an injunction—Does Paul promote Jewish women's practices of head-veiling? Does he criticize "pagan" women's loose hair and/or prophetic chaos leading to Dionysian-like abandon for women?—none is convincing, largely because we cannot know for certain the variety of veiling practices in Roman Corinth. We do know that Roman men *and* women covered their heads when engaged in pious practices, as we see in a statue of Octavian found at Corinth; were his right hand preserved, we would see it pouring a libation to the gods (see also Oster).

If we cannot fix a social context that explains Paul's injunction, we can glean several things about prayer and prophecy in the community at Corinth. First, men and women alike were praying and prophesying; as we think about the letter as a whole, we see that wisdom and spiritual gifts are key to the community (11:1-4, 12-14). Second, Paul wishes to change this practice in some way, perhaps especially through insisting on women's veiling and grounding this practice in a logic of women's subordination to men. Third, given the scattershot of logics he offers, it is likely that he is aware he faces a tough crowd, for whom only one reason for his argument will not suffice. Paul argues according to cosmology and creation: man as God's image and glory; woman as glory of the man; the Genesis 2 story that woman was made from man, with a concessive realization that men are born from women in verse 12. He argues according to "the angels," either indicating that the Corinthians understood angels to be present in their community practices and/or that he was alluding to the danger of angels' attraction to human women, as is hinted at in the biblical reference to angelic intercourse with female humans (Gen. 6:1-2; Wire; BeDuhn). Paul argues based on the logic of propriety (11:13), from nature (11:14), and from general practice in the *ekklēsiai* (11:16).

Paul proceeds to another practice that has to do with Corinthians' gathering (11:17-34): that of eating and drinking. When they gather to eat, he says, they do not engage in "the Lord's supper" (11:20). One concern, according to the text, is that "those who have nothing" (11:22) are humiliated. From Paul's perspective, something in meal practices has broken down. Scholars have speculated that perhaps this breakdown has to do with social status: some have access to food or the ability to come when they wish, leaving out or disregarding others with less status, such as slaves. Paul's final word is to "wait" lest condemnation fall (11:34).

Paul's discussion of what he "received from the Lord" about the supper is the earliest evidence we have of such a practice; although the traditions contained in the Gospels may be earlier, the Gospels themselves postdate the writing of Paul's letters. The meal is grounded with a historical etiology ("on the night he was handed over," 11:23): it is understood as a repetition of the practices of that first supper. The eschatological aspect of the meal is highlighted, as it is a proclamation of the death of the Lord "until he comes." For Paul, the Lord's Supper has potential dangers associated with it; interpreters influenced by the anthropology of religion have noted Paul's attribution of quasi-magical properties to the supper, since it can cause weakness, illness, and death if misused (11:30).

Those in Christ were not the only ones to gather at meals or to be warned about their behavior while doing so. Contemporaneous associations were well known for their practices of gathering to eat and to celebrate a god, and for regulating those gatherings. The second-century Iobacchoi inscription found in Athens, for instance, regulates participation and membership in their association to honor the god Bacchus (Dionysus) and states fines for poor behavior while in a gathering together (IG II² 1368 = PHI 3584) as well as the financial contributions necessary to participate in the meal (Ascough, et al.).

Comments regarding meal practices in 1 Corinthians 11 should make us wonder not only about the ritual nature of the meal but also about food and hunger in the community. The majority of the population of the Roman Empire was poor (recent hypotheses extend from 68 to 99 percent), with poverty defined in this way by Peter Garnsey and Greg Woolf: "the poor are those living at or near subsistence level, whose prime concern it is to obtain the minimum food, shelter, and clothing necessary to sustain life, whose lives are dominated by the struggle for physical survival" (Garnsey and Woolf, 153; Meggitt). Various famines occurred in mid-first-century Greece and the Greek East, including perhaps one at Corinth in the early 50s CE (Winter, 6, 216–25). Corinth's economy depended on trade, and the city and its environs could not supply enough food for its urban population (Williams, 31–33, 38; Strabo, *Geog.* 8.6.23).

▌ THE TEXT IN THE INTERPRETIVE TRADITION

Paul's assertion that women should be veiled when praying or prophesying and his arguments supporting this change in practice may have met with instant controversy. It also created controversy in the late second or early third century, as evidenced in the writings of Tertullian. The North African writer is famous for his pithy statement that "you [women] are the devil's gateway" (*On the Apparel of Women* 1.1). In *On the Veiling of Virgins*, Tertullian discusses 1 Corinthians 11 and the way in which it is being interpreted in his day. Some, he indicates, argue from 1 Corinthians 11 that, while women should veil while praying or prophesying, virgins should not; thus, virgins in those Christian communities in North Africa remain unveiled when they gather with others in church. These interpreters, Tertullian disgustedly says, ground their argument in Paul's statement about the unmarried woman being concerned about the affairs of the Lord, while the married woman worries about worldly affairs and how to please her husband (1 Cor. 7:34; Tertullian, *Virg.* 4.4).

Tertullian cites 1 Cor. 11:3 and its language of man as head of woman—a term in Greek that can also be translated "wife," but which Tertullian insists must be understood as a general classificatory term under which female virgin falls as a particular instance of "woman." He continues to argue that virgin women should also be veiled by appealing to the assertion in 1 Cor. 14:34-35 that women should be silent in the assembly. Is a virgin, he wonders acerbically, something of a third sex (*Virg.* 7.2), which can escape such regulations? In the end, he supports his argumentation by referring to a vision of a woman in his community to whom an angel appeared, rapping on her bare neck and sarcastically suggesting that she expose more of her body (*Virg.* 17.6). The issue of women and veiling in religious practice is a long-standing one, and some among earliest Christians argued strongly for women's veiling in religious community.

▮ The Text in Contemporary Discussion

Scholars today debate whether the Greek *kephalē* in 1 Cor. 11:3 should be translated "head" (as in RSV) or "source"; the latter might allow for a nonhierarchical interpretation of the passage, with the term "source" indicating the order of creation. At stake is the role of women in Christian community. Does 1 Corinthians provide a biblical foundation for the idea of women's subordination to men, especially with regard to women's roles in religious leadership in Christian ministry?

Mimi Haddad, president of Christians for Biblical Equality, along with many who participate in the organization, argues that 1 Corinthians 11 refers to the order of creation. Paul states in 1 Cor. 11:8-9, 11-12, that, despite the order of creation (man first, then woman, according to Genesis 2), men are now born from women. Haddad and others cite this as evidence of Paul's recognition of the roles of both sexes and the interdependence of men and women. She concludes: "Rather, in Christ both males and females are equal heirs of God's New Covenant community. Both are born of the Spirit, and both are gifted for leadership which is first and foremost service" (Haddad).

Haddad's perspective is one among many who debate whether Paul argued for women's egalitarian status in assemblies in Christ or argued for women's subordination (Elliott). Other feminist approaches would emphasize the clear role of women in the earliest Jesus movement, from accounts that Mary Magdalene was the first to greet Jesus after his resurrection to Paul's own list of women who were coworkers and even a woman apostle in Romans 16. Still others would add that the texts we associate with earliest Christianity, like all writing, are rhetorically constructed in order to persuade, and would ask why Paul here insists on a hierarchy that is in part gendered, while elsewhere in Paul's writings and other texts we find evidence of egalitarian tendencies in the early *ekklēsiai*.

1 Corinthians 12:1-26: Being the Body of Christ

▮ The Text in Its Ancient Context

Paul introduces the topic with the statement, "Now concerning spiritual gifts [or "spiritual things," *pneumatika*], brothers and sisters, I do not want you to be uninformed" (12:1). This statement may have been a surprise to those at Corinth who heard these words: with their interest in wisdom and knowledge, the Corinthians likely understood themselves to be quite well informed about spiritual gifts. The Corinthians, with their interest in *pneumatika*, were on the cutting edge of an emerging medical and philosophical debate in the first and second centuries, including medical debates over whether "spirit" runs through the blood and philosophical debates about the materiality of *pneuma*. From the fourth to the first centuries BCE, terms etymologically related to *pneumatika* are found approximately thirty-six times in extant literary writings. In writings from the first century CE, however, we find at least 104 uses of the term, and in the second century CE, a shocking 990 uses; a good many of these are Christian, emerging because of discussion of 1 Corinthians (Nasrallah 2003).

Nevertheless, even as Paul likely mirrors the Corinthians' own interest in and discussions of *pneumatika* and their participation in a broader cultural fascination with the topic of *pneuma*, he asserts that they do not understand spiritual gifts particularly well. He ranks spiritual gifts and seeks to reconfigure the importance of prophecy and glossolalia in the Corinthian community.

Paul embeds his ranking of spiritual gifts in a discussion of the body. First Corinthians is full of advice on the discipline and control of the individual body in relation to the "one body" of the *ekklēsia*. Paul uses the image of many members making up that one body (12:12-27). He uses the term *sōma* in two primary ways. The first is the *sōma* as the individual body, which can be transformed (1 Cor. 15:35-50) and, as we recall, can be bought (6:20; 7:23a). Paul folds this image of body into an image of "one body" as community ("For just as the body is one and has many members, and all the members of the body, though many, are one body, so it is with Christ," 12:12), joking that the foot shouldn't compete with the hand nor the ear complain that it isn't an eye. This language of one body derives from the political discourse of the day.

The image of "one body" and the idea of communal benefit are powerful tools of deliberative rhetoric, and present an argument that few would want to dispute. Who wants to damage the common body? The first-century-CE Stoic philosopher Epictetus enjoins: "you are a citizen of the world, and a part of it," and urges his hearers "to treat nothing as a matter of private profit . . . but to act like the foot or the hand, which, if they had the faculty of reason and understood the constitution of nature, would never exercise choice or desire in any other way but by reference to the whole" (*Diatr.* 2.10.1–4 [Oldfather, 275]). By the second century, the cities of Asia Minor aggressively minted coinage representing *homonoia*, the unity between these bodies politic, even as at the same time they fiercely competed with each other to secure Roman imperial attention and funds (Price; Kampmann).

Along with the rhetoric of one body, Paul employs the political language of "general benefit," often employed in deliberative rhetoric, to persuade the audience: all spiritual gifts must be for the general benefit (*to sympheron*, 12:7; Mitchell 1991). Paul's statement that all spiritual gifts are from the same spirit (12:11), moreover, further underscores his emphasis on unity and sameness over and against or in the midst of the diversity of spiritual gifts.

Paul's emphasis in chapter 12 on the common benefit and one body reorders and marginalizes those spiritual gifts that are connected to wisdom and knowledge, and that the Corinthians may have most valued. The general list of spiritual gifts in verses 8-10 is ranked in 12:28: "And God has appointed in the church first apostles, second prophets, third teachers; then deeds of power, then gifts of healing, forms of assistance, forms of leadership, various kinds of tongues." While 1 Cor.

12:14–26 argues for the significance of every member of the body, both the "weaker" and those given more "honor," this argument is undercut by the ranking and ordering of *pneumatika* in 12:28. This ranking erodes the emphasis on wisdom and knowledge—and concomitantly glossolalia and prophecy, gifts the Corinthians held dear. Paul admits the importance of prophets, but subordinates them to apostles; he also disaggregates prophecy from glossolalia, and ranks the latter last, perhaps as part of his strategy of challenging the Corinthians' understanding of Wisdom. After all, she was associated with eloquence and speech: "wisdom opened the mouth of the dumb, and made the tongues of babes speak clearly" (Wis. 10:21). Even infants (recall Paul's accusation in 3:1) benefit from Wisdom.

▌ The Text in the Interpretive Tradition

Christian communities have long struggled with questions of how the divine is manifest in different historical periods. Some early Christians believed that the Spirit and its gifts were relegated to a past time; the beginning of the *Martyrdom of Perpetua and Felicitas* (1.4) argues that new witnesses may still be found, and indeed may be greater than past ones: "Let those then who would restrict the power of the one Spirit to times and seasons look to this: the more recent events should be considered the greater, being later than those of old, and this is a consequence of the extraordinary graces promised for the last stage of time" (Musurillo). This is followed by a citation of Acts 2:17/Joel 2:28, which refers to the Lord pouring out "my spirit upon all flesh." The passage continues with allusions to ideas of Spirit, community benefit, and distribution of gifts also found in 1 Corinthians: "So too we hold in honour and acknowledge not only new prophecies but new visions as well, according to the promise. And we consider all the other functions of the Holy Spirit as intended for the good of the Church; for the same Spirit has been sent to distribute all his gifts to all, as the Lord apportions to everyone" (1.5; Musurillo).

In earliest Christianity, some groups celebrated new manifestations of the Spirit. This was certainly the case for those who edited and used the *Martyrdom of Perpetua and Felicitas*, a community that may have been associated with the prophetic renewal movement, sometimes called Montanism, that arose in Asia Minor in the late second century CE and flourished for some time around the Mediterranean basin. Of course, such prophetic renewal movements were not limited to ancient times, but can be found in a figure like Joachim of Fiore in the twelfth century or the movement, sparked at Azusa Street in Los Angeles in the early twentieth century, that came to be called Pentecostalism.

▌ The Text in Contemporary Discussion

We find a comparable phenomenon in the Shakers or the United Society of Believers in Christ's Second Coming, which began in the mid-eighteenth century and was characterized by women's leadership, ideas of the equality of the sexes, an understanding of an unfolding Parousia or appearance of Christ, and ecstatic experiences of spiritual gifts, including speaking in tongues. The community was known for "shaking" and speaking in tongues and prophesying. The 1816 biography of one key leader, Ann Lee, talks about the gifts of the Holy Ghost and the current time when people can be filled "with visions, revelations and gifts of God" (Bishop and Wells, v; 7). Although much of their understanding of revelation is grounded in interpretations of the book of Revelation, some Shaker writings combine references to Saul of Tarsus with reference to gifts (and 1 Cor. 2:11) in order to argue for a new, Spirit-filled dispensation (see the 1848 edition of *A Summary View of the Millennial Church, or United Society of Believers, Commonly Called Shakers* 5.5). The Spirit's working was sometimes manifest in "gift drawings" and in "gift music" (Morin).

Debate about dispensations of time and the Spirit have not ceased. Global Pentecostalism, in all its variegated forms, is a growing force in Christianity, especially in the so-called two-thirds world, while academic engagement with such ideas is ongoing (*The Journal of Pentecostal Studies*; J. K. A. Smith; Miller and Yamamori). Different Christian communities use the very same text, 1 Corinthians, to argue for the effervescence of the Spirit's inbreaking in community *and* to argue, to the contrary, that true Christian community gathers in a unified way in which all speech is comprehensible and the use of tongues is barred.

1 Corinthians 12:27—13:13: Love and the Ranking of *Charismata*

▮ THE TEXT IN ITS ANCIENT CONTEXT

Chapter 13 seems like a digression because some of these materials are pre-Pauline, a kind of aretalogy of love derived from Jewish wisdom traditions (Conzelmann, 218). Yet its contents are intimately linked to the foregoing and following chapters on *pneumatika*: the themes of prophecy and tongues in particular, and the question of who is a spiritual person in general.

Chapter 13 begins by citing spiritual gifts significant at Corinth, but then relativizes their importance: "If I speak in the tongues of mortals and of angels, but do not have love, I am a noisy gong or a clanging cymbal. And if I have prophetic powers, and understand all mysteries and all knowledge, and if I have all faith, so as to remove mountains, but do not have love, I am nothing" (13:1–2). Paul emphasizes that these three things the Corinthians value (tongues, prophecy, faith) will all pass away, while "love never ends" (13:8). Returning to the theme of perfection (*to teleion*) raised in chapter 2, in which Paul contrasted the perfect person or initiate with the faulty Corinthians, Paul insists, "Our knowledge is imperfect and our prophecy is imperfect; but when the perfect comes, the imperfect will pass away" (13:9-10). Using the metaphors of being an infant and of gazing into a dim mirror, 1 Corinthians 13 emphasizes the immaturity and partialness of any sort of present knowledge and wisdom.

Verses 4-8a may present a pre-Pauline aretalogy—that is, a list of virtues or qualities—of love that is used to relativize the importance of wisdom in the Corinthian community. Aretalogies of Wisdom (as well as of Isis, who has qualities similar to Wisdom) are well known from the ancient world, and it is possible that the Corinthians knew these and celebrated Wisdom in their midst. First Corinthians 13 may seek to redirect the community's interest in wisdom by celebrating love instead, just as chapters 1–4 attempted to upend expectations about what true wisdom and knowledge are.

THE TEXT IN THE INTERPRETIVE TRADITION

Later Christian commentators connected Paul's comment, "If I deliver my body to be burned, but have not love, I gain nothing" (1 Cor. 13:3), to martyrdom. (Note that here lies one of the text-critical debates of 1 Corinthians: is the word "burn" or "boast" original to Paul's letter? They differ by only one letter in Greek.) In late second-century Alexandria, Clement argued: "You see that martyrdom for love's sake is taught" (*Strom.* 4.7). To celebrate the idea of the glory of a noble death, Clement cites Pindar, Aeschylus, Heraclitus, the words of Indian sages meeting Alexander the Great, and even Plato's *Republic*, among other sources. His discussion culminates with an argument about Christians displaying a true understanding of death for true love, a death that leads to glory, in a mix of Pauline verses from 1 Corinthians 13 about enduring love and 1 Cor. 4:9-13 about apostolic suffering. In heresiological debates, the verse is used to denigrate Christians with whom one disagrees. For instance, Tertullian argues that if Praxeas's body had been burned (in martyrdom)—Praxeas being another Christian whom Tertullian considered heretical—it would have profited him nothing since he did not have the love of God (*Prax.* 1.4).

First Corinthians 13 had a powerful afterlife as well in Augustine's *On Christian Doctrine*. All Scripture should be interpreted in light of "faith, hope, and love" while knowledge and prophecies fall away. Even a mistaken interpretation of Scripture, if it builds up love, argued Augustine, still goes in the right direction, even if the interpreter needs to be put correctly on the right path of interpretation (*On Christian Doctrine* 1.36–40). A person who has "faith, hope, and love" (1 Cor. 13:13) does not even need Scripture, except to instruct others (*On Christian Doctrine* 1.39). Dale Martin powerfully suggests that this principle of interpretation be applied to passages by Paul and those writing in his name that are used to condemn what some might today call homosexuality, especially in view of the quite different sex-gender system of the ancient world (Martin 2006, 49–50).

THE TEXT IN CONTEMPORARY DISCUSSION

In a sermon given on November 4, 1956, in Montgomery, Alabama, Martin Luther King Jr. delivered "Paul's Letter to American Christians." In it, "Paul" wonders at the "fascinating and astounding advances that you have made in the scientific realm" but states, "It seems to me that your moral progress lags behind your scientific progress" (M. L. King, 415), quoting Henry David Thoreau to support his argument. He offers an economic critique of capitalism's excesses, while arguing that America cannot turn to communism. He critiques American Protestantism, Roman Catholicism, and segregation in American society, particularly in the churches. He concludes by calling love the "most durable power in the world," and declares that it is "at bottom the heartbeat of the moral cosmos" (M. L. King, 420). He reaches this conclusion by interpreting 1 Corinthians 13, arguing that American Christians' "eloquence of articulate speech," "heights of academic achievement," and philanthropy are nothing if devoid of love: "I must bring my writing to a close now. Timothy is waiting to deliver this letter, and I must take leave for another church. But just before leaving, I must say to you, as I said to the church at Corinth, that I still believe that love is the most durable power in the world" (419). Martin Luther King, Jr., uses 1 Corinthians 13 to offer a cultural critique and to navigate the troubled waters of American politics by foregrounding a love that expels inequalities, whether of economics, race, or education.

1 Corinthians 14:1-40: Spiritual Gifts and Building up Community

▮ THE TEXT IN ITS ANCIENT CONTEXT

In 1 Cor. 14:1, Paul picks up the themes of the previous chapters and continues to work out his arguments about spiritual gifts, especially prophecy and glossolalia. "Pursue love," Paul insists, referring back to the contents of chapter 13; and "strive for the spiritual gifts," reminding his readers/ hearers of chapter 12, "especially that you may prophesy." This last phrase reminds us that Paul highlights prophecy over against tongues. Paul may have invented this division; it is possible that the Corinthian community had not categorized and ranked the *pneumatika* received at baptism.

Paul offers a series of arguments that deconstruct the importance of tongues. These arguments hinge on the concepts of "building up" (*oikodomē*)—as we recall, a key term in political rhetoric of the first century—and intelligibility. In 1 Corinthians 14, by his own admission, Paul seeks to rein in tongues, which are a primary means of accessing the divine and divine knowledge: "For those who speak in a tongue do not speak to other people but to God; for nobody understands them, since they are speaking mysteries in the spirit" (14:2). Yet Paul admits in 1 Corinthians 14 that he too speaks in tongues. He thus asserts that he can match the high status of any Corinthian who exhibits glossolalia, but chooses not to. By the time of the writing of 2 Corinthians 12, Paul feels forced to argue again on the Corinthians' terms, especially over against the "super-apostles" with their spiritual gifts. Thus Paul circuitously talks about his own "visions and revelations" (2 Cor. 12:1). In his famous "fool's speech," Paul insists that the Corinthians' resistance to him has compelled him to enter into a sort of performance competition where he must demonstrate that he too has experienced rich charismatic experiences.

Because of passages like 1 Corinthians 12–14, because of Paul's discussion of his own ecstatic experience in 2 Corinthians 10–12, and because of Paul's references to bearing Christ's body or to having the spirit of God (7:40), some have understood Paul as a mystic (Schweitzer) or a shaman (Ashton). Others have pointed to spirit-possession as an important characteristic of the religious lives of Corinthians (J. Z. Smith; Mount).

▮ THE TEXT IN THE INTERPRETIVE TRADITION

First Corinthians 14:33b-34, with its comments on women (or, less likely, wives; the Greek *gynaikes* can mean either) being silent in the *ekklēsia*, clearly raised issues for later Christians. This can be seen from the way in which various manuscripts treat the verses. We have none of Paul's "autographs," or original manuscripts; thus variations from text to text in the manuscripts we do have often indicate early Christian interpretations of those now-lost origins. In several manuscripts, verses 34-35 are displaced to after verse 40; in other manuscripts, including the early P[46] (third century), these verses appear as following verse 33 (Thiselton, 1148). Some have hypothesized that because this text "wanders," it may not have been original, but a scribal gloss (Fee), but Wire demonstrates that the "wandering" nature of the passage traces back only to one manuscript, thus strengthening the argument that this is *not* an interpolation (Thiselton, 1148–49). While Paul mentions prominent women leaders in the earliest *ekklēsiai* (see Romans 16), in 1 Corinthians 11 he also offers a subordinationist logic for women's veiling. In addition, that passage, as well as 1 Corinthians 15, relies on the account in Genesis 2 of man's creation first, and woman's creation from man; it may be that the Corinthians (as with other, later Christian communities) relied instead on the idea in Gen. 1:27 that God created the human in God's image, "male and female God created them." We cannot know Paul's intentions, and his letters offer contradictory indications regarding the role of women in earliest Christian communities. What we can know is that Paul's letters indicate women's leadership and voice in earliest in-Christ communities, and both his support for and ambivalence about this phenomenon. His arguments for veiling and women's silence indicate that they were praying and prophesying in community unveiled, on the one hand, and that they were vocal in the community, on the other. Looking in 1 Corinthians and to other texts, especially Romans 16, we find a panoply of women in communication with Paul and leading in communities. Those who draw from Paul's letters the justification for subordinating women's leadership in worship have grounds to do so, and those who use Paul's letters to argue for women's leadership have grounds to do so as well.

■ THE TEXT IN CONTEMPORARY DISCUSSION

The story of the origins of Pentecostalism at Azusa Street in Los Angeles, California, is replete with references to Acts 1–2 and the story of *heteroglossia*—speaking in other languages—in those passages. References to 1 Corinthians 12–14, with its emphasis on *glossolalia*, speaking in tongues, are puzzlingly less utilized, perhaps precisely because of how Paul cites his own speaking in tongues yet also downgrades and relativizes the importance of this spiritual gift among others.

One contemporary Pentecostal treatment of 1 Corinthians 14 comes in a sermon by Rev. David Yonggi Cho, pastor of the Yoido Full Gospel Church in South Korea (Myung and Hong). In 2007, this Pentecostal church claimed approximately a million members. In a sermon titled "The Benefits of Speaking in Tongues," preached on February 15, 2009, Cho began by narrating the origins of global Pentecostalism at Azusa Street. His sermon, grounded in 1 Cor. 14:18 ("I thank God that I speak in tongues more than all of you"), emphasizes the ongoing importance of this spiritual gift. Cho provides five reasons for speaking in tongues to encourage his audience to continue in the practice. He argues that speaking in tongues benefits the individual, who can pray in the spirit with the help of the Paraclete (the term used for the Holy Spirit in John's Gospel). It allows for prayers to well up when the person praying is sufficiently despairing that she or he cannot find a way to pray. It allows for all-night prayer vigils since, without the Holy Spirit, Christians would be unequal to the task of praying all night. Speaking in tongues, he asserts, can cast out a devil, and the Christian who speaks in tongues needs no psychologist as tongues have a healing function. Speaking in tongues, Cho further states, can calm nightmares and allows God to speak through humans. Finally, speaking in tongues is a privately edifying phenomenon that should be practiced *before* teaching or preaching a sermon; it leads to greater clarity and purpose in public speaking and preaching. Some Christian communities today continue to think of glossolalia as a powerful, expansive, and indispensable spiritual practice that can encourage, advocate, heal, and spur the growth of church ministry.

1 Corinthians 15:1-58: Transformations: From "Psychic Body" to "Spiritual Body"

∎ THE TEXT IN ITS ANCIENT CONTEXT

Some have debated whether 1 Corinthians 15 belongs in this letter or is a segment of another writing with the theme of the resurrection. Most agree, however, that themes of the body, spirit, baptism, Christ's role, and the resurrection have been drawn from earlier in the letter and find their culmination in this, the final section of the body of the letter.

The chapter starts (vv. 1-11) with a defense and explanation of Paul's role in preaching the gospel, a role we know from Gal 1:11—2:10 was a matter of debate, even if the Acts of the Apostles solders into place Paul's authority in going to the gentiles (although not before giving Peter the primacy of place). Issues of Paul's identity and authority often surface in different ways in his letters—we need only to glance at the beginning of Galatians to see that he strongly defines his role as apostle with *no* connections to human authority there; in Romans, a community he does not know, he begins more cautiously with an unqualified self-designation as "apostle" and by describing himself more humbly as "slave of Christ." In 1 Cor. 15:1-11, Paul traces a proto-creedal statement that predates him (he uses a form of *paradidōmi*, a verb used to indicate the transmission of knowledge from a teacher, or by tradition, in his statement "what I in turn had received," 15:3) and links it to an authoritative line of transmission. Of "first importance" is that "Christ died for our sins in accordance with the scriptures, and that he was buried, and that he was raised on the third day in accordance with the scriptures" (vv. 3-4). Paul began his letter by emphasizing the crucifixion of Christ. Here, near the letter's end, he returns to the theme of Christ's death and elaborates on the theme of resurrection and the idea of death's overthrow.

Paul then traces the authoritative line of eyewitnesses, beginning with Cephas, then the Twelve, and the line continues "to all the apostles," then to James. Paul does not mention women in this list, though later sources would name Mary Magdalene and others. Paul states that he is "last of all": "as to one untimely born, [Christ] appeared also to me" (15:8). Paul locates his unfitness to be called an apostle *not* in the lack of ties he has to the historical Jesus or his lack of training in Jerusalem, but in his persecution of the *ekklēsia* of God. The proto-creedal statement recedes as Paul articulates that it does not matter whether it was "I or those" who preached and "so you believed," reprising the theme of various leaders at the beginning of his letter.

In verses 12 and following, Paul accuses the Corinthians of saying that "there is no resurrection of the dead" and argues the futility of this point of view (vv. 12-19) to those who are in Christ. We cannot know if the Corinthians actually claimed that there was no resurrection of the dead; indeed, this seems unlikely given that they baptize on behalf of the dead. Perhaps the Corinthians were emphasizing the power of resurrection in the present, even as they also emphasized Wisdom's power evidenced in their community through spiritual gifts. Paul then proceeds to defend the idea that Christ has been raised from the dead. He does so by turning to the story of creation and a typology that pairs Adam and Christ, with the first bringing death ("for as all die in Adam") and the second life ("so all will be made alive in Christ," v. 22).

Arguments from creation and arguments about Adam were commonplace at the time of Paul's writing of 1 Corinthians. Commentaries and philosophical debates over Plato's *Timaeus*, a story of the origins and structure of the cosmos, were penned; so, too, we find interpretations of Genesis that result in texts like the radical retelling of Genesis 1–2 in the *Hypostasis of the Archons* (perhaps second century CE). Jews contemporary with Paul engaged in debate over Genesis, sometimes with quite different interpretations, as we find in Philo's comment that all humans are a degeneration from the first human, who was "beautiful and good" and "lovely of body," compounded from the most pure and refined earthly substance (*Opif.* 137–40).

Portions of 1 Corinthians 15 remix 1 Thess. 4:13—5:11, with its eschatological themes. Here, as there, Paul offers an image of the Parousia or appearance of Christ in power (15:23). Paul employs language of the "reign of God" (15:24) and the destruction of "every ruler and authority and power." Given that the last of these to be destroyed is death, we can understand that, for the Corinthians hearing this letter, both temporal and cosmological rulers would be brought to mind, providing a coda to Paul's mention of "rulers of this age" crucifying "the Lord of glory" (2:8). Paul indicates that Christ's role should be understood in light of the Jewish Scriptures (Pss. 8:6; 110:1). Understanding this death-slaying Christ in relation to the psalmist's phrase "all things are put in subjection under his feet" might raise the question of whether he who subjected things is then superior or equal to God. Paul reassures the community that the Son is subject to God (15:28), dispelling any concerns or ideas that his theology involved "two powers in heaven," as did other, debated Jewish theologies of antiquity (Boyarin 2010; 2001).

Paul had begun this elaboration of the resurrection of the dead by stridently accusing the Corinthians of claiming there is no resurrection of the dead. He abruptly shifts back to them and to their practices, namely, baptism on behalf of the dead. This is the earliest and only reference in the Letters of Paul to such a practice, and it has raised many questions. The Corinthians may have been concerned about incorporating their ancestors into their new cult, and so baptism was a mechanism for initiating not only the living but also the dead (DeMaris). This practice becomes the grounds for Paul to insist on the truth of resurrection of the dead—not just of Christ but also of Christ as first evidence of a greater transformation.

In verse 35, Paul either paraphrases or caricatures a question from someone at Corinth: "How are the dead raised? With what kind of body do they come?" The answer is a full-scale blast in which Paul combines theories from religion and physics. Paul uses the metaphor of a kernel of grain, and argues that there are different kinds of flesh (*sarx*) and different kinds of bodies (*sōmata*), which themselves have different glories (*doxai*). We should think about this, as well as other aspects of 1 Corinthians, in light of scientific theories of the first century, a time when philosophical and theological speculation were often one and the same, and when theories from physics and medicine informed such speculation. For instance, while we may think of "spirit" as immaterial, Stoic philosophers of antiquity thought of it as a purer form of matter (Engberg-Pedersen).

This speculation from physics becomes the ground for further defining the "resurrection of the dead" and the particular problematic of the body. Paul lists a set of hierarchical binaries: weakness, power; physical, spiritual; first Adam, last Adam. Again, Paul argues from the creation story that the first Adam was a living soul, while the last Adam is a life-giving spirit. This language of *psychikon* versus *pneumatikon* echoes the hierarchical use of the terms in chapter 4 and may indicate some debate over the evolution or development of bodies from one kind of coarse matter to a finer kind of matter associated with spirit or *pneuma* (Engberg-Pedersen, 39–74). Certainly this language was quickly taken up and discussed by Paul's later interpreters. Origen tried to resolve the fact that Paul insisted the resurrected body was not flesh and blood, yet was a body (*De princ.* 2.10–11), while other early Christians, concerned about the continuation of the appetites after death, debated whether the resurrected body would have teeth or genitalia (Petrey).

Paul reprises and develops a vision of the end that he articulated in an earlier letter, 1 Thessalonians. This letter uses language of "putting on" (15:53) imperishability and immortality, imagery of clothing and unclothing, that probably called to mind baptismal practices (see 2 Cor. 5:1-5; Gal. 3:27).

■ THE TEXT IN THE INTERPRETIVE TRADITION

Paul's claim to have met Jesus "by revelation" (*apokalypsis* or cognates: Gal. 1:12, 16) and his lack of a familial or historical link to the earliest Jesus traditions or Jesus himself was a bone of contention among those in Christ in the first and second centuries and beyond. The Corinthians, among other communities, may have wanted to hear from an apostle who visited them a recital and confirmation of the "tradition" that Paul mentions in 1 Cor. 15:1-11; that is, they may have preferred someone who had known Jesus "in the flesh." Paul instead presents to them in writing "what I also received" (15:3) and explains how Christ appeared to him (15:6), using this revelation both to authorize his role as apostle and to present himself as called and chosen, echoing language of the Jewish prophets (Gal. 1:15)—not as a convert to a new religion (Stendahl).

This self-presentation would have many effects in the interpretive tradition. First, some would take up Paul's language of call, apocalypse, and visionary experience (see also 2 Cor. 12:1-13) and produce a text like the *Apocalypse of Paul*, found among the documents at Nag Hammadi, in which Paul is caught up into the heavens as he travels on his way to Jerusalem. Others, whose stance is represented in the Pseudo-Clementine literature (compiled in the fourth century CE but including sources that date to the second century CE), implicitly criticized Paul's claims as illegitimate, attributing to Jesus the saying that the "evil one" would also send apostles (*Clementine Hom.* 11.35.3). A fictional scene is set: The apostle Peter argues with "Simon"—a *magus*-figure whom Christians often evoked to represent their opponents—who is a lightly veiled stand-in for Paul. Peter challenges the truth of the sort of knowledge that comes through visionary experience, demonstrates that visions often occur to the impious rather than to the blessed, and finally spurts out: "So even if our Jesus did appear in a dream to you, making himself known and conversing with you, he did so in anger, speaking to an opponent. That is why he spoke to you through visions and dreams—through revelations which are external" (*Clementine Hom.* 17.19.1 [Meeks and Fitzgerald]). While it is clear that Paul's letters are very influential today, especially in Protestant Christianity, ancient texts also indicate a strong ambivalence about Paul's letters, on the one hand—letters that were, after all, much interpreted among Christians who would come to be called heretics (followers of Valentinus, for instance) as well as those who would come to be considered orthodox (John Chrysostom, for example). In addition, some ancient texts show a strong skepticism regarding claims for revelation, questioning whether a visionary experience of Christ (like Paul's) could be false. Many of those who heard Paul's message in antiquity were more skeptical of it than most Christians, and those who use Paul's thought for political theology, are today. Those who understand Christ primarily through the lens of Paul (some do call themselves Paulinists!) or who would argue, with Slavoj Žižek, that "There is no Christ outside Saint Paul," miss early Christian controversy and even rejection of Paul and his letters. The versions of Christianity prevalent today, especially in North American Protestantism, make it hard to picture what a Christian identity that rejects Paul would look like, or even to engage in the work of historical reconstruction of the voices of the Corinthians or others who may have debated or rejected Paul's teachings in the first century.

■ THE TEXT IN CONTEMPORARY DISCUSSION

Colossians 3:1-3, a pseudepigraphic text that claims to have been penned by Paul, offers the idea: "So if you have been raised with Christ, seek the things that are above, where Christ is . . . For you have died, and your life is hidden with Christ in God." As we have seen, some at Corinth may have understood themselves to have been living already, through the initiatory ritual of baptism, in a transformed, resurrected type of life. Colossians 3:1 takes up the themes of Paul's writings and transforms them more explicitly into the idea that Christians have already died and been raised with Christ, even in their present lives.

Karl Barth's 1924 *Die Auferstehung der Toten* decidedly rejects the idea that the resurrection occurs in the present: "It is not we who are the risen ones!" he exclaimed (Janssen, 65). Barth understood 1 Corinthians 15 as "the very peak and crown of this essentially critical and polemically negative Epistle" (Barth, 101) and "a clue to its meaning" (Barth, 5). It is a doctrine of last things, for Barth, which points to the gap between humans and God and the gap between now and then.

> Because it is *thus within* our existence, even our Christian existence, and must always be, however high we climb, because the "then" is really a *Then* and *There*, no Now and Here, the *reality* of the resurrection is exclusively the reality of the *resurrection*, the truth of Christianity is exclusively *God's* truth, its absoluteness is exclusively *God's* absoluteness. (Barth, 210–11)

In contrast, Rudolf Bultmann's appreciative 1926 response to Barth emphasizes that "our resurrection is reality, now that Christ is risen" (Janssen, 76). He explains: "in a certain sense, i.e. in so far as we belong to Christ, we are the resurrected, are the 'first fruits' . . . , are a 'new creation'" (Bultmann, 93–94). In this contrast between Barth and Bultmann we may see an echo of Paul's and some Corinthians' differing interpretations of the resurrection: Paul with Barth would insist on perfection or completion and resurrection as happening *then*, not now; think of his insistence, for example, in 1 Cor. 13:12: "For now we see in a mirror, dimly, but then we will see face to face." Some of the Corinthians, in contrast, may have delighted in spiritual gifts and in demonstrating the *now* of the new creation.

1 Corinthians 16:1-23: Epistolary Closing

▌ THE TEXT IN ITS ANCIENT CONTEXT

First Corinthians 15, with its crescendo of criticism of the Corinthians for their questions about the resurrection of the dead and compelling and varied arguments about the truth of the resurrection of the dead, its connection to the first and last Adam, and its ability literally to transform individuals and the cosmos, thundered at the end. Chapter 16, the closing of the letter, offers a quiet denouement and a glimpse of everyday life.

The letter first reminds its readers about the "contribution for the holy ones" (or "saints") and indicates that Paul has some expectation of equity among communities, since he has written the same to the *ekklēsiai* of Galatia. We also find, in 2 Corinthians 8 and 9, more letters about this contribution (see Georgi). We glimpse something of travel and social networks as Paul explains how to collect money and that he will send some emissary/ies, whom the Corinthians approve, with a letter—and funds—to Jerusalem.

Paul concludes with travel plans, as is typical of his letters, and reveals that he is likely in Ephesus as he writes. The social networks that Paul hints at or reveals earlier in the letter here arise again: the question of when Timothy and Apollos will visit Corinth is raised; the visit of Stephanas and Fortunatus and Achaicus to Paul, making up for the absence of the entire community, is mentioned, and their authority is enforced with the injunction to "be subject" to them and to "everyone who works and toils with them" (16:16). The epistle began with Paul's mention of Stephanas and "those in his household." The names Fortunatus and Achaicus hint at their servile or freedperson status, since one is nicknamed "fortunate," and the other is named after the region of his origin; we can wonder if they were Stephanas's slaves or freedpersons. Social networks are further highlighted as Paul offers greetings from *ekklēsiai* of Asia and mentions Aquila and Priscilla, whose names also appear in Romans 16.

Certain rituals and mechanics are exposed at the end of the letter. Perhaps like Romans—we know from Rom. 16:22 that the scribe Tertius wrote the letter—1 Corinthians was penned by a scribe, since Paul emphasizes his own writing at the end of the letter, probably in a note and signature, as was common in ancient letter writing.

▌ THE TEXT IN THE INTERPRETIVE TRADITION

Paul ends 1 Corinthians by reprising his mention of Stephanas and household at the beginning of the letter and names them "the first converts in Achaia." This may have aided in the invention of 3 Corinthians. This text is known from the Armenian Bible and the commentary of Ephrem; it also seems to have circulated as part of a larger *Acts of Paul* (Schneemelcher, 217). Third Corinthians consists of a fragmentary letter purporting to be from Stephanas "and the presbyters (or ambassadors) who are with him," and Paul's reply. The Corinthians' letter to Paul expresses concern about the teachings of two men in Corinth who are introducing new ideas, such as that one should not appeal to the prophets, that there is no resurrection of the flesh, that Christ was not born of Mary nor came in the flesh, that the creation is not God's work. A brief narrative element before "Paul's" reply claims that Stephanas's letter was delivered to Paul in Philippi, where he was in prison, and he sent a reply to the theological confusion introduced by these false teachers.

From the fictive correspondence of 3 Corinthians we see the staying power of certain names, like Stephanas's, in what became the Christian tradition. We also learn more of the ancient context in which early Christians wrote letters in Paul's name and imaginatively responded to new social and theological crises in "Paul's" voice. Such responses in Paul's name, but not by Paul, include New Testament writings like Colossians, Ephesians, and the Pastoral Epistles (1 and 2 Timothy, Titus), as well as "letters" to and from Paul, like 3 Corinthians. The epistle was a powerful literary tool not only among early Christians. This phenomenon, called "epistolary narrative" or "epistolary fiction" (Rosenmeyer), burgeoned in antiquity; letters of Plato, Socrates, and others were invented to provide biographical details or to tease out the philosophical importance of famous figures. In using pseudepigraphical letters to create new narratives, early Christians were taking part in a larger cultural phenomenon that we need not understand as forgery or deception. Rather, Christians (among others) were in their writings creating possible worlds in which a figure like Paul, even after his death, was wielded to support Christian communities' responses to theological difference with "his" authoritative voice. These pseudepigraphical letters represent the multiple and even opposing directions in which Paul's teachings could be taken.

▌ THE TEXT IN CONTEMPORARY DISCUSSION

First Corinthians 16:2 discusses raising funds for a gift to be carried to Jerusalem: "On the first day of every week, each of you is to put aside and save whatever extra you earn, so that collections need not be taken when I come." The seeming conditional link between storing up money for the Jerusalem collection, on the one hand, and prosperity, on the other, makes the verse a possible source for those debating the "prosperity gospel."

Creflo Dollar, a famous pastor associated with the prosperity gospel, uses 1 Cor. 16:2, among other texts, to discuss the idea of prosperity in Bible study notes titled "The Secret Combination for True Prosperity" (Dollar). His Bible study notes argue that definitions of prosperity changed over time in biblical writings, and that 1 Cor. 16:2 is evidence of prosperity as "success in profitability and material gain." Although he reframes prosperity in terms of the total wholeness of the person, with money as only one aspect of prosperity, Dollar nonetheless reveals a larger debate going on among those who adhere to the prosperity gospel: which scriptural passages promise prosperity, and what do the same verses enjoin in terms of contributions (understood in contemporary churches as weekly tithes) that individuals may make?

This use of 1 Cor. 16:2 in the context of a broad range of biblical passages on "prosperity" reminds us, too, of how this strategy of interpretation is both fair use and misuse of Paul's letters. It is fair use because Paul's letters are indeed now part of a canon and as such can be juxtaposed with texts in a different language, from a different time period and context, in a creative theological way. But such a strategy is also misuse, because Paul's letters were in their first instantiation occasional, rather than works of systematic theology, to be picked over and juxtaposed with other "Scriptures." They were produced and received in an ad hoc, improvisational context by those who did not bear the name Christian, much less know that the letters would emerge into a canon of Pauline Letters or that some would put pen to papyrus to "imitate" Paul as he had enjoined (but perhaps not as he would have wished), writing letters in his name. The Letters of Paul were produced and received by those who could not imagine them embedded within a canon. It is our responsibility to pursue a letter like 1 Corinthians with a disciplined intimacy that calls us to see the text first as stranger, not at all written to us, or about us, and only later to see the text as intimate, as a fruitful interlocutor for the theological imagination, for political action, for religious practice today.

Works Cited

Agamben, Giorgio. 2005. *The Time That Remains: A Commentary on the Letter to the Romans.* Translated by Patricia Dailey. Stanford: Stanford University Press.

Ascough, Richard S., Philip A. Harland, and John S. Kloppenborg. 2012. *Associations in the Greco-Roman World: A Sourcebook.* Waco: Baylor University Press.

Ashton, John. 2000. *The Religion of Paul the Apostle.* New Haven: Yale University Press.

Badiou, Alain. 2003. *Saint Paul: The Foundation of Universalism.* Translated by Ray Brassier. Stanford: Stanford University Press.

Bagnall, Roger S., and Bruce W. Frier. 2006. *The Demography of Roman Egypt.* Cambridge: Cambridge University Press.

Bartchy, S. Scott. 1973. *Mallon Chrēsai: First Century Slavery and the Interpretation of 1 Corinthians 7:21.* Atlanta: Scholars Press.

Barth, Karl. 1933. *The Resurrection of the Dead.* Translated by H. J. Stenning. London: Hodder and Stoughton.

Baur, F. C. 1831. "Die Christuspartei in der korinthischen Gemeinde, der Gegensatz des petrinischen und paulinischen Christentums in der ältesten Kirche, der Apostel Petrus in Rom," *Tübinger Zeitschrift für Theologie* 4:61–206.

BeDuhn, Jason David. 1999. "Because of the Angels: Unveiling Paul's Anthropology in 1 Corinthians 11." *JBL* 118, no. 2:295–320.

Bishop, Rufus, and Seth Youngs Wells, eds. 1816. *Testimonies of the Life, Character, Revelation and Doctrines of Our Ever Blessed Mother Ann Lee.* Hancock, MA: J. Tallcott and J. Deming, Junrs.

Bookidis, Nancy, and Ronald S. Stroud. 1997. *Corinth XVIII, Part III: The Sanctuary of Demeter and Kore: Topography and Architecture.* Princeton: ASCSA.

Boyarin, Daniel. 2001. "The Gospel of the Memra: Jewish Binitarianism and the Prologue to John." *HTR* 94, no. 3:243–84.

———. 2010. "Beyond Judaisms: Metatron and the Divine Polymorphy of Ancient Judaism." *Journal for the Study of Judaism* 41:323–365.

Buell, Denise Kimber. 2005. *Why This New Race: Ethnic Reasoning in Early Christianity.* New York: Columbia University Press.

Bultmann, Rudolf. 1987. *Faith and Understanding.* Vol. 1. Translated by Louise Pettibone Smith. Edited by Robert W. Funk. Minneapolis: Fortress Press.

Cadbury, Henry J. 1934. "The Macellum of Corinth." *JBL* 53, no. 2:134–41.

Calvin, John. 1981. *Commentary on the Epistles of Paul the Apostle to the Corinthians.* Translated by John Pringle. Grand Rapids: Baker.

Castelli, Elizabeth A. 1991. *Imitating Paul: A Discourse of Power*. Louisville: Westminster John Knox.

Clement of Alexandria. 1994. "The Stromata, or Miscellanies." In *ANF* 2:299–568.

Cohen, Shaye J. D. 1999. *The Beginnings of Jewishness: Boundaries, Varieties, Uncertainties*. Berkeley: University of California Press.

Concannon, Cavan. 2014. *"When You Were Gentiles": Specters of Ethnicity in Roman Corinth and Paul's Corinthian Correspondence*. New Haven: Yale University Press.

Conzelmann, Hans. 1975. *1 Corinthians: A Commentary on the First Epistle to the Corinthians*. Hermeneia. Philadelphia: Fortress Press.

"Decree on Ecumenism, *Unitatis redintegratio*." 1964. Documents of the II Vatican Council. http://www.vatican.va/archive/hist_councils/ii_vatican_council/documents/vat-ii_decree_19641121_unitatis-redintegratio_en.html. Deissmann, Adolf. 1908. *Licht vom Osten: das Neue Testament und die neuentdeckten Texte der hellenistisch-römischen Welt*. Tübingen: Mohr.

DeMaris, Richard E. 1995. "Corinthian Religion and Baptism for the Dead (1 Corinthians 15:29): Insights from Archaeology and Anthropology." *JBL* 114, no. 4:661–82.

Dollar, Creflo. 2006. "The Secret Combination for True Prosperity." *Creflo Dollar Ministries*. http://www.creflodollarministries.org/BibleStudy/StudyNotes.aspx?id=62.

Douglas, Mary. 1970. *Natural Symbols*. London: Barrie & Rockliff.

Eisenbaum, Pamela. 2009. *Paul Was Not a Christian: The Original Message of a Misunderstood Apostle*. New York: HarperCollins.

Ekroth, Gunnel. 2007. "Meat in Ancient Greece: Sacrificial, Sacred or Secular?" *Food and History* 5:249–72.

Elliott, Neil. *Liberating Paul: The Justice of God and the Politics of the Apostle*. Maryknoll, NY: Orbis, 1994.

Engberg-Pedersen, Troels. 2010. *Cosmology and Self in the Apostle Paul: The Material Spirit*. New York: Oxford University Press.

Fee, Gordon D. 1987. *The First Epistle to the Corinthians*. NICNT. Grand Rapids: Eerdmans.

Fitzmyer, Joseph A. 2008. *First Corinthians: A New Translation with Introduction and Commentary*. AYB. New Haven: Yale University Press.

Frilingos, Christopher A. 2004. *Spectacles of Empire: Monsters, Martyrs, and the Book of Revelation*. Philadelphia: University of Pennsylvania Press.

Gaca, Kathy L. 2003. *The Making of Fornication: Eros, Ethics, and Political Reform in Greek Philosophy and Early Christianity*. Berkeley: University of California Press.

Gager, John G. 2000. *Reinventing Paul*. New York: Oxford University Press.

Garnsey, Peter, and Greg Woolf. 1989. "Patronage of the Rural Poor in the Roman World." In *Patronage in Ancient Society*, edited by Andrew Wallace-Hadrill, 153–70. London: Routledge.

Georgi, Dieter. 1992. *Remembering the Poor: The History of Paul's Collection for Jerusalem*. Nashville: Abingdon.

Glancy, Jennifer A. 2002. *Slavery in Early Christianity*. Oxford: Oxford University Press.

Gooch, Peter David. 1993. *Dangerous Food: I Corinthians 8–10 in Its Context*. Waterloo, ON: Wilfrid Laurier University Press.

Grabbe, Lester L. 1997. *Guide to the Apocrypha and Pseudepigrapha*. Vol. 3, *Wisdom of Solomon*. Sheffield: Sheffield Academic.

Haddad, Mimi. 2013. "Male Rule a Biblical Ideal? Part Two." *CBE International*. http://www.cbeinternational.org/?q=content/2013-09-12-male-rule-biblical-ideal-part-two-arise-e-newsletter.

Harrill, J. Albert. 1995. *The Manumission of Slaves in Early Christianity*. Tübingen: Mohr Siebeck.

Hodge, Caroline Johnson. 2007. *If Sons, Then Heirs: A Study of Kinship and Ethnicity in the Letters of Paul.* Oxford: Oxford University Press.

Horsley, Richard A. 1979. "Spiritual Marriage with Sophia." *VC* 33:30–54.

———. 1998. *1 Corinthians.* ANTC. Nashville: Abingdon.

Janssen, Claudia. 2000. "Bodily Resurrection (1 Cor. 15)? The Discussion of Resurrection in Karl Barth, Rudolf Bultmann, Dorothee Soelle and Contemporary Feminist Theology." *JSNT* 79:61–78.

Johnson-DeBaufre, Melanie. 2005. *Jesus among Her Children: Q, Eschatology, and the Construction of Christian Origins.* Cambridge, MA: Harvard University Press.

Johnson-DeBaufre, Melanie, and Laura S. Nasrallah. 2011. "Beyond the Heroic Paul: Toward a Feminist and Decolonizing Approach to the Letters of Paul." In *The Colonized Apostle: Paul Through Postcolonial Eyes*, edited by Christopher Stanley, 161–74. Minneapolis: Fortress Press.

Kampmann, Ursula. 1998. "Homonoia Politics in Asia Minor: The Example of Pergamon." In *Pergamon, Citadel of the Gods: Archaeological Record, Literary Description, and Religious Development*, edited by Helmut Koester, 373–93. Harrisburg, PA: Trinity Press International.

Kent, J. H. 1966. *Corinth VIII, Part III: The Inscriptions, 1926–1950.* Princeton: ASCSA.

King, Karen L. 2005. *What Is Gnosticism?* Cambridge, MA: Harvard University Press.

King, Martin Luther, Jr. 1956. "Paul's Letter to American Christians." *The King Center.* http://www.thekingcenter.org/archive/document/pauls-letter-american-christians-0.

Kloppenborg, John. 2013. "Membership Practices in Pauline Christ Groups." *Early Christianity* 4, no. 2:183–215.

Kocar, Alexander. 2013. "'Humanity Came to Be According to Three Essential Types': Ethical Responsibility and Practice in the Valentinian Anthropogony of the Tripartite Tractate (NHC I, 5)." In *Jewish and Christian Cosmogony in Late Antiquity*, edited by Lance Jenott and Sarit Kattan Gribetz, 193–221. Tübingen: Mohr Siebeck.

Koester, Helmut. 1990. *Ancient Christian Gospels: Their History and Development.* Harrisburg, PA: Trinity Press International.

Kovacs, Judith L. 2005. *1 Corinthians: Interpreted by Early Christian Medieval Commentators.* The Church's Bible. Grand Rapids: Eerdmans.

Lamp, Jeffrey S. 2000. *First Corinthians 1–4 in Light of Jewish Wisdom Traditions: Christ, Wisdom, and Spirituality.* Lewiston, NY: Mellen.

Lieu, Judith. 2002. *Neither Jew Nor Greek? Constructing Early Christianity.* London: T&T Clark.

Luther, Martin. 1973. *LW* 28.

Marchal, Joseph A. 2011. "The Usefulness of an Onesimus: The Sexual Use of Slaves and Paul's Letter to Philemon." *JBL* 130, no. 4:749–70.

Martin, Dale B. 1990. *Slavery as Salvation: The Metaphor of Slavery in Pauline Christianity.* New Haven: Yale University Press.

———. 1995. *The Corinthian Body.* New Haven: Yale University Press.

———. 2006. *Sex and the Single Savior.* Louisville: Westminster John Knox.

Meeks, Wayne A. 2003. *The First Urban Christians: The Social World of the Apostle Paul.* 2nd ed. New Haven: Yale University Press.

Meeks, Wayne A., and John T. Fitzgerald. 2007. *The Writings of St. Paul: Annotated Texts, Reception and Criticism.* New York: Norton.

Meggitt, Justin J. 1998. *Paul, Poverty, and Survival.* Edinburgh: T&T Clark.

Miller, Anna C. 2013. "*Not with Eloquent Wisdom*: Democratic *Ekklēsia* Discourse in 1 Corinthians 1–4." *JSNT* 35:323–54.

Miller, Donald E., and Tetsunao Yamamori. 2007. *Global Pentecostalism: The New Face of Christian Social Engagement.* Berkeley: University of California Press.

Millis, Benjamin W. 2010. "The Social and Ethnic Origins of the Colonists in Early Roman Corinth." In *Corinth in Context: Comparative Studies on Religion and Society*, edited by Steven J. Friesen, Daniel N. Schowalter, and James C. Walters, 13–36. Leiden: Brill.

———. 2013. "The Local Magistrates and Elite of Roman Corinth." In *Corinth in Contrast: Studies in Inequality*, edited by Steven J. Friesen, Sarah A. James, and Daniel N. Schowalter, 38–53. Leiden: Brill.

Mitchell, Margaret M. 1991. *Paul and the Rhetoric of Reconciliation: An Exegetical Investigation of the Language and Composition of 1 Corinthians.* Tübingen: Mohr Siebeck.

———. 2002. *The Heavenly Trumpet: John Chrysostom and the Art of Pauline Interpretation.* Louisville: Westminster John Knox.

Morin, France. 2001. *Heavenly Visions: Shaker Gift Drawings and Gift Songs.* Minneapolis: University of Minnesota Press.

Mount, Christopher. 2005. "1 Corinthians 11:3-16: Spirit Possession and Authority in a Non-Pauline Interpolation." *JBL* 124, no. 2:313–40.

Mouritsen, Henrik. 2011. *The Freedman in the Roman World.* Cambridge: Cambridge University Press.

Musurillo, Herbert, trans. 1972. *The Acts of the Christian Martyrs.* Oxford: Clarendon Press.

Myung, Sung-hoon, and Yonggi Hong, eds. 2003. *Charis and Charisma: David Yonggi Cho and the Growth of Yoido Full Gospel Church.* Oxford: Regnum.

Nabers, Ned Parker. 1967. *Macella: A Study in Roman Archaeology.* Princeton: Princeton University Press.

Naiden, F. S. 2013. *Smoke Signals for the Gods: Ancient Greek Sacrifice from the Archaic through Roman Periods.* New York: Oxford University Press.

Nasrallah, Laura Salah. 2004. *An Ecstasy of Folly: Prophecy and Authority in Early Christianity.* Cambridge, MA: Harvard University Press.

———. 2012. "Grief in Corinth: The Roman City and Paul's Corinthian Correspondence." In *Contested Spaces: Houses and Temples in Roman Antiquity and the New Testament*, edited by David L. Balch and Annette Weissenrieder, 109–40. Tübingen: Mohr Siebeck.

———. 2013. "'You Were Bought with a Price': Freedpersons and Things in 1 Corinthians." In *Corinth in Contrast: Studies in Inequality*, edited by Steven J. Friesen, Sarah A. James, and Daniel N. Schowalter, 54–73. Leiden: Brill.

———. Forthcoming (2014). "Archaeology and the Pauline Letters." In *Oxford Handbook of Pauline Studies*, edited by Barry Matlock. New York: Oxford University Press.

Neyrey, Jerome. 1986. "Body Language in 1 Corinthians: The Use of Anthropological Models for Understanding Paul and His Opponents." *Semeia* 35:129–70.

Økland, Jorunn. 2010. "Ceres, Κόρη, and Cultural Complexity: Divine Personality Definitions and Human Worshippers in Roman Corinth." In *Corinth in Context: Comparative Studies on Religion and Society*, edited by Steven J. Friesen, Daniel N. Schowalter, and James C. Walters, 199–229. Leiden: Brill.

Oldfather, W. A., trans. 1925. *Epictetus: Discourses, Books 1–2.* LCL 131. Cambridge, MA: Harvard University Press.

Oster, Richard. 1988. "When Men Wore Veils to Worship: the Historical Context of 1 Corinthians 11.4." *NTS* 34, no. 4:481–505.

Pétrement, Simone. 1990. *A Separate God: the Christian Origins of Gnosticism.* Translated by Carol Harrison. San Francisco: HarperSanFrancisco.

Petrey, Taylor. 2010. "Carnal Resurrection: Sexuality and Sexual Difference in Early Christianity." ThD diss., Harvard University Divinity School.

Pervo, Richard I. 2008. *Acts: A Commentary.* Hermeneia. Minneapolis: Fortress Press.

Price, S. R. F. 1985. *Rituals and Power: The Roman Imperial Cult in Asia Minor.* Cambridge: Cambridge University Press.

Robinson, Elizabeth A. 2011. *Histories of Peirene: A Corinthian Fountain in Three Millennia.* Princeton: ASCSA.

Rosenmeyer, Patricia A. 2001. *Ancient Epistolary Fictions: the Letter in Greek Literature.* Cambridge: Cambridge University Press.

Ruyt, Claire de. 1983. *Macellum, marché alimentaire des romains.* Louvain-la-Neuve: Institut supérieur d'archéologie et d'histoire de l'art, College Érasme.

Schmithals, Walter. 1971. *Gnosticism in Corinth: An Investigation of the Letters to the Corinthians.* Nashville: Abingdon.

Schneemelcher, Wilhelm, ed. 1992. *New Testament Apocrypha.* Vol. 2, *Writings Relating to the Apostles, Apocalypses and Related Subjects.* Rev. ed. Cambridge: James Clarke & Co.

Schüssler Fiorenza, Elisabeth. 1983. *In Memory of Her: A Feminist Theological Reconstruction of Christian Origins.* New York: Crossroad.

———. 1987. "Rhetorical Situation and Historical Reconstruction in 1 Corinthians." *NTS* 33:386–403.

———. 1993. *Discipleship of Equals: A Critical Feminist Ekklesia-logy of Liberation.* New York: Crossroad.

———. 1994. *Jesus: Miriam's Child, Sophia's Prophet: Critical Issues in Feminist Christology.* New York: Continuum.

———. 1999. *Rhetoric and Ethic: The Politics of Biblical Studies.* Minneapolis: Fortress Press.

Schweitzer, Albert. 1931. *The Mysticism of Paul the Apostle.* Translated by William Montgomery. New York: Henry Holt.

Shaner, Katherine. 2012. "Religion and the Civic Life of the Enslaved: A Case Study in Roman Ephesos." ThD Dissertation, Harvard University Divinity School.

Shewring, W. H., trans. 1929. *The Passion of Perpetua and Felicity.* London: The Fleuron. Modernized translation by Paul Halsall. 1996. "Medieval Sourcebook: St. Perpetua: *The Passion of Saints Perpetua and Felicity* 203." Internet Medieval Source Book. Fordham University Center for Medieval Studies. http://www.fordham.edu/halsall/source/perpetua.asp.

Skogen, Dan. 2009. "The Battle Continues For Nebraska Church Formerly Affiliated With the ELCA." *Exposing the ELCA.* http://www.exposingtheelca.com/exposed-blog/the-battle-continues-for-nebraska-church-formerly-affiliated-with-the-elca.

Slane, Kathleen Warner. 2000. "East-West Trade in Fine Wares and Commodities: the View from Corinth." *RCRFActa* 36:299–312.

Smith, James K. A. 2010. *Thinking in Tongues: Pentecostal Contributions to Christian Philosophy.* Grand Rapids: Eerdmans.

Smith, Jonathan Z. 2004. "Re: Corinthians." In *Relating Religion: Essays in the Study of Religion,* 340–61. Chicago: University of Chicago Press.

Spawforth, A. J. S. 1996. "Roman Corinth: The Formation of a Colonial Elite." In *Roman Onomastics in the Greek East: Social and Political Aspects,* edited by A. D. Rizakis, 167–82. Paris: Diffusion de Boccard.

Stang, Charles M. 2012. *Apophasis and Pseudonymity in Dionysius the Areopagite: "No Longer I."* New York: Oxford University Press.

Stendahl, Krister. 1976. *Paul Among Jews and Gentiles and Other Essays.* Minneapolis: Fortress Press.

Sterling, Gregory E. 1995. "Wisdom among the Perfect: Creation Traditions in Alexandrian Judaism and Corinthian Christianity." *NovT* 37, no. 4:355–84.

Still, E. Coye, III. 2002. "The Meaning and Uses of *EIDOLOTHYTON* in First Century Non-Pauline Literature and 1 Cor 8:1—11:1: Toward Resolution of the Debate." *Trinity Journal* 23, no. 2:225–34.

Stowers, Stanley K. 2011a. "Kinds of Myth, Meals, and Power: Paul and the Corinthians." In *Redescribing Paul and the Corinthians*, edited by Ron Cameron and Merrill P. Miller, 105–50. Atlanta: Society of Biblical Literature.

———. 2011b. "Does Pauline Christianity Resemble a Hellenistic Philosophy?" In *Redescribing Paul and the Corinthians*, edited by Ron Cameron and Merrill P. Miller, 219–44. Atlanta: Society of Biblical Literature.

———. 2011c. "The Concept of 'Community' and the History of Early Christianity." *Method and Theory in the Study of Religion* 23, nos. 3–4:238–56.

Svebakken, Hans. 2012. *Philo of Alexandria's Exposition of the Tenth Commandment.* Atlanta: Society of Biblical Literature.

Theissen, Gerd. 1982. *The Social Setting of Pauline Christianity: Essays on Corinth.* Edited and translated by John H. Schütz. Philadelphia: Fortress Press.

Thiselton, Anthony C. 2000. *The First Epistle to the Corinthians.* NIGTC. Grand Rapids: Eerdmans.

United Society of Believers, Commonly Called Shakers. 1848. "A Summary View of the Millennial Church." *Pass the Word Services.* http://www.passtheword.org/shaker-manuscripts/Millennial-Church/mchrch4x.htm.

Weissenrieder, Annette. 2012. "'Do You Not Know That You Are God's Temple?' Towards a New Perspective on Paul's Temple Image in 1 Corinthians 3:16." In *Contested Spaces: Houses and Temples in Roman Antiquity and the New Testament*, edited by David L. Balch and Annette Weissenrieder, 377–412. Tübingen: Mohr Siebeck.

West, A. B. 1931. *Corinth VIII, Part II: Latin Inscriptions, 1896–1926.* Cambridge, MA: ASCSA.

Wilckens, Ulrich. 1959. *Weisheit und Torheit: Eine exegetisch-religionsgeschichtliche Untersuchung zu 1 Kor 1 und 2. BHTh*, 26. Tübingen: Mohr.

Williams, Charles K., II. 1993. "Roman Corinth as a Commercial Center." In *The Corinthia in the Roman Period (JRASup 8)*, edited by T. E. Gregory, 31–46. Ann Arbor: JRA.

Winter, Bruce W. 2001. *After Paul Left Corinth: The Influence of Secular Ethics and Social Change.* Grand Rapids: Eerdmans.

Wire, Antoinette Clark. 1990. *The Corinthian Women Prophets: A Reconstruction through Paul's Rhetoric.* Minneapolis: Fortress Press.

World Council of Churches. 2014. "Week of Prayer for Christian Unity." World Council of Churches. http://www.oikoumene.org/en/press-centre/events/week-of-prayer-for-christian-unity.

Žižek, Slavoj. 2000. *The Fragile Absolute: or, Why is the Christian Legacy Worth Fighting For?* London: Verso.

2 CORINTHIANS

David E. Fredrickson

Introduction

Second Corinthians has impressed itself on scholars as a collection of originally separate Pauline writings, a quilt made of several letter fragments. The integrity of the letter has so been put in doubt that even Paul's authorship in the case of one passage (6:14—7:1) has, for plausible reasons, been called into question. The letter as we read it today appears to have seams, to have been sown together at a time unknown by an editor unnamed. Note the abrupt and, by current standards, inexplicable transitions between 2:13 and 14; 6:13 and 14; 7:1 and 2; 7:16 and 8:1; 8:24 and 9:1; and 9:15 and 10:1. For many interpreters, these appear to be awkwardly stitched together texts hinting at a history of compilation. And so it is frequently said that 2 Corinthians lacks argumentative flow. The simplest explanation is that the letter never possessed rhetorical unity since it was not in the strict sense *a* letter penned by Paul. This is the dominant scholarly opinion today, and it renders naïve any questions about the meaning of the letter considered as a whole, either in the first century, in the history of interpretation, or for modern readers.

Yet there is another way of reading 2 Corinthians, one that is not alarmed when letters written in or near the first century shift from topic to topic or change tone without warning (for the "mixed" type of letter, see Malherbe 1988, 73, 81). This approach bolsters the case for integrity by highlighting the continuity of themes and key terms across the letter. Along these lines, we might observe that the contrast Paul draws between himself and his opponents over severity and gentleness in leadership style runs throughout the letter, from 1:12 to 13:10 to be precise. Most importantly, this alternative way of reading defers final judgment concerning the letter's unity until it reconstructs events and emotions between Paul's sending of 1 Corinthians and his composition of 2 Corinthians. This present approach *presumes* the letter's unity and uses passages throughout to imagine a complicated situation between Paul and the church at Corinth, which only a complex letter, appearing to some readers as having seams, could even hope to address.

It appears, then, that we have arrived at a method of reading the letter. First, there is a need to discern the situation and then observe what Paul has to say to it. But a word of warning is in order: not only must our reconstruction remain tentative and open to revision, but we must also admit that the story of Paul and the Corinthians is entirely a Pauline fiction. (Actually, it is my fiction about Paul's fiction.) That is, there is no way for us to see through the letter to "what really happened" between the two Corinthian letters. All we have is the way *Paul* wants his readers to see what happened and what it all means. A clear division between context and text or between occasion and rhetoric is therefore an illusion. Paul's construal of persons, events, and emotions is rhetorical from the very start. That does not make the backstory of 2 Corinthians narrated below any less interesting. It does demand, however, that any interpretation, and that certainly includes this essay, confess that it is a fiction, provisional, and risks being taken in unanticipated directions. I emphasize this demand at the beginning of the essay, since habits of the biblical commentary genre will induce me to write as if I had forgotten it.

So where to begin in *imagining* the events and emotions as Paul wants his first readers to think of them? Second Corinthians 1:8-9 tells a dismal tale of Paul's journey in Asia, one of melancholy and thoughts of suicide. Christian writers of the fourth century, perhaps alarmed at the sadness of the apostle, thought Paul was describing external events: his arrest, a court's death sentence, and the apprehension anyone would feel in such circumstances (see Fredrickson 2000). But the phrase "we ourselves in ourselves had the sentence of death" (here and below, my own translation) would more likely have been understood in the first century as self-condemnation, the feelings that overwhelm the soul with regret or remorse. Regret arose from the paradox of the stern judge and convicted offender inhabiting the same body.

What did Paul have to regret? In 2 Cor. 7:8, he speaks plainly about the matter: he had written a letter to the church powerful enough to induce pain in the readers. He refers to this letter in 2:3-4 as he denies that it was his intention to cause grief, thus, of course, reinforcing our sense that he did. This is the so-called letter of tears, which has puzzled interpreters for centuries. John Chrysostom thought this letter was 1 Corinthians itself. Today some scholars identify it as 2 Corinthians 10–13, although a third opinion, one the present essayist shares, holds that the letter is lost and not to be identified with any extant Pauline writing and therefore a bit of a mystery (see Furnish, 163–68). But thanks to Ps.-Libanius and Ps.-Demetrius, unknown authors of the two surviving ancient epistolary handbooks, there are some helpful clues (see Malherbe 1988, 30–41, 66–81). These handbooks gave instructions on how to write a grieving letter (*epistolē lypētikē*), and when the many actual letters of grief in antiquity (e.g., Ps.-Demosthenes, *Ep.* 2) are also consulted, we learn that a letter writer's grieving self-presentation was intended, and understood by recipients, as stinging moral reproof (see Fredrickson 2001). To paraphrase the critical portion of these letters: "The tears through which I write are evidence of the grief your behavior has caused me."

What did the church at Corinth do to cause Paul pain? Paul hints in 2:1 at an unplanned visit to Corinth. He made this trip presumably because 1 Corinthians, the letter carried by Timothy, did not have its desired effect of discouraging the elite from displaying their social status, the main problem addressed in that letter. During this impromptu visit, Paul was injured or treated unjustly by some member of the church (Barrett 1970). He alludes to this event tactfully in 2:5 and mentions the offender directly in 7:12 ("the one who injured"), though still without naming him. He refers to himself as "the one injured." Here is the point: the church, for its part, took no action against the one who had treated Paul unjustly during his unplanned visit. So Paul fled to Ephesus and from a distance wrote the "letter of tears," rebuking the community for its indifference to the injury he suffered. Titus took this epistle to Corinth.

As Paul tells this story, when the letter arrived in Corinth under Titus's care it had a double effect. On the one hand, it caused the Corinthian church grief, yes, but a "grief according to God," as Paul assures his readers, since the letter's severity issued in their repentance. That is, it aroused the readers' zeal for Paul (7:7, 11-12). On the other hand, the community's newfound resolve to discipline the offender was excessive; note the term "vengeance" (*ekdikēsis*) in 7:11. In its response to the letter of tears, then, it seems that the church swung around wildly from its former indifference to the offense committed against Paul. The harshness of their treatment of the offender is indicated in the term *epitimia*, which stands behind the English term "punishment" in 2:6. *Epitimia* held a special place in Greco-Roman moral exhortation. It was moral chastisement intended to cause shame, a particularly extreme measure in the honor-seeking society of the first century, especially if it was delivered in public (see Malherbe 1983). It was a commonplace worry for ancient moral guides in antiquity, except among harsh Cynics (see Malherbe 1989), that public reproof, particularly of young men, might result in suicide (see, e.g., Plutarch, *How to Tell a Flatterer from a Friend* 70F–71C). It is no wonder, then, that Paul expresses concern for the offender; he is liable to being "drunk down by excessive grief" (2:7), a euphemism for suicide.

The letter of tears had one more effect, though if we are to understand it, one more set of players in Corinth must be introduced. As if the relationship between Paul and the church were not complicated enough, missionaries critical of Paul's manner of ministry entered Corinth, most likely after his flight to Ephesus. In his absence, they competed with him (and with one another? see 2 Cor. 10:12) for the community's allegiance. Paul calls them "super-apostles" (2 Cor. 11:5 and 12:11) and characterizes them in terms reminiscent of harsh Cynic philosophers who sought to dominate those they led (Malherbe 1970). Again, it must be emphasized that this depiction of his rivals is Paul's: his portrayal of them as severe moralists accentuates his own image as conciliatory, gentle, and gracious. Yet the issue of Paul's free speech was far broader than Paul and his relationship with the Corinthians. A fundamental disagreement about the nature of frank speech raged (sometimes within the same author) from the Hellenistic period well into late antiquity: Was it to be viewed as the verbal expression of the wise man's moral independence, or was it to be regarded as a means to improve others in the context of friendly relations? (For a study in *parrēsia* as display of freedom and as the art of moral improvement, see John Chrysostom's encomium of Babylas, *De sancto hiero-martyre Babyla* [PG 50:541–46]).

What did these rival apostles think of the letter of tears? They praised it for its severity; but they also contrasted the letter's power at a distance with Paul's deficient physical presence and his ironic and deceptive spoken words. In what might be regarded as the earliest commentary on the Pauline Epistles, 2 Cor. 10:9-10 describes the characterization of Paul's own letters that he attributes to his rivals. The passage is saturated with terminology from ancient rhetorical handbooks and treatises. "To frighten," "weighty," and "strong" are the markers of "forcefulness" (*deinotēs*), a style of speaking in which orators, most notably in the ancient world Demosthenes (see Dionysius of Halicarnassus, *Demosthenes* 22), overwhelmed audiences. Two additional phrases indicate the super-apostles' familiarity with ancient rhetorical and literary criticism: "presence of the body" and "attenuated speech" (*ho logos exouthenēmenos*, my translation: see Fredrickson 2001). "They say" Paul's physical presence, a reference in rhetorical terms to oratorical delivery, is weak, and that he intentionally makes his speech less forceful than he could (as judged by the letters) and more like the utterings of persons of low esteem, much in the style of Socrates, whose ironic self-depreciation pricked holes in puffed-up dialogue partners. So the letter of tears was just one more piece of evidence that Paul in the church's presence was deceptive and lacked the frank speech, the quality of *deinotēs*, that marked true apostles. This charge of disparity between words and deeds Paul vigorously disputes in 10:10 and throughout the letter, as we will see below.

So here are the issues facing Paul on the eve of 2 Corinthians. First, Paul is in an impossible position. He must assert that he possesses frank speech, but the medium for his apology is a letter, and as he writes from a distance, he runs the risk of convicting himself of the very charges summarized in 10:9-10. This problem he takes up in 2 Cor. 2:14—4:6. Second, the individual who wronged Paul has been isolated from the community; Paul exhorts the community to bring him back in 2:5-11. Third, even though the church responded to the letter of tears positively by disciplining the offender, the grief (or was it resentment or vexation?) lingered on; Paul confronts this issue in 4:7—7:16 as he places his frank speech into the ancient tradition of friendship, stresses his love for the church, and appeals for reconciliation. To further assuage hard feelings, he accentuates his regret for ever having written the letter (1:8-9 and 7:8). The final purpose of 2 Corinthians, if the present reconstruction of the letter's occasion is at all plausible, is to dissuade the church from recognizing the legitimacy of the super-apostles and their harsh form of leadership; this he does sporadically in 2 Corinthians 1–7 and pointedly in chapters 10–13.

Nothing has yet been said about 2 Corinthians 8–9. These chapters deal with the collection for the saints in Jerusalem. In 1 Cor. 16:1-9, Paul had tailored his travel plans around his pivotal role in organizing a fund from the churches of Galatia, Macedonia, and Corinth for the relief of communities in Jerusalem. The problem for Paul was how to encourage the Corinthians to make good on their promise to contribute without reinforcing the patron-client ideology that permeated all charitable activities in the Roman period. Gift-giving in general symbolized the social difference between giver and recipient and announced the former's power and superiority while emphasizing the latter's neediness and obligation to repay the gift through public glorification of the giver. This is precisely the problem Paul attacks so energetically in 1 Corinthians. It also explains why Paul shuns the financial support of the Corinthian elite in 2 Corinthians 10–13: simply put, he doesn't want to be owned (see Marshall). Finally, it is worth considering that domination hidden in the gift-giving of ancient society and potentially, Paul fears, in the collection for the saints in Jerusalem resembles the sovereignty in disciplinary matters that the super-apostles exhibit. In other words, patronal power and super-apostle severity are two instances of domination. Paul's opposition to any form of lordship that is not inhabited by the crucified Messiah is a central feature in all of his letters and especially here in 2 Corinthians. This makes him a sharp, if indirect, critic of empire.

2 Corinthians 1:1-7: The Sound of P

▌THE TEXT IN ITS ANCIENT CONTEXT

The Greek letter *pi* (*p*) is repeated twenty-six times in these verses. There is comfort in the repetition of sounds, as in the sincere utterance of "there, there." Each time the letter *pi* is pronounced, lips meet, puffing a bit of breath toward the other person. An intimacy adheres to these hesitant vocalizations, a gentle insistence of breath. *Parakalō* and its noun cognate *paraklēsis* together occur ten times. Perhaps Paul entreats, or does he exhort? *Parakalō* could mean either, and it is impossible to say with certainty which is meant here. Another word starting with *pi* in this passage is *pathēma*. This word bears a double character also: it meant suffering, but included both exterior and interior aspects. Thus it signifies pain inflicted on Paul from without (beatings or maltreatment, for example), or it could refer to emotions themselves, like love, or regret (cf. Rom. 8:18; Phil. 3:10). It, with its cognate *paschein* ("to suffer"), occurs four times.

Paul clearly departed from his usual practice of beginning a letter by thanking God for the very issues he addresses in the rest of the text (e.g., 1 Cor. 1:4-9; Phil. 1:3-11). Does this mean that 1:3-7 is unrelated to the rest of the letter? Not at all. *Parakalō* ("I exhort" or "entreat") in its second sense anticipates the grace, gentleness, and forgiveness in Paul's manner of leadership in contrast to the severity of the super-apostles. Yet the dueling meaning within the one word also anticipates the movement of Paul between the reproof of the letter of tears and his begging for reconciliation.

Note further that in 1:3 Paul links his manner of ministry to divine names: the father of compassionate feelings (*oiktirmos* suggests the vocalizations of ritual lament, "keening" in other words) and the God of all exhorting/entreating. The association of Paul's grace in ministry with God's grace is the primary form of Paul's apology through the letter (e.g., 5:18—6:2). Similarly, in 1:5, Paul and Christ are, insofar as emotions (*pathēmata*) are concerned, indistinguishable (cf. Phil. 1:8), and that goes a long way to defending his form of ministry. Paul develops the motif of his sharing of emotions/suffering with Christ throughout the letter and includes the Corinthians in 1:6-7. Finally, in verse 7, he states his hope about the community; this is yet another way of exhorting/begging. The content of his hope (there is, incidentally, another *pi* in the middle of *elpis*) is unstated at this point, but the position of *paraklēsis* at the end of the sentence suggests the church has its own comforting to do by restoring the offender (2:7) and continuing to mend fences with Paul (1:13-14; 4:14-15; 6:20—7:4).

▌THE TEXT IN THE INTERPRETIVE TRADITION

Early Christian commentators took from these first verses clues to the nature of the whole letter and emphasized the "consolation" in the midst of suffering that Paul proclaims. Pelagius, however, focused on Paul's setting his name before his recipients, adopting "the custom of secular judges," because "he is an apostle who is writing to those who are accountable to him"; he thus emphasized the element of correction throughout the letter (*Commentary*).

It is also the case that commentators diminished the passionate side of many Pauline terms in this letter (e.g., see below on "weakness" in 13:4). Their treatment of *pathēmata* in 1:1-7 is no exception. I translated the word above as "emotions." The English "sufferings" expresses the view of early commentators that Paul has in mind things done to him, shipwreck or imprisonment for example, not stirrings within his soul difficult or impossible to control like grief or desire (see John Chrysostom, *In epistulam ii ad Corinthios* [*homiliae 1–30*, PG 61:579]; but for a combination of the inner and outer aspects see Theodorus Studites, *Epistulae* 252.15). A similar downplaying of passion can be seen in the case of *oiktirmos* (1:3). In the interpretive tradition, the word came to be defined by the benefactor and his *philanthropia* ("love for humanity"). This redefinition dulled the sharp edge of violent emotion conveyed by the word in the case, for example, of the widow or childless mother keening the death of her loved one (see John Chrysostom, *De corruptoribus virginum* [PG 60:744]). The New Testament itself is partly responsible for adding a sense of condescension to this term (see Luke 6:36), but beginning with Clement of Alexandria (*Protrepticus* 1.8.4), the Christian tradition substituted a philanthropic wish on God's part to save humanity and show it mercy for a divine desire for communion with humanity.

▌ The Text in Contemporary Discussion

The "Father of all compassionate feelings and the God of all entreaties" (2 Cor. 1:3) is a weak and unsuitable God for those who, like the super-apostles, see church leadership in terms of issuing divine commands from a position of dispassionate invulnerability. The adequacy of the philosophical idea of impassibility for the representation of God in the Old Testament has been called into question by biblical interpreters (see, e.g., Fretheim). Christian theology's comfort with a self-constituting and self-sufficient God has been sharply critiqued by Jürgen Moltmann (1974) as he put a question to the tradition seldom asked in Christian theology: What did the death of the Son mean for the Father?

2 Corinthians 1:8-13: Reconciliation as Resurrection

▌ The Text in Its Ancient Context

As previously noted, in 1:8-9 Paul uses the ancient rhetoric of regret to communicate to the church his turbulent emotional state after he sent the letter of tears but before he met up with Titus in Macedonia. Such self-disclosure might have itself been seen as a gesture of reconciliation (see Aristotle, *Nicomachean Ethics* 1110b 18–30), since Paul implies that he did not delight in criticizing the church. In fact, the uncertainty of his relationship with the community after he wrote severely weighs Paul down to the point of considering suicide, if his readers are to believe these self-revelations, as he makes his way through Asia.

Unlike those whose confidence is based on themselves (perhaps a dig at the super-apostles; see 3:5 and Phil. 3:2-4), Paul's boldness for life and ministry resides in his relationship to the church (see 1:14; cf. Phil. 4:1; 1 Thess. 2:19-20). For this reason, his report of rescue by the God who raises the dead is a theological interpretation of the Corinthians' change of heart reported by Titus (see 7:6-7). The church's (tentative?) steps toward Paul are portrayed as the working of God (cf. Phil 2:13), and in verses 10-11 he hopes for further rescue/reconciliation. Finally, it is significant that, located between two theologically rich understandings of the church as communion (1:11 and 14), we find the charge of "fleshly wisdom" leveled at Paul by the super-apostles. What Paul understands as a ministry growing out of the bonds of friendship, whose speech embodies "openness" and "sincerity" (both synonyms for *parrēsia*) and exhibits "the grace of God," his opponents characterize as rhetorical trickery. That fundamental tension between Paul and his rivals runs through 2 Corinthians from beginning to end.

▌THE TEXT IN THE INTERPRETIVE TRADITION

Early Christian commentators took Paul at his word when he declares his sincerity (*eilikrineia*), a term that in conjunction with *haplotēs* ("frankness," NRSV) in rhetorical theory was a matter of straightforward and clear language in contrast to artificiality and the concealment of figured speech (see Smiley, 219–24). John Chrysostom praised Paul for this very reason (*Homilies in 2 Cor.* [PG 61:405–6]). Theodoret of Cyrus was likewise impressed: Paul "teaches only what he has been taught by the grace of God, adding nothing of his own to it. . . . The facts speak for themselves and prove that he is right" (*Commentary*). The fathers' enthusiasm for Paul's *eilikrineia* may have come from the central role this term played in ancient rhetorical handbooks, where it connoted the opposite of irony, flattery, and particularly the moral criticism carried out under cover of rhetorical figures (Fiore). In short, early interpreters thought Paul's sincerity was synonymous with his *parrēsia*.

▌THE TEXT IN CONTEMPORARY DISCUSSION

One dramatic difference between early Christian commentary on Paul's letters and contemporary scholarship is the attention given in the latter to Paul's persuasive speech, that is, rhetoric. Rather than presuming, for example, that Paul really has despaired of life and seeking to identify the "affliction" he suffered (1:8), scholars ask about the rhetorical effect of such claims. While this approach has proven very fruitful, and is employed in this essay, it sometimes raises the question of whether Paul was manipulative, since today's readers often associate "rhetoric" with speech that gets its way dishonestly. That there is no easy response, or perhaps no response at all, to this modern doubt about Paul is indicated by the undeniable similarity between his self-revelations in 1:8 (and in 7:8-12) and the contemporary rhetoric of domestic violence: "I know I hurt you; it pains me that I hurt you; but I only wanted to show my love; I will harm myself if you do not forgive me." Rhetorical analysis cannot by itself determine whether Paul meant what he said, only how it *might* have been heard by a first-century audience.

2 Corinthians 1:15—2:4: If I Am a Flatterer, Then So Is God

▌THE TEXT IN ITS ANCIENT CONTEXT

A pattern in Paul's argumentation is emerging. Paul's style of ministry mimics God's; his emotions are indistinguishable from Christ's. To fault him is to fault God. To oppose him is to oppose Christ.

In this passage Paul deflects the super-apostles' charge of flattery by implicating God in the same yes-saying that he, Silvanus, and Timothy make the core of their preaching (for the "light touch" in 1:17 as a sign of flattery see Plutarch, *How to Tell a Flatterer from a Friend* 65B; 71F). The topic of flattery here is not in question, since from Cicero (*De amicitia* 93) we learn that the phrase "Yes, yes and No, no" had broad circulation as early as the first century BCE. It was a proverbial expression for the flatterer's malleability and desire to please and had been lifted from its original literary context of a play by Terence. The flatterer is devious; he wins victims over by posing as a friend and telling them what they want to hear. Flatterers transform themselves into the ones they seek to please, a behavior Paul's adaptability in 1 Cor. 9:19-23 dangerously approaches. Paul, however, argues that his change of travel plans (1:15-16) is not evidence of flattery but proof of his desire to spare the church further grief, a point he reiterates in 1:23—2:4.

In 1:18-22, Paul presents himself and God not as flatterers, though they do say only "yes," but as friends, as the term *pistos* ("faithful") in verse 18 and the verb *bebaioō* (lit., "I make firm or constant") in verse 21 indicate. These two terms were commonly associated with the motif of friendship (see Xenophon, *Memorabilia* 2.6.20; and Lucian, *Toxaris* 6–7, 9, 20, 35, 63) and now in Paul's use define the relationship of God with the community and the community with Paul.

▮ The Text in the Interpretive Tradition

What did the early church make of Paul's letter of tears (2:4)? John Chrysostom made a proposal that persuaded many later commentators: the letter of tears is actually 1 Corinthians. Chrysostom thought the offender mentioned in 2 Cor. 2:5-11 was the same person singled out for discipline in 1 Cor. 5:1. While this solution has several obvious deficiencies, which modern commentaries do not fail to point out, one cannot keep from admiring its simplicity. But the chief problem with the proposal is this: in 1 Corinthians, Paul does not present himself as grieving. There is no reason to categorize it as a grieving letter (*epistolē lypētikē*).

▮ The Text in Contemporary Discussion

Some scholars have suggested that we look no further than 2 Corinthians 10–13 to find Paul's "letter of tears" (see Watson). This would be a simple solution if it were not the case that in this portion of the letter Paul does not present himself as grieving, aside from the possibility of lament he mentions in 12:31. Furthermore, the "letter of tears" dealt with an individual's unjust act, but 2 Corinthians 10–13 concerns the super-apostles' rivalry with Paul. (For additional reasons to doubt identification of the "letter of tears" with chapters 10–13, see Amador.)

2 Corinthians 2:5-11: Shame and Satan

▮ The Text in Its Ancient Context

This passage is the gateway to the rest of 2 Corinthians 1–7. Later arguments are anticipated as Paul seeks to persuade the community to forgive and accept the offender who had been disciplined and put to shame. Paul turns the injury from himself (2:5, 10) and stresses that now the community must forgive and confirm love. Here Paul is performing, and asking the church to enact, the inconsistency that the super-apostles perceive in Paul's ministry. A true apostle, they would assert, is severe (see 13:3), and the true church would enforce discipline without reprieve. But Paul detects the bullying and begrudging Satan (2:11) in such a one-sided approach to pastoral care. Paul sees the face of Christ, however, in the act of forgiveness (2:10). And then, in order to ground his ministry in Christ's lordship (which does not exclude weakness) and God's grace, Paul takes his readers on an extensive literary digression in 2:12—7:4, which echoes his painful procession to reunite with Titus in Macedonia.

■ THE TEXT IN THE INTERPRETIVE TRADITION

Paul's characterization of Satan as an envious bully (2 Cor. 2:11) would become a stock theme in early Christianity. Envy (!) entered the garden to corrupt Adam and Eve and their descendants (see Theophilus, *Ad Autolycum* 2.29; Epiphanius, *Panarion* 3.416.1; Antiochus Monachus, *Pandecta scripturae sacrae* 55). In this regard, there is an intriguing overlap in Christian and Hellenistic traditions as they grow and influence one another in late antiquity. Envy, understood as begrudging the happiness of another, was a prominent *theological* explanation among Greeks for human disappointment and loss (see Plutarch, *Consolatio ad Apollonium* 105B). In erotic relationships, personified Envy was blamed for separations (see Chariton, *Chareas and Callirhoe* 1.1.16; Nicetas Eugenianus, *Drosilla and Charicles* 1.52–53).

■ THE TEXT IN CONTEMPORARY DISCUSSION

Readers interested in connecting Paul's concern about the shaming and isolating effects of punishment with current criticism of the American criminal justice system might consult the recently adopted social statement of the Evangelical Lutheran Church in America (see "The Church and Criminal Justice: Hearing the Cries," at http://www.elca.org/en/Faith/Faith-and-Society/Social-Statements/Criminal-Justice). The complicity of some Christian beliefs in the needless worsening of offenders' lives is slowly coming into general consciousness. For centuries, Christians have promoted biblical texts that view the purpose of punishment to be the isolation and destruction of offenders (see, e.g., 2 Peter). Christians elect state and federal legislators who pass laws requiring or enabling mass incarceration, mandatory sentencing, the location of prisons far removed from families and other systems of support, solitary confinement, and other collateral punishments that work through the harsh logic of isolation. It is sobering to think that Paul regards the self-destructive results of enforced isolation as the work of Satan.

2 Corinthians 2:12—3:3: Topography of an Apostle's Heart

■ THE TEXT IN ITS ANCIENT CONTEXT

This is a provocative definition of the rhetorical unit since, as I noted above, many scholars detect a seam between verses 13 and 14. They suggest that 2:14—7:5 (with the possible exception of 6:14—7:1) was taken from another Pauline epistle and inserted into an opening created by cutting between 2:13 and what is now 7:5. Attractive as this theory might be (it accounts for what would otherwise be a delayed thanksgiving period in 2:14), there are thematic continuities that make the proposal of interpolation unnecessary. Note the place names in verses 12-13 (Troas and Macedonia) and Paul's reference to "every place" in verse 14. Along these lines, the term *thriambeuein* ("to lead in triumphal procession") suggests movement, while in verses 12-13 Paul discuss his travel in some detail. But the most striking connection between the writing before and after the conjectured seam is the resonance between Paul's having "no relief" at not finding Titus and the apostle's being led in a triumphal procession. A brief explanation of the Roman triumph, and of its adaptation by ancient erotic writers (primarily in poetry and ancient romance), is in order.

Roman generals had the practice of degrading foreign nobility captured in military campaigns by parading them as slaves through the streets of Rome. For poets and novelists, Eros conquered, enslaved, and forced the rejected lover, or the one uncertain of the beloved's response, to march in an equally humiliating procession (see Ovid, *Amores* 1.2.19–52; and Miller). Two other motifs, both of which figure prominently in 2 Corinthians, were often allied with the lover led in triumph. *Servitium amoris* (the slavery of love; see Murgatroyd) depicted the lover's paradoxical "voluntary slavery" (e.g., Plato, *Symposium* 184C), degrading loss of self-control (Zagagi), and lovesickness even to the point of death (Xenophon, *Symposium* 4.14; Achilles Tatius, *Leucippe and Clitophon* 1.7.2–3). Paul deploys the other popular motif, *Amor vincit omnia* ("Love conquers all"), in 2:14 and extensively in 2 Corinthians 10–13.

So, how does Paul turn the erotic connotations of the triumph motif to his rhetorical aim of conciliating the Corinthians to himself? The metaphor presents Paul suffering a lover's pain, the grief of separation from his beloved community, and, more significantly, apprehension over its response to his stinging reproof in the letter of tears. He presents himself suffering with self-accusation and worry, not unlike the unrequited lover of Latin elegy, whose every thought is about the beloved's rejection. Moreover, note that *God* leads Paul in this triumphal procession. This is striking not only because readers knew that Eros plays the part of conquering general in love poetry but even more because knowledge of God is apparent for all who see into Paul's experience, which he has been narrating since "our affliction" in 1:4. Some, of course, will smell nothing but the odor of death; presumably Paul wants readers to think of the super-apostles here. Paul's readers, however, *if and as they remain true to him*, will perceive the fragrance of life in his socially demeaning and soul-draining love for them.

▉ THE TEXT IN THE INTERPRETIVE TRADITION

For over a thousand years, "Love conquers all" lay dormant, but when it awoke in the Middle Ages it was applied to Pauline texts with vigor. Even God is vanquished by love for humanity, according to Bernard of Clairvaux (*Sermon* 64.10 [PL 183:1088]). Hadewijch of Antwerp thought so too.

> What seems to the loved soul the most beautiful encounter
> Is that it should love the Beloved so fully
> And so gain knowledge of the Beloved with love
> That nothing else is known by it

Except: "I am conquered by Love"
But he who overcame Love was rather conquered
So that he might in love be brought to naught
God the lover is victim of love. (*Poems in Stanzas* 8.71–77)

In the fourteenth century, the Byzantine theologian Nicholas Cabasilas, writing about the christological topic of *kenosis* ("emptying"), likens the God emptied by *erōs* first to the "locked out lover," perhaps the most popular ancient cliché depicting the slave of love, and then to the "lover led in a triumphal procession" (*thriambeuein erastēn*: *The Life in Christ* 6.3). Even though it took over a thousand years, the erotic motif of triumph in 2 Cor. 2:14 opened a way into the passion of God that had been foreclosed by the philosophically inspired doctrine of divine impassibility.

2 Corinthians 3:1-18: Frank Speech and Moses' Face

▌ THE TEXT IN ITS ANCIENT CONTEXT

This section is a carefully crafted argument resting to a great degree on Paul's playfulness with the Greek language, and therefore difficult to appreciate in English translation. Nevertheless, some points can be made. In 3:12, Paul claims to use the very *parrēsia* ("frank" or "free speech," not "boldness" as the NRSV translates; see Fredrickson 1996) that his opponents charge that he lacks. Paul's rhetorical predicament lies in the fact that he makes this claim at a distance, through a letter; for Paul simply to assert his free speech would be to confirm the criticism directed against him. His solution is this: rather than giving proof of his confidence based on his own power (3:5), Paul appeals to the Spirit, whose work was to inscribe the Corinthians in his heart (3:2-3; for the eroticism of such writing, see *Greek Anthology* 12.57).

The Spirit is life-making precisely in this way, by its deepening of *philia* ("friendship") to the point of love (*erōs* or *agapē*). *Parrēsia* of this kind is the language of friendship, as Plutarch once remarked (*How to Tell a Flatterer from a Friend* 51C), not the verbal expression of an individual's freedom attained through self-control and moral accomplishment, as many philosophers (and most likely the super-apostles) taught. If *parrēsia* is a function of friendship, Paul argues, then the new covenant (literally "new arrangement"), which is love and longing for communion kindled by gazing at another's face and being looked upon (cf. 1 Cor. 13:12), guarantees free speech to all, wherever the Spirit is. The covenant of death, though having a glory of its own, is the application of written laws and commands; it does not create friendship and is unable to kindle the gaze upon the face of another and experience the other in his or her singularity, as the sons of Israel discover (3:7).

Moses' face plays an equally important role in the second of the proofs of Paul's *parrēsia* (3:12-18). The argument here is structured according to the rhetorical technique of comparison (*synkrisis*), using negative and positive examples. Paul is not like Moses, who covered his face, a movement in Greek culture associated with shame. Moses veiled his face so that the "sons of Israel" might not gaze upon the *telos* ("end," in the sense of intended result) of "that which is being nullified," presumably the old covenant. The shaming effect of that which is written on stone was alluded to in 3:9 in two ways. First, the word Paul uses to describe the end result of the new covenant, *glory*, was generally understood as the opposite of shame. Second, the old covenant is described as a ministry of condemnation. It is tempting to think that Paul is describing the situation of the disciplined offender in 2:5-11. He, Moses, the "sons of Israel" (3:14-15), and perhaps Paul himself—as he made his way through Asia to Macedonia, despairing of life over the alienation he feared his *grammata* ("letters") had worked on the Corinthian church—they are all caught up in the ministry of death.

But Moses' face does not remain veiled. Verse 16 should be translated, "whenever he [not "one"] turned to the Lord, the veil was taken away." The "he" is Moses in his role as positive example. Paul, indeed the whole church, is *just like* Moses, who in that moment of face-to-face intimacy with the Lord, an intimacy created by the Spirit, is free, and if free, then bold of speech, since the two words *eleutheria* and *parrēsia* were nearly synonymous. So once again Paul bases his free speech not on individual power or accomplishment but on a Spirit-made intimacy in which "we all" (3:18) are free in the moment of an uncovered face, as in the climactic instant of the ancient Greek wedding when the bride—her veil swept aside in the moment of *apokalypsis*—and groom gazed without shame on each other's face. The political consequences of 3:18 are staggering when contrasted with the ancient world's limitation of freedom and frank speech to elite male citizens. In the phrase "we all," Paul envisions a community of any and all persons, all equally free to speak their minds, as they simultaneously gaze upon one another as if in a mirror and in this way are transformed into what they see, Christ the image of God (cf. 4:4).

■ The Text in the Interpretive Tradition

"For the letter kills, but the Spirit gives life" (3:6). No other Pauline phrase so profoundly set the course of Christian biblical interpretation and theology. Early on, Paul's distinction between letter and Spirit, in which he clearly prefers Spirit over letter, was interpreted as the difference between text and the author's intention (see Grant). At least three consequences flowed from this reading: first, it paved the way for the phonocentrism of Greek philosophy to overtake Christian theology. What is phonocentrism? Jacques Derrida has analyzed texts in the Western intellectual tradition, from Plato (see especially *Phaedrus* 275C–276E) to the twentieth century, and has pointed out the tradition's unjustified preference for voice over writing. Yet it is not Derrida's point simply to reverse the two by awarding to writing a privileged status over voice. Rather, he shows that what philosophers understand as the deficiencies (Derrida would not use this term) of writing affect the voice as well, but very few thinkers ever admit this. For example, it is generally agreed that writing inevitably destabilizes meaning, since the mortality of the author and that of the reader leave no enduring witness to what was meant when the text was composed. The move that characterizes phonocentrism is to claim that the everyday experience of hearing oneself think or the perceived immediacy of speaking one's thoughts proves that voice mitigates the danger of contaminating one's thoughts. The voice holds and protects the idea from contamination, so it is claimed in phonocentrism, as it travels from one's mind through the external world through another's ear and ultimately to his or her own interiority. In short, phonocentrism thinks of voice as a somewhat successful substitute for the thinking one does silently in one's head; but writing, in this view, as a phonetic system representing voice in the speaker's absence, is merely a substitute for a substitute and thus two steps removed from self-present thought (see Culler, 89–110). From the phonocentric perspective, then, the letter kills in the sense that it fails to live up to the voice's power to deliver the speaker's thoughts. Second, the misconstrued distinction between letter and Spirit enabled Christians to appropriate the allegorical method employed by Stoics (and others) in the interpretation of Homer and thus created a special class of spiritual persons who presumed they could read past the literal meaning of texts into God's mind. Third, the distinction between letter and Spirit contributes to animosity against Jews, who, according to the Christian interpretation of Paul's distinction, are incapable of knowing the meaning of their own Scriptures.

■ THE TEXT IN CONTEMPORARY DISCUSSION

Paul's reasoning from friendship and the face here bears an intriguing resemblance to recent approaches to ethics by writers influenced by Jacques Derrida and Emmanuel Levinas (see, e.g., Caputo 1993; for the related idea of *perichōrēsis* in recent trinitarian theology and ecclesiology, see Moltmann 2000). Nevertheless, Derrida's wariness of the reduction of friendship to brotherhood in Western political philosophy, which buys the communion of some at the price of excluding others, must be kept in mind (Derrida). Does Paul himself fall into the trap of building a community on the backs of others, that is, on the exclusion of "the sons of Israel" (3:7)? This question, which can only be raised here and not answered, is crucial in light of the comparison Paul makes between the two covenants in 3:4-18. It is not possible to rescue Paul from the charge of anti-Judaism simply by pointing out that it is the old covenant that is nullified (3:14) and not Judaism itself. Is there a difference between covenant and Judaism, or enough of a difference between the two so that Christ's nullification of the former does not mean the destruction of the latter?

2 Corinthians 4:1-6: Your Slaves

■ THE TEXT IN ITS ANCIENT CONTEXT

In 4:1-3, Paul reiterates his claim that he possesses all the boldness and openness necessary for an apostle of Christ, and if anyone (think super-apostles here) thinks his gospel is hidden or that he is playing tricks on the Corinthians with his talk of grace and forgiveness, then it must be that the god of this age (think Satan here) has blinded their minds. A word about the two major ancient theories of vision might be helpful at this point. One theory, which posits that very small bits of objects break off and pass through the air into the soul via the eyes, plays no role here. The other imagines a light in the soul or mind, burning like a lamp and sending out its rays through the eyes to illumine external objects. From this latter perspective, to be blinded is to have one's internal fire extinguished. That is what Paul says the god of this age has done to his opponents. They have no fire. In them, no beams of light proceed from an internal fire, and this suggests that they lack love or desire, which was also conceptualized as burning within the innards (cf. 1 Cor. 7:9; 2 Cor. 11:29). They do not love the Corinthians as Paul does; rather, Paul implies, they preach themselves as lords over the community (cf. 2 Cor. 1:24; 11:20).

In contrast, Paul preaches himself as the community's slave (4:5). Paul once more alludes to the *servitium amoris* motif so popular in the erotic literature of the ancient world (see comments on 2:14 above). He loves the Corinthians madly and without regard for his own dignity, and he does so in imitation of Jesus ("on account of Jesus"), who took the form of a slave (see Phil. 2:7).

▌THE TEXT IN THE INTERPRETIVE TRADITION

The Christian tradition by and large has suppressed Paul's vision of a lovesick, servile Christ who is here Paul's model for imitation. The authors of Colossians and Ephesians, for example, eliminated the motif of Christ as slave as they revised Paul's theology and substituted their philosophically influenced gospel of self-control. But there are moments in the tradition when poetry returns Christology to Paul's daring appropriation of the slavery motif, which we find in Phil. 2:7 as well. Guerric of Igny (1080–1157) is a good example of a writer turning Christ's slavery away from obedience to God the Father and toward humanity.

> "I will not serve," man says to his Creator. "Then I will serve you," his Creator says to man. "You sit down. I will minister, I will wash your feet. You rest; I will bear your weariness, your infirmities. Use me as you like in all your needs, not only as your slave but also as your beast of burden and as your property." (*Sermon* 29.1; Monks of Mount Saint Bernard Abbey, 2:55–56)

At the end of the thirteenth century or the beginning of the fourteenth, the Italian mystic Jacopone da Todi spoke to Jesus in a way that likely would not have displeased Paul.

> You went about the world as if you were drunk,
> Led by Love as if you were a slave . . .

▌THE TEXT IN CONTEMPORARY DISCUSSION

Paul's introduction of slavery into his discourse about Christ and about his own ministry have not gone unnoticed by contemporary scholars. Some quite correctly criticize the way the idea of Jesus as a slave (to God, as it is almost always assumed) has legitimated various forms of domination within the church and in secular social institutions influenced by Christianity (Briggs). Recognition that the figure of the popular leader (demagogue) in ancient democracies was frequently described in servile terms (Martin 1990) goes some distance in undermining the oppressive potential of this motif. For many other scholars, however, Jesus' slavery to God is not at all problematic—quite the opposite, since they think his obedience as the "new Adam" reverses the disobedience of the first Adam, thereby offering salvation and a model of Christian behavior to the church (see Barth, 63–64).

The erotic motif of *servitium amoris* in 2 Cor. 4:5 and throughout the epistle has important consequences for the interpretation of Paul's Christology, understanding his hopes for the political culture of the churches he established and, ultimately, the contemporary appropriation of Pauline thought for contemporary Christianity. First, the "work of Christ" (a standard phrase used by theologians to speak of the role of Jesus in their theological systems) will have to include his passionate longing for communion, his slave-like devotion to humanity. Second, church leaders, who often claim to pattern themselves after Paul, would have to question the prevalent view of Paul as an authoritarian leader and imitate instead his imitation of Christ as a slave of love. Finally, ecclesiastical regimes of oppression that legitimate themselves by an appeal to Jesus' obedience to the Father, or in the case of secular institutions by obedience to higher authority, would have to be challenged (see Fredrickson 2013).

2 Corinthians 4:7—5:10: More Body

▌THE TEXT IN ITS ANCIENT CONTEXT

To review: in the face of charges that he is a deceptive flatterer lacking courage to speak his mind, Paul asserts his *parrēsia* (3:12, 4:1), placing it in the context of friendship and love but also contrasting it with the speech of the super-apostles who, like the Cynics, are harsh moral critics. In 4:7—5:10, he further develops the idea of frank speaking based on friendship. In language that anticipates the weakness he will describe as his experience in the aftermath of his abduction into paradise in 12:1-10, Paul's hardships in 4:8-12 remind him that the power he possesses in excess is not the force of command but the enslaving power of love, which God has enkindled in his heart to illumine the glory of God that Paul sees on the face of Christ (4:6). The slavery motif is developed in 4:10-12, where the bearing of the master's death in one's own body goes to the heart of servitude, as verse 12 powerfully states. Paul's *servitium amoris* to Christ is inseparable from his slavery to the church in Corinth. It is out of this relationship with the church, not his own moral virtue, that his speech flows freely (4:13).

The topic of 4:14—5:10 is increased intimacy in the *parrēsia*-generating relationship Paul has with the Corinthians. He begins in 4:14-15 by repeating the topics of resurrection and transformation (see 1:10-11, 14, 21; 3:18). Abruptly, however, as if Paul had a conversion to the philosophic doctrine of the immortality of the soul, 4:16—5:1 introduces stock themes about the afterlife as it was described in Platonism and accepted by a few of the later Stoics. These themes include the inner and outer human being; the insignificance of present suffering in comparison with the soul's perfection; the eternality of things unseen; and, most significantly, the body as prison or temporary dwelling place of the soul (See Seneca, *Ep.* 102.23; 120.14). New Testament scholars have for decades pointed out the profound difference between immortality of the soul and resurrection of the body. So why has Paul conflated the two notions here? Quite possibly Paul speaks like a philosopher in 4:16—5:1 in order to undermine philosophy's commitment to the survival of the separated self that lives in unchanging and serene contemplation of the universe when the external influence of its body has been removed. By temporarily passing as a philosopher in 4:16—5:1, he gives his attack on philosophical reason all the advantages of stealth.

Having drawn his readers' attention to the isolated self-sufficiency of the wise man's soul (see 3:5), note in 5:2-5 how powerfully Paul rejects the philosophical idea of death as the soul stripped of flesh (see Seneca, *Ep.* 102.24–25). He groans and longs for more clothing, for more body, not less. Life after death for Paul is not the eradication of death (that is philosophy's delusion in the teaching of the immortal, bodiless soul), but the drinking down of death by life (NRSV "swallowing up," cf.

1 Cor. 15:53-57), an unimaginable event and an impossible possibility (5:4) rightly given over by Paul to the name of God, who gives the Spirit (cf. 1:20-22).

▌ THE TEXT IN THE INTERPRETIVE TRADITION

Interpreters up to the tenth century understood the "inner person" (4:16) as Paul's reference to the soul just as the "outer person" designated the body (Suda, *Lexicon* Epsilon 3170). Yet if it is the case, as discussed above, that Paul *plays* with the philosophical commonplace of body as the house (or prison, or crypt) of the soul in order to challenge the very notion of a bodiless soul, the interpreters of the early church and the Byzantine period mistook his rhetorical strategy in 4:16—5:1. They thought he was advocating asceticism as the path to spiritual perfection. In fact, with great regularity, they slightly misquoted the Pauline text as follows: "*as much as* the outer person is destroyed, *to this extent* the inner person is renewed" (emphasis mine: see Basil, *Quod deus non est auctor malorum* [PG 31:337]; Ephraem Syrus, *In sermonem, quem dixit dominus, quod: In hoc mundo pressuram habebitis, et de perfectione hominis* 335; Michael Choniates, *Epistulae* 2.132.269).

▌ THE TEXT IN CONTEMPORARY DISCUSSION

In recent years there has been a growing interest in possible intersections of Pauline thought and contemporary philosophy (see Caputo and Alcoff; Frick). Second Corinthians 4:16—5:10, in its complex engagement with Platonic themes, is a natural site for these modern conversations to take place. Three Pauline themes (there are certainly others) in this passage invite comparison with postmodern philosophy, which has its own complex engagement with Platonism that at least on some points runs parallel to Paul's. First, the thought of death swallowed down by life, discussed above, and the accompanying thought of resurrection did not fall on an unsympathetic ear in the case of Jacques Derrida (Kearney); indeed, for Derrida, dreaming the impossible is always the way to start any undertaking whatsoever, but especially in the case of philosophy, theology, and justice (see Caputo 1997, 20–26). Second, the famous Pauline phrase "for we walk by faith not by sight" (5:7) reads almost as a motto for some postmodern critiques of foundationalism (Caputo 1997, 41–48). Third, the eschatological desire for a future that cannot be known or described is indicated by the groaning, longing, and wishing of 5:2, and this passion correlates with the aim of deconstruction: to impassion a wish for something totally other in those of us whom tradition, theology, and social systems have trained not to expect the unexpected and not to welcome surprises (Caputo 1997, 134–49).

2 Corinthians 5:11-19: The Madness of Saint Paul

▌ THE TEXT IN ITS ANCIENT CONTEXT

In 5:13, Paul admits that he went insane (*exestēmen*), a moment of candor whose significance is not apparent. The present essay has stressed Paul's consistent description of the opponents' Cynic-like moral severity and their complaint against him that he is bold in letters but deceptively weak in the church's presence. If this is the situation, then 5:13 might be read as Paul's admission of inconsistency and his explanation of it. Going mad with violent emotion in rhetorical performance was, in fact, an important element in the style of speech called *deinotēs* (see the comments above on 2 Cor. 10:9-10; and Voit), and presumably the opponents would have approved of Paul's blast of anger in the letter of tears. The style of speech contrasting with *deinotēs* was known as "grace" (*charis*). To achieve this style, the speaker must do precisely what Paul says he did when he returned from his madness and is still doing as he writes: "we are temperate" (*sōphronoumen*: see Van Hook, 32). The purpose of this calm self-presentation was to persuade and win over (as Paul says he aims to do in 5:11) rather than to overwhelm hearers as in the case of *deinotēs*.

Following on Paul's confession of madness are two applications of the motif of friendship, one to Christ (5:14-17) and the other to God (5:18-19). In each instance, the point is to distance Paul's ministry from flattery and associate it as closely as possible with divine grace (cf. 1:12). The "love [*agapē*] of Christ" in 5:14 will be misunderstood if readers interpret it through the influential but problematic work of Anders Nygren's *Agape and Eros*, which rules out of order the porous border between *agapē* and *philia* running throughout the present commentary (for a trenchant critique of Nygren, see McGinn). There is one point about friendship in antiquity, however, that Nygren properly underlines: its exclusivity. There was in Paul's day the widespread opinion that friendship was dyadic; if anyone had more than one, or possibly two friends, that person might well be thought of as a flatterer and guilty of *polyphilia*, the vice of having many friends (see Plutarch, *On Having Many Friends* 93B–97B). Read against this aversion to *polyphilia*, the quasi-hymnic writing in 5:14-15 trades on the commonplace that "friends have all things in common" (how else would all die or all live unless all share all things with Christ?). There is a "new creation" (5:17) in which having many friends is the very nature of things, not a symptom of flattery and deception.

Paul shifts in 5:18-19 from a christo-logic to a theo-logic, but the point remains the same. The new, many-friended creature that Paul is legitimates his manner of ministry in which reconciliation (in the sense defined below) and forgiveness take center stage. This new creation applies to God also, although interpreters rarely notice this. The Greek word translated "reconcile" does not refer to a restoration of a previous relationship so much as the initiation of new friendship (see Fredrickson 1997, 171–74) in which all things are shared. God's yes-saying in Christ (1:18-20) is matched by God's having all things in common with the *kosmos* and placing in "us" (Paul? Paul and his cowriters? the readers, too? the world?) the *logos* (word? logic?) of reconciliation.

▌ THE TEXT IN THE INTERPRETIVE TRADITION

Various commentators have wanted to protect Paul from the meaning of his own words. Typical is John Chrysostom, who rendered the sense of Paul's statement hypothetical: "What Paul means is that *even if* people think he is mad, everything he does is for the glory of God" (*Homilies on the Epistles of Paul to the Corinthians* 11.2, emphasis added). Other interpreters have construed Paul's madness as prophetic truth-telling, since they read *exestēmen* in 5:13 in light of Ps. 116:11: "I said in my consternation [*en tē ekstasei mou*] 'Everyone is a liar'" (see Eusebius, *Commentaria in Psalmos* [PG 23:353]). The latter reading supports the explanation given above. Finally, in the early church there was another interpretation of Paul's madness, and this one plays an important role in present-day discussions. It is that 2 Cor. 5:13 refers to Paul's vision of the Lord recounted in

12:1-10 (see Athanasius, *Expositiones in Psalmos* [PG 27:301]; and Cyril of Alexandria, *Expositio in Psalmos* [PG 69:1156]).

◼ THE TEXT IN CONTEMPORARY DISCUSSION

Paul's madness (5:13) is difficult to understand. An influential explanation among today's scholarly readers is that Paul's opponents, influenced by Gnosticism or by the ideal of the "divine man," had accused him of *not* having ecstatic experiences, validations in their view of an apostle of Christ (Schmithals, 187–89; Georgi, 252, 280–83). This verse would thus be Paul's rebuttal. As we have seen, there is indeed support in the early church for one portion of this claim, Paul's possible allusion to visionary experience. Yet the larger assertion, that a demand had been placed on Paul, depends on our viewing the opponents as seekers of ecstatic visions or speaking in tongues, for which there is scant evidence in 2 Corinthians and silence in the interpretive tradition (see Barrett 1973, 166–67; Furnish, 324–25).

2 Corinthians 5:20—7:4 God Entreating through Us, Not Them

◼ THE TEXT IN ITS ANCIENT CONTEXT

In a tender and urgent reminiscence of 1:3-7, where it was likewise not possible to distinguish between God's entreaty or exhortation and Paul's, so also in 5:20—6:2 Paul pleads for the community to be reconciled (in the full sense of the term) to him. If the Corinthians withhold forgiveness, then Paul's ministry itself becomes the cause of offense (6:2) in spite of the proof of its validity provided by the hardships he suffers (6:4-10). With an open mouth (6:11), an allusion to *parrēsia* (see Isocrates, *Oration* 12.96), he entreats the church, calling them by name ("Corinthians"). His heart is wide, a sign of joy and the holding of another in one's heart as in 3:2-3. Holding another in one's heart is a sign of friendship, according to John Chrysostom (PG 61:491), but the community's grief has narrowed (6:12) their souls (see Diogenes Laertius, *Lives of Illustrious Philosophers* 7.118) and forced Paul out of their "innards" (*tois splanchnois*). He pleads with them (6:13) to make room for him.

Paul then pleads with the church in Corinth not to align itself with the super-apostles. Scholars have correctly identified "mismatched" (*heterozygountes*) as nuptial imagery. Their assessment is confirmed by the terms denoting union, which follow in verses 15-16, especially *koinōnia*, which was widely employed; marriage was defined, in fact, as a *koinōnia* of bodies, wealth, and children. And yet the way the same scholars deal with *apistois* (translated by the NRSV as "with unbelievers") leads them to conclude that Paul here warns church members not to marry outside the community (cf. 1 Cor. 7:12-16 for a more complex view on the matter held by Paul himself). There is another way to read this text. The term *apistos* in 4:4 likely refers to the *disloyal* super-apostles. Moreover, not only did the yoke (*zygos*) function in marital contexts, but it was also a metaphor for the pulling together of friends. Paul uses it in Phil. 4:3 to persuade the readers of that letter to financially support the missionary work of Euodia and Syntyche as the church had supported him. Paul's plea, then, not to be "otherwise-yoked" with the unfaithful ones might be interpreted as his warning not to support the super-apostles.

■ The Text in the Interpretive Tradition

Interpreters in the early church sometimes found themselves in the uncomfortable position of making sense of texts that, from the perspective of the tradition's adherence to the *apatheia* (impassibility) of God, could not mean what they say. "The word *became* flesh" (emphasis added) in John 1:14 is a good example. Here the threat to the unchangeable, eternal Word comes not from heretical teaching but from the biblical text itself. The recourse of substituting "take on flesh" for "become flesh" was the preferred solution to this problem (see Theodoret of Cyrus, *Eranistes*, passim). Another famous example is Gal. 3:13, where we read that Christ "became a curse for us"; Jerome explained (*Commentarius in Epistolam S. Pauli ad Galatas* 2 [PL 26:387–88]) that this should not be taken literally—to Luther's irritation (*Lectures on Galatians* [*LW* 26:276]). This brings us to 2 Cor. 5:21, which Athanasius (*Oratio II contra Arianos* 47.2) recognized was as problematic as John 1:14 and Gal. 3:13. The stakes are high, however, since this verse undergirds Paul's plea for reconciliation in 5:20 and presents readers with a shocking idea: God made Christ "to be sin." Gregory of Nyssa (*Contra Celsum* 1.69) softened the offense by claiming that Paul wrote *sin* but meant *flesh*. Eutherius (*Confutationes quarundam propositionum* 4) took a different approach and applied what interpreters in the tradition had learned in dealing with John 1:14: Christ was not altered to be sin but "took our sin and caused it to disappear" (*aphanisai*). Theodorus Studites (*Parva Catechesis* 30) similarly emphasized that Christ "put on" human nature corrupted by sin.

■ The Text in Contemporary Discussion

What do love (*agapē*, 5:14) and justice (*dikaiosynē*, 5:21) have to do with one another? This important question, especially in the context of Christian responses to the criminal justice system in the United States, has been sidelined by Nygren's approach to love and by translators insisting on using "righteousness" to represent *dikaiosynē*. Even when the question is asked, however, justice is often reduced to calculation or the equitable enforcement of rules, and love is reduced to mercy's smoothing the rough edges of justice. But Paul holds the two tightly together, each indeed as an example of the other, not only in 2 Corinthians 5 but also in Gal. 5:5-6 and, by extension through nuptial imagery, in Phil. 3:7-11. Justice and love share at least two things in Paul. First, each is constituted by openness to the future (see especially Gal. 5:5-6). Just as one would never say of a beloved, "I have loved enough," so justice forbids saying, "justice has been done." The second thing love and justice share is that they spring from the singularity of the other; it is always the face of *this one* that calls forth my love just as it is the call of *this one* that moves me to response. For these reasons, both love and justice are pure gifts.

2 Corinthians 8:1—9:15: By Poverty Enriched

■ The Text in Its Ancient Context

In the ancient world, gift-giving displayed social status and obligated recipients to repay benefactors with gratitude and honor (see Danker). While Paul challenges the elite of the Corinthian church in these two chapters to contribute to the fund for the saints in Jerusalem, he nevertheless seeks to persuade them not to participate in a system of benefaction that would shame the poor in the Corinthian church (since they had nothing to give) and would establish the churches of Greece and Asia as patrons of the struggling client church in Jerusalem. Paul has a difficult task in front of him: to disrupt the circle of gift and gratitude without ruining the collection itself.

Paul shames the Corinthians by praising the generosity of the impoverished Macedonians (8:1-6). Yet there is more to it than this. First, an impossible logic about the Macedonian gift loosens, if not dissolves, the connection between giving and the display of social status. How so? In verse 2, the strange condition that makes gift-giving possible is "profound poverty." It is not the case, then, as it is with Corinth's wealthy elite, that the Macedonians give out of their fullness, as if their gift testified to their invulnerability. Like the widow in Mark 12:41-44, the Macedonians give out of their emptiness.

In 8:9, the "gift [*charis*] of our Lord Jesus Christ" follows the same unexpected pattern of giving out of poverty, in language that echoes the Christ hymn in Phil. 2:5-11. Paul writes, "by the poverty of that one you got rich." Next, in 8:13-15, Paul tries a second strategy, manipulating the well-known philosophical topic of proportional equality (Aristotle, *Nicomachean Ethics* 1130b–1132b). Instead of the expected notion of equality as distribution according to status (that is, equality is achieved when superior persons receive more), however, Paul implies that the very act of giving is the admission that one might one day be in need. Equality understood in this way exposes human frailty, even that of the elite, within any system of economic exchange.

To the ears of modern readers, chapter 9 simply repeats chapter 8. One prominent scholar has argued that the two chapters circulated independently before the final compilation of 2 Corinthians (see Betz). But to repeat oneself was not necessarily a fault in ancient letters (see Phil. 3:1). And although it is the case in chapter 9 that Paul again undermines the patron-client structure that had monopolized the act of giving in the ancient world, he does so in a different way, using a theological argument: God's justice *is* God's scattering, and this is good news for the poor, as the quotation of the Psalm in 9:9 suggests. Such a definition of justice (NRSV translates "righteousness") must have been shocking, since in the wake of Plato (*Republic* 433B–435B), justice was understood as a harmony of interests or a strict limitation on individuals to perform assigned roles within an unchallenged gradation of social power. In short, 2 Corinthians 8 and 9 does not credit God with preserving the patron-client relationship, but with deconstructing it. The wildly unaccountable dissemination in verses 10-11, just another instance of scattering, does indeed produce gratitude to God, but what is one to be grateful for (note the "indescribable gift" in 9:15) at the scene of such dispersion accomplished by God's giving? Might it be the generosity (*haplotēs*), made possible by God's grace, of shaking things loose? Thus, in the end, it is not gratitude that Paul imagines the poor in Jerusalem will feel toward the church in Corinth: it is longing for communion (vv. 13-14).

▌The Text in Contemporary Discussion

Paul's probing of the ideology of the gift (*charis*), which might also be translated as "grace," bears a remarkable resemblance to recent philosophical and theological discussions of gift-giving (see

Horner; Walters) that have been inspired, at least in part, by Derrida's critical analysis of Marcel Mauss's 1925 anthropological study *The Gift: The Form and Reason for Exchange in Archaic Societies*. What is the connection between the first-century apostle and recent philosophers, at least the ones for whom the language of religion has proven indispensable? Very briefly stated, for Derrida, the gift in a pure sense is impossible: it refuses to let itself be intended by the giver or perceived by the recipient. In the moment that a gift either generates the expectation of repayment or a feeling of obligation, it ceases to be a gift. Thus the very possibility of a gift (for which there needs to exist a giver, a gift, and a recipient) also makes gift-giving impossible (see Caputo 1997, 160–64). This is not a mere word game, as Paul's ingenious and impassioned attempt to free the collection from the ancient system of benefaction shows. Christ's poverty, God's disseminative justice, and the gift's indescribability all reflect Paul's efforts to keep the elite from capitalizing on the collection and dominating the Corinthian church.

2 Corinthians 10:1-18: *Miles Gloriosus: Militia Amoris*

▌THE TEXT IN ITS ANCIENT CONTEXT

In the first five words of 10:1, Paul manages to say "I" three times and to write "Paul" once for good measure. His audacity, mentioned in 7:16 but kept under wraps in chapters 8 and 9, now bursts forth: Paul is a warrior! But unlike the stock figure of the *miles gloriosus* of Roman comedy (see Plautus, *The Swaggering Soldier*), whose penchant for comparing himself to others and commending himself (see 10:12-18) sets the stage for Paul's appearance in chapters 10–12, and in whose image Paul creates the super-apostles, Paul is a soldier in Love's campaign. Rather than boasting in personal power, he swaggers in his weakness (10:10; 11; 21, 29, 12:9-10; 13:3-4, 9). This is not, however, weakness in a general sense, that is, an incapacity that could be remedied with extra effort or training. Rather, the erotic motifs woven into the discourse of these chapters suggest that Paul's weakness is the kind ancient love poets wrote about: desire for a communion that appears impossible. Second Corinthians 10–13 is a complex argument, ironies captured within ironies, a pretended and demented bragging about those desperate emotions about which no one but a crazed lover would ever boast. Paul's boasting in his weakness was intended to expose his opponents' severity and to commend Christ's gentleness and reasonableness that the apostle seeks to emulate.

Once again, the charge of duplicity rears its head: 10:1 incorporates into its own discourse the opponents' complaint that Paul is bold at a distance but *tapeinos* ("lowly," connoting, from the perspective of elites, marginalized persons of low social class) when present. Fighting words! Note the military terms marching forward: "I am bold" (10:2), "daring" (10:2), "wage war" (10:3), "weapons of our warfare" (10:4), "take down strongholds" (10:4) and "elevated heights" (10:5), "taking captive" (10:5), "obedience" (10:5,6), and "avenge disobedience" (10:6). Paul is conducting a campaign, to be sure, but first-century readers, especially those who remembered the motif of the triumphal procession in 2:14 and its association with the motif *servitium amoris*, would see the amatory point: Paul portrays himself as Eros taking captive and subjecting to servitude the high-minded, philosophical despisers of love, who in ancient amatory literature often reversed course and fell especially hard in love through Eros's avenging intervention (see the opening chapter of Xenophon of Ephesus, *An Ephesian Tale*; Philostratus, *Ep.* 12; *Greek Anthology* 5.294). Verse 6 marks a pause in the general campaign; only when the Corinthians' obedience to Christ (obedience of love, that is, another instance of *servitium amoris*) is complete will Paul turn to the others. Yet, lest anyone take his feigned belligerence in 10:1-6 seriously, in 10:8 he denies intent to pull anything or anyone down. He wouldn't want to frighten anyone (10:9)!

▌ THE TEXT IN THE INTERPRETIVE TRADITION

According to 10:9-10, Paul's letters written before 2 Corinthians had already entered an interpretive tradition of considerable sophistication. As I noted in the introduction, the super-apostles evaluated Paul's letters and speech according to the literary and rhetorical standards of the time; his speech in the presence of the community, they said (10:10), was "attenuated" (*exouthenēmenos*). The *Rhetorica ad Herennium* (4.11.16) equated attenuated speech with the simple style that employed everyday language and could, if handled skillfully, achieve elegance. If mishandled, however, it was debased and merely ordinary, and as Cicero noted (*De oratore* 20; see also Quintilian, *Institutio oratoria* 9.2.3), it was furthest from the forceful style (*deinotēs*). In short, we might infer the opponents charged that Paul in the presence of the church used irony (*eirōneia*), not in the modern sense of saying the opposite of what one means but in the ancient sense. That is, he talked the way poor people and slaves talked (cf. 1 Cor. 1:28), although he was capable of much more, and did so in order to ridicule others (see Dio Chrysostom, *Oration* 42.1–3). John Chrysostom (*In illud: Utinam sustineretis modicum* [PG 51:304]) had no doubt that Paul's opponents accused him of irony. In fact, Chrysostom's reading of 2 Cor. 10:9-10, and particularly his detailed explanation of Paul's "attenuated speech," lines up with the discussion of this topic in rhetorical handbooks and literary treatises (for a deep appreciation of Chrysostom as a Pauline interpreter, see Mitchell).

▌ THE TEXT IN CONTEMPORARY DISCUSSION

Such talk about lowliness, weakness, love, and slavery in Christian discourse forced Friedrich Nietzsche to cry out, "Bad air! Bad air!" (Nietzsche, 24). Hatred, revenge, envy—these terms taken together translate *ressentiment*, the word Nietzsche deployed against what he perceived to be the stench of Jewish and Christian souls deformed by the "revaluation of values." In a "slave revolt," he complained, the weak of the world seek "spiritual revenge" against the strong and their spontaneous affirmation of life; by promoting guilt, pettiness, and duties, the priestly class prevails by sullying the heroic embrace of life (Nietzsche, 19–33). This is not the place to assert or deny that Paul's weakness or the *servitium amoris* motif were examples of *ressentiment*, but the question might at least be raised whether the eroticism Paul weaves into his self-presentation and into his Christology entails a spontaneous and infinite affirmation of the other and thus even a slight chance for a rapprochement with Nietzsche's "yes-saying." (For a reading of the philosopher that might facilitate such an unexpected meeting of minds, see Caputo 1993, 42–68.)

2 Corinthians 11:1-4: Zealous to Preserve Christ's Marriage Bed

THE TEXT IN ITS ANCIENT CONTEXT

Here Paul raises the stakes on the church's flirtation with the super-apostles. He has married the Corinthians off to Christ; for them now to shift their allegiance to his rivals would be the same as abandoning their nuptial union with Christ. Paul makes a similar move in his letter to the Galatians (1:6-9), where a note similar to verse 4 can be heard.

THE TEXT IN THE INTERPRETIVE TRADITION

Paul, in unconscious cooperation with the Song of Songs, had perhaps no more profound influence on later doctrine than in the nuptial imagery he employs here for the relation of Christ and the church (for the early church, see Elliott; for a medieval example, see Gilbert of Hoyland, *Sermons* 2.5). Luther's notion of the "joyous exchange" comes out of this tradition (see, e.g., his *The Blessed Sacrament of the Holy and True Body of Christ and the Brotherhoods* [*LW* 35]).

THE TEXT IN CONTEMPORARY DISCUSSION

Unlike their medieval counterparts, today's readers are no doubt bewildered or put off by the conceptual framework of Christ as bridegroom and the church as bride. To be sure, definite risks accompany this way of imagining Christian doctrine and piety. First of all, there appears to be a bias toward heterosexual marriage that abets heterosexism in contemporary culture (on which see Jung and Smith). To counter this impression that Paul is a champion of heterosexual marriage, one need only read his tepid commendation of marriage in 1 Thess. 4:3-8 and 1 Corinthians 7 (see Martin 2006). Moreover, nuptial imagery actually has the potential of deconstructing the binary opposition of male and female—think of Corinthian manbrides! (See Fredrickson 2013, 129–49). Finally, a clear distinction must be made between Paul's use of nuptial imagery in his genuine epistles and that found in the pseudonymous letters (Colossians, Ephesians, and the Pastorals). In the former, Paul emphasizes the ritual of marriage, the wedding, and does so in the context of eschatological expectation. Furthermore, standard motifs of friendship (the theme of *koinōnia*, for example) define what it means to get married. In the pseudonymous letters, however, marriage is placed within the ancient Greek household (see Balch) and illustrates the same hierarchical relation that obtains between head and body and Christ and church, the very relations of power and authority that the genuine Paul says Christ is presently nullifying (see 1 Cor. 15:24; for the brazen misconstrual of this verse to legitimate hierarchy, see Eph. 1:20-23).

2 Corinthians 11:5—12:10: Dog Apostles, Hardships, and Weakness

THE TEXT IN ITS ANCIENT CONTEXT

As God is his witness, Paul loves the Corinthians (11:11). For that reason, they should take his refusal of financial support not as an insult but rather as witness of his affection. But there is more to his refusal than this. Paul is setting up an extended comparison between himself and the super-apostles in 11:12—12:13, just what he said in 10:12 he would not do. The comparison hinges on the opponents' Cynic-like behavior. In this connection, note in 11:9 that he refuses the Corinthians' aid in order that he might keep himself in every way "without weight" (*abarē*). The term "weighty" (*baros*) was often associated with Cynic philosophers (Malherbe 1970) whose harsh criticism was felt to be oppressive. Cynics also had the reputation of throwing their weight around in another way: by demanding lodging from the very people they rebuked. And then they ate them out of house and home (see 11:20: "preys upon you" might also be translated "eats up" or "devours"). Cynics, in short, had big jaws (see Billerbeck, 113).

Paul compliments himself perhaps too much (or is his sense of humor very dry?) when he explains the reason for this comparison with the super-apostles: he wants to prevent them from "being found as he is" (11:12). It turns out that Paul is a wreck, but before he enumerates his hardships (11:23-33) and exposes his weaknesses (12:8-10), he alludes in 11:13-15 and 20-21 to behavioral traits frequently associated with Cynic behavior. (The name "Cynic" is related to the Greek word for dog; for these traits, see Epictetus, *Diatr.* 2.12.24; 3.22.23–25, 45–50; 4.8.6–20; Lucian, *Fugitivi* 12–19; *Piscator* 31; Aelius Aristides, *Oration* 3.663–68, 671, 676, 682–83; Julian, *Oration* 6.201A.) He implies that the Corinthians ought to be horrified in discovering the super-apostles' real identity and ashamed not to have seen it before. Perhaps most important here is that the dog-like apostles are portrayed as minions of Satan (11:14-15), whom we have encountered before in this letter when severity threatens to drive an individual through shame to suicide (2:5-11).

Ancient philosophers listed their hardships for three reasons: to display their moral virtue; to describe training in moral virtue; and, less frequently, to show their kindly attitude (*philanthrōpia*) toward the ignorant masses they sought to improve (see Fitzgerald). In 11:23-33, Paul mimics the philosopher's occupational hazards; but in verses 28-29 he slips in sentiments illustrative not of a moralist's day-to-day troubles but of the emotions of those who care for and fret over a beloved, even to the point of burning (cf. 1 Cor. 7:9).

Second Corinthians 12:1-10 is a tour de force in which Paul makes the following point, representative of the entire letter, by having the Lord himself say it (12:9): weakness—the lover's sickness of body and soul when separated from the beloved—perfects divine power. The Lord should know of what he speaks, since he was crucified "out of weakness" (13:4). But why, from first-century perspectives, does Paul stage the event of his abduction into paradise in such dramatic terms? It is not an overstatement to say that in the ancient Greek world, anyone who had something important to say, especially about the great transitions of individual or community life, what anthropologists call liminality, told a story of erotic abduction. Consider Homer's *Iliad*, the founding of Europe, Zeus's love for Ganymede, Eos's desire for Tithonos, the educational experience of the young men of Sparta and Crete, the tolerance of forced marriages by abduction, and the bitterly protested marriages to Hades at death. It is not unreasonable to suppose that Paul could not have told the most important story of his life and of his ministry without narrating rapture into paradise (for erotic abduction and sexual violence in ancient culture, see Fredrickson 2013, 85–104). But in this mysterious event, this apocalypse, he refuses to boast. Of course, by saying that he won't talk about it, he speaks volumes.

■ THE TEXT IN THE INTERPRETIVE TRADITION

The eroticism of these verses has faded from view in the modern period, but some readers, especially medieval mystics and monastics, experienced a reawakening of friendship in theology and in their communal life and treasured Paul's abduction (*harpagenta* in v. 2 and *hērpagē* in v. 4) into paradise, the unspeakable, wordless intimacy, and his disorienting and grief-filled return to earth. Paul's story matched their brief ecstasies and then the long and hollow periods of Christ's absence. There was a particular interest in Paul's experience of hearing "wordless words" (*arrēta rēmata*, 12:4), which was understood as erotic and an example of apophaticism (see John of Ford, *Sermons* 4.1; 45.2, 5; 94.9; 100.5).

■ THE TEXT IN CONTEMPORARY DISCUSSION

Apophaticism, or negative theology, is a kind of theological discourse that denies, inconsistently, that it is possible to speak about God. God is beyond being, it is claimed, and therefore to speak about God violates God, and yet this very impossibility impassions more and more words spoken and written about God. Robust in the medieval period, when Paul's loquacious silence about his encounter with Jesus in 2 Cor. 12:4 served as a kind of proof text, apophaticism is making a comeback in postmodern philosophy and theology thanks to the fascination the contradiction between speaking and not speaking held for Jacques Derrida. Derrida did not, however, share negative theology's confidence that it could *rest* in the God beyond being, beyond linguistic signification. Quite the opposite. In an uncanny and certainly unintended parallel to Paul's return to earth (12:7-10), where divine power happens in weakness, that is, in Paul's troubled, loving relation to the Corinthians, Derrida generalized the impossibility and passion of the speaking about God to the speaking about every other. "Deconstruction is rather the thought, if it is a thought, of an absolute heterogeneity that unsettles all the assurances of the same within which we comfortably ensconce ourselves. That is the desire by which it is moved, which moves and impassions it, which sets it into motion, toward which it extends itself" (Caputo 1997, 5).

2 Corinthians 12:11—13:10: A True Apostle

■ THE TEXT IN ITS ANCIENT CONTEXT

The letter is coming to an end. Paul must first extricate himself from his pretense of boasting and comparison with the super-apostles. This he accomplishes in 12:11-13 by shifting blame: the Corinthians themselves forced him to act the part of a bragging fool.

In 12:13-15, he deals one last time with the implications of his refusal of financial support. First, he seeks (the Greek term *zēteō* has erotic connotations and might also be translated "desires") them, not their things. Second, he is their parent (cf. 1 Cor. 4:14-15). The last reason (v. 15) can of course be read in terms of economics, but the words carry an erotic connotation as well, which should not be unexpected given the emphasis on love at the end of the verse. The words in question here are *dapanaō* and *ekdapanaō* (NRSV: "spend and be spent"). The first term might reasonably carry only economic meaning, but the fact that the second is used in the passive voice means that Paul himself is expended for their lives. There is continuity with the motif of *servitium amoris* running throughout the letter. Two obvious parallels are 1 Thess. 2:8 and Phil. 2:17. A more subtle parallel is Phil. 2:7, in which Christ is said to have "emptied himself." In Greek and Latin love literature, longing for communion with a beloved causes the lover to melt and then drain away, in other words to be poured out or expended (see Fredrickson 2013, 45–83; for a much later example of *dapanaō* used in this erotic sense, see Theodorus Prodromus, *Rhodanthe and Dosicles* 8.179: "the hearts of those who long are expended").

Before he bids farewell in a proto-trinitarian formula (13:13), which is itself significant in its repetition of Paul's emphasis throughout the letter on love, grace, and communion, Paul concludes the body of the letter with three final contrasts between himself and the super-apostles. First, in 12:20, as he returns to the ethical and social class issues he had addressed in 1 Corinthians (likely linked through elite male privileges), Paul makes a surprising turn: the church's bad behavior will be the occasion of God driving him once again into melancholy and causing him to lament. Reading verse 21 first and then going back to the first half of verse 20 raises a question: Is Paul suggesting that their finding him "not as they wish" means that they will find him weak and lacking in the severity of the super-apostles? Second Corinthians 13:3 hints that this was the case. The second contrast is the oblique criticism in 13:5-10 that Paul's rivals engage in moral exhortation in order to burnish their own reputations for frank speaking. Paul claims to have no stake in the Corinthians' progress other than their improvement. The final contrast, which ends the body of the letter, has Paul locating the purpose of his authority not in harsh criticism (the Greek phrase connotes "cutting") but in building up.

■ The Text in the Interpretive Tradition

In a stunning turn, the very weakness (*asthenia*) Paul seeks mightily to preserve in the face of the super-apostles' harshness, even to the point of his adopting the guise of a warrior, became an embarrassment to the apostle's later interpreters. But Paul plainly *does* connect his weakness to Christ's in 13:4: "he [Christ] was crucified from weakness" and "we are weak in him." The subtle adjustments made to the first phrase by exegetes betray their nervousness over its dogmatic implication that weakness pertains to the whole Christ, a view that the fathers worried the uneducated reader might erroneously entertain (John Chrysostom, *In epistulam ii ad Corinthos* [PG 61:598–600]).

One solution to the perceived threat to the *apatheia* of God, a nonnegotiable point in Christian theology as soon as ancient philosophy was let in, was to assign the weakness mentioned in 13:4 to Christ's "human part" or "nature" or to his "flesh." His resurrection, power, and life were referred to the divine (see Gregory of Nyssa, *Contra Eunomium* 3.4.10). A related strategy was to deny any passivity in Christ. In Eusebius's words, "He himself made himself weak, not being conquered by another" (*Commentaria in Psalmos* 23.309). Christ's *voluntary* weakness made it not weakness in the usual sense (see Cyril of Jerusalem, *Catacheses ad illuminandos* 14.8). Finally, weakness might be understood simply as a matter of suffering persecution or plots (see John of Damascus, *Commentarii in epistulas Pauli* [PG 95:773).

■THE TEXT IN CONTEMPORARY DISCUSSION

Second Corinthians begins (1:3) and ends (13:4) with divine suffering. The interpretive tradition's discomfort with Paul's straying outside the lines drawn for theology by the doctrine of the *apatheia* of God, a doctrine inspired by Greek philosophy, make Paul's weakness, his passions, all the more interesting. On several occasions in this essay, it was pointed out that Paul's subtle use and critique of Greek philosophical ideas make his writings a site of exploration for postmodern philosophers, especially those, like John Caputo, influenced by Jacques Derrida.

If we shift from God to Paul, a distinction that Paul himself obscures throughout the letter (see, e.g., 5:20-21), we note that the interpretive tradition generally characterized Paul's suffering as his endurance of hardships or opposition not unlike the wise man's training in virtue. Yet here are good reasons to think that his suffering was in fact the vulnerability opened up in him by loving the Corinthians: weakness, in other words. We have seen that Paul aligns himself with the weakness of Christ, and this leads him to a pastoral practice of adaptability, grace, and forgiveness, none of which compromises frank speech from Paul's perspective, as the harsh super-apostles charge, but that works in concert with truth-telling and justice. Paul insists on the "slavery of love" (*servitium amoris*) and related motifs drawn from erotic literature to unify the argument of the letter and persuade the Corinthians to accept his ministry and to reject that of his rivals. Finally, we observed how the letter's critique of the severe disciplinary practice that had the effect of isolating the individual who wronged Paul challenges the contemporary church to examine its understanding of punishment and the isolating practices of the American system of criminal justice.

Works Cited

Amador, J. D. H. 2000. "Revisiting 2 Corinthians: Rhetoric and the Case for Unity." *NTS* 46:92–111.

Balch, David L. 1981. *Let Wives Be Submissive: The Domestic Code in 1 Peter*. SBLMS 26. Chico, CA: Scholars Press.

Barrett, C. K. 1970. "Ο ΑΔΙΚΗΣΑΣ (2 Cor. 7.12)." In *Verborum Veritas: Festschrift für Gustav Stählin*, edited by Otto Böcher and Klaus Haacker, 149–57. Wuppertal: Rolf Brockhaus.

———. 1973. *A Commentary on the Second Epistle to the Corinthians*. HNTC. New York: Harper & Row.

Barth, Karl. 2002. *The Epistle to the Philippians*. Translated by James W. Leitch. 40th anniversary ed. Louisville: Westminster John Knox.

Betz, Hans Dieter, and George W. MacCrae. 1985. *2 Corinthians 8 and 9: A Commentary on Two Administrative Letters of the Apostle Paul*. Philadelphia: Fortress Press.

Billerbeck, Margarethe. 1978. *Epiktet: Vom Kynismus*. Philosophia Antiqua 34. Leiden: Brill.

Briggs, Sheila. 1989. "Can an Enslaved God Liberate? Hermeneutical Reflections on Phil 2:6-11." *Semeia* 47:137–53.

Caputo, John D. 1993. *Against Ethics: Contributions to a Poetics of Obligation with Constant Reference to Deconstruction*. Bloomington: Indiana University Press.

———. 1997. *The Prayers and Tears of Jacques Derrida: Religion without Religion*. Bloomington: Indiana University Press.

Caputo, John D., and Linda Martin Alcoff. 2009. *St. Paul among the Philosophers*. Bloomington: Indiana University Press.

Culler, Jonathan D. 1982. *On Deconstruction: Theory and Criticism after Structuralism*. Ithaca, NY: Cornell University Press.

Danker, Frederick W. 1982. *Benefactor: An Epigraphic Study of a Graeco-Roman and New Testament Semantic Field*. Saint Louis: Clayton.

Derrida, Jacques. 2005. *The Politics of Friendship*. New York: Verso.

Elliott, M. W. 2000. *The Song of Songs and Christology in the Early Church, 381–451*. Studien und Texte zu Antike und Christentum 7. Tübingen: Mohr Siebeck.

Fitzgerald, John T. 1988. *Cracks in an Earthen Vessel: An Examination of the Catalogues of Hardships in the Corinthian Correspondence*. SBLDS 99. Atlanta: Scholars Press.

Fiore, Benjamin. 1985. "'Covert Allusion' in 1 Corinthians 1–4." *CBQ* 47:85–102.

Fredrickson, David E. 1996. "*Parrēsia* in the Pauline Epistles." In *Friendship, Flattery, and Frankness of Speech: Studies on Friendship in the New Testament World*, edited by John T. Fitzgerald, 163–84. NovTSup 82. New York: Brill.

———. 1997. "The Presence of Jesus in 2 Corinthians 1–7." In *The Quest for Jesus and the Christian Faith*, edited by Frederick J. Gaiser, 163–74. Word and World Supplements 3. St. Paul: Word and World.

———. 2000. "Paul's Sentence of Death (2 Corinthians 1:9)." In *God, Evil, and Suffering: Essays in Honor of Paul R. Sponheim*, edited by Terence E. Fretheim and Curtis L. Thompson, 99–107. Word and World Supplements 4. St. Paul: Word and World.

———. 2001. "'Through Many Tears (2 Cor 2:4)': Paul's Grieving Letter and the Occasion of 2 Corinthians 1–7." In *Paul and Pathos*, edited by Thomas H. Olbricht and Jerry L. Sumney, 161–79. Atlanta: Society of Biblical Literature.

———. 2013. *Eros and the Christ: Longing and Envy in Paul's Christology*. Minneapolis: Fortress Press.

Fretheim, Terence E. 1984. *The Suffering of God: An Old Testament Perspective*. OBT 14. Philadelphia: Fortress Press.

Frick, Peter, ed. 2013. *Paul in the Grip of the Philosophers: The Apostle and Contemporary Continental Philosophy*. Minneapolis: Fortress Press.

Furnish, Victor Paul. 1984. *2 Corinthians*. AB. Garden City, NY: Doubleday.

Georgi, Dieter. 1987. *The Opponents of Paul in Second Corinthians*. Studies of the New Testament and its World. Edinburgh: T&T Clark.

Grant, Robert M. 1957. *The Letter and the Spirit*. London: SPCK.

Horner, Robyn. 2001. *Rethinking God as Gift: Marion, Derrida, and the Limits of Phenomenology*. Perspectives in Continental Philosophy 19. New York: Fordham University Press.

Kearney, Richard. 2005. "Deconstruction, God, and the Possible." In *Derrida and Religion: Other Testaments*, edited by Yvonne Sherwood and Kevin Hart, 297–308. New York: Routledge.

Jung, Patricia B., and Ralph F. Smith. 1993. *Heterosexism: An Ethical Challenge*. Albany: State University of New York Press.

Malherbe, Abraham J. 1970. "'Gentle as a Nurse': The Cynic Background to I Thess II." *NovT* 12:203–17.

———. 1983. "Exhortation in First Thessalonians." *NovT* 25:238–56.

———. 1988. *Ancient Epistolary Theorists*. SBLSBS 19. Atlanta: Scholars Press.

———. 1989. *Paul and the Popular Philosophers*. Minneapolis: Augsburg Fortress.

Marshall, Peter. 1987. *Enmity in Corinth: Social Conventions in Paul's Relations with the Corinthians*. WUNT 23. Tübingen: J. C. B. Mohr.

Martin, Dale B. 1990. *Slavery as Salvation: The Metaphor of Slavery in Pauline Christianity*. New Haven: Yale University Press.

———. 2006. *Sex and the Single Savior: Gender and Sexuality in Biblical Interpretation*. Louisville: Westminster John Knox.

McGinn, Bernard. 1996. "God as Eros: Metaphysical Foundations of Christian Mysticism." In *New Perspectives on Historical Theology: Essays in Memory of John Meyendorff*, edited by Bradley Nassif, 189–209. Grand Rapids: Eerdmans.

Miller, John F. 1995. "Reading Cupid's Triumph." *Classical Journal* 90:287–94.

Mitchell, Margaret. 2002. *The Heavenly Trumpet: John Chrysostom and the Art of Pauline Interpretation*. HUT 40. Louisville: Westminster John Knox.

Moltmann, Jürgen. 1974. *The Crucified God: The Cross of Christ as the Foundation and Criticism of Christian Theology*. New York: Harper & Row.

———. 1981. *The Trinity and the Kingdom: The Doctrine of God*. San Francisco: Harper & Row.

Monks of Mount Saint Bernard Abbey. 1970–1971. *Guerric of Igny: Liturgical Sermons*. 2 vols. Cistercian Fathers 8, 32. Spencer, MA: Cistercian.

Murgatroyd, Paul. 1980. "*Servitium Amoris* and the Roman Elegists." *Latomus* 40:589–606.

Nietzsche, Friedrich. 1998. *On the Genealogy of Morality: A Polemic*. Translated by Maudemarie Clark and Alan J. Swensen. Indianapolis: Hackett.

Smiley, Charles Newton. 1906. *Latinitas and Hellēnismos: The Influence of the Stoic Theory of Style as Shown in the Writings of Dionysius, Quintilian, Pliny the Younger, Tacitus, Fronto, Aulus Gellius, and Sextus Empiricus*. Madison: University of Wisconsin.

Schmithals, Walter. 1971. *Gnosticism in Corinth: An Investigation of the Letters to the Corinthians*. Nashville: Abingdon.

Stowers, Stanley K. 1986. *Letter Writing in Greco-Roman Antiquity*. LEC 5. Philadelphia: Westminster.

Van Hook, Larue. 1905. *The Metaphorical Terminology of Greek Rhetoric and Literary Criticism*. Chicago: University of Chicago Press.

Voit, Ludwig. 1934. ΔΕΙΝΟΤΗΣ: *Ein antiker Stilbegriff*. Leipzig: Dieterich.

Walters, Gregory. 2013. *Being Promised: Theology, Gift, and Practice*. Sacra Doctrina. Grand Rapids: Eerdmans.

Watson, Francis B. 1984. "2 Cor. X–XIII and Paul's Painful Letter to the Corinthians." *JTS* 35:324–46.

Zagagi, Netta. 1980. *Tradition and Originality in Plautus: Studies in the Amatory Motif in Plautine Comedy*. Hypomnemata 62. Göttingen: Vandenhoeck & Ruprecht.

GALATIANS

Brigitte Kahl

Introduction

Paul's epistle to the "assemblies [*ekklēsiais*] of Galatia" (1:2) is a circular letter dating from the early fifties CE. Its recipients are Pauline Christ communities in the Roman province of Galatia, a vast, multiethnic territory in central Asia Minor, whose inhabitants—among them a sizable Jewish population—were subject and tributary to Rome, collectively unified and naturalized as Roman Galatians. The terms *Galatians* and *Galatia* at Paul's time thus connoted a hybrid identity and location that, first and foremost, spelled out Roman victory and the power to name foreign nations and tribes (*ethnē*). More specifically, the common "surname" commemorates the successful subjugation and cooptation of the Celtic tribes, as the terms *Galatae/ai* ("Galatians"), *Galli* ("Gauls"), and *Keltoi* ("Celts") were widely synonymous in ancient Latin and Greek. Spread all over Europe, they had clashed with Rome for centuries and once even sacked the city itself (387 BCE). Greco-Roman political mythology and art stylized them as prototypical barbarians and archenemies of civilization, for example, in the Great Altar of Pergamon (Kahl 2010). In 279–278 BCE, three of their migrant tribes, after an assault on Delphi, had established the easternmost outpost of Celtic presence in the ancient Mediterranean by crossing over to Anatolia. They settled in what is today Turkey, around Ankyra. Following a century of severe clashes with Pergamon and a devastating Roman massacre in 189 BCE, they gradually changed from enemies to allies and power brokers of Rome. Ankyra in 25 BCE became the capital of the newly founded Galatian province, with a magnificent imperial temple to the goddess Roma and the god Augustus that featured a monumental Greek and Latin inscription of the emperor's worldwide achievements (the *Res Gestae*). Paul's Galatians could be either living in these northern tribal territories of the province, or further to its south, where Rome made its presence felt through roads (*Via Sebaste*), massive building activities, and numerous veteran colonies like Pisidian Antioch, Iconium, and Lystra (see Acts 13:13—14:23). Yet no matter which geographic or ethnic part of the province they inhabited, their identity was overlaid with a hybrid Romanized "Galatian-ness" and their everyday existence shaped by the imprint of colonization (Mitchell 1993a; Kahl 2010).

This Roman contextuality, although never explicitly addressed by Paul and entirely eclipsed in traditional interpretations, might be key to rethinking some of the most troublesome questions that Galatians—arguably Paul's most influential letter—raises for a twenty-first-century reading. In response to an acute crisis among his messianic communities, Paul tried to convince their non-Jewish Christ-followers that they should not adopt Jewish circumcision because they were fully legitimate Jewish children of Abraham already through Christ (3:1—4:31). This focal message was driven home as Paul recapitulated the formative events around Damascus, Jerusalem, and Antioch that established the coequality of circumcised and uncircumcised people "in Christ" (1:10—2:21). A new diverse commonality of oneness-in-difference was thus created that operated through love and mutuality (5:1—6:18). The uniformity of an all-circumcised *ekklēsia*, as demanded by Paul's opponents, was anathema (1:6-9).

From within this fervent confrontation between "foreskin" and "circumcision," Paul developed his signature theology of justification by grace and faith rather than by works of the law (Gal. 2:15-21), embedded in dramatic confrontations with the gospel-falsifiers (1:6-9; 5:12), "false brothers" (2:1-10), Peter (2:11-14), the allegorical "Hagar" (4:21-31), and the "stupid Galatians" themselves (3:1). This unrelenting antithetical force of Galatians has propelled its history of interpretation and often eclipsed Paul's great emancipatory manifesto about baptismal oneness across split-lines of race, religion, class, and gender (3:28), as well as his visionary statements about self and other reconciled through love and bearing one another's burdens (6:2). The polarization of "law versus gospel" and "faith versus works" prevailed, powerfully, not only molding Galatians into the core document of the Protestant Reformation but also helping to generate Christian anti-Judaism, patriarchal authoritarianism, and dogmatic policies of "zero tolerance" against others of all kinds—those (de) classified by wrong faith, inferior gender or status, or aberrant sexual orientation or social practice.

This standard reading of Galatians as the prototype of Christian conservatism and master script for the separation between Christianity and Judaism has been challenged over the past fifty years in the context of post-Holocaust, feminist, liberationist, womanist, empire-critical, and postcolonial approaches (Ehrensperger; Zetterholm). The "New Perspective on Paul" has entirely reconfigured the debate by pointing to the continuing Jewishness of Paul even after "Damascus" (Stendahl; Dunn; Wright 2005). Jewish scholars joined the discussion (Boyarin 1994; Nanos; Le Cornu and Shulam); feminist interpreters have either scrutinized Galatians for emancipatory traits (Gaventa; Osiek; Kahl 1999; Wiley; Lopez) or employed a hermeneutics of suspicion strongly critical of Paul (Fatum; Briggs; Schüssler Fiorenza 1999, 149–73); the native Anatolian context has been searched for hermeneutical clues (S. Elliott 2004; Arnold), and African American as well as African perspectives have been used for constructive rereadings (Braxton, Niang, Kamudzandu). Feminist Lutheran theologians have entered into the debate (Streufert). At the same time, empire-critical and postcolonial reconstructions have remapped the interpretational debates by pointing to the Roman rather than exclusively Jewish or Hellenistic contexts of Paul's theology (Horsley 1997; 2000; Stanley).

Right now, the interpretation of Galatians is shifting. The circumcision conflict at the heart of the letter appears as having been codetermined by Roman and civic pressures on the Galatians to conform to standard norms, apart from questions of the value or significance of the Torah itself (Winter, 124–43; Nanos, 257–71). The long-neglected phenomenon of Roman emperor worship, which was in fact massively present in provincial Galatia at the time of Paul (Hardin), points to the political idolatry of empire as potentially the primary target of Paul's polemics (Kahl 2010). And a new debate about the term "Christianity"—a term Paul himself never used—is emerging. Paul's messianic converts in Galatia defy our attempts at labeling or categorizing them (Boyarin 2004; Johnson Hodge; Campbell; Garroway), Instead of neatly categorized identities, we encounter here a messianic hybridity of multiply shaped identities, practiced as the commonality of love "in Christ." This hybridity mimics and mocks, summons and subverts the hybrid imperial identity imposed by Rome and her false gods.

At the beginning of the twenty-first century, appropriations of Galatians are being reoriented toward entirely new types of dialogue and interaction across all kinds of boundaries that dissect the body of humanity—and, for Christian interpreters, the body of Christ.

Galatians 1:1-9: The Other Gospel and the End of Otherness

▌THE TEXT IN ITS ANCIENT CONTEXT

Tied into his signature greeting of "grace . . . and peace," Paul in the prescript of his letter highlights the key elements of the message he is entrusted with as God's ambassador (*apostolos*). The strong emphasis on a family-related terminology of God, Father, sonship, and siblinghood in Gal. 1:1-5 is noteworthy, as is the transition from the language of "I," "he," and "you" to the inclusive "we" and "our" over the first four verses, leading into the liturgical imperative collectively to worship and glorify "our" God and father (1:5). This concluding doxology is sealed by a participatory "Amen," to be pronounced in unison by the extended multiethnic family of God. The prominent placement of the resurrection event in 1:1 indicates that these new kinship affiliations are based on God's fatherhood, made manifest in raising Jesus Messiah (= Christ) as his son "out of the dead" (cf. Rom. 1:4). As children of "our God and Father" (1:4), "we" are reborn as siblings of Jesus into God's diverse patchwork family of Jews and non-Jews together, a topic further explored in Galatians 3–4.

Read before the Roman backdrop, the political overtones of this ecumenical family construct are noteworthy. The establishment of empire-wide affiliations among diverse subject nations like Jews and Galatians, all of them united through a common fictive father (*pater patriae*), God (*divus*), son of God (*divi filius*), and Lord (*dominus*), was at Paul's time the prerogative of the emperor alone. It was he who claimed universal worship and fatherhood, especially in Galatia, where, around 50 CE, the lure of imperial religion was omnipresent as never before (Hardin). Furthermore, the liberation out of this "present evil age" (1:4) in the apocalyptic key of a new age lasting "forever and ever" (1:5), starkly clashed with the Roman ideology of a present "golden age"; it evoked a new exodus out of Roman slavery that was initiated when God's Son—*another* divine son, of a supreme God and Father other than Caesar—was resurrected from a Roman cross. In light of this Roman contextuality, the contours of a conflict between Paul's gospel of "grace . . . and peace" (1:3) and Roman peace (*Pax Romana*), between Christ-faith and imperial religion, are tangible from the outset, although Paul never addresses them directly—possibly in order to protect his addressees, whose names and locations he never discloses either (see Wright 2000; N. Elliott 2008, 25–43; Kahl 2010, 250–58).

What Paul makes more than explicit, however, is his stern disagreement with an "other gospel" that has gained ground in Galatia (1:6-9). Neglecting the most basic epistolary etiquette of his day, Paul abruptly moves from greeting to accusation as he indicts the Galatians of swift defection to this "other gospel." A double curse is hurled against anyone violating the integrity of the *euangelion* ("gospel") that Paul had preached to them (1:8-9). Full of hurt, anger, and sarcasm, Paul tries to disentangle the Galatians from whatever draws them toward those "who are confusing you and want to pervert the gospel of Christ" (1:7 NRSV).

Yet Paul is highly confusing himself. While he on the one hand anathematizes the proponents of an "other gospel," he simultaneously and with perplexing ambiguity declares this difference to be nonexistent. The Greek text of 1:6-7 says literally: "I am astonished that you are so quickly deserting . . . to a different gospel [*eis heteron euangelion*] which is not an other [*ho ouk estin allo*]." This sounds as if he is talking about two kinds of otherness, one that he fiercely contests, and one that he embraces as "not other." Nowhere else in the New Testament is the term *euangelion* so programmatically discussed as in Gal. 1:6—2:22. Is the "gospel according to Paul" thus *one*, or is it *one and other*? With this enigma, the whole interpretation of Galatians is at stake.

▍ THE TEXT IN THE INTERPRETIVE TRADITION

Traditionally, most translators and commentators have assumed that the "other gospel" was the Jewish gospel of circumcision that Paul wanted to leave behind. They thus saw fit to "correct" his paradoxical statement about difference and not-difference into an unambiguous rejection of the "other gospel" as being false or nonexistent: "I am astonished that you are so swiftly turning to a different gospel—*not that there is another*" (NRSV, emphasis added). With this, the "gospel of Christ" right from the beginning was cast into the "iron cage" of a binary construct that set Christianity off against the cursed other, whether Judaism or paganism or, in later centuries, heresy, or Islam, or other "opponents." During the Reformation, Luther redrafted the root binary in Galatians between Christ-gospel and the false circumcision gospel as the antithesis between Protestantism and Catholicism: his opposition of the "gospel" of faith righteousness to the "law" of works righteousness became foundational for Protestant and evangelical interpretations until today (Kahl 2010, 11–16).

But what if Paul contested, rather than (re)inscribed, this binary order, and what if he saw it primarily "at work" in Roman law rather than in Jewish Torah? What if his theology of the other is much more complex and subversive than our (falsely) simplified translations of Gal. 1:6-7 have led us to believe? Krister Stendahl, spearheading the New Perspective already in the 1970s, showed that the core of Paul's theology is not about excommunication of the other but community-building with the other—not about Christians versus Jews, rather about Jews together with gentiles (Stendahl, 1–7). More recently, J. Louis Martyn has done groundbreaking work regarding the apocalyptic "antinomies" or "pair of opposites" that were constitutive parts of the old cosmos but that were dissolved for Paul, through the Christ event, including the polarity of circumcision versus foreskin (Martyn 1997, 393–400). Thinking along these lines, we might regard Paul as criticizing the Galatians for applying an outdated binary model of otherness and oneness by moving toward circumcision; they act as if their difference (foreskin) still made them "other" to the Jews, or vice versa. This, the present entry proposes, is the basic deception of the "other gospel which is not another." The Galatians cannot be circumcised because this would reestablish the oppositional structure of the world as self over and against other. That opposition for Paul is the essence not of Torah (cf. 5:14), but rather of the worldwide "combat order" codified as Roman *nomos*. In this reading, the "other gospel" Paul rejects is essentially the Roman gospel of peace through war and victory, although it is disguised as "Jewish gospel" of strict obedience to the requirements of Torah, that is, circumcision. This issue of misleading appearance and of "hypocrisy"—making the deceptive claim to represent nothing but God's law while in reality following the logic of empire—is addressed throughout Galatians (e.g., 2:13; 6:12).

■ The Text in Contemporary Discussion

Present-day examples abound for this dynamic of "othering," which, in the name of God, tacitly replicates the law of imperial or colonial domination. We might take a look at Africa, where HIV has become a pandemic that affects millions of people and tears the social fabric of communities apart. One of the aggravating factors is the attitude of many Christian churches that stigmatize people with HIV/AIDS as "sinners," rightly punished for their sexual promiscuity and needing to be cast out from churches, social life, and families to prevent further infection. In the name of Christ, taboos are imposed that not only cause enormous additional trauma for people with HIV but also prevent effective education about the spread of the disease and proper prevention. African theologians like Musa Dube and others have spoken up against the devastating self-righteousness in this "false gospel" that divides the body of Christ into a healthy and virtuous self over and against a sick and sinful other. This split, in fact, reproduces and reinscribes the law and logic of the colonial powers. Under the disguise of "rigorous Christianity," a distorted, moralistic understanding of human sexuality is perpetuated that was once preached by Western missionaries who condemned African sexuality as the evil other, to be colonized and civilized by the superior Christian self (Dube, 77–92; Mligo). As in Paul's day, the "other gospel" shape-shifts from allegedly proper faith to a law of domination, comparable to what Paul fiercely contested as irreconcilable with the coequal oneness and solidarity in God's universal family.

Galatians 1:10-21: Damascus: Defecting from the Culture of Enmity

■ The Text in Its Ancient Context

As if he were acknowledging the confusion among his readers regarding the "otherness" of the messianic gospel, Paul declares that it is indeed alien to all human traditions and teachings. Nor is it accountable to any religious authority apart from the divine revelation (*di' apokalypseōs*) of Jesus

Christ (1:12). God's verification of Jesus as Messiah (*Christos*) struck Paul himself like a flash of lightning, unhinging his whole world. According to all human standards and norms, he had been impeccable and a model of religious superachievement, practicing Judaism flawlessly and with a competitive edge in his zeal for the "traditions of the fathers," violent in his conduct of holy warfare against dissidents like the Jesus-assemblies (1:13-14).

At this point, the divine intervention, or rather interruption, hit him. God not only revealed (*apoka-lypsai*) the persecuted other as "God's Son" to him but also charged Paul to proclaim (*euangelizōmai*) this "other" reality of God as "good news" (*euangelion* = "gospel") among the non-Jews: the sinners, gentiles, infidels whom he had previously seen as the irreconcilable other to God, to Judaism, and to himself (1:15-16). This was a complete transvaluation of all values and belief systems to which Paul had adhered. He had become a new, other-defined self and was in a vulnerable position now, unable to "consult with flesh and blood" about the nature of his transformation (1:16)—a different person unknown to his former allies and victims alike, and probably to himself too. Initially staying away from Jerusalem (1:17, 22), he visited Peter and James only after three years and for a brief period of fifteen days. Arabia, Damascus, Syria, and his native Cilicia were the places where he was "now proclaiming the faith that he once tried to destroy" (1:23). He was out among the gentile others, an other himself, proclaiming the one God of Israel who is with the other (Isa. 2:1-4).

■ THE TEXT IN THE INTERPRETIVE TRADITION

"Damascus" over the millennia has become shorthand for the foundational event of Christianity and the beginning of the Christian world mission, which was all too often closely aligned with world-wide occidental colonialism and cultural imperialism. Once Paul's experience was understood as a "conversion" from Judaism to Christianity, a transition from a narrow-minded Jewish particularism to the wide-open, transethnic universalism of a new world religion, Christianity was framed in a binary way and turned into an inevitably anti-Jewish self-construct. Furthermore, Martin Luther's "tower experience" (*Turmerlebnis*) and search for a "gracious God," which occasioned his break with Catholicism, was often anachronistically collapsed with Paul's transformation from Jewish "Saul" to Christian "Paul." Following Krister Stendahl and the New Perspective, however, this antithetical view was challenged, reframing the "conversion" to another religion as a prophetic call *within* Judaism (Segal) and emphasizing the lasting Jewishness of Paul (Dunn, 341–60; Nanos; Eisenbaum).

Another question concerns the relationship between Paul's "firsthand" report of his "revelation" in Galatians and its noticeably divergent, later counterparts in Acts. Paul's famous "fall from his horse" is mentioned in neither Acts nor Galatians, and the name change from "Saul" to "Paul" occurs only in Acts 13:9 (and is unrelated to Damascus). Other facets of the different accounts are plainly incompatible and have led to perennial scholarly debates regarding the basic chronology and key coordinates of Paul's life and of early church history. Different from Paul's own more guarded account in Galatians, Acts makes his post-Damascus conflicts with the Roman order very explicit (e.g., Acts 17:6-7), while simultaneously trying to minimize their importance and to present Paul as a Roman model citizen (e.g., 16:37), inflating instead clashes with Judaism—an interpretive pattern that has been prevalent up to today (Kahl 2008).

THE TEXT IN CONTEMPORARY DISCUSSION

"Damascus" in our language still stands for a profound life-changing experience. What happens if we realize that the whole construct we have used to validate ourselves while devalidating the other is no longer valid? Can strangers, aliens, competitors, adversaries, and even the fiercest enemies turn into neighbors? The terrorist attacks of September 11, 2001, on the World Trade Center and Pentagon, cost three thousand lives. For weeks afterward, New York City became a sanctuary of mourning and shared grief, while an international outcry against violence and a strong wave of sympathy reached out to the United States from all over the world. Yet what could have become a decisive turning point—a "Damascus" of sorts—toward sustainable global peace after the end of the Cold War was incinerated in the fire of retaliatory strikes and military counterviolence. In their book on restorative justice and peacemaking, Elaine Enns and Ched Myers report how members of the 9/11 family "made poignant pleas that violence not be done in their loved ones' names; instead, they turned their grief into actions for peace." Venturing on peace-building missions to countries like Afghanistan, they "transgressed the strictures of wartime's absolute demand for national loyalty by traveling to war zones to seek the human face of the 'enemy'" (Enns and Myers, 71–72).

What if a similar audacity "to defect from the culture of enmity" was at the core of Paul's Damascus experience, which demobilized him as a "holy warrior"? Prior to Damascus, he had seen the churches as compromising national and religious loyalty in the face of perpetual gentile (including Roman) onslaught against Israel. Might his post-Damascus "world mission" be described as journeying into the foreign "war zones" of otherness, not to plant "Christianity" in opposition to Judaism or paganism but to convey the Good News of Christ (*euangelizōmai auton en tois ethnesin*, 1:16) that deconstructs enmity and establishes viable peace? If so, then "Damascus" today could be taken not simply to mean the birth but rather the rebirth of Christianity as a comprehensive movement toward reconciliation with the enemy-other as the core of one's self-in-Christ.

Galatians 2:1-10: Peace Council at Jerusalem

THE TEXT IN ITS ANCIENT CONTEXT

After many years of journeying, it took a second revelation (*apokalypsis*, 2:2) to make Paul finally return to Jerusalem. He returns as someone other from whom he was before, seeking the consensus of the Jerusalem leaders regarding "the gospel that I proclaim among the Gentiles"—clearly an "other gospel" in their eyes. Paul brings two mismatched "brothers" along, the Jew Barnabas and the Greek Titus (2:1). The textual hints at the drama surrounding their visit are cryptic, but clear enough to understand the key issue: From the standpoint of the Jerusalemites, the uncircumcised Titus (2:3) and the new mode of gentile-Jewish community he embodies are an anomaly threatening the integrity of the Christ proclamation. Conflicts pop up instantaneously. Paul mentions false brothers, infiltration of his communities, spying (2:4)—but he also passionately reports that eventually Titus was not forced to be circumcised and the "truth of the gospel" was preserved (2:3-5). Finally, in a somewhat miraculous reversal, the Jerusalem leaders concede the legitimacy of Paul's *other* gospel. Galatians 2:8-10 is a statement of groundbreaking importance: "On the contrary, when they saw that I had been entrusted with the gospel of the foreskin [*euangelion tēs akrobystias*], as Peter with the one of the circumcision [*tēs peritomēs*], . . . they gave to me and Barnabas the right hand of fellowship [*koinōnia*] . . . Only that we remember the poor" (my translation). The "gospel of Christ" (1:7) is authorized in two different versions that are applicable to two different groups, previously divided by an insurmountable boundary: Jews and gentiles. The "truth of the gospel" (2:5) is not uniformity but pluriformity; it reconfigures difference from enmity toward community and commonality (*koinōnia*). Yet this transformation is not encoded in a dogmatic statement, nor through erasing diversity (the foreskin of the male gentiles), but through concrete bodily and material practices of sharing—a handshake of solidarity and the collection of money from the gentile communities for the poor in Jerusalem, which became Paul's signature project.

▌ THE TEXT IN THE INTERPRETIVE TRADITION

In line with the dominant reading, which sees in Galatians the appearance of a new unified and distinct phenomenon, Christianity, most translators and interpreters have eclipsed the notion of the "one" gospel of Christ being two different gospels. The phrases "gospel *of* the foreskin" and "gospel *of* the circumcision" were rendered as "gospel *for* the Gentiles" and "gospel *for* the Jews" by the majority of translations, thus acknowledging only the difference between the audiences, but not the differentness within the gospel itself. Indeed, Hans Dieter Betz went so far as to assume that the notion of the two gospels was essentially un-Pauline and "may very well [have] come from an underlying official statement" (Betz, 97, 82). Most striking is Marcion's rendering in the second century, which simply omitted "gospel of the circumcision" from the text, as he saw it as an illicit compromise with outdated Jewish law-observance on Paul's side; therefore also the term "community" in 2:9 and the reference to the collection as "remembering of the poor" were removed (Riches, 103). Once the Jerusalem agreement became a merely tactical concession and the diversity of foreskin and circumcision that Paul envisioned was erased into the foreskin-only uniformity of gentile Christianity, the concrete practices of "difference-management" that integrated the diverse body of Christ lost their foundational importance as well. Not surprisingly, the importance of the collection as a church-founding antipoverty campaign is usually played down as a theologically irrelevant "kind of philanthropic gesture" (Betz, 101), although Paul mentions it as a primary act of economic and spiritual community-building, not only in Gal. 2:10 but also in 1 Cor. 16:1-4; 2 Corinthians 8–9; and Rom. 15:25-32 (Georgi 1992; 2005; Wan 2000; Longenecker).

▌ THE TEXT IN CONTEMPORARY DISCUSSION

Identifying the Jerusalem Council as the declaration of mutual acceptance (*koinōnia*) of formerly exclusive and hostile identities raises fascinating questions of unity and diversity in the early Jesus movement and today. Paul's radically inclusive messianic praxis of reconciling the nonuniform bodies of foreskin (gentileness) and circumcision (Jewishness) through concrete practices of solidarity "in Christ" might challenge contemporary notions of a uniform Christianity, to be defined over and against Judaism, Islam, Buddhism, or atheism. What would it mean for Christians to think

Christianity outside the binary opposition of self-versus-other that has shaped Christian theology and ecclesiology throughout the centuries? In the contemporary landscape, what might be new ways of embodying a sort of Christian "both/and" identity that might correspond to what Jared Garroway describes when he refers to Paul's "Jew-Gentiles" (Garroway, 1–10)?

Paul Knitter is one of the leading voices in interreligious dialogue today. Formerly a Catholic priest, trained at Rome during the Second Vatican Council, he identifies himself as both a Christian and a Buddhist. For him, Christ remains central in his spiritual practice, but this doesn't mean that Buddha is secondary. The Buddhist concept of the No-Self, for example, enabled him to understand Christ in a new way. Meditating on a regular basis, the traditional Christian practices of Eucharist, worship, and scriptural reflection have lost none of their importance for him. While he wants to share the message of the kingdom with non-Christians, he doesn't necessarily aim at "converting" them; rather, he understands the living, resurrected Christ to urge him to find the presence of the Spirit in others. Knitter frames his interreligious creed in the provocative book title *Without Buddha I Could Not Be a Christian*. Might the discussion above suggest that Paul of Tarsus could have pointed to Titus with an equally border-transgressive claim: "Without the gentiles I couldn't be a Jew true to Christ"? Does Paul's model of a bridge-identity through rigorous deconstruction of self and other contain new impulses to peace-building practices in the interreligious arena today that need to be unearthed?

Galatians 2:11-21: Eating (Dis)orders at Antioch and Justification by Faith

■ THE TEXT IN ITS ANCIENT CONTEXT

The clash between Peter and Paul at Antioch was harsh and somewhat traumatic; again, concrete bodily markers and practices of community (*koinōnia*) were at stake. Jews including Peter had been eating together with the gentiles, but after the arrival of emissaries from James in Jerusalem, they withdrew from the common table "for fear of those from the circumcision." Boundaries were then reinstalled, visible to everyone (2:11-14). Paul calls this a collective hypocrisy of Peter and the Antiochene Jews (*synypekrithēsan*) and is shocked that even his companion Barnabas, witness of the Jerusalem agreement, joined them.

As his rebuke of Peter seamlessly leads into an extended exposition of justification theology, Paul links the Antioch table crisis with the present circumcision conflict in Galatia. The separation that originally set "us," Peter and Paul as "Jews by birth," apart from "gentile sinners" is no longer valid because sin is on "our" side as well (2:15). Doesn't Peter the Jew live like a gentile (i.e., as a sinner, too, betraying his Jewishness: 2:14)? It might well be that Paul here thinks in particular of the Roman order, which has made both Jews and gentiles/nations subservient to and compliant with global structures of injustice and power divinization, which from a radically Torah-based perspective is sin. In this situation, the whole hierarchical split between righteous selves and sinful others is made obsolete, no matter how carefully one tries to fulfill the requirements of Torah by doing "works of the law" (2:16). Paul fully concedes the challenge this commonality of both Jewish and gentile sin poses to the entire system of social categorization and distinction that provides status and recognition. The Antioch episode demonstrates how the temptation to "rebuild" the old, law-based divisions of "us" (righteous) versus "them" (sinful) is almost irresistible (2:17). Yet to actually put trust, or faith (*pistis*), in the righteousness of these new practices that reconfigure the relationship between self and other is what makes people just (or righteous) in their relations to both God and neighbor, according to Paul (2:16, 18).

This inevitably leads into social conflicts where these faith practices defy the required practices (*erga* = "works") of the established law (*nomos*) and turn the messianic communities into transgressors and "sinners" (2:16-17). In first-century Roman Antioch, the "mixed" table community of circumcised and uncircumcised, under the auspices of Jesus as Messiah, probably represented a political anomaly bordering on civil disobedience. It meant practicing an alternative *oikoumenē* among the conquered nations that acknowledged, not the triumphant Caesar, but his lawfully executed convict as supreme peacemaker, Lord, lawgiver, and divine presence. Since certain exemptions from the expectation of worship and subservience to Caesar were granted to Jews alone, Paul's Jewish antagonists in Antioch may well have been troubled by the blurring of boundaries as non-Jews joined with Jews at the common table. Would they be seen as inciting non-Jews to withdraw from normal civic honors to the emperor? Did they consequently either plead to avoid the common table (2:12) or seek to impose circumcision on the non-Jewish believers (2:14) as an "evasive action" to establish some minimal compliance with law and order (Winter, 141–42; Nanos, 257–71; Kahl 2011, 219–22)? Either explanation might make clearer the connection between the situation in Antioch and subsequent events in Galatia.

For Paul, this going back to "works of the law" means "nullifying" the grace of God and the crucifixion event (2:21)—a collective "hypocrisy" (2:13) that claims as Torah-obedience what, in fact, is subservience to *Caesar's* law, which has "hijacked" Torah. Jews and gentiles alike, formerly justified or unjustifiable by the criterion of law, are now together justified by Christ-faith, thus forging a new type of coequal community in tension with the established law of "divide and rule" that perpetually outlaws the other. There is no going back. Rather, the self has to accept its "death to the law" as death to itself, in an act of co-crucifixion with Christ that leads to an entirely new mode of life (2:19-20). Sin is overcome, not by law-works that set each one apart from the other, but by love-works of self-giving for the other that are embodied in Christ. This is the core of God's grace and of Paul's justification apart from the law (2:21).

▌ THE TEXT IN THE INTERPRETIVE TRADITION

One of the most perennial problems around Gal. 2:15-21 has been the theological split that detached the Protestant emphasis on justification by faith as core doctrine from the circumstances of the Antiochene incident itself. Paul's grand community manifesto was long read as an abstract theological declaration, without its concrete scriptural context. "Faith" became reduced to its vertical and personal component, as the individual act of belief "alone," while its horizontal and social dimension was eclipsed and often disqualified as "works of the law." The "dogmatic" and "conservative" Paul became the antagonist of the socially involved, liberating practice of Jesus. The seeming indifference of justification theology toward ethics led many Christians to question its theological relevance or to sidestep it as a "subsidiary crater" of Paul's theology (Schweitzer, 225). The following insights provided the decisive turning points in these debates: first, the Greek genitive *pistis Christou* could be translated either as "faith *in* Christ" or "faith *of* Christ," that is, pointing to the model faithfulness and obedience of Jesus (Hays); second, "works of the law" in Paul might not mean meritorious "good deeds," but rather exclusivist and boundary-marking practices to maintain a distinct status (Dunn, 140); third, "law" is not simply Torah but can also imply *nomos* in a more general sense, including Roman and civic *nomos* (Taubes, 24; Georgi 1997, 153); and, fourth, *nomos* can also be defined in terms of competition for honor and status (Jewett, 298), or of antithetical binaries (Martyn 1997, 406), or of the hierarchical antagonism between a dominant self and an inferior other (Kahl 2010, 23).

▌▍ THE TEXT IN CONTEMPORARY DISCUSSION

"Law" in this latter perspective is the normative order that systemically negates the worth of countless people on a global and local scale by "ranking" them, based on their economic or social status, their gender, ethnicity, religion, education, bodily (dis)ability, age, or other criteria. The poor, black, Hispanic, immigrant, indigenous, old, or underachieving part of humanity is disqualified as the loser and "undeserving," becoming dispensable or even disposable. Feminist liberation theologian Elsa Tamez, from Costa Rica, sees this "logic of alienation" and "out-casting" as the primary economic and social context for efforts to retrieve the transformative power of justification by grace and faith for today, efforts that mean affirming the humanity and dignity of those treated as "human trash." For Tamez, as for the Argentinian Néstor Oscar Míguez, the most powerful present-day embodiment of the "law" as an order of exclusion is the "law of competition" that is imposed globally by the neoliberal market economy and that justifies boundless self-interest and greed. "Sin" in this perspective is both personal and structural evil; it applies to us simultaneously as accomplices and as victims of injustice. Justification is inseparable from justice, opening a new logic of life and empowerment. It requires not only the renunciation of self-aggrandizement on the part of those in power but also the cessation of self-denigration on the part of those who see their marginalization as inevitable, natural, or God-willed punishment for their sin.

Galatians 3:1-29: "Queering" the Human Family

▌ THE TEXT IN ITS ANCIENT CONTEXT

The principal topic of Galatians 3, with 3:28 as its climactic statement, is the "genealogy" of the *ekklēsia* as messianic commonality that dismantles and reconfigures all established self- constructs emerging from exclusivist, hierarchical identity markers—like nation, race, class, or gender. The chapter starts with another angry rebuke of the Galatians. They have lost their messianic clear-sightedness for the meaning of "Christ crucified" and have gone back to "works of the law" (3:1-5).

If this means Christ-believing gentiles accepting circumcision to make them less prone to accusations of civil disobedience (compare the discussion of 2:11-21 above), Paul sees this seemingly Torah-based "accommodation" as entirely anti-Jewish.

Already in Gen. 12:3, the "proto-gospel" (*proeuēngelisato*, 3:8) had declared the Jewish progenitor Abraham as the future "body" incorporating God's transethnic blessing for every nation and tribe. One singular "seed" alone (*spermati, henos*) is carrying what might metaphorically be called the "genetic information" needed to generate this exceptional body of a collective self in communion with the other—"who is Christ [Messiah]" (3:16). This unique messianic seed was activated through the event of crucifixion and God's life-giving act of resurrection that claims life "out of the dead" (1:1; 3:13-14). The resurrected divine Son embodies God's universal fatherhood by granting new life in his own body to all those living in the shadow of Roman crosses, and a new identity as children of God and seed of Abraham. Becoming "one in Christ Jesus," Jews and non-Jews together are made heirs to Abraham's promise of a blessing that is color-blind, status-blind, and gender-blind (3:26-29).

The theological backbone of Paul's argument is a discourse of law and oneness that draws on the oneness of God as core-commandment of Torah (Exod. 20:1-5; Deut. 6:4). Oneness in the Messiah (3:28), however, is not the absence of diversity, but the contestation of an enslaving uniformity imposed by Caesar as the supreme "mediator" of the law, including Torah. Through his power to grant or revoke Jewish privileges, among them the privilege of nonparticipation in imperial cult, the emperor can bend Torah into a hybrid misrepresentation of God's will and oneness (3:19-20; Kahl 2010, 227). Although Rome did not suppress religious (including Jewish) diversity per se, it "united" all conquered nations and religions in a collective submission that prominently featured worship of Caesar as the one lord, God, son of God, and father in a kind of "imperial monotheism"—a horrendously idolatrous practice and anathema, from a Jewish perspective (Kahl 2010, 138–44). Despite their exemption from the expectation of emperor religion proper, Jews had to make every effort to show their subservience to and reverence for Caesar in other ways. However, accepting uncircumcised non-Jews who didn't worship Caesar, like Paul's messianic gentiles in Galatia, might have easily looked like making Judaism a hotbed of rebellion against Rome (Winter, 141–42; Nanos, 257–71). Ultimately, it was Caesar as "mediator of the law" (3:19) who determined that Paul's interpretation of Torah was "lawless."

"The mediator is not of the one [*henous ouk estin*], but God is one [*heis estin*]," Paul counters (3:20). His model of oneness radically challenges a construct of God and humanity that unifies the worldwide imperial "family" of the nations through oppressive imperial patriarchy and the idolatrous divinization of power. Contrariwise, the messianic family is derived from the (pro)creative power of a "seed" that generates life "out of the dead" (1:1) and is thus resistant to the dehumanizing, consent-producing power of Roman crosses. Baptism means reincorporation, through the generative power of the messianic "seed," that ends any form of patriarchal lineage. Humanity is no longer segregated into descendants of "our clan" or "their clan," highborn or lowborn, rich or poor fathers—or the absence of "documented" fathers altogether. In Paul's vision, the old, ghettoized self vanishes as humans are "reclothed" as new human beings in Christ: children of God and of Abraham, but siblings to one another and to Christ without any human father present, in this all-inclusive community where there is no longer Jew or Greek, slave or free, male and female, "for all of you are one in Christ Jesus" (3:26-28).

◼ THE TEXT IN THE INTERPRETIVE TRADITION

As the climactic summary of Galatians 3, Paul's words in 3:26-28 constitute one of his most influential and controversial statements. There is a broad consensus that it originated from a pre-Pauline baptismal tradition, as attested elsewhere (1 Cor. 12:13; Col. 3:9-11; *2 Clem.* 12.2; *Gos. Thom.* 22; *Gospel of the Egyptians* 3.91; MacDonald). Its egalitarian implications, however, are matters of much debate. Does the "baptismal formula" mainly attest to emancipatory practices in the congregations prior to and at odds with Paul (Schüssler Fiorenza 1985, 208–11; Briggs)? Or is it exemplary of Paul's fear and erasure of difference in terms of "repressive sameness" or "coercive universalism" (Boyarin 1994, 234–35; Castelli, 124)? Would the baptismal oneness chiefly point to a future eschatological entity or a secluded spiritual reality "in Christ," without real-life implications, as much of the interpretational tradition has implicitly assumed? Is therefore the demand of subordination for women, children, slaves, and political subjects elsewhere in the (deutero-)Pauline letters (e.g., Eph. 5:21—6:9) compatible with Gal. 3:28; or, contrariwise, is the demand of subordination the "canonical betrayal" of Paul, that is, his conservative "gentrification" (N. Elliott 1994, 25–54)? In terms of "male and female," would Paul's oneness formula imply a primordial androgyny (Meeks), or the critique of the order of marriage and procreation (Schüssler Fiorenza 1985, 211), or might it rather signal severe "gender trouble" in Galatia due to Paul's deconstruction of dominant masculinity paradigms that were linked to circumcision as an established marker not just of Jewishness but also of maleness? (Kahl 1999; 2000; Wiley; cf. Lieu).

◼ THE TEXT IN CONTEMPORARY DISCUSSION

How might Paul's baptismal oneness of Gal. 3:28 translate into today's society that is no longer split into "Jew" or "Greek/gentile," but into black and white, poor and rich, aliens and citizens, inmates and free people? Around eight million people in the United States are presently incarcerated, on probation, or on parole. Compared to the overall population, this is not only by far the largest number in any country of the world but also includes a disproportionally high number of poor people, African Americans, and immigrants. Two key markers of Gal. 3:28—race/ethnicity and social location in terms of class, the lingering heritage of slavery, and immigration status—are involved in creating a hierarchical division of society that separates "us" as the law-abiding citizens, preferably perceived as white, from "them" who are the righteously incarcerated lawbreakers: dangerous and dark "others." According to Mark Taylor, a part of the "surplus population" needs to be sacrificed to keep the others complacent and under control, and this sacrifice is enacted by a theatrical spectacle of control that keeps viewers both in fear and fascinated by state power (Taylor, 49, 60, 105–6; cf. Wacquant).

From Paul's perspective, this status quo might look like another version of the dehumanizing and therefore godless imperial model of "divide and rule" he was confronted with in his own day. The waters of baptism for him have "drowned" this entire system, washing away the distinction markers that give "us" (the nonimprisoned) a sense of self-righteousness and legitimate superiority, which is derived from the existence of unrighteous others: This is how for Bob Ekblad the Pauline theology of justification by faith rather than through works of the law starts to develop its transformative power. Ekblad reads Paul, including Galatians 3, with people in jail, in particular with undocumented immigrants at the US-Mexican border who know all too well the "curse of the law" (Gal. 3:10) that perpetually condemns them as illegal. For him, Jesus is the "Good Coyote" who crosses people over the border into the kingdom of God, against the law, despite the law. "In the waters of baptism into Jesus' death and resurrection the borders are brought down, and there are no longer distinctions between the law-abiding and criminal, US citizens and foreigners, legals and illegals, brown and white, chemically dependent and clean and sober, poor and rich, male and female—all are one in Christ. . . . We're all wetbacks, and must even count ourselves as fellow 'criminal aliens'" (Ekblad, 192).

Galatians 4:1-31: Mother Paul: Giving Birth to Messianic Solidarity

▌ The Text in Its Ancient Context

In chapter 4, Paul continues the messianic reconfiguration of family, genealogy, and identity. Consistent with the nonpatriarchal messianic "seed logic" of his midrashic discussion in Galatians 3, female concepts of mothering and birth-giving start to invade Paul's language with surprising consistency, making its gender dichotomies porous all throughout—most strikingly in Paul's "unmanly" depictions of himself as an inglorious missionary and a birth-giving mother in labor pains (4:12-20). In the subsequent allegory of the two competing archmothers (4:21-31), it is no longer Abraham's biological fatherhood, but an exclusively female differential—paradoxically spelled out as the "barren motherhood" of a childless and abandoned woman (4:27; Isa. 54:1)—that defines kinship and belonging, including citizenship in the metropolis ("mother city") of Jerusalem "above" (4:26, 31).

This highly irregular family construct is introduced in the opening section (4:1-7) by a strong appeal to "come of age" as children of God who recognize their adoption into an entirely new kin group, a transition tantamount to redemption from slavery. Collectively invoking God as *Abba*-Father (4:6), Paul says, "we" transition from slaves or minors to God's children (4:1). This change in legal status is achieved through God's Son, "born by a woman" and "under the law." His lawful death and his law-defying resurrection deflects the force of the law that defines people on the one hand as either Jew or Greek/gentile/Roman, and on the other as subservient/slaves to Rome, which in the common Roman perception "naturally" entails feminization and demasculinization (Lopez, 26–54). Persons are no longer confined by these attributions, nor by the codes of behavior (including circumcision) they entail. Rather, they are redeemed, that is, "bought out" (*exagorazein*), from "under the law" and its legal grip on their allegiance, conduct, and perception of themselves as opposed to others (4:4-5). It is noteworthy that in 4:1-7, "law" is equated with the "elemental spirits of the world" (*stoicheia tou kosmou*), which according to Martyn (1997, 393–406) are the (binary) "pairs of opposites" that antithetically constitute the cosmos as its basic building blocks and function as universal agents of enslavement for both Jews and gentiles ("us": 4:3, 5). This is strong evidence of the peculiar hybridity in Paul's law terminology, which excludes any clear alignment of *nomos* with Torah alone and rather points toward the worldwide governance through Roman law.

In 4:8-10, Paul admonishes the Galatians ("you") not to step back into their prior enslavement and underage status by resubscribing to the former gods that are "non-Gods." Recent scholarship has pointed out that in this passage Paul's antithetical stance against imperial religion, rather than Judaism and paganism in general, surfaces most visibly (Hardin, 116–47). The imperial gods that have co-opted all other civic deities are present among Roman subjects in a ceaseless sequence of "special days, and months, and seasons, and years" (4:10). These observances throughout the calendar year define civic time and space through a never-ending flurry of public festivals, processions, sacrifices, concerts, meals, benefactions, and rituals of all kinds (Mitchell 1993b, 10). Returning to at least minimal forms of participation on the side of the Galatians would restore political conformity as a matter of prudence; otherwise, they might imagine that they should take on a fully Jewish status through circumcision and thus hope to be excused from civic worship, as were the Jews.

Paul disagrees passionately. Rather than blending into the imperial *oikoumenē* of the imperial father and god on Caesar's terms, he tries to realign the Galatians with the generative body of Christ that brought them forth in the new shape of a humanity no longer split into two; that is, to *disalign* them from the destructive and all-devouring law of competition, combat, conquest that he sees embodied in the imperial idols who all claim falsely to be gods (4:8). His description of the birthing process that brought forth the new messianic (Christ-)identity among the Galatians and of the birth labors he himself is again enduring on their behalf (3:19) is one of the most moving passages in Paul's letters. He reminds the Galatians of their initial encounter, when they practically picked him up from the garbage pile of "human trash"—the embodiment of otherness in its plainest shape, as disposable and despicable nothingness (*exoutheneō*, "despise, regard as nothing," 4:14; cf. 1 Cor. 1:28). Yet it was precisely in this solidarity with the destitute human other, stripped of all human dignity, that the Galatians accepted the Messiah, the embodiment of an alternative world order (cf. Matt. 28:31-46). It is to this shape (*morphē*) of humanity as one alongside or in solidarity with another that Paul tries to rebirth his converts in his messianic labor pains (*ōdinō*): "My children with whom I am again in the pain of childbirth until Christ is formed [*morphōthē*] in you" (4:19).

It is only in this overall logic that the concluding passage (4:21-31) makes sense. All depends on taking seriously Paul's clues demanding a strictly "allegorical" and coded reading of "Hagar." Hagar is not a "real" woman, nor is she identical with her counterpart in Genesis 16 and 21. Rather, she represents what Paul "allegorically" attaches to her as a "correspondence" (*allegoroumenos, systoichei*): the blasphemous cooptation of the exodus-Torah ("Mount Sinai"), by the Roman law of colonial slavery, including the compliant birth of children into the enslaving master order as its subjects and soldiers (4:24-25). What Paul wants to "drive out" (*ekbale*, 4:30) is not Hagar the slave woman as a person, but on the contrary, "Hagar" as the mental and social imprint of Roman slavery on Jewish practices and mind-sets in Paul's time that she allegorically embodies as "Jerusalem now" (4:25). Hagar stands for the deceptive self-perception of those whom the Roman "father" claims as slaves, in continuous appellation to them as either *his* "children" or as subservient females who give birth to these children. The metaphorical Hagar's son, similar to the pre-Damascus Paul and the Antiochene Peter, personifies an enslaved body using aggressive self-assertion (*ediōken*, 4:29; 1:13; *anagkazeis*, 2:14) against other enslaved bodies. This delusional practice of "freedom" makes the conquered violently reenact against each other the law of conquest and combat that continues to enslave them all.

Hagar's allegorical counterpart is the "free woman." She is "our mother" (4:26)—the new body of one-with-another (3:28) that is generated out of "barren mothers" (like Paul), through the generative power of the messianic seed (3:16) and Abraham's transethnic blessing (3:8). This whole genealogical/birth narrative strongly draws on the theological deep structures of the Genesis accounts, with their entirely irregular construction of birthrights for second-born sons in opposition to existing patriarchal law. It brings all those parents not capable of bringing forth "proper" children together with all "other" children of God whom the law doesn't entitle to their share of the "inheritance" (4:31). Together, "we" are children of the promise like Isaac, citizens of the "Jerusalem above" as universal metropolis of peace and freedom (4:26). Yet "our" messianic reaffiliation requires clear dissociation (4:30) from the forces represented by "Hagar": forces that maintain the self-destructive and fratricidal binaries opposing "self" to "other" (Kahl 2004; 2013; Lopez, 153–63).

▌ THE TEXT IN THE INTERPRETIVE TRADITION

One of the biggest interpretational liabilities of Galatians has been the binary reading that took the Hagar allegory as a "proof text" for a violent and supersessionist Christian disalignment from the other of Judaism. This polarity is famously depicted in the defeated and blindfolded female body of the "Synagogue," opposed by the triumphant woman "Ecclesia," in many churches in Europe. In line with Genesis 16 and 21, Gal. 4:21-31 has been read as another "text of terror" (Trible) that canonized the "legitimate" oppression and exclusion of Hagar not only as "Jew" but also as the abused and traded woman, the exploited African American (sex) slave, the single mother, the disposable foreigner (Williams 1993; 2006; Briggs, 224). Furthermore, the equally relentless stance of Gal. 4:30 against Hagar's son Ishmael, who was according to Qur'an 2:121 the cofounder of the Kaaba in Mecca, could very well preconfigure contemporary anti-Islamism (Hassan). Without a Roman "reading lens," the harsh verdict against Hagar can indeed all too easily change into the epitome of Christian anti-Judaism, patriarchy, xenophobia, and "kyriarchal" social master codes as they are commonly attributed to Paul (Schüssler Fiorenza 1999, 163–65).

▌ THE TEXT IN CONTEMPORARY DISCUSSION

As a theological text, Galatians 4 is strikingly concrete in talking about able and defective human bodies. When the Galatians received and restored the weak, perhaps disfigured body of Paul as if he were Christ (*hōs Christon Iēsoun*, 4:14), rather than "spitting" (*exeptysate*) at him, they themselves became the "seed" (3:16) of the Messiah in his disabled and reenabled shape, as crucified and resurrected (4:12-15). This "form" and body of Christ is now in danger of being aborted (4:19) under the censorship of "standard" expectations regarding circumcised and noncircumcised bodies.

The pressure of normative body images in our contemporary society is strongly felt by people who don't conform to established standards of "ability." Bioethicist Adrienne Asch (1947–2013) was a pioneer in feminist disability studies who passionately spoke against prenatal testing as a means to detect disabilities in unborn children and terminate those pregnancies. Blind all her life and a passionate pro-choice advocate, she nonetheless strongly condemned such targeted abortions, arguing that life with disabilities was not "worthless" life (Parens and Asch). That might strongly resonate with Paul, who himself experienced the life-giving power of the messianic "seed" (3:16) in Galatia as a disabled, perhaps (vision)-impaired (cf. 4:15) missionary who received solidarity—and as the birth-giving mother of a human shape accused of being an intolerable misfit (4:12-20). His theology of the "body of Christ" suggests the integration (not necessarily the "mending") of broken and non-normative bodies in a healing, supportive community where they can thrive in their diversity. Could Paul's expulsion of the metaphorical body of "Hagar" be read, in a contemporary version, as the exorcism of compulsive, self-destructive (body) images of perfection and "normalcy" that we impose on ourselves and others? This "law" of accomplishment keeps people enslaved to the established master order by instilling constant anxiety, competition, and relentless "persecution" (cf. Gal. 4:29) of imperfection, in a never-ending race toward adequate performance and conformity. Ultimately, the "stigmatization of disability drives power mechanisms of capitalism" (Tataryn and Truchan-Tataryn, 14; cf. Isherwood).

Galatians 5:1—6:18: Old Cosmos and New Creation: The Ecology of Interdependence

■ THE TEXT IN ITS ANCIENT CONTEXT

The last section of Galatians shifts the emphasis to the concrete conflicts in Galatia. For the first time, the pressure to be circumcised is actually made explicit (5:3, 11; 6:11). And in candid language, Paul addresses issues of ethical norms and community rules that specifically target divisive behavior like "biting and devouring one another" or "competing against one another, envying one another" (5:15, 26). The catalog of vices and virtues in 5:19-23, though using a conventional pattern of ancient moral discourse, nonetheless is specifically tailored toward internal strife as signaled in eight out of the fifteen vices listed: enmity, rivalry, jealousy, anger, quarrels, dissensions, factions, envy. All of these for Paul reflect an inflated sense of self-entitlement that damages the relationship between oneself and the other.

In contrast, love is the first item in the list of virtues. These all uniformly emphasize community-building "fruits of the spirit" like joy, peace, patience, kindness, generosity, faithfulness, gentleness, self-control (5:22). The term "one another" (*allēlōn*), derived from *allos-allos* ("other-other"), occurs no less than seven times in the brief section (5:13—6:2), pointing to the messianic movement from self-against-other to self-with-another that dissolves all binaries and divisions. The "law of Christ" is to "bear one another's burdens" (6:2); this fulfills Torah, which is "summed up" (*peplērōthei*) in the *one* commandment of Lev. 19:18 to love your neighbor as yourself (Gal. 5:14). In all these ethical admonitions, "faith that 'works' through love" (*energoumenē*, 5:6) is the key concept: the indicative, that is, the Christ-reality of a new life "through the spirit," is inseparable from the imperative of "walking according to the norm of the spirit" (5:25).

"Spirit" in this context is the opposite of "flesh." The antithesis "spirit versus flesh" first came up in 3:2-3, together with the juxtaposition "works of power" or "faith" versus "works of the law" (3:5); it structures the whole passage, alongside the parallel polarity of "freedom versus slavery." The spirit-engendered life in conformity with the law of Christ/Spirit embodies the "freedom" of the Galatians to withdraw from their slavish allegiance to the dominant law. Chapter 5 starts with a passionate plea that the Galatians "stand firm" in their freedom and not "submit again to a yoke of slavery" (5:1). Slavery was linked to the allegorical Hagar and the flesh in the preceding passage—and to the imperial law of divisiveness and submission that Paul sees creeping up in the circumcision conflict as well as in other internal combats and competitions.

Does this strongly antithetical structure in fact reinscribe the old dichotomies as structuring principle and basic building blocks of the cosmos (*stoicheia tou kosmou*, cf. 4:3, 9)? Is the assertion of freedom for ourselves on its underside inevitably the affirmation of slavery for others? These are valid questions. Paul dispels them with a carefully worded paradox: Messianic freedom is enacted as mutual slavery. It is not the unrestricted pursuit of self-interest from a master position as licensed by imperial law; rather, it is that law's perpetual subversion by "serving as slaves (*douleuete*) to one another through love" (5:13). Unlike manumission by civic and imperial law, Christ-freedom thus is the undoing of slavery rather than its tacit reinscription as licit.

What if a member of the congregation fails to live according to the law of love? How should the community respond, without the backup of established law, "if anyone is detected in a transgression" (6:1)? One might think that at this point, finally, a strong hand is needed to restore order and accountability. Yet in the final section (6:1-10), Paul carefully avoids the recourse to any hierarchical authority (including his own) that judges, sanctions, and corrects misbehavior. Judgment and setting things right is strictly mutualized as task of the spirit-guided (*pneumatikoi*, 6:1) community. Any transgressor must be held accountable indeed, but in a "spirit of meekness." Mindfulness of the judge's own fallibility has to counterbalance the constant temptation to reestablish oneself in a master position over and against a sinful other (6:1). The "law of Christ" is not fulfilled through sanctioning the other's lapses, but through "bear[ing] one another's burdens" (6:2).

Paul here seems to be concerned about the judges more than the transgressor. The urge of the self to display its own righteousness before the dark foil of another's offenses is sarcastically derided: After examining their own works, those who want to be important (but are not) should acclaim their merits strictly to themselves alone (*pros seauton monon*, 6:4). They should avoid the sort of "competitive boasting" (Jewett, 296) that reproduces the whole falsehood and deception (*phrenapatā*, 6:3) of social status, distinction, and superiority. God is the only judge, and only in the final judgment will each one have to carry their "own burdens" (6:5). Yet investing one's life into the "Spirit" by "working for the good of all" (6:10) will reliably bring forth eternal life, whereas "sowing into the flesh" of self-obsession (and circumcision) will engender the harvest of death (6:8).

At the end, Paul adds a postscript in his own "large letters" (6:11-18). Circumcision in Galatia does not mean what it ordinarily does, namely, a seal of Jewish allegiance; its advocates are not really concerned about Torah (6:13). Rather, the "persecution" that they fear from the outside enforces the pressures to conform to established norms and identity markers (6:12; Winter, 123–43; Hardin, 85–115). At this point, Paul makes a final declaration: It is exactly this death-dealing conformity to a commonly accepted world order (*kosmos*) of divisive binaries that is dead through the cross. The universal logic that breeds violence, war, and subjugation, while claiming to be without alternative, has been deactivated. Paul is "crucified to the old *kosmos*" and the old *kosmos* to him (6:14). Yet the power of the resurrection emerges as the life-giving manifestations of the "new creation." It is not yet fully present, but tangible reality wherever the old antitheses of self versus other, or circumcision versus foreskin, are invalidated (6:15). This is the "canon" of peace and mercy (6:16). It continuously dissolves enmity and polarity (which continuously keep building up again) within a community practice of dynamic mutuality and peace-building propelled by the transformative power of the Spirit and "the grace of our Lord Jesus Christ/Messiah" (6:18). With this concluding testimony framed as a farewell greeting to his Galatian brothers and sisters followed by a final "Amen," Paul summarizes and closes his letter.

▌The Text in the Interpretive Tradition

Rather than being understood as the climax of Galatians, Paul's condensed reflection about love and community practice in Galatians 5–6 has often been disavowed as a mere afterthought to the letter, as it was seen as being in tension with its main theological thrust of "faith (alone)" versus "works" (see Barclay, 7–16). The question of how Paul's theology and ethics are related has been widely debated, including the complex issue of "indicative" and "imperative"—that is, the paradoxical relationship between justification as the state of already achieved freedom from sin on the one hand and the demand to actively "work" against sin in line with faith, love, and Spirit on the other, as expressed in Gal. 5:1, 5-6, 25 (Horrell, 10–15). Another disputed topic has been the opposition of "flesh" (*sarx*) versus "spirit" (*pneuma*). The term "flesh" was often falsely identified as the inferior and sinful materiality of the human body, specifically with regard to sexuality. On the opposite side, "spirit" came to be understood as the superior and immaterial sphere of the "soul" and of "spiritual discernment," defined in entirely individualistic categories. Instead, as has been rightly stated, "flesh" in Paul stands for the "radical inclination to self-centeredness," in conjunction with the general biblical notion of flesh as the sphere of sin, that is, "human existence [seen] from the aspect of its being hostile to God and other human beings because it is essentially turned in on self" (Byrne , 45).

▌The Text in Contemporary Discussion

Galatians as Paul's probably most consequential letter has been discussed from a variety of perspectives, but rarely in light of the current ecological crisis. While the phenomenon of a global, life-threatening devastation of the earth's habitat didn't exist yet in the ancient world, and Paul certainly was not a "green" theologian, one might rightly ask whether the cosmic scope of his antidualistic thinking and the strong concern for the social, religious, and cultural other as key signatures of his messianic theology might have implications for the nonhuman other of nature as well. Does the "new creation" (*kainē ktisis*) in Gal. 6:15 as a condensed statement of the messianic transformation refer to humans alone, or is the conversion of ourselves in relation to the other of earth, water, and air implied?

As the *Sydney Morning Herald* reported in June 2013, a church in Queensland, Australia, has twenty-four solar panels bolted to its roof in the shape of a Christian cross. And a mosque in Bursa, western Turkey, is projected to have a vertical-axis wind turbine (without the big revolving blades) installed on a minaret. Should one read the "solar cross" on a Christian church as a crude trivialization, a fad, a blasphemous persiflage on Paul's august theology of the cross, or as one of its valid and urgent contemporary recontextualizations? The cross obviously features prominently all throughout Galatians, including the final handwritten postscript in 6:11-18. In 6:14-15, Paul boldly declares that he is crucified to the (old) *kosmos* and the *kosmos* to him, because the dichotomies on which the established world order (*kosmos*) rests (like the antithesis of circumcision/Jews versus foreskin/gentiles) have been dissolved and left behind. The cross thus opens up an ongoing transformation of self and other toward reconciliation and mutuality that clearly transcends the realm of humans. Paul is crucified to the entire *kosmos* with its multiple polarities, not just its faith-based, ethnic, and social divisions (Martyn 1985). Echoing the biblical creation accounts in Genesis 1–3 and Isa. 43:18-19; 65:17-25, the "new creation" in Gal. 6:15 that is born out of the cross, then, would be more than simply a new society or religion, it would rather comprise the entirety of the human and nonhuman world (Kahl 2010, 272–73).

The polar (dis)order that over the centuries has become formative for Western philosophy, theology, and civilization excludes and exploits not only the human other in terms of gender, race, religion, and class, but also the other of nature and earth. Paul's radical regard for the other and his messianic model of a "corporate solidarity" in Christ, as perceptively outlined by David Horrell (274), for our time thus inevitably have an ecological dimension as well—for example, where our mutual interdependence within overarching ecosystems and the rights of nonhuman species need to be acknowledged (Horrell, Hunt, and Southgate, 190–94). "Greening" Paul and his theology of faith-justification is one of the most cutting-edge tasks ahead for Pauline interpretation. And maybe the "solar cross" and the "wind energy minaret" mentioned above could allow us to envision a nonbinary creation (Gal. 6:15) as the forging of new coalitions toward a universally sustainable connectivity across all kinds of religious and other boundaries that was as vital to Paul's world as it is to ours.

Works Cited

Arnold, Clinton A. 2005. "'I Am Astonished That You Are So Quickly Turning Away!' (Gal 1:6): Paul and the Anatolian Folk Belief." *NTS* 51:429–49.

Barclay, John M. G. 1988. *Obeying the Truth: Paul's Ethics in Galatians*. Edinburgh: T&T Clark.

Betz, Hans Dieter. 1979. *Galatians*. Hermeneia. Philadelphia: Fortress Press.

Boyarin, Daniel. 1994. *A Radical Jew: Paul and the Politics of Identity*. Berkeley: University of California Press.

———. 2004. *Border Lines: The Partition of Judaeo-Christianity*. Philadelphia: University of Pennsylvania Press.

Braxton, Brad R. 2002. *No Longer Slaves: Galatians and African American Experience*. Collegeville, MN: Liturgical Press.

Briggs, Sheila. 1994. "Galatians." In *Searching the Scriptures*. Vol. 2, *A Feminist Commentary*, edited by Elisabeth Schüssler Fiorenza. New York: Crossroad.

Byrne, Brendan. 2010. *Galatians and Romans*. Collegeville, MN: Liturgical Press.

Campbell, William S. 2006. *Paul and the Creation of Christian Identity.* New York: T&T Clark.

Castelli, Elizabeth A. 1991. *Imitating Paul: A Discourse of Power.* Louisville: Westminster John Knox.

Dube, Musa, ed. 2007. *Theology in the HIV and AIDS Era Series: Reading the New Testament in the HIV and AIDS Contexts.* Geneva: World Council of Churches.

Dunn, James D. G. 2005. *The New Perspective on Paul: Collected Essays.* WUNT 185. Tübingen: Mohr Siebeck.

Ehrensperger, Kathy. 2004. *That We May Be Mutually Encouraged: Feminism and the New Perspective in Pauline Studies.* New York: T&T Clark.

Eisenbaum, Pamela. 2009. *Paul Was Not a Christian: The Original Message of a Misunderstood Apostle.* New York: HarperOne.

Ekblad, Bob. 2005. *Reading the Bible with the Damned.* Louisville: Westminster John Knox.

Elliott, Neil. 1994. *Liberating Paul: The Justice of God and the Politics of the Apostle.* Maryknoll, NY: Orbis.

———. 2008. *The Arrogance of Nations: Reading Romans in the Shadow of Empire.* Minneapolis: Fortress Press.

Elliott, Susan M. 2004. *Cutting Too Close for Comfort.* JSNTSup 248. Sheffield: Sheffield Academic.

Enns, Elaine, and Ched Meyers. 2009. *Ambassadors of Reconciliation.* Vol. 2, *Diverse Christian Practices of Restorative Justice and Peacemaking.* Maryknoll, NY: Orbis.

Fatum, Lone. 1989. "Women, Symbolic Universe and Structures of Silence." *ST* 43:61–80.

Garroway, Joshua D. 2012. *Paul's Gentile-Jews: Neither Jew Nor Gentile, But Both.* New York: Palgrave Macmillan.

Gaventa, Beverly Roberts. 1990. "The Maternity of Paul: An Exegetical Study of Galatians 4:19." In *The Conversation Continues: Studies in Paul and John in Honor of J. Louis Martyn*, edited by Robert T. Fortna and Beverly Roberts Gaventa, 189–210. Nashville: Abingdon.

Georgi, Dieter. 1992. *Remembering the Poor: The History of Paul's Collection for Jerusalem.* Nashville: Abingdon.

———. 1997. "God Turned Upside Down." In *Paul and Empire: Religion and Power in Roman Imperial Society*, edited by Richard Horsley, 148–157. Harrisburg, PA: Trinity Press International.

———. 2005. "Is There Justification in Money? A Historical and Theological Meditation on the Financial Aspects of Justification by Christ." In *The City in the Valley: Biblical Interpretation and Urban Theology*, 283–207. Atlanta: Society of Biblical Literature.

Hardin, Justin K. 2008. *Galatians and the Imperial Cult: A Critical Analysis of the First-Century Social Context of Paul's Letter.* Tübingen: Mohr Siebeck.

Hassan, Riffat. 2006. "Hagar in African American Biblical Appropriation." In *Hagar, Sarah, and Their Children: Jewish, Christian, and Muslim Perspectives*, edited by Phyllis Trible and Letty M. Russell, 149–67. Louisville: Westminster John Knox.

Hays, Richard. 1983. *The Faith of Jesus Christ: An Investigation of the Narrative Substructure of Galatians 3:1–4:11.* Chico, CA: Scholars Press.

Horrell, David G. 2005. *Solidarity and Difference: A Contemporary Reading of Paul's Ethics.* London: T&T Clark.

Horrell, David G., Cheryl Hunt, and Christopher Southgate. 2010. *Greening Paul: Rereading the Apostle in a Time of Ecological Crisis.* Waco, TX: Baylor University Press.

Horsley, Richard A., ed. 1997. *Paul and Empire: Religion and Power in Roman Imperial Society.* Harrisburg, PA: Trinity Press International.

———. 2000. *Paul and Politics: Ekklesia, Israel, Imperium, Interpretation: Essays in Honor of Krister Stendahl.* Harrisburg, PA: Trinity Press International.

Isherwood, Lisa. 2008. *The Fat Jesus: Christianity and Body Image.* New York: Seabury.

Jewett, Robert. 2007. *Romans: A Commentary.* Hermeneia. Minneapolis: Fortress Press.

Johnson Hodge, Caroline. 2007. *If Sons, Then Heirs: A Study of Kinship and Ethnicity in the Letters of Paul.* Oxford: Oxford University Press.

Kahl, Brigitte. 1999. "Gender Trouble in Galatia? Paul and the Rethinking of Difference." In *Is There a Future for Feminist Theology?* Edited by Deborah F. Sawyer and Diane M. Collier, 57–73. Sheffield: Sheffield Academic.

———. 2000. "No Longer Male: Masculinity Struggles Behind Galatians 3.28?" *JSNT* 79:37–49.

———. 2004. "Hagar between Genesis and Galatians: The Stony Road to Freedom." In *From Prophecy to Testament: The Function of the Old Testament in the New*, edited by Craig A. Evans, 219–32. Peabody, MA: Hendrickson.

———. 2008. "Acts of the Apostles: Pro(to)-Imperial Script and Hidden Transcript." In *In the Shadow of Empire: Reclaiming the Bible as History of Faithful Resistance*, edited by Richard A. Horsley, 137–56. Louisville: Westminster John Knox.

———. 2010. *Galatians Re-Imagined: Reading with the Eyes of the Vanquished.* Paul in Critical Contexts. Minneapolis: Fortress Press.

———. 2011. "Galatians and the 'Orientalism' of Justification by Faith: Paul among Jews and Muslims." In *The Colonized Apostle: Paul through Postcolonial Eyes*, edited by Christopher Stanley, 206–22. Minneapolis: Fortress Press.

———. 2013. "Krieg, Maskulinität und der imperiale Gottvater: Das Augustusforum und die messianische Re-Imagination von 'Hagar' im Galaterbrief." In *Doing Gender—Doing Religion*, edited by U. Eisen, C. Gerber, and A. Standhartinger, 273–300. WUNT 302. Tübingen: Mohr Siebeck.

Kamudzandu, Israel. 2013. *Abraham Our Father: Paul and the Ancestors in Postcolonial Africa.* Minneapolis: Fortress Press.

Knitter, Paul. 2009. *Without Buddha I Could Not Be A Christian.* London: Oneworld.

Le Cornu, Hilary, and Joseph Shulam. 2005. *A Commentary on the Jewish Roots of Galatians.* Jerusalem: Academon.

Lieu, Judith. 1994. "Circumcision, Women and Salvation." *NTS* 40:358–70.

Longenecker, Bruce W. 2010. *Remember the Poor: Paul, Poverty, and the Greco-Roman World.* Grand Rapids: Eerdmans.

Lopez, Davina. 2008. *Apostle to the Conquered: Reimagining Paul's Mission.* Minneapolis: Fortress Press.

MacDonald, Dennis R. 1987. *There Is No Male and Female: The Fate of a Dominical Saying in Paul and Gnosticism.* Philadelphia: Fortress Press.

Martyn, J. Louis. 1985. "Apocalyptic Antinomies in Paul's Letter to the Galatians." *NTS* 31:410–24

———. 1997. *Galatians: A New Translation with Introduction and Commentary.* AB. New York: Doubleday.

Meeks, Wayne A. 1974. "The Image of Androgyne: Some Uses of a Symbol in Earliest Christianity." *HR* 13:165–208.

Míguez, Néstor Oscar. 2004. "Galatians." In *Global Bible Commentary*, edited by Daniel Patte, 463–72. Nashville: Abingdon.

Mitchell, Stephen. 1993a. *Anatolia: Land, Men, and Gods in Asia Minor.* Vol. 1, *The Celts and the Impact of Roman Rule.* Oxford: Clarendon.

———. 1993b. *Anatolia: Land, Men, and Gods in Asia Minor.* Vol. 2, *The Rise of Christianity.* Oxford: Clarendon.

Mligo, Elia Shabani. 2011. *Jesus and the Stigmatized: Reading the Gospel of John in a Context of HIV/AIDS-Related Stigmatization in Tanzania.* Eugene, OR: Pickwick.

Nanos, Mark. 2002. *The Irony of Galatians: Paul's Letter in First-Century Context.* Minneapolis: Fortress Press.

Niang, Aliou Cissé. 2009. *Faith and Freedom in Galatia and Senegal: The Apostle Paul, Colonists, and Sending Gods*. Biblical Interpretation Series 97. Leiden: Brill.

Osiek, Carolyn. 1992. "Galatians." In *The Women's Bible Commentary*, edited by Carol A. Newsome and Sharon H. Ringe, 333–37. Louisville: Westminster John Knox.

Parens, Erik, and Adrienne Asch, eds. 2000. *Prenatal Testing and Disability Rights*. Washington, DC: Georgetown University Press.

Riches, John Kenneth. 2008. *Galatians through the Centuries*. Malden, MA: Blackwell.

Schüssler Fiorenza, Elisabeth. 1985. *In Memory of Her: A Feminist Theological Reconstruction of Christian Origins*. New York: Crossroad, 1985.

———. 1999. *Rhetoric and Ethic: The Politics of Biblical Studies*. Minneapolis: Fortress Press.

Schweitzer, Albert. 1931. *The Mysticism of Paul the Apostle*. London: Black.

Segal, Alan. 1990. *Paul the Convert: The Apostolate and Apostasy of Saul the Pharisee*. New Haven: Yale University Press.

Stanley, Christopher D., ed. 2011. *The Colonized Apostle: Paul through Postcolonial Eyes*. Paul in Critical Contexts. Minneapolis: Fortress Press.

Stendahl, Krister. 1976. *Paul among Jews and Gentiles, and Other Essays*. Minneapolis: Fortress Press.

Streufert, Mary J., ed. 2010. *Transformative Lutheran Theologies: Feminist, Womanist, and Mujerista Pespectives*. Minneapolis: Fortress Press.

Tamez, Elsa. 1993. *The Amnesty of Grace*. Nashville: Abingdon.

Tataryn, Myroslaw, and Maria Truchan-Tataryn. 2013. *Discovering Trinity in Disability: A Theology for Embracing Difference*. Maryknoll, NY: Orbis.

Taubes, Jacob. 2004. *The Political Theology of Paul*. Stanford: Stanford University Press.

Taylor, Mark Lewis. 2001. *The Executed God: The Way of the Cross in Lockdown America*. Minneapolis: Fortress Press.

Trible, Phyllis. 1984. *Texts of Terror: Literary-Feminist Readings of Biblical Narratives*. Philadelphia: Fortress Press.

Wacquant, Loic. 2009. *Punishing the Poor: The Neoliberal Government of Social Insecurity*. Durham: Duke University Press;

Wan, Sze-Kar. 2000. "Collection for the Saints as Anticolonial Act." In *Paul and Politics: Ekklesia, Israel, Imperium, Interpretation. Essays in Honor of Krister Stendahl*, 191–215. Edited by Richard A. Horsley. Harrisburg, PA.: Trinity Press International.

Wiley, Tatha. 2005. *Paul and the Gentile Women: Reframing Galatians*. New York: Continuum.

Williams, Delores. 1993. *Sisters in the Wilderness: The Challenge of Womanist God-Talk*. Maryknoll, NY: Orbis.

———. 2006. "Hagar in African American Biblical Appropriation." In *Hagar, Sarah, and Their Children: Jewish, Christian, and Muslim Perspectives*, edited by Phyllis Trible and Letty M. Russell, 171–84. Louisville: Westminster John Knox.

Winter, Bruce. 1994. *Seek the Welfare of the City: Christians as Benefactors and Citizens*. Grand Rapids: Eerdmans.

Wright, N. T. 2000. "Paul's Gospel and Caesar's Empire." In *Paul and Politics*, edited by Richard Horsley, 160–83. Harrisburg, PA: Trinity Press International.

———. 2005. *Paul: In Fresh Perspective*. Minneapolis: Fortress Press.

Zetterholm, Magnus. 2009. *Approaches to Paul: A Student's Guide to Recent Scholarship*. Minneapolis: Fortress Press.

EPHESIANS

Jennifer G. Bird

Introduction

It is important to keep in mind that, when the Letter to the Ephesians was written in the first century, many of its ideas might have been new and perhaps somewhat startling to the people who read or heard it. When we consider the letter's content from this angle, we can see not just what is unique to Ephesians but also how striking some of the letter's components are, despite the fact that the letter has become part and parcel of Christian thought.

We find a surprising array of topics and issues in the letter. Written near the end of the first century, Ephesians shows evidence of several components of what became Gnostic thought ("every spiritual blessing in the heavenly places," 1:3; "made known to us the mystery of his will," 1:9; "fullness of time," 1:10; "spirit of wisdom and revelation," 1:17; "fullness of him who fills all in all," 1:23; "mystery," "perceiving," and "understanding" language in 3:3-4; "renewed in the spirit of your minds," 4:23; dualistic language in 5:6-16). Here as well are traces of an internal struggle among the various strands of thought within Judaism regarding who belongs to the covenant and which observances are legitimate (1:3-14; 2:11-22). And here are marked distinctions from several ideas found in the genuine Pauline Letters, which contribute to some scholars labeling Ephesians as deuteropauline instead of genuine. (The various strands of thought in Judaism went beyond just what Josephus named as the "schools" of the Essenes, Pharisees, Sadducees, and Zealots. Jesus' own disciples were Jews, and some of them had some differences of opinion from what Paul was saying, for instance. Any time we see New Testament texts claiming that Christ is the fulfillment of God's true covenant, we can pause to consider how this stands in contrast with other Jewish beliefs at the time. At the very least, there were proponents of Jewish observances visiting some of Paul's churches offering different instructions than he did [Acts 15; 2 Corinthians 10–13; Galatians 1–2].)

Though there are significant topics throughout the letter, the overarching and most important aspect of it for us today is perhaps the focus on the spiritual realm. Not only does this focus foster beliefs in a literal and embodied devil as a spiritual evil being (6:10-16), but it also creates a worldview primarily interested in spiritual warfare and attending to people's souls or spirits more than addressing the needs of this physical world. This in turn can lead to a form of escapism, if not simply a seemingly depoliticized or apolitical perspective on the world. In the twenty-first century, we cannot afford to live such disinterested and disconnected lives. Rather, however spiritually we experience the world, we also need to be intimately involved in making it a more humane and just place to live.

That this heavenly realm is discussed, as we shall see, in terms suggesting a mirror or counter to the empire of this world raises significant questions for us in terms of how we ought to be reading this letter, or any such imperial language, today. The source of power and control within any kingdom draws on the elements of fear and highly rigid roles for a majority of the people. Thus we do well to pay attention to the relationship that is encouraged here between "citizens" and the lord or king in the spiritual kingdom of heaven. Similarly, the passage giving instructions to persons occupying different roles in the household, customarily called the "household code" (or *Haustafel*: 5:21—6:9), must be seen as making deliberate sociopolitical claims, which restrict and control at times or grant relative freedom to the various people within the household structure. In light of this element of the letter, members of the church today would do well to consider carefully how or whether to use this paradigm to help define family relationships.

Among the other topics to be addressed in discussing this letter are an at least partially realized eschatology (1:14), fully realized at times, meaning that the spiritual salvation available because of Christ is already at work in us (e.g., 1:7); the main New Testament references to predestination (1:3-11; 2:10); the imagery of the church as the bride of Christ (5:22-32); and fodder for the idea that followers of Christ are "soldiers for the Lord," which comes from the quasi-military rhetoric found here (6:10-17).

Ephesians plays a role in the stark distinction one sees between churches that focus on the "Christ of salvation" rather than the "Jesus of the Gospels." A focus on high Christology is underwritten by letters such as Ephesians, at the expense of potentially losing touch with the humanity of Jesus.

Ephesians 1:1—2:10: Spiritual Blessings and Riches in Christ

▌ THE TEXT IN ITS ANCIENT CONTEXT

Though we do not know who the original recipients were, as *en Ephesō* was likely added into the letter from a marginal notation, it was most likely written for a church in the vicinity of Ephesus. This opening section discusses the Christ in a way that Jesus himself might not have identified with (1:3-14; see also 2:11-22). Here, references to being chosen by God, to inheritance as sons, and to redemption through Christ's blood all resonate with aspects of Judaism's belief system as much as with Greco-Roman religious traditions. It is also a passage resplendent with the language of predestination. The author declares that God "chose us" before the foundation of the world (1:4); in love he "destined us" to adoption (1:5); our inheritance is according to his purpose (1:11); and there are good works prepared for us to accomplish in Christ (2:10). There is great comfort for the recipients in such promises and assurances.

Throughout, this letter resonates with elements of what would become Gnosticism. Terminology such as "riches" and "spiritual blessings"; "heavenly places," "mysteries," and "the mystery of God's will"; "fullness" and "fullness of time"; "spirit of wisdom"; "knowledge"; "enlightenment"; and "spiritual powers" are all later developed in Gnostic worldviews. It is somewhat striking to see such proto-Gnostic ideas in the canon, given both how different it is from the perspective of the genuine Pauline writings and that the Gnostic traditions would later come to be deemed heretical by church fathers. In another deuteropauline move, we see the idea of having *already* obtained the inheritance in Christ, what we now refer to as "realized eschatology." The "sealing with the Holy Spirit" (1:13) perhaps draws on the way emperors, rulers, or other people of great importance would "mark" a letter with their seal. This idea resonates with royal importance, though Christ, not the Roman emperor, is the "lord" whose seal is placed on these recipients.

▌ THE TEXT IN THE INTERPRETIVE TRADITION

Ephesians 1:4-11, and to a much lesser degree 3:8-10, has played heavily in the church's discussion of predestination over the centuries. It was first made a significant focus in what is now referred to as the Pelagian controversy in the early fifth century. The basic beliefs promulgated by Pelagianism, all deemed heretical by the Council of Carthage (418), focus on the concept we have come to refer to as original sin and the early church's reading of the story of Adam and Eve in Genesis 2–3. Pelagius denied that there was ever a pristine state that is so often read into Genesis 2; he denied that there was a moment in time when sin entered into human actions, and thus that there was ever a time when humans were perfect and would have had immortality. He also insisted that our bodies dying is a natural event, and not something caused or brought about by "Adam and Eve" in the garden. Finally, his claim that we are born not in our full development, "but with a capacity for good and evil; we are begotten without virtue as much as without fault, and before the activity of the individual will there is nothing in humans other than what God has placed in them," suggests that he wanted to reject the idea of humans being born tainted. This is also backed up by his claim that newborn children need not be baptized, which is the second of his beliefs that was denounced at the Council of Carthage. Pelagius's ideas significantly downplayed the need for the Christ event, and placed a great deal of agency with humans instead of salvation stemming only from God and God's grace through Christ.

Church fathers, in particular Augustine, responded to Pelagius's ideas with claims that put the efficacy of salvation squarely on God and God's grace, though humans were thought to be called on to participate. For the early church fathers, giving humans any level of responsibility for salvation in this way was explained by the idea of divine foreknowledge of humans' actions, here drawing on Eph. 1:4-11. It was Augustine who made the obvious conclusion clear, that if one was chosen or elected to be a child of God, then one was also chosen or elected to salvation. As one might imagine, taking this idea to its next logical step would cause problems for later theologians of the church.

It was John Calvin who built on Augustine's idea of predestination to salvation to include the implied other component: predestination to sin and damnation as well. This idea, double predestination, was rejected by other Reformers, however. Still drawing on this passage in Ephesians, Huldrych Zwingli and Martin Luther focused on the chosenness in Christ, and God's goodness and righteousness. Within the Roman Catholic tradition, the discussion of predestination engendered two extremist positions, which were eventually both permitted by Pope Paul V. They are represented by Thomism and Molinism, beginning with grace and free will, respectively, with significant debate regarding the nature of grace, both as sufficient and as efficacious. Karl Barth (1957) interpreted this divinely predestined election as entirely focused on Christ, as we would expect from him: election to salvation is ascribed to humankind through Christ, and Christ took on himself the election to damnation. The "grace versus free will" discussion remains somewhat unresolved in many, perhaps all, Christian denominations.

The phrase "by nature, children of wrath" (2:3) also received attention over the centuries. In response to Pelagius's denial of original sin, this passage helped early church fathers formulate the belief in the inherent corruption of human nature, an essential component of the belief in original sin.

■ THE TEXT IN CONTEMPORARY DISCUSSION

In Eph. 1:7 we see the first reference to a realized redemption, as opposed to the idea espoused in the genuine Pauline Letters that it will be fulfilled at the Parousia. The metaphor for atonement used here, "redemption through his blood," is based on ideas about sacrifice that call for reconsideration. The redemption-through-blood metaphor is also used in 5:2, which refers to the pleasant aroma of an offering and sacrifice. This is, no doubt, one of the main reasons ancient peoples thought such offerings would be pleasing for their god(s). But the insistence on the necessity of the blood that comes from death, and the violence implied by it, in order to restore life or to bring about reconciliation between two parties, has been problematized by numerous theologians, in particular in the last few decades (Terrell; Weaver).

The idea that apart from Christ, all people live "in the lusts of [their] flesh, indulging the desires of the flesh and senses, and were by nature children of wrath" (2:1-4; see also 1:3) is one that warrants our thoughtful consideration. Though it may be familiar to many people, it does draw on a dualistic worldview, wherein the spirit is good, but all things to do with the body are bad. Many contemporary scholars of religion or biblical studies have commented on the detrimental effects of such dualisms on the ways we relate to others (see Ruether). What we see, specifically here in Ephesians, also underscores a belief that only in Christ can people be moral, disciplined people. There is very little in the adult world of continuums and variety that can be so simply labeled. Dualisms are necessary for children in order to help them establish good judgment and healthy, respectful behaviors, but these dualisms are best left behind as one matures in mind, body, and faith.

On the topic of predestination, suggested by 1:4-8 and 2:8-10, I offer a few caveats for the thoughtful reader today. First, the concept of predestination was originally only about being saved, where our souls would go after dying, contrasted with ideas of who or what we are "destined" to be in this life. As such, predestination came to be intimately connected to the idea of original sin. But the basic idea of "original sin," contrary to popular belief, is not an inherent component of Genesis

2–3; rather, it is a belief read *into* that passage that requires taking the narrative as a literal account instead of as it was intended: as a myth. There is much theological content of the early church that is based on a literal reading of this story, perhaps often to our detriment. The assertion of the reality of "original sin," and thus the manifold ways that have subsequently been developed to describe God's saving us from it, are among the most far-reaching ideas within Christian doctrine. The system of thought that has been built up around these texts, including the ideas of election to salvation, election to damnation, and total human depravity without Christ; that humans are by nature disobedient and that it is Adam and Eve's fault that we need salvation; how salvation is conferred to humans, even simply the preoccupation with the relation of divine grace to human free will—are all dependent on the early (mis)readings of Genesis 2–3. The early intense focus on the belief in human inadequacy, depravity, and disobedience, not to mention the disparagement of our bodies and anything that is natural to them, has left its mark on the collective consciousness of the church and its doctrine. One does not have to agree with these early, eager, earnest church leaders. There are more beneficial and life-supporting ways to read those biblical passages that do not end up denigrating the value and beauty of our bodies or our humanness itself.

The second caveat is directly related to the first. If the God who created us also gave us our minds to use, it is not a transgression of God's will or grace to suggest that the conversation regarding salvation, as debated and deliberated over the centuries, simply went painfully awry. Saying that God would create all humans, but would choose in advance some to be saved and others to receive eternal damnation, goes against all moral sensibility. Some people counter this claim by saying that God's ways are higher than ours. This response asserts that what seems unjust to us is somehow reasonable, given God's love for us and simultaneous need for justice in response to our sin.

It is the effort to make something unique of the Christ event that prepared the way for the early church writers to apply God's foreknowledge and "choosing" to salvation, now only in Christ. Prior to the Christ event, election was a matter of God's having chosen the Jews, through their ancestors the Israelites, which is represented in the covenant. Election and salvation are intertwined in the Jewish context, though the focus is on salvation in this life, not what happens after dying. "Salvation" has been understood in numerous ways within the church over the centuries, not to mention what it means to people of other faiths. Given how deeply rooted in dualistic thinking the traditional Christian ideas of salvation and predestination are, the reevaluation of it, to which a number of contemporary theologians call the church, will present a considerable, but perhaps beneficial, challenge.

Ephesians 2:11—3:21: Mystery, Power, and Oneness in Christ

▌ THE TEXT IN ITS ANCIENT CONTEXT

The writer here makes it clear that he is writing as a member of Israel to people who, while formerly gentiles, are now considered a part of the covenant promises given to Israel. The reference to two groups of people, those of "the uncircumcision" in contrast to those of "the circumcision," recalls the dilemma that Paul often addressed for the young communities: Do gentiles need to uphold the tenets of the law in order to be fully included in the covenant? Paul's consistent response was no: The law was Israel's means to the covenant; gentiles trying to uphold the law had missed the whole point. In Ephesians, however, we see Paul's idea taken one step further. The writer claims in 2:14-15 that Christ broke "down the dividing wall, that is, the hostility between us. He has abolished the law with its commandments and ordinances." Ephesians says that it is not simply that the law was only intended for Israel, as Paul suggested, but also that the law is what is causing the enmity between Jews and gentiles within the *ekklēsia*, and that because of Christ the law is abolished. One might imagine that this idea would not have sat well with some Jews in the first century.

Though it may seem reassuring to many today, in the author's claim that Christ "established peace" we perhaps ought to hear something more along the lines of the imposition of the *Pax Romana* by the Roman emperors. It would have been heard as abruptly as this by those who were not convinced by the gospel or who did not embrace gentiles within Judaism. Similarly, the author draws on "strangers and aliens" terminology, which would resonate with Israel's past, when the Israelites were strangers and aliens in Egypt. We see this label used in one other New Testament letter, 1 Peter. Both letters, written near the end of the first century, simultaneously draw on Israel's past and speak of how it is no longer needed or valid. For instance, in 3:9-10, there is a suggestion that God's wisdom had been kept hidden until the establishment of the church, even though this church is built on the "foundation" of Israel's prophets and the apostles. It is important to note that these claims were being made within the early church, in particular in light of what they imply about the people of Israel and the validity of their belief system.

The building imagery in 2:20-22 is perhaps an intentional move away from the body metaphors Paul so often uses (e.g., Romans 12; 1 Corinthians 12) to something more tangible and durable, even permanent.

Whether one sees 2:11-22 as similar to encomiums attributed to emperors (Perkins), or finds in 1:20—2:22 the application of the general structure of ancient Near Eastern divine warfare mythology (Gombis), in either case it is clear that praise and exaltation of rulers or other gods is being adapted here in praise of Christ. For instance, the latter passage includes an exaltation of the God or divine king (1:20-2), naming a threat (2:1-3), describing the battle or victory (2:4-7), ascribing lordship to the victor (mostly prior to this section, in 1:3-11; 2:6), and the building of a house or temple to the god (2:19-22), ending with a celebration. Since this paradigm already existed, applying it to Christ would place him in competition with the deified emperor in addition to other gods.

In 3:3-21, we see more ideas that diverged from genuine Pauline ideas. The author writes, "the mystery was made know to me by revelation," but here the previously undisclosed "mystery" is that "the Gentiles have become fellow heirs" with Jews (3:6). Paul himself regarded this as the clear message of scripture, however (e.g., Rom. 4:1-15), and used the language of "mystery" to refer to the paradoxical course that God's purposes had taken in the temporary "hardening" of Israel (Rom. 11:25-26). Those nuances are absent from Ephesians. Further, references to fullness (*plērōma*), knowledge, wisdom, and riches, all employed in this section, are used in ways that are foreign to the Pauline Letters. Through and through, Ephesians affirms the need for the spiritual knowledge that can only be revealed through Christ.

Interestingly enough, 3:20-21 sounds like a benediction, as we would expect at the end of such a letter. Thus some scholars suggest that this letter was, as many others in the New Testament are, pieced together from more than one source.

THE TEXT IN THE INTERPRETIVE TRADITION

Ephesians 2:11-22 has been important throughout the centuries in terms of Jewish-Christian relations. It was a helpful passage for Tertullian to reference in denouncing one of the men he considered heretics, Marcion. Since Marcion believed the God of Jewish Scripture was a different God from the one of Christian Scripture (which meant, for him, a few of the writings we consider the New Testament), Tertullian and others emphasized the continuity between the "Old" and "New" Testaments and the belief that the two groups of people being brought together, Jews and gentiles, would be brought together under the same God (Tertullian, *Apology* 37, 50). Much has been made of this passage over the centuries, with interpretations ranging from maintaining Israel's place of prominence as God's chosen people (Barth) to a dismissal of Israel's relevance altogether for Christianity (Lindemann).

Luther used 2:20-22, the church as God's building, to speak against papal primacy. He suggested that the papacy is one part of the church, of which only Christ is the head. Thus all parts of the church are equal to each other, and final authority rests with Christ, not the pope.

THE TEXT IN CONTEMPORARY DISCUSSION

A careful biblical theologian today will turn to Romans 9–11, in addition to Eph. 2:11-22, for textual support for the discussion of the relationship between the church and Israel. I wish to draw attention to supersessionism and the irrelevance of Israel or Judaism that several passages in Ephesians appear to endorse. Saying that Christ "abolished the enmity" between Jews and gentiles, the enmity that was the law of commandments (2:14-15), sets up the Scripture that is sacred to Jews as a problem that needs to be eradicated. The very belief espoused here, that God has extended the covenant to all people, is embraced by some Jews but certainly not all, both then and now. Thus any and all attempts to "make peace" between the church and Judaism today that do not take this point into account will ultimately be of no avail. But there can be no doubt that there is fodder in the texts of the New Testament to support both ideas: that the coming together of all Jews and gentiles in the covenant is God's will, and that there is only one special sect of Judaism that "counts" as the correct one of the covenant, which is the one that became what we know as Christianity.

Two striking developments in this section of Ephesians are worth consideration. The first is the change from the very human Jesus of Nazareth, who is the central character in the Synoptic Gospels and is seen mingling with and relating to the masses, to the elevated and mighty Christ, who is above all earthly powers and is enthroned in the heavenly realm. As such, he might appear out of reach of the people who need him (2:20-22). The other is the contrast between the kind of *ekklēsia* Paul's genuine letters describe and the communities as they are defined here. When Paul first employed the terminology to gatherings of followers of Jesus, an *ekklēsia* was an assembly or gathering of the *polis*, one that would address physical, daily concerns of the people allowed into the gatherings. In Ephesians, the realm in which their *ekklēsia* takes effect is the spiritual, cosmic realm. Perhaps both are needed, but a one-sided focus on the spiritual realm can lead to apathy in the face of the problems in the tangible world.

Another aspect of the spiritual or heavenly kingdom described in Ephesians is that while it may be seen to offer a counterempire or kingdom to the Roman Empire, all of the roles of dominance and subjectivity are maintained, but simply applied to a new ruler (Bird). For some, this idea of God as almighty ruler is comforting; certainly it has pervaded Christian thought, doctrine, and hymns for two thousand years. But that does not mean that understanding our world in those terms is the most beneficial way to conceive it. For instance, when we speak of the powers of this world being subject to Christ (1:20-22), we set up a system that turns the former oppressors into the oppressed, and vice versa. In other words, we imply a divine sanction of the cycle of domination of one power over another. Though Ephesians speaks of this in the "spiritual" realms, when a person is subject to this victorious Christ/ruler, one assumes either that only the next life or spiritual realm is important, or that claiming that Christ is above all justifies whatever action one undertakes in order to establish "peace" on his behalf. The former situation tends to lead to withdrawing from the world; the latter mind-set leads to tragedies such as the Crusades, but also to a sense that "might makes right."

Similarly, when we see the claim in Ephesians that the peace of Christ is established among his followers, we should consider how such things happen. Within the Roman Empire, the rule and reign of the emperor were established by means of terror, intimidation, and military action. What happens when we view the empire of God and the heavenly rule of Christ through the same lens? This perspective highlights a tension between *offering* the peace of Christ and *imposing* it on others. Those who, as members of the cosmic *ekklēsia*, presume to be members of this new empire may be reassured by the dominance and rule of Christ. But what fearsome implications for those "outside"! The image constructed of those who continue to live in disobedience and ignorance (4:17-22; 5:5-8, 11-12) does not encourage including them, but of distancing oneself and one's group from such others. The demonizing of the "other" continues in this new empire—as an act of intimidation, at the very least—and, as history has shown us again and again, can set the stage for violent military attacks once this *ekklēsia* is also embraced by worldly emperors. While many people today may enjoy the language in Eph. 3:18-19 about knowing the great extent of God's love and the love of Christ that surpasses knowledge, responsible handling of Scripture requires that we remember the context of such encouraging words.

Ephesians 4:1—5:20: Unity in the Body of Christ and Living Wisely

▌ THE TEXT IN ITS ANCIENT CONTEXT

Clearly, 4:1-16 is concerned with creating unity, an issue alluded to in other parts of the letter as well. Here the issue seems to be that people spoke of things such as baptism or "faith" with different purposes, or as being symbolically meaningful in different ways, and that there is consequently some confusion regarding spiritual gifts. Thus the author asserts that there is only one God, from whom all these things (faith, baptism, hope, gifts, etc.) come to them. Having a common understanding of such important matters would have been crucial to the sustainability of the movement.

The next section of the letter, 4:25—5:20, resonates with much of the basic content of Paul's earlier letters, in particular charging people to do their own work, to help others in need, to speak only words of edification, to not be deceived by foolish or misguided beliefs, and to put away wrath and anger. There is also a significant presence of dualistic thought, making dark/light and foolish/wise distinctions, and referring to the recipients as "children of light."

Speaking of Jesus as the Christ who gave himself up for them, "a fragrant offering and sacrifice to God" (5:2), draws on the common practice of animal sacrifice that would have been a part of Jewish and pagan worship alike in the first century. Here the metaphor serves to highlight the execution of Jesus, symbolized as a "sacrifice," as the most important aspect of who he is and what he did for the church.

◼ THE TEXT IN THE INTERPRETIVE TRADITION

In seeking to create unity, as the beginning of this section does, the author endorses the idea that there is only *one* way, *one* hope, *one* faith, *one* baptism, and so on. While we may see the importance of such unity, it has also led to divisions over the centuries, for example, in understanding the intention, meaning, and symbolic efficacy of Christian baptism. Though the diversity belies the claim, different traditions have and will continue to understandably identify their own practice with the "one baptism" to which the text refers.

The primary references in church fathers' writings to this part of the letter are to 4:7-16, which discusses specific roles and gifts, all given freely by Christ as a gift of grace (4:7). While early writers seemed content simply to note that various roles (apostles, prophets, evangelists, pastors, and teachers) are listed, and just as often referred to Acts 6:2 or 20:28 as to this passage for edification regarding how to be a Christian leader, for the sixteenth-century Reformers the distinction between different roles was of great importance. Their primary concern regarded where, within the hierarchy of the church, each role was intended. Most notably, the role of bishop is not mentioned in this list, yet the bishop held a position of primacy at that time; were some of the roles named in Ephesians to be identified with specifically episcopal duties? Also, if the then-current role and function of the papacy had been intended by Christ, why does this passage not even allude to it? Throughout the ages, there has been agreement on the idea that all spiritual gifts are intended to serve the Word, and to build up the congregation. In present-day ecumenical dialogues, Romans 12 and 1 Corinthians 12 feature more prominently than Ephesians in discussions of spiritual gifts and their relative importance.

◼ THE TEXT IN CONTEMPORARY DISCUSSION

The generalized language in 4:17-24 serves to perpetuate the denigration or demonizing of people who are not in the fold. All descriptions suggesting that outside of Christ people are callous and constantly "give themselves over to sensuality," practicing every kind of impurity and greed, is dangerous for us today. The reference to people's being objects of God's wrath prior to their becoming members of the church, and to their being ignorant and foolish apart from Christ can lead to judgmental views of "others" on the part of Christians. We see this clearly in 4:17-19, which says that the gentiles "live, in the futility of their minds. They are darkened in their understanding, alienated from the life of God because of their ignorance and hardness of heart." Not only does this kind of talk belittle people outside of the church, but it also suggests that apart from Christ all people are incapable of being moral and loving. We should not be surprised, then, to hear that many Christians believe, for instance, that atheists are by definition immoral people. If Christians are teaching their children to see non-Christians in this way, there is very little space for understanding others and much precedent for judging.

While the concomitant charge to be renewed in the spirit of our minds (4:23) is lovely, it comes at a great cost. If we could frame the positive ideas about living well and being "children of light" without demonizing those who do not align with our worldview, we would make great strides toward productive dialogues within various segments of our world today. If, however, we continue to speak with language implying that "if you're not with us you're against us," we will continue to see our leaders and politicians struggling to "be right" instead of struggling to be understood and to understand others. The dualistic mind-set that undergirds this letter is not helpful for navigating the diversity of belief systems and worldviews of our global community.

Ephesians 5:21—6:9: Household Code

■ The Text in Its Ancient Context

This section is one of the three clear examples in the New Testament (see also Col. 3:18—4:1; 1 Pet. 2:18—3:7) of the "household codes" that appear in ancient Greek and Latin writings; Martin Luther called these *Haustafeln*, "tables" of household duties. It is worth noting that all three cases appear near the end of the first century, and that the implications for women and slaves stand in stark contrast to the words of encouragement Paul himself gave several decades earlier (Gal. 3:28; as well as Rom. 16:1-16, or even the implications of equality between husband and wife in 1 Cor. 7:1-16). We should not be surprised to see this move, however, since the household codes endorse the patriarchal Roman family ideals. Since the rules of the household were understood to undergird economics and politics within a city, the household is the key to sociopolitical control (Schüssler Fiorenza 1997; D'Angelo). While many scholars have argued that the household ideals were adapted in a way that is kinder toward women, children, and slaves than the non-Christian archetype, others have described this relative "kindness" as "love-patriarchalism" (MacDonald). The worldview endorses what is culturally expected, namely patriarchy; but the commands are laced with love or kindness, which, presumably, softens the harshness of the domination and control.

The *Haustafel* section begins with a call to the entire community to "be subject to one another out of reverence for Christ" (5:21). Similarly, the wives are to submit to their husbands, in all things, as they do to the Lord (5:33), and the slaves are to obey their human masters with fear and trembling (6:5). Though the other typical members of the household are also addressed, their exhortations are not buttressed by obedience out of fear as is the case for wives and slaves (the NRSV translates *phobētai* with "respect" in 5:33, but the Greek literally says "that the husband may be feared"; the word is a cognate of *phobos*, "fear," in 6:5). We do well to ask why such strong language is used for these two groups of people in particular. Not only were women and slaves central to the economic productivity of the household, and thus were essential in supporting the empire; but their sheer numbers also made their control by others important to maintaining the social order. To be sure, the freedom and empowerment that women and slaves had experienced in the early movement, which had been fully endorsed by Paul in his letters, might well have been perceived by outsiders as a threat to social and political order. The shrewd reader of New Testament writings can see political power plays at work in and behind them.

One striking comparison that is particular to the Ephesian *Haustafel* is that the Christian community is constructed in terms of two images: the body of Christ and the subject status of a wife (Osiek; Sampley). Thus the *ekklēsia* is seen as both Christ's body and Christ's bride, in contrast with Paul's use of just the body metaphor (Romans 12; 1 Corinthians 12). Perhaps neither surprising—as the endorsement of the married-with-children state would earn favor with Roman officials—nor new—we see in Hosea and elsewhere in Hebrew Scriptures references to Israel as the bride of Yahweh—the effect of claiming that the church is the bride of Christ is nevertheless far-reaching.

In spite of the focus on the heavenly realms throughout this letter, the *Haustafel* section is grounded in everyday life with its attendant sociopolitical concerns. Just as in the Roman Empire the married-with-children state was encouraged by legislation, now the married state is encouraged in the *ekklēsia* by this letter.

█ THE TEXT IN THE INTERPRETIVE TRADITION

Men from all ages of Christendom have found two components of this section of the letter important and useful. First is the striking comparison between a marriage between and man and a woman and the "union" of Christ and his bride, the church. Second is the related phrase "this is a great mystery" (5:32). Interpreters have questioned what, exactly, the author intended by the term *mysterion*; and because this term was translated into Latin as *sacramentum*, this became a key passage for the Scholastic and Reformation debates regarding the sacraments.

As to the first point, we must note that, with few exceptions, the church fathers read Gen. 2:24 as an indication that marriage itself was established by God, as a part of creation, and thus was something sacred and holy. Building on this assumption, then, there were various claims made regarding the unique importance of marriage, often implying that physical or sexual love within a marriage ought to be on par with a spiritual, holy love. Marriage between a man and a woman was declared a *typos*, or a visual example, of the union between Christ and the church. Given marriage's divine endorsement, Augustine and others were able to defend the goodness of marriage against those who generally saw anything to do with the "flesh" as evil and corrupt. Augustine countered his contemporaries in his claim that the marriage alluded to in Genesis 2 was a sexually active marriage, and that had there been no sin (in Genesis 3), then sexual desires within marriage today would be without lust, since Augustine deemed lustfulness to be shameful (*De nuptiis* 54).

As to the matter of marriage constituting a sacrament, since the belief developed that sacraments bring about what they indicate (Hugh of St. Victor, *de sacramentis* 9.2; Peter Lombard, *Sententiarum libri quatuor* 4.1.4, 2.1), Aquinas concluded that the way marriage brought about participation in grace was that entering into marriage was symbolic of belonging to Christ. We see in writings beginning with the Reformation, and as recently as the Pastoral Constitution of the Second Vatican Council, an interest in speaking of Christian marriage as a special form of the worldly institution, simply because Christians are connected to Christ through salvation.

The final section of this passage, Eph. 6:5-9, along with the similar passages of Col. 3:22—4:1 and 1 Pet. 2:18-25, have played a significant role historically in justifying the inhumane treatment of enslaved African people in the United States. First Peter's discussion of masters and slaves is lengthier and declared that suffering made a person Christlike. These elements made it more popular than Ephesians on this topic.

■ THE TEXT IN CONTEMPORARY DISCUSSION

The theme of being subject to God or Christ out of fear (5:21) deserves some reconsideration. While there is much within the sacred writings of the Jews, and no small amount within the New Testament, that refers to devotion to God in terms of "fear," which is typically defended as meaning "reverence," we may still ask whether the terminology is positive or helpful. Fear and control go hand in hand. Fearing the power of the emperor is one thing; (re)importing such fear into the religious realm is simply ascribing the same dominant, and thus oppressive, relationship with the deity that the people have with the emperor. These may be structures and relations people can understand, and thus they may be effective, but that does not mean that they are beneficial for us today.

Describing the *ekklēsia* in terms of both Christ's body and Christ's bride is problematic for many scholars today (Merz), in part because the images are mutually exclusive and thus confusing. Beyond that, however, calling the church the bride of Christ feminizes the church (as "she") in a way that cannot be undone. Based on the initial application of the label in a heteronormative, patriarchal setting, "she" must be led by a man, and "she" is fully subservient to her "husband," the Christ. It only follows, of course, that the same dominant/submissive roles would then be applied between men and women within the *ekklēsia*. It is important to consider how starkly different this image is from what we see in the genuine Pauline writings, where Paul urges his readers not to behave according to the social, familial, and cultural gender roles of the wider culture (Gal. 3:28). Seeing the author of Ephesians intentionally adopting the androcentric, patriarchal political ideals for men and women ought to give the reader pause. This move not only encourages the married state for all people in the church, as the Augustan legislation of the first century BCE did for the people of the Roman Empire, but also places extraordinary focus on women's married status. The patriarchal, heterosexual marriage becomes the ultimate, if not the only, representation of the church's relation to Christ (Merz). Further, only heterosexual marriages would be considered "normal" or approved of by God.

The purity required or implied in 5:27 may make sense in context, but it also serves to perpetuate a double standard between men and women in terms of purity, and ultimately makes a detrimental connection between sex and purity. If it is the bride who needs to be pure, then it is the woman in the male/female couple who is expected to be "pure" today. The early church fathers had no difficulty identifying sexuality as impure, and hanging the responsibility for sexual "impurity" on women. We have inherited several components of their way of thinking that are detrimental to the way we view and value our bodies, sexuality, and women in general.

The metaphor of a "marriage" between Christ and the church has also been wielded in conversations regarding sex before marriage. These conversations might be reframed once we note that in Eph. 5:31, Gen. 2:24 has been pulled out of context, both in the Christian tradition and in current English translations, and interpreted as implying that Adam and Eve were *married* in the Garden of Eden. The NRSV, for example, represents the Greek *gynē* with "wife" rather than "woman" (compare the translation of *anēr* as "man" rather than "husband"). In the context of Genesis, however, we are only told why two people who are drawn to each other are to go out from their parents and start their own family. There is no mention of "marriage," and the Hebrew terms used throughout this passage, *'îš* and *'iššâ*, can just as easily be translated "man" and "woman" as "husband" and "wife." Though subtle, the distinction has far-reaching implications. It is in part on the basis of the translation "wife," as well as the commands and suggestions made by Paul in 1 Corinthians 7 (especially 7:9), that some Christians today claim that sex before marriage is a sin. The special significance attributed to marriage here may inform the harsh judgment some Christians pass on divorce as a sin as well, and may help to underwrite a worldview that says marriage is to be only between a man and a woman. Remarkably, the analogy between marriage and the relationship between Christ and his church appears to break down when some churches assert that only *men* can be the leaders or representatives of the (feminized) church, which is (symbolically) married to Christ, a male.

This Ephesians passage is often read today and embraced without hesitation by men and women alike. Suggesting that a husband is to his wife as Christ is to the Church, however, puts an inordinate, entirely unfair pressure on men. For centuries, Christians have sought to embrace this "ideal," but in doing so have only perpetuated the social and cultural confusion of healthy gender roles. If Christ's self-sacrificial "love" for the church is the primary model for men in marriage, it would seem to follow that men must protect and provide for their wives to a potentially limitless extent. It should be no wonder, then, that so many people expect women to need to be cared for, or that men as "breadwinners" should receive higher salaries and earlier promotions than equally qualified women. Similarly, suggesting that women are to be as subordinate to their husbands as they are *to Christ* seems extraordinary, in that it is not balanced with a similar injunction to men; yet, again, because it is in Scripture, many people today seek to abide by it as a way of showing faithfulness to Christ, assuming that it is what God intended.

Moreover, there can be no question that the racial, economic, educational, emotional, and spiritual effects of four hundred years of slavery in the United States continue to this day. This reality permeates cultural and social realities in the United States to the point that people who are conscious of it do not know where to begin to address it, and people unaware of it can easily carry on with life as they know it, with clear consciences. Many people today also try to claim that slavery no longer happens in our world, a belief all the more stunning since so much of our global, political, and trade relations are dependent on child labor for the production of goods and on child and female bodies for support of the highly lucrative international sex slave trade. Some scholars even push us to reconsider the value we place on child-rearing and housework, since so much of it is done "for free," yet disproportionately by women and often at great expense to them in terms of their careers or influence outside of the home (Engels; Hartsock; Schüssler Fiorenza, 1987).

Ephesians 6:10-24: Spiritual Battle and Benediction

▌ THE TEXT IN ITS ANCIENT CONTEXT

In 6:10-17 (see also 4:8), we see a specific parallel between serving in the military and living the Christian life, though one cannot miss that the comparison is entirely spiritualized through the reference to the "rulers," "cosmic powers of this present darkness . . . spiritual forces of evil in the heavenly places" (6:12). The author suggests that as a follower of Christ, one can count on being prepared for the "battle" ahead, fully clothed in God's spiritual protection. We may also see the author responding to early persecution, even the prospect of martyrdom, in referring to the "evil day" and "standing firm" in the face of it. The letter itself ends with a typical greeting and benediction.

▌ THE TEXT IN THE INTERPRETIVE TRADITION

Because of the spiritualized language of struggles and battles in this section of the letter, we ought not be surprised at the wide range of interpretive contexts in which the church fathers applied it. In addition to evoking the context of gruesome battlefields, which made this a prime passage in the construction of *militia Christi* (military service for Christ), it was also adapted to discuss—and at times encourage—martyrdom, monastic lifestyles, and mysticism.

The struggle against one's own passions and "carnal desires" is perhaps the most common application of this spiritual battle into everyday life, intimately connecting an ascetic life with a moral one (Clement of Alexandria, *Strom.* 2.109–10; 7.20). The early fathers equated our passions and desires with the enemy, the ruler of the spiritual realm of evil that all Christians are to fight and conquer. Interestingly, several church fathers wrestled with the implications that there are many real battles that take place within the First (Old) Testament. Origen concluded that God commanded such physical battles, in books such as Joshua, in order to foreshadow the spiritual battles of Christians. Just as soldiers were expected to put their military service and performance in battle above their own lives and families, so too many church fathers (Tertullian, Clement, Origen) discussed the calling to be a disciple of Christ as something that deserved highest regard, even claiming that the Christian's battle serves Christ's message of peace. In this way, the *militia Christi* is well grounded. The connection between devotion to Christ and fighting a *spiritual* battle led to a view of martyrdom as the ultimate way to prove one's worth to Christ: since victory "consists in achieving that for which one has fought," that is, salvation, a Christian martyr is victorious (Tertullian). Erasmus of Rotterdam's *A Handbook for the Christian Soldier* (1501) makes clear that the Christian's daily battle is a spiritual one, which will best be fought with God's armor, with knowledge and prayer being the two primary weapons.

▌ THE TEXT IN CONTEMPORARY DISCUSSION

The idea of the armor of God is simultaneously familiar to many Christians but somewhat offensive to some modern sensibilities. Though this armor is fully "spiritualized" and described in terms of beneficent and loving actions, it is nevertheless preparing the community *for battle.* They are to be prepared at all times to figuratively "slay" their enemies with the words of their God, knowing that because of God they are invincible. There is a divine sanction for violence and a conquering mentality; it is embedded in church liturgy and hymns because they draw on the language present in the texts of the Christian tradition (Russell). Just because the imagery is now deployed within the spiritual realm does not neutralize the violent, aggressive, and bloody battle imagery associated with being Christ's soldier. At the same time, many theologians over the centuries have suggested that the Christian is only to fight defensively.

While many websites today will offer content for vacation Bible schools based on the theme of the "Soldier for Christ," we do well to keep in mind that in Ephesians, this metaphor is significantly, if not primarily, framed as soldiers fighting against the "powers and principalities" within the spiritual realm. The exhortation to be "strong in the Lord" (6:10) can be helpful, in particular when people are up against persecution or an unrelenting "foe." The notion that there is a literal devil lurking out there, supported by his demons and evil spirits, all of which constitute the forces of darkness, is still embraced by some Christians today. The realistic quality of the popular Christian novels *This Present Darkness* and *Piercing the Darkness* (Peretti 1986; 1989) indicates that the predilection for waging "spiritual wars" continues to this day, and that people are willing to spend a great deal of time and energy focused on the heavenly realm instead of on the tangible world we all live in. While focusing on the spiritual realm can be a palliative for real, physical discomfort or oppression, it can also promote a seemingly depoliticized worldview, which can neutralize the motivation for social change.

With many of our governmental leaders being faithful Christians who endorse this way of thinking, is it any wonder that our governments tend toward military action more often than to peace talks? Again, according to Russell, "Those who live in nations that shape the principalities of our day cannot afford triumphal hymns" (Russell, 68). The ideals of one's faith will dictate how one behaves in the world.

When we see terminology used in Ephesians (or in the New Testament in general) that is adopted from imperial pronouncements, political labels and ideas, household code ideals, and even from the imagery of preparation for battle, we would do well to stop and consider the inherent political implications in that terminology instead of moving quickly to spiritualize it. There is no question that the author of Ephesians is speaking in highly spiritualized terms, but even those spiritual ideas about a heavenly realm will influence how people behave politically. These dimensions are intertwined, and it is our responsibility to be aware of the political implications of such commingling. It is time to take seriously the detrimental results of blind adherence to such biblical texts and to consider why we often conveniently try to overlook some aspects of them. For some readers today, theological responsibility means courageously declaring the ideal that the Word of God leads to life, fulfillment, and liberation from oppression; it must not be oppression's cause. This is where reason and thoughtful reflection meet. Perhaps by challenging a focus solely on the heavenly realm and the rhetoric of battle, we may be inspired toward loving mutuality and a spirituality that enriches the world in which we live.

Works Cited

Barth, Marcus. 1959. *Israel und die Kirche im Brief des Paulus an die Epheser*. Theologische Existenz heute. Munich: Kaiser.

Bird, Jennifer. 2009. "Ephesians." In *A Postcolonial Commentary on the New Testament Writings*, edited by R. S. Sugirtharajah and Fernando F. Segovia, 265–80. New York: T&T Clark.

D'Angelo, Mary Rose. 1993. "Colossians." In *Searching the Scriptures*. Vol. 2, *A Feminist Commentary*, edited by Elisabeth Schüssler Fiorenza, Ann Brock, and Shelly Matthews, 313–24. New York: Crossroad.

Engels, Frederick. 2001. *The Origin of the Family, Private Property and the State*. Translated by Ernest Untermann. Honolulu: University Press of the Pacific.

Gombis, Timothy G. 2004. "Ephesians 2 as a Narrative of Divine Warfare." *JSNT* 26, no. 4:403–18.

Hartsock, Nancy. 1983. *Money, Sex, and Power: Toward a Feminist Historical Materialism*. Boston: Northeastern University Press.

Lindemann, Andreas. 1975. *Die Aufhebung der Zeit*. Gutersloh: Gerd Mohn.

MacDonald, Margaret. 1988. *The Pauline Churches: A Socio-historical Study of Institutionalization in the Pauline and Deutero-Pauline Writings*. Cambridge: Cambridge University Press.

Merz, Annette. 2000. "Why Did the Pure Bride of Christ (2 Cor. 11.2) Become a Wedded Wife (Eph. 5:22-33)?" *JSNT* 79:131–47.

Osiek, Carolyn. 2002. "The Bride of Christ (5:22-23): A Problematic Wedding." *BTB* 32:29–39.

Peretti, Frank. 1986. *This Present Darkness*. Wheaton, IL: Crossway.

———. 1989. *Piercing the Darkness*. Wheaton, IL: Crossway.

Perkins, Pheme. 1997. *Ephesians*. ANTC. Nashville: Abingdon.

Ruether, Rosemary Radford. 2011. "Rejection of Dualism." In *Creating Women's Theology: A Movement Engaging Process Thought*, edited by Monica Coleman, Nancy Howell, and Helene Russell, 60–70. Eugene, OR: Pickwick.

Russell, Letty. 1984. *Imitators of God: A Study Book on Ephesians*. New York: General Board of Global Ministries, United Methodist Church.

Sampley, J. Paul. 1974. *"And the Two Shall Become One Flesh": A Study of Traditions in Ephesians 5:21-33*. London: Cambridge University Press.

Schüssler Fiorenza, Elisabeth. 1987. *Women, Work and Poverty*. Concilium: Religion in the Eighties. Edinburgh: T&T Clark.

———. 1997. "The Praxis of Co-Equal Discipleship." In *Paul and Empire: Religion and Power in Roman Imperial Society*, edited by Richard A. Horsley, 224–41. Harrisburg, PA: Trinity Press International.

Terrell, JoAnne Marie. 1998. *Power in the Blood? The Cross in the African American Experience*. Maryknoll, NY: Orbis.

Weaver, J. Denny. 2009. "Forgiveness and (Non)violence: The Atonement Connections." *Mennonite Quarterly Review* 83, no. 2:319–47.

PHILIPPIANS

Julia Lambert Fogg

Introduction

Paul's letter to the "saints in Christ Jesus who are in Philippi" (1:1, translations are the author's, unless otherwise indicated) is not a systematic treatise on theology, but rather a work of theological and pastoral reflection. The letter interprets the Philippians' friendship with Paul and one another as their participation in and partnership with Christ. Paul calls this embodied participation of shared community practices *koinōnia*. Through this *koinōnia* they are experiencing salvation (2:13). Paul shows the believers at Philippi that, together with himself and Timothy (1:1), they are practicing being Christ to each other in their shared ministry. In this way, they are "working out [their own] salvation" (2:12). Paul's rhetorical strategy for community building (literally a kind of bodybuilding to embody Christ), reveals Paul's understanding of salvation as corporate participation in the representative and resurrected body of Christ.

Paul writes to the Philippians from prison (1:13). But what city? We don't know much more about Paul's imprisonment than that he was more than a few days travel from Philippi (2:26-8), in a city with imperial guard (4:22), and that he had been away long enough for multiple trips and correspondence to take place (2:25-30) and for Paul's preaching to affect the local community (1:13-17). In the ancient world, prisons were spare holding tanks at best, and dungeons at worst. Paul would have had to use his own resources to eat, to write, or to bribe the guard for any favors. Paul's physical discomfort and suffering in prison are magnified by those who ridicule him on the outside (1:15-16), and by the uncertain outcome of his imprisonment (2:23). Timothy assisted Paul through this suffering (1:1; 2:19), and Paul expected to be released from prison "soon" (2:23) to see the Philippians again (2:24). Some scholars have proposed to identify the city of Paul's imprisonment, following one or another externally reconstructed chronologies that synthesize Paul's letters with matching events or geographical movements in Acts. This work yields three main hypotheses.

Philippians was written from Rome, accounting for multiple trips (2:19-30) and references to the imperial guard (1:13) and Caesar's household (4:22). Ephesus also fits these criteria. Another possibility is Caesarea. Such identifications based on Acts are problematic, however, because Acts, like Paul, has its own rhetorical strategy for choosing particular geographical locations to tell Paul's story, and because Acts leaves out so much of what Paul reports firsthand. For those reasons, other scholars are reluctant to specify either a city of origin or a date (ranging from the 50s to early 60s), and that is the approach taken here.

Philippians contains a pre-Pauline liturgical tradition in 2:5-11, often called the "Christ hymn." Paul may borrow this tradition because it illustrates Christ's humble and obedient character (2:8) and specifically refers to Christ's attitude—his "mind-set" and the way he "thinks" (2:6). Rather than seizing equality with God, he embodies a humble disposition and assumes the form of a servant or "slave" (2:7). Christ's character and way of thinking anchor Paul's exhortation to the Philippians to "think like Christ" and act out of Christ's dispositions in 2:5. Most scholars agree in the identification of this pre-Pauline liturgical piece, but disagree on how to interpret another seam, a change in tone or logic, at 3:1-2. Although this shift suggests an interruption in the text, it actually works rhetorically to highlight the series of exemplars in chapter 2 (Christ, Paul, Timothy, and Epaphroditus) in contrast with the anonymous and negative examples of missionaries Paul calls "dogs" in 3:2.

Philippians stands out among Paul's letters for its joyful tone (e.g., 1:18, 4:1-4) and its effusive affirmation of friendship. Studies of ancient friendship language and themes have demonstrated the coherence of the letter and illuminated Paul's unique relationship to the Philippians. Such friendship themes include partnership in ministry (1:5; 1:7; 1:25; 2:22; 4:2-3), a common attitude and mind (1:27; 2:2-5; 3:15; 4:2), a shared struggle (1:27; 4:14), shared love and joy (1:7, 16; 2:2, 17-18), exchange of help and goods (2:19, 25-30; 4:10, 15-18), the same enemies (1:27-28; 3:2-4), and a shared offering to God (2:17-18; 4:15-20). Other studies focus on the form of ancient friendship letters, which begin with the sender expressing longing for the recipient (1:3-11), updating them on the sender's affairs (1:12-26; 2:19—4:1), expressing an interest in the recipient's affairs (1:26; 2:19), and an exhortation to continue the mutual friendship (1:27—2:18; 3:2—4:1). To this epistolary form, Paul adds a celebration of God's work in their friendship, their *koinōnia*. The theme of mutuality additionally shapes the rhetorical structure of Paul's letter. As Paul shifts between news about himself and interest in the Philippians' affairs, he is interpreting their mutual longing, shared thinking, prayer, and service to one another as an imitation of Christ's character. In this way, Paul's Letter to the Philippians is a theological demonstration of how to embody Christ's mind in the community body. And, as they literally conform their friendship to the shape of Christ, they partake in God's saving work among them.

Paul's Letter to the Philippians does not appear very often in discussions of Paul's theology. This is partly because Paul does not expound here on traditional systematic topics (redemption, salvation, creation, sin), and partly because of the way contemporary discussions have defined theology. If theology is the logical presentation of key concepts in a fully developed system of thought, then Philippians is not theological. But if theology is a sustained reflection on and an articulation of the divine-human relationship, then Paul is one of the most profound theologians, and this letter is deeply significant for Christians struggling to faithfully understand what it means to live in an increasingly complex, interconnected, and technologically dependent world.

Philippians 1:1-11: Sharing in Thanksgiving with Joy

■ THE TEXT IN ITS ANCIENT CONTEXT

Paul begins the Letter to the Philippians with a traditional but lengthy greeting (1:1-2), followed by an effusive thanksgiving (1:3-8) that leads into a pastoral prayer (1:9-11). Paul recognizes his cosender, Timothy, as well as the "holy" believers in Philippi and the leaders among them. Paul does not yet name Epaphroditus, the Philippians' own minister who has carried this letter from Paul (2:25, 4:18) and now reads the letter aloud to the gathered assembly in Philippi.

The effect of such a generous epistolary opening is to affirm Paul's long relationship with the Philippians in the past (1:5), their mutual support in the present (1:7), and God's ongoing work in them for the future (1:6). Paul highlights the Philippians' sharing in his practice of prayer and his work in the gospel through their support of his ministry (1:7), and he uses the language of Greek friendship between two equals, and then extends this friendship to the entire community and to Christ; it is "Christ's love" that Paul has for the Philippians (1:8).

In addition to the Greek topos of friendship, Paul also draws on the ancient understanding of virtue ethics, that the mind controls the passions and the actions of the body. "It is right," then, for Paul to think about the Philippians with thanksgiving, and to "long for" them with the "passion of Christ" (1:8) since they, too, share his "heart" for them (1:7). Following these affirmations of shared affection, Paul will show how his mind shapes the actions he takes in friendship with Christ, and with the Philippians. One action is sending this letter with Epaphroditus to encourage them. Paul's words remind them that "the one who began a good work among you" will also bring that work to completion (1:6). When Epaphroditus arrives in Philippi and reads the letter aloud, Paul's words in 1:9-11 put the rhetorical aim of the letter into action: "that your love abound more and more in all knowledge" (author's translation), to discern the things that matter most in Christ (1:9-10). Paul will next exemplify this discernment of love abounding in his active friendship (*koinōnia*) with the Philippians.

Finally, Paul's reflection on and interpretation of *koinōnia* functions to counteract his physical and mental suffering in prison. The richness of positive, emotional language communicates Paul's confidence in God, to whom he gives thanks, and also his confidence in the Philippians, that they are standing firm, sharing with Paul in his suffering (1:7; 4:10-11), as Paul shares Christ's suffering (1:13).

■ THE TEXT IN THE INTERPRETIVE TRADITION

Many interpretations of Phil. 1:1-11 have focused on the development of early Christian governance, the role of "overseers" and "deacons" (1:1 NIV) in Paul's time. Ecclesiastical and denominational differences have influenced the variety of translations of this phrase: "bishops and deacons" appears in translations as varied as that of John Wycliffe, the Geneva Bible, the Douay-Rheims translation, and the NRSV; meanwhile, the Contemporary English Version renders the phrase "church officials and officers." The Greek *episkopoi*, literally "overseers," traveled into Latin (*episcopus*), Spanish (*obispo*), and English (*bishop*).

Other recent interpretations have questioned the unity of the letter, suggesting that Paul wrote multiple letters to the Philippians, portions of which have been combined into the existing canonical letter. This argument partly rests on the observation that Paul doesn't "thank" the Philippians for the gift they sent, but only briefly mentions the gift at the end of the letter (4:16-17) (Peterman 1991).

▮ THE TEXT IN CONTEMPORARY DISCUSSION

Paul's Letter to the Philippians is known in churches today as the "joyful letter." From the first verses of thanksgiving, where he sets out the themes of "love" (1:7-9), "grace" (1:7), and "joy" (1:4), the language is bright and effusive. Paul affirms their friendship by recounting instances of shared reciprocity (1:5, 7). Recent scholarship has given special attention to the rhetorical function of friendship language here. As contemporary churches search for ways to be community in a culturally and politically diverse, and at times divisive, global context, Paul's letter to this most beloved, faithful, and unique church appears especially pertinent. Faith communities may find in Philippians a way forward through mutuality and humility in Christ (1:1). As individual members draw closer to each other by sharing each other's suffering and joy, progress and setbacks, loss and abundance, the letter suggests, they draw closer to Christ.

Philippians 1:12-26: Embodying the Mind of Christ: Paul's Example

▮ THE TEXT IN ITS ANCIENT CONTEXT

Paul not only celebrates the Philippians' friendship in chapter 1 but also aims to anchor that friendship in Christ's example of humility and obedience in chapter 2. In 1:12-26, Paul prepares the Philippians to see Christ's perfect mind by demonstrating how he has shown forth Christ's mind in prison.

First, Paul identifies the Christlike motivation that follows from a Christlike mind-set. Those who think like Christ are Paul's "friends" who love Christ and preach the gospel out of love (1:16). Then, typical of friendship speech, Paul contrasts these friends with "enemies" who are competing with Paul and preach the gospel out of "envy and rivalry" (1:15 NRSV). This rhetorical move is similar to the use of polarizing language of friends and enemies in the Fourth Gospel and James. Each instance of friend and enemy language functions to unite "us" over against "them." Thus Paul reinforces the common practices and mind-set that he shares with the Philippians, his friends.

Second, it is critical to note that Paul, most known for his polemical stances and ad hominem arguments, does not condemn the enemies who seek to hurt him. Instead of matching their boastful words or competitive motivations, Paul demonstrates a humility of mind and willingly bears their "intentions to increase my suffering" (1:17). "So what?" asks Paul (1:18 NRSV reads "what does it matter?"). He will endure "false motives or true" as long as Christ is preached (1:18 NRSV). Then Paul grounds his humility in joy—celebrating the Philippians' humility in continuing to stand with

Paul. Putting the mind of Christ into action, Paul can also claim the powerful presence, or "supply" (NRSV reads "help") of "the Spirit of Jesus Christ" (1:19).

Next, Paul shifts from the friendship categories of "friends and enemies" to what many contemporary scholars have read as an existential choice. But this description misses the way Paul continues his rhetorical point: that the discerning, Christlike mind (2:5) operates with humility. Paul presents his impending court sentencing as a rhetorical choice: "to live or to die" (1:21-23). Then he shows the Philippians how to think like Christ when they are discerning such choices. Ultimately, in Paul's example, the criterion for discerning the best choice is not "what is best for me" (after all, both choices offer a benefit to Paul, for "to live is Christ and to die is gain," 1:21), or "what I most desire" (to be released and "be with Christ," 1:23), but "what is best for you all" (1:24). Paul puts his friends first. To think like Christ is to look to the concerns of the other. Thus the Christian process of discernment, according to Paul, is not about one's own "desires," but rather about what one's friends need most in Christ. Indeed, when Paul chooses "to remain and continue in the flesh" for the Philippians, Christ is glorified (1:26).

▌THE TEXT IN THE INTERPRETIVE TRADITION

One of the difficult questions in the long interpretive history of Philippians has been where Paul was imprisoned. This letter does not seem to fit any of the Acts chronology. Nor do the hints about the "praetorian guard" (1:13) or Caesar's household (4:22) help us to pinpoint Paul's location.

Another question arises because Paul seems overly optimistic in 1:12-26. He is in prison and unsure of the outcome (2:23), but believes Christ is "revealed in my chains" (1:13). He is hungry, thirsty, and suffering (4:11-12), yet he affirms that his situation is furthering the "progress of the gospel" (1:12). Yet, understood pastorally, Paul's epistolary optimism functions to reassure the Philippians and to encourage those who stand in solidarity with him through their financial and emotional support.

In the end, Philippians steps free of such historical questions aimed at understanding Paul's imprisonment. The letter has, again and again, lent itself more readily as a model for the letters of prisoners of faith who follow in Paul's footsteps. Letters from other martyrs and prisoners of faith have reflected theologically on suffering (Dietrich Bonhoeffer, imprisoned Quakers, Stephen Biko) and on injustice (Martin Luther King Jr., Oscar Romero), and have striven to comfort their friends as Paul also does in 1:12-13 and 1:24-26, 30. But Philippians is also a *public* letter from prison. And, like Dietrich Bonhoeffer's *Letters and Papers from Prison* and Martin Luther King's "Letter from a Birmingham Jail," Paul's letter "to all the saints in Christ who are in Philippi" is rhetorically constructed to model Christ's way of thinking and acting.

▌THE TEXT IN CONTEMPORARY DISCUSSION

In the end, Paul dismisses the power of his jailors and presumes that the choice of a life-or-death sentence is his—not because he necessarily thinks he is in control, but precisely to exemplify how one should regard one's situation, whether one is in control or not. Thus the rhetorical construction of a life-or-death choice is not a literal consideration of suicide, but a way to model Christ's humble regard for others. Paul humbles his own desire to be with Christ now (1:23) in order to put the Philippians' needs first (1:24), thus demonstrating how they, too, may embody Christ's way of thinking in the midst of affliction, and in solidarity with others who suffer.

To observe Paul's interpretation of his prison situation does not address the state of prison systems today. Paul's friends had access to him; he wrote letters, socialized with the civil servants, received guests and gifts. Today, prison inmates suffer prolonged stays in solitary confinement without visitors. Maximum-security prisons are designed to minimize human contact. In such a situation, there is little possibility of articulating, let alone sharing, one's suffering, despair, or mental deterioration. For Paul, human relationships modeled on Christ's example and participation in one another's lives are part of a saving process. Prison activists today are asking if isolating prisoners from human contact doesn't disconnect them from restorative social communion and even the possibility of healing the whole community, inside and outside of the cell.

Philippians 1:27—2:18: Embodying the Mind of Christ: Christ's Example

▮ THE TEXT IN ITS ANCIENT CONTEXT

As Rome transitioned from a city-state to a world empire in the first century BCE, Roman soldiers colonized Philippi and citizenship became an important social distinction among residents. Some had the "green card" of belonging, either Roman citizenship or, at least, citizenship within the city. But other residents were not so privileged. The "saints in Philippi" (1:1) whom Paul addresses did not necessarily share the same social or political status with one another. To correct this imbalance, Paul levels the playing field. He challenges the Philippians' investment in their own sociopolitical status. Instead of competing for higher social and political recognition by Roman officials, they are to "be worthy citizens" (*politeuesthe*) of Christ (1:27). The Greek verb *politeuesthe* is related to our language of "politics" and, through Latin, the language of "civic" responsibility and therefore "citizenship." With this language, Paul reorients the Philippians' personal and community identity: they are not vying to be citizens of the empire on earth, but are "striving side by side with one mind for the faith of the gospel" (1:27) to be citizens of Christ in heaven (3:20). This "heavenly citizenship" defines their humble *koinōnia* through the practices of servant friendship, rather than political favors for social advancement. Thus Paul delivers the Philippians from the constant race for honorary titles and beneficial political affiliations. He anchors their social and political identity in christological friendship "with one another" and with Christ (1:27—2:4). Now, because of their *koinōnia* with Christ, the Philippians' citizenship credentials are even greater than the emperor's (2:10).

To further impress on the Philippians that Christ's character is one of humility that leads to emptying oneself of status, not seizing it, Paul introduces a liturgical hymn (2:5-11). Perhaps the assembly sang together before or after the reading of Paul's letter, thus connecting their worship of Christ to their ethical practice of Christ's humility and emphasizing the embodied experience of sharing Christ.

Paul closes the section with an expanded exhortation (2:12-18) to obedience (2:12) and reminds the Philippians that God is the one working in them (2:13, 1:28) to bring them to completion (1:6).

With this exhortation comes a warning from the exodus. The Philippians are not to "murmur and argue" (2:14) like God's people did in the wilderness. But when they strive to be "worthy citizens" (1:27), and to share Christ's sufferings (1:29), they will also share in Christ's cosmic glory (as Lord, 2:10-11) and "shine like stars" (2:15). Their honor thus comes from Christ's cosmic lordship, not their individual status in the Roman Empire.

◼ THE TEXT IN THE INTERPRETIVE TRADITION

Catholics and Protestants have often debated Paul's stance on "faith and works." Catholic readings of Philippians therefore emphasize 2:12, where Paul writes, "work out your faith," while Protestant theologians emphasize verse 13, "for God is at work in you." For Paul, both theological points are true at the same time: Empowered by divine grace, the faithful must live out their faith by actively participating in divine grace.

Scholars have long perceived in 2:6-11 a Christ hymn, sometimes designated by the Latin phrase *carmen Christi* (Martin). Extracted from the letter, the hymn seems to point to a more ancient and traditional concept, perhaps Hellenistic, of a heavenly being who comes to earth and then returns to heaven. Scholars have continued to look for the social setting—*Sitz im Leben*—of this pre-Pauline Christology. The hymn also offers a glimpse into the liturgical life of the early church. Further examination suggests that Paul has emended the preexisting hymn in verse 8, by adding "until death on a cross." The reason for this emendation becomes clear in the letter's current form, when Paul presents Epaphroditus as imitating Christ's obedience "until death" (2:30). Additionally, Paul has recontextualized the hymn to illustrate Christ's way of thinking: "Have this mind among you" (2:5). Now it is Christ's way of thinking that enacts his humility and obedience (2:6-8), receives honorary titles from God (2:10), homage from earth (2:11), and ultimately results in God's glory (2:11). Thus Paul uses the hymn to connect Christ's character and behavior with Christ's "mind."

Philippians 2:6-11 has been a critical text for the development of the theology of *kenōsis*, or self-emptying, highlighted in verse 7. In kenotic theology, Christ empties himself of all divinity, taking on the lowest form of existence by becoming human, and then by taking the lowest human form in the ancient social hierarchy, a slave. Thus the divine's servant nature effects salvation, and therefore Christ's followers are to imitate this self-emptying, servant nature as they participate in God's saving work.

◼ THE TEXT IN CONTEMPORARY DISCUSSION

Today kenotic theology offers a helpful contrast to consumerist approaches to life. Rather than amassing as much as possible, or buying into the consumer's arms race for more and better, kenotic theology, which is constantly "pouring out" rather than "taking in," offers an alternative for Christians in the world. It emphasizes a way of "being" over "having." Read this way, the Christ hymn is perhaps as countercultural today as it was in the first-century Roman Empire. Whereas Paul's first-century audience heard his challenge to relinquish human status in order to share in Christ's glorified servanthood, today's readers may hear a challenge to relinquish consumption and ownership of more "stuff" in order to share and preserve our increasingly limited resources.

Hearing the exhortation to share in the divine *kenōsis* and Paul's political discourse about citizenship may challenge churches today to reflect on the broken US immigration system. Those who wish to immigrate legally wait decades for permission. Others fleeing economic desperation arrive only to live in fear of being separated from their US-born children. Undocumented immigrants are often denied legal rights because of their limbo status—they don't belong here or there. And children who arrived at an early age grow up thinking they are "American" only to discover they don't have access to the same "firsts" as other teens—first job, first car, first generation to go to college. Paul is not writing political policy, but advising a church how to live in a state that values some residents over others. In Philippi, Paul levels the playing field—you are all citizens of Christ. Churches today must reflect on Paul's pastoral approach to holding a community of differently documented members together as one body of Christ.

Philippians 2:19—4:1: Examples of Embodying the Mind of Christ

▌ THE TEXT IN ITS ANCIENT CONTEXT

In the ancient Mediterranean world, letters were not the primary source of communication. Personal visits were. Because the ancients preferred to network and conduct business in person, they developed a philosophical understanding of the letter as the author's presence (M. Mitchell, 650; Malherbe 1988). Paul thus chooses and sends first Epaphroditus (carrying this letter, 2:25-30), and then Timothy (2:19-24), to be his ambassadors—his physical voice and presence in Philippi.

But Paul's recommendation of Timothy and Epaphroditus in 2:19-30 functions in another critical way: they exemplify Christ's pattern of living in the flesh. Ancient philosophers often used the concept of a mirror to focus their students' gaze on the character after which they would pattern themselves (Johnson 1988). Instead of looking at their own image in the mirror, students would focus on their teacher as a mirror and shape themselves according to the lived pattern their teacher embodied. For Paul, Christ is this mirror and pattern for how he and the Philippians should think and reason, with humility and obedience, before God. But the Philippians cannot "see" Christ in action. So Paul utilizes the philosopher-teacher's refrain of "imitate me" (3:17; 4:9) and focuses the Philippians' gaze on how he embodies Christ's pattern. Now that he is in prison, Paul points to Epaphroditus and Timothy, who will provide the Philippians additional mirrors (2:19-30).

Timothy embodies Christ by being "genuinely concerned for your [the Philippians'] welfare." Paul contrasts Timothy's selflessness with the others who "are seeking their own interests, not those of Jesus Christ" (2:20-21 NRSV). Simply by sending Timothy, Paul too demonstrates his humble concern for the Philippians, who are anxious about Paul's welfare. Epaphroditus is the Philippians' ambassador to Paul. When he falls ill on the journey, Paul likens him to Christ, offering himself "until death" in service to Paul and the Philippians. In this way, Epaphroditus, too, exemplifies the humility of "putting others' concerns first" (2:19-21). Now, when the Philippians "welcome [Epaphroditus] then in the Lord with all joy, and honor such people" (2:29 NRSV), they are embracing Christ in their midst.

Paul reinforces his point in 3:1-4. Once students have seen how their teacher embodies Christ, they, too, can discern the un-Christlike patterns in other teachers. Thus Paul's abrupt criticism of competing teachers in 3:2 (the "dogs"), like his own mock boasting in 3:4-6, negatively illustrates Christ's pattern of humility. Scholars have tried to reconstruct the identity of these teachers, but this is not necessary to understanding Paul's rhetorical point (Kurz).

Next, Paul demonstrates how embodying the mind of Christ leads to fellowship, or *koinōnia*, with Christ. He begins with his own example in 3:4-11. Like Christ (2:6a), Paul acknowledges that he could boast in his own "human form" and origin, "circumcised on the eighth day, of the people of Israel, of the tribe of Benjamin" (3:5) and could rightfully claim superior status over others (3:6). But, also like Christ, Paul refuses to seize hold of this status (2:6b-8; 3:7-8). By rejecting such "confidence in the flesh," Paul gains something far greater: fellowship with Christ. When Paul shares Christ's "sufferings" and his obedience in death (3:10), he is participating in Christ's faithfulness and righteousness (3:9) and hopes to know "the power of his resurrection" (3:10).

Finally, Paul turns to the Philippians in 3:15 and exhorts them to embody the mind of Christ with him. This is not a finished process, but a shared striving "toward the goal for the prize of the heavenly call of God in Christ Jesus" (3:14). God is at work in the community as they "join in imitating Paul, and observe all of those who live according to" Christ's example in Paul, Epaphroditus, and Timothy. In this way, the community of Christ is "conformed to the body of his glory" (3:21 NRSV).

▮ THE TEXT IN THE INTERPRETIVE TRADITION

For much of the modern interpretive history, Phil. 2:19—3:1 was understood as a "travel narrative," a common way for friends to tell their listeners where they have been and where they are going. Taking the passage at face value, scholars have worked to interpret it in relation to that other narrative of Paul's travels, Acts, removing the passage from its rhetorical context in this letter and comparing it to information gleaned from Acts regarding where Paul was imprisoned, for how long, and in what situation.

There is a sharp rhetorical break in 3:2, and on the premises of source-critical method many scholars posit that the travel narrative was inserted beside the exhortative material that begins in 3:2 (e.g., O'Brien, 352). Read this way, the letter seems to be, at worst, disparate pieces of a conversation stitched together from multiple letters, some time after Paul wrote them, and at best, an incongruent argument on the part of Paul himself, perhaps due to the arrival of another letter from Philippi, causing Paul to change his tone of voice here to address the problem of false teachers he calls "the dogs."

The latter possibility further led scholars such as Ronald Hock to argue that "the dogs" and the "circumcision" refer to competing missionaries like those who evangelized the Galatian churches. These "circumcision parties" may have wished to convert the Philippians to Judaism, or to a more strict form of Torah observance. While this interpretation does explain Paul's enumeration *and rejection* of his Jewish credentials, according to Torah, in favor of "knowing Christ" (3:8), it loses sight of the rhetorical context and tone of the letter as a whole. That is, rather than boasting in his own credentials in 3:4-6, Paul is again demonstrating the humility that shapes how one "regards," "considers," and "thinks" according to Christ's humility and pattern of "thinking" (2:5), also illustrated by Timothy and Epaphroditus in chapter 2 (see above).

Another important question for Paul's interpreters arises in 3:9. Does the Greek phrase *pistis Christou* mean that Christ is the object of faith (i.e., the Philippians' *faith in Christ*), or the subject of faith (*Christ's faithfulness* to God)? Most translators have favored the objective translation, putting the emphasis on human belief in Christ. This leads to a Christianity defined by individual assent that privileges personal belief. But Philippians concentrates not on what the community believes, but on how they live out Christ's example. In 3:8, immediately preceding the problematic phrase, Paul uses a parallel genitive construction that is also ambiguous. The phrase *gnōsis Christou Iēsou* could be translated "knowing Christ" (objective) or "Christ's way of knowing" (subjective). In this case, *both* phrases fit Paul's meaning. Paul wants the Philippians to develop Christ's mind—Christ's way of knowing, thinking, discerning. But Paul is also describing a relational way of "knowing Christ" by participating in Christ's humility, suffering, and obedience to God in relation to community. The interpretive question is not easily solved, since decades of Christian theology have depended on one translation or the other. Still, Paul is perhaps best read as a proponent of "both/and." (For a more extensive argument advocating the subjective reading, see Hays; Stegman.)

◼ THE TEXT IN CONTEMPORARY DISCUSSION

To contemporary Christian communities, both local churches and national denominations, that are fragmenting over discussions of sexual identity, arguing about how to reach the next generation, and stalemating over environmental policies, Philippians may be read to address the toll that individualism is taking on the very idea of community. To this situation, Paul holds up the ideal of a dynamic, shared, saving body. Christian community is not about worshiping in a church on Sunday, simply believing in Christ, or even converting one's neighbors. For Paul, healthy Christian community cultivates humility and obedience to God so that members are transformed in relationship with one another and conformed to Christ.

Philippians also challenges contemporary discussions in some Christian churches about salvation. Does salvation begin the moment one accepts Jesus Christ as Lord and Savior? Is salvation a lived, present reality, or something realized only in the future? Do we participate in our salvation, and if so, how? What is the role of the individual, the community, creation? For Paul, salvation is not an end or a beginning: it is a complex, dynamic, corporate relationship—the process of being conformed to Christ through fellowship with others. Such complexity makes today's question, what would Jesus do? seem facile. Asking about Jesus' actions only in the moment when one is making a specific decision misses a central piece of Paul's argument in Philippians: character. In Philippians, following Christ is not a series of actions, but an immersion in Christ's character, attitudes, and experiences. In salvation, the question is not, what would Jesus *do*? but rather, *how* would Jesus do it?

Philippians 4:2-23: Embodying the Mind of Christ in Life and Worship

◼ THE TEXT IN ITS ANCIENT CONTEXT

Philippians 4:2-9 contains Paul's final exhortations to the community in Philippi. He begins by publicly exhorting two high-profile women by name (4:2). In their disagreement, they are not exhibiting the humility and shared mind of Christ that Paul has just exemplified (3:15-17). Paul does not take sides in their disagreement, which may be disrupting the community. Instead, Paul recognizes that while disagreements occur among the saints, with Christ's humility, Euodia and Syntyche should seek God's revealed solution rather than victory in the argument. Syntyche and Euodia are to "imitate Paul" and those with Paul (3:17) so that their behavior unites rather than divides, exemplifying the mind of Christ.

In 4:10-20, Paul finally includes the Philippians themselves as examples of Christ's mind for their sharing a gift with Paul in his suffering (4:10). Paul refers to a gift that Epaphroditus carried from the Philippians, perhaps financial aid, clothes, books, or a blanket Paul might need in prison. In the logic of the ancient system of patronage, *do ut des* ("I give in order that you will give"), there is no "free" gift (Stowers 1994, 110, 115). But each exchange between people created a relationship of dependency. When Paul accepts the Philippians' gift, he is now in debt to them. Paul acknowledges that the gift was of great benefit, but refuses to be in their debt. Such a social debt would restrict Paul's claim to be "self-sufficient" (4:11) and to depend only on God (4:13). So Paul deflects the benefit of the gift from himself and attributes the benefit to the Philippians. That is, through their gift they share in his "affliction" (4:14). And by "giving and receiving" with him (4:15-16), they practice the ethics of *koinōnia*, or community fellowship, that leads to salvation in Christ.

Some scholars have argued that Philippians is a letter of "thankless thanks" (Peterman 1991; 1997). Others have argued that Paul is quite conscious of the social conventions of thanksgiving, and that he seems to be walking a fine line between affirming the Philippians' gift and incurring the social debt of reciprocity that comes with the gift (White). The position taken here is that Paul reinterprets the Philippians' gift as a practice of *koinōnia* or community fellowship in Christ (Fogg). He does this by quickly moving through three different characterizations of the gift. First, Paul begins with friendship language, which invokes the ancient conventions of reciprocity (4:15-16). Next, instead of reciprocating with a material gift in return, or thanking them in a conventional way and thereby acknowledging that he has incurred a debt, Paul interprets the Philippians' gift as a contribution to their heavenly account with God (4:17). This introduces financial banking language, "your account" (v. 17), and, "I have been paid in full . . ." (v. 18), from which Paul immediately moves to the language of worship, "now that I have received from Epaphroditus the gift you sent, a fragrant offering" (v. 18). Finally, having received the offering, Paul takes up the role of priest and presents the "sacrifice" to God (v. 18). In this way, Paul transforms the Philippians' financial gift *to him* into "a sacrifice acceptable and pleasing *to God*" (4:18). It is therefore not the Philippians' material gift that Paul celebrates, but rather the relationship with him that their material gift signifies. In other words, their communion with Paul and with each other becomes their corporate offering and worship of God. So Paul has written, "I am being poured out as a libation on the offering of your faith" (2:17-18). The result of this communion is shared joy in Christ (2:18; 3:1; 4:4) and glory to God (4:20).

▍THE TEXT IN THE INTERPRETIVE TRADITION

Paul names only three members of the Philippian community: one man, Epaphroditus (2:25), and two women, Euodia and Syntyche (4:2). (He does, intriguingly, leave a fourth member unnamed in 4:3.) Paul recommends Epaphroditus, "my brother and coworker and fellow soldier, your messenger and minister to my need" (2:25). Then he recommends the women "who have struggled beside me in the work of the gospel" and "whose names are in the book of life" (4:3). What roles did these women have in Philippi? Are they founders of the church? Are they significant patrons of Paul's ministry? Are they local teachers whose divided leadership in the community might disrupt unity, as occurred in the Corinthian churches? Whatever their role, Euodia and Syntyche are important enough in their church community to require Paul's attention and, apparently, to lead the church by example to embody Christ's mind together.

■ THE TEXT IN CONTEMPORARY DISCUSSION

Philippians is consciously liturgical. Paul gives thanks to God (1:3-8), prays (1:9-11), quotes a hymn (2:6-11), exhorts the community, and closes with an offering to God (4:10-20). Paul conducts himself as a priest, officiating for the Philippians at God's altar (2:17; 4:18-19). This liturgical work both describes the Philippians' service to God and enacts their shared life in Christ. Such liturgical rhythms remind today's readers that ancient letters were read aloud in early church gatherings. What letters edify our communities today? How is contemporary worship woven into our common life? And where are congregations living out their shared Christology? In attempting to answer to these questions, emergent church communities may have much to offer.

The interdependence of Paul's vision for the body of Christ is especially challenging for today's church. On the one hand, our global society understands what it means to be deeply dependent on one another economically and to be intimately entwined electronically in the social marketplace. Yet on the other hand, we cling fiercely to our independence and self-determination. As we have seen above, Paul's own theological reflection on practice suggests a both/and approach that we might consider as we wrestle with this existential situation.

Finally, living Christ's pattern of humility and obedience is a community effort, not an individual one. One's relationship with God is "worked out" (2:12) precisely in the ways one embodies Christ to fellow believers, and to those outside the community. For Paul, the theologically weighted word *salvation* means being in fellowship with Christ through one's fellowship with members of Christ's body. As believers practice Christ's humility and obedience in their shared suffering, joys, afflictions, and trials, as well as their shared practices of friendship and proclamation of the gospel, they *together* participate in God's salvation. This salvation in which they participate is the very "work" that God is bringing to completion (1:6; 2:13) in the Philippians as they live out Christ's pattern of social and relational humility and obedience now. Paul's assertion that their salvation is already coming to completion is both their hope and their witness in the world (1:28; 3:17-21), until they "shine like stars" in the cosmos (2:15).

Works Cited

Alexander, Loveday. 1989. "Hellenistic Letter-Forms and the Structure of Philippians." *JSNT* 37:87–101.

Cassidy, Richard J. 2001. *Paul in Chains: Roman Imprisonment and the Letters of Saint Paul*. New York: Crossroad.

Croy, N. Clayton. 2003. "'To Die Is Gain' (Philippians 1:19-26): Does Paul Contemplate Suicide?" *JBL* 122, no. 3 (September 1): 517–31.

Fee, Gordon D. 1994. *God's Empowering Presence: The Holy Spirit in the Letters of Paul*. Peabody, MA: Hendrickson.

———. 1995. *Paul's Letter to the Philippians*. NICNT. Grand Rapids: Eerdmans.

Fitzgerald, John T. 1996. *Friendship, Flattery, and Frankness of Speech: Studies on Friendship in the New Testament World*. Leiden: Brill.

Fogg, Julia Lambert. 2006. "Koinonia Is Soteria: Paul's Theological Reading of Practices in His Letter to the Philippians." PhD diss., Emory University.

Fowl, Stephen. 1990. *The Story of Christ in the Ethics of Paul: An Analysis of the Function of the Hymnic Material in the Pauline Corpus*. Sheffield: JSOT Press.

Gorman, Michael J. 2009. *Inhabiting the Cruciform God: Kenosis, Justification, and Theosis in Paul's Narrative Soteriology*. Grand Rapids: Eerdmans.

Hays, Richard B. 2002. *The Faith of Jesus Christ: The Narrative Substructure of Galatians 3:1–4:11*. 2nd ed. Grand Rapids: Eerdmans.

Hock, Ronald F. 1980. *The Social Context of Paul's Ministry: Tentmaking and Apostleship*. Philadelphia: Fortress Press.

Hooker, Morna D. 2000. "The Letter to the Philippians." In *The New Interpreter's Bible*. Vol. 11, *2 Corinthians–Philemon*, edited by Leander E. Keck, 469–549. Nashville: Abingdon.

Johnson, Luke Timothy. 1986. *The Writings of the New Testament: An Interpretation*. Philadelphia: Fortress Press.

———. 1988. "The Mirror of Remembrance (James 1:22-25)." *CBQ* 50:632–45.

———. 1993. "The Social Dimensions of Soteria in Luke-Acts and Paul." *SBLSP* 32:520–36.

Karris, Robert. 2000. *Prayer and the New Testament*. New York: Crossroad.

Kurz, William. 1985. "Kenotic Imitation of Paul and of Christ in Phil 2 and 3." In *Discipleship in the New Testament*, edited by Fernando Segovia, 103–26. Philadelphia: Fortress Press.

Malherbe, Abraham J. 1987. *Paul and the Thessalonians: The Philosophic Tradition of Pastoral Care*. Philadelphia: Fortress Press.

———. 1988. *Ancient Epistolary Theorists*. Atlanta: Scholars Press.

———. 1996. "Paul's Self-Sufficiency (Philippians 4.11)." In *Friendship, Flattery, and Frankness of Speech*, edited by John T. Fitzgerald, 125–39. Leiden: Brill.

Martin, Ralph P. 1997. *A Hymn of Christ: Philippians 2.5-11 in Recent Interpretation and the Setting of Early Christian Worship*. Downers Grove, IL: InterVarsity Press.

Martin, Ralph P., and Brian J. Dodd. 1998. *Where Christology Began: Essays on Philippians 2*. Louisville: Westminster John Knox.

Meggitt, Justin J. 1998. *Paul, Poverty and Survival*. Edinburgh: T&T Clark.

Mitchell, Alan. 1997. "Greet the Friends by Name: New Testament Evidence for the Greco-Roman *Topos* on Friendship." In *Greco-Roman Perspectives on Friendship*, edited by John T. Fitzgerald, 225–62. Atlanta: Scholars Press.

Mitchell, Margaret. 1992. "New Testament Envoys in the Context of Greco-Roman Diplomatic and Epistolary Conventions: The Example of Timothy and Titus." *JBL* 111:641–62.

O'Brien, Peter Thomas. 1991. *The Epistle to the Philippians: A Commentary on the Greek Text*. NIGTC. Grand Rapids: Eerdmans.

Peterman, Gerald W. 1991. "Thankless Thanks: Philippians 4.10-20." *TynBul* 42:261–70.

———. 1997. *Paul's Gift from Philippi: Conventions of Gift-Exchange and Christian Giving*. Cambridge: Cambridge University Press.

Secret, Mosi. 2012. "Prisoners' Letters Offer a Window into Lives Spent Alone in Tiny Cells." *New York Times*, October 2, A25 of the New York edition.

Stegman, Thomas D. 2009. *Second Corinthians*. Catholic Commentary on Sacred Scripture. Grand Rapids: Baker Academic.

Stowers, Stanley Kent. 1986. *Letter Writing in Greco-Roman Antiquity*. Library of Early Christianity 5. Philadelphia: Westminster.

———. 1994. "Friends and Enemies in the Politics of Heaven: Reading Theology in Philippians." *Pauline Theology*. Vol. 1, *Thessalonians, Philippians, Galatians, Philemon*, edited by Jouette Bassler, 105–22. Minneapolis: Fortress Press.

White, L. Michael. 1990. "Morality between Two Worlds: A Paradigm of Friendship in Philippians." In *Greeks, Romans, and Christians: Essays in Honor of Abraham J. Malherbe*, edited by David L. Balch, Everett Ferguson, and Wayne A. Meeks, 201–15. Minneapolis: Fortress Press.

Wiles, Gordon P. 1974. *Paul's Intercessory Prayers: The Significance of the Intercessory Prayer Passages in the Letters of St. Paul*. Cambridge: Cambridge University Press.

COLOSSIANS

Sylvia C. Keesmaat

Introduction

The ancient city of Colossae was located in the Lycus Valley (modern-day Turkey), less than fifteen miles from the more prominent cities of Laodicea, an important imperial center, and Hierapolis, famous for its healing springs. Due to Roman resettlement and its location on a trade route, the population of Colossae was quite diverse, including a Jewish community. An earthquake destroyed Colossae between 60 and 64 CE, and it appears that the city was not rebuilt for some time.

The letter itself suggests that Epaphras was the founder of the community (1:7-8) and that Paul was not personally known to them. Although the opening of the letter indicates that Paul wrote the Letter to the Colossians, there is some debate among scholars as to whether he indeed did. Those who argue against Paul's authorship point out that the vocabulary and theological emphases of Colossians differ from the letters that are universally accepted as Pauline. Not only does Colossians seem to have a more exalted view of Christ, but there is also less of an emphasis on the Spirit, as well as a turn to a more authoritarian and hierarchical social structure. Those who argue in favor of Paul's authorship point out that the different circumstances of this community could have resulted in differences in vocabulary and emphasis; that an exalted Christology is also found in Philippians; and that the perception of a more hierarchical social structure is a misunderstanding of the text in its original context. Some scholars argue that the letter was written in the presence of Paul by an associate and that that this accounts for differences of style and theological emphasis.

Given the occasional nature of Paul's letters, and the diversity of vocabulary and theology found in his other letters (for instance, justification by faith is central in both Galatians and Romans, but not in Corinthians), differences of style and theology are not a sufficient argument against authenticity. In fact, the theology of Colossians fits squarely with that of the other Pauline letters. In addition, the rich theology, evocative poetry, and clear familiarity with both the Scriptures of Israel and wider imperial culture are overwhelmingly consistent with Paul's other writings and suggest that Paul was indeed the author of this letter.

Paul's reference to his chains in Col. 4:3 suggests that he was in prison at the time of writing. Possible locations for this imprisonment are Ephesus (inferred from 1 Cor. 15:32; 2 Cor. 1:8), Caesarea (Acts 24:27), and Rome (Acts 28:16). Traditionally, the "Prison Epistles" (Philippians, Ephesians, Colossians, and Philemon) were thought to have been written during Paul's imprisonment in Rome. More recently, others have suggested that Paul was imprisoned in Ephesus when he wrote Colossians, since the proximity of the two cities would have facilitated the presence of both Epaphras and Onesimus with Paul at the time of writing. However, it is not clear that Luke (referred to in Col. 4:14) was with Paul in Ephesus. Although arguments are strong for both Rome and Ephesus, the balance of the evidence is slightly stronger for Ephesus. This would mean that the letter was written between 52 and 55 CE.

A few scholars have suggested that the close connection between Philemon and Colossians could provide a specific context for the letter. The letter itself indicates that it was carried to Colossae by Tychicus and Onesimus (4:7-9). If the latter is the slave Paul discusses in the Letter to Philemon (see commentary on 4:9 below), this could provide the occasion for Paul's extended comments on the relationship between masters and slaves in Col. 3:22—4:1.

The Colossian community was undoubtedly shaped by the strongly hierarchical character of Roman society, particularly the household unit, structured under the control of the *paterfamilias* (literally, "the father of the family"). The paterfamilias had economic and moral authority over the women of the household, slaves, and his own children, even after they reached adulthood. As we shall see, Paul's comments on the role of masters, women, children, and slaves in 3:18—4:1 provide insight into how this community struggled with what it meant to be followers of Jesus while negotiating their identities in the context of the story and hierarchy of the Roman Empire.

The closing of the letter indicates that Paul expected it to be read in neighboring church communities (4:15-16). The corporate address suggests that while it contained advice specific to the Colossians, this letter was also more widely applicable to other believing communities. Since these communities lived, moved, and had their being in cities that were shaped architecturally, liturgically, and economically by the historical realities of the Roman Empire, the following reading of Colossians will draw on recent research to show the ways early believing communities negotiated their identity in light of imperial realities (Horsley; Walsh and Keesmaat; Maier). In addition, the story of Israel deeply shaped Paul's understanding of the work of Jesus and God in the world. Hence, Paul's many allusions to the Scriptures of Israel will also be highlighted in this reading.

It is important to note that Paul's imagery and metaphors in this letter are rooted in the stories and symbols of his world. The overarching story of Rome with its myths, symbols, and images provided a rich cultural context for both Paul and the believers in Colossae. In addition, the story of Israel was the primary symbolic world for Paul and perhaps some of this letter's recipients. It is no surprise, therefore, to discover throughout this letter not only the metaphors and imagery of Rome but also those of Judaism.

Colossians 1:1-14: Greeting and Description of the Colossians' Story

▌THE TEXT IN ITS ANCIENT CONTEXT

At the outset of this letter, Paul roots the identity of the Colossian believers in the story of both Jesus and Israel. As people who lived under the powerful rule of Rome, the Colossians would have been aware of the need to be faithful to the emperor, Nero, a faithfulness rooted in the widespread hope that Nero's gospel would unite the whole of the known world under the civilizing influence of Roman culture and law. Paul, however, not only describes a different identity, one of faithfulness to Jesus, but also a hope in a different gospel, one that also bears fruit in the whole world (1:2, 5-6). In fact, the imagery of bearing fruit is a direct challenge to Rome, since the fertility and abundance of the empire was celebrated as a result not only of Roman rule in general but also of the new age inaugurated by Nero. Paul, in contrast, asserts that it is the gospel of Jesus Christ that is bearing fruit not only in the whole world but also in the life of this particular community (1:6, 10).

Paul describes this fruit in a number of ways: it is the love that the Colossians have in the Spirit (1:7); it is connected to growing in the knowledge and understanding of God (vv. 9-10); and it is the fruit of "good work" as they walk in ways that are holy to the Lord (v. 10). All of this will be unpacked as the letter unfolds.

Throughout Jewish Scriptures, not only is fruitfulness a sign of Israel's obedience, but Israel is also the one called to bear the good fruit of justice and righteousness (Isa. 5:1-7; 2 Kgs. 19:30 // Isa. 37:31; Hos. 9:10-17). This fruit, moreover, is the way in which Israel would be a blessing to the nations (Isa. 42:6; 49:6). Paul evokes that story not only in his reference to bearing fruit but also in verses 12-14, where he describes the actions of Jesus, the beloved Son, who has rescued the Colossians from the power of darkness and transferred them to his kingdom. By referring to inheritance, redemption, and forgiveness, Paul is alluding to the exodus, where Israel was redeemed from the powerful kingdom of Egypt and welcomed into an inheritance and redemption by God.

By the end of this introduction, the recipients of this letter have been grounded in love and called to wisdom, knowledge, and the fruit of good works, all shaped by the story of Jesus.

▌THE TEXT IN THE INTERPRETIVE TRADITION

In a later time, when the early church was exploring the implications and parameters of Christian faith, both Tertullian and Augustine appealed to Col. 1:6 to emphasize the universal nature of the true gospel, in contrast to heresies that, they asserted, tended to be limited in both time (in that they were recent doctrinal innovations) and location (for instance, the Donatists in Africa: Gorday, 4).

John Calvin (148), writing in a context where the mediating presence of the church was understood to be required for salvation, noted Paul's emphasis on faith in Jesus Christ in verses 4 and 7, along with the redemption and forgiveness found in Jesus, the beloved Son (v. 14), as evidence of the need for Christ alone for salvation. These verses, then, constituted a challenge to the papacy, which, in Calvin's opinion, undermined the sufficiency of Christ.

◾ The Text in Contemporary Discussion

For much of church history, the emphasis on the all-sufficient character of Christ's salvation was comfort in the face of uncertain circumstances. In a postmodern context, however, the overwhelmingly masculine and all-encompassing nature of Paul's claims in these verses may evoke a totalizing character that is experienced as oppressive. If this letter is addressed to those who are faithful and who are holy, how can this letter speak to others who make no such claims to holiness or faithfulness? Similarly, is Paul not making a totalizing claim about the story of Jesus that rivals the totalizing hegemonic claims made by the Roman Empire? Does this story not then function in what is potentially a similarly oppressive way as any hegemonic metanarrative? (Walsh and Keesmaat, 17–18).

Other questions arise in light of recent research into the importance of slavery as a context for this letter. Do the references to being made strong and enduring everything with patience (v. 11) indicate that even those who are followers of Jesus in this community suffer not only at the hands of the wider culture but also at the hands of masters who may or may not be believers? Can the reference to sharing the inheritance of the saints (v. 12) nevertheless provide a word of hope for those who are enslaved to imperial powers, both in Paul's time and today?

Colossians 1:15-23: Who Is Lord: Jesus or Caesar?

◾ The Text in Its Ancient Context

The poem found in Col. 1:15-20 describes the "beloved Son" of verse 13, into whose kingdom the Colossians have been transferred. It begins with an allusion to both the story of Israel and the story of Rome: "He is the image of the invisible God." In keeping with the theme of creation that permeates this passage, these words echo the biblical creation account of humankind's being created in the image of God (Gen. 1:26-27), an echo Paul picks up again in 3:10, where he describes the new nature of the Colossian believers as "renewed in knowledge according to the image of its creator." Throughout Israel's history, the language of humanity's being created in the image of God carried polemical weight in the face of mythologies that portrayed humanity as slaves who do the menial labor of the gods (Middleton). In the Roman Empire, where the emperor embodied the glory of the gods and where the images of the emperor dominated public space, Paul's appeal to the story of Adam would have sounded a subtle challenge to the superiority of the emperor.

The references to creation in these verses find their context not only in Genesis but also in the wisdom traditions of Israel, where Wisdom is described as the image of God (Wis. 7:26), the first-born of creation (Prov. 8:22; Sir. 24:9), the one who designed all things and permeates all things (Wis. 7:24; Prov. 3:19-20; 8:22-30), and the one in whom all things are made new (Wis. 7:37). Paul has taken these rich wisdom traditions and applied them to Christ (Moule, 59–67; D'Angelo, 317–18). Later they become explicit in his argument (1:28; 2:3).

Paul's language concerning the powers is also rooted in Israel's Scriptures, where the terms "thrones" (*thronoi*), "dominions" (*kyriotētai*), and "powers" (*exousiai*) commonly referred to kings and their dynasties, their realms, and the power that they exercised. While "rulers" (*archai*) could be used to refer to spiritual entities, it also referred to earthly rulers (Wink, 11–18). There is some debate as to whether these verses refer to spiritual powers or earthly institutions. Paul, however, insists that he is talking about all things in heaven and *on earth*, *visible* and invisible, suggesting that "thrones or dominions or rulers or powers" cannot simply be a reference to "invisible" or "heavenly" realities; they must also have a visible and earthly reference. In the Roman Empire, thrones, dominions, rule, and powers referred above all to Rome; to her *ruler*, Caesar, on the *throne* established by the gods; to his *dominion* over all of the known world; to his military *power* and might. In a few short words, Paul draws deeply on Israel's traditions to undermine the whole mythic structure of the empire: its ruler, its throne, its dominion, its power. Jesus is the one who created these structures and holds them together.

For those surrounded by the imagery and symbolism of Rome, Paul's language continued to sound familiar themes in a jarring way. In a world where Caesar was the head of the body politic, the empire, Paul describes Jesus as the head of a new body politic, the church (1:18).

Paul brings these verses to a climax with the claim that in Jesus, all things in heaven and earth are reconciled, for he has made peace through the blood of the cross (1:20). Making peace is nothing new in the empire. In fact, making peace is the language used "in Roman political discourse to celebrate the universal *pax* or military pacification arising from imperial rule" (Maier, 333). In striking contrast to Rome, where peace was brought through violent military might, economic oppression, and cultural domination, Colossians proclaims a peace achieved through the bearing of violence. This is not the violent hegemony of Rome. This is the reconciliation of all things, even the things that wound by a self-sacrificial love.

This reconciliation continues in the lives of the Colossian believers, who have heard the gospel proclaimed to them as it was proclaimed to every creature under heaven. It is this good news to every creature that rounds out the creation language of the poem, and it is this good news for which Paul became a servant (1:23, 25).

▮ THE TEXT IN THE INTERPRETIVE TRADITION

In the face of the Arian assertion that Christ was not preexistent with the Father, but was a creature who was later exalted, the fourth-century church fathers appealed to these verses as the basis for the eternal preexistence of Christ and, in the fifth century for the doctrine of the two natures of Christ. Later, Calvin (149) pointed out that because they had been struggling with Arianism, the church fathers had missed the chief point of this text, which is that the Father is made visible to believers in Jesus. In so doing, he shifted the focus from Jesus' relation to God to Jesus' relation to believers.

More recently, Paul's description of "thrones, dominions, rulers and authorities" in verse 16 has played a central role in the debate on the meaning of the principalities and powers. Some argue that this language refers to heavenly spiritual beings who are identified with the powers of darkness in verse 13 (Arnold, 251–55). Others argue that these powers also include human systems and structures (Wink; Sumney, 67), an argument that is convincing in light of the political overtones of "thrones, dominions, rulers and authorities" in the first century.

The Text in Contemporary Discussion

Colossians 1:15-20 has become a central text in discussions of environmental theology. In that context, Paul's allusions to the story of creation, the centrality of the wisdom tradition with its emphasis on creation, Paul's description of the reconciliation of all things, whether on earth or in heaven (v. 20), and the proclamation of the gospel to all creatures (v. 23) provide a basis for a message of good news and redemption for all of creation (Bouma-Prediger, 105–10; Wilson, 309). This stands in contrast to the creation-denying asceticism that Paul critiques in 2:16-23.

Postmodern and postcolonial readers might also question, however, whether in these verses Paul continues to reinscribe the violent and totalizing character of the Roman Empire itself. His description of Jesus appropriates imperial language so powerfully that it seems that Jesus functions like any other imperial ruler. This is reinforced by the repetition of the phrase "all" and "all things" throughout the passage (vv. 15-16 [×2], 17 [×2], 18, 19, 20), and by the language of Jesus triumphing over his enemies in 2:15.

Interpreters struggle with this dynamic. Some argue that a ruler who makes peace by bearing rather than inflicting violence is engaging in self-sacrificial love rather than violent hegemony. Others argue that by imitating the language of empire, the text provides a basis for the sort of hierarchical and authoritative control that has often characterized Christendom. In such a context, the nonviolent character of Jesus' actions has been lost in the oppressive dynamic of the language of the "kingdom."

Colossians 1:24—2:6: The Mystery of Christ

The Text in Its Ancient Context

In light of Paul's other letters, the assertion that Paul is "completing what is lacking in Christ's afflictions for the sake of his body, that is, the church" is an unusual concept, because it suggest that Paul's suffering adds to or completes the suffering of Christ. Some argue that because the identification of Christ and the church is so close, the suffering of believers is the suffering of Christ (MacDonald 2000, 79); others argue that Paul is referring to the messianic woes, the sum of suffering that God's people must fulfill before the end times; and others argue that Paul is referring to the tradition of noble death in Greco-Roman literature, where the death of martyrs vicariously provides an example for the benefit of others (Sumney, 101).

However it is interpreted, in the context of participation in the story of Jesus' death and resurrection, which runs throughout this letter (see 2:10-13; 3:1-4), this verse serves to root Paul's experience more deeply in the story of Jesus. By implication, any suffering that those in this community might be experiencing is also rooted in that story.

In the imperial story, the mystery that is revealed, and the glory that is celebrated, is that of the glorious rule of the emperor himself. Instead, Paul asserts that wisdom and knowledge are hidden in God's mystery, Christ, who is, in Roman eyes, a failed Messiah who died at Roman hands. For the Colossians, however, he is the hope of glory (1:27). This Messiah, Jesus, who is Lord (while the slogan of the empire is that *Caesar* is Lord), is the one in whom they should walk. The language of "walking in the Lord" is rooted in Torah observance, in the story of Israel. Moreover, the Colossians not only walk in him but also are rooted and built up in him. These are images from the empire, usually applied to the way in which Nero gives root to, binds together, and builds up the whole of Roman society (Maier, 328). Rather than Nero, however, the Colossians are rooted and built up in a different Lord.

▮ THE TEXT IN THE INTERPRETIVE TRADITION

In light of Paul's assertion that his sufferings complete what is lacking in Christ's suffering, interpreters from the church fathers to the present have been concerned to defend the sufficiency of Christ Jesus' death for salvation. In the sixteenth century, the Catholic Church taught that the blood of the martyrs played a role in the expiation of sins, using this verse to argue that the suffering of the saints has redemptive power (Gorday, 36). In opposition to this, Calvin argued that the suffering of the saints had no redemptive role; rather, their suffering confirmed the faith of the church. Since Christ lived in Paul, his suffering is the suffering of Christ; as a result, Paul's suffering edifies the church, rather than redeems it (Calvin, 165–67).

▮ THE TEXT IN CONTEMPORARY DISCUSSION

The question of the place and role of suffering in the life of believers continues to dominate the interpretation of this passage. In the North American context, where the church has been shaped by a theology of blessing and prosperity, what meaning does Paul's language of suffering carry? Do these verses suggest that the church in North America has something to learn from the suffering of believers in other parts of the world?

Furthermore, in light of the legacy of suffering inflicted by Christians, in contexts like residential schools for native peoples in Canada and the United States, is there a way theologically to interpret this suffering in light of the suffering of Christ? Moreover, if Christians are the ones inflicting this suffering, have they abandoned the story of Jesus?

Colossians 2:8—3:4: Paul's Challenge to Idolatry

▮ THE TEXT IN ITS ANCIENT CONTEXT

What is at stake in this letter is the very freedom of the believers at Colossae. If, as we have suggested, this community is struggling with the roles of both masters and slaves, Paul's allusions and ethical exhortations in the next section suggest that life shaped by the story and structures of empire is fundamentally an experience of being taken captive. His argument begins by showing the Colossian believers that their story is rooted in the story of Jesus: they have come to fullness in him (2:10); they were spiritually circumcised in him (2:11); they were buried with him in baptism (2:12); they were raised with him (2:12, 3:1); and they were made alive with him (2:13). All of this was made possible because Jesus, the head of every ruler and authority, erased the legal record against them, setting it aside.

The irony is complete: Jesus was stripped by the Roman authorities and held up to contempt as they celebrated their triumph over him. Now the tables are turned. Those rulers and authorities who were known to conquer and take captive the peoples of the world were disarmed by Jesus on the cross and made a public example (2:15). First-century hearers would have discerned an allusion to the victory parades that formed part of Roman triumphal celebrations, where conquered peoples, now Roman slaves, were paraded as a public example of what happens to those who resist the benefits of Roman imperial rule (Wright, 116). Rather than violently triumphing over and then parading conquered and enslaved losers, Jesus triumphed over the rulers and authorities by *disarming* them on a *cross*. This nonviolent suffering is not only a challenge to Roman power but also a word of hope to those who were enslaved under this empire. Jesus is not someone who glories in violence and the demeaning humiliation of captives.

There is much debate about what sort of "philosophy" and "empty deceit" Paul is referring to in these verses, especially since in 2:16-23, he describes religious restrictions and practices that could relate to Judaism (festivals, new moons, Sabbaths [v. 16]; angelic visions [v. 18]; and food restrictions [v. 21]). Others have found references to pagan ascetic religious practices in these verses.

Some have suggested that Paul is not referring to any one specific problem in the Colossian community but rather that he has in mind a range of possible challenges that these new disciples could face (Hooker). Others have explored Paul's allusions in these verses to the prophetic critique of idolatry found in Israel's Scriptures (Walsh). Just as idolatry is worthless, vain, and nothing (Pss. 97:7; 115:4-7; 135:15-18; Isa. 44:9; 57:13; Jer. 2:5), so the philosophy to which Paul refers is described as "empty deceit" (2:8) and a shadow without substance (2:17). Just as idols are constructed by human hands (Ps. 115:4; Isa. 2:8; 41:6-7; 44:11; Jer. 10:1-10; Hosea 8:4, 6; 13:2; Hab. 2:18), so the philosophy is a human tradition (2:8), and a human way of thinking (2:18) that imposes human commands and teachings (2:20). Just as idolatry results in a deluded mind and a fundamental lack of knowledge (Isa. 44:18-20; Hosea 4:6) and just as an idol is a teacher of lies (Hab. 2:18), so the philosophy is puffed up without cause (2:18) and deceives people by employing supposedly plausible arguments (2:4, 8). Just as idolatry is impotent, without value, and does not profit (Pss. 115:4-7; 135:15-18; Isa. 4:20; 46:1-2; Jer. 2:11; Hosea 7:16; Hab. 2:19), so the philosophy is of no value in checking self-indulgence (v. 23). And just as idolatry is a matter of exchanging glory for shame (Ps. 106:20; Jer. 2:11; Hosea 4:7; 7:16; 13:1-3; Rom. 1:23), so the philosophy disqualifies, insists on self-abasement (2:18), and promotes severe treatment of the body (2:23).

Of course, in biblical tradition, the critique of idolatry is rooted in the confession that Yahweh is the creator of heaven and earth (Pss. 115:16; 135:5-7; Isa. 40:12-26; 44:9-28; 45:12, 18; Jer. 10:11-16; 51:15-19). Paul also grounds his critique of the philosophy in the assertion that Jesus is the one through whom and for whom all things were created (Col. 1:15-17). And, of course, Jesus triumphs over all rulers and authorities on the cross (2:15), just as Yahweh triumphs over other gods.

Throughout the Jewish Scriptures, it is when the people of Israel forget their story that they succumb to the idolatry of the surrounding peoples. Paul, too, frames this whole section with the story that provides a context for the life of the Colossian believers. Picking up the narrative thread of Col. 2:12 in 3:1, he continues: "If, then, you have been raised with Christ, seek the things that are above, where Christ is seated at the right hand of God." In an empire where the deified imperial rulers were considered to continue to rule with the gods after their death, Paul asserts that Christ—who has been raised to new life—is seated at the right hand of God. Paul is not advocating an otherworldly dualism, but rather raising the question of ultimate authority. Who is really in control? Is the whole body of the empire held together by the emperor who nourishes and upholds it, or by Jesus? In using the imagery of the body politic in 1:18 and 2:19, Paul has already challenged the rule of Caesar. By stating that the whole fullness of the deity dwells bodily in Jesus (2:9), and placing Jesus at the right hand of God (3:1), Paul has undermined the sacred canopy of Roman rule. Not only are the religious practices of paganism characterized as idolatry, but Paul is also reminding this community that throughout Israel's Scriptures, the religious practices of Judaism were considered idolatrous when they were used in service of injustice and captivity (i.e., Isaiah 58). Paul's language reminds the community at Colossae that their practices reveal whom they worship and the story of which they are a part.

■ THE TEXT IN THE INTERPRETIVE TRADITION

In a later context, where Christianity was engaged in differentiating itself from both Judaism and other religious and civic associations, the early church fathers emphasized how these verses undermined the rituals of both Judaism and pagan mystery religions. As time went on, these verses were also used to challenge the body-denying practices and beliefs of Gnosticism.

For those in Christian traditions who practiced asceticism and taught its importance as a form of Christian discipleship, however (for instance, the desert fathers), these verses were problematic because they appear to condemn the ascetic practices that shaped early monasticism. As a result, these commentators emphasized that it was not the ascetic practices themselves that were the problem but rather the *intention* of the practitioner, who must ensure that such discipline is grounded in Christ and reflects a reliance on grace rather than human achievement (Gorday).

Later, in the face of Catholicism, with its emphasis on the intervention of saints and martyrs for salvation, Calvin identified Paul's reference to the worship of angels not only with the worship of saints in his own time but also with the practice of relying on the mediating role of those who had died. He argued that these verses assert that no mediator other than Christ is necessary to approach God (Calvin, 194–96).

■ THE TEXT IN CONTEMPORARY DISCUSSION

Paul's critique of the practices of the Colossian community has raised a number of questions in the minds of readers. Most prominent is the question of whether Paul is engaging in a supersessionist strategy here, denigrating the practices of Judaism and equating them with the elemental spirits of the universe that have the appearance of wisdom. Given Paul's allusions to the prophetic critiques of idolatry, along with his allusions and echoes of Israel's story and Scriptures in this letter, supersessionism seems unlikely. There is no doubt, however, that these verses have lent themselves to antisemitic purposes in the past.

It is also difficult to discern the precise nature of the beliefs and practices that Paul is critiquing, given the fact that we have only Paul's allusions to them, and these may be pejorative and emotive rather than entirely accurate (Caird, 162). How much can we trust Paul's depiction of "the philosophy" here?

Some have also asked whether Paul is describing his opponents in ways that can be applied just as easily to his own teaching. He describes the opponents' belief as "human tradition" (2:8) and "simply human commands and teachings" (2:22). In short, he says, "Do not let anyone condemn you" (2:16), and then proceeds with his own words of condemnation. The text invites us to identify with Paul's perspective here. But what is it about Paul's teaching that makes it more acceptable than that of his opponents (Walsh and Keesmaat, 102–14)?

Colossians 3:5-17: Living as Image Bearers

▌ THE TEXT IN ITS ANCIENT CONTEXT

In light of this story, how then are the Colossians to live? In light of the creation-affirming language in Col. 1:15-23, it is unlikely that Paul is referring to a dualist rejection of the body when he tells the Colossians to "put to death whatever in you is earthly" (3:5). Instead, he lists examples that include not only sexual sins (sexual immorality, impurity, passion, evil desire) but also sins that tear apart community: covetousness, greed, anger, wrath, malice, slander, abusive language, and lying (3:5, 8-9). Moreover, he explicitly links greed with idolatry, suggesting that it is the consumptive economic practices of the empire that reveal the idolatry at its very heart. Sexual immorality, impurity, passion, evil desire, and covetousness all demonstrate the way in which greed manifests itself, both sexually and more generally.

Paul's language here again links the story of the Colossian Christians with that of Jesus. The new self with which they are clothed is being renewed in knowledge according to the image of its Creator. This is the knowledge that Paul has been praying for this community since the outset (1:9-10; 2:2), a knowledge that causes the Colossians to look more like this image of God found in Jesus, who suffered the violence of the empire in order to bring peace.

Paul again challenges the claims of imperial rule to bring pacification to all the peoples of the world by asserting that in the renewal Jesus brings there is "no longer Greek or Jew, circumcised and uncircumcised, barbarian, Scythian, slave and free," but that "Christ is all and in all" (3:11). Even those most marginalized and oppressed in the far-flung reaches of the empire (barbarian, Scythian), the most marginalized and abused in the households of the Colossians along with those who control them (slave and free), and those most easily dismissed as unworthy by the other (Jews and gentiles) participate in the story of Jesus and are being renewed in his image. It is an audacious claim in a context where only the civilizing influence of Rome was thought to bring renewal to the world.

In the face of the community-destroying practices that the Colossians are to put to death, Paul calls the community to be clothed with those virtues that instead build up community: compassion, kindness, humility, meekness, and patience (3:12). Paul, however, also recognizes the need—particularly in this community, where people are just learning to negotiate their old power structures and relations in light of their new identity in Christ—to bear with one another and to forgive. Not only will love be needed, but also the peace of Christ, to make such forgiveness possible. The reconciliation that comes from self-sacrificial love is the only thing that is to rule them. Paul winds up these admonitions with a call to thankfulness that permeates all they do: teaching, admonishing, singing, and learning. Such love, forgiveness, peace, and gratitude will be necessary to negotiate the complicated relationships that Paul alludes to in the next section.

◼ THE TEXT IN THE INTERPRETIVE TRADITION

The central debate over these verses has been whether Paul considers the body to be evil. More Platonic interpretations of this text throughout history have associated that which is "earthly" with the body and its passions. John Chrysostom and others have challenged that view, arguing that it is our moral choices that determine what is earthly. Following Platonism, gnostics argued that true spirituality meant an escape from the body; once again, the church fathers strove to affirm the goodness of the created order. This temptation to denigrate the body and its desires has continued to plague Christian tradition through the ages, right up until the present time. It is striking that the church fathers, surrounded by a culture that was permeated with otherworldly spirituality, continued their emphasis on the goodness of the created order (Gorday, 42).

◼ THE TEXT IN CONTEMPORARY DISCUSSION

What does Paul's assertion that there is no longer Greek and Jew, circumcised and uncircumcised, barbarian, Scythian, slave and free mean in a world where identity is constantly being negotiated and renegotiated? In the Roman Empire, all races and people were to be brought under the all-encompassing sway of Roman culture. In our own world, where cultural identity is rapidly being erased by the pervasive nature of global technology and culture, what are the implications of cultural and social differences being erased "in Christ"? Is this a denial of cultural difference? Or does the language of reconciliation hint at a different kind of cultural equality in Christ?

Colossians 3:18—4:1: Submission and Inheritance— A Jubilee for Slaves

◼ THE TEXT IN ITS ANCIENT CONTEXT

The household code, as Col. 3:18—4:1 is known, has been the focus of much recent scholarly work (other household codes are found in Eph. 5:21—6:9 and 1 Pet. 2:18—3:7). No longer interpreted as an unequivocally oppressive text, these verses—in particular their nuanced character and the socially complex context in which they were written—have received more attention than in the past. As a result, there is a growing acknowledgment that they contained a subversive and liberating message in their ancient context (MacDonald 2000; Standhartinger; Sumney; Walsh and Keesmaat).

In the first place, while the language of these verses appears to uphold the status quo in directing women to be subject to their husbands, children to be obedient to their parents, and slaves to be obedient to their masters, it also subtly undermines the absolute authority of the head of the household. Not only are women, children, and slaves addressed in these verses; but the husbands, fathers, and masters are also uncharacteristically given commands to love (3:12), forgo provocation and harsh treatment (3:19, 21), and act justly and fairly (4:1).

It is difficult, however, to know how these commands were heard in Colossae. Within the Colossian community, there were complex and overlapping identities: slaves may have been parents, wives may have been masters, children may have been freeborn or slave and may have had parents who were believers or not, or have been the product of a mixed marriage between a believer and a nonbeliever (MacDonald 2010). In addition, a child may have been the offspring of the master of the house and a slave (McDonald 2012). How these commands were heard would have varied widely amongst the hearers themselves.

Second, when slaves are told that they are to obey their *masters according to the flesh* (v. 22, translated often as "earthly masters"), a question arises. In Pauline writings, the flesh (*sarx*) often has negative overtones, referring to a way of being that is opposed to the Spirit of God. Are these negative overtones present here?

Moreover, the language of these verses plays on the Greek word for "lord" and "master" (*kyrios*). If we translate all occurrences of *kyrios* in these verses as "master," capitalizing those occurrences that refer to Christ (and are usually translated "Lord"), the sense is much clearer. Paul tells slaves that they are to fear the Master, and do their work as if it is done for the Master, not for their masters. He tells them that they serve the messianic Master (usually translated "the Lord Christ").

This last phrase is important, because it concludes a sentence where slaves are told that from the Master they will receive an inheritance (3:24). It was not normal in Roman law for slaves to expect to inherit. However, in Israelite tradition, there is a time when slaves are released to receive their inheritance. This was known as the year of Jubilee (Leviticus 25). In the shifting sands of Jewish messianic expectation, there were certainly those who linked the coming of the Messiah with Jubilee expectation. When the Messiah came to establish God's kingdom, debts would be forgiven and slaves would be freed. It may be that this reference to the messianic Master refers to that tradition (Walsh and Keesmaat, 207–8). In addition, masters are called to treat their slaves justly and with equality; this last word, *isotēs*, denotes the equality of different social groups before Roman law. It has been suggested that this verse is the key to the passage as a whole, undermining the dominant ethos of subordination (Standhartinger, 13).

This careful language with regard to slaves likely reflects the complexity of slave relationships in the first century. Slaves at this time, whether children, adolescents, or adults, were simply assumed to be sexually available to their masters (MacDonald 2007, 95). If some of the slaves listening to Paul's letter had masters who were unbelievers, the possibility of following Paul's commands to put off immorality (3:5) would have been difficult. Even if their masters were believers, it is not immediately clear that sexual use of their slaves would have ceased, given cultural assumptions (MacDonald 2007,101–3). However, it has been suggested that the fact that Paul warns masters of their accountability before their Lord, and the fact that "the relinquishing of past patterns of life is an ethical priority in the work (cf. Col. 1:21-23; 2:20; 3:5-7)" (MacDonald 2007, 101) means that masters were to cease their use of slaves for sexual relations.

The fact that Paul has already referred to the cancellation of the debtor's bond in 2:14 would have subtly undermined Paul's commands in these verses. So would his reference to the way in which Jesus had triumphed over those who gloried in parading slaves and conquered men, women, and children from around the empire in 2:15. In addition, in an empire where slaves comprised mainly those people who had been conquered and taken from their own lands, Paul's assertion that there is no slave and free, alongside no Greek or Jew, barbarian or Scythian, would have painted a picture of a world where the structures of slavery were called into question (Sumney, 254).

▌ THE TEXT IN THE INTERPRETIVE TRADITION

For much of the interpretive tradition, these verses have garnered relatively little attention, primarily because Paul's commands here were seen as self-evident in the predominantly patriarchal culture of Christendom. The church fathers acknowledged that Paul was merely describing the natural order in relation to husband and wives, fathers and children. On the vexing issue of slavery, some asserted that while slavery was an inequity, the wise person is always free, even when outwardly enslaved (Ambrosiaster, cited in Gorday, 53).

In the 1800s, both sides in the heated debate over slavery appealed to these verses as a justification for slavery on the one hand (since Paul does not here judge the institution of slavery) and as providing a challenge to it on the other (for if masters were to treat their slaves justly and fairly, slavery as we know it would disappear [Swartley]).

▌ THE TEXT IN CONTEMPORARY DISCUSSION

For many, Paul's commands in these verses provide an interpretive crux for the letter as a whole. Is Paul here upholding the authority and power of the patriarchal household, and therefore upholding the power structures of the empire? Do these verses demonstrate that Paul's all-encompassing language about Jesus as the one with ultimate authority and power in 1:16-20; 2:9, 15; and 3:1 provide the basis for a model of totalitarian control that is founded on male authority and hierarchy?

These are important questions to bring to the text, not only because they force us to ask what the theology of the letter looked like in the actual lives of first-century believers (especially those who were most vulnerable) but also because they compel us to realize how our own contemporary assumptions can affect our reading. In the context of modern feminism, and in a culture where slavery is considered morally repugnant, these texts seem oppressive. When read in their own nuanced and complex circumstances, it is apparent that Paul is carefully attempting to speak a word of liberation and hope into a situation of complex power structures.

If this letter does indeed explore the difficulty of faithful living in complex circumstances, then questions of discipleship come front and center. What are the contexts in which followers of Jesus find themselves negotiating different power relationships as they strive to be faithful? On the one hand, how do Western Christians, who benefit from slave-like working conditions prevalent in the two-thirds world, read these texts? Is there a need to heed the call to justice and equality in Col. 4:1? What does the biblical call for Jubilee look like in contemporary contexts? On the other hand, how does an abused young man who has to sell his body to live on the streets hear this message of the renewal in Jesus in a way that can possibly be lived in his situation? What is the word of hope to those who find themselves working as sharecroppers for North American companies in Colombia, knowing that the working conditions will likely kill them? Or the women working in a maquila who must endure sexual abuse in order to feed their families? How can those who are powerless and at the mercy of those who control their lives be faithful followers of Jesus?

Colossians 4:2-18: The Shape of the Community

▋ THE TEXT IN ITS ANCIENT CONTEXT

The closing section of this letter provides insight into the social context of this letter. In the first place, it is clear that Paul is urging those in this community to be careful in their walk, particularly in relation to outsiders. By urging them to walk in wisdom (*sophia*), Paul is alluding to the beginning of the letter (1:9; 2:3); however, the reference to outsiders makes it clear that such wisdom requires discernment. Similarly, and in light of Paul's somewhat coded language throughout the letter, his call to gracious speech, seasoned with salt, indicates a need for appropriate speech in different contexts. This is strengthened by the fact that there is more for Tychicus and Onesimus to tell the community than what has been put in the letter (4:9), suggesting that there are some things that Paul did not want to entrust to writing.

Paul's language in 4:7-9 alludes to some of the central tensions in this community. It is clear from the content of Colossians that the issue of slavery has been front and center throughout, as seen in the reference to both Epaphras and Tychicus as fellow slaves (1:7; 4:7), the references to the philosophy as that which enslaves (2:8), the overturning of the patterns of slavery (2:15; 3:11; 3:24—4:1), and the clear linking in the last verses of this letter with the Letter to Philemon. The author suggests that this letter has been brought to the Colossian community by Tychicus and Onesimus. Onesimus is described as part of this community by Paul (v. 9); it is likely that this is a reference to Onesimus the runaway slave mentioned in Philemon (MacDonald 2000, 188; Sumney, 269; Thompson, 106; cf. Wilson, 296; Lincoln 2000, 580). This makes it all the more astounding that Paul describes both Tychicus and Onesimus as beloved and *faithful*. How can a runaway slave possibly be faithful? By describing Onesimus this way, Paul is suggesting that previous commitments have changed for Onesimus. He is faithful in serving another Master, and this faithfulness is more important than faithfulness to his earthly master. More than that, however, Paul describes Tychicus as both a brother and a fellow slave (*doulos*) in the Lord, while Onesimus, who is an actual slave, is described as a brother. If the hearers of this letter haven't realized before this point that the categories have shifted, Paul now makes it explicit.

The greeting to Nympha and the church in her house (4:15) suggests that Nympha was the leader of the Christian community in Laodicea, raising the interesting question of how the commands of 3:18—4:1 would have been heard in a context where a woman exercised leadership over the community. There is such a similarity between the Christian communities in Colossae and Laodicea that they are encouraged to read each other's letters.

Paul's last request, "remember my chains," reminds the Colossians not only to pray for Paul (see 4:3) but also to remember where this gospel can lead. Participation in the story of Jesus leads to the same suffering that Jesus endured (1:11, 24). Even in that context, Paul hopes for grace for this community: grace as they remember the story of which they are a part, and grace as they discern how to live out that story in the complexities of life in the empire.

◼ The Text in the Interpretive Tradition

Paul's presence in prison as he writes this letter has provided an important context for interpreting his words. The church fathers highlighted the importance of prayer in situations of suffering, particularly as a guard against sin and as a way to overcome adversaries. In a time when many Christians were facing persecution, it was acknowledged that prayer, rather than weaponry, was the way believers fought against their adversaries; through prayer, they acknowledged that God provided strength to bear suffering (Gorday, 55).

◼ The Text in Contemporary Discussion

In a postmodern context, which acknowledges the coded nature of language, Paul's reference to gracious, seasoned speech that seeks to be appropriate in context highlights our need to be attentive to the way in which Paul's language may be guarded in this letter (Walsh and Keesmaat, 209). In a situation of oppression, what might Paul have been careful about articulating? How might his context in prison have affected his ability to write freely? Might his allusions to Jubilee and equality in the household code, for instance, be embedded in seemingly usual commands for obedience because it was too dangerous for this vulnerable community to be perceived as undermining the social structures of imperial society? For those with ears to hear, the references to a new social structure are present in these verses and throughout the letter. For those who expect allegiance to accepted social codes, that language is present as well. In the same way, Paul is telling this community to be attentive to how their language will be perceived by those who have power over them.

In addition, when interpreting this letter, should readers perhaps privilege the hermeneutical insights of those who speak from a social location similar to Paul's? Should we question our own ability to interpret the letter well if we read from a position of privilege? Perhaps readers need to remember not only Paul's chains but also the chains of those in the present world before they can truly fulfill the task to which this letter calls them in the Lord (4:17).

Works Cited

Arnold, Clinton E. 1996. *The Colossian Syncretism: The Interface between Christianity and Folk Belief at Colossae.* Grand Rapids: Baker.

Bouma-Prediger, Steven. 2001. *For the Beauty of the Earth: A Christian Vision of Creation Care.* Grand Rapids: Baker Academic.

Caird, G. B. 1976. *Paul's Letters from Prison (Ephesians, Philippians, Colossians, Philemon) in the Revised Standard Version: Introduction and Commentary.* Oxford: Oxford University Press.

Calvin, John. 1860. *Commentaries on the Epistles of Paul the Apostle to the Galatians, Ephesians, Philippians, and Colossians.* Translated by John Pringle. Edinburgh: Calvin Translation Society.

D'Angelo, Mary Rose. 1994. "Colossians" in *Searching the Scriptures.* Vol. 2, *A Feminist Commentary*, edited by Elisabeth Schüssler Fiorenza. New York: Crossroad.

Francis, Fred O. 1962. "Humility and Angelic Worship in Col. 2:18." *Studia Theologica—Nordic Journal of Theology* 16, no. 2:109–34.

Gorday, Peter, ed. 2000. *Colossians, 1–2 Thessalonians, 1–2 Timothy, Titus, Philemon.* Ancient Christian Commentary on Scripture, New Testament 9: Downers Grove, IL: InterVarsity Press.

Hooker, Morna D. 1973. "Were There False Teachers in Colossae?" In *Christ and Spirit in the New Testament*, edited by Barnabas Lindars and Stephen S. Smalley, 315–31. Cambridge: Cambridge University Press.

Horsley, Richard A., ed. 1997. *Paul and Empire: Religion and Power in Roman Imperial Society.* Harrisburg, PA: Trinity Press International.

Lincoln, Andrew T. 1999. "The Household Code and the Wisdom Mode of Colossians." *JSNT* 74:93–112.

———. 2000. "The Letter to the Colossians." In *The New Interpreter's Bible.* Vol. 11, *2 Corinthians, Galatians, Ephesians, Philippians, Colossians, 1 and 2 Thessalonians, 1 and 2 Timothy, Titus, Philemon*, edited by Leander E. Keck, 553–669. Nashville: Abingdon.

Maier, H. O. 2005. "A Sly Civility: Colossians and Empire." *JSNT* 27, no. 3:323–49.

MacDonald, Margaret Y. 2000. *Colossians and Ephesians.* Sacra pagina. Collegeville, MN: Liturgical Press.

———. 2007. "Slavery, Sexuality and House Churches: A Reassessment of Colossians 3.18—4.1 in Light of New Research on the Roman Family." *NTS* 53:94–113.

———. 2010. "Beyond Identification of the Topos of Household Management: Reading the Household Codes in Light of Recent Methodologies and Theoretical Perspectives in the Study of the New Testament." *NTS* 57:65–90.

———. 2012. "Reading the New Testament Household Codes in Light of New Research on Children and Childhood in the Roman World." *SR* 41, no. 3:367–87.

Middleton, J. Richard. 2005. *The Liberating Image:* Imago Dei *in Genesis 1.* Grand Rapids: Brazos.

Moule, C. F. D. 1957. *The Epistles of Paul the Apostle to the Colossians and to Philemon.* Cambridge: Cambridge University Press.

Standhartinger, Angela. 2000. "The Origin and Intention of the Household Code in the Letter to the Colossians." *JSNT* 79:117–30.

Sumney, Jerry L. 2008: *Colossians: A Commentary.* Louisville: Westminster John Knox.

Swartley, Willard M. 1983. *Slavery, Sabbath, War and Women: Case Issues in Biblical Interpretation.* Scottdale, PA: Herald.

Thompson, Marianne Meye. 2005. *Colossians and Philemon.* Two Horizons New Testament Commentary. Grand Rapids: Eerdmans.

Walsh, Brian. 1999. "Late/Post Modernity and Idolatry: A Contextual Reading of Colossians 2.8—3.4." *ExAud* 15:1–17.

Walsh, Brian, and Sylvia Keesmaat. 2004. *Colossians Remixed: Subverting the Empire.* Downers Grove, IL: InterVarsity Press.

Wilson, R. McL. 2005. *A Critical and Exegetical Commentary on Colossians and Philemon.* ICC. London: T&T Clark.

Wink, Walter. 1984. *Naming the Powers: The Language of Power in the New Testament.* Minneapolis: Fortress Press.

Wright, N. T. 1986. *Colossians and Philemon.* TNTC. Grand Rapids: Eerdmans.

1 THESSALONIANS

Edward Pillar

Introduction

The Roman Empire was not a distant and inconsequential authority on the horizon of the Thessalonians' life. Having been founded in 316 BCE by the amalgamation of a number of small settlements, Thessalonica was defeated in battle by the Romans in 197 BCE and from then began its comprehensive imperialization. The Thessalonians drank freely of imperial ethos, philosophy, and culture, which together were a dominant influence on every aspect of their existence.

Thus, when Paul and his companions entered the city and began to proclaim the gospel concerning the Lord Jesus Christ, it is inevitable that the interpretative lens through which their message was heard and understood would have been one profoundly influenced by imperial ideas, ethos, and culture. It is this that we need to consider if we are to hear Paul as the Thessalonians heard him.

Moreover, we should allow the possibility that even if Paul did not directly intend to make references that might be understood as challenges to the imperial ethos and culture, the Thessalonians themselves, from where they stood in this extraordinary blend of Greek and Roman imperial culture, may well have drawn conclusions that engaged with their situation politically as well as spiritually.

At the heart of Paul's gospel, accepted by the Thessalonians, was the announcement that God had raised Jesus from the dead. The implications of this suggestion, more than any other, must be taken seriously if we are to appreciate the significance of this letter—the earliest Christian writing that we have. Emphasis on the resurrection should not simply be seen by readers in the twenty-first century as a precursor to the Parousia—the anticipated reappearance of Jesus Christ, but rather as bearing profound implications for how the Thessalonians were to live in the present and how they were to view and relate to their rulers, the imperial authorities.

1 Thessalonians 1:1-10: The Gospel in Thessalonica

▌ THE TEXT IN ITS ANCIENT CONTEXT

Paul begins the letter with a foundational statement of how he sees the Thessalonians. First, he refers to them as the church, the *ekklēsia*. However, rather than the Athenian model of *ekklēsia* as essentially a forum for democracy, Paul seems to see the Thessalonian *ekklēsia* as a gathering to share what was common among them, to support, challenge, and encourage one another in their newfound discipleship of Jesus Christ. Nonetheless, there remains a political nuance in the very act of adopting the name *ekklēsia*, for the Thessalonians are joined together in a new anti-imperial assembly. Conversion to God would have involved massive social, cultural, and political reorientation. A strong, supportive, and encouraging *ekklēsia*, or "church," would have been vital for the survival of each convert. Paul makes clear that this new "church" is rooted in relationship to God the Father and to the Lord Jesus Christ. Paul's reference to God as Father may highlight the fact that this *ekklēsia* is no longer dependent on the imperial father—the emperor—as *Pater Patriae* ("father of the country"). In addition, the reference to the Lord Jesus Christ may be Paul's way of saying that the Lord of this *ekklēsia* is specifically not the emperor; the reference to Jesus as the Christ may hint at the fulfillment and priority of the narrative of Israel over against the imperial story.

Paul then reflects back to the Thessalonians three key elements essential to understanding the visit of Paul and Silas to Thessalonica. First, the gospel was announced in Thessalonica. Here, Paul adopts another imperial term—"gospel," normally reserved for good news concerning the emperor or the imperial family—as an encompassing description of his message. Paul's gospel comprised news of the resurrection of Jesus from the dead. The practical significance of the news of the resurrection for the Thessalonians is that the immense power of the empire—epitomized by crucifixion—has been usurped and upended by a greater power: that of the living and true God. Second, the gospel announcement included mention of the reappearance of Jesus (his Parousia, hinted at in 1:10 and made clear at 2:19; 3:13; 4:15; 5:23). Once again, Paul is taking up a term familiar in the imperial context, normally used, for example, at the appearance and entry of a king into a city. Third, Paul's gospel makes clear that Jesus will rescue the Thessalonians from or defend them against wrath.

A second key element is that of the suffering of the Thessalonians as they receive the gospel. It is clear from 1:6 that the Thessalonians have endured persecution in the process of accepting the gospel (cf. 2:14 and 3:3). It is also likely that Paul speaks about wrath (1:10) precisely because there was a readily perceived and present awareness of suffering. Moreover, the Thessalonians' own expectation of wrath, and thus of suffering, would be linked to the neglecting of the gods and idols inherent in their social, cultural, and political context. Thus, while the Thessalonians would interpret the wrath as having its origin in the anger of the pagan gods, its precise form may well encompass both official and informal harassment and persecution. While the Thessalonians anticipated that Jesus would rescue or defend them both in their present context of suffering but also as persecution continued, it is made clear that they suffered at the hands of their "own compatriots" (2:14). Paul later encourages the Thessalonians that they are not destined for wrath (5:9).

The response of the Thessalonians is highlighted by the welcome given to Paul and Silas (1:9) and their joyous reception of the gospel (1:6). Their confidence in the gospel is underscored by their willingness to reorient their lives away from idols and toward God while waiting for the appearance of Jesus, the resurrected Son. Paul's use of an unusual term to describe this "waiting" is one used by the Jewish historian Josephus to portray waiting for the emperor (*J.W.* 7.68, 71).

◼ THE TEXT IN THE INTERPRETIVE TRADITION

Scholars have seen 1:9-10 as an example of Paul's mission preaching, perhaps adopted from other evangelists before him or employed by Jewish apologists in their contacts with gentiles (although Friedrich considered it to be part of a baptismal hymn: Friedrich, 502–16). Georg Strecker agrees and points out that it contains two of the affirmations fundamental to Christian faith: (a) worship of the true God and (b) the expectation of the return of Jesus the Son of God, who had been raised from the dead (Strecker, 65). However, it is unlikely that Paul would have been bound by a previous kerygma and more likely would have announced a gospel relevant to and contemporary in each context (Hooker, 435). The "wrath to come" has often been assumed to originate with God (e.g., Calvin 1960a, 339; Best, 85; Fee, 50)—although the text does not support this. Moreover, while the wrath is often taken to be eschatological, Martin Luther argued that the destruction of Jerusalem by Vespasian and Titus and the subsequent expulsion of the Jews is sufficient evidence for the "ruthless wrath of God" (Luther 1971, 138). Robert Jewett (37–41) suggests massacres, famine, or expulsion may have been in view here.

◼ THE TEXT IN CONTEMPORARY DISCUSSION

The experience of the Thessalonians highlights the transformative challenges of the gospel for every cultural, social, and political context. The close relationship between church and state in contemporary democratic societies and the normalization of consumerism have often left the demands of the gospel as little more than the requirement of slight moral and ethical adjustment, while the changes required by the gospel in the Thessalonian context involved a radical social and political metamorphosis.

1 Thessalonians 2:1-12: Paul's Defense of his Ministry

◼ THE TEXT IN ITS ANCIENT CONTEXT

This section begins with the first in a series of reminders—"you know" (*oidate*)—perhaps alerting the Thessalonians to what Paul and Silas had taught them during their visit to the city. Paul wants to remind the Thessalonians of what he considers they know to be true. First, he takes up the theme of suffering and reminds them that he and Silas suffered for the gospel prior to arriving in Thessalonica. In this there is a clear attempt to identify himself with the Thessalonians' own situation and to show empathy. So begins Paul's defense. Why Paul feels he has to defend himself is not entirely clear, but most likely it relates to the struggle and suffering that the Thessalonians are presently experiencing, and may relate to the grief to which Paul later refers regarding the deaths among the group (4:13). Paul's defense entails reference to their relation to God, an appeal to the evidence of their character, refuting rumors about their motives, and repeated references to the gospel. However, at the end of this section Paul returns to the theme inherent in his gospel, that of the subversion and arrogation of all other powers and authorities as he reminds the believers of the call on their lives.

First, Paul stresses that he and his companions consider themselves approved by God (2:4); their priority in speaking is to please God (2:4); and he maintains that God has been their witness (2:5). Second, Paul highlights the character that was evident while they were with the Thessalonians. They were gentle, "like a nurse" (2:7), which points also to the fatherly relationship they had with them (2:11). They sought to engage deeply with the Thessalonians, sharing "our own selves" (2:8), and moreover worked hard in order not to be a burden to them (2:9), insisting that they were never less than pure, upright, and blameless (2:10).

Third, he challenges accusations that appear to have arisen among some in the believing community. Paul's insistence that they did not come to Thessalonica with deceit or impure motives (2:3), nor with words of flattery (2:5), nor with any pretext for greed (2:5) makes clear that suspicions and concerns had arisen with the believing community as to the authenticity of Paul's mission among them.

Finally, he emphasizes his own sense of responsibility to present the gospel to them. He and Silas had shown great courage in declaring the gospel (2:2), believing that it had been entrusted to them (2:4). They shared (2:8) and proclaimed (2:9) the gospel, all the while urging, pleading, and encouraging the Thessalonians to live a life worthy of God (2:12).

▌ THE TEXT IN THE INTERPRETIVE TRADITION

John Huss, who after being accused of heresy was persecuted and burned at the stake, emphasized Paul's stress on integrity in the announcement of the gospel (Huss, 106), while Calvin considered that Paul reminds his readers of his integrity in order to stress the divine origin of their call to faith (1960a, 342).

▌ THE TEXT IN CONTEMPORARY DISCUSSION

At the heart of contemporary discussion is the validity of the gospel and those who proclaim it for every culture and context. The gospel concerning the resurrection of Jesus Christ from the dead continues to challenge and subvert structures that lay claim to power and authority over those called into God's kingdom. The gospel belongs to God and is founded on God's action in Jesus Christ. Those who proclaim his gospel are called to do so in the same humble and self-effacing spirit that was evident in Jesus himself. Moreover, Paul's own emphasis on how he and his companions lived their own lives as key aspects of the proclamation of the gospel is a timely call to authenticity and integrity for all to whom the gospel has been entrusted.

1 Thessalonians 2:13—3:11: Persecution, Suffering, and Wrath

▌ THE TEXT IN ITS ANCIENT CONTEXT

The theme of suffering persecution continues through this section. Paul and Silas give thanks to God for the way in which the Thessalonians received the word of God. First Thessalonians 2:13-14 echoes 1:6 in its reference to imitation. In 1:6, the Thessalonians are said to be imitators of Paul, Silas, and the Lord. The reference to "the Lord" is noteworthy and seems to suggest that the apostles and the Thessalonians share with the Lord the experience of receiving the word of God in the midst of suffering. In 2:13-14, they are described as receivers of the word of God in the midst of persecution, but on this occasion they are imitators of their Judean brothers and sisters.

The element of imitation Paul highlights is that of suffering at the hands of one's compatriots. Just as the Judean believers suffered persecution at the hands of their compatriots, so too the Thessalonians are experiencing persecution by their own neighbors. Moreover, Paul appears to suggest that suffering incurred from compatriots is becoming typical for followers of the Lord Jesus, for not only are the Lord's disciples being persecuted, but the Lord Jesus himself and the prophets before him also suffered in this way. In 2:15-16, Paul highlights how the Jews (*hoi Ioudaioi*) had apparently and unfortunately adopted this malevolent habit over many centuries (see below).

Paul then appears to suggest that the Jews were presently experiencing "wrath," although he elaborates neither on the source nor on the nature of the wrath. However, as wrath in the ancient world was normally associated with the neglect of appropriate cultic activity, then we may tentatively consider that Paul views the Jews' present experience of wrath to have its source in God, whom they neglect in their rejection of the Lord Jesus, the prophets, and the Christian disciples.

Although Paul had made clear that there would be persecution (3:3-4), the depth of Paul and Silas's concern over the Thessalonians becomes apparent. There is the concern that the Thessalonians' fledgling faith and the newly formed *ekklēsia* may have dissipated under the pressure of the suffering brought about by the persecutions.

The longing "with great eagerness" (2:17) that Paul expresses to travel again to Thessalonica and to strengthen and encourage the church arises out of this concern for the persecuted Thessalonians. Moreover, the profound personal investment that Paul and Silas have made in the Thessalonians is unmistakable in their description of the new church as "our glory and joy" (2:20) and additionally in their apprehension lest their labor had been in vain. Thus Timothy is sent to visit them. It is not made clear at this point why Timothy was able to make the journey while Paul was not, other than the enigmatic reference to Satan (2:18). Although some argue that Paul intends Satan and "the tempter" to be understood as one and the same (Fee, 120), Paul himself does not make the identity of "the tempter" clear, nor does he make the supposed link with Satan explicit.

Timothy's task in journeying to Thessalonica is at least twofold. First, he is to strengthen and encourage them (3:2). Clearly some of them have been disturbed by the persecutions and may even have begun to doubt the veracity of Paul's message to them. The extent of the persecutions may have led some to question Paul's teaching that Jesus would rescue or defend them against wrath (1:10). Additionally, the impact of the persecutions on the young church and possibly even Paul's awareness of it is made clear in two ways: First, in his expression of fear that the tempter had tempted them and all of Paul and Silas's hard work in the city had come to nothing (3:5); and second, in his saying again that he longs to see them face-to-face and to restore or to mend what is lacking in their faith (3:10). Such a comment would be superfluous unless it was evident that the Thessalonians' immature faith had in some measure been fragmented in the ongoing persecutions.

Timothy's second task was to bring an account to Paul and Silas of the condition of the Thessalonian church (3:5). Timothy's report involved good news. The Thessalonians still have kind memories of the apostles and also long to see them again (3:6). This positive report brings great encouragement to Paul and Silas, who respond with hopefulness. Paul's affirmation, "For we now live" (3:8) is cautiously optimistic. As long as the Thessalonians "continue" to stand firm, then Paul and Silas can assess that their work is bearing fruit.

Paul concludes this section of his letter with a blessing for abundance in love and strength in their lives of holiness as they look to the appearance of the Lord Jesus.

■ THE TEXT IN THE INTERPRETIVE TRADITION

First Thessalonians 2:14-16 is among those passages "repeatedly used to demonize the Jewish people" (Hagner, 70). Thomas Aquinas clearly considered the Jews responsible for the killing of the Lord Jesus, and argues that they were also antagonistic, prohibiting and impeding the preaching to the gentiles, and that all this was by "divine permission . . . that they fill up the measure of their sins" (1969, 19). Luther was convinced that "this work of wrath is proof that the Jews, surely rejected by God, are no longer his people, and neither is he any longer their God" (1971, 139). Calvin comments here that God "strips the Jews of all honor, so as to leave them nothing but hatred and ill repute" (Calvin 1960a, 348).

■ THE TEXT IN CONTEMPORARY DISCUSSION

While Raymond E. Brown raises the possibility that the polemic against the Jews may be an interpolation, as it resembles pagan polemic and is "scarcely characteristic of Paul" (Brown, 463), Ernest Best is an example of those who argue that Paul held "an unacceptable anti-Semitic position" (Best, 122), and F. F. Bruce considered that just because Paul himself was a Jew did not rule out the possibility of anti-Jewishness here (Bruce, 51). However, Ben Witherington III considers that Paul has in view here a "temporal and temporary judgment which has already come in full" on those who opposed the gospel in Judea. At most, Paul may well have seen the wrath come upon the Jews as "poetic justice" in the light of the execution of Jesus and the persecution of Jesus' earliest followers (Witherington, 87). Hatred and racism have no place in Paul or the contemporary church, but rather we can see this passage as deep encouragement for those suffering persecution.

1 Thessalonians 4:1-12: Sanctification as a Mark of Community

■ THE TEXT IN ITS ANCIENT CONTEXT

There is considerable evidence for the presence of voluntary associations in Thessalonica established on the basis of professional or religious affinities (Ascough, 316). Each of these associations would obligate its members to a common ethos, values, and rules. Both the regularity and the content of the gatherings would differ from group to group. It seems likely that the *ekklēsia* in Thessalonica would have been recognizable as a voluntary association with its own distinctive ethos. In this section, Paul follows his words of blessing (3:13), which seek to encourage holiness among the believers, by reminding them of the values and ethos that he and Silas had insisted should mark the *ekklēsia* (4:1-2). As far as Paul is concerned, the Thessalonians know very well what these values are. Paul then makes reference to two key elements of the distinctive ethos of the Thessalonian *ekklēsia*.

The initial concern is for their sanctification. Here Paul reminds the believers of three specific elements, each regarding sexual purity. The first aspect is that they should abstain from fornication. Second, that they should all learn to discipline their sexual desires, controlling themselves in a manner worthy of God and of course adopting the values they were instructed in and that should be espoused by the group of believers themselves. Moreover, they should not reflect the values of those outside the group or in other associations. Third, Paul reminds them that they should not use sexuality as a tool of power or exploitation.

It may be that the believers previously belonged to groups where there was a degree of sexual freedom or where, as a generalized aspect of Roman culture, power and status were expressed through sexual dominance. Indeed, Paul's reminder may have been prompted by rumors of inappropriate activity, but that was not to be a mark of the Thessalonian Christian *ekklēsia*. Paul insists that rejecting the instruction to pure and holy behavior was a rejection of God's authority, perhaps hinting that this would lead to exclusion from the Christian association.

Paul's second reminder listed above seems to concern the impression made on outsiders by the loving nature of the group of believers. Having reiterated the primacy of love as the key aspect of their ethos, Paul then encourages them to ensure that the life they share together be marked by honesty and freedom from dependence on those who do not share their ethos and values. Rather than individualizing the instructions in 4:11-12, we should rather see them as admonishments intended to be understood corporately. In particular, Paul speaks of living together "quietly" (4:11). This is probably a reference to living without selfish ambition and without the striving for honors that may have prevailed in other associations that were profoundly influenced by values of the empire-inclined city. The group is to look after their own affairs and not be dependent on outsiders for their regulation and direction.

▮ THE TEXT IN THE INTERPRETIVE TRADITION

Tertullian cited 1 Thess. 4:3-5 in arguing "in defense of modesty, of sanctity, of chastity: they all aim their missiles against the interests of luxury, and lasciviousness, and lust" (1870a, 101). Whereas Jerome references 1 Thess. 4:7 in his treatise questioning marriage, "for God called us not for uncleanness, but in sanctification" (1892, 1.16), Augustine spoke more positively of marriage for purposes of procreation, not "in the passion of lust like the Gentiles who do not know God" (1955, 13). Scholarly debate here has often centered on the meaning of *skeuos* (here translated "body") in verse 4, while almost equal weight throughout history has been placed on the translation "wife" as on "body." Both alternatives are theoretically possible, but the use of *ktasthai* ("control, acquire") seems to point to "body" as the preferred option.

▮ THE TEXT IN CONTEMPORARY DISCUSSION

In an era when the power of sexuality seems to prevail in public and private, religious and political arenas, this passage from Paul is a timely reminder of the robust challenge to followers of the Lord

Jesus to live lives that are defined by the values of Christ and not to be enslaved by the dominant ethos of the day.

1 Thessalonians 4:13—5:11: Confidence in the Gospel

▌ THE TEXT IN ITS ANCIENT CONTEXT

Paul elucidates the meaning of salvation in answer to profound concerns that have arisen among the Thessalonian believers. He then urges them to encourage one another (4:18; 5:11).

The first stimulus to mutual encouragement (4:18) is accompanied by a restatement of the gospel, "Jesus died and rose again" (4:14). However, while Paul's previous reiteration of the gospel in 1:10 was set in the context of courage, confidence, and hopefulness, here there is ignorance, grief, and hopelessness (4:13). It is likely that "those who have died" were killed during the substantial and ongoing persecution suffered by the Thessalonians from their compatriots. The expectation of the Thessalonians was that they would be rescued or defended against such wrath (1:10), and thus it appears that these bereavements have led to a serious reassessment of the veracity of Paul's teaching and perhaps even the gospel itself. Therefore, Paul has to reiterate the gospel on which their hope is based: "we believe that Jesus died and rose again" (4:14). Moreover, Paul then gives his confident assessment of what this gospel hope means for both the living and dead in Thessalonica and elsewhere. Because Jesus has been raised from the dead, he is Lord over against the claims of the emperor. Thus Paul anticipates that Jesus will appear as a conquering king in a manner reminiscent of the *parousia* of imperial victors. As with the familiar imperial custom, those who accept Jesus and accede to his lordship will go out to greet him—whether presently dead or alive. It is in no way necessary to insist that this was intended to be an exact prediction of the events that will accompany the appearance of Jesus, but Paul appears to blend imperial practice with war imagery from the Qumran community (1QM 1:4-17) and prophetic oracles from Zechariah 9 to paint a picture of a dramatic and decisive salvific event.

The second stimulus to mutual encouragement (5:11) again draws on the key aspects of the gospel: the death of Jesus leading to resurrection, "who died for us, so that . . . we may live with him" (5:10). However, 5:9 also appears to mirror 1:10. It goes perhaps to the heart of the motive for the letter, that of reassurance within a present experience of severe suffering under persecution and a restatement of the trustworthiness of the gospel and the deep hope that it provides, "For God has destined us not for wrath but for obtaining salvation through our Lord Jesus Christ."

Although Paul says, "you do not need to have anything written to you," he nevertheless considers it necessary to restate his teaching about "the times and the seasons" (5:1). From the perspective of awareness of the chronology of the narrative of God's people and the anticipation of the fulfillment of God's purposes, Paul sets up a direct challenge to the assertion of Roman imperial ideology that the empire can guarantee "peace and security." Rather, just as the Israelites were protected in Egypt against the angel of death, so the Thessalonians will be safe against the "sudden destruction," while those outside the *ekklēsia* will discover that "there will be no escape" (5:3). Paul then juxtaposes the lifestyle of the believers over against that of those who continue to live under the values and ethos of the empire: the believers are children of light over against those of the darkness; of the day over against the night; awake rather than asleep; and sober instead of drunk (5:4-7). Moreover, Paul appears to highlight once again the church/imperial contrast by adopting two elements of the dress of the soldier, who was commissioned to keep a contrived "peace and security" under the imperial banner. The Christian will put on the breastplate of faith and love and the helmet as the hope of salvation. Paul's final assertion here highlights his deep confidence that the destiny of the believer, whether presently alive or dead, is salvation through the death and resurrection of the Lord Jesus Christ.

Throughout this letter Paul has had his eyes on the anticipated appearance of the Lord Jesus. One element of his concern for the Thessalonian believers is that holiness might be the distinctive feature of their group. Paul's encouragement that this holiness should be maintained and strengthened in practical ways as the central ethos of the group is encapsulated in his final blessing (5:23). Previously he has spoken of sexual purity and mutual love as distinguishing marks (4:1-12). Now Paul highlights respectful internal relationships, thankful prayer, and openness to the Spirit. First, Paul emphasizes the need for a deep respect and profound love for those who have spiritual responsibility. Second, they are all to ensure peaceful relationships within the group. This peace has to extend to warning those who might be idle or cause trouble, strengthening those who are discouraged, and helping those who may be weak in the face of the persecutions. They are to be patient with one another. Third, thankfulness is to define their life together. Moreover, their continuous expression of prayer is to be distinguished by joy.

Finally, Paul expresses his desire that the Thessalonians should be open to the activity of the Holy Spirit among them and particularly that they cherish and appreciate prophetic words. It may be that hasty contempt has been shown when prophecies that might have strengthened or admonished the community have been shared. Rather, they are to test everything to make sure that nothing that might be profitable to their growth and strength is lost. Paul assures them all that God is faithful and will prepare them well for the appearance of Jesus.

▌ The Text in the Interpretive Tradition

Discussions around eschatology have inevitably dominated consideration of this passage. The early church appeared to be particularly concerned with the individual context of eschatology, countering suggestions that it is only the soul that survives death. Tertullian, for example, tackled the thorny issue of the decomposition of the body in the interval before resurrection, arguing for "the integrity of the whole substance of man" at the resurrection (1922, 57). Origen stressed the transformation of the body at the resurrection into a state of incorruptibility (*Against Celsus* 5.19), while Augustine considered the possibility that those who are alive at the resurrection might pass through death into immortality as they were "carried aloft" to meet Christ in the air (1963, 20.20). Calvin speaks of the transformation into "an entirely new nature" while reminding us of the inevitable judgment that awaits (1960b, 2:17). In more recent times, the dispensationalist views popularized by J. N. Darby and published in the Scofield Bible have dominated in some quarters. The rapture, interpreted from 1 Thess. 4:17, whereby the faithful were snatched away from the earth upon the Parousia of Jesus, became a central tenet in this belief system. Each interpretive strategy ultimately concerns the meaning of salvation: will it take place in the present or the future; is it for the individual or for a corporate body; does it involve apocalyptic destruction of creation or its restoration?

■ THE TEXT IN CONTEMPORARY DISCUSSION

N. T. Wright is among those who have critiqued the escapist rapture theologies prevalent among the evangelical wing of the church, as popularized by Hal Lindsey in *The Late Great Planet Earth* and by Tim LaHaye and Jerry B. Jenkins's *Left Behind* series. Wright has argued that such theologies' acceptance of the subsequent cataclysmic destruction of the earth deny the need to put things right in this world as it will all be destroyed anyway (Wright, 119). Helmut Koester emphasizes the significance of the believing community in the context of the Parousia (Koester, 159) and concludes, "Paul envisions a role for the eschatological community that presents a utopian alternative to the prevailing eschatological ideology of Rome" (166). The transformation of all creation is predicated on the resurrection of Jesus Christ from the dead. This in turn supports a robust understanding of the resurrection of all believers as life in community and cooperation with God putting things right on the earth as a more balanced and ecologically friendly view.

2 THESSALONIANS

Edward Pillar

Introduction

Although the Pauline authorship of this second letter is sometimes questioned, more often scholarship accepts its authenticity (Malherbe, 349–74). Scholars who observe differences in language, style, and theology do not always take into account the changed circumstances of the Thessalonians. The believing community based in Thessalonica continues to suffer considerable persecution and perhaps even a significant increase in persecution as they seek to live out their calling to be followers of the Lord Jesus Christ. Paul speaks specifically and carefully into the Thessalonian context at this precise time to encourage them. Their imperially dominated context seems to be a more acute backdrop for Paul than was the case in the first letter. The focus of encouragement for the believers is set against an awareness of the clash of kingdoms—God's and Caesar's. In order to affirm the believers' stance in the face of their suffering, Paul adopts apocalyptic imagery to inspire and to strengthen.

2 Thessalonians 1:1-12: Steadfastness in Suffering

▌THE TEXT IN ITS ANCIENT CONTEXT

The greetings at the head of this letter are almost identical to the first letter, but there is emphasis in the repetition of "God our Father and the Lord Jesus Christ." There are three key elements here that may arise from a subtle countercultural stance Paul is taking and supporting in the church in Thessalonica. First, true peace has its source in God the Father contra Caesar as *Pater Patriae* ("father of the country"). Second, the true Lord is Jesus the Risen One. And third, the prevailing narrative is not the imperial story (e.g., Virgil's *Aeneid*), but God's story that finds its fulfillment in the Christ.

583

In the light of the evidently significant persecution of the Christians in Thessalonica, there is the possibility that Paul draws inspiration from the account of the suffering of the Jews in the face of the persecution at the hand of Antiochus IV Epiphanes. Two centuries prior to Paul, the Jewish people had been ordered to forsake their laws and traditions and to defile the temple in Jerusalem. Although their suffering was interpreted as discipline, their resistance and steadfastness in the face of tyrannical oppression was celebrated. Moreover, there was a clear belief that the Lord would punish the unrighteous to the full measure of their sins (2 Macc. 6:14). If indeed Paul is alluding to this account, then it is most likely that he is simply seeking to encourage the Thessalonians to remain faithful against whoever persecutes them.

Paul advocates the vengeance of God's kingdom over Caesar's kingdom. While Paul assures the Thessalonians of prayers in the face of their struggle against persecution, it is not clear whether he intends to affirm their accentuated suffering or their steadfastness and faith as signs of the judgment of God and as creative preparation of the believers for the kingdom of God (1:5). Moreover, Paul sees God's response to the suffering of the Thessalonians as decisive and definitive, affirming God's response as "just" (1:6). This goes so far as eternal punishment (1:9), hinting that Paul advocates an "eye-for-an-eye" rejoinder from God. Paul affirms his confidence that the coming of the Lord Jesus will be the conclusive day of judgment (1:9-10).

■ THE TEXT IN THE INTERPRETIVE TRADITION

The apocalyptic nature of this passage was important for John Chrysostom, who passionately argued for the justice of God against the wicked. However, while he stressed, "Let us not remember the kingdom so much as hell. For fear has more power than the promise" (Chrysostom, 477) and "If we always think of hell we shall not soon fall into it" (476), he also counseled that believers should not rejoice at the punishment of others (475).

■ THE TEXT IN CONTEMPORARY DISCUSSION

Just as those described in 2 Maccabees anticipated that resurrection would bring both vindication of the righteous and God's judgment whereby there would be a putting things to right, there is also a challenge here to actualize God's righteousness in the face of suffering. The impact of the insidious, life-sapping values evident in modern economic and militaristic empires must be countered with a confidence in God's ultimate conquest. However, those suffering persecution and seeking vengeance against the perpetrators should not deny the love, mercy, and justice that lie at the heart of God's kingdom.

2 Thessalonians 2:1-17: Avoiding Deception— the Day of the Lord

■ THE TEXT IN ITS ANCIENT CONTEXT

This passage is ultimately about deception. Paul is concerned that the believers should not be deceived by those who say the day of the Lord has already come. Paul also speaks of the deception that clouds the perception of the unbeliever. Paul's intuition seems to be that the previous narrative of Israel under persecution is the template for what the Thessalonians should expect in the future. Just as Antiochus defiled the temple in his day, so Paul may also now be drawing on the account of Gaius Caligula, who promoted himself as divine and insisted upon setting up a statue to himself within the Jerusalem temple in 41 CE. However, while we might seek to interpret "the lawless one" as Antiochus or Caligula, Paul hints that neither their coming (*parousia*) nor any previous or present tyrant (2 Thess. 2:9) is necessarily direct evidence that they are the "lawless one," and the anticipated direct confrontation between the "lawless one" and the Lord Jesus has yet to take place. The momentous "day of the Lord" has not yet dawned. Nonetheless, we can at least surmise that, set within the Thessalonian imperial context, Paul does intend his readers to infer that an imperial tyrant is the target for annihilation at the magnificent splendor of the Lord's coming. Moreover, Paul assures the Thessalonians that their persecutors are operating under a powerful delusion—possibly that they refuse to accept the revelation of God in Jesus Christ—that will lead to their ultimate punishment.

Paul makes plain his desire to encourage the Thessalonians: they are loved and have been chosen. God called them, through a gospel that countered imperial claims, to serve the new Lord. And Paul is confident that their present experience of being tested will prepare them for salvation. Again Paul seems to hint at those who had suffered under Antiochus as they had resolutely held to their ancestral traditions, and he encourages the believers in Thessalonica to hold decisively to the traditions they had been taught (2:15) while offering a blessing that is steeped in the confident hope of the resurrection. Moreover, Paul references the elusive figure of the one who "restrains," but as Gordon Fee makes clear, "we can describe what it is they know, but with almost no insight as to what it meant to them" (Fee, 285).

▌THE TEXT IN THE INTERPRETIVE TRADITION

Following Tertullian's assertion that the "lawless one" of 2 Thess. 2:3 was the antichrist (Tertullian, 1870b, 463), scholars throughout history have presented various individuals as the antichrist. Among others, Calvin (1960b, 4.2.11) considered the pope to be a candidate, as did Luther, who also included "the Turk" in his designation (Luther 1857, 193). However, Augustine was a little more circumspect, suggesting something of a communal nature to the antichrist, referring to "all who are wicked . . . the multitude of men who belong to him" (1963, 20.19). Perhaps the earliest example of the identification of a living figure with antichrist may be found in the late first-century-BCE *Ascension of Isaiah* 3:13—4:22, where some have interpreted the language as code suggesting that Nero was antichrist (Charles 1900, li–lxxiii). Augustine considered this and also the hypothesis that the "restrainer" is the Roman Empire but finally concludes, "for myself, I confess, I have no idea what is meant" (1963, 20.19).

▌THE TEXT IN CONTEMPORARY DISCUSSION

For a long time people have pulled together different elements of apocalyptic texts, including 2 Thessalonians, fusing the figure of the antichrist and the lawless one, seeking to identify them with present individuals in order perhaps to give these texts a sense of literal veracity and in addition to further particular viewpoints. This can be done clearly in service to imperial agendas, as when Saddam Hussein invaded Kuwait or when Osama Bin Laden was held responsible for the attacks on the United States in 2001. Such identification justified, for some, the American invasion of Iraq and latterly of Afghanistan. It's possible *in this way* for readers to be "deceived"; today and here we have some analogy with what Paul wants to say. The important thing is to remain focused on the establishment of God's kingdom in the midst of suffering and all the while holding firmly to the values, ethos, and traditions of the Lord Jesus.

2 Thessalonians 3:1-18: Warning the Idle

▌ THE TEXT IN ITS ANCIENT CONTEXT

Just as Paul appeals for prayer for himself and his companions, he confidently asserts the faithfulness of the Lord. There are wicked and evil people from whom Paul and his companions need defending, and there is evil itself (literally "the evil one") from which they all need protection. The values of the kingdom to which the believers have been called are evident as Paul prays that they might be directed to the love of God and to the steadfastness of Christ—no doubt a reminder of Christ's patient endurance under suffering (note the Thessalonians' patient waiting in 1 Thess. 1:9).

Again, Paul is concerned that the believers should hold to the traditions they have been taught (3:6). There is to be a clear delineation between those who hold to the traditions and those who idly let things slip. It is not clear whether the idlers are casually awaiting the appearance of the Lord or whether they have given up working in anticipation of what they see as their inevitable demise at the hands of their persecutors. Certainly this latter case would be seen as a betrayal of a living confidence in God and a capitulation to the demands of their persecutors. The strength of Paul's reprimand denotes the seriousness with which he takes the need for all to continue working hard in the confident assurance of the appearance of the Lord Jesus.

Paul demonstrates his pastoral commitment to the church in Thessalonica once again as he encourages the believers to treat the idlers not as enemies but as fellow believers in need of warning and admonishment. The extent of the persecution suffered by the believers that is evident throughout this letter might easily divide the group and cause it to slowly disintegrate. However, Paul's encouragement to continue to treat those who have become lax as brothers and sisters is a clear sign of his pastoral determination to see this fledgling group shine radiantly as evidence of the power of the gospel to transform lives and communities. Paul's final salutation—repeated in 1 Cor. 16:21 and Col. 4:18—here both emphasizes his authorship of the letter and his concern noted in 2 Thess. 2:2 about false doctrine circulating in his name.

▌ THE TEXT IN THE INTERPRETIVE TRADITION

Augustine critiqued those monks who refused to work and who insisted that "they must be free for prayer, chanting psalms, for reading and for the word of God" (1952, 362) and cited 2 Thess. 3:10 against them. Aquinas quotes Augustine and affirms "that religious are bound to manual labour" (Thomas Aquinas 1973, 2.2, 187.3). Luther, however, suggests that this passage had been quickly corrupted by "lay people" and prefers, "let the minister of the Word be more intent on godliness than on the work of his hands," and as far as eating is concerned, "let God worry about that" (Luther 1973, 324). Calvin argued that those who excused themselves from the "common rule" (of work) should forfeit their sustenance as the reward of their work (1960a, 418).

■ The Text in Contemporary Discussion

Bruce Winter suggests that the idle busybody might be a reference to those who have not yet moved on from being beholden to the benefaction of a patron but instead are politicking and all the while trying to influence the believing community in the favor of the patron. Those who might be in a position to support such an idle busybody should not do so (Winter, 57–58). Best indicates that the community may be tempted to eject the idle ones in order to purify it and "relieve themselves of an intolerable burden" (Best, 333), although Néstor Míguez highlights the possibility that there may have been a class of idle rich, the traders and landowners, in Thessalonica who did not need to work with their hands, but relied on their servants (Míguez, 67). Furthermore, it is striking that while Vladimir Lenin adopted, "He who does not work neither shall he eat" as a principle of socialism (Lenin, 85), this slogan is also heard on the lips of those representing the American right-wing movement such as US Representative Michele Bachmann (Volsky).

Works Cited

Ascough, R. S. 2000. "The Thessalonian Christian Community as a Professional Voluntary Association." *JBL* 119, no. 2:311–28.

Augustine. 1952. *The Work of Monks*. In *Treatises on Various Subjects*, 323–94. Edited by R. J. Deferrari. Translated by Mary Sarah Muldowney. FC 16. Washington, DC: Catholic University of America Press.

———. 1955. *The Good of Marriage*. In *Treatises on Marriage and Other Subjects*, 9–51. Translated by Charles D. Wilcox et al. FC 27. New York: Father of the Church.

———. 1963. *City of God*. Translated by J. W. C. Wand. London: Oxford University Press.

Best, Ernest. 1972. *A Commentary on the First and Second Epistles to the Thessalonians*. BNTC. London: Black.

Brown, Raymond E. 1997. *Introduction to the New Testament*. New York: Doubleday.

Bruce, F. F. 1982. *1 and 2 Thessalonians*. WBC 45. Waco, TX: Word.

Calvin, John. 1960a. *The Epistles of Paul to the Romans and to the Thessalonians*. Edited by D. W. Torrance and T. F. Torrance. Translated by R. Mackenzie. Edinburgh: Oliver and Boyd.

———. 1960b. *Institutes of the Christian Religion*. Edited by John T. McNeil. Translated by Ford Lewis Battles. Louisville: Westminster John Knox.

Charles, R. H., ed. 1900. *The Ascension of Isaiah*. London: Black.

Chrysostom, John. 1879. *Homilies on Thessalonians*. In *The Homilies of St. John Chrysostom, Archbishop of Constantinople: On the Epistles of St. Paul the Apostle to the Philippians, Colossians, and Thessalonians*. Oxford: James Parker.

Fee, Gordon D. 2009. *The First and Second Letters to the Thessalonians*. NICNT. Grand Rapids: Eerdmans.

Friedrich, G. 1965. "Ein Tauflied Hellenistischer Judenchristen, 1 Thess. 1:9f." *TZ* 21, 502-16.

Hagner, Donald A. 2000. "Anti-Semitism and the New Testament." In *Eerdmans Dictionary of the Bible*. Edited by D. N. Freedman, A. C. Myers, and A. B. Beck. Grand Rapids: Eerdmans.

Hooker, Morna D. 1996. "1 Thessalonians 1:9-10: A Nutshell—But What Kind of Nut?" In *Frühes Christentum*. Vol. 3, *Geschichte–Tradition–Reflexion: Festschrift für Martin Hengel zum 70*, edited by Hubert Cancik, Hermann Lichtenberger, and Peter Schäfer, 435–48. Tübingen: Mohr Siebeck.

Huss, John. 1953. *On Simony*. In *Advocates of Reform*, edited by M. Spinka, 196-278. London: SCM.

Jerome. 1892. *Against Jovinianus*. In *NPNF²* 6:346–86.

Jewett, Robert. 1986. *The Thessalonian Correspondence: Pauline Rhetoric and Millenarian Piety*. Philadelphia: Fortress Press.

Josephus. 1927–1928. *Jewish War*. Translated by H. St. J. Thackeray. 3 vols. LCL. Cambridge, MA: Harvard University Press.

Koester, Helmut. 1997. "Imperial Ideology and Paul's Eschatology." in *Paul and Empire*, edited by Richard A. Horsley, 158–66. Harrisburg, PA: Trinity Press International.

Lenin, Vladimir. 1992. *The State and Revolution*. London: Penguin.

Luther, Martin. 1857. "Of Antichrist." In *The Table Talk of Martin Luther*, 193–225. Translated and edited by W. Hazlitt. London: Bohn.

———. 1955. *The Catholic Epistles*. *LW* 30. H. T. Lehmann, ed. St. Louis: Concordia.

———. 1971. *The Christian in Society*. *LW* 47. F. Sherman and H. T. Lehmann, eds. Philadelphia: Fortress Press.

———. 1973. *Select Pauline Epistles*. *LW* 28. St. Louis: Concordia.

Malherbe, Abraham J. 2000. *The Letters to the Thessalonians*. AB 32B. New York: Doubleday.

Míguez, Néstor O. 2012. *The Practice of Hope: Ideology and Intention in 1 Thessalonians*. Paul in Critical Contexts. Minneapolis: Fortress Press.

Origen. 1965. *Contra Celsum*. Translated by Henry Chadwick. Cambridge: Cambridge University Press.

Strecker, Georg. 2000. *Theology of the New Testament*. Berlin: de Gruyter.

———. 1870a. *On Modesty*. In *ANF* 4:56–122.

———. 1870b. "On the Second Epistle to the Thessalonians." In *Against Marcion*. In *ANF* 3:269–476.

Tertullian. 1922. *Concerning the Resurrection of the Flesh*. Translated by A. Souter. London: SPCK.

Thomas Aquinas. 1969. *Commentary on Saint Paul's First Letter to the Thessalonians and the Letter to the Philippians*. Translated by F. R. Larcher and M. Duffy. Albany, NY: Magi.

———. 1973. *Summa Theologiae*. Vol. 47. Translated by J. Aumann. London: Blackfriars.

Volsky, Igor. 2011. "Michele Bachmann: 'If Anyone Will Not Work, Neither Should He Eat.'" *Thinkprogress.org*. November 7. http://thinkprogress.org/lgbt/2011/11/07/362845/michele-bachmann-if-anyone-will-not-work-neither-should-he-eat/

Winter, Bruce W. 1994. *Seek the Welfare of the City: Christians as Benefactors and Citizens*. Carlisle: Paternoster.

Witherington, Ben, III. 2006. *1 and 2 Thessalonians: A Socio-Rhetorical Commentary*. Grand Rapids: Eerdmans.

Wright, N. T. 2008. *Surprised by Hope*. San Francisco: HarperOne.

1 TIMOTHY

Deborah Krause

Introduction to the Pastoral Epistles

The Pastoral Epistles (PE) comprise a corpus of pseudepigraphical teachings attributed to the apostle Paul and ostensibly written to his closest followers, Timothy and Titus. These books were likely compiled in the early second century CE. Written several generations after the death of the historical Paul, the PE represent a part of the early church's interpretation of Paul. As an evangelist to the gentiles and leader of churches, the historical Paul saw his letters as a means to an end. As such, he likely did not think of himself predominantly as a "letter writer." By the second century, however, his letters (copied and redistributed) had become widely known, and his ministry (heroically recounted in Luke's Acts of the Apostles) had become legendary. First and Second Timothy and Titus take their place in relation to this period of remembering and reinterpreting Paul. As such, they pose as the Pauline voice of authority about matters related to church leadership (hence the name "Pastoral Epistles"), and they seek to define the Pauline legacy for the church in a particular direction. Importantly, they were but one venture in the struggle to define that legacy. Other writings, such as the canonical Acts of the Apostles and the noncanonical Acts of Paul, engaged in the interpretation of the Pauline tradition in remarkably different directions. Such divergent interpretations mark a moment in the contentious period of early Christian origins in which the Pauline legacy was deeply contested (e.g., 2 Pet. 3:16). In particular, the PE represent the effort to codify and manage the written teachings of Paul into a set of resources for guiding and directing not simply local communities but also the universal church.

Most historical scholars of early Christian literature argue that the PE were composed as a corpus. They do not appear in the earliest artifacts of the process of canonization (e.g., Marcion's list of early Christian writings, c. 144 CE, or the earliest extant manuscript of Paul's letters, P46), and thereby likely represent a singular performance of Paul's voice and insight as an intervention into early Christian disputes about the interpretation of Paul. As a corpus their likely original order would have concluded with 2 Timothy, the final writing offering a poignant glimpse of Paul as he provides his last testament to his entrusted colleague and friend. In this historical perspective, the corpus may have been composed to appear as a trove of recently (and miraculously) discovered Pauline insight and the key to the overall interpretation of Paul's occasional letters (i.e., 1 Thessalonians, 1–2 Corinthians, Philippians, Philemon, Galatians, and Romans).

One of the important elements of reading the PE in light of their likely historical origins is the awareness that they are not really letters. Their letter form is a part of their construction of a Pauline voice and authority. As such, the PE present perspectives on church order and governance in the guise of personal letters between Paul and his closest companions. Ironically, in attempting to direct Paul's wisdom more broadly for a diversifying and growing movement, the PE mimic a personal and privileged space of communication. Such layers of rhetoric make the interpretation of these writings a fascinating study in navigating the construction of authority in the interpretation of Paul and the early church.

While the historical-critical perspective on the PE described in this introduction has revolutionized their interpretation in the last century, it is important to remember that for the vast majority of the church's history, the authorship of the letters was not questioned. For that reason, for most of the church's history, 1 and 2 Timothy and Titus have not been distinguished as a particular interpretation of the Pauline tradition from the late or early second century. Rather, the writings have been seen as authentic communication between Paul and his closest companions in ministry—a continuation of Paul's correspondence. As such, these writings have been remarkably successful in achieving their original intent—to influence and direct the Pauline tradition as it has informed the life and ministry of the church. The form of this current commentary, with its emphasis on ancient, interpretive, and contemporary aspects of the text, offers an excellent opportunity to engage in an exploration of the PE in ways that honor their various contexts and perspectives of interpretation.

Introduction to 1 Timothy

The intimate tone struck by 1 Timothy prepares its readers/hearers for unfettered, trustworthy, and "genuine" access to Paul's thinking about the matters he is about to discuss with one whom the tradition (and Paul's historical letters) present as one of his most trusted coworkers in the ministry. Imagine how the gathered leadership would have responded upon the first reading of these writings! From a context several generations removed from Paul's ministry and in the midst of controversies about his teaching and the church, the reading of his communication to his friend Timothy would come across as a rare opportunity to overhear his voice and glean his perspective. No doubt, the gathered faithful were on the edge of their seats.

1 Timothy 1:1-2: Opening Salutation

■ THE TEXT IN ITS ANCIENT CONTEXT

The naming of writer and sender is a stock element of the greeting of the Greco-Roman letter. Such greetings are also characterized by a blessing. The naming of Paul as sender and Timothy as his "genuine child in the faith" frames the relationship of the sender and recipient as intimate.

■ THE TEXT IN THE INTERPRETIVE TRADITION

Paul's association with Timothy is certainly referenced in his likely historical writings where he is named as a cowriter (2 Cor. 1:1; Phil. 1:1; 1 Thess. 1:1; Philem. 1:1), an emissary (1 Cor. 4:17; 16:10; 1 Thess. 3:2), and a coprisoner (Phil. 2:19), but the connection became legendary within the Pauline interpretive tradition. For Luke, Timothy is narrated in the Acts of the Apostles as the child of a pious Jewish mother and a Greek (likely pagan) father (Acts 16:1). As such, his genealogy literally embodies the Pauline mission of the reconciliation of Jew and Greek. Additionally, Luke recounts that Paul circumcised Timothy prior to embarking on a missionary journey throughout Greece (Acts 16:3), an act that hardly seems to square with Paul's own boast regarding Titus's resistance to circumcision in Jerusalem (Gal. 2:3). Finally, the likely pseudonymous Pauline superscription at the conclusion of Hebrews references Timothy and his recent release from prison (Heb. 13:23).

■ THE TEXT IN CONTEMPORARY DISCUSSION

Much contemporary ecclesial interpretation of Timothy and Titus in relation to Paul focuses on the mentor-mentee relationship in developing leaders in ministry. The chapel of Concordia Seminary in St. Louis, Missouri, the flagship school for the ordained leadership of the Lutheran Church–Missouri Synod, is named for Timothy and Titus. Practical theologians refer to the PE as an example of Paul's careful stewardship of upcoming leaders for the church (e.g., Hoehl). Other scholars now question the authenticity of the canonical, legendary portrayal of Paul's relationship with Timothy and Titus. Some have advanced the hypothesis that Timothy and Titus (as referenced in Paul's historical letters) are the same person, an example of ancient heteronymity, the practice of ascribing multiple names to the same person (e.g., Fellows). Whatever the historical relationship of Timothy and Titus to Paul (or to one another), it is clear that the enduring interpretive tradition understands that they are linked in the act of imparting and receiving sound teaching and wisdom. Certainly the PE bear an important place in characterizing this relationship.

1 Timothy 1:3-11: Call to Proper Instruction

■ THE TEXT IN ITS ANCIENT CONTEXT

After its terse greeting, the writing takes up the context of interreligious conflict that may be the catalyst for the PE. The writer casts Paul in the role of instructing Timothy to remain in Ephesus in order to teach "certain people" not to teach "false teachings." The immediate preoccupation with the potential threat of "false teaching" and the caricature of it as "empty words" offers potential insight into the overall purpose of the PE, namely to establish an authoritative interpretation of Paul's teachings and set clear lines between correct and false instruction in the faith.

Within the ethos of the PE writer, proper instruction begins with proper interpretation of sacred tradition. Likewise, "false teachings" begin with misguided interpretation. For the PE writer as he performs Paul, this sacred tradition would be Israel's scriptural tradition. Far from being contrary to the law, the writer is chiding interpreters who miss the point of the law and "promote useless speculations." The particular malpractice in view in these verses arises out of what the writer characterizes as an overemphasis on "myths" and "endless genealogies."

▌ THE TEXT IN THE INTERPRETIVE TRADITION

While the historical context of this particular characterization has been difficult for historical scholars to label, it is noteworthy that other Greco-Roman rhetoricians (such as Plutarch and Philo) also warn against overly esoteric speculation on sacred or traditional origins (Wall, 63). While there is no way to know precisely what interpretations are in view in 1 Timothy, it is noteworthy that the canonical genealogical traditions in Matthew (1:1-17) and Luke (3:23-38) represent divergent interpretations of Israel's scriptural tradition for the sacred and salvation-historical origins of Jesus. Could it be that this kind of diversity was even further multiplied within the PE writer's context, and that such divergences and arguments about them bred conflict and division within the church?

▌ THE TEXT IN CONTEMPORARY DISCUSSION

Contemporary liberation theologian, poet, and activist Elsa Tamez has written a commentary on 1 Timothy in which she traces lines of connection between struggles for power at work between the PE writer and his opponents and the challenges of Roman Catholic women in the barrios of Costa Rica. Tamez argues that those who hold ecclesial, economic, and social power within the church often use rhetoric to disparage and demean those who threaten their power and authority. First Timothy offers her a ground from which to explore these contested relationships in the church and to validate the experience of women in her community who struggle every day to survive and to claim their God-given dignity in the midst of global socioeconomic and political oppression and ecclesial domination.

1 Timothy 1:12-20: Christ's Mercy—An Example from Paul's Biography

▌ THE TEXT IN ITS ANCIENT CONTEXT

The PE writer offers thanks to Jesus Christ for the merciful experience of his calling to Christ's service. This particular element of Paul's biography—whether it be characterized as a call to mission or a "conversion"—offers a powerful insight into the development of the PE writer's Christology.

In Paul's seven likely authentic letters (i.e., Romans, 1 and 2 Corinthians, Galatians, Philippians, 1 Thessalonians, Philemon), he often refers to his "revelation" (*apokalypsis*) as an event in which God is the agent, Jesus Christ is the subject ("God was pleased to reveal his Son in me"), and the content is a mission to proclaim the gospel of Jesus Christ among the gentiles (e.g., Gal. 1:15-16). The fact that Paul had persecuted the churches prior to this event is mentioned (Gal. 1:13), but it is not a part of the content or experience of his revelation. In the Acts of the Apostles, likely written at least forty years after Paul's own letters, Luke narrates this event (Acts 9:4) as one in which Jesus himself, after a flash of heavenly light, asks, "Saul, Saul, why do you persecute me?" The PE writer continues the characterization of the event in this vein. The writer describes Jesus, not God, as the source of the experience, and the primary content of the phenomenon is the dramatic reversal of Paul's work from persecuting the churches to proclaiming the gospel within them. No doubt Luke and the PE writer had much to do with the legendary characterization of Paul's "Damascus road" experience as a "conversion" more than, in his own words, a theological "revelation." In the interpretive trajectory of Luke and the PE writer, Paul's primary connection is with Jesus (in contrast to God), and the content of the experience is not so much a theological vision of how Paul's mission to the gentiles relates to God's saving purpose for the world, but rather how he has been mercifully saved from his "unbelief" (1:13). Furthermore, Paul is portrayed not so much as a collaborator with God in the mission to the gentiles, as an example of Christ's mercy and redemption for those who are to believe in him (1:16). He has become the chief sinner whose own salvation is the proof that "Christ came into the world to save sinners" (1:15).

THE TEXT IN THE INTERPRETIVE TRADITION

The characterization of Paul as the first or chief among sinners has captured the imagination of the Christian interpretive tradition. One prominent interpreter of this motif, Augustine, noted that Paul's conversion was powerful testimony to Christ's saving power precisely because the devil held him so tightly. As Augustine notes, "the enemy is more overcome by wringing a man from him of whom he had more hold" (St. Augustine's Confessions I, 8.4, The Loeb Classical Library, 423). No doubt the personal appeal of the Pauline example inspired Augustine in his own journey toward conversion, and offered him an archetype for understanding and teaching the process of conversion in general.

THE TEXT IN CONTEMPORARY DISCUSSION

The topic of whether the historical Paul "converted" to a new faith tradition (i.e., "Christianity") or responded to a theological calling consistent with his own Jewish belief and practice is a prominent subject of debate within the contemporary critical scholarly engagement of the historical Paul in the "Newer Approaches to Paul." At stake in this debate is the question of whether Paul understood himself to remain a Jew in his experience of his revelation or changed his religious identity in response to it. Pamela Eisenbaum summarizes the historical research that informs this debate, and well outlines her sense of how the characterization of Paul's "conversion" from his Jewish faith has had tremendously negative ethical and moral consequences in terms of anti-Judaism within

Christian theology. No matter where one stands in this debate in Pauline scholarship, one must acknowledge the formative role of the PE in representing Paul as a converted sinner who identifies his life prior to his religious experience as "unbelief."

1 Timothy 2:1-15: The Call to a Quiet Life

■ THE TEXT IN ITS ANCIENT CONTEXT

The PE are well known for their promotion of a proto-orthodoxy. Throughout the corpus, the writer calls for adherence to "sound doctrine" and for guarding the "deposit of faith." The opening instructions of 1 Timothy identify the danger of "false teachings" (1 Tim. 1:3) in the church. Over-all, however, the PE corpus seems preoccupied more with orderly behavior (i.e., orthopraxy) than belief. In this vein, 1 Tim. 2:1-15 takes up the call to challenge the church leadership to promote a "peaceful and quiet" life.

The opening verses of this section relate to offering prayers, intercessions, and thanks on behalf of all people, kings and all who are in authority (2:1-2). In relationship to those in political author-ity, the goal of a "peaceful and quiet life" is characterized by acknowledging the hierarchies of power that frame the social experience of the churches. In this sense, the opening verses of this section offer an implicit call for the readers and hearers of the PE to know their place within the sociopo-litical order, and as leaders of the churches, to do what is necessary to ensure ongoing peace and har-mony between those in governing authority and the church. As the section goes on to address the behavior of men and women in worship (2:8-15), the writer continues with the theme of "proper" behavior within the social hierarchy for the good of the community. Throughout the section, images of speaking and language continue to tie back to the initial goal of a peaceful and quiet life.

While the writer addresses both the behavior of men and women in worship, the majority of the discussion is devoted to women. This imbalance is telling regarding the PE writer's energy for instruction and reproof. While the behavior of men can be generally addressed, women, it seems, require more specific and repeated calls to "learn in silence" (v. 11), "not to teach or have authority over men" (v. 12), and "to keep silent" (v. 12). Some scholars argue that this focus on the prevention of women's speech likely signals a context in which women were already actively at work teaching and leading in the church. It is, in other words, prescriptive rather than descriptive rhetoric (e.g., Schüssler Fiorenza, 310).

The writer summarizes his prohibition of women's speech and leadership within the community with an argument based on a midrashic interpretation of Genesis 2–3. As the PE writer applies the story of Adam and Eve to his prohibition of women's teaching and leadership, he offers Eve as the prototypical woman who is easily deceived (ostensibly, by the serpent). One explanation for this is that the author focuses on deception in the Genesis text in order to speak to the deceptive teach-ings at work in the community, where women are particularly susceptible to such teachings (2 Tim. 3:6-7; see Bassler, 60). This interpretation helpfully contextualizes the prohibitions and mitigates concerns about how the author's appeal to "origins" seems to imply that all women are inherently untrustworthy.

▌THE TEXT IN THE INTERPRETIVE TRADITION

Early church interpreters of 1 Tim. 2:15-16 discerned a christological claim in this text's connection between childbearing and salvation. Given that the term "childbearing" is preceded in 1 Tim. 2:15 by the definite article ("the"), interpreters such as Justin Martyr and Ignatius of Antioch argued that the singular act of Mary's childbearing of Jesus Christ reversed the curse of Eve's original transgression (Witherington, 240). This messianic interpretation has not endured in the church. By and large, the technical matter of the presence of the definite article has been taken to mean childbearing in general as interpreters have promoted an understanding of the text as an ontological statement on the secondary and untrustworthy nature of women, and their consignment to positions within the church and household in which they are supervised and controlled.

▌THE TEXT IN CONTEMPORARY DISCUSSION

The prohibition in this text of women's teaching and leadership has served as a key proof text in the church's structural exclusion of women from leadership in general and from offices that include ordination in particular. While the call to silence and the relegation of women to positions of submission within the community may sound antiquated, it is remarkable to see how broadly this text is cited as an authority in current manuals of church administration and polity, for example in the teaching of the Roman Catholic Church, the Lutheran Church–Missouri Synod, and the Southern Baptist Convention (Krause, 50–52).

1 Timothy 3:1-16: Qualities for Church Leadership

▌THE TEXT IN ITS ANCIENT CONTEXT

The list of qualities for bishops (*episkopoi*) and deacons (*diakonoi*) found in 1 Tim. 3:1-13 provide the corpus of 1 and 2 Timothy and Titus with the traditional characterization of "pastoral" letters. Namely, they are concerned with matters of church leadership and administration. From a historical-critical perspective, this emphasis locates the writings within the realm of an administrative discourse on leadership and how it is ordered properly within the church. In this sense, these writings stand apart from the rest of the Pauline canon as they are framed as an intramural discussion, by leaders and for leaders, rather than the address of a leader to a given community or set of communities. The two lists, while separate (first bishops, then deacons), are coordinated by the rhetorical use of "likewise" in 1 Tim. 3:8. While each office requires different characteristics, they are like one another in anticipating the most exemplary elements of Greco-Roman moral virtue—the highest quality of character imaginable.

In this sense, the lists seem to be framed ideally and perhaps in contrast to false teachers within the midst of the community. Indeed, several of the qualities of bishops and deacons are framed negatively (e.g., "not a drunkard, not violent, not quarrelsome, no lover of money," v. 3; or "not double-tongued, not addicted to much wine, not greedy," v. 8). This element may support the understanding that this portion of the writing is not simply a manual on leadership but also a way of framing the conflict besetting the church regarding leadership. The list makes plain that not all leaders are created equally, and the current crisis over competing leaders ("false teachers") within the church provides the opportunity to set the standards and expectations of the church's leadership high while simultaneously maligning its opponents.

▌ THE TEXT IN THE INTERPRETIVE TRADITION

The intramural leadership emphasis of the PE was attractive to generations of church leaders into the third and fourth century. Early church fathers offered commentary and sermonic amplification of the corpus (e.g., Clement, Polycarp, Theodore of Mopsuestia, and Chrysostom: Witherington, 168). While the text of the PE shies away from offering a "job description" for bishops and deacons and concentrates instead on characteristic virtues of the positions, there is a sense in which the PE represent a developmental step in defining offices of leadership (bishop, elder, deacon) rather than mere functions of different leaders in the community (oversight, teaching, and service). The emphasis on virtues rather than duties for leaders no doubt proved valuable to generations of church leaders who followed in different contexts and circumstances.

▌ THE TEXT IN CONTEMPORARY DISCUSSION

In the midst of the list of qualities for deacons, there is an enigmatic passage that is of particular interest to contemporary interpreters within settings where the leadership and ordination of women is debated. First Timothy 3:11 marks an abrupt change in the flow of the PE writer's list of expectations for deacons. Until this point, the list does not identify whether men or women are in view. Suddenly, at verse 11 the writer states that "women" (Greek *gynai*, translated "wives" in a few translations such as the NIV) are "likewise" expected to behave virtuously. When this verse is understood to refer to women (rather than wives) it stands as a testimony to the presence of women within the designated (and likely financially compensated) offices of the early church. While there is a great deal of evidence for the leadership of women in the seven likely authentic letters of Paul (e.g., Rom. 16:1), and in other traditions of the early Jesus movement (e.g., Mark 15:41), the fact that these late first- or early second-century writings of the church reference women's leadership challenges all forms of the church today to acknowledge that women's leadership in the church is not a recent mark of human progress but an original expression of the church's vision for community.

1 Timothy 4:1-16: Sound Teaching

▌ THE TEXT IN ITS ANCIENT CONTEXT

This portion of the writing draws on the mentor-mentee relationship between Paul and Timothy. The writer evokes the wisdom and experience of Paul as he encourages Timothy to "let no one despise your youth" (v. 12). The pseudepigraphical and pseudepistolary framework (mimicking the form of a letter) of the writing's composition offers the chance to see this relationship as paradigmatic of a problem within the late first- and early second-century church. The historical Paul would likely not have been in much of a position to encourage his mentees in the command of authority and respect, given his own particular struggles in attaining these things for himself (e.g., 2 Corinthians 10–12). However, by the early second century, Paul's leadership had been lauded in both the reinterpretation and use of his teaching and in legendary traditions found in the Acts of the Apostles and the *Acts of Paul*. In this sense, the church leaders of the PE corpus no doubt faced the anxiety of establishing the authority of a new generation of leaders and teachers of the tradition. The call to claim one's authority within the rising generation, and to lead with conviction and purpose, resonates with the structural institutional developments at work within the second-century church. One striking element of the genius and innovation of the PE corpus is that it positions this call in the person and voice of the legendary leader himself.

▌THE TEXT IN THE INTERPRETIVE TRADITION

One poignant element of the mentor-mentee relationship drawn in this unit is the challenge to carry on the work of ministry and the life of the church in the midst of Paul's absence. In verse 13, the writer states: "Till I come, attend to the public reading of scripture, to preaching, and to teaching." These are practices of ministry as they relate to corporate worship. Such practices have parallels within the worship practices of early Judaism. Early church fathers such as Justin demonstrate that this list of activities continued to describe much of the shape of corporate Christian worship into the second and third centuries, and liturgies of the Western and Eastern traditions and the Reformation show that such practices are prominent elements of corporate worship even to the present day.

▌THE TEXT IN CONTEMPORARY DISCUSSION

In outlining the contours of "sound teaching," the text also characterizes the false teachers' practices. The identification of the "liars" with those who "forbid marriage and abstain from certain foods" (v. 3.) is somewhat surprising in light of common practices of a celibate clergy and fasting within parts of the contemporary church. Importantly, Paul's likely authentic letters reflect positively on the gift of celibacy within the life of the church (e.g., 1 Cor. 7:1, 8). In light of these discrepancies with both the historical Paul and the contemporary church, it is clear to see that the PE corpus defines orthopraxy and orthodoxy at times more narrowly than can be seen within either more ancient or contemporary expressions of the church.

1 Timothy 5:1—6:3: Clarifying Roles and Responsibilities

▌THE TEXT IN ITS ANCIENT CONTEXT

In this section, the writer addresses roles within the church and homes in on widows, elders, and slaves. It is not clear why these three groups are treated together and why elders, for instance, are not discussed earlier in chapter 3 along with the qualifications for bishops and deacons. One clue to the connection between widows, elders, and slaves in this unit is the common use of the term "honor" (meaning financial payment) in each case. Widows, on the one hand, are discussed in terms of limiting their draw on the financial resources of the community. Elders, on the other hand, are recommended for a significant raise (a double portion). Slaves are reminded that their service to their masters benefits beloved believers. In sum, compensation for widows is curtailed, while that for elders is raised. Slaves, whose labor is uncompensated, are called to regard their masters as "worthy of all honor." Far from an equitable distribution of resources among all groups (such as is envisioned by Luke in Acts 2:44-45 and Acts 4:32-35), this writer calls for a redistribution of the financial resources of the community toward a particular constituency (elders), and away from others (widows and slaves).

The writer's process of identifying "authentic" or "real" widows is instructive. Where the practice of the church had become that of providing for all women whose husbands had died, the letter writer is redirecting the responsibility for care back to private family units and away from the church (1 Tim. 5:16). In this process, the writer calls for the community to honor (compensate financially) those widows who are "real," that is, who meet criteria that would ensure that there was no private familial community of support, as well as those widows who would be considered beyond the age of remarriage. Given the limits the writer sets (over the age of sixty, the wife of only one husband, who has raised children, but has none that can financially support her), one might wonder if any widow in the ancient world would be considered "real," or if the only "real" widow in the eyes of the writer might be a dead widow! Certainly, the position of widow as the writer has constructed it is populated by women who would have very little social power (few familial relationships and no access to financial resources other than the support received from the church). In this sense, the writer's agenda may be seen as surpassing simply trimming the budget and more along the lines of consolidating and managing relations of power within the church. Such a perspective on the social dynamics of this text helps to clarify that, far from a natural evolution in Paul's thought, the claims of 1 Timothy represent a marked reorientation of power in the church, and a striking reinterpretation of Paul's legacy.

▌ The Text in the Interpretive Tradition

Most of the history of the church's interpretation of this passage has read these instructions regarding widows, elders, and slaves as the teaching of the apostle Paul. In this perspective, interpreters have argued that Paul, by the time of this writing, has seen the unsustainable nature of the vision of the church he upheld in places such as 1 Thess. 5:14; Gal. 3:28; and 1 Cor. 11:17-22. Moreover, he has seen the error of his commitment to "preach the gospel free of charge," and not to collect on his right as an apostle to compensation (1 Cor. 9:18). On this reading, in 1 Timothy, Paul advocates for the professional compensation of elders (1 Tim. 5:17-18) even while he argues for the church's financial support of widows to be curtailed. What such theories miss is that far from a linear development of Paul's thought and practice, the PE writer's instructions involve a complete reorientation of Paul's priorities. Scholarship that takes seriously the pseudepigraphic nature of the writing offers an understanding of how this writing has appropriated Paul's persona and authority to structure the church in remarkably alternative ways to his vision of community found in the likely authentic letters of the Pauline corpus. These ways centralize power and financial resources in the newly constructed offices of bishops, elders, and deacons, and limit the authority of other classes within the church that have grown in significance in the community (such as widows and slaves).

The Text in Contemporary Discussion

In many contemporary contexts of the church, the rhetoric of 1 Tim. 5:1—6:3 appears to be complicit with histories of the subjugation of women and slaves and the marginalization of certain classes from professional ministry. In particular, the writer's attack on the character of women in his community as "idlers, gossips, and busybodies" (5:13) and his paternalistic chide for slaves not to disrespect their masters (6:2) place him on the wrong side of movements for human liberation and struggles for justice within the church and world. Once again, an appreciation of the pseudepigraphical nature of this writing helps to locate this rhetoric not in the natural evolution of Paul's thought and the growth of the church but rather in late first- and early second-century struggles to determine the social construction of the church in the world. The rhetoric of the PE writer offers insight into how those struggles transpired. Women increased in stature and presence within the church, and other elements of the church resisted. The text's misogyny and paternalism do not need to be seen as prescriptive of contemporary church polity but as descriptive of the kinds of struggles that arose in the face of the social mobility of the early church. In these descriptions, we certainly hear the perspective of the letter writer; however, we also learn that women and slaves were enough of a concern in their emerging roles to merit the writer's concern and calls for their submission. Far from needing to honor all the writer's expectations, contemporary readers can appreciate that the writing contains witnesses to those women and slaves who dared to network socially and resist the confines of traditional households in order to pursue their vocations and engage in ministry.

1 Timothy 6:4-19: False Teaching and the Call to Guard the Good Confession

The Text in Its Ancient Context

One of the remarkable challenges to Paul's apostolic identity and leadership was that he did not know the historical Jesus. In his correspondence with churches, Paul references this embarrassing datum as being "untimely born" (1 Cor. 15:8). While he affirms his own religious authority as immediate and from God, as opposed to human teaching (Gal. 1:12), it is clear that his opponents capitalized on this fact and insinuated that his apostolic identity was not legitimate (2 Corinthians 11–12). In this light, it is powerful to witness how the PE writer develops the Pauline tradition to clarify and originally authorize the church's leadership (e.g., Timothy) in relation to the historical Jesus. In verse 12, the writer presents Paul connecting Timothy's good confession at his ordination to the "good confession" Jesus Christ made in his trial before Pontius Pilate. In this sense, the PE writer (much like Luke in his Acts of the Apostles) has solved for the Pauline tradition what for Paul was an enduring challenge in his ministry—suspicion about the source of his authority. Connecting Timothy's confession at his ordination with that of Jesus in his trial before Pilate provides an original and indisputable ground of authority, identity, and purpose for the leaders of the church.

■ The Text in the Interpretive Tradition

The connection between the confession of church leaders at ordination and the confession of Jesus at his trial before Pontius Pilate provided the early Christian martyrological tradition the opportunity of calling leaders to stand firm in their faith in times of religious persecution. Jerome Quinn notes the connection between 1 Tim. 6:12 and the late second-century North African text of the *Acts of the Scillitan Martyrs* (Quinn and Wacker, 542–43). The leader of the twelve Christians in this text, Speratus, testifies in his hearing using language similar to the claims of the dominion and sovereignty of God (as opposed to the emperor) in doxological affirmation of 1 Tim. 6:16: "he alone is immortal and dwells in unapproachable light, whom no one has seen or can see, to him be honor and eternal dominion."

■ The Text in Contemporary Discussion

This unit of text bears an aphorism that has had a long interpretive history and is broadly referenced in North American popular culture. In verse 10, the PE writer states, "love of money is the root of all evil." The most widely referenced version of this saying is shortened in popular rhetoric to "Money is the root of all evil." Needless to say, there is an important distinction between the *love* of money (in Greek, *philargyria*) and money itself (*argyria*). Nonetheless, Christian faith has often been characterized, on account of this misquotation, as promoting an impossible standard in practical worldly terms. Moreover, defenders of capital have chided that the institution of the church is hypocritical, because it obviously needs money to operate. One prominent example of the defense of money against this misquotation is Ayn Rand's presentation of Francisco D'Anconia's apologia for money in the novel *Atlas Shrugged*. In the novel, D'Anconia passionately outlines Rand's philosophy of "capital" as far from "evil," but rather the source of all creativity, power, and good in the world. Ironically, while the PE writer may represent an early church leader with whom Rand might have some affinity regarding values of self-sufficiency, this treatise would illustrate the essential problem of the "love of money," which is indeed maligned in the text. As the PE writer sees it, the problem with the *love* of money is the elevation of human productivity above a theological framework that would identify God as the source of all goodness and creative power.

2 TIMOTHY

Deborah Krause

Introduction

Second Timothy takes a different form than 1 Timothy. Rather than a simple continuation of instructions for church leadership, 2 Timothy is structured as a final testament from Paul to one of his most trusted emissaries. As such, the writing presupposes Paul's imprisonment in Rome rather than his Aegean travels and ministry as envisioned in 1 Timothy and Titus. In this light, scholars of the corpus have proposed that the canonical order may not have been the original design of the corpus, but rather that Titus and 1 Timothy would have preceded the poignant last testament of Paul to Timothy in 2 Timothy.

2 Timothy 1:1-18: The Good Treasure Entrusted to You

▌THE TEXT IN ITS ANCIENT CONTEXT

Overall, the opening verses of 2 Timothy build a sense of poignancy by referring to Paul as one who "suffers" for his calling as preacher, apostle, and teacher, with the implication that those who lead in his stead should and will do the same.

The writing opens with words of affirmation for Timothy in his faith and with a reminder of the deep bond between Timothy and Paul in light of Paul's authorization of Timothy through the laying on of hands (v. 6).

▌THE TEXT IN THE INTERPRETIVE TRADITION

Luke presents the story of Paul's meeting of Timothy in Lystra and adds a detail of his lineage, namely, that he is the son of a Jewish mother and a Greek father (Acts 16:1). For Luke, this tradition of Timothy's Jewish and Greek ethnic heritage makes him an ideal companion of Paul as he carries the gospel of Jesus Christ into Macedonia, literally embodying the reconciliation of Jew and Greek. For the PE writer, the mixed ethnic heritage is not as important as the enduring (multigenerational) faithfulness of Timothy's family, encompassing both his mother and his grandmother. As such, he is a model of steadfast faithfulness for which the PE writer is calling throughout the PE corpus. In both interpretive contexts (Luke and the PE), Timothy lives as a model of faithfulness, and his heritage is claimed in support. How that heritage is characterized offers insight into what in particular is being valued about Timothy's faith in each interpretive context.

Later interpreters of the Pauline tradition, such as John Chrysostom, continued to make theological meaning out of Timothy's foreign biological heritage and the PE writer's representation that he is Paul's "beloved son." In his *Homily 19 on Romans* 11.7 Chrysostom notes that if Paul could call Timothy (of Lystra) his "son" (which Paul also claims in 1 Tim. 1:2), then all people of faith have the capacity to be God's children. As such, claims to ethnic heritage as either a point of privilege or dishonor have no place in the life of faith.

▌The Text in Contemporary Discussion

The PE writer presents Paul encouraging Timothy in his faith with these words: "for God did not give us a spirit of timidity but a spirit of power and love and self-control." In their ancient context, these words served as a challenge to church leaders to stand firm on the foundation of the faith and to claim the authority of their ordination and leadership to guide the church. Not surprisingly, however, the call to courage has been found useful by rhetoricians in many different contexts. Far from the confines of challenging church leaders, President Barack Obama used this text as a rallying cry to console and encourage the citizens of Boston and the United States at a memorial service after the Boston Marathon Bombing on April 18, 2013. Toward the end of his address, speaking directly to the yet unknown perpetrators of the violence, the president noted that their goal may have been to spread terror, but "our fidelity to our way of life, to our free and open society, will only grow stronger. 'For God did not give us a spirit of timidity but a spirit of power and love and self-control.'" As these words from the Pauline tradition were reanimated for the encouragement and hope of a city and a nation, the hundreds of attendees of the memorial service rose to a standing ovation.

2 Timothy 2:1-26: Dedication to Service and Sound Teaching

▌The Text in Its Ancient Context

In chapter 2, the PE writer presents Paul directly charging Timothy and other leaders with him to be strong and to share in suffering (presumably with Paul, and foremost with Jesus Christ). In addition to using Paul's own biography and circumstances to compel and to inspire to greater dedication, the PE writer draws on three models of Greco-Roman masculinity in the persons of the soldier, the athlete, and the farmer. The purpose of these brief and somewhat enigmatic portraits is to challenge church leaders to be trustworthy in their tasks. The lessons seem to call listeners to focus wholly on the work of ministry. They are to avoid outside entanglements (like a good soldier), follow the rules (like a victorious athlete), and work hard (like a successful farmer). On the one hand, this call to focus and discipline seems to challenge leaders to function as "professional" ministers (in contrast to the tent-making historical Paul). On the other hand, the work of the clergy is cast in comparison to secular pursuits, and the expectations of church leaders can be identified in the Greco-Roman cultural mainstream values of hard work, discipline, and integrity.

▊ THE TEXT IN THE INTERPRETIVE TRADITION

The conclusion of the chapter raises the question of how we should characterize an apparent heretical teaching about the resurrection within the church. In 1 Corinthians 15, Paul himself battled with what he considered a misunderstanding of the resurrection: the denial of the efficacy of a general resurrection of the dead following, and separate from, Christ's resurrection. It is clear that a similar denial may have been present decades later, in the PE writer's context in the late first or early second century CE. Quinn and Wacker comment on the tenacity of this heretical teaching over this period, and in the following decades of early patristic interpretation and leadership as well: for example, Origen was compelled to argue for a "double resurrection," that is, of Jesus and of the faithful in general, in his commentary on Rom. 5:9. As Quinn and Wacker note, such a double understanding of the resurrection—apparently a very early development in Christian belief, though never receiving wide acceptance in Judaism—was an offense against the intellect of the Greco-Roman world. Moreover, the expectation of a judgment of all humankind on the "day of the Lord" offered a sin-focused eschatology that was difficult to square with the proclamation of a gospel in which the death and resurrection of Christ were proclaimed as the good news that sin had been forgiven (Quinn and Wacker, 683). Seen in this light, the challenges of understanding the resurrection in the PE are merely a way station between Paul's original challenge in Corinth and Origen's enduring challenge to maintain the general resurrection. What these three moments have in common is the purpose of reinforcing how God's work in the death and resurrection of Jesus relates to God's sovereign plan to save the world.

▊ THE TEXT IN CONTEMPORARY DISCUSSION

At the end of chapter 2, the PE writer returns to the overarching theme of challenging church leaders to carry out their ministries with discipline and care. The disposition of peacemaking is attributed to leaders. In verses 23-25, the writer declares that a servant of the Lord must not be quarrelsome, must be kindly to everyone, an apt teacher, patient, correcting opponents with gentleness. This list of expectations places the work of church leadership in the realm of navigating difficult (conflicted) social relationships. While much of the PE corpus has the ring today of antiquated structures and outdated paradigms, this call for ministers to lead with charity and openness to others is rhetoric straight out of many contemporary "boundary training" and conflict resolution seminars for clergy. When it comes to ministry, the PE writer seems to embrace that sound teaching and doctrine can only go so far. Often what is most important in the formation of faithful Christian communities is the capacity for leaders to show and be shown compassion, and to embrace ways of serving that make for peace.

2 Timothy 3:1-17: Avoid the Unholy and Adhere to Paul's Example

▌THE TEXT IN ITS ANCIENT CONTEXT

Commentators have long struggled to identify the particular beliefs and practices of the opponents who are in view in the PE. Whether they should be characterized as "Gnostic," antinomian, libertine, and so on is difficult to determine from the PE writer's rhetoric. This opacity of theological and social problems is hard to understand in the PE. If the writer were targeting particular opponents, why would not their errant beliefs and practices be enumerated clearly for church leadership to see and understand? Several options are possible. It may be that the PE writer and his audience are completely aware of the theological and ethical specifics of the opponents' beliefs and practices and therefore do not need to rehearse them. On the other hand, it may be that the PE writer has crafted the PE to characterize ecclesial and social ills more generally, so that the corpus will have more of an enduring role in guiding the ministry of the church in a variety of contexts and situations.

The vice list that opens 2 Tim. 3:1-9 seems to support the thesis that the PE writer has intentionally framed the opponents in generic terms. Here the eschatological framework of the "last days" sets up the expectation that people will fall into numerous social ills. The list of vices is extensive (superseded in the New Testament only by Rom. 1:28-32, which may serve as a base of tradition for the present list). Together they offer an overwhelming rhetorical demonstration that in the "last days" one can expect the world "to go to hell." Importantly, the vices listed provide the opposite extreme of the idealized virtues of the soldier, athlete, and farmer of 2 Tim. 2:4-6. As such, the PE writer offers broad cartoons of good and bad men among whom his churches' leaders can easily locate themselves and their opponents.

▌THE TEXT IN THE INTERPRETIVE TRADITION

In contrast to the generic portrait of bad leaders in 2 Tim. 3:1-9, the PE writer presents a portrait of Paul's suffering and persecution in 2 Tim. 3:10-17. The legend of Paul's suffering is one that finds broad appeal in the interpretive tradition. Luke, in the Acts of the Apostles, narrates the obstacles, angry crowds, trials, torture, and shipwrecks that Paul encounters. Likewise, the early Christian noncanonical writing the *Acts of Paul* presents Paul (and companions like Thecla) facing imprisonment, mob violence, wild beasts, and persecution (Taussig, 337–44). Luke's characterization serves to draw Paul into a line of "witnesses" (including Jesus) who suffer on behalf of the way of the gospel. The *Acts of Paul* characterizes Paul as a model of chaste devotion who eschews the trappings of culture and devotes himself wholly to the preaching and teaching of the Word. The PE writer's characterization of Paul's suffering offers a model of leadership with which to challenge and encourage the leaders of the church. Overall, the original call of Paul to "imitate me as I imitate Christ" (1 Cor. 11:1) is well heard in the interpretive tradition, and Paul's various commitments are reflected in its multifaceted expressions.

◼ The Text in Contemporary Discussion

One element of the PE writer's characterization of his opponents that does not bear a generic tone is his description of those, among the perpetrators of various vices, who "make their way into households and captivate silly women, overwhelmed by their sins and swayed by all kinds of desires, who are always being instructed and can never arrive at any knowledge of the truth" (2 Tim. 3:6-7). No doubt this rhetoric is filled with hyperbole; however, the subject of women and their particular vulnerability to doctrinal error is present at several points in the PE corpus (e.g., 1 Tim. 2:12-14; 5:13). While scholars debate the historical circumstances that gave rise to this rhetoric, contemporary feminist biblical critics have challenged that the writer's characterizations of women bear a misogynistic tone—in particular, demeaning women's activities and ways of knowing as frivolous, weak, and untrustworthy. Critics have countered to the PE writer, if these women are of such little account, why do their words and activities preoccupy so much of your concern?

2 Timothy 4:1-22: Presenting Paul's Final Requests

◼ The Text in Its Ancient Context

In many ways, the source of much of the rhetorical power of the overall PE corpus is lodged in the closing words of this chapter. While this trove of writings, presented to church leaders as lost letters of Paul, would no doubt have had profound impact within the late first- and early second-century church, that impact could only be compounded by the framing of the letters as personal correspondence between Paul and two of his most trusted emissaries in ministry, and furthermore as the last words of Paul written from prison prior to his death in Rome. The conclusion of 2 Timothy provides the forum for this presentation of Paul. He knows his death is imminent (4:6), and in this position he is able to dispassionately model the kind of leadership he is calling for from others. Needless to say, this is a compelling setting from which to impart wisdom to the church's leadership: "proclaim the message; be persistent whether the time is favorable or unfavorable; convince, rebuke, and encourage, with the utmost patience in teaching" (2 Tim. 4:2); "be sober, endure suffering, do the work of an evangelist, carry out your ministry fully" (2 Tim. 4:5).

◼ The Text in the Interpretive Tradition

The particulars of Paul's death are a shadowy mystery in Christian origins. The canon of the Christian New Testament does not record the event of his death. Luke chooses to conclude the Acts of the Apostles with Paul under arrest in Rome and yet preaching openly to the close of the story. The only other canonical reference to Paul's Roman imprisonment and impending death come in these verses of 2 Timothy. In the mid- to late second century, Ignatius of Antioch in his *Letter to the Ephesians* refers to Paul's death as a martyrdom in chapter 12, where he lionizes Paul as "the holy, the martyred, the most deservedly happy" (The Ante-Nicean Fathers, vol. 1, 55). Beyond these few specifics, other sources hold that Paul was beheaded (in contrast to Peter's more brutal upside-down crucifixion).

◼ THE TEXT IN CONTEMPORARY DISCUSSION

In the midst of the heroic portrait of Paul and the gentle admonishing of Timothy in his leadership, the PE writer manages to get in one last parting shot at those within the community who are susceptible to false teaching. It is in this sense that the PE likely originated as the parts of an intramural manual on leadership in ministry and have endured as such throughout much of church history. Only among teachers does such lampooning of bad teaching make sense. It emerges from the camaraderie of shared struggle. Acknowledging the "last days," the PE writer speaks to the condition of "itching ears" among the members of the church who seek teachers who will tell them what they want to hear. In the contemporary interpretation of this passage within twenty-first-century North American Christianity, this concept of itching ears has been used to characterize a progressive attitude toward tradition. In the midst of a culture and church polarized around issues of human sexuality, women's rights, environmental degradation, and the relationship of church and state, some church leaders appeal to the rhetoric of the PE writer as a demonstration that the "last days" are upon us and that "fundamentals" of the Christian faith, such as the authority of Scripture, the virgin birth, the bodily resurrection, and other tenets are "under negotiation" by those who have "itching ears" and who seek teachers who will tell them what they want to hear instead of the truth. In such contexts of rhetoric, it is important to recall that the PE themselves were forged in the midst of the early church's struggles over leadership, theology, and social structure. As such, their deployment to characterize one expression of ecclesial structure, belief, or practice as in error as opposed to another tends more to mirror their rhetorical origins than accomplish a definitive statement of orthodoxy.

TITUS

Deborah Krause

Introduction

While the canonical shape of the PE corpus places Titus at the end (being the shortest of the writings), it is quite likely that the corpus was originally intended to conclude with what is now called 2 Timothy, which takes the form of a final testament from Paul before his death (see above).

Titus 1:1-16: Opening Words of Paul to Titus

▌THE TEXT IN ITS ANCIENT CONTEXT

Titus parallels the scenario envisioned in 1 Timothy; Paul is writing during the period of his Aegean ministry (prior to his departure to Rome) to one of his trusted emissaries, in this case Titus on the island of Crete.

▌THE TEXT IN THE INTERPRETIVE TRADITION

Titus plays a prominent role in Paul's own recounting of the origins of his relationship with the Jerusalem church and his ministry to the gentiles. Paul notes that his second journey to Jerusalem was in the company of Barnabas and Titus. What is remarkable about Titus, as Paul describes it, is that he was a gentile and uncircumcised. During the visit to Jerusalem, he was not compelled to be circumcised, and through this detail Paul seems to want to communicate that the Jerusalem church leadership were at this point convinced of the authority of his calling and understanding of the gospel (Gal. 2:1-3). Elsewhere, Titus plays a significant role in serving as an intermediary and negotiator of Paul's unraveling relationship with the Corinthian church. At several points in that correspondence, Paul references Titus and his reconciling role (2 Cor. 2:13; 7:6, 13; 8:6, 16,

23). Finally, Paul seems to imply that Titus may have more credibility with the church than Paul himself (2 Cor. 12:18). Given his significance to Paul, both as an archetype of the faithful Greek and as an effective emissary, it is remarkable that Luke does not mention Titus in the Acts of the Apostles. While the PE writer clearly reanimates the place of Titus in the Pauline legacy through the PE corpus, Luke and other Pauline interpreters are more likely to reference the role of Timothy as trusted emissary of Paul.

■ THE TEXT IN CONTEMPORARY DISCUSSION

Along with Timothy, Titus has come to represent the church in the generations after Paul. While Paul found them to be important partners in his ministry in the Aegean, the PE corpus solidified their role in the Christian imagination as the torchbearers of the ongoing tradition. During Paul's historical ministry, Timothy and Titus bore the message of the gospel and stood in Paul's stead to strengthen and encourage the churches when he could not. After his death, and as Paul's legend and interpretation developed, they stand as examples of those faithful followers who uphold the tradition and pass it on to the next generation. In this sense, Timothy and Titus stand for those leaders who work to keep the church alive as it moves forward and finds its shape and purpose in each succeeding generation.

Titus 2:1-15: Enforcing the Social Order

■ THE TEXT IN ITS ANCIENT CONTEXT

As mentioned above, much of the traditional material found in 1 and 2 Timothy is also present in Titus. While this may appear to be the PE writer "repeating" himself, it is a device by which to reiterate the important message of the corpus and the relevancy of the same message for various contexts. As such, it is a means of underlining the universal applicability of the Pauline tradition. One element of the traditional material in Titus 2 is the "household code," in which the expectations of social order common in the Greco-Roman milieu are outlined. In contrast to Paul's use of the metaphor of the "body of Christ" to say that everyone in the community, no matter their role, has a place (1 Corinthians 12), the PE writer in Paul's name establishes a clear social hierarchy in Titus 2 (parallel to 1 Tim. 5:3—6:3), in which the overarching message is that everyone in the community should know his or her place.

■ THE TEXT IN THE INTERPRETIVE TRADITION

The representation of the Pauline tradition as one that establishes the theological basis and ecclesiological command for the social hierarchy of the household code has had significant consequences in numerous contexts. One powerful consequence has been a widespread ambivalence toward Paul in the African American Christian heritage. The teaching in Titus 2:9, "tell slaves to be submissive to their masters and give satisfaction in every respect: they are not to talk back" (an eerie echo of the mandate for women's silence in 1 Tim. 2:12), has played a role in casting all of Paul's teachings in a negative light. The great twentieth-century North American theologian Howard Thurman recounts the story that his grandmother (who was enslaved as a child) would ask him to read the Scripture to her, but rarely asked for the writings of Paul. When Thurman asked why, she noted that the slave master's preacher would often remind the slaves that Paul said slavery was God's will and several times a year would quote, "slaves should submit to and honor their masters" (Thurman, 30–31).

▌THE TEXT IN CONTEMPORARY DISCUSSION

Feminist interpreters work to excavate the rhetorical tactic in the PE writer's use of household codes. In the *Women's Bible Commentary*, Joanna Dewey engages Titus with historical-critical analysis to unveil the anxiety that underlies the PE writer's maintenance of the household code in the corpus. Dewey notes, for instance, that a driving force behind the PE writer's rigid social order is the sense that God, who is imagined as the paternal overlord of this hierarchal social structure, could be discredited by the misbehavior of his subjects (Titus 2:5). One particular strategy of the PE writer in Titus 2 that Dewey uncovers is the conscripting of older women to "encourage" younger women in their submission to this patriarchal social order and their subordinate role within it (Titus 2:3-5; see Dewey, 361). This strategy has a long history in the implementation of patriarchy. Often, within women's struggle for equality in ecclesial structures over the course of the twentieth and twenty-first centuries, some of the most vociferous and effective opponents of women's ordination have been powerful women in the existing structures of church hierarchy. No doubt, power manifests itself complexly in social organizations of the church and society. The struggle for women's full inclusion in church leadership (which in spite of advances in different quarters continues to this day) offers insight into the complexity of power at work in the midst of a hierarchically ordered and transforming social structure.

Titus 3:1-15: Avoiding Controversy for the Whole Church

▌THE TEXT IN ITS ANCIENT CONTEXT

The PE writer's concern for "the quiet life" continues into chapter 3 with a call for members of the church to be "subject to rulers and authorities, to be obedient, to be ready for every good work, to speak evil of no one, to avoid quarrelling" (Titus 3:1-2). The call to be subject to governing authorities echoes Paul's from Rom. 13:1-7. While the historical authenticity of that text has been debated, it provides a more robust theological justification for the connection between those with human sovereignty and God. The rhetoric of Titus 3:1-2 stands as shorthand of the earlier argument of Rom. 13:1-7. Given that the PE writer was likely addressing a group of leaders already familiar with Paul's teachings, it may be that the broader theological justification can be assumed between the writer and his audience. This context of the representation of Paul in the PE provides a helpful insight into why the PE overall seem to present such an abbreviated, and less nuanced, form of instruction than that found in Paul's likely authentic letters. Given that all the correspondence now resides within a canonical context under the label of "Paul," however, the work of interpretation involves the challenging step of attending to the differences between texts like Rom. 13:1-7 and Titus 3:1-2, and allowing the particularities of their rhetoric to be heard even in the midst of the similarities of their themes.

◼ THE TEXT IN THE INTERPRETIVE TRADITION

In the midst of the call for obedience among church members both to governing and familial leaders, the PE writer challenges his audience to positively "devote themselves to good works," to "avoid stupid controversies, genealogies, dissensions, and quarrels about the law," and "to have nothing more to do with anyone who causes divisions" (Titus 3:9-10). Note that the writer does not deny the existence of such controversies and divisive ideas, but he nonetheless calls his readers to avoid such things. In this sense, the writing stands within the church's tradition of promoting ecumenical engagement even in the midst of acknowledging doctrinal differences. The concept is captured well in the phrase (often attributed to Augustine) "in necessary things, unity; in unnecessary things, liberty; in all things, charity."

◼ THE TEXT IN CONTEMPORARY DISCUSSION

Titus 3 offers a glimpse into what has become a debate in contemporary Christianity regarding the nature of salvation. In Paul's similar historical correspondence, the concept of salvation is articulated as the work of God (in and through Jesus Christ), and is most often cast within a global context. God's saving work, in other words, is articulated as the work of redeeming all creation. Paul articulates his ministry to the gentiles as one component of this overarching plan of God for the salvation of the world (Romans 9–11). In Titus 3, the PE writer articulates a view of salvation that is more personal. In fact, the PE writer, writing in the name of Paul, proclaims that when he was "saved" (something that, as a pious Jew, the historical Paul would not have imagined he needed), he was delivered from involvement in division, argument, and controversy (Titus 3:3-7). Theological differences over the global and personal dimensions of soteriology continue to this day. What is captured in the Pauline interpretive tension between Romans 9–11 and Titus continues to be a tension at the heart of contemporary faith and practice. In this sense, the interpretive expression of Paul in the PE is an impetus still at work in Christian faith and practice.

Works Cited

Augustine. 1912. *Confessions*. Book 1. LCL. edited by T. E. Page and W. H. D. Rouse. New York: Macmillan.

Bassler, Jouette M. 1996. *1 Timothy, 2 Timothy, and Titus*. Nashville: Abingdon.

Dewey, Joanna. 1992. "1 Timothy, 2 Timothy, and Titus." In *The Women's Bible Commentary*, edited by Carol A. Newsom and Sharon H. Ringe. Louisville: Westminster John Knox.

Eisenbaum, Pamela. 2009. *Paul Was Not a Christian: The Original Message of a Misunderstood Apostle*. San Francisco: HarperOne.

Fellows, Richard G. 2001. "Was Titus Timothy?" *JSNT* 81:33–58.

Hoehl, Stacy. 2011. "The Mentor Relationship: An Exploration of Paul as Loving Mentor to Timothy and the Application of This Relationship to Contemporary Leadership Challenges." *Journal of Biblical Perspectives on Leadership* 3:34–47.

Ignatius. 1999. "Letter to the Ephesians." *Ante-Nicene Fathers*, vol. 1., edited by Alexander Roberts and James Donaldson. Peabody, MA: Hendrickson.

Krause, Deborah. 2004. *1 Timothy*. New York: T&T Clark.

Pervo, Richard I. 2010. *The Making of Paul: Constructions of the Apostle in Early Christianity*. Minneapolis: Fortress Press.

Quinn, Jerome, and William Wacker. 2000. *The First and Second Letters to Timothy*. Eerdmans Critical Commentary. Grand Rapids: Eerdmans.

Schüssler Fiorenza, Elisabeth. 1998. *In Memory of Her: A Feminist Theological Reconstruction of Christian Origins*. 2nd ed. New York: Crossroad.

Tamez, Elsa. 2007. *Struggles for Power in Early Christianity: A Study of 1 Timothy*. Translated by Gloria Kinsler. Maryknoll, NY: Orbis.

Taussig, Hal, ed. 2013. *A New New Testament: A Bible for the 21st Century Combining Traditional and Newly Discovered Texts*. New York: Houghton Mifflin Harcourt.

Thurman, Howard. 1949. *Jesus and the Disinherited*. Nashville: Abingdon.

Wall, Robert. 2012. *1 and 2 Timothy and Titus*. Two Horizons New Testament Commentary. Grand Rapids: Eerdmans.

Witherington, Ben, III. 2006. *Letters and Homilies for Hellenized Christians*. Vol. 1, *A Socio-Rhetorical Commentary on Titus, 1–2 Timothy and 1–3 John*. Downers Grove, IL: IVP Academic.

PHILEMON

Eric D. Barreto

Introduction

The twenty-five verses of Philemon have had an outsized influence on our culture and history. Curiously, its influence has been perhaps most resonant beyond the walls of the church rather than within, as this diminutive correspondence became a site of contestation over the morality of slavery in the United States. Philemon has unfortunately been too frequently and tragically misread. At the same time, this correspondence is a powerful witness of the ways the gospel demands we reimagine how we relate to one another, especially in light of wider societal pressures to embrace destructive hierarchies.

The shortest of Paul's letters, Philemon appears to be full of practical and personal matters but not much theological reflection, especially in comparison to a letter like Romans. Such initial impressions are incorrect, for in this short letter we discover the epitome of Paul's pastoral and theological work. The letter is a vivid illustration of the careful cultural negotiations people of faith must grapple with in a complex world. Most importantly, however, this letter revolves around a critical theological question. If God has drawn people together into communities of faith, how then are we to relate to one another when the dictates of the wider culture lead us toward division and social stratification rather than toward unity and equality?

The letter deals with a seemingly personal matter, which nonetheless evokes deep theological and communal questions. Somehow, Philemon's slave Onesimus has come to be in Paul's presence and provided succor to him in his time in prison. The letter itself does not make clear how Onesimus and Philemon came to be separated. Most interpreters have theorized that Onesimus escaped his master's house and yet somehow ended up becoming a Christian under the tutelage of Paul, Philemon's friend. Perhaps more likely is that Philemon himself sent Onesimus to Paul as a helper during his imprisonment. Prisoners in antiquity relied on the kindness of the free—whether friends or family—to provide for their daily needs. There was no cafeteria or commissary in an ancient prison. One's provisions came from those faithful friends who deigned to visit one in prison (see Matt. 25:36).

In light of Onesimus's kind service to Paul as well as Paul's deep affection for him as a believer (v. 10), Paul sends Onesimus back to his master's household with this letter. What does Paul hope for his dear "child" Onesimus?

The whole letter will be explored as one sense unit, though the section on the letter's "ancient context" does provide an outline based on sections of the letter.

◼ The Text in Its Ancient Context

No exegetical question about Philemon is more important than determining what precipitating event led Paul to write this letter. What are the relational dynamics among Paul, Philemon, and Onesimus? How this question is answered often predetermines a great deal of the conclusions interpreters will reach about the import of this letter for contemporary Christians.

The difficulty is that the letter itself provides few solid clues about the nature of the conflict Paul seeks to address. Key to the background of this letter are four verses, though they each prove difficult to interpret: verses 11, 15, 16, and 18.

First, verse 11 notes that Onesimus appeared to Philemon to be "useless," while he has now proven "useful" to Paul and thus to Philemon too. That is, Paul intimates that Onesimus's utility has shifted in Philemon's eyes. But how exactly has this shift occurred? Second, Paul recounts in verse 15 that some separation has grown between Philemon and Onesimus, a separation Paul now hopes to help heal. However, what is the nature of this separation? Third, Paul seems to allude to Onesimus's status as a slave (*doulos*) in verse 17. Despite the importance of Onesimus's identification as a slave in the history of this letter's interpretation, this is the only time that the word is used in the whole letter. Why? Last, verse 18 seems to allude to some debt Onesimus may owe Philemon. And yet, what exactly is the nature of this debt?

From these few strands of data, interpreters have long sought to reconstruct the background to this letter. Most common has been the conclusion that Onesimus was a runaway slave who somehow came into Paul's circle of influence. Onesimus thus became a Christian, but Paul is now sending him back to his owner, Philemon. Paul seeks to reconcile these conflicted individuals who are now brothers in Jesus. This interpretation can be found throughout Christian tradition, starting with John Chrysostom and continuing through Reformers like Luther and Calvin and the majority of modern study Bibles and commentaries.

Challenges to this regnant conclusion have emerged. For instance, Allen Dwight Callahan has contended that Philemon and Onesimus were actually brothers caught in a bitter rivalry. Moreover, Philemon is now being reexamined by a growing number of African American scholars in particular (see Johnson, Noel, and Williams). These are important critiques of the traditional interpretation, though the view that Onesimus was a runaway slave remains influential.

Behind all these interpretive questions lies an ethical query. Did Paul hope that Philemon would liberate Onesimus? Did Paul in this letter question slavery at its core? Did Paul take the gospel to its liberative end and declare—even if subtly—that the ownership of humans has no place in the church? Often, interpreters have highlighted Paul's willingness to abide by the status quo of antiquity. There were laws regulating slavery, and Paul fully abided by them, these interpreters insist, even sending a runaway slave back to his owner. His submission to the status quo is often seen as commendable, something Christians should imitate. This view depends in significant part on the view that passages enjoining slaves' subordination to masters in other letters (Ephesians, Colossians, 1 Timothy, Titus) are genuine epistles of Paul, a judgment seriously challenged today (see the introductions to those letters and the essay "Situating the Apostle Paul in His Day and Engaging His Legacy in Our Own"). Others, however, have argued that a more robust rejection of slavery resides in Paul's rhetoric. How then do we make sense of these disparate possibilities?

In the end, the best interpretation of Philemon may lean on an ancient tradition of interpretation as more recent scholarship has questioned and reframed it. That is, Onesimus probably was Philemon's slave. He was likely sent to Paul by Philemon to care for Paul's needs in prison; Paul now sends Philemon back to Onesimus. In his letter, however, Paul develops a subtle but no less powerful rationale for reconfiguring how Christian community is conceived. He thus forwards a theological argument that could, if embraced, collapse the all-too-frequent oppressions that mar our world still today. Onesimus returns to Philemon no longer as a slave but a sibling, no longer a piece of property but a beloved brother. Their relationship has been irretrievably changed by the gospel.

Slavery Then and Today

Also critical to the interpretation of Philemon is the very practice of owning another person for economic gain. It would be incorrect simply to equate the practice of slavery in antiquity with its many modern forms today and in the recent past. The commodification of human bodies has taken a wide number of forms throughout history. Two errors ought to be avoided. Modern slavery does not coincide precisely with ancient slavery. Neither is it true that these forms of slavery are wholly distinct.

Several key differences are evident when studying slavery in antiquity and in the history of the United States. First, slavery in antiquity was not based on phenotype, skin color, or other visible identity markers. Peoples were not lumped together as slaves simply because of their cultural attachments or their race. Instead, a variety of misfortunes such as debt or defeat in military conflict could imprison individuals in long-term though not necessarily lifetime servitude. Second, therefore, slavery was not an inevitable and inescapable condition of a particular people. Emancipation was possible, and slavery was not necessarily seen as an inheritance passed from generation to generation.

At the same time, there are some commonalities that ought to be noted. First, both systems converted people into commodities, products that could be owned and used for the benefit of an owner. The dehumanization present in such economic systems is inescapable, no matter the other rationales tied into these systems of slavery. Second, both systems lean on the stratification of a hierarchical society in which some are owners and others are slaves. Some are inherently superior, and others must defer to them. Such hierarchy is antithetical to the gospel as enunciated by Paul in Philemon.

Ancient and modern practices of slavery are not identical. Despite differing practices and assumptions governing and justifying it, slavery remains a theological and ethical scandal. Thus interpretations of Philemon cannot dwell solely on Paul's character or matters of abstract dogma about freedom. At its core, this letter is about how we structure our relationships to one another and how the gospel must shape and reshape these webs of belonging.

Introductory Matters (vv. 1-7)

Like many of Paul's letters, the opening provides a number of interpretive clues for hearers. First is Paul's self-identification as "a prisoner of Christ Jesus" (v. 1). In this way, Paul casts his lot with the broken and despised of the world and thus approaches Philemon not as a spiritual superior but as a dedicated servant of Christ and a friend. Rhetorically, Paul is establishing his equality with Philemon, a sense of equality he will nonetheless use as leverage in the body of the letter.

Moving from the sender to the recipient of the letter, we discover that this epistle is misnamed. Though Philemon was certainly the primary recipient, the addressees include a certain Apphia and Archippus (who may have been the wife and son of Philemon) but also the whole church that gathers in his home. That is, this is not just a personal but a communal letter. Paul makes a request of Philemon but calls on the witness of the whole community to ensure the proper result. The contents of this letter do not include only matters of personal business between the apostle Paul and Philemon the head of his household but a mutual discourse among all of God's children in this congregation.

The thanksgiving section (vv. 4-7), however, returns to a second-person singular address. Paul turns to Philemon in particular, though the opening makes clear that there is a wider audience for this message. In these verses, Paul praises Philemon's faithfulness and witness to the gospel and begins to suggest that there may be something that he might do in order to share in "all the good that we may do for Christ" (v. 6). This initially cryptic reference takes form in the body of the letter.

The Body of the Letter (vv. 8-21)

Paul continues to emphasize not his power over Philemon but the relationship they share. But notice that Paul continues to point glancingly to his power even as he *says* he is subsuming it. Thus, for example, Paul states that he could demand Philemon's compliance (v. 8), and yet he appeals to a brother in the faith, not an inferior person (v. 9). We learn in verse 10 the primary concern of Paul's letter: he is interceding on behalf of Onesimus, who has become like a son to Paul. As noted above, however, it is not immediately clear what the backstory is between Onesimus and Philemon. There is clearly a profound relational tie between Paul and both Onesimus and Philemon. His concern seems to be to align the relationship between the latter two.

In verse 11, a pun in the Greek is lost in English translation. When Paul distinguishes that Onesimus was "useless" but is now "useful" to Philemon, he plays on Onesimus's name, which in Greek means "useful" or "beneficial." In short, the rules by which Philemon relates to Onesimus have changed; his worth, as Paul will detail later, is not based on his utility but on the kinship these followers of Jesus now share. Paul follows this language of persuasion with language of adoption.

This new relationship is embodied by Paul's description of Onesimus as "my own heart." Though he was certainly a help to Paul during his imprisonment (v. 13), Paul's love for Onesimus extends beyond the service he provides. In subtle language, Paul is exhorting Philemon to receive Onesimus in the same spirit, to inhabit this "good deed" (see v. 6). After all, it was Onesimus who had stood in the gap for Philemon, serving an imprisoned Paul in his stead.

But why was Onesimus with Paul in the first place? In verse 15, Paul seems to allude to a period of separation between Philemon and Onesimus. Why were they separated? Was it because Onesimus happened to flee his captivity? Was it because Philemon and/or the church who met in his home sent Onesimus to care for Paul's needs while in prison (see v. 13)?

It seems most likely that Onesimus was not a runaway slave. The encounter of a runaway Onesimus and an imprisoned Paul seems all too serendipitous. What are the chances that they would meet and develop a close relationship only to discover that Paul knew Onesimus's aggrieved master? Such a striking coincidence would certainly need to be mentioned in the letter. Instead, Paul assumes that Philemon knew Onesimus was in his presence. Paul never explains how he came to know Onesimus. Thus it seems most likely that Onesimus was sent by Philemon to care for him in prison. During that time, Paul has to come see Onesimus in a new way. Now Paul invites Philemon to do the same.

Verses 15-16 mark the transformation of Onesimus and a reinvention of the relationship between him and Philemon. Paul theorizes in verse 15 that Onesimus's separation from Philemon (whatever the reason) was a divine initiative so that their bonds would be extended but also transformed. Onesimus is much more than a slave now, Paul tells Philemon; he has become your brother, your kin, a part of you (v. 16).

Just as Onesimus previously stood in Philemon's stead, Paul now asks Philemon to receive his erstwhile slave as if Paul himself were his guest (v. 17). When Philemon sees Onesimus, he ought to imagine the face of Paul. Paul offers to fulfill any debt he might have incurred, even taking the scribe's pen in his own hand to state this (v. 19). And yet, the very next verse is an even more powerful rhetorical stroke: "I say nothing about your owing me even your own self." In saying nothing of this indebtedness, Paul nonetheless raises it. In these renewed communities of faith, it seems, debt is ever present, never discharged, but its payment also never demanded.

Perhaps the debt Paul offers to repay in Onesimus's place is not a straightforward offer. Previous interpreters have suggested that these debts may have been the reason for Onesimus's slavery or that he incurred a debt in running away from his master. But what if the mention of the debt is rhetorical? Between brothers and sisters in faith, no such thing could exist. It may be that, in light of how verse 19 concludes, the debt Paul speaks about is figurative.

As the body of the letter draws to a close starting in verse 20, Paul once again alludes to Onesimus's name by asking Philemon to provide him this "benefit" (*onaimēn*). And when he refers to having "his heart" refreshed, Paul must be pointing back to verse 12. Caring for Onesimus is caring for Paul himself. Here, a powerful model of mutual belonging is present. Paul concludes with words of confidence of Onesimus's "obedience" (v. 21). Paul's rhetoric of persuasion hits its peak here. Paul is not forcing Philemon's hands, but neither is he leaving this critical matter to chance. The witness of the community and the clarity of the good news require a new form of community and belonging.

Final Greetings (vv. 22-25)

These closing words of greeting are not just appendages to the letter. Though we know little about the people Paul names in these closing verses, the rhetoric of persuasion is clearly still evident. The letter is bracketed both in its opening and closing with language of mutuality. Thus, for instance, Paul refers in verse 1 to Philemon as a coworker (*synergos*) and in verse 2 to Archippus as a "fellow soldier" (*systratiōtēs*). Both words share a common Greek prefix (*syn*). That same prefix reemerges again in these closing verses when he refers to Epaphras, "my fellow prisoner" (v. 23, *synaichmalōtos*) and a list of other companions as "fellow workers" (v. 24, *synergos*). Mutual belonging is thus the primary rhetorical stance of the letter of Philemon. There is a flattening of hierarchies. At the same time, Paul is more than willing to deploy the power he has over Philemon. After stating that he is "confident of [his] obedience," Paul follows this note of surety with a not-so-subtle reminder in verse 22. When he asks Philemon to make his household ready for a visit, Paul is not just making necessary travel arrangements or being a polite guest. He is promising to visit this household of sisters and brothers to ensure their community reflects the gospel in all its fullness. Even in this brief letter, the rhetoric of persuasion is consistent and at the center of Paul's argumentation.

▌ THE TEXT IN THE INTERPRETIVE TRADITION

Because of its brevity and the seemingly personal nature of the correspondence, Philemon has suffered from scholarly and exegetical neglect. As detailed above, most interpreters of Philemon have reconstructed the letter's background around a runaway slave and his aggrieved owner. This interpretation was advocated as early as John Chrysostom in his *Homilies on Philemon* in the fourth century. Near unanimity has prevailed ever since. So, in nearly every study Bible and commentary available today, Onesimus is assumed to be a runaway slave whom Paul is returning to his proper master. In many cases, Paul's decision is read as acquiescence to the status quo of his day. According to these interpreters, the letter does not contain a full embrace of ancient slavery, but neither does it seem to oppose it in a full-throated way.

Demetrius K. Williams (12) has argued that when scholars have paid attention to the letter, three primary interpretive questions have guided the tradition. First, interpreters posit what the letter reveals about Paul, not Philemon or Onesimus. In this way, Paul himself becomes an exemplar of humble and measured leadership.

Second, interpreters have had to grapple with the ethical and theological implications of slavery both in antiquity and today. Some found in Paul's subtle rhetoric sanction to continue modern forms of slavery, while others read in the letter a call for liberation. Proponents of slavery saw in Philemon a commitment to a cultural status quo. If Paul did not explicitly condemn slavery, they averred, why should we? In fact, if Paul was willing to send back a fugitive slave to his owner, ought not good citizens to have done the same in the antebellum United States? In contrast, slavery's detractors dwelled on the transformed status of Onesimus in the letter. As Paul himself concludes, Onesimus is "no longer as a slave but more than a slave, a beloved brother" (v. 16).

Last, Philemon has become embroiled in questions about Colossians and its authenticity as a composition of Paul himself because of the reference to Archippus in Col. 4:17 (see also Fitzmyer, 8–9).

Most recently, Philemon has reemerged as a critical instance of the destructive power that flawed exegesis can work and also of how readings from diverse social locations can reveal theological blind spots. Reading from the perspective of Onesimus and privileging the perspective of the enslaved reveal an entirely new way to understand this letter. In short, such a fresh reading can open up new possibilities. As a recent book concluded, "We are interested in hearing from Onesimus and reading from his marginalized position and find that the newer reading perspectives give him voice and agency. However, these newer readings and interpretations will not traverse the same worn and tired territory that has kept Onesimus enslaved and silent. To liberate Onesimus, Paul's letter to Philemon must be read anew or reread from this totally different basis and perspective" (Johnson, Noel, and Williams, 7).

◼ The Text in Contemporary Discussion

Reading Philemon in light of this interpretive history and today's pressing questions requires that we reinterpret Paul's rhetorical strategy in Philemon and its continued significance in theological reflection. Specifically, the composition and theology of Philemon ought to be set alongside the purported heights of Paul's other correspondence. Philemon is likely an exemplar of the kind of pastoral work Paul engaged in on a daily basis. Such quotidian conflicts probably absorbed most of Paul's attention. Philemon thus exemplifies the merging of a particular theology with a particular mode of belonging in community. If we have caught a glimpse of God's character in Jesus, how then ought we live together in faith? This is the question that resonates in Philemon and Romans alike, and the response Philemon provides is no less vital in our world today.

We might begin by asking how we understand Onesimus's role in this triangle of relationships. Interpreters have often focused largely on the relationship between Paul and Philemon, between the great apostle and the slave master, thus excluding from consideration the one individual whose life would be most affected by the outcome of this correspondence. Onesimus's very life and identity are at stake in the rhetorical negotiation Paul outlines. Of course, we can know very little about Onesimus's perspective on these matters. His voice is never directly heard in the letter.

But what we can glimpse are the difficult but necessary ways that Paul sought to stitch together communities composed of all kinds of people: poor and rich, powerful and weak, free and slave. In a hierarchical and highly structured culture, Paul sought to create small spaces of belonging, where these conventions might not hold absolute sway. Perhaps these small, largely powerless communities could not change the political status quo of the day. Perhaps they could not overturn the moral and cultural logics that ruled their society. Perhaps they could not even escape these basic assumptions about the functioning of human civilizations. However, in this letter, Paul invites Philemon and the church around him to imagine a new way to relate to one another. Thus Paul's mode of instruction here is not primarily by dictate or merely listing a new set of rules for everyday life; instead, he posits a theological imagination around kinship and belonging, the implications of which he invites Philemon and the church to embody in their own community. In short, what does it mean to receive one another as beloved sisters and brothers? What effect does this mutual reception have on the ways in which our culture marks us as superior or inferior?

Key to such interpretive efforts will be questioning received assumptions about this letter. Though the notion that Onesimus was a runaway slave has long been sanctioned by interpreters of the letter, recent studies have demonstrated ably how critical it is to revisit even this seeming consensus. Such seeming unanimity often imports unquestioned assumptions into interpretations that too easily become destructive and discordant with the text itself. Onesimus's story may have yet to be told because regnant assumptions have limited exegetical possibilities.

In short, Philemon is an exhortation to communities of faith to bond as kin, to embrace one another as children of God. The gospel reconstitutes our relationships and our communities at a fundamental level. The gospel also calls us, then, to give ear to those who are normally voiceless in our midst. Our communities must have wide boundaries and an eagerness to invite other voices to speak along with an equal yearning to listen carefully to these marginalized voices.

In light of these new relational ties, Philemon ought to propel its readers to rethink slavery again, both its historical legacies and contemporary iterations. Philemon's history of interpretation should remind us of the great harm that can be wielded by the exegete. Today, we ought to remain humble about our own interpretations of Scripture but also prophetic as we strive to invite the liberating reign of God in our midst.

How then do we live in the light of this witness today? How do we resist the siren calls of our own highly structured and demarcated social structures? How do we develop new lines of kinship even as so much of the wider culture draws us toward isolation and homogeneity? The Letter to Philemon suggests that the gospel has reordered our societal structures even as we live within them. Even as we feel the constraints of the ways we relate to one another, God has declared a new order in which the primary way we relate to one another is not based on inferiority and superiority but kinship, sisters and brothers adopted by a loving and just God. This was true for Philemon and Onesimus, no matter their relationship and conflicts. The same remains true for us today.

Works Cited

Callahan, Allen Dwight. 1997. *Embassy of Onesimus: The Letter of Paul to Philemon*. *The New Testament in Context*. Valley Forge, PA: Trinity Press International.

Fitzmyer, Joseph A. 2000. *The Letter to Philemon*. AB 34C. New York: Doubleday.

Johnson, Matthew V., James A. Noel, and Demetrius K. Williams, eds. 2012. *Onesimus Our Brother: Reading Religion, Race, and Culture in Philemon*. Paul in Critical Contexts. Minneapolis: Fortress Press.

Williams, Demetrius K. 2012. "'No Longer as a Slave': Reading the Interpretation History of Paul's Epistle to Philemon." In Johnson, Noel, and Williams, 11–45.

INTRODUCTION TO HEBREWS, THE GENERAL EPISTLES, AND REVELATION

Neil Elliott

The transition from the Letters of Paul to the "Epistle to the Hebrews" and the General Epistles that follow offers an opportunity to reflect on the organization of writings that we call the New Testament. Although early Bible manuscripts show a number of different ways of organizing the collection, from the fourth century onward the pattern began to take hold in different codices that we see in our current New Testament.

First appear the four Gospels, then the Acts of the Apostles (though this followed the Epistles of Paul in the fourth-century Codex Sinaiticus). Note that the gathering together of Gospels means the separation of the two-volume work Luke and Acts. Then come the Letters of Paul—arranged roughly in order of length, rather than chronology, with 1 and 2 Corinthians and 1 and 2 Thessalonians being put together, and with letters to churches preceding letters apparently written to individuals (though note that Philemon, the last of the Pauline Epistles, is also addressed to a church). Hebrews was often included among Paul's letters, following Romans (for example, already in P[46], c. 200), presumably on the assumption, held for example by Augustine and Jerome, that Paul had written it. Its present position following Paul's letters (as it appears already in Sinaiticus) may be the result of its dislocation from that collection as doubts about its authorship gradually arose. (The third-century theologian Origen quipped that "God only knows" who penned the epistle, but he usually quoted the letter as if it came from Paul, and commended churches who held it to be from the apostle. He also knew of a tradition that the epistle had been written by Clement of Rome: Eusebius *Hist. eccl.* 6.25.)

In the Syriac Peshitta (c. second century CE), the letters appearing under the names of the most prominent of the apostles—James, 1 Peter, and 1 John—appear immediately after Acts, before the Pauline Epistles. Other epistles that appear in our New Testament today—2 Peter, Jude, and 2 and 3 John—gained currency relatively late in the first centuries of Christianity; they were not included in the Peshitta or in early lists of the New Testament writings. The fourth-century Codex Vaticanus arranges all the General Epistles before the Epistles of Paul; Sinaiticus puts Acts and the General Epistles together, but following Paul's letters.

The nomenclature of "General" or "Catholic" Epistles (from the Greek *kath' holikos*, "general" or "universal") was first used by Alexandrian scholars to refer to 1 Peter and 1 John, then by the fourth-century bishop and historian Eusebius to refer to James; 1 and 2 Peter; 1, 2, and 3 John; and Jude—though Eusebius acknowledged that several of these were "disputed" by different churches (*antilegomena: Eccl. hist.* 2.23; 3.25.1–3). Referring to these as "Catholic" Epistles implies a distinction from Paul's letters: if Paul wrote to specific congregations, these epistles are written to the church "Catholic" or universal. The distinction cannot be maintained, of course, once we recognize that Paul's letters are also directed to multiple congregations (e.g., the "churches" of Galatia, Gal. 1:2) and consider that early manuscripts of Ephesians do not include the address "in Ephesus" (1:1); indeed, the collection of Paul's letters shows that they were perceived by some Christians, at least, as relevant and useful for churches beyond their original addressees. Colossians 4:16 assumes an interchange of letters between churches. And the probability that some of those letters are pseude-pigrapha, created after Paul's death to extend his legacy (or claim his authority) to new audiences, shows a "catholicizing" impulse at work in that collection.

Meanwhile, the Epistle of James and the First Epistle of Peter explicitly address more general audiences ("to the twelve tribes in the Dispersion," James 1:1; "to the exiles of the Dispersion in Pontus, Galatia, Cappadocia, Asia, and Bithynia," 1 Pet. 1:1), but these letters were nonetheless written in specific circumstances with particular goals in mind. Furthermore, the characterization of addressees in terms of "exile" and Diaspora may have a particular rhetorical function. It hardly distinguishes these as the only two writings in our New Testament written to communities of immigrants or "rootless" people, as Margaret Aymer shows in her article in this volume ("Rootless-ness and Community in Contexts of Diaspora," 47–61).

Neither should we assume that the reference to Diaspora is evidence that these writings both addressed Jews (see the introductions to each epistle). Similarly, the title "To the Hebrews" may well be secondary; it neither indicates that this "word of exhortation" (Heb. 5:11; 6:1) was intended for Jewish readers or that it enjoyed particular popularity among them. To be sure, the status of the law, the temple, and the covenant with Israel are prominent topics in several of these writings, but as Lawrence M. Wills shows, these were paramount concerns in numerous early churches, over many decades ("Negotiating the Jewish Heritage of Early Christianity," 31–45).

In short, all of these writings give important glimpses into the convictions and concerns of early believers in Jesus. We can well imagine that their authors and intended readers shared particular knowledge and assumptions that are lost to us now. Their collection into a loose and rather ill-fitting category, "General Epistles," may obscure important historical connections (for example, between the Johannine Epistles and the Gospel according to John). At any rate, that category, and the place of these epistles and Hebrews "in between" Paul's letters and the Revelation to John, should not be taken to indicate that their various authors actually aimed these writings at churches "in general." As the introduction to each of the following entries will indicate, we can make reasonable judgments about the specifics of place, time, and situation surrounding each letter. Taken together, they offer us additional glimpses of the diversity, no less than the commonality, of early churches. But their being grouped together in one part of our New Testament labeled "General Epistles" is little more than a matter of organizational convenience, and readers today should not for that reason consider themselves more included in the implied audience of any of these than of any other New Testament writing. The responsibility for how any of us read ourselves "into" these ancient writings, or read them "into" our own time, remains, at last, with us.

HEBREWS

David A. deSilva

Introduction

"The Epistle of Paul the Apostle to the Hebrews," as the KJV names this book, is a misnomer in every respect. First, the author does not present this text as an epistle. The opening sentence does not reflect the standard letter-opening formula, but the beginning of a well-crafted oration. He labels his own text a "word of exhortation" (13:22), a term for a "sermon" in early Judaism (see Acts 13:15). Hebrews is best read as an example of early (and expert) Christian preaching. The author closes with the elements of an epistolary postscript (13:18-25), in keeping with the fact that he has, of necessity, had to commit his sermon to writing to be read aloud to the audience by a third party.

The sermon is anonymous. The mention of Timothy (Heb. 13:23) and Paul's reputation as a letter-writer led early scribes to attribute the text to Paul. This is unlikely on several grounds. Paul vehemently insists that he came to faith in Christ without human mediation (Gal. 1:11-17; 1 Cor. 15:3-10), whereas this author came to faith through the preaching of other apostles (Heb. 2:3-4). Paul's undisputed letters exhibit none of the attention to rhetorical ornamentation that one finds in Hebrews. Indeed, Paul avoids rhetorical polish in principle, lest persuasion come through the speaker rather than the Spirit (1 Cor. 2:1-5), a reluctance this author did not share. The author does seem to belong to the large circle of teachers that constitute the Pauline team (Heb. 13:23).

Debates in the early church concerning authorship (Apollos and Barnabas were also suggested) show that it was consistently regarded as Pauline, prior to Jerome's and Augustine's championing of Pauline authorship (in connection with their promoting its canonical status). Although it has become popular to suggest Priscilla as a candidate, the author's use of a self-referential masculine participle in 11:32 argues against this. Arguments that this was intended to hide the author's gender founder on the fact that addressees clearly know the author's identity (13:19, 23) and on the Pauline churches' openness to female leadership (see, e.g., Rom. 16:1-3; Col. 4:15).

The author mastered both the Jewish scriptural heritage and the art of rhetoric, giving the clearest signs of formal training, at least at the level of elementary rhetorical education, of any New Testament author (deSilva 2012, 3–19). He writes Greek like a native speaker and shows a broad familiarity with elements of Greek culture (like athletic practices, philosophy of education, and popular ethics). The text has some connection with Christianity in Italy (Heb. 13:24), though it is unclear whether the author sends greetings from Italy abroad (which seems more likely) or back home to fellow Italian Christians. Clement of Rome's use of the sermon in 95–96 CE confirms some connection with Roman Christianity and also sets the latest possible date of composition. The author's references to the Levitical sacrifices as ongoing (e.g., Heb. 10:2-3) most naturally suggest a date prior to 70 CE, when the temple was destroyed by the Roman armies.

The audience is not made up of "Hebrews," at least as Acts 6:1-6 understands the term. The recipients speak Greek and know the Jewish Scriptures primarily in the Greek translation rather than Hebrew (the author makes several points that rely on details found only in the former). If the audience was part of the Pauline mission, the goal of which was to take the good news to non-Jews and to establish congregations in which Jewish and gentile believers worshiped together, it was likely of mixed ethnicity (Attridge, 10–13; deSilva 2000, 2–7; Eisenbaum, 8–9). The author's extensive use of the Jewish Scriptures is no argument against this, as these were the authoritative oracles of God for both gentile and Jewish Christians.

The text provides three windows into the audience's past: their initial conversion, in which a new experience of divine power cemented their commitment to a new group (2:1-4); their socialization into the worldview of the Christian group, in which they learned some of the foundational convictions on which the author will build throughout his sermon (6:1-3); and their experience of rejection by their neighbors, who used a variety of tactics to shame them into abandoning their new way of life and returning to a more acceptable one (10:32-34). While they had successfully resisted those pressures in the past, their current behavior suggests that the loss of status and honor had begun to make some disciples, at least, question whether God's nonmaterializing promises were worth enduring continued alienation from the way of life and social networks of support they once enjoyed. Some individuals have already ceased to associate openly with the Christian group (10:25).

The author perceives that others may be in danger of doing the same (hence the recurring warnings in 2:1, 3; 3:12; 4:11; 6:4-6; 10:26-31; 12:15) and writes to stave off any such course of action. He seeks to confirm the hearers in their commitment to persevere in their Christian practice and to invest in one another's perseverance as well, countering society's negative pressures (3:6, 14; 4:11; 6:9-12; 10:23-25, 35-36, 39; 12:1, 3, 12-13; 13:12-14). He pursues several strategies to advance this agenda. He "normalizes" the experience of rejection and disgrace and turns endurance of the same into an opportunity for honor in God's sight. He taps into the foundational social codes of reciprocity, presenting Jesus as a supremely generous mediator of God's patronage and setting before the audience's eyes the insuperable advantages of continuing to nurture this relationship through appropriate loyalty and gratitude (rather than incurring divine wrath through ingratitude). He uses the authoritative Scriptures and the basic convictions of the Christian community (for example, final judgment, the passing away of the present age, and the imminence of God's kingdom) to locate the audience on the very threshold of encountering Jesus at his return and entering into God's unshakable realm, thus promoting consideration of the "eternal" over the "temporal" by stressing the former's imminence.

The sermon alternates between exposition and exhortation, the former consistently providing the warrant for the latter. Scholars formerly questioned whether chapter 13, with its relatively brief and practical instructions, was originally a part of the sermon, but Floyd Filson's study effectively ended the debate in favor of the text's unity.

Clement of Rome and Justin Martyr used and valued Hebrews, but the book was slow to gain recognition as a canonical authority in the West. It was more widely used and embraced among Eastern Christians. The question of apostolic authorship was important to some early church teachers, but not to others (like Origen, who could accept both the sermon's authority and anonymity). Hebrews provided, nevertheless, an important resource for the development of Christology (e.g., the question of the relationship of Jesus to God as "Son" and the idea of the two natures of Christ) and for reflection on the meaning of Jesus' death and the mechanics of atonement. Its acceptance into the canon of Paul's letters finally facilitated its acceptance into the canon of the New Testament.

Contemporary readers question the appropriateness of the author's interpretation of the Jewish Scriptures, taking these texts almost solely as a witness in some way to the person and work of Jesus, showing no interest in the text's meaning in its own right. While this is integral to the sermon's contribution to the formation of Christology, it also flies in the face of the practice of modern biblical criticism. Closely related to this is the theological problem of supersessionism—the replacement of the Mosaic covenant with the new covenant—that runs throughout the sermon. Other major issues revolve around the author's apparent impositions of limitations on repentance and God's mercy (no less a problem for ancient Christians than modern ones) and his sublimation of a brutal execution through the language of sacrifice and atonement. On the other hand, there is a growing appreciation for the anti-imperial rhetoric in Hebrews and its function as resistance literature (both sociopolitically and culturally).

Hebrews 1:1-14: The Ultimate Revelation in God's Son

■ THE TEXT IN ITS ANCIENT CONTEXT

In an artfully crafted antithesis, the author opens by emphasizing the ultimacy, completeness, and finality of the word spoken by God in the Son, the word around which his hearers were shaped into a new community. This opening sentence sounds the "indicative" that underscores every "imperative" to keep giving this word its due weight and to continue to respond properly to this announcement (e.g., 2:1-4; 3:7-8, 14-15; 5:11; 12:25-29). The Son's exalted status remains an important datum throughout the sermon, underscoring both the value of remaining connected with Jesus and the danger of dishonoring such a being. Locating the hearers "in the later part of these days" (1:2, my translation) heightens the importance of responding well. The imminence of the end, portending eternal deliverance for the Son's loyal clients and eternal judgment for the Son's enemies (1:13-14), intensifies the importance of the choices made in the present moment. The author's use of Ps. 110:1 (1:3) foreshadows the author's use of the Jewish Scriptures throughout: these texts are so completely a witness to the Son, Jesus, that they can be read to speak of events in his story prior to his birth and after his ascension (events for which there could be no human witnesses).

Hebrews 1:5-14 provides a sampling of how the author sees the "many pieces" (*polymerōs*, 1:1) of God's prior words spoken through prophets (here including David, the traditional author of royal psalms such as Pss. 2; 45; and 110; see Heb. 1:5, 8, 13) coming together in the revelation of the Son. The true significance of those many "pieces" emerges as they are read as though spoken *to*, *about*, or even *by* the Son. The author's focus on the Son's superiority to angels has given rise to the mistaken view that the author addressed some heresy involving an inferior view of Christ or a strange fascination with angels. The rhetorical questions of 1:5, 14, however, presuppose agreement between the author and the recipients on these points. Angels were seen as mediators and messengers: as intercessors in the heavenly temple (*T. Levi* 3:4-8; Tob. 12:12, 15; Matt. 18:10; Rev. 8:3-4) and also as the couriers who brought the law to Israel (see *Jub.* 1:27-29; 2:1; Acts 7:38, 53; Gal. 3:19). The Son will be presented throughout the sermon as a superior mediator and superior messenger, thus more to be held on to and heeded than any previous ones (see the comparisons with Moses and with the Levitical priesthood). Here, the scriptural "proof" of Jesus' superiority to angels (1:5-14) serves to establish the premise (1:4) on which the hortatory conclusion drawn in 2:1-3a will depend.

A second major point is the unchangeableness—the constancy—of the Son vis-à-vis the mutable angels and the temporary material creation (1:7-12). The latter introduces us to the author's cosmology, which is of great importance to the whole of his sermon. The cosmos is divided into two principal parts: the visible, material earth and heavens (skies, stars, etc.) and the invisible realm beyond creation ("heaven itself," 9:24). The first is transitory and will eventually be removed (1:10-12; 12:26-28). The second existed prior to creation and will last forever. Everything belonging to God's realm, therefore, is of infinitely greater quality and value than anything in the material realm—hence, "better," because "lasting" (thematic words in the sermon). This cosmology undergirds the author's exhortations to act with a view to keeping hold of the invisible, eternal goods that God has promised, and not to sacrifice these for short-lived relief in the present age.

Christ's exaltation to God's right hand carries both promise and menace (1:13-14). The author strategically frames the hearers' consideration of their presenting challenges with the "larger" challenge: How should they respond to this Son so as to remain in his favor rather than return to the ranks of his enemies (2:1-4)?

▌ THE TEXT IN THE INTERPRETIVE TRADITION

The author ascribed attributes of Wisdom known from Proverbs 8 and Wisdom of Solomon 7–9 (see especially 7:22, 26-27; 8:1; 9:9) to the preincarnate Son, who gives Wisdom a new face. Hebrews 1:1-14 thus became an important resource for early Christian reflection on the relationship of Jesus to God. The analogy of the relationship of "radiance" to "glory" figured prominently in discussions of the Son's sharing in the essence of the Father (Origen, Athanasius, against Arius) and his coexisting with God for eternity: to declare that there was a time when the "radiance" was not would imply that there was a time when the "glory" was not (Gregory of Nyssa).

The comparison of the Son with the angels fed early Christian fascination with the latter. Early theologians were also concerned with how each of these statements applied to each of the two natures of Christ: the divine nature was unchanging and unending in every way; the human nature could experience exaltation to God's right hand (Theodoret of Cyr). These readers accepted without question the Christ-centered interpretation applied to the Hebrew scriptural texts recited by the author, a mode of interpretation they embraced completely (patristic commentary on Hebrews has been conveniently compiled in Heen and Kray 2005).

▌THE TEXT IN CONTEMPORARY DISCUSSION

Questions abound about the integrity of biblical interpretation in the early church such as Hebrews exhibits. The author does not ground his interpretations in a consideration of the "original meaning" of many of the texts he uses and has therefore been accused of co-opting them for his own group-forming and ideology-sustaining agenda. It is worth noting, however, that his reading also reflects an implicit criticism of his own tradition. For example, his reading transcends the nationalism and the legitimation of a particular system of domination (the Davidic monarchy) inherent in the context of the royal psalms' composition.

The author's cosmology also raises questions. Is it, as many since Bultmann would aver, a relic of a more primitive stage in human thinking? Or does it represent, conversely, a persistent and needful challenge to contemporary philosophical materialism, as well as its practical manifestations in contemporary priorities and practices?

There are strong trends in contemporary scholarship that resist making Jesus more than human. This author's assertions about the "Son" and his place at God's right hand could again seem to reflect a more mythologically driven understanding of the man Jesus. The author will go on to speak about Jesus' complete humanness with the same energy as he speaks of Jesus' proximity to the divine. The fundamental connection between reflecting God's image and being truly human (Gen. 1:26-27; Heb. 1:3) may lead Christians to reexamine the author's language from the point of view that Jesus is *the* Human One (the "son of man") par excellence, the one in whom the image of God is seen fully and without distortion. Jesus reminds his followers of what it means to be human and to show God's image in one's being and doing, as well as revealing something important about the character and commitments of God. Readers may also appreciate the politically subversive overtones of speaking of Jesus as "Son of God" in an environment in which the emperor Tiberius, for example, was named "son of the deified Augustus." The author again is seen to address and oppose the sort of mythic language that legitimated domination systems in favor of an alternative vision of how the divine reaches into and nurtures human community.

Hebrews 2:1-18: God's Son and the Many Sons and Daughters

▌THE TEXT IN ITS ANCIENT CONTEXT

Hebrews 2:1-4 presents the argumentative point toward which Heb. 1:1-4 and 1:5-14 have been leading. God has spoken a definitive word in the Son (1:1-4); the Son's honor is greater than that of the angels (1:5-14); therefore, since God expected the earlier message articulated through angels (the Torah) to be obeyed and enforced this with the death penalty, the hearers would do well to respond to the Word they heard from the Son with even greater diligence and commitment (2:1-4). The author strategically presents as "drifting away" the course of action that the Christians' neighbors would have urged as "getting back on course," namely, dissociation from the Christian gospel and the group that promoted it. This is the first of several such calls to keep responding to the gospel in a manner befitting the supreme dignity of the Son who enacted and announced it (see also 4:1-11; 6:4-8; 10:26-31; 12:25-29). The author's specific recommendations concerning *how* to keep responding appropriately center mostly on ongoing investment in the lives of one's fellow disciples and ongoing witness—through both speech and action—to the value of Jesus' friendship and God's promises.

The author recalls the hearers' experience of the presence of the supernatural as a divine confirmation of the truth of the gospel, reminding them how their new way of life brought them in line and in contact with God. The description resembles Paul's own reminiscences about his congregations' experiences of conversion (see 1 Cor. 2:1-5; Gal. 3:1-5). Religious experience was an important element in the hearers' process of converting to this new faith.

The discussion returns to the person of the Son, this time focusing on his complete sharing in human nature and experience (2:5-18). The author recites Ps. 8:4-6, called to mind perhaps by the shared interest between this text and Ps. 110:1 in the subjection of "enemies" or "all things" under someone's "feet." While the divine realm (designated by the author as the *oikoumenē* at 1:6; 2:5, informed perhaps by the opposition of the shakable "earth," *gē*, to the unshakable *oikoumenē* in, e.g., Ps. 96:9-10) has been subjected to the Son, not all things have yet been brought under his dominion. But the story *is* unfolding as God indicated: the disciples have witnessed Jesus' humiliation in his incarnation and death and his exaltation, so the remainder must just be a matter of time. The author may show awareness of the fact that the psalm was originally a text about humanity in general. What we "see" in Jesus is the foretaste of what we will yet see when the many sons and daughters share in the glory and honor that the Son now enjoys (2:10).

The author interjects that suffering death on behalf of others, as a manifestation of God's favor (2:9), was the precondition to exaltation. Such costly beneficence supports the author's call for costly gratitude on the hearers' part (see, e.g., 13:12-14). Moreover, the course of Jesus' life through suffering to glory was the result of God's forethought for the hearers in the struggles that God knew *they* would have to endure on *their* journey to lay hold of God's promises. It was "fitting" for God to "perfect" the pioneer—that is, to bring him to the appointed goal of his own journey—through sufferings because God knew that the many sons and daughters would have to journey through sufferings themselves (see, e.g., 10:32-34). Thus God charted out Jesus' path specifically so that he would become fully sympathetic with his followers, and thus be fully committed to helping them in their own struggles to respond faithfully to God, as Jesus had (2:16-18). Speaking of the hearers' experience of rejection as "trials" or "tests" is also strategic: their neighbors' hostility becomes an opportunity to prove themselves, and yielding to such hostility means failing the test (2:18).

Jesus' solidarity with his followers is also exhibited using a string of Scripture citations (2:11-13; see Ps. 22:23; Isa. 8:17-18), where, once again, the author finds the ancient texts' meaning by referring them to—or even placing them on the lips of—Jesus himself. The fact that such an exalted figure (1:1-14) would associate himself so closely and confidently with the marginalized disciples should bolster their own self-respect and repair their esteem.

◼ THE TEXT IN THE INTERPRETIVE TRADITION

Discussing the nature of the "salvation" or "deliverance" provided through the Son (2:1-4), early theologians focused their readers' expectations not on deliverance from temporal ills or enjoyment of earthly rewards, but rather on deliverance from the power of death and the devil over human beings in this life and the next (John Chrysostom). They were also sensitive to the warning given in this passage, reading it as a stern admonition to be watchful over one's own heart and life, so as not to throw away Jesus' deliverance (Origen, John Chrysostom).

These theologians were also interested in the text's focus on the two natures of Christ who, as God, was always superior to the angels but, as a human being, lived for a short while below them in the order of being (Theodoret of Cyr, Theodore of Mopsuestia)—and that *genuinely* as a human being, against docetist claims to the contrary (Cyril of Alexandria). The fact that not everything was yet subjected to Christ explained the ongoing suffering of his followers: both Christ's own experience of suffering and the promise of his eventual triumph over all things provided encouragement to the many sons and daughters (John Chrysostom).

◼ THE TEXT IN CONTEMPORARY DISCUSSION

Contemporary readers might find themselves alienated from the author's assumption of a future visitation of divine judgment, from which "deliverance" is needed (2:1-3a). On the other hand, many people still believe in some kind of accountability beyond death and hope for "deliverance" resulting in a better postmortem existence (2:10). A belief in divine judgment is often an important ideological prop for continued resistance to cultural and religious imperialism, such as the Christian group experienced at the hands of the dominant Roman culture and the better-empowered Jewish culture.

In an era in which theological violence (inscribed, for example, in satisfaction or substitutionary theories of atonement) has become more highly problematic than in centuries past, the author's interpretation of the cross as Jesus' confronting and destroying the power of death to distort and constrain human life (2:14-15; this was also of interest to early theologians) can provide a constructive alternate model. The fear of death remains a basic datum of the human psyche (Becker, 11–24). It threatens to distort life by driving people to finding ways to "make their mark," to prioritizing their own enjoyment of this brief span over the concerns of others, to avoiding confrontations with the powers that be on behalf of the oppressed, and to more obvious neuroses. The promise of "deliverance" from its power is a great desideratum.

The passage challenges the modern Western allergy to suffering, whether one's own or another person's, making suffering the focal point of God's interest, Jesus' experience, and the experience of humanity, as well as the locus for encountering Jesus' help. The robust theology of the incarnation promoted by the author of Hebrews challenges Western Christians (in particular) not to embrace their culture's avoidance of suffering, but to look more bravely at the plight of the suffering and allow that vision to transform their priorities and practices. On the other hand, many in the Western and in the majority world cannot escape suffering, marginalization, and deprivation. The author of Hebrews holds out a vision in which the God of the universe took a particular interest in them and others like them, conforming the experience of the Son of God to their experience, indeed making people in their plight the chief focal point of the divine redemptive intervention. While this perspective never legitimates the infliction of deprivation or suffering, it lends an empowering dignity to the experience of the same that may assist both endurance and resistance.

Hebrews 3:1-19: The Dangers of Responding with Distrust

▌ THE TEXT IN ITS ANCIENT CONTEXT

First Samuel 2:35 spoke of God's raising up "a faithful priest" *and* "a faithful house," which may account for the author's transition from the former (2:18) to the latter (3:1-6). The author compares Jesus favorably now with Moses: while the latter was faithful in God's house (see Num. 12:7) as a servant (like the angels, 1:7, 14), the former was faithful *over* God's house as a Son. Both possess the positive virtue of reliability, but Jesus' proximity to God remains closer and his status greater (Attridge, 105). Moses, like the angels, was regarded as a mediator figure (see Exod. 32:7-14, 30-34; *T. Mos.* 11.17; Pseudo-Philo, *L.A.B.* 19.11). The hearers have in Jesus the best-placed mediator of God's favor and promises possible, and should for no reason relinquish that relationship. Their continuing place in God's household depends on it (3:6).

Repeating the pattern of 1:1—2:4, this comparison leads to an exhortation to heed the word spoken by the Son, comparing the audience's situation with that of Moses' generation (3:7-19). The author uses Ps. 95:7-11, with its summons to listen for and heed the divine voice, as a principal scriptural resource. While the original Hebrew recalls three separate incidents of failure to respond well to God's voice (at Massah, Meribah, and Kadesh-barnea), the Greek version focuses only on the episode in Numbers 14, which is essential background for this chapter. With the exceptions of Caleb and Joshua, the exodus generation gave more weight to the hostility and power of the Canaanites than to the promise and power of God, with the result that they disobeyed God's command to take Canaan and were condemned to wander in the desert till they dropped dead (3:8-11, 15-19). The author places his audience in an analogous situation, standing on the very threshold of the greater promised land of the divine realm. Hostile people stand in their way (see, e.g., 10:32-34), but God has given God's assurance of victory and possession. They should, therefore, learn from the exodus generation's example (3:19; 4:11) to persevere in moving forward in trust and obedience to God's call, rather than turn aside (3:12).

▌ THE TEXT IN THE INTERPRETIVE TRADITION

Calling Jesus an "apostle" (Heb. 3:1), when many people were called "apostles," seemed not to suit Jesus' unique dignity. Justin Martyr and Theodoret of Cyr read this in terms of the incarnation and Jesus' unique sense of having been "sent" by the Father in the Fourth Gospel. Patristic commentators also recognized that the comparison with Moses stems from the genuine esteem in which the author and audience held Moses (Theodoret of Cyr, John Chrysostom).

While acknowledging the warning inherent in 3:7-19, particularly to the first hearers who found themselves in a situation like that of the wilderness generation (Theodore of Mopsuestia), early commentators also found the emphasis on "Today" to be a source of ongoing encouragement to those who stood in need of repentance. As long as this age lasted, there was hope for the sinner's recovery (John Chrysostom).

▌THE TEXT IN CONTEMPORARY DISCUSSION

The author's reading and application of the example of the exodus generation conforms quite closely with modern standards of exegesis, maintaining the distance between the original situation and the situation of application, deriving principles more by analogy than direct application to the new situation. Many modern Christians may have difficulty, however, with the suggestion that belonging to God's household or of remaining Christ's partners is conditional (3:6, 14), because of the theological domination of certain post-Reformation interpretations of *Pauline* texts that negate the contributions of human effort or actions to salvation. Hebrews challenges these interpretations, and could helpfully even raise questions about their correctness in regard to Paul himself.

The text challenges contemporary presuppositions in other important respects. The author presupposes a degree of intimacy and interaction that runs counter to ecclesiastical practices nurtured in a context of Western individualism and of Western conceptualizations of the lines between private and public, insiders and outsiders. The community as a whole is charged with looking out for signs that individuals might be wavering in their commitment and acting to shore up that commitment (3:12-13; see also 4:1; 5:12; 10:24-25; 12:15), as well as investing themselves fully to relieve the pressures that weigh on other members (6:9-10; 13:1-3, 15-16), creating a strong alternative social body (Filson, 69; deSilva 2012, 139–49). Each member of the community bears some responsibility for the perseverance or nonperseverance of the other members. The author does not address his audience as "brothers and sisters" (3:1, 12) because of superficial religious convention, but because he truly expects them to take on the same obligations toward one another (as members of God's household) as they would undertake for their natural family.

This passage is based on a segment of a deeply problematic narrative within the Hebrew Bible, namely, the conquest of the land of Canaan and the genocide that essentially accompanied this conquest. This is a narrative that has repeated itself in the New World in regard to its indigenous peoples as well as within other episodes of colonial conquest throughout the globe. While the author of Hebrews does not explicitly critique this aspect of his own heritage, he offers a delegitimating perspective on the narrative as a call to conquest in the geopolitical sphere of this world. In his understanding, the conquest of Canaan did not accomplish God's purposes for God's people, for Joshua did not, in fact, lead Israel into "God's rest." Similarly, he leaves no room for such a crusade in the visible, material world, for God's people "are seeking a better, that is a heavenly," homeland (11:16). The divine narrative and call is, in his view, not one that invites us into conflict and the quest for the domination of territory. The history of Western and other colonization, however, has shown the author's reinterpretation not to be influential.

Hebrews 4:1-13: Entering God's "Rest"

▐ THE TEXT IN ITS ANCIENT CONTEXT

"Entering God's rest" is thematic throughout 3:7-19 (see 3:11, 18-19) and becomes even more prominent in 4:1-11 (4:1, 3 [2×], 5, 6 [2×], 10, 11). This drums into the hearers' ears the importance of succeeding in "entering God's rest," drowning out, for the moment at least, other potential agenda items. The author crafts an argument based on Scripture passages related to God's "rest" to establish exactly what this destiny entails. Based on the fact that "David" speaks of a promise to enter God's rest centuries after Joshua led the children of the exodus generation into Canaan (Ps. 95:11; Heb. 4:7-8), the author concludes that the destined "rest" had nothing to do with entry into Canaan. This "rest," furthermore, must exist outside of creation—it was the place where God "rested" after creation, the place where God's full presence dwells eternally (Gen. 2:2; Heb. 4:3-5). Entering God's rest, therefore, speaks of the same reality as the many other images the author uses to speak of the divine realm beyond the visible creation ("glory," 2:10; "the inner side of the curtain," 6:20; "the better, heavenly homeland," 11:16; the "unshakable kingdom," 12:28; the "city that is to come," 13:14). Other texts also conceived of the coming age as an eschatological "sabbatical" (4:9; see *Barn.* 15.3-6; *L.A.E.* 51.2–3). Hebrews 4:10 is an ambiguous verse, but it might be read as an oblique reference to Jesus (Vanhoye, 99–100), who has indeed already entered into God's rest, that is, into "heaven itself," at his ascension (9:12, 24-25) as the forerunner for the hearers (2:10; 6:19-20; 12:2-3).

The author places the hearers at the threshold of this "rest": they "are entering" (3:3a), but still must "make every effort to enter" (4:11; see also 10:19-22, 35-36). The thing to fear is failing to enter, falling into the exodus generation's pattern on the threshold of their own inheritance (4:1, 11). This is a strong ideological move, as some members of the congregation clearly "fear" other losses, which has already led some to defect (10:25). If they accept the author's framing of their position in terms of Numbers 14, they will be more likely to persevere in their commitment to the group and to the cost of continued identification with Jesus in the midst of an unsupportive society.

The passage concludes with a strong warning. Hebrews 4:12 is often quoted as a triumphant testimony to the power of Scripture, but 4:12 and 4:13 together really paint a fearsome image. They compare God's Word, in its power to cut through our psychological defenses and rationalizations, to a two-edged sword—a familiar accoutrement of the omnipresent Roman soldiers that could slice through any part of a human body and send the "soul" to Hades and the "spirit/breath" back to God (4:12). They further compare the hearers to naked victims, whose throats are exposed (Gk. *tetrachēlismena*) to the executioner's blade, awaiting the word from the Judge (4:13). The author's use of wordplay is once again masterful, as he poses the implicit question: What kind of "account" (*logos*, 4:13) will the hearers be able to give in regard to their response to the Word (*logos*, 4:12) announced in the Son?

◼ THE TEXT IN THE INTERPRETIVE TRADITION

Patristic- and Reformation-era commentators emphasized the different kinds of "rest" envisioned in Scripture, with the people of faith looking ahead to the perfect tranquility of God's eternal kingdom rather than any earthly kingdom that would always be subject to war and unrest. They were also keenly interested in what 4:12-13 had to say about the power of the Word, usually understood as the Scriptures (with Augustine even relating the double-edged quality to the two testaments), and about the human desire to hide oneself from God's all-searching Word (Ambrose). John Chrysostom and Martin Luther viewed 4:12-13 as a warning concerning the judgment of the ungodly.

◼ THE TEXT IN CONTEMPORARY DISCUSSION

More objections could be raised concerning the author's exegesis in 4:1-11 than 3:7-19, most notably the fallacy of claiming that Ps. 95:11 actually speaks of a "rest" other than the one denied the exodus generation at Kadesh-barnea. The psalmist himself uses the Numbers 14 incident to illustrate a poor response to God's word, urging worshipers to be more attentive to God's voice than were their ancestors, and the oath (Ps. 95:11) is just part of that example. Nevertheless, by the canons of first-century biblical interpretation (notably the application of the rule of *gezera shawa*, the use of one verse, like Gen. 2:2, to interpret a second verse, like Ps. 95:11, linked by a common lexical element, like "rest"), the author's argument has integrity. He is also ultimately pointing to a conceptual reality (God's realm) that is amply attested elsewhere, so that his exegesis aligns with his contemporaries' cosmology.

A more pressing question concerns the author's appeals to fear here and elsewhere throughout his sermon. Many contemporary people of faith would not regard fear to be an adequate—or a spiritually mature—motivator of religious commitment. They would critique a theology that incorporated notions of God as a more powerful being willing to exercise that power in violent, punitive ways intending harm—the potential that is prerequisite to "fear." The text might challenge these readers in return, however, asking whether the modern discomfort with "fear" reflects their failure to apprehend the power and holiness of the divine and, thus, the demands placed on their response, if that response is to be appropriate.

Hebrews 4:14—5:10: God's Son as Sympathetic Mediator

◼ THE TEXT IN ITS ANCIENT CONTEXT

Arousing particular emotions in an audience was an integral part of the ancient art of persuasion (see, e.g., Aristotle, *Rhet.* 2.1–11). While the author crafted images designed to arouse fear in 4:12-13, he turns immediately in 4:14-16 to craft an appeal designed to instill confidence in the hearers. This pattern recurs throughout the sermon (6:4-8 // 6:9-12; 10:26-31 // 10:32-36), with the author associating cause for fear with drifting away from commitment to the group and its confession, and cause for confidence with perseverance in commitment to Christ and one another.

While the audience endured significant losses as a result of their conversion (10:32-34), the author dwells extensively on what they also now "have" as a result—here the help of Jesus, God's Son, to keep them connected with God and God's favor. The author urges the hearers to deal with the pressures they face not by acquiescing (and thus withdrawing from the group), but by going confidently before God in prayer (and thus drawing closer to the center of the group), seeking God's resources and support to meet any and every challenge to perseverance (4:16).

The concept of a mediator or "broker" whose main gift was providing a connection with a better-placed patron was well known in the Hellenistic-Roman world. Priests were de facto brokers of divine patronage (5:1). Like other priests (ideally), Jesus was sympathetic toward his clients' weaknesses, having experienced the same trials and tests himself (2:14, 17-18; 4:15). Unlike other priests, however, Jesus was not overcome by any of those tests, such that he himself affronted God by transgression and had first to make peace between himself and God before he could secure God's favors for others (4:15; 5:2-3; 7:27). While the author will affirm Jesus' complete identification with the readers in their shared humanity (2:14-18), he also will not allow them to forget his distance from them (both in terms of proximity to God and sinlessness)—a distance that proves, in the end, to be to their ultimate advantage.

The Scriptures provide "proof" of Jesus' legitimate appointment to serve as such a mediator: the author finds this proof in Ps. 110:4, a little further on in the same psalm that spoke of the Son's exaltation (Ps. 110:1; see Heb. 1:13; 8:1; 10:12; 12:2). Again, he discovers the significance of the ancient text by hearing it as if spoken *to* Jesus. The significance of this appointment to serve "in the order of Melchizedek" (5:6, 10) will occupy Heb. 7:1-28.

Readers tend to identify the portrait of Jesus in 5:7-9 with the account of Jesus' agony in Gethsemane (Mark 14:32-42 and parallels), even though the author otherwise shows no signs of familiarity with the Synoptic tradition. The author's portrait also closely aligns with depictions of righteous petitioners and intercessors in other Jewish texts (e.g., 2 Macc. 11:6; 3 Macc. 1:16; 5:7, 25; Attridge, 151). Jesus emerges here more as a model of offering pious, committed prayer. It is unclear whether the phrase "although he was a Son" qualifies what precedes or follows (a question raised as early as the ninth century by Photius of Constantinople). The majority of translations favor reading this in connection with Jesus learning through suffering, as if this should *not* be expected for a "Son." However, in 12:5-11, the author will argue precisely that legitimate sons and daughters *should* expect to experience formative discipline. It may thus be preferable to read the concessive clause ("although he was a Son") as qualifying what precedes: it was Jesus' *piety* that led to his being heard by God, and thus an example of what any pious follower could hope for; it was not a case of preferential treatment.

The language of "perfection" and "being perfected" pervades this sermon. This word group appears generally to speak of a person or thing having arrived at its final state or goal (such that it describes the child who has reached adulthood, or an ordinary person when the rite of consecration to priesthood is complete). Here, Jesus' perfection relates to his having entered God's realm after the completion of his course, from which vantage point he is able to exercise his mediation (deSilva 2000, 194–204).

■ THE TEXT IN THE INTERPRETIVE TRADITION

Early commentators tended to read this text (particularly 5:7-9) through the lens of Christ's two natures, stressing how it applied to the human nature but not to the divine, which was not subject to suffering (Theodoret of Cyr, John Chrysostom). At the same time, they highly valued what this passage has to say about Jesus' subjection to every manner of trial and temptation that might afflict his followers, making him sympathetic to the plight of the human beings who seek refuge in him now and in the judgment (Theodoret of Cyr), and also about Jesus' sinlessness, making him an empowering example and a suitably blameless offering (Leo the Great).

■ THE TEXT IN CONTEMPORARY DISCUSSION

It is important to remember, when reading material that seems at the surface to be so otherworldly and theological, that the author of Hebrews writes, essentially, to equip members of a voluntary counterculture to maintain the will to resist cultural, religious, and other forms of domination and repression. Holding on to their "confession" (4:14) is an act of resistance against the dominant culture's religious practices, against their more empowered neighbors' attempts to enforce conformity to the same, and against the prevailing mythos that legitimates power relations within the Roman Empire. It is, similarly, an act of resistance against a tolerated subculture's (Judaism's) attempts to enforce conformity among Jewish converts to the Christian movement. Keeping the original setting and challenges of the sermon firmly in our minds helps us remain attentive to how the author uses theological and traditional resources in settings where resistance is costly but necessary, if one's integrity is to remain intact.

The summons to prayer (4:14-16) and the portrait of Jesus' engaging in prayer to equip him to run his course (rather than to allow him to avoid unpleasantness) also challenges the expectations of many modern people of faith, for whom prayer and God represent ways *out* of suffering rather than ways to persevere *through* suffering. The experience of suffering is, for the author of Hebrews, neither the result of failed or unanswered prayer, nor a cause to question God's goodness or existence. Rather, Jesus' example suggests that suffering—here, particularly suffering endured as a result of responding faithfully to God's call—becomes an opportunity for deepening obedience and for discovering God's ability to provide the resources required to persevere in faithfulness so as to experience not deliverance *from* death, but deliverance *on the other side of* death.

Hebrews 5:11—6:20: Summons to Respond Honorably and Appropriately

■ THE TEXT IN ITS ANCIENT CONTEXT

The author pauses in his exploration of Jesus as "high priest in the order of Melchizedek" (5:10) to attend to his hearers' disposition. He wants to ensure that they will listen attentively and commit to invest themselves fully in their response to Jesus' investment in them. He chides them for not having yet taken up the responsibility for keeping one another steadfast in their commitment ("becoming teachers"), acting instead like children waiting for him to come alongside and administer the needed instruction and discipline. "Milk" and "meat" (or "solid food") were common metaphors for the stages of instruction through which a person passed in any educational process. In keeping with Greco-Roman philosophical discourse, the author uses these metaphors to shame the hearers into taking responsibility for living up to their potential and to what they already knew to be true (cf. Epictetus, *Diatr.* 2.16.39; *Ench.* 51.1).

The author urges the hearers to invest themselves in persevering together toward the final goal (the "perfection" or "completion," 6:1) of the pilgrimage that began with their conversion and instruction in the fundamental tenets of the Christian worldview (6:1-2). The metaphor of growing into maturity (becoming *teleios*) in 5:11-14 is morphed into the metaphor of moving forward to the end of a journey (*teleiōtes*). This exhortation is supported with an argument from the contrary: failure to move forward amounts to desertion of one's benefactor and a trampling on his gifts (6:4-6). Repentance here refers not to the act of contrition (see on 12:15-16), but to restoration—in effect, "starting over" with God from step one (cf. the place of "repentance" in 6:1). The audience will likely accept the claim that restoration to favor is "impossible" based on their cultural knowledge of the expectations of patron-client relationships (the social context of "grace" relationships; deSilva 2000; 2012): "those who insult their benefactors will by nobody be esteemed to deserve a favor" (Dio Chrysostom, *Or.* 31.65).

The author further supports this warning with an argument from analogy taken from agricultural practice. Sowing, reaping, and quality of soil were frequently used metaphors in ancient discussions of giving benefits and responding to a benefactor's kindness (see Seneca, *Ben.* 1.1.2; 2.11.4-5; 4.8.2; 4.33.1-2; Pseudo-Phocylides, *Sentences* 152). The gifts that God has lavished on the congregation (6:4-5) ought to produce a suitable return that will please the divine Patron who has "cultivated" this relationship with them. If the hearers return insult for grace by choosing friendship with the non-Christian society over a friendship with God in which God has invested so much, they should expect fiery retribution (6:8; 10:26-31).

Up to this point, however, the hearers have largely responded well. The author recalls their investment of themselves and their resources in one another, helping one another persevere in the face of hostile neighbors. Because they have responded nobly to God's favor, God, being just, will continue to favor them (6:9-10). The warning of 6:4-8 serves, in the end, to sustain the hearers' "long obedience in the same direction" (Nietzsche), their responsiveness to God's call (6:11-12).

Abraham naturally comes to mind as an example of "those who inherited the promises through trust and perseverance" (6:12; see *Jub.* 17:17-18; 19:3, 8). Oaths are a common feature in courtrooms and other contexts where added assurances of truthfulness are called for (see Aristotle, *Rhet.* 1.15.27–32). While human beings might indeed take such oaths deceptively, they tended nevertheless to carry considerable weight (6:16; see Philo, *Dreams* 1.12). God gave such an assurance to Abraham (Gen. 22:17), but the author avers that God gave such an oath to the hearers as well. This promise and oath are both found in Ps. 110:4 and depend on reading this verse as *addressing* Jesus (like Ps. 110:1). Describing the hearers as people who have "fled" subtly reminds them of the greater dangers that they have escaped (viz., "eternal judgment," 6:2) by joining the Christian movement, and thus of the advantage of persevering. Jesus is consistently described as going where the hearers would one day enter, and thus their connection with Jesus remains an assurance of their own entrance into the divine realm (see 2:9-10; 12:2).

This brings the author back to the place from which he will resume his exploration of Jesus' priesthood (cf. 5:10 with 6:20).

THE TEXT IN THE INTERPRETIVE TRADITION

Interpreters have long struggled with the author's claims about the impossibility of restoration to favor through repentance after some grievous—but unspecified—sin. Tertullian (*Pud.* 20) and the Novatians (see Epiphanius, *Pan.* 59.1.1–3.5) argued that the passage barred those who, after having been baptized, committed serious sins (like apostasy and adultery) from restoration. Those who favored restoration of the penitent argued, in turn, against the authority of Hebrews on the basis of its non-Pauline authorship (e.g., Gaius the Elder; see Eusebius, *Hist. eccl.* 6.20.3).

Another stream of interpretation focused on reading this passage primarily as a warning intended to spur Christians on in their commitment to discipleship, calling them to take the consequences of willful persistence in sin seriously enough to avoid such paths and to match God's gifts with earnest striving to make progress in the new life (see Clement of Alexandria, *Strom.* 2.13; 4.20; Origen, *Hom. Jer.* 13.2; Erasmus, *Paraphrase*, 227–28). Ambrose (*Paen.* 2.2) and John Chrysostom (*Hom. Heb.* 9.5–10.1) solved the problem by reading the passage not as a prohibition against readmitting the penitent, but merely against rebaptism, essentially turning the passage *into* an exhortation to repent speedily, lest one alienate God further and further (so also Luther and Calvin). Whether a person's repentance was effective would be evident in his or her amendment of life.

Luther used the language of Heb. 6:4-6 to denounce the view that the Mass was a repetition of Christ's sacrifice, since this would amount to crucifying Jesus anew (*Misuse of the Mass, LW* 36:147), and the quest to establish one's own righteousness apart from Christ, which meant trampling Christ underfoot (cf. Heb. 10:29; *LW* 52:282), though he did not deny that such people could repent of such practices.

THE TEXT IN CONTEMPORARY DISCUSSION

Contemporary Christian readings of Heb. 6:4-8 often continue the historical patterns of interpretation, forcing it to speak in conformity with particular theological positions. For example, the passage's meaning and challenge are frequently limited by an interpreter's adherence to the doctrine of "eternal security," the idea that once a person has trusted in Jesus and been "saved," that person cannot then fall away (Gleason; Oberholtzer). Such approaches fail to do justice to the fact that the author of Hebrew conceives of "salvation" or "deliverance" as something still ahead of himself and his audience (1:14; 9:28), thus not something already possessed so as to be "lost." Alternatively, the passage can be applied at face value where the "unpardonable sin" has been committed, usually identified as a decisive moment of apostasy (Lane 1991a:142).

Other Christian scholars are reluctant to apply the passage beyond situations analogous to the situation specifically addressed by the author and outside his own rhetorical purpose, which was to motivate perseverance in commitment to the Christian faith, practice, and community, even when such commitment carried an unwelcome price tag. Thus the passage has force as an exhortation to believers, but not as case law to be applied to those who have "fallen away," to whom the author might indeed have addressed himself differently. The author thus does not make an absolute statement about the limits of God's beneficence, but about the parameters within which recipients of God's costly gifts must act and the considerations they should keep before them as they weigh any courses of action (deSilva 2000). The author of Hebrews is thus understood to preach "costly grace," the necessity of responding nobly and justly, whatever the cost, to a God who has given so much (Bonhoeffer). If the author's real intent was to suggest that it would be unthinkable for persons who have received such great gifts from God to respond in any way that showed a lack of valuing the gifts and dishonored the giver, readers might take issue with the way he has couched this argument in terms of what God might or might not forgive.

Hebrews 7:1-28: The "Better" High Priestly Mediator

▌ THE TEXT IN ITS ANCIENT CONTEXT

This passage begins the "long and complicated message" about Jesus' high priesthood, which extends through 10:18. The author opens by considering the founder of the priestly "order of Melchizedek" named by Ps. 110:4. Every detail of (or silence concerning!) Melchizedek's story (see Gen. 14:17-20) is interpreted in such a way as makes this shadowy figure a prototype for Jesus, legitimating Jesus' unconventional appointment to priestly office. "Peace" and "righteousness" were attributes of the Messiah's government (e.g., Isa. 9:6-7; 11:1-9; *4 Ezra* 13:37-39; *T. Levi* 18.2–4). The silence concerning Melchizedek's genealogy established the possibility of a priesthood based not on pedigree (descent from Levi, 7:13-14), but on some other quality—here, the quality of a life without beginning or ending (7:3, 15-17, 23-25). The author finds this intimated in the phrase "a priest *forever*" (Ps. 110:4; Heb. 7:16-17)—not just made a priest permanently (i.e., for life), but a priest eternally ("forever").

Melchizedek's priestly line is not just different, however, but superior, as demonstrated from Abraham's giving the tribute of a tithe to Melchizedek. Because an ancestor was thought of as holding within himself his entire line, the author can assert that Levi and his priestly descendants paid the tithe to Melchizedek (and *his* successor, Jesus), acknowledging the latter's superiority (7:4-10). Jesus' priestly mediation, moreover, is supported by God's oath ("the Lord has sworn and will not change his mind," Ps. 110:4), giving the new covenant, of which Jesus is the guarantor, a more certain foundation than the old (Heb. 7:20-22; see 6:13-20).

The author employs another argument from chronology (Spicq, 1:365): the fact that God spoke through David about appointing a new priest (Ps. 110:4) demonstrates that the earlier priesthood and the covenant that regulated it—and that it, in turn, sustained—had been superseded (7:11-12, 18-19). Why would God set aside the former covenant? The Levitical priesthood and its covenant were not able to "perfect" the worshipers, meaning, to fit them to enter into God's presence. Indeed, these worshipers were not fitted even to enter the inner chambers of the *copy* of God's realm, the tabernacle and temple, let alone "heaven itself," by the Levitical mediators (7:11, 19; 9:1-10). The author presupposes here that God's ultimate goal for God's people was not a static situation in which the majority were kept at a safe distance from God's holy dwelling but a dynamic process by which they would be brought into God's dwelling forever, such that God would indeed "dwell in their midst" (see Ezek. 37:27; Zech. 2:11; 2 Cor. 6:16b; Rev. 21:3-4, 22; 22:3b-4).

■ THE TEXT IN THE INTERPRETIVE TRADITION

Melchizedek drew the attention of patristic commentators who were predisposed to such typological forays into the Hebrew Bible. Some early voices regarded Melchizedek as a divine being, but Epiphanius employed this passage to refute their position. These commentators also embraced the arguments concerning the insufficiency of the provisions of the Mosaic covenant for accomplishing God's purposes for human beings, seeing in the advent, ministry, and death of Jesus the perfection of those imperfect types that came before (Theodoret of Cyr, John Chrysostom). Discussions of Jesus' death as a sacrifice naturally occasion discussions of the Eucharist, which is seen as a remembrance and not a reenactment of Jesus' unique and all-sufficient priestly act (Theodoret of Cyr, Bede).

■ THE TEXT IN CONTEMPORARY DISCUSSION

Particularly in a world where people make competing claims concerning how best to relate to God (or the gods), how do Christians know that they can trust what the church says about Jesus and the consequences of his mediation between human beings and God? How do Christians know that God looks on Jesus and his mediation the way the church *says* God does? The author and his congregation certainly lived in such a world, and the author's attempts to construct tightly reasoned arguments from Scripture in this chapter reflect his interest in answering these questions for his audience. Whether or not his particular arguments (or the data on which they are based, like Jesus' ascension) "work" for contemporary Christians, the question remains.

Some Christians readers have decided that they cannot trust the claims made about Jesus in Hebrews—that he was, at best, a remarkable teacher with a compelling vision for human community that still merits our attention, even commitment. His death revealed his own commitment to that vision and perpetually reminds his followers of the potential cost of pursuing that vision, but does not directly impinge on one's relationship with God. For such Christians, the author of Hebrews' arguments will not carry weight. In the end, however, such arguments were not the starting point even for the author and his audience themselves. Rather, their starting point was the experience of God opened up for people in Jesus' name (2:3-4; 6:4-5; 10:22; cf. Gal. 3:1-5; 4:6-7). Again, this raises the issue for people of all faith traditions of the importance of valuing religious experience over arguments concerning religious truth in an increasingly naturalistic environment.

Hebrews 8:1-13: The "Better" Covenant

■ THE TEXT IN ITS ANCIENT CONTEXT

Hebrews 8:1-13 advances the discussion in two respects. First, it establishes the existence of a divinely made, heavenly tabernacle and the superiority of the same to the terrestrial, material, human-made copy, based on a widely held exegesis of Exod. 25:40 (see also Wis. 9:8; Acts 7:44; *2*

Bar. 4:1-7). Jesus' ascension is interpreted as his relocation to officiate in this greater sanctuary (Heb. 8:1-5; 9:24), where God is fully present. Second, it identifies an authoritative text in which God, speaking in God's own voice, invalidates the former covenant with its arrangements in favor of a "new" covenant (Jer. 31:31-34; Heb. 8:7-13). The essential element of this new covenant is God's promise decisively to remove the worshipers' sins even from God's *own* memory, thus enabling them to approach God's holy presence without fear of being consumed on account of their defilements. The author will return to this in 10:17 after showing how Jesus is the agent through whom this decisive purification takes place.

▌ THE TEXT IN THE INTERPRETIVE TRADITION

Patristic theologians read the author's interpretation of Jeremiah 31:31-34 as an authoritative declaration concerning the invalidation of the Mosaic covenant on account of its perceived limitations. This, in turn, reinforced their prejudices against Judaism in general and its sacrificial cult in particular (Bede). Nevertheless, these authors also regarded the author of Hebrews to validate the importance of the old covenant as "type" and prophetic prefiguring of what would be accomplished in Jesus, thus affirming the connection between the covenants (Theodoret of Cyr).

▌ THE TEXT IN CONTEMPORARY DISCUSSION

Hebrews 8 acutely raises the problem of supersessionism (the idea that Christianity has *replaced* Judaism in God's dealings with humanity, not merely grown up alongside it), particularly in a post-Holocaust environment (as in any setting in which the church is empowered and the synagogue more marginal and disempowered). This is exacerbated by the author's use of Septuagint Jeremiah, which renders the Hebrew "although I was their husband" (a clause attesting to intimate involvement and concern) as "I ceased to be concerned about them," which contrasts with other voices expressing their own and God's ongoing concern for Israel (e.g., Paul's heartfelt wrestling with the question in Romans 9–11).

Even while asserting a radical discontinuity between an old and a new covenant and priesthood, the author nevertheless grounds the new fully in, and legitimates it fully on, the old. Continuity with the earlier revelations of the God of Israel remains essential to his enterprise. In this regard, he challenges post-Holocaust Christians to continue to search out this continuity in their own attempts to extend their understanding of God's work in an ever-changing world.

Hebrews 9:1—10:18: The "Better" Sacrifice

▌ THE TEXT IN ITS ANCIENT CONTEXT

The author focuses now on the ritual that both inaugurates the new covenant and effects the decisive cleansing of sin's defilement from the worshipers' consciences and God's presence. While the author evokes pictures of a sequence of ritual acts ostensibly played out in the heavenly sanctuary, these pictures are meant collectively to interpret the significance for the divine-human relationship of this-worldly events: the crucifixion of Jesus and its aftermath.

The primary templates ("types") for framing the discussion are the Day of Atonement ritual (Leviticus 16, an essential chapter for understanding this section) and, less prominently, the covenant inauguration ritual (Exod. 24:1-8; see Heb. 9:15-22). The former involves ritual acts "outside the camp" (the sending of the scapegoat to die in the desert and the burning of the bodies of the sacrificial animals; Lev. 16:20-22, 27) and a ritual act involving the taking of blood into the holy of holies (Lev. 16:15-19). These acts now provide the meaning behind Jesus' crucifixion "outside the city" (Heb. 9:14; 13:12) and ascension into the heavenly holy of holies (Heb. 9:11-14, 23-26): the worshipers' consciences on earth are cleansed, and the defilement of the heavenly place of intercession by the worshipers' sins is removed, thus wiped clean as far as God is concerned (Nelson, 76–78, 148–52).

The author offers, as further evidence for the inefficacy of the sacrifices performed in the earthly tabernacle, their annual repetition (10:1-3). The layout of the earthly tabernacle/temple and the ongoing limitations of access to the inner sanctum signify the failure of the Levitical sacrifices to bring God and human beings as closely together as God intended (9:6-7), proof once again of the need for new cultic arrangements. He attributes this ineffectiveness, in part, to the reliance on the blood of animals as the medium for reconciliation and purification, drawing on popular philosophy (Thompson, 103–15) and the Jewish prophetic critiques of animal sacrifices as inadequate for any spiritual or ethical purpose (9:13; 10:4; cf. Isa. 1:11-13, 16-17; Hosea 6:6). He finds scriptural support for his claims (which contradict such key texts as Lev. 16:30; 17:11) in the Greek version of Ps. 40:6-8, read as if spoken by Jesus himself. The Hebrew original speaks of God's preferring obedience to Torah to the sin offerings that followed disobedience. While the Greek translator probably had the same intent, the author of Hebrews finds in the Greek version now a warrant for "a body"— the human body that the Son took on in his incarnation—as the sacrifice that God appointed to be offered in place of the ineffective animal sacrifices (10:5-10).

That Jesus' priestly work was decisively accomplished after his unique offering of himself is demonstrated through an inference drawn from the thematic Ps. 110:1. Priests performed their duties while standing (Deut. 10:8; 18:7); the fact that Jesus, the priest in Melchizedek's line, was invited by God to "sit" (Heb. 10:11-14) signals the successful accomplishment of reconciliation, the decisive removal of sins promised as part of the "new covenant" (10:15-18). As the final act of the Levitical high priest on the Day of Atonement was to return from the holy of holies to declare forgiveness to the people, so the author speaks once more of Jesus' forthcoming return from "heaven itself" to bring final deliverance to his followers (and subjection to his enemies; 9:28; 10:13).

▍THE TEXT IN THE INTERPRETIVE TRADITION

The author of Hebrews restrained himself in regard to the symbolic significance of each item in the sanctuary, but the same was not true of early Christian commentators, who interpreted the layout of the tabernacle and its accoutrements allegorically as representations of elements of the cosmos or of the human psyche (Origen, John Cassian, Bede, Luther). Again, Jesus' one-time sacrifice is related to the regular remembrance of the same in the Eucharist (John Chrysostom, Luther). This lengthy passage also served to reinforce early Christian discourse concerning the relationship of the Mosaic covenant and Hebrew Scriptures to the new covenant as type of fulfillment or shadow to the reality casting the shadow (Origen, John Chrysostom, Symeon the New Theologian, Bede). These commentators continue to embrace the author's Christocentric lens as the appropriate resource for interpreting particular Old Testament texts like Psalm 40 (John Chrysostom).

■ THE TEXT IN CONTEMPORARY DISCUSSION

The author of Hebrews provides the earliest thoroughgoing interpretation of the significance of Jesus' death and ascension for humanity's relationship with the divine. Contemporary theologians have been moving away from thinking about Jesus' reconciliation of humankind with God in terms of sacrificial metaphors (with their emphasis on the spilled blood and the death of a victim). This is motivated not just by a growing distaste with images involving the actual slaughter of a victim, but also by a desire not to sanction an act of political injustice and oppression (the brutal execution of a dissenting voice) with a theological overlay and not to continue to attribute to God the desire for blood and death.

We should not lose sight, however, of the fact that the author of Hebrews was using this language figuratively as a means of helping his hearers appropriate for themselves the significance of Jesus' death for their relationship with God. He could not have imagined Jesus carrying physical blood into "heaven itself": the blood is a metonym for Jesus' absolute obedience and commitment to God, undeterred by the prospect of a bloody death. Jews reflected on the deaths of the martyrs for Torah in similar terms, positing that such extreme commitment to the covenant acted as the equivalent of an effecting atonement offering on behalf of the nation: but again it was their obedience, not their blood, that satisfied the alienated Deity and restored God's favor toward the nation (2 Macc. 7:37-38; 8:5; 4 Macc. 6:29-31; 17:21-22; see deSilva 1998, 137–41). Jesus' death can be similarly understood as an offering of representative obedience that restores God's favor—as well as redirects humanity's hearts back to God and pursuing what pleases God out of a desire to maintain this restored relationship.

Hebrews 10:19-39: Summons to Persevere in Faithful Response

■ THE TEXT IN ITS ANCIENT CONTEXT

The author concludes his sermon with a climactic exhortation to persevere in the course of action that shows proper gratitude and loyalty toward God (10:19-13:25). The "long and complicated word" about Jesus' high-priestly mediation (7:1-10:18) provides the basis for an exhortation to hold on to the advantages this mediation has gained, which includes nothing less than the "boldness" to enter God's very presence when "the Day" of Christ's visitation and the eschatological removal of the visible, material creation arrives (10:25; see 9:28; 12:26-28).

This course of action involves group-sustaining practices. "Drawing near" to their destiny (10:22; the opposite of "shrinking back," 10:37-39) means continuing to meet together and engage in community- and identity-maintaining activities such as public witness to their hope and mutual encouragement and care (10:23-25). English translations since the KJV often err in regard to 10:24. The Greek does not speak of considering *how to provoke* other disciples to do good and to show love (CEB; NIV; NLT; NRSV); rather, the author urges his hearers to consider their fellow believers with the result that they themselves will be motivated by what they see to show love and do good

(NJB; Lane 1991b, 273; Ellingworth, 526). The author would have the hearers feel confidence in regard to continuing in this path.

If some are disposed to throw it all away because they have a greater concern for what they have lost in this transitory world (10:25a), what are the implications of doing so? The author answers this in 10:26-31 (strongly reminiscent of 6:4-6). By describing the alternative course of action as "sinning willfully" (10:26; see Num. 15:22-31), the author reminds the audience that there is *always* a choice to be made between bearing up under their neighbors' disapproval and hostility and giving in, thus betraying their commitments to God and one another. He employs another "lesser-to-greater" argument to propose that the fate of those who break faith with the Son will be worse than the fate of those who broke faith with the Mosaic covenant (10:28-29; cf. 2:1-4), that is, a fate worse than death (reciting Deut. 17:6). Preferring their neighbors' friendship to the continuing friendship of God means trampling God's Son (who awaits all things to be subjected under *his* feet, Heb. 1:13; 10:13) and meeting favor with insult (10:29). The stark impropriety of such images is calculated to shock the audience into seeing defection as an absurd, and ultimately more dangerous, choice with much more frightful consequences than persevering in faith (10:27, 30-31).

The author returns to topics that will arouse confidence in place of fear in 10:32-36. Like a general pointing out his troops' former victories, the author recalls the audience's former investment in and commitment to their cause (10:32-34) as the best model for them to imitate in the future (10:35-36). Their former courage in the face of their neighbor's repressive pressure exhibited *parrhēsia*—the boldness to declare one's convictions and commitments in the face of power and violence, an ancient political value. The author urges them, after giving such testimony to the value of Jesus, his gifts, and his promises, not to be cowed into silence now. Maintaining "boldness" in the face of society's hostility is intimately connected with retaining their "boldness" to enter God's presence at last (10:19, 35).

◼ THE TEXT IN THE INTERPRETIVE TRADITION

Hebrews 10:26-31 posed many of the same problems and concerns as 6:4-8, and thus received similar attention. Most read the passage as a call to repentance (Oecumenius) and as a call to take seriously the need to turn from sin rather than continue to indulge it (Theodore of Mopsuestia). The ongoing possibility of repentance, however, was not to become an excuse for a continuous cycle of sin and repentance, which was no better than apostasy with a conscience (Clement of Alexandria, *Strom.* 2.13.56–57).

John Chrysostom recognized the rhetorical force of speaking of events meant by the Christians' neighbors to shame them into conforming once again with their former lives as a "contest" (10:32). Victims become contestants, and resisting pressures to conform becomes the path to an honorable victory in God's sight.

◼ THE TEXT IN CONTEMPORARY DISCUSSION

The theological problems concerning the place of fear in mature discipleship and the positing of unpardonable sins (10:26-31) were already discussed in regard to 4:12-13; 6:4-8. The author's use of Scripture again raises issues for the modern reader. At 10:37-38, the author combines a phrase from Isa. 26:20 with Hab. 2:3-4 in order to stress the imminence of God's visitation, and further rearranges the phrases of the Habakkuk passage in order to craft an antithesis between persevering in faith and shrinking back in fear. Eusebius, who recognized these changes, affirmed this as an appropriate correction of that which was obscure in the older text. Modern readers might be more willing to question how far one can go to shape a text to address the need of a situation before one has done violence to it and undermined the integrity of one's argument.

The author's selective introduction of Isa. 26:20 into this recitation also raises the issue of the early Christian belief in the imminent return of Jesus to dispense judgment and rewards. While Christians may still affirm that "he will come again to be our judge" (Nicene Creed), they may justifiably ask—after two millennia passing without the Day, which may still be "drawing nearer," actually arriving—what "in just a very little while" was supposed to mean and whether the author ought rather to have prepared his congregation for resistance over the long haul. This question remains relevant to Christian leaders' seeking to encourage congregations in repressive environments throughout the world.

These potential limitations, however, do not negate the force of the author's challenge to contemporary Christians to exercise "boldness" in regard to their witness in the face of modern systems of domination built on values and goals different from, and in many instances antithetical to, the values and goals for human community attested in the Scriptures. To the extent that people of any faith tradition are bound to temporal goods and enjoyments, are geared toward seeking acceptance by their neighbors, and fear hostile confrontation, they will be cowed into not bearing witness— both in speech and in living practice—to those latter values and goals. The author would consider this a gross failure in Christians' obligation to their divine Patron.

Hebrews 11:1—12:3: Encomium on Faith

▐ THE TEXT IN ITS ANCIENT CONTEXT

Hebrews is probably best known for its portrait of "faith" in action, the encomium (a laudatory, celebratory speech) on the "heroes of faith" and how they responded to God's word and promise in the midst of challenging circumstances. The author shapes these examples to address the specific challenges facing the addressees (deSilva 1995, 165–208; Eisenbaum, 178–83), providing them with a model (see 6:11-12) of how to respond advantageously in light of Christ's imminent visitation (10:37-39).

One recurring theme is that people of faith respond to the challenges and circumstances of the moment with a view to God's future intervention and to the invisible realities beyond this world (11:1). Noah orients his whole activity around meeting a disaster yet to come (11:7); Abraham moves throughout his life with his eyes fixed on the promise of receiving a homeland in the future (11:8-22); Joseph gives instructions about his burial on the basis of God's future acts on behalf of the Hebrews (11:22); Moses chose his allegiances with a view to God's future acts of liberation and the future reward (11:23-27), and so forth. People of faith take their bearing in this life from the invisible Cause of the visible world (11:3), as did Moses (11:27). Looking to the future acts of

God and to the invisible realm are vitally important components of the author's program for his audience, who must conduct themselves now in such a way as to encounter future crises successfully (1:13; 2:3; 10:30-31, 37-39) and to maintain their grasp of goods as yet not seen (3:6, 14; 6:12; 10:34-35; 11:16; 12:28; 13:14).

A second recurring theme is that the person of faith accepts temporal loss and deprivation for the sake of eternal ("abiding," "lasting") gain (deSilva 2012, 64–83). Such acceptance gives the person of faith freedom to pursue this greater hope and calling. The author particularly crafts certain examples in such a way as to resonate as strongly as possible with the addressees' plight in their setting. Abraham leaves behind his place in his homeland, accepting the lower status of sojourner and alien in Canaan, mirroring the audience's loss of status within their native cities (11:9, 13). The patriarchs' rejection of being "at home" in their native land becomes a source of witness to the "better, heavenly homeland" that they seek (11:14-16). Moses relinquished his status in Pharaoh's household, choosing to identify with God's marginalized people and the reproach that befalls God's people and God's "Anointed" in this world (11:24-26; cf. 10:32-34; 13:3, 13). Prophets and martyrs (see *Liv. Pro.*; 2 Maccabees 6–7; 4 Maccabees 5–17) accepted being driven into the margins of society and even being subjected to the degradation of torture and death for the sake of loyalty to God and the "better resurrection" God would bestow on God's faithful clients (10:32-34; 11:35-38; 13:3).

Jesus crowns the list of examples as the "perfecter of faith" (not, as in many translations, the "perfecter of *our* faith"), such that one needs to read the exhortation of 12:1-3 in connection with 11:1-40. Jesus showed faith to the utmost degree by "enduring a cross, despising shame." The path of responding obediently to God and attaining the reward God set before him involved embracing the most abject humiliation (including the "verbal abuse" with which so many of the addressees could relate, 12:3) and suffering, showing that faith looks not to human approval but only to God's approval and, in so doing, attains eternal honor and place. The addressees' past behavior also falls into this commendable pattern (10:32-34), and the author shapes his exhortations simply to urge them to continue to exhibit that kind of commitment to God and to one another, deliberating with a view to holding on to God's promises, not temporal goods.

▐ THE TEXT IN THE INTERPRETIVE TRADITION

Patristic authors give ample attention to these heroes of faith as moral examples of a foundational virtue in Christian culture, with the example of Jesus crowning the series. In dying for our sake, Jesus obligates us all the more to endure for his sake and to be willing to despise temporal honor in order to attain the lasting honor in God's sight (John Chrysostom). These authors also tend to interpret these figures as "types" prefiguring Jesus in some way, reading chapter 11 as if the author himself were continuing to appeal to Hebrew scriptural narratives typologically, as he had in regard to Moses, Joshua, and the Levitical cult and its staff. Their own penchant for a typological reading of the Hebrew Bible takes over, as it were. This is especially true in regard to Abraham's near-sacrifice of Isaac (Athanasius, Theodoret of Cyr, Augustine), Moses and the Passover (Theodoret of Cyr, John Chrysostom), and Rahab's scarlet thread (Justin Martyr, John Chrysostom). This same connection between the heroes of faith and Christ, however, assures their enjoyment of the same rewards as Christian disciples, all of whom look ahead together to Christ's second coming for the rewards of their perseverance in faith (Origen, John Chrysostom).

◼ THE TEXT IN CONTEMPORARY DISCUSSION

The author's descriptions of faith in action, like his description of the challenges faced by his audience throughout their existence as a faith community, may seem remote to contemporary Western Christians and to people of other faith traditions where theirs is the majority religion. However, these descriptions are quite immediately relevant to many who profess allegiance to Jesus in openly repressive societies or societies where Christians constitute a disempowered minority culture. Some Western Christians have read this text as a challenge to think and look beyond their borders and to include Christians in hostile contexts in their plans for relief and political activism.

The passage also serves as a check on the practice of making Christian faith a means to the end of the enjoyment of temporal gain, seen most egregiously in the "prosperity gospel." The promotion of Christianity as a means of tapping into God's endless supply for the sake of the material enrichment of one's life and its associated enjoyments not only is only rampant in popular culture in the United States but has been exported throughout the world and been embraced as particularly appealing in situations of significant poverty. Nothing could be more antithetical to the author's vision of faith-in-action or the attitudes toward the temporal and its rewards that he seeks to inculcate. This chapter challenges any interpretation of Christianity that makes of it a means to attain consumerist or materialist ends.

The author's choice of subjects to include in his parade of praiseworthy and exemplary persons also critiques popular fascination with the lives of celebrities, whose basic claim to hold people's attention is wealth, glamour, and notoriety. Where such people hold a prominent place in a person's focus, that person's sense of what is desirable and what is valuable will be shaped accordingly. The "heroes of faith," however, include both those who were "success stories" by temporal standards as well as abject failures who died in disgrace, and, more often than not, people who were characterized more by "downward mobility" than the reverse. Freedom from attachment or attraction to the rewards over which the domination systems of this world have control is essential to the exercise of the *parrhēsia*, the prophetic witness to alternative values and practices that the author so values in the Christian movement.

Hebrews 12:4-29: Challenge to Endure and Show Gratitude

◼ THE TEXT IN ITS ANCIENT CONTEXT

While separating 12:1-3 from 11:1-40 is problematic insofar as Jesus is the climactic example of faith-in-action, separating 12:1-3 from what follows is also problematic in that it is the transition back to direct exhortation. Indeed, 12:1-4 works in tandem with 12:5-11, as the author uses two powerful images to reinterpret the unpleasant experience of the Christians' neighbors' rejection and abuse in a manner that empowers and encourages continued resistance rather than abdication. Hebrews 12:1-3 used the image of the footrace, with the stadium filled with the heroes of faith who now watch how the audience will perform in the event they have successfully completed. Hebrews 12:4 shifts this to the image of the wrestling match, where the addressees are matched against "sin," the impulse to choose the temporary rewards of friendship with society over friendship with God. Both images implicitly shame the hearers into perseverance, the first by convening a court of reputation before whom failure would be truly disgraceful, the second by suggesting that the hearers have not yet begun to endure for Jesus what he endured for them (12:2), so how could they be so cowardly and faithless as to contemplate abandoning their obligations to their benefactor (Petersen 1982, 174)?

Hebrews 12:5-11 shifts further to the image of parental discipline (*paideia*, 12:5, 7-8, 11): what their neighbors inflict with a view to shaming them is interpreted as something God uses to shape them, contributing to their positive formation as committed, courageous, virtuous citizens of their heavenly country (12:10-11; see Croy). The negative experience, moreover, becomes a proof of their adoption by God as God's legitimate sons and daughters (12:7-8; cf. 5:7-8). While the author uses a quotation from Proverbs (3:11-12) to launch this exhortation, nearly every line is paralleled in Seneca's *De providentia*. Moreover, he concludes this paragraph with an expanded paraphrase of a popular classical maxim attributed to Isocrates—"the roots of education [*paideia*] are bitter, but its fruits are sweet"—showing the author to be drawing on well-established topics to reinterpret hardship and empower continued endurance of repressive measures.

Esau's example (12:16-17), like that of the exodus generation (3:7—4:11), reinforces the danger of choosing poorly between temporary relief and long-term goods—thus, in the audience's situation, between securing escape from their neighbors' disapproval (and its negative effects on their lives and psyches) and holding securely onto God's friendship and promises through perseverance (see also 2:1-4; 6:4-8; 10:26-31). Esau's story has been reshaped somewhat to conform more closely to the author's purposes in using it (cf. Gen. 25:29-34; 27:30-40; deSilva 2000, 461–63).

The author has been strategically arousing both fear and confidence throughout the sermon; his work climaxes with a pair of images that continue the alternation. Using many scriptural allusions to the event, he paints a picture of the encounter with God at Sinai that is dark, fearsome, and dangerous (12:18-21). This is the encounter with God that the hearers do *not* have to endure because of the Son's mediation, which opens up for them a festive and confident approach to God at the heavenly Zion (12:22-24).

Recalling the Sinai event leads the author to another warning, using another "lesser-to-greater" argument to suggest that greater danger awaits those who reject the message spoke in the Son (and, even more specifically, the Son's death, 12:24) than befell those who cast off the Sinai covenant (12:25; cf. 2:1-4). Similarly, the earthquake that traditionally accompanied God's appearance at Sinai (Judg. 5:4-5; Ps. 68:7-8) leads the author to consider the future, decisive shaking and removal of the entire material creation (12:26-27, reciting and interpreting Hag. 2:6), revealing the way into the (already extant) unshakable kingdom, the divine realm, which God wishes to share with the faithful (12:28). The author's cosmology and eschatology continue to suggest the lesser value of all that pertains to this present, visible world (as opposed to "the coming world," 2:5)—an estimation that is essential to his advice concerning what course of action is ultimately advantageous.

In light of God's plan to confer such a benefit on the audience, the only appropriate response is to "show gratitude" (12:28; deSilva 2000, 473–77). Gratitude toward a more powerful patron generally took on the forms of witness (increasing the patron's reputation by praising his or her generosity), loyalty (when faced with a choice between standing by and deserting one's patron), and service (that is, doing whatever the patron might ask). This well encapsulates the response the author hopes his audience will continue to make in regard to God and God's Son in their present circumstances.

■ THE TEXT IN THE INTERPRETIVE TRADITION

Patristic readers appreciated the author's discussion of trials and hardships as the exercise regimen and diet for God's athletes being trained in virtue (Basil). Basil thought the passage to apply to such experiences as illness, and not merely social opposition for the sake of one's commitment to Jesus. John Chrysostom recognized the pastoral value of this passage, since the typical human reaction to suffering or ill-fortune is to read it as a sign of divine displeasure or abandonment. On the contrary, encountering trials may still be an opportunity to experience God's love.

Early church commentators also focused on the virtue of peace extolled in 12:14, agreeing with the author that communal harmony was indeed prerequisite to enjoying the divine presence (Augustine, Gregory the Great). They understood the "all" here to denote fellow believers, since "peace" would only be made with unbelievers by defecting from the group. Once again, these authors tended to interpret the author's warnings in such a way as promoted the perpetual availability of repentance during this life (Theodoret of Cyr, Theodore of Mopsuestia); for example, suggesting reasons why Esau's repentance was rejected and describing, on that basis, what kind of repentance ought to be nurtured.

The contrast between the approach to God at Sinai and at the future, heavenly Zion in 12:18-24 fed Christian criticisms of the old covenant (for example, John Chrysostom interpreted the "darkness," "gloom," and "tempest" as indications of "the obscurity of the Old Testament and the shadowy and veiled character of the Law") and celebrations of the more positive community of angels and righteous disciples formed around the new covenant, brought together like "living stones" in the new kingdom of God (Ambrose).

■ THE TEXT IN CONTEMPORARY DISCUSSION

This passage has raised disturbing questions about God's relationship to experiences of suffering. It is important to note what the text does *not* say. The author does not say that God inflicts suffering in response to something the addressees have done wrong (Croy, 196–214). He distances himself, in fact, from Prov. 3:11-12 on this point. God may *use* suffering as a crucible for character, but the suffering is still born of the "hostility of sinners" (12:3). The author also does not say that human beings are divinely sanctioned to inflict punishment on those whom they "love" in order to correct them (as some spousal-abusers will claim). In its original context, the passage speaks only of the deprivations and hardship endured from human beings who regard the Christians as deviants on account of their religious commitments. Applying the passage to suffering beyond this is risky business (Croy, 222). Within these limits, Heb. 12:5-11 still speaks a word of encouragement to many Christians across the globe, whose experience may match or outdo that of the original audience in many respects (10:32-34), empowering resistance and, therefore, the freedom and integrity of each believer in a repressive environment.

The example of Esau challenges contemporary allegiances to the values and practices of gratification, consumption, and materialism. The author would ask many Christians how often their choices reflect a hunger and love for God or a desire to serve as God's instruments in this world and how often, to the contrary, their choices reflect their obsession with this world's trivial entertainments, pursuits, and rewards. He would call such Christians to examine the folly of being rich in the moment, but bankrupt in eternity.

The portrayal of the Sinai theophany in 12:18-21 is fair enough, but it is not an adequate representation of the experience of God known by persons who approached God through the Torah prior to, or apart from, Jesus. One thinks of the rapture of the psalmists, for whom the presence of God is peace, safety, and refreshment, for whom the law is light and joy. One thinks also of the representatives of the Jewish wisdom tradition like the authors of Proverbs, Wisdom of Solomon, and Ben Sira, for whom God and God's instruction are ever-present guides to walk in secure and stable paths. The author's contrast between the approach to God at Sinai and the approach to God through the new covenant aligns too readily with the ongoing Christian assumption that the "God of the Old Testament" (a fearsome and vindictive deity) is somehow different from the "God of the New Testament" (a deity of love and acceptance), which is a gross caricature of the image of God in both.

One of the author's foundational assumptions, shared with his host society, is that costly gifts call forth costly response. This dynamic of favor and gratitude, of gift and response, potentially reconnects grace and Christian discipleship, the experience of God's favor, and the investment of one's whole self in responding. It challenges the contemporary Christian commodification of God's gift (or of "salvation") as something enjoyed independently of an ongoing, dynamic response to the Giver in the way of testimony, loyalty, and obedient service.

Hebrews 13:1-25: Specific Exhortations for Making a Grateful Response

◼ THE TEXT IN ITS ANCIENT CONTEXT

The author concludes his sermon with practical instructions on how to "show gratitude" and live "in a manner well-pleasing to God" (12:28; cf. 13:16, 21). These focus chiefly on group-sustaining practices (13:1-6, 15-17). The willingness of Christians to open up their homes to the group for worship and study or to traveling teachers and missionaries was essential to the Christian movement (13:2). Reaching out to support those members who were most targeted by their neighbors for "corrective discipline" was similarly essential to sustaining commitment (13:3). The most intimate human relationships needed to be safeguarded against erosive behavior (13:4). Attachment to temporal goods—when deprivation of such goods is a major tool for pressuring deviants into conformity—is also assiduously to be avoided (13:5-6; see 10:32-34). High regard to leadership, both those who currently exercise their office (13:17) and those who have passed (13:7), gives a strong internal focus for the group. In every way, the author seeks to stimulate a strong sense of mutual commitment and investment—the kind that would normally be reserved for one's natural brothers and sisters—within the group, such that they will put themselves out to meet one another's need and, thus, sustain one another's commitment (13:1, 3, 16).

The declaration "Jesus Christ is yesterday and today the same—and forever" (13:8) activates a topic familiar from discussions of trust (see, notably, Dio Chrysostom, *Or.* 74.4, 21–22). This is less an ontological statement than an ethical one: the hearers can count on Jesus to be constant and reliable in their relationship. What he was for them in the past, he will yet be for them in the future. This was the basis for their departed leaders' faith (13:7) and can be for theirs as well. The author contrasts this basis for trust one final time with elements of the Levitical system of mediation (13:9-11; see Lev. 16:27), recalling in a summary way the surer mediation the hearers have in Jesus, and therefore the firmer foundation for continued trust.

The author returns to the theme of making an appropriate return to God and to Jesus for their costly favor. Since Jesus suffered "outside the camp" for the hearers, the author urges them similarly to "go out of the camp"—that is, willingly to leave behind their place in their society—to meet him in the margins of society, being willing to bear temporary disgrace for their association with him (13:12-13). Such loyalty is a component of a grateful response. But the way "out" of the camp is also the way "in" to the unshakable realm of God, into which they are being welcomed (13:14). They are also urged to continue to bear witness to the value of Jesus' mediation and God's promises (13:15) and to invest in one another's perseverance (13:16). These acts of bringing honor to the Patron and offering service are also recognized elements of gratitude toward superiors. They are painted in cultic terms: such enactments of gratitude, and not animal sacrifices, are now the language of and means of expressing their ongoing relationship with God (see also 6:9-10).

The sermon ends with the typical elements of a letter's closing (13:18-25; cf. 1 Thess. 5:23-28; 1 Pet. 5:10-14).

▮ The Text in the Interpretive Tradition

John Chrysostom appreciated the practical guidance for disciples, particularly as regards the proper accumulation and use of property (promoting keeping oneself from superfluities and prioritizing charity). Hebrews 13:8 became a frequent text invoked in conversations about Christology, especially the divine nature of Christ that undergoes no change in the incarnation, passion, death, and ascension.

▮ The Text in Contemporary Discussion

Hebrews 13 brings together many of the themes encountered throughout the sermon, and hence raises once again many of the issues already discussed—the state of Christians in restricted nations and the obligations of Christians in free (and often prosperous) nations toward them; the author's challenge to contemporary boundary lines between "family" and "outsiders," private and public; the notion of "grace" as a relationship of ongoing mutual exchange and obligation rather than a commodity simply to be received.

The text challenges the fundamental logic of Western economic practice, which is to amass capital and, in a sense, "build bigger barns" for the future in the form of investment portfolios and retirement accounts. The author of Hebrews would not take issue with this, were it not for the fact that many lack the daily necessities of life *this* day and are not being relieved. Allowing Heb. 13:5-6 to take deeper root in Western Christian practice would enable more "capital" to be directed toward meeting such needs (13:2-3, 16).

This closing chapter also challenges the tendency of Christian people in the West to prioritize insulating themselves against suffering or hardship, avoiding negative circumstances as if they were an absolute evil. Where do "Christ followers" in West *not* go, *not* dare to follow Christ and his call, out of this deep-rooted unwillingness to lose face or temporal advantages, or to fail to attain what our socialization has taught us to value?

Works Cited

Attridge, Harold W. 1989. *The Epistle to the Hebrews*. Hermeneia. Philadelphia: Fortress Press.

Becker, Ernst. 1973. *The Denial of Death*. New York: Free Press.

Bonhoeffer, Dietrich. 1966. *The Cost of Discipleship*. New York: Macmillan.

Bultmann, Rudolf. 1953. *Kerygma and Myth*. London: SPCK.

Croy, N. Clayton. 1998. *Endurance in Suffering: Hebrews 12:1-13 in Its Rhetorical, Religious, and Philosophical Contexts*. Cambridge: Cambridge University Press.

deSilva, David A. 1998. *4 Maccabees*. Sheffield: Sheffield Academic Press.

———. 2000. *Perseverance in Gratitude: A Socio-Rhetorical Commentary on the Epistle "to the Hebrews."* Grand Rapids: Eerdmans.

———. 2012. *The Letter to the Hebrews in Social-Scientific Perspective*. Eugene, OR: Cascade.

Eisenbaum, Pamela Michelle. 1997. *The Jewish Heroes of Christian History: Hebrews 11 in Literary Context*. SBLDS 156. Atlanta: Scholars Press.

Ellingworth, Paul. 1993. *The Epistle to the Hebrews*. NIGTC. Grand Rapids: Eerdmans.

Filson, Floyd Vivian. 1967. *"Yesterday": A Study of Hebrews in the Light of Chapter 13*. London: SCM.

Gleason, Randall C. 1998. "The Old Testament Background of the Warning in Hebrews 6:4-8." *BSac* 155:62–91.

Heen, Eric M., and Philip D. W. Krey, eds. 2005. *Hebrews*. Ancient Christian Commentary on Scripture. Downers Grove, IL: InterVarsity Press.

Lane, William L. 1991a. *Hebrews 1–8*. WBC 47A. Dallas: Word.

———. 1991b. *Hebrews 9–13*. WBC 47b. Dallas: Word.

Nelson, Richard D. 1993. *Raising Up a Faithful Priest: Community and Priesthood in a Biblical Theology*. Louisville: Westminster John Knox.

Oberholtzer, Thomas Kem. 1988. "The Thorn-Infested Ground in Hebrews 6:4-12. *BSac* 145:319–28.

Petersen, David G. 1982. *Hebrews and Perfection: An Examination of the Concept of Perfection in the "Epistle to the Hebrews."* SNTSMS. Cambridge: Cambridge University Press.

Spicq, Ceslaus. 1953. *L'Épitre aux Hébreux*. 2 vols. Paris: Gabalda.

Thompson, J. W. 1982. *The Beginnings of Christian Philosophy: The Epistle to the Hebrews*. CBQMS. Washington, DC: Catholic Biblical Association of America.

Vanhoye, Albert. 1963. *La structure littéraire de l'Épitre aux Hébreux*. Paris: Desclée de Brouwer.

JAMES

Timothy B. Cargal

Introduction

Little can be said with certainty about the origins of the Letter of James. Although there has been widespread agreement for associating the letter with James the Just, the brother of Jesus and a leader of the early church in Jerusalem (Matt. 13:55; Acts 15:13; Gal. 1:19; 2:9), there has been just as widespread disagreement over the centuries as to whether the letter was actually written by him or by someone else using his name. The argument that the literary quality of its Greek surpasses the likely ability of a Galilean laborer is just as strong as the argument that the book lacks specific biographical references such as are usually found in pseudonymous writings that establish the connection with the person named as the author. Since the name James (Greek, *Iakōbos*, from the Hebrew name Jacob; James 1:1) was common among Jews of the first century, it is as likely that the association with James the Just is a result of misidentification as it is of authentic authorship or even pseudepigraphy.

Beyond the name James/Jacob, other characteristics of the letter associate it with what has been called "early Jewish Christianity," although some of this evidence is more ambiguous than sometimes asserted. Imagery linking gentile Christians with Israel as now people of God, such as the description of this letter's recipients as the "twelve tribes in the Dispersion" (1:1), was not uncommon (see, e.g., 1 Pet. 1:1). Similarly the use of the Greek word *synagōgē* ("synagogue") to refer to the recipients' Christian "assembly" (James 2:2) is also found in such non-Jewish writers as Hermas, Justin, Origen, and Eusebius, who use *synagōgē* and *ekklēsia* ("church") interchangeably for gentile Christian communities. While the letter clearly has a positive view of "the law" (*nomos*, corresponding to Hebrew *tôrâ*; see 1:25; 2:8-12; 4:11), it does not address controversies between "Jewish Christians" and "gentile Christians" over circumcision or other aspects of Torah observance.

Evidence from literary dependence suggests the letter was written in the 60s or 70s CE. It seems likely that the assertion people are "not [justified] by faith alone" (2:24) is indirectly related to Paul's statement, "a person is justified by faith apart from works prescribed in the law" (Rom. 3:28), which would set the late 50s or early 60s as an earliest possible date. Sections of *1 Clement* are likely reliant on material in this letter (cf. *1 Clem.* 29.1; 30.1–5; 31.2 with James 2:14-26; 4:1-10), which would establish the early to mid-90s as a latest possible date. This general time period, which encompasses the run-up to and aftermath of the first Jewish War with Rome (66–73 CE), also provides a fitting historical setting to the letter's imagery of social dislocation and expectation of an imminent "coming of the Lord" (5:1-8). The economic and cultural disruption of the war might also have prompted the letter's strong interest in social justice concerns (see, e.g., 1:27; 2:5; 5:1-5). If indeed the first Jewish War provides some of its historical background, this would preclude the current form of the letter from being an authentic writing of James the Just, who was executed by the high priest Ananus II in 62 CE (Josephus, *Ant.* 20.9.1).

There has been a tendency, particularly since the Protestant Reformation, to read the Letter of James as in direct conflict with the apostle Paul's understanding of the relationship between faith and works in establishing a person's relationship with God (that is, one's "justification"). The likely literary dependence of James 2:24 on Rom. 3:28 has already been noted, and there is also the striking similarity in how the two letters employ Abraham as an example in their discussions of this issue—albeit to opposite conclusions (cf. Rom. 4:1-25 with James 2:20-24). More recently, however, many interpreters have moved toward seeing libertine Pauline enthusiasts as the more likely catalysts for James's statements about the necessity of both faith and works. Both Paul and James understand faith in terms of trust in God (rather than, say, holding certain beliefs about God; cf. Rom. 4:5 with James 1:5-6). Additionally, Paul himself had both anticipated and argued against those who might conclude that, having been justified by faithful trust in God, their actions did not matter (Rom. 2:13; 3:31; 6:1-2; Phil. 2:12-13; and cf. James 2:18). Even more beneficial has been the trend to see the doctrine of justification as an important but not all-consuming concern within the Letter of James. Read as a whole, James's primary interest centers on encouraging consistency in living out "the implanted word" (1:21) both individually (1:19-21, 26; 3:13-18) and communally (2:2-4; 4:11-12), particularly as it gives rise to the social justice themes already mentioned.

James 1:1-21: Obtaining Wisdom from God

▌The Text in Its Ancient Context

James describes himself as "a servant of God and of the Lord Jesus Christ" (1:1a). The word "servant" might also be translated as "slave." Surprising as it may seem today, to describe oneself as a "slave of God" could actually be a claim of status and authority in the letter's Greco-Roman context, where slaves could be used as their masters' personal representatives and so receive a kind of ancillary authority. This social reality led to Israel's prophets also being referred to as "God's servants." Nevertheless, slaves did lose all independence to the will of their masters—and the idea that God's will should supplant our own desires and will is a recurring theme within the letter that will be firmly established in this opening section.

Before turning to that, we need to consider how James characterizes the audience to whom he is writing. He addresses the "twelve tribes in the Dispersion" (1:1b). Clearly the language is metaphorical because Israel had lost any real twelve-tribe structure since at least the Assyrian conquest of the northern kingdom in 722 BCE. The question is, then, how far does the metaphorical aspect extend? The metaphor may simply identify ethnic Jews ("the twelve tribes") living outside Roman Palestine ("in the Dispersion"). However, the fact that the author closes the letter by suggesting some "among you" have "wander[ed] from the truth" and so need to be brought back (5:19-20) opens a broader possible meaning: the recipients are people of God ("the twelve tribes") who have departed from ("in the Dispersion") a proper understanding of their relationship with God ("wandered from the truth") and so need James's correction.

Following a pattern often used in letters of this period, James lays out this purpose in a twofold introduction. This relationship between the key ideas can be illustrated by presenting the two subsections of 1:2-12 and 1:13-16 in parallel columns.

1:2-4: "trials" (*peirasmoi*) and tests	1:13-16: temptation (*perirazein*)
1:5-8: God's gift is "wisdom"	1:17-19a: God's "perfect gift" is the "word of truth"
1:9-12: culminates with a "crown of life"	1:19b-21: culminates with the salvation of the soul

Thus James identifies what he believes is the problem in the recipients' current understanding (how they view "trials" and being "tempted"), offers a correction (God's "perfect gift" of "wisdom"/"the word of truth"), and concludes with the benefit it promises ("life" for the "soul").

In order to see the corrective aspect of his opening paragraph (1:2-4), it is necessary to challenge the customary translation of the word "consider" (*hēgēsasthe*) in verse 2. Most Greek verbs have quite distinct forms and spellings when they are used as simple statements (the indicative mood) as compared to being used as commands (imperative mood). Some, however, have exactly the same forms, and the verb *hēgesthai* is one of them. Since the Letter of James has more than fifty imperative verbs in its 108 verses, most translations take it as an imperative here in 1:2; thus James is encouraging the recipients to respond to "trials of any kind" as an occasion for "nothing but joy" because "the testing of . . . faith produces endurance," which in the end will make them "mature and complete, lacking in nothing" (1:3-4). This idea that trials make one's faith stronger was common in the first century (and even today).

But notice that James immediately says that if one "is lacking in wisdom," it can only be received as a gift from God (1:5); thus, at least for James, "endurance" *cannot* cure every "lack" because being "lacking in wisdom" is only resolved by God's gift. This point suggests that James makes an observation in the previous paragraph about how they have been thinking about "trials" (thus "you consider," in the indicative mood) that is in fact different from how he wants them to think about trials. That James is indeed trying to correct their views is reinforced by the parallel subsection in 1:13-18. Whereas some believe they are being "tempted by God" (using the cognate verb for the noun translated as "trials" in 1:2)—perhaps identifying these temptations as "trials" meant to strengthen faith through "endurance"—James emphatically insists God can neither be tempted nor tempts anyone else. Rather, God is the unvarying source of "every generous act of giving" and "every perfect gift" (1:17).

Trusting in God's unvarying goodness is the essence of "faith," as distinct from "doubt," which is tossed back and forth between trust and uncertainty (1:7-8) since it can never be sure whether God will provide a "perfect gift" or "trials" and temptations. It is the "implanted word" (1:21) that unifies God's wisdom and will *within* the individual that "has the power to save [one's] soul" (1:21) and bestow "life" (1:12), so that one is no longer "double-minded" (1:7-8) and "lured and enticed" by one's own improper "desire" (1:14).

▋THE TEXT IN THE INTERPRETIVE TRADITION

The Letter of James has often been described as "the New Testament's Proverbs"; that is, many have seen it as a collection of sayings expressing conventional wisdom without an overarching structure or argument. Especially in its opening chapter, the view has been that sayings have been strung together by "catchwords": the occurrence of a word in a saying calls to mind another saying with the same word, which is then placed immediately after it without developing the idea. Over the last several decades, that view has been challenged by studies employing a variety of literary-critical and linguistic approaches. Though there is variation in the details of the analysis, there is an emerging consensus that a twofold introduction sets out the key themes that will be given further development later in the letter.

▋THE TEXT IN CONTEMPORARY DISCUSSION

James's insistence that "God cannot be tempted by evil and he himself tempts no one" (1:13) serves his rhetorical and theological purposes well. It clearly establishes a reason why someone could ask God for whatever they need without doubting either God's generosity or the goodness of God's response (cf. Matt. 7:9-11). But the assertion is not without its difficulties in light of the broader scriptural tradition, as James himself must have known. After all, he will later refer to one of the most important stories about God's testing someone when he says, "Abraham [was] justified by works when he offered his son Isaac on the altar" (James 2:21; notice how James avoids using the word *test* in this passage, even though it opens the story in Gen. 22:1-19). He also will allude to "the endurance of Job" (James 5:11b), a story often seen as God's testing of Job even if at the instigation of the Satan (Job 1:1–2:10). And in Exodus, Moses persuades God to take a different course of action lest the Egyptians accuse God of having acted with "evil intent" (Exod. 32:11-13). The narrator's summary comment in Exod. 32:14 goes so far as to flatly state that God not only can be but also has been tempted to do evil, leading God to repent, where (the Hebrew behind the NRSV's "the Lord changed his mind about the disaster that he planned" can be translated more bluntly, "the Lord repented of the evil").

But in a post-Holocaust world, the challenge to James's assertion goes beyond just conflicting Bible stories. Theodicy—how an all-good and all-powerful God can allow evil to exist—may well be the preeminent theological issue of our age. True, James is not engaging in a philosophical discussion of theodicy; but it is an issue that moderns cannot avoid when confronted with assurances about God's unvarying goodness. At the risk of gross oversimplification, process theologians (such as Charles Hartshorne, John Cobb, and Marjorie Suchocki, who hold that God is changed by and develops though relationship with creation) might say that God is striving to become a God worthy of James's trust/faith, but the evidence suggests that neither God nor the world has yet arrived at that point.

James 1:22—2:13: Doing the Word

▌The Text in Its Ancient Context

Two concepts, one theological and the other sociological, provide the foundations for this section of the Letter of James. The "piety of the poor" was a conviction within Judaism and early Christianity, that God had "chosen the poor in the world" (2:5b)—not because they were more religiously or spiritually pious, but because "the rich" and powerful have "oppressed" and defrauded them (see 2:6b; 5:1, 4). This theological concept stood in marked contrast to the Greco-Roman cultural system rooted in honor and shame. Those cultural values provided the sociological framework for an extensive patronage system through which the rich and powerful received honor, in part, from the beneficence they showed to others. By showing honor to upper classes, the lower classes hoped to become beneficiaries of the patronage from the rich.

Having in the opening section of the letter focused on the need to receive God's "wisdom" expressed within the "word of truth" (1:5, 18, 21), James now emphasizes that his readers must become "doers of the word, and not merely hearers" (1:22). To be a "doer of the word" is to be a person who brings to reality God's will for the world. For that reason he defines "religion" not merely in holiness language ("pure and undefiled," "unstained by the world") but also in terms of acting on the basis of God's choice in favor of the poor by "car[ing] for orphans and widows in their distress" (1:27).

But to the degree that his readers had chosen anyone for special attention, James charges they have shown "favoritism" toward those "with gold rings and in fine clothes" (2:1-2). Beyond even the demands for displays of honor required by the patronage system, they have come to identify with the rich against the poor whom God has chosen. Notice how he alleges the readers would direct those "wearing the fine clothes . . . [to] 'Have a seat *here*, please'" (that is, *here among us*), whereas "to the one who is poor [they] say, 'Stand there,' or, 'Sit at my feet'" (that is, *away from us or in a place that illustrates your subordination to us*, 2:3). In a string of rhetorical questions, James expresses his amazement at their choice because their actions have not brought them the patronage they might have expected but rather further abuse (2:6b-7).

In James's view, such "partiality" is the very antithesis of the "royal law" (2:9), the "law of liberty" (2:12). And that "law" must be understood as a unified whole; a person can no more violate only one of its provisions than one can break *only* the stem of a crystal goblet.

▌The Text in the Interpretive Tradition

Because the Letter of James has been associated with "early Jewish Christianity," there has been a particular interest in its use of the phrase "the law of liberty" (2:12). Some have suggested that it draws on the Stoic ideal of life in accord with the rule of reason (the *Logos*), others with Jewish descriptions of the Torah as providing joy and freedom, and still others with Christian conceptions of Jesus' ethical teachings as a "new law" that either replaces or "fulfills" the mandates of Torah (cf. Matt. 5:17-48). But given the way James links the images of "law" and "word" in 1:22-25, and the image of the "implanted word" in 1:21, it may be that the best antecedent is to be found in Jeremiah's "new covenant," whereby God promises to "put my law within them, and . . . write it on their hearts" (Jer. 31:31-34). As Leonard Goppelt (2:206) described it, "For James, the Law was not an objectively prescribed norm . . . but the will of God that was written in the heart."

Keeping this "perfect law, the law of liberty" (1:25) for James required a consistency between one's speech and actions ("bridle their tongues," 1:26), and attention to what later Christian moral tradition would refer to as "sins of commission" (improper actions) and "sins of omission" (failure to do those things that God desires). Often Christian communities have tended to emphasize one or the other. James's admonition "to keep oneself unstained by the world" has been emphasized within certain holiness movements as the core of the religious life. His charge to "care for orphans and widows in their distress" has been emphasized by social gospel movements. But James calls for a "both . . . and" rather than an "either . . . or." Just as God's will/law is characterized by a unifying wholeness, James calls for "keep[ing] the whole law" (2:10) even as he also reminds his readers that "mercy triumphs over judgment" (2:13).

The Text in Contemporary Discussion

The discussion of "favoritism" and "partiality" in terms of economic distinctions has a special relevance in terms of modern concerns regarding classism, but also calls to mind all forms of discrimination. In some ways, though, classism has grown as a problem in our society even as more overt forms of discrimination based on gender, racial, or other physical distinctions are openly criticized. While people increasingly accept others who are physically different from them, they still tend toward "favoritism" and "partiality" for those who are like them in terms of educational attainment and socioeconomic status. And as work on the social structures of "white privilege" in Western societies and corollary forms of privilege in other cultures has demonstrated, we are often blind to the "favoritism" we both bestow on others and benefit from ourselves.

The way in which James unmasks the real allegiances of his readers is instructive. Although they would certainly have called on the "piety of the poor" to associate themselves with those whom God has "raised up" in contrast to "the rich" who are "brought low" (see 1:9-11), their actions demonstrate they strive to be "the rich" ("Have a seat *here*"; 2:3). James repeatedly reminds his readers to assess all progress toward becoming the just world that he believes God desires not by declarations about inclusivity but by concrete actions. His admonition continues to be a warning to any who speak more about God's "preferential option for the poor" than act in ways to make it a lived reality.

James 2:14-26: A Living Faith

The Text in Its Ancient Context

A repetition of keywords establishes the concern and the limits of this section of the letter: For "faith" to be any "good" in the sense of "sav[ing] you" it must "have works," because "without works" faith is "dead" (2:14, 26). But James structures the argument in a way that makes clear that the "good" (or "benefit") that comes from being "save[d]" will respond to material needs as well as spiritual ones.

Just as the discussion of "favoritism" (2:1), in the previous section, was rooted in values of honor and shame and the Greco-Roman patronage system, so also the discussion throughout this section presupposes cultural expectations regarding hospitality (2:15, 25). The idea that someone might refuse to assist a "brother or sister" in need of material assistance would have been shocking to everyone in that society; when almost everyone struggles at subsistence for themselves, they know in the most pragmatic ways why providing for others is a communal responsibility. But for James, hospitality is more than a social obligation. The invocation of blessing ("Go in peace") especially when joined with what are in Greek passive imperative verbs—more literally, "Be warm and be well fed" (2:16)—are indications that the speaker recognizes that it is God's will that these material needs be met (see 1:27). Jews often used passive voice verbs to avoid naming God directly. To use such constructions to tell another to "keep warm and eat your fill" was to invoke God to keep them warm and fed. Such knowledge of God's goodness ("faith"), if it produces only words ("has no works"), accomplishes no "good" and is in fact "dead" (2:16-17).

That one's knowledge about God should determine one's actions is the central point of the diatribe (a literary device involving an imagined exchange with a person holding a different view) in 2:18-26. Given a text that originally had no punctuation at all and certainly no quotation marks, it has proven difficult definitively to assign certain words to James and others to his rhetorical partner. What is clear, however, is that James insists not only that heroes of the "faith" like Abraham (2:21-23) and Rahab (2:24) act on what they believe about God, but so do "even the demons," who "shudder" (2:19). He is astounded that any sensible person (2:20), then, could think "faith" and "works" are separable in any way.

Close attention needs to be given to the word order in James's summarizing analogy: "just as the body without the spirit is dead, so faith without works is also dead" (2:26). Notice the "body" correlates to "faith," and the "spirit" to "works"—*not* "body" to "works" and "faith" to "spirit." As the "spirit" animates the "body," so "works" animate (that is, "bring to life" or "live out") "faith" (2:26).

■ THE TEXT IN THE INTERPRETIVE TRADITION

During the great debates of the Protestant Reformation about the means by which people are "justified" by God (see 2:21, 24-25) and "save[d]" (2:14; see also 1:21; 5:19-20), considerable attention was given to the fact that Gen. 15:6, "[Abraham] believed the LORD; and the LORD reckoned it to him as righteousness," is employed as a proof text by both James (2:23) and Paul (Rom. 4:3; Gal. 3:6). Whereas Paul uses the Abraham example in support of the view "that a person is justified by faith apart from works prescribed by the law" (Rom. 3:28), James uses Abraham to show "that faith apart from works is barren" (2:20).

In the view of many interpreters, Paul and James held contradictory views. More traditional theologians argued that James demonstrated that both faith *and* works contribute to justification. Martin Luther and some other Reformers agreed that James contradicted Paul, but held that Paul was correct in insisting that works contribute nothing to justification. Luther went so far as to state that James's letter had "nothing of the nature of the Gospel about it" (Luther, 362).

John Calvin, however, was not convinced that James and Paul truly contradicted one another. He argued Paul was concerned exclusively with "the ground on which our hope of salvation ought to rest," whereas James was concerned only with "the manifestation of righteousness by conduct" that follows from having been "justified" by God. For Calvin, this distinction was seen clearly in James's statement, "faith was brought to completion by the works" (2:22), about which he commented, "the question here is not respecting the cause of our salvation, but whether works necessarily accompany faith" (Calvin, 314–15).

■ THE TEXT IN CONTEMPORARY DISCUSSION

The common tendency among interpreters to construe Abraham and Rahab as examples for us to follow can create problems. If Abraham is said to *epitomize* faith in "offer[ing] his son Isaac on the altar" (perhaps, as Heb. 11:19 suggests, trusting "God could even raise him from the dead") and "Rahab the prostitute" to *embody* hospitality that spares others from destruction (see also Heb. 11:31), then emphasizing Abraham's *faith* and Rahab's *work of hospitality* serves to reinscribe her primarily as "the prostitute." Too easily, Abraham and Rahab come to exemplify two extremes: God justifies not only the venerated Abraham but also the lowest of sinners, the prostitute Rahab.

It is possible to read this letter, however, in a way that resists debasing Rahab. James states she not only "welcomed the messengers" but also "sent them out by another road" or "way" (the word used in 1:6-8 and in 5:20 of one's manner of life [the NRSV's "wandering" is more literally "error of one's way"]). Her story in Joshua 2 relates how she encouraged the spies and, through them, all the Israelites to adopt a manner of life that ended their wilderness wanderings by believing in God's promises (especially Josh. 2:8-11). As distinguished from the so-called hospitality of a harlot, Rahab can exemplify those whom James describes as "bringing back" others who "wander from the truth" and so "will save" them "from death" (5:19-20).

James 3:1—4:12: Humbly Preparing for Judgment

■ THE TEXT IN ITS ANCIENT CONTEXT

The central theme of this third section in the letter is expressed through the contrast between the readers' desire to obtain for themselves power and high social standing—the reason for James's warning, "Not many of you should become teachers" (3:1; see the earlier discussion of 1:22–2:13)—and what is for James a proper attitude of humility: "Humble yourselves before the Lord, [so that] he will exalt you" (4:10). Such humility is required because of the coming judgment, which is again explicitly mentioned at the beginning and end of the section—teachers "will be judged with greater strictness" (3:1) by the "one lawgiver and judge who is able to save and to destroy" (4:12a).

James believes that his readers perceive the role of teachers as being to exercise authority over errant members of the community (possibly punitively: "So who, then, are you to judge your neighbor?" 4:12b). Rather than being dispensers of punitive "judgment," he argues, "teachers" will be the recipients of "stricter judgment." Within the overall context of the letter, James considers teachers "servant[s] of God and of the Lord Jesus Christ" (1:1) who "save the sinner's soul from death and will cover a multitude of sins" (5:19-20), thereby sparing errant members of the community from harsh judgment rather than inflicting judgment on them.

The question of proper and improper speech plays an important role in the development of this section. In 3:2, James describes the "perfect" person as one who "makes no mistakes in speaking"; such a person stands in stark contrast to one who "speaks evil against or judges another" and so "speaks evil against the law" (4:11). But improper speech is only a symptom, one of "many" ways in which people sin (3:2). The origins of evil behavior and speech, James argues, reside in the "cravings that are at war within you" (4:1; cf. 1:14-15). The true problem, in his view, is desire for social status (3:1), "envy and selfish ambition" (3:16), and arrogance (4:6).

James contrasts the fact that "all of us make many mistakes" (3:2; see 3:14-16 for some of his examples) with the many things that should typify one "who is wise and understanding" (3:13) in terms of "the wisdom from above [that] is pure, then peaceable, gentle, willing to yield, full of mercy and good fruits, without a trace of partiality or hypocrisy" (3:17). True "wisdom" is demonstrated not by what one says but by "works" that display "gentleness born of wisdom" (3:13).

What is true of individuals is also true of communities. "Conflicts and disputes" arise between members of the community because of their covetous "cravings" that James alleges have even led to "murder" (4:1-3). While some argue James is alluding here to Jesus' saying that links anger with "murder" (see Matt. 5:21-22), it is possible James uses the word in a more literal sense. If a failure "to care for orphans and widows" (James 1:27) and other indigent members of the community (2:15-16) results in unnecessary deaths, then the evil desire to "spend what you get on your pleasures" (4:3) would be a kind of murder.

The promise in the proverb that God "gives grace to the humble" (4:6; see Prov. 3:34) provides the basis for James's call to "submit yourselves . . . to God" (James 4:7) and to "humble yourselves before the Lord, and he will exalt you" (4: 10; cf. 1:9-10). The "laughter" and "joy" that come from "friendship with the world" must be replaced with the grief, mourning, and gloom of realizing that one has "become an enemy of God" (4: 4, 9). Genuine humility and repentance—both turning away from evil and turning to God—is the only way to prepare oneself to come before the "one lawgiver and judge" (4:12).

▌ The Text in the Interpretive Tradition

Some commentators have argued that James uses his metaphors about bridles and ship rudders (3:2b-4) to illustrate the influence of teachers over the "body" of the community. Ralph Martin (103–7) went so far as to argue that not just these particular metaphors but all of 3:1-12 presents "a discussion where (i) 'the body' [see 3:2b] in question is the ecclesial one, not the anatomical one, and (ii) the tongue is used in a setting of the congregation at worship" where "'praising God' is the chief component" (see 3:9-10). This communal reading seeks to resolve the difficulty that the human tongue does not actually control human actions in the way that a bit does a horse or a rudder does a ship. Others argue that the allegorical relationship is more general, perhaps even alluding to Jesus' statement, "out of the abundance of the heart the mouth speaks" (Matt. 12:34;

Luke 6:45). One's speech is a clear indicator of the internal desires that control all one's actions (notice James explicitly mentions that "ships ... are guided by a very small rudder *wherever the will of the pilot directs*" [3:4]).

THE TEXT IN CONTEMPORARY DISCUSSION

How does one square the view of God as "the one lawgiver and judge," able both to "save" or "exalt" (4:10) and to "destroy" (4:12), with James's conviction that God is the source of "every perfect gift" and nothing bad or evil (1:17)? Could recognizing God as such a "judge" lead to "doubt" and "double-mindedness" (1:7-8), since one does not know whether to expect salvation or destruction from God? It seems likely that James would respond that while "judgment" is clearly a bad thing for those who will be destroyed, that does not mean God's destructive judgment is a bad thing in itself. Moreover, no one should have any "doubt" about what awaits them (even the demons "shudder" in their certain knowledge of God's judgment, 2:19). Those who have asked for, received, and lived out God's gift of wisdom can trust they will be saved (see 1:21-22).

But theologies—whether Christian or of another tradition—that depend on the destruction not only of evil but also of those caught under its control and who do its bidding have had terrible effects in the world. Those who are sure they know whom God will ultimately "destroy" in judgment often have little regard for James's admonition that they should not judge their neighbors (cf. 4:12). James will himself later advise patience while God's harvest is reaped (5:7; cf. Matt. 9:37-38; 13:24-30), but if God were to show a bit more patience—tending the fields for as long as it might take—could it be possible to "save" the whole crop? Perhaps James, like Moses, should have worked harder at persuading God to turn aside from any "evil intent" to destroy as an act of judgment (see discussion of James 1:1-21 in "The Text in Contemporary Discussion" above).

James 4:13—5:20: Restoring One's Neighbor—and Self

THE TEXT IN ITS ANCIENT CONTEXT

James concluded the previous section of the letter by calling his readers to repentance (4:7-10). As he draws the letter itself to a close, he challenges them to follow his example by bringing back others within their community who may be "wander[ing] from the truth" (5:19-20). He again reminds them that the standard of judgment will be whether they have accepted the divine will as their own (see especially 4:13-17), and creates a sense of urgency by asserting, "the Judge is standing at the doors!" (5:9b). He insists that they cannot restore others by "grumbl[ing] against one another" (5:9a); rather, they must encourage "patience" and "endurance" (5:10-11) by directing the attention of those who are "suffering" to God's goodness and provision through communal prayer, praise, and confession (5:13-18).

In the midst of this summons to his readers to bring back anyone who "wanders from the truth," James once more calls "the rich" to account (5:1-6) and encourages "patience" on the part of those who suffer at their hands (5:7-11). The unmistakable harshness of the imagery he employs against the rich (the corrosion that consumes their hoarded goods will likewise "eat [their] flesh like fire,"

5:3) may on the one hand seem justified since their abuse of others (5:4) is once again said to have resulted in deaths (5:6) but on the other hand seems overly strident from one who advises against judging others (4:11-12). Notice, however, that James calls on the rich to "weep and wail for the miseries that are coming" (5:1). James has earlier associated weeping with repentance (4:9), and the decay of their possessions calls to mind the demise of their way of life in 1:11. It is likely that rather than taking joy in their "miseries," James hopes these events will awaken the rich to their dependence on God and lead them to repent of their past sins. The prospect that they too might yet be "brought back" is the only reason to counsel patience.

Although we have seen that 5:19-20 provides a key insight into how James understands his purpose for writing the letter, there is an ambiguity that lies at the heart of these verses. The NRSV flags the issue with its textual note in 5:20 that the word translated as "sinner's" is in Greek simply "his" (*autou*). The problem resides in identifying the antecedent of "his." Is it the "sinner's soul" that is saved (as the NRSV has it), or is it the soul of "whoever brings back a sinner"? Perhaps James intends the ambiguity because it is in doing such things consistent with God's will that people are "blessed" (1:22-25) and that their "faith" is able to save them from spiritual death (2:14, 26).

▌The Text in the Interpretive Tradition

James 5:14-16 has been a key passage in the development of the Catholic "sacrament of the sick," commonly referred to as "the last rites." While the "call[ing] for the elders of the church," prayer, "anointing . . . with oil," and confession and forgiveness of sins mentioned in those verses are widely recognized aspects of that liturgical practice, some may be surprised that a ritual so closely associated with death (at least in the popular imagination) is rooted in a passage that holds out the hope of healing.

A deeper insight into this relationship between the "last rites" and "healing" can be found by carefully considering the specific words James uses for God's response to the act of anointing the sick with oil: "The prayer of faith will *save* the sick, and the Lord will *raise* them up" (5:15). While the Greek verbs *sōzein* and *egeirein* were commonly used to refer to healing and restoration to wholeness, they also have specialized uses within Christian theology. All the other uses of "save" (*sōzein*) in the Letter of James (1:21; 2:14; 4:12; 5:20) have the sense of salvation and eternal life. Although "raise" (*egeirein*) is not used elsewhere in this letter, it is widely used in reference to resurrection, and specifically of Jesus being "raised" from the dead (see, e.g., 1 Cor. 15:12-14). Thus the "sacrament of the sick" holds out the hope that even if physical healing does not come, there remains God's promise of wholeness in the life to come.

▌The Text in Contemporary Discussion

Two aspects of James's discussion of prayers for healing open possibilities for abuse. First, relating healing and forgiveness reflects a traditional view that connected sin and sickness (cf. John 9:1-2) and leads some to conclude that every disease is a result of sin, either as a natural consequence or even as an act of divine judgment (but see John 9:3). Second, James's assertion, "The prayer of the righteous is powerful and effective" (James 5:16), leads some to affix blame for unanswered prayers by impugning the righteousness either of the sick person or of those who pray on her or his behalf.

To the degree that James offers any explanation as to why some prayers for healing do not result in physical restoration, it is that the elders are to pray "in the name of the Lord" (5:14). The invocation of "the name of the Lord" is both an appeal to the power and authority of God, and a recognition that our desires—even in prayer—must be conformed to God's will (cf. 4:3). But once again it seems that James is sidestepping the problem of theodicy that we in the twenty-first century cannot so easily avoid (see the discussion on 1:1-21). Therein may lie the single greatest theological challenge for the Letter of James in contemporary discussion.

Works Cited

Calvin, John. 1855. *Commentaries on the Catholic Epistles.* Translated and edited by John Owen. Edinburgh: The Calvin Translation Society.

Goppelt, Leonard. 1982. *Theology of the New Testament.* 2 vols. Translated by John E. Alsup. Grand Rapids: Eerdmans.

Luther, Martin. 1960. "Preface to the New Testament of 1552." In *LW* 35.

Martin, Ralph P. 1988. *The Epistle of James.* WBC 48. Dallas: Word.

1 PETER

David L. Bartlett

Introduction

The First Epistle of Peter claims to be written by the apostle Peter to a group of churches in Asia Minor. Some scholars believe that the letter was written, as claimed, by Simon, one of Jesus' first four disciples, whose nickname, given by Jesus, was Peter. Others, including this author, believe that the letter was written after Peter's death, in the sixties of the common era, by another Christian writing in Peter's name and trying to apply the principles of apostolic faith to a new generation.

There are several reasons why many doubt that this letter was originally written by Peter. First, the letter is written in quite sophisticated Greek, and when it quotes Scripture it quotes from the Greek Old Testament, the Septuagint. From what we know of Peter, that he was an Aramaic-speaking fisherman, it seems unlikely that he would have written in this language and this style.

Second, the letter seems to be appropriate to the situation of the churches in the later part of the first century, after Peter would have been martyred. The sense that the church is undergoing widespread opposition from society looks more appropriate to the latter part of the century than to the fifties and sixties. While such judgments are always a matter of guesswork, it is a plausible guess that the kind of church order that 1 Peter implies, with a group of leaders designated as elders, was a development as the original apostles were passing away. Indeed, 1 Peter 5 is in many ways most reminiscent of Acts 20, probably also a late first-century composition, where Paul gives orders to the elders of Ephesus concerning their leadership of the church after he has departed.

Third, there are enough hints that the author of 1 Peter knows Paul's writings, and in particular the letter to the Romans, to suggest that our letter is written after Paul's letters have already begun to circulate among the churches.

Because the author says in 5:12 that he has written this letter "though Silvanus [Silas]," some have thought that the letter was written in its final form by Silas, either as he took instructions from Peter or on the basis of Peter's notes. This is not impossible, but seems like a stretch in order to preserve the conviction that Peter wrote the letter himself.

The letter is written from "Babylon," almost certainly a code name for Rome. We know that from early in the church's history, Peter was especially associated with Rome. So perhaps the letter comes from leaders of the Roman church writing in the name of their favorite apostle.

The letter is directed to the churches in seven communities in Asia Minor. The list of areas may represent the order in which a courier would have carried this circular letter through Asia Minor. A glance at a map will indicate that such a route would have been a plausible way to make such a journey.

We will see the themes of the letter as we go through its claims. Clearly there is concern for rebirth, regeneration. The letter claims that the church has become Israel: that all the promises of the Old Testament were really promises for the church. There is considerable concern with the conduct of new Christians in the midst of their pagan neighbors, but also considerable encouragement for living with opposition—whether that consists of actual persecution or constant disrespect, it is hard to know. The author expresses a strong belief that the end of the ages is at hand and that God in Christ will come to judge the living and the dead and to reward those who have proved faithful to the end.

1 Peter 1:1-12: The Foundation of Christian Hope

▌ THE TEXT IN ITS ANCIENT CONTEXT

This letter begins, as do other letters written in the first century, with the simple formula: From ____ To ____. The letter purports to be from Peter the apostle, and it is written to a group of churches in Asia Minor. I suggested above that the letter is probably written by a later follower of Peter, in Peter's name.

The information in the address goes far beyond the simple listing of the churches to which the letter is sent. Those who are to receive the letter are called "exiles of the Dispersion." This reference to exile compares the churches to the people of Israel and Judah who were exiled from their homelands in the eighth and sixth centuries BCE. As they are cut off from their homeland, so the Christians who receive this letter are cut off from a homeland too. The reference also compares the recipients to the Jewish people of the late first century CE who have been exiled from the Holy City, Jerusalem, which was destroyed by the Roman armies in 70 CE. It is likely that the Christians who receive this letter were not historically Jewish at all. We see this especially in the references to the readers' pre-Christian life in 1 Pet. 1:14, 18; 2:10, 35; 4:3-4. We will need to ask, therefore, why they are to identify with Jewish exiles far from home. Our letter will give us some clues. In addition to the kind of imaginative description of the letter's audience, we have a theologically rich description of who they are. They are a people entirely defined by their relationship to God in Jesus Christ. That relationship has both a present and a future dimension. In the present, these Christians hope in the care of God. For the future, they hope for God's glory to be revealed. What they now know in part they will then know entirely.

Some students of this letter think part of it was originally a sermon for a baptism service. Certainly the references to a "new birth into a living hope" fit the theme of baptism, now as much as in the first century. As Christians await what is hoped for, they need to choose how to live in the meantime, even though that time may be filled with tests and tribulations. The way the Christians are to live is by loving God and hoping for God's future.

We do not know for sure what kind of tribulations these people were facing, but we do know that the author sees those tribulations as a test and as a strengthening. He uses the analogy of gold being refined by fire to suggest the way in which trouble can refine the faith of these early Christians (1:6-7).

A major theme of 1 Peter is that it is Christians who are the true inheritors of the promises of Scripture (what Christians now call the Old Testament). Contemporary scholars tend to believe that when the prophets of Israel and Judah wrote, they wrote of promises fairly close at hand. From the beginning, however, Christians have read those promises as pointing to their own situation: prophecies about the people of God are read as foreshadowings of the church; prophecies of a Messiah or of a greater prophet are read as pointing to Jesus Christ. So for 1 Peter, promises to Abraham and his descendants are not so much a witness to the story of Israel as a witness to the story of Jesus Christ. We shall see throughout this letter that because the Scripture he inherits is always looking ahead, Peter can affirm that the church is now the real Israel: not just Israel-like, but Israel itself, Israel in the flesh.

◼ THE TEXT IN THE INTERPRETIVE TRADITION

This letter grows out of an interpretive tradition at least as much as it funds one. The authority of the letter may originally have depended on the identification of the author with Simon, traditionally one of the first four disciples called by Jesus (Mark 1:16-20). Simon is renamed "Peter" (Cephas in Aramaic; see Gal. 2:11-14), "the Rock." In the book of Acts, he is the interpreter of the events of Pentecost and therefore the homiletical father of the emerging church. In both Acts and the Letters of Paul, we discover that Peter was designated the apostle to the Jews as Paul was to the gentiles. This is one of the reasons John Calvin assumed Peter writes this letter to Jewish exiles.

Catherine Gunsalus González helpfully points out that though the full doctrine of the Trinity was a later development of the church, these early verses of 1 Peter help give us an insight into a very early emerging affirmation about the way in which the one God is evident in Father, Son, and Holy Spirit. These three are all affirmed in verse 2, and then in succeeding verses the author testifies that the Father gives new birth through the Son; that the Father and the Son will judge the world; and that the Spirit inspired the prophets and now inspires the church (González, 15).

◼ THE TEXT IN CONTEMPORARY DISCUSSION

Much of the discussion of these verses still focuses on the question of authorship and in a related question, the date of the letter. (For a thorough presentation of the details see Achtemeier, 1–43; more briefly, Bartlett, 234–36.)

Contemporary readers are appropriately concerned about the ethical implications of a letter written in someone else's name. While our ethical queasiness has some rationale, it seems unlikely that the readers of this letter thought it had actually been written by Peter. By the time the letter was written, he had been martyred. More likely they read it as a kind of tribute to him, written by someone trying to bring faithful understanding to new and challenging circumstances. If "Babylon" is a code word for "Rome" in this text, it seems likely that the letter was written from Roman churches early associated with Peter. (For a much fuller discussion, see Achtemeier, 42–43.)

1 Peter 1:13-25: The Shape of New Christian Life

▌THE TEXT IN ITS ANCIENT CONTEXT

Again in verse 17, the author refers to the time of the Christians' "exile." It may be helpful to try to understand what that exile might mean.

Some scholars have thought that this letter was written with a particular socioeconomic group in mind, those resident aliens who were not citizens of the lands in which they live but were there on a kind of green card. The letter is written to help them live in a land where they, under an emperor far away, have little power (see Elliott). Other scholars think these people are exiles because they are exiled from their heavenly home, and that when Christ comes in his glory, the Christians will be returned to their rightful destination, with God in Christ. While both these insights may be valid, it is also fairly clear that the people who received this letter are exiled from their own former lives as pagans. "You know that you were ransomed from the futile ways inherited from your ancestors" (1:18; on the options for exiles, see Achtemeier, 125). We will see time and again that 1 Peter distinguishes the Christians from the world around them, which is also the world where they used to live. They are in the world of pagan values and practices, but they are not of that world: they are exiles.

Like the apostle Paul, 1 Peter emphasizes again and again that the central act which redeems people from their past in idolatry is the death and resurrection of Jesus Christ. Here Christ's death is seen as comparable to the sacrifice of a lamb in the Old Testament; it brings the curtain down on past sins and opens a future for redemption. Christ's resurrection is the ground of Christian faith for now and of Christian hope for the future, when God will consummate God's will.

But as we might expect for an author who thinks that Israel's Scripture points entirely to Christ, this sacrifice and triumph of Jesus Christ was not a second thought on God's part. It was the plan from before the foundation of the world. "He was destined before the foundation of the world but was revealed at the end of the ages for your sake" (1:20). One could almost say that for the author, as the purpose of Israel's Scripture is to reveal Christ, the purpose of creation is to make possible the new creation.

When in 1:16 the author quotes from Lev. 4:44, "You shall be holy, for I am holy," he seems to understand that both Moses and God had the early Christian church in mind. For our author (at 1:24-25), when the book of Isaiah says that "the word of the Lord endures forever" (Isa. 40:6-8), the text refers to the Christian gospel, the word that these early Christians have heard and that they now read in this letter.

In his discussion of 1:17, Richard Vinson quotes at some length from a sermon John Donne preached on this text to seventeenth-century British magistrates. While Donne's talk about "judgment" is clearly particularly pertinent to judges, it is also a word for all Christians, who have to make judgments daily. Our life in the world, says Donne, is not just a passing through, "but such a stay as upon it our everlasting dwelling depends." And Donne tells the magistrates to live in such a way that they can pray: "'God be such to me at the last day, as I am to his people this day,' and for that day's justice in thy public calling, God may be pleased to cover many sins of infirmity" (Donne, sermon number 13, quoted in Vinson, 81–82).

Catherine González finds in these verses the ancient but always contemporary discussion of the relationship between faith and works.

> "Therefore." . . . *Because* these Christians have been chosen by God the Father, *because* by baptism they have been joined to Jesus Christ the Son and redeemed by him, and *because* they have been strengthened by the Holy Spirit, *therefore* they are to be holy. On their own, by their own strength, without the involvement of the triune God, they could not be holy. (González, 33)

For our author as for Paul, the first mark of holiness is belonging in the community of the holy, the community of saints. It is the church in its entirety that is a royal priesthood and a holy people (2:9). At the same time, individual Christians now live a life that is different from the life they lived in their "pagan" years; in particular, they move away from idolatry to faithful worship of the one God revealed in Jesus Christ.

1 Peter 2:1-10: The Royal Priesthood

In this section of the letter, the author reminds his readers of the radical newness of their lives in Christ. This is yet another instance of the emphasis on rebirth and regeneration that has led some scholars to believe that at least the first portion of 1 Peter may have been a baptismal homily.

As individuals, Christians are called to their new identity. But they find that identity in part by looking back—by becoming like infants, trusting in God as an infant trusts a parent. They are to drink spiritual milk, the formula for beginnings, first things.

Of course, new beginnings require re-formation, so readers are encouraged to give up the trappings of what seemed like maturity in their pagan days: guile, malice, insincerity, envy, slander. Though he does not explicitly say so, the author calls his hearers away from those particular vices and sins that might destroy Christian community. Again, as is so often the case, he has a scriptural citation to underline this call to newness: "O taste and see that the Lord is good" (Ps. 34:8).

Being born anew does not mean simply adding a belief in Jesus to one's established patterns of thought and action. Being born anew means giving up a whole host of comfortable habits, including guile, malice, insincerity, envy, and slander: the ways of the world. No wonder these Christians seem like exiles.

Notice, too, that while these Christians have been born again, born anew, their pilgrimage as Christians has not yet reached its goal. The milk of the childlike Christian is the beginning of a process of maturity—"so that by it you may grow to salvation."

The call for a new life is a call for a new community as well, but again Peter looks ahead by looking back. Now he looks not to the images of childhood but to the images of Israel—the covenant with God's people now extended to God's new people, the Christians.

The mélange of images is also a mélange of biblical texts. The image of the stone is applied both to Jesus and to the believers. Jesus is the stone who is chosen, the stone who provides the foundation for the new household of faith, the stone on which unbelievers will stumble. The richness of the image depends on the combination of scriptural texts: Isaiah 28, Psalm 118, Isaiah 8. All these texts are cited elsewhere by Christian writers (see Matt. 21:32; Acts 4:11; Rom. 9:33).

The image of the stone is also applied to believers: Christ is a living stone, but so are believers living stones. Christ is the cornerstone of the new building, but all the faithful are built into that new edifice. The edifice is a new temple, and references to temple, priesthood, race, nation now affirm what Peter has already insisted on. The Church is now Israel. God's promises to Israel are fulfilled in the life of the church. "But you are a chosen race, a royal priesthood, a holy nation, God's own people" (2:9). As the Christian moves from unbelief to belief, from the old life to the new, so the whole community moves out of darkness to light.

The author ends this section by recalling one of the most moving narratives of the Old Testament—Hosea's reconciliation with his wife and with his children (see Hosea 2:23). Hosea gives his children new names when their new lives begin. The author gives the Christian community new names as well: "a chosen race, a royal priesthood, a holy nation, God's own people."

▌ THE TEXT IN THE INTERPRETIVE TRADITION

Not surprisingly, pietistic Christianity has played down the heavily apocalyptic theme in 1 Peter and, to some extent, the radically communal theme as well. Charles Spurgeon, in a sermon on this text, talks about "coming to Jesus" and about the Christian hope in ways that are probably more individualistic and less eschatological than Peter had in mind: "Coming to Christ . . . is, in one word, a trusting in and upon him. He who believes Jesus Christ to be God and to be the appointed atonement for sin, and relies upon him as such, has come to him, and it is this coming which saves the soul."

Every interpretation of a text is of course also a reinterpretation, but we can see Spurgeon's sermon a move away from the strongly communal and future-oriented themes of 1 Peter. For our author, people come to Christ by coming to the community, and Christ comes to them on the last day. For Spurgeon, people come to Christ by trusting in him, and in that moment, Christ also comes to the believer.

■ THE TEXT IN CONTEMPORARY DISCUSSION

It is striking that in 2:9-10, the language traditionally applied to Israel is now applied to Christians. But there is no claim here that this represents any revocation of the Old Testament promises. Rather, the author simply reads the words as applicable to the church (too?).

> There is no trace of polemic in this practice, however, but only a curious appearance of naiveté. Nowhere in 1 Peter are the readers addressed as a new Israel or a new people of God as if to displace the Jewish community. . . . If there is an "anti-Jewish" polemic here, it is a polemic that comes to expression simply by pretending that the "other" Israel does not exist. (Michaels, 197)

1 Peter 2:11-17: Living Honorably among the Gentiles

■ THE TEXT IN ITS ANCIENT CONTEXT

When the author calls the Christians to become a new temple for God, he also calls them to be part of a new house, and a new household. In the portions of the letter that we now discuss, Peter talks about what life in that new household looks like. We will see that much of the discussion assumes a kind of hierarchical society, ordered from the top-down, which is difficult for twenty-first-century Christians to affirm—often with good reason.

Note, however, that the author, like many other first-century Christian writers, has two main concerns. First is that the church should be ordered according to the will of God. The author interprets that will in ways more highly structured and even authoritarian than some would affirm, but nonetheless he thinks that his orderliness reflects the orderliness of God.

Second, the church should be a peaceful and respected part of the larger community in which it lives. Already our author's people must seem like "exiles" to the very friends, families, and institutions that they have left behind to become part of the church. This letter is concerned that Christians be respected as good citizens, good householders, orderly family members. If they are to be immigrants and aliens, at least let the larger community admire them for their exemplary behavior.

Such behavior starts with the civil authorities. The emperor is both the pinnacle of civil authority and its most visible symbol. Included in the injunctions to honor the emperor is the injunction to honor local and provincial officials as well.

Yet even in this fairly staid view of a submissive community, there are important distinctions to be drawn—distinctions that in other circumstances might well lead Christians to other, less polite behavior.

First of all, though Christians are under government authority, that authority does not take away from their freedom, which is grounded in God. Christians should be good citizens only because they choose freely to do so; they are under no compulsion to obedience save obedience to God.

Second, notice how the last sentence makes a kind of rhetorical, almost poetic point. There are four injunctions for Christians. The first and last injunction go together and so do the middle two. (The technical word for this device is *chiasmus*.) The first and last injunctions tell Christians how to get along as members of the community. They urge a kind of prudence: "Honor everyone. . . . Honor the emperor." In the world of the first century, "honor" is a kind of social convention in which one promotes civic harmony by giving honor to those to whom honor is due.

The second and third injunctions tell Christians who they are as a new community, a royal priesthood. "Love one another" instructs regarding how to attend to the fellow Christian. "Fear God, reverence God" tells how to attend to the Creator. Notice that these Christians, who face some kind of persecution or slander, are *not* told either to fear the emperor and his deputies, or to reverence them (see, e.g., Kelly, 113).

▌THE TEXT IN THE INTERPRETIVE TRADITION

John Calvin writes about honoring the ruler in ways that reflect his situation in Reformation-era Geneva and have influenced a good deal of theology since.

> We ought to respect the civil authority because it has been appointed by the Lord for the common good of mankind, for we must be utterly barbarous and brutal, if the public good is not close to our hearts. This, in short is what Peter means, that since God keeps the world in order by the ministry of magistrates, all those who detract from their authority are the enemies of mankind. (Calvin, 12:270)

Of course the situation becomes more complicated if the magistrate is not devoted to the common good. Both our letter and the Reformers tend to assume that rulers promote good order. For 1 Peter, any thought of overturning the governmental order would have seemed impracticable, and in the face of the coming end of the age, pointless. Calvin sought to establish good order where magistrates ruled according to Christian principles.

The struggle of the contemporary church has often been how to be faithful when the civil authority seems to contradict the precepts of the faith. Dietrich Bonhoeffer finally turned to plot against the authorities; Martin Luther King Jr. was willing to break the laws in the hope of changing them.

▌THE TEXT IN CONTEMPORARY DISCUSSION

These verses have provided crucial resources both for contemporary biblical studies and in the United States, especially, for contemporary theological reflection.

John Elliott is among the American scholars who has paid special attention to the social location of New Testament writings, and he has argued that 1 Peter was written for Christians who were legally and socially—and not simply metaphorically—exiles in their place and time. Much recent discussion of the text has been in response to Elliott's claim (see Elliott; Bartlett).

Stanley Hauerwas and William Willimon have argued that the picture of the church as a community of "resident aliens" provides a proper description for the church in America. The influence of the church has waned as Christendom has given way to a more diverse and secular society. For them, the claims and values of Christian faithful are now not those of the culture but of a counter-culture. Church is and should be less an institution and more a movement.

Other Christians, often inspired by Calvin, see a more complicated relationship between the society and the church. For them, Christians live both as citizens of this world and as citizens of God's rule, and faithfulness consists in balancing those demands.

1 Peter 2:18—3:7: Living Honorably in the Household

▌The Text in Its Ancient Context

In these verses, the author continues to present his version of good order. The standards he suggests for Christians are not very different from the standards that upstanding "pagan" citizens of Asia Minor would have suggested for the right ordering of a household. (See Bartlett, 278; I use "pagan" as a shorthand for those who were neither Jews nor Christians.) Here a powerful christological formulation is drawn in to buttress a widespread social practice and institution. The more general exhortation to endure suffering that follows is finally in the service of the instructions to slaves. "Slaves, accept the authority of your masters with all deference, not only those who are kind and gentle but also those who are harsh" (2:18).

The christological passage powerfully provides one reading of Christ's suffering and death, which are rightly designated by the church's theology as both essential and mysterious. Not surprisingly, 1 Peter looks at the mystery through the lens of the Old Testament. First Peter 2:22-25 is in many ways a Christian commentary on the meaning of Isaiah 53.

In 3:1, the author shifts the focus from slaves to wives, but makes clear by his sentence structure that the obedience of wives is another example of his vision of right order for a Christian household. "In the same way"—in the same way as slaves, that is—"wives, accept the authority of your husbands" (NRSV). In fact, in both the instance of slaves and wives, the Greek imperative would better be translated: "Be obedient" or "be subject."

Appropriate wifely conduct includes a kind of dress code. Most likely the standards for appropriate dress are the standards that right-thinking non-Christians would also uphold. If Christians are to stand out, it is for the beauty of their lives, not the luxury of their attire. We notice that the description of the obedient Sarah is a considerably sanitized version of the Sarah we meet in Genesis, where her wifely obedience is considerably more ambiguous (see Kittredge, 618).

Strikingly, in 3:7 husbands are not told to live in mutual obedience or subjection to their wives but to "show [them] consideration . . . as the weaker sex" (NRSV). (See Eph. 6:21 for a somewhat more egalitarian alternative.) However, there is no license given here for a husband to harm a wife, physically or psychologically. Husbands are enjoined to honor their wives.

▌The Text in the Interpretive Tradition

Calvin provides the kind of reading that has informed much Christian understanding of this passage from the first century until today.

> [Peter] proceeds now to another instance of subjection, and bids wives to be subject to their husbands. Since those who are married to men who are unbelievers seem to have more reason for shaking off the yoke, he expressly reminds them of their duty, and shows particular reason why they ought to obey more faithfully, so that by their honesty they may attract their husbands for faith. If wives ought to obey ungodly husbands, those who have believing husbands ought to obey even more readily. (Calvin, 12:280)

◼ THE TEXT IN CONTEMPORARY DISCUSSION

While considerable helpful scholarship has suggested some of the differences between slavery in the Roman Empire and slavery in pre–Civil War America, the appropriate consensus among Christians in our time is that slavery is an unacceptable human practice and that the defense of slavery is an unacceptable use of Scripture. It would simply be unethical and unfaithful for people to live in the twenty-first century as Peter enjoined Christians to live in the first.

For some Christians, this discrepancy leads them to reinterpret the text to try to soften its impact. For many Christians, this involves arguing against the text, acknowledging that other parts of Scripture read slavery far less favorably (e.g., Philemon), or arguing that we must sometimes distinguish the gospel for our time from the Scripture of another.

In understanding the relationship between men and women, too, this is a difficult chapter. Cynthia Kittredge reminds us how problematic this portion of 1 Peter is for Christians who want to move toward an egalitarian vision both of marriage and of the church.

> [First] Peter presents difficult interpretive issues for women today because its rhetoric constructs the female gender as the "weaker sex" (3:7) and both assumes and reinforces the social structures of masters and slaves. Its injunctions . . . have inflicted harm when perceived as universal instruction to the weak to endure injustice and abuse. (Kittredge, 616)

Many Christians would argue both from a theological and from a humane point of view that the center of Christian practice should be Gal. 3:28: "[in Christ] there is no longer Jew nor Greek, there is no longer slave nor free, there is no longer male and female" (NRSV).

1 Peter 3:8-22: Faithful Suffering

◼ THE TEXT IN ITS ANCIENT CONTEXT

Now the exhortations for right Christian conduct move from the household to the church and then to the larger community. Verse 8 seems to be directed toward the Christian community itself and seems almost a mirror image of 1 Pet. 2:1. There, new Christians are called to reject "malice, guile, insincerity, envy, slander." Here, new Christians are called to embrace "unity of spirit, sympathy, love for one another, a tender heart, and a humble mind."

With verse 9, we move to the question of the conduct of Christians in the larger society and especially Christian interaction with nonbelievers who may abuse them. These verses may provide some insight into the circumstances of these first-century churches. The issue does not (yet at least) seem to be persecution and martyrdom, but slander and abuse.

The proper Christian response to evil is good, and the proper Christian response to abuse is blessing (see also Matt. 6:38-42; Rom. 12:17-18). The author seems here to draw on a widespread Christian ethic of nonretaliation. His own addition to this tradition is his citation of Ps. 34:12-16.

As in previous exhortations, the author gives two reasons for such peaceful behavior. The first is that Christians want to have a good reputation in the larger community. The second reason is that Christians are to live their lives according to the shape of Jesus' own passion, resurrection, and ascension. It is not only that Christ's sacrificial acts are worthy of imitation but also that these acts are atoning. "For Christ also suffered . . . in order to bring you to God" (3:18).

There follows a description of the passion and resurrection of Christ that has puzzled Christian commentators through the ages. The first part is clear enough. Jesus was "put to death in the flesh but made alive in the spirit" (3:19). The claim is not strikingly different from that in Rom. 1:3-4. Peter is not arguing that only Jesus' spirit was made alive, but that he was made alive in the power of the Spirit.

Now comes the particularly puzzling description of what the living Jesus did after his resurrection: "he went and made a proclamation to the spirits in prison" (v. 19). The connection of these spirits with the flood (Genesis 6–9) suggests one of two possibilities. Perhaps these spirits are those of the disobedient people who perished in the flood. Or perhaps these spirits are the offspring of the "sons of God" and mortal women described in the puzzling passage Gen. 6:1-4. William Joseph Dalton argues persuasively that this passage fits with other first-century texts that speculate on the fate of these human/divine offspring. He further suggests that when the risen Christ preaches to these spirits, they are imprisoned in a kind of holding place located between earth and the upper heaven, where God the Father dwells. Jesus preaches to the spirits as part of his ascent.

The author now uses the reference to the ark and the flood to remind the readers of their own baptism. The flood prefigures baptism, but of course only in a kind of striking reversal. Noah and his family were actually saved from water; Christians are saved through water.

▌The Text in the Interpretive Tradition

Karl Barth drew on 1 Peter 3 along with other texts in his discussion of Christian suffering and Christian hope.

> The true analogy of the resurrection of Jesus Christ in the existence of oppressed Christians, the true might and power of the future which already in their present is appointed for them in their fellowship with Jesus Christ . . . simply consists in the fact that the Christian in affliction is a man who is absolutely secured by the goal appointed for him in Christ. (*CD* IV/3, 644–45)

▌The Text in Contemporary Discussion

Catherine González reads the text in ways that are clear and pertinent for contemporary North American and Western European Christians.

> Christians in the ancient world were at risk of being persecuted for their faith. In the midst of such suffering, they gave witness to the power of that faith. The same is true of Christians in some parts of our world today. . . . But that is not usually our situation. . . . What is it that Christians do in our culture that makes them stand out enough that others ask what is the source of their strength and joy? (González, 102)

For those who live in countries where Christian faith is perfectly acceptable and sometimes even assumed, there may be a temptation to use the dangerous situation of first-century Christians in

Asia Minor as an inappropriate analogy for the so-called War on Christmas, for example, or for the anxiety Christians may feel at having soccer practice compete with Sunday school. We would do well to distinguish the diminution of cultural hegemony in our era with genuine persecution and shunning in that earlier era.

Furthermore, the text reminds us that there are still many parts of the world where being a Christian is not only unpopular but also dangerous. In churchly concerns and with regard to national foreign policy alike, we should continue to oppose any genuine religious persecution of Christians (and, it goes without saying, *by* Christians, too).

1 Peter 4:1-11: Christ's Suffering as Example

■ THE TEXT IN ITS ANCIENT CONTEXT

The author continues to reflect on Christ's suffering as a guide to the current situation of those who hear his letter. Now, however, Christ's suffering "in the flesh" becomes a paradigm for first-century Christians to understand their new conduct as Christian believers.

For the author of 1 Peter, as for Paul, the distinction between "flesh" and "spirit" does not relate to two different aspects of the personality but to two different ages in God's dealing with humankind. In the time of the flesh, people live selfishly, competitively; in the time of the spirit, people live selflessly and cooperatively. Until their baptism, these Christians of Asia Minor have lived according to the flesh—in licentiousness and idolatry. In these behaviors, they have linked their lives not only to the old age of the flesh, which is passing away, but also to the environment around them of "gentiles," pagans, those who have not become part of God's Israel, God's true people.

The consequences of citizenship, whether people choose to live in the time and community of the flesh or in the time and community of the Spirit, will be judgment. Again, as so often, we realize that 1 Peter is written with the impending end of the world very much in mind.

Yet in a somewhat mysterious verse, our author seems to hint that at least for those who have gone before and lived lives according to the flesh, it is not too late to repent and become part of the community of the Spirit. "For this is the reason the gospel was proclaimed even to the dead, so that, though they have been judged in the flesh as everyone is judged, they might live in the spirit as God does" (4:6). It is unclear whether the "dead" are those who preceded Christ and are now included in the proclamation of the gospel, or believers who have died between Christ's resurrection and his return, or perhaps even those unbelievers who have died more recently. It is not even clear that it is Christ who preached the gospel in this passage. What is clear is that not even the dead are separated from the love of God, forever.

The reference to the glory of God leads the author to move into a kind of doxology, a poem that might almost be better sung than read: "To God be the power and the glory forever and ever. Amen." Not only does this hymn of praise end this part of the letter's exhortation, but also some have thought that it marks an end to an earlier, shorter writing that was basically a sermon on baptism.

■ THE TEXT IN THE INTERPRETIVE TRADITION

Some early Christian theologians (including Clement of Alexandria and Augustine) allegorically understood the dead to whom the gospel was preached to be the spiritually dead (see Kelly, 173). Calvin understood the preaching to the dead as a word of comfort to the (already) faithful who die in Christ: "It is a remarkable consolation to the godly that death itself brings no loss to their salvation. Even if Christ does not appear as deliverer in this life, yet His redemption is not void, or without effect, for His power extends even to the dead" (Calvin, 12:302).

■ THE TEXT IN CONTEMPORARY DISCUSSION

Catherine González, while acknowledging the obscurity of the reference to preaching to the dead, has a more generous view of what the text might imply than Calvin's. "There is some hope at the end of verse 6 that those who had been judged and condemned at the end of their earthly lives might be given the ability to live in the spirit just as God lives. . . . The former companions of these converts have been judged on the basis of their earthly life, but there is hope that they will be able to live a new life, just as these Gentile converts have begun to do" (González, 118).

We might wish that we could use this text answer the question, which goes back at least to the third century, whether God intends finally to redeem everyone. There are passages in the New Testament that suggest the hope of universal salvation (see Rom. 5:18, for instance). The meaning of this text, however, is too uncertain for the text to be of much help in discussing this disputed issue.

1 Peter 4:12-19: The Coming Crisis

■ THE TEXT IN ITS ANCIENT CONTEXT

Partly because our letter seems to come to a kind of full stop at 4:11 and partly because the mood of the letter shifts and intensifies with 4:12, some have thought that from 4:12 to the end of the epistle we have a real and urgent letter appended to what was originally some kind of sermon. We notice, however, that in other letters like Paul's Letter to the Romans, an author is perfectly capable of moving into a doxological hymn right in the middle of things and then moving on to the next part of his argument (see, e.g., Rom. 11:34-36). And it may be that the injunctions of 1 Pet. 4:12 do not indicate a new situation but a new perspective on the situation in view throughout the letter—where Christians are subject to some kind of slander and abuse from the very gentile communities they have left behind.

In this passage, the exemplary behavior is particularly straightforward. We can paraphrase: "do not be a criminal or a busybody" (4:15). Whether this injunction represents a real danger or a rhetorical flourish we cannot know. What is clear is that here the question of the law is not about idolatry or emperor worship. Christians are commanded not to be murderers or thieves.

Furthermore, in this passage the sufferings of the present time are explicitly linked to the final judgment. It is not just that judgment is coming but also that these very sufferings are themselves the firstfruits of that judgment, the small tribulation that points toward the great and fearful Day of the Lord, when the faithful will be redeemed and the unfaithful will suffer desolation greater than these passing trials.

▌THE TEXT IN THE INTERPRETIVE TRADITION

In commenting on this (and several similar texts), Karl Barth writes:

> Thus those who, like Christians, suffer something corresponding in their little passions as a reflection and likeness of His great passion, may rest assured that their suffering takes place in the light of the Easter revelation toward which He moved in His great passion. . . . Hence they can and may expect no other than their existence in fellowship with the One who rose again and lives as the crucified and slain. (*CD* IV/3, 372)

▌THE TEXT IN CONTEMPORARY DISCUSSION

J. Ramsey Michaels resists the claim that the tone and focus of the letter change radically with 1 Pet. 4:12. Rather, he suggests that these verses provide a kind of retrospective look at the claims about the difficulty of Christian life that have preceded these verses in our epistle.

> Although it has often been suggested that there is an intensification or a heightening of the urgency between 4:11 and 4:12 (as if Peter had just heard of a sudden crisis or disaster) there is no real evidence of this. . . . The difference in tone between 1:6-8 and 4:12-19 on the one hand, and most of 2:11—4:6 on the other, is the difference between a rhetorical summary of the Christian community's position in a hostile world and a series of directives on how to respond to specific aggravations or challenges. (Michaels, 258)

1 Peter 5:1-11: Instructions for Community Order

▌THE TEXT IN ITS ANCIENT CONTEXT

With 5:1, the author shifts from addressing the congregations at large to devote particular attention to church leaders. Whether the "elders" of the church are to be understood as designated offices or as more informal leaders is impossible to tell. What we do know is that from the beginning of the church, the different gifts of members suggested different functions. The issue becomes even murkier with the reference to those Christians who are younger (5:5). Are the "elders" always older members of the church? Or is the distinction between those who have been Christians for a time and those who are younger in faith? In any case, whatever their age and however they are chosen, the pastoral and ethical responsibilities of the elders are clear enough. Their pastoral responsibility is to provide oversight for the congregation and to do so with proper humility. Their ethical responsibility is not to do so for personal gain. (For similar injunctions to church elders, see Paul's address to the elders of Ephesus in Acts 20). The author puts before the elders of Asia Minor two examples of the right exercise of the pastoral, shepherdly role. The first example is the person whose identity he takes on for the writing of this letter—Peter, who knew Christ's glory. The second example is Christ, the great shepherd of all the flock—including the elders.

In 5:5b-11, the author turns from the distinction between elders and younger to address again all the members of the congregations, returning to the theme of suffering and distress but elaborating on his portrayal of this stressful situation in two ways. First of all, the present tribulations are not simply the consequence of human opposition to the believers, they are signs of the continuing devouring strategies of Satan. It is a general feature of Christian and Jewish apocalyptic expectation for the future that the present time is an age of warfare between God and God's great enemy. God of course will emerge victorious, but in the present moment the battle is joined.

Second, it is made clear to each of the congregations that what they suffer is not their unique and local difficulty but part of the ongoing tribulation of the whole church. This is presented not only to provide the comfort of community but also as one more reminder that all the world is caught up in the struggle between Satan and God—a further sign that the end must be near.

The good news is that the end will be God's gracious end. First Peter 5:1-10 is not only a prophecy but also a benediction. And as with the first part of this letter (4:11), this second section of the letter ends with doxology: "To him be the power forever and ever. Amen."

▌The Text in the Interpretive Tradition

Augustine of Hippo of course assumed that 1 Peter was written by the apostle Peter, and he therefore connects this passage with Jesus' dialogue with Peter in John 21, where Peter is commanded by Jesus to "feed his sheep" (*Homily on the Feast of St. Peter and St. Paul*). Here, as Augustine reads our text, Peter, himself a shepherd and elder, tells other elders that they are to be good shepherds too.

▌The Text in Contemporary Discussion

In 1973, a group of Lutheran and Roman Catholic scholars completed a series of discussions of the apostle Peter by publishing a book called *Peter in the New Testament*. The hope was that by better understanding the biblical portrait of Peter, Catholics and Lutherans—and presumably other Protestants as well—might come to a more nuanced and even ecumenical understanding of the relationship of Peter to the bishopric and especially to the bishopric of Rome. In their discussion of 1 Peter, the authors present both sides of the discussion about authorship, but in looking at these verses from 1 Peter 5 they come to a kind of consensus.

> In 5:1 the author of 1 Peter, introducing himself to the presbyters (elders) of the communities of Asia Minor assumes the title of "fellow presbyter" or "co-presbyter." We should not be deceived by this modest stance as if the author were presenting himself as their equal. He has already identified his authority as "apostolic" (1:1); and so the use of "fellow presbyter" is a polite stratagem of benevolence, somewhat as when a modern bishop of a diocese addresses his "fellow priests." (Brown, Donfried, and Reumann, 152–53)

1 Peter 5:12-14: Final Greetings

▌The Text in Its Ancient Context

We have discussed in the introduction the issue of who wrote this letter and where it was written. What becomes clearer at the letter's end is that the purpose of the letter is not finally instruction about morals or warnings about last things, but encouragement. If the Christians have heard this letter right, they have found courage (though the Greek word translated as "encourage" [*parakalein*] is rich enough that it can mean that they have found exhortation and instruction as well).

Whether the author of our letter knew a Christian named Mark, or uses the name "Mark" (and perhaps, Silvanus, Silas) to connect "Peter" with other another first-generation Christian, we cannot know.

The exhortation for the holy kiss strengthens our conviction of the importance of communal love and fellowship for the first churches and probably gives us a glimpse into a liturgical practice common to their assemblies. The final word of this sometimes tumultuous discourse is, blessedly, "Peace."

∎ THE TEXT IN THE INTERPRETIVE TRADITION

These last verses have not been at the center of any basic theological discussion over the centuries, nor are their themes subject to much debate even now.

What they provide is a hint or two of church life toward the end of the first century. The church in Babylon/Rome is sufficiently connected to these churches in Asia Minor to join in greeting.

∎ THE TEXT IN CONTEMPORARY DISCUSSION

The citation of "Silvanus/Silas" and Mark provides fuel for the ongoing discussion of authorship and, in recent years, the tricky question of pseudonymity. Some scholars have tried to hold to Peter's authorship of this letter by suggesting that his work was edited and presumably improved literarily by his companion Silvanus.

Certainly for centuries—certainly as early as Polycarp's *Letter to the Philippians* in the early second century CE—Christians assumed this was written by Jesus' companion Peter. Early on, it was treated as part of the canon, as part of Sacred Scripture, probably in part because of its assumed apostolic authorship.

From at least the beginning of the twentieth century, many scholars have suspected that 1 Peter was written in Peter's name. Perhaps it was written by late first-century Christians devoted to Peter and hoping to provide the kind of perspective he might have offered for the new situations of their own age.

In any case, 1 Peter has continued through the centuries to provide, above all, a word of encouragement for Christians suffering for their faith, and a thoughtful attempt to wrestle with the relationship between the church and the world that is sometimes both its opponent and its home.

Works Cited

Achtemeier, Paul. 1996. *First Peter*. Hermeneia. Minneapolis: Fortress Press.

Augustine. *Homily on the Feasts of St. Peter and St. Paul*. www.onbehalfofall.org/2013/06/29.

Barth, Karl. 1963. *Church Dogmatics*, trans. G.W. Bromiley et al., Edinburgh: T&T Clark.

Bartlett, David. 1998. "First Peter." In *The New Interpreter's Bible*. Vol. 12, *Hebrews–Revelation*, edited by Leander E. Keck, 229–301. Nashville: Abingdon.

Brown, Raymond A., Karl Donfried, and John Reumann. 1973. *Peter in the New Testament: A Collaborative Assessment by Protestant and Roman Catholic Scholars*. Minneapolis: Augsburg, 1973.

Calvin, John. 1970. *Commentaries*. 12 volumes. Translated by William B. Johnson. Grand Rapids: Eerdmans.

Dalton, William Joseph. 1989. *Christ's Proclamation to the Spirits: A Study of 1 Peter 3:18—4:6*. 2nd ed. Rome: Pontifical Biblical Institute.

Elliott, John H. 1990. *A Home for the Homeless: A Social-Scientific Criticism of 1 Peter, Its Situation, and Strategy, with a New Introduction*. Minneapolis: Fortress Press.

Gonzáles, Catherine Gunsalus. 2010. *First and Second Peter and Jude*. Louisville: Westminster John Knox.

Hauerwas, Stanley, and William Willimon. 1989. *Resident Aliens*. Nashville: Abingdon.

Kelly, J. N. D. 1976. *Epistles of Peter and of Jude*. London: Black.

Kittredge, Cynthia Briggs. 2012. *1 Peter* in *The Women's Bible Commentary* 3rd edition, pp. 616–19. C. Newsome, S. Ringe, and J. Lapsley, eds. Louisville: Westminster John Knox,

Michaels, J. Ramsey. 1998. *First Peter*. WBC. Waco, TX: Word.

Spurgeon, Charles H. 1916. "Coming to Christ: A Sermon." The Spurgeon Archive. April 27. www.spurgeon.org/sermons/3509.htm.

Vinson, Richard B., with Richard F. Wilson and E. Mills Watson. 2010. *First and Second Peter and Jude*. Macon, GA: Smyth & Helwys.

2 PETER

Pheme Perkins

Introduction

Faced with growing skepticism over belief in the second coming of Christ and the consequences of that view for the ethical conduct of believers, a pseudonymous author invoked the authority of the apostle Peter to confirm established teaching. The transfiguration of Jesus (2 Pet. 1:16-18), establishes both Jesus' divine identity and belief in his parousia. This focus on Jesus as God is reflected in the opening verse (1:1) of the letter as well as its concluding doxology (3:18). Since Jesus is their benefactor and divine Savior (1:11; 2:20; 3:2), Christians must hold fast to the true knowledge of the Lord (Kistemaker, 221–26). The divine power and goodness of the Savior enables the faithful to participate in the divine nature (1:4; Craddock, 88).

The author reinforces the Petrine voice by employing a Semitic version of the apostle's name, "Simeon" instead of "Simon" (v. 1), and referring back to an earlier epistle written in Peter's name, our 1 Peter (3:1). By suggesting that in this letter one also possesses Peter's "testament," his final teaching at the point of death (1:12-15), the author invokes the authority of a revered figure delivering final instructions and warnings as Moses does in Deuteronomy. The reference to Jesus' prediction of Peter's death in 1:14 reflects a tradition attested in John 21:18-19. In addition to these Petrine echoes, 2 Peter also insists that "our beloved brother Paul" presented the same teaching, despite the attempt by false teachers to use the complexity of his letters in support of their theological innovations (3:15-16).

Although the reference to the transfiguration does not quote any one of our written Gospels, it seems reasonable to conclude that 2 Peter expects Christians to know one or more of the Gospels and a collection of apostolic letters that includes several from Paul as well as 1 Peter. When we compare the Old Testament examples used to support the teaching of divine judgment in 2 Peter 2 with Jude 4-13, it becomes clear that the author has employed that writing as well without appealing to Jude as apostolic. Although 2 Peter does not identify either its place of origin or the locale of its audience, several features of the work suggest that it may have been composed in Rome in the early second century CE. In addition to the traditional association of Peter with that city, 1 Peter was dispatched from Rome to believers in Asia Minor. Toward the end of the first century, *1 Clement* invoked the authority of both apostles, Peter and Paul, in writing to Corinth (*1 Clem.* 5.4-5). In addition to the traditional link between Peter and the city, some scholars find a clue in the ethical teaching of 2 Peter. Christian faith as commitment to purity and holiness of life that distinguishes believers from their pagan surroundings is characteristic of Roman Christianity (Bauckham, 158–61).

Though it is difficult to untangle the logic of an opponent's argument from a well-crafted polemical response, scholars have detected traits of Epicurean philosophy that could have supported the false teaching opposed here (Neyrey, 122–25). Epicureans argued against any belief in intervention by or punishment from the gods and held that the universe reflects the eternal, random interactions of various sorts of atoms moving in a void. Death is the dissolution of the atoms that make up the person. Therefore there is no such thing as a divine providence in the world or divine punishment and reward. By following this philosophy, humans liberate themselves from fear of the gods, the future, or death. Exactly how the false teachers adapted Epicurean principles to distort Christian faith is unclear. Presumably the opposition must have held out some view of salvation, perhaps a divinization of the soul similar to that envisioned in 2 Peter. At the same time, they may have used Epicurean cosmology to reject as mythology all teaching about an end-time judgment. Perhaps they also adopted an ethic of the pleasant life, which 2 Peter interprets as freedom for immorality or caving in to the passions (2:2, 10a, 13-14, 18).

2 Peter follows the structure of a letter.

> Greeting (1:1-2)
> Opening, purpose for writing (1:3-15)
> Summary of the faith shared by believers (vv. 3-11)
> Peter's testament to endure beyond his death (vv. 12-15)
> Body of the letter; the certainty of divine judgment (1:16—3:13)
> The transfiguration confirms the truth of the Lord's coming in glory (1:16-18)
> True prophecy is inspired by God (1:19-21)
> False teachers are comparable to false prophets (2:1-3)
> Examples of divine punishment and rescue of the righteous (2:4-10a)
> Application to the false teachers and their followers (2:10b-22)
> Exhortation to the readers (3:1-13)
> Body closing (3:14-18a)
> Final doxology (3:18b)

2 Peter 1:1-15: Christ's Calling

▌THE TEXT IN ITS ANCIENT CONTEXT

The greeting and opening of 2 Peter adopt the voice of the apostle Peter in defense of a shared faith that is summarized in verses 3-11. By casting this work as a testament of the apostle intended to enable future believers to recall Peter's teaching after his death, the author has crafted a piece intended to transcend the historical particulars of Peter's life (Harrington and Senior, 250–52). Verses 3-11 summarize the faith shared by believers, which forms the basis of "entry into the eternal kingdom of our Lord and Savior" (v. 11). "Knowledge of our Lord Jesus" refers to the moral goodness, separation from the passions, and mutual love appropriate to persons who will share the divine nature.

▌THE TEXT IN THE INTERPRETIVE TRADITION

Doubts about its Petrine authorship based on the obvious difference in style between 1 and 2 Peter led fourth-century authors to treat it as marginal to the canon (Eusebius, *Hist. eccl.* 3.3.1; Jerome, *Vir. ill.* 1). John Calvin defends reading this letter despite such doubts by suggesting that even if written by another it reflects Peter's teaching.

▌THE TEXT IN CONTEMPORARY DISCUSSION

Though 2 Peter does not develop the reference to sharing divine nature in 1:4, divinization would become the centerpiece of Christ's saving work in the fourth-century-CE Greek fathers. The Son of God became man so that we might become God. This transformation could be expressed as participating in divine immortality (Novatian, *Trin.* 15.1) or linked with receiving a divine nature by participating in the Eucharist (Cyril of Jerusalem, *Cat. Lect.* 4.3). Contemporary theologians look to the insights of the Greek fathers in formulating a soteriology of human transformation into the new being envisaged by God.

2 Peter 1:16—2:3: The Example of the Prophets

▌THE TEXT IN ITS ANCIENT CONTEXT

An indirect reference to John's Gospel may have been intended by the comment that Jesus had predicted Peter's death (v. 14). This section makes a more explicit allusion to the story of Jesus' transfiguration in the Synoptic Gospels (Matt. 17:1-8; Mark 9:2-13; Luke 9:28-36) by referring to a group of apostolic witnesses ("we"), the glory of Jesus, and the words of God's voice. Most of the details of the Gospel stories have been omitted from this précis. The divine words are closest to Matt. 17:5.

The transition to a discussion of authentic prophecy points to a specific crisis behind the composition of 2 Peter. How affirming the validity of Old Testament prophecy as it points forward to Christ in verse 19a relates to the transfiguration is not entirely clear. Perhaps 2 Peter expects readers to treat the presence of Moses and Elijah as prophetic witnesses. The metaphor of a shining lamp and the morning star rising in the heart recalls such earlier Christian language about awaiting the day of judgment as 1 Thess. 5:5-8 (Neyrey, 183). Second Peter insists that the prophets neither invented their oracles nor fabricated interpretations of their visions, since they spoke under the guidance of the Holy Spirit (vv. 20-21). This argument could be directed against an Epicurean skepticism concerning all oracles or against claims on the part of the false teachers to divine inspiration.

Since biblical prophecy is divinely inspired, the author will connect ancient examples of divine punishment with the fate that awaits false teachers who delude believers and corrupt their morals (2:1-3). Greed is often invoked as a motive in polemical rhetoric along with the standard items of moral depravity. Second Peter employs the polemic of Jude 4 in depicting the false teachers, but it adds an ironical turn. Though they point to the apparent delay as evidence against a day of judgment, the condemnation of these false teachers has been fixed in God's plan, and is not suspended (v. 3b; Kraftchick, 121–23).

▌The Text in the Interpretive Tradition

Justin Martyr may be alluding to 2 Pet. 2:1 when he compares the false prophets of the Old Testament to the many false teachers of his own day (*Dial.* 82.1).

▌The Text in Contemporary Discussion

Although Christians reaffirm their belief in the Hebrew prophets as witnesses to Christ and in the Lord's coming in judgment whenever they recite the creed, many consider that language a mythological or poetic holdover from a more naive time. The transfiguration story presents the presence of God in the Son as the culmination of a story of God's saving presence with humanity that began with creation. To use the language of end-time judgment as a way of underlining the moral seriousness required of believers (1:3-11) is one way of holding on to a biblical heritage that no longer matches scientific or popular media scenarios for the end of planet earth. Since 2 Peter clearly retains the early Christian tradition that this world will come to a cataclysmic end when the divine Christ appears as judge, its explanation of the delay (3:5-10) does not imply that the phrase "until he comes again" should be dropped from the creed.

2 Peter 2:4-22: Lessons from the Biblical Past

Second Peter 2:4-10a has modified the language and content of Jude 4-13. It omits Jude's references to Jewish apocryphal material, such as the contest between Satan and Michael over the body of Moses in Jude 9 or the citation of Enoch as an authoritative prophet in Jude 14-16. These omissions may reflect an awareness that such apocrypha are not inspired Scripture. However, the author might simply have dropped material unfamiliar to the intended audience (Bauckham, 260). In another striking modification, the author adds the dimension of salvation to the judgment and punishment motif in the examples of the flood ("Noah, a herald of righteousness, with seven others") and Sodom and Gomorrah ("Lot, a righteous man"). This shift helps readers to view their own situation in these ancient stories. Second Peter even stresses the distress of a righteous man like Lot faced while living among the ungodly (vv. 7-8). Therefore the lesson that his audience is to learn includes God's ability to rescue the righteous who suffer trials (v. 9a; Bauckham, 257).

Second Peter harangues the opposition (vv. 10b-22) under two heads, the depravity of persons driven by fleshly desires and their arrogant disregard for authority. The latter is picked up first in an ambiguous charge that they engage in some form of slander against heavenly beings that not even angels would attempt (vv. 10b-11). Subjection to fleshly passions reduces the opponents to the level of irrational animals, destined to be the hunter's prey (v. 12). This section culminates in two proverbial sayings about the filth of irrational animals: dogs that lick their own vomit and pigs that go from water to rolling in mud (v. 22). Disgusting animalistic behavior reflects the dissipation that characterizes the life of the opponents and their followers (vv. 13-14, 18).

With characteristic irony, the invective points out that the freedom promised by the opposition is nothing less than slavery. To adopt false moral teaching is worse than living as the unbelievers do because it undermines the liberating power of Christ (vv. 18-21).

■ THE TEXT IN THE INTERPRETIVE TRADITION

First Clement 11.1–2 also uses the rescue of Lot to drive home the point that God never abandons the godly. Lot's wife becomes a warning to believers who might begin to doubt God's power.

■ THE TEXT IN CONTEMPORARY DISCUSSION

Second Peter 2:5-9 emphasizes God's power to preserve the moral character of the faithful even when they live in situations that are shot through with evil. It acknowledges the spiritual suffering that causes righteous people to keep themselves apart from the wicked but does not advocate sectarian isolation. Christians can bear witness to the gospel in such a world by refusing to accept its moral relativism.

2 Peter 3:1-18: Salvation and Judgment

Second Peter invites the audience to apply two sources of insight to their situation: the holy prophets and the commandment of the Lord handed on through the apostles (vv. 1-3; cf. Jude 17-18). The author then defends Christian belief in divine judgment. Those who deny it ignore the truth that the same power by which God created all things preserves them until the day of judgment (vv. 5-7). Another argument points to the psalm text that distinguishes the human and divine perceptions of time (v. 8; Ps. 90:4). Once again, 2 Peter includes God's saving power in the discussion, since new creation follows judgment (vv. 11-13). To account for the delayed end-time, verse 9 invokes a familiar Jewish treatment of the question of divine punishment. God withholds it to provide opportunity for the wicked to repent (Exod. 34:6; Joel 2:12-13; Sir. 5:4-7; Bauckham, 312). God's merciful forbearance does not mean that judgment has been canceled. The traditional Christian conviction that the Day of the Lord will come suddenly remains true (v. 10; cf. 1 Thess. 5:2-6).

Therefore Christians should appreciate the delayed judgment as an opportunity for salvation, not license (vv. 14-15). Second Peter insists that the letters of Paul teach the same understanding of the Christian life despite the use false teachers make of them and other Scriptures. A final exhortation to remain steadfast in faith concludes with a doxology to Jesus as Lord and Savior rather than God, as in Jude 25, "to the only God our Savior, through Jesus Christ." Praising Jesus in this fashion suggests that at least in its worship, the community perceives him as fully divine.

▌ The Text in the Interpretive Tradition

A rabbinic tradition that the arrival of the end time is somehow correlated with Israel's repentance (*b. Sanh.* 97b–98a) raises an interesting possibility for verse 9b ("... is patient with you, not wanting any to perish"). The delay could reflect a lack of repentance among Christians. Bede reads this passage with Rev. 6:11 as indicating the time for God to gather all those elect predestined before creation.

▌ The Text in Contemporary Discussion

The balance 2 Peter exhibits in revising the apocalyptic traditions adapted from Jude—namely, incorporating salvation of the faithful along with condemnation of the wicked—highlights the deficiency of our secular apocalypses. Unlike the postapocalyptic world in contemporary films, which leaves a few humans wandering amid the ruins of civilization, the Christian hope extends beyond judgment to the new creation no longer marred by evil (v. 13; Rom. 8:21; Rev. 21:1).

However, the methodological problem still engages Christian theology. How can traditional Christian belief address the skepticism generated by scientific descriptions of the universe? Though cast as a form of polemic that most Christians today find distasteful, the ethical emphasis in 2 Peter points to the key area of dispute. Scientific theories about the world are not a threat. It is the moral consequences that opponents of religion such as the "new atheists" attach to them that believers must resist.

Works Cited

Bauckham, Richard J. 1983. *Jude, 2 Peter.* WBC 50. Waco, TX: Word.

Craddock, Fred. 1995. *First and Second Peter and Jude.* Louisville: Westminster John Knox.

Kistemaker, Simon. 1996. *Exposition of James, Epistles of John, Peter, and Jude.* Grand Rapids: Baker.

Kraftchick, Steven J. 2002. *Jude, 2 Peter.* Nashville: Abingdon.

Neyrey, Jerome H. 1993. *2 Peter, Jude.* AB 37C. New York: Doubleday.

Senior, Donald, and Daniel J. Harrington. 2008. *1 Peter, Jude and 2 Peter.* Sacra Pagina 15. Collegeville, MN: Liturgical Press.

1, 2, 3 JOHN

Jaime Clark-Soles

Introduction

The Johannine Epistles, along with the Gospel of John, occupy a substantial position in the canon, constituting "The Johannine literature" and perhaps indicating a "Johannine school of thought" from which they all emerged, akin to the notion of a "Pauline school of thought." Certainly 1 John has provided the church ample liturgical material with its insistence on confession of sin and assurance of pardon (1:8-9); the call to prayer (4:14-15), especially intercessory prayer (4:16); and its proclamation that "God is love." The epistles raise and inform the following issues:

- *Ecclesiology*: How is the group to form and maintain a cohesive communal identity? How should it handle church discipline when conflict arises? Who has the authority to instruct the church in matters of theology and praxis? Does the "elder"? On what is this authority based?
- *Hospitality:* Who deserves hospitality from Christians and who does not? On what basis is this decision made?
- *Ethics*: What is the shape of a Christian praxis based on the preeminent commandment from Jesus to "love one another"? How does this cohere with denying hospitality to certain individuals? How should the Christian interact with "the world"?
- *Theology*: What is the nature of sin? Who is Jesus and how has his blood cleansed the Johannine Christian?

Unlike 2 and 3 John, the author of 1 John remains entirely unnamed, but claims to be an eyewitness to the earthly Jesus (1:1-4). Due to apparent knowledge of and dependence on the traditions evinced by the Fourth Gospel, some assume that the same author penned both texts. Based on differences in theology and style, however, others attribute 1 John to a different author, perhaps the "elder" referred to in 2 John 1 and 3 John 1 (though the epistles may well come from different

691

hands). The composition history of the Fourth Gospel itself is quite complex and probably reflects various stages of the community in which it arose (see the entry on the Gospel), and more than one authorial or editorial hand. As a result, theories concerning the authorship and dating of the Gospel and each epistle abound. If, as seems likely, the epistles were composed after the Gospel, they should be dated to around 100 CE. (For a thorough treatment of the composition history of the Johannine material, see von Wahlde.)

Also unlike 2 and 3 John, 1 John is more a hortatory address or essay than an epistle. It lacks the conventional features of a letter, including the names of the sender and recipient, opening and closing greetings, or a thanksgiving. Second John is written to "the elect lady and her children" and 3 John, to Gaius. First John does not designate its audience, but its rhetoric, allusions, and assumptions indicate that the audience is part of the same community from which the Fourth Gospel arose. In each case, the author is concerned with both the theology and the ethics of the community. Whereas the Gospel of John devotes much attention to the relationship between the Johannine community and other entities outside of it (the parent Jewish tradition, Rome, other Christian groups: Clark-Soles), the Johannine Epistles focus internally. The letters share a common language, outlook, and social setting. They instruct their readers regarding how to deal with those who have abandoned the community (and thereby apostatized) as well as those who espouse false teachings. The tensions felt in the community with respect to those members who have become a problem raise questions about the nature of Christian hospitality and inclusivity. In addition to building up the faithful who remain by demonizing those who departed, the epistles also reiterate the importance of binding the community together through active, sacrificial love.

"God is love [*agapē*]." This central, climactic assertion provides shape to the Johannine Epistles. Inseparable from this main theme are two others: proper Christology and the avoidance of sin, especially the sin that leads to death (5:16). As an act of love, God sent Jesus (1) to reveal the nature of love, which is always concrete and other-oriented (if sectarian), and (2) to free people from the power of sin by his sacrificial act through his blood (1:6—2:2; 4:10).

First John appears concerned to combat what historians call docetic Christology. The term *docetism* derives from the Greek verb *dokeō*, "to seem." Broadly speaking, it refers to a form of Christianity, known to us chiefly from the writings of other Christians who condemned it, that maintained Jesus was not really human but only appeared to be. He was not truly subject to the vicissitudes of embodied fleshly existence and therefore only "appeared" to suffer physically. Docetism is usually described as related to Gnosticism, another modern name for a number of early Christian movements that until the mid-twentieth century were also known only through the writings of polemicists like Irenaeus. Bishop of Lyons in the late second century, Irenaeus mocked certain other Christian teachers as "falsely so-called 'knowers' [*gnōstikoi*]." As conventionally understood, both docetism and Gnosticism malign the material order and denigrate the usefulness of the flesh; both were declared heresies in the early centuries of the church.

Curiously, "gnostic" thinkers such as Valentinus drew heavily on the Gospel of John. Indeed, the renowned theologian Ernst Käsemann detected what he called a "naïve docetism" in the Fourth Gospel, generated by the author's heavy emphasis on Jesus' divinity, not to mention the aplomb with which Jesus manages his passion as compared to the Synoptic Gospels. But the author of 1

John castigates docetic Christologies, and was followed by numerous subsequent theologians (see Ignatius's *Letter to the Smyrnaeans* 1–7; *Letter to the Trallians* 9.1–2; Irenaeus's *Against Heresies*).

Although the authors of the epistles remain anonymous, all three became associated with "John" in the early church, whether that John was identified as the son of Zebedee or "John the Elder." Eventually, Revelation, the one text that actually names its author as John (but does not give any more identifying details), becomes associated with the Gospel and the three epistles. From the outset there were doubts about the authenticity of the material, especially of 2 and 3 John (Eusebius, *Hist. eccl.* 6.25.9–10). The letters are cited unevenly among the church fathers, and the reception of each varies geographically (Lieu 2008, 25–28). While 1 John appealed widely early, 2 and 3 John experienced rockier paths to canonization. Their survival and final inclusion in the canon signifies that, regardless of their authorship or original audience, the contents of the letters were and are useful to the wider Christian church.

1 John

1 John 1:1-4: The Prologue

No two commentaries agree on the structure of 1 John. The epistle does not present a clear thesis that drives forward to a compelling conclusion. Rather, it is marked by repetition, a spiral-like collection of themes, and self-referential habits (e.g., 1 John 3:24 and 4:13 make the same statement; 4:1-6 picks up on 2:18-28). Like the Fourth Gospel, 1 John begins with a prologue that introduces key themes and terms: word, life, revealed, testify, declare, fellowship, and the relationship between God and Jesus as Father and Son. Authority is justified by a claim to eyewitness status. The prologue also anticipates a major theme of the epistle, namely, the incarnation, the embodiedness of the Messiah, such that he could be perceived by the senses: he was seen, heard, and touched. In addition, the transmission of the Gospel involves attending to the embodiedness of one's brothers and sisters (3:16-18) and abiding with another in love; as the text demonstrates, this ideal can be elusive.

1 John 1:5—2:17: Walk in the Light

▌THE TEXT IN ITS ANCIENT CONTEXT

After declaring that "God is light" (v. 5), the author continues to solidify bonds with the listeners by drawing them into "we" rhetoric and indicating what behavior and beliefs they should espouse and what they should eschew. The audience is to walk in the light. The language of walking (Greek *peripatein*) as a metaphor for ethical behavior is common in the Hebrew Bible and stems from the Hebrew verb *halak*, to walk. Hence, even today the collection of rabbinical ethical teachings is called the halakah.

First John 1:6-10 enjoins the audience to walk in the light, for those who do so testify to truth; enjoy fellowship with one another; confess that they have sin; and have been forgiven their sin and cleansed from all unrighteousness by the blood of Jesus, God's Son. Those who walk in the darkness can enjoy none of these benefits. As parents assume the role of moral formation in their children, so the author addresses them as "my little children" (note that the "we" language has receded here). With respect to sin, one must confess that one has sin in order to receive forgiveness (1:9). Although the author wants the audience to behave ethically and avoid sin (indeed, this is a main point of the sermon as indicated in 2:1), he makes allowance for it by noting that if anyone does sin, Jesus Christ provides the solution. How?

First John 2:2 deserves further explication. The sentence reads: "And he himself is a *hilasmos* on behalf of our sins, but not only on behalf of our [sins] but also on behalf of the whole cosmos." It is difficult to translate *hilasmos* because apart from here and 1 John 4:10, it appears nowhere else in the New Testament. The NRSV translates it as "atoning sacrifice"; Judith Lieu (2008, 64) as "forgiveness"; and John Painter (146) and D. Moody Smith (52) as "expiation." Unfortunately, the word appears only six times in the Septuagint (Lev. 25:9; Num. 5:8; 2 Macc. 3:33; Ps. 129:4; Amos 8:14; Ezek. 44:27; Dan. 9:9) and does not always have the same meaning. It can refer to the effects of cultic (or sacrificial) action, such as expiation (which emphasizes the subjective agency of God in removing sin) or propitiation (which emphasizes the human action in appeasing God's wrath); or it can refer to the action itself, specifically a sin offering; or it can simply refer to forgiveness. Those who argue for a cultic meaning in 1 John point to Lev. 25:9 and the context of the Day of Atonement. They also note the phrase "on behalf of our sins" in 2:2 and link this verse with 1:7-9, which refers to Jesus' blood and cleansing. Lieu 64 disagrees with this approach and argues that the scant evidence does not bear out such specificity as a translation such as "atoning sacrifice" would imply. Those Christian scholars who do see a cultic meaning are careful to translate *hilasmos* as "expiation," not "propitiation," because God and Jesus the just (*dikaios*) are the actors and agents in dealing with sin.

A connection is sometimes made between 2:2 and the martyr traditions found in 4 Maccabees and the Suffering Servant of Isa. 52:13—53:11. The servant is just (*dikaios*; Isa. 53:11); his death is "on behalf of sin" (Isa. 53:10); and he "bore the sins of many and was handed over on account of their sins" (Isa. 53:12 LXX; Lieu 2008, 63–64). The Maccabees, as just martyrs, may present a parallel: "the tyrant was punished, and the homeland purified—they having become, as it were, a ransom [*antipsychon*] for the sin of our nation. And through the blood of those devout ones and their death as an atoning sacrifice [*hilastērion*], divine Providence preserved Israel that previously had been mistreated" (4 Macc. 17:21-22). If martyrdom is the notion the author has in mind, it raises doubts about 1 John's containing a developed doctrine of atonement at all.

Whatever one decides, it is important to be clear that (1) God and Jesus provide the solution for sin; (2) Jesus continues to solve sin in the present as a living, active agent; and (3) Jesus' action was and is part of God's original plan, not, so to speak, an improvisation. That is, we should not imagine that in the author's view, God had devised a plan A for the Jews, through the Torah and covenants, which failed so that God was forced to scramble to initiate a plan B in the form of Jesus. Jesus' work implements God's initial plan. There are at least three problems with imagining that atonement in Jesus is in any way an innovation or improvisation. First, it divorces Jesus from his own Jewish identity and tradition. Second, it postulates Christianity as a solution to the failure of atonement in Judaism and is therefore supersessionist and, potentially, antisemitic. Third, it appears gnostic; that is, it seems to see the Old Testament as evidence of a lesser God of a lesser religion and the New Testament as evidence of Jesus who frees the believer from the gnostic demiurge.

The proclamation that Jesus' justifying work is on behalf of "the whole cosmos" is noteworthy and, when combined with 4:14, where Jesus is denoted "the savior of the world," sounds quite hopeful and expansive. As it turns out, however, this is probably the exception to the general rule of 1 John (and the Gospel of John); the world represents opposition to God and God's children. In this way, 1 John may be described as sectarian and dualistic.

It is not surprising in a hortatory address to find the author moving from a discussion of sin to that of obeying Jesus' commandments and imitating Jesus' behavior. Though the author speaks of commandments in the plural at 2:3-4, he really has only one commandment in mind: "Love your brother [*adelphos*]." This commandment may well allude to John 13:34: "I give you a new commandment, that you love one another. Just as I have loved you, you also should love one another." In both cases, the author calls the audience to love fellow believers (this use of sibling language for church relationships is typical for early Christians). Those familiar with the Synoptic Gospels will miss the charge to "love your enemies" (Matt. 5:44; Luke 6:27, 35) or "love your neighbor as yourself" (Matt. 19:19; 22:39; Mark 12:31; Luke 10:27), neither of which appears in the Gospel of John. Instead, Johannine Christians are to love the other members of the group, but they are to do so specifically by imitating Jesus' own way of loving. The author is trying to create a household of love where the family ties are strong enough to maintain group cohesion: note the familial language in 2:12-14—fathers, children (*teknia*), young people (*paidia*), and that the family ties that bind also liberate (1 John 3:17-18).

At 2:15, the author warns the listeners that one can either love the world or love God; the two are mutually exclusive. Scholars debate extensively the meaning of the triad presented in 2:16, which the NRSV translates: "the desire [*epithymia*] of the flesh [*sarx*], the desire [*epithymia*] of the eyes [*ophthalmōn*], the pride [*alazoneia*] of riches [*tou biou*]." Some consider the first two to refer specifically to sexual issues; others consider all three to relate to greed, a lust for wealth. Desire in and of itself may not be problematic, but deformed desire always is. William Loader suggests that the author signifies "the depraved excesses of the rich at their often pretentious banquets" where money, drunkenness, and sexual immorality inevitably coalesce (forthcoming, 6). This passage relates to a fundamental ethical concern that runs throughout the epistle: the care of the poor. The Roman Empire in the first century had nothing like "the middle class" of today; the vast majority of people lived in poverty at a bare subsistence level and depended on handouts from the state or wealthy persons. The passage immediately preceding demands that the Christians love one another, referring not to a mere feeling but to concrete action as defined in 3:16-18. Faithful Christians will resist greed and exploitation of others, both of which are tantamount to "hate" and even "murder." In 2:14, the author declares that true Christians have "overcome the evil one."

▌THE TEXT IN THE INTERPRETIVE TRADITION

First John 2:1-2 has given rise to christological debates about the work accomplished by Jesus in solving the problem of sin. This includes attention to various hotly debated theories of atonement.

Many Christians unjustifiably assume penal substitutionary atonement theories when reading any New Testament texts. In this view, God's justice demands a legal payment as the penalty for human sin. Rather than each sinful person having to pay that price, Jesus is substituted. First John should challenge that assumption. In fact, the issue already arises in the Gospel of John itself, when Jesus is referred to as "the Lamb of God who takes away the sin of the world" (John 1:29), and where Jesus dies a day earlier in the Gospel of John than in the Synoptics, at the time when the sacrifice of the Passover lambs occurred in the temple. Technically speaking, the Passover lamb was not a sacrifice *for sin* (so no particular theory of atonement is in view), but symbolized deliverance from death. Most likely, the Gospel's language of the "Lamb of God" represents a merger of Passover-lamb symbolism with imagery of the Suffering Servant in Isaiah 53. Rather than presenting a notion of penal substitutionary atonement, John depicts Jesus as dying to reconcile an alienated world to its God by overcoming the world's hostility through belief. "*When the love of God, conveyed through the death of Jesus, overcomes the sin of unbelief by evoking faith, it delivers people from the judgment of God by bringing them into true relationship with God.* This is atonement in the Johannine sense. . . . There is no suggestion that dying 'for' the people equals paying the legal penalty for sin. The Fourth Gospel has a different understanding of sacrifice" (Koester 2008, 115–16). This understanding is probably what the author of 1 John also has in mind.

Others debate whether *hilasmos* means expiation or propitiation (see above). Still others argue that 1 John may have both expiation and propitiation in mind (Painter, 146–47).

■ THE TEXT IN CONTEMPORARY DISCUSSION

From purely academic contexts to popular Christianity today (e.g., Rob Bell, Brian McClaren, Emergent Christianity), atonement theology has recently come under scrutiny. Feminists and others raise deep concerns about the marriage of religion and violence in sacrificial language. Did God will the death of God's own child? Is child sacrifice ever warranted? Does God ever perpetrate violence and demand it as an act of faith from God's followers? If so, by what standards does one judge a violent act done in the name of God as faithful or evil? How does voluntary or involuntary martyrdom relate to these themes, if at all? If Jesus' act was performed on behalf of the whole world, does this imply that, finally, the whole world will be saved?

Though nuances inhere, there are currently five primary views of atonement in play in modern Christianity.

1. The first is *Christus Victor* or "Ransom." Human beings used their free will to rupture their relationship with God, and Satan used this opportunity to imprison us in sin and death. Sinless Jesus was sent as a "ransom" and won the victory over sin, death, and Satan.

2. The "satisfaction theory of atonement" was championed most famously in the eleventh century by Anselm the archbishop of Canterbury in his book *Cur Deus Homo* ("Why did God become human?"), and furthered by Thomas Aquinas in the thirteenth century. God created the universe in an orderly manner in which human beings are meant to honor and obey God. In the Garden of Eden episode, God's honor was offended and the universe was thrown off balance. Someone must satisfy the debt due God's offended honor. That someone has to be

infinite since God is infinite. Enter Jesus, the one who is both human and infinite. "By dying on the cross, Jesus, as a man, satisfied God's honor. As God, he provided the infinite payment necessary to satisfy an infinite debt" (Baker, 57).

3. The third model of atonement, Jesus as moral example, is associated with Peter Abelard (1079–1142) and employs the metaphor of courtly love. "Abelard wanted his listeners to think about God as loving, compassionate, and merciful. Consequently, Jesus lived, died, and rose again in order to reveal God's love to us. Everything Jesus said or did served as an example not only of how God behaves, but how we should behave too" (Baker, 60).

4. The model popularized by John Calvin (1509–1564), and the one probably most familiar to contemporary Christians, is penal substitution. Those familiar with or committed to the so-called Romans Road to Salvation will consider it the singular version of atonement theology: (a) "All have sinned and fall short of the glory of God" (Rom. 3:23); (b) the wages of sin is death (Rom. 6:23); (c) though all deserve eternal punishment, Jesus "acts as our substitute, taking on our sin and suffering our punishment so we don't have to" (Baker, 63).

5. Finally, the model of atonement made popular by authors such as Sharon Baker and Raquel St. Clair may be called an "antiviolent atonement theory." It lays the blame of Jesus' violent, unjust death at the feet of all of us human beings (rather than God or Satan) who are addicted to violence in the name not only of barbarous entertainment but also of political expediency. The salient features of this view of atonement (as enumerated by Baker) are as follows:

   a. "Jesus emptied himself of the right to live selfishly and gave his life in service to all creation" (Baker, 158).
   b. Jesus died as a consequence of human sin.
   c. Jesus asked God to forgive that sin, and God complied with Jesus' prayer.
   d. Jesus' salvific work undoes the sin of Adam and brings salvation on a cosmic level (Baker, 159).
   e. "Through his life, death, and resurrection, Jesus reveals to us the incomprehensible love of God . . . toward all creation. . . . God forgave all people universally, without condition and without exception" (Baker, 159). When human beings embrace this forgiveness, reconciliation and justice abound.

The evidence in 1 John (and the Gospel itself) probably cannot bear the weight imposed on it by those who would argue for a "theory of atonement," and certainly not a singular one. Lieu is wise to warn against overinterpreting the *hilasmos* language. Of the five models mentioned above, the Johannine Epistles (and Gospel) may have most in common with the fifth. "In 1 John, however, there is nothing to demand a sacrificial understanding . . . particularly as not only did God *send* (aorist) Jesus as a *hilasmos* (4:10), but he *is* (present) one (2:2)—past act and present reality. In all the emphasis is probably on the reconciliation thus made possible and not on any precise model of its method" (Lieu 1991, 64).

First John 2:15-17 may be less about asceticism than it is about care for the poor. Though readers are often tempted to focus on sexual lust in the passage, the better question is, how do sex and greed and lust combine to promote injustice? As Philo already noted: "For strong drink and gross eating accompanied by wine-bibbing, while they awaken the insatiable lusts of the belly, inflame also the lusts seated below it" (*Spec. Laws* 1.192). In our world as well, insatiable sexual lust and economic injustice are intertwined. Loader's depiction of the gluttonous banquets of the rich relates directly to the staggering enormity of human slavery and sex trafficking worldwide at present. The text lends urgency to our consideration of such issues by setting it in an eschatological context, noting that one's choices have ultimate consequences before God.

1 John 2:18—3:24: Love in Action

▋The Text in Its Ancient Context

Those who have left the community are antichrists and liars and do not love God. While they are not directly equated with "the world," by denying God they show that they love the world. What makes these apostates antichrists? Their Christology. Not only do they deny the Father and the Son and that Jesus is the Messiah (2:22), but they also deny the flesh of Jesus. For the author, it appears to be a short step from denying the importance of Christ's fleshly embodiedness to denying the importance of a fellow Christian's bodily needs. When one does this, one walks in the footsteps of Cain, who is associated with the evil one and traffics in fratricide (3:12-15). Wealthy Christians are to care for poorer Christians.

The ethical exhortation is set in an eschatological context. It is "the last hour" (2:18). The faithful community is able to do right because they are "christs" (2:20; 27), having been anointed by the Holy One. They know everything they need to know to abide and love; even more will be revealed to them when Jesus comes again (2:28; 3:2; cf. 1 Corinthians 13). They are on an ethical journey that has not yet been brought to fruition; in the end, they will be like Jesus. Jesus is pure, holy, and just (2:20; 3:3, 7).

It is clear, however, that the author of 1 John holds an apocalyptic worldview (like most New Testament authors). Like Paul, he understands that Christians live in a "middle period," the time between Christ's effective work on the cross and the full unveiling of the eschaton. There is a cosmic battle being waged between the forces of good and evil. Human beings can enlist with one or the other, but they cannot remain neutral. While the devil's days are numbered, he still wanders to and fro about the earth causing trouble for the faithful (cf. the figure of "the adversary," *ha-Satan*, in Job, and the devil in 1 Pet. 5:8). Even Christians must be on guard lest they inadvertently lend their energies to the work of the devil. When they slip up, they confess and are righted; this distinguishes them from those who have departed and abandoned Jesus entirely.

The leitmotif of 1 John is love. God loves us, as shown through the way Jesus has loved us (by laying down his life) and continues to love us (including advocating for us in our weakness). This love commandment dominates as it has "from the beginning." The latter is a favorite phrase of the author and is multivalent. Surely it means, at least, from the beginning of everything, since it defines God's character (1 John 4:16); from the beginning of creation; from the beginning of humanity's story (Cain and Abel are representative of the fruits of love and hate); from the beginning of the Son's particular work in the incarnation (cf. the Gospel of John); and quite possibly, from the beginning of the Johannine community, likely in Palestine, and continuing in the author's day: in Ephesus, according to some traditions. Love is foundational. It is also generative: note both the mention of God's seed (*sperma*) in 1 John 3:9 as well as the language of birth, children, and life throughout. Love is eternal and abiding. As noted earlier, the practical expression of love involves trusting in the name of Jesus and loving one another (3:23).

▌THE TEXT IN THE INTERPRETIVE TRADITION

First John 3:2 has been beloved by the mystics who longed to attain illumination and the beatific vision (Murphy, 59–60), while 1 John 3:3 (sometimes in concert with 2:16) has inspired asceticism among many church fathers, such as Tertullian and Augustine (Greer, 21–26).

First John 3:4-10 is one of the most difficult passages in 1 John. Verses 4-6 have appeared in debates both about the doctrine of the sinlessness of Jesus and about the doctrine of original sin. Furthermore, in it the author declares that Christians do not do sin (*ou poiei hamartian*) and cannot sin (*ou dynatai harmatanein*). Those who sin are children of the devil, do not do justice, and do not love. This proclamation is puzzling, given the author's insistence that one must not deny having sin (1:5-10) and his assurance that if they sin, Jesus will advocate for them (2:1-2). How is this apparent contradiction to be explained? Some suggest that the earlier discussion refers to a person's pre-Christian life as if that were in the past tense, whereas 3:4-10 refers to a person who has become a Christian. This fails to convince, however, because both the having sin in 1:8 and the doing sin in 3:4 are in the present tense. Another proposed solution depends on the language of abiding (*menō*). As long as one abides, one does not sin; when one does not abide, one sins. This notion of moving in and out of the state of abiding, however, does not make sense in Johannine terms. The word "abide" denotes stability and something God and Jesus are said to do as well. A third suggestion is to consider that, while the abiding might be stable, it is incomplete until the eschaton. Others find this explanation wanting, arguing that it applies to the cosmic level but not the individual (Lieu 2008, 132).

▌THE TEXT IN CONTEMPORARY DISCUSSION

The emphasis on care for those in poverty draws the contemporary reader's attention to gender, race, and disability concerns. Who is poor and why? Faith and love belong together and coalesce in a concern for economic justice. While the author may have only the Christian poor in mind, doesn't morality compel modern readers to both acknowledge the sectarian impulse in the text and move to universalizing the principle of concern for the poor? Johannes Beutler declares: "Christians living in affluence must share their material goods with their brothers and sisters beyond the boundaries of their Christian communities on a worldwide scale and challenge unjust social structures. . . . For the nations of the northern hemisphere, this responsibility means sharing their wealth with the nations of the south. But this commandment also applies to the developing nations that are characterized by vast inequality in material wealth. A rich ruling class often exploits the masses of the poor" (556–58).

1 John 4:1-6: Incarnation and Antichrists

▌THE TEXT IN ITS ANCIENT CONTEXT

First John 4:1-6 returns to the theme of 2:18-28. There the subjects were the last hour and the antichrists associated with it, who deny that Jesus is the Messiah and deny the Father and Son;

those who went out (from the Greek verb *exerchomai*) from the community (19); and a warning to abide and not fall under the spell of deceivers. Likewise, 1 John 4 depicts an urgent eschatological scenario (4:3) characterized by the activity of false prophets (4:1) who have "gone out [from *exerchomai* again] into the world." (Recall that in 1 John, "the world" represents a sphere where God's values are not regnant.) There are antichrists who apparently deny that Jesus has come in the flesh and do not confess Jesus (4:2-3). For this author, having the right Christology is not merely an academic exercise but is essential for acting justly, which is to say, loving in the way that God loves (*agapē* language occurs forty-eight times in 1 John). The denial of Jesus' fleshly existence along with the overwhelming use of "knowing" language (*ginōskō*, twenty-five times; *oida*, fifteen times) immediately raises the specter of docetic or gnostic Christology among opponents. It is no accident that the noun "knowledge" never appears in 1 John; the emphasis is on action. Knowing is doing, and knowing rightly is tied to acting rightly. Those who disembody Jesus easily disembody their neighbor. Certain ways of "knowing" cause arrogance and disdain of others in the community.

▌ THE TEXT IN THE INTERPRETIVE TRADITION

The insistence on proclaiming that Jesus came in the "flesh" (*sarx*; 1 John 4:2; 2 John 7) indicates that the opponents deny Jesus' flesh or separate the human Jesus from his role as the Christ.

Not surprisingly, docetic Christology also has implications for eucharistic theology, with its emphasis, in some traditions, on consuming Jesus' flesh and blood. First John 4:2 (and 2 John 7) also appear in debates about the virgin birth, the doctrine that Jesus was miraculously conceived by the Holy Spirit and that Mary remained a virgin until after he was born. In 1 John, the emphasis is on the fact of Jesus' physical birth, not on Mary's virginity (which is never mentioned). That is to say, docetic Christologies, with their disparagement of the flesh, would not tolerate a literal incarnation; clearly the author of 1 John insists on it and, therefore, lends support to those who argue for an actual human birth (if by miraculous conception: Sweeney).

▌ THE TEXT IN CONTEMPORARY DISCUSSION

First John's focus on the incarnation implies that Christians ought to be concerned with ecological matters (Lee). The prologue to John proclaims: "The Word became flesh [*sarx*] and tabernacled among us." Though Jesus is the unique Son of God, he is related to us insofar as we have become children of God through his blood. As the Son, he has authority over all flesh (*pas sarx*; 17:2). Since the prologue narrates the Word's participation in the creation of everything (John 1:3), "all flesh" presumably includes the whole created order, not just human beings (cf. Romans 8). First John eschews docetist theologies that denigrate the material order. Do we? Should human beings relate to the earth in a hierarchical, dominating fashion by which the earth exists merely as an object to be used in the gratification of human greed and gluttony as described in 1 John 2:16?

Ecofeminists argue that denigration of creation is usually connected to denigration of female bodies. The power dynamic of patriarchy involves a system of hierarchy where the male rules as lord (Latin *dominus*, tied to the word "dominate") and the female (and children) are subjects (objects, really) to be used as the male sees fit. Rape, of the earth or of people, is inherent in such a system. Postcolonialism extends the conversation to other bodies, colonized bodies.

The Gospel of John draws heavily from creation language in Genesis. There God created the first earth creature (*'adam*) from the ground (*'adamah*). The fall points to the tragic disruption of the synergistic relationship between humans with each other and humans with the earth (Trible). Jesus redeems this problematic situation from the prologue to the Garden, where Jesus and Mary become a new Adam and Eve. Given 1 John's apparent frustration with "the world," some might argue that ecological concerns are not in its purview. On the contrary, since the "world" signifies those ignorant of or in opposition to God's values, then

> this attitude of the world, to find its own answers and to create its own security outside the realm of light and truth, is the real cause for the exploitation of the earth in a manner that shows no concern for the commandment of neighbourly love. The endless ravaging of the earth for economic progress, and the consequential pollution of the earth, the atmosphere and the oceans, are all symptoms of the world's blindness, its mindless quest to establish a security of its own, to erect its own modern Tower of Babel. . . . Neighbourly love must take on a concrete form, and there is no way that people can continue to ravage their neighbour's environment and pollute the air that they must breathe and still say that they are walking in the light, that they are keeping the commandment of neighbourly love. (Pretorius, 273, 277)

1 John 4:7—5:12: The Church Defined by Love

■ THE TEXT IN ITS ANCIENT CONTEXT

This section of 1 John repeats numerous themes and images from earlier:

- The mark of being a child of God is to love one another.
- To love God is to obey God; to obey God is to love one another.
- God's love was "revealed" (1:2; 2:28; 3:2, 5, 8, 10) by sending his son Jesus to provide life (*zōē*) for God's children.
- Jesus is an "atoning sacrifice" (4:10; cf. 2:2).
- The ability to love depends on the abiding relationship that involves the believer, the Holy Spirit, God, and Jesus (4:13-15).
- God's love precedes and is the basis for the love that Christians manifest for one another (4:19).
- God is not visible to the human eye at this point in history except through acts of love (4:20); until the eschaton (and the full unveiling of God's face), the only way to surely connect to God is to practice loving with the expectation that practice will make perfect, eventually.
- Love and God go together; hate and God do not (20); fear and God do not (18).
- Proper christological confession is important and entails these beliefs about Jesus:
- He is the Messiah (5:1).
- He is the Son of God (5:5).
- He came in the flesh (5:6-7).
- Proper belief empowers one to overcome "the world" (5:4).

Thus no new topics are introduced except perhaps the water and blood (5:6-7). This may refer to John 19:34, where Jesus was stabbed in his side with the spear and water and blood came out. Even apart from that possible allusion, the language fits well in 1 John, where all the "begetting" language implies birth language, which involves both blood and water (cf. the woman in labor in John 16:21 and the womb [*koilia*] and water language in John 3:4; 7:38). Furthermore, the blood of Jesus has already been mentioned in chapter 1 in relation to his salvific death. By insisting on this earthy, earthly, wet, and bloody reality that Jesus experienced, the author may be emphasizing his actual death, thus countering once again a docetic Christology that insists that Jesus only "seemed" human. As often happens with the passage in John 19, some find baptismal and eucharistic allusions in the language. While this is possible, 1 John does not mention either ritual explicitly.

▌THE TEXT IN THE INTERPRETIVE TRADITION

As noted earlier, many over the centuries have interpreted the Gospel of John docetically. It may be that some in the community of 1 John already made this docetic move, thereby provoking the vitriol of the elder who considers these docetic Christians to be opponents and even antichrists.

Study Bibles note that some early Latin manuscripts insert the following just before the phrase "and these three are one": "There are three that testify in heaven, the Father, the Word, and the Holy Spirit." This is referred to as "The Johannine Comma" and reflects a later stage in textual transmission in which a scribe, familiar with trinitarian debates, makes a marginal note that subsequently enters the body of the text in some later Greek manuscripts and thus into the Authorized Version of the English Bible of 1611. It does not appear in most ancient texts and should not be considered original. Martin Luther dismissed it as an addition by "an ignoramus," by which he meant to refer to an early Catholic Christian who opposed Arianism (Posset, 247).

The capacious proclamation at 4:16 complexifies the epistle because, on the one hand, it has been interpreted as highly sectarian and dualistic, but now it appears to be the most expansive and universal of all New Testament literature. The latter accounts for its appeal over the centuries to Indians and its repeated translation into Sanskrit. Commenting on a new "presentation of the first letter of St. John in Sanskrit poetry and Indian symbolic idiom," G. Gispert-Sauch declares: "The text has a clear mystical resonance that cannot but appeal to all religious people specifically those nurtured in Indian religions, and the nature of its teaching has a certain universality that can be applied to different doctrinal contexts" (422).

▌THE TEXT IN CONTEMPORARY DISCUSSION

First John 4:16 may be the most famous verse in the epistles, if not the New Testament: "God is Love." As such, it touches on everything, from the individual-psychological to the radically communal. Writing from the perspective of a therapist, William Clough draws on 1 John 4. He concludes:

> 1 John 4:19 is the ultimate summation of the process of sanctification, and, one might suggest, the best possible outcome of counseling, therapy, or spiritual direction. We love because he first loved us. . . . The Logos shows itself therapeutically as love: the deep energy that motivates us to

seek spiritual direction, therapy, counseling, mentoring, education, advice, sermons, worship, and community. It lives in our affection for our children; our debt to our parents; our concern for one another; and our responsibility to the earth, to other species, and to God. Love challenges and convicts us. It is the living reality that drives and can ground "discourse" and "meaning-making" in existential psychotherapy and post-modernist psychology: It is the basic motivation which must be addressed in counseling. (Clough, 30)

Throughout this study, I have noted the author's tendencies toward dualistic, binary categories. This philosophical habit typically quickly degenerates into systems of hierarchies where one element is valued and empowered at the expense of the other: male versus female; white versus black; rich versus poor; this culture versus that culture; this religion versus that religion. Many contemporary thinkers (e.g., Fr. Richard Rohr of The Rohr Institute) are calling for unitive ways of thinking, replacing either/or modalities with both/and. Such approaches have great potential for addressing oppressive divisions of all kinds and invite readers to contemplate the challenging tension that Miroslav Volf has identified between "Johannine Dualism and Contemporary Pluralism."

1 John 5:13-21: Final Verses

▮ The Text in Its Ancient Context

First John 5:13 echoes the thesis statement of John 20:31 and connects back to 1:4. The author writes to engender belief, knowledge, and eternal life. He reminds the readers to be confident, even bold in prayer (cf. 3:21-22) and to pray for any fellow Christian who is sinning, but not "sinning to death." What is the difference? The author indicates that all injustice (*adikia*) is sin. When a Christian does not "do justice," does not love a brother or sister, she is not acting in accordance with God's will or loving the way God loves. That person needs to recognize that she is out of step with God and the community and is thereby affecting the whole group negatively. She needs to recognize her sin, rely on Christ's advocacy (2:2), and move back into harmonious relationship with God and neighbor. The result will be, as usual, life.

But there is a different kind of sin that leads to death: apostasy. Those who leave the Johannine community abandon their church and enlist with the world, which lies under the power of the evil one (5:19). They have not simply faltered momentarily but have severed their connection to life; their end is destruction. Those who abide with the community by definition do not sin in this way. As long as one abides, life is inevitable; as soon as one apostatizes, death is inevitable. The same distinction is made in 3:9. Again, there is a cosmic battle going on between God and Satan; as long as the readers remain in the Johannine community, they are protected by Jesus.

First John 5:21 may seem like a strange way to close the epistle, but it aptly concludes not only what immediately precedes it but also the whole letter. The readers have a choice: serve the true God or serve idols. This is reminiscent of the Old Testament, when Israelites were tempted to worship the gods of other nations or apostatize. The language is a trope and is often described in the metaphorical imagery of sexual immorality ("play the harlot," "commit adultery"). It is clear throughout 1 John that those who remain in the Johannine community do serve the true God (5:20), which leads to life and to "conquering the world"—a typically Johannine phrase that is never defined but that points to the Johannine understanding of the world as oppositional. In contrast, those who go out from the community serve Satan. Since he has power over the whole world (5:19), those who leave oppose Christ (i.e., they are antichrists) and instead adopt the values of Satan and his world: desire of the flesh, desire of the eyes, the pride in riches (2:16). The author closes by asking the readers: "Whom will you serve?"

■ THE TEXT IN THE INTERPRETIVE TRADITION

The textual transmission of 5:18 reveals that it has caused some consternation: Who is protecting whom? It makes the most sense to argue that Jesus, the Son of God, does the protecting. He is like those he is protecting because he is born of God as they are (both are described using a participle of the verb *gennaō ek tou theou*), but he is unique in that he is the only Son of God, whereas they are children. The concept that Jesus was "born of God" offended some thinkers as the christological debates of the later centuries developed, so one finds glosses in some manuscripts that make the text say that the believer protects himself (*heauton*); but that obviates the essential role played by Jesus in 1 John. A third option suggests that God is the protector: "This connection with John 17:15 seems close enough to lead to the conclusion that somehow 1 John 5:18 means that God keeps the believer" (Painter, 324).

Due to later trinitarian debates, some have tried to distinguish between Jesus' birth from God and the believer's birth from God by noting that the perfect participle of the verb is used for believers (*gegennēmenos*) and the aorist tense (*gennētheis*) for Jesus. That is, the perfect tense, on the one hand, is used for an action that occurred in the past but has continuing effect in the present (those who have been begotten, the effects of which are continuing). The aorist tense, on the other hand, refers to a single completed action in the past, without reference to an ongoing process. Centuries later, post-Nicene Christianity would resolve the debate by using the phrases "eternally begotten" and "begotten not made" to refer to the Son.

The reference to mortal sins calls Christians to serious reflection about sin, confession, and repentance, both individually and corporately. The later church distinguished between "mortal" sins (pride, covetousness, lust, envy, gluttony, anger, and sloth) and "venial" sins. Tertullian claims that John refers to murder, idolatry, injustice, apostasy, adultery, and fornication (Smith, 134).

■ THE TEXT IN CONTEMPORARY DISCUSSION

A number of important questions for contemporary Christians arise from this passage. Does the contemporary church adhere to a notion of mortal sin? If so, what should be added or deleted from the lists above, if anything?

How vital is intercessory prayer? "How seriously does the Church take its responsibility to intercede on behalf of a sinning brother or sister? What formal means of reconciliation and forgiveness are available and utilized with the Church?" (Thomas, 281–82).

Finally, what constitute idols in our contemporary context? Do wealth, status, power, ego, vanity, and nationalism qualify? Are there other false teachings or gods that tempt people away from God?

2 John

Introduction

This short book follows some of the themes addressed in 1 John (see the introduction to 1 John). For example, the call to love one another is an ancient command present from the beginning. It also warns of practicing this love with some caution; receiving or welcoming those who deceive can compromise the faith of both individuals and the community. The whole of this epistle is treated as a single sense unit.

■ THE TEXT IN ITS ANCIENT CONTEXT

Written in letter form, 2 John opens with the identification of the sender and receiver followed by a greeting that, in this case, appears as a benediction. But the atypical immediately captivates: Who is the "elder"? The author never names himself but assumes authority of some kind on the basis of advanced age or, perhaps, by virtue of an office. Verse 12 indicates that he plans to educate them more deeply in person (cf. Paul).

And what of the recipients, the *eklektē kyria* and her "children"? *Eklektē* (whence we derive the word "eclectic") means "chosen" or "elect." *Kyria* is the feminine form of *kyrios*, which means "sir" or "lord" or "master." Usually *eklektē kyria* is translated "elect lady" and assumed to refer metaphorically to the gathered church receiving the letter (as opposed to being addressed to a woman named Eclecta or Kyria), particularly because the letter closes with reference to "your elect sister," likely a reference to the author's own church community. The "children" of the elect lady probably refers to church members. The intimate, relational, familial language, quite typical of the Johannine literature, strikes the reader immediately. Furthermore, the personal tone, signified especially by the abundance of first-person constructions, is remarkable and lends a sense of immediacy to the letter.

The immediate preoccupation with truth looms large, as the word *alētheia* ("truth") appears five times in the first four verses. This author links truth and love together from the start (1, 3, 5-6) and assumes that these attributes tie Christians together into a cord that cannot be easily broken. To love one another is to walk in the commandment(s) (cf. John 15:12; 1 John 1:7). This does not imply a generalized love but rather a choosy love that embraces only those who agree with the author's vision of truth. Based on the author's language, one can delineate the characteristics of the two opposing groups: those who abide (who believe correctly) and those who are antichrists (those who oppose truth and promote falsehood).

Led by figures such as Irenaeus and Hippolytus, subsequent readers of the Johannine Epistles have expressed consistent fascination with the antichrist language, identifying characters from the historical to the fantastic and mythical as "*the* Antichrist." For the elder, however, "the antichrist" was not an individual character; rather, it described anyone who expressed a Christology incommensurate with the elder's own. Specifically, it denoted "those who do not confess that Jesus Christ has come in the flesh" (v. 7; cf. 1 John 2:18, 22; 4:3). These antichrists are deceivers; they are "many" (v. 7); and they are former members of this very community, known personally by the readers and elder (cf. 2:18, 22). Antichrists are probably Christian, since non-Christians are unlikely to deal in the details of various Christologies. Any Christian, then, can remain a christ (2:20, 27) or become an antichrist at any time (Koester forthcoming).

To summarize this dualistic picture: the elder and his sympathizers abide with the community and the inherited tradition, are marked by truth and love and obedience, have the Father and the Son, and deny hospitality to those deemed unorthodox in their Christology. The opponents are deceivers and antichrists who depart and who "go beyond" the christological tradition (v. 9) and try to tempt others to do the same; they do not have God.

The elder forbids the readers to extend hospitality to anyone espousing an alternative Christology. To receive that person is to become an antichrist; it has eschatological ramifications, namely, the loss of all heretofore accumulated rewards.

▉ The Text in the Interpretive Tradition

Although Polycarp (*Phil.* 1 34) followed the elder's lead in construing the antichrist as pluriform (using the term to refer to docetists, for example), the habit of envisioning a single political or religious figure as *the* Antichrist began early in Christian history and continues today. By combining traditions such as "the lawless one" of 2 Thessalonians and the beast described in Revelation 13, Christians have imagined a single person who represents pure evil, serving in the army of Satan in an apocalyptic eschatological battle between God and Satan. Sometimes the figure is Jewish (Hippolytus), sometimes Muslim, sometimes this or that Roman emperor. The pope as antichrist has enjoyed a long tenure beginning in the fourth century. Indeed, in the Middle Ages, Emperor Frederick II Hohenstaufen's publicists "gained an advantage by showing how the numerical value of the name *Innocencius papa* was 666, concluding that there can be no doubt that Innocent IV is the 'true Antichrist!'" (McGinn, 154). Luther, Calvin, Increase and Cotton Mather, and Jonathan Edwards all capitalized on this tradition. Those named as the Antichrist throughout history are too many to list, but include Hitler, Reagan, Elvis, and Saddam Hussein (Nichols, 81–83). The impetus of the original text, whose purpose was to insist on the humanity of Jesus and to emphasize the incarnation, has largely been eclipsed by the construction of the later Antichrist myth and rapture theology.

The insistence on embodiedness described in verse 7 has also fueled enduring and sometimes vociferous debates in Christian tradition about the virgin birth, the incarnation, and the real presence of Christ in the Eucharist (Painter, 350).

▉ The Text in Contemporary Discussion

The phrase identifying the addressee, *eklektē kyria*, may refer to a church leader named either Kyria ("lady") or Eclecta ("the elect"). If either word is a proper name, this would show the importance of female leadership in the early church. More likely, however, the phrase is a metaphor imaging the church as a lady (*kyria*) in relationship with her lord Jesus (*kyrios*). This image may offer a liberating trajectory regarding women, their value, and their experience. However, such language might simply entrench patriarchy where the male elder becomes "lord" over "lady church" (O'Day, 467).

The insistence on incarnation is important. Womanists and feminists know that theologies that view the body and soul as binary categories (as in docetism and Gnosticism) are always detrimental to women. The soul is valued and the body is denigrated as a hindrance to the soul (summarized in the pithy saying, *sōma sēma*—"the body is a tomb"). Women are associated with the bodily, which is to be controlled and subdued.

Second John's injunction against hospitality and his promotion of exclusionary practices toward opponents raise deep concern regarding current ethno-religious conflicts, whether it is the Catholic-Protestant conflict in Northern Ireland or Catholic-Muslim-Orthodox fighting in Yugoslavia (Slater, 511). However, our reading of 2 John today may evoke important questions about how to maintain group cohesion and draw healthy boundaries when destructive persons are allowed to wreak havoc on a community with impunity.

3 John

Introduction

See the introduction to 1 John for additional commentary regarding the connection of the three Johannine Epistles. Here again, the theme of discerning truth and being coworkers with the truth is emphasized. Gaias and Demetrius are commended for walking in the truth, while Diotrephes is accused of spreading false rumors. Again, the whole of this brief letter is treated as one sense unit.

▌ THE TEXT IN ITS ANCIENT CONTEXT

If one were to title this letter, it might be "Good Gaius, Dastardly Diotrephes, and Devoted Demetrius." Like 2 John, 3 John is a letter written by "the elder," but in this case to an individual, Gaius, "whom I love in truth" (cf. 2 John 1, where the same language is used of "the elect lady and her children"). The elder uses *agapē* language twice in the opening sentence. It is almost as if "Beloved" were the author's nickname for Gaius (1, 2, 5, 11) since he begins the next sentence with it as well.

As is customary in an epistle, the author follows the introduction with a prayer on behalf of Gaius and words of praise about his "walking in truth" (3, 4). The language of "walking" as a metaphor for ethical behavior is typical for the Johannine Epistles (cf. 1 John 1:6, 7; 2:6, 11; 2 John 4, 6). As in all of the epistles bearing the name of John and in the Gospel of John, concern for *truth* predominates (1, 3, 4, 8, and 12).

The body of the letter comprises verses 5-12. Immediately we learn that just as Gaius is beloved, he also loves fellow believers (v. 6), in accordance with the commandment of Christ so fundamental to the Johannine community (John 13:34; 1 John 3:11). Thus walking in truth is synonymous with loving. Gaius expresses his love in practical terms by showing hospitality to Christian missionaries: feeding, housing, and financially supporting them. This model was common in the early church.

Third John testifies to a power struggle in the church between the elder and Diotrephes. The elder has written to the church requesting that the church receive the missionaries and show them hospitality as Gaius has previously done. Diotrephes, however, does not recognize the elder's authority;

instead, he commands the community to reject hospitality to the missionaries or be expelled. Many details remain obscure, including whether or not Gaius is subject to Diotrephes' power. Since he implies that Gaius is his child (v. 4), one wonders if the elder converted him. No specific church offices are mentioned in the letter, but it attests to the struggle regarding the best way to structure Christian communities both locally and at a broader level.

Unlike 1 and 2 John, 3 John does not refer to false teachings or particular christological claims. In fact, neither the word *Jesus* nor *Christ* appears in the letter (NRSV fills it in at v. 7, but the Greek word *Christos* is not there). The author exhorts Gaius not to imitate evil (associated with Diotrephes), but good (modeled by Demetrius, who may be the bearer of the letter).

The letter concludes with almost identical words as 2 John 12 about not writing more but meeting in person. This is followed by a word of peace, greetings from the elder's church, and a request that Gaius share the elder's greetings with those whom he knows personally.

▋ The Text in the Interpretive Tradition

Citations of 3 John are rare, though verse 2 has appeared occasionally. Some imagine in verse 2 a distinction between the prosperity of the body and the prosperity of the soul and quickly move to asceticism (Tertullian and Augustine). The Benedictine Bede saw prosperity as a communal category so that prosperity was a way to gift others in need. Debates arise about the relationship between spiritual health and physical health, in some cases leading to the founding of medical institutions or healing movements, as in the case of Carrie Judd Montgomery. Montgomery (1858–1946), was a leader in the Divine Healing movement and an influence in Pentecostalism. She began opening healing homes in the 1880s. The translation of the phrase *peri pantōn* leads to different stances. Those who translate it as "above all things" see God as supporting an emphasis on financial prosperity (Oral Roberts); those who translate it as "with respect to all things" do not (Landrus).

▋ The Text in Contemporary Discussion

Third John addresses questions about hospitality as an ethical imperative for Christians. Christians are called to love not only those whom they know but also those who are "strangers" to them. It also raises questions about how Christians are to support financially those who are called to teach and preach the gospel near and far.

Third John also demands that individual Christians and communities guard against those who have a "passion for preeminence" (Jones, 272), who "love being first" (*philoproteuō*) in church leadership. Conflict is inevitable, but is there a better way to address it than the elder's strategy of vituperation (v. 10, "talking nonsense about us with evil words," author translation).

Finally, the interpretation of verse 2 raises questions about the relationship between faith and physical well-being as well as faith and financial well-being. Those committed to the "prosperity gospel" (also known as "the health and wealth gospel") suggest that faithful believers should expect physical and financial deliverance. Others link holiness with poverty. Are Christians free or even obligated to succeed financially? Does wealth necessarily cause spiritual injury? Is poverty a sign of a lack of faith or a sign of blessedness?

The field of disability studies has taught us to ask these questions about physical health as well. Should those who have physical or mental disabilities seek physical healing to conform to "normal" bodies, or does physical suffering bring holiness (cf. 2 Corinthians 12)?

Works Cited

Baker, Sharon. 2013. *Executing God: Rethinking Everything You've Been Taught about Salvation and the Cross.* Louisville: Westminster John Knox.

Beutler, Johannes, SJ. 2004. "1, 2, and 3 John." In *Global Bible Commentary*, edited by Daniel Patte, 553–58. Nashville: Abingdon.

Clark-Soles, Jaime. 2003. *Scripture Cannot Be Broken: The Social Function of the Use of Scripture in the Fourth Gospel.* Leiden: Brill.

Clough, William R. 2006. "To Be Loved and to Love." *Journal of Psychology and Theology* 34, no. 1:23–31.

Gispert-Sauch, G., S.J. 1987. "St John's Nectar in Indian Flavour." *Vidyajyoti* 51:421–24.

Greer, Rowan A. 2005. "Sighing for the Love of Truth: Augustine's Quest." In *God, Truth, and Witness: Engaging Stanley Hauerwas*, edited by L. Gregory Jones, Reinhard Hütter, and C. Rosalee Velloso Ewell, 13–34. Grand Rapids: Brazos.

Hill, Charles E. 2004. *The Johannine Corpus in the Early Church.* Oxford: Oxford University Press.

Jones, Peter Rhea. 2009. *1, 2 & 3 John.* Macon, GA: Smith & Helwys.

Koester, Craig R. 2008. *The Word of Life: A Theology of John's Gospel.* Grand Rapids: Eerdmans.

———. Forthcoming. "The Antichrist Theme in the Johannine Epistles and Its Role in Christian Tradition." In *Communities in Dispute: Current Scholarship on the Johannine Epistles*, edited by R. Alan Culpepper and Paul N. Anderson. Atlanta: Society of Biblical Literature.

Landrus, Heather L. 2002. "Hearing 3 John 2 in the Voices of History." *Journal of Pentecostal Theology* 11, no. 1:70–88.

Lee, Dorothy. 2010. "Ecology and the Johannine Literature." *St. Mark's Review* 212, no. 2:39–50.

Lieu, Judith. 1991. *The Theology of the Johannine Epistles.* New Testament Theology. Cambridge: Cambridge University Press.

———. 2008. *1, 2, and 3 John: A Commentary.* Louisville: Westminster John Knox.

Loader, William. 1992. *The Johannine Epistles.* London: Epworth.

———. Forthcoming. "The Significance of 2:15-17 for Understanding the Ethics of 1 John." In *Communities in Dispute: Current Scholarship on the Johannine Epistles*, edited by R. Alan Culpepper and Paul N. Anderson. Atlanta: Society of Biblical Literature.

McGinn, Bernard. 1994. *Antichrist: Two Thousand Years of the Human Fascination with Evil.* San Francisco: HarperSanFrancisco.

Murphy, Francis X. 1984. "The Patristic Origins of Orthodox Mysticism." *Mystics Quarterly* 10, no. 2:59–63.

Nichols, Stephen J. 2001. "Prophecy Makes Strange Bedfellows." *JETS* 44, no. 1:75–85.

O'Day, Gail. 2012. "1, 2, and 3 John." In *Women's Bible Commentary*, edited by Carol A. Newsom, Sharon H. Ringe, and Jacqueline Lapsley, 622–24. 2nd ed. Louisville: Westminster John Knox.

Painter, John. 2002. *1, 2, and 3 John.* Sacra Pagina. Collegeville, MN: Liturgical Press.

Posset, Franz. 1985. "John Bugenhagen and the *Comma Johanneum.*" *CTQ* 49, no. 4:245–51.

Pretorius, N. F. 1998. "Redemption of the Earth or from the Earth? The Gospel of John and the Johannine Epistles." *Scriptura* 66:269–78.

Rensberger, David. 2001. *The Epistles of John*. Louisville: Westminster John Knox.

Slater, Thomas B. 2007. "1–3 John." In *True to Our Native Land: An African American New Testament Commentary*, edited by Brian K. Blount, Cain Hope Felder, Clarice J. Martin, and Emerson B. Powery, 496–517. Minneapolis: Fortress Press.

Smith, D. Moody. 1991. *First, Second, and Third John*. IBC. Louisville: Westminster John Knox.

St. Clair, Raquel. 2008. *Call and Consequences: A Womanist Reading of Mark*. Minneapolis: Fortress Press.

Sweeney, James P. 2003. "Modern and Ancient Controversies over the Virgin Birth of Jesus." *BSac* 160:142–58.

Thomas, John Christopher. 2004. *Pentecostal Commentary on 1 John, 2 John, 3 John*. Cleveland: Pilgrim.

Trible, Phyllis. 1986. "A Love Story Gone Awry." In *God and the Rhetoric of Sexuality*, 72–143. Minneapolis: Fortress Press.

Volf, Miroslav. 2005. "Johannine Dualism and Contemporary Pluralism." *Modern Theology* 21:189–217.

Von Wahlde, Urban C. 2010. *The Gospel and Letters of John*. 3 vols. Grand Rapids: Eerdmans.

JUDE

Pheme Perkins

Introduction

A warning against the false teachers who would arise at the end of days concludes the collection of seven letters in the Christian canon attributed to Peter, James, the brother of the Lord, John, the son of Zebedee, and Jude, the brother of James (Mark 6:3). Though the author of 2 Peter employed its material, Jude is rarely mentioned in early Christian authors or read in worship services today. Unlike the Pauline Epistles, which are targeted to specific churches or individuals, the so-called Catholic Epistles are addressed to churches in a broad region. Those attributed to brothers of Jesus give voice to a Greek-speaking Jewish Christianity that had become marginalized by the second century (Perkins, 1–2, 141–45).

Visions of the end of days connected with the figure of Enoch (Gen. 5:22) circulated widely among first-century Jews, so it is not surprising that Jude adopts a prophecy from Enoch (v. 15; *1 En.* 1:9). The author also knows popular Jewish legends about the fallen angels responsible for the evils of the preflood generation, as well as a tale that the devil attempted to wrest the body of Moses from the archangel Michael (v. 9). In that episode, Satan, acting out his role as prosecutor (Job 1:6-7), apparently charged Moses with the murder of the Egyptian (Exod. 2:12). No murderer should enjoy divine burial (Deut. 34:5-6). By using these dramatic stories, Jude underlines the serious evil at work in the false teachers (vv. 8, 10, 12, 16; Painter and deSilva, 208–17). This polemical rhetoric (vv. 5-16) makes it difficult to determine what the specific points of dispute were (Thurén). Certainly, Jude's demand that readers exclude false teachers from the communal meal (*agapē*) because their presence defiles indicates that the opponents are part of the local church (v. 12). Matthew 18:15-17 has such a ban on sinners who will not listen to the voice of the community, as does 1 Cor. 5:3-5, 11, in a case of extreme immorality. Therefore most interpreters conclude that the false teaching more likely involved Christian conduct than points of doctrine (Painter and deSilva, 183–84).

Several phrases in the letter's appeal to the audience envisage the difficulty that a postapostolic generation may have in preserving a tradition ("faith") entrusted to them (vv. 3, 20; Kraftchick, 62–65). In addition to the warnings embedded in familiar stories from the Torah, Jude reminds readers that "the apostles of our Lord Jesus Christ" had predicted the rise of such scoffers at the end of days (vv. 17-18). By presenting this exhortation in the form of an apostolic letter, the author suggests that its message enjoys comparable authority. The concluding doxology (vv. 24-25) follows a familiar liturgical pattern already employed in the Pauline Epistles (Rom. 16:25-27; Phil. 4:20; 1 Tim. 1:17; 6:15-16). However, Jude lacks the concluding greetings that ordinarily precede the liturgical-sounding phrases that conclude those letters. That omission suggests that this piece was intended for general circulation.

Jude follows a standard pattern (Bauckham, 3).

Greeting (vv. 1-2)

Opening stating the occasion for writing (vv. 3-4)

Body of the letter, establishing judgment awaiting the impious (vv. 5-19)

Three examples: wilderness generation, Sodom and Gomorrah, death of Moses

Three additional examples: Cain, Balaam, Korah

Two prophecies of judgment against false teachers: Enoch, the apostles

Conclusion, exhortation to the recipients (vv. 20-23)

Doxology (vv. 24-25)

Jude 1-25

Because the book of Jude is just one chapter, all verses will be dealt with as a single sense unit.

▌ THE TEXT IN ITS ANCIENT CONTEXT

The greeting of the letter (vv. 1-2) identifies the sender as "brother of James" rather than "brother of the Lord," as James was commonly known (Gal. 1:19), suggesting that this work is directed to Jewish Christian churches that revered James (Mark 6:3). Instead of the familiar "grace and peace" of the Pauline letter, Jude has an augmented Jewish formula, "mercy, peace, and love," but retains the two-part reference to the Father and Jesus Christ. The expression "kept safe" in Jesus Christ strikes the ominous note that believers must be protected against the end-time ravages of the wicked (Fuchs and Reymond, 155).

In verses 3-4, the author suggests that the danger of false teachers infiltrating the community has forced him to break off an exposition of Christian salvation to compose this warning. He telegraphs the two sections that follow: (a) evidence from ancient Scripture and prophecy for the condemnation of such persons; and (b) appeal to the recipients to resist their influence. The charges, turning grace into the occasion for immorality and denial of "the only Master," probably meaning God (v. 25), and the Lord Jesus, reflect a general disdain for God's commandments (cf. Titus 1:16).

Verses 5-8 describe divine judgment against the rebellious. The first three examples of destruction employ a schema in which those who had experienced God's salvation rebel and are destroyed: the

Israelites in the wilderness, through lack of faith (Num. 14); the fallen angels, who desert their proper place (Gen. 6:1-4) out of lust for human women; and the people of Sodom and Gomorrah, who are punished for unnatural sexuality. Imprisonment of the angels prior to judgment belongs to the Enoch material (*1 En.* 6–19). Verse 8 applies the examples to the present by providing three corresponding vices, though not in the same order, "defile flesh" (= fallen angels); "reject authority" (= that of Moses), and "slander glorious ones" (= the demand that Lot turn over his angelic visitors; Bauckham, 48–55).

In verses 9-11, the woe against those who are acting like irrational beasts and who are primed to reap the consequences that befell those led astray by Balaam (Deut. 23:3-6), or the rebellious Israelites at Korah (Num. 16:1-3), invokes an apocryphal tradition concerning the burial of Moses. Satan attempts to snatch the body of this murderer (Exod. 2:11-15) from the archangel Michael. Patristic sources (Clement of Alexandria, Didymus the Blind, Origen) attribute the story to a *Testament of Moses* that is no longer extant. Michael's response, a phrase from Zech. 3:2 (LXX), charges Satan with blasphemy for putting himself forward as judge against the Lord (Bauckham, 60–67).

Verses 12-13 include a warning to guard against false teachers, whose presence in the community corrupts its most sacred ritual, the "love feasts" or communal meal. A catalog of striking images builds to the rhetorical climax, eternal confinement in darkness for such brazen individuals.

Readers should not be taken off guard, according to verses 14-19, since God's judgment against such impiety has been prophesied from the earliest days, from "the seventh from Adam, Enoch," up to the apostles themselves. The rhetorical climax, which declares this wickedness evidence of the end-time and describes the schismatics as "without Spirit," suggests that Jude is not an appeal for their conversion.

However, all are not lost. The final words of encouragement and ethical advice to the community in verses 20-23 include the possibility that some can be rescued from the fiery judgment, which otherwise awaits them. Ancient scribes found verses 22-23a problematic: the three-clause exhortation to "convince, save, and have mercy" found in some manuscripts appears to be a clarification of a problematic two-clause sentence, "saving from fire, having mercy," that alluded to Zech. 3:1-5 (LXX).

Jude 24-25 concludes with a traditional doxology (cf. Rom. 16:25) that has been modified to underline the author's concern that his audience remain firm in their faith until the Lord's coming in judgment.

▌THE TEXT IN THE INTERPRETIVE TRADITION

Both its attribution to a little-known figure and the treatment of Jewish Christianity as heretical by later church fathers may explain why Jude plays no role in later Christian worship or theology. Doubts about its place in the canon focused on the appeals to the legend about the death of Moses and to the authority of Enoch. John Calvin bolstered the apostolic authority of Jude by identifying its author as the apostle mentioned in Luke 6:16 and Acts 1:13.

▌THE TEXT IN CONTEMPORARY DISCUSSION

The theological emphasis on a "deposit of faith" received from the apostles coupled with polemic invective against "false teachers" whose views are never directly confronted makes Jude problematic for modern readers who seek churches that welcome diversity. Some respond by highlighting comparable positions in Paul's Epistles and emphasizing the need for Christians to retain an ethical holiness that could be undermined by pluralism (e.g., Bauckham). Jude also provides an opening to the Jewish matrix in which Christianity was born. Instruction in piety does not stop with the Jewish canon but extends to the apocryphal Jewish traditions concerning Moses and Enoch.

Works Cited

Bauckham, Richard J. 1983. *Jude, 2 Peter*. WBC 50; Waco, TX: Word.

Fuchs, Eric, and Pierre Reymond. 1980 *Le deuxième épitre de Saint Pierre. L'épître de Saint Jude.* Commentaire du Nouveau Testament Deuxième série XIIIb. Neuchâtel: Delachaux et Niestlé.

Kraftchick, Steven J. 2002. *Jude, 2 Peter*. Nashville: Abingdon.

Painter, John, and David deSilva. 2012. *James and Jude.* Grand Rapids: Baker Academic.

Perkins, Pheme. 1995. *First and Second Peter, James, and Jude.* Louisville: Westminster John Knox.

Thurén, Lauri. 1997. "Hey Jude! Asking for the Original Situation and Message of a Catholic Epistle." *NTS* 43:451–65.

REVELATION

Barbara R. Rossing

Introduction

The apocalyptic book of Revelation is one of the most disputed books of the Bible. Full of mysterious and bizarre symbolism, its visions have inspired artists and musicians as well as doomsday prophets and activists. Revelation was one of the latest books to be included in the biblical canon.

The book consists of a series of visions experienced by a prophetic leader, John, while he was on the island of Patmos, off the coast of western Turkey. Early tradition dates this book to the end of the first century, late in the reign of the emperor Domitian (95 CE; Irenaeus, *Against Heresies* 5.30.3). This was a time when other Jewish apocalypses such as *2 Baruch* and *4 Ezra* were also being written, in response to the trauma of Rome's destruction of Jerusalem in 70 CE. Revelation's label of "Babylon" for Rome—invoking the ancient empire that had destroyed Jerusalem six hundred years earlier—offers the strongest internal evidence, albeit implicit, for a date later than 70 CE (Collins 1984, 85).

The author's name, John, is the same as that of several other New Testament figures. In later Christian tradition he came to be identified with the apostle John as a way of affirming the book's place in the canon. From early times, however, interpreters realized he was likely not the same person as the author of the Gospel of John, since his Greek style of writing is so different. He makes no claim to be an apostle; his references to the apostles (18:20, 21:14) do not include himself. He is certainly Jewish, as evidenced by his hundreds of scriptural allusions and his advocacy of strict observance of Jewish purity laws (Frankfurter 2011). John's idiosyncratic Greek leads some scholars to suggest Greek may not be his first language. He may have been a Jewish refugee from Palestine who settled in Asia Minor in the aftermath of the Roman-Jewish war.

Writing at the height of imperial prosperity in Asia Minor, John proclaims the message of hope that Rome's unjust reign would last only a little while longer, and that Rome had already been defeated by the nonviolent victory of Jesus the Lamb. Unlike other ancient apocalypses, John's message is not a secret to be sealed up until the end (in contrast to the apocalyptic book of Daniel; see Dan 12:4). Rather, as a public prophetic letter, Revelation is to be "read aloud" in the communities to which it is addressed (Rev. 1:3).

Several literary genres characterize Revelation. The first word of the book, "apocalypse," literally means revealing, or pulling back a curtain. Apocalypses were a popular type of literature for Jews and others in the ancient world. Apocalypses communicate their message not by logical proofs or arguments but by means of visionary journeys and pictures, creating an alternative "world of vision" (Schüssler Fiorenza 1991, 22). They typically use exaggerated imagery in order to heighten a sense of urgency and call readers to commitment and action.

The book also calls itself "prophecy," a second genre, which may reflect a circle of itinerant or resident Christian prophets in the cities of Asia Minor (as evidenced by other early Christian texts such as the *Ascension of Isaiah*; Bauckham 1993a, 84–85). Like other biblical prophets, John's primary purpose in writing prophecy was not to predict future events but rather to wake people up to the peril of their present situation. In John's view, faithfulness to God necessitated uncompromising resistance in the midst of the Roman Empire. Rival Christian prophets in these same communities apparently preached a very different message, permitting greater participation in Roman culture. John wants the audience to accept his prophetic interpretation of their situation.

A third genre is that of epistle or letter. John employs the format of a letter to communicate his prophetic message, much like the letters of the apostle Paul. From the island isolation of Patmos, John could not visit Christian communities in cities of Asia Minor (Turkey). So he communicates by writing a letter to them. The epistolary framework at the beginning and end (Rev 1:4-6; 22:10-12) underscores the book's character as a prophetic letter.

Because Revelation does not unfold in linear fashion, it can be difficult to outline. Numbered sequences of seven seals, seven trumpets, and seven bowls, as well as messages to seven churches, may have provided a structure helpful for those listening to the oral performance of the book. The book may follow a concentric or chiastic structure, a model popular in antiquity, in which the end of the book reprises the beginning (Schüssler Fiorenza 1998, 175). The book's chronology includes flashbacks to earlier events, such as the battle in heaven narrated in chapter 12. Revelation unfolds in cyclical or spiral fashion, often showing the same series of judgments from different angles, rather like a kaleidoscope. Each cycle of visions includes warnings as well as hymns, blessings, and promises.

Like other apocalypses, the book has a narrative framework. It tells a story (Barr 1998, 1)—the story of the Lamb Jesus who defeats evil and leads the community on a great exodus out of the unjust empire, personified as a dragon. The narrative journey ends in a utopic new city, the bridal new Jerusalem, with a river of life and a healing tree in a renewed creation. The entire book draws on prophetic cadences from the Hebrew Bible, without ever quoting Scripture directly. Stories of the exodus plagues, Danielic beasts, exile in Babylon, and other biblical narratives are remapped onto John's own time.

Creation and the earth play a central role in the dramatic conflict. In one of the most spectacular scenes in chapter 12, earth itself becomes a hero—coming to the aid of a mythic woman who represents God's people. Revelation's plagues of bloody oceans, giant hailstones, and other ecological catastrophes can give the impression that the book condemns the earth to destruction at the hands of a wrathful God. Such destruction has been the focus of many interpretations, including the recent best-selling *Left Behind* novels. But Revelation is clear that God created the world and everything in it. The book describes not the destruction of the earth but earth's liberation and renewal, with the proclamation that "the time has come . . . for destroying those who destroy the earth" (Rev. 11:18; my translation, here and throughout, unless otherwise noted).

Interpretive History

No other book of the Bible has had such a profound and wide-ranging impact on literature, art, music, theology, liturgy, politics, psychology, spirituality, and popular culture. Throughout the centuries, interpreters have disagreed about whether the visions refer to John's own time or to future ages, or whether they are timeless truths for all ages.

From earliest times, many have attempted to "figure out" the mysterious symbols of Revelation as if they were a timetable of future events. Beginning in the second century, followers of the New Prophecy, or Montanist movement, predicted the descent of the new Jerusalem in their own area of Asia Minor, while other early interpreters expected a future millennial paradise on earth.

Augustine and others critiqued such movements as "chiliast" (from the Greek word for one thousand, a reference to the millennium) and successfully shifted interpretations in a more timeless, spiritual direction. Allegorical readings predominated for the next five hundred years, with the understanding that the church was already living in the millennium.

Futurist interpreters resurfaced again in the Middle Ages and Reformation. Some even predicted specific dates when Christ would return. The landscape of futurist interpreters included Joachim of Fiore, followers of St. Francis of Assisi, Anabaptists, and even Martin Luther, who correlated specific images of Revelation with enemies in his own time. Two recent American denominations have origins tied to futurist interpretations of Revelation: the Seventh-Day Adventists (founded by William Miller, who predicted the return of Christ in the 1840s) and the Jehovah's Witnesses.

The premillennialist dispensationalist line of interpretation was developed in the nineteenth century by British preacher John Nelson Darby and popularized by the *Scofield Reference Bible*. Premillennialists view the millennium as a literal event still to happen in the future (disagreeing with Augustine and others who view the church as already living in the millennium); they view history as divided into distinct dispensations or epochs, with the present time a "parenthesis" between dispensations that will end with the so-called rapture of Christians up to heaven.

One of the key tenets of premillennialists since 1948 has been that the nation of Israel plays a pivotal role in what they view as God's prophetic plan. Revelation's suggestion of a battle of

Armageddon provides the playbook for their understanding of a future World War III, read through zealously nationalistic and sometimes violent lenses. Today's radio preachers, televangelists, prophecy novels, and rapture websites correlate current political events with Revelation according to Darby's system, based also on his reading of Daniel 9.

Most scholars reject premillennialism. They point out that the book's images have multiple meanings, and were not intended as a futurist script or timetable for geopolitical events in this century. The Greek word for what Revelation "shows" or "makes known" in the very first verse of the book is the same as the word for "signs" in John's Gospel. The whole book may be intended to be read at a deeper sign level, more like poetry or art than any predictive script. Essayist Kathleen Norris makes the case for poetic interpretation.

> This is a poet's book, which is probably the best argument for reclaiming it from fundamentalists. It doesn't tell, it shows, over and over again, its images unfolding, pushing hard against the limits of language and metaphor, engaging the listener in a tale that has the satisfying yet unsettling logic of a dream. (Norris, ix)

Among the many poets, artists, liturgists, and musicians who have loved Revelation and whose interpretations continue to be influential are Hildegard of Bingen, Emily Dickinson, Christina Rossetti, William Blake, George Friedrich Handel, Charles Wesley, as well as Thomas Dorsey and many anonymous composers of African American spirituals and blues music. Some interpreters critique pietistic and poetic interpretations as collapsing Revelation into nothing but a privatistic message of personal salvation. But the book's power as public liturgy also resonates in churches and communities through their work, especially in situations of suffering. The liberationist poetry of Guatemalan Julia Esquivel and others shows that poetic interpretations can also foster liberation. Liberationist voices have turned to Revelation as a message of hope for justice overcoming oppression, as evidenced by the African American and feminist interpretations, and voices from South Africa and Latin America.

Triumphalistic, even violent readings have also played a role in history. Again and again, the book has proved irresistible to those in power, sometimes providing biblical justification for attacks on their enemies. After 2001, for example, Revelation's critique of "Babylon" was used by some to make the case for the United States' invasion of Iraq, noting that ancient Babylon is located in today's Iraq. Fanatical self-proclaimed prophets such as David Koresh of the Branch Davidians and others have also laid claim to the book.

No single interpretive strategy can encompass the richness of Revelation. Rhetorical readings of Revelation that investigate its persuasive power in its original first-century context may provide the most promising criteria for interpretive communities adjudicating competing readings today. Seeking analogies to John's rhetorical situation can bring certain readings to the fore while problematizing others. I especially encourage reading from the perspective of marginalized people, and with communities and movements who have found in this book a profound message of hope—including ecological hope for our life together on this earth. John's emphasis that God is the one who creates the world—and who will not leave the world behind—makes a hermeneutics of hope appropriate for reading the book today.

Revelation 1:1-8: Prologue

■ THE TEXT IN ITS ANCIENT CONTEXT

John writes as a visionary. The book gives testimony to "what he saw" (1:2). The literary prologue of 1:1-8 has strong echoes in the epilogue of 22:6-21.

John sets up a chain of authority that validates the book. He claims he is not writing for himself but on behalf of God, who gave the revelation to Jesus Christ. An angel delivers the revelation to God's "slaves," or servants—perhaps a reference to early Christian prophets (Schüssler Fiorenza 2001, 40), among whom John names himself.

John intends his apocalypse to be read aloud to the community, as a prophetic letter. The blessing for the person who "reads aloud" (1:3) underscores the oral character of Revelation. Revelation contains seven such blessings (1:3; 14:13; 16:15; 19:9; 20:6; 22:7, 14). "How fortunate" may be a better translation than "blessed." Blessings were prophetic forms familiar from the Hebrew Scriptures, with the power to enact what they describe. Together, "the seven beatitudes comprise a kind of summary of Revelation's message" (Bauckham 1993a, 30).

The characterization of the book as "prophecy" (1:3) situates it in the tradition of Hebrew Bible prophets. John may also be contrasting his message with that of Rome's official political prophets, such as Virgil and Horace, who prophesied about the Roman Empire's eternal destiny and divine favor (Georgi 1986). John in effect says no to the claim by Roman prophets that Emperor Augustus's reign had already ushered in a new eschatological age of peace for the whole world.

Beginning in 1:4-6, John follows the typical letter format used also by the apostle Paul, marking the entire book as a letter. The sender first identifies himself (John), then names the recipients (the seven churches that are in Asia), and then gives a greeting, followed by a doxology. "Grace and peace" is the typical Pauline greeting. The greeting is threefold: from God, the seven spirits, and Jesus.

John's use of peculiar Greek grammar in 1:4 is probably deliberate. Literally translated, the greeting from God is "from He the Is and He the Was" (incorrectly using a nominative case following the preposition *apo*). John often defies grammatical rules in ways that would have sounded strange to Greek ears (see also Rev. 1:11, 13, 15; 2:13, 20; 3:12; 4:1; 8:9; 14:7, 19; 19:6, 20). English translations that smooth out his Greek may do John a disservice, since his use of nonstandard Greek appears intentional. He may be calling attention to scriptural allusions to create a "biblical effect" (Beale, 103), or he may be subverting grammar rules of the dominant culture as a form of protest or resistance (Callahan 1995).

Jesus is the faithful "witness" (1:5), a term of crucial importance throughout the book. The Greek word "witness" (*martys*) can also mean "martyr." John aims to inspire hearers themselves to become witnesses, even to the point of martyrdom. Jesus was martyred ("by his blood," 1:5). John may expect martyrdom for his followers, although he is able to name only one actual martyr, Antipas, in the church of Pergamum (2:13).

Jesus also is "the one ruling the kings of the earth" (1:5)—a daring claim in the face of the Roman Empire's hegemonic rule, and expressed already in the present tense. John also ascribes political values of "glory" and "dominion" (1:6) to Jesus, values ascribed to Rome in imperial hymns and celebrations.

Throughout the book, John continually shapes the Christian community as a countercultural community. God's people are called a "kingdom of priests" (1:6; a theme that will recur in 5:10 and 20:6; see also 1 Pet. 2:5, 9). John draws this imagery from the exodus story in which God liberates Israel from Egypt to be a "priestly kingdom" (Exod. 19:6), and from Isaiah's description of God's people as priests in the return from exile in Babylon (Isa. 61:6).

Two liturgical exclamations of "Amen!" bracket a description of Jesus' coming with the clouds (based on Dan. 7:13). "Look! He is coming" is present tense, suggesting a coming already underway.

Only twice in Revelation does God speak directly (1:8; 21:5-7). "I am the Alpha and Omega" uses the first and last letters of the Greek alphabet to underscore God's all-encompassing presence. God is the first and the last, the beginning and the end (see also 1:17; 21:6; 22:13).

■ THE TEXT IN THE INTERPRETIVE TRADITION

In the sixteenth century, Reformer Martin Luther drew his doctrine of the priesthood of all the baptized from the proclamation of God's people as a "kingdom of priests" (Rev. 1:6), similar to the "royal priesthood" of 1 Pet. 2:5 and 2:9. Luther's notion that "we are all priests" (*Babylonian Captivity of the Churches*) became a central tenet for Protestants, countering the medieval Catholic division of Christians into separate estates of clergy (the "religious") and laity.

The Alpha and Omega of Rev. 1:8 have inspired visionary art and music throughout Christian history. The fourth-century Latin hymn "Of the Father's Love Begotten" describes Christ as "Alpha and Omega," the source, the ending. The prevalence of the Alpha and Omega in earliest Christian art, including catacomb art, may reflect its use as an anti-Arian symbol in christological controversies (Kinney, 202). A mosaic of Christ as the Alpha and Omega adorns the late fourth-century Church of St. Pudenziana in Rome, along with other images from Revelation (Klein, 160). In the twelfth century, the most influential medieval interpreter of Revelation, Joachim of Fiore, used the Alpha and Omega in the "psaltery with ten strings," a figure that came to him in a mystical vision (Kovacs and Rowland). Methodist hymnist Charles Wesley used the Alpha and Omega image in his "Love Divine, All Loves Excelling" ("Take away the love of sinning / Alpha and Omega be").

■ THE TEXT IN CONTEMPORARY DISCUSSION

Scholars differ on how Revelation understands Jesus' "coming" (1:7). John switches freely among past, present, and future tenses throughout the book in a manner typical of the visionary language of apocalypses.

A traditional view has seen Revelation as primarily referring to Jesus' "second coming" (a term never used in Revelation), an eschatological future event when Jesus will come to judge. The apocalyptic vision of the figure coming on the clouds lends support to such a view, drawing on traditional Jewish eschatology from Daniel.

Recent scholars also emphasize Jesus' sacramental coming—as evidenced by numerous "Amens" and other liturgical acclamations, as well as the setting of the book within the Sunday worship service ("on the Lord's day," 1:10). The antiphonal call-and-response invitations to "come" in Rev.

22:17 may be part of a eucharistic dialogue between lector and hearers (Vanni, 363; Ruiz 1992). Some even argue that the book's "eschatology is realized" in the worship setting, via the book's journey into another reality (Barr 1984, 46). The book sweeps hearers up into a dramatic experience of apocalyptic transformation, leading to a new way of life (Rhoads). The ritual setting enables worshipers' experience of the coming of Jesus in a way that "brings the future into the present" (Barr 1998, 174).

Most scholars reject a fully "realized eschatology" that collapses Jesus' coming primarily into a liturgical event, however, since this would leave in place the unjust Roman system. Revelation is unquestionably anti-Roman—and this may shed light also on the book's eschatology, if John is critiquing Rome's own eschatology embodied in slogans such a *Roma Aeterna*. References to Jesus' future coming in judgment may herald God's judgment against the unjust Roman Empire much more than the end of the world. Increasingly, scholars think the comment that the "time is near" (1:3) may proclaim the impending end of Rome, not the end of the cosmos itself.

Revelation 1:9-16: Introducing John of Patmos

▌THE TEXT IN ITS ANCIENT CONTEXT

Revelation 1:9 sets the narrative context for the entire book. John does not claim authority as an apostle. Instead, he introduces himself by expressing solidarity with his hearers, calling himself a "brother" and a "partner" (*synkoinōnos*).

Three key words in 1:9 describe the situation John shares with the communities. The first word, "tribulation" or "persecution" (*thlipsis*), can have a wide range of meanings. We know of no historical evidence of state-sponsored persecution at the time of the emperor Domitian, the time Irenaeus assigns for the book's writing and the consensus of most scholars. The "persecution" (*thlipsis*) of Revelation's audience was likely the local harassment or social marginalization experienced by a few of John's communities for refusing to participate in the Roman imperial economic system or imperial cult worship. John anticipates that if the communities are faithful to Jesus, their witness may provoke some kind of persecution in the future.

"Kingdom," or *basileia*, the second term John says he shares with his communities in 1:9, likely refers to both the kingdom of God and the kingdom of Rome. "Kingdom" is a political term used frequently in Revelation with profound religious power.

The third term, *hypomonē*, becomes a core ethical imperative for Revelation's strategy of resistance (2:2, 3, 19; 3:10; 13:10; 14:12). Translations as "patient endurance" (RSV, NRSV) are too passive for this word. John champions a more active engagement, rooted in the radical Jewish apocalyptic tradition of nonviolent resistance to idolatrous empires. A better translation might be "nonviolent resistance" (Blount 2009, 42), or "resistance" (Richard 1995).

John gives his location: the island of Patmos, about sixty miles off the coast of modern Turkey. He is on the island "because of the word of God and the testimony of Jesus" (1:9). There is no historical evidence for the Roman use of Patmos as a place of banishment or exile, although that became the understanding of John's situation in later Christian tradition (Eusebius, *Hist. eccl.* 3.18;

Boxall). "Because of the word of God" could have a range of meanings. What is important is that John identifies himself as unable to visit his communities in person. So he writes to them. Like the apostle Paul, he wants his letter to embody his physical presence.

John dates his letter "on the Lord's day" (1:10), anchoring it in the church's gathering for liturgy and the sacraments. Revelation was written to be read aloud in the worship service on Sunday. John wants hearers to join in the "Amens" and "Alleluias" of the book.

John "turned to see the voice" (1:12), an example of the Apocalypse's mixing of hearing and seeing. John had never seen Jesus in the flesh, but he saw Jesus as "one like a son of humanity," drawing on images from Daniel that combine the heavenly Ancient of Days with the human "son of humanity" figure. With hair "as white as white wool" (Dan. 7:9) and feet "like burnished bronze" (Dan. 10:6), Jesus looks African (Blount). The two-edged sword issuing from his mouth is the word of God (Isa. 49:2). Jesus' all-seeing eyes "like a flame of fire" (1:14; 2:18; 19:12) alert hearers to Jesus' power to scrutinize them.

This vision, like John's other visions, is beyond description in words. John uses the words "as" and "like" (*hōs, homoios*) more than seventy times in this book, a reminder that the images are metaphorical. John "gropes to find the language to convey adequately" what he sees (Rowland, 566), appealing to readers' imaginations more than to logic or literal representation.

John falls down when he sees Jesus, almost terrified to death. But Jesus stoops to touch him, telling him not to be afraid. This scene is modeled on Daniel's call story in Dan. 8:15-18.

In addition to allusions from Hebrew Scripture, John also situates Jesus in terms of Greco-Roman imagery familiar to his first-century audience, as a way of underscoring Jesus' sovereignty. The seven stars may challenge the emperor Domitian's own use of astral imagery, as depicted on a coin from 83 CE commemorating his son's death, showing seven stars and proclaiming the "Divine Caesar" (Barr 1998, 47; Kraybill). The image of Jesus holding the keys to death and Hades may reference the Greek goddess Hecate, often depicted as holding the keys to Hades. John's point is that Jesus—not Roman emperors or deities—holds power over life and death, and over the cosmos itself.

John is called to communicate the vital message that the risen Jesus is alive and present, personally walking among the seven churches (2:1, depicted as seven lampstands), with a message for each one.

▌The Text in the Interpretive Tradition

From earliest times, readers longing for more information about John have filled in additional information not found in the text itself. Some imagined John sentenced to hard labor in the mines of Patmos. Tertullian (*Praescr.* 36) and subsequent interpreters (including Albrecht Dürer) depicted John as being boiled in oil, unscathed, before his exile to Patmos (see Smith; Boxall).

John provides the only physical description of Jesus in the Bible, a description that has inspired many artists through the centuries. Yet the Jesus of Revelation is impossible to depict. If Jesus has a sword literally coming from his mouth—as in illuminated manuscripts such as the eleventh-century Bamberg Apocalypse, as well as Albrecht Dürer's late-fifteenth-century woodcut—he would not be able to speak. In some artistic depictions, the two-edged sword becomes two swords.

The command to "write" has inspired many Christian mystics and visionaries. Hildegard of Bingen's twelfth-century *Scivias* is introduced by a voice from heaven telling her to "write what you see and hear" (Huber, 98). John's apocalyptic vision inspired William Blake's visionary world during England's Industrial Revolution, furnishing a template for both artistic appropriation and social critique (Blake's hymn "Jerusalem" from *Milton* critiqued the "Satanic Mills" of industry). Hildegard and Blake encourage their audience themselves to "envision," in part to encourage reform in their own times (Huber).

■ THE TEXT IN CONTEMPORARY DISCUSSION

Did John really see things? John's statement that he was "in the spirit" (1:10; 4:2; 17:3; 21:10) has generated much debate. Did his visions occur in an altered state of consciousness, in an ecstatic trance of divine possession? Or are his visions more interior hallucinations brought on by mental illness, or even hallucinogens?

Visionary experiences were understood to be a genuine channel for divine revelation in the ancient Greco-Roman context, in contrast to our post-Freudian understandings of dreams as private phenomena (Aune 1983; Flannery, 105). John's visionary claims situate him in a Jewish visionary tradition with other prophets who are described as experiencing heavenly revelations, including Ezekiel and Daniel, and even the apostle Paul. The question whether these depictions are literary motifs or based on visionary experiences—or both—is raised concerning other writings as well, including *1 Enoch*, the *Sibylline Oracles*, *4 Ezra*, *2 Baruch*, and the *Testament of Levi*. John is deeply immersed in the Scriptures, yet his visions are more than simply a mosaic of scriptural images (deSilva, 121–24). Speaking in the spirit, John claims to represent the voice of Jesus (Barr 1998, 36).

In 2 Cor. 12:1-4, the apostle Paul himself narrates an experience of visionary travel to the third layer of heaven, a description that gives important details even if Paul's intention in this passage is to be ironic. In 1 Corinthians 12–14, Paul makes clear that many early Christians experienced a mantic state of prophetic speech, and that prophetic gifts were both revered and contested in the community. Richard Bauckham compares John's experiences narrated in Revelation with the *Ascension of Isaiah*, another early Christian apocalypse that was also influenced by Jewish Merkabah mysticism, where a circle of prophets gather to experience inspiration and then interpret visionary experiences through the Scriptures (Bauckham 1993b, 89, 141). Falling into a trance, the prophet Isaiah is invited up through an open door into seven heavens, where "the mind in his body was taken up from him. But his breath was in him, for he was seeing a vision. . . . And the vision which he saw was not from this world, but from the world which is hidden from the flesh" (*Ascension of Isaiah* 6:10-15).

Early Christian prophecy was also influenced by Hellenistic oracular and revelatory traditions (Aune 1983). Visionary travel into the underworld or the realm of the divine was a familiar vehicle for receiving divine revelations, as described in literary sources such as Cicero's *Dream of Scipio* (Flannery). The presence of two well-known oracular sanctuaries of the Greek god Apollo in the same region of Asia Minor as John's cities, in Claros and Didyma, as well as a sanctuary of Asclepius at Pergamum, where people went for dream incubation, make it likely that John's communities would have known traditions about revelatory experiences.

What is important is that John does not want to undertake the transformative apocalyptic journey alone. His visions are not private. He takes readers along with him on his time-travel journey (Maier, 56), conducting his audience also into an altered state of consciousness, a new reality (Barr 2002, 35). His first-person narrative is like on-the-scene reporting, inviting hearers into the journey in the spirit. Through this shared experience, the audience itself, "by subtle degrees, is brought around to a new way of seeing and understanding" (Maier, 58).

John's goal in sharing "in the spirit" is to recount not an ecstatic experience but rather a prophetic experience. The visionary journey is meant to be transformative, both for John and for his communities. John's primary focus in narrating his visionary experiences is "not spiritual fervor but ethical awareness" (Blount 2009, 42).

Revelation 2–3: Seven Churches on Earth; Seven Messages

■ The Text in Its Ancient Context

The so-called letters to the seven churches function as prophetic messages, similar to imperial edicts (Aune 1990). All seven messages are intended to be heard by all the churches—a point made explicit in the message to Thyatira (2:23), the longest of the seven messages. The messages give the risen Christ's assessment of each church's situation.

The seven messages furnish our most detailed historical information about each church in late first-century Asia Minor. These seven churches were quite different from one another, economically and socially, some with leaders who did not agree with John's uncompromising perspective. Most of the cities named had official Roman imperial altars or temples, promoting worship and allegiance to the empire and emperors (Thompson). The seven cities form a geographical circuit northward and inland from the port city of Ephesus on the Aegean coast.

All seven messages are addressed to the "angel" or "messenger" of the church—probably the corporate spirit of the congregation (Wink, 3). The seven messages follow a similar pattern, in differing order: Each begins with a description of Jesus, echoing some aspect of the inaugural vision (2:1, 8, 12, 18; 3:1, 7, 14). Next comes a performance review, introduced by "I know"—a reminder of the all-seeing eye of Christ, who walks among the churches (imaged as seven golden lampstands, 2:1). "Works" (*erga*) set a standard by which the churches are measured. Four churches are told to repent, and five churches experience sharp rebuke. John uses rhetoric of innuendo to vilify rival prophetic leaders with biblical labels ("Jezebel," "Balaam"), criticizing what he considers overly assimilationist practices such as eating food that has been sacrificed to pagan deities. The call to "hear" resembles Jesus' call in the Gospels (Matt. 11:15; Mark 4:9, 23; Luke 8:8). Finally comes a wondrous promise from the Spirit to the "conquerors" (from the Greek verb *nikaō*), motivating hearers to remain faithful so they can "conquer" as Jesus conquered.

A promise-fulfillment compositional structure ties the seven messages to the final vision of the book in a concentric pattern (Schüssler Fiorenza 1998). The promises will be fulfilled in the final vision of the new Jerusalem, in chapters 21–22.

Ephesus, the largest city and closest to the island of Patmos, receives high praise for its "resistance" (*hypomonē*, 2:2) and for its strict standards in judging of false teachers, including the "Nicolaitans," a group whose identity and "works" are uncertain. But the church has forgotten to love. The tree of life (2:7; 22:2, 14, 19), the most famous of the promises of future blessing, draws on the paradise traditions from Gen. 2:9.

The messages to Smyrna and Philadelphia introduce the difficult question of the relationship of the churches to Judaism. We cannot know why John labels opponents in both cities the "synagogue of Satan" (2:9; 3:9). Since John is clearly a Jew himself who identifies strongly with the traditions of Israel, his criticism should be viewed as a sibling dispute within the Jewish family rather than as anti-Judaism. Given the great diversity of first-century Christian communities in Asia Minor, it is even possible that John is critiquing not Jews at all, but Christian gentiles in the same cities who followed the teachings of Paul—those who think they can inherit the promises of Israel without following Jewish dietary law (Pagels). Alternately, if the word "synagogue" refers to actual Jews, then these two churches may have been experiencing separation from local Jewish communities—thereby risking loss of official legitimacy negotiated by Jewish communities within the empire. Within the diverse landscape of early Christianity and Judaism in the cities of late first century Asia Minor, multiple scenarios are possible for reconstructing the history of Revelation's seven churches.

The message to Pergamum (2:12-17) brings up two issues that also concern Thyatira: eating food offered to idols and participating in "fornication" (*porneia*), probably a metaphor for participation in the imperial cult (2:14, 20). Food was a divisive issue for early Christians, as evidenced by the many New Testament debates about eating meat offered to idols (Rom. 14:13-23; 1 Cor. 10:23-33). John's strict vegetarian line prohibiting all meat sacrificed to pagan gods in the city markets would have meant social marginalization, especially for wealthier Christians seeking to move up socially by participating in civic banquets.

John's polemic reveals intense theological debate within the churches. John labels a leader in Pergamum who was apparently advocating a more lenient position as "Balaam," the name of a notorious false prophet (Numbers 22; 31:16). Similarly, in Thyatira, John labels a rival prophet who permits Christians to eat meat as "Jezebel"—a pejorative link to the queen of Israel who promoted pagan worship (1 Kgs. 18:19). The woman prophet in Thyatira is clearly influential, with many followers whom John calls her "children." Accusation of "deceit" (2:20) links her to Roman figures who practice deceit later in the book (the whore of Babylon, 17:23; the two beasts, 12:9; 13:14; 14:17).

The sixth church, Philadelphia, receives only praise. This church will be kept from the "hour of trial coming upon the whole empire [*oikoumenē*]"—probably a reference to God's impending judgment against the whole Roman Empire rather than to general end-times tribulation (Rossing 2003; Richard 1995). That judgment or legal trial will happen in the Babylon vision of chapter 18.

The Laodiceans receive the harshest critique. Prosperous Laodicean church members who may feel secure in their wealth do not "see" that their situation nauseates God. To persuade the church to repent of its complacency, John gives the image of Jesus knocking at the door and promising to eat with the church—possibly a reference to the Lord's Supper. The "conqueror" receives the promise of sharing a throne with Jesus, as Jesus shares a throne with God.

◼ THE TEXT IN THE INTERPRETIVE TRADITION

Although addressed to the Laodicean community corporately, the image of Jesus knocking at the door in 3:20 is frequently interpreted by mystics and pietists as the door of the individual's heart. Hildegard of Bingen heard 3:20 as an invitation to the spiritual life. For St. John of the Cross (1542–1591), when Christ knocks on the soul's door he brings the supper of "his own sweetness" (Wainwright, 203). Warner Sallman's nineteenth-century painting *Christ at the Heart's Door*, displayed in many churches, exemplifies the popularity of this understanding.

Premillennial dispensationalists use Rev. 3:10 as proof of the so-called rapture, a word not mentioned in Revelation. Their interpretive system, developed by John Nelson Darby in the nineteenth century, undergirds modern fundamentalist "prophecy" writings such as Tim LaHaye and Jerry Jenkins's *Left Behind* (1995) and Hal Lindsey's *The Late Great Planet Earth* (1970). Proponents claim that being saved "from the hour of trial coming upon the whole world" (3:10) means that born-again Christians will be snatched up to heaven for seven years while others suffer a period of tribulation (Boyer; Rossing 2004).

Elaborate dispensationalist charts interpret Revelation 2–3 as depicting seven stages, or "dispensations," of church history "from AD 96 to the end" (the *Old Scofield Reference Bible)*.

In these charts, Ephesus is viewed as the apostolic church of the first century; Smyrna as the persecuted church until the time of Emperor Constantine; Pergamum as the church "where Satan's throne is," after the conversion of Constantine; Thyatira as the church of the Roman Catholic papacy; and Sardis as the Protestant Reformation that became "the Dead Church" when it retained rituals such as infant baptism (LaHaye, 50). Laodicea is viewed as the present lukewarm, mainline church.

Contrary to such "futurist" interpretations, most scholars consider it highly unlikely that John wrote the seven letters with any predictive system of future church history in mind. To claim that Revelation was written in order to predict events hundreds or thousands of years later in the United States or the Middle East detracts from its original meaning to communities in the first century.

◼ THE TEXT IN CONTEMPORARY DISCUSSION

Scholars debate whether the intra-Christian polemic against rival prophetic leaders is primary or secondary to the overall anti-imperial polemic of the book. John fights on multiple fronts at once, using innuendo and even death threats ("I will strike her children dead," 2:23) to discredit fellow leaders with whom he disagrees. The question is whether it is this rivalry among Christian prophets, rather than the critique of Rome, that constitutes John's principal purpose in writing (Thompson; Duff). Recent consensus among scholars that there was no systemic persecution of Christians may lend support to this perspective, although other scholars point to the all-pervasive pressure to participate in Roman imperial cult (Friesen).

John clearly views Roman imperial cults and Rome's military and economic hegemony as demonic. But aspects of the rhetoric of Revelation complicate the perception that we might read the book today as supporting a straightforward anti-imperial agenda. The book's rhetoric of gender further complicates the issue, as does the antisemitic legacy of the phrase "synagogue of Satan" (2:9;

3:9) in Christian history. John's violent polemic against the woman he labels "Jezebel" and other scenes of violence against women (17:16) may make any liberating reading impossible for women today (Pippin). On the other hand, John critiques "Jezebel" not because she is a woman per se, but because John disagrees with her teachings (Schüssler Fiorenza 1998). We know that other women prophets were revered in nearby Christian communities in Asia Minor in the first and second centuries. (The historian Eusebius lauds the four prophesying daughters of Philip [Acts 21:9] in Hierapolis, as well as later women prophets Quadratus and Ammia, *Hist. eccl.* 5.17). What John seems to be advocating is a "rigorous priestly purity" of Jewish dietary practices (Frankfurter 2011, 468) over against those who permit intermingling with Greco-Roman culture. It may even be that all John's attacks concern the same issue: his "synagogue of Satan" label for Pergamum and Smyrna, as well as his "Balaam" and "Jezebel" labels for leaders in Pergamum and Thyatira, may all represent thinly veiled attacks on Christian communities that abandoned Jewish dietary law, perhaps the heirs of Paul's gentile-Christian churches (Pagels; for history of this view see Rowland, 545).

Revelation 4–5: Heavenly Throne Room, the Lamb, All Creation's Worship

▮ THE TEXT IN ITS ANCIENT CONTEXT

A voice summons John to "come up" to heaven. The vision takes place "in the spirit" (the same terminology as in 1:10; 17:3; 21:10). Many ancient apocalypses contain such visionary journeys involving travel into layers of heaven or time travel into the future. The seer returns from the transformative journey with an urgent message for readers, typically calling for repentance and faithfulness.

John borrows imagery from the prophets Ezekiel and Isaiah to describe what he sees in heaven. The divine throne looks as the prophets saw it (Isa. 6:2; Ezek. 1:4-28), with concentric circles of worshipers including Ezekiel's four mysterious living creatures. Too holy to be named, God is simply the "One seated on the throne." Peals of lightning and thunder recall God's theophany at Sinai. John adds a rainbow, connecting the throne to God's covenant with Noah and all creation (Gen. 9:20-21).

Power is the key to this scene. The throne is the central symbol of power in Revelation. The central questions addressed by Revelation are questions of power: "Who is the true Lord of this world?" "To whom does this earth belong?" (Schüssler Fiorenza 1991, 58, 120). Dueling thrones throughout Revelation represent the struggle between God's agents and evil that is at the heart of the book. Satan (2:13), represented as the dragon (13:2), and his agent the beast (16:10) are both portrayed symbolically as having thrones. As representatives of imperial evil, they must be dethroned, giving way to the final vision of God's throne from which flows the river of life at the center of the renewed earth (22:1).

As political imagery, the heavenly throne-room scene evokes comparisons with the Roman emperor's throne-room ceremonies (Aune 1983). In Roman imperial throne rooms, worshipers threw their crowns before the emperor as a sign of allegiance, singing hymns and liturgies of praise. With the image of the elders casting their crowns before God's magnificent throne (4:10), John in effect trumps Roman court liturgies. The message is that only God, not the emperor or the empire, is worthy of worshipers' allegiance.

More than fifteen hymns or hymnlike compositions occur throughout Revelation, all giving encouragement to God's people on earth from the perspective of heaven. In the book's three-tiered cosmology (heaven, earth, and the Abyss or underworld), events in heaven give direction for how things should be on earth. Revelation's frequent use of hymns, doxologies, and descriptions of heavenly liturgies is "not for the sake of persuading his audience to participate in the daily or weekly liturgy," but rather "for the sake of moving the audience to political resistance" (Schüssler Fiorenza 1991, 103).

Revelation 5:5 introduces Jesus into the throne-room scene via a surprising plot development. The sealed scroll God holds must be opened. But no one can be found worthy to open the scroll's seals and learn its secrets. John invites readers to "weep much" (5:4) with him, employing pathos as part of his persuasive strategy (Maier, 57). One of the elders tells John not to weep because "the Lion of the tribe of Judah, the Root of David, has conquered" (5:5). Two words—"lion" and "conquer"—lead us to expect a fierce animal to open the scroll, like the fierce animals of other apocalypses (compare the lion that conquers the Roman eagle in 2 Esdras 12).

Yet John delivers an amazing surprise. In place of the expected lion comes a Lamb: "Then I saw . . . a Lamb standing as if it had been slaughtered" (5:6). The Greek word John uses for "lamb" (*arnion*) actually is a diminutive form, suggesting vulnerability. This is one of a number of passages where hearing and seeing reveal two different and paradoxical dimensions of the same reality. John "hears" a lion but "sees" a Lamb.

This powerful image of Jesus as "the Lamb that was slaughtered" (Rev. 5:12) becomes the central symbol of Jesus for all of Revelation. No other apocalypse portrays its divine hero as a lamb (Johns). This depiction reveals Jesus in the most vulnerable way possible, as a victim who is slaughtered but standing upright—crucified, yet risen to life. The image links Jesus to the Passover lamb that saved the Israelites in the exodus story. Reminiscent also of the servant-lamb of Isaiah 53 who "is led to the slaughter," the Lamb of Revelation becomes the victor not by militaristic power and bloodshed but rather through being slaughtered. Evil has been conquered not by overwhelming force or violence, but by the Lamb's victory on the cross.

Singing breaks out in heaven for a second time when the Lamb is introduced. John of Patmos envisions a liturgy where animals and all creatures in heaven, on earth, and under the earth join in exuberant singing. The four living creatures and twenty-four elders now take up their harps to sing a "new song," this time praising Jesus, the Lamb (Rev. 5:8-14). The emphasis on "new" hints at the way everything will be renewed at the end of Revelation, in the vision of the new heaven and the new earth (Revelation 21–22).

■ THE TEXT IN THE INTERPRETIVE TRADITION

Since the second century (Irenaeus, *Against Heresies* 3.11.8), Christian tradition has associated the four living creatures with the four Evangelists, identified by Jerome (*Preface to the Commentary on Matthew*) as Matthew (the human); Mark (the lion); Luke (the ox); John (the eagle).

The Lamb, the most important image of Jesus in Revelation, figures prominently in Christian imagery from the time of the catacombs. The Moravian church's emblem is the Lamb carrying a flag of victory, held in its right foreleg and resting on its shoulder. The church's motto is "Our Lamb has conquered; let us follow him." Liturgically, the Lamb of Revelation became combined with Jesus as "Lamb of God who takes away the sin of the world" from John's Gospel, although the words for lamb differ (*arnion* in Revelation, *amnos* in John 1:29, 36) and Revelation's Lamb is not described as "Lamb of God." The most notable difference between the lamb Christologies of the two books is that Revelation lacks the Gospel of John's expiation model of the Lamb "taking away" or atoning for sin (Schüssler Fiorenza 1998, 95–97; Johns; Blount 2005, 78).

No book of the Bible has had more influence on Western music and art than Revelation. The hymns of Revelation are familiar to Christian worshipers from the liturgy (the Sanctus, "Holy, Holy, Holy"; "This is the Feast of Victory for Our God") and choral works such as Handel's *Messiah* ("Worthy Is the Lamb Who Was Slain"). Alfred Lord Tennyson acclaimed Reginald Heber's hymn "Holy, Holy, Holy," based on Rev. 4:8-11, as "the world's greatest hymn."

The hymns are not intended to be understood literally. Their symbolic dimension is precisely what gives these songs their power. Songs connect God's people to something deeper. Songs serve to "unbind a people from their fear" (Blount 2005). That is why so many African American spirituals are based on Revelation ("Shall We Gather at the River?," "I Want to Be Ready to Walk in Jerusalem Just like John," "Down by the Riverside"). Often using a call-and-response format, they evoke hearers' capacity for solidarity and resistance. They give courage and hope.

▊ THE TEXT IN CONTEMPORARY DISCUSSION

"Does the Lion lie down with the Lamb?" asks one scholar (Moyise 2001). The question is important because of implications for the representation of divine violence. Scholars differ regarding the extent to which the figure of Jesus as "Lamb" supersedes that of "Lion" in 5:5 or what relationship is intended between lionlike and lamblike elements in Revelation's Christology. In biblical and apocalyptic tradition, the lion symbolized ferocity and destructive strength (Bauckham 1993a, 183). The lion was interpreted messianically as a devouring lion at Qumran (1QSb 5:29) and in *4 Ezra* 11–12, where the lion destroys the Roman eagle.

John hears of a Lion but sees a Lamb. For many scholars, this means the nonviolent Lamb image has replaced the violent Lion (Caird 1966, 75; Johns; Barr 1997, 161; Kraybill). Even a scholar who argues that hearing normally interprets seeing in Revelation, not vice versa (Resseguie), thinks that seeing reinterprets hearing in Rev. 5:5. Yet Steve Moyise and others make the case that the Lion/Lamb juxtaposition may instead necessitate the two images mutually interpreting each other (Moyise 2001, 194).

All scholars agree there is no textual basis for dispensationalist claims, like those made by San Antonio preacher John Hagee and others, that Jesus will return the second time as a violent "Lion of the tribe of Judah, who will trample His enemies until their blood stains His garments," replacing Jesus' first Lamblike incarnation (Hagee 1999, 239).

The hymn of 4:8 also raises an ecological question for scholars. The hymn draws closely on the "Holy, Holy, Holy" of Isa. 6:3. But why does John omit the line of Isaiah, "The whole earth is full of God's glory"? This change suggests John does not yet consider earth to be filled with God's glory (Bauckham 2011, 179; Stephens, 178). God does not intend to destroy the creation, however; the repeated emphasis in Revelation's hymns on God as creator and allusions to the rainbow of the flood narrative (4:3; 11:8) make that clear. Yet the earth must be liberated from the "destroyers of the earth" (11:8) before it can be filled with God's glory. In this way, John's change in the use of Isaiah reveals an earth-focused dimension of his eschatology.

Revelation 6: The Seven Seals: Diagnosing the Crises of Empire

■ THE TEXT IN ITS ANCIENT CONTEXT

The journey up into heaven (begun in Rev. 4:1) continues with the opening of the seven seals. The seals interpret events on earth from a heavenly perspective, giving John an apocalyptic view of causality and consequences. The four living creatures represent the whole cosmos (Bauckham 2011). One by one, the living creatures call out "Come," unleashing scenes of destruction rampaging across the world. The command "Come," addressed to the four horses and riders, may also be addressed to John himself. ("Come and see" is the sense in a few later manuscripts that add the word "see" in verses 1, 3 5, and 7.)

Like an urgent wake-up call, the first four seal visions deliver God's exposé of the evils of the Roman imperial system. John sees vivid pictures of war, famine, and the pathologies of empire, drawing on the prophet Zechariah's visions of horses of different colors patrolling the earth's four directions (Zech. 1:7-11; 6:1-8).

As a quartet, the four horsemen most likely portray the imperial system gone awry. The first horseman who "conquers" mimics Christ in appearance, leading some interpreters to identify him as Christ. But the resemblance to the figure of Christ on the white horse in Rev. 19:11 is more mimicry, not identification. The Lamb Jesus and his followers conquer only nonviolently, whereas this rider on a white horse conquers with killing.

The second horseman represents a critique of Rome's own internal "peace," the *Pax Romana*. This rider of the red horse wields a sword to instigate civil war so that people slaughter "one another." This verse also introduces the difficult image of these calamities being "permitted," a passive verb used frequently in the book. The presumed subject who permits these disasters is God.

The third horseman brings food insecurity and inflation, symbolized by the commercial scales (literally, "yoke") that he carries for measuring. An unidentified voice uses irony to underscore the pointedly economic critique: Grain has become so expensive that a whole day's wage buys only a measure of staple food. Cropland is used to grow export crops of wine and oil, which must not be harmed. Rome's predatory economy causes food insecurity for the poor.

The fourth horse, the color of grass and vegetation, represents the consequences of the first three calamities for the whole creation. Personified figures of Pestilence (Death) and Hades follow war, bringing power to kill and devour one fourth of the world with a lethal mix of natural and human-caused calamities.

With the fifth and sixth seals, the pattern shifts. John sees an altar in heaven, sheltering Rome's victims who had been "slaughtered." (The same word as was used to refer to Jesus' death in 5:12.) "Souls" (*psychai*) can also be translated as "lives," with slaughtered victims including even the creation itself (see 8:9 for the "souls" of sea creatures among those killed). The altar signifies the promise of restoration to life for those who, like Jesus, have been slaughtered for their active witness (see 20:4; Blount 2005).

"How long, O Lord?" is the cry of ancient Israel throughout the Hebrew Bible, especially in the Psalms (Pss. 13:1; 35:17). This prayer for vindication underscores Revelation's call to readers to identify with those who have suffered for their testimony. "Just a little longer" assures victims of the nearness of Rome's end, in contrast to Rome's own claims of eternal rule. God's justice will soon be "fulfilled" or made "complete" (*plērōthēnai*) by the community's defiant witness.

The whole cosmos undergoes cataclysms with the opening of the sixth seal, unleashing terrifying visions of the sun darkening, stars falling, and the moon turning to blood. Such imagery is conventional, recalling the Hebrew prophets' descriptions of the "Day of the Lord" (Isa. 13:6, 10; Joel 2:31). It also resembles the Synoptic Gospels' apocalypses (Matt. 24:29; Mark 13:24). The imagery is hyperbolic, not literal. The cosmic Day-of-the-Lord cataclysms envelop everyone, from rich to poor. All seek to hide from God's judgment. The attribution of the earthquake to the "wrath of the Lamb" (6:16) is the only reference in Revelation to the Lamb's wrath. The sixth seal concludes with the ominous question, "Who is able to stand?"

▌ THE TEXT IN THE INTERPRETIVE TRADITION

From earliest times, interpreters have debated the meaning of the seals, as well as the two other numbered sequences of sevens, the seven trumpets (Revelation 8–9) and seven bowls (Revelation 16). Those who interpret the sequences as providing a detailed map of history or ages of the church tend to view themselves as living in the time between the fifth and sixth seals. During the Crusades of the twelfth century, Joachim of Fiore believed the opening of the sixth seal was imminent (Daniel). A similar perspective has been taken by others, such as David Koresh and his Branch Davidian sect at the end of the twentieth century. Some contemporary fundamentalists read the series of numbered sevens as a step-by-step chronology of twenty-one future calamities, all scheduled to happen after a supposed rapture. Most interpreters, however, have recognized that attempts to make sense of these visions in a strict linear chronology do not work logically. For example, the stars fall from heaven after the sixth seal is opened (6:13), yet the stars are back in the sky again for the trumpet visions (8:12). Since the time of Joachim, most interpreters have recognized that the visions of the seven seals, trumpets, and bowls recapitulate one another in spiral-like fashion, diagnosing deeper and deeper aspects of the same structures of evil in the world.

The four horsemen figure prominently in interpretive history. Albrecht Dürer's 1517 woodcuts of the four horsemen rampaging across the earth furnished a pattern for many subsequent artists and interpreters, including Lucas Cranach and William Blake. Dürer's portrayal of the third horseman swinging his scale like a weapon against the poor in the center of the scene, and the huge sword and bow of his other three horsemen, have engendered reinterpretation in many contexts, especially in times of war (Smith).

▌ THE TEXT IN CONTEMPORARY DISCUSSION

Most contemporary scholarship seeks the meaning of the seals not by attempting to figure out a chronology but by analyzing the literary and rhetorical structure. Rhetorically, the seals, trumpets, and bowls all function as warnings, with the aim of strengthening an ethic of resistance on the part of the audience. The warnings intensify with each sequence. The trumpets and bowls are modeled on the Exodus plagues of the Hebrew Scriptures, whereas the seal sequence does not follow one specific biblical pattern.

The violence of the seal sequence poses troubling ethical questions for contemporary interpreters. Most scholars argue that the violence of the seals represents Rome's own violence, not God's violence. John is not glorifying war, but rather unmasking structural violence and the consequences of militarism. The sixth seal becomes harder to explain in terms of such Roman imperial violence, however, since it seems to portray natural calamities as divinely authorized. Recent comparative scholarship on the Jewish apocalypses of Daniel and *1 Enoch* makes the case that even such "cosmic catastrophe" imagery of earthquakes functions politically, as a critique of imperial terror and brutality so severe that the very ordering of the world is "de-created" (Portier-Young, xxiii).

Liberation scholars read Revelation's seals as proclaiming a judgment against empires and a vision for justice for all victims. God's assurance that it will be "just a little while" before oppression ends has brought hope to marginalized peoples throughout history. In the 1980s, Allan Boesak interpreted the cry of the souls under the altar, "How long, O Lord," as a voice of protest to bring hope for liberation to South Africans, while in the 1990s Pablo Richard drew on the seals to expose violence of the rich against the poor in Latin America. The four horsemen elicit rich analogies among scholars and commentators. Employing the methodology of ecological hermeneutics, some scholars find analogies to the seals in environmental-justice crises today. One classical historian likens the four horsemen to "climate change, famine, state failure and disease" (Morris). If the seals function to diagnose crises today, Harry Maier and others underscore that in the logic of Revelation's sense of urgency, there is still time for repentance and hope.

Revelation 7: First Interlude: The People of God

▮ THE TEXT IN ITS ANCIENT CONTEXT

Instead of the expected seventh seal, there is now a delay. The scene shifts. Four angels stand at the four corners of the earth, holding back destructive winds of judgment until God's people can be "sealed" (7:1-8).

Even in the most difficult sections of Revelation, judgment is not unrelenting. A similar interlude will interrupt the trumpet sequence, between the sixth and seventh trumpets (Revelation 10–11). These interludes employ the ancient rhetorical model of a "digression," presenting material that is set apart from—and even sometimes more urgent than—the body of the narrative. Revelation's interludes function rhetorically to shape the identity of God's people as "protected, separated, praising, persecuted, and vindicated" (Perry 2009, 217), preparing the community to persevere in its prophetic witness even in the midst of hardship.

The "sealing" that marks God's people on their foreheads is the same word used to identify the seven seals on the scroll in chapter 6. Sealing may be baptismal imagery (as in 2 Cor. 1:22; Eph.

1:13; 4:30), though there is no actual mention of baptism in Revelation. "Sealing" recalls Ezekiel's description of the mark on the forehead that saved a remnant from judgment (Ezek. 9:4) as well as the Passover story in Exodus, when the angel seals the Israelites' doorposts with the blood of the Passover lamb so their children will be spared (Exodus 12). The seal on God's people's foreheads suggests ownership, like a brand. It contrasts with the symbol of the imperial "mark" followers of the beast receive on their foreheads or right hands (representing some aspect of Roman economic participation) in 13:16-17; 14:9.

Two visions describe the community of followers of Jesus. The first vision, introduced with "I heard" (Rev. 7:4), gives the number of 144,000 Israelites, consisting of 12,000 people from each of twelve tribes. The second vision, introduced with "I saw" (7:9), describes a gentile multitude that no one can count. Since hearing and seeing often show the same thing in different ways in Revelation (In 5:5–6, for example, John "heard" about a Lion but "saw" a Lamb—both referencing Jesus), both visions probably depict the same group of people. As in 5:5-6, the second vision reinterprets the first.

At a time when followers of Jesus were few in number, the huge symbolic number 144,000 would have encouraged an expansive vision for the people of God. The number 144,000 will recur in Revelation 14, as a description of those who "follow the Lamb wherever he goes" (14:4).

The second vision (7:9-16) portrays the multiethnic multitude standing before the throne of God. Variations of the phrase "from every nation, from all tribes and peoples and tongues" (Rev. 7:9) occur seven times in Revelation (5:9; 7:9; 10:11; 11:9; 13:7; 14:6-7; 17:15; González 1999), underscoring the multiethnic character of God's people. The white-robed multitude sings songs and waves palm branches. "Salvation," "blessing," "glory," and "power" were imperial terms common in Roman propaganda, used in the songs here to make counterimperial claims for God alone. Palm branches in the hands of these worshipers allude to the Feast of Tabernacles, one of Revelation's many exodus links (Lev. 23:40-43). For Revelation, a dramatic new exodus is being undertaken "not in Egypt but in the heart of the Roman Empire" (Richard 1995, 77).

After the vision, one of the elders gives its interpretation. The question-and-answer section also helps cement John's identity with his community. Like them, he has to ask for interpretive help. People who belong to the Lamb's multitude are those who have come out of the great *thlipsis* ("persecution," "tribulation"; see the discussion of 1:9).

In an incongruous combination of colors, the multicultural multitude wash their robes in the Lamb's blood to make them white. This may be a reference to the washing away of sin commanded in Isa. 1:16-18 ("though your sins are like scarlet, / they shall be like snow").

God tenderly cares for the people. The verb "shelter" (*skēnōsei*) invokes tabernacle imagery, the sense of God's radiant presence or dwelling (see Ezek. 37:27) as a canopy or tent over the community. The Lamb Jesus now becomes also the shepherd, tending the flock, leading people to springs of water, and wiping away all their tears (a quotation from Isa. 25:8, cited again in 21:4).

"Who is able to stand?" was the ominous question at the end of the dreaded sixth seal (Rev. 6:17). The interlude of Revelation 7 gives God's people their answer to that question by depicting their identity as a redeemed community. By the end of the interlude of Revelation 7, God's people can confidently answer: "With God's help, *we* are those who are able to stand."

▌THE TEXT IN THE INTERPRETIVE TRADITION

The question of the identity of the 144,000 has had a lively interpretive history. The Jehovah's Witnesses, founded in the late nineteenth century, argue that the 144,000 form the new nation who will rule with Christ in the millennium (Wainwright), while the larger multitude of 7:9—a different group of people—will not rule but will share in a blessed life on earth. Most interpreters agree that since those who belong to the Lamb are said to be a multitude "that no one could count" (Rev. 7:9), any literalistic fixation on the number 144,000 in the earlier vision of twelve tribes (Rev 7:4) is thus undermined.

When Revelation 7 is read at funerals and on All Saints' Day, the white-robed host of saints waving palms and praising God becomes a consoling vision of the heavenly afterlife. In her devotional commentary, poet Christina Rossetti interpreted the tribulation out of which the saints have come in 7:14 as the chastening or "sifting" that believers experience in their daily life (Rossetti, 236). The imagery of God wiping away all tears (from Isa. 25:8, also read for All Saints' Day), as well as the tabernacling God and springs of water, comforts believers with the assurance of God's living presence.

▌THE TEXT IN CONTEMPORARY DISCUSSION

Rhetorical critics point to the importance in Revelation's interludes of the use of pathos or emotion to shape the confidence and identity of God's people (deSilva, 217; Perry 2009). The interludes of chapters 7 and 10–11 give the audience strong, positive characters with whom to identify. After the wrath of the sixth seal, hearers are drawn to see themselves in the great multitude in white robes, as those who have courage to endure further tribulation and follow the Lamb. The interlude also develops John's own ethos in relation to the audience.

The multitude is strikingly multicultural, from many tribes and nations. Cuban scholar Justo González compares the multicultural perspective of Revelation to mestizo literature, addressed to people of a mixed cultural heritage. John may have been a recent refugee to Asia Minor from Palestine following the trauma of the Roman-Jewish War. For González, John's dual identity as a Jew writing to Greek-speaking people in Asia Minor, in a land and language not his own, places him in a situation similar to those of people with hybrid identities today (González 1999, 59).

Revelation 8–9: Woes, Seven Trumpets: Alas for the Earth

▌THE TEXT IN ITS ANCIENT CONTEXT

At the end of the interlude, the Lamb opens the seventh seal. The result brings silence in heaven for half an hour (8:1), like the silence of the seventh day of creation (Aune 1988). The foreboding silence does not last long. More calamities will follow, as seven angels receive seven trumpets that unleash seven more terrifying visions of judgment.

But first, an opening scene in heaven functions to give assurance to the community, identified with the "saints" (8:3). The altar in heaven connects the trumpet sequence back to the fifth seal of

6:10 and the cry of "How long, O Lord?" The urgent prayers of the saints that rise before God serve as a catalyst to set in motion the series of trumpet judgments on earth (Talbert). This message is that prayers matter, and that God hears their prayers.

The seven trumpets follow a pattern similar to that of the seven seals (Revelation 6): the first four elements form a quartet, followed by the fifth and sixth elements intensifying the destruction, and then an interlude of hope (Revelation 10–11) before the seventh element. The first four elements reflect a fourfold division of creation: earth, sea, rivers and springs, and heaven (Bauckham 2011).

John models the trumpets of Revelation on trumpet passages from the Hebrew Scriptures. In Ezekiel 33, the primary model, the prophet blows the trumpet to warn people so that the wicked "turn from their ways and live" (Ezek. 33:11). Trumpets can also function militarily (Joshua 6; 2 Chron. 13:12), as priestly announcements of festivals (Num. 10:1-10), or eschatologically to announce the Day of the Lord (Joel 2:1; Zeph. 1:16).

The calamities announced by trumpet borrow their imagery primarily from the Exodus plagues, although the word "plague" is not used until the sixth trumpet (9:18, 20). The trumpet visions will be closely paralleled by the seven bowls in Revelation 15–16, where each calamity is called a "plague." Together, the trumpet and bowl sequences function to evoke a sense of a new exodus for God's people, this time from the Roman Empire. Like the plague sequence leading up to the exodus of Israel from Egypt, the judgments announced by the trumpets elicit both hope and terror—enacting a cosmic judgment that brings justice and liberation. The trumpet and bowl sequences recapitulate the seal sequence, with ever-increasing intensity of destruction.

The first trumpet's rain of hail and fire on the earth, mixed with blood, is modeled on the seventh Exodus plague (Exod. 9:22-26). Narration of the action in the passive voice suggests God as the one permitting the calamity. The destruction of one-third of the earth and its trees intensifies the one-fourth destruction of the seal visions (6:8)—yet, two-thirds of the creation is still spared. John may even be critiquing Rome's destructive practices of over-logging the forests of conquered nations, a practice lauded by Rome's own propagandists (see Aelius Aristides, *Orations* 26.12).

The second trumpet's killing of one-third of the sea creatures echoes the first Exodus plague (Exod. 7:20-21; cf. Ps. 105:29). John also weaves in creation motifs with the description of the sea creatures as "having souls" (8:9, another example of John's defying grammatical rules, similar to 1:4). He alludes to Gen. 1:20-21, where sea creatures and mammals also are called "living souls" (Perry 2010). John adds a sharp element of economic critique of Roman maritime trade by stating that one-third of the ships are also destroyed. Judgment on Roman maritime trade will be taken up in chapter 18, the Babylon vision.

The poisoning of one-third of the springs and rivers sounded by the third trumpet, caused by a falling star named Wormwood, has no Exodus antecedent. John likely draws imagery from the prophet Jeremiah ("Because they have forsaken my law . . . Behold I will feed this people with wormwood and give them poisonous water to drink," Jer. 9:13-18; cf. Lam. 3:15). In Hebrew Scriptures, a falling star heralds the death of a tyrant (Isa. 14:12; Richard 1995).

The fourth trumpet resumes the reworking of the Exodus calamities with darkness wiping out one-third of the sunlight, moon, and stars, similar to the darkness brought on Egypt in the ninth plague (Exod. 10:21; cf. Ps. 105:28).

While the first four trumpets are broadly modeled on Exodus plagues, John also makes important changes. Absent from Revelation is any element similar to the hardening of Pharaoh's heart in Exodus, thus keeping open the possibility for repentance—a theme underscored in 9:20-21, albeit negatively (in actuality "they did not repent"). The consequences of the trumpets are more cosmic than the Exodus plagues, falling on the entire creation rather than on a specific nation, Egypt. In effect, the trumpets' destruction functions as a cosmic "de-creation," reversing the order of Gen. 1:1-25, where stars, sun, moon, sea creatures, and plants are created in sequence (Maier, 106).

After the fourth trumpet, the imagery shifts. An eagle flies through mid-heaven crying out, "Woe, woe to the inhabitants of the earth" (8:13). The eagle was a familiar symbol of the Roman Empire, ironically used here to proclaim the empire's demise. The Greek word translated "woe" (*ouai*) voices an untranslatable sound expressing lamentation or mourning as well as horror (Alexiou). In chapter 18, the same word is usually translated "Alas, alas, alas," 18:10, 16, 19 NRSV, RSV). The translation "alas" rather than "woe" may be better here as well, in which case the "woes" declare not so much a curse or woe *against* the inhabitants and the earth as God's grief-stricken lament *on behalf of* the earth and its inhabitants (Rossing 2002, 181–83). These verses also introduce the peculiar use of *ouai* as a noun in 9:12, constituting the final three blasts of the trumpets ("the first woe/ alas," 9:12; "the second woe/alas," 11:14). Although the third woe is never identified, it is likely the seventh trumpet, blown in 11:14-15.

With the fifth and sixth trumpets, Exodus imagery gives way to more sinister destruction, magnifying the horror of de-creation. A falling star (see also 8:10) breaks the locked boundaries between heaven and the underworld, resulting in smoke that darkens the cosmos. The underworld is allowed to invade the realm of earth with mutant creatures worse than any biblical plague. Monstrous locusts recall the locusts of the Exodus story (Exod. 10:1-20), but now with the supernatural power of scorpions and the military appearance of war horses (Joel 2:4).

Yet a word of assurance is given to the audience in 9:4, in the midst of the locusts: God's people who received the seal on their foreheads will continue to be protected (9:4), as will the grass and trees. This verse reminds the audience that longs for justice to view the trumpets with hope rather than dread, since they herald the collapse of the unjust imperial system.

Apollyon, the name of the commander of the locusts (literally, "the destroyer"), likely alludes to the Greek god Apollo, whose identity was claimed by some Roman emperors. The Euphrates River was both the boundary of ancient Israel and the boundary of the Roman Empire, from where the dreaded Parthians threatened invasion. The sixth trumpet's demonic cavalries, of 200,000 surreal horses that kill one-third of the world's population (9:13–19), evoke potent anti-Roman overtones (similar also to the anti-Kittim or anti-Roman polemic in the Habakkuk pesher among the Dead Sea Scrolls).

The verses about repentance immediately following the description of this sixth deadly plague (9:20-21) underscore that the goal of the entire sequence is repentance: The rest of humanity "did not repent of the works of their hands." A similar warning about the lack of repentance will be noted in the bowl plagues (Rev. 16:11). These verses suggest the purpose of such horrific imagery is not to inflict cruelty but to "shock the audience" into changing their lives (Schüssler Fiorenza 1991, 73).

Suspense builds as hearers await the seventh trumpet.

The Text in the Interpretive Tradition

The series of horrible plagues (trumpets, bowls) that constitute the middle chapters of the book are unquestionably the most difficult section, giving rise to highly problematic interpretations.

For Martin Luther, the trumpets correlated to spiritual tribulations—encompassing the history of heresies in the church. Unlike the seals, which to him represented persecution and injustice on earth, Luther related the trumpet angels to doctrinal heretics such as Marcion, the Manicheans, Montanists, the medieval Cathars, and even Thomas Müntzer "and the fanatics" in his own time. Luther viewed the fifth angel, or first woe, as Arius. The sixth angel, or second woe, was "the shameful Mohammed, with his companions, the Saracens, who inflicted a great plague on the church."

Others who have tried to understand Revelation as a code with one-to-one correspondences to contemporary events likewise "discover" in the trumpets and woes almost limitless possibilities for correlations. One contemporary blogger interpreted the burning Deepwater Horizon oil rig in the Gulf of Mexico as the "great mountain" that was thrown, burning, into the sea in Rev. 8:8 (Miller). Today's dispensationalists interpret the trumpets militaristically, likening the monstrous locusts with scorpion-like powers to attack helicopters and other military vehicles. Since they plan to be in heaven, watching the destruction from a safe distance, adherents of the so-called rapture have little to fear from the ghoulish violence.

The Text in Contemporary Discussion

Scholars debate whether the primary purpose of the trumpets is to elicit repentance, or whether they serve more to inaugurate end-times calamities. Those who emphasize repentance see the closest analogy to the trumpet of Ezekiel 33, whereas those who see predictions of judgment call attention to other trumpets in the Hebrew Scriptures. Liberation scholars view the trumpets and bowls as calling for a new exodus on the part of the Christian community, an exodus out of participation in the Roman imperial system.

Some scholars who emphasize repentance note that the strategy of using plagues and threats in the sequences of the trumpets ultimately resulted in failure, because it did not elicit the desired response of repentance (Koester, 101). In light of the trumpets' failure to persuade people to repent, God will now change strategies in the interlude of chapters 10–11, turning to the two witnesses—a strategy that will prove to be more persuasive than the plagues in eliciting repentance.

Revelation 10–11: Second Prophetic Interlude; the People of God

The Text in Its Ancient Context

Before the expected seventh trumpet, an interlude interrupts the narrative. The seventh trumpet will be delayed until 11:15.

This interlude's many images can be confusing, combining descriptions from the book of Daniel and other texts. The overall goal is to encourage prophetic witness. John's hearers are not just passive spectators in the cosmic drama. Two witnesses show the audience its urgent prophetic role. Like the interlude between the sixth and seventh seals (chapter 7), this interlude uses delay to strengthen the audience for prophetic testimony and resistance.

The interlude consists of two parts: renewal of John's call to prophecy (chapter 10) and the story of two witnesses (chapter 11). Both together make up a single vision introduced by "I saw" in 10:1.

A mighty angel, wrapped in cloud and rainbow, straddles sea and earth, indicating God's dominion over both realms. The rainbow recalls the promise to Noah that God will not destroy creation. The angel holds a little scroll, representing the prophetic call. Amid thunder, the angel swears a solemn oath by God the Creator: There shall be no more delay, no more time for repentance. The focus is on the present moment, announcing (*euangelizein*) the mystery of God's judgment as "good news" that will now be "fulfilled" or completed (*telesthēnai*). Yet John is told *not* to write down the prophecy—a departure from the book's many commands to "write."

John's authority is underscored through the renewal of his own prophetic call, symbolized in three actions: swallowing, prophesying, and measuring. By swallowing the scroll, John internalizes its message into his own life, in the tradition of Ezekiel (Ezek. 2:8—3:3). His prophecy is to be "concerning many peoples, nations, tongues, and kings" (10:11).

Measuring the temple, a symbolic action, recalls the prophet Ezekiel (Ezek 40:3). Since the physical temple in Jerusalem had long since been destroyed by the Romans, "temple" and "holy city" probably refer not to the former Jerusalem temple or to a heavenly temple, but rather to John's own community. "Temple" recalls the promise to the Philadelphian community that they would become pillars in the temple (3:12). Measuring symbolizes divine protection (Zech. 2:1-5; *1 En.* 61:1-5).

The story of the two witnesses (11:3) serves as a kind of parable (Bauckham 1993b). Described as two "lampstands" (the same name given to the churches in 1:20), the two witnesses likely represent the community as it is called to engage in prophetic confrontation with the idolatry of Rome. John models the two witnesses on Elijah and Moses. Like Elijah confronting Jezebel, they exercise power over fire and rain (1 Kings 17:1); and like Moses confronting Pharaoh and his magicians (Exodus 8–12), they can turn water to blood and strike the earth with plagues.

The symbolic period of time for the two witnesses' prophetic testimony, 1,260 days, is the same finite period in which the holy city is to be trampled (forty-two months, 11:2). This "Danielic time-period" of three and a half years (Bauckham 1993b, 284) occurs in different forms in 11:2, 3; 12:6, 14; and 13:5, drawing on Dan. 9:25-27. It represents the present time in which the community is now living. It is a time of limited duration, "the period just before the destruction of the empire" (Friesen, 159).

The monstrous beast from the bottomless pit, introduced here for the first time, represents Rome's power to kill. The community's prophetic testimony may lead to martyrdom, as portrayed in the beast's killing the two witnesses. But God's breath of life raises the two witnesses to stand again on their feet (see Ezek. 37:5), vindicating their testimony.

An earthquake accompanying the two witnesses' resuscitation decimates one-tenth of the great city, killing seven thousand people. The symbolism of this city is debated. Most important is that the earthquake now persuades the other nine-tenths of the city's people (presumably more than sixty thousand) to give glory to God (11:13). Nine-tenths of the city is saved. The story of the two witnesses thus assures John's churches that their prophetic testimony will succeed where the trumpets' violent plagues failed: namely, in converting the world to give glory to God. The vision of 11:3 anticipates the announcement of 15:4 that "all nations" will worship God (Schüssler Fiorenza 1991).

The seventh trumpet finally sounds at the end of the interlude. The third "woe" is most likely the seventh trumpet (11:14). Unlike the first six trumpets that brought disaster, this trumpet brings rejoicing, celebrating the reign of God.

The antiphonal victory song of the elders praises God that the "time" (*kairos*) has finally come. The time is not for destroying the earth but for destroying earth's destroyers (11:18)—that is, the Roman imperial system of military conquests and client kings that enslaves lands and peoples. God's will is for the fulfillment of creation, not its destruction.

More destruction is still to come in the second half of the book, as Satan and his agents continue to stalk the earth. But the hymn celebrates in advance that "the kingdom of this world has become the kingdom of our Lord" (11:15).

A theophany in 11:19, with lightning and thunder and a vision of God's temple in heaven, underscores the solemnity of this moment.

▐ THE TEXT IN THE INTERPRETIVE TRADITION

Many throughout Christian history have identified themselves and their communities with the two witnesses. Early interpretations of the two witnesses expand on the expected return of Elijah (Mal. 4:5) combined with Enoch, who had never experienced death (Gen 5:24).

The beast from the abyss became a potent symbol, especially as it coalesced with legends of the "Antichrist" (a word not found in Revelation). Illustrations of the two witnesses preaching to the Antichrist were common in medieval illuminated manuscripts. In the twelfth century, Franciscans and other fraternal orders identified themselves and their leaders as the two witnesses. Medieval interpreters often used the image of the beast to critique popes and church practices they viewed as illegitimate.

During the Reformation, Protestants and Catholics traded polemics back and forth, using the two witnesses of Revelation 11. In one of the most famous woodcuts from Luther's 1522 September Bible, artist Lucas Cranach depicted the beast of Revelation 11 wearing the three-tiered crown of the pope—a visibly anti-Catholic polemic. Cranach softened the anti-Catholic image in the December reprint of the Bible by eliminating the two upper levels of the tiara. In both depictions, however, the temple sanctuary being measured is clearly Luther's Wittenberg Castle Church, and the two witnesses tormented by the beast are Reformers.

In the eighteenth century, William Blake identified the two witnesses as founders of Methodism, John Wesley and George Whitefield (*Milton* 22.52–62; Jeffrey, 231), praising them for their social concern as well as their signs and miracles.

The time span of 42 months, or 1,260 days, and the reference to the temple have given rise to elaborate timetables for supposed end-times events. Dispensationalist proponents of the rapture theology of Darby argue that the temple in Jerusalem must be rebuilt in modern times for a period of 42 months, so that it can then be desecrated by an "Antichrist," fulfilling their interpretation of the seventieth week in Dan. 9:27 and precipitating a final battle of Armageddon. In this view, time periods of Revelation 11 spell out a predictive chronology of violent geopolitical events in the Middle East that must happen before Jesus is able to return to earth.

◼ THE TEXT IN CONTEMPORARY DISCUSSION

Scholars discuss whether the open little scroll of Revelation 10 is the same scroll as the sealed scroll in 5:2. Although different words describe the two scrolls (*biblion* in 5:2; *biblidarion* in 10:2, 8) and the little scroll is "open," contrasting with the "sealed" scroll of 5:2, John may understand them as the same scroll (Bauckham 1993b, 243; Blount 2009, 190; contra Schüssler Fiorenza 1991, 73).

The phrase in 10:11, "peoples, nations, languages, and kings," can be understood positively or negatively, depending on whether the preposition *epi* means "against" these nations or "about" these nations. The addition of "kings"—not found in previous listings of peoples, tongues, and nations (5:10; 7:9)—suggests the negative connotation of "against" (Schüssler Fiorenza 1991, 76; Aune 1998, 571). González, however, makes the grammatical argument on the basis of the dative case that John is to speak positively to his own communities "about" God's multicultural mission that includes Gentiles—a task he finds bitter to the taste (González 1999, 91).

A related question is whether John truly envisions the repentance and conversion of the nations in 11:13. Bauckham makes a convincing case that the terms "fear God" and "give glory to God" are always positive in Revelation, and that the conversion of the nations is at the center of John's prophetic message (1993b, 238). Others caution that the nations' worship is motivated only by fear. "Nothing about coming and worshiping implies conversion or redemption" (Carey 1999, 161–62).

Recent ecological scholarship underscores the centrality of God's declaration to "destroy the destroyers of the earth" (11:18). The term "destroyers" (*diaphtheirontes*) also refers to "corruption," a likely allusion to the flood story of Genesis 6–9, applied to the Roman Empire's violence also in 19:2. John makes an important change from the original flood story. Whereas in Genesis the intent was to destroy the earth along with evildoers (Gen 6:13), John underscores that only the destroyers themselves—not the earth—will be destroyed. The declaration of Rev. 11:18 sets the program for the entire second half of the book (Stephens, 197–98). The judgment that will subsequently unfold in chapters 12–20 is the judgment God pronounces on the violent systems that destroy peoples and the earth.

Revelation 12: Witness to Hope: The Woman, the Dragon, and Earth's Daring Rescue

◼ THE TEXT IN ITS ANCIENT CONTEXT

Beginning with chapter 12, the second half of the book is about the defeat of evil. Different aspects of the unjust Roman imperial system—personified as Satan and his agents—are defeated in reverse order of their introduction (Bauckham 1993a, 20; Koester). Satan is introduced in chapter 12 and defeated in chapter 20. The beast from the sea and the beast from the earth, together representing Rome's military/political system and its local collaborators, are introduced in chapter 13 and then defeated in chapter 19. The whore of Babylon, representing Rome's predatory economic system, is introduced and defeated in chapters 17–18.

Revelation 12 takes the form of an inclusion, with a central story of the war in heaven (Rev. 12:7-12) sandwiched between two stories about the cosmic woman and the dragon (12:1-6 and 12:13-17; Schüssler Fiorenza 1991, 80). These deeply symbolic stories represent the life-and-death struggle against evil that is at the heart of the book. They give hearers hope and courage to persevere in witness.

Revelation does not proceed chronologically. Even though these stories come in the middle of the book, they are most likely flashbacks to the past—to Jesus' victory on the cross—in which Satan and evil were already defeated. Revelation uses highly pictorial and visionary language to communicate spiritual truths.

In the first story (Rev. 12:1-6 and 12:13-17), a pregnant woman in the throes of labor gives birth to a son, then acquires two wings of a great eagle to escape the dragon. Both the woman and the dragon are called "signs" (*sēmeia*, 12:1, 3), underscoring the symbolic character of the stories.

John borrows and subverts a popular mythological story of his day, familiar from multiple Roman, Egyptian, and Hellenistic variations (Collins 1976 and 1993). The story of the birth of the god Apollo to the goddess Leto, and their escape from the dragon Python, was a favorite of Roman emperors who identified themselves with Apollo. By scripting the emperor as the dragon, John used the story to assert Jesus' lordship rather than the emperor's.

John reworks the story to make it a story about Jesus. The child is depicted as the Messiah of Psalm 2, who will "rule all the nations with a rod of iron" (Rev. 12:5; see also 2:27; 19:15). The heavenly woman probably does not represent the Virgin Mary (since John does not appeal to other stories of Jesus' mother or family) but is a larger symbolic depiction of Israel, the whole people of God, imaged in cosmic terms. Jesus is born of the people of God.

John models the dragon on earlier political references to foreign nations as "dragons" (Egypt as a dragon, Ezek. 32:2; the Roman general Pompey who conquered Jerusalem as an "arrogant dragon," *Pss. Sol.* 2:25), combined with the deceptive serpent from Genesis 3 and the ten horns from Daniel's fourth beast (Dan. 7:7). The woman flees from the dragon into the wilderness, a familiar biblical place of refuge for the Israelites as well as for Hagar (Gen. 21:14-21).

Into this story of the woman's childbirth and rescue in the wilderness, John sandwiches the epic heavenly battle of the "dragon-slayer" (Sánchez), with overtones of a legal courtroom trial (Schüssler Fiorenza 1991, 81). The angel Michael is familiar from Daniel (Dan. 10:21; 12:1). Satan is familiar as a biblical name given to the personification of evil and deceit as an "accuser," especially in Job. In 12:9, John lists other names for the dragon, culminating in "deceiver of the whole empire [*oikoumenē*]." Michael and his angels defeat the dragon and his angels, throwing them down from heaven to earth. But although heaven is now become a "Satan-free zone" (Smith, 65), Satan still temporarily prowls the earth. Readers live in the in-between time, symbolically pictured as the time and space between Satan's expulsion from heaven and his being thrown down into the abyss (20:3, 10).

Even though earth cannot yet rejoice, a voice calls out in heaven, celebrating Satan's defeat. The victory hymn (12:10-12) makes the surprising declaration that it is God's people themselves who have "conquered" Satan, both by the blood of the Lamb (underscoring nonviolent resistance) and by the power of their witness or martyrdom (two possible translations of the same Greek word, *martyria*). "Conquer" recalls the promises to the churches in Revelation 2–3 that they would become "conquerors," just as Jesus conquered. The victory song concludes with a lament ("Alas" or "woe," 12:12) on behalf of the earth and sea, similar to 8:13.

Earth plays a heroic role as the mythic story resumes. Personified as a feminine figure (the feminine noun *gē*) with a mouth, the earth rescues the heavenly woman by swallowing the dragon's river. Heroic swallowing by Earth is a motif found also in the anti-Roman apocalypse *2 Baruch* (*2 Bar.* 6:6-10). Earth's heroic swallowing recalls the Exodus victory song after the crossing of the Red Sea, when the Israelites gave thanks that the earth "swallowed" up the Egyptians (Exod. 15:12).

Chapter 12 closes on an ominous and deeply symbolic note. The woman and child have been rescued, but the dragon is angry that he has been thrown out of heaven. Since he cannot devour Jesus, he goes off to make war against the "rest of [the woman's] children, those who keep the commandments of God and hold the testimony of Jesus" (12:17). Things will get worse under Rome's rule before they get better. During the time visualized by the sequence of the seven bowls (Revelation 16), the suffering will be twice as intense as it was during the seven trumpets sequence.

◼ THE TEXT IN THE INTERPRETIVE TRADITION

Battles and characters from Revelation 12 feature prominently in interpretive history and art. In some Western churches the Feast of the archangel Michael and All Angels is celebrated on September 29 (with lectionary readings from Dan. 12:1; Rev. 12:7-9). The Feast of the Virgin of Guadalupe on December 12, celebrated by many throughout Latin America and North America, also assigns Revelation 12 as the lectionary reading.

The woman clothed with the sun has shaped the self-understanding of many Christian women prophets, beginning with Maximilla and Priscilla, the leaders of the New Prophecy ("Montanist") movement popular in Asia Minor and North Africa in the late second century. Mother Ann Lee (1736–1784), founder of the Shakers, also saw herself in the woman of Revelation 12 (Wainwright, 96). Women mystics such as Hildegard of Bingen and Hadewijch of Brabant drew on imagery of the heavenly woman to narrate their own visionary experiences (Huber).

The Virgin Mary became associated with the woman of Revelation 12. Sixth-century commentator Oecumenius interpreted the woman's flight into the desert as the flight into Egypt to escape Herod's plot and the "wings of the great eagle . . . given to the all-holy Virgin" as the angel who exhorted Joseph to take the child and his mother to Egypt (Suggit 2006, 116). Pope Sixtus IV's approval of the Feast of the Immaculate Conception of Mary in the fifteenth century further strengthened the identification of Mary, as the Queen of Heaven, with the woman of Revelation 12 (Kovacs and Rowland, 135).

The Virgin of Guadalupe, who appeared to indigenous Mexican peasant Juan Diego Cuauhtlatoatzin on December 12, 1531, took the form of the woman of Revelation 12, with the moon and stars around her head. Indigenous resistance to Spanish conquest both appropriated and subverted apparition accounts of the Virgin—drawing on traditions brought to the Americas by the Spaniards, who were themselves steeped in Franciscan apocalyptic spirituality (Sánchez).

Protestants view the woman of Revelation 12 either as the church or as Israel. Martin Luther's hymn "My Bride, the Church, Is Dear To Me" (trans. Samuel Janzow [St. Louis: Concordia, 2004]) sings a love song about the church portrayed as the woman of Revelation 12. The bridal church wears a crown of gold with twelve stars, and "brings forth her noble Son."

Many artists have illustrated the woman of Revelation 12. Inspired by the fourteenth-century Angers Apocalypse Tapestry, French artist Jean Lurcat's huge 1950 tapestry in the church in Plateau d'Assy depicts the woman and dragon facing each other, in red, black, and white. The worshiper's eye is drawn to the victorious woman enclosed in the sun's flaming orb, her arm raised in triumph. Red and green panels on either side show the tree of life and the Jesse tree of Christ's genealogy.

▌THE TEXT IN CONTEMPORARY DISCUSSION

Feminist scholars debate the feminine symbolism of Revelation, including whether the heavenly woman of Revelation 12 is the same figure as the bridal new Jerusalem of Revelation 21 (Humphrey 1995). From a history of religions approach, the woman is portrayed as a strong goddess figure, in contrast to the imperial goddess Roma (Collins 1993). Yet both of Revelation's positive feminine figures—the woman of Revelation 12, who is exiled, and the bride of 19:17, who is transformed into a city—can become overshadowed by the stereotypically evil feminine portraits. Elisabeth Schüssler Fiorenza cautions against a reading approach that focuses single-mindedly on a dualistic gender framework, since gendered language is symbolic, not natural (Schüssler Fiorenza 1998). The legacy of Revelation's gendered imagery, including its bride/whore polarity, is ambiguous at best (Pippin).

"Earth," another positive personified feminine character well-known from Greek mythology, should not be overlooked (Friesen, 186). Earth plays a heroic role in Revelation's cosmic drama. While Revelation's ecological "texts of terror" (Stephens, 216) can give the impression that the book predicts destruction for the earth, the rescuer role given to the earth in 12:16 underscores a positive valuation for it.

Revelation 13: Sea Beast and Earth Beast: Allies of the Dragon

▌THE TEXT IN ITS ANCIENT CONTEXT

In chapter 13, John critiques a "web of empire-worship institutions" (Kraybill, 53) by portraying the Roman Empire as a tool of Satan—a bold portrayal, since Rome was still very much in power. Specifically, John links the leaders of the empire with the images of two monstrous beasts in order to critique Rome's ideology of power.

Daniel 7 provides the model for the beasts, with its succession of four world empires. John's beast from the sea incorporates aspects of all four of Daniel's beasts. Its seven heads and ten horns are identical to those of the dragon in 12:3. The head that has suffered a mortal wound (13:3) should probably be identified with the emperor Nero. After Nero's death in 69 CE, the Roman Empire had fallen into chaos but then recovered, becoming even more invincible with the Flavian emperors, including Domitian. People became enthralled by Rome's power; thus John depicts them crying out, "who is like the beast?" (13:4).

Imagery of the throne and worship is central to John's critique of Rome. The whole earth now follows the monstrous beast and "worships" (*proskynei*, 13:4, 8) its imperial system, along with the dragon whose throne is given to the beast. The beast's throne and worship constitute a direct affront to God's throne and the worship scene of chapter 4. Imagery of the beast mimics that of the Lamb, with the same word group (*esphagmenon*, "wounded"; *sphazein*, "to slaughter") used for the mortal "wound" marking the deathblow of both the beast and the Lamb (5:6, 9, 12; 13:3, 8). A demonic "trinity" of Satan, the beast from the sea, and the beast from the earth (the false prophet) is a hideous distortion, parodying the divine trinity of God, the Lamb Jesus, and the spirit (Koester).

Rome rules through military power and also through deception. The first beast, representing the government of Rome and its military and political system of conquest, "is allowed to make war on the saints and to conquer them" (13:7). The second beast likely represents Asia's elite local leadership that "deceives" (13:14). Imperialism requires indigenous collaboration (Carey). The second beast is able to perform prophetic signs to deceive people (13:13), perhaps a reference to the cult statues of emperors and divinities that could be made to speak. The beast from the earth is also called the false prophet (16:13; 19:20; 20:10).

The "mark of the beast" (13:17) probably refers to the image of the emperor on Roman coins, or to some other economic aspect of empire. Rome's predatory economic system will be critiqued as the whore of Babylon in chapters 17–18. The numerical reference to the satanic dragon as "666" (13:18; 616 in some manuscripts) is a riddle that may have multiple meanings, including that of imperfection. (Since seven was considered the number of perfection, six would have implied imperfection.). However, a Hebrew practice of assigning numerical value to transliterated letters of the alphabet, called gematria, may be intended to calculate the sum of numbers to refer to a specific emperor's name—most likely Nero Caesar. (The Latin transliteration for Nero would explain the variant 616; Aune 1998, 769–71).

▋The Text in the Interpretive Tradition

The two beasts of Revelation fueled interpretive imagination, especially as they became associated with the "Antichrist" (a figure not found in Revelation or Daniel). In the tradition of Augustine, most interpreters understood the beasts as general manifestations of evil (Reeves). Joachim of Fiore broke from tradition, however, labeling each of the beast's heads as specific historical tyrants, including the Muslim Saladin and a final Antichrist still to come. Influenced by Joachim, radical Franciscan Peter Olivi correlated the first beast to Islamic power and the second beast to false prophets and a false pope within the Christian church (McGinn 1994). Many reformers in subsequent centuries, including John Wycliffe and Jan Hus, seized on Olivi's identification of the papacy with the beasts, a tradition that had intensified during the fourteenth-century split of the papacy between Avignon and Rome. Reformer Martin Luther simply appropriated this already-existing critique and applied it to the papacy of his own time in the sixteenth century.

Various interpreters today claim to have "figured out" the symbolism of 666, whether in universal product bar codes, credit cards, or in world leaders whom they detest. Mary Stewart Relfe's

When Your Money Fails: The "666 System" Is Here, published in 1981, sold more than 600,000 copies (Boyer). Fears of the number 666 remain widespread in popular culture.

▌THE TEXT IN CONTEMPORARY DISCUSSION

Scholarly debates have focused on particular issues such as the meaning of 666 as an anti-Roman economic symbol, and the critique of the local imperial cult leadership in Asia Minor as the second beast.

Revelation 13 has played an important role in liberation movements and their contribution to New Testament scholarship. In John's view, the Roman government was satanic; it must not be honored or obeyed. Revelation 13 gives a different view of government from Paul's counsel in Romans 13 that government is "God's servant for your good" (Rom. 13:4), and from 1 Pet. 2:13-17 and other passages that exhort Christians to honor government. The 1985 South African "Kairos Document" critiqued the use of Rom. 13:1-7 to justify the apartheid system, instead lifting up Revelation 13, where "the State becomes the servant of the dragon (the devil) and takes on the appearance of a horrible beast. Its days are numbered." In Brazil, a landless peasants' protest encampment was inspired by the depiction in Revelation 13 of the state as the beast (Westhelle).

Recent New Testament scholarship on Paul's epistles and the Gospels has moved in major anti-imperial directions (Horsley 1997; 2003), in part thanks to Revelation 13. In John's view, Rome itself was the primary perpetrator of satanic violence in the world—and that is why the entire Roman Empire must come to an end.

Revelation 14: Followers of the Lamb, Harvest of the Earth: The Alternative Community

▌THE TEXT IN ITS ANCIENT CONTEXT

Revelation 14's vision of the people of God constitutes a bold response to the realities depicted in chapter 13. Satan's two agents—the beast from the earth and beast from the sea—may seem to have the upper hand. But on Mount Zion, "the Lamb of God holds the high ground" (Koester, 136).

This chapter shapes the identity of the people of God as an alternative community of followers of the Lamb, in contrast to the community of the beast. Like the interludes after the sixth seal and sixth trumpet, Revelation 14 functions to encourage the churches to see their role in God's spiritual battle of salvation and judgment. This chapter may even be viewed as the literary and theological center of Revelation (Richard 1995, 117).

Several images draw on Joel 3, including Mount Zion, the imagery of holy war, and a two-stage harvest. In biblical tradition, Zion evokes a place of safety and protection (Isa. 24:23; Joel 3:21), where the remnant is gathered. It is not clear whether John envisions Mount Zion as a gathering on earth (Richard 1995, 117) or in heaven (Talbert, 59; Koester, 136). The Lamb "standing" (resurrected) hearkens back to 5:6. John depicts the Lamb's community as "standing strong" (Blount 2009, 265) against the community of the beast.

John uses multiple metaphors to depict the community. The number 144,000 is familiar from Revelation 7 as the 12,000 sealed from each of Israel's twelve tribes. Now this same group of 144,000 is imaged as "those who follow the Lamb wherever he goes" (14:4)—that is, those who resisted Roman assimilation and obeyed the call for endurance and faith (13:9-10). As in Revelation 7, the number 144,000 is not meant literally. That the community is imaged as an army is suggested by the word "thousands" (*chiliades*), a military term. This army's weapons are not violence but endurance and faithfulness (14:12).

The "new song" represents the spirituality of resistance on earth that God's people learn from heaven (5:9). Only followers of the Lamb can learn to sing the new song, in contrast to worshipers of the beast who "cannot sing" (Richard 1995, 119).

To further shape the identity of the alternative community as a spiritual army, John draws on holy war metaphors of purity and virginity (Deut. 23:9-10; 1 Sam. 21:5), as well as a Sinai holiness tradition requiring men not to defile themselves with women (Exod. 19:5). "Defile" is figurative language for idolatry, as in the message to Sardis (3:4), perhaps alluding to Enoch's Watchers who "defiled" themselves (*1 En.* 7:1; 9:9; 10:11; Stenstrom). Holy war imagery is employed metaphorically to portray a war of religious commitments—the Lamb's community versus the army of the beast.

In 14:4, John draws on additional metaphors to portray the Lamb's followers as an alternative community: They are "first fruits," dedicated to God (Exod. 23:19), the first offering without blemish. Harvest metaphors for the community will be used again in 14:14-16. The community is "redeemed" or "purchased," a metaphor for buying a slave's freedom (recalling 5:9).

Three angels with messages fly through the air in quick succession, similar to the eagle of 8:13. The angels' exhortations and threats summarize Revelation's entire argument (deSilva, 258). The first angel proclaims the "gospel" that the hour of God's judgment has come. This judgment is good news: God is the one "who made the earth," and God's desire is for the whole world to give God glory and worship.

The second angel announces the fall of "Babylon the great" (Isa. 21:9), using a prophetic funerary dirge to preview the portrayal of Babylon's destruction in Revelation 17–18. The label "Babylon" links Rome and its recent destruction of Jerusalem to the hated empire that destroyed Jerusalem six centuries earlier, in 587 BCE.

The third angel's proclamation brings terrifying threats. Those tempted to worship the beast are threatened with God's cup of wrath, a contrast to Babylon's wine of wrath (*thymos*, the same word in 14:8 and 10, drawing on Jer. 25:15). The message to readers is that neutrality is not possible. People must worship either God or the beast. Graphic threats of eternal torment in the presence of the Lamb and God's angels function as warnings, shocking the audience.

Exhortation is also the goal of the next two prophetic utterances. Revelation 14:12 calls for hearers' resistance (*hypomonē*) and faithfulness, similar to 13:18. The beatitude for those who die (14:13) is the second of Revelation's seven beatitudes. Deeds (*erga*) are the crucial measure of faith, underscored in 20:12 with the image of books recording the deeds of the dead.

The two-stage harvest (grain harvest followed by grapes) draws on Joel 3:13. The first stage—the grain "harvest of the earth" (14:15)—is likely a positive image for the community's ingathering, similar to Mark 4:29 and John 4:35-37, recalling the Lamb's community as "first fruits" of the harvest (14:4). John reflects the positive, even joyful, usage of the term "harvest" (*therismos*). The vision of one "like a Son of Humanity" (14:14) hearkens back to 1:13 and Dan. 7:13. John adds the sickle as a positive image of harvest, not an image of destruction (Bauckham 1993a, 96–98).

By contrast, the second stage of grape harvest and grape-pressing inaugurated by a different angel brings terrifying judgment. The image of treading the winepress of the fury of God's wrath draws on Isa. 63:3-6. The judgment is executed not by God but by an angel—thus tempering the Isaiah imagery. The bloodbath up to the horse's bridle is a standard apocalyptic image (*1 En.* 100:1-3; *4 Ezra* 15:35).

▊ THE TEXT IN THE INTERPRETIVE TRADITION

The identity of the Lamb's followers as 144,000 "virgins" (a number mentioned also in 7:4) evokes diverse interpretation. The virgins were sometimes understood literally as Christian virgins (Tertullian), or as Jewish Christians (Victorinus; Wainwright, 28). Drawing on the "first fruits" imagery, some Roman Catholics interpreted them as a special group of celibates within the larger group of the church (Murphy, 314). Protestants understood them symbolically as the whole church, imagined as a priestly people. For Jehovah's Witnesses, founded in the late nineteenth century, a literal interpretation of Rev. 14:1-4 means that a special class of exactly 144,000 people will rule with Christ in the millennium (Wainwright)—although their identity as "virgins" is not literal.

During the Civil War, Julia Ward Howe applied the violent imagery of the trampling of the grapes of wrath in 14:17-20 to what she viewed as God's judgment on citizens of the United States for their tolerance of slavery. Her 1862 abolitionist hymn "The Battle Hymn of the Republic" interpreted the bloody Civil War as a loosing of God's "terrible swift sword" against a bloody institution of her day—slavery. In majestic cadences, she portrayed the imagery of grape harvest as bringing justice and liberation. John Steinbeck drew on her imagery in *The Grapes of Wrath* to critique the economic injustice of the effects of the Dust Bowl in the 1930s.

The image of the blood flowing as high as horses' bridles is prominent in the *Left Behind* novels. Authors Tim LaHaye and Jerry B. Jenkins, like other premillennialists, understand the image literally, as the bloody future battle in Israel after Christ's "glorious appearing" when Christ and his forces return to earth to kill his enemies with the sword of his mouth (19:15).

In his *German Requiem*, composed in 1865, Johannes Brahms gives one of the most moving and beautiful musical interpretations of the beatitude in 14:13, "Blessed are those who die . . . their works follow them" ("Selig sind die Toten").

▊ THE TEXT IN CONTEMPORARY DISCUSSION

Many interpreters grapple with the misogyny implicit in the description of the followers of the Lamb as 144,000 male "virgins who have not defiled themselves with women." Taken literally, the language depicts a community of only celibate males—no women or married men. Such a misogynist view that all women are defiling is not likely John's intent, however, since elsewhere he uses positive feminine metaphors for marriage and the community (the mother, Revelation 12; the bride's marriage, 19:7; 21:2; Schüssler Fiorenza 1991). If John intends the celibacy language literally, he may mean a temporary or priestly celibacy, perhaps analogous to the Essenes (Collins 1984).

The language of defilement makes this gendered metaphor especially problematic, with its legacy of excluding women as "defiled" throughout Christian history (Pippin).

Chapter 14 also raises ethical questions about divine violence. The scene of eternal torture (14:9-11), carried out "in the presence of the Lamb," furnishes some of the most graphic imagery of the book. Even if John uses imagery of fire and sulfur hyperbolically, for the purpose of exhortation rather than prediction—effectively shocking the audience into repentance (Schüssler Fiorenza 1991, 91; Koester, 139)—the language is terrifying. Its function may also be cathartic, preventing Christians from engaging in any actual violence themselves (Collins 1984, 156–75).

Revelation 15: The Song of Moses and the Lamb

▌ THE TEXT IN ITS ANCIENT CONTEXT

John introduces a new vision by the word "sign" or "portent" (*sēmeion*, 15:1), the same word used for the heavenly woman and the dragon in 12:1, 3. Seven angels with seven bowls containing plagues are the "last," after which the wrath of God will end. But first, as with the seven trumpets, John lifts the community's eyes to the heavenly throne room to give assurance, in advance of the terrifying plagues to come.

The Exodus link is now made explicit: Those singing the Song of the Lamb in heaven also sing the "Song of Moses" (15:3). John remaps the story of the Exodus onto his own community. Those who have refused to participate in Roman worship are metaphorically likened to the Israelites who crossed through to the other side of the Red Sea. The community stands at the shore of the sea of glass (4:6), like the Israelites standing on the shore of the Red Sea. Jesus the Lamb is scripted in the role of Moses. Bestial Rome becomes the new Egypt, from which God's people escape. Their "new song" of victory hearkens back to the song Moses and Miriam taught the Israelites (Exodus 15), combined with imagery from the Psalms (Pss. 86:8-10; 98:1-2).

The reference to those who "conquered" the beast makes a bold claim for God's people, as does their "standing." In contrast to Rome's violent conquest, God's people have conquered by their faith and endurance.

This song, like the other heavenly songs of Revelation, functions to give direction and interpretation to the community, "like the chorus in a Greek drama" (Schüssler Fiorenza 1991, 92).

Judgment means justice for victims. "All nations" will worship god, a universalizing of the Exodus song (Bauckham 1993a, 100–101).

The reference to the heavenly temple as the tent of witness (15:5) constitutes another Exodus link, corresponding to the tent sanctuary or tabernacle on Mount Sinai (Exod. 25:9). A living creature holds golden bowls, as in 5:8. Here the bowls contain not the prayers of the saints but the wrath of God that will be poured out upon the earth.

▌ THE TEXT IN THE INTERPRETIVE TRADITION

The richness of the worship scene is reflected in Christian hymnody drawing on imagery from the scene of the worshipers singing beside the sea of glass, often combined with imagery from worship before God's throne in chapters 4–5. Most famous is "Holy, Holy, Holy," written by Reginald Heber, with the image of the saints "casting down their golden crowns upon the glassy sea." Isaac Watts's hymn "Babylon Falling" includes the line "The Christian church unites the songs of Moses and the Lamb." Activist and war protester Daniel Berrigan titled his 1978 book of prayers *Beside the Sea of Glass: The Song of the Lamb*, drawing on imagery from this chapter.

The earliest artistic representation of the glassy sea of 15:2 (also 4:6) is in the apse mosaic in the Church of Sts. Cosmas and Damian, from the sixth or seventh century (McGinn 1992, 207, and 105 fig. 1).

◼ THE TEXT IN CONTEMPORARY DISCUSSION

What is the function of heavenly liturgies and hymns in Revelation such as 15:3-4? Older scholarship saw Revelation's hymns as reflecting the church's actual liturgies. Most scholars now agree that John composed the hymns himself, as part of his rhetorical program.

The hymns of Revelation, including the hymns of chapter 15, likely function as correctives against praise offered to gods and emperors, more than as forming a new cultic liturgical experience for Christians (Schüssler Fiorenza 1976; Ruiz 2001). The cities of Asia Minor were replete with imperial cult liturgies and celebrations including hymns, liturgical processions, altars, and other cultic features, all fostering patriotic allegiance to the empire (Friesen; Thompson). Revelation challenges the imperial cult's liturgies and claims to allegiance by hearkening back to the Psalms and hymns of liberation from Israel's past.

John does not simply adopt biblical hymns but transforms them. By juxtaposing the "Divine Warrior" victory hymn of Exodus 15 with the song of the Lamb, John may be underscoring that God's people conquer nonviolently, through the Lamb's death rather than by divine acts of aggression (Friesen, 190). John calls it the Song of Moses, but the words of the song in fact draw more from Psalms 96 and 98 than Exodus 15. John's intertextuality sets the hymns in "dialogical tension" (Moyise 2004). Perhaps most importantly, John shifts the focus of the hymn from praising God for victory over enemies (Exodus 15) to celebrating the universal worship and praise of God by all nations, thereby developing "the most universalistic form of the hope of the Old Testament" (Bauckham 1993a, 306, 311; contra Beale, 799).

Revelation 16: Seven Bowls, Seven Plagues, and the Angel of the Waters

◼ THE TEXT IN ITS ANCIENT CONTEXT

The seven bowl plagues recapitulate the seven trumpets of Revelation 8–9, with even more destructive intensity. Their effects target the four elements of the cosmos, including earth, sea, rivers and springs, and air. Their destruction is double that signaled by the trumpets. Yet it is important to note that these are not universal plagues against all of humankind, but only targeted against the beast and its followers (Richard 1995, 84).

Like the seven trumpets, the bowl plagues come from the heavenly temple. They follow the same 4-2-1 pattern as the seals and trumpets, but with a much shorter interlude (or no interlude at all) between the sixth and seventh element.

The word "plague" (Greek *plēgē*) literally means "strike" or "blow." The parallel use of the same verb "pour out, shed" (*ekchein*) to refer to both a crime and its consequences underscores the logic of reciprocity, using legal language. The "pouring out" of each bowl's contents of judgment (16:1, 2, 3, 4, 8, 10, 12, 17) reciprocates Rome's own "shedding" of blood (16:6), both described by the same verb. Measure for measure, God's judgments against evildoers match their offense (Blount 2009, 293).

The first bowl plague of boils reflects a brutal symmetry: Those who accepted the mark of the beast are now branded with gruesome sores by God (Blount 2009, 295). The second bowl poured out on the seas recalls the Exodus plagues, turning the water to blood and killing every creature. As in 8:9, sea creatures are described as "souls" (*psychai*), hearkening back to Genesis.

With the third bowl, the logic of consequences is made explicit in a lengthy liturgical doxology about blood by the angel of the waters (16:6). The angel explains that it is precisely because oppressors "shed" the blood of saints and prophets that the waters have turned to blood, and God now gives them blood to drink. As in Isa. 49:26, the bloodthirsty are made to choke on the very blood they shed (Blount 2009, 97). These consequences are "worthy" or appropriate (*axios*; compare "axiomatic," in the sense "self-evident")—reflecting the logic of the action itself. Antiphonal liturgy breaks in at this point in the narrative "so that the community can be actively present" (Richard 1995, 83). A personified talking altar responds to affirm the just judgments of God.

The fourth plague darkens the sun, similar to the fourth trumpet. The function of the plagues to elicit repentance is made clear, by noting that people should have repented (16:9). Instead of acknowledging their Creator and giving God glory, however, recipients curse God. The case is similar with the fifth bowl, poured onto the "throne" of the beast, the seat of the monstrous empire's power. Reminiscent of the Exodus plagues, the beast's kingdom is plunged into darkness. Still, the people curse God and again refuse to repent (16:11).

The sixth bowl, like the sixth trumpet, affects the River Euphrates, the eastern border of the Roman Empire. The Euphrates was familiar from the biblical traditions of enemy nations amassing from the East. The river dries up, facilitating the invasion of demonic foreign nations. Frog-like evil spirits represent the demonic evil trinity of the dragon, the beast, and the false prophet. The false prophet lures kings of the earth into attacking, using "deception" to bring about the collapse of the dragon's entire political system.

Interjected into this scene is the prophetic warning of the third beatitude, urging readers to keep awake (16:15). There is no lengthy interlude between the sixth and seventh elements as in the sequences of seals and trumpets. The brief interjection of Jesus in 16:15, "Behold, I am coming soon! Blessed is the one who stays awake and is clothed," fits the pattern of interludes, although much briefer. Like the other interludes, it shapes the identity of the community. This interlude is so short because the emphasis is now on the imminence of the end, rather than its delay.

"Armageddon" is probably a reference to the ancient site of Megiddo in Israel, where a number of battles in the Hebrew Scriptures were fought (Judg. 5:19; 2 Kgs. 23:29–30; *har* means "mountain" in Hebrew, so *Har-Megiddo* would mean "mountain of Megiddo"). While Armageddon is popularly imagined as a battle, it is striking that no battle is described in 16:16. Instead, the battle is delayed—most likely until 19:19-21—although even there, no battle is narrated. This is typical of John's use of delay, to allow time for repentance, and to temper the threats of violence. The armies amass at the mountain of Megiddo. But instead of a battle, the scene shifts to the judgment of Babylon (16:19).

When the seventh bowl is poured out, the voice from God's throne pronounces the end, accompanied by a theophany and earthquake greater than at any previous time (Dan. 12:1). The seventh bowl targets the air, one of the four elements of creation. God "remembers" Babylon, and forces the unjust city to drink the hated cup of wrath (recalling 14:8 and Jeremiah 25). Even in the face of huge hailstones and cosmic destruction of mountains and islands, people still refuse to repent.

▌ THE TEXT IN THE INTERPRETIVE TRADITION

Those who view Revelation as a road map for world history tend to see themselves as living between the fifth and sixth bowl. In the eighteenth century, Jonathan Edwards viewed Revelation's sixth bowl as coming to fulfillment in the decline of Catholicism, with the "drying up" of the Euphrates (16:12) referring to the evaporation of financial revenue to the Vatican (Thuesen, 47).

Armageddon has engendered more focus than any image of Revelation, even though the word appears only once (16:16) and, as we have seen, no battle is actually narrated there. Some have assumed it is a battle already past (the siege of Masada in 70 CE: Wainwright, 132). For today's premillennialists, it will be a future World War III, centered on the plains of northern Israel, where Christ will defeat the Antichrist and establish a literal thousand-year kingdom in Jerusalem. Ronald Reagan famously speculated about Armageddon in a 1971 dinner speech, pointing to a coup in Libya: "that's a sign Armageddon isn't far off. . . . It can't be long now." For Reagan, the fire and brimstone of Ezekiel and Revelation referred to nuclear weapons (Boyer, 142).

▌ THE TEXT IN CONTEMPORARY DISCUSSION

The angel of the waters and the extended judgment doxology of 16:16 raise the question of how Revelation understands the solidarity between humans and the natural world. John understands natural elements to be represented by messengers or angels (see also the angel of fire in 14:18) who speak out on their behalf against oppressors. John may be drawing on an older tradition that represents the four Hellenistic "elements of the cosmos" (earth, air, fire, and water: Betz, 1969), here made to speak out against human oppression, similar to Enochic literature and to the Egyptian *Kore Kosmou* from the *Corpus Hermeticum*. The angel interprets the plague sequence in a way that can also be understood ecologically: oppressors who commit acts of violence will unleash their own destructive consequences against themselves. A similar ecological logic of consequences can be seen in the Exodus plagues (Fretheim, 1991), the antecedent for John's bowls. The response from the personified altar affirms the judgment as the just consequence, engaging the community in active liturgical response to the empire's own violence that de-creates the very fabric of the world.

Liberation scholar Pablo Richard likens the bowl plagues to multiple forms of contemporary imperial oppression, identifying the plagues of Revelation today as "the disastrous results of ecological destruction, the arms race, irrational consumerism, the idolatrous logic of the market" (Richard 1995, 86).

Revelation 17:1—19:8: Courtroom Trial, Judgment, and Funeral for Babylon/Rome

▌THE TEXT IN ITS ANCIENT CONTEXT

Revelation culminates in a tale of two cities, with a call to make a choice between them. Like a tour guide, John leads the audience on contrasting tours of the two rival political economies. The same angel issues the invitation, "Come, I will show you," and carries John "in the spirit" to a location where he is shown each city (cf. 17:1 and 21:9). Readers must make the urgent choice to "come out" of the imperial system of Babylon (18:4), so that they can "come in" to God's new Jerusalem, the city of blessing and promise (22:14).

Both cities are personified metaphorically as feminine figures, reflecting the grammatically feminine gender of the noun "city" (*polis*) in Greek, a trait of the Hebrew Bible as well. The city of Babylon is labeled a "whore" or "prostitute," whereas new Jerusalem is called a "bride" (Rev. 17:1; 21:2). John may be structuring the ethical contrast according to the binary structure of two feminine figures, good and evil, from Proverbs 5–9, or from the familiar story of the choice between Pleasure and Virtue posed to Heracles (Rossing 1998). He applies feminine personifications of cities, as we find in the Hebrew prophets, to political economies.

The first tour shows the judgment of the evil city, Babylon (Revelation 17–18), representing Rome's seductive economic system. Babylon is clad in luxurious jewelry and scarlet, riding astride the seven-headed Roman beast (familiar from Revelation 12–13). The refrain of "purple and scarlet," gold, and "jewels and pearls" unites the entire Babylon vision (17:4; 18:12; 18:16).

The label "Babylon" triggers biblical memories of the hated Babylonian empire that destroyed Jerusalem in 587 BCE, analogous to Rome's destruction of Jerusalem in 70 CE. Other Jewish and Christian texts also call Rome "Babylon" (1 Pet. 5:13; *2 Bar.* 11:1; *Sib. Or.* 5.143, 158–59; *4 Ezra* 2:36-40).

The charge of "fornication" against Babylon/Rome is metaphorical; the offense is economic exploitation, modeled on biblical critiques of the ancient maritime empire of Tyre. Isaiah labeled Tyre's trade and economic gain as "fornication" (Isa. 23:15–18); John attacks Rome's trading alliances.

Rome's golden cup, modeled on the biblical cup of wrath (Jeremiah 25), contains an intoxicating poison—symbolizing "desire" that is at the heart of the entire Babylon vision (Callahan 1999). Nations have become drunk on Rome's wine of fornication (17:4; 18:3). John even uses the imagery of "sorcery" (*pharmakeia*, 18:23) to describe the "deceptive" spell cast by Rome's economic system, linking Babylon to Jezebel, the beast, and other deceitful characters in Revelation.

The image of "mother" of whores (17:5) refers to Rome as a "mother city" or metropolis, capable of founding daughter colonies. The beast's seven horns are to be identified as the famed seven hills of Rome (17:9).

Babylon/Rome's downfall is launched by its own client kings who turn against the empire in 17:16. Taken literally, the punishment of Babylon in 17:16 can sound like a horrific scene of gang rape (Pippin). A better translation of 17:16 may be "they will make it a wasteland and denuded," to emphasize the language primarily as imagery of a city besieged rather than of torture of a woman's body (Rossing 1998, 87–97). That Babylon is an empire, not a woman, is made explicit in 17:18: "The woman you saw is the great city that rules over the kings of the earth."

With powerful Exodus language, echoing Jer. 51:45, John calls on the community to "come out" (Rev. 18:4) of the empire before it is too late. Their exodus is not to be a physical departure but rather an economic and social departure, as a call to "create alternatives" (Richard 1995, 135). The punishments of 18:4-6 are carefully structured to show that the judgments against the empire are what it brought on itself by its own violence against others. "Double" restitution is a biblical principle (Isa. 40:2; 47:9; 51:19), now extended into international relations.

The arrogant boast, "I rule as a queen . . . I will never see grief" (18:7), reflects Rome's idolatrous claims of eternal dominance; John also draws on Isaiah's satire of Babylon (see Isa. 47:8).

John portrays the fall of Rome's unbridled economic system through a series of funeral dirges voiced by three groups who profited from Babylon's wealth: kings, merchants, and seafarers. Each group cries "Alas! Alas!" (or "Woe," *ouai*, 18:9, 16, 19), lamenting their fallen city. The central dirge is that of the merchants, lamenting the loss of shipments of cargo they can no longer buy and sell (Rev. 18:9, 16, 19).

The cargo list of Revelation 18:12-13 encompasses the span of Rome's extractions from the land and sea: gold, precious stones, pearls, exotic hardwoods and wooden products, ivory, metals, marble, luxury spices, food, armaments and war horses, and "slaves—even human lives" (18:13). The list draws from Ezekiel's critique of Tyre (Ezek. 27:12-22), updated to critique Rome's economy (Bauckham 1993a). The final two items in the cargo list—"slaves, even human lives" (18:13)—furnish the most explicit critique of slavery and slave trade in the New Testament. John denounces the lucrative slave trade that was the economic backbone of the Roman Empire (Martin). John underscores that slaves are not just "bodies" (*sōmata*) but living people, "human souls" (*psychai*).

Rome's crimes extended beyond crimes against humanity even into crimes against creation. Deforestation, erosion, the silting of rivers, and extinctions of animals and habitats were significant problems caused by the Roman extractive economy, as evidenced by archaeology and by numerous ancient sources (Hughes, 1996). With the cargo list of 18:12-13, John connects the overconsumption of the empire with ecological devastation of lands and peoples.

John portrays the final defeat of Babylon/Rome not on a battlefield but in a court scene, as of a legal class action (Schüssler Fiorenza 1991; Richard 1995, 134). The plaintiffs are the saints, representing all Rome's victims who have been killed on earth. The charge is murder: "In you was found the blood of prophets and of saints, and of all who have been slaughtered on earth" (Rev. 18:24). The cargo list of 18:12-13 serves as the list of exhibits in the lawsuit (Callahan 1999, 60). The judge is God. An angelic voice explains the verdict and sentence, pronouncing Babylon guilty on all charges, and sentencing the empire to receive a like measure of its own unjust medicine at the hands of its victims (18:6–8).

The vision culminates with a dramatization of Babylon's fall (18:21), modeled on a similar scene from Jer. 51:63-64. An angel takes up a large millstone and throws it into the sea, proclaiming Babylon's destruction.

Joy breaks out in heaven and on earth when the sentence is announced, with the posttrial celebration of plaintiffs extending to the celebration of God's angels in heaven (18:20).

The judgment scene closes with a heavenly liturgy, 19:1-8. Four hallelujah choruses and acclamations praise God for bringing the great harlot city to justice. Salvation, glory, and power (19:1) are Roman political terms, now reclaimed by God. The saints' cry from under the altar for recompense or "vindication" (6:9-11) is finally fulfilled in 19:2.

After the judgment of Babylon/Rome, a brief preview introduces the bride of the Lamb (19:7), wearing the righteous deeds of the saints. As with the brief preview of Babylon in 14:7, a beatitude follows ("Blessed are those invited to the marriage supper of the Lamb," 19:9). The invitation to the Lamb's marriage feast will be fulfilled in the new Jerusalem vision of Revelation 21–22, when the bride is transformed into a city.

▌ THE TEXT IN THE INTERPRETIVE TRADITION

The image of Rome as the garish "whore of Babylon," wearing gold jewelry and a scarlet dress, and seducing victims with her cup of fornication (17:3-6), is one of the most unforgettable images of Revelation. Throughout the history of art and literature, the whore of Babylon has become the ultimate evil woman in cultural imagination—linked also to "Jezebel" of Rev. 2:20 via the vocabulary of "deception" (2:20; 18:23). Nathaniel Hawthorne's *The Scarlet Letter* speaks of Hester Prynne as "a scarlet woman and worthy type of her of Babylon" (Bond).

Both the violence and incongruity of interpreting the whore and bride as literal human women, and the Lamb as a literal sheep, can be seen in the sixteenth-century Brussels tapestry *The Marriage of the Lamb*, depicting Rev. 19:7-10. On his hind legs, the lamb stands on the dining table, being cradled by a beautiful woman, his bride, who "looks adoringly at him" (Pippin, 14). Above their heads another woman—Babylon the whore—is consumed by flames as she is being burned alive.

Elizabeth Cady Stanton critiqued the image of the whore of Babylon in her 1902 *Women's Bible*, lamenting Revelation's "painfully vivid" pictures and including much of Revelation 17–18 among texts that should "no longer be read in churches" (Callahan 1999, 54).

Novelist D. H. Lawrence critiqued the "endless envy" embodied in the cargo list of the Babylon vision of 18:12-13, embodying the "Christian desire to destroy the universe" that he saw reflected throughout Revelation (Lawrence, 48).

Yet Revelation's anti-empire critique is vital to liberation theology, especially the condemnation of the Roman economic system. Classicist Ramsay MacMullen sees Revelation 18 as the most daring anti-Roman polemic written by any ancient author during the empire's rule. Most important has been Revelation's critique of the slave trade, the clearest articulation of slave trading as evil in the New Testament. In the nineteenth century, abolitionists, including the Reverend Uzziah C. Burnap and others, lifted up Rev. 18:13 in denouncing slavery and the slave trade in the United States (Callahan 1999, 60n45).

During twentieth-century liberation struggles in Latin America and South Africa, Revelation's analysis and critique of the violent Roman economic system inspired analyses and critiques of modern-day empires and economic systems. In the Caribbean, an indigenized Rastafarian reading of the

Bible developed in response to the brutality of conquest, depicting Babylon as the colonial system of oppression (Murrell). The practice of "chanting down" Babylon is reflected in the lyrics of songs by Bob Marley and others: "Get up! Stand up!" "Let's get together to fight this Holy Armageddon" ("One Love") and "We're leaving Babylon, we're going to our Father's land" ("Exodus").

◼ THE TEXT IN CONTEMPORARY DISCUSSION

Feminist liberationist scholars debate how to interpret the destruction of Babylon/Rome in 17:16, since it is presented as the destruction both of a city and of the metaphorical body of a woman. In chapter 17, imagery of the feminine figure is foregrounded, whereas in chapter 18 the emphasis shifts primarily to the metaphorical description of a city. Whether the pronouns for Babylon are translated as "she" or "it" and whether translations are applied consistently to both the Babylon and new Jerusalem visions, affect how the balance between woman and city are interpreted. Unfortunately, English translations typically use "she" for most references to Babylon but "it" for the new Jerusalem (RSV, NRSV), effectively inscribing the duality as that of an evil woman versus a good city, rather than a pair of cities.

What does it look like to "come out" of Babylon? Part of the answer depends on whether the addressees of all the imperatives of 18:6-7 are "my people." The first command to "come out" is clearly addressed to the audience ("my people"). But there has been a reluctance to see the audience as the addressee of the four additional plural commands to "give back" and "double" the punishment Babylon gave to others, and to "mix" and "give" to Babylon a dose of its own torture and grief. To solve the problem, some scholars have introduced hypothetical divine "ministers of justice" (Swete 1911), "heavenly beings" (Collins 1984, 193), or even God (Talbert) as the addressee. The question is important for understanding how the audience (of "my people") plays an active role—not only in coming out of empire but also in "divesting" itself of Babylon/Rome's cup, and even participating in the empire's demise. A few later manuscripts added "to you" to make clear the identification as "my people" for all the imperatives of 18:4-7. The audience's role is "vindication," not vengeance (Callahan 1999, 63; deSilva, 266), actively handing back Babylon's cup in order to divest themselves of all participation in empire. If so, this poses interesting questions for churches and communities of faith today about how to actively "come out" of empire.

Revelation 19:11—20:15: Satan Bound: The Millennium Interlude

◼ THE TEXT IN ITS ANCIENT CONTEXT

Revelation 19–20 presents multiple visions of the defeat of evil. The purpose of these scenes is to show that God's justice wins in the end. Systems of oppression must be brought to judgment. Babylon/Rome's economic system has already been tried and sentenced in the divine courtroom (Revelation 18). Other aspects of Rome and its systemic oppression, represented as Satan and his other agents, must also be defeated. Each different vision begins with "I saw" (19:11, 17; 20:1, 4, 11; 21:1). The multiple visions are symbolic, defying any literal chronology.

Heaven is opened and Jesus comes out, riding on a white horse, to "judge with justice and make war." The imagery may draw from the Wisdom of Solomon, where the personified Word of God is imaged as a mighty warrior, wielding God's commandment as a sword (Wis. 18:15). The sword from Christ's mouth symbolizes the power of his word (Isa. 11:4; 49:2).

A number of features make this scene highly unusual. The garment Jesus wears is already stained with blood before the battle even starts (19:11-13). The source is Isa. 63:1-3, a battle scene in which the blood on the rider's garments is that of Israel's enemies. John changes the imagery so that the blood on the rider's robe most likely is Jesus' *own* blood, shed on the cross—not the blood of his enemies (Caird, 243–44; Boring, 196; Metzger 1993, 91). For Revelation, the key battle was already won in the crucifixion, not some future battle of "Armageddon."

A heavenly army on horses accompanies Jesus, but they have no weapons. Robed in white linen garments, they do not fight. This is different from other texts' image of eschatological battles, as in the Qumran *War Scroll* (1QM 1). In Revelation, the saints do not participate in the final battle.

The picture of the return of Jesus as a heavenly warrior has led to the idea of Christ's second coming, or *parousia*. But "second coming" is not a biblical phrase, nor does Revelation use the word *parousia*. The picture of Christ's arrival on a white horse, wearing diadems and inscription of his titles, resembles a post-battle "triumph," a well-known Roman celebration after a victory in which the victorious general and his army parade home with the spoils of war (Aune 1998, 1050–51). If this is the model, the triumph may celebrate the judgment and defeat of Babylon that already took place in chapter 18, or the defeat of Satan that happened in chapter 12, rather than a future end-times return of Christ for war.

No actual battle is ever narrated. Instead, preparation for war leads immediately to the aftermath: the grisly supper of God's enemies (19:17-21). On the menu are the defeated military leaders and nations, modeled on Ezekiel's portrait of the mythical warrior nations of Gog and Magog being eaten by wild animals (Ezek. 39:17-20). This meal serves as the revolting counterpart to the Lamb's marriage supper, to which readers were invited in 19:7-9. If the angel calling the birds from "mid-heaven" (19:17) is the same as the angel of mid-heaven in 14:16, then this scene has a similar function of "urgent warning" (Schüssler Fiorenza 1991, 106).

The defeat of evil continues with the capture and imprisonment of Satan's two beasts (20:1-3), familiar from chapter 13. "False prophet" is another name for the second beast, which "deceived" people (13:14; 19:20), probably representing local imperial elites in Asia Minor. John makes clear that the lies and deceptions by which the empire dominates the world must come to an end (20:3, 10). The lake of fire represents the threat of punishment (20:14; 21:8).

The defeat of oppression and evil culminates when Satan himself is tied up and imprisoned in the underworld, completing the expulsion from heaven begun in chapter 12. Satan symbolizes all the forces of evil in the world, represented by his many names—"the dragon, that ancient serpent, who is the Devil and Satan" (20:2)—the same list as 12:3. The image of shutting up evil in a pit echoes Isa. 24:22 (cf. *1 En.* 10:4-6; 53–54). The point is to remove imperial evil from any further deceiving of the nations. But for reasons that are not made clear, Satan's defeat happens in two steps, with an interlude between them. Satan must be released one more time before his final defeat.

In the interlude, between the first binding of Satan for one thousand years and his final capture and judgment, John introduces the notion of the "first resurrection" (20:4-6), in which those martyred are raised to life to sit on thrones and reign with God. This scene functions as an answer to 6:9, where the souls of the slaughtered cried out from under the altar for vindication (Blount 2005, 59). Now they get their vindication by being raised to life to reign with Christ.

Other Jewish apocalypses such as *2 Baruch* and *4 Ezra* similarly depict a temporary messianic kingdom between the destruction of the Roman Empire and the final judgment, with a duration of four hundred years specified in *4 Ezra* 7:28.

The symbolic millennium is not meant to furnish a literal chronology of linear time. The entire book follows a kind of journey-like "vision time" (Friesen, 158) in which the thousand years represents "vindication time" for the victims of Roman imperial rule. Although the location is not specified as earth or heaven, most likely this picture is intended as a vision of hope for life on earth after the fall of the Roman Empire. The scene ends with the fourth of Revelation's beatitudes, calling "blessed and holy" those who share in the first resurrection (20:6). They are priests of God (reprising the priestly image for the community from 1:6 and 5:10; drawing on Isa. 61:6; Exod. 19:6).

After the thousand years, Satan is released from the Abyss to deceive the mythical nations of Gog and Magog (from Ezekiel 38–39). That these nations apparently survived the previous destruction of hostile nations in 19:11-21 underscores that these visions are not to be understood chronologically. Fire from heaven defeats them, and Satan is thrown into the same lake of fire as the two beasts.

Only the final scene of judgment, 20:11-15, focuses on the judgment of individuals rather than judgment of systems of oppression. God is seated on a great white throne, with all the dead standing before the throne. Books are opened, including the book of life inscribed with people's names from the foundation of the world (13:8; 17:8; 21:27). Each person is judged according to the ledger of his or her "deeds" (*erga*). The last enemy to be destroyed is the personified figure of Death, thrown into the lake of fire along with Hades, to join the rest of Satan's agents. No actual humans are depicted as being thrown into the lake of fire.

Earth and heaven flee from God's presence (20:11)—presumably because they represent the world corrupted by life-destroying forces and imperial oppression (see 21:1).

█ THE TEXT IN THE INTERPRETIVE TRADITION

Disputes about the millennial reign of a thousand years almost kept the book of Revelation out of the Bible, and continue to play an inordinate role in discussions about Revelation. No other New Testament passage mentions a temporary messianic reign before the last judgment, nor is the millennium part of any of the early church's creeds. The brevity of the millennium passage makes clear that it is not the center of Revelation (Murphy).

Early interpreters such as Papias, Justin Martyr, and Irenaeus understood the millennium as a literal time of earthly bliss, combining it with Isaiah 65 and other Scriptures about the renewal of the earth, even though John himself does not make such paradisiacal connections. Irenaeus's hyperbole included descriptions that "vines will grow, each having ten thousand shoots . . . and in each cluster ten thousand grapes, and each grape when crushed will yield twenty-five measures of wine" (*Against Heresies* 5.33.3). Such earthly interpretations came about in part as a way of counteracting gnostic anti-earth tendencies. The thousand years were not necessarily literal years, however, since "the day of the Lord is as a thousand years" (Ps. 90:4; cited by Justin, *Dialogue with Trypho* 80).

Tyconius and Jerome shifted the millennium in a timeless, spiritual direction. The battle depicted in Revelation became the spiritual battle within the individual soul. Augustine completed the turn by claiming Christians are already living symbolically in the millennial age, in the church. The binding of Satan had happened in the first coming of Christ, embodied in Jesus' exorcisms when Satan was bound, and it would last until Jesus' second coming. The first resurrection happened in baptism, with the second resurrection being identified with the final raising of the dead for the judgment at the end of the age.

Augustine's became the dominant interpretation until Joachim of Fiore (1132–1202), when futurist interpretations once again emerged. Today's premillennial dispensationalists continue to critique Augustine's symbolic interpretation of the church as living already in the millennium.

Throughout history, social movements have drawn on Revelation's idea of an earthly millennium in order to promote reform. From the People's Crusade of 1095 (Cohn, 61–68) to the Taborites in fifteenth-century Bohemia to the attempt to establish new Jerusalem in Münster, Germany, in the 1530s (Moore, 298) to the nonviolent communal life of sixteenth-century Anabaptists to Franciscan and Jesuit missionaries pursuing millennial dreams in the New World to the "Diggers" movement advocating for restructuring land ownership in England in the seventeenth century or the Shakers and their Millennial Laws in early nineteenth-century New England, popular movements throughout the centuries have read their own history in light of the millennial vision of Rev. 20:4-6 (Reeves). Even Sir Isaac Newton, a prolific commentator on Daniel and Revelation, gave extensive interpretations of the millennium.

The great white throne of judgment from Revelation 20, combined with the judgment of the sheep and goats from Matt. 25:31-46, has shaped Christian imagination about the last judgment. Medieval cathedrals portrayed this scene over the entrance tympanum, threatening worshipers with judgment as they entered. The twelfth-century sculpture at the Cathedral of St. Lazare in Autun, France, by Giselbertus shows a terrified crowd waiting for the weighing of souls, with tiers of graphic punishments for the damned on Christ's left side, and the blessings of eternal life for those on his right side. Dante Alighieri's late-thirteenth-century Italian poem *The Inferno* depicts the last judgment as one of the church's teachings of "four last things" (death, judgment, hell, and heaven), detailing tortures far surpassing Revelation's lake of fire. Michelangelo's painting of the last judgment before the great white throne, influenced by Dante, occupies the most prominent wall in the Sistine Chapel in Rome. William Blake's allegorical painting *The Day of Judgment* (1808) retains the traditional right/left division between heaven and hell, including vivid rewards and punishments, with the great white throne in the center. He adds the element of earth convulsed with the resurrection life of the dead rising up from their graves.

The mysterious nations of Gog and Magog (Rev. 20:8; Ezekiel 38–39), prevalent in Jewish apocalypticism (cf. *3 En.* 45.5; *Sib. Or.* 3.319), have fueled multiple attempts to correlate Revelation with geopolitical events unfolding in interpreters' own times. Josephus (*Ant.* 1.6.1) identified Gog with the Scythians. Some medieval maps such as the thirteenth-century "Psalter" even pictured a wall in northeastern Europe behind which Gog and Magog were imprisoned (Boyer). Joachim of Fiore identified them as the Saracens; Martin Luther identified them as the Turks (Kovacs and Roland, 213). One British legend combined them into a single figure of a giant named Gogmagog (Jeffrey of Monmouth's *History of Britain*; Emmerson and McGinn, 312).

Twentieth-century premillennial dispensationalists identified Russia as Magog, an identification made popular by Cyrus Scofield's best-selling 1909 *Scofield Reference Bible*. Hal Lindsay's original *The Late Great Planet Earth* includes an entire chapter titled "Russia Is Gog," expanded more recently to include Islamic nations (*Planet Earth: The Final Chapter*, 1998, 280). John Hagee in 2014 interpreted the crisis in Ukraine as a signal that biblical prophecies about Gog and Magog will be fulfilled in an imminent invasion of Israel by Russia, along with Iran, Libya, and other Muslim nations.

▪ THE TEXT IN CONTEMPORARY DISCUSSION

Much scholarly debate focuses on how to interpret the violence and judgment of these final scenes. Whereas Jesus has been depicted as a Lamb since chapter 5, here he is depicted as a warrior, wielding the sword of his word as a weapon. The question is whether Jesus now uses violence to kill his enemies—a departure from the nonviolent Lamb—and how John employs the violent imagery of Isaiah 63. Liberation scholars do not all agree. Brian Blount has changed his position from understanding the blood on his garments to be Jesus' own blood to understanding it now as the blood of his enemies (Blount 2009, 352; contra Blount 2005, 82), although he still underscores that "John depicts the Lamb as a nonviolent resister." In Blount's view, John closely follows Isaiah, working with the imagery of a warrior and the trodden winepress (Isa. 63:1-6; Rev. 20:15), including Isaiah's depiction of the robe dipped in enemies' blood. Other liberation scholars such as Pablo Richard counter that John radically changes the imagery of Isaiah so that the blood is Jesus' own (Richard 1995, 147).

Justice is the focus of all the scenes in Revelation 19–20. When the victims of Rome's injustice are raised to sit on thrones, Richard translates their role as "doing justice" (20:4), with "justice" as a preferred translation rather than "judgment" for the Greek word *krisis* throughout the book. For Richard, the millennium must be reclaimed from the two poles of a fundamentalist literalist interpretation on the one hand or a "spiritualizing" ecclesiastical approach on the other hand that collapses the millennium into the church. The millennial vision's importance for mobilizing poor and oppressed people throughout history needs to be reclaimed as a vision for justice for victims on earth.

The location of the thousand-year reign of the resurrected martyrs is also an important question. While the location has sometimes been understood as heaven (Beale, 998), if it is on earth, as liberation scholars argue, then Revelation gives one of the most important visions for helping us imagine life after empire, on earth—an important element also for ecological hermeneutics.

Revelation 21:1—22:5: New Jerusalem and the Renewed Earth

▌ THE TEXT IN ITS ANCIENT CONTEXT

The promise of a "new heaven and new earth" offers the most earth-centered eschatological picture of the entire Bible, a countervision to Babylon/Rome. Contrary to the escapism or "heavenism" of some interpretations today, the picture of Revelation promises God's future dwelling with people in a radiant, thriving cityscape located on a renewed earth. Heaven is not mentioned again after 21:2.

The entire book leads up to this wondrous vision of renewal and joy. The Lamb's bride (introduced in 19:7) now becomes transformed into a magnificent bridal "city" (*polis*). Images of radiance and beauty persuade readers who have "come out" of empire (18:4) to "enter in" (22:14) as citizens of this landscape of blessing and healing.

Repetition of the word "new" (21:1-2) underscores the distinction between God's renewed world and the Roman imperial world that has gone before. The first earth and the sea have "passed away" (*apēlthon*, 21:1). The identity of the "first earth" that passes away is debated. It likely represents the earth as dominated by Roman imperial violence and exploitation. While some scholars interpret the word "new" (*kainos*) as implying cosmic catastrophe and discontinuity of the new earth from the present earth, similar to 2 Pet. 3:10 (Roloff; Adams), John's point is probably not that the whole cosmos will be annihilated and then replaced (Stephens). Rather, it is the Roman imperial world and the world of sin that must be replaced.

Belief in a heavenly Jerusalem was widespread in biblical times (see Gal. 4:26, "Jerusalem above . . . is our mother"; Heb. 12:22; *2 Bar.* 3:1; 5Q15). Isaiah 54 imagines the renewed Jerusalem as made of precious stones and "married" to God in covenantal love. What is so striking in Revelation—unlike any other Jewish apocalypse—is that this heavenly city descends from heaven to earth.

The radiant new city that descends to earth fulfills Isaiah's promises of newness (Isa. 43:19, 65:17) as well as covenantal promises from Ezekiel and Zechariah, and promises from Revelation's seven letters (Schüssler Fiorenza 1991, 111). Greco-Roman utopian hopes about the ideal city are also fulfilled in the vision's majestic processional street and verdant green space (Georgi 1980).

The repeated phrase "no more" (*ouk eti*, Rev. 21:1, 4) underscores new Jerusalem's contrasts with the toxic city of Babylon/Rome (Revelation 17–18). Mourning, pain, and death—all found in Babylon—come to an end in God's holy city. With great tenderness, God wipes away people's tears. The most pointed contrast between the political economies of Babylon and new Jerusalem is John's declaration that "the sea was no more" (21:1). Although this declaration may reflect biblical chaos traditions associated with the sea (Boring), more likely it serves as part of the political critique of Rome (Wengst), a perspective shared also by the *Sibylline Oracles* 5.447–49. The Mediterranean Sea was the location of Rome's unjust trade, condemned in the cargo list of Rev. 18:12-13. Therefore, in God's new Jerusalem, there will be no more sea trade.

God's presence will have its "dwelling" or will "tabernacle" (*skēnē*, *skēnoō*, Rev. 21:3) in the midst of the bridal city, recalling God's "tabernacling" with Israel in the wilderness (Lev. 26:11-12; Ezek. 37:27; Zech. 2:10-11). The descent of God's dwelling to earth draws on the descent of the personified feminine figure of Wisdom in Sir. 24:4-8, 10-11.

Readers who have come out of Babylon/Rome now are named "victors" or "conquerors" who will inherit all the promises of God (Rev. 21:7). The designation brings to fulfillment the promise to each of the seven churches in Revelation 2–3 ("to the one who conquers," 2:7, 11, 17, 26; 3:5, 12, 21).

God speaks for the first time since Rev. 1:8, not through angelic intermediaries but directly, "Behold, I make all things new." God promises water of life for all who thirst, free of charge. This twice-repeated promise of the water of life *dorean*, "without price" (Rev. 21:6; 22:17), underscores the economic contrast between God's political economy and Rome's. Unlike the unjust commerce of Babylon/Rome, in God's new Jerusalem the essentials of life are given to all who thirst as a free gift, "without money" (Isa. 55:1; Sir. 51:25), even to the poor who cannot pay for them.

The city's descent is narrated a second time, this time as an architectural tour of new Jerusalem (21:9—22:5). The same angelic guide who showed John the judgment of Babylon (17:1) now takes him to a high mountain to "show" him features of God's radiant city. The city is huge (1,500 miles in each direction), shaped as a cube, with golden streets, twelve pearly gates, and foundations of precious stones.

The tour is modeled on the angel's tour of the new temple in Ezekiel 40–48. Revelation makes important changes to open up Ezekiel's priestly vision to everyone. One striking modification is that the new Jerusalem has "no temple" (21:22). God's presence now extends to the entire city's landscape, with all of God's people serving as priests (Rev. 1:6; 5:10; 20:6; 22:3, 5). New Jerusalem is a welcoming city, not a gated community. Ezekiel's temple gate was shut so that "no one shall enter by it" (Ezek. 44:1-2), but the gates into new Jerusalem are perpetually open (21:26). Even foreigners are invited to enter into this radiant city, whose lamp is the Lamb, Jesus. Nations will walk by its light, streaming in through its open gates (21:24, 26).

The bridal city represents the entire renewed world, not just the church (Schüssler Fiorenza 1991, 112; Richard 1995, 164; Krodel, 359). Whereas in the Pauline tradition the bride is the church (2 Cor. 11:2; Eph. 5:25), in Revelation the bride is much more. The city's walls, whose twelve foundations are the twelve apostles, likely represent the church. But the size of the city itself is much larger than the walls and foundations.

Only those whose names are written in Jesus' book of life may enter as citizens into God's new Jerusalem. A lengthy vice list (21:27), similar to other vice lists (21:8, 22:15), warns those excluded from the city. The function of such threats is exhortation, in the tradition of a prophetic wake-up call. John's goal is to persuade readers to be faithful, so that their names will be written in God's book of life.

The final section of this city vision (22:1-6) features paradise-like images of nature and healing. God, nature, and human beings all become reconciled (Georgi 1980).

The image of the "throne" recurs twice in this section (Rev. 22:1, 3). Although it is not explicitly stated, Rev. 22:1, 3 suggests that God's throne will now move down from heaven to earth, in the midst of the city. God's river of life and green space fill out the final description of the city. Revelation 22:1-5 recreates the Garden of Eden in the center of a thriving urban landscape, drawing on Ezekiel's vision of a river flowing out from the temple (Ezek. 47:1-12). In Revelation the river of life flows not from the temple but from the throne of God and the Lamb, through the center of the processional street of the city. Ezekiel's fruit trees on both banks become the wondrous "tree of life" in Revelation (Rev. 22:2), invoking paradise traditions. The fruit of the ever-bearing tree of life satisfies the hunger of all in need, overcoming the prohibition of Gen. 3:22.

Most importantly, the tree's leaves provide healing. In contrast to the toxic *pharmakeia* ("sorcery," Rev. 18:23) of Babylon, God's tree of life gives medicine—*therapeia*—for the world. Healing for the earth is an important apocalyptic theme also in *1 Enoch* ("Heal the earth, announce the healing of the earth," *1 En.* 10:7). The prophet Ezekiel described trees with leaves for healing; Revelation universalizes Ezekiel's vision by adding the "healing of the *nations*" to the tree's healing leaves (Rev. 22:2; cf. Ezek. 47:12). Revelation's medicinal leaves offer a vision of a political economy that heals the entire world. Healing comes not directly from God but through the creation, from a tree.

The tour of the city concludes with reference to God's servants who offer service and worship (*latreusousin*) before the throne (Rev. 22:3). God's servants shall reign forever and ever. At a time when Rome claimed to reign forever, Revelation boldly proclaimed that it is God who reigns—not the empire—and that God's servants will also reign with God. There is no object of the verb "reign." God's servants do not reign over anyone else.

▮ THE TEXT IN THE INTERPRETIVE TRADITION

The vision of the city with the gleaming golden street and pearly gates, where death and tears are no more, has given form and voice to the dreams of God's people through the ages. From Augustine's *City of God* through William Blake's "Jerusalem" and Martin Luther King's "I Have a Dream," Revelation's holy city has promised life and healing, reconciliation and justice.

A prophet of the New Prophecy ("Montanist") movement in the second century, Priscilla, taught that the new Jerusalem would descend in rural Pepuza in Asia Minor (Epiphanius, *Pan.* 49.1.2–3). Partly in reaction to such apocalyptic speculation, Augustine and Tyconius identified the church itself as the new Jerusalem, and baptism as the water of life.

Many have looked for the new Jerusalem as an actual city of hope within history, overturning injustice. African American spirituals and gospel songs inspire hope by evoking imagery of the golden holy city and its river of life. "Blow Your Trumpet, Gabriel" longs for the trumpet to "blow me home" to the new Jerusalem, with its tree of life:

> Blow your trumpet, Gabriel
> Blow louder, louder
> And I hope dat trumpet might blow me home
> To the new Jerusalem.

For Martin Luther King Jr., the new Jerusalem was an ethical vision, offering a view of "what we have to do." King appealed to this vision in his 1968 speech "I See the Promised Land."

> It's all right to talk about "streets flowing with milk and honey," but God has commanded us to be concerned about the slums down here, and his children who can't eat three square meals a day. It's all right to talk about the new Jerusalem, but one day, God's preacher must talk about the new New York, the new Atlanta, the new Philadelphia, the new Los Angeles, the new Memphis, Tennessee. This is what we have to do. (Washington, 282)

Revelation's tree of life gave rise to a rich interpretive history, especially in art. The twelfth-century apse mosaic of the basilica of San Clemente in Rome depicts Christ's crucifix as a life-giving tree for nesting birds and other creatures, from which flows a stream of water giving drink to two deer. The foliage of the tree is portrayed as a new Jerusalem cityscape, with vignettes of people's vocations in daily life encapsulated in the branches of the tree. The tree of life tradition is also present in the "green cross" of the stained glass windows at Chartres cathedral.

Revelation's healing tree inspired the Nobel Peace Prize–winning Green Belt work of Wangaari Maathai in Kenya. She situated her work of planting hundreds of thousands of trees in the tradition of John and other biblical prophets who ask "why we do this to the earth," and she responded that "they are commanding us to heal and replenish it now" (Maathai, 125). Revelation's tree and river also inspired US poet laureate Maya Angelou's poem "On the Pulse of the Morning," invoking the invitation of "a rock, a river, and a tree," read at President Bill Clinton's inauguration in 1993.

The new earth imagery of Revelation 21 became Christopher Columbus's inspiration for his explorations in the vision of the new earth of Revelation 21: "Of the new heaven and earth which our Lord made, as St John writes in the Apocalypse . . . he made me the messenger thereof and showed me where to go" (Kovacs and Rowland, 226).

C. S. Lewis based his "New Narnia" image on Revelation 21, envisioning "new" in terms of both continuity and transformation. In *The Last Battle*, the New Narnia where Lucy and her companions find themselves at the end of their journey is not an escape from old Narnia, but rather an entry more deeply into the very same place. Everything is more radiant. It is "deeper country." New Narnia is "world within world," where "no good thing is destroyed" (Lewis, 181).

◼ THE TEXT IN CONTEMPORARY DISCUSSION

Continuity or discontinuity between the present earth and the eschatological future is a subject of scholarly debate. Traditionally, scholars thought of apocalyptic literature as reflecting a pessimistic outlook of "cosmic dissolution and annihilation" of the present world as a precondition for any new creation (Adams). But recent scholarship has made the convincing case that what was viewed as "cosmic catastrophe" may in fact be more political than cosmic. Apocalypses are resistance literature (Portier-Young, xxii). In times of imperial oppression, Jewish apocalyptic authors employed hyperbolic imagery of the earth rent asunder, followed by a "new heaven" (*1 En.* 91:16), as a way of assuring the audience that oppressive rule will be terminated. The new heaven of *1 Enoch* "consists in the restoration of divine governance" and renewal for the people (Horsley, 2003, 76, 79). Similarly, Revelation's language of the new heaven and the new earth reflects renewal and radical transformation, not replacement or annihilation of the present earth (Stephens; Bauckham 2010, 175).

For ecological hermeneutics, Revelation 21–22 is the most important vision of the book. Revelation suggests that our future dwelling with God will be on a radiant earth. Revelation's declaration of water given "without cost" (*dorean*) can be an important corrective to modern capitalist tendencies to commodify or "festishize" everything (Richard 1995, 130), where even water must be bought and sold. The world's rivers of life and trees of life are not for sale.

As a biblical image common also to many other religions, the tree of life can be an important resource for interreligious dialogue, including "the menorah of Judaism, the tree pattern on an Islamic prayer carpet, the kadamba tree of Krishna in Hinduism, the bodhi tree in Buddhism . . . and the Lakota tree of life at the center of the world" (Ramshaw, 118; Rasmussen, 195–207). Revelation's nation-healing tree of life can invite us into interreligious dialogue with people of other faiths.

Scholars disagree as to the function of the threats of 21:8 and 21:27, and whether John envisions the possibility of universal salvation. If these threats are modeled on Ezekiel 44, they may delineate those forbidden to enter the new Jerusalem. Yet Revelation makes numerous changes to open up the city, especially the proclamation in 22:3 that nothing shall be accursed any longer—perhaps even intending an end to the lake of fire. John depicts a "radically inclusive city" (Boring, 221). Even kings, previously condemned, contribute positively to the splendor of the city in 21:24. These and other verses lead a few scholars (Georgi 1980, 183; Rissi, 80–81) to suggest that Revelation implies the salvation of all. The new Jerusalem vision's proclamation of healing for the nations "brings to fulfillment the conversion of the nations" (Bauckham 1993a, 318). Possibly, what John hopes for is the conversion and salvation of everyone—although most scholars stop short of claiming that John envisions such universalism.

Revelation 22:6-21: Epilogue: Closing Blessings and Exhortations

■ THE TEXT IN ITS ANCIENT CONTEXT

Revelation 22 concludes the prophetic letter with formulaic blessings, warnings, and exhortations. Frequent changes in speaker between the sayings make it difficult to know whether an angel, or John, or the risen Christ is speaking.

Eschatological and ethical urgency underlie this chapter, with the repeated proclamation that Christ will come "soon" (*tachy*, Rev. 22:6, 7, 12, 20) and the declaration that he is the first and the "last" (*eschatos*), the Alpha and Omega (22:13). These themes parallel the opening verses, 1:1-8. The proclamation that Christ would come soon was good news for those who cried out "How long, O Lord?" (Rev. 6:10).

Revelation's journey ends as it began, pronouncing as blessed everyone who "keeps" what is written. Two references to "keeping" (22:7, 9; recalling 1:3) underscore a sense of ethical urgency. The two blessings or beatitudes in verses 7 and 14 are the last of Revelation's seven beatitudes, a typical form of speech used by Christian prophets (see Rev. 1:3; 14:13; 16:15; 19:9; 20:6; 22:7, 14). Recalling the promises to Ephesus and Philadelphia (2:7; 3:12), the beatitude of Rev. 22:14 promises the tree of life and citizenship in the holy city as a reward ("so that they may have the right to come into the city by the gates"). The beatitude assures those who have come out of Babylon (18:4) that they will "come into" God's city of blessing as citizens and heirs. Repetition of imagery of the tree of life and holy city both in this beatitude and in the closing threat of 22:19 underscores their centrality. John invites readers to desire a share (*meros*, 22:19) in the holy city and its tree of life rather than a share (*meros*) in the lake of fire (21:8).

Authentication is one function of the entire closing section. John establishes the book's authority by his claims to have seen the visions (22:8). Even here (as in 19:10), he has to be corrected to worship God alone. The directive not to seal up the vision contrasts with 10:4, where John was directed to seal up the vision (echoing Dan. 8:26).

Multiple threats and warnings also underscore a sense of urgency in this final section. The vice list of 22:15, listing those "outside" the city, like the other vice lists (21:8, 27), may be read as exhortation rather than prediction. It is harder to know what is meant by the imperatives of 22:11. They may indicate that it is too late for repentance—although the beatitude of 22:14 suggests otherwise (Harrington 1993, 222).

Jesus is the bright morning star of Balaam's oracle in Num. 24:17, a text that was already interpreted messianically by the time of the New Testament. "Washing their robes" recalls the vision of the community in 7:14.

Revelation concludes with a liturgical dialogue (Vanni). The entire book has brought hearers on a transformative journey, through hearing the book read aloud in the worship service. This final scene is the homecoming. The antiphonal "Come" (Rev. 22:17) may be part of a eucharistic liturgy in which the Spirit and the bridal new Jerusalem call the community to participate. The reference to "manna" in 2:17 also hints at Eucharist, as does the gift of water for those who thirst—perhaps analogous to some early churches' Eucharists that included water along with wine (Hippolytus, *Apostolic Tradition* 23; Daly-Denton). The invitation to "take the water of life" (Rev. 22:17) draws the new Jerusalem vision to a sacramental close. Drinking and eating at the eucharistic table transport readers in some measure into God's future holy city, to glimpse the throne of God and taste its life-giving water. As in Rev. 21:6, God gives the water of life *dorean* ("without cost"), contrasting the Lamb's gift-economy once again to the ruthless economies of all of Babylon/Rome.

The threats in verses 18-19 against "anyone who adds to" or "takes away from" the words of this book may reflect the prophetic dispute between John and other Christian leaders evidenced in the seven letters of chapters 2–3. Distinguishing true and false prophets was a concern also in other early Christian texts such as the *Didache*.

The closing invocation of 22:20, "Come, Lord Jesus," translates the Aramaic expression *maranatha*, which also appears in *Didache* 10.6 and 1 Cor. 16:22. The letter closing, like the opening, resembles a Pauline letter, with a final announcement of grace (22:21; cf. Gal. 6:18). Ancient manuscripts of Revelation differ by one word as to whether this is a final grace given to "all" or simply to "all the saints"—again raising the question of how far Revelation pushes toward universalism (Boring, 226).

▌THE TEXT IN THE INTERPRETIVE TRADITION

The threats of chapter 22 led Martin Luther, in his 1522 preface to Revelation, to criticize Revelation as "neither apostolic nor prophetic." John "seems to be going much too far when he commends his own books so highly . . . and threatens that if anyone takes anything from it, God will take away from him." By the time of his second preface (1530), Luther had come to see more value in the book.

Many other interpreters have found resonances in this concluding section of Revelation. Hildegard of Bingen appealed to John's threats and pronouncements of authority in order to claim authority for her own book of mystical interpretations, *Scivias* (Kovacs and Rowland, 243). Johnny Cash quoted 22:11 in his 2002 song "The Man Comes Around," the title track of the album. In addition to the pessimistic "let the filthy still be filthy," other images from Revelation fill Cash's song about the Christ's coming in judgment, including Armageddon, the white horse, "It's Alpha and Omega's kingdom come" (21:6; 22:13), and the elders' casting of golden crowns. Cash's song is deeply personal and also dark, perhaps reflecting the sense of his own approaching death.

■ THE TEXT IN CONTEMPORARY DISCUSSION

Four times in this chapter, Jesus says he is coming "soon." His coming means not a terrible final battle at Armageddon or inevitable doomsday for the world, but rather an end to oppression—a radical apocalyptic hope that still resonates today.

Revelation's apocalyptic hope can be read in multiple ways, evoking a broad range of ethical responses. In the area of public policy, for example, when Interior Secretary James Watt was asked by the US House of Representatives in 1981 about the importance of preserving the environment for future generations, he qualified his "yes" with the now-famous remark, "I do not know how many future generations we can count on before the Lord returns." Belief in Christ's imminent coming can lead some people to a disregard for environmental issues and denial of global warming (Northcott; Barker and Bearce). For many others, however, the hope of Christ's coming empowers their commitment to stewardship of God's earth, and even their nonviolent resistance against systems of domination.

Revelation's sense of time can sound threatening. But hope, not threat, is the book's central message. When musician Olivier Messiaen composed his *Quartet for the End of Time* from a Nazi prison camp in 1941, he inscribed the score with words borrowed from Rev. 10:6: "In homage to the Angel of the Apocalypse, who lifts his hand toward heaven, saying, 'There shall be time no longer.'" Revelation's sense of time can sound threatening. But hope, not threat, is the book's central message. Messiaen, like many before him, was able to articulate the radical eschatological hope of Revelation that has been proclaimed through centuries by artists, musicians, poets, reformers, activists, prophets, mystics, and many others.

John's Apocalypse has led hearers through 22 chapters, including dire diagnosis of their situation. His mission has been to help communities see the inevitable end that lies ahead, and then to give them the courage and hope to follow the Lamb, to "come out" of empire before it is too late (Rev. 18:4).

The hope John proclaims is that unjust empires and systems will soon come to an end—in fact, they have already been defeated. The message of hope assures communities thirsting for justice that God hears their cries and that God dwells with them. The hope of Revelation centers on a slain Lamb and a radiant city with gates open to all, with a river of life and a tree that gives healing for the whole world, and healing for each one of us. It is this hope that John intends in the final, summative words, "Amen. Come, Lord Jesus."

Works Cited

Adams, Edward. 2007. *The Stars Will Fall From Heaven: Cosmic Catastrophe in the New Testament and Its World*. New York. T&T Clark.

Alexiou, Margaret. 1974. *The Ritual Lament in Greek Tradition*. Cambridge: Cambridge University Press.

Aune, David E. 1983. "The Influence of Roman Imperial Court Ceremonial on the Apocalypse of John." *BR* 18:5–26.

———. 1990. "The Form and Function of the Proclamations to the Seven Churches (Rev 2–3)." *NTS* 36:182–204.

———. 1997–1998. *Revelation*. 3 vols. WBC 52. Dallas: Word.

Barker, David, and David H. Bearce. 2012. "End-Times Theology, the Shadow of the Future, and Public Resistance to Addressing Global Climate Change." *Political Research Quarterly* 66:267–79.

Barr, David L. 1984. "The Apocalypse as Symbolic Transformation of the World." *Int* 38:39–50.

———. 1997. "Towards an Ethical Reading of the Apocalypse." *SBLSP*, 358–73. Atlanta: Scholars Press.

———. 1998. *Tales of the End: A Narrative Commentary on the Book of Revelation*. Santa Rosa, CA: Polebridge.

Bauckham, Richard. 1977. "The Eschatological Earthquake in the Apocalypse of John," *NovT* 19:216–25.

———. 1993a. *The Theology of the Book of Revelation*. New Testament Theology. Cambridge: Cambridge University Press.

———. 1993b. *The Climax of Prophecy: Studies on the Book of Revelation*. Edinburgh: T&T Clark.

———. 2010. *The Bible and Ecology: Rediscovering the Community of Creation*. Waco: Baylor University Press.

———. 2011. *Living with Other Creatures: Green Exegesis and Theology*. Waco: Baylor University Press.

Beale, G. K. 1999. *The Book of Revelation: A Commentary on the Greek Text*. NIGTC. Grand Rapids: Eerdmans.

Betz, Hans Dieter. 1969. "On the Problem of the Religio-Historical Understanding of Apocalypticism." *Journal of Theology and Church* 6:134–56.

Blount, Brian. 2005. *Can I Get A Witness? Reading Revelation through African American Culture*. Louisville: Westminster John Knox.

———. 2009. *Revelation: A Commentary*. NTL. Louisville: Westminster John Knox.

Boesak, Allan A. 1987. *Comfort and Protest: Reflections on the Apocalypse of John of Patmos*. Philadelphia: Westminster.

Bond, Ronald. 1992. "Whore of Babylon." In *A Dictionary of Biblical Tradition in English Literature*, edited by David Lyle Jeffrey, 26-28. Grand Rapids: Eerdmans.

Boring, M. Eugene. 1989. *Revelation*. IBC. Louisville: Westminster John Knox.

Boyer, Paul. 1992. *When Time Shall Be No More: Prophecy Belief in Modern American Culture*. Studies in Cultural History. Cambridge, MA: Harvard University Press.

Boxall, Ian. 2013. *Patmos in the Reception History of the Apocalypse*. Oxford: Oxford University Press.

Caird, G. B. 1966. *The Revelation of Saint John*. Black's New Testament Commentaries. London: A. & C. Black.

Callahan, Allen. 1995. "The Language of Apocalypse." *HTR* 88:453–70.

———. 1999. "Apocalypse as Critique of Political Economy: Some Notes on Revelation 18." *HBT* 21:46–65.

Carey, Greg. 1999. *Elusive Apocalypse: Reading Authority in the Revelation to John*. StABH 15. Macon, GA: Mercer University Press.

———. 2008. "The Book of Revelation as Counter-Imperial Script." In *In the Shadow of Empire: Reclaiming the Bible as a History of Faithful Resistance*, edited by Richard A. Horsley, 157-75. Louisville: Westminster John Knox.

Cohn, Norman. 1970. *The Pursuit of the Millennium: Revolutionary Millenarians and Mystical Anarchists of the Middle Ages.* Oxford: Oxford University Press.

Collins, Adela Yarbro. 1976 *The Combat Myth in the Book of Revelation.* HDR 9; Missoula, MT: Scholars Press.

———. 1980. "Revelation 18: Taunt-Song or Dirge?" in Jan Lambrecht (ed.) *L'Apocalypse johannique et l'apocalyptique dans le Nouveau Testament.* Gembloux: J. Duculot.

———. 1984. *Crisis and Catharsis: The Power of the Apocalypse.* Philadelphia: Westminster.

———. 1993. "Feminine Symbolism in the Book of Revelation." *BibInt* 1:20–33.

Daniel, E. Randolph. 1992. "Joachim of Fiore: Patterns of History in the Apocalypse." In *The Apocalypse in the Middle Ages*, edited by Richard Emmerson and Bernard McGinn, 72–88. Ithaca, NY: Cornell University Press.

Daly-Denton, Margaret. 2011. "To Hear What Water Is Saying to the Churches." In *Water: A Matter of Life and Death*, edited by Norman Habel and Peter Trudinger, 111–25. *Interface* 14, no. 1. Hindmarsh, Australia: ATF Press.

DeSilva, David. 2009. *Seeing Things John's Way: The Rhetoric of the Book of Revelation.* Louisville: Westminster John Knox.

Duff, Paul B. 2001. *Who Rides the Beast? Prophetic Rivalry and the Rhetoric of Crisis in the Churches of the Apocalypse.* Oxford: Oxford University Press.

Emmerson, Richard Kenneth, and Bernard McGinn, eds. 1992. *The Apocalypse in the Middle Ages.* Ithaca, NY: Cornell University Press.

Flannery, Frances. 2014. "Dreams and Visions in Early Jewish and Early Christian Apocalypses and Apocalypticism." In *Oxford Handbook of Apocalyptic Literature*, edited by John J. Collins, 104–20. Oxford: Oxford University Press.

Frankfurter, David. 2001. "Jews or Not? Reconstructing the 'Other' in Rev 2:9 and 3:9." *HTR* 94:403–25.

———. 2011. "Revelation to John." In *The Jewish Annotated New Testament*, edited by Amy-Jill Levine and Marc Zvi Brettler, 463–98. Oxford: Oxford University Press.

Fretheim, Terrence. 1991. "The Plagues as Ecological Sign of Historical Disaster." *JBL* 110:385–96.

Friesen, Steven J. 2001. *Imperial Cults and the Apocalypse of John: Reading Revelation in the Ruins.* Oxford: Oxford University Press.

Georgi, Dieter. 1980. "Die Visionen vom himmlischen Jerusalem in Apk 21 und 22." In *Kirche: Festschrift fur Gunther Bornkamm*, edited by Dieter Luhrmann and Georg Strecker, 351–72. Tübingen: Mohr Siebeck. ET: "John's Heavenly Jerusalem." In *The City in the Valley: Biblical Interpretation and Urban Theology.* Atlanta: Society of Biblical Literature, 2005.

———. 1986. "Who Is the True Prophet?" *HTR* 79:100–126.

González, Justo L. 1999. *For the Healing of the Nations: The Book of Revelation in an Age of Cultural Conflict.* Maryknoll, NY: Orbis.

Hagee, John. 1999. *From Daniel to Doomsday: The Countdown Has Begun.* Nashville. Thomas Nelson.

Harrington, Wilfrid J. 1993. *Revelation.* Sacra Pagina 16. Collegeville, MN: Liturgical Press.

Horsley, Richard A. 2003. *Jesus and Empire: The Kingdom of God and the New World Disorder.* Minneapolis: Fortress Press.

———, 2010. *Revolt of the Scribes: Resistance and Apocalyptic Origins.* Minneapolis: Fortress Press.

———, ed. 1997. *Paul and Empire: Religion and Power in Roman Imperial Society.* Harrisburg, PA: Trinity Press International.

Huber, Lynn R. 2013. *Thinking and Seeing with Women in Revelation.* New York: T&T Clark.

Hughes, Donald. 1996. *Pan's Travail: Environmental Problems of the Greeks and Romans.* Baltimore: Johns Hopkins University Press.

Humphrey, Edith M. 1995. *The Ladies and the Cities: Transformation and Apocalyptic Identity in Joseph and Aseneth, 4 Ezra, the Apocalypse, and the Shepherd of Hermas.* Sheffield: Sheffield Academic Press.

Jeffrey, David Lyle, ed. 1992. *Dictionary of Biblical Tradition in English Literature.* Grand Rapids. Eerdmans.

Johns, Loren. 2003. *The Lamb Christology of the Apocalypse of John: An Investigation into Its Origins and Rhetorical Force.* WUNT. Tübingen: Mohr Siebeck.

Keller, Catherine. 1996. *Apocalypse Now and Then.* Boston: Beacon.

Kinney, Dale. 1992. "The Apocalypse in Early Christian Monumental Decoration." In *The Apocalypse in the Middle Ages*, edited by Richard Kenneth Emmerson and Bernard McGinn, 200–216. Ithaca, NY: Cornell University Press.

Klauck, Hans-Joseph. 2001. "Do They Never Come Back? Nero Redivivus and the Revelation of John." *CBQ* 63:683–98.

Klein, Peter K. 1992. "The Apocalypse in Medieval Art." In *The Apocalypse in the Middle Ages*, edited by Richard Kenneth Emmerson and Bernard McGinn, 159-99. Ithaca, NY: Cornell University Press.

Koester, Craig R. 2001. *Revelation and the End of All Things.* Grand Rapids: Eerdmans.

Kovacs, Judith, and Christopher Rowland. 2004. *Revelation: The Apocalypse of Jesus Christ.* Oxford: Blackwell.

Kraybill, J. Nelson. 2010. *Apocalypse and Allegiance: Worship, Politics, and Devotion in the Book of Revelation.* Grand Rapids: Brazos.

Krodel, Gerhard. 1989. *Revelation.* ACNT. Minneapolis: Augsburg.

LaHaye, Tim. 1973. *Revelation Illustrated and Made Plain.* Rev. ed. Grand Rapids: Zondervan.

Lawrence, D. H. 1988. "Apocalypse." In *The Revelation of Saint John the Divine*, edited by Harold Bloom, 45–53. Modern Critical Interpretations. New York: Chelsea House.

Lewis, C. S. 1956. *The Last Battle.* New York: MacMillan.

Luther, Martin. 1530. "Preface to the Revelation of St. John." In *LW* 35:398–99.

———. 1972. *Luther's "September Bible" In Facsimile. Part I. Das Newe Testament Deutzsch. Part II. Brief Historical Introduction by Kenneth A. Strand.* Ann Arbor, MI: Ann Arbor Publishers.

Maathai, Wangari. 2010. *Replenishing the Earth: Spiritual Values for Healing Ourselves and the World.* New York: Doubleday.

Maier, Harry O. 2002. *Apocalypse Recalled: The Book of Revelation after Christendom.* Minneapolis: Fortress Press.

Martin, Clarice. 2005. "Polishing the Unclouded Mirror: A Womanist Reading of Revelation 18:13," in David Rhoads, ed., *From Every People and Nation: The Book of Revelation in Intercultural Perspective.* Minneapolis: Fortress Press. 82-109.

McGinn, Bernard. 1994. *Antichrist: Two Thousand Years of the Human Fascination with Evil.* San Francisco: HarperSanFrancisco.

———, ed. 1998. *The Encyclopedia of Apocalypticism.* Vol. 2, *Apocalypticism in Western History and Culture.* New York: Continuum.

Metzger, Bruce M. 1993. *Breaking the Code: Understanding the Book of Revelation.* Abingdon.

Miller, Lisa. 2010. "Some Say BP's Oil Spill Heralds the Apocalypse." *Newsweek* June 3, 2010. http://www.newsweek.com/some-say-bps-oil-spill-heralds-apocalypse-73117.

Moore, Rebecca. 2011. "European Millennialism." In *The Oxford Handbook of Millennialism*, editd by Catherine Wessinger, 284–303. Oxford: Oxford University Press.

Morris, Ian. 2010. *Why the West Rules—for Now: The Patterns of History, and What They Reveal about the Future.* New York: Farrar, Straus and Giroux.

Moyise, Steve. 2001. "Does the Lion Lie Down with the Lamb?" In *Studies in the Book of Revelation*, edited by Steve Moyise, 181–94. New York: T&T Clark.

———. 2004 "Singing the Song of Moses and the Lamb: John's Dialogical Use of Scripture," *Andrews University Seminary Studies* 42: 347–60.

Murphy, Frederick. 1998. *Fallen Is Babylon: The Revelation to John.* Harrisburg, PA: Trinity Press International.

Murrell, Nathaniel. 2001. "Wresting the Message from the Messenger: the Rastafari as a Case Study in the Caribbean Indigenization of the Bible." In *African Americans and the Bible*, edited by Vincent Wimbush, 558–76. New York: Continuum.

Norris, Kathleen. 1999. *Introduction to Revelation.* Pocket Canon Series. New York: Grove.

Northcott, Michael. 2009. "Earth Left Behind? Ecological Readings of the Apocalypse of John in Contemporary America." In *The Way the World Ends? The Apocalypse of John in Culture and Ideology*, edited by William John Lyons and Jorunn Økland, 227–39. Sheffield: Sheffield Phoenix.

Pagels, Elaine. 2012. *Revelations: Visions, Prophecy, and Politics in the book of Revelation.* New York: Viking.

Perry, Peter Soren. 2009. *The Rhetoric of Digressions: Revelation 7:1-17 and 10:1–11:13 and Ancient Communication.* WUNT 2/268. Tübingen: Mohr Siebeck.

———. 2010. "Things Having Lives: Ecology, Allusion and Performance in Revelation." *CurTM* 37: 105–33.

Pippin, Tina. 1992. *Death and Desire: The Rhetoric of Gender in the Apocalypse of John.* Literary Currents in Biblical Interpretation. Louisville: Westminster John Knox.

Portier-Young, Anathea. 2011. *Apocalypse against Empire: Theologies of Resistance in Early Judaism.* Grand Rapids: Eerdmans.

Ramshaw, Gail. 1995. *God beyond Gender.* Minneapolis: Fortress Press.

Rasmussen, Larry. 1996. *Earth Community, Earth Ethics.* Maryknoll, NY: Orbis.

Reeves, Marjorie. 2008. "Dragon of the Apocalypse." In *A Dictionary of Biblical Tradition in English Literature*, edited by David Lyle Jeffrey, 210–13. Grand Rapids. Eerdmans.

Resseguie, J. L. 1998. *Revelation Unsealed: A Narrative Critical Approach to John's Apocalyptic.* Leiden: Brill.

Rhoads, David, ed. 2005. *From Every People and Nation: The Book of Revelation in Intercultural Perspective.* Minneapolis: Fortress Press.

Richard, Pablo. 1995. *Apocalypse: A People's Commentary on the Book of Revelation.* Maryknoll, NY: Orbis.

Rissi, Matthias. 1972. *The Future of the World: An Exegetical Study of Revelation 19:11—22:15.* SBT 23. London: SCM.

Roloff, Jürgen. 1993. *Revelation.* CC. Minneapolis: Fortress Press.

Rossetti, Christina. 1892. *The Face of the Deep: A Devotional Commentary on the Apocalypse.* London: SPCK.

Rossing, Barbara. 1999. *The Choice Between Two Cities: Whore, Bride and Empire in the Apocalypse.* HTS 48. Harrisburg, PA: Trinity Press International.

———. 2002. "Alas for the Earth: Lament and Resistance in Revelation 12." In *The Earth Bible.* Vol. 5, *The Earth Story in the New Testament*, edited by Norman Habel and Shirley Wurst, 180–92. Sheffield: Sheffield Academic Press.

———. 2003. "(Re)Claiming *Oikoumene*? Empire, Ecumenism and the Discipleship of Equals." In *Walk in the Ways of Wisdom: Essays in Honor of Elisabeth Schüssler Fiorenza*, edited by Shelly Matthews, Cynthia Briggs Kittredge, and Melanie Johnson-DeBaufre, 74–87. Harrisburg, PA: Trinity Press International.

———. 2004. *The Rapture Exposed: The Message of Hope in the Book of Revelation.* Boulder, CO: Westview.

Rowland, Christopher C. 1998. "Revelation: Introduction, Commentary, and Reflections." In *Hebrews–Revelation*. Vol. 12, *The New Interpreter's Bible*, edited by Leander E. Keck, 503–736. Nashville: Abingdon.

Ruiz, Jean-Pierre. 1992. "Betwixt and Between on the Lord's Day: Liturgy and the Apocalypse." *SBLSP* 31. Ed. Eugene H. Lovering. 654–72.

———. 2001. "Praise and Politics in Revelation 19:1-10." In *Studies in the Book of Revelation*, edited by Steve Moyise, 69–84. New York: T&T Clark.

Sánchez, David. 2008. *From Patmos to the Barrio: Subverting Imperial Myths*. Minneapolis: Fortress Press.

Schüssler Fiorenza, Elisabeth. 1991. *Revelation: Vision of a Just World*. Proclamation Commentaries. Minneapolis: Fortress Press.

———. 1998. *The Book of Revelation: Justice and Judgment*. 2nd ed. Minneapolis: Fortress Press.

———. 2001. "The Words of Prophecy: Reading the Apocalypse Theologically." In *Studies in the Book of Revelation*, edited by Steve Moyise, 1–20. New York: T&T Clark.

Smith, Robert H. 2000. *Apocalypse: A Commentary on Revelation in Words and Images*. Collegeville, MN: Liturgical Press.

Stenstrom, Hanna. 2013. "'They Have Not Defiled Themselves with Women . . .': Christian Identity According to the Book of Revelation." In *A Feminist Companion to the Apocalypse of John*, edited by Amy-Jill Levine. New York: T&T Clark.

Stephens, Mark B. 2011. *Annihilation or Renewal? The Meaning and Function of New Creation in the Book of Revelation*. WUNT 2/307. Tübingen: Mohr Siebeck.

Suggit, John N. 2006. *Oecumenius: Commentary on the Apocalypse*. Fathers of the Church. Washington, DC: Catholic University of America Press.

Swete, Henry B. 1911. *The Apocalypse of St. John*. 3d ed. London: MacMillan.

Talbert, Charles H. 1994. *The Apocalypse: A Reading of the Revelation of John*. Louisville: Westminster John Knox.

Thompson, Leonard L. 1990. *The Book of Revelation: Apocalypse and Empire*. Oxford: Oxford University Press.

Thuesen, Peter, ed. 2008. *The Works of Jonathan Edwards*. Vol. 26, *Catalogues of Books*. New Haven: Yale University Press.

Vanni, Ugo. 1991. "Liturgical Dialogue as a Literary Form in the Book of Revelation." *NTS* 37:348–72.

Wainwright, Arthur W. 1993. *Mysterious Apocalypse: Interpreting the Book of Revelation*. Nashville: Abingdon.

Washington, James M., ed. 1986. *Testament of Hope: The Essential Writings and Speeches of Martin Luther King, Jr.* New York: HarperCollins.

Wengst, Klaus. 1987. *Pax Romana and the Peace of Jesus Christ*. Philadelphia: Fortress Press.

Westhelle, Vitor. 2005. "Revelation 13: Between the Colonial and the Postcolonial, a Reading from Brazil," in David Rhoads, ed., *From Every People and Nation: The Book of Revelation in Intercultural Perspective*. Minneapolis: Fortress Press, 183–99.

Wink, Walter. 1998. *The Powers That Be: Theology for a New Millennium*. New York: Doubleday.